D0110591

Contents

R03253 24749

BELIZE 227
Belize City 229
The Northern Cayes... 236
Caye Caulker.....236
Ambergris Caye & San Pedro 240
Northern Belize..... 245
Bermudian Landing 245
Altun Ha.....245
Lamanai.....246
Orange Walk 246
Corozal.....248
Western Belize 250
Belmopan 251
San Ignacio (Cayo) 254
Mountain Pine Ridge Area.....258
Southern Belize 261
Hummingbird Highway .. 261
Dangriga 261
Villages of Toledo 272
Understand Belize 274
Belize Today 274
History 274
The Culture 275
Arts..... 275
Landscape & Wildlife.... 276
Survival Guide..... 277

EL SALVADOR..... 283
San Salvador..... 285
Cihuatán 302
El Boquerón.....303
Ruinas de San Andrés...303
Joya de Cerén.....303
Los Planes de Renderos .303
Panchimalco.....303
La Libertad 303
La Costa del Bálsamo ...305
Western El Salvador... 307
Parque Nacional Los Volcanes.....308
Lago de Coatepeque 308
Santa Ana 309
Metapán..... 312
Parque Nacional Montecristo–El Trifinio .. 313
Ruinas de Tazumal..... 314
Ahuachapán 314
Tacuba 316
Ruta de las Flores 316
Sonsonate 320
Parque Nacional El Imposible..... 321
Eastern El Salvador ... 322
San Vicente.....323
Alegría 324
Carretera del Litoral ... 325
Isla Montecristo 325
Usulután 325
Bahía de Jiquilisco.....326
San Miguel.....327
La Unión.....330
Beaches near La Unión.....332
Golfo De Fonseca Islands 332
Morazán.....333
El Mozote.....336
Northern El Salvador.. 336
Suchitoto.....336
Chalatenango 339
La Palma 340
Understand El Salvador 342
El Salvador Today.....342
History 342
The Culture 345
Religion 345
Arts.....345
Landscape & Wildlife....346
Survival Guide..... 348

HONDURAS..... 355
Tegucigalpa 357
Western Honduras 369
Comayagua.....369
La Esperanza..... 371
Marcala 372
Cuevas de Taulabé.....373
Lago de Yojoa 373
San Pedro Sula.....374
Parque Nacional Cusuco 378
Copán Ruinas 378
Copán Archaeological Site 384
Santa Rosa de Copán ...388
Gracias.....390
Parque Nacional Montaña de Celaque 392
San Juan 393
Nueva Ocotepeque 393
Northern Honduras ... 393
Puerto Cortés.....394
Omoa 394
Tela 395
La Ceiba.....398
Trujillo.....406
Bay Islands 408
Roatán 410
Utila 417
La Moskitia 423
Laguna de Ibans.....424
Reserva de la Biosfera del Río Plátano 424
Palacios 425
Brus Laguna 425
Puerto Lempira & Around 425
Southern Honduras ... 426
Isla El Tigre 426
Understand Honduras... 426
Honduras Today 426
History 428
The Culture 430

DISCARD

ON THE ROAD

Religion 431
Arts 431
Landscape & Wildlife 432
Survival Guide 433

NICARAGUA 438

Managua 442
Granada & the Masaya Region 456
Granada 456
Masaya 467
Parque Nacional Volcán Masaya 469
Southwestern Nicaragua 470
Isla de Ometepe & Around 470
Southern Pacific Coast 476
San Juan del Sur 476
León & Northwestern Nicaragua 481
León 482
Poneloya & Las Peñitas Beaches 489
Cosigüina Peninsula Beaches 489
Northern Nicaragua ... 491
Estelí 491
Área Protegida Miraflor ... 495
Área Protegida Cerro Tisey-Estanzuela 495
Somoto 496
Jinotega 497
Matagalpa 498
Caribbean Coast 500
Bluefields 501
Pearl Lagoon 503
Corn Islands 504
Bilwi (Puerto Cabezas) .. 507
San Carlos & Around 508
Understand Nicaragua 512

TIER UND NATURFOTOGRAFIE J. UND C. SOHNS / GETTY IMAGES ©

ROATÁN, HONDURAS P410

Nicaragua Today 512
History 513
The Culture 517
Arts 518
Landscape & Wildlife 519
Survival Guide 520

COSTA RICA 528

San José 532
Central Valley & Highlands 546
Alajuela 546
Parque Nacional Volcán Poás 550
Heredia 550
Parque Nacional Braulio Carrillo 551
Cartago 552
Río Orosi Valley 553
Parque Nacional Volcán Irazú 554
Turrialba 554
Caribbean Coast 556
Tortuguero 557
Puerto Limón 560
Cahuita 562
Puerto Viejo de Talamanca 566
Manzanillo 571
Sixaola 571
North Central Costa Rica 571
Monteverde & Santa Elena 572
Tilarán 579
La Fortuna & Volcán Arenal 580
Los Chiles 583
La Virgen 583
Puerto Viejo de Sarapiquí 584
Guanacaste 585
Cañas 585
Parque Nacional Palo Verde 586
Liberia 586
Parque Nacional Rincón de la Vieja 589
Santa Rosa 589
La Cruz 590
Península de Nicoya ... 591
Playa del Coco 591
Playa Tamarindo 594
Playas Avellanas & Negra 598
Playa Sámara 599
Playa Naranjo 600
Paquera 600
Montezuma 601

Contents

Reserva Natural Absoluta Cabo Blanco 603
Mal País & Santa Teresa .. 604
Central Pacific Coast ... 605
Puntarenas 605
Parque Nacional Carara .. 605
Jacó 605
Quepos 607
Manuel Antonio 610
Dominical 611
Uvita 613
Southern Costa Rica & Península de Osa ... 613
San Isidro de El General . 613
San Gerardo de Rivas ... 615
Parque Nacional Chirripó 616
Palmar 617
Sierpe 617
Bahía Drake 617
Puerto Jiménez 619
Parque Nacional Corcovado 620
Golfito 622
Pavones 622
Neily 622
Paso Canoas 623
Understand Costa Rica 623
Costa Rica Today 623
History 624
The Culture 627
Landscape & Wildlife 628
Survival Guide 629

PANAMA 637
Panama City 639
Panama Canal 657
Monumento Nacional Isla Barro Colorado 660
Isla Taboga 660
Pacific Coast & Highlands 661
El Valle 662
Chitré 663
Pedasí 663
Playa Venao 665
Santa Catalina 666
Santa Fé 668
Chiriquí Province 668
David 668
Golfo de Chiriquí 671
Punta Burica 672
Playa Las Lajas 672
Boquete 672
Parque Nacional Volcán Barú 677
Cerro Punta 678
Parque Internacional La Amistad 678
Bocas del Toro Province 679
Isla Colón 680
Isla Carenero 689
Isla Bastimentos 689
Almirante 692
Changuinola 692
Colón Province 693
Colón 693
Portobelo 695
Isla Grande 697
Comarca de Kuna Yala 698
Darién Province 702
Metetí 705
Yaviza 706
El Real 706
Rancho Frío 707
La Palma 707
Reserva Natural Punta Patiño 707
Sambú 709
Understand Panama ... 709
Panama Today 709
History 709
Culture 713
Arts 715
Sports 715
Landscape & Wildlife 715
Survival Guide 717

SURVIVAL GUIDE

Directory A-Z 728
Transportation 738
Language 743
Index 754
Map Legend 766

SPECIAL FEATURES

Itineraries 28
Off the Beaten Track ... 34
Chichén Itzá, Mexico, 3D illustration 52
Tikal, Guatemala, 3D illustration 202

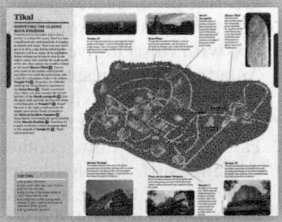

Welcome to Central America

From clear, turquoise seas to magnificent Maya ruins, lush cloud forests, bustling markets and coffee farms, Central America can be as chilled out or as thrilling as you wish.

Outdoor Adventures

In Central America, nature is all about discovery. Explore the ruins of Spanish forts on the Caribbean coast or boat deep into indigenous territories in a dugout canoe. Wildlife is incidental: a resplendent quetzal on the highland trail, the unruly troupe of howler monkeys screeching through the canopy or the breaching whale that turns your ferry ride into an adrenaline event. Adventure tourism means zipping through rainforest canopies, swimming alongside sea turtles or trekking to sublime cloud forest vistas. Eight countries with 300-plus volcanoes and two long tropical coasts make for a pretty big playground.

Ruins

With a culture that hearkens back 4000 years, the Maya are widely considered the greatest pre-Columbian civilization. Their territory sprawled from Mexico to Honduras, with ruins in five present-day Central American countries: from the lost temples of Tikal, soaring above the Guatemalan jungle canopy, to Mexico's otherworldly Palenque and Tulum, perched above the crashing surf. See life-like carved jaguars in Honduras' Copán, and find out why Chichén Itzá was voted one of the new seven wonders of the world.

Culture

Central America may be the size of Texas, but its tapestry of cultures has created a diverse and dynamic society. With more than 20 Maya languages spoken, Guatemala is the region's true indigenous heartland, though traditions are still held fast in many other groups throughout the region. The Spanish left their mark with gorgeous colonial plazas and silent hours of siesta. African culture permeates many parts of the Caribbean coast, from Congo rebel traditions to Garifuna drumbeats. And the last century brought the rest of the world, including Asians, Europeans and North Americans. Cosmopolitan nightlife marks Panama City, where colonial charm now mingles with skyscrapers.

Beaches

With a spate of deserted islands, chill Caribbean vibes on one side and monster Pacific swells on the other, Central America can deliver the best of all beach worlds. Scuba dive the Pacific with whale sharks, snorkel the world's second-largest coral reef off Belize or set sail in Panama's indigenous territory of Kuna Yala, where virgin isles wear nary a footprint. World-class breaks lure surfers psyched to have them all to themselves. Hello, paradise.

Why I Love Central America

By Carolyn McCarthy, Author

Trekking through rainforests, seeing indigenous culture and sailing between pristine Caribbean islands here opened up my sense of wonder. The wildlife viewing is astounding, from world-renowned parks to urban outskirts housing an errant sloth. For me, the region is a confluence – an explosion of nature, cultures and beliefs in a messy, musical arrangement that's everyday life in Latin America.

For more about our authors, see p768

Above: Little Corn Island (p506), Nicaragua

Central America

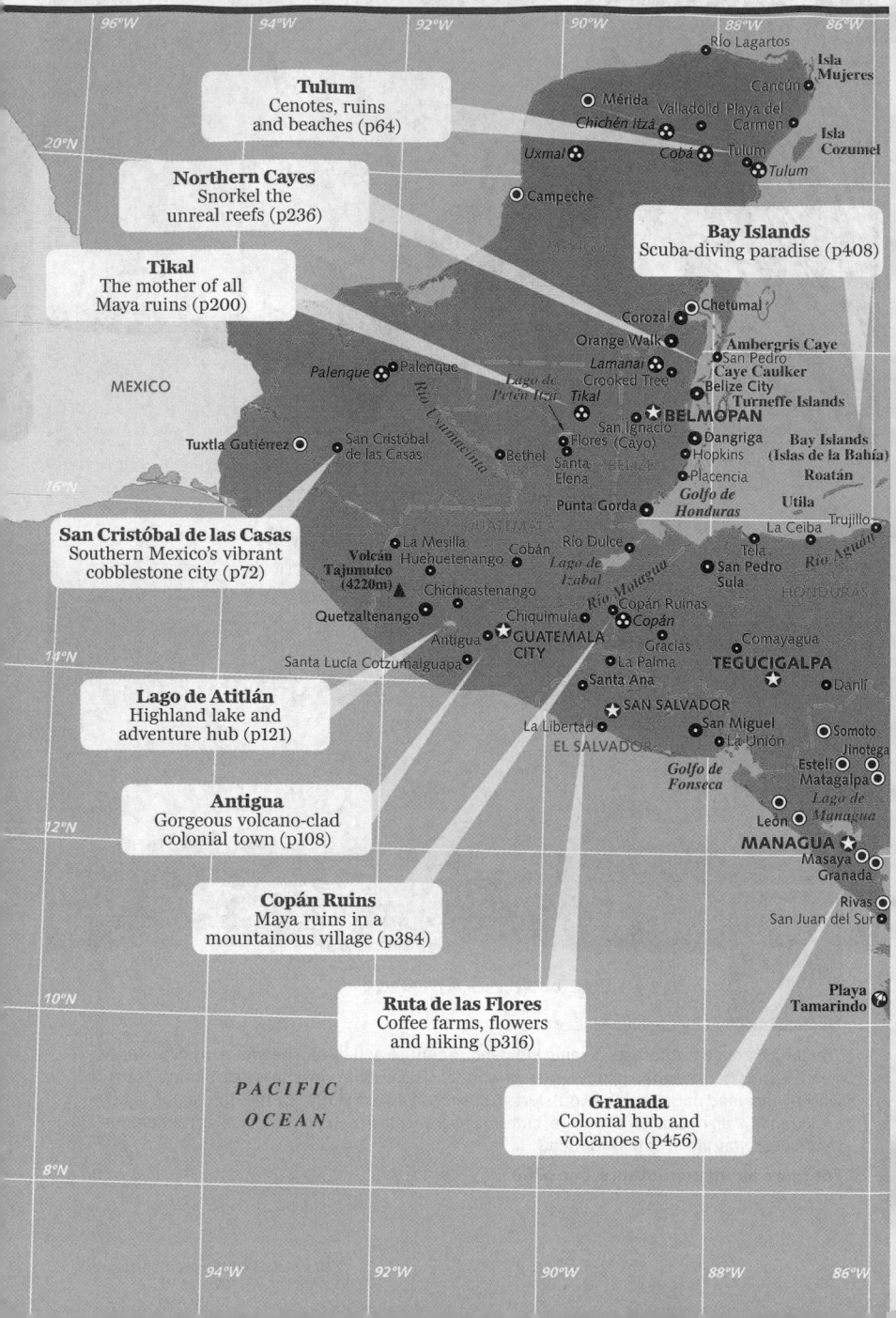

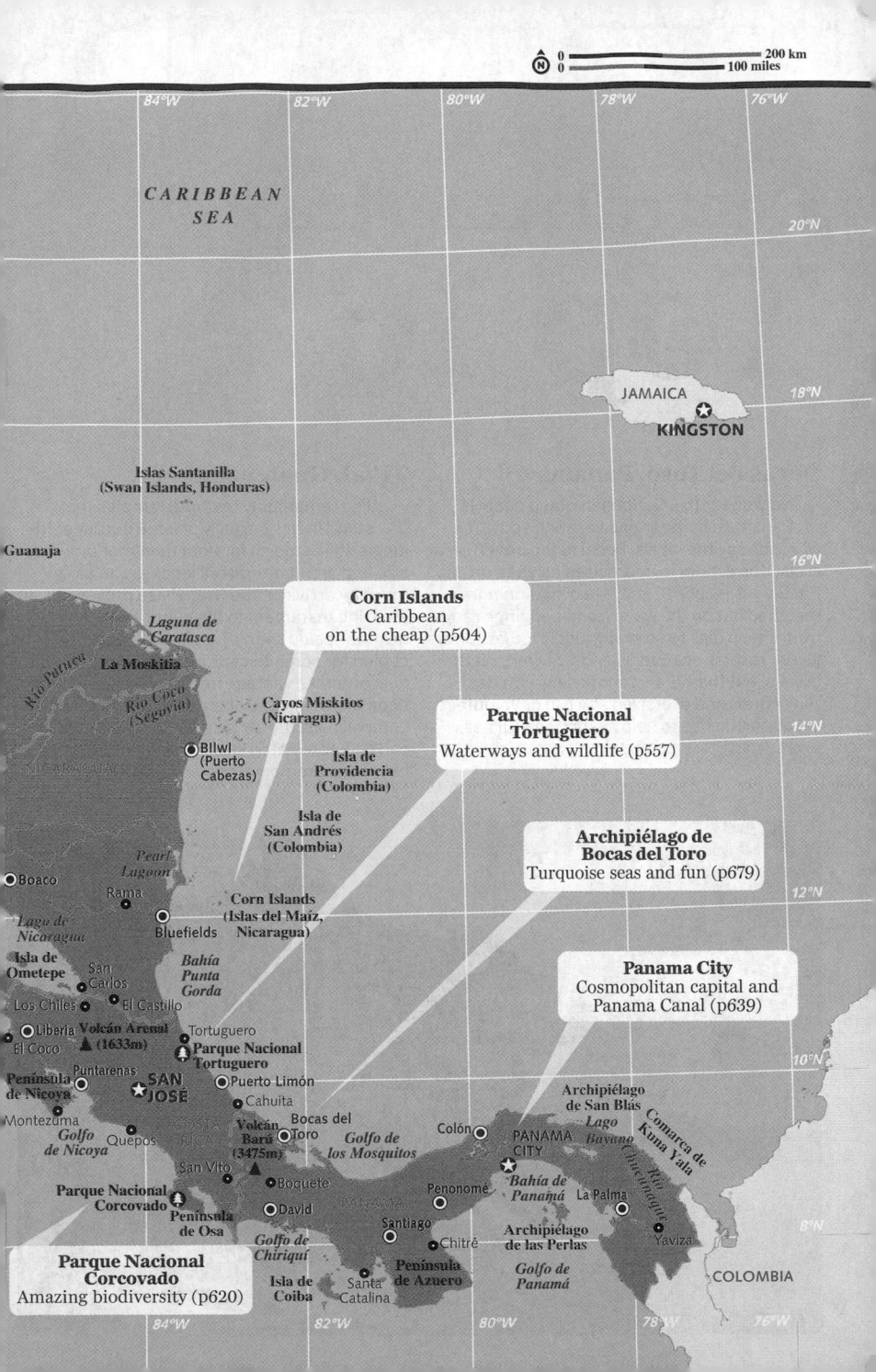
0 200 km
0 100 miles
84°W
82°W
80°W
78°W
76°W
20°N
18°N
16°N
14°N
12°N
10°N
8°N
CARIBBEAN SEA
JAMAICA
KINGSTON
Islas Santanilla (Swan Islands, Honduras)
Guanaja
Corn Islands
Caribbean on the cheap (p504)
Parque Nacional Tortuguero
Waterways and wildlife (p557)
Archipiélago de Bocas del Toro
Turquoise seas and fun (p679)
Panama City
Cosmopolitan capital and Panama Canal (p639)
Parque Nacional Corcovado
Amazing biodiversity (p620)
Laguna de Caratasca
La Moskitia
Río Patuca
Río Coco (Segovia)
Cayos Miskitos (Nicaragua)
Bilwi (Puerto Cabezas)
Isla de Providencia (Colombia)
Isla de San Andrés (Colombia)
NICARAGUA
Pearl Lagoon
Boaco
Rama
Corn Islands (Islas del Maíz, Nicaragua)
Bluefields
Lago de Nicaragua
Isla de Ometepe
San Carlos
Bahía Punta Gorda
Los Chiles
El Castillo
Liberia
Volcán Arenal (1633m)
Tortuguero
El Coco
Parque Nacional Tortuguero
Puntarenas
Puerto Limón
Península de Nicoya
SAN JOSÉ
Cahuita
Montezuma
Golfo de Nicoya
Quepos
COSTA RICA
Volcán Barú (3475m)
Bocas del Toro
Golfo de los Mosquitos
San Vito
Boquete
Parque Nacional Corcovado
Península de Osa
David
PANAMA
Golfo de Chiriquí
Isla de Coiba
Santa Catalina
Santiago
Chitré
Península de Azuero
Colón
PANAMA CITY
Bahía de Panamá
Penonomé
Archipiélago de San Blás
Lago Bayano
Río Chucunaque
Comarca de Kuna Yala
La Palma
Archipiélago de las Perlas
Golfo de Panamá
Yaviza
COLOMBIA

Central America's Top 16

Bocas del Toro, Panama

1 No wonder this Caribbean island chain is Panama's number-one vacation spot. *'It's all good,'* say the locals. Pedal to the beach on a cruiser bike, hum to improvised calypso on Isla Bastimentos (p689) and laze over dinner in a thatched hut on the waterfront. Lodgings range from cheap digs to stunning jungle lodges and luxury resorts on outer islands. Surfers hit the breaks, but there's also snorkeling with dazzling corals and oversized starfish or volunteering opportunities to help nesting sea turtles.

Cayos Zapatillas (p688), Bocas del Toro

Tikal, Guatemala

2 The remarkably restored temples that stand in this partially cleared corner of the jungle still astonish for both their monumental size and architectural brilliance, as an early morning arrival at the Gran Plaza proves. It's an amazing testament to the cultural and artistic heights scaled by this jungle civilization, occupied for some 16 centuries. A highlight is the helicopterlike vantage from towering Temple IV on the west edge of the precinct. Equally compelling is the abundance of wildlife, which can be appreciated strolling ancient causeways between ceremonial centers. (p200)

ALFREDO MAIQUEZ / GETTY IMAGES ©

NEIL SETCHFIELD / GETTY IMAGES ©

Granada, Nicaragua

3 Granada (p456) is a town of immense and palpable magnetism. At the heart of the city's charms are the picture-perfect cobblestone streets, polychromatic colonial homes and churches, and a lilting air that brings the city's spirited past into present-day focus. Most trips here begin and end on foot; simply dawdling from gallery to restaurant to colonial church can take up the better part of a day. Nearby, myriad wild areas, islands, volcanoes and artisan villages await.

Bay Islands, Honduras

4 Imagine living the Caribbean dream – swimming in balmy, turquoise water off a white-sand beach then sipping a sundowner – but on a backpacking budget. Well Honduras' Bay Islands offer that opportunity. Blessed with a fascinating British and buccaneering heritage, today these islands are renowned for their fabled coral reefs and scuba diving. Search for the world's biggest fish, the whale shark, off the island of Utila (p417) or explore shipwrecks in Roatán (p410). Then feast on surf-fresh seafood and investigate the bars. Underwater Roatán (p412)

MLENNY PHOTOGRAPHY / GETTY IMAGES ©

STEPHEN FRINK / GETTY IMAGES ©

MANUEL ROMARIS / GETTY IMAGES ©

CHRISTER FREDRIKSSON / GETTY IMAGES ©

CHRISTOPHER P BAKER / GETTY IMAGES ©

Palenque, Mexico

5 Gather all your senses and dive headfirst into these impressive ruins (p79), some of the Maya world's finest. Here pyramids rise above jungle treetops and howler monkeys sound off like monsters in the dense canopy. Wander the maze-like Palacio gazing up at its unique and iconic tower. Scale the stone staircase of the Templo de las Inscripciones, the lavish mausoleum of Pakal (Palenque's mightiest ruler) and survey the sprawling ruins from atop. Then head downhill, following the Otulum river and its pretty waterfalls, and finish by visiting Palenque's excellent museum.

Panama City, Panama

6 Panama City (p638) is high-octane Latin America: think *ceviche* (marinated seafood), casinos and a stacked skyline. For this city of nearly a million, transformation is in the air: a new coastal green space, a biodiversity museum soon to open and a subway system under construction. Sure, the traffic resembles a boa constrictor digesting one megalithic meal, but its appeal persists. People are real here and nature is never very far away. Beauty lives in the skewed rhythms, incongruous visions and fiery sunsets.

Panama City skyline from Casco Viejo (p639)

Parque Nacional Manuel Antonio, Costa Rica

7 It's easy to understand why Parque Nacional Manuel Antonio (p610) is Costa Rica's most popular national park: this green gem is blessed with stunning beaches, accessible trails and bountiful wildlife. A perfect day at Manuel Antonio entails a leisurely morning of navigating the trails and scanning the canopy for wildlife, and an even more leisurely afternoon of picnicking under swaying beach palms and swimming in the turquoise Pacific. To end, dinner is served at a cliff-side restaurant, as the sun sets the horizon ablaze. *Pura vida*, indeed.

CHRISTER FREDRIKSSON / GETTY IMAGES ©

WAYNE WALTON / GETTY IMAGES ©

Monteverde, Costa Rica

8 To explore the Reserva Biológica Bosque Nuboso Monteverde (Cloud Forest Reserve; p572) is to arrive at the pinnacle of Costa Rica's continental divide. Warm humid trade winds from the Caribbean sweep up forested slopes where they cool and condense into clouds that congregate here and over the nearby Reserva Santa Elena. What that means is a blast of swirling misty euphoria as you take in two forests rich in diversity and oxygen, where lichen-draped trees soar, exotic birds sing, and orchids and bromeliads bloom.

Caye Caulker, Belize

9 Take the plunge from island docks, discover the rush of kite surfing or explore the big blue of Belize's barrier reef. Relaxed Caye Caulker (p236) seduces everyone from backpackers to families with its paradisiacal airs. Its famed Blue Hole is a brilliant sinkhole where divers plunge under the stalactites amid tiger sharks and hammerheads. Hungry diners delight on coconut-fused kebobs, grilled lobster and dinner hot off the streetside grills. As destinations go, it's more central than Placencia and more chilled out than Ambergris Caye.

BRENDA THARP / GETTY IMAGES ©

JEAN-PIERRE LESCOURRET / GETTY IMAGES ©

Lago de Atitlán, Guatemala

10 Possibly the worthiest destination in Guatemala, Atitlán (p121) elicits poetic outbursts from even the most seasoned traveler. Of volcanic origin, the alternately placid and turbulent lake is ringed by volcanoes and villages like Santiago Atitlán (p130), with a thriving indigenous culture, and San Marcos La Laguna (p135), a haven for those wishing to plug into the lake's cosmic energy. And there are enough activities – paragliding from Santa Catarina Palopó, kayaking around Santa Cruz La Laguna or hiking the glorious lakeshore trails – to make a longer stay viable.

Chichén Itzá, Mexico

11 Ever since Chichén Itzá (p51) was named one of the 'new seven wonders of the world,' it has become all the rage. The massive El Castilo pyramid, the Maya site's most iconic structure, will knock your socks off, especially at spring and autumn equinoxes when the sunlight casts a shadow of a feathered serpent on the staircase. If you can't make it then, Chichén Itzá will wow you nonetheless – after all, the remains left behind are a testament to one of the most brilliant pre-Hispanic civilizations in Latin America.

FABIENNE ROSSEZ / ALAMY ©

STEFANO PATERNA / ALAMY ©

AFP / GETTY IMAGES ©

Copán, Honduras

12 There may be hundreds of Maya sites dotted around Central America but few can rival the beauty of Copán (p384). Its location in an idyllic river valley, home to scarlet macaws and other outstanding bird life, surrounded by pine-forested hills, is simply sublime. The site itself is also very special indeed, with a towering hieroglyphic stairway and a great plaza dotted with imposing, fabulously carved stelae and altars. When you've had your fill of exploring Maya temples you'll find the charming little neighboring town of Copán Ruinas (p378) a delightful base. Carvings at Copán's Ball Court

Ruta de las Flores, El Salvador

13 Driving through coffee plantations and small mountain villages may seem like a fairly sedate affair, but the Flower Route (p316) traverses the volcanic Apaneca Range and is packed with waterfalls, night markets, food fairs and hiking trails. At the northern end of the 60km highway ascent is Tacuba (p316), a gateway town to the spectacular Parque Nacional El Imposible (p321) on the Guatemalan border. Near the southern tip is Lago de Coatepeque (p308), a pristine volcanic lake where the ancients used to swim.

Church in town of Juayúa (p317)

Playa El Tunco, El Salvador

14 Playa El Tunco (p305) is the most famous beach in El Salvador. Known for its throbbing weekend party scene, world-class beach breaks and relatively large international crowd, El Tunco delivers in black sandy spades. If you want to chill, many surrounding beach hamlets are far less hectic. At the western reaches, Barra de Santiago (p320) is wild and windswept and sea turtles hatch along its shores. Plug further east and find bliss beaches you can have all to yourself.

Altun Ha, Belize

15 Though not the largest Maya site in Belize, Altun Ha (p245) is definitely the country's most well known. An easy trip from Belize City, the 1500 acre site contains a central ceremonial precinct of two plazas surrounded by two temples, including the Temple of the Green Tomb and the Temple of the Masonry Altars (that's the one you'll recognize from both the Beliken Beer label and Belizean banknote). After a day of exploring, have your weary muscles pampered at the Maruba Spa, 15 miles north of the ruin.

Isla de Ometepe, Nicaragua

16 Lago de Nicaragua's beloved centerpiece, this laid-back island has it all. Archaeological remains, waterfalls, bird life and monkeys are at your doorstep, as are the lapping waves. Activity-seekers can take to the twin volcanoes, lush hillsides and zip lines, or kayak, bike and climb their way through this lost paradise found again. At the heart of the island's charms are the cool hostels, camping areas and peaced-out traveler scenes. Custom-fit your experience from high-end lodges to hippie huts; Ometepe is big enough for all kinds. (p471)

DENNIS MACDONALD / ALAMY ©

JOHN COLETTI / GETTY IMAGES ©

Need to Know

For more information, see country Survival Guides

Planes
Each country has an international airport, regional and charter flights via national airlines.

Buses
The main form of regional transport. Quality ranges from comfortable, air-conditioned long-haul buses to run-down former school buses.

Cars
Rentals are usually not allowed to leave the country.

Boat
Regional boats range from dugout canoes to ferries; motorboats and chartered sailboats go to Colombia from Panama.

Bicycle
Rentals available in most tourist areas.

Trains
Limited to the Panama City–Colón route in Panama.

When to Go

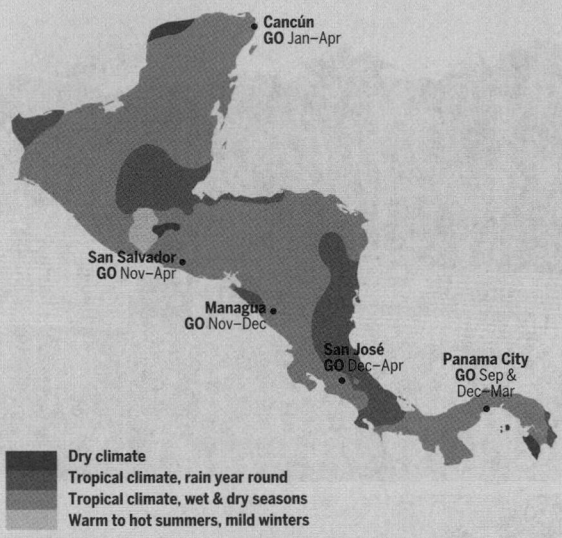

High Season
(summer: mid-Dec–mid-Apr)

➡ Pacific-side dry season.

➡ Higher rates and demand for hotels.

High Season Peak
(holidays)

➡ Includes Christmas, New Year and Easter week.

➡ Hotel rates may be up to double that of normal rates.

➡ Resorts, festival towns and beaches are crowded with national vacationers.

Low Season
(winter: mid-Apr–early Dec)

➡ Rainy season in most of the region; hurricane season between June and November.

➡ Many destinations can still be enjoyed – check regional climate charts.

➡ Lodging rates and resorts are better priced.

Websites

Mundo Maya (www.mayadiscovery.com) Articles on Maya heritage and travel information.

Planeta (www.planeta.com) Regional articles, events, reference material and links, with an emphasis on sustainable travel.

OAS (Organization of American States; www.oas.org) Covers regional issues and cultural events.

Lonely Planet (www.lonelyplanet.com/central-america) The popular Thorn Tree forum, travel news and links to useful sites.

Visas

Generally not required for stays under 90 days. Visitors entering Belize are authorized 30 days.

Centro America 4 (CA-4) A regional agreement between Nicaragua, Honduras and El Salvador, gives travelers a 90-day stay for *the entire region*, with extensions possible.

Money

ATMs are widespread except for in remote areas we have noted.

Credit cards are accepted only by some midrange and high-end hotels, restaurants and adventure tour outfitters.

Bargaining is OK in markets and informal transactions.

Daily Costs

Costs vary by country, with the cheapest being Guatemala and the most expensive Mexico or Belize.

Budget: US$18–US$43

➡ Dorm bed: from US$7

➡ Dine on *comida corriente* (set meals), visit markets and street stalls

Midrange: US$44–US$180

➡ Double room in a midrange hotel: from US$30

➡ Some fine dining, activities like canopy zip lines or surf lessons and regional flights

Top End: From US$180

➡ Double room in a high-end hotel, resort or lodge: from US$120

➡ Guided trips with bilingual naturalist guides, internal flights and car rental

Money-saving Tips

➡ Consider low-season travel

➡ Plan sightseeing via bus, DIY visits to beaches, and walks

➡ In lodgings forgo private bathrooms or air-con if nights aren't sweltering

➡ Eat at low-priced *cafeterias* or *comedores*, street stalls and bakeries

Arriving in Central America

Belize Belize City Philip SW Goldson International Airport (BZE)

Costa Rica San José Aeropuerto Internacional Juan Santamaría (SJO; p634)

El Salvador San Salvador Aeropuerto Internacional Comalpa (SAL; p300)

Guatemala Guatemala City Aeropuerto Internacional La Aurora (GUA; p104) or Flores Aeropuerto Internacional Mundo Maya (FRS; p198)

Honduras San Pedro Sula (SAP; p376), Tegucigalpa (TGU; p367) or Roatán (RTB; p417)

Mexico Cancun Aeropuerto Internacional de Cancún (CUN; p48)

Nicaragua Managua Augusto C Sandino (MGA; p452)

Panama Panama City Tocumen International Airport (PTY; p655) or David Aeropuerto Enrique Malek (DAV; p671)

Responsible Travel

Go overland Take buses, not planes

Give right Handouts to kids encourage begging; give directly to schools or clinics

Buy local Try to eat and stay at family-owned places and use community-owned services

Volunteer Make a difference by preserving turtle-nesting sights, teaching English or working with reputable nonprofits

Reduce waste Buy only larger bottled water and get refills where available

Respect local traditions Dress appropriately when visiting local churches or traditional communities

Be curious Interacting and making an effort to use the local language benefits both hosts and travelers

For much more on Transportation, see p738

First Time Central America

For more information, see chapter Survival Guides

Checklist

- Check the validity of your passport
- Check the visa situation and government travel advisories
- Organize travel insurance
- Check flight restrictions on luggage and camping or outdoors equipment
- Check your immunization history
- Contact your credit card company to see if your card includes car rental insurance

What to Pack

- Phrasebook
- Flip-flops
- Poncho or rain jacket
- Binoculars
- Bug repellent with DEET
- Refillable water bottle
- Driver's license, if you plan to rent a car
- Field guide of local fauna and/or flora
- Batteries and chargers
- Flashlight

Top Tips for Your Trip

- Pack half of what you think you need. Laundry service is cheap.
- Outside the cities, many perfectly good lodgings don't have a handle on email and websites. Don't get frustrated if no one sees your reservation. If you have even basic Spanish, call ahead.
- Central Americans are used to foreigners dissing local idiosyncrasies – like drivers not using signals, or crowds that can't form lines. But, instead, ask why it is the way it is and you'll have a lively conversation.

What to Wear

Locals rarely wear shorts if not at the beach. Bring lightweight pants or skirts and tops with short sleeves. Dining and nightlife can be formal in the capital. Bring proper dress shoes or sandals for women, pants and a dress shirt for men and a skirt or dress for women. Pack a light sweater for over air-conditioned restaurants and bus rides. A fleece and lightweight shell are necessary for highlands. For hiking, long sleeves and quick-drying pants help keep bugs away.

Sleeping

It is rarely necessary to book lodgings ahead except during high peak times. For these dates it's best to book two to six months out, particularly for beach destinations.

- **Hotels** Come in every stripe; for a cheap option check out private doubles in hostels.
- **Camping** Organized campgrounds are not that common, though there are facilities in national parks and reserves.
- **Guesthouses/B&Bs** A good midrange option, usually family-run and small.
- **Hostels** Not necessarily just for young travelers, hostels range from quiet digs to party central.
- **Lodges** Running the gamut from rustic to high-end, these are good places to commune with nature, mostly in jungle or highland locations.

Bargaining

It's OK to bargain in markets and at street stalls, but educate yourself first by asking around to get an idea of the pricing of different items and the specific factors that contribute to the quality of what you're bargaining for.

Tipping

➡ **Restaurants** Tip 10%; check first to see if it's included in the bill.

➡ **Taxis** Tipping is optional but you can round up, especially at night.

➡ **Guides** Tip US$1 to US$2 per person for day tours, with more substantial tips for specialized guides.

Central America Soundtrack

Think Central America and salsa, calypso, soca and steel drums may come to mind. But these days, it's a lot more. Reggaetón and punta are huge here, heavily influenced by Afro-Caribbean drumming. Look for the following:

➡ **Rubén Blades** The Panamanian salsa icon and ex-presidential candidate; see his collaboration with Calle 13

➡ **Café Tacvba** A Mexican rock band with modern beats

➡ **Gaby Moreno** Singer-songwriter from Guatemala with a lush Latin sound

➡ **Sonido Gallo Negro** Fun party rhythms; try *Cumbia Salvaje*

➡ **Rodrigo y Gabriela** Fast, rhythmic acoustic guitarists

➡ **Aurelio Martínez** Musician/politician, Martínez is the star of the punta scene. His *Garífuna Soul* and *Laru Beya* albums have received rave reviews

JEREMY WOODHOUSE / GETTY IMAGES ©

Guatemalan woman in traditional dress

Etiquette

➡ **Asking for help** Say *disculpe* to get someone's attention; *perdón* to ask for an apology.

➡ **Personal space** Don't be surprised if locals have fewer boundaries about personal space than what's customary in North America and Europe.

➡ **Visiting indigenous communities** Ask permission to take photos, particularly of children, and dress more modestly than beachwear; bargaining may be appropriate for buying crafts but not for lodging and food; the best gifts for children are those that are useful (pens, paper, notebooks, creative games or books).

➡ **Surfing** Novice surfers should be aware of 'dropping in' on more-experienced surfers and of swimmers crossing your path.

Language

Beyond English-speaking Belize, Spanish is the primary language of Central America. Knowing some very basic Spanish phrases is not only courteous but also essential. Parts of the Caribbean coast speak English. If you visit indigenous communities, pick up a few words in the local language beforehand, it's the best way to warm relations.

For more information, see the Language chapter p743.

If You Like...

Snorkeling

Isla Holbox, Mexico An offbeat Gulf island surrounded by sea turtles, barracuda and manta rays (p48).

Utila, Honduras For the ultimate snorkeling experience seek out the gargantuan whale shark in the big blue (p417).

Belize Mile upon mile of the western hemisphere's finest reef makes Belize a snorkeling paradise (p236).

Bocas del Toro, Panama From giant starfish to a rainbow of corals, this tropical archipelago is the perfect spot to strap on your flippers (p680).

Manzanillo, Costa Rica When conditions are right, you can snorkel straight off the beach at this picturesque Caribbean outpost (p571).

Hiking

Volcán Mombacho, Nicaragua Accessible cloud forest with great hiking and even better birdwatching (p465).

Parque Internacional La Amistad, Panama True wilderness hiking without the drama of the Darién; access via the highlands or Caribbean coast (p678).

Parque Nacional Cusuco, Honduras Dramatic and mountainous, with trails laced with giant ferns, dwarf forest and hidden quetzals (p378).

Parque Nacional Chirripó, Costa Rica Peak-baggers can't resist Cerro Chirripó, the highest point in Costa Rica. The trail to the top is a thrilling, chilling adventure (p616).

Volcán Tajumulco, Guatemala Central America's highest point is a relatively easy climb, especially if you take two days and camp overnight (p147).

Juayúa, El Salvador Perfect for day hikes and intimate cafe nights. Take in coffee *fincas* (plantations) and waterfalls with friendly local guides (p317).

Wildlife Watching

Península de Osa, Costa Rica Monkeys and macaws, sloths and snakes – wildlife is prolific all around the Osa (p613).

Refugio de Vida Silvestre Los Guatuzos, Nicaragua Perfectly preserved wetlands with fantastic bird-watching by day and action-packed crocodile spotting by night (p509).

Isla Bastimentos, Panama From July to August, loggerheads, hawksbills, greens and leatherbacks – half the world's turtle species – hatch on the north shore (p689).

Moskitia, Honduras Vast wetlands, savannah and tropical forest, it's the best place in the nation for searching for jaguar and tapir (p423).

Monterrico, Guatemala Save a turtle, spot a whale or go bird-watching in the mangroves from this Pacific coast village (p168).

Playa El Cuco, El Salvador Baby sea turtles hatch in the dry season. Dolphin pods and eagles watch on (p332).

Scuba Diving

Parque Nacional Coiba, Panama Dive with hammerheads and swim through enormous schools of fish – wildlife here is epic (p667).

Roatán, Honduras Outstanding wall dives on the edge of the Cayman trench, flourishing hard and soft corals and prolific sea life (p410).

The Blue Hole, Belize This deep blue sinkhole has you swimming under stalactites with bull sharks and hammerheads (p240).

Isla Cozumel, Mexico The famed reefs off this island draw diving aficionados from all over the world (p61).

GREG JOHNSTON / GETTY IMAGES ©

VISUALS UNLIMITED, INC. / ANDRES MORYA / GETTY IMAGES ©

(Above) The Blue Hole, Belize

(Below) Two-toed sloth, Costa Rica

Isla del Caño, Costa Rica Sea turtles and humpback whales make this island a popular destination for dive trips from Bahía Drake and Quepos (p617).

Off the Beaten Track

Pearl Keys, Nicaragua Live out your shipwreck fantasies beneath the coconut palms on this group of tiny, idyllic Caribbean islands (p503).

Bahía de Jiquilisco, El Salvador Pounding surf, lush mangroves, fishing villages and a biosphere make for *Survivor*-style wonder stuff (p144).

The Darién, Panama Steeped in indigenous culture and exotic wildlife – with required permits, checkpoints and delays, the real trouble is arriving (p702).

Mal País, Costa Rica Make your way to the tip of the Península de Nicoya for pristine beaches, blood-pumping surf and good vibes (p604).

La Campa, Honduras An incredibly pretty heartland *pueblo*. Zip-line over canyons, seek out authentic ceramics and set up highland hikes (p392).

Tilapita, Guatemala A one-hotel Pacific beach town where the pace of life slows waaay down (p166).

Colonial Cities

Antigua Guatemala's colonial show pony is a riot of gorgeous cobblestoned streets, crumbling ruins and noble churches (p108).

Granada Charge your batteries, Nicaragua's wonderfully preserved colonial showpiece lays on the charm from the moment you get off the bus (p456).

Suchitoto, El Salvador The real deal. This picture-book town is littered with war history and art galleries. Festivals reign most weekends (p336).

Casco Viejo, Panama City Super hot for a night out but ditch the stilettos, since you'll be darting the cobblestones between underground bar, brew pub, wine bar and live-music venue (p639).

Comayagua, Honduras Relaxed and prosperous, with a historic core of elegant churches and buildings dotted around its lovely parque central (p369).

Surfing

Dominical, Costa Rica Bring your board and you may never want to leave this easygoing town (p611).

Santa Catalina, Panama No souvenir shops in this dusty village – it's all about world-class waves, and hostels boast front-row seats (p666).

Pavones, Costa Rica Surfers travel here to catch the longest left-hand break on the planet (p622).

Playa Hermosa, Nicaragua Charge the waves and hang out in one of the best beach hostels around (p481).

Las Flores, El Salvador Tucked into El Salvador's untrodden east, it's as good as anywhere in Latin America (p332).

Ruins

Tikal, Guatemala This regional superstar is well on the tourist trail but totally worth the visit for its soaring, jungle-shrouded temples (p200).

Chichén Itzá, Mexico Recently named one of the 'new seven wonders of the world'. Enough said (p51).

Copán, Honduras Exquisite with some of the most intricate carvings in the Maya world, an acropolis and dozens of temples and monuments (p384).

Tulum, Mexico Maya ruins perched atop a cliff with jaw-dropping views of the Caribbean below (p64).

Caracol, Belize The view from the top of the Ka'ana pyramid alone is worth the trek (p258).

Tazumal, El Salvador The name of El Salvador's most impressive Maya ruins translates as 'the place where the victims burned' (p314).

Volcanoes

Volcán Rincón de la Vieja, Costa Rica Trails crisscross the volcanic slopes, leading to multihued fumaroles, soothing springs, bubbling mud pots and a sputtering *volcancito* (small volcano; p589).

Volcán Masaya, Nicaragua Watch parakeets nest among clouds of sulfuric gases above visible pools of lava (p469).

Volcán Arenal Costa Rica's celebrated volcano has gone quiet, but it still looks threatening with smoke curling out of its conical top (p580).

Pacaya, Guatemala An easy day trip from Antigua, this smoking, lava-dribbling peak is an all-time favorite for hikers (p113).

Volcán Barú, Panama Terribly steep, hard, and invariably foggy and muddy, but how else can you view both oceans at once? (p677)

El Salvador Known as the Land of Volcanoes: Santa Ana may be the largest, but conical-shaped Izalco is the most dramatic (p308).

Beaches

Kuna Yala, Panama Known for perfect postage-stamp islets with turquoise waters (p698).

Playa Grande, Las Baulas The water is warm, the waves are powerful and the sand at this Costa Rican beach attracts sea turtles, who carry on the cycle of life (p594).

West Bay, Roatán Honduras' classic Caribbean beach of the white sand and coconut palm persuasion, with the added bounty of a coral reef offshore (p415).

Little Corn Island, Nicaragua Brilliant turquoise waters meet snow-white sand in secluded coves on this enchanted isle (p506).

Hopkins How much longer will Belize's best beach town remain semi-secret? (p264)

Playa El Tunco, El Salvador Mix it up at bonfires on black-sand beaches with pro surfers and young revelers from the capital (p305).

Month by Month

TOP EVENTS

Día de los Muertos, November 1

Carnaval, February or March

Semana Santa, March or April

Bolas de Fuego, August 31

Garifuna Settlement Day, November 19

January

With the dry season and tourist season at their peaks, this is a big month for travel throughout the region. It's prime for kitesurfing and swimming, since Pacific Ocean temperatures are at their warmest, but the wind is up. Quetzal-viewing season begins in Costa Rica's Monteverde (through July).

Nicaraguan Baseball Championship

The national pastime of Nicaragua culminates in the National Baseball Championship, an action-packed series that comes to a head during mid-January. (p450)

Panama Jazz Festival

The week-long jazz festival is a blast and one of the biggest musical events in Panama, drawing top-caliber international musicians from jazz, blues, salsa and other genres. Held all over the city, the open-air events are usually free. (p645)

February

It's prime time for surfing both on Pacific and Caribbean swells. High season is winding down. Carnaval, a feature of all Central American countries, takes place in February or March.

Carnaval in Mexico

A big street bash preceding the 40-day penance of Lent, Carnaval is festively celebrated in Mérida, Campeche and Isla Cozumel with parades, music, dancing and lots o' fun.

Festival de Diablos y Congos, Panama

Held every two years, this festival in Portobelo celebrates rebellious slave ancestors with spirited public dancing featuring beautiful masks and costumes. Participants assume the role of escaped slaves and take captives on the street.

March

Easter celebrations may take place in March or April. Semana Santa (Holy Week) offers reenactments of the crucifixion and resurrection of Christ. On Good Friday, religious processions are held across Central America.

Desfile de Bufos, Guatemala

Guatemala City university students take to the streets during the Parade of Fools on the Friday before Good Friday to mock the government and make other political statements.

April

The tail end of the dry season for most of Central America. In the jungle lowlands of Guatemala, March and April are scorchers, while it's the best time to see whale sharks off Honduras' Utila or Placencia in Belize.

Día de Juan Santamaría, Costa Rica

April 11 commemorates Costa Rica's national hero, who died driving William Walker out of Costa Rica in 1856. The week-long national holiday features parades, parties and other celebrations, especially in Santamaria's hometown of Alajuela.

May

The rainy season is here. May begins a five- to six-month nesting season for both loggerhead and green sea turtles in the Caribbean.

Fería de Cultura de las Flores y las Palmas, El Salvador

Near San Salvador, this colorful extravaganza stars beauty queens and gauche floral arrangements in Panchimalco.

Toledo Cacao Festival, Belize

Brings together folks who grow chocolate, sell chocolate and just plain love chocolate in mid-May. Also showcases Toledo's history and culture.

La Feria de San Isidro

Honduras' largest fiesta takes place in the streets and clubs of La Ceiba, culminating in late May with 250,000 attending parades. Costumed dancers and revelers fill the city to bursting point.

Palo de Mayo, Nicaragua

Bluefields celebrates fertility with a series of neighborhood block parties leading to the bright and boisterous carnival on the last Saturday of the month. The closing Tulululu features a midnight romp through the streets complete with brass band. (p502)

SEMANA SANTA IN GUATEMALA

Although Semana Santa is celebrated all over Guatemala, nowhere is more alive than Antigua during this Holy Week leading up to Easter. Hundreds of people dress in purple robes to accompany the most revered sculptural images from the city's churches in daily street processions remembering Christ's crucifixion and the events surrounding it. Dense clouds of incense envelop the parades and the streets are covered in breathtakingly elaborate *alfombras* (carpets) of colored sawdust and flower petals.

The fervor and the crowds peak on Good Friday, when an early morning procession departs from La Merced church, and a late afternoon one leaves from Iglesia de la Escuela de Cristo. There may also be an enactment of the crucifixion in Parque Central. Have ironclad Antigua room reservations well in advance of Semana Santa, or plan to stay in Guatemala City or another town and commute to the festivities.

Processions, *velaciones* (vigils) and other events actually go on every weekend through Lent, the 40-day period prior to Holy Week. Antigua's tourist office has schedules of everything, and the booklet *Lent and Holy Week in Antigua*, written by Elizabeth Bell, gives explanations.

It seems that Guatemala City's entire population of pickpockets decamps to Antigua for Semana Santa; they target foreign tourists especially.

June

June to November is hurricane season, though big weather events are sporadic and hard to predict. Forty days after Easter, Corpus Christi features colorful celebrations throughout the region, held in May or June.

Lobsterfest, Belize

The world's favorite crustacean along with spirits and libations galore. Takes place in San Pedro in mid-June, Placencia in the last week of June, then Caye Caulker in early July.

July

Though it's the middle of rainy season in Central America, weather is relatively dry on the Caribbean side; Belize can be uncomfortably hot. It's off-peak for visitors and hotels offer better rates.

Rabin Ajau

Guatemala's most impressive indigenous festival, this folkloric gathering takes place in Cobán in late July or early August.

August

Breeding humpback whales can be observed in the Pacific. Rainy season continues.

Festival de Invierno, El Salvador

For the Winter Festival, hip, lefty students flood the small mountain town of Perquín and party like the war has just ended.

Sun Jam, Honduras

In search of the perfect rave? Held in early August, this tech-no-prisoners party features DJs of global repute. The setting is a tiny desert island off Utila.

Bolas de Fuego, El Salvador

Local scallywags paint their faces like devils and throw fireballs at each other. Just a bit of potentially harmful fun, held on August 31 in Nejapa.

September

It's peak hurricane season in the north; Panama City is drier; flooding in Honduras is possible.

Costa Rican Independence Day

Action centers on a relay race that passes a 'Freedom Torch' from Guatemala to Costa Rica. The torch arrives at Cartago in the evening of September 14, when the nation breaks into the national anthem.

October

In most of the region October 12 is Día de la Raza (Columbus Day); a dubious legacy nonetheless celebrated by every high-school brass band letting loose. Loggerhead turtles nest on the Pacific coast from now until March.

Nogapope, Panama

In Panama, Kunas converge on Isla Tigre for three days of tireless traditional dancing. It's visually engaging and fully authentic. From October 10 to 12, followed by a three-day fair with art shows and canoe races.

Noche de Agüizotes, Nicaragua

This spooky festival held on the last Friday in October in Masaya brings to life characters from horror stories of the colonial period with elaborate costumes.

November

Seasonal rains have tapered off in most of the region, except for Honduras' north coast, where flooding is possible through to February. In Panama, the whole country takes off to celebrate multiple independence-related holidays.

Día de Todos los Santos, Guatemala

In Santiago Sacatepéquez and Sumpango, just outside of Antigua, celebrations include the flying of huge, technicolor kites while in the tiny highlands town of Todos Santos Cuchumatán, November 1 is celebrated with drunken horse races through the main streets of town.

Día de los Muertos, Mexico

On November 2, families build altars in their homes and visit graveyards to commune with their dead, taking garlands and gifts.

Garifuna Settlement Day, Belize

Celebrates the arrival of the first Garifuna people to Belize by canoe. The best spots to partake in the three Ds (dancing, drinking and drumming) are Dangriga and Hopkins. On November 19.

December

One of the coolest months on the Pacific coast, from Nicaragua to the jungle lowlands of Guatemala. The Christmas holidays disrupt the region's work schedule, cities empty out and beaches are full.

Las Fiestas de Zapote, Costa Rica

For one week, this celebration embraces all things Costa Rican – from rodeos to fried food and a whole lot of drinking – in Zapote, southeast of San José.

Plan Your Trip
Itineraries

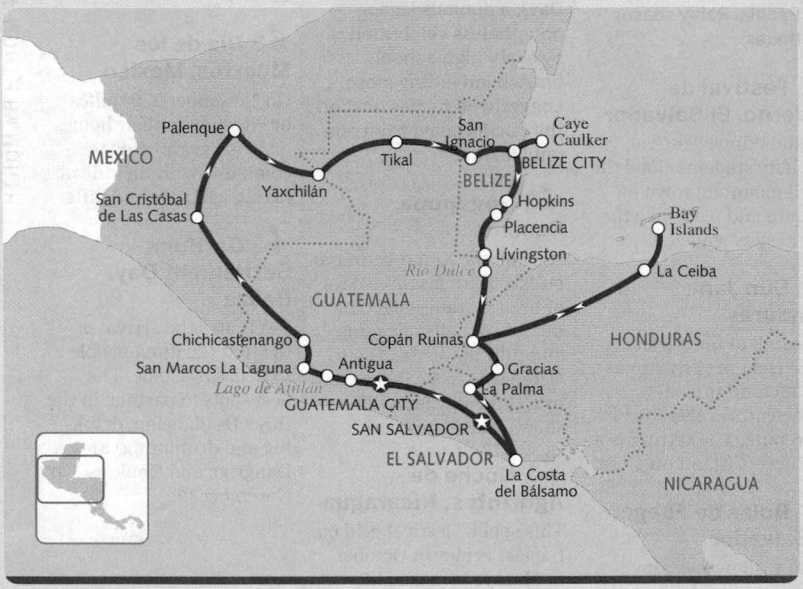

DOELAN YANN / GETTY IMAGES ©

5 WEEKS Guatemala, Mexico, Belize, Honduras & El Salvador

This route takes in many of the northern region's natural and cultural highlights, including Maya ruins, markets, caving and jungle exploration. Go just before or after peak season (December to April) to miss most of the crowds and tropical storms.

Start from **Guatemala City**. Head straight to colonial **Antigua** for a few days, doing a volcano climb and perhaps a crash course in Spanish. Then get a chicken bus to other highland sites; at stunning **Lago de Atitlán** skip the touristy bustle of Panajachel for a few days of hiking and swimming in the beautiful lake village and New Age magnet **San Marcos La Laguna**, before moving on to **Chichicastenango** to see the famous Maya market.

Pad your budget and venture north to Mexico on a Chiapas loop. Explore the colonial city of **San Cristóbal de Las Casas** and nearby Maya villages, stopping to explore the Maya ruins of **Palenque** set in jungle haunted by the screech of howler monkeys. Back in Guatemala, visit the riverside ruins of **Yaxchilán** en route to the mother of all Maya sites, **Tikal**, best soaked up with an overnight stay. Bus east

Chichicastenango market (p138), Guatemala

to Belize, stopping to go river tubing or caving outside hilly **San Ignacio**, before splashing into the Caribbean's wonderful reefs at laid-back **Caye Caulker**.

Cay-hop south, stopping at offbeat **Hopkins** or more mainstream **Placencia**, before boating to Guatemala's **Lívingston** to take a serious jungle boat trip along the Río Dulce. Cross into Honduras and head for the cobblestone town of **Copán Ruinas**, which offers river-tubing trips, horseback rides over mountains, and the namesake ruins. After Copán, detour via La Ceiba to the region's star diving destination – the **Bay Islands**. Utila offers the chance to spot enormous whale sharks suspended in the silent waters of the big blue. When you're chilled to the max, head back to Copán and continue your journey through Honduras on a bus to **Gracias**, and thank the colonial town for its proximity to Parque Nacional Celaque and its gorgeous long-tailed resplendent quetzals.

Southward in El Salvador, stop in kitschy mountain town **La Palma** for adventure hikes that cross rivers on teetering log bridges. Bypass San Salvador for the Pacific 'surf villages' of **La Costa del Bálsamo**. Catch a Guatemala City bus from San Salvador.

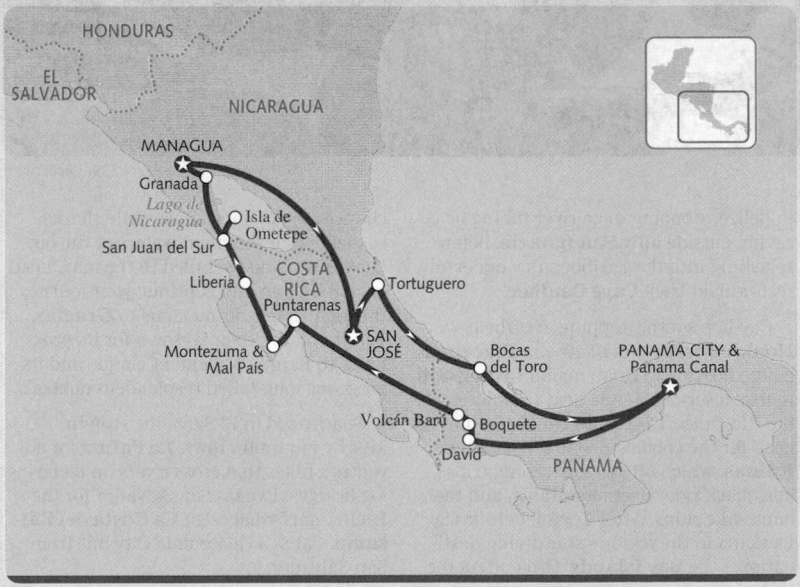
HONDURAS
EL SALVADOR
NICARAGUA
MANAGUA
Granada
Lago de Nicaragua
Isla de Ometepe
San Juan del Sur
Liberia
COSTA RICA
Puntarenas
Tortuguero
SAN JOSÉ
Montezuma & Mal País
Bocas del Toro
PANAMA CITY & Panama Canal
Volcán Barú
Boquete
David
PANAMA

CHRISTIAN HEEB / GETTY IMAGES ©

ROY TOFT / GETTY IMAGES ©

Top: Volcán Barú (p677), Panama
Bottom: Strawberry poison dart frog, Tortuguero (p557), Costa Rica

Costa Rica, Panama & Nicaragua

From volcano climbs to barefoot, sun-soaked beach towns, southern Central America offers equal parts adventure and R&R. Most travelers first target green giant Costa Rica, but neighboring Nicaragua and Panama offer a strong complement with vibrant culture, colonial character and off-the-beaten-path attractions.

Starting in **San José**, take the bus-and-boat trip to the English-speaking Caribbean coast and **Tortuguero**, where you can wander the boardwalk Afro-Caribbean village and paddle a maze of lush canals in search of manatees and poison-dart frogs.

Bus south into Panama and boat out to the Caribbean archipelago of **Bocas del Toro** for snorkeling and island-hopping, sugar-sand beaches and turquoise waters. When you've achieved total relaxation, dust off your best duds to hit Central America's cosmopolitan capital, **Panama City**, where you can soak up the funky nightlife, explore the cool colonial area of Casco Viejo and admire the expansion of the **Panama Canal**.

Head west, via David, to the cool cloud forests around **Boquete** for adventure. Whitewater raft, tour coffee farms and slog up **Volcán Barú** to earn gaping 360-degree views of both the Pacific and Caribbean. Bus back to Costa Rica, taking the ferry from Puntarenas to check out the boho beach hangout of **Montezuma**, the ideal base to explore the area. Head further off-track to Península de Nicoya's swimming holes, wilderness beaches and the wicked waves of **Mal País**.

Bus to Liberia and continue north to Nicaragua. Sip rum, test the surf and swing in a hammock in kicked-back **San Juan del Sur**, where you can plot your next adventure on **Isla de Ometepe**, a volcano island in a sea-sized lake with hikes that take you to the clouds and beyond. Follow up with a trip to colonial **Granada**, with more volcanoes on tap, this time with eerie night hiking. End your journey by motoring to Managua to grab a direct bus back to San José.

2 WEEKS Pacific Coast: El Salvador to Panama

This sinuous coastline has something to suit everyone, from beach-lovers to surfing pros and dedicated first-time boarders. Hit the monster curls and long-breaking lefts, or simply wend your way from one beach town to the next searching for the ultimate spot in the sun.

Arrive in San Salvador and beam to the nearby **La Costa del Bálsamo**, El Salvador's surf mecca and home to world-class breaks just off La Libertad. Playas El Zonte and Sunzal offer reasonable seaside digs and lessons for budding boarders. Then cross the Nicaragua border to Managua and catch a shuttle to **San Juan del Sur,** a hip international scene ringed by beaches catering to both high-end surf campers and bare-bones backpackers.

Continue south to Liberia, where you'll veer to the famed tip of the Península de Nicoya. Chill out under palm trees, work on your yoga wheel and if you're here for the surfing, take on the raved-about waves of **Mal País** and **Santa Teresa**. Take a shortcut to the mainland with a ferry to Puntarenas. Hardcore surfers should keep heading south to meet the wicked waves of **Dominical**. Otherwise, you can bus to Panama, where you will find a scene that's more up-and-coming than prime time. Veer off the Interamericana at Santiago; from here a couple of small coaster buses will get you to **Santa Catalina** in Panama, a highlight for surfers that is reverently compared with Hawaii.

If you still have time, hit the mellow **Playa Venao** on the Península de Azuero, a rural region renowned for the wild, street-stomping festivals in colonial villages. From Las Tablas, grab a bus to **Panama City** or head north to David to take a long-haul bus back to San Salvador.

Need a break from the tubes? Add a few days to your trip and bolt to the highlands slightly east of the coast, with places like El Salvador's **Ruta de los Flores**, Costa Rica's **Monteverde** and Panama's **Boquete** offering cooler mountain air, coffee farms and hiking trails.

Plan dates to coincide with surf season to feel the full vibe of this trail. In El Salvador and Nicaragua, peak time is March to December, while further south it's February to March. Beginners should visit when the surf isn't at its peak.

RYAN CREARY / GETTY IMAGES ©

REBECCA E MARVIL / GETTY IMAGES ©

Top: San Juan del Sur (p476), Nicaragua
Bottom: Boquete (p672), Panama

Ruta de los Flores
SAN SALVADOR
HONDURAS
La Costa del Bálsamo
EL SALVADOR
NICARAGUA
MANAGUA
San Juan del Sur
Liberia
Monteverde
Puntarenas
Peninsula de Nicoya
Mal País & Santa Teresa
COSTA RICA
Dominical
PANAMA CITY
Boquete
PANAMA
David
Santiago
Las Tablas
Santa Catalina
Playa Venao

Central America: Off the Beaten Track

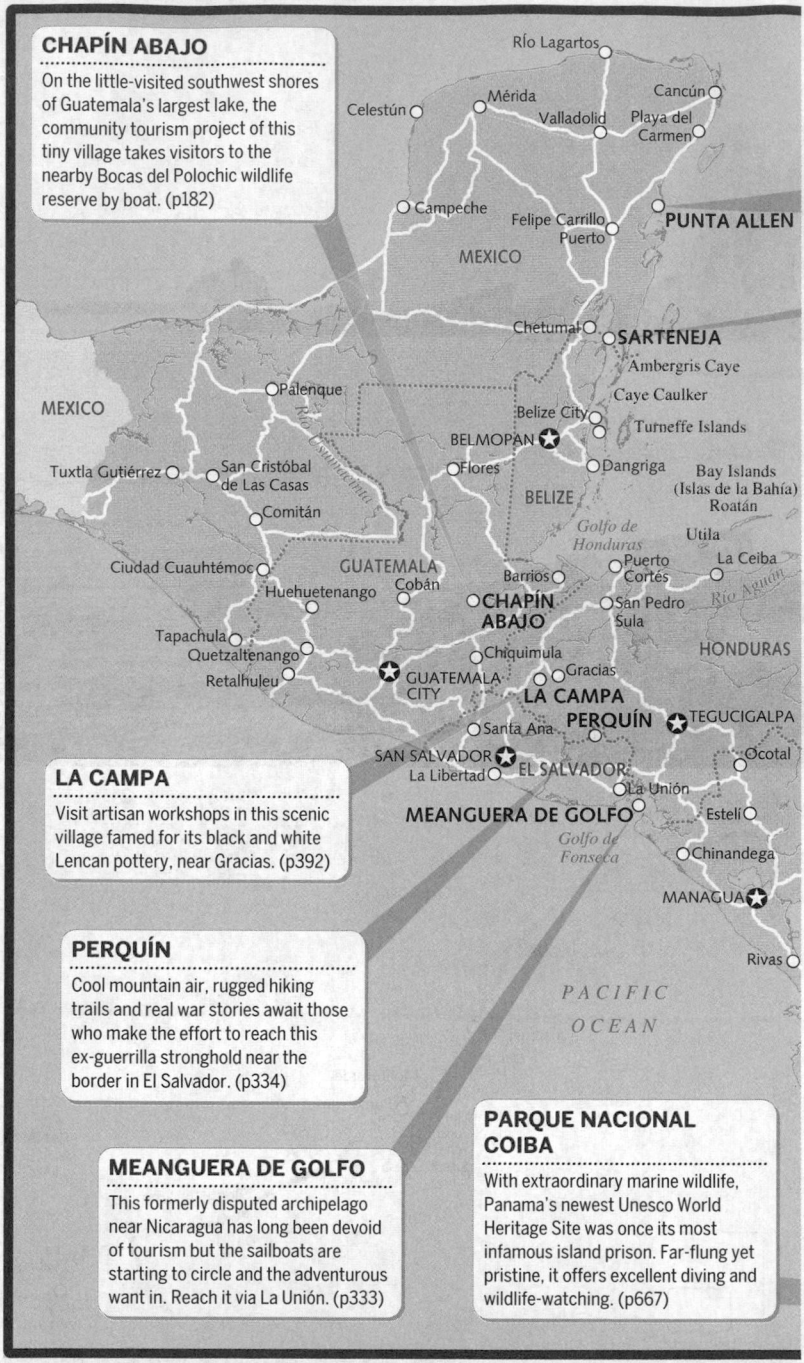

CHAPÍN ABAJO

On the little-visited southwest shores of Guatemala's largest lake, the community tourism project of this tiny village takes visitors to the nearby Bocas del Polochic wildlife reserve by boat. (p182)

LA CAMPA

Visit artisan workshops in this scenic village famed for its black and white Lencan pottery, near Gracias. (p392)

PERQUÍN

Cool mountain air, rugged hiking trails and real war stories await those who make the effort to reach this ex-guerrilla stronghold near the border in El Salvador. (p334)

MEANGUERA DE GOLFO

This formerly disputed archipelago near Nicaragua has long been devoid of tourism but the sailboats are starting to circle and the adventurous want in. Reach it via La Unión. (p333)

PARQUE NACIONAL COIBA

With extraordinary marine wildlife, Panama's newest Unesco World Heritage Site was once its most infamous island prison. Far-flung yet pristine, it offers excellent diving and wildlife-watching. (p667)

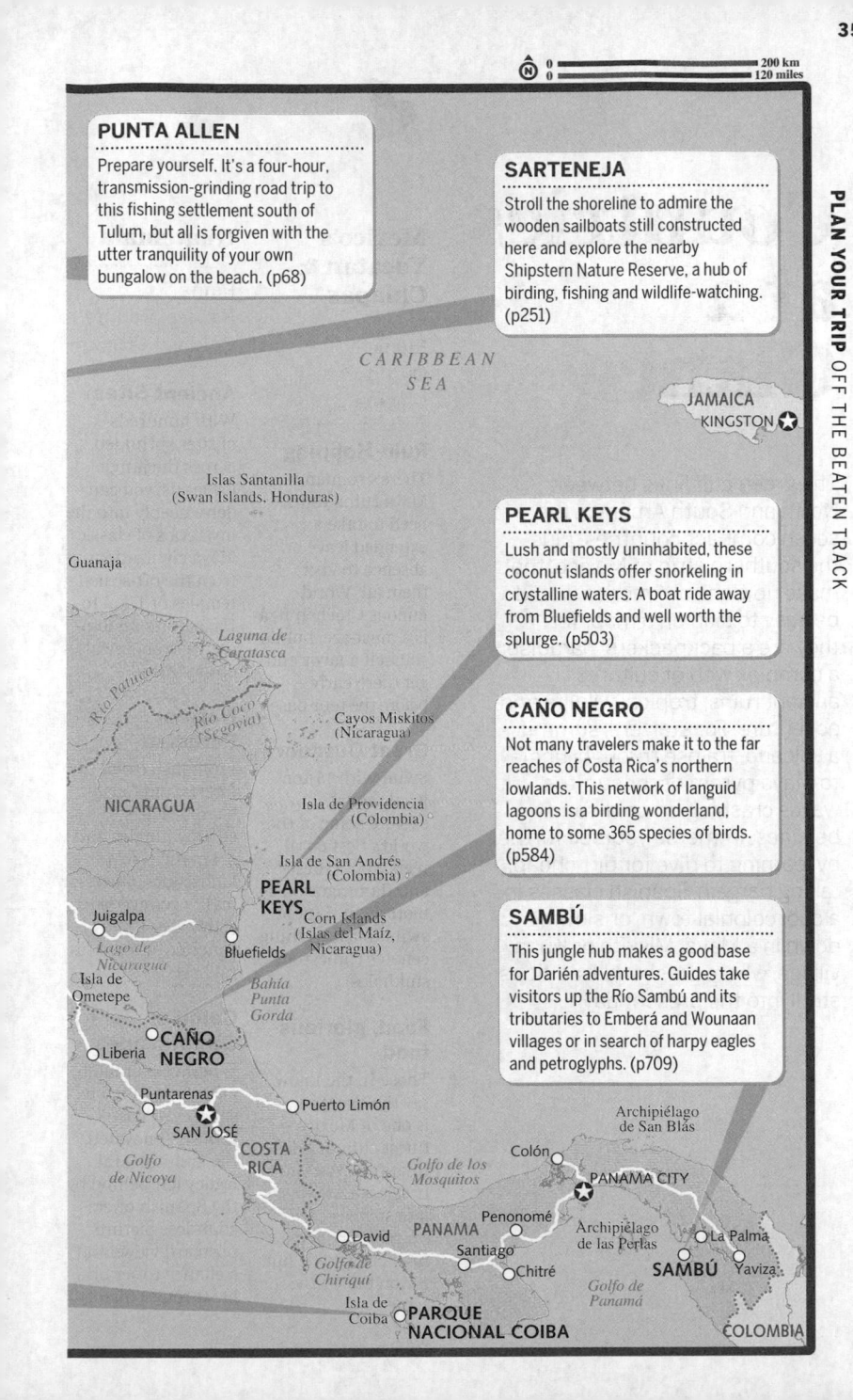

PUNTA ALLEN

Prepare yourself. It's a four-hour, transmission-grinding road trip to this fishing settlement south of Tulum, but all is forgiven with the utter tranquility of your own bungalow on the beach. (p68)

SARTENEJA

Stroll the shoreline to admire the wooden sailboats still constructed here and explore the nearby Shipstern Nature Reserve, a hub of birding, fishing and wildlife-watching. (p251)

PEARL KEYS

Lush and mostly uninhabited, these coconut islands offer snorkeling in crystalline waters. A boat ride away from Bluefields and well worth the splurge. (p503)

CAÑO NEGRO

Not many travelers make it to the far reaches of Costa Rica's northern lowlands. This network of languid lagoons is a birding wonderland, home to some 365 species of birds. (p584)

SAMBÚ

This jungle hub makes a good base for Darién adventures. Guides take visitors up the Río Sambú and its tributaries to Emberá and Wounaan villages or in search of harpy eagles and petroglyphs. (p709)

Countries at a Glance

The green cuff links between North and South America, the seven compact countries, plus the southern strip of Mexico, that make up Central America would be easy to skip on a map. Yet they are a backpackers' paradise: a complex web of cultures, ancient ruins, tropical wildlife and adventure. For starters, summit a volcano, traipse through jungle to Maya pyramids, or surf the waves crashing on gold-sand beaches. Immerse yourself further by learning to dive for dirt cheap, taking bargain Spanish classes in a cool colonial town, or slowing down in a Maya, Miskito or Kuna village, where old-world traditions stroll into the present day.

Mexico's Yucatán & Chiapas

Ruins
Outdoors
Cuisine

Ruin-Hopping

There's so many Maya ruins you'd need to take an extended leave of absence to visit them all. World-famous Chichén Itzá is a must-see, but do yourself a favor and get there early – before the tour buses.

Great Outdoors

Swim with 15-ton whale sharks, explore some of the world's best coral reefs, spot crocs and flamingos on a motorboat tour, or swim in astonishing cenotes (limestone sinkholes).

Food, glorious food

Those in the know say the Yucatán is one of Mexico's finest culinary destinations. You can try classic *yucateco* fare such as *cochinita pibil* or *sopa de lima* elsewhere, but it won't taste the same.

p40

Guatemala

Ruins
Natural Beauty
Colonial Cities

Ancient Sites

With hundreds of sites sprinkled across the jungle lowlands, you can delve deeply into the mysteries of classic Maya civilization, from the oft-scaled temples of Tikal to Uaxactún's seldom-seen astronomical observatory.

Natural Paradise

From lush cloud forests and Caribbean beaches to steamy jungles and dramatic volcanic landscapes, Guatemala's countryside showcases Central America at its natural best.

Colonial Streetscapes

Whether crumbling gracefully in town squares or gorgeously renovated, the architectural legacy left behind by the Spanish offers countless picture postcard views and a chance to scramble through history.

p91

Belize

Water Sports
Ruins
Cuisine

Nautical Adventure

With miles of coastline, scores of islands and the Western Hemisphere's most spectacular reef, this one's a no-brainer. From sailing to kite-surfing, Belize offers endless opportunity for water fun.

Exploring the Maya World

After surviving 2012, there's no better time to visit major Maya ruins such as Caracol and Lamanai or the smaller sites around San Ignacio and Toledo. For modern Maya culture, explore the villages of the deep south.

Culinary Traditions

From Mexican-inspired *ceviches* to Maya chicken soup, Garifuna specialties and lobster on the cayes, Belizean cuisine is as varied and unique as the nation itself.

p227

El Salvador

Landscapes
History
Surfing

Small Wonders

The fast track to your Central American fix, El Salvador has black-sand beaches, volcanic lakes, Maya ruins, hip coffee towns and cranking nightlife all within 130km.

Civil War Stories

See the tide of history turning in remote mountain villages where the civil war was most fiercely fought. To fill in the blanks, visit excellent regional museums and the galleries of San Salvador.

Wicked Waves

Surf the smoothest and most uncrowded waves in Latin America, from the international flavor of La Costa del Bálsamo to the more remote eastern breaks. The secret may be out but most folks just don't listen.

p283

Honduras

Diving/Snorkeling
National Parks
Colonial Cities

Get Deep for Cheap

Few places are as inexpensive as the Bay Islands to learn to dive. Boasting outstanding reefs, famous wrecks and bountiful sea life, Utila and Roatán offer memorable marine time.

Tropical & Biodiverse

Highlights from Honduras' 20-plus national parks include the cloud forests of Parque Nacional Cusuco, wetland and mangrove reserves near Tela and the Río Plátano region in La Moskitia, a World Heritage Site.

Old-World Appeal

Explore the colonial grandeur of the graceful former capital of Comayagua, the delightful highland settlement of Gracias and the attractive university town of Santa Rosa de Copán.

p355

Nicaragua

Surfing
History
Adventure

Surf's Up

You don't get better surf in many other places. Best of all, after you hit dawn patrol at legendary spots such as Playas Hermosa and Maderas, you can chill out with cool tunes and companionship in your beachfront hammock paradise.

Colonial Charms

Nicaragua's history is as complex and nuanced as it gets. It's evidenced in colonial cities like Granada and León, where you'll see it in the architecture, festivals, art and living culture.

Island Life

Isla de Ometepe and Nicaragua's slice of the Caribbean Coast are paradises lost... that have yet to be found. Discover petroglyphs, climb volcanoes, kayak to lost coves and relax in cool travelers' enclaves on the edge of the wild.

p438

Costa Rica

Surfing
Wildlife
Forests

Ride a Wave

Point and beach breaks, lefts and rights, reefs and river mouths – warm water and year-round waves make Costa Rica a legendary surf destination.

Tropical Safari

The biodiversity is astounding: 850 species of birds, 380 kinds of reptiles and amphibians, six species of wild cats, four of monkeys, three of anteaters, two kinds of sloths and one bumbling Baird's tapir. How many can you tick off?

Storybook Cloud Forest

Covering only one-quarter of 1% of the planet's land surface, this rare habitat is a mysterious neverland, dripping with mist and mossy vines, sprouting with ferns and bromeliads, gushing with creeks and blooming with life.

p528

Panama

Engineering feat
Wildlife
Islands

Panama Canal

The expansion of this 80km marvel means even more reason to visit. It's a mammoth jigsaw puzzle of engineering, but few know there's also wildlife-watching, fishing and kayaking off the shipping lanes.

Jungle Love

Rainforest adventure and some of the best wildlife-watching can be had just outside Panama City. Think canopy towers and birding hotspots. For nature on steroids, explore the Darién or Parque Nacional Coiba.

Kuna Yala Archipelago

It would be hard to beat these idyllic islands with technicolor turquoise waters. Resort islands comprise little more than thatched huts with sandy floors and hammocks, but what more do you need?

p637

On the Road

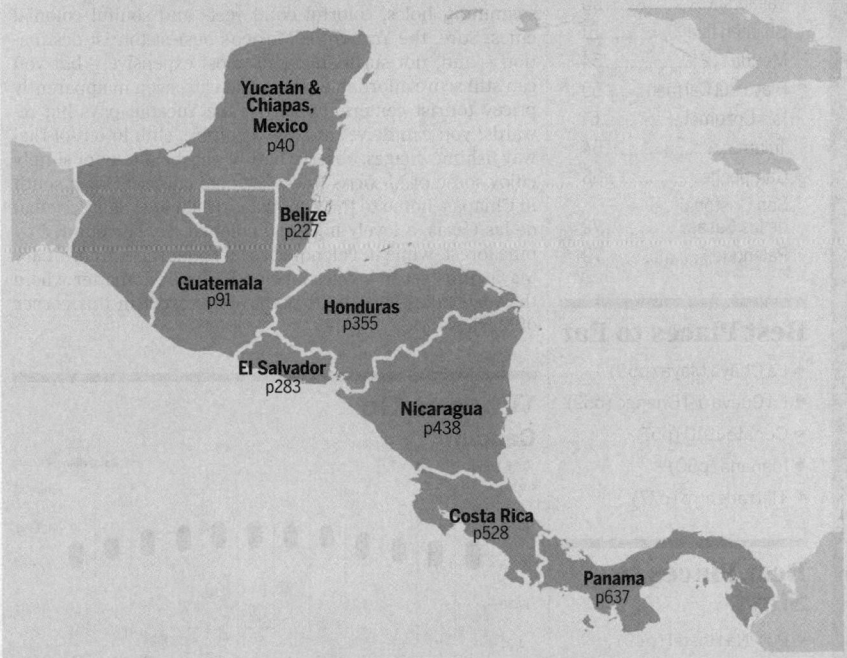
Yucatán & Chiapas, Mexico
p40
Belize
p227
Guatemala
p91
Honduras
p355
El Salvador
p283
Nicaragua
p438
Costa Rica
p528
Panama
p637

Mexico's Yucatán & Chiapas

52 / POP 8.9 MILLION (YUCATÁN, QUINTANA ROO, CAMPECHE AND CHIAPAS STATES)

Includes ➡

Cancún 43
Isla Mujeres 49
Valladolid 50
Chichén Itzá 51
Mérida 54
Playa del Carmen 59
Isla Cozumel 61
Tulum 64
Campeche 68
San Cristóbal de las Casas 72
Palenque 79

Best Places to Eat

- ➡ La Chaya Maya (p58)
- ➡ La Cueva del Chango (p59)
- ➡ Conato 1910 (p51)
- ➡ Mañana (p50)
- ➡ Tierradentro (p77)

Best Places to Stay

- ➡ Poc-Na Hostel (p49)
- ➡ Nómadas Hostel (p55)
- ➡ Hotel López (p69)
- ➡ El Jardín de Frida (p65)
- ➡ Posada La Media Luna (p75)

Why Go?

Flanked by the turquoise waters of the Caribbean and the wildlife-rich Gulf coast, the steamy Yucatán Peninsula is a wonderland of Maya jungle ruins, picturesque limestone swimming holes, colorful coral reefs and soulful colonial cities. Sure, the Yucatán is Mexico's busiest tourist destination – and, not surprisingly, its most expensive – but you can still score affordable sleeps and eats, even in apparently pricey tourist centers. Exploring the Yucatán pays big rewards: you can delve into Maya culture, chill in out-of-the-way fishing villages, observe nature on a boat tour, or simply enjoy some of Mexico's finest regional cuisine. Down south in Chiapas, home to the Zapatistas, you'll love San Cristóbal de las Casas, a lovely highland colonial city surrounded by pine forest, while in Palenque it's all about the extraordinary Maya ruins set in a celestial cloud forest. No matter where the road takes you, life is pretty darn sweet in this corner of Mexico.

When to Go

Cancún

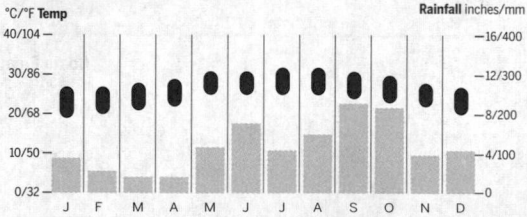

Mar Don't miss the shadowy serpent's appearance in Chichén Itzá at vernal equinox.

May-Sep Swim with gigantic whale sharks at Isla Holbox.

Oct-Nov Cooler climes and cheaper accommodations make low season an ideal time to visit.

Connections

From Mexico you can loop into Guatemala – from San Cristóbal de las Casas to Quetzaltenango, or to Tikal via Palenque – and into Corozal, Belize, from Chetumal, south of Tulum. The best way into Guatemala is from Ciudad Cuauhtémoc, near La Mesilla, Guatemala. Another option is crossing into Guatemala from the Mexican border town of Tapachula, further southwest. For more detailed information, see Survival Guide on p90.

FIRST TIME IN MEXICO'S YUCATÁN AND CHIAPAS

One Week

Greet the first day with a splash in the turquoise waters of **Cancún's** Zona Hotelera, then hit downtown for affordable eats and some nocturnal mischief. Cancún makes a good base to visit nearby **Isla Mujeres**, which arguably has the most beautiful beaches in the Mexican Caribbean. Return to the mainland and head south for **Playa del Carmen**, an ultrachic party town and the jumping-off point for **Isla Cozumel**, a world-famous diving destination. Next, check out **Tulum**, known for its spectacular oceanfront Maya ruins, and if time allows, head inland to **Cobá**, a Maya archaeological site set in the jungle.

Two Weeks

From Cobá head to **Valladolid**, a colonial city with a small-town feel. West of Valladolid awaits **Chichén Itzá**, the mother of all Maya ruins. Continue on to the peninsula's cultural capital, **Mérida**, and spend several days indulging in yucateco cuisine and taking in the city's ample entertainment offerings. Then go south to the immaculately preserved walled city of **Campeche**. Stop at the archaeological sites of **Edzná** and **Calakmul** as you make your way down to the southern state of Chiapas. Even if you're all ruined-out at this point, still drop by **Palenque**, where unforgettable Maya structures sit pretty in a dreamlike cloud forest. For the last leg of the trip, hit **San Cristóbal de las Casas**, a pleasant highland colonial town.

Essential Food & Drink

- **Cochinita pibil** Slow-cooked pork marinated in citrus juices and a spice made from annatto seed.
- **Sopa de lima** Soup with shredded turkey, lime and tortilla.
- **Papadzules** Diced hard-boiled eggs wrapped in tortilla and topped with pumpkin seed and tomato sauces.
- **Panuchos** Fried tortilla filled with beans and topped with chicken, lettuce and pickled red onion.

AT A GLANCE

Currency Mexican Peso (M$)

Language Spanish and Maya

Money ATMs in most towns

Visas Not required for many countries (see p89)

Time GMT minus six hours; minus five hours during daylight-saving time

Fast Facts

- **Area** Yucatán Peninsula and Chiapas 220,700 sq km
- **State capitals** Chetumal (Quintana Roo), Tuxtla Gutiérrez (Chiapas), Campeche (Campeche), Mérida (Yucatán)
- **Emergency** ☎066

Set Your Budget

- **Hostel bed/budget room** M$150/M$500
- **Evening meal** M$100
- **Bus ticket** M$180 (three-hour trip)
- **Ruins admission** M$50 to M$180

Resources

- **Yucatán Today** (www.yucatantoday.com) Covers Yucatán and Campeche
- **Yucatán Tierra de Maravillas** (www.yucatan.travel) All things Yucatán
- **Campeche Travel** (www.campeche.travel) Campeche tourism board

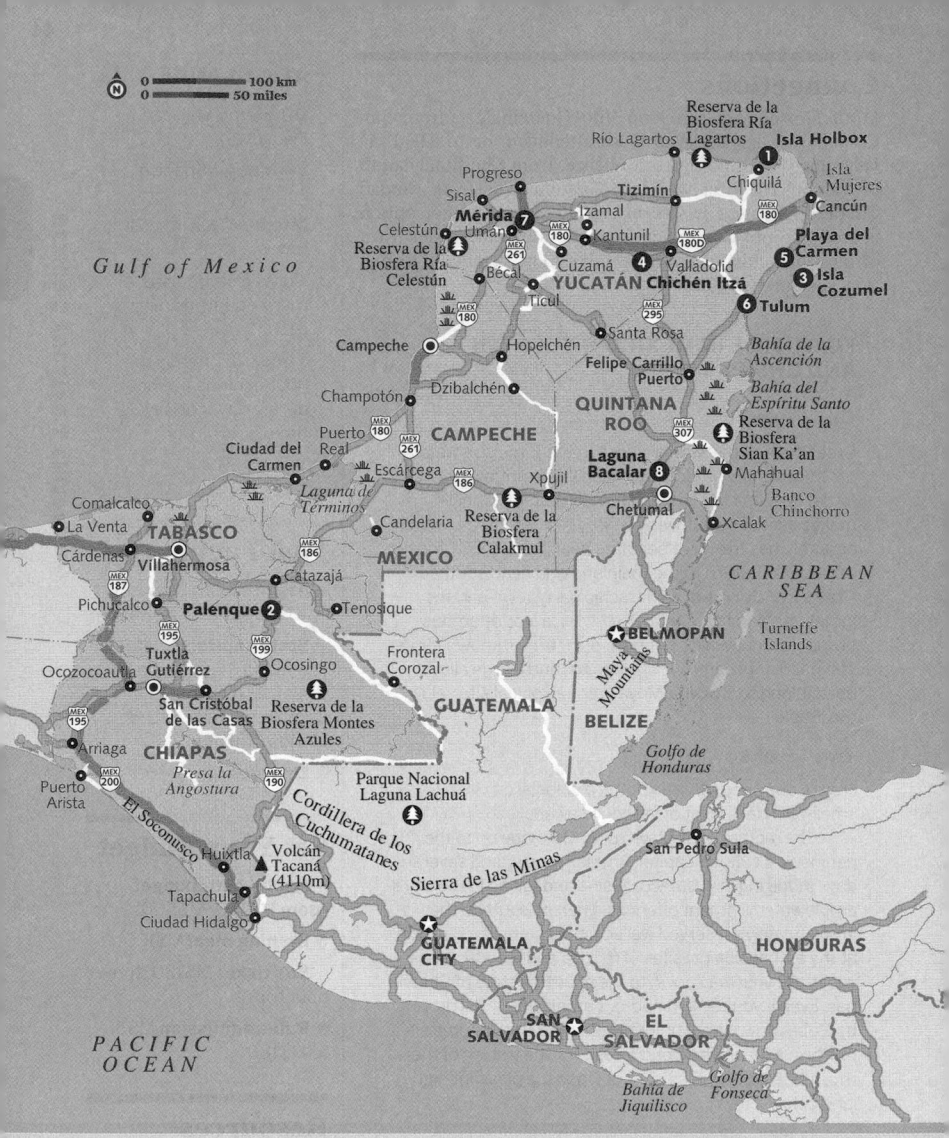

Mexico's Yucatán & Chiapas Highlights

1. Snorkel with massive whale sharks at **Isla Holbox** (p48)
2. Explore **Palenque's** (p80) astonishing jungle ruins
3. Immerse yourself in the colorful underwater world of **Isla Cozumel** (p63)
4. Marvel at **Chichén Itzá's** (p51) famed Maya ruins
5. Party in ultrachic beach town **Playa del Carmen** (p59)
6. Swim at oceanfront Maya ruins at **Tulum** (p65)
7. Delight in delicious regional cuisine in **Mérida** (p57)
8. Plunge into the deep blue at **Laguna Bacalar** (p65)

THE YUCATÁN

Chock-full of fun and thrilling surprises, the Yucatán is brimming with Maya ruins, postcard-perfect Caribbean beaches, old-world colonial cities, famed diving destinations and a host of natural wonders.

Cancún

998 / POP 628,300

Cancún is a tale of two cities. There's the glitzy Zona Hotelera with its famous white-sand beaches, unabashed party scene and sophisticated seafood restaurants. Then there's the actual city itself, which gives you a taste of local flavor at, say, a neighborhood bar or taco joint.

That's what keeps Cancún interesting. If you've had your fill of raucous discos in the Zona Hotelera, you can easily escape to a downtown salsa club. Or if you're tired of lounging around poolside in Ciudad Cancún, simply hop on a bus and head for the sapphire waters of the hotel zone.

Cancún also makes a great base to venture out to the islands of Holbox, Contoy and Mujeres.

Beaches

Under Mexican law, travelers have the right to walk and swim on every beach throughout the country, except those within military compounds. In practice, it is difficult to approach many stretches of beach without walking through a hotel lobby, particularly in the Zona Hotelera – just pretend you own the place. You'll find public access points to the beaches at Km 6.5, Km 9.5 and Km 18.

The most beautiful Caribbean-blue waters lie south of **Punta Cancún** (Km 9), however, be careful as the currents can be strong at times; Cancún's north-facing beaches are more swimmer-friendly. Many hotels in the Zona Hotelera rent snorkeling gear, body boards and kayaks.

Water Sports

Museo Subacuático de Arte DIVING, SNORKELING

(MUSA Underwater Museum; www.musacancun.com; snorkeling tour M$380, 1-tank dives M$700-1145) Built to divert divers away from deteriorating coral reefs, this one-of-a-kind aquatic museum features 403 life-size sculptures in the waters of Cancún and Isla Mujeres. Scuba Cancún does several tours to the sculpture gardens.

Scuba Cancún DIVING

(849-7508; www.scubacancun.com.mx; Blvd Kukulcán, Km 5.2; 1-/2-tank dives M$702/884, equipment rental extra) Family-owned operation offering snorkeling, fishing and dive excursions (including cenote and night dives).

Sights

Ruins

San Miguelito ARCHAEOLOGICAL SITE

(885-3842; Blvd Kukulcán Km 17; admission incl Museo Maya de Cancún M$57; R-1) Cancún's newest archaeological site contains more than a dozen restored Maya structures, including the 8m-high Gran Piramide (Grand Pyramid). The price of admission includes entry to the shiny new Museo Maya (Maya Museum).

Museo Maya de Cancún MUSEUM

(Maya Museum; www.inah.gob.mx; Blvd Kukulcán Km 17.5; admission incl San Miguelito M$57; 10am-7pm Tue-Sun; R-1) Housing one of the most important collections of Maya artifacts in Mexico, this new, modern museum is a welcome sight in a city known more for its party scene than cultural attractions. On display are some 350 pieces found at key sites in and around the peninsula.

Zona Arqueológica El Rey ARCHAEOLOGICAL SITE

(Blvd Kukulcán Km 17.5; admission M$42; 8am-5pm; R-1) In El Rey, on the west side of Blvd Kukulcán between Km 17 and Km 18, there's a small temple and several ceremonial platforms. The ruins here are compact and easy to explore but lack the wow factor of some of the bigger Maya sites around the region.

Yamil Lu'um ARCHAEOLOGICAL SITE

(off Blvd Kukulcán Km 12.5; R-1) FREE A weathered Maya temple sits atop a beachside knoll in the parklike grounds between the Park Royal and the Westin Lagunamar hotels. Visit via the hotels or approach it from the beach – there is no direct access from the boulevard.

Sleeping

The area around Parque de las Palapas has numerous hostels and other budget digs on offer.

Hostel Mundo Joven HOSTEL $

(898-2104; www.mundojovenhostels.com; Av Uxmal 25; dm/d incl breakfast from M$180/550; ; R-1) Common-area offerings at this

The Yucatán

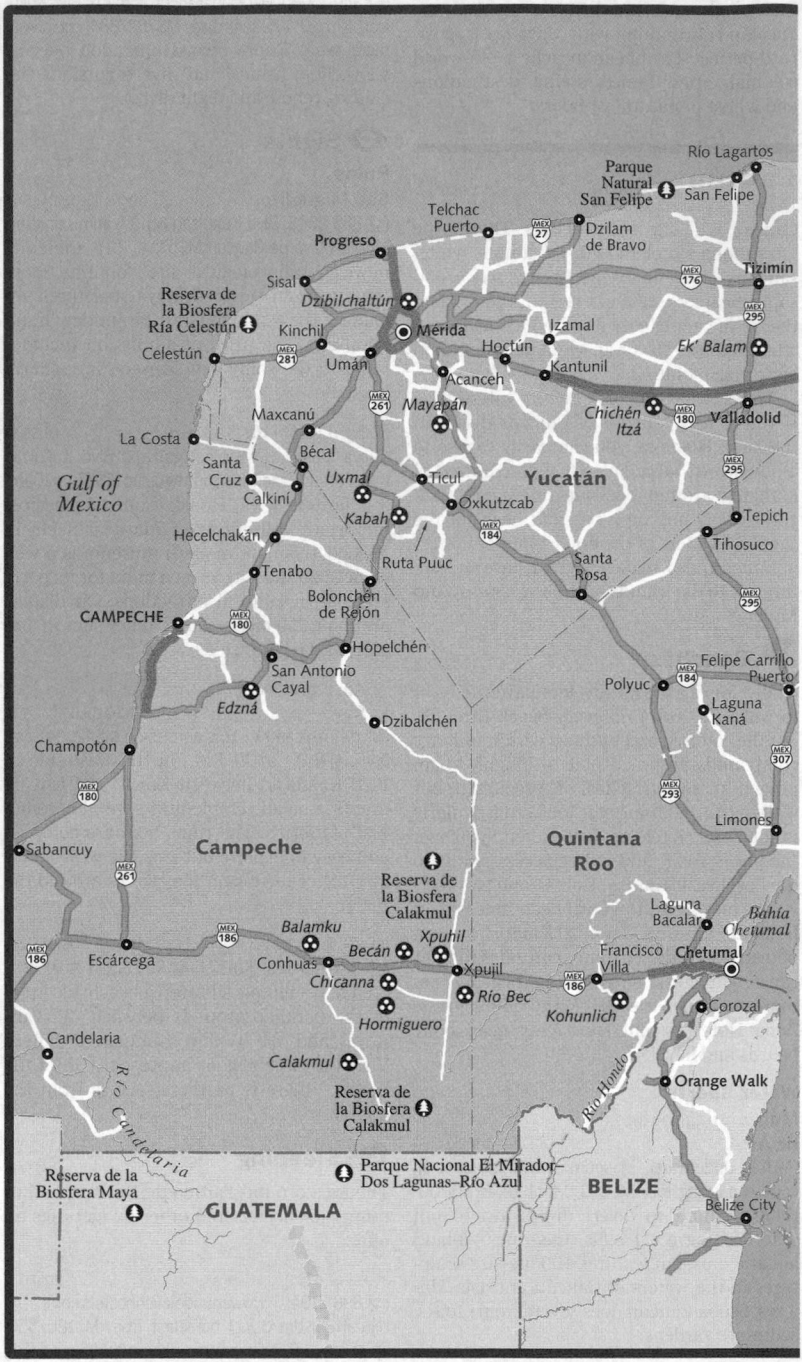
Río Lagartos
Parque Natural San Felipe
San Felipe
Telchac Puerto
MEX 27
Dzilam de Bravo
Progreso
Tizimín
MEX 176
Sisal
Dzibilchaltún
Reserva de la Biosfera Ría Celestún
Mérida
MEX 295
Kinchil
Izamal
Celestún
MEX 281
Umán
Hoctún
Ek' Balam
Kantunil
Acanceh
MEX 261
Mayapán
Chichén Itzá
MEX 180
Valladolid
Maxcanú
La Costa
Bécal
MEX 295
Santa Cruz
Uxmal
Ticul
Yucatán
Gulf of Mexico
Calkiní
Oxkutzcab
Kabah
Tepich
MEX 184
Hecelchakán
Tihosuco
Ruta Puuc
Santa Rosa
Tenabo
Bolonchén de Rejón
MEX 295
CAMPECHE
MEX 180
Hopelchén
San Antonio Cayal
Felipe Carrillo Puerto
MEX 184
Polyuc
Edzná
Laguna Kaná
Dzibalchén
Champotón
MEX 307
MEX 180
MEX 293
Limones
Sabancuy
Campeche
Quintana Roo
MEX 261
Reserva de la Biosfera Calakmul
Laguna Bacalar
Bahía Chetumal
MEX 186
Balamku
Xpuhil
MEX 186
Escárcega
Becán
Francisco Villa
Chetumal
Conhuas
Xpujil
Chicanna
Río Bec
MEX 186
Kohunlich
Corozal
Hormiguero
Candelaria
Calakmul
Río Hondo
Orange Walk
Río Candelaria
Reserva de la Biosfera Calakmul
Parque Nacional El Mirador–Dos Lagunas–Río Azul
Reserva de la Biosfera Maya
GUATEMALA
BELIZE
Belize City

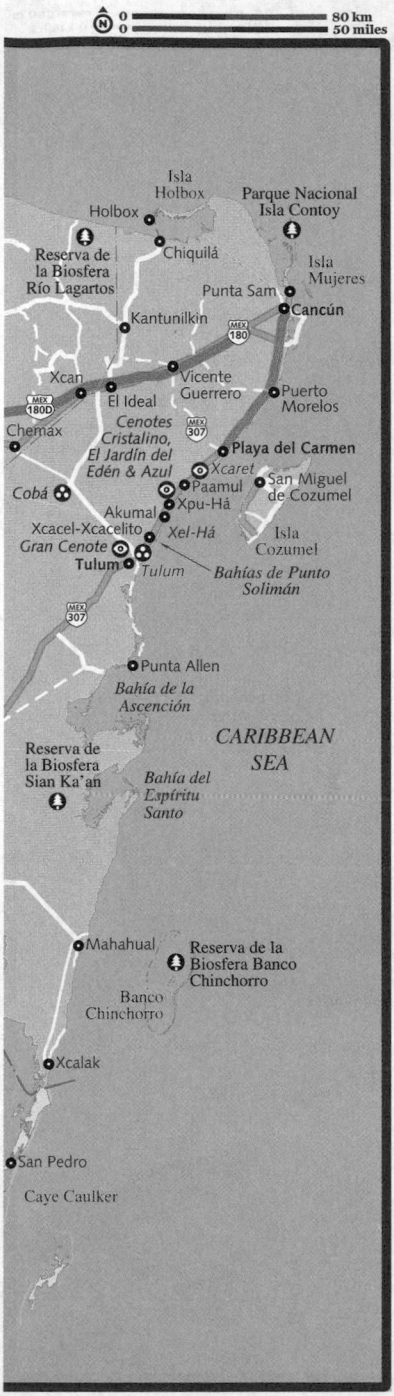

HI affiliate include a rooftop bar and hot tub. Need we say more? Dorm rooms are tidy and cost slightly more with air-conditioning. If you feel like living big, Mundo Joven has a private room with your very own Jacuzzi (M$750).

Hostal Mayapan HOSTEL $
(☎ 883-3227; www.hostalmayapan.com; Blvd Kukulcán Km 8.5; dm incl breakfast M$200-240, r M$600; ❄ @ 📶; 🚌 R-1) Located in an abandoned mall, this is the only budget spot in the Zona Hotelera. The dorms and private rooms are superclean and there's a little hangout spot in an atrium upstairs (the old food court?).

Hostel Ka'beh HOSTEL $
(☎ 892-7902; www.facebook.com/hostelkabeh; Alcatraces 45; dm incl breakfast from M$150; ❄ @ 📶; 🚌 R-1) A central option off the buzzing Parque de las Palapas, this small hostel has a lived-in feel (some might say cluttered), which goes hand-in-hand with the relaxed vibe. Expect many social activities at night, most organized around food and drink.

Soberanis Hotel HOTEL $$
(☎ 884-4564, 800-101-0101; www.soberanis.com.mx; Av Cobá 5; dm/d incl breakfast M$200/595; @ 📶; 🚌 R-1) Good value with a nice location and a fun place to meet friends. All rooms have very comfortable beds, cable TV and nicely appointed bathrooms. Though primarily a midrange hotel, the Soberanis also has four-bed 'hostel' rooms.

Eating

Cancún's downtown area has lots of good budget eats, many clustered in Mercados 23 and 28. For groceries, hit **Comercial Mexicana** (cnr Avs Tulum & Uxmal), a supermarket close to the bus terminal.

El Paisano del 23 MEXICAN $
(Mercado 23; tacos M$12, tortas M$30; ⏲ 6am-3pm; 🚌 R-1) A local favorite for more than 40 years, the *paisano* marinates *pierna* (pork leg) in red wine and slow-cooks it to perfection. The *tortas* (sandwiches) go fast on weekends.

Los de Pescado SEAFOOD $
(Av Tulum 32; tacos & tostadas M$24-26, ceviche M$78-117; ⏲ 9am-6:30pm; 🚌 R-27) Order ceviche or fish tacos along with a beer or two at one of downtown's best budget spots.

Cancún Centro

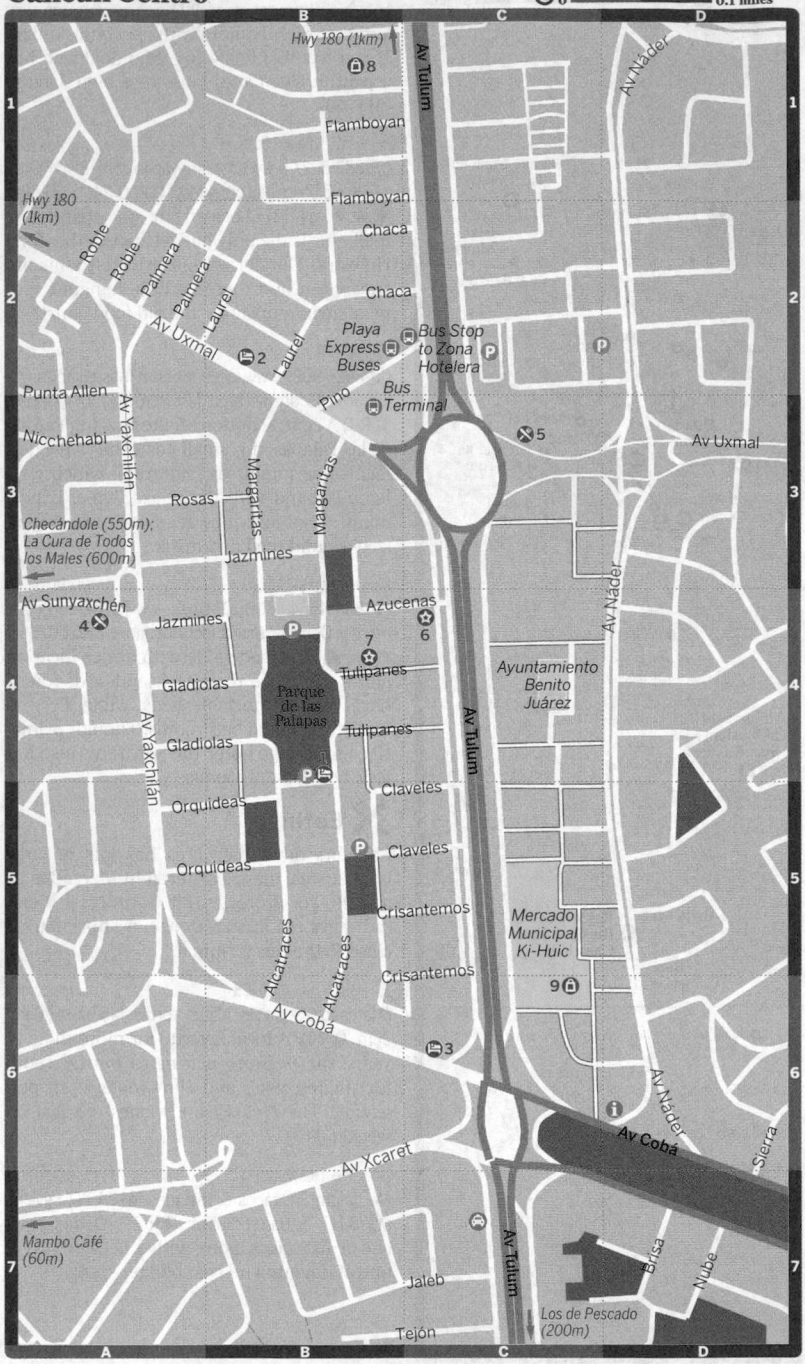

Cancún Centro

Sleeping
1 Hostel Ka'beh B4
2 Hostel Mundo Joven B2
3 Soberanis Hotel C6

Eating
4 100% Natural A4
5 Comercial Mexicana C3
El Paisano del 23 ..... (see 8)

Entertainment
6 Karamba C4
7 Roots B4

Shopping
8 Mercado 23 ..... B1
9 Mercado Municipal Ki-Huic C6

Surfin' Burrito FAST FOOD $
(Blvd Kukulcán Km 9.8; M$49-75; 24hrs; R-1) In the Zona Hotelera, where cheap eats come few and far between, this small burrito joint prepares beef, shrimp, fish and vegetarian burritos with a choice of tasty fixings.

★Checándole MEXICAN $$
(884-7147; Av Xpujil 6, cnr Av Tankah; mains M$59-128; noon-8pm Mon-Sat; R-2) If you can only eat at one restaurant in Cancún, you should eat here. The *menú del día* (fixed three-course meal) is just M$50 – great value.

100% Natural MEXICAN $$
(Cien Por Ciento Natural; 884-0102; www.100natural.com.mx; Av Sunyaxchén 62; mains M$64-136; 7am-11pm;) Vegetarians and health-food nuts delight at this health-food chain near Av Yaxchilán.

Drinking & Nightlife

Ciudad Cancún clubs are mellower than those in the rowdy Zona Hotelera, which often charge pricey open-bar covers. Downtown, stroll along Av Yaxchilán down to Parque de las Palapas and you are sure to run into something (or somebody) you like.

La Cura de Todos los Males BAR
(Mercado 28, Av Xel-Ha, cnr Erizo; 2pm-1am Mon-Sat, 6pm-1am Sun; R-2) Paying tribute to Mexican pop culture and all things retro, this hip *mezcal* bar draws a young, mostly local crowd.

Roots JAZZ
(884-2437; www.rootsjazzclub.com; Tulipanes 26; 7pm-2am Thu-Sat; R-1) Pretty much the coolest bar and best live music in Ciudad Cancún.

Mambo Café CLUB
(884-4536; www.mambocafe.com.mx; cnr Avs Xcaret & Tankah; 10:30pm-6am Wed-Sat; R-2) Shake your booty to groups playing Cuban salsa and other tropical styles.

Karamba GAY
(884-0032; www.karambabar.com; Av Tulum 9, cnr Azucenas; 10:30pm-6am Tue-Sun; R-1) Come here for a varied crowd of gays, lesbians and cross-dressers.

Coco Bongo CLUB
(883-5061; www.cocobongo.com.mx; Forum Mall, Blvd Kukulcán Km 9.5; 10pm-4am; R-1) A huge disco in the Zona Hotelera with a year-round spring-break-like party atmosphere.

Dady'O CLUB
(800-234-9797; Blvd Kukulcán Km 9.5; 10pm-4am; R-1) One of Cancún's more elaborate dance clubs. In the Zona Hotelera.

Shopping

Mercado 23 MARKET
(Av Tulum s/n; R-1) Locals head to Mercado 23 for clothes, shoes and inexpensive food stalls.

La Europea DRINK
(www.laeuropea.com.mx; Blvd Kukulcán Km 12.5; 10am-9pm Mon-Sat, 11am-6pm Sun; R-1) Reasonable prices, knowledgeable staff and hands down the best liquor selection in Cancún. Salud!

Mercado Municipal Ki-Huic MARKET
(Av Tulum; R-1) This warren of stalls and shops carries a wide variety of souvenirs and handicrafts.

Information

Cancún's Zona Hotelera, home to the resorts and beaches, is set along Blvd Kukulcán, which curves around an L-shaped sandy spit (actually an island). Ciudad Cancún, just west, is home to *el centro* (downtown). Internet cafes in downtown Cancún are plentiful, speedy and cheap. There are several banks with ATMs on Av Tulum, between Avs Cobá and Uxmal. Cancún's Visitors Bureau has an informative website, www.cancun.travel.

City Tourism Office (887-3379; www.cancun.gob.mx; Av Náder s/n, cnr Av Cobá; 8am-4pm Mon-Fri, 9am-12:30pm Sat)

Hospital Playa Med (140-5258; Av Náder 13, cnr Av Uxmal; 24hr; R-1) Modern medical facility with 24-hour assistance.

WORTH A TRIP

ESCAPE FROM CANCÚN

Here are two wonderful low-key island getaways near Cancún:

➡ **Parque Nacional Isla Contoy** A bird-watcher's paradise, this uninhabited island is only accessible via a tour, receives just 200 visitors a day and makes for a great side trip from Cancún. **Asterix** (☎886-4270; www.contoytours.com; Blvd Kukulcán Km 5.2; adult/child 5-11yr M$1300/750; ⏲tours 9am-7pm Tue, Thu & Sat) offers tours departing from the Marina Scuba Cancún in the Zona Hotelera; they include guide, breakfast, lunch, open bar and snorkeling gear.

➡ **Isla Holbox** Swimminig with whale sharks (from mid-May to mid-September) is all the rage these days and you really can't beat the island's mellow vibe if you just want a place to chill for several days. **Hostel Tribu** (☎875-2507; www.tribuhostel.com; Av Pedro Joaquín Coldwell; dm/r M$150/400; ❄📶) is your best budget bet, or try **Hostel Ida y Vuelta** (☎875-2358; www.holboxhostel.com; Av Paseo Kuka; campsites & hammocks M$80, dm M$100, bungalows M$390, house with kitchen M$500; 📶). Ferries headed to Isla Holbox depart frequently from Chiquilá. Chiquilá-bound buses (M$86) leave from the Cancún bus terminal at 7:50am and 12:40pm.

Main Post Office (☎884-1418; cnr Avs Xel-Há & Sunyaxchén; ⏲8am-6pm Mon-Fri, 9am-1pm Sat)
Tourist Police (☎885-2277)

Getting There & Away

See p50 for details on getting to Isla Mujeres.

AIR

Aeropuerto Internacional de Cancún (☎848-7200; www.asur.com.mx; Carretera Cancún-Chetumal Km 22) About 8km south of the city center.

BUS

The **bus terminal** (cnr Avs Uxmal & Tulum) offers 1st- and 2nd-class service and it's within walking distance of most downtown accommodations. Across from the bus terminal, a few doors from Av Tulum, is the ticket office and miniterminal of **Playa Express** (Calle Pino). It runs shuttle buses down the Caribbean coast to Tulum approximately every 30 minutes until early evening.

DESTINATION	COST (M$)	DURATION (HR)
Chetumal (to Belize)	302-362	5½-6
Chichén Itzá	119-194	3-4
Mérida	180-490	4-7
Mexico City	1536-1788	24-26
Palenque	684-816	12-13½
Playa del Carmen	34-45	1-1¼
Tulum	80-104	2½-3
Valladolid	150-158	2-3

Getting Around

ADO (☎800-009-9090; www.ado.com.mx) buses to Ciudad Cancún (M$52) leave the airport every 30 minutes between 8:15am and 11pm. They depart from a parking lot next to the international arrivals terminal in the Aeropuerto Internacional de Cancún.

Once in town, the buses travel up Av Tulum and will stop most anywhere you ask. Going to the airport from Ciudad Cancún, the same ADO airport buses (Aeropuerto Centro) leave regularly from the bus terminal.

Yellow Transfers (☎800-021-8087; www.yellowtransfers.com), with ticket booths in each airport terminal, runs shuttles to and from Ciudad Cancún and the Zona Hotelera for M$160 per person.

Colectivos (shared taxis) head to the airport from a stand in front of the Hotel Cancún Handall on Av Tulum, about a block south of Av Cobá. These operate from 2am to 3pm (hours may vary), charge M$40 per person and they leave when full. Private taxis to the airport from town charge M$170.

Cab rides within the Zona Hotelera or downtown area cost around M$25 to M$50.

For city bus service, to reach the Zona Hotelera from downtown catch any bus displaying signs with 'R1,' 'Hoteles' or 'Zona Hotelera' as they travel along Av Tulum toward Av Cobá, then eastward on Av Cobá. The one-way fare is M$8.50.

To reach Puerto Juárez and the Isla Mujeres ferries, hop on a Ruta 13 ('Pto Juárez' or 'Punta Sam') bus heading north on Av Tulum. Some R1 buses make the trip as well.

Isla Mujeres

☎998 / POP 12,600

If you are going to visit just one of Quintana Roo's islands, consider Isla Mujeres. It's not too crowded and has plenty to see and do. Sure, there's quite a few ticky-tack tourist shops, but folks still get around by golf cart and the crushed-coral beaches are sublime.

The name Isla Mujeres (Island of Women) goes at least as far back as Spanish buccaneers, who (legend has it) kept their lovers in safe seclusion here. Archaeologists say a more plausible explanation is that the island was a stopover for the Maya en route to worship their goddess of fertility, Ixchel, on Isla Cozumel.

Sights

Isla Mujeres Turtle Farm FARM

(Isla Mujeres Tortugranja; ☎888-0705; Carretera Sac Bajo Km 5; admission M$30; ⏲9am-5pm; 👪) For a change of scenery, head south from town to Isla Mujeres Tortugranja. The sanctuary, which liberates tens of thousands of the little guys each year, has pools and protected shores for turtles and their eggs.

Punta Sur LOOKOUT/GARDEN

(ruins admission M$30) The dramatic Punta Sur, at the southern tip of the island (8km from town), has a romantic lighthouse and a severely weather-beaten Maya ruin.

Activities

Swimming

The best swimming on the island is conveniently found in town at **Playa Norte** (North Beach; northwest to be precise). The lagoon separating the Avalon Reef Club from the rest of the island has a great shallow swimming spot known as **Yunque Reef**.

Diving & Snorkeling

Within a short boat ride of the island there's a handful of lovely dives, such as Ultrafreeze and Manchones. You can expect to see sea turtles, rays and barracuda, along with a wide array of hard and soft corals.

Snorkeling with whale sharks (M$1500, from mid-May to September) is the latest craze. Folks at the following dive shops offer various diving and snorkeling outings.

Aqua Adventures DIVING

(☎cell 998-236-4516; www.diveislamujeres.com; Av Juárez, cnr Morelos; 1-/2-tank dives M$850/1100, whale-shark tour M$1500; ⏲9am-7pm) Great option for snorkeling with whale sharks and reef dives.

Mundaca Divers DIVING

(☎999-2071; www.mundacadiversisla.com; Zazil Ha s/n, at Avalon Reef Club; 1-/2-tank dives M$650/800, snorkeling tours M$455-585) Does everything from shark-cave dives to snorkeling trips at unique underwater sculpture museum, MUSA (p43).

Fisherman's Cooperative Booth TOUR

(☎877-1363; Av Rueda Medina, cnr Madero; snorkeling incl lunch M$330-450; ⏲8am-5pm) You can get reasonably priced snorkeling trips at the Fisherman's Cooperative booth in a *palapa* (shelter with a thatched, palm-leaf roof and open sides) near the gas station. Its boats also go to Isla Contoy (M$750) from 9am to 3pm.

Hotel Garrafón de Castilla SNORKELING

(☎877-0107; Carretera Punta Sur Km 6; admission M$50; ⏲9am-5pm) About 7km south of town, the beach club at Hotel Garrafón de Castilla provides a pleasant spot to do some snorkeling and it's relatively affordable as well, especially if you bring your own gear.

Sleeping

★Poc-Na Hostel HOSTEL $

(☎877-0090; www.pocna.com; Matamoros 15; dm with fan/air-con M$115/175, r with/without bathroom & air-con M$300/400; ❄📶) Moments away from one of the island's nicest beaches and decorated with shells and hibiscus flowers, Mexico's oldest youth hostel also ranks among the country's best.

Apartments Trinchan APARTMENT $

(☎cell 998-166-6967; atrinchan@prodigy.net.mx; Carlos Lazo 46; r M$400-450, apt M$450-500; ❄📶) Since it has no website, you'll have to take our word for it when we say this is one of the best budget-deal outfits in town – and the beach is right around the corner.

Hotel D'Gomar HOTEL $

(☎877-0541; Av Rueda Medina 150; d from M$500; ❄📶) A friendly, old-school place facing the ferry dock, this has four floors of well-maintained rooms with double beds, minibars and cable TV. The mirror in the stairway gives warped, funhouse-style reflections as you head to your room.

Eating

★Mañana CAFE $
(☎877-0555; cnr Matamoros & Guerrero; dishes M$40-85; ⏲8am-4pm;) A good-vibe place with colorful hand-painted tables, super-friendly service and some excellent veggie options.

Mercado Municipal MARKET $
(Guerrero; ⏲6am-4pm) Outside the remodeled market are several stalls selling regional food at low prices (M$30 to M$70).

Pita Amore MEDITERRANEAN $
(Guerrero; sandwiches M$35-45; ⏲12:30-10pm Mon-Sat;) This unassuming shack does just three varieties of pita sandwiches and does them extremely well. The chicken, beef and vegetarian pitas are the creation of a New York Culinary Institute alum.

Mininos SEAFOOD $$
(Av Rueda Medina; mains M$70-150; ⏲noon-9pm) A tiny, colorfully painted shack with a sand floor, right by the water. It's the best of the seafood joints along this strip and there's marimba music to boot.

Olivia MEDITERRANEAN $$
(☎877-1765; www.olivia-isla-mujeres.com; Matamoros; mains M$88-180; ⏲5-9:30pm Tue-Sat) This delightful, Israeli-run restaurant makes everything from scratch, from Moroccan-style fish to chicken shawarmas.

Drinking & Nightlife

Isla Mujeres' highest concentration of nightlife is along Calle Hidalgo.

Fenix Lounge BAR
(☎274-0073; www.fenixisla.com; Zazil-Ha; ⏲11am-midnight Tue-Sun;) Catch DJ sessions or live reggae, salsa and jazz acts here at this waterfront lounge bar.

Poc-Na Hostel BAR
(www.pocna.com; Matamoros 15; ⏲11pm-3am Mon-Sat;) A popular beachside joint with bonfires and booze to bring out your inner pagan.

Information

HSBC Bank (Av Rueda Medina, cnr Morelos)
Internet Cafe (cnr Matamoros & Guerrero; per hr M$10; ⏲9am-10pm Mon-Sat)
Medical Center (Guerrero btwn Madero & Morelos)
Police (☎877-0082)
Post Office (☎877-0085; cnr Guerrero & López Mateos; ⏲9am-4pm Mon-Fri)
Tourist Information Office (☎877-0767; Av Rueda Medina; ⏲8am-8pm Mon-Fri, 9am-2pm Sat & Sun)

Getting There & Away

There are several points of embarkation to reach Isla Mujeres from Cancún by boat. Ferries from Puerto Juárez (M$70 one way; 4km north of Ciudad Cancún) depart frequently; departures are less frequent from the Zona Hotelera and more expensive, ranging from M$110 to M$140. For more information, see www.granpuerto.com.mx.

The R1 'Ultramar' bus, which runs along Av Tulum and Blvd Kukulcán, serves all Zona Hotelera docks and Puerto Juárez.

Getting Around

A number of shops rent bikes, scooters and golf carts.

Local buses depart about every 25 minutes from the ferry dock and head along Av Rueda Medina, stopping along the way. Taxi rates are set by the municipal government and posted at the taxi stand just south of the passenger ferry dock.

Fiesta (Av Reuda Medina btwn Morelos & Bravo; per hour/day M$30/100; ⏲8am-5pm) Has mountain bikes and beach cruisers.
Gomar (☎877-1686; Av Rueda Medina, cnr Bravo; golf carts per hour/day M$180/600, scooter M$250 per day) For golf carts and scooters.

Valladolid

☎985 / POP 49,000

Also known as the Sultaness of the East, Yucatán's third-largest city is known for its quiet streets and sun-splashed, pastel walls. It certainly is sultry, and it's worth staying here for a few days or even a week, as the provincial town makes a great hub for visits to Río Lagartos, Chichén Itzá, Ek' Balam, and a number of nearby cenotes.

Sights & Activities

Templo de San Bernardino & Convento de Sisal CHURCH
(Church of San Bernardino; cnr Calles 49 & 51; convent admission M$30; ⏲9am-6pm Mon-Fri, to 3pm Sat) About 700m southwest of the plaza, these buildings were constructed between 1552 and 1560 to serve the dual functions of fortress and church. The church's decoration includes beautiful rose-colored walls, arches and some 16th-century frescoes.

Museo de San Roque MUSEUM
(Calle 41; ⏲8am-8pm Mon-Fri, 9am-6pm Sat & Sun) FREE A small museum with models and exhibits on the history of the city and the region. Between Calles 38 and 40.

Cenote Zací SWIMMING
(www.cenotezaci.com.mx; Calle 36; admission M$15; ⏲7am-6pm) There are prettier cenotes on the outskirts of town, but Zací is worth visiting nonetheless.

Cenote Dzitnup SWIMMING
(Xkekén & Samulá; admission M$56; ⏲8am-5pm) A massive limestone formation with stalactites hanging from the ceiling, this is an impressive swimming hole, though it could certainly do without the artificial lighting. It's 7km west of the plaza.

Cenote Samulá SWIMMING
(admission M$56; ⏲8am-5pm) Take a dip at this lovely cavern pool with *álamo* (poplar) roots stretching down the walls. To get here, hire a taxi, rent a bike from **Rudy Tours** (☎985-113-1565, 856-2026; Calle 40, btwn Calles 37 & 39; tours M$250, bike rental per hr M$20), or catch a shared van departing from the corner of Calles 41 and 44 for M$20.

Sleeping & Eating

La Aurora HOTEL $
(☎856-1219; www.hotelcoloniallaaurora.blogspot.mx; Calle 42 No 192; s/d/tr M$420/490/570; P ❄ 📶) If only more budget hotels were like the colonial-style Aurora. Well-appointed rooms overlook a pretty courtyard with a pool and potted plants. At last visit the hotel was installing a rooftop hot tub. Avoid the noisier street-facing rooms.

Hostel La Candelaria HOSTEL $
(☎856-2267; www.hostelvalladolidyucatan.com; Calle 35 No 201F; dm/r incl breakfast M$120/330; @ 📶) A friendly place right on a quiet little square, this hostel can get a little cramped and hot, but there are two kitchens, a cozy garden area complete with hammocks, a female-only dorm, and plenty of hangout space.

★Conato 1910 MEXICAN $
(Calle 40 No 226; mains M$50-80; ⏲5pm-midnight Wed-Mon; ✎) Once a meeting spot for revolutionaires in the early 20th century, this historic building now houses an atmospheric restaurant with a vegetarian-friendly menu.

Bazar Municipal MARKET $
(cnr Calles 39 & 40; breakfast M$30-50; ⏲6am-10pm) This place at the plaza's northeastern corner is a collection of market-style shops, popular for big, cheap breakfasts.

Getting There & Away

The main **bus station** (cnr Calles 39 & 46) is two blocks west of the plaza. Frequent buses go to Cancún (M$90 to M$150, two to three hours), Mérida (M$90 to M$150, two to three hours) and Chichén Itzá (M$23 to M$62, 45 minutes).

Colectivos for Pisté and Chichén Itzá (M$23, 40 minutes) leave just north of the ADO bus terminal, and for Tizimín (M$30, 40 minutes) from Calle 40, beween Calles 35 and 37. *Colectivos* for Ek' Balam (M$40) leave from Calle 44, between Calles 35 and 37.

Chichén Itzá

The most famous and best restored of the Yucatán Maya sites, **Chichén Itzá** (Mouth of the Well of the Itzáes; off Hwy 180, Pisté; admission M$182, parking M$22, sound & light show M$75, guide M$600; ⏲8am-6pm Apr-Sep, to 5:30pm Oct-Mar), while tremendously overcrowded – every gawker and their grandmother is trying to check off the new seven wonders of the world – will still impress even the most jaded visitor. Many mysteries of the Maya astronomical calendar are made clear when one understands the design of the 'time temples' here.

Chichén Itzá was a modest late-Classic town before war-torn Toltecs from Tula, in central Mexico, conquered it in AD 987. An unlikely harmony followed, with experienced Maya architects masterfully adhering to the imagery of the Toltec feathered-serpent cult of Quetzalcóatl (Kukulcán in Maya). The city was abandoned around 1224.

To explore the site, start from the **Great Plaza**, about 100m beyond the gate. In the middle, the imposing **El Castillo** (The Castle) pyramid is designed to represent the Maya calendar in stone. The four stairways have 91 steps each; add the top platform and the total is 365, the number of days in the year. It's also famous for the moving serpent illusion on its staircase, visible during the spring and autumn equinoxes. Inside the pyramid is a pre-Toltec pyramid with a red jaguar throne, reached by a sweatbox chamber – now closed.

Chichén Itzá

It doesn't take long to realize why the Maya site of Chichén Itzá is one of Mexico's most popular tourist draws. Approaching the grounds from the main entrance, the striking castle pyramid **El Castillo** 1 jumps right out at you – and the wow factor never lets up.

It's easy to tackle Chichén Itzá in one day. Within a stone's throw of the castle, you'll find the Maya world's largest **ball court** 2 alongside eerie carvings of skulls and heart-devouring eagles at the Temple of Jaguars and the Platform of Skulls. On the other (eastern) side are the highly adorned **Group of a Thousand Columns** 3 and the **Temple of Warriors** 4. A short walk north of the castle leads to the gaping **Sacred Cenote** 5, an important pilgrimage site. On the other side of El Castillo, you'll find giant stone serpents watching over the High Priest's Grave, aka El Osario. Further south, marvel at the spiral-domed **Observatory** 6, the imposing Nunnery and Akab-Dzib, one of the oldest ruins.

Roaming the 47-hectare site, it's fun to consider that at its height Chichén Itzá was home to an estimated 90,000 inhabitants and spanned approximately 30 sq km. So essentially you're looking at just a small part of a once-great city.

THE LOWDOWN

» **Arrive** at 8am and you'll have a good three hours or so before the tour-bus madness begins. Early birds escape the merchants, too.

» **Remember** that Chichén Itzá is the name of the site; the actual town where it's located is called Pisté.

ADINA TOVY/GETTY IMAGES ©

El Caracol
Observatory
Today they'd probably just use a website, but back in the day priests would stand from the dome of the circular observatory to announce the latest rituals and celebrations.

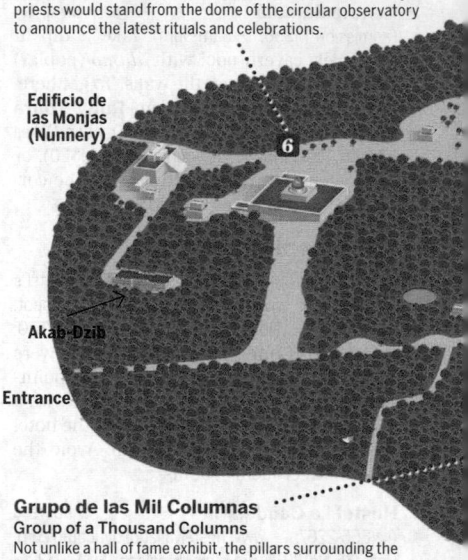

Grupo de las Mil Columnas
Group of a Thousand Columns
Not unlike a hall of fame exhibit, the pillars surrounding the temple reveal carvings of gods, dignitaries and celebrated warriors.

ROSS BARNETT/GETTY IMAGES ©

LONELY PLANET/GETTY IMAGES ©

El Castillo

The Castle

Even this mighty pyramid can't bear the stress of a million visitors ascending its stairs each year. No climbing allowed, but the ground-level view doesn't disappant.

AFP/GETTY IMAGES ©

Gran Juego de Pelota

Great Ball Court

How is it possible to hear someone talk from one end of this long, open-air court to the other? To this day, the acoustics remain a mystery.

Entrance

Parking Lot

Visitors Center

Templo de los Jaguares (Temple of Jaguars)

Tumba del Gran Sacerdote (High Priest's Grave)

1

2

3

4

5

Plataforma de los Cráneos (Platform of Skulls)

Cenote Sagrado

Sacred Cenote

Diving expeditions have turned up hundreds of valuable artifacts dredged from the cenote (limestone sinkhole), not to mention human bones of sacrificial victims who were forced to jump into the eternal underworld.

Templo de los Guerreros

Temple of Warriors

The Maya associated warriors with eagles and jaguars, as depicted in the temple's friezes. The revered jaguar, in particular, was a symbol of strength and agility.

EDUCATION IMAGES/UIG/GETTY IMAGES ©

JUAN CARLOS MUNOZ/GETTY IMAGES ©

Just northeast (back to the left as you enter the plaza) is the **Gran Juego de Pelota**, the biggest ball court in Mesoamerica. The acoustics are terrific: try chatting with a friend on opposite sides.

Across the plaza from El Castillo is a 300m path north to **Cenote Sagrado** (Sacred Cenote), where sacrificial victims were forced to plunge into the underworld.

Back in the plaza, on the eastern end, stands the impressive **Templo de los Guerreros** (Temple of the Warriors), with a reclining *chac-mool* (Maya sacrificial stone sculpture) at the top of the temple looking over the warrior-carved columns. Behind is the shady **Grupo de las Mil Columnas** (Group of a Thousand Columns). Beyond, a path leads through the forest past the **Mercado** (Market), with a sunken courtyard rimmed by columns.

The path leads past a replica of a **traditional home**, then another goes a few hundred meters south to the unusual **Caracol** (Snail), once used as an observatory. Just beyond is the **Edificio de las Monjas** (Nunnery).

Getting There & Away

Oriente has ticket offices near the east and west sides of Pisté, the nearest town to the Chichén Itzá site. Most 2nd-class buses passing through town stop almost anywhere along the way; 1st-class buses usually make stops at the ruins and the west side of town, close to the toll highway.

Oriente's 2nd-class buses pass through Pisté bound for Mérida (M$64, 2½ hours, hourly), Valladolid nine times daily (M$22, 50 minutes) and Cancún seven times daily (M$115, 4½ hours). There's also one daily 2nd-class bus to Tulum (M$85, three hours), Playa del Carmen (M$123, four hours) and Cobá (M$58, two hours).

First-class buses serve Mérida (M$120, 1¾ hours, 5:15pm), Cancún (M$202, three hours, 4:30pm) and Tulum (M$148, 2½ hours, 8:25am and 4:30pm).

Shared vans to Valladolid (M$20, 40 minutes) pass through town regularly.

Mérida

☎999 / POP 830,700

Since the Conquest, Mérida has been the cultural capital of the entire peninsula. At times provincial, at others very cosmopolitan, it is a town steeped in colonial history, with narrow streets, broad central plazas, and the region's best museums. It's also a perfect hub city to explore the rest of Yucatán state. There are cheap eats, good hostels and hotels, thriving markets, and goings-on just about every night in the downtown area.

Sights

Try coordinating your visit to Mérida on Sunday for the weekly food and crafts market on the main square, Plaza Grande.

Plaza Grande PLAZA

Plaza Grande is rimmed by Mérida's main historic buildings, most built from disassembled Maya pyramids.

Catedral de San Ildefonso CATHEDRAL

(Calle 60 s/n; ⏲6am-1pm & 4-7pm) The most obvious of Mérida's historic buildings are the 42m towers of the Catedral de San Ildefonso (Mesoamerica's oldest cathedral, dating from 1598) – much of its interior was destroyed during the Mexican Revolution (1910–29).

Casa de Montejo MUSEUM

(Museo Casa Montejo; www.casasdeculturabanamex.com/museocasamontejo; Calle 63 No 506, Palacio de Montejo; ⏲10am-7pm Tue-Sat, 10am-2pm Sun) FREE At the south end of Plaza Grande, Casa de Montejo is the home of the founding conquistadors. Dating from 1549, it now houses a museum with Victorian, neo-recoco and neo-renaissance furnishings on display.

Palacio de Gobierno PUBLIC ART

(Calle 61; ⏲8am-9.30pm) FREE Go past the guards at the 1892 Palacio del Gobierno, facing the plaza's northeast corner, to see Fernando Castro Pacheco's impressive wall-sized murals upstairs.

Iglesia de Jesús CHURCH

(Calle 60) Just beyond shady Parque Hidalgo rises the 17th-century Iglesia de Jesús, also called Iglesia de la Tercera Orden. Built by Jesuits in 1618, this is the sole surviving edifice from a complex of buildings that once filled the entire city block. The church was built from the stones of a destroyed Maya temple that once occupied the same site. On the west wall facing Parque Hidalgo, look closely and you can see two stones still bearing Maya carvings.

Mercado Municipal Lucas de Gálvez MARKET

(cnr Calles 56A & 67) Mérida's main market is an ever-evolving mass of commerce, with stalls selling everything from *panuchos* (fried tortillas stuffed with beans and topped with meat and veggies) to ponchos.

The surrounding streets are all part of the large market district.

Museo Regional de Antropología MUSEUM
(Regional Anthropology Museum of the Yucatán; ☎923-0557; www.palaciocanton.inah.gob.mx; Paseo de Montejo No 485; admission M$46; ⏲8am-5pm Tue-Sun) Nine blocks north of the plaza and housed in the ornate Palacio Cantón, this great museum explains why the Maya deformed their children's skulls, plus it displays jewelry, carvings and artifacts (with explanations in English).

Gran Museo del Mundo Maya MUSEUM
(www.granmuseodelmundomaya.com; Calle 60 Nte No 299E; adult/child under 12yr M$150/50; ⏲8am-5pm Wed-Mon) A new Maya-themed museum showcasing a permanent exhibit of 500 artifacts ranging from stone sculptures and jewelry to ceramics and etchings. It's divided into six sections: ancient Maya, modern Maya, culture and nature, art and science, society, and cosmovision. It's about 12km north of downtown. Buses departing from Calle 58, between Calles 57 and 59, head to the Gran Plaza mall, which is a short walk to the museum.

Sleeping

★Nómadas Hostel HOSTEL $
(☎924-5223; www.nomadastravel.com; Calle 62 No 433; dm incl breakfast M$129, d incl breakfast with/without bathroom M$420/320; P @ ❄ ≈) This is Mérida's backpackers' central, and the best hostel in the city. There are mixed and women's dorms, as well as private rooms. It even has free salsa classes and an amazing pool out back.

Hostel Zocalo HOSTEL $
(☎930-9562; hostal_zocalo@yahoo.com.mx; Calle 63 No 508; dm incl breakfast M$100, r incl breakfast with/without bathroom M$330/280; @ ❄) A great location and a beautiful old colonial building make this hostel unique. It has firm beds, and a big buffet breakfast is included. You may have problems getting hot water.

Hotel Santa Lucía HOTEL $
(☎928-2672; www.hotelsantalucia.com.mx; Calle 55 No 508; s/d/tr M$410/490/550; P ❄ ❄ ≈) Across from the park of the same name, this centrally located hotel is clean, secure and popular, and has an attractive lobby. The pool is small but clean, and the rooms have TV, phone and so-so beds. Someone here really likes potted plants.

Álvarez Family Guest House GUESTHOUSE $
(☎924-3060; www.casaalvarezguesthouse.com; Calle 62 No 448 btwn Calles 51 & 53; d with fan/aircon M$500/600, ste M$700; P ❄ ❄ ≈) Impeccably clean and in a family home, this 'hostel plus' offers a friendly, one-of-the-family ambiance, nice showers, spotless bathrooms and in-room fridges.

Casa Ana B&B B&B $
(☎934-0005; www.casaana.com; Calle 52 No 469; r incl breakfast from M$520; ❄ ❄ ≈) Though out of the way, Casa Ana is an intimate escape and the best budget B&B in town. It features a nice pool surrounded by an overgrown garden complete with Cuban tobacco plants (memories of home for the Cuban owners).

★Luz en Yucatán BOUTIQUE HOTEL $$
(☎924-0035; www.luzenyucatan.com; Calle 55 No 499; r M$700-850, house M$1800; P ❄ ❄ ≈) For

LOCAL KNOWLEDGE

QUICK TRIPS FROM MÉRIDA

We asked a local in the know where to go for the best quick trips out of Mérida. For more tips, check out www.redecoturismo.com.mx or www.yucatantoday.com.

➡ **Celestún** For an amazing bird-watching tour, head to this coastal biosphere reserve, where flamingos and other waterfowl abound.

➡ **Cuzamá** A horse-drawn railcart takes you to spectacular cenotes with ethereal shafts of light beaming down into deep blue water.

➡ **Dzibilchaltún and Progreso** En route to the coastal town of Progreso, stop at the Maya ruins of Dzibilchaltún and take a refreshing dip in a 40m-deep cenote.

➡ **Uxmal and Ruta Puuc** First hit Uxmal, one of the Maya world's finest sites, then check out less-visited ruins in the rolling hills of the Ruta Puuc. Cap off the trip exploring **Loltún**, one of the peninsula's largest dry cave systems.

Mérida

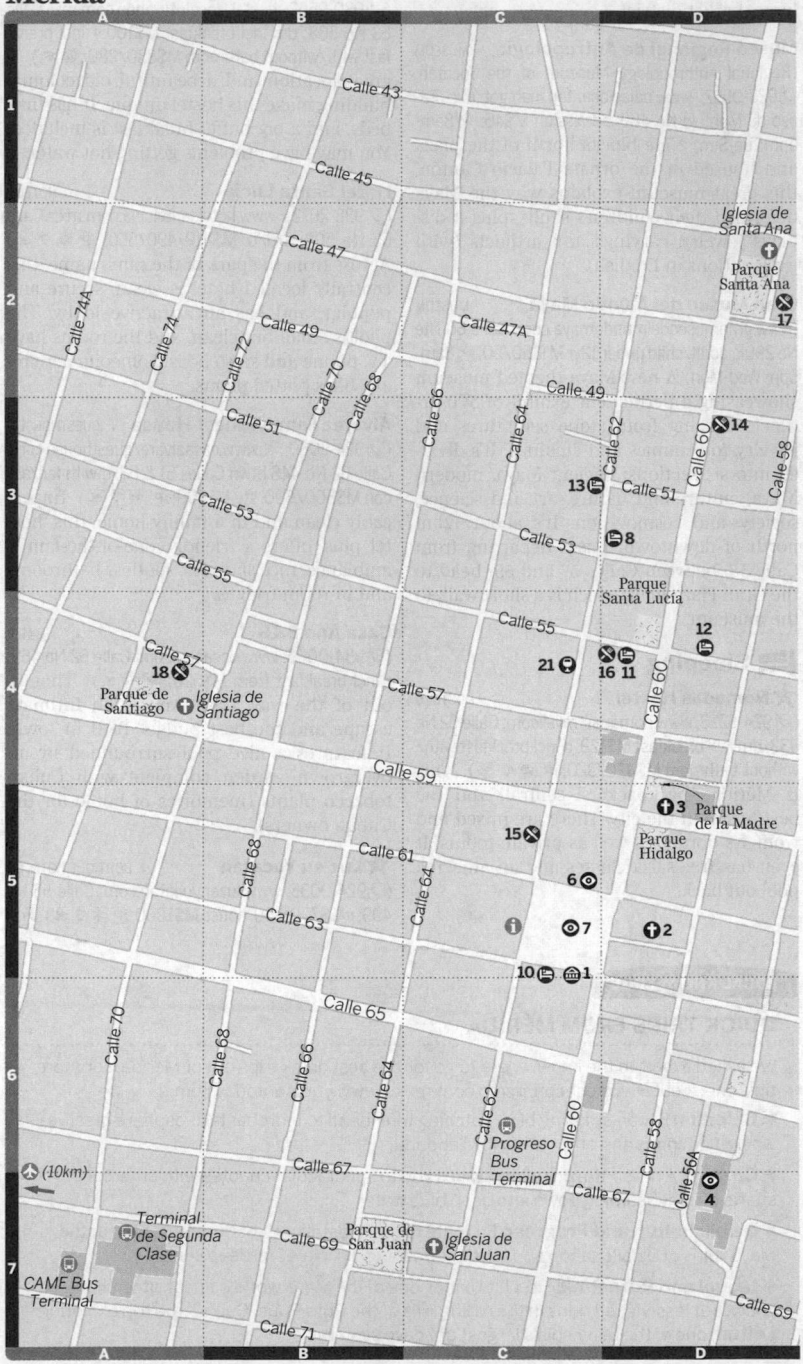
A
B
C
D
1
2
3
4
5
6
7
Calle 43
Calle 45
Calle 47
Calle 49
Calle 51
Calle 53
Calle 55
Calle 57
Calle 59
Calle 61
Calle 63
Calle 65
Calle 67
Calle 69
Calle 71
Calle 74A
Calle 74
Calle 72
Calle 70
Calle 68
Calle 66
Calle 64
Calle 62
Calle 60
Calle 58
Calle 56A
Calle 47A
Iglesia de Santa Ana
Parque Santa Ana
Parque Santa Lucía
Parque de Santiago
Iglesia de Santiago
Parque de la Madre
Parque Hidalgo
Progreso Bus Terminal
(10km)
Terminal de Segunda Clase
CAME Bus Terminal
Parque de San Juan
Iglesia de San Juan
1
2
3
4
6
7
8
10
11
12
13
14
15
16
17
18
21

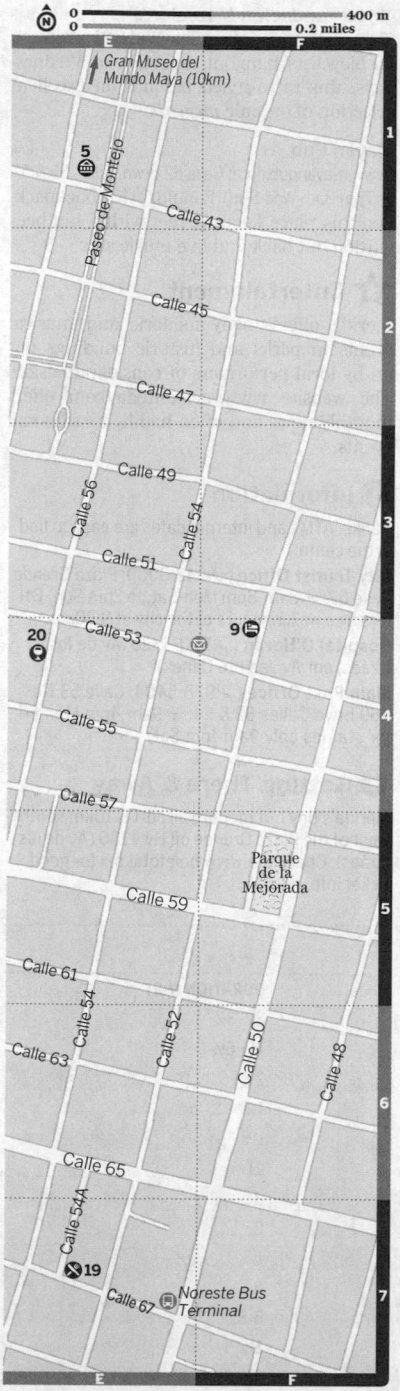

Mérida

Sights

1 Casa de Montejo C5
2 Catedral de San Ildefonso D5
3 Iglesia de Jesús D5
4 Mercado Municipal Lucas de Gálvez D7
5 Museo Regional de Antropología E1
6 Palacio de Gobierno C5
7 Plaza Grande C5

Sleeping

8 Álvarez Family Guest House D3
9 Casa Ana B&B F4
10 Hostel Zocalo C5
11 Hotel Santa Lucía D4
12 Luz en Yucatán D4
13 Nómadas Hostel C3

Eating

14 Café Chocolate D3
15 El Trapiche C5
16 La Chaya Maya D4
17 La Socorrito D2
Mercado Municipal Lucas de Gálvez ..... (see 4)
18 Mercado Municipal No 2 ..... A4
19 Super Bodega E7

Drinking & Nightlife

20 La Fundación Mezcalería E4
21 Mayan Pub C4

a worthwhile splurge, this downtown hotel is a great deal with individually decorated rooms, fabulous common areas and a wonderful pool/patio area out back. The hotel also has a wonderful house across the road that sleeps seven.

Eating

A few blocks east of the Plaza Grande are side-by-side supermarkets (on Calle 56) as well as a branch of **Super Bodega** (cnr Calles 67 & 54A), a market-department store chain.

Mercado Municipal Lucas de Gálvez MARKET $

(cnr Calles 56A & 67; mains & ceviche M$60; ⏲ 6am-5pm) This is where Mérida's least expensive eateries are located. Choose between all your favorite *yucateco* dishes, maybe even some *cochinita pibil* (pork marinated in annatto-seed paste and pit-cooked or baked).

La Socorrito MEXICAN $
(Calle 47 btwn Calles 58 & 60; tortas M$17; ⏲6am-2pm) These old pros started slow-cooking *cochinita* in underground pits more than six decades ago and they're still at it.

Mercado Municipal No 2 MARKET $
(Calle 70; mains M$40-60; ⏲8am-4pm) 'Número Dos' is a less crowded, but still good and cheap, market on the north side of Parque de Santiago.

El Trapiche MEXICAN $
(Calle 62 No 491; mains M$26-90; ⏲8am-midnight; ✎) A great, centrally located place, El Trapiche has cheap Mexican eats in a casual environment.

Café Chocolate CAFE $
(www.cafe-chocolate.com.mx; Calle 60 No 442; breakfast buffets M$69, mains M$69-89; ⏲7am-midnight Mon-Sat; 📶✎) The food is excellent at this colonial cafe. Sandwiches and paninis are prepared with homemade bread and the menu features interesting local concoctions, such as baked ham rubbed with a white recado marinade.

★La Chaya Maya MEXICAN $$
(Calle 55 No 510; mains M$57-175; ⏲7am-11pm) In a lovely downtown colonial building, consider La Chaya Maya your introduction to classic *yucateco* fare like *relleno negro* (a unique turkey stew).

Drinking & Nightlife

You need not look far to find a friendly neighborhood bar.

★La Fundación Mezcalería BAR
(Calle 56 No 465; ⏲8pm-3am Wed-Sat) A popular bicyclists' hangout, especially on Wednesdays, this retro-styled bar has an excellent selection of organic *mezcals*.

Mayan Pub BAR
(www.mayanpub.com; Calle 62 btwn Calles 55 & 57; ⏲7pm-3am Wed-Sun) Popular with backpackers, this place keeps it real with a big beer garden out back and live music acts.

Entertainment

Mérida offers many folkloric and musical events in parks and historic buildings put on by local performers of considerable skill. The website www.yucatantoday.com offers monthly news and often highlights seasonal events.

Information

Banks, ATMs and internet cafes are easy to find in the center.

City Tourist Office (☎942-0000; Plaza Grande, Calle 62; ⏲8am-8pm Mon-Sat, to 2pm Sun) Offers free walking tours of the city at 9:30am.

Hospital O'Horán (☎930-3320; Av de los Itzáes, cnr Av Jacinto Canek)

Main Post Office (☎928-5404; Calle 53 No 469 btwn Calles 52 & 54; ⏲9am-4pm Mon-Fri, for stamps only 9am-1pm Sat)

Getting There & Away

Mérida's tiny but modern airport is 10km southwest of the Plaza Grande off Hwy 180 (Av de los Itzáes). Check out www.boletotal.mx for good ticket info.

BUSES FROM MÉRIDA

DESTINATION	COST (M$)	DURATION (HR)
Campeche	122-180	2½-3½
Cancún	180-290	4½-6½
Celestún	49	2½
Chichén Itzá	68-114	1½
Izamal	23	1½
Mexico City	1322-1558	21
Palenque	242-366	8
Playa del Carmen	446	8
Progreso	16	1
Ruta Puuc (round trip)	187	8
Tulum	152-220	5-8
Uxmal	47	1½
Valladolid	90-150	2½-3½

CAME Bus Terminal (☎ reservations 920-4444; Calle 70 btwn Calles 69 & 71) Mérida's main bus terminal has mostly 1st-class buses.

Noreste Bus Terminal (Calle 67 btwn Calles 50 & 52) Second-class Noreste, Sur and Oriente bus lines use this terminal.

Progreso Bus Terminal (Calle 62 No 524) A separate terminal serving Progreso.

Terminal de Segunda Clase (Calle 69) ADO, Mayab and Oriente run mostly 2nd-class buses to various points in the state and around the peninsula.

Playa del Carmen

☎ 984 / POP 150,000

Once a small fishing town, Playa del Carmen is now Quintana Roo's third largest city. Sitting coolly on the lee side of Cozumel, its beaches are jammed with superfit Europeans. The waters aren't as clear as those of Cancún or Cozumel, but this ultrachic playground just continues to grow.

Activities

In addition to great ocean diving, most outfits offer cenote dives. Prices are similar at most shops: resort dives (M$1400); one-/two-tank dives (M$630/900); cenote dives (M$1400); snorkeling (M$450); whale-shark tour (M$2500); and open-water certification (M$5000).

Dive Mike DIVING
(☎ 803-1228; www.divemike.com; Calle 8; tour M$455) Offers snorkeling tours to reefs and a secluded beach.

Scuba Playa DIVING
(☎ 803-3123; www.scubaplaya.com; Calle 10) A PADI five-star instructor development dive resort with technical diving courses available.

Courses

Playa Lingua del Caribe LANGUAGE COURSE
(☎ 873-3876; www.playalingua.com; Calle 20; 1 week without/with homestay M$2925/5200) Offers Spanish and Maya classes, plus homestays.

Sleeping

Hostel Playa HOSTEL $
(☎ 803-3277; www.hostelplaya.com; Calle 8; dm/d/tr incl breakfast M$160/420/630; P) This place was made for mingling with its central common area, cool garden area and nice rooftop terrace. The private rooms are simple but decent enough and the staff is extremely helpful.

Hostel Río Playa HOSTEL $
(☎ 803-0145; see www.hostelworld.com; Calle 8; dm incl breakfast M$245-270, r without bathroom incl breakfast M$450-500;) A fine budget buy, the Río offers easy access to the beach and a women's-only dorm. It also has a shared kitchen, a rooftop bar and hangout area – with a remarkably shallow pool – and air-con in all rooms.

Hostel Quinta Playa HOSTEL $
(☎ 147-0428; www.quintaplaya.com; Calle 2 btwn Quinta Av & beach; dm with/without air-con M$200/170;) It's all about the location here. Just 30m from the beach, one block from the bus station and two blocks from the ferry to Isla Cozumel. Now that's convenience.

Hotel Casa Tucán HOTEL $$
(☎ 873-0283; www.casatucan.com.mx; Calle 4; r with fan/air-con M$600/720, ste M$1200; P) This German-run hotel is a warren of 30 rooms of several types. Rooms have fans or air-con, a couple have kitchenettes, and some come with a minibar. The café serves good, affordable food.

Eating

For cheap eats, head away from the tourist center, or try the small **market** (Av 10 btwn Calles 6 & 8; mains M$30-70; ⏲ 9am-4pm) for some economical homestyle cooking.

Don Sirloin MEXICAN $
(10 Av; tacos M$13; ⏲ noon-7am) *Al pastor* (marinated pork) and sirloin beef are sliced right off the spit at this popular all-night taco joint.

★La Cueva del Chango MEXICAN $$
(www.lacuevadelchango.com; Calle 38 btwn Quinta Av & the beach; breakfast M$60-68, lunch & dinner M$74-158; ⏲ 8am-11pm) The Monkey's Cave uses fresh, natural ingredients and it's remarkably affordable.

100% Natural VEGETARIAN $$
(Cien Por Ciento Natural; www.100natural.com.mx; cnr Quinta Av & Calle 10; mains M$64-136; ⏲ 7am-11pm;) The trademarks of this quickly establishing chain – fresh juices, salads, various vegetable and chicken dishes and other healthy foods – are delicious and filling.

Entertainment

The party generally starts on bustling Quinta Av, then heads down toward the beach on Calle 6.

Playa del Carmen

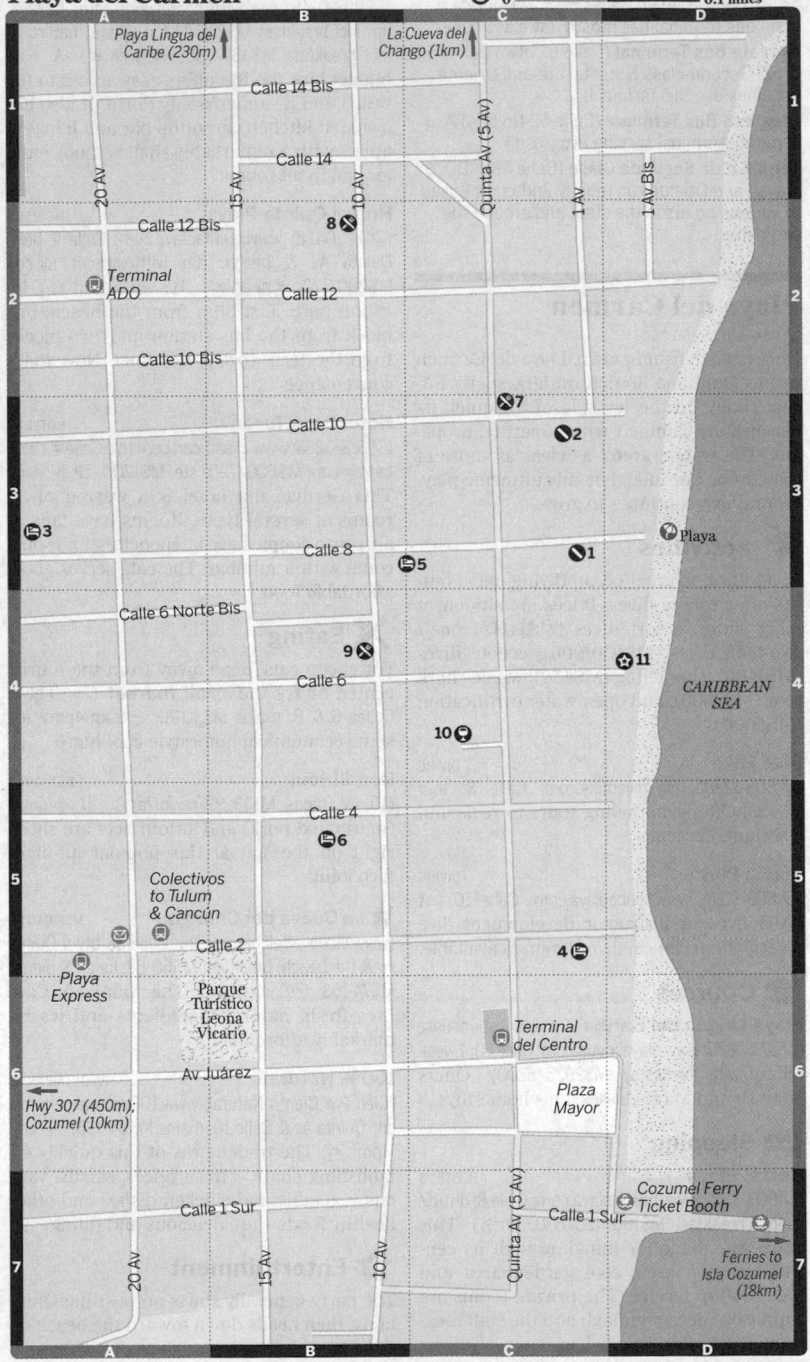

Playa del Carmen

Activities, Courses & Tours
1 Dive Mike C3
2 Scuba Playa C3

Sleeping
3 Hostel Playa A3
4 Hostel Quinta Playa C5
5 Hostel Río Playa C3
6 Hotel Casa Tucán B5

Eating
7 100% Natural C3
8 Don Sirloin B2
9 Market B4

Drinking & Nightlife
10 Playa 69 ..... C4

Entertainment
11 Fusion D4

★Fusion LIVE MUSIC
(www.fusionhotelmexico.com; Calle 6; ⏲7am-2am) Groove out by the beach under the Playa moon at Fusion.

Playa 69 GAY
(www.rivieramayagay.com; Callejón off Quinta Av btwn Calles 4 & 6; ⏲8pm-2am Tue, 8pm-6am Wed-Sun) A happening gay-friendly dance club.

Information

Banamex (cnr Calle 12 & 10 Av)

Clinic & Hyperbaric Chamber (Playa International Clinic; ☎803-1215; cnr 10 Av & Calle 28; ⏲9am-8:30pm) Excellent medical clinic with hyberbaric chamber.

Lavandería & Internet Estrella (Calle 2 No 402; per hr M$10; ⏲8am-10pm Mon-Sat) Conveniently has both an internet cafe and a laundry.

Post Office (cnr 20 Av & Calle 2; ⏲9am-4pm Mon-Fri)

Tourist Police Kiosk (☎873-2656; Plaza Mayor; ⏲24hr)

Getting There & Away

BOAT

Ferries depart frequently to Isla Cozumel (M$156 one way), usually from 7am to 9pm. For schedules of the two ferry operators, see www.granpuerto.com.mx and www.mexicowaterjets.com. **Ticket booths** are on Calle 1 Sur.

BUS

Playa has two bus terminals. The newer one, **Terminal ADO** (20 Av), just east of Calle 12, is where most 1st-class buses arrive and depart. The old bus station, **Terminal del Centro** (cnr Av Juárez & Quinta Av), gets all the 2nd-class (called *intermedio* by lines such as Mayab) services. **Playa Express** (Calle 2 Norte) offers quick service to downtown Cancún for M$34.

COLECTIVOS

Colectivos are a great option for cheap travel southward to Tulum (M$40, 45 minutes). They depart from Calle 2 near Av 20 about every 15 minutes from 5am to 10pm. They will stop anywhere along the highway between Playa and Tulum, charging a minimum of M$20. Luggage space is somewhat limited. From the same spot, you can grab a *colectivo* to Cancún (M$30).

Isla Cozumel

☎987 / POP 77,200

Some 70km south of Cancún, Cozumel is Mexico's largest island, measuring 53km by 14km. Called Ah-Cuzamil-Peten (Island of Swallows) by its earliest inhabitants,

BUSES FROM PLAYA DEL CARMEN

DESTINATION	COST (M$)	DURATION (HR)
Aeropuerto Internacional de Cancún	120	1
Chetumal (to Belize)	190-252	5-5½
Chichén Itzá	130	4
Cobá	72-92	1¾-2
Mérida	334-404	4¼-5
Palenque	448-750	11-12
San Cristóbal de las Casas	540-796	16½-18
Tulum	38-66	1
Valladolid	106-150	2½-3½

San Miguel de Cozumel

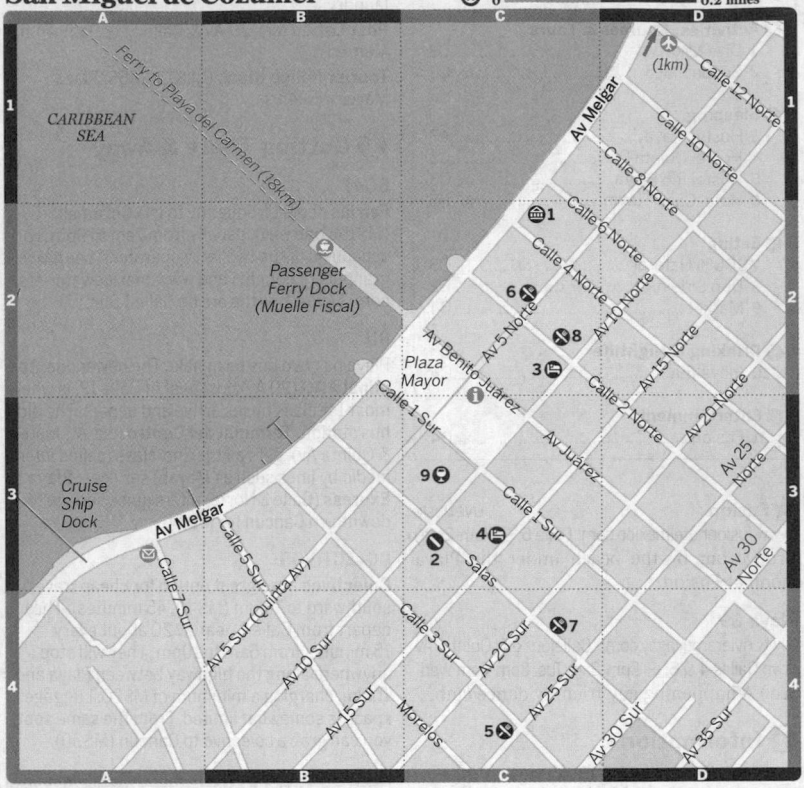

San Miguel de Cozumel

Sights
1 Museo de la Isla de Cozumel C2

Activities, Courses & Tours
2 Deep Blue C3

Sleeping
3 Hostelito C2
4 Hotel Pepita C3

Eating
5 Cocina Económica Las Palmas C4
6 Kinta C2
7 Mercado Municipal C4
8 Taquería El Sitio C2

Drinking & Nightlife
9 Ambar C3

Cozumel has become a world-famous diving and cruise-ship destination.

Maya settlement here dates from AD 300. During the Postclassic period, Cozumel flourished as a trade center and, more importantly, as a ceremonial site. Every Maya woman living on the Yucatán Peninsula and beyond was expected to make at least one pilgrimage here to pay tribute to Ixchel, the goddess of earth, fertility and the moon, at a temple erected in her honor.

Sights

It's easy to make your way on foot around the island's only town, San Miguel de Cozumel. The waterfront boulevard is Av Melgar and the Plaza Mayor is opposite the ferry dock.

In order to see most of the island you will have to rent a vehicle or take a taxi; cyclists will need to brave the regular strong winds.

The eastern shoreline is the wildest part of the island and presents some beautiful seascapes and many small blowholes. Swimming is dangerous on most of the east coast because of riptides and undertows.

Museo de la Isla de Cozumel MUSEUM
(☎872-1434; www.cozumelparks.gob.mx; Av Melgar; admission M$50; ⏲9am-5pm) Exhibits at this fine museum present a clear and detailed picture of the island's flora, fauna, geography, geology and ancient Maya history. It's a good place to learn about coral before hitting the water, and it's one not to miss before you leave the island.

El Cedral ARCHAEOLOGICAL SITE
FREE About the size of a small house and with no ornamentation, El Cedral is the oldest Maya ruin on the island. It's thought to have been an important ceremonial site; the small church standing next to the tiny ruin today is evidence that the site still has religious significance for locals. The turnoff for the site is between Km 17 and Km 18 on the southern coastal highway. It's best reached by vehicle or taxi.

Playa Palancar BEACH
About 17km south of town, Playa Palancar is a great beach, where you can rent snorkel gear and kayaks.

Parque Punta Sur NATURE RESERVE
(☎872-4014; www.cozumelparks.gob.mx; Carretera Costera Sur Km 27; adult/3-11yr M$156/104; ⏲9am-4pm Mon-Sat) On the island's southern tip, this ecotouristic park offers a nautical museum, lighthouse, beach restaurant and three midday boat tours that allow you to spot crocs and migratory birds. A taxi to get here costs M$300.

San Gervasio ARCHAEOLOGICAL SITE
(www.cozumelparks.gob.mx; admission M$90; ⏲8am-4pm) The Maya complex of San Gervasio contains Cozumel's only preserved ruins. San Gervasio is thought to have been the site of the sanctuary of Ixchel, goddess of fertility, and thus an important pilgrimage site at which Maya women worshipped.

Activities

The top dives in the area include **Santa Rosa Wall**, **Punta Sur Reef**, **Colombia Shallows** and **Palancar Gardens**. Prices vary, but in general expect to pay about M$1000 to M$1600 for a two-tank dive, M$910 for an introductory 'resort' course and M$5500 to M$6000 for PADI open-water certification. The best snorkeling sites are reached by boat; a half-day outing will cost M$400 to M$650.

Deep Blue DIVING
(☎872-5653; www.deepbluecozumel.com; Calle Rosado Salas 200; 2-tank dives M$1000-1200, resort courses M$910) Diving and snorkeling trips.

Parque Chankanaab AMUSEMENT PARK
(☎872-4014; www.cozumelparks.gob.mx; Carretera Costera Sur, Km 9; adult/3-11yr M$273/182; ⏲8am-4pm Mon-Sat; 👪) Great for kids, this park is a popular snorkeling spot and botanical garden 7km south of town. A taxi from town costs M$130 one way.

Sleeping

Hostelito HOSTEL $
(☎869-8157; www.hostelcozumel.com; Av 10 Norte btwn Av Benito Juárez & Calle 2 Norte; dm M$150, d/q with air-con from M$450/650; ❄📶) The hostel's tagline says it all: affordable *and* clean. There's one shared dorm room downstairs for guys and gals and amazingly clean showers. (How's that for truth in advertising?) Upstairs you'll find a great terrace, a shared kitchen and private rooms that sleep up to nine people.

Hotel Pepita HOTEL $
(☎872-0098; www.hotelpepitacozumel.com; Av 15 Sur No 120; r with air-con M$400; ❄📶) The owner, Maria Teresa, takes pride in her work, and it shows. This is the best economical hotel in the city. It's friendly, with well-maintained rooms grouped around a garden.

Amigo's Hostel HOSTEL $
(☎872-3868; www.cozumelhostel.com; Calle 7 Sur No 57; dm/r incl breakfast M$156/585; ❄@📶🏊) Unlike some cramped budget digs, here you get a large garden, an inviting pool and a good lounge area. Some guests say it's too far removed from the tourist center, others like the distance from the cruise-ship crowds.

Eating

The cheapest eating options are the little market *loncherías* (lunch stalls) next to the **Mercado Municipal** (Calle Rosado Salas btwn Avs 20 & 25 Sur; ⏲7am-4pm).

WORTH A TRIP

CRISTALINO CENOTE

On the west side of the highway south of Playa del Carmen is a series of wonderful cenotes. Among these is **Cristalino Cenote** (admission M$40; ⏲6am-5:30pm), just south of the Barceló Maya Resort. It's easily accessible, only about 70m from the entrance gate, which is just off the highway. Two more sinkholes, Cenote Azul and El Jardín del Edén, are just south of Cristalino along the highway, but Cristalino is the best of the three.

Taquería El Sitio MEXICAN $
(Calle 2 Norte; tacos & tortas M$10-33; ⏲7:30am-12:30pm) Head over here for scrumptious tacos and *tortas* (sandwiches).

Cocina Económica Las Palmas MEXICAN $
(cnr Calle 3 Sur & Av 25 Sur; set meals M$60; ⏲9am-7pm Mon-Sat) This place overflows with locals come lunchtime. And while it gets hotter than Hades, you'll love the *chicharrones* (fried pork rinds) and Maya favorites like *poc-chuc* (grilled pork) on offer.

★Kinta MEXICAN $$
(☎869-0544; www.kintacozumel.com; Av 5 Nte; mains M$120-195; ⏲5:30-11pm Tue-Sun) Putting a gourmet twist on Mexican classics, this chic bistro is one of the best restaurants on the island. The grilled scallops and shrimp with tomato-corn salsa and cilantro pesto are delightful.

☆ Entertainment

Cozumel's nightlife is fairly subdued, though you can always find some late-night action in and around the Plaza Mayor.

Ambar BAR
(Av 5 Sur; ⏲8am-midnight Mon-Fri, 8am-4am Sat, noon-midnight Sun) Good tunes, a pool table and a beer garden out back – what more can you ask for from a drinking establishment?

La Hach LIVE MUSIC
(www.lahachcozumel.com; Av Melgar Km 2.9; ⏲10am-1am Sun-Tue, 10am-3am Wed-Sat) Cozumel doesn't have much of a live-music scene, so the cover bands playing here are about as good as it gets. That said, the ocean view rocks. It's a 10-minute cab ride from the town center.

ℹ Information

San Miguel de Cozumel is the island's main town. There are ATMs, banks and internet joints on the plaza.

Cozumel International Clinic (Hyperbaric Chamber; ☎872-1430; Calle 5 Sur btwn Av Melgar and Av 5 Sur) Medical clinic and hyperbaric chamber.

Tourist Office (2nd fl, Plaza Mayor; ⏲8am-3pm Mon-Fri)

ℹ Getting There & Away

AIR

American, Delta, Frontier and United Airlines fly direct from the US; European flights are usually routed via the US or Mexico City.

BOAT

Passenger ferries run to Isla Cozumel from Playa del Carmen. Unless you're driving your own car, take the Playa passenger ferries offered by **México Waterjets** (www.mexicowaterjets.com) or **Ultramar** (www.granpuerto.com.mx). The service costs M$155 one way, and there's normally a ferry every hour to and from Cozumel from 6am to 9pm.

ℹ Getting Around

BICYCLE

Shark Rider (Av 5 Norte btwn Av Benito Juárez & Calle 2 Norte; mountain/racing bikes per day M$130/195; ⏲8am-7pm) On an alley off Av 5, rents beach cruisers and mountain bikes, or slightly more expensive racing bikes.

CAR & SCOOTER

Car-rental rates are generally around M$500 all-inclusive. For scooters and motorcycles, you'll pay anywhere from M$250 to M$500 per day.

Rentadora Isis (☎872-3367; rentadoraisis@prodigy.net.mx; Av 5 Nte; ⏲8am-6:30pm) Rents VW Beetles for around M$400 per day and scooters for M$250.

TAXI

Fares in and around town are M$40 per ride; a day trip around the island costs M$700 to M$1000.

Tulum

☎984 / POP 18,200

Tulum's spectacular coastline – with its confectioner-sugar sands, jade-green water, balmy breezes and laid-back, international vibe – make it one of the top beaches in Mexico. Where else can you get all that and a dramatically situated Maya ruin? Cheap eats and sleeps abound in Tulum Pueblo, the inland town center, and though in much shorter supply, you can still find budget accommodations on the coast, too. Nearby cenotes, the Maya ruins of Cobá and the massive Reserva de la Biosfera Sian Ka'an all make great day trips.

Sights

Tulum Ruins ARCHAEOLOGICAL SITE
(admission M$57; ⏲8am-5pm; P) As far as Maya ruins with a view go, you can't beat the mesmerizing oceanfront scenery of Tulum. It's true that the site doesn't have the grandiose structures of other ancient Maya cities, but its privileged cliffside location certainly makes up for that, as does the beach down below, where visitors can go for a refreshing swim.

Tulum is believed to have been an important port town during its Postclassic heyday (AD 1200–1521). Named by the Spanish, Tulum means 'wall'. The site's original Maya name was Zama, or 'Dawn' – watch the sunrise here to realize why. Tulum was one of Mexico's last ancient cities to be abandoned, about 75 years after the Spanish conquest.

A M$20 train takes you to the ticket booth from the entrance, or just hoof the 300m. Taxis from town charge M$50. There's a less-used foot entrance from the north side of the Zona Hotelera. To explore the ruins, pass the ticket booth and enter the compact rectangular site near its northeastern corner.

The first structure you'll see is the **Casa del Cenote** (House of the Cenote), named for the small pool at its southern base. Above, you can look over the site – set just south on a waterfront bluff is the **Templo del Dios del Viento** (Temple of the Wind God). Past it is the biggest site, **El Castillo** (The Castle), whose Toltec-style *kukulcanes* (plumed serpents) are evidence of the late Postclassic period. Just south are the steps down to the beach, and above are many ocean-view vantage points for your camera.

West, roughly in the middle of the site, the interesting two-story **Templo de las Pinturas** (Temple of the Paintings) features relief masks and murals on its unapproachable inner wall.

Activities

Cave and reef diving, snorkeling trips or surfing – it's all here for the taking in Tulum.

Xibalba Dive Center DIVING
(☎871-2953; www.xibalbadivecenter.com; Andromeda 7; 1-/2-tank cenote dive M$940/1500, snorkeling M$390-585) Known for its safety-first approach to diving, this dive shop specializes in cave and cavern diving, but you can also arrange reef dives and snorkeling trips here. Xibalba doubles as a hotel and offers attractive diving/lodging packages.

Sian Kite Watersports KITESURFING
(☎cell 984-127-1125, cell 984-116-3774; Carretera Tulum-Boca Paila Km 4.5, at Papaya Playa Project; surfing/kiteboarding per hr M$520/900) Offers one-hour introductory kiteboarding lessons (ask about cheaper group rates). You can take surfing classes here, too.

Sleeping

You can choose to stay in the pricier Zona Hotelera on the coast or in Tulum Pueblo; some hostels in Tulum town have free bikes for their guests or offer transport to the beach for a nominal fee.

El Jardín de Frida HOSTEL $
(☎871-2816; www.fridastulum.com; Av Tulum, Tulum Pueblo; dm/r incl breakfast M$200/600; P) Dorms and private rooms surround a pleasant garden area out back, while in front the

WORTH A TRIP

LAGUNA BACALAR & AROUND

If you're making your way down south, Laguna Bacalar (aka the 'lake of seven colors') is a must-see. There you can swim in a 90m-deep sinkhole at **Cenote Azul** (www.cenote-azul.com; Hwy 307; life vests M$35; ⏲8am-6pm; P), then check out the sleepy town's imposing colonial fortress.

Further south, the fishing villages of **Mahahual** and **Xcalak** appeal to diving enthusiasts and beach bums seeking a chilled-out, low-rise coastal town experience.

ADO has a daily bus departure to Laguna Bacalar from Tulum; for Mahahual, take a bus to Felipe Carrillo Puerto (95km south of Tulum), then transfer (there are two daily departures to Mahahual).

OFF THE BEATEN TRACK

EXPLORE MORE OF YUCATÁN STATE

There are a lot of gaps on the maps of this vast state. Here are some DIY ideas to get you started.

➡ **Río Lagartos** Head to this little fishing village on the Gulf coast to kick off adventures into a nearby nature reserve. On your way down, stop at the well-preserved archaeological site, **Ek' Balam** (adult/child 7-12yr M$98/6, guides M$600; ⏲8am-5pm; Ⓟ).

➡ **Izamal** The yellow city has heaps of unexplored ruins nearby.

➡ **Ticul to Tihosuco** Part of the route is called Ruta de los Conventos (Route of the Convents), as each of these tiny villages has a cathedral or church, many in beautiful disrepair.

hostel has a cool little scene at its open-air, roadside restaurant/bar.

Cabañas Playa Condesa CABINS $
(Carretera Tulum-Boca Paila Km 3, Zona Hotelera; r with/without bathroom M$500/400) Just 1km north of the T-junction (take Av Cobá to the coast road and turn left), this group of thatched *cabañas* (cabins) is a great deal. Along with the basic rooms – which are rather clean – you also get mosquito nets (believe us, you'll need them).

Cabañas Xbalamque CABINS $
(☎984-146-6021; xbalamquetulum@hotmail.com; Carretera Tulum-Boca Paila Km 10, Zona Hotelera; dm M$150, campsite with tent M$150, cabin with shared bathroom M$500; ❄) The cheapest budget buy on the coast, with dorms, private cabins and a campsite. There's a large onsite cenote (watch out for the crocs!) and the beach is just 50m away.

Weary Traveler HOSTEL $
(☎871-2390; www.wearytravelerhostel.com; Av Tulum, Tulum Pueblo; dm/r incl breakfast from M$150/375; ❄@📶) A great place to meet friends, the Weary Traveler is known for its full breakfast and a great central courtyard with hammocks and picnic benches.

Diamante K CABINS $$
(☎984-876-2115; www.diamantek.com; Carretera Tulum-Boca Paila Km 2.5; cabin with/without bathroom M$1200/600; 📶) A fine midrange option on the beach, cabins here go from budget-rustic to rustic-chic. Those with bathrooms vary hugely in size and design – check out a few if you can.

Eating

You'll find more affordable eats in Tulum Pueblo. In the Zona Hotelera, some budget and midrange hotels have reasonably priced menus. For groceries, hit the **Súper Express** (Av Tulum 81, cnr Luna; ⏲7am-10pm) in town.

Los Aguachiles SEAFOOD $$
(☎802-54-82; Av Tulum, cnr Palenque; tostadas M$33, mains M$89-159; ⏲noon-7pm Tue-Sun; Ⓟ) Done up in Mexican-cantina style yet with one big difference: the menu offerings, such as fish tacos and artfully prepared tuna *tostadas*, go above and beyond your typical bar grub.

El Camello SEAFOOD $$
(Av Tulum, cnr Av Kukulcán; mains M$90-150; ⏲10:30am-9pm Mon, Tue & Thu-Sat, 10:30am-6pm Sun) Founded by a local fishermen's co-operative, you're guaranteed fresh fish and seafood at this immensely popular roadside eatery. It's all about the fish or mixed seafood ceviches.

La Nave ITALIAN $$
(☎871-2592; Av Tulum; mains M$95-170; ⏲7am-11pm Mon-Sat) Perched over Av Tulum, this open-air Italian joint is perpetually packed.

Drinking & Nightlife

Curandero BAR
(www.facebook.com/curandero.tulum; Av Tulum, cnr Beta; ⏲7am-3pm Mon-Sat) Bands play four nights a week in a cool interior space fashioned almost entirely from recycled objects.

Papaya Playa Project BAR
(www.facebook.com/papayaplayaproject; Carretera Tulum-Boca Paila Km 4.5) Design hotel Papaya Playa Project regularly hosts festive parties and music events at its beachside venue Tribal Room. From town, take Av Cobá to the coast road T-junction, then head 1km south.

Information

Tulum Pueblo has internet cafes, currency-exchange booths and ATMs.

HSBC bank (Av Tulum; ⏲8am-5pm Mon-Sat; 📶) Offers good exchange rates and a 24-hour ATM.

Post Office (Orión, cnr Venus; ⏲8am-4:30pm Mon-Fri, 8am-noon Sat) On the corner of Orión and Venus.

Getting There & Away

The bus terminal is toward the southern end of town.

If you're headed for Valladolid, be sure your bus is traveling the short route through Chemax, not via Cancún.

Colectivos leave from Av Tulum for Playa del Carmen (M$35, 45 minutes) and Punta Allen (at 2pm; M$240, four hours).

DESTINATION	COST (M$)	DURATION (HR)
Cancún	98	2
Chetumal (to Belize)	142-194	3½-4
Chichén Itzá	92-148	3½
Cobá	44	45min
Mérida	228	4
Playa del Carmen	62	1
Valladolid	84	2

Getting Around

Except for the shuttles operated from the youth hostels, there are no *colectivos* out to the beach. Taxi fares are fixed and pretty cheap; a ride from town to the ruins costs M$50 and fares to the coast (aka Zona Hotelera) run M$80 to M$130. Alternatively, you can get around on bike; **I Bike Tulum** (Av Cobá; per day incl gear M$100; ⏲9am-6pm) rents mountain bikes and beach cruisers.

Around Tulum

Gran Cenote

A taxi from downtown Tulum to this **limestone sinkhole** (snorkeling M$100; ⏲8am-5pm) costs around M$60 one way, or it's an easy bike ride.

Cobá

A Classic-era Maya city set deep in tropical jungle, the fascinating **Cobá ruins** (www.inah.gob.mx; admission M$57, guides M$500-750; ⏲8am-5pm; P), 48km northwest of Tulum, are more linked with distant Tikal than Tulum or Chichén Itzá. Cobá was home to 55,000 Maya at its peak (AD 800–1100). Many amazing regional *sacbeob* (stone-paved avenues) led here. The longest one runs 100km to Yaxuna, near Chichén Itzá. The name – from the Maya word *koba* (believed to mean 'ruffled waters') – likely refers to the reedy, croc-filled lakes in the area.

Be at the gates when they open and you'll see very few people for several hours. Be prepared to walk several kilometers on paths, depending on how much you want to see. A short distance inside is a concession renting bicycles for M$35 per day. These can only be ridden within the site, and are useful if you really want to get around the further reaches.

Only a few of the estimated 6500 structures have been excavated. The four principal groups are spaced apart. Approximately 100m along the main path is **Grupo Cobá**, with an enormous pyramid and corbelled-vault passages. After 500m, the road forks: the left leads to the Nohoch Mul pyramid, the right to Grupo Macanxoc. Either way passes the **Conjunto Pinturas** (Collection of Paintings), 100m further, which has a couple of stelae.

If you're pressed for time, skip **Grupo Macanxoc**, 500m away (which has a few eroded stelae depicting women from Tikal) and head northeast past the **Grupo Nohoch Mul** and continue to the right (east) to the semicircular Xaibé structure, the juncture of four *sacbeob*. To the north, past a couple of structures, you'll see the 42m-high **Nohoch Mul** (Big Mound), a pyramid you can climb to look over the jungle canopy.

Sleeping

You'll find two unremarkable budget hotels along the main drag in Cobá town, both within walking distance of the ruins. Consider staying in nearby Tulum if you prefer a town with more nightlife and eating options.

Hotel Sac-bé HOTEL $
(☎984-144-3006; r with fan/air-con M$350/450; ❄) The best digs in town. Clean and friendly, the Sac-bé is on the the main road heading into town. The chickens are a bit noisy in the morning, but the hotel has a restaurant, hot water and mediocre beds.

Hotel El Bocadito HOTEL $
(☎984-807-2071; r with fan/air-con M$200/450; ❄) Very basic rooms – only go here if Hotel Sac-bé is full.

Getting There & Away

Most buses serving Cobá swing down to the ruins to drop off passengers at a small bus station; some only go as far as Hotel El Bocadito, the town's other bus station. Buses run six to eight times daily between Tulum and Cobá (M$36 to M$44, 45 minutes) and Playa del Carmen (M$66 to M$86, 1¾ hours). Buses also run to Valladolid (M$40 to M$62, 45 minutes) and Chichén Itzá (M$68 to M$90, 1½ hours).

Reserva de la Biosfera Sian Ka'an

More than 5000 sq km of tropical jungle, marsh, mangroves and islands on Quintana Roo's coast have been set aside by the Mexican government as a large biosphere reserve. In 1987 the UN classified it as a World Heritage Site – an irreplaceable natural treasure.

Entering the reserve by land on the road to Punta Allen, you pass **Boca Paila Camps** (Cesiak; ☎984-871-2499; www.cesiak.org; Carretera Tulum-Boca Paila; r from M$1470; P), where you can go bird-watching on a five-hour kayak tour (M$650). About 1km further south is the **Centro de Visitantes Reserva de la Biosfera Sian Ka'an**, where you'll find some natural history exhibits along with a watchtower.

At the end of the road, **Punta Allen** (40km south from Tulum) is a quiet beach town getaway known for its catch-and-release bonefishing; tarpon and snook are very popular sportfish as well. An hour's tour of the lagoon there, which includes snorkeling and turtle- and bird-watching, costs M$700 to M$800. Ask at your hotel about tour operators. There are no ATMs or internet cafes in town.

At the entrance to town, the beachfront **Hotel Costa del Sol** (☎984-113-2639; reservaciones@bungaloscostadelsol.com; campsites M$200, r M$1100) has quaint fan-cooled bungalows and a laid-back feel. The restaurant is pretty decent, and there's karaoke on weekend nights.

Getting There & Away

Community Tours Sian Ka'an (☎871-2202; www.siankaantours.org; Osiris cnr Sol; ⏲office 7am-8pm) runs tours from Tulum that include pickup in the Zona Hotelera; trips cost about M$1300. You can also enter the reserve by taking **colectivos to Punta Allen** (☎984-115-5580) out of Tulum; one leaves daily from downtown at 2pm and arrives about four hours later.

Campeche

☎981 / POP 259,000

Campeche is a colonial fairyland, its walled city center a tight enclave of perfectly restored pastel buildings, narrow cobblestoned streets, fortified ramparts and well-preserved mansions. Added to Unesco's list of World Heritage Sites in 1999, the state capital has been so painstakingly restored you wonder if it's a real city.

Sights & Activities

Plaza Principal & Around

Shaded by spreading carob trees, and ringed by tiled benches and broad footpaths radiating from a belle-epoque kiosk, Campeche's appealingly modest Plaza Principal started life in 1531 as a military camp.

Catedral de Nuestra Señora de la Purísima Concepción CATHEDRAL
(⏲6:30am-9pm) Dominating the plaza's east side is the two-towered cathedral. Statues of Sts Peter and Paul occupy niches in the baroque facade; the sober, single-nave interior is lined with colonial-era paintings.

Centro Cultural Casa Número 6 HISTORIC BUILDING
(☎816-1782; Calle 57 No 6; admission M$10, audio guide M$15; ⏲8am-9pm Mon-Fri, 9am-9pm Sat & Sun) This prerevolutionary-era mansion is worth the visit for an idea of how the city's high society lived. The front sitting room is furnished with Cuban-style pieces of the period.

Ex-Templo de San José HISTORIC BUILDING
(Former San José Church; cnr Calles 10 & 63) Built in the early 18th century by Jesuits who ran it as an institute of higher learning until they were booted out of Spanish domains in 1767. It now serves as an exhibition space.

Baluartes

After a particularly blistering pirate assault in 1663, the remaining inhabitants of Campeche set about erecting protective walls around their city. Following the wall around is a great way to visit a number of museums and sites in one day. Among the favorite stops are two main entrances which connected the walled compound with the outside world – the **Puerta del Mar** (Sea Gate; cnr Calles 8 & 59), which opens onto a wharf, and the **Puerta**

de Tierra (Land Gate; Calle 18; admission M$10; ⏲9am-6pm), now the venue for a sound-and-light show.

★Museo de la Arquitectura Maya
MUSEUM, RAMPART

(Calle 8; admission M$35; ⏲9am-5:30pm Tue-Sun) The Baluarte de Nuestra Señora de la Soledad contains this fascinating must-see museum. It provides an excellent overview of the archaeological sites around Campeche state and the key architectural styles associated with them.

Baluarte de San Pedro
RAMPART, MUSEUM

(cnr Avs Circuito Baluartes Este & Circuito Baluartes Nte; ⏲9am-9pm) FREE Behind Iglesia de San Juan de Dios, the Baluarte de San Pedro houses the **Galería y Museo de Arte Popular**, which displays beautiful indigenous handicrafts.

Sleeping

Hotel Guarandocha Inn
HOTEL $

(☎811-6658; rool_2111@hotmail.com; Calle 55 btwn 12 & 14; d incl breakfast M$350-450, tr incl breakfast M$600; ❄ @ 📶) One of the better-value rooms in town is at this modest but pleasant hotel. Rooms are nice and spacious, and the newer ones upstairs come brighter and more open (and will cost a bit more).

Hostal La Parroquia
HOSTEL $

(☎816-2530; www.hostalparroquia.com; Calle 55 No 8; dm M$95, d/q without bathroom incl breakfast M$250/400; 📶) Conveniently located half a block from the Plaza Principal, this basic hostel resides in a crumbling late-1500s mansion. The hangout areas desperately need help, but at least there's breakfast and bike rental.

★Hotel López
HOTEL $$

(☎816-3344; www.hotellopezcampeche.com.mx; Calle 12 No 189; d/tr/q/ste M$620/670/720/900; ❄ 📶 🏊) This elegant hotel is one of Campeche's best midrange options. Small but modern and comfortably appointed rooms open onto curvy art-deco balconies around oval courtyards and pleasant greenery.

Eating

Café La Parroquia
MEXICAN $

(☎816-2530; Calle 55 No 8; mains M$45-150, lunch specials M$70-80; ⏲24hr) Appeals to both locals and foreigners with a wide-ranging menu of everything from fried chicken and grilled pork to turkey soup and regional specialties.

Chef Color
MEXICAN $

(☎811-4455; cnr Calles 55 & 12; half/full lunch platters M$30/50; ⏲12:30-5:30pm Mon-Sat) This cafeteria-style eatery serves up large portions of cheap and tasty, Central American–influenced Mexican dishes from behind a glass counter; just point at what you want.

Cafetería Atrapa Sueño
VEGETARIAN $

(☎816-5000; Calle 10 No 269; mains M$30-80; ⏲8am-8pm Mon-Sat, also Sun from Dec-Mar; ✎) A German-run, new-age eatery featuring a good selection of vegetarian fare such as sandwiches and soups. There are meditation and yoga classes, too.

★Luz de Luna
INTERNATIONAL $$

(☎811-0624; Calle 59 No 6; mains M$75-110; ⏲8am-10pm Mon-Sat) Carved, painted tables and

WORTH A TRIP

EXPLORE MORE OF CAMPECHE STATE

Leave the guidebook behind and head out into the less explored corners of Campeche. If you don't have a vehicle, **Xtampak Tours** (☎811-6473; www.toursencampeche.com; Calle 57 No 14; ⏲8am-8pm Mon-Sat, to 2pm Sun) offers excursions to all of the following places:

➡ **Chenes Sites** Northeastern Campeche state is dotted with more than 30 sites in the distinct Chenes style, recognizable by the monster motifs around the doorway.

➡ **Calakmul** (☎555-150-2073; admission M$46; road maintenance fee per car M$56 plus per person M$28, Biosphere Reserve entrance fee per person M$54; ⏲8am-5pm) It's tough to get to this remote Maya site, which is surrounded by Mexico's largest biosphere reserve, but it's well worth the extra expense.

➡ **Edzná** (admission M$46; ⏲8am-5pm) The closest major ruins to Campeche – and some of the most impressive in the entire peninsula – are easy to reach on a day trip from town. **Combis** (minibuses; M$35, one hour) to the site leave from Campeche's Calle Chihuahua near the market.

Campeche

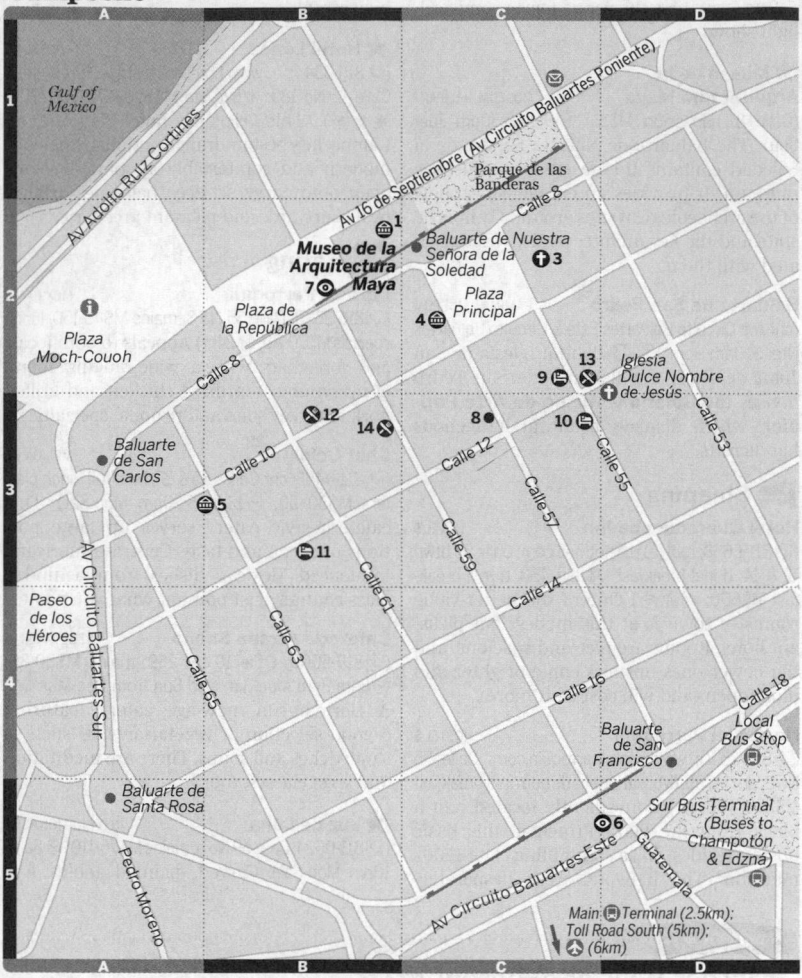

folksy decor add a creative atmosphere to this popular restaurant on a pedestrian street. The menu choices are equally interesting – try the shrimp salad or vegetarian burrito.

☆ Entertainment

There's invariably someone performing on the Plaza Principal every Saturday and Sunday evening from around 6:30pm. For Campeche's hottest bars and clubs, head 1km south of the city center along the *malecón* (waterfront promenade) past the Torres del Cristal.

ℹ Information

There are several *'cibers'* (internet cafes) in the town center. You'll find banks and ATMs just south of the plaza on Calle 10.

Central Post Office (cnr Av 16 de Septiembre & Calle 53; ⏲ 8:30am-4pm Mon-Fri, 8-11:30am Sat)

Hospital Dr Manuel Campos (☎ 811-1709; Av Circuito Baluartes Nte)

Secretaría de Turismo (☎ 127-33-00; www.campeche.travel; Plaza Moch-Couoh; ⏲ 8am-9pm Mon-Fri, 8am-8pm Sat & Sun)

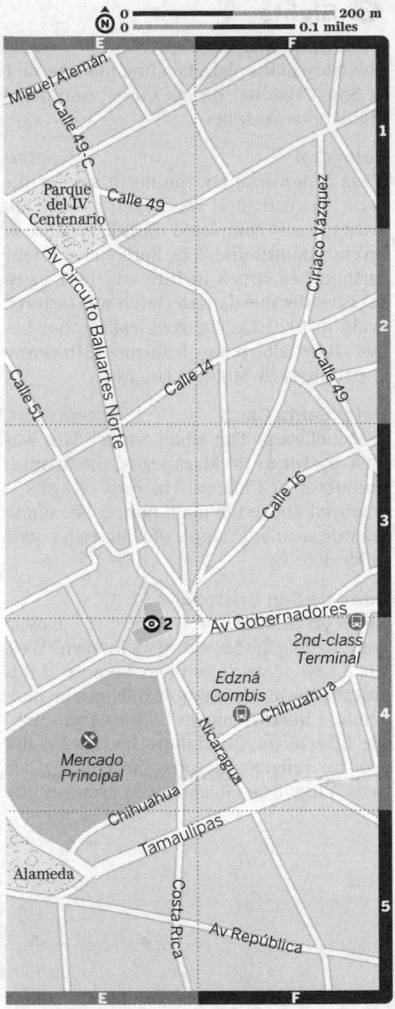

Campeche

Top Sights

1 Museo de la Arquitectura Maya B2

Sights

2 Baluarte de San Pedro E4
3 Catedral de Nuestra Señora de la Purísima Concepción C2
4 Centro Cultural Casa Número 6.....C2
5 Ex-Templo de San José.....B3
6 Puerta de Tierra.....D5
7 Puerta del Mar B2

Activities, Courses & Tours

8 Xtampak Tours C3

Sleeping

9 Hostal La Parroquia.....C2
10 Hotel Guarandocha Inn.....C3
11 Hotel López.....B3

Eating

Café La Parroquia..... (see 9)
12 Cafetería Atrapa Sueño B3
13 Chef Color C2
14 Luz de Luna.....B3

Getting There & Away

AIR

The airport is 6km southeast of the center. **Aeroméxico** (☎800-021-4010; www.aeromexico.com) provides service to Mexico City.

BUS

Campeche's **main bus terminal** (☎811-9910; Av Patricio Trueba 237), usually called the ADO or 1st-class terminal, is about 2.5km south of Plaza Principal via Av Central.

The **2nd-class bus terminal** (☎811-9910; Av Gobernadores 289), often referred to as the 'old ADO' station, is 1.5km east of the Mercado Principal.

To get to the new terminal, catch any 'Las Flores,' 'Solidaridad' or 'Casa de Justicia' bus by the central post office. To the 2nd-class terminal, catch a 'Terminal Sur' bus from the same point.

DESTINATION	COST (M$)	DURATION (HR)
Cancún	450-550	7
Mérida via Bécal	136-162	2½
Mérida via Uxmal	94-105	4½
Mexico City	1175-1400	18
Palenque	300	6
San Cristóbal de Las Casas	435	10

Getting Around

Most local buses (M$5.50) have a **stop** at or near the market.

Consider seeing the sights by pedaling along the *malecón*; get bike rentals at **Buenaventura** (☎144-3388; www.viajesbuenaventura.com.mx; Av 16 de Septiembre 122 Local 3; bike rentals M$30 for the first hr, then M$20 per hr thereafter, per day incl helmet & lock M$150; ⏲9am-3pm & 5-8pm Mon-Sat). Taxis around town charge from M$25 to M$50.

CHIAPAS

Chilly pine-forest highlands, rainforest jungles and well-preserved colonial cities exist side by side within Mexico's southernmost state, a region awash with the legacy of Spanish rule and some fabulous remnants of ancient Maya civilization. The state has the second-largest indigenous population in the country, and the modern Maya of Chiapas form a direct link to the past, with a traditional culture that persists to this day. The fine city of San Cristóbal de las Casas is at the heart of this region and was once the central bastion for the Zapatistas, now much less influential than in the 1990s.

San Cristóbal de las Casas

☎ 967 / POP 185,900 / ELEV 1940M

Set in a gorgeous highland valley, the colonial city of San Cristóbal has been a popular travelers' destination for decades. It's a pleasure to explore its cobbled streets and markets, soaking up the unique ambiance and the wonderfully clear highland light. Medium-sized San Cristóbal also boasts a comfortable blend of city and countryside, with restored century-old houses giving way to grazing animals and fields of corn. Surrounded by dozens of traditional Tzotzil and Tzeltal villages, San Cristóbal is a great base for local and regional exploration.

Sights

Plaza 31 de Marzo PLAZA

The leafy main plaza is a fine place to take in San Cristóbal de las Casas' unhurried highland atmosphere.

Cathedral CATHEDRAL

(Plaza 31 de Marzo) On the north side of the plaza, the cathedral was begun in 1528 but wasn't finally completed till 1815 because of several natural disasters. Sure enough, new earthquakes struck in 1816 and 1847, causing considerable damage, but it was restored again in 1920-22. The gold-leaf interior has five gilded altarpieces featuring 18th-century paintings by Miguel Cabrera.

Hotel Santa Clara HISTORIC BUILDING

(SE cnr of plaza) The Hotel Santa Clara was built by Diego de Mazariegos, the Spanish conqueror of Chiapas. His coat of arms is engraved above the main portal. The house is a rare secular example of plateresque style in Mexico.

Cerro de San Cristóbal & Cerro de Guadalupe LOOKOUT

Want to take in the best views in town? Well, you'll have to work for them, because at this altitude the stairs up these hills can be punishing. Churches crown both lookouts, and the **Iglesia de Guadalupe** becomes a hot spot for religious devotees around the Día de la Virgen de Guadalupe (December 12).

WORTH A TRIP

EXPLORE MORE OF CHIAPAS STATE

Try out some of these DIY adventures:

➡ **Agua Azul and Misol-Ha** These spectacular water attractions – the thundering cascades of Agua Azul and the 35m jungle waterfall of Misol-Ha (www.misol-ha.com) – are both short detours off the Ocosingo–Palenque road.

➡ **Lagos de Montebello** The temperate pine and oak forest along the Guatemalan border east of Chinkultic is dotted with more than 50 small lakes of varied hues. The nearby **Chinkultic ruins** add to the mystery.

➡ **Ocosingo** A respite from both the steamy lowland jungle and the chilly highlands, the bustling regional market town of Ocosingo sits in a gorgeous valley between San Cristóbal and Palenque. The impressive Maya ruins of **Toniná** (☎ 919-108-22-39; admission M$41; ⏲ 8am-5pm) await a few kilometers away.

➡ **Reserva de la Biosfera la Encrucijada** This large biosphere reserve protects a 1448-sq-km strip of coastal lagoons, sand bars and wetlands.

➡ **Sima de las Cotorras** (☎ 968-689-0289; simacotorras@hotmail.com) A dramatic sinkhole punching 160m wide and 140m deep into the earth and a habitat for thousands of parrots. It's about 1½ hours' drive from Tuxtla Gutiérrez.

Beware: these areas are not considered safe at night.

Templo & Ex-Convento de Santo Domingo CHURCH
(⏲6:30am-2pm & 4-8pm) FREE Just north of the center, the 16th-century Templo de Santo Domingo is San Cristóbal's most beautiful church. The baroque frontage, with its outstanding filigree stucco work, was added in the 17th century and includes the double-headed Hapsburg eagle, symbol of the Spanish monarchy in those days. The interior is lavishly gilded, especially the ornate pulpit.

Around Santo Domingo and the neighboring **Templo de la Caridad** (built in 1712), Chamulan women and bohemian types from around Mexico conduct a colorful daily crafts market. The ex-monastery attached to Santo Domingo contains two interesting exhibits: one is the weavers' showroom of Señora Jolobil; the other is the **Centro Cultural de los Altos** (☎678-16-09; Calz Cárdenas s/n; admission M$46; ⏲9am-6pm Tue-Sun), which contains a Spanish-language museum on the history of the San Cristóbal region.

Na Bolom HISTORIC BUILDING
(☎678-1418; www.nabolom.org; Guerrero 33; admission M$40, with tour M$50; ⏲7am-7pm) An atmospheric museum and research center, Na Bolom is dedicated to the study and support of Chiapas' indigenous cultures and natural environment, and has community and environmental programs in indigenous areas. Its library of more than 9000 books and documents is a major resource on the Maya.

Mercado Municipal MARKET
(⏲ outside shops 6am-6pm, inside stalls 8am-3pm) For a closer look at local life – and an assault on the senses – visit San Cristóbal's busy municipal market, eight blocks north of the main plaza.

Museo de la Medicina Maya MUSEUM
(☎678-5438; Av Salomón González Blanco 10; admission M$20; ⏲9am-5pm Mon-Fri, to 4pm Sat & Sun; P) This award-winning museum introduces the system of traditional medicine used by many indigenous people in the Chiapas highlands. It's a 20-minute walk north from the plaza.

Centro Cultural El Carmen CULTURAL BUILDING
(Hermanos Domínguez s/n; ⏲9am-6pm Tue-Sun) FREE The **Arco del Carmen** dates from the late 17th century and was once the city's gateway. The ex-convent just east is a wonderful colonial building, with a large, peaceful garden. It's now a cultural center, hosting art and photography exhibitions and the occasional musical event.

Café Museo Café MUSEUM, CAFE
(☎678-7876; MA Flores 10; admission M$30; ⏲7am-10pm) This cafe and coffee museum is a venture of Coopcafé, a grouping of more than 17,000 small-scale (mainly indigenous) Chiapas coffee growers.

Museo del Ámbar de Chiapas MUSEUM
(☎678-9716; www.museodelambar.com.mx; Plazuela de la Merced; admission M$20; ⏲10am-2pm & 4-8pm Tue-Sun) Come here for an explanation of all things amber; it displays and sells some exquisitely carved items and insect-embedded pieces.

Courses

El Puente Spanish Language School LANGUAGE COURSE
(☎678-3723; www.elpuenteweb.com; Real de Guadalupe 55) Learn *español* here; homestays available.

La Casa en el Árbol LANGUAGE COURSE
(☎967 674-52-72; www.lacasaenelarbol.org; Real de Mexicanos 10; classes-only individual/group per hr M$143/91, 7 days family accommodations M$1885) Socially committed school that teaches Tzeltal and Tzotzil as well as Spanish. It offers lots of out-of-school activities and is also a base for volunteer programs.

Tours

Explora ADVENTURE TOURS
(☎674-6660; www.ecochiapas.com; Calle 1 de Marzo 30; ⏲9:30am-2pm & 4-8pm Mon-Fri, 9:30am-2pm Sat) Specializes in three- to six-day river kayaking and rafting adventures to the Lacandón jungle communities.

Jaguar Adventours BICYCLE RENTAL
(☎631-5062; www.adventours.mx; Av Belisario Domínguez 8A; bicycle rentals per hr M$40, per day M$200; ⏲9am-2:30pm & 3:30-8pm Mon-Sat, 9am-2:30pm Sun) Bicycle tours to Chamula (20km) and Zincantán (32km), plus longer expeditions of up to 80km.

Festivals & Events

Feria de la Primavera y de la Paz RELIGIOUS
(Spring & Peace Fair) Easter Sunday is the start of the weeklong town fair, with parades, musical events, bullfights and so on.

Chiapas

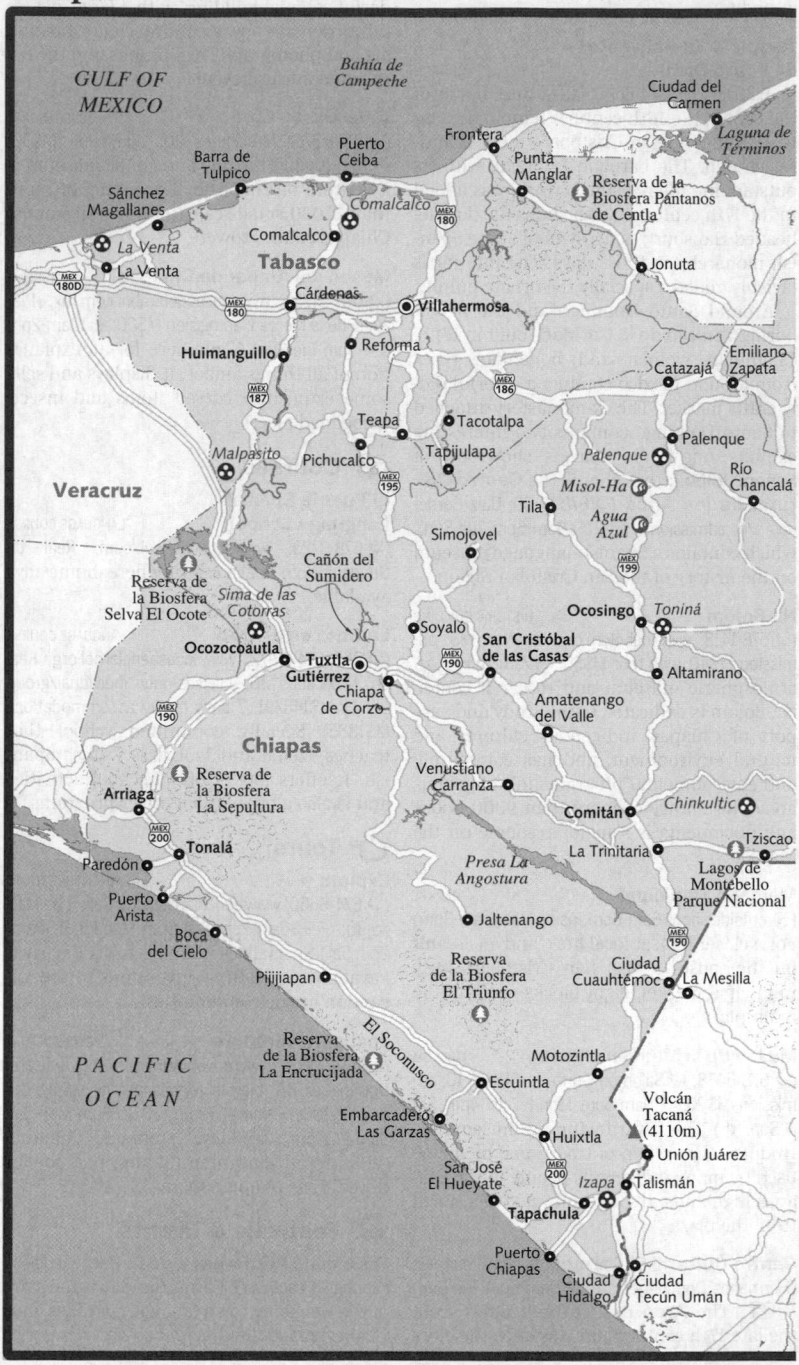
GULF OF MEXICO
Bahía de Campeche
Ciudad del Carmen
Laguna de Términos
Frontera
Puerto Ceiba
Barra de Tulpico
Punta Manglar
Reserva de la Biosfera Pantanos de Centla
Sánchez Magallanes
Comalcalco
MEX 180
La Venta
Comalcalco
Tabasco
Jonuta
MEX 180D
La Venta
Cárdenas
MEX 180
Villahermosa
Reforma
Huimanguillo
Catazajá
Emiliano Zapata
MEX 187
MEX 186
Teapa
Tacotalpa
Palenque
Malpasito
Pichucalco
Tapijulapa
Palenque
Río Chancalá
Veracruz
MEX 195
Misol-Ha
Tila
Agua Azul
Simojovel
MEX 199
Cañón del Sumidero
Reserva de la Biosfera Selva El Ocote
Sima de las Cotorras
Ocosingo
Toniná
Soyaló
San Cristóbal de las Casas
Ocozocoautla
Tuxtla Gutiérrez
MEX 190
Altamirano
Chiapa de Corzo
Amatenango del Valle
MEX 190
Chiapas
Reserva de la Biosfera La Sepultura
Venustiano Carranza
Arriaga
Comitán
Chinkultic
MEX 200
Tonalá
La Trinitaria
Tziscao
Paredón
Presa La Angostura
Lagos de Montebello Parque Nacional
Puerto Arista
Jaltenango
Boca del Cielo
MEX 190
Reserva de la Biosfera El Triunfo
Ciudad Cuauhtémoc
La Mesilla
Pijijiapan
El Soconusco
Reserva de la Biosfera La Encrucijada
Motozintla
PACIFIC OCEAN
Escuintla
Volcán Tacaná (4110m)
Embarcadero Las Garzas
Huixtla
Unión Juárez
San José El Hueyate
MEX 200
Izapa
Talismán
Tapachula
Puerto Chiapas
Ciudad Hidalgo
Ciudad Tecún Umán

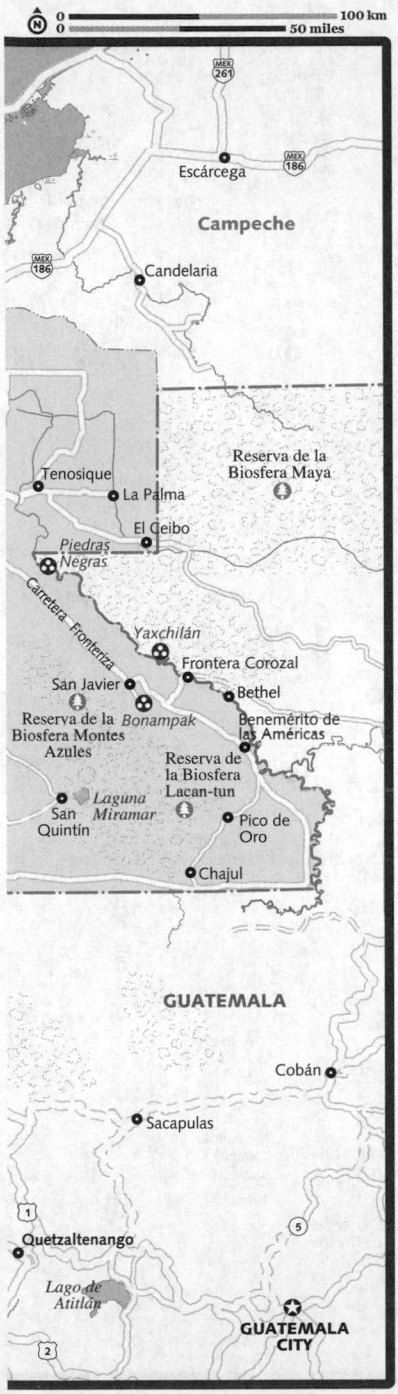

Festival de las Culturas CULTURAL
(www.conecultachiapas.gob.mx) In mid- to late-October, this free weeklong cultural program stages interesting music, dance and theater performances.

Sleeping

Posada La Media Luna HOTEL $
(☎631-5590; www.hotel-lamedialuna.com; Hermanos Domínguez 5; s/d/tr/q M$400/500/600/700, apt M$1300; @) This friendly, Italian-owned place is a great budget choice. It's well-maintained and offers comfortable and pretty rooms with cable TV, all set around a covered patio with potted plants. But beware of nearby church bells!

Rossco Backpackers HOSTEL $
(☎674-0525; www.rosscohostel.com; Real de Mexicanos 16; dm incl breakfast M$165-185, d/tr/q incl breakfast M$500/700/800; P @) Wonderful hostel in an old building with rooms surrounding a lovely garden. Dorms are good though tight, and spacious privates are hotel-quality and come with rustic furniture and towel animals, and some have skylights.

México Hostel HOSTEL $
(☎678-0014; www.himexico.com; Josefa Ortiz de Domínguez 12; dm M$160, r with shared/private bathroom M$400/440; P @) A large courtyard compound with stunning mountain views, this HI-affiliated hostel has pretty gardens, good, bright rooms and dorms (one for women only), a kitchen and lots of comfy common areas.

Hostal Rincón de los Camellos HOSTEL $
(☎967 116-0097; www.loscamellos.over-blog.com; Real de Guadalupe 110; dm M$80, s/d/tr/q without bathroom M$160/220/270/340, with bathroom M$220/280/330/400) A clean, tranquil little spot run by a welcoming French-Mexican trio. The brightly painted rooms are set around two patios, with a grassy little garden out back.

Hotel Posada Tepeyac HOSTEL $
(Real de Guadalupe 40) A neat, small hotel in the heart of the Real de Guadalupe travelers' scene. The 33 clean rooms, around a couple of pretty little patios and a lovely stained-glass foyer, sport zingy color schemes.

Eating

Stock up on groceries at the centrally located **Super Más** (Real de Guadalupe 22; ⏲8am-9:30pm) market.

San Cristóbal de las Casas

San Cristóbal de las Casas

Sights

1 Arco del Carmen C5
2 Café Museo Café C3
3 Cathedral C4
4 Centro Cultural de los Altos C2
5 Centro Cultural El Carmen C5
6 Hotel Santa Clara C4
7 Mercado Municipal D1
8 Museo del Ámbar de Chiapas A4
9 Na Bolom F2
10 Plaza 31 de Marzo C4
11 Templo & Ex-Convento de Santo Domingo C2
12 Templo de la Caridad C2

Activities, Courses & Tours

El Puente Spanish Language School ..... (see 24)
13 Explora B3
14 Jaguar Adventours D4
15 La Casa en el Árbol B2

Sleeping

16 Hostal Rincón de los Camellos F4
17 Hotel Posada Tepeyac D4
18 México Hostel D4
19 Posada La Media Luna C5
20 Rossco Backpackers B2

Eating

21 Arez D4
22 El Caldero C4
23 El Horno Mágico C4
24 La Casa del Pan Papalotl D4
25 Tierradentro C4
26 Trattoria Italiana D3

Drinking & Nightlife

27 Kakao Natura C5
28 La Viña de Bacco C4

Entertainment

29 Cafe Bar Revolución C3
30 Cocoliche D4

Shopping

31 Super Más C4

Tierradentro MEXICAN $

(674-6766; Real de Guadalupe 24; set menu M$65-100; 8:15am-10:30pm;) A popular gathering center for coffee-swigging, laptop-toting locals, this large indoor courtyard restaurant and cafe is a comfortable place to while away the hours. It's run by Zapatista supporters, who hold frequent cultural events and conferences on local issues here. A simple yet delicious *menú del día* (set menu M$65 to M$100) rotates daily.

Arez MIDDLE EASTERN
(☎967 678-6308; Real de Guadalupe 29; wraps M$25-45, mains M$60-90; ⏲noon-11pm) Lamb shawarma and other delicious dishes grace the menu of this Lebanese falafel spot. Try the 'barbecue Arez,' with grilled beef, chicken, onions and peppers.

La Casa del Pan Papalotl MEXICAN $
(☎678-7215; Real de Guadalupe 55; mains M$50-100; ⏲8am-10pm Mon-Sat; ✉) This excellent courtyard vegetarian restaurant does a particularly filling buffet lunch from 1:30pm to 4:30pm (M$100). Fresh bread and locally grown organic ingredients are staples here.

El Caldero MEXICAN $
(Insurgentes 5; soups M$49; ⏲11am-10pm) Simple, friendly little El Caldero specializes in delicious, filling Mexican soups like *pozole* (shredded pork in broth) and *mondongo* (tripe and beef) – all with sides of tortillas, onions and spices.

El Horno Mágico BAKERY $
(Utrilla 7; bread & pastries under M$25; ⏲8:30am-8:30pm) Offering some of the best French bread in town, it bakes delicious pastries as well.

Trattoria Italiana ITALIAN $$
(☎678-5895; Dr Navarro 10; mains M$120-145; ⏲2-10pm Mon & Thu-Sat, 2-5:30pm Sun) A mother and daughter–run Italian eatery specializing in ravioli, handmade fresh every day. The sauces are divine – don't miss the mango, chipotle and gorgonzola sauce if it's available.

Drinking

La Viña de Bacco WINE BAR
(☎119-1985; Real de Guadalupe 7; ⏲2pm-midnight Mon-Sat) San Cristóbal's most popular wine bar serves international *vino*, beer, tequila and coffee. On warm nights, the sidewalk tables are hot spots.

Kakao Natura CAFE
(Moreno 2A; ⏲8am-10pm Mon-Sat) For something different, melt into a hot chocolate at this *chocolatería*. Order a classic, semibitter or bitter, and add cardoman, vanilla or even chilis for a few pesos.

Entertainment

Cafe Bar Revolución LIVE MUSIC
(1 de Marzo 11; ⏲noon-3am) With live music daily from 8:30pm, every day brings new sounds – Monday features blues and electronica, Tuesday is salsa and Wednesday you get reggae and jazz. Cocktails like mojitos and caipirinhas add joy.

Cocoliche LIVE MUSIC
(Colón 3; ⏲noon-midnight) By day it's a funky bohemian restaurant, come nighttime the live music starts up – expect Mexican bands with the occasional international guest musician.

Information

Banamex (⏲9am-4pm Mon-Sat) Has an ATM; exchanges dollars and euros.

Main Post Office (☎678-0765; Allende 3; ⏲7:30am-7pm Mon-Fri, 8:30am-3:30pm Sat)

Municipal Tourist Office (☎678-06-65; Palacio Municipal, Plaza 31 de Marzo; ⏲8am-9pm)

Getting There & Away

A fast toll *autopista* (expressway; M$45 for cars) zips here from Chiapa de Corzo. An increased military and police presence has reduced the number of highway holdups on Hwy 199 between Ocosingo and Palenque, but it's still best to avoid traveling at night.

AIR

San Cristóbal's airport, about 15km from town on the Palenque road, has no regular passenger flights; the main airport serving town is at Tuxtla Gutiérrez. Five daily OCC minibuses (M$170, 1¼ hours) run between Tuxtla's airport and San Cristóbal's main bus terminal; book in advance.

BUS, COLECTIVO & VAN

The main bus terminal is the 1st-class **OCC terminal** (☎678-0291; cnr Pan-American Hwy & Insurgentes). Bus tickets are also sold in the center of town at **Boletotal** (☎678-0291; www.boletotal.mx; Real de Guadalupe 16; ⏲7:30am-10:30pm).

First-class AEXA and 2nd-class Ómnibus de Chiapas share a terminal on the south side of the highway. Also, various *combi* and *colectivo* taxi companies to Ocosingo, Tuxtla and Comitán have depots on the highway in the same area (it's a frenzied madhouse with shouting operators competing for passengers).

DESTINATION	COST (M$)	DURATION (HR)
Campeche	415	11
Cancún	795-950	18
Ciudad Cuauhtémoc (Guatemalan border)	95	3½
Mérida	532	14
Mexico City (TAPO)	350-1060	13-14
Palenque	80-166	5
Villahermosa	232	6

CAR

San Cristóbal's only car-rental company, **Optima** (☎674-5409; optimacar1@hotmail.com; Mazariegos 39), rents VW Beetles for M$500 per day and M$3000 per week, but has other car makes too. It's located inside Hotel Mansión del Valle; ask for a discount if paying with cash.

ℹ Getting Around

San Cristóbal is very walkable, with straight streets rambling up and down several gentle hills. The Pan-American Hwy (Hwy 190, Bulevar Juan Sabines) runs through the southern part of town, and nearly all transportation terminals are on it or nearby. *Combis* (M$5) go up Crescencio Rosas from the Pan-American Hwy to the town center.

From the OCC bus terminal, it's six blocks north up Insurgentes to the central square, Plaza 31 de Marzo.

Taxis cost M$25 to M$30 within town and about M$35 at night.

Croozy Scooters (☎683-2223; croozyscooters@live.com.mx; Belisario Domínguez 7; scooters per 3hr/day M$250/400; ⏲10am-6pm, later by appointment) rents bicycles and well-maintained scooters; passport and deposit required. Jaguar Adventours (p73) also rents quality mountain bikes with helmet and lock.

Around San Cristóbal

The inhabitants of the beautiful Chiapas highlands are descended from the ancient Maya and maintain some unique beliefs, customs and costumes.

During the day, walking or riding by horse or bicycle along the main roads to San Juan Chamula and San Lorenzo Zinacantán should not be risky; however, it's not wise to wander into unfrequented areas or down isolated tracks.

Transportation to most villages goes from points around the Mercado Municipal in San Cristóbal. *Combis* to San Juan Chamula (M$12) leave from Calle Honduras frequently from 4am to about 6:30pm; for Zinacantán, *combis* (M$12) and *colectivo* taxis (M$14) go at least hourly, from 5am to 6pm, from a yard off Robledo.

San Juan Chamula

POP 3300 / ELEV 2200M

The Chamulans are a fiercely independent Tzotzil group, more than 80,000 strong. Their principal village is San Juan Chamula, located 10km northwest of San Cristóbal. There's a weekly market on Sundays, when people from the hills stream into the village to shop, trade and visit the main church. Many tour buses also visit on Sundays, so expect crowds then.

The white **Templo de San Juan**, Chamula's pretty main church, is vividly accented in green and blue. Step inside and you'll instantly notice hundreds of flickering candles, clouds of copal incense and worshipers kneeling with their faces to the pine needle–carpeted floor. Chanting medicine men or women may be rubbing patients' bodies with eggs or bones, and you might even see a chicken or two being sacrificed. As you can imagine, it all makes for a powerful impression.

As an outsider, you're allowed to enter the church, but you must obtain a ticket first (M$20). There's usually someone at the church door selling them, or you can get one at the **tourist office** (⏲7am-6pm) in the orange building in front of (and to the side of) the church's front courtyard.

No photography is allowed inside the church.

San Lorenzo Zinacantán

POP 3800 / ELEV 2558M

The orderly village of San Lorenzo Zinacantán, about 11km northwest of San Cristóbal, is the main village of the Zinacantán municipality (population 36,500). Zinacantán people, like Chamulans, are Tzotzil.

A small **market** is held on Sundays until noon, and during fiesta times. The huge central **Iglesia de San Lorenzo** (admission M$15) was rebuilt following a fire in 1975. Photography is banned in the church and churchyard. The small thatch-roofed **Museo Jsotz' Levetik** (admission by donation), three blocks below the central basketball court, covers local culture and has some fine textiles and musical instruments.

Palenque

☎916 / POP 42,900

The soaring jungle-swathed temples of Palenque are a national treasure and one of the best examples of Maya architecture in Mexico. Modern Palenque town, a few kilometers to the east, is a sweaty, humdrum place without much appeal except as a jumping-off point for the ruins, though a recent makeover has spiffed up a few blocks of the main road near the park.

Hwy 199 meets Palenque's main street, Av Juárez, at the Glorieta de la Cabeza Maya, an intersection with a large statue of a Maya chieftain's head, at the west end of the town. From here Av Juárez heads 1km east to the central square, El Parque. The main bus stations are on Av Juárez just east of the Maya statue.

A few hundred meters south from the Maya statue, the paved road to the Palenque ruins, which are 7.5km away, diverges west off Hwy 199. This road passes the site museum after about 6.5km, then winds on about 1km further uphill to the main entrance to the ruins.

History

The name Palenque (Palisade) is Spanish and has no relation to the city's ancient name, which may have been Lakamha (Big Water). Palenque was first occupied around 100 BC, and flourished around AD 630–740. The city rose to prominence under the ruler Pakal, who reigned from 615 to 683. Archaeologists have determined that Pakal is represented by hieroglyphics of sun and shield, and he is also referred to as Escudo Solar (Sun Shield). He lived to the then-incredible age of 80.

Pakal's son Kan B'alam II (r 684–702), who is represented in hieroglyphics by the jaguar and the serpent (and is also called Jaguar Serpent II), continued Palenque's expansion and artistic development. During his reign, Palenque extended its zone of control to the Río Usumacinta, but was challenged by the rival Maya city of Toniná, 65km south.

Kan B'alam's brother and successor, K'an Joy Chitam II (Precious Peccary), was captured by forces from Toniná in 711, and probably executed there. Palenque enjoyed a resurgence between 722 and 736, however, under Ahkal Mo' Nahb' III (Turtle Macaw Lake), who added many substantial buildings. After AD 900, Palenque was largely abandoned.

Sights

Palenque Ruins ARCHAEOLOGICAL SITE
(admission M$57; ⏲ 8am-5pm, last entry 4:30pm)
Just eight kilometers from Palenque city, the ruins of ancient Palenque stand at the precise point where the first hills rise out of the Gulf coast plain. The dense jungle covering these hills forms an evocative backdrop to Palenque's exquisite and unique Maya architecture. Hundreds of ruined buildings are spread over 15 sq km, but only a fairly compact central area has been excavated. The forest around these temples is still home to howler monkeys, toucans and ocelots.

The ruins and surrounding forests form a national park, the Parque Nacional Palenque, for which you must pay a separate M$27 admission fee at Km 4.5 on the road to the ruins.

Don't miss Palenque's extraordinary **Museo de Sitio** (☎ 345-26-84; Carretera Palenque-Ruinas Km 7; admission free with ruins ticket; ⏲ 9am-4:30pm Tue-Sun), which displays finds from the site and interprets Palenque's history. The highlight here is the life-size reproduction of Pakal's (Palenque's greatest leader) carved stone sarcophagus lid.

Official site **guides** (2hr tour for up to 7 people in English M$960) hang out near the entrance and can be identified by their official badges. Unofficial guides are also around and charge less.

Transportes Chambalú (☎ 345-2849; Hidalgo) and **Transportes Palenque** (cnr Allende & Av 20 de Noviembre) run *combis* to the ruins about every 15 minutes from 6am to 6pm daily (M$10 each way). They will pick you up or drop you off anywhere along the town-to-ruins road.

As you enter the site, a line of temples rises in front of the jungle on your right, culminating about 100m ahead at the **Templo de las Inscripciones** (Temple of the Inscriptions), the tallest and most stately of Palenque's buildings. From the top, interior stairs lead down into the **tomb of Pakal** (closed indefinitely to avoid further damage from the humidity exuded by visitors). This is where, in 1952, Pakal's jewel-bedecked skeleton and jade mosaic death mask were finally uncovered by Alberto Ruz Lhuillier (whose **tomb** is in front of Templo XIII). It was one of the greatest Maya archeological finds in history.

Diagonally opposite the Templo de las Inscripciones is **El Palacio** (The Palace), a large structure divided into four main courtyards, with a maze of corridors and rooms. Keep following the path over a bridge and up some stairs; go left at the 'Y' and you'll soon reach the **Grupo de las Cruces** (Group of the Crosses). Soon after the death of his father, Pakal's son Kan B'alam II (684–702) started designing the temples here. The **Templo del Sol** (Temple of the Sun), on the west side of the plaza, has the best-preserved roofcomb at Palenque. Nearby, steep steps

Palenque Ruins

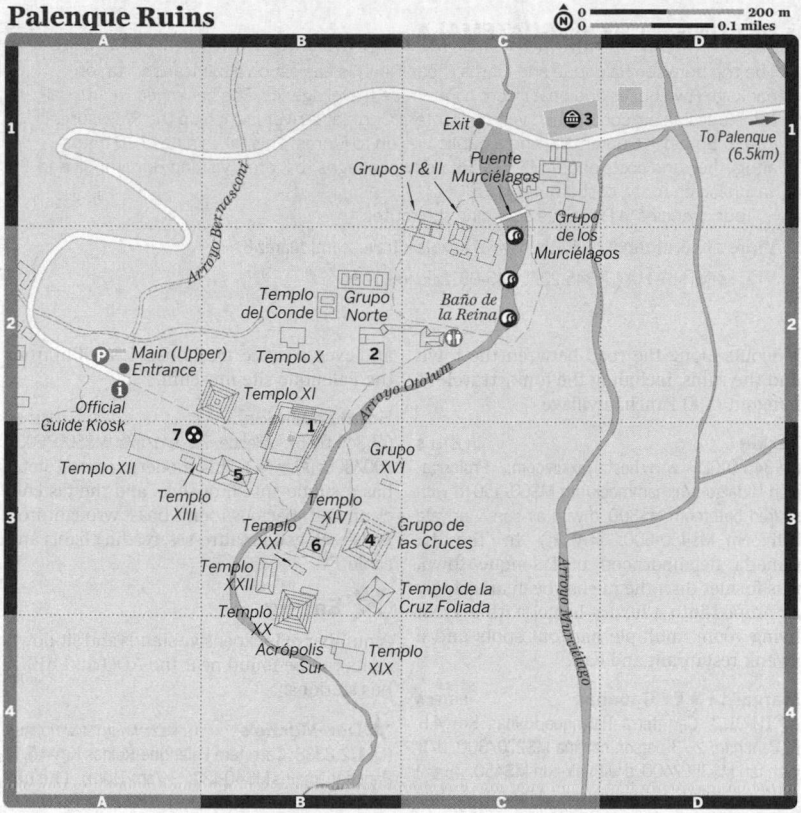

climb to the **Templo de la Cruz** (Temple of the Cross), the largest and most impressive in this group.

South of the Grupo de las Cruces is the **Acrópolis Sur**, where archaeologists have recovered some terrific finds in recent excavations. It appears to have been constructed as an extension of the Grupo de las Cruces, but this area was closed at research time and unfortunately will probably remain closed for a few more years.

Follow the path north and back down to the river; you'll eventually reach the **Juego de Pelota** (Ball Court) and, behind it, the handsome and blissfully souvenir-free buildings of **Grupo Norte** (Northern Group). After a visit here you can follow a steep path down to mildly interesting Grupos II, but better yet double back to the original path and take it across the river again and down a series of steep stairs, eventually reaching the **Grupo de los Murciélagos** (Bat Group).

Palenque Ruins

Sights

1 El Palacio B3
2 Juego de Pelota B2
3 Museo de Sitio C1
4 Templo de la Cruz B3
5 Templo de las Inscripciones Group B3
6 Templo del Sol B3
7 Tomb of Alberto Ruz Lhuillier A3

You'll then cross a pretty bridge with view of a small rocky waterfall – now head up a short way to Grupos II if you'd like – and finally exit via the back way (this exit is open until 4pm).

Sleeping

The first choice to make is whether to stay in or out of Palenque town. Many people prefer to base themselves at one of the forest

GETTING TO TIKAL, GUATEMALA

The trip between Palenque and Flores (near Tikal) is easiest on a full-transportation package (two buses and boat) from a Palenque travel agency. The packaged tour usually includes an air-conditioned van to Frontera Corozal, a river launch up the Río Usumacinta to Bethel in Guatemala, and a public bus on to Flores. This takes nine or 10 hours altogether, and costs about M$350. Two-day packages to Flores, visiting Bonampak and Yaxchilán en route, cost around M$1200.

Tour agencies in Palenque servicing the route:

Viajes Kukulcán (☎345-1506; www.kukulcantravel.com; Juárez 8)

Viajes Misol-Ha (☎345-2271, 345-0911; Juárez 148)

hideouts along the road between the town and the ruins, including the funky travelers' hangout of El Panchán village.

Yaxkin HOSTEL $

(☎345-0102; www.hostalyaxkin.com; Prolongación Hidalgo s/n; hammock/dm M$60/150, d with shared bathroom M$300, d with air-con & private bathroom M$450-600; ❄@📶) In the La Cañada neighborhood of Palenque town, this former discotheque has been amazingly revamped into a luxury hostel with a great living room, multiple hangout spots and a swank restaurant and bar.

Margarita & Ed Cabañas HOTEL $

(☎111-9112; Carreterra Palenque-Ruinas Km 4.5, El Panchán; 2-/3-person cabaña M$270/300, d/tr with fan M$350/400, d with air-con M$450; P❄) Full of local information, Margarita has welcomed travelers to her homey place in El Panchán for nearly 20 years. A variety of clean and cheerful rooms have good mosquito netting, and the more rustic, screened *cabañas* are well kept too.

Hotel Canek HOTEL $

(☎345-0150; www.hotelcanek.com; 20 de Noviembre 43; r with fan/air-con M$450/550; ❄📶) Good, well-maintained budget choice in Palenque town with simple, good-sized rooms, though some are dark – get one facing the street if you can. It has a nice rooftop terrace with a *palapa* and hammocks.

Mayabell HOTEL, CAMPING $$

(☎341-6977; www.mayabell.com.mx; Carretera Palenque-Ruinas Km 6; hammock rental M$20, campsites per person M$60 plus per car M$30, vehicle site with hookups M$180, r with fan/air-con M$750/950, treehouse M$120-150; P❄📶🏊) There's something for everyone at this spacious, grassy complex – camping, hammocks, a trailer park, regular hotel rooms and even a rustic 'treehouse.' It's 400m from the Palenque site museum.

Hotel Lacandonia HOTEL $$

(☎345-00-57; Allende 77; s/d/tr/q M$500/600/700/800; P❄📶) This modern, central hotel has a subtle splash of style, and the tasteful, clean and spacious rooms boast wrought-iron beds with good mattresses, reading lights and cable TV.

Eating

A number of inexpensive stands and sit-down spots can be found near the ADO and AEXA bus stations.

★Don Mucho's MEXICAN, INTERNATIONAL $

(☎112-8338; Carretera Palenque-Ruinas Km 4.5, El Panchán; mains M$40-120; ⏲7am-11pm) The hot spot of El Panchán, Don Mucho's provides great-value meals in a jungle setting, with a candlelit atmosphere at night. There's wide menu variety, from Mexican specialties to home-made pastas and wood-fired pizzas.

Café de Yara CAFE $

(☎345-0269; Hidalgo 66; breakfasts M$38-70, tourist menus M$65-100; ⏲7am-11pm) A sunny start to the day, this modern and beautiful vegetarian-friendly cafe has great breakfasts and excellent Chiapas-grown organic coffee.

El Huachinango Feliz SEAFOOD $

(☎345-4642; Hidalgo s/n; mains M$70-120; ⏲9am-11pm) Popular, atmospheric restaurant in the leafy La Cañada neighborhood. It has an attractive front patio with tables and umbrellas, and there's also an upstairs covered terrace. Seafood is the specialty here.

Restaurant Las Tinajas MEXICAN $

(☎345-4970; cnr Av 20 de Noviembre & Abasolo; mains M$50-100; ⏲7am-11pm) It doesn't take long to figure out why this open-sided, corner restaurant is always busy. It slings large portions of excellent homestyle food, and the menu has a little bit of everything.

La Selva MEXICAN $$
(☎345-03-63; Hwy 199; mains M$70-175; ⏲11:30am-11:30pm; P) Palenque's most upscale restaurant serves well-prepared traditional and specialty dishes under an enormous *palapa* roof. There's a Sunday afternoon buffet (M$155). It's 150m south of the Maya head statue, on the road to the ruins.

Information

There are several internet cafes and banks with ATMs in town.

Clínica Palenque (☎345-0273; Velasco Suárez 33; ⏲8:30am-1:30pm & 5-9pm)

Post Office (Independencia; ⏲8am-8:30pm Mon-Fri, to noon Sat)

Tourist Information Kiosk (El Parque; ⏲9am-2pm & 6-9pm Mon-Fri)

Tourist Office (☎345-0356; Carretera Catazajá-Palenque Km 27.5, cnr Dr Manuel Velasco Suárez; ⏲8am-4pm Mon-Fri)

Getting There & Away

Highway holdups are more a thing of the past, but it's still best not to travel Hwy 199 between Palenque and San Cristóbal at night.

Palenque's airport has no commercial flights. The closest major airport is in Villahermosa.

ADO (☎345-1344; Av Juárez) has the main bus terminal, with deluxe and 1st-class services, an ATM and left-luggage facilities; it's also used by OCC (1st-class) and TRT (2nd-class). **AEXA** (☎345-2630; Av Juárez 159), with 1st-class buses, and Cardesa (2nd-class) are 1½ blocks east. Transportes Palenque runs vans to Tenosique, which has onward connections to Guatemala.

Getting Around

Taxis charge M$50 (M$70 at night) to El Panchán and M$60 to the ruins. *Combis* (M$10) head to the ruins from 6am to 6pm and can stop anywhere along the way.

Bonampak, Yaxchilán & the Carretera Fronteriza

The ancient Maya cities of Bonampak and Yaxchilán, southeast of Palenque, are easily accessible thanks to the Carretera Fronteriza. This good, paved road runs parallel to the Mexico–Guatemala border all the way from Palenque to the Lagos de Montebello, and goes around the fringe of the Lacandón Jungle.

Bonampak, famous for its frescoes, is 152km by road from Palenque. The bigger and more important Yaxchilán, with a peerless jungle setting beside the broad and swift Río Usumacinta, is 173km by road, then about 22km by boat. Both can be visited in one long day.

Tours

If you don't have wheels, the easiest way to see both Bonampak and Yaxchilán is by taking a tour from Palenque. This is more much time-efficient, less stressful and actually cheaper than dealing with public transport – and gives enough time at each site for most people. Various tour agencies in Palenque organize this tour, and each charges the same – M$550 to M$650 per person, depending on the season. Entry fees, two meals and all transportation (except a M$15 dock fee at Yaxchilán) is included, but there's no tour guide (these can be hired at each site).

Be aware that a cooperative requires all travelers to take a Lacandón van through their jungle to Bonampak. This happens about 3km into the side road towards the ruins; all travelers must stop at a checkpoint (whether they're in private vehicles or tour vans) and switch into a Lacandón van. The charge is high – M$70 per person for essentially a 19km roundtrip ride. This charge is already included in the price for travelers taking the day tour from Palenque.

DEPARTURES FROM PALENQUE

DESTINATION	COST (M$)	DURATION (HR)
Campeche	285-300	5
Cancún	470-685	13
Mérida	425-450	8
San Cristóbal de las Casas	90-160	5
Tulum	478-566	11
Villahermosa	120	2½

For private vehicles, on the Carretera Fronteriza there's a Pemex gas station at Chancalá and another at Benemerito. Because of the highway's proximity to Guatemala, expect a few military checkpoints looking for illegal immigrants or drugs; it's best not to drive this road at night.

Mesoamerican Ecotourism Alliance TOUR (www.travelwithmea.org) Organizes all-inclusive trips to the region, including the Lacandón villages of Nahá and Metzabok.

Bonampak

The site of **Bonampak** (admission M$46; ⏲8am-4:30pm) spreads over 2.4 sq km, but all the main ruins stand around the rectangular Gran Plaza. Never a major city, Bonampak spent most of the Classic period in Yaxchilán's sphere of influence. The most impressive surviving monuments were built under Chan Muwan II, a nephew of the Yaxchilán's Itzamnaaj B'alam II, who acceded to Bonampak's throne in AD 776. The 6m-high **Stele 1** in the Gran Plaza depicts Chan Muwan holding a ceremonial staff at the height of his reign. He also features in **Stele 2** and **Stele 3** on the Acrópolis, which rises from the south end of the plaza.

However, it's the vivid frescoes inside the modest-looking **Templo de las Pinturas** (Edificio 1) that have given Bonampak its fame – and its name, which means 'Painted Walls' in Yucatec Maya.

The Bonampak site abuts the Reserva de la Biosfera Montes Azules, and is rich in wildlife.

ℹ Getting There & Away

To reach Bonampak from Palenque via public transport, take an hourly *combi* bound for either Frontera Corozal or Benemerito and ask to be let out at San Javier (M$60, two hours). This is the 12km turnoff for Bonampak; from here you'll have to take a Lacandón vehicle to the ruins (M$70 to M$80 per person roundtrip with two hours waiting time).

The *combis* that drop you at San Javier leave from a small van depot just south of the Maya Head statue at the entrance to Palenque; look for the black grate fence next to the 'Carne Suprema' sign. They also leave from the Transportes Montebello bus terminal, which is a few blocks northwest of Palenque's center, on Velasco Suárez near the corner of Calle 4A Poniente Norte.

Yaxchilán

Jungle-shrouded **Yaxchilán** (admission M$49; ⏲8am-4:30pm, last entry 3:30pm) has a terrific setting above a horseshoe loop in the Río Usumacinta. The control this location gave it over river commerce, and a series of successful alliances and conquests, made Yaxchilán one of the most important Classic Maya cities in the Usumacinta region. Archaeologically, Yaxchilán is famed for its ornamented facades and roofcombs, and its impressive stone lintels carved with conquest and ceremonial scenes. A flashlight is helpful for exploring some parts of the site.

Howler monkeys (saraguates) inhabit the tall trees, and are an evocative highlight. You'll almost certainly hear their visceral roars, and you stand a good chance of seeing some. Spider monkeys, and occasionally red macaws, can also be spotted here at times.

Yaxchilán peaked in power and splendor between AD 681 and 800 under the rulers Itzamnaaj B'alam II (Shield Jaguar II, 681–742), Pájaro Jaguar IV (Bird Jaguar IV, 752–68) and Itzamnaaj B'alam III (Shield Jaguar III, 769–800). The city was abandoned around AD 810. Inscriptions here tell more about its 'jaguar' dynasty than is known of almost any other Maya ruling clan. The shield-and-jaguar symbol appears on many Yaxchilán buildings and steles; Pájaro Jaguar IV's hieroglyph is a small jungle cat with feathers on its back and a bird superimposed on its head.

As you walk toward the ruins, a signed path to the right leads up to the **Pequeña Acrópolis**, a group of ruins on a small hilltop – you can visit this later. Staying on the main path, you soon reach the mazy passages of **El Laberinto** (Edificio 19), built between AD 742 and 752, during the interregnum between Itzamnaaj B'alam II and Pájaro Jaguar IV. Dozens of bats find shelter under the structure's roof today. From this complicated two-level building you emerge at the northwest end of the extensive **Gran Plaza**.

Though it's difficult to imagine anyone here ever wanting to be any hotter than they already were, **Edificio 17** was apparently a sweathouse. About halfway along the plaza, **Stele 1**, flanked by weathered sculptures of a crocodile and a jaguar, shows Pájaro Jaguar IV in a ceremony that took place in AD 761. **Edificio 20**, from the time of Itzamnaaj B'alam III, was the last significant structure built at Yaxchilán; its lintels are now in Mexico City. **Stele 11**, at the northeast corner of the Gran Plaza, was originally found in front of Edificio 40. The bigger of the two figures visible on it is Pájaro Jaguar IV.

An imposing stairway climbs from Stele 1 to **Edificio 33**, the best-preserved temple at Yaxchilán, with about half of its roofcomb intact. The final step in front of the building is carved with ball-game scenes, and splendid relief carvings embellish the undersides of the lintels. Inside is a statue of Pájaro Jaguar IV, minus the head, which it lost to treasure-seeking, 19th-century timber cutters.

From the clearing behind Edificio 33, a path leads into the trees. About 20m along this path, fork left uphill; go left at another fork after about 80m, and in 10 minutes or so, mostly going uphill, you'll reach three buildings on a hilltop: **Edificio 39**, **Edificio 40** and **Edificio 41**.

Getting There & Away

To reach Yaxchilán from Palenque, take an hourly *combi* bound for Frontera Corozal (M$100, 2¾ hours), where you'll have to pay a M$15 per person charge to enter the *embarcadero* (dock) area.

From here it's a 40-minute *lancha* (motorboat) ride to the ruins.

All boat operators charge the same. Round trip with 2½ hours waiting time costs M$700 for one to three people. The boats usually leave frequently from 7am until 1:30pm or so, and it's sometimes possible to hook up with other travelers or a tour group to share costs.

It's possible to take a *combi* between the two ruins. Visit Yaxchilán first, then wait for a *combi* heading back to Palenque and ask to be let off at San Javier. Always check when the last *combi* back to Palenque is – usually it's around 4pm or 5pm, depending on the season.

UNDERSTAND MEXICO'S YUCATÁN & CHIAPAS

Mexico's Yucatán & Chiapas Today

Tourism is the driving force behind life in the Yucatán. It shapes politics, economics and many of the region's important social issues. The peninsula's two busiest gateway cities, Cancún and Mérida, saw international arrivals increase by about 5% in 2012, which was great news for the many hotels, restaurants and tour companies that depend on a steady flow of dollars pouring in each year.

Yet despite the tourism boom, poverty remains a pressing concern. An estimated 51% of Mexico's population lives below the poverty line and the poorest of the poor are often indigenous people who live in rural communities, where food, medical services and work are hard to come by. Income inequality is especially a hot-button topic in the Yucatán state, home to one of the largest indigenous populations in the nation.

After a 12-year hiatus the former ruling party, known as the PRI, stormed back to power in 2012. The PRI's telegenic presidential candidate Enrique Peña Nieto defeated leftist Andrés Manuel López Obrador in an election allegedly marred with widespread fraud. The PRI also governs in all three peninsular states. Prior to 2000, the PRI ruled Mexico for 70 consecutive years. The Peña Nieto government has vowed to implement sweeping reform in key sectors such as telecommunications, education and energy.

THE ZAPATISTAS

To learn more about the Zapatistas, check out www.ezln.org.mx (in Spanish). Further background is available in *The Zapatista Reader*, an anthology of writers from Octavio Paz and Gabriel García Márquez to the Zapatista leader Marcos himself, as well as at the **SiPaz** (www.sipaz.org) and **Radio Zapatista** (www.radiozapatista.org) websites.

History

The Maya set up many city-states across the broad south of Mexico, though the population and activity had declined before the Spanish arrived. A couple of Spaniards – Diego de Mazariegos in present-day Chiapas, and Francisco de Montejo in the Yucatán – had the area under Spanish control by the mid-16th century. Mexico won independence from Spain in 1821, and pulled in Chiapas from the United Provinces of Central America in 1824.

Long oppressed by Spaniards and *criollos* (Latin Americans of Spanish lineage), the Maya rose in the Caste War in 1847, leading to destroyed churches and many massacres. The brimming sense of inequality didn't settle with peace in 1901. As the North American Free Trade Agreement (NAFTA) kicked into effect in 1994, the mainly Maya Zapatistas stormed San Cristóbal de las Casas. Their struggle has quieted down in recent years, now that they run five autonomous zones (called *caracoles*, literally 'snails') outside San Cristóbal.

The Culture

Travelers often comment on the open, gentle and gregarious nature of the people of the Yucatán, especially the Maya. Here, more than elsewhere in Mexico, it seems, you find a willingness to converse and a genuine interest in outsiders. This openness is all the more remarkable when you consider that the people of the Yucatán Peninsula have fended off domination by outsiders for so long. The situation persists today – much of the land is foreign-owned and the Maya generally don't get any say in the big infrastructure decisions.

SURVIVAL GUIDE

Directory A–Z

ACCOMMODATIONS

If you're dorming it, a bunk runs from M$100 to M$170; if you go 'private,' Quintana Roo rates are higher than in the rest of the Yucatán Peninsula and Chiapas. You'll need a towel and soap for some cheap stays and some budget digs lack mosquito nets (but not mosquitoes). Places on the beach and in Palenque charge around M$100 for campsites or hammocks.

ACTIVITIES

Diving in the Yucatán is a big highlight, with great dives off the entire Quintana Roo coast, especially Isla Cozumel. Also fun is snorkeling or diving in cenotes between Playa del Carmen and Tulum. You can rappel into one at Ek' Balam. There are kayak trips at the Reserva de la Biosfera Sian Ka'an. In the highlands you can arrange good bike trips from San Cristóbal de las Casas.

BOOKS

If you're venturing to Oaxaca, Mexico City or further inland on the Yucatán Peninsula, pick up Lonely Planet's *Mexico* or *Cancún, Cozumel & the Yucatán* guides.

CLIMATE

It's always hot in the Yucatán and around Palenque. The wet season, from May to October, makes the air sticky and hot. The hurricane season lasts from June to November, with most of the activity from mid-August to mid-September. In the Chiapas highlands, temperatures cool considerably, hovering between 10°C (50°F) and 20°C (68°F) all year.

CUSTOMS

The normal routine when you enter Mexico by air is to complete a customs declaration form (which lists duty-free allowances), then place it in a machine. If the machine shows a green light, you pass without inspection. If a red light shows, your baggage will be searched.

DANGERS & ANNOYANCES

Despite often alarming media reports and official warnings for Mexico in general, the Yucatán Peninsula and Chiapas remain safe places to travel, and with just a few precautions you can minimize the risk of encountering problems.

Be wary of your belongings on night buses, on the beach and in crowded markets.

Women traveling alone, even pairs of women, should be cautious about going to remote beach and jungle spots. Take *sitio* (stationed) taxis rather than hailing cabs on the street, especially at night.

Cocaine and marijuana are prevalent in Mexico, and possession of small amounts for personal consumption has been legalized – that said, there's still a lot of violence that goes along with drug trafficking so you're better off avoiding drugs. Drug trafficking and illicit northbound immigration are concerns along the border regions with Guatemala, and military checkpoints are frequent on the highway along the Guatemalan border from Palenque to the Lagos de Montebello. These checkpoints generally increase security for travelers, though it's best to be off the highway before dark. For similar reasons all border crossings with Guatemala are places you should aim to get through early in the day.

Indigenous villages are often extremely close-knit, and their people can be suspicious of outsiders and particularly sensitive about having their photos taken. In some villages cameras are, at best, tolerated – and sometimes not even that. You may put yourself in physical danger

SLEEPING PRICE RANGES

We list prices for high season, generally December to March. Unless otherwise stated, prices are for doubles with private bathroom.

$	Less than M$550
$$	M$550–1200
$$$	More than M$1200

by taking photos without permission. Always ask first.

DISCOUNT CARDS

The ISIC student card, the IYTC card for travelers under 26, and the ITIC card for teachers can help you obtain reduced-price air tickets to or from Mexico at student- and youth-oriented travel agencies. Staying at hostels affiliated with Hostelling International (HI) saves about M$10 per night.

EMBASSIES & CONSULATES

Most embassies are in Mexico City; Cancún is home to several consulates, and there are some diplomatic outposts in Mérida as well.

Belizean Consulate (☎983-285-35-11; Génova 369, Colonia Benito Juárez)

Canadian Consulate (☎984-803-2411; playadelcarmen@canada.org.mx; Av 10 Sur btwn Calles 3 & 5 Sur, Playa del Carmen)

Dutch Consulate (☎998-884-8672; Av Nichupte, in Pabellón Caribe, Cancún)

French Consulate (☎998-147-74-48; consulatcancun@aol.com; Blvd Colossio 760, SM 311, Mérida)

German Consulate (☎998-884-15-98; Punta Conoco 36, SM24, Cancún)

Guatemalan Consulate (☎962-626-12-52; 5a Nte 5, Tapachula)

UK Consulate (☎998-881-01-84; Royal Sands, Blvd Kukulcán Km 13.5, Zona Hotelera, Cancún)

US Consulate (☎998-883-02-72; Despacho 301, Torre La Europea, Blvd Kukulcán Km 13, Zona Hotelera, Cancún)

FOOD

Look for *comidas corridas* or *comidas económicas* – these basic set meals, served for lunch (and into the afternoon), are widespread and cheap. They usually come as soup, a meat dish with rice, a drink and dessert.

GAY & LESBIAN TRAVELERS

Cancún and Playa del Carmen are the biggest destinations. Here are some good online resources:

- **Gay Mexico Map** (www.gaymexicomap.com)
- **GM** (www.gaymexico.com.mx)
- **Out Traveler** (www.outtraveler.com)
- **IGLTA** (www.iglta.com)

INTERNET ACCESS

Internet cafes are easy to find in most places in the Yucatán and Chiapas, other than Punta Allen and the far-flung ruins. It costs about M$10 to M$15 per hour.

LEGAL MATTERS

Mexican law presumes an accused person is guilty until proven innocent. If you're arrested, you have the right to notify your embassy or consulate.

Road travelers should expect occasional police or military checkpoints. They are normally looking for drugs, weapons or illegal migrants.

EATING PRICE RANGES

In this chapter, price indicators denote the cost of a main meal:

$	Less than M$80
$$	M$80 to M$150
$$$	More than M$150

MAPS

Quality regional maps include the highly detailed **ITMB** (www.itmb.ca) 1:500,000 *Yucatán Peninsula Travel Map.*

Guía Roji (www.guiaroji.com.mx) publishes an annually updated national road atlas called *Mapa Turístico Carreteras de Mexico* (M$99). It's widely available throughout Mexico and can be bought from the website.

A good internet resource is **Maps of Mexico** (www.maps-of-mexico.com), with detailed maps of all the states.

MONEY

The Mexican peso (M$) is divided into 100 centavos.

The best way to get pesos in Mexico is from readily available ATMs *(cajeros automáticos)*, which use the Cirrus and Plus systems. You can cash money or traveler's checks at banks or at many *casas de cambio* (exchange offices). It's generally possible to change US and Canadian dollars, euros and British pounds.

Not many cheap accommodations or restaurants accept credit cards, but most travel agencies selling air tickets do.

At most restaurants, a 10% to 15% tip is expected.

OPENING HOURS

Most stores geared to locals (not tourists) are open from 9am to 7pm, with an hour or two off for lunch, Monday to Saturday. Musuems often close Monday and most archaeological sites receive vistors from 8am to 5pm. Post offices are typically open Monday to Friday, and some work Saturday morning hours.

PUBLIC HOLIDAYS

The chief holiday periods are Christmas to New Year, Semana Santa (the week leading up to Easter and up to a week afterward) and mid-July to mid-August. Other national holidays:

- **Día de la Constitución** (Constitution Day) February 5
- **Día de Nacimiento de Benito Juárez** (Anniversary of Benito Juárez' birth) March 21
- **Día del Trabajo** (Labor Day) May 1
- **Día de la Independencia** (Independence Day) September 16
- **Día de la Revolución** (Revolution Day) November 20

RESPONSIBLE TRAVEL

Travelers can help protect the Yucatán's environment by taking the following steps:

- Pack a water purifier or purifying tablets (chlorine dioxide) to avoid unnecessary waste of plastic bottles.
- Don't buy souvenirs made from endangered plants and animals that have been acquired illegally.
- Don't carry off anything that you pick up at the site of an ancient city or out on a coral reef.
- When snorkeling or scuba diving, be careful what you touch and where you place your feet.
- Keep water use down. Most of the Yucatán Peninsula has limited water reserves.
- Don't use sunblock, lotions, perfumes, insect repellent or any other pollutants when swimming in a cenote.

STUDYING

Spanish-language schools are more expensive in Mexico than in the rest of Central America. San Cristóbal de las Casas has the most developed language-school scene, but there are also schools in Playa del Carmen.

TELEPHONE

Casetas de teléfono (call offices) are quite widespread and can be cheaper than card phones. Voice Over Internet Protocol (VOIP) calling such as Skype is a great money-saver.

Area codes have three digits and local numbers have seven. To call a Mexican landline from abroad, dial your international access code, the Mexican country code (52), plus the 10-digit number. Add a 1 before the 10-digit number if you're calling a cell phone.

To make international calls from Mexico, dial the international prefix (00), followed by the dialing code, area code and local number.

To call a town or city in Mexico other than the one you're in, dial the long-distance prefix (01) followed by the area code and number.

Cell Phones

The most widespread cell-phone system in Mexico is **Telcel** (www.telcel.com). Cell phones are cheap in Mexico – you're better off buying one here than bringing one from home. You can get phone credit at most convenience stores and some newsstands.

Phone Cards

To use a Telmex pay phone, you need a phone card called a *tarjeta Ladatel*. These are sold at kiosks and shops everywhere.

Calls from Telmex card phones cost M$3 for unlimited time for local calls (M$1.50 per minute to cell phones); M$2.50 per minute for long-distance within Mexico (M$3 per minute to cell phones); M$5 per minute to the continental US, Canada and Central America; and M$10 per minute to anywhere else.

TOURIST INFORMATION

Just about every town of interest to tourists in the Yucatán has a state or municipal tourist office. You can also call the Mexico City office of the national tourism ministry **Sectur** (☎078; www.sectur.gob.mx) at any hour of the day for information or help in English.

State-run websites include the following:

Campeche (☎981-811-9229, 800-900-2267; www.campeche.travel)

Chiapas (☎961-617-0550, 800-280-3500; www.turismochiapas.gob.mx)

Quintana Roo (☎983-835-0860; http://sedetur.qroo.gob.mx)

Tabasco (☎993-316-3633, 800-216-0842; www.visitetabasco.com)

Yucatán (☎999-930-3760; www.yucatan.travel)

PAID YOUR 'NONIMMIGRANT FEE' YET?

The fee for the tourist permit, called the *derecho para no inmigrante* (DNI; nonimmigrant fee), is M$294, but it's free for people entering by land who stay less than seven days. If you enter Mexico by air, however, the fee is included in your airfare.

If you enter by land, you must pay the fee at a bank in Mexico at any time before you reenter the frontier zone on your way out of Mexico (or before you check in at an airport to fly out of Mexico). Most Mexican border posts have on-the-spot bank offices where you can pay the DNI fee. When you pay at a bank, your tourist permit will be stamped to prove that you have paid.

Look after your tourist permit because it may be checked when you leave the country. You can be fined for not having it.

VISAS & DOCUMENTS

Every tourist must have an easily obtainable Mexican government tourist permit. Some nationalities also need to obtain visas.

Citizens of the USA, Canada, EU, Australia, New Zealand, Iceland, Israel, Japan, Norway and Switzerland are among those who do not require visas to enter Mexico as tourists. The website of the **Instituto Nacional de Migración** (INM, National Migration Institute; ☎800-004-6264; www.inm.gob.mx) lists countries that must obtain a visa to travel to Mexico.

US citizens traveling by land or sea can enter Mexico and return to the US with a passport card, but if traveling by air will need a passport. Non-US citizens passing (even in transit) through the US on the way to or from Mexico should check well in advance on the US's complicated visa rules. Consult a US consulate (p87), or the **US State Department** (www.travel.state.gov) or **US Customs and Border Protection** (www.cbp.gov) website.

The Mexican tourist permit (tourist card; officially the *forma migratoria multiple* or FMM) – is a brief paper document that you must fill out and get stamped by Mexican immigration when you enter Mexico and keep till you leave. It's available at official border crossings, international airports, ports, and often from airlines and Mexican consulates. At land borders you won't usually be given one automatically – you have to ask for it.

A tourist permit only allows you to engage in what are considered tourist activities. The maximum possible stay is 180 days for most nationalities but immigration officers might put a much lower number (as little as 15 or 30 days in some cases) unless you tell them specifically what you need.

VOLUNTEERING

Volunteering is an amazing way to give back and learn from your trip. There are volunteer opportunities in a sea-turtle conservation program offered by **Flora, Fauna y Cultura** (☎984-871-5244; www.florafaunaycultura.org; turtle observation M$390; ⏲9pm-3am Mon-Fri Jul-Sep) in Xcacel-Xcacelito. And you can always look for opportunities at your local hostel or language school. Most programs require a minimum commitment of at least a month, and some charge room and boarding fees.

Getting There & Away

AIR

Most visitors to the Yucatán arrive by air. Direct flights normally originate from an airline's hub city and connecting flights often go through Mexico City. The majority of flights into the peninsula arrive at busy Aeropuerto Internacional de Cancún (p48). The region's other gateways are **Cozumel** (CZM; ☎987-872-2081; www.asur.com.mx; Av 65 & Blvd Aeropuerto; 📶), **Mérida** (MID; ☎999-940-6090; www.asur.com.mx) and Campeche (CPE).

Flights from other parts of Mexico arrive at the airports of Cancún, Campeche, Cozumel, Mérida and **Tuxtla Gutiérrez** (☎961-153-6068), which services San Cristóbal de las Casas in Chiapas.

Airlines

Mexico's major airline for domestic and international flights is **Aeroméxico** (☎Mexico 800-021-4000; www.aeromexico.com), which is usually more expensive than low-cost carriers **VivaAerobus** (☎Mexico City 55-4777-5050, US 888-935-9848; www.vivaaerobus.com), **Volaris** (☎800-122-8000; www.volaris.com) and **Interjet** (☎800-011-2345; www.interjet.com).

The following are just some of the many carriers serving the Yucatán:

Air France (☎Mexico 800-123-1628; www.airfrance.com)

AirTran Airways (☎USA 800-247-8726; www.airtran.com)

American Airlines (☎Mexico 800-904-6000; www.aa.com)

British Airways (☎USA 866-835-4133; www.britishairways.com)

Delta Airlines (☎866-0660; www.delta.com)

Frontier Airlines (☎USA 800-432-1359; www.flyfrontier.com)

United Airlines (☎Mexico 800-900-5000; www.united.com)

BUS

Mexico's bus system is luxurious, with frequent services (unlike much of Central America's); many buses have air-con, toilets, reserved seating and movies. And you pay for it – prices are

DEPARTURE TAX

A departure tax equivalent to about US$48 is levied on international flights from Mexico. It's usually included in the price of your ticket, but if it isn't, you must pay in cash during airport check-in.

There are two taxes on domestic flights: IVA, the value-added tax (16%), and TUA, an airport tax of about US$16. In Mexico, the taxes are normally included in quoted fares and paid when you buy the ticket. But if you bought the ticket outside Mexico you will have to pay the TUA when you check-in at the airport in Mexico.

substantially higher than in the rest of Central America.

Most cities and midsize towns in and around the peninsula have one main bus terminal where all long-distance buses arrive and depart. If there is no single main terminal, different bus companies will have separate terminals scattered around town. **Grupo ADO** operates most of the bus lines serving the Yucatán and Chiapas. *Segunda* (2a) *clase* (2nd-class) buses serve small towns and villages, and provide cheaper, slower travel.

BORDER CROSSINGS

Mexico borders Guatemala and Belize to the south, and there is an array of border crossings between them.

Belize

From Quintana Roo, travelers can connect to buses to Belize (or on to Flores, Guatemala) via Chetumal, just north of Corozal, Belize. Frequent buses run between Chetumal and the Belizean towns of Corozal (M$35 to M$40, one hour) and Orange Walk (M$35 to M$50, two hours). The buses depart from the **Nuevo Mercado Lázaro Cárdenas** (Calzada Veracruz) and some continue on to Belize City. Alternatively, **Gibson's Tours & Transfers** (☎501-423-8006; www.gibsonstoursandtransfers.com; Santa Elena-Corozal border) provides ground transportation to Corozal for M$290 and goes to other Belizean destinations as well. Be prepared to show evidence of the payment of your 'nonimmigrant fee' to leave Mexico.

Each person leaving Belize for Mexico needs to pay a BZ$30 exit fee for stays less than 24 hours and BZ$37.50 for longer stays. All fees must be paid in cash (in Belizean or US currency) and officials usually won't have change for US currency.

Guatemala

From Chiapas, there are three major border crossings to Guatemala.

Southeast of Palenque, at Frontera Corozal, it's possible to boat over to Bethel and get a bus; tour packages ease the uncertainties of this journey. See the box on p82 for more.

South of San Cristóbal de las Casas, the best way into Guatemala is via the convenient Ciudad Cuauhtémoc–La Mesilla, Guatemala border. A few OCC buses run to Ciudad Cuauhtémoc from San Cristóbal de las Casas (M$100, three hours) from 11:30am to 5:30pm, or you can get to Comitán and pick up onward transportation there. Frequent vans, *combis* and buses from Comitán run about every 20 to 30 minutes, 5am to 5pm. From La Mesilla, mototaxis can drop you off at the bus depot. Buses leave frequently for Huehuetenango and Quetzaltenango, where you can find onward connections to Guatemala City. There are banks and money changers on both sides of the border.

Agencies in San Cristóbal also offer daily van service to Guatemala's Quetzaltenango (M$350, eight hours), Panajachel (M$350, nine hours) and Antigua (M$450, 11 hours).

Another option is crossing into Guatemala from the Mexican border town of Tapachula, further southwest. Bus line **Trans Galgos Inter** (www.transgalgosinter.com.gt) has three daily departures from Tapachula to Guatemala City (M$290, six hours).

Getting Around

BOAT

Ferries connect Cancún with Isla Mujeres and Playa del Carmen with Isla Cozumel. Ferries also go to Isla Holbox from Chiquilá, several hours north of Cancún. Most visitors heading to Yaxchilán go by boat.

BUS

Buses in the Yucatán rarely fill, but try to reserve ahead for night buses between the Yucatán and Chiapas. You can book some 1st-class buses through **Boletotal** (☎800-009-9090; www.boletotal.mx).

ADO GL (☎800-900-0105; www.adogl.com.mx) and **OCC** (☎800-900-0105; www.occbus.com.mx) provide luxury services. **ADO** (☎800-900-0105; www.ado.com.mx) sets the 1st-class standard. The biggest 2nd-class companies are Mayab, Oriente and **Noreste** (☎800-280-1010; www.noreste.com.mx).

First-class buses typically cost around M$60 to M$70 per hour of travel (70km to 80km). Deluxe buses may cost just 10% or 20% more than 1st class, or about 50% more for super-deluxe services. Second-class buses cost 20% less than 1st class.

Note that there have been occasional highway robberies on overnight buses over the years. You can store bags in the secure luggage hold.

CAR & MOTORCYCLE

To rent a car or scooter you'll need to show a valid driver's license (your country's license is OK) and a major credit card.

LOCAL TRANSPORTATION

Many locals prefer piling into vans or *colectivos* (shared taxis or minibuses), which travel on shorter routes. They cost about the same as a 2nd-class bus, but *colectivos* go more frequently.

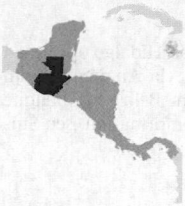

Guatemala

☎502 / POP 16.2 MILLION

Includes ➡

Guatemala City 93
Antigua 108
Lago de Atitlán 121
Chichicastenango 138
Nebaj 143
Quetzaltenango 145
Huehuetenango 158
Cobán 171
Lago de Izabal 181
Lívingston 187
Flores & Santa Elena 194
Tikal 200

Best Places to Eat

- ➡ Restaurante Buga Mama (p189)
- ➡ Xkape Koba'n (p174)
- ➡ Tienda La Canche (p116)
- ➡ Taberna El Pelicano (p169)
- ➡ La Fonda de la Calle Real (p117)

Best Places to Stay

- ➡ Quetzalroo (p99)
- ➡ Earth Lodge (p121)
- ➡ Hotel Kangaroo (p183)
- ➡ Posada del Cerro (p200)
- ➡ Finca Santa Elena (p163)

Why Go?

Guatemala is a magical place. If you're into the Maya, the mountains, the markets, kicking back lakeside or exploring atmospheric pre-Columbian ruins and gorgeous colonial villages, you're bound to be captivated.

Want to surf in the morning and learn Spanish in the afternoon? No problem. Descend a volcano, grab a shower and hit the sushi bar for dinner? You can do that. Check out a Maya temple and be swinging in a beachside hammock by sunset? Easy.

Guatemala's got its problems, but they mainly keep to themselves (although if you go looking for trouble, who knows what you'll find). Travel here – once fraught with danger and discomfort – is now characterized by ease; you can do pretty much whatever you want, and your experience will only be limited by your imagination and time.

When to Go

Guatemala City

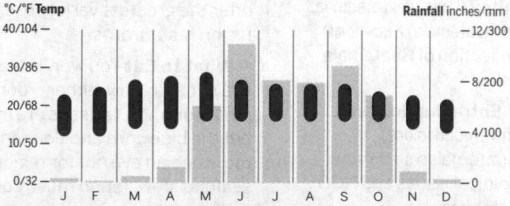

Dec–May Festivities such as Christmas and Easter are celebrated with gusto.

Apr–Sep Prices drop and crowds thin out as the rainy season starts in earnest.

Oct–Nov Rains begin to ease up, making for good hiking weather.

AT A GLANCE

Currency Quetzal (Q)

Language Spanish (official), 21 Maya languages, Garífuna

Visas Generally not required for stays up to three months.

Money ATMs widely available. Credit cards accepted in higher-end places.

Time North American Central Standard Time (GMT/UTC minus six hours)

Fast Facts

- **Area** 108,890 sq km
- **Capital** Guatemala City
- **Emergency** English ☎1500, Spanish ☎110

Set Your Budget

- **Hostel bed** Q60-100
- **Set meal** Q25-40
- **Three-hour 'chicken bus' ride** Q20

Resources

- **Lanic Guatemala** (http://lanic.utexas.edu/la/ca/guatemala) Excellent collection of Guatemala links.
- **EntreMundos** (www.entremundos.org) Guatemalan social and political issues and NGO database.
- **Lonely Planet** (www.lonelyplanet.com/guatemala) Information, hotel bookings, traveler forum and more.

Connections

From Mexico enter Guatemala at Ciudad Hidalgo or Ciudad Cuauhtémoc. From El Salvador enter via Anguiatú; from Honduras via Agua Caliente; and from Belize via Benque Viejo del Carmen. For more detailed information, see Survival Guide on p224.

FIRST TIME IN GUATEMALA

One Week

With a week up your sleeve you won't see it all, but you can at least catch the Big Three. Make a beeline for **Antigua** and spend a couple of days wallowing in colonial glory and climbing volcanoes before heading off to **Lago de Atitlán**. Choose which village suits you, from bustling Panajachel to out-of-the-way San Juan, and explore the lake and its surrounds by boat, kayak, horseback, bike or whatever else takes your fancy. From there, head back to **Guatemala City** and catch a bus or plane to **Flores**, your stepping off point for the mother of all Maya ruins, **Tikal**.

Two Weeks

Add another week and you'll have time for a quick dip in the lovely limestone pools at **Semuc Champey** and a boat ride down the lush **Río Dulce**. Try to set a day aside for Guatemala City's fantastic collection of museums and galleries.

Essential Food & Drink

- **Where to Eat** The cheapest eats are to be found at food stalls around the central plaza or bus terminal – exercise common sense when buying food at these places. Family-run *comedores* (eating halls) are the next up the budget scale, often serving good-value set meals for a pittance. Towns with large tourist populations, such as Antigua and Panajachel, offer the greatest variety of eats, all the way up to world-class fusion restaurants.
- **What to Eat** You won't be able to avoid corn tortillas, and you shouldn't try, either – done right they're delicious. The most common varieties are made with yellow or white corn, but the blue corn and flour ones are worth looking out for, too. Keep an eye out for regional specialties like *tapado* (a seafood stew, found mostly on the Caribbean coast), *pepián* (spicy sesame-seed sauce served with chicken or turkey) and *jocón* (a stew of chicken or pork with green vegetables and herbs), found in the highlands; and boxbol (maize dough and chopped meat or chicken), a staple in the Ixil Triangle area.
- **What to Drink** The best drinks for miles around are *licuados*, fresh fruit juice blends made with milk or water.

GUATEMALA CITY

POP 1.1 MILLION / ELEV 1500M

Depending on who you talk to, Guatemala's capital (known universally as 'Guate') is either big, dirty, dangerous and utterly forgettable or big, dirty, dangerous and fascinating. Either way, there's no doubt that there's an energy here unlike that found in the rest of Guatemala, and the extremes that characterize the whole country are in plain view.

It's a place where dilapidated buses belch fumes next to BMWs and Hummers, where skyscrapers drop shadows on shantytowns, and where immigrants from the countryside and the rest of Central America eke out a meager existence, barely noticed by the country's elite.

This is the cultural capital of Guatemala – the writers, the thinkers, the artists mostly live and work here – and all the best museum pieces go to the capital. While nearly every city-dweller dreams of getting away to Antigua or Monterrico for the weekend, this is where they spend most of their time – a fact reflected in the growing sophistication of the restaurant and bar scenes.

Sights & Activities

The major sights are in Zona 1 (the historical center) and Zonas 10 and 13, where the museums are grouped. If you're here on a Sunday, consider taking the Transmetro's **SubiBaja** (9am-2pm) FREE hop-on, hop-off self-guided tour. Air-con Transmetro buses run a circuit every 20 minutes, passing 10 stops including the Parque Central, Centro Cívico, La Aurora Zoo (and museums), the Zona Viva, Pasos y Pedales, Cuatro Grados Norte and Mapa en Relieve. Volunteer guides give on-board commentary and each bus is staffed by a member of the Transit Police. It's an excellent way to see sights without worrying about public transportation or taxis.

Zona 1

Parque Central PLAZA

(Plaza de la Constitución; Map p98; Parque Central) Most of the notable sights in Zona 1 are near the Parque Central, which is bounded by 6a and 8a Calles and 6a and 7a Avs.

Every town in the New World had a plaza used for military exercises, reviews and ceremonies. On the plaza's northern side would be the *palacio de gobierno* (colonial government headquarters). On another side, preferably east, was a church (or cathedral). The other sides of the square could house additional civic buildings or imposing mansions. Parque Central is a good example of this classic town plan.

Visit on Sunday, when locals stroll, play in the fountains, gossip, neck and groove to salsa music. Otherwise, try for lunchtime or late afternoon. You'll be besieged by shoeshine boys, Polaroid photographers and sellers of kitsch.

Palacio Nacional de la Cultura HISTORIC BUILDING

(Map p98; 2253-0748; cnr 6a Av & 6a Calle; admission Q30; 9-11:45am & 2-4:45pm Mon-Sat) The magnificent Palacio Nacional de la Cultura was built at enormous cost during the dictatorial rule of General Jorge Ubico (1931–44). It's the third palace to stand here. It often hosts revolving exhibitions featuring contemporary Guatemalan artists.

You can go wandering independently, or else free tours take you through a labyrinth of gleaming brass, polished wood, carved stone and frescoed arches (painted by Alberto Gálvez Suárez). Notable features include the 2-ton gold, bronze and Bohemian-crystal chandelier in the reception salon, and two Moorish-style courtyards.

Centro Cultural Metropolitano CULTURAL CENTER

(Map p98; 7a Av 11-67; 9am-5pm Mon-Fri) This surprisingly avant-garde cultural center hosts art exhibitions, book launches, handicraft workshops and film nights.

Casa MIMA CULTURAL CENTER

(Map p98; 8a Av 14-12; 10am-5pm Mon-Sat) This wonderfully presented museum and cultural center is set in a house dating from the late 19th century. The owners of the house were collectors with eclectic tastes ranging from French neo-Rococo, Chinese and art deco, to indigenous artifacts. The place is set up like a functioning house, filled with curios and furniture spanning the centuries.

Museo de Ferrocarril MUSEUM

(Railway Museum; Map p98; www.museofegua.com; 9a Av 18-03; 9am-4pm Tue-Fri, 10am-4pm Sat & Sun) FREE This is one of the city's more intriguing museums. Documented here are the glory days of the troubled Guatemalan rail system, along with some quirky artifacts, such as hand-drawn diagrams of derailments and a kitchen set up with items used in dining cars. You can go climbing around the passenger carriages, but not the locomotives.

Guatemala Highlights

1. Ignore the tour groups – **Tikal** is Guatemala's number-one attraction for good reason (p200)
2. Eat, drink and sleep well, study Spanish and climb volcanoes in cosmopolitan and picturesque **Antigua** (p108)
3. See another side of Guatemala in the Garífuna enclave of **Lívingston** (p187)
4. Hike the country's best trekking routes in the **Western Highlands** (p147)
5. Find out why people call **Semuc Champey** the most beautiful spot in the whole country (p176)
6. Take a spectacular boat ride down a jungle-walled canyon between **Río Dulce** and **Lívingston** (p190)
7. Explore the lovely, traditional lakeside village of **San Juan La Laguna** (p136)
8. Investigate beguiling stone sculptures from a pre-Mayan culture in **Santa Lucía Cotzumalguapa** (p165)

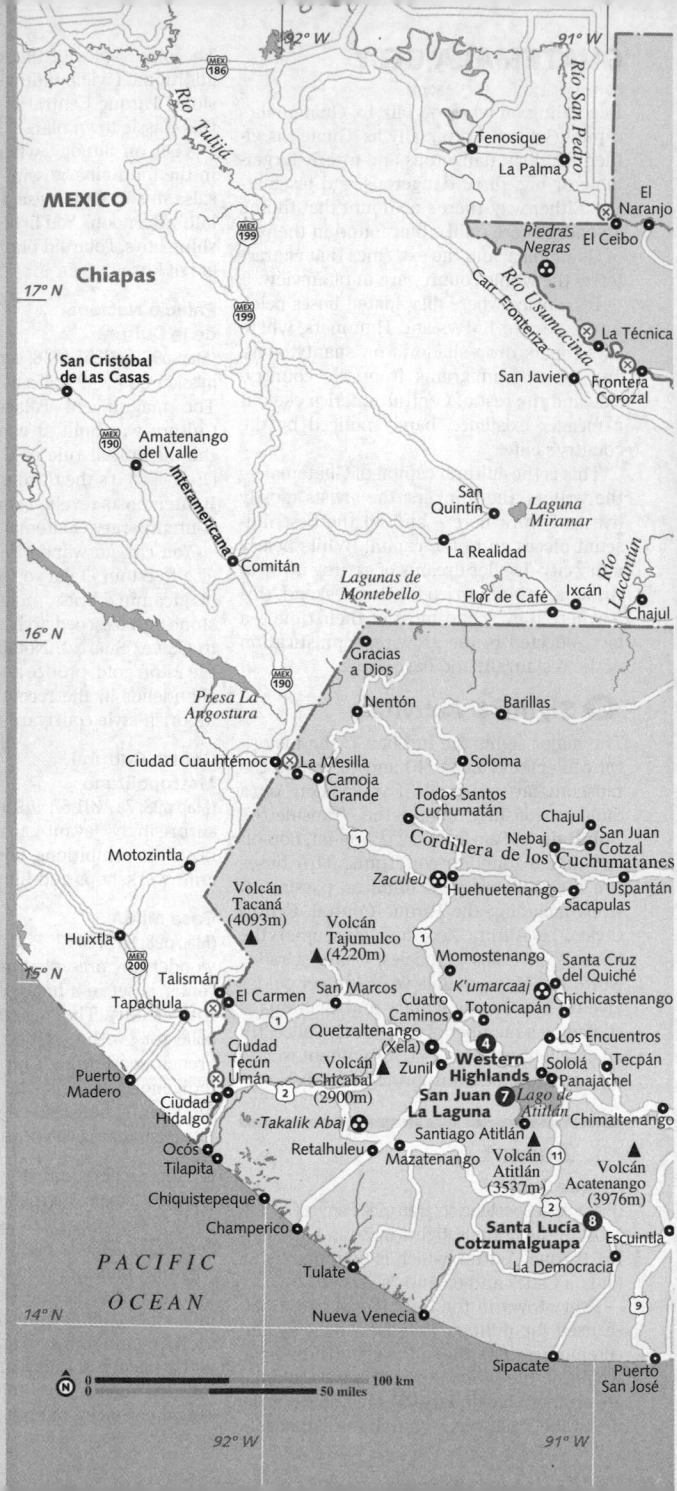

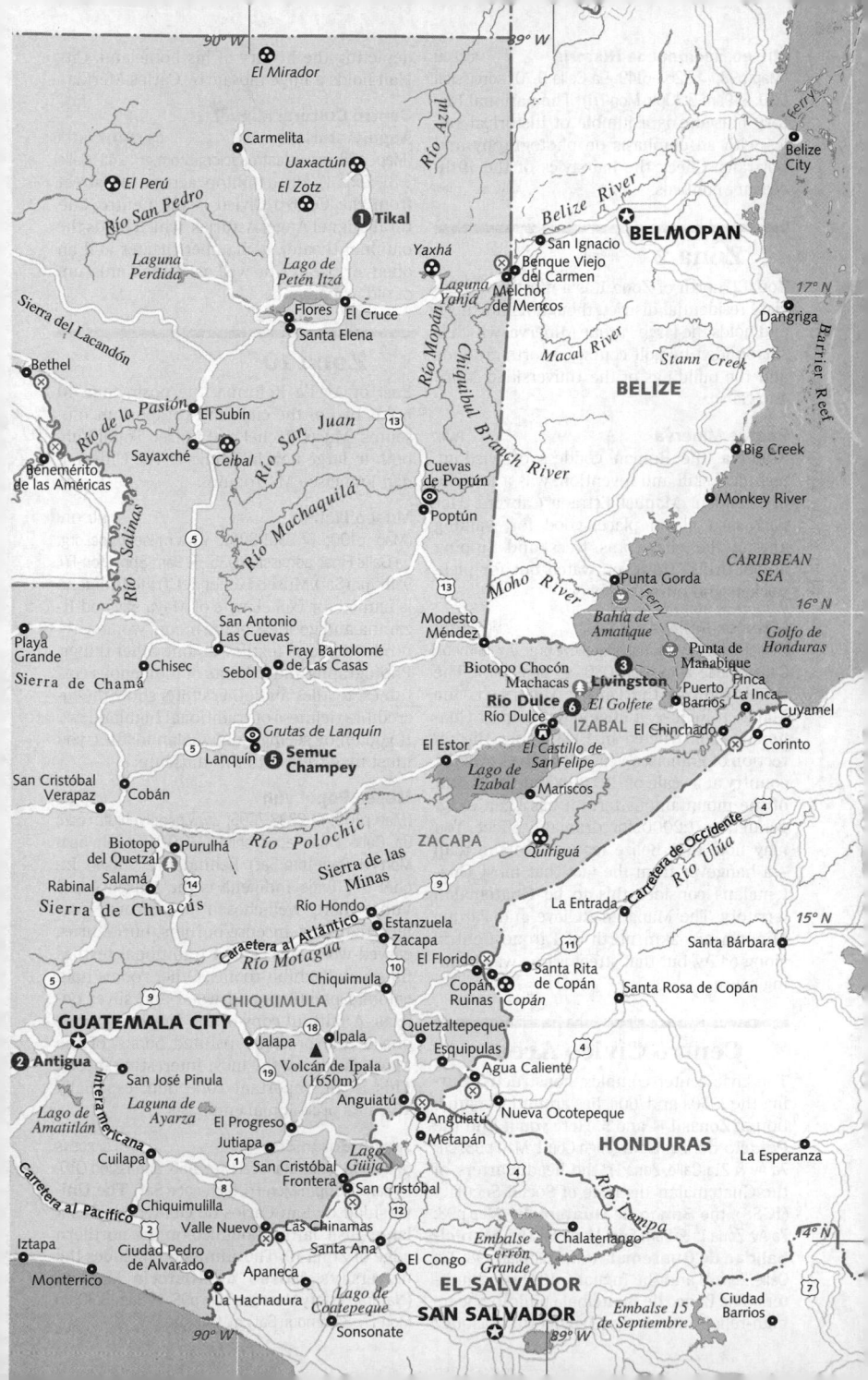
90° W
89° W
El Mirador
Carmelita
Uaxactún
El Zotz
El Perú
Río San Pedro
1 Tikal
Río Azul
Belize River
BELMOPAN
Belize City
ferry
San Ignacio
Benque Viejo del Carmen
Melchor de Mencos
Yaxhá
Laguna Perdida
Lago de Petén Itzá
Laguna Yaxhá
Flores
El Cruce
Santa Elena
Río Mopán
Chiquibul Branch River
Sierra del Lacandón
Bethel
Río de la Pasión
El Subín
Sayaxché
Ceibal
Río San Juan
Benemérito de las Américas
Río Salinas
Río Machaquilá
Cuevas de Poptún
Poptún
Macal River
Stann Creek
BELIZE
17° N
Dangriga
Barrier Reef
Big Creek
Monkey River
CARIBBEAN SEA
Moho River
Punta Gorda
Ferry
Bahía de Amatique
16° N
Golfo de Honduras
Modesto Méndez
San Antonio Las Cuevas
Fray Bartolomé de Las Casas
Playa Grande
Chisec
Sebol
Sierra de Chamá
Biotopo Chocón Machacas
3 Livingston
Punta de Manabique
Puerto Barrios
Finca La Inca
Río Dulce
6 El Golfete
Río Dulce
IZABAL
El Chinchado
Cuyamel
Corinto
Grutas de Lanquín
Lanquín
5 Semuc Champey
El Estor
El Castillo de San Felipe
Lago de Izabal
Mariscos
San Cristóbal Verapaz
Cobán
Río Polochic
ZACAPA
Quiriguá
Carretera de Occidente
Río Ulúa
Biotopo del Quetzal
Purulhá
Salamá
Rabinal
Sierra de Chuacús
Sierra de las Minas
Río Hondo
Estanzuela
Zacapa
La Entrada
15° N
Santa Bárbara
Carretera al Atlántico
Río Motagua
El Florido
Chiquimula
Copán Ruinas
Copán
Santa Rita de Copán
Santa Rosa de Copán
CHIQUIMULA
GUATEMALA CITY
Jalapa
Ipala
Volcán de Ipala (1650m)
Quetzaltepeque
Esquipulas
Agua Caliente
2 Antigua
San José Pinula
Interamericana
Laguna de Ayarza
Lago de Amatitlán
Anguiatú
Nueva Ocotepeque
El Progreso
Jutiapa
Cuilapa
Metapán
HONDURAS
La Esperanza
Lago Güija
San Cristóbal Frontera
San Cristóbal
Carretera al Pacífico
Chiquimulilla
Valle Nuevo
Las Chinamas
Río Lempa
Chalatenango
Iztapa
Ciudad Pedro de Alvarado
Santa Ana
Embalse Cerrón Grande
14° N
Monterrico
Apaneca
El Congo
EL SALVADOR
La Hachadura
Lago de Coatepeque
SAN SALVADOR
Ciudad Barrios
Embalse 15 de Septiembre
Sonsonate
90° W
89° W

Museo Nacional de Historia MUSEUM
(Map p98; ☎2253-6149; 9a Calle 9-70; admission Q50; ⏲9am-5:30pm Mon-Fri) The national history museum is a jumble of historical relics with an emphasis on photography and portraits. Check the hairstyles of the 19th-century politicos.

Zona 2

Zona 2, north of Zona 1, is a mostly middle-class residential district, though its northern end holds the large Parque Minerva, which is surrounded by golf courses, sports grounds and the buildings of the Universidad Mariano Gálvez.

Parque Minerva PARK
Minerva, the Roman goddess of wisdom, technical skill and invention, was a favorite of President Manuel Estrada Cabrera. Her park is a placid place, good for walking among the eucalyptus trees and sipping a cool drink. However, watch out for pickpockets and purse-snatchers.

Mapa en Relieve MONUMENT
(Relief Map; www.mapaenrelieve.org; Av Simeón Cañas Final; admission Q30; ⏲9am-5pm) The prime sight at the Parque Minerva is the Mapa en Relieve, a huge relief map of Guatemala. Constructed in 1904 under the direction of Francisco Vela, the map shows the country at a scale of 1:10,000, but the height of the mountainous terrain has been exaggerated to 1:2000 for dramatic effect. You may note that Belize features on the map – a hangover from the fact that most Guatemalans consider this to be Guatemalan territory. The Mapa en Relieve and Parque Minerva are 2km north of Parque Central along 6a Av, but that street is one way heading south.

Centro Cívico Area

The civic center complex, constructed during the 1950s and '60s, lies around the junction of Zonas 1, 4 and 5. Here you'll find the **Palacio de Justicia** (High Court; Map p98; cnr 7a Av & 21a Calle, Zona 1), the headquarters of the Guatemalan Institute of Social Security (IGSS), the **Banco de Guatemala** (Map p98; 7a Av, Zona 1; ⏲9am-5pm Mon-Fri), the **Municipalidad de Guatemala** (City Hall; Map p98; 22a Calle, Zona 1) and the Inguat (p104) headquarters. The Banco de Guatemala building bears high-relief murals by Dagoberto Vásquez depicting the history of his homeland. City Hall holds a huge mosaic by Carlos Mérida.

Centro Cultural Miguel Ángel Asturias CULTURAL CENTER
(Map p98; www.teatronacional.com.gt; 24a Calle 3-81, Zona 1) On a hilltop across the street from the Centro Cívico is the Centro Cultural Miguel Ángel Asturias, which holds the national theater, a chamber theater and an open-air theater, as well as a small museum of old armaments.

Zona 10

East of Av La Reforma, the posh Zona 10 holds two of the city's most important museums, Museo Ixchel and Museo Popol Vuh, both in large new buildings at the Universidad Francisco Marroquín.

Museo Ixchel MUSEUM
(Map p100; ☎2361-8081; www.museoixchel.org; 6a Calle Final; admission Q35; ⏲9am-5pm Mon-Fri, 9am-1pm Sat) Museo Ixchel del Traje Indígena is named for Ixchel, wife of Maya sky god Itzamná and goddess of the moon, women, reproduction and textiles, among other things. Photographs and exhibits of indigenous costumes, textiles and other crafts show the incredible richness of traditional highland art. If you enjoy seeing Guatemalan textiles, you must make a visit to this museum.

Museo Popol Vuh MUSEUM
(Map p100; ☎2338-7896; www.popolvuh.ufm.edu; 6a Calle Final; adult/child Q35/10; ⏲9am-5pm Mon-Fri, 9am-1pm Sat) Behind the Museo Ixchel del Traje Indígena is the Museo Popol Vuh, where well-chosen polychrome pottery, figurines, incense burners, burial urns, carved-wood masks and traditional textiles fill several exhibit rooms. Other rooms hold colonial paintings and wood and silver objects. A faithful copy of the Dresden Codex, one of the precious 'painted books' of the Maya, is among the most interesting pieces. This is an important collection, especially given its precolonial emphasis.

Jardín Botánico GARDENS
(Map p98; Calle Mariscal Cruz 1-56; admission Q10; ⏲8am-3:30pm Mon-Fri, 8am-noon Sat) The Universidad de San Carlos de Guatemala has a large, lush Jardín Botánico on the northern edge of Zona 10. The admission includes the university's **Museo de Historia Natural** (Natural History Museum; Map p98; ⏲8am-3:30pm Mon-Fri, 8am-noon Sat) at the site.

Pasos y Pedales WALKING
(Map p100; www.pasosypedales.com; ⏲10am-2pm Sun) If you're here on a Sunday, check out Pasos y Pedales, a wonderful municipal initiative that sees the Av de las Americas (Zona 10) and its continuation, Av la Reforma in Zona 13, blocked off to traffic for 3km and taken over by jugglers, clowns, in-line skaters, dogwalkers, food vendors, t'ai chi classes, skate parks and playgrounds for kids. It's a great place to go for a walk (or you can hire bikes or in-line skates on the street) and a very relaxed, sociable side of the city that is rarely otherwise seen.

Zona 13 & Around

The major attraction in the city's southern reaches is Parque Aurora, with its zoo, children's playground, fairgrounds and several museums.

Museo Nacional de Arqueología y Etnología MUSEUM
(Map p100; ☎2475-4399; www.munae.gob.gt; Sala 5, Finca La Aurora; admission Q60; ⏲9am-4pm Tue-Fri, 9am-noon & 1:30-4pm Sat & Sun) One of the museums at Parque Aurora, the Moorish-looking Museo Nacional de Arqueología y Etnología, has a collection of Maya artifacts from all over Guatemala, including stone carvings, jade, ceramics, statues, stelae and a tomb. Models depict the ruins at Tikal and Zaculeu. Exhibits in the ethnology section highlight the various indigenous peoples and languages in Guatemala, with emphasis on traditional costumes, dances and implements of daily life.

Museo Nacional de Arte Moderno GALLERY
(Map p100; ☎2472-0467; Sala 6, Finca La Aurora; admission Q30; ⏲9am-4pm Tue-Fri, 9am-12:30pm & 2-4pm Sat & Sun) Facing the Museo Nacional de Arqueología y Etnología is the Museo Nacional de Arte Moderno, which holds a collection of 20th-century Guatemalan art, especially paintings and sculpture.

Museo Nacional de Historia Natural Jorge Ibarra MUSEUM
(Map p100; ☎2472-0468; 6a Calle 7-30; admission Q50; ⏲9am-4pm Tue-Sun) Near the Museo Nacional de Arte Moderno is the Museo Nacional de Historia Natural Jorge Ibarra, whose claim to fame is its large collection of dissected animals. Several hundred meters east of these museums is the city's official handicrafts market, the **Mercado de Artesanías** (Crafts Market; Map p100; ☎2475-5915; cnr 5a Calle & 11a Av, Zona 13; ⏲9:30am-6pm), just off the access road to the airport. It's a sleepy place where shopkeepers display the same items available in hotel gift shops.

La Aurora Zoo ZOO
(Map p100; ☎2472-0507; www.aurorazoo.org.gt; 5a Calle; adult/child Q25/10; ⏲9am-5pm Tue-Sun) La Aurora Zoo is not badly kept as zoos in this part of the world go, and the lovely, parklike grounds alone are worth the admission fee.

X-Park ADVENTURE SPORTS
(☎2380-2080; www.xpark.net; Av Hincapié Km 11.5; admission Q15; ⏲10am-7pm Mon-Fri, 10am-9pm Sat, 10am-7pm Sun) About 10-minutes' drive south of the airport is X-Park, a very well-constructed 'adventure sports' park. A taxi here from Zona 10 should cost around Q30.

Sleeping

Zona 1

Shoestringers tend to head straight for Zona 1. Prices in Guate are higher than in the rest of the country, but there are a few bargains. Many of the city's cheaper lodgings are 10 to 15 minutes' walk south from Parque Central.

Hotel Ajau HOTEL $
(Map p98; ☎2232-0488; hotelajau@hotmail.com; 8a Av 15-62; s/d Q160/205, without bathroom Q85/120; @📶) If you're coming from or going to Cobán, the Ajau's the obvious choice, being right next door to the Monja Blanca bus station. It's still a pretty good deal, anyway, with lovely polished floor tiles and cool, clean rooms.

Hotel Spring HOTEL $
(Map p98; ☎2230-2858; www.hotelspring.com; 8a Av 12-65; s/d from Q160/200, without bathroom Q110/140; @📶) With a beautiful courtyard setting, the Spring has a lot more style than other Zona 1 joints. It's central and has quiet sunny patios. The 43 rooms vary greatly, but most are tall, spacious and clean. Have a look around if you can. All rooms have cable TV. It's worth booking ahead.

Hotel Fenix HOTEL $
(Map p98; ☎2232-2839; 15a Calle 6-56; s/d Q100/160) Zona 1's classic budget hotel has found a new home, just around the corner

Guatemala City North

Guatemala City North

Sights
1 Banco de Guatemala B4
2 Casa MIMA C3
3 Centro Cultural Metropolitano C2
4 Centro Cultural Miguel Ángel Asturias B4
5 Jardín Botánico C7
6 Municipalidad de Guatemala B4
7 Museo de Ferrocarril C4
8 Museo de Historia Natural C7
9 Museo Nacional de Historia C2
10 Palacio de Justicia C4
11 Palacio Nacional de la Cultura C1
12 Parque Central C1

Sleeping
13 Hotel Ajau C3
14 Hotel Capri C3
15 Hotel Fenix B3
16 Hotel Quality Service B1
17 Hotel Spring C2

Eating
18 Café de Imeri B1
19 Café-Restaurante Hamburgo B3
20 Fu Lu Sho B2
21 Picadilly B2
22 Restaurante Rey Sol B2

Drinking & Nightlife
23 El Gran Hotel C2
24 Las Cien Puertas C1

Entertainment
25 Black & White Lounge B2
26 Centro Cultural de España B2
Centro Cultural Miguel Ángel Asturias ..... (see 4)
27 Genetic B6
28 La Bodeguita del Centro B2
29 Los Lirios C2
30 TrovaJazz B6

Shopping
31 Mercado Central C1
32 Plaza El Amate B4

from where it used to be. The reasonably spacious, straightforward budget rooms here are a very good deal.

Hotel Capri HOTEL $
(Map p98; ☎2232-8191; 9a Av 15-63; s/d Q150/195, without bathroom Q95/140) A modern four-story number in a decent location. Get a room away from the noisy street out front.

Hotel Quality Service HOTEL $$
(Map p98; ☎2251-8005; www.qualityguate.com; 8a Calle 3-18; s/d Q180/240; @) There's a pleasing, old-timey feel about this place, which is balanced perfectly by the modern-but-not-overly-so rooms. It is the best pick near the park.

Zonas 10 & 13

Guesthouses are springing up all over the place in a middle-class residential area in Zona 13. They're very convenient for the airport, and staff will pick you up or drop you off there. There are no restaurants out here, but these places offer breakfast and have the complete lowdown on home-delivery fast food in the area.

Quetzalroo HOSTEL $
(Map p100; ☎5746-0830; www.quetzalroo.com; 6a Av 7-84, Zona 10; dm/s/d without bathroom Q140/200/280; @) Guatemala City's best downtown hostel has reasonable rooms and dorms, a cramped kitchen area and a great rooftop terrace. The location's handy for the Zona Viva eating and nightlife scene. Call for free pickup from the airport or bus terminal.

Patricia's Guest House GUESTHOUSE $
(☎2261-4251; www.patriciashotel.com; 19 Calle 10-65, Aurora II; r per person without bathroom Q115; @) Relaxed and comfortable, with a sweet little backyard where guests can hang out. Also offers private transportation around the city and to bus stations.

Hostal Los Lagos HOSTEL $
(☎2261-2809; www.loslagoshostal.com; 8a Av 15-85, Aurora I; dm/s/d Q120/Q200/320; @) The most hostel-like of the near-the-airport options. Dorms are airy and spacious and there are a couple of reasonable-value private rooms.

Eating

Cheap eats are easily found, as fast food and snack shops abound. To really save money, head for Parque Concordia, in Zona 1 bounded by 5a and 6a Avs and 14a and 15a Calles, whose west side is lined with stalls serving sandwiches and snacks at rock-bottom prices from early morning to late evening. Fine dining is concentrated in Zona 10.

Guatemala City South

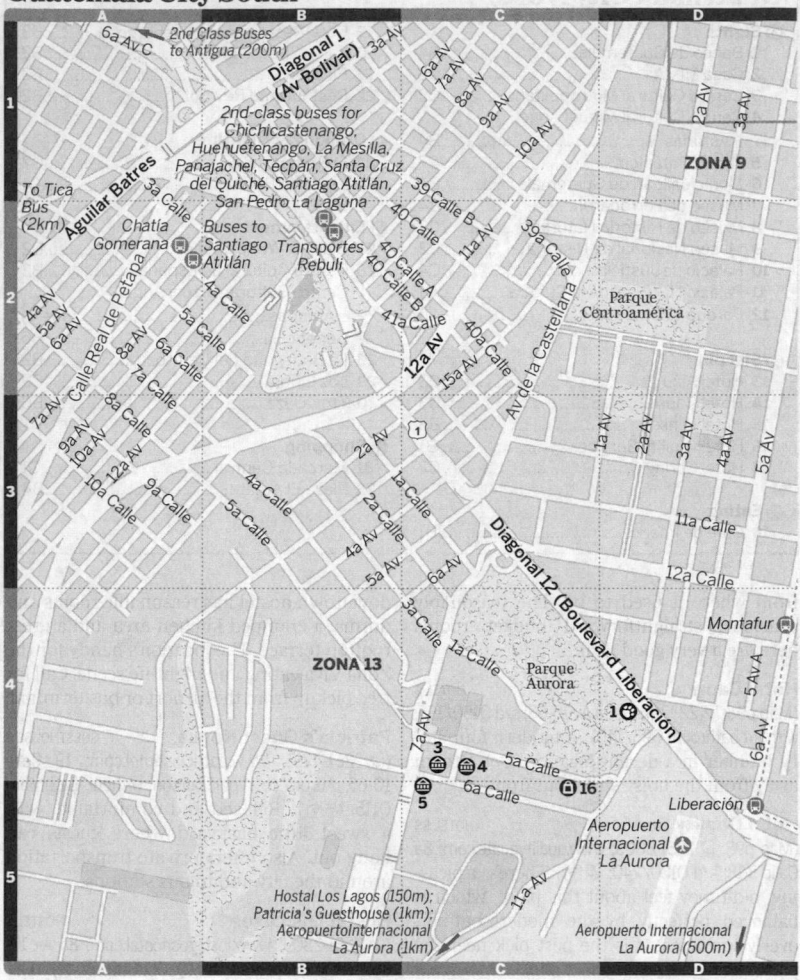

Zona 1

Dozens of restaurants and fast-food shops are strung along and just off 6a Av between 8a and 15a Calles.

Café de Imeri CAFE $

(Map p98; 6a Calle 3-34; mains Q30-50; ⏲8am-7pm Mon-Sat;) Completely out of step with the majority of Zona 1 eateries, this place offers interesting breakfasts, soups and pastas. The list of sandwiches is impressive and there's a beautiful little courtyard area out the back.

Restaurante Rey Sol VEGETARIAN $

(Map p98; 11a Calle 5-51; mains Q20-30; ⏲7am-7pm Mon-Sat, 7am-4pm Sun;) Good, fresh ingredients and some innovative cooking such as soy pâté and vegetarian tamales keep this strictly vegetarian restaurant busy at lunchtimes.

Café-Restaurante Hamburgo GUATEMALAN $

(Map p98; 15a Calle 5-34; set meal Q30-50; ⏲7am-9:30pm) This bustling spot facing the south side of Parque Concordia serves good Guatemalan food (including some extremely tasty *chiles rellenos* – stuffed bell peppers),

with chefs at work along one side and orange-aproned waitresses scurrying about. At weekends a marimba band adds some atmosphere.

Fu Lu Sho CHINESE $

(Map p98; 6a Av 12-05; mains Q30-60; ⏲8am-11pm) This classic Zona 1 Chinese joint has been going for years and is a reliable, if somewhat unexciting, choice. It's straight-up Chinese with a few Guatemalan staples thrown in, but for late-night cheap eats, it's definitely hard to beat.

Picadilly INTERNATIONAL $$

(Map p98; cnr 6 Av & 11a Calle; mains Q45-90; ⏲11am-9:30pm) Right in the thick of the 6a Av action, this bustling restaurant does OK pizzas and pastas and good steak dishes. The place is clean and street views out of the big front windows are mesmerizing.

Zona 10

La Chapinita GUATEMALAN $

(Map p100; 1 Av 10-24; ⏲breakfast, lunch & dinner) Down-home Guatemalan food served in more or less formal surrounds can be hard

Guatemala City South

Sights
1 La Aurora Zoo D4
2 Museo Ixchel H2
3 Museo Nacional de Arqueología y Etnología C4
4 Museo Nacional de Arte Moderno C4
5 Museo Nacional de Historia Natural Jorge Ibarra C5
6 Museo Popol Vuh H2

Activities, Courses & Tours
7 Pasos y Pedales F2
8 Productos Mundiales H4

Sleeping
9 Quetzalroo F2

Eating
10 Cafetería Patsy F3
11 Kacao F4
12 La Chapinita F3

Drinking & Nightlife
13 Bajo Fondo F5

Entertainment
14 Kahlua E5
15 Rattle & Hum F5

Shopping
16 Mercado de Artesanías C5
17 Oakland Mall G4
18 Sophos F4

to come by in Zona 10, but this place does it well at good prices. Tables out front on the shady terrace are cool and breezy and the *churrasco* (flame-grilled steak) hits the spot for a simple, honest feed.

Cafetería Patsy CAFE $
(Map p100; Av La Reforma 8-01; set lunch from Q35; ⏲7:30am-8pm) A bright, cheerful place popular with local office workers, offering subs, sandwiches and good-value set lunches, perfect for the showstring traveler.

Kacao GUATEMALAN $$$
(Map p100; 2a Av 13-44; mains Q70-120; ⏲12-3pm & 7-11pm Mon-Sat, 12-4pm Sun) Set under a *palapa* (thatched palm-leaf shelter), and with a soft marimba soundtrack, this is Zona 10's best *típica* (regional) food restaurant. The atmosphere and food are both excellent. The *subanick* (a spicy pork, beef and chicken stew), a traditional Kaqchikel dish, is the standout.

Drinking & Entertainment

Centro Cultural de España (Map p98; ☎4752-7226; www.centroculturalespana.com.gt; 6a Av 11-02, Zona 1; ⏲9:30am-1pm & 2-5pm Mon-Fri, 10am-2pm Sat) and **Centro Cultural Miguel Ángel Asturias** (Map p98; ☎2332-4041; www.teatronacional.com.gt; 24a Calle 3-81, Zona 1), both in Cuatro Grados Norte, host regular theatrical performances and other artistic events. It's always worth dropping in or checking their websites to see what's on.

The English-language *RevueMagazine* (www.revuemag.com) has events details, although it focuses more on Antigua. Your hotel should have a copy, or know where to get one. Free events mags in Spanish come and go. At the time of writing, *El Azar* (www.elazarcultural.blogspot.com) had the best info. Pick up a copy at a cultural center. Movie and other listings can be found in the *Prensa Libre* newspaper.

There are a couple of clubs worthy of mention for gay men, and nothing much for women.

Zona 1

Staggering from bar to bar along the darkened streets of Zona 1 is not recommended, but fortunately there's a clutch of good drinking places all within half a block of each other just south of Parque Central.

Las Cien Puertas BAR
(Map p98; 9a Calle 6-45, Pasaje Aycinena 8-44; ⏲12pm-1am) This superhip (but not studiously so) little watering hole is a gathering place for all manner of local creative types and other colorful characters. It's in a shabby colonial arcade that is sometimes closed off for live bands.

El Gran Hotel PUB
(Map p98; 9a Calle 7-64; ⏲6pm-1am Tue-Sun) The down-market renovated lobby of this classic ex-hotel is one of downtown's better-looking bars. There's poetry, live music and film nights throughout the week – check the website for details.

Los Lirios CLUB
(Map p98; 7a Av 9-20; ⏲7pm-1am Wed-Sat) One of the most reliable dance floors in the downtown area. The crowd is mostly young, and the music is mostly Latina, along the

lines of salsa, merengue and reggaetón. Occasional live music.

La Bodeguita del Centro LIVE MUSIC
(Map p98; 12a Calle 3-55; ⏲9pm-1am Tue-Sat) There's a hopping, creative local scene in Guatemala City, and this large, bohemian hangout is one of the best places to connect with it. There's live music of some kind almost every night from Tuesday to Saturday, usually starting at 9pm.

Black & White Lounge GAY
(Map p98; www.blackandwhitebar.com; 11a Calle 2-54; ⏲7pm-1am Wed-Sat) A well-established gay disco-bar located in a former private house right near the downtown area, often with strippers.

Zona 4

TrovaJazz LIVE MUSIC
(Map p98; www.trovajazz.com; Vía 6 No 3-55) Jazz, blues and folk fans should look into what's happening here.

Genetic GAY
(Map p98; Ruta 3 3-08; admission from Q30; ⏲9pm-1am Wed-Sat) This used to be called Pandora's Box, and has been hosting Guatemala's gay community since the '70s, though it gets a mixed crowd and is one of the best local venues for trance/dance music. It has two dance floors, a rooftop patio and a relaxed atmosphere. Friday is 'all you can drink'.

Zona 10

The best place to go bar-hopping is around the corner of 2a Av and 15a Calle – there's plenty of places to choose from – check and see who's got the crowd tonight.

Bajo Fondo BAR
(Map p100; 15a Calle 2-55; ⏲7pm-1am Wed-Sat) One of the more atmospheric little bars in the area, this place has good music and the occasional spontaneous jam session.

Kahlua CLUB
(Map p100; 15a Calle & 1a Av; admission from Q30; ⏲7pm-1am Thu-Sat) For electronica and bright young things.

Rattle & Hum LIVE MUSIC
(Map p100; cnr 4a Av & 16 Calle; ⏲12pm-1am) One of the last places left in Zona 10 to still be hosting live music, this Australian-owned place has a warm and friendly atmosphere.

Shopping

For fashion boutiques, electronic goods and other developed-world paraphernalia, head for the large shopping malls such as **Oakland Mall** (Map p100; www.oaklandmall.com.gt; Diagonal 6 13-01, Zona 10; ⏲8am-8pm).

For a more everyday Guatemalan experience, check out the stalls at **Plaza El Amate** (Map p98; cnr 18a Calle & 4a Av, Zona 1; ⏲8am-6pm) where you can find cheap copied CDs, shoes, underwear, overalls and pretty much everything else under the sun.

Mercado Central MARKET
(Map p98; cnr 8a Av & 8a Calle, Zona 1; ⏲9am-6pm Mon-Sat, 9am-noon Sun) Until it was destroyed by the earthquake of 1976, the central market, east of the cathedral, was where locals bought food and other necessities. Reconstructed in the late 1970s, the new *mercado* specializes in touristy items such as cloth, carved wood, worked leather and metal, basketry and other handicrafts. Except for the odd tour group, not that many tourists make it here – if you're a hard bargainer, you might get a good deal. Vegetables and other daily needs are on sale on the lower floor – check it out for a sensory overload. The city's true 'central' food market is in Zona 4.

Sophos BOOKS
(Map p100; ☎2419-7070; www.sophosenlinea.com; 4a Av 12-59, Plaza Fontabella, Zona 10; ⏲9am-9pm Mon-Sat, 10am-7pm Sun) Relaxed place to have a coffee and read while in the Zona Viva. A good selection of books in English on Guatemala and the Maya, including guidebooks and maps.

Orientation

Guatemala City, like almost all Guatemalan towns, is laid out according to a logical grid system. Avenidas run north–south; calles run east–west. Streets are usually numbered from north and west (lowest) to south and east (highest); building numbers run in the same directions, with odd numbers on the left side and even on the right heading south or east. In addition, Guatemala City is divided into 25 *zonas*, each with its own version of the grid. Thus 14a Calle in Zona 10 is a completely different street several miles from 14a Calle in Zona 1, though major thoroughfares such as 6a Av and 7a Av cross several zones.

Addresses are given in this form: '9a Av 15-12, Zona 1,' which means '9th Av above 15th St, No 12, in Zona 1.' The building will be on 9th Av between 15th and 16th Sts, on the right side as you walk south. Beware of anomalies, such as diagonal *rutas* and *vías* and wandering *diagonales*.

Short streets may be suffixed 'A,' as in 14a Calle A, running between 14a Calle and 15a Calle.

MAPS

Intelimapas' *Mapa Turístico Guatemala*, Inguat's *Mapa Vial Turístico* and International Travel Maps' *Guatemala* all contain useful maps of Guatemala City.

Instituto Geográfico Nacional (IGN; ☎2248-8100; www.ign.gob.gt; Av Las Américas 5-76, Zona 13; ⏲9am-5pm Mon-Fri) Sells 1:50,000 and 1:250,000 topographical maps of all parts of Guatemala (Q140 each).

Information

DANGERS & ANNOYANCES

Street crime, including armed robbery, has increased in recent years. Use normal urban common sense: don't walk down the street with your wallet bulging out of your back pocket, and avoid walking downtown alone late at night. Work out your route before you start so you're not standing on corners looking lost or peering at a map; pop into a cafe if you need to find your bearings. It's safe to walk downtown in the early evening, as long as you stick to streets with plenty of lighting and people. Stay alert and leave your valuables in your hotel. Don't flaunt anything of value, and be aware that women and children swell the ranks of thieves here. The incidence of robbery increases around the 15th and the end of each month, when workers get paid.

Pretty much anywhere in Zona 1 off the 6a Av pedestrian strip is troublesome at night – a taxi is a worthwhile investment after a night on the town. The more affluent sections of the city – Zonas 9, 10 and 14, for example – are safer but crimes against tourists and street crime in general is on the rise in these areas, too. The Zona Viva, in Zona 10, has police patrols at night. But even here, going in pairs is better than going alone. Never try to resist if you are confronted by a robber.

EMERGENCY

Proatur (☎toll free, in English 1500; ⏲24hr)

MEDICAL SERVICES

Guatemala City has many private hospitals and clinics. Public hospitals and clinics provide free consultations but can be very busy. To reduce waiting time, try to be there before 7am.

Hospital Centro Médico (☎2361-1649, 2361-1650; 6a Av 3-47, Zona 10) Recommended private hospital with some English-speaking doctors.

Hospital General San Juan de Dios (☎2256-1486; 1a Av 10-50, Zona 1) One of the city's best public hospitals.

MONEY

Card skimming is rife in Guatemala City – try to use ATMs that are under some sort of watch at all times, such as those inside stores or shopping malls.

Visa/Mastercard ATM, Zona 1 (18 Calle 6-85, Zona 1) Inside the Paiz Supermarket.

Visa/Mastercard ATMs, Zona 10 (16a Calle, Zona 10) Inside Los Proceres mall.

American Express (☎2331-7422; 12a Calle 0-93, Centro Comercial Montufar, Zona 9; ⏲8am-5pm Mon-Fri, to noon Sat) In an office of Clark Tours.

Banco de la República (Aeropuerto Internacional La Aurora; ⏲6am-8pm Mon-Fri, 6am-6pm Sat & Sun) Currency-exchange services. On the airport departures level.

POST

Main Post Office (Palacio de Correos; 7a Av 11-67, Zona 1; ⏲8:30am-5pm Mon-Fri, 8:30am-1pm Sat) In a huge yellow building at the Palacio de Correos. There's also a small post office at the airport.

TOURIST INFORMATION

The **main tourist office** (☎2421-2854; www.visitguatemala.com; 7a Av 1-17; ⏲8am-4pm Mon-Fri), located in the lobby of the Inguat (Instituto Guatemalteco de Turismo) headquarters in the Centro Cívico, has limited handout material, but staff are extremely helpful. There's also a branch at **Aeropuerto Internacional La Aurora.** (☎2322-5055; in the arrivals hall; ⏲6am-9pm)

Getting There & Away

AIR

Guatemala City's **Aeropuerto Internacional La Aurora** is the country's major airport. All international flights to Guatemala City land and take off here. At the time of writing, the country's only *scheduled* domestic flights are between Guatemala City and Flores. **Grupo TACA** (☎2470-8222; www.taca.com; Avenida Hincapié 12-22, Zona 13) makes two round-trip flights daily (one in the morning, one in the afternoon). **TAG** (☎2380-9494; www.tag.com.gt; cnr Av Hincapie & 18 Calle, Zona 13) offers one flight daily, leaving Guatemala at 6:30am.

Tickets to Flores cost around Q1330/2300 one way/round trip with Grupo TACA and Q1250/2100 with TAG, but some travel agents, especially in Antigua, offer large discounts on these prices.

BUS

Buses from here run all over Guatemala and into Mexico, Belize, Honduras, El Salvador and beyond. Most bus companies have their own terminals, some of which are in Zona 1. The city council has been on a campaign to get long-haul bus companies out of the downtown area, so it may be wise to double check with Inguat or your hotel about the office location.

Departures for Central and Eastern Guatemala and the Petén mostly leave from CentraNorte.

International Bus Companies

The following companies offer daily 1st-class bus services to international destinations. Many longer-distance trips require a compulsory overnight stop in one of the other Central American capitals, which can add to the overall price. Check the websites for departure times and details.

Hedman Alas (☎2362-5072; www.hedmanalas.com; 2a Av 8-73, Zona 10) For multiple destinations in Honduras.

King Quality & Comfort Lines (☎2337-2991; www.king-qualityca.com; Biltmore Hotel, 15 Calle 0-31, Zona 10) For most Central American capitals.

Línea Dorada (☎2415-8900; www.lineadorada.com.gt; cnr 10a Av & 16a Calle, Zona 1) Has a service to Tapachula, Mexico. Also has luxury domestic buses to the Petén region, Quetzaltenango, Huehuetenango, Río Dulce etc.

Pullmantur (☎2495-7000; www.pullmantur.com; Holiday Inn, 1a Av 13-22, Zona 10) Covers El Salvador and Honduras.

Tica Bus (☎2473-3737; www.ticabus.com; Calzada Aguilar Batres 22-55, Zona 12) Covers all of Central America and Mexico.

Transportes Galgos Inter (☎2232-3661; www.transgalgosinter.com.gt; 7a Av 19-44, Zona 1) Runs to Tapachula, Mexico and can book connections to as far north as the US and south to El Salvador.

National Pullman Companies

The following bus companies have Pullman services to Guatemalan destinations. It is strongly advised that solo female travelers not catch buses at night time.

ADN (☎2251-0610; www.adnautobusesdelnorte.com; 8a Av 16-41, Zona 1) For Flores and Quetzaltenango.

Fortaleza del Sur (☎2230-3390; CentraSur, Zona 12) Covers the Pacific Coast.

Fuente del Norte (☎2238-3894; www.grupofuentedelnorte.com; 17a Calle 8-46, Zona 1) Covers the whole country.

Litegua (☎2220-8840; www.litegua.com; 15a Calle 10-40, Zona 1) Covers the east and Antigua.

Los Halcones (☎2433-9180; Calzada Roosevelt 37-47, Zona 11) For Huehuetenango.

Monja Blanca (CentraNorte, Zona 18) For Cobán and points in between.

INTERNATIONAL BUSES FROM GUATEMALA CITY

DESTINATION	COST (Q)	DURATION (HR)	FREQUENCY	COMPANY
Copán, Honduras	520	5	2 daily	Hedman Alas
La Ceiba, Honduras	700	12	2 daily	Hedman Alas
Managua, Nicaragua	450-1500	16-35	3 daily	King Quality & Comfort Lines, Tica Bus
Panama City, Panama	1220	76	2 daily	Tica Bus
San José, Costa Rica	640-1200	40-63	3 daily	King Quality & Comfort Lines, Tica Bus
San Salvador, El Salvador	120-720	5	7 daily	King Quality & Comfort Lines, Tica Bus, Pullmantur, Transportes Galgos Inter
San Salvador, El Salvador	120-720	5	7 daily	King Quality & Comfort Lines, Tica Bus, Pullmantur, Transportes Galgos Inter
Tapachula, Mexico	170-293	5-7	4 daily	Tica Bus, Línea Dorada, Transportes Galgos Inter
Tegucigalpa, Honduras	270-1370	10-35	6 daily	Hedman Alas, King Quality & Comfort Lines, Tica Bus, Pullmantur

NATIONAL PULLMAN BUSES FROM GUATEMALA CITY

DESTINATION	COST (Q)	DURATION (HR)	DEPARTURES	FREQUENCY	COMPANY
Antigua	64-70	1	daily	4 times per day	Litegua, Hedman Alas
Chiquimula	50-60	3	4:30am-6pm	every 30 mins	Rutas Orientales
Cobán	50-60	4½	4am-5pm	hourly	Monja Blanca
El Carmen	80	7	12:15am-6:30pm	every 30 mins	Fortaleza del Sur
Esquipulas	50-60	4½	4:30am-6pm	every 30 mins	Rutas Orientales
Flores/ Santa Elena	100-220	8-10	daily	26 times per day	Fuente del Norte, Línea Dorada, ADN
Huehuetenango	60-110	5	daily	4 times per day	Los Halcones, Línea Dorada
La Mesilla	170	7	daily	3 times per day	Línea Dorada
Panajachel	50	3	5:15am daily	once per day	Transportes Rebuli
Poptún	150-190	8	daily	3 times per day	Línea Dorada
Puerto Barrios	60-100	5	3:45am-7pm	every 30 mins	Litegua
Quetzaltenango	65-70	4	daily	11 times per day	Transportes Galgos, Alamo, Línea Dorada, ADN
Retalhuleu	80	3	daily	5 times per day	Fuente del Norte
Río Dulce	65	5	6am-4:30pm	every 30 mins	Litegua
Amatitlán	5	30 min	7am-8:45pm	every 5 min	CentraSur
Antigua	9	1	7am-8pm	every 5 min	Calz Roosevelt btwn 4a Av & 5a Av, Zona 7
Chichicastenango	25	3	5am-6pm	hourly	Parada, Zona 8

Rapidos del Sur (☎2232-7025; CentraSur, Zona 12) For the Pacific coast and El Petén.

Rutas Orientales (☎5481-2946; CentraNorte, Zona 18) Covers the east.

Transportes Álamo (☎2471-8646; 12a Av A 0-65, Zona 7) For Quetzaltenango.

Transportes Galgos (☎2253-4868; 7a Av 19-44, Zona 1) For Quetzaltenango and Retalhuleu.

Transportes Rebuli (☎2230-2748; 41 Calle btwn 6a & 7a Av, Zona 8) For Panajachel.

SHUTTLE MINIBUS

Shuttle services from Guatemala City to popular destinations such as Panajachel and Chichicastenango (via Antigua – both around Q230) are offered by travel agencies in Antigua.

Getting Around

TO & FROM THE AIRPORT

Aeropuerto Internacional La Aurora is in Zona 13, in the southern part of the city, 10 to 15 minutes from Zona 1 by taxi, or 30 minutes by bus.

Taxis wait outside the arrivals exit. 'Official' fares are Q60 to Zona 9 or 10, Q85 to Zona 1, but in reality you may have to pay a bit more. Be sure to establish the destination and price before getting in. Prices for taxis *to* the airport, hailed on the street, are likely to be lower – around Q60 from Zona 1.

BUS

Due to an alarming increase in (often violent) crime on Guatemala City's red city buses, it is pretty much universally accepted that tourists should only use them in case of dire emergency. The major exceptions are the TransMetro and TransUrbano buses which are most useful for getting to the CentraSur and CentraNorte bus terminals, respectively.

For the thrillseekers out there, listed below are the most useful red bus routes. Buses will stop anywhere they see a passenger, but street corners and traffic lights are your best bet for hailing them – just hold out your hand. Buses should cost Q1 per ride in the daytime (but this can as much as quadruple on public holidays or the driver's whim). You pay the driver or his helper as you get on. Don't catch them at night.

Zona 1 to Zona 10 (Bus No 82 or 101) Travels via 10a Av, Zona 1, then 6a Av and Ruta 6 in Zona 4 and Av La Reforma.

Zona 10 to Zona 1 (Bus No 82 or 101) Travels via Av La Reforma then 7a Av in Zona 4 and 9a Av, Zona 1.

Airport to Zona 1 (Bus No 82) Travels via Zonas 9 and 4.

Zona 1 to Airport (Bus No 82) Travels via 10a Av in Zona 1 then down 6a Av in Zonas 4 and 9.

TransMetro

In early 2007, in answer to growing concerns about traffic congestion and insecurity on urban buses, Guatemala City inaugurated the **TransMetro** (http://transmetro.muniguate.com) system. TransMetro buses differ from regular old, red urban buses because they are prepaid (the driver carries no money, thus reducing risk of robberies), travel in their own lanes (not getting caught in traffic jams), only stop at designated stops and are new, comfortable and bright green.

There are currently two routes in operation: one connects Zona 1's Plaza Barrios with the CentraSur bus terminal where the majority of

2ND-CLASS BUSES FROM GUATEMALA CITY

Most 2nd-class ('chicken bus') Pacific Coast services leave from CentraSur, a large terminal on the southern outskirts of the city which is connected to the center by Transmetro buses. Buses for the Western Highlands leave from a series of roadside *paradas* (bus stops) on 41a Calle between 6a and 7a Avs in Zona 8.

DESTINATION	COST (Q)	DURATION (HR)	DEPARTURES	FREQUENCY	COMPANY
Ciudad Pedro de Alvarado	45	2½	5am-4pm	every 30 min	CentraSur
Escuintla	20	1	6am-4:30pm	every 30 min	CentraSur
Huehuetenango	60	5	7am-5pm	every 30 min	Parada, Zona 8
La Democracia	20	2	6am-4:30pm	every 30 min	CentraSur
La Mesilla	90	8	8am-4pm	hourly	Parada, Zona 8
Monterrico	40	3	daily	3 times	CentraSur
Panajachel	30	3	7am-5pm	every 30 min	Parada, Zona 8
Puerto San José	20	1	4:30am-4:45pm	every 15 mins	CentraSur
Salamá	45	3	5am-5pm	every 30 min	17a Calle 11-32, Zona 1
San Pedro La Laguna	40	4	2am-2pm	hourly	Parada, Zona 8
Santa Cruz del Quiché	40	3½	5am-5pm	hourly	Parada, Zona 8
Santiago Atitlán	35	4	4am-5pm	every 30 min	Parada, Zona 8
Tecpán	15	2	5:30am-7pm	every 15 min	Parada, Zona 8
Rivas *ordinario*	2	2	4am-6pm	every 30min	Huembes
San Carlos	7.50	9	5am-1pm	6 daily	Mayoreo
San Juan del Sur	3.25	2½	10am & 4pm	–	Huembes
San Marcos minibus	1	1	4am-6pm	when full	Huembes
Siuna	9	10-12	4:30am, 3pm & 5pm	–	Mayoreo
Somoto	4	4	7:15am, 9:45am, 11am, 12:45pm, 1:45pm, 2pm, 3:45pm & 4:45pm	–	Mayoreo
Ticuantepe minibus	0.35	40 min	4am-6pm	when full	Huembes

GETTING TO ANTIGUA

The classic exit strategy on arrival at Guatemala City airport is to make a beeline for elsewhere, usually Antigua. Door-to-door minibuses run to any address in Antigua (usually Q80 per person, one hour). Look for signs in the airport exit hall or people holding up 'Antigua Shuttle' signs.

The first shuttle leaves for Antigua about 7am and the last around 8pm or 9pm, although there's often one hanging around to meet the last flight (around midnight). For groups, the other option is a taxi (around Q250), but if there are only one or two of you, shuttle minibuses are more economical (if a bit slower and less comfortable).

buses for the Pacific coast now depart. The other runs south from Plaza Barrios through Zonas 9 and 10.

Crime has got so bad on Guate's regular red buses that travelers are advised not to use them, but TransMetro buses are safe, fast and comfortable. All rides cost Q1, payable with a Q1 coin at the bus stop before boarding.

TransUrbano

A more recent improvement to Guatemala City's bus scene is **TransUrbano** (www.transurbano.com.gt), a much wider network of buses that aren't quite as slick as TransMetro but still safe, reliable and comfortable. They're slower because they don't have a dedicated lane, but safer than the old red buses because to board you need a magnetic rechargeable card (card and first ride free) which can only be obtained by showing your passport or Guatemalan ID card. The rechargeable cards are available from special booths, the most useful for travelers being in Zona 1's Plaza Barrios, the CentroNorte bus terminal and the Zona 10 office on Avenida Reforma.

TAXI

Plenty of taxis cruise most parts of the city. Fares are negotiable; always establish your destination and fare before getting in. Zona 1 to Zona 10, or vice versa, costs around Q40 to Q60. If you want to phone for a taxi, **Taxi Amarillo Express** (☎1766) has metered cabs that often work out cheaper than others, though true *capitaleños* (capital-city residents) will tell you that taxi meters are all rigged and you get a better deal by bargaining.

ANTIGUA

POP 58,150

Guatemala's tourism showpiece, Antigua, remains far more than a tourist attraction. A place of rare beauty, major historical significance and vibrant culture, it's the country's one must-visit destination.

A former capital – the seat of government was relocated to Guatemala City following several major earthquakes during the colonial period – Antigua boasts an astonishing catalog of colonial relics in a magnificent setting. Its streetscapes of pastel facades under terracotta roofs unfold amid three volcanoes: Agua (3766m), Fuego (3763m) and Acatenango (3976m). Designated a Unesco World Heritage Site and with an ideal climate, it's a splendid place for walking (though it can get chilly after sunset). While many old ecclesiastical and civic structures are beautifully renovated, others retain tumbledown charm, with fragments strewn about parklike grounds and sprays of bougainvillea sprouting from the crumbling ruins.

Thanks to the dozens of Spanish language schools that operate here, Antigua has become a global hot spot as well, boasting fine dining, plenty of colonial-chic accommodations and an aggressively cosmopolitan nightlife. But the foreign presence by no means dominates the atmosphere. Antigua remains a vibrant Guatemalan town, its churches, plazas and markets throbbing with activity.

Perhaps the real miracle of Antigua is its resilience. Despite the destructive forces that have conspired against it – earthquakes, volcanic eruptions and floods, followed by virtual abandonment and centuries of neglect – the town has reemerged with a vengeance, buoyed by the pride of its inhabitants.

History

Antigua was founded on March 10, 1543, and served as the colonial capital for 233 years. The capital was transferred to Guatemala City in 1776, after Antigua was razed in the earthquake of July 29, 1773.

The town was slowly rebuilt, retaining much of its traditional character. In 1944 the Legislative Assembly declared Antigua a national monument, and in 1979 Unesco declared it a World Heritage Site.

Most of Antigua's buildings were constructed during the 17th and 18th centuries, when the city was a rich Spanish outpost and the Catholic church was ascending to power. Many handsome, sturdy colonial buildings remain, and several impressive ruins have been preserved and are open to the public.

Sights

Once glorious in their gilded baroque finery, Antigua's churches have suffered indignities from both nature and humankind. Rebuilding after earthquakes gave the churches thicker walls, lower towers and belfries, and bland interiors, and moving the capital to Guatemala City deprived Antigua of the population needed to maintain the churches in their traditional glory. Still, they are impressive. In addition to those noted here, you'll find many others scattered around town in various states of decay.

Parque Central

The gathering place for locals and visitors alike, on most days the plaza is lined with villagers selling handicrafts to tourists; on Sunday it's mobbed and the streets on the east and west sides are closed to traffic. Things are cheapest late Sunday afternoon, when the peddling is winding down.

The plaza's famous fountain was built in 1738. At night, mariachi or marimba bands play in the park.

Palacio de los Capitanes Generales HISTORIC BUILDING
Begun in 1558, the Palace of the Captain's General was the governmental center of all Central America from Chiapas to Costa Rica until 1773. The stately double-arcaded facade, which marches proudly along the southern side of the Parque, was added in the early 1760s.

Catedral de Santiago CATHEDRAL
(ruins admission Q3; ⏲ruins 9am-5pm) On the park's east side, Catedral de Santiago was founded in 1542, damaged by earthquakes many times, badly ruined in 1773 and only partially rebuilt between 1780 and 1820.

In the 16th and early 17th centuries, Antigua's churches had lavish baroque interiors, but most – including this one – lost this richness during post-earthquake rebuilding. Inside, a crypt contains the bones of Bernal Díaz del Castillo, historian of the Spanish conquest, who died in 1581. If the front entrance is closed, you can enter at the rear or from the south side.

Museo del Libro Antiguo MUSEUM
(Old Book Museum; ☎7832-5511; admission Q30; ⏲9am-4pm Tue-Fri, 9am-noon & 2-4pm Sat & Sun) Housed in the Palacio del Ayuntamiento is the Museo del Libro Antiguo, with exhibits of colonial printing and binding, including a replica of Guatemala's first printing press, which began work here in the 1660s.

Museo de Arte Colonial MUSEUM
(admission Q50) Now in Guatemala City, San Carlos University was founded in Antigua in 1676. What used to be its main building, half a block east of the park, houses the Museo de Arte Colonial, with some expressive sculptures of saints, and paintings by leading Mexican artists of the era, such as Miguel Cabrera and Juan de Correa.

West of Parque Central

Iglesia y Convento de Nuestra Señora de la Merced CHURCH, MONASTERY
(monastery ruins Q5; ⏲monastery ruins 8:30am-5:30pm) At the north end of 5a Av is La Merced; the Iglesia y Convento de Nuestra Señora de la Merced is Antigua's most striking colonial church. Construction began in 1548 and improvements continued until 1717, when the church was ruined by severe earthquakes.

Reconstruction was completed in 1767, but in 1773 an earthquake struck again and the convent was destroyed. Repairs to the church were made from 1850 to 1855; its baroque facade dates from this period. Inside the **monastery ruins** is a fountain 27m in diameter – possibly the largest in Central America.

Iglesia y Convento de la Recolección RUIN
(Av de la Recolección; admission Q40; ⏲9am-5pm) A massive ruin at the west end of 1a Calle Poniente, the Iglesia y Convento de la Recolección, is among Antigua's most impressive monuments. Built between 1701 and 1708, it was destroyed in the 1773 earthquake.

Colegio de San Jerónimo RUIN
(Real Aduana; cnr Calz de Santa Lucía & Calle de la Recolección; adult Q30; ⏲9am-5pm) Built in 1757 by friars of the Merced order, Colegio de San Jerónimo did not have royal authorization and was therefore was taken over by Spain's Carlos III in 1761. In 1765 it was designated for use as the Royal Customhouse, but, along with many of the area's most important buildings, was destroyed in the 1773 earthquake.

Antigua

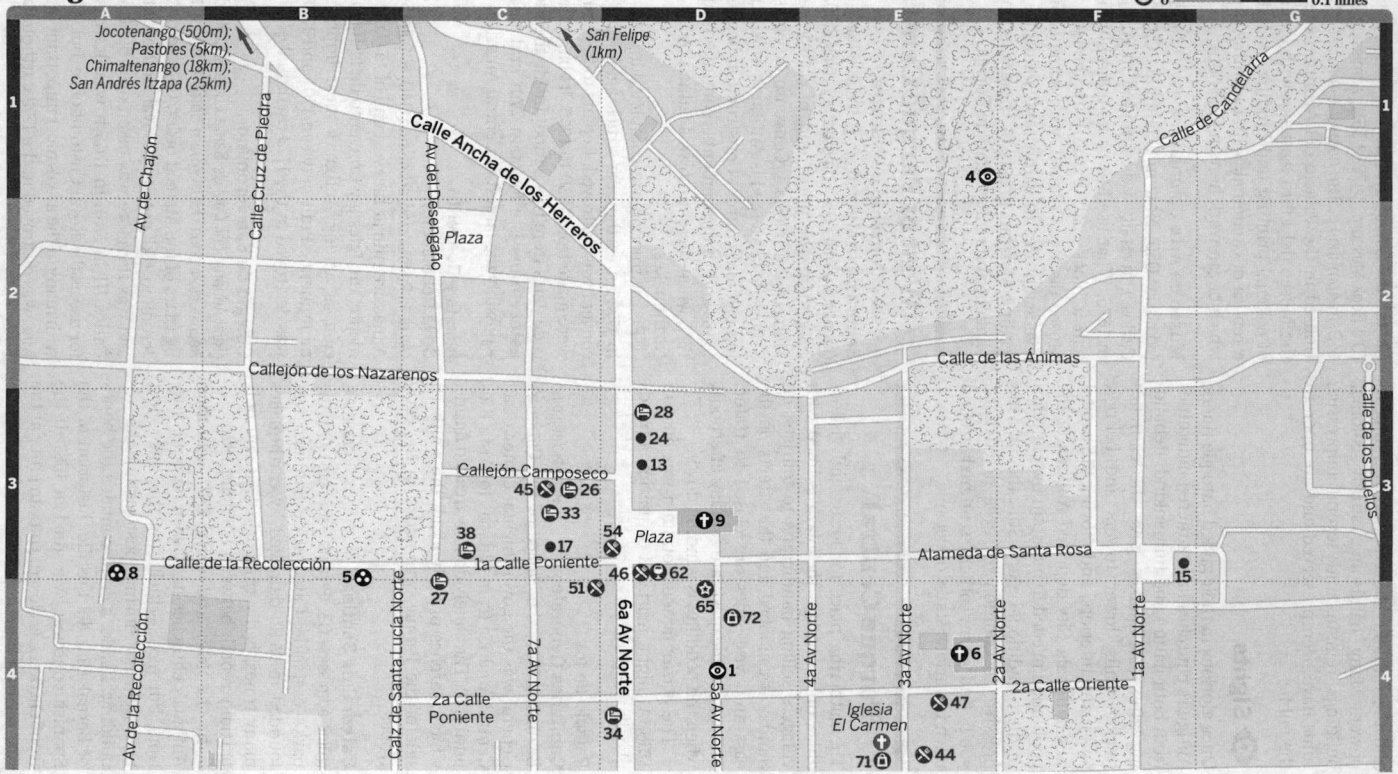
0 200 m
0 0.1 miles
A B C D E F G
1 2 3 4
Jocotenango (500m);
Pastores (5km);
Chimaltenango (18km);
San Andrés Itzapa (25km)
San Felipe
(1km)
Calle Ancha de los Herreros
Av de Chajón
Calle Cruz de Piedra
Av del Desengaño
Plaza
Calle de Candelaria
Calle de las Ánimas
Calle de los Duelos
Callejón de los Nazarenos
Callejón Camposeco
Calle de la Recolección
1a Calle Poniente
Plaza
Alameda de Santa Rosa
Av de la Recolección
Calz de Santa Lucía Norte
7a Av Norte
6a Av Norte
5a Av Norte
4a Av Norte
3a Av Norte
2a Av Norte
1a Av Norte
2a Calle Poniente
2a Calle Oriente
Iglesia
El Carmen
4
28
24
13
45
26
33
9
38
17
54
8
5
27
51
46
62
65
72
15
6
1
47
34
71
44

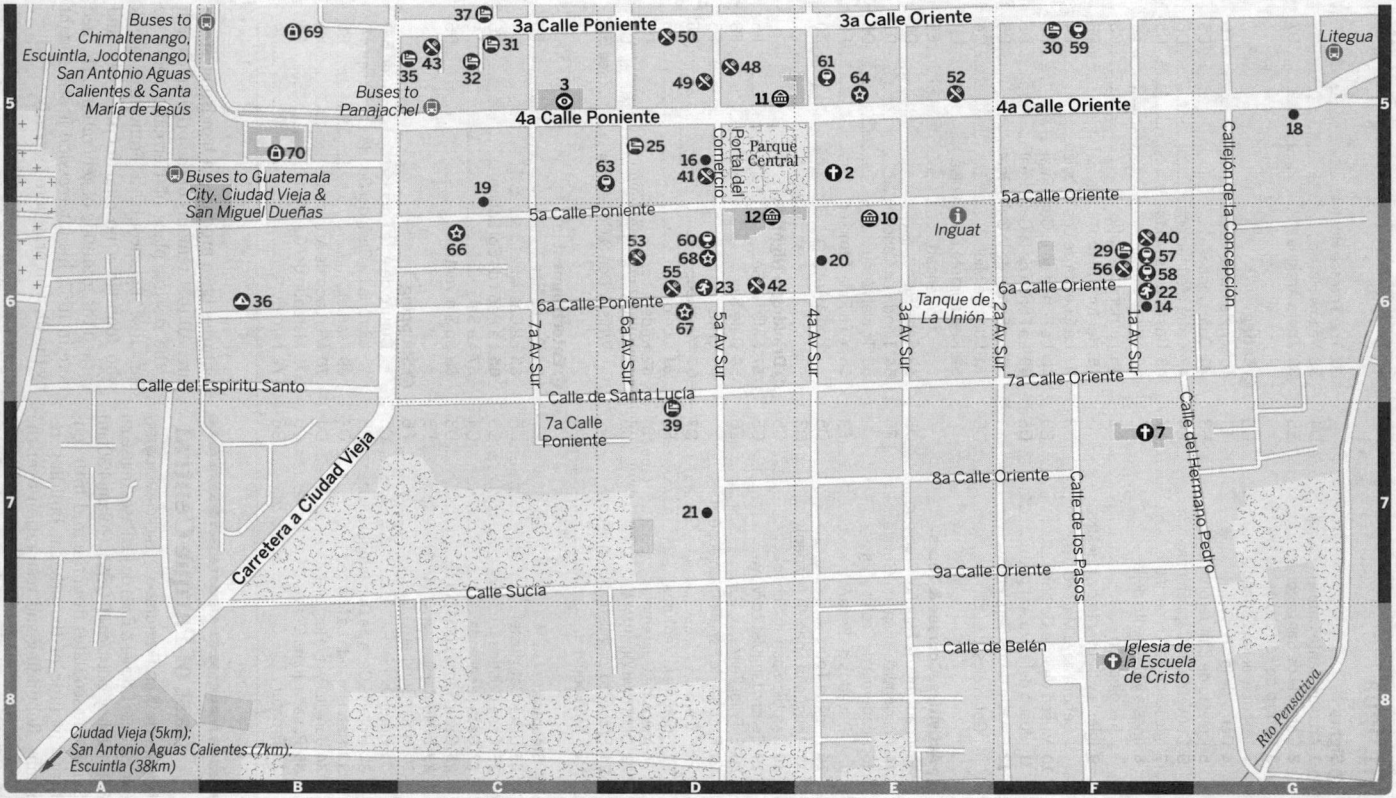
Buses to Chimaltenango, Escuintla, Jocotenango, San Antonio Aguas Calientes & Santa María de Jesús
Buses to Panajachel
Buses to Guatemala City, Ciudad Vieja & San Miguel Dueñas
3a Calle Poniente
3a Calle Oriente
4a Calle Poniente
4a Calle Oriente
5a Calle Poniente
5a Calle Oriente
6a Calle Poniente
6a Calle Oriente
7a Calle Poniente
7a Calle Oriente
8a Calle Oriente
9a Calle Oriente
Parque Central
Portal del Comercio
Inguat
Tanque de La Unión
Litegua
Callejón de la Concepción
Calle del Hermano Pedro
Calle de los Pasos
Calle de Belén
Iglesia de la Escuela de Cristo
Calle de Santa Lucía
Calle del Espíritu Santo
Calle Sucia
Carretera a Ciudad Vieja
7a Av Sur
6a Av Sur
5a Av Sur
4a Av Sur
3a Av Sur
2a Av Sur
1a Av Sur
Río Pensativo
Ciudad Vieja (5km); San Antonio Aguas Calientes (7km); Escuintla (38km)

Antigua

Sights
1 Arco de Santa Catalina D4
2 Catedral de Santiago E5
3 Centro de Formación de la Cooperación Española C5
4 Cerro de la Cruz E1
5 Colegio de San Jerónimo B3
6 Convento de Capuchinas E4
7 Iglesia de San Francisco F7
8 Iglesia y Convento de la Recolección A3
9 Iglesia y Convento de Nuestra Señora de la Merced D3
10 Museo de Arte Colonial E6
11 Museo del Libro Antiguo D5
12 Palacio de los Capitanes Generales D6

Activities, Courses & Tours
13 Academia de Español Probigua D3
14 Academia de Español Sevilla F6
15 Academia de Profesores Privados de Español F3
16 Antigua Tours D5
17 Antigüeña Spanish Academy C3
18 Cambio Spanish School G5
19 Centro Lingüístico Maya C5
20 El Frijol Feliz E6
21 Escuela de Español San José el Viejo D7
22 Guatemala Ventures F6
Niños de Guatemala ..... (see 18)
23 Old Town Outfitters D6
24 Proyecto Lingüístico Francisco Marroquín D3

Sleeping
25 Black Cat Hostel D5
26 Casa Cristina C3
27 Casa Jacaranda C4
28 Casa Santa Lucía No 1 ..... D3
29 El Hostal F6
30 Hotel Burkhard F5
31 Hotel Dionisio C5
32 Hotel la Casa de Don Ismael C5
33 Hotel Posada La Merced C3
34 Jungle Party Hostal D4
35 Posada Juma Ocag C5
36 Proatur B6
37 The Terrace Hostel C5
38 Yellow House C3
39 Zoola Antigua D7

Eating
40 Angie Angie F6
41 Café Condesa D5
42 Caffé Mediterráneo D6
43 Casa de las Mixtas C5
44 Epicure E4
45 Fernando's Kaffe C3
46 Hector's Bistro D3
47 La Cuevita de Los Urquizú E4
48 La Fonda de la Calle Real D5
49 La Fonda de la Calle Real D5
50 La Fonda de la Calle Real D5
51 Luna de Miel C4
52 Restaurante Doña Luisa Xicotencatl E5
53 Sabe Rico D6
54 Tienda La Canche D3
55 Travel Menu D6
56 Y Tu Piña También F6
Zoola Antigua ..... (see 39)

Drinking & Nightlife
57 Café No Sé F6
58 Café Sky F6
59 El Muro F5
60 Monoloco D6
61 Ocelot Bar E5
62 Reds D3
63 Reilly's D5
Whisky Den & Coffee Bar ..... (see 61)

Entertainment
64 Circus Bar E5
65 La Casbah D4
66 La Peña de Sol Latino C6
67 La Sala D6
68 La Sin Ventura D6

Shopping
Centro de Arte Popular ..... (see 64)
Librería La Casa del Conde ..... (see 41)
69 Market B5
70 Mercado de Artesanías B5
71 Mercado del Carmen E4
72 Nim Po't D4

East of Parque Central

Iglesia de San Francisco CHURCH, MONASTERY
(cnr 8a Calle Oriente & Calle do los Pasos; museum & monastery adult/child Q5/2; ⏲ 9am-4:30pm) San Francisco dates from the mid-16th century, but little of the original building remains. Rebuilding and restoration over the centuries have produced a handsome structure. All that remains of the original church is the resting place of Hermano Pedro de San José Betancourt, a Franciscan monk who founded a hospital for the poor and earned the gratitude of generations. He died here in 1667; his intercession is still sought by the ill, who pray here fervently.

Convento de Capuchinas CONVENT
(Iglesia y Convento de Nuestra Señora del Pilar de Zaragoza; cnr 2a Av Norte & 2a Calle Oriente; adult/student Q30/15; ⏲9am-5pm) Las Capuchinas was founded in 1736 by nuns from Madrid. Destroyed repeatedly by earthquakes, it is now a museum with exhibits on religious life in colonial times. The building has an unusual structure of 18 concentric cells around a circular patio.

Cerro de la Cruz HILL
(Hill of the Cross) On the town's northeast side is the Hill of the Cross, offering fine views over Antigua and south toward Volcán Agua. Don't come here without a tourist police escort, as it's notorious for muggers. The tourist police was formed because of robberies here; reportedly no crime against tourists has taken place on the hill since.

Activities

Two professional, established and friendly outfits offering a big range of activities are Old Town Outfitters and Guatemala Ventures. Drop by either place to chat about possibilities.

Climbing the Volcanoes

All three volcanoes overlooking Antigua – Agua, Acatenango and Fuego – are tempting challenges. How close you can get to Fuego depends on recent levels of activity. In many ways the twin-peaked Acatenango (3976m), overlooking Fuego, is the most exhilarating summit. For an active-volcano experience many people take tours to Pacaya (2552m), 25km southeast of Antigua (a 1½-hour drive).

Old Town Outfitters leads strenuous hikes up Volcán Acatenango, traversing four ecosystems to reach the summit (Q980, including lunch and transport to the trailhead in the village of La Soledad). The expedition departs at 5am.

Most agencies run seven-hour Pacaya trips daily for Q80 (leaving Antigua at 6am and 2pm); food or drinks are not included, nor is the Q50 admission to the Pacaya protected area. It takes about 1½ hours to make the steep ascent to the simmering cleft black cone. (If you're out of breath, kids will rent you horses on the way up.) From the summit there are stupendous views west to Agua and northeast to Lago de Amatitlán. The descent is quicker as you slide down the powdery slope.

To climb Volcán de Agua, travel to the village of Santa María de Jesús on the volcano's northeast slopes (Q3.50 from bus terminal). From the tourist office on the Parque Central of Santa María, you can hire Inguat-authorized guides (Q175 to Q250 per person, plus park entry fee of Q40).

Cycling

Old Town Outfitters ADVENTURE SPORTS
(☎5399-0440; www.adventureguatemala.com; 5a Av Sur 12C) Offers a range of guided half-day mountain bike rides (Q380 per person) in the hills around Antigua, at varying levels of difficulty. The two-day Pedal and Paddle Tour (Q1960 to Q2270) includes kayaking and hiking at Lago de Atitlán.

Guatemala Ventures MOUNTAIN BIKING
(fax 7832-3383; 1a Av Sur 15) Offers bike tours, from half-day rides through the Antigua valley (Q235) to week-long jaunts encompassing volcanic slopes, highland forest and Pacific mangroves, as well as Lago de Atitlán. Another, lazier, option is the trip up Cerro Alto in a minibus with a coast back down on a mountain bike (Q275).

Horseback Riding

Ravenscroft Riding Stables HORSEBACK RIDING
(☎7830-6669; 2a Av Sur 3, San Juan del Obispo) This stable, 3km south of Antigua on the road to Santa María de Jesús, offers English-style riding, with scenic rides of three, four or five hours in the valleys and hills around Antigua. Rides cost Q195 per hour per person for experienced riders, Q235 for beginners. You need to be fairly fit. Reach the stables on a bus bound for Santa María de Jesús.

Volunteering

Many Spanish schools can help you find volunteer work, even if you're not studying there. **EntreMundos** (www.entremundos.org) and **Idealist** (www.idealist.org) both have free, searchable databases listing Antigua opportunities.

Courses

Antigua is world-famous for its many Spanish-language schools. Prices, teacher quality and student satisfaction vary greatly, so shop around. Ask for references and talk to ex-students. Inguat has a list of reputable schools.

Language classes start Mondays at most schools, though you can usually be placed with a teacher any day of the week. The busiest seasons are January, and April to August – some schools request advance reservations for these times. Instruction is usually one-on-one and costs between Q750 to Q1515 per week for four hours of classes daily, five days per week. You can enroll for up to 10 hours a day of instruction. Most schools offer room and board with local families, where you'll often have your own room, usually with shared bathrooms, for around Q700 per week (including three meals daily except Sunday). Homestays are supposed to promote the 'total immersion' concept of language learning, but often there are several foreigners staying with one family and separate mealtimes for students and the family. Make a point of inquiring about such details if you really want to be totally immersed.

Antigua is not for everyone who wants to study Spanish; there are so many foreigners about, it takes some real discipline to converse in Spanish rather than your native tongue. Many enjoy this social scene, but if you think it will bother you, consider studying in Quetzaltenango (Xela), El Petén or elsewhere, where there are fewer foreign students and more opportunities to dive into Spanish.

Academia de Español Probigua LANGUAGE COURSE
(☎7832-2998; www.probigua.org; 6a Av Norte 41B) Well-regarded, nonprofit school that donates profits to establish and maintain libraries in rural villages.

Academia de Español Sevilla LANGUAGE COURSE
(☎7832-5101; www.sevillantigua.com; 1a Av Sur 17C) This school has a good free activity program, and offers a shared student house as a sleeping option.

Academia de Profesores Privados de Español LANGUAGE COURSE
(☎7882-4284; www.appeschool.com; Alameda de Santa Rosa 15) Also offers courses for tourism, educational and healthcare personnel, and an opportunity to study in the outlying village of San Juan del Obispo.

Antigüeña Spanish Academy LANGUAGE COURSE
(☎5375-4638; www.spanishacademyantiguena.com; 1a Calle Poniente 10) A highly recommended school, only hiring experienced teachers. It can arrange volunteer work in the area.

Cambio Spanish School LANGUAGE COURSE
(www.cambiospanishschool.com; 4a Calle Oriente 41) Supports **Niños de Guatemala** (☎7832-8033; www.ninosdeguatemala.org; 4a Calle Oriente 41), an educational program for underprivileged kids.

Centro Lingüístico Maya LANGUAGE COURSE
(☎7832-0656; www.clmaya.com; 5a Calle Poniente 20) Large, professionally managed, slightly pricier institute with 30 years' experience training diplomatic personnel and journalists.

Escuela de Español San José el Viejo LANGUAGE COURSE
(☎7832-3028; www.sanjoseelviejo.com; 5a Av Sur 34) Professional school accredited by Guatemalan Ministry of Education, set in superb gardens with tennis court, pool and own tasteful accommodations.

Proyecto Lingüístico Francisco Marroquín LANGUAGE COURSE
(☎7832-1422; www.spanishschoolplfm.com; 6a Av Norte 43) Antigua's oldest Spanish school, run by a nonprofit foundation working to preserve Maya languages and culture. Also offers instruction in Maya languages.

El Frijol Feliz COOKING COURSE
(☎7832-5274; www.frijolfeliz.com; 4a Av Sur 1; 3hr class Q360) Offers hands-on instruction on preparing Guatemalan meals; students may choose their own menu.

Tours

Inguat-authorized guides around the Parque Central offer city walking tours, with visits to convents, ruins and museums, for Q100 to Q200. Similar guided walks are offered daily by Antigua travel agencies such as **Adventure Travel Center** (www.adventravelguatemala.com; 5a Av Norte 25B) and Atitrans (p120). Also on offer are trips to the surrounding villages and coffee plantations for around Q200.

Tours to more distant places – including Tikal, the Cobán area, Monterrico, Chichicastenango and Lago de Atitlán – are also possible. Two-day trips to Tikal, flying from Guatemala City to Flores and back, start at Q3000 per person. Two-day land tours to Copán (some including Quiriguá and Río Dulce) run around Q1140 per person.

CATours (☎7832-9638; www.catours.co.uk; 6a Calle Oriente 14) offers two-day motorbike tours to Lago de Atitlán or Monterrico from Q1175.

Antigua Tours WALKING TOUR
(☎7832-5821; www.antiguatours.net; Portal del Comercio) Elizabeth Bell, a local scholar of Antigua history, or one of her knowledgeable associates, lead three-hour cultural walking tours of the town (in English and/or Spanish) on Tuesday, Wednesday, Friday and Saturday at 9:30am, and on Monday and Thursday at 2pm. The cost is Q160. Reservations can be made through Antigua Tours, inside Café El Portal (Portal del Comercio 6) off the Parque Central; groups congregate at the park's fountain at the appointed hour. Bell's book, *Antigua Guatemala: The City and Its Heritage*, is well worth picking up: it has extensive descriptions of all the monuments and neatly encapsulates the history and fiestas. Bell and company also do tours to the nearby villages of San Antonio Aguas Calientes and San Andrés Itzapa to investigate weaving workshops and Maya shrines, respectively.

As Green As It Gets VOLUNTEERING
(☎5663-9764; www.asgreenasitgets.org) As Green As It Gets offers tours of coffee plantations around San Miguel Escobar, a suburb of Ciudad Vieja, with local growers demonstrating cultivation, harvesting and processing techniques. Tours (Q200 per person) depart daily at 9am and 2pm from the central plaza of San Miguel Escobar.

Festivals & Events

Semana Santa RELIGIOUS FESTIVAL
(Holy Week; ⊙Easter weekend) The week leading up to Easter, when hundreds of people dress in purple robes in daily street processions.

Sleeping

When checking a budget establishment, look at several rooms, as some are much better than others. Antigua hotels can fill up fast, particularly on weekends and festival days.

El Hostal HOSTEL $
(☎7832-0442; www.elhostal-antigua.com; 1a Av Sur 8; dm Q80, s/d without bathroom Q130/260;) Half a dozen neatly kept rooms and dorms with sturdy single beds or well-spaced bunks, set around a cheery little patio/cafe.

Posada Juma Ocag HOTEL $
(☎7832-3109; Calz de Santa Lucía Norte 13; s/d Q120/160) Comfortable and creatively decorated. Good rooftop patio and well-tended little garden. Reservations in person only.

Zoola Antigua HOSTEL $
(☎7832-0364; www.zoola-antigua.com; Calle de Santa Lucía 15; dm/r incl breakfast Q75/200;) Such was the success of its flagship hostel on Lago de Atitlán that the Israeli-run Zoola opened an Antigua branch in 2012. The concept successfully translates to the new colonial setting: sparely furnished dorms surround an open courtyard where global travelers chill and nosh on healthy Middle-Eastern snacks beneath a rainbow canopy.

Yellow House HOSTEL $
(☎7832-6646; yellowhouseantigua@hotmail.com; 1a Calle Poniente 24; dm/d without bathroom incl breakfast Q80/190; @) Simple but thoughtfully designed and ecologically conscious, this makes a superior budget choice. Rooms vary, but comfy beds, recessed lighting, and mosquito-screened windows are the norm.

Hotel Dionisio HOSTEL $
(☎7832-6078; hoteldionisioantigua.net; 3a Calle Poniente Callejón 19A; dm 50, r with/without bathroom Q200/150; @) The most relaxed of four guesthouses along a little cul-de-sac, featuring spanking clean and nicely decorated rooms along a sunny terrace, a well-supplied kitchen and a cozy lounge area.

Hotel la Casa de Don Ismael HOTEL $
(☎7832-1932; www.casadonismael.com; 3a Calle Poniente 6, Lotificación Cofiño 2a Callejón; s/d Q120/175, incl breakfast Q160/225;) This homey, humble guesthouse is hidden down a small side street and overseen by its kind, cordial namesake. Seven rustic rooms share three hot-water bathrooms, and there's a pleasant roof terrace.

Black Cat Hostel HOSTEL $
(☎7832-1229; www.blackcathostels.net; 6 Av Norte 1A; dm/d/tr Q65/160/240) Though the dorms are cramped and you can't use the kitchen, this place is always hopping. Plenty of tours are on offer, plus free movies and good local advice.

Jungle Party Hostal HOSTEL $
(☎7832-0463; www.junglepartyhostal.com; 6a Av Norte 20; dm Q60;) With bar service, hammock hangouts and the famous all-you-can-eat Saturday barbecue, the Jungle Party has a great atmosphere, and the smiling staff know exactly what's needed by travelers.

The Terrace Hostel HOSTEL $
(☎7832-3463; www.terracehostel.com; 3a Calle Poniente 24; incl breakfast dm Q65, r with/without bath Q275/200) The key feature at this fun-filled establishment is the rooftop terrace, a fabulous perch for both volcano views and Q10 Brahvas (happy hour starts at noon). Below deck, rooms are fairly bare but kept tidy. Don't miss the Monday pub crawl, taking off from here at 3pm.

Casa Santa Lucía No 1 HOTEL $
(☎7832-1386; 6a Av Norte 43; r Q183) Step back in time, down arched hallways with heavy exposed beams, to reach the well-maintained paint-dappled rooms equipped with blasting hot showers. Though the staff could be a tad more communicative, it's a great location, just north of La Merced.

Hotel Burkhard HOTEL $
(☎7832-4316; hotelburkhard@hotmail.com; 3a Calle Oriente 19A; r Q110; 📶) Tiny hotel with a dozen compact, fancifully decorated rooms on two levels.

Proatur CAMPGROUND
(☎5978-3586; 6a Calle Poniente Final; 📶) FREE
You can park an RV or pitch a tent on the grounds of Proatur, the tourist police. There's no charge, but it's appreciated if campers contribute items such as tools or bug spray. There are toilets, showers and electric hookups.

★Casa Jacaranda HOSTEL $$
(☎7832-7589; www.hosteljacaranda.com; 1a Calle Poniente 37; incl breakfast dm Q95, s/d without bathroom Q120/240; @📶) Rooms at this original, mellow new hostel are simple but pleasing. Four-bed dorms leave plenty of elbow room, and the shared bathrooms are thoughtfully designed. A grassy patio under a jacaranda tree makes for a tranquil retreat.

Casa Cristina BOUTIQUE HOTEL $$
(☎7832-0623; www.casa-cristina.com; Callejón Camposeco 3A; s/d downstairs Q200/240, upstairs Q320/360; 📶) There are just a dozen rooms at this comfy little two-story hotel on a pretty backstreet near La Merced. All are quaintly appointed with indigenous bedspreads, brushed-on pastels and wood-stained furniture, and the roof terrace (only open till 8pm) makes a nice retreat. *Muy tranquilo.*

Hotel Posada La Merced HOTEL $$
(☎7832-3197; www.posadalamercedantigua.com; 7a Av Norte 43A; s/d from Q265/340; 📶) Behind the big wooden doors, La Merced sports a modern interior. Rooms in the rear section have a bit more pizzazz, with *típico* (traditional) weavings and colonial furniture. Bonuses include a rooftop terrace, well-appointed guest kitchen, morning coffee and gracious staff.

Eating

For global gourmands, Antigua is a banquet. Within 10 minutes' walk of Parque Central you can dine well and inexpensively on Italian, Belgian, French, Thai, Indian, Irish, Israeli, German, Danish, Chinese, Mexican and Salvadoran cuisines.

Saturday and Sunday evenings, tables are set up in front of Convento La Merced, serving, among other snacks, chicken salad sandwiches, *rellenitos* (refried black beans in mashed plantain dumplings), *enchiladas* (fried tortillas covered with refried beans, avocado and crumbly cheese), tamales and *chuchitos* (small tamales) laced with hot sauce and pickled cabbage, along with bowls of *atol blanco* (corn-based hot beverage). Talk about comfort food!

Note that most formal restaurants in Antigua whack on a 10-percent tip before presenting the bill. It should be itemized, but if in doubt, ask.

★Tienda La Canche GUATEMALAN $
(6a Av Norte 42; set lunch Q20) A hole in the wall if there ever was one, the restaurant, behind a 'mom and pop' store, consists of two tables with floral tablecloths. It prepares a couple of traditional options daily, such as *pepián de pollo,* a hearty chicken stew containing chunks of potato and huizquil, a yucca-like tuber, accompanied by a tray of thick tortillas. *Frescos,* home-squeezed fruit beverages, are served alongside.

Restaurante Doña Luisa Xicotencatl CAFE $
(☎7832-2578; 4a Calle Oriente 12; sandwiches & breakfast dishes Q30-40; ⏲7am-9:30pm) Probably Antigua's best-known restaurant, this is a place to enjoy the colonial patio ambience over breakfast or a light meal. The attached bakery sells all kinds of bread and rolls: banana bread comes hot from the oven around 2pm daily.

Café Condesa CAFE $
(☎7832-0038; Portal del Comercio 4; cakes & pastries Q18-26; ⏲7am-8pm Sun-Thu, 7am-9pm Fri & Sat) Go through the Librería La Casa del Conde bookstore to reach this restaurant, set around the patio of a 16th-century

mansion. Baked goods are the strong suit – pies, cakes, quiches, scones and housebaked whole-wheat sandwich bread. The Sunday buffet, from 9am to 1pm, a lavish spread for Q78, is an Antigua institution.

Sabe Rico DELI $
(☎7832-0648; 6a Av Sur 7; sandwiches & salads Q40; ⏲8am-7pm Mon & Wed, 11am-3pm Tue, 8am-8pm Thu-Sat, 9am-4pm Sun) For tasty salads and sandwiches, freshly baked breads, brownies and fine wines.

Fernando's Kaffe CAFE $
(cnr 7a Av Norte & Callejón Camposeco; ⏲7am-7pm; 📶) Antigua has no shortage of coffee or cafes, but Fernando's is the sort of place where you could end up hanging out all day, munching your way through the menu of salads and empanadas and sipping some of the best coffee in town.

Zoola Antigua ISRAELI $
(www.zoola-antigua.com; Calle de Santa Lucia 15; ⏲8am-10pm; ✉) The restaurant component of Zoola hostel whips up highly authentic Israeli fare. Nosh on felafel, kebabs or a *sabich* sandwich, stuffed with hummus, eggplant and salad. Seating is at low coffee tables surrounded by pillows. Friday evenings Zoola offers a buffet-style spread of salads.

Luna de Miel CREPERIE $
(www.lunademielantigua.com; 6a Av Norte 40; ⏲10am-10pm; 📶) Loungey Luna de Miel does dozens of variations on the classic crepe – the *chapín* version is stuffed with avocado, cheese and fried tomatoes – plus tropical smoothies. As if that weren't enough, the graffitied roof deck makes a remarkably relaxing place to enjoy them, then kick back with a hookah.

Y Tu Piña También SANDWICHES $
(1a Av Sur 10B; sandwiches & salads Q30-35; ⏲7am-8pm Mon-Fri, 8am-9pm Sat & Sun; 📶✉) A tempting array of healthy sandwiches (served on wholewheat, pita or bagel), salads and crepes. Good breakfasts, too: omelets, waffles and abundant fruit salads, plus excellent coffee.

Casa de las Mixtas GUATEMALAN $
(3a Callejón; mains Q20-30; ⏲breakfast, lunch & dinner Mon-Sat) For down-home Guatemalan fare with a bit of style, try this family-run operation on a quiet backstreet across from the market. Aside from their namesake snack – *mixtas* are Guatemalan-style hot dogs, wrapped in tortillas – it also does *paches* (like tamales, but made of mashed potatoes instead of corn dough) and offers a range of set breakfasts.

Travel Menu INTERNATIONAL $
(6a Calle Poniente 14; mains Q28-32; ⏲noon-7:30pm; ✉) Not nearly as unimaginative as the name would imply, this little bar-restaurant serves food that you may have been craving (chow mein, curry, etc) in an intimate candlelit environment. Its motto: 'small place, big portions'.

★Caffé Mediterráneo ITALIAN $$
(☎7882-7180; 6a Calle Poniente 6A; mains Q90-130; ⏲lunch & dinner Wed-Mon) Here you'll find the finest, most authentic Italian food in Antigua – if not all Latin America – in a lovely candlelit setting with superb service. Hailing from Calabria, chef Francesco does a tantalizing array of salads and pasta, using seasonally available ingredients.

La Fonda de la Calle Real GUATEMALAN $$
(5a Av Norte 5: mains Q70-80, ⏲noon-10pm Tue-Sun; 3a Calle Poniente 7: ☎7832-0507, 3a Calle Poniente 7, ⏲noon-10pm Tue-Sun; 5a Av Norte 12: 5a Av Norte 12, ⏲8am-10pm) This restaurant, with three branches, all in appealing colonial style, has a good menu ranging from generous salads and sandwiches (Q40) to grilled meats (up to Q99). The specialty is *caldo real,* a hearty chicken soup that makes a good meal. The branch at 3a Calle Poniente 7 is the most attractive, with several rooms and patios.

Hector's Bistro FRENCH $$
(☎7832-9867; 1a Calle Poniente 9A; mains Q85-110) A hit with the expat community, this tiny salon across the way from La Merced has just a few tables, with the kitchen behind the bar. Guatemala City native Hector has garnered acclaim for his versions of beef bourguígnon, grilled duck breast and so on. There's no proper sign: check the chalkboard for daily specials and the quiche of the week.

Angie Angie ARGENTINE $$
(1a Av Sur 11A; pastas Q65-80) Equal parts Southern Cone eatery, art gallery and social club, Angie's place is always worth stopping into, if only to lounge around the tropically abundant back garden. Besides the *empanadas*, mixed grills and homemade pastas, there's a good-value set lunch. Bonfires nightly plus live blues and jazz on weekends.

Epicure DELI $$
(3 Av Norte 11B; sandwiches Q50-58, mains Q65-100) A good place to stock up on sandwiches

for the volcano climb is this Euro-standard deli, with all kinds of gourmet items. Offers elegant open-air dining under the rear arbor.

La Cuevita de Los Urquizú GUATEMALAN $$
(☎4593-5619; 2a Calle Oriente 9D; lunch combo Q80; ⏲lunch & dinner) Sumptuous *típico* food is the draw here, all kept warm in earthenware pots out front, making it almost impossible to go past. Choose from *pepián, kaq'ik* (spicy turkey stew), *jocón* (green stew of chicken or pork with green vegetables and herbs) or other such Guatemalan favorites, and you'll get two accompaniments.

Drinking & Entertainment

Antigua's bar scene is jumping, except for the nationwide law that says that all bars must close at 1am. Many people roll into town from Guatemala City for a spot of Antigua-style revelry on Friday and Saturday nights.

The **Centro de Formación de la Cooperación Española** (☎7932-3838; www.aecid-cf.org.gt; 6a Av Norte; ⏲9am-6pm) FREE runs thematic series of documentaries or foreign arthouse films on Wednesday nights.

For North American and European sports on TV, check the programs at Reds or Monoloco.

Café No Sé and Angie Angie host folk, rock and jazz performances.

Reilly's BAR
(6a Av Norte 2) Antigua's Irish pub packs them in from afternoon onwards during its extended happy hour. The music is loud, the pub grub tasty and the Guinness pricey, at Q66. The Monday evening trivia quiz (7pm) is a pretty big deal.

El Muro BAR
(3a Calle Oriente 19D; ⏲7-11pm Mon-Sat) 'The Wall' is a friendly neighborhood pub with a range of beers, an eclectic menu of snacks and plenty of comfortable sofas to lounge around on. The music, which tends toward '70s and '80s rock (think Pink Floyd), is kept low enough for conversation.

Café No Sé BAR
(cafenose.com; 1a Av Sur 11C) This downbeat little bar is a point of reference for Antigua's budding young Burroughs and Kerouacs. It's also the core of a lively music scene, with players wailing from a corner of the room most evenings.

Monoloco PUB
(5a Av Sur 6, Pasaje El Corregidor) The atmosphere can get pretty rowdy here after hours, with plenty of newcomers filing in. The two-level place (open-air upstairs, with benches and long tables) has scores of TVs tuned to the big game.

Café Sky BAR
(☎7832-7300; 1a Av Sur 15) The rooftop is deservedly popular for sunset drinks and snacks, weather permitting. Below deck, there's a candlelit tiki bar with freaky warrior outfits covering the walls.

Reds BAR
(1a Calle Poniente 3) Across the way from La Merced, Reds is a low-key clubhouse that draws a refreshingly mixed crowd, often more Guatemalan than gringo. Come here to shoot pool (tourneys on Thursday nights), drink cut-rate mojitos and/or watch sports TV.

La Sala LIVE MUSIC
(6a Calle Poniente 9; ⏲Tue-Sun) Crowds pour into this boisterous hall, with murals of frenetic dancers, for live rock, blues or reggae – or maybe it's the cheap liquor. Bands hit the stage nightly around 9pm.

La Peña de Sol Latino LIVE MUSIC
(☎7882-4468; www.lapenaantigua.com; 5a Calle Poniente 15C) This supper club is named after its headlining band, who play their distinctive brand of Andean progressive music Wednesday to Sunday night from 7pm.

La Casbah CLUB
(☎7832-2640; 5a Av Norte 30; admission Q30; ⏲8:30pm-1am Tue-Sat) This two-level disco near the **Arco de Santa Catalina** (5a Av Norte) has a warm atmosphere, is reportedly gay-friendly and quite a party most nights.

La Sin Ventura CLUB
(5a Av Sur 8; ⏲Tue-Sat) The liveliest dance floor in town is packed with Guatemalan youth toward the weekend. There's live salsa and merengue on Thursday nights.

Circus Bar LIVE MUSIC
(www.circusbar.com.gt; 4a Calle Oriente 10; ⏲noon-midnight) On the upper level of the Casa Antigua El Jaulón shopping center, the balconied nightspot hosts flamenco sets Friday and Saturday evenings.

Ocelot Bar BAR
(4a Av Norte 3; ⏲noon-midnight) Just off the Parque Central, the Ocelot feels like a large living room, with wall-length sofas, rock posters and board games, not to mention the best-stocked bar in town. It's highly popular with the mature expat crowd; the Sunday evening pub quiz really packs them in.

Whisky Den & Coffee Bar CAFE
(4a Av Norte 3) This little lounge, next to the Ocelot Bar, highlights two great pick-me-ups: there's an all-star lineup of world whiskies and coffee produced by a local cooperative whose members take turns setting up espressos and lattes.

Shopping

Antigua's **market** (Calz de Santa Lucía Sur) – chaotic, colorful and always busy – sprawls north of 4a Calle. The best days are the official market days – Monday, Thursday and Friday – when villagers from the vicinity roll in and spread their wares north and west of the main market building. Immediately south, the **Mercado de Artesanías** (4a Calle Poniente; ⏲8am-7pm) displays masses of Guatemalan handicrafts. While they're not at the top end of quality, you'll find colorful masks, blankets, jewelry, purses and more. Don't be afraid to bargain. The **Mercado del Carmen**, next to the ruins of the Iglesia del Carmen, is a good place to browse for textiles, pottery and jade, particularly on weekends, when activity spills out onto 3a Av.

Nim Po't HANDICRAFTS
(☎7832-2681; www.nimpot.com; 5a Av Norte 29) This shop boasts a huge collection of Maya dress, as well as hundreds of masks and other wood carvings. This sprawling space is packed with *huipiles* (long embroidered tunics), *cortes* (wraparound skirts), *fajas* (waist sashes) and more, all arranged according to region, so it makes for a fascinating visit whether you're in the market or not.

Centro de Arte Popular ART
(4a Calle Oriente 10; ⏲9:30am-6:30pm) Inside the Casa Antigua El Jaulón, a courtyard shopping arcade, this shop/museum displays Tz'utujil oil paintings, cedar figurines, masks and other crafts in four galleries.

Librería La Casa del Conde BOOKS
(Portal del Comercio 4) Excellent selection of Central American history, politics and nature guides in English, literature in Spanish, and Lonely Planet guides.

Orientation

Volcán Agua is southeast of the city and visible from most points; Volcán Acatenango is to the west; and Volcán Fuego – easily recognizable by its plume of smoke and red glow – is to the southwest. These three volcanoes (which appear on the city's coat of arms) provide easy reference points.

In Antigua compass points are added to the avenidas and calles. Calles run east–west, so 4a Calle west of Parque Central is 4a Calle Poniente; avenidas run north–south, so 3a Av north of Parque Central is 3a Av Norte.

Most buses arrive at the Terminal de Buses, a large open lot just west of the *mercado*, four blocks west of Parque Central along 4a Calle Poniente.

Information

DANGERS & ANNOYANCES

Antigua generally feels safe to walk around but muggings do occur, so don't let your guard down completely. This holds doubly true after the bars close at 1am, when muggers are on the lookout for inebriated visitors. After 10pm, consider taking a taxi back to your lodging, especially if you're female. Pickpockets work the busy market, doing overtime on paydays at the middle and end of the month. December (bonus time) brings a renewed wave of robberies.

Some of the more remote hiking trails have been the scene of muggings, though stepped-up police patrols have reduced the likelihood of such incidents in recent years. If you're planning on hiking independently to any of the volcanoes, check with Proatur (p119) about the current situation.

EMERGENCY

Proatur (☎5578-9835; operacionesproatur@inguat.gob.gt; 6a Calle Poniente Final; ⏲24hr) The helpful tourism assistance agency acts as a police liaison for tourists.

MEDIA

The Antigua-based **Revue Magazine** (www.revuemag.com) runs about 90% ads, but has reasonable cultural events information. It's available everywhere. **La Cuadra** (www.lacuadraonline.com), also Antigua-based, mixes politics with irreverent commentary.

MEDICAL SERVICES

Farmacia Ivori Select (☎7832-1559; 6a Av Norte 19) Pharmacy.

Hospital Nacional Pedro de Bethancourt (☎7831-1319) A public hospital in San Felipe, 2km north of the center, with emergency service.

Hospital Privado Hermano Pedro (☎7832-1190; Av de la Recolección 4) Near the bus station, a private hospital that offers 24-hour emergency service and accepts foreign insurance.

MONEY

Banco Industrial (5a Av Sur 4; ⏲9am-7pm Mon-Fri, 9am-1pm Sat) Has a reliable ATM and changes US dollars (cash and traveler's checks). Another useful BI ATM is inside Café Barista, across the square.

Citibank (cnr 4a Calle Oriente & 4a Av Norte; ⏲9am-4:30pm Mon-Fri, 9:30am-1pm Sat) Gives Visa (not MasterCard) cash advances. A second branch, one block east, changes US dollars and euros.

Visa & MasterCard ATM (Portal del Comercio) Facing Parque Central.

POST

Post Office (cnr 4a Calle Poniente & Calz de Santa Lucía Norte) West of Parque Central, near the market.

TOURIST INFORMATION

Inguat (☎7832-0787; info-antigua@inguat.gob.gt; 5a Calle Oriente 11; ⏲8am-5pm Mon-Fri, 9am-5pm Sat & Sun) The tourist office has free city maps, bus information and helpful, bilingual staff.

TRAVEL AGENCIES

Everywhere you turn in Antigua, you'll see travel agencies offering tours to interesting sites around Antigua and elsewhere in Guatemala, international flights, shuttle minibuses and more.

Atitrans (☎7832-3371; www.atitrans.com; 6a Av Sur 8)

LAX Travel (☎7832-2674; laxantigua@intelnett.com; 3a Calle Poniente 12) International flight specialist.

Onvisa Travel Agency (☎5226-3441; onvisatravel@hotmail.com; 6a Calle Poniente 40) Operates shuttles to Copán and elsewhere.

National Travel (☎7832-8383; antigua@nationalgua.com; 6a Av Sur 1A) Offers one-way flights, including student and teacher fares.

Rainbow Travel Center (www.rainbowtravelcenter.com; 7a Av Sur 8) Student and teacher air fares are their specialty.

ℹ Getting There & Around

BUS

Buses from Guatemala City, Ciudad Vieja and San Miguel Dueñas arrive and depart from a street just south of the market, alongside the Mercado de Artesanías. **Buses to Chimaltenango, Escuintla, San Antonio Aguas Calientes and Santa María de Jesús** go from a lot behind the main market building. If you're heading out to local villages, go early in the morning and return by mid-afternoon, as bus services drop off dramatically as evening approaches.

To reach highland towns such as Chichicastenango, Quetzaltenango, Huehuetenango or Panajachel, take one of the frequent buses to Chimaltenango, on the Interamericana Hwy, then catch an onward bus. Making connections is easy, as many folks will jump to your aid as you alight from one bus looking for another. But stay alert and watch your pack.

Litegua (☎7832-9850; www.litegua.com; 4a Calle Oriente 48) offers Pullman service to Guatemala City (Q45) from its office at the east end of town at 10am and 4pm. To Panajachel, Transportes Rebulli has one Pullman bus daily (Q36, 2½ hours) departing at 7am from Panadería Colombia on 4a Calle Poniente, half a block east of the market.

SHUTTLE MINIBUS

Numerous travel agencies offer frequent and convenient shuttle services to places such as Guatemala City, Aeropuerto Internacional La Aurora, Panajachel and Chichicastenango. They also go less frequently (usually on weekends) to places further afield, including Río Dulce, Copán Ruinas (Honduras) and Monterrico. These services cost a lot more than ordinary buses (for example, around Q80 to Guatemala City, as opposed to Q9 on a chicken bus), but they are comfortable and convenient, with door-to-door service at both ends.

BUSES FROM ANTIGUA

DESTINATION	COST (Q)	DURATION	DEPARTURES	FREQUENCY
Chimaltenango	5	45 min	5am-6:30pm	every 10 min
Ciudad Vieja, take a San Miguel Dueñas bus	3	20 min	3am-8pm	every 15 min
Escuintla	7	1 hr	5am-4pm	every 30 min
Guatemala City	9	1 hr	5am-7:30pm	every few minutes
San Antonio Aguas Calientes	3.50	30 min	6am-8pm	every 30 min

WORTH A TRIP

BEYOND ANTIGUA

There's enough in Antigua to keep you going for weeks, but the surrounding countryside has its attractions, too. It's well worth the 25-minute bus ride northwest to soak in the popular hot springs at **San Lorenzo El Tejar**, and if you're in the market for leatherwork, nearby **Pastores** is ground zero for handmade cowboy boots, stock whips and the like.

Near the village of San Lucas Sacatepéquez is **Cerro Alux** (www.cerroalux.com), a hilltop ecopark with interpretive trails and good bird-watching opportunities.

Set on a 16-hectare avocado farm in the hills above Jocotenango, the **Earth Lodge** (☎5664-0713; www.earthlodgeguatemala.com; dm Q50, cabin s/d/tr Q100/170/195) is fast becoming a backpacker must-do. See the website for transportation details.

TAXI & TUK-TUK

Taxis and tuk-tuks wait where the Guatemala City buses stop and on the east side of Parque Central. An in-town taxi ride costs around Q25; tuk-tuks are Q10. Note that tuk-tuks are not allowed in the center of town; you'll have to hike a few blocks out to find one.

THE HIGHLANDS

Guatemala's most dramatic region – the highlands – stretches from Antigua to the Mexican border northwest of Huehuetenango. Here the verdant hills sport emerald-green grass, cornfields and towering stands of pine, and every town and village has a story.

The traditional values and customs of Guatemala's indigenous peoples are strongest in the highlands. Maya dialects are the first language, Spanish a distant second. The age-old culture based on maize (from which the Maya believe that humans were created) is still alive; a sturdy cottage set in the midst of a thriving *milpa* (cornfield) is a common sight. And on every road you'll see men, women and children carrying burdens of *leña* (firewood), to be used for heating and cooking.

Dramatic scenery, traditional villages, excellent hiking and the travelers' oasis of Quetzaltenango are what really shine in the west of this region. Roads and buses are some of the worst in the country, making travel tough but rewarding. Contained within the highlands is also the department of Quiche – a largely forgotten little pocket of the country. Most visitors to this region are on a quick in-and-out for the famous market at Chichicastenango. Further to the north is Santa Cruz del Quiché, the departmental capital; on its outskirts lie the ruins of K'umarcaaj (or Gumarcaah), also called Utatlán, the last capital city of the K'iche' (Quiché) Maya. More adventurous souls come for the excellent hiking around Nebaj.

Getting There & Around

The curvy Interamericana Hwy, also known as Centroamérica 1 (CA-1), passes through the highlands on its way between Guatemala City and the Mexican border at La Mesilla. Driving the 266km between Guatemala City and Huehuetenango can take five hours, but the scenery is beautiful. The lower Carretera al Pacífico (Hwy CA-2), via Escuintla and Retalhuleu, is straighter and faster; it's the better route if you're trying to reach Mexico as quickly as possible.

The Interamericana is thick with bus traffic. As most places you'll want to reach are off the Interamericana, you may find yourself waiting at junctions such as Los Encuentros and Cuatro Caminos to connect with a bus or pickup. Travel is easiest on market days and in the morning. By mid or late afternoon, buses may be scarce, and short-distance local traffic stops by dinnertime. On remote routes, you'll probably be relying more on pickups than buses for transportation.

Lago de Atitlán

The poster child for Guatemala's natural beauty, the volcano-ringed Lago de Atitlán, has been attracting tourists for decades. Surrounded by small villages, the lake deals with its popularity well, although a major bacteria outbreak in late 2009 alerted inhabitants to the perils of rapid growth. The only place that feels really played out is Panajachel – the other villages maintain a quiet air, while offering a reasonable degree of comfort.

Information

DANGERS & ANNOYANCES

The most frequent sites for robberies are unfortunately some of the most beautiful – the paths that run around Lago de Atitlán. The security situation is forever changing here – some

Lago de Atitlán

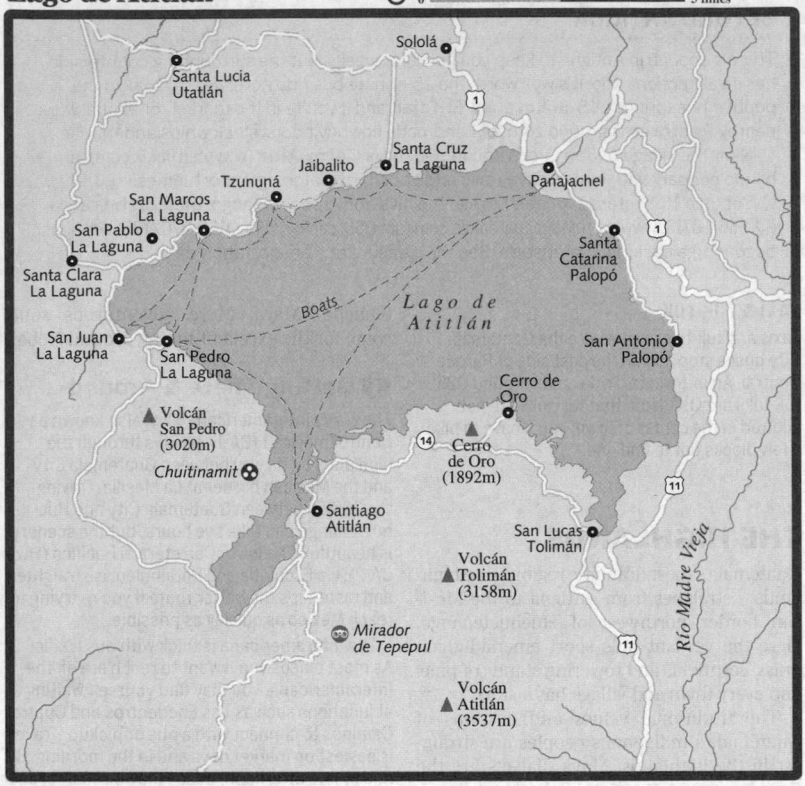

months it's OK to walk between certain villages, then that route suddenly becomes dangerous. Proatur (p129) have the most up-to-date independent advice on troublesome walking trails in the area.

If you do plan to go walking, use common sense and don't take any more money than you need or anything that you really don't want to lose.

Getting There & Around

Following the Interamericana 32km west from Chimaltenango, you'll reach the turnoff for the back road to Lago de Atitlán via Patzicía and Patzún. The area around these two towns has been notable for bandit activity in the past (as has the other back road, which runs from Cocales on the CA-2 to San Lucas Tolimán), so stay on the Interamericana to Tecpán, the starting point for a visit to the ruined Kaqchiquel capital of Iximché (*eesh*-im-chay).

Another 40km west along the Interamericana from Tecpán is the Los Encuentros junction. It's a new town serving people waiting to catch buses. The road to the right heads north to Chichicastenango and Santa Cruz del Quiché. From the Interamericana a road to the left descends 12km to Sololá and another 8km to Panajachel, on the shores of Lago de Atitlán.

If you are not on a direct bus, you can get off at Los Encuentros and catch another bus or minibus, or flag a pickup, from here down to Panajachel or up to Chichicastenango; it's a half-hour ride to either place.

The road from Sololá descends through pine forests, losing more than 500m in elevation on its 8km course to Panajachel. Sit on the right for breathtaking views of the lake and volcanoes.

Panajachel

POP 23,500 / ELEV 1595M

The busiest and most built-up lakeside settlement, Panajachel ('Pana' to pretty much the entire country) has developed haphazardly and, some say, in a less than beautiful way. Several different cultures mingle on Panajachel's dusty streets.

Ladinos and gringos control the tourist industry. The Kaqchiquel and Tz'utujil Maya from surrounding villages come to sell their handicrafts to tourists. Tour groups descend on the town by bus for a few hours or overnight.

Its excellent transportation connections and thumping nightlife make it a favorite for weekending Guatemalans. During the week, things quiet down, but the main street, Calle Santander, remains the same – internet cafe after handicrafts store after restaurant after travel agent, but you need only go down to the lakeshore to understand why Pana attracts so many visitors.

Sights & Activities

Lago de Atitlán offers phenomenal **hiking** and **cycling**. You can walk from Panajachel to Santa Catarina Palopó in about an hour, continuing to San Antonio Palopó in about another hour; it takes only half as long by bicycle, on hilly roads. Or take a bike by boat to Santiago Atitlán, San Pedro La Laguna or another village to start a tour of the lake. Several places along Calle Santander rent bicycles.

Kayaks are available for rent from the pier at the foot of Calle del Rancho Grande.

If you're pressed for time, a boat tour of the lake, stopping at a few villages, is a fine idea. Boats leave the Playa Pública quay daily at 8:30am and 9am for tours to San Pedro La Laguna (where you stop for about 1½ hours) and Santiago Atitlán, returning at 3pm and 3:30pm respectively. The earlier tour also takes in San Antonio Palopó, the later one San Marcos La Laguna, and cost Q100 and Q150 respectively. Travel agencies offer more expensive tours (around Q540 per person), which may include weaving demonstrations, visits to the shrine of Maximón in Santiago (p127), and so on.

The women's empowerment organization Oxlajul B'atz' (p129) offers day tours (Q240) of Panajachel and other lakeside villages with visits to its member weaving cooperatives.

Roger's Tours CYCLING
(☎7762-6060; www.rogerstours.com; Calle Santander) Roger's Tours rents quality mountain bikes for Q30/120 per hour/day and leads a variety of cycling tours (Q440 per person including helmet, guide and lunch).

Realworld Paragliding GLIDING
(☎5634-5699; realworldparagliding.jimdo.com; Calle Santander, Centro Comercial San Rafael) Paragliding is Atitlán's latest growth industry – in Pana you can hook up with the highly recommended Realworld Paragliding, who charges Q700 per flight, which takes 20 minutes to an hour, depending on wind conditions and passenger preferences.

Reserva Natural Atitlán PARK
(☎7762-2565; www.atitlanreserva.com; adult/child Q45/25; ⏲8am-5pm) The Reserva Natural Atitlán is down the spur leading to Hotel Atitlán and makes a good day trip. The well-designed nature reserve has trails, an interpretive center, zip lines, camping, a butterfly farm, small shade coffee plantation, lots of monkeys and an aviary. For longer stays, there are some excellent rooms with private decks, and camping.

Courses

Panajachel has a niche in the language-school scene. Two well-run schools are **Jardín de América** (☎7762-2637; www.jardindeamerica.com; Calle del Chalí) and **Jabel Tinamit** (☎7762-6056; www.jabeltinamit.com; cnr Av de Los Árboles & Callejón Las Armonías). Four hours of one-on-one study five days per week, including a homestay with a local family, will cost around Q1500 per week. The latter institute also offers courses in Kaqchiquel and Maya weaving.

Sleeping

Budget travelers here will rejoice at the profusion of family-run *hospedajes* (guesthouses). They're simple – perhaps two rough beds, a small table and a light bulb in a bare boarding room – but cheap. Most provide clean toilets and some have hot showers. More expensive hotels offer generous discounts for longer stays.

★Hotel Larry's Place HOTEL $
(☎7762-0767; Calle 14 de Febrero; s/d Q100/150) Set back from the road behind a wall of vegetation, Larry's Place offers good-sized, cool rooms in a sylvan setting. Furnishings are tasteful and the balconies welcome, though they lack views.

Mario's Rooms HOTEL $
(☎7762-2370; www.mariosrooms.com.gt; Calle Santander; s/d incl breakfast Q100/160, without bathroom Q60/120; @) A long-time favorite with return visitors, Mario's smallish rooms are arranged on two floors facing a plant-filled courtyard, and have blasting-hot showers.

Panajachel

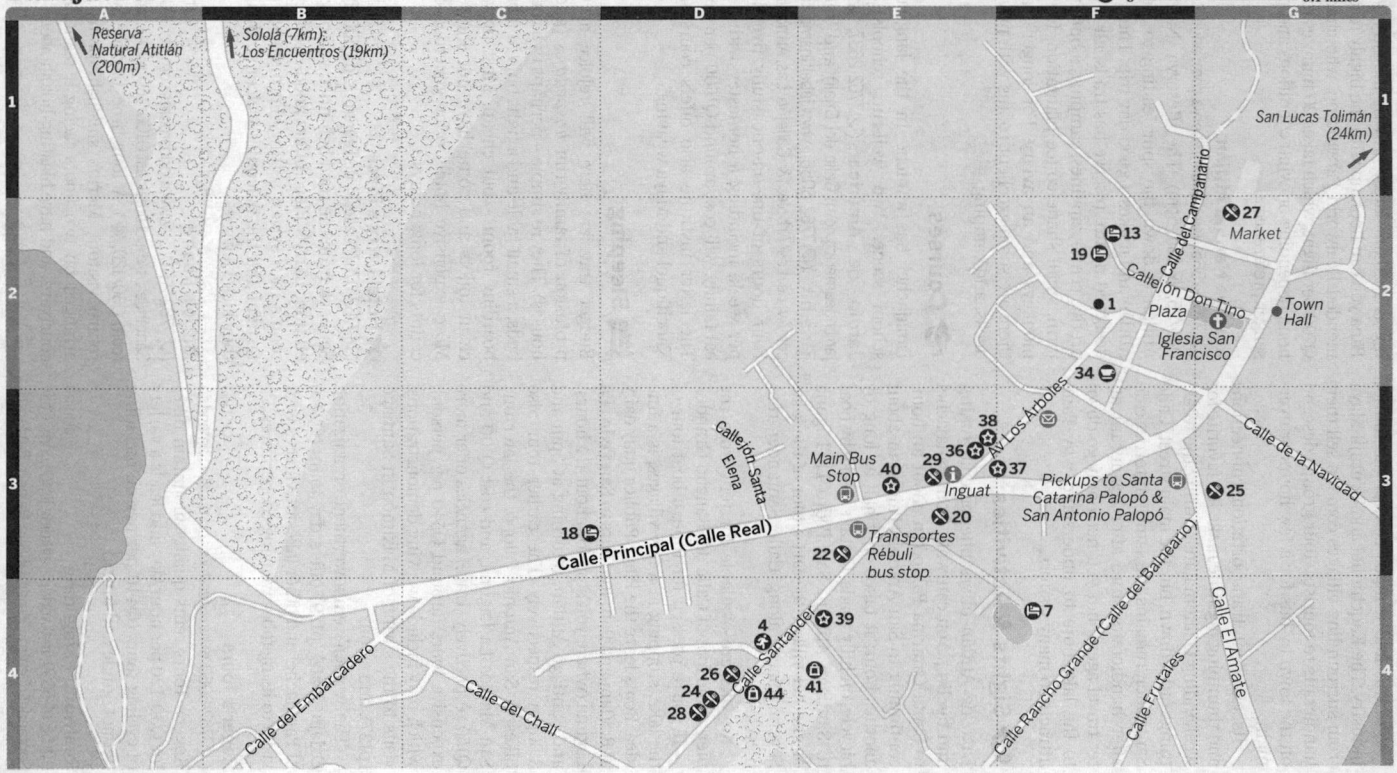
0 200 m
0 0.1 miles
A B C D E F G
1 2 3 4
Reserva Natural Atitlán (200m)
Sololá (7km); Los Encuentros (19km)
San Lucas Tolimán (24km)
Calle del Campanario
27 Market
13
19
Callejón Don Tino
1
Plaza
Town Hall
Iglesia San Francisco
34
38
Av. Los Árboles
Calle de la Navidad
Callejón Santa Elena
Main Bus Stop
40
29
36
37
Inguat
Pickups to Santa Catarina Palopó & San Antonio Palopó
25
20
18
Calle Principal (Calle Real)
Transportes Rébuli bus stop
22
7
Calle Rancho Grande (Calle del Balneario)
Calle El Amate
Calle Frutales
4
Calle Santander
39
41
26
24
44
28
Calle del Chalí
Calle del Embarcadero

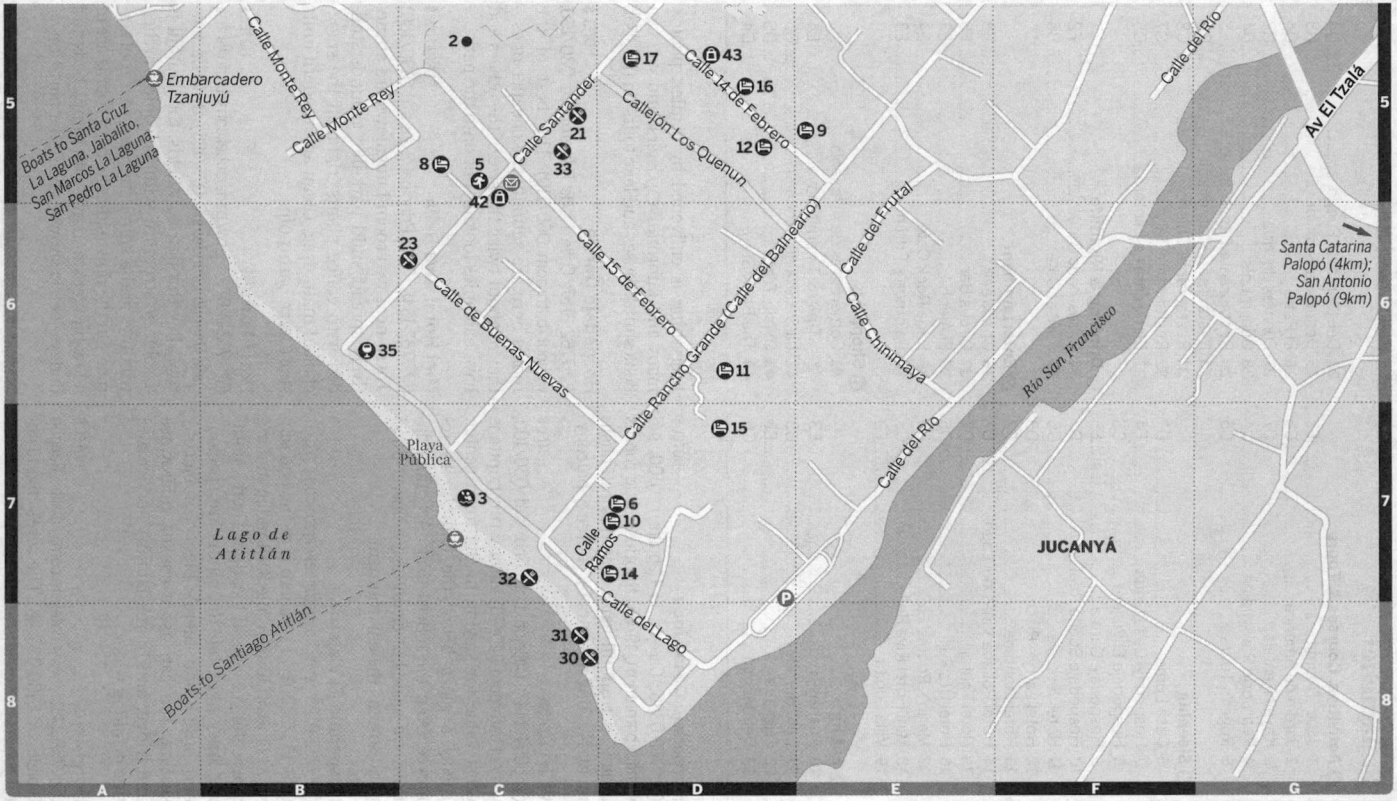
Embarcadero Tzanjuyú
Boats to Santa Cruz La Laguna, Jaibalito, San Marcos La Laguna, San Pedro La Laguna
Calle Monte Rey
Calle Monte Rey
Calle Santander
Callejón Los Quenun
Calle 14 de Febrero
Calle del Río
Av El Tzalá
Calle del Frutal
Calle 15 de Febrero
Calle de Buenas Nuevas
Calle Rancho Grande (Calle del Balneario)
Calle Chinimaya
Calle del Río
Calle Ramos
Calle del Lago
Rio San Francisco
Santa Catarina Palopó (4km); San Antonio Palopó (9km)
Playa Pública
Lago de Atitlán
Boats to Santiago Atitlán
JUCANYÁ
2
17
43
16
9
12
21
33
8
5
42
23
35
11
15
3
6
10
14
32
31
30
A
B
C
D
E
F
G
5
6
7
8

Panajachel

Activities, Courses & Tours
1 Jabel Tinamit F2
2 Jardín de América C5
3 Kayak Rentals C7
4 Realworld Paragliding D4
5 Roger's Tours C5

Sleeping
6 Casa Loma D7
7 Hospedaje Casa Linda F4
8 Hospedaje El Viajero C5
9 Hospedaje García E5
10 Hospedaje Sueño Real D7
11 Hotel Jere D6
12 Hotel Larry's Place D5
13 Hotel Montana F2
14 Hotel Posada Viñas del Lago D7
15 Hotel Tzutujil D7
16 Hotel Utz Rajil D5
17 Mario's Rooms D5
18 Mini Hotel Riva Bella C3
19 Villa Lupita F2

Eating
20 Atlantis E3
21 Café Bombay C5
22 Chez Alex E3
23 Deli Jasmín C6
24 Deli Llama de Fuego D4
25 Despensa Familiar G3
26 El Patio D4
27 Fuentes de Vida G2
28 Guajimbo's D4
29 Restaurante Casablanca E3
30 Restaurante Catamarán C8
31 Restaurante Chichoy C8
32 Restaurante Taly C7
33 Ristorante La Lanterna C5

Drinking & Nightlife
34 Crossroads Café F2
35 Sunset Café B6

Entertainment
36 Chapiteau E3
37 Circus Bar F3
38 El Aleph E3
39 Pana Rock Café E4
40 Salomon's Porch E3

Shopping
41 Comerciales de Artesanías Típicas Tinamit Maya E4
42 La Señora de Cancuén C5
43 Oxlajuj B'atz' D5
44 The Book Store D4

Hospedaje Casa Linda HOTEL $
(☎7762-0386; Callejón El Capulín; r Q100, s/d without bathroom Q49/85) Spotless little rooms around a tranquil garden at this establishment. Get one upstairs for a breezy balcony.

Villa Lupita HOTEL $
(☎5054-2447; Callejón Don Tino; s/d Q50/100, without bathroom Q40/75) Family-run Lupita is great value for staying in the town center. Facing a plaza below the church, it's removed from the tourist drag. Accommodations are basic but clean and a flower-filled patio softens the environment.

Hospedaje El Viajero HOTEL $
(☎7762-0128; www.hospedajeelviajero.com; s/d/tr Q80/150/220;) El Viajero is at the end of a short lane off lower Calle Santander, making a peaceful yet central location. There's nothing fancy here, but the rooms are spacious and bright and there's plenty of balcony seating. You can use a cooker, microwave and fridge, and there's laundry service and free drinking water.

Hotel Jere HOTEL $
(☎7762-2781; www.hoteljere.com; Calle Rancho Grande; s/d Q100/125; @) The Jere's big, tasteful rooms are a class act in this part of town. Everything is enlivened by textiles, photos, maps and informative posters, and you can book shuttle buses and lake tours on the spot.

Hospedaje García HOTEL $
(☎7762-2187; Calle 14 de Febrero; s/d Q80/160, without bathroom Q60/110) The best of the rooms here are actually the cheaper ones – they're about twice the size of the others and have balconies looking out onto the patio.

Mini Hotel Riva Bella BUNGALOW $
(☎7762-1348; Calle Principal 2-21; s/d Q130/180) These neat two-room bungalows are attractively spread amid park-like grounds studded with coffee plants, right off the smog-choked main drag. Clean and modern units sport huge bathrooms.

Hotel Tzutujil HOTEL $
(☎7762-0102; www.panajachel.com/tzutujil.htm; Calle Rancho Grande; s/d Q75/125) Down a narrow alley through cornfields, the Tzutujil is a solitary structure with balconies, arched windows and a spiral staircase to a roof terrace. On the downside, the boxy rooms are of a low-budget standard, with lumpy beds and dodgy electric showers behind a partition.

Hotel Posada Viñas del Lago HOTEL $
(☎7762-0389; Playa Pública; s/d/tr Q75/125/175; 📶) This garishly painted hotel, just steps from the lakefront, offers basic rooms with great views (the best are units 21 to 23).

Casa Loma HOTEL $
(☎7762-1447; Calle Rancho Grande; s/d Q75/150, without bathroom Q50/100; 📶) Basic wood-plank rooms and a sweet grassy lawn area.

Hotel Montana HOTEL $$
(☎7762-0326; Callejón Don Tino; s/d Q150/250) Down a narrow street near the church, the Montana is an old-fashioned establishment with wonderful plant-laden balconies. Choose a room on the upper level for brilliant views of the mountainside through large windows.

Hospedaje Sueño Real HOTEL $$
(☎7762-0608; suenorealhotel@hotmail.com; Calle Ramos; s/d Q150/225; @📶) Better than most of the budget options along this lane, the Sueño Real has cheerfully decorated, if cramped, rooms with TV and fan. The best are the upstairs triples, opening on a plant-festooned, lakeview terrace.

Hotel Utz Rajil HOTEL $$
(☎7762-0303; gguated@yahoo.com; Calle 14 de Febrero; s/d/tr Q125/200/275) A modern, three-story hotel with large, well-maintained rooms and quality furniture, the Utz Rajil (Kaqchiquel for 'good deal') features cool balconies for photo ops of the street activity below. (Don't expect to get any sleep past 6am, though.)

THAT'S ONE SMOKIN' GOD

The Spanish called him San Simón, the *ladinos* (persons of mixed indigenous and European race) named him Maximón and the Maya know him as Rilaj Maam (ree-lah-*mahm*). By any name, he's a deity revered throughout the Guatemalan highlands. Assumed to be a combination of Maya gods, Pedro de Alvarado (the Spanish conquistador of Guatemala) and the biblical Judas, San Simón is an effigy to which Guatemalans of every stripe go to make offerings and ask for blessings. The effigy is usually housed by a member of a *cofradía* (Maya religious brotherhood), moving from one place to another from year to year, a custom anthropologists believe was established to maintain the local balance of power. The name, shape and ceremonies associated with this deity vary from town to town, but a visit will be memorable no matter where you encounter him. For a small fee, photography is usually permitted, and offerings of cigarettes, liquor or candles are always appreciated.

In Santiago Atitlán, Maximón is a wooden figure draped in colorful silk scarves and smoking a fat cigar. Locals guard and worship him, singing and managing the offerings made to him (including your Q10 entry fee). His favorite gifts are Payaso cigarettes and Venado rum, but he often has to settle for the cheaper firewater Quetzalteca Especial. Fruits and gaudy, flashing electric lights decorate his chamber; effigies of Jesus Christ and Christian saints lie or stand either side of Maximón and his guardians. Fires may be burning in the courtyard outside as offerings are made to him.

In Nahualá, between Los Encuentros and Quetzaltenango, the Maximón effigy is à la Picasso: a simple wooden box with a cigarette protruding from it. Still, the same offerings are made and the same sort of blessings asked for. In Zunil, near Quetzaltenango, the deity is called San Simón but is similar to Santiago's Maximón in custom and form.

San Jorge La Laguna on Lago de Atitlán is a very spiritual place for the highland Maya; here they worship Rilaj Maam. It is possible that the first effigy was made near here, carved from the *palo de pito* tree that spoke to the ancient shamans and told them to preserve their culture, language and traditions by carving Rilaj Maam (*palo de pito* flowers can be smoked to induce hallucinations). The effigy in San Jorge looks like a joker, with an absurdly long tongue.

In San Andrés Itzapa near Antigua, Rilaj Maam has a permanent home, and is brought out on October 28 and paraded about in an unparalleled pagan festival. This is an all-night, hedonistic party where dancers grab the staff of Rilaj Maam to harness his power and receive magical visions. San Andrés is less than 10km south of Chimaltenango, so you can easily make the party from Antigua.

Eating

The cheapest places to eat are by the beach at the mouth of the Río San Francisco. The cook shacks on the shore have rock-bottom prices, as do the food stalls around the parking lot. Across the street, you can fill up for Q30 at any of several little restaurants, all of which offer priceless lake views. Taco and fried-chicken stalls also proliferate along Calle Santander every afternoon and evening. You might try the appropriately named Humo en Tus Ojos, last spotted near the intersection of Calle Principal and Calle Santander; this is where the cops eat.

For food shopping, there's the **Despensa Familiar** (Calle El Amate), at the north end of Calle El Amate.

If you're looking for cheap with a view, check out the touristy restaurants crowding the east end of Calle del Lago, such as **Restaurante Taly** (Calle del Lago), **Restaurante Catamarán** or **Restaurante Chichoy**, all with decks overlooking the lake. All the beach restaurants serve seafood and *caldo de mariscos* (shellfish stew), though lake fish has not been served since an outbreak of bacteria in late 2009.

Deli Llama de Fuego ORGANIC $
(☎7762-2586; Calle Santander; items Q25-45; ⏲7am-10pm Thu-Tue) Offering a variety of healthy food and drink, this natural-foods haven revolves around a *llama de fuego* (African tulip) tree.

Fuentes de Vida GUATEMALAN $
(lunch Q15) This is the largest of a group of cook stalls at the rear of the market building, near the pork vendors in a bright courtyard surrounded by tall trees. It offers half a dozen menu options daily, all of which come with beans, tortillas and a fiery salsa made from dried red chilies.

Deli Jasmín ORGANIC $
(☎7762-2585; Calle Santander; items Q25-45; ⏲7am-6pm Wed-Mon) This tranquil garden restaurant serves a range of healthy foods and drinks to the strains of soft classical music. Breakfast is served all day, and you can buy whole-wheat or pita bread, hummus or mango chutney to take away.

Guajimbo's STEAKHOUSE $$
(Calle Santander; mains Q50-90; ⏲7:30am-11pm) This Uruguayan grill is one of Pana's best eateries, serving generous meat and chicken dishes with vegetables, salad, garlic bread and rice or boiled potatoes. You won't leave hungry. There are vegetarian dishes too, good-value breakfasts, and bottomless cups of coffee.

El Patio GUATEMALAN $$
(☎7762-2041; Plaza Los Patios, Calle Santander; mains Q35-65; ⏲7am-10:30pm) Popular with locals for lunch. Try to make it on a Monday for the *caldo de res* (a broth with large chunks of meat and veggies), served with all the trimmings.

Café Bombay VEGETARIAN $$
(☎7762-0611; Calle Santander; mains Q45; ⏲11am-10pm Wed-Mon; ✎) This cozy joint plays up the international angle, with creative vegetarian dishes from 14 countries: everything from spinach lasagna to miso to curries, and there's even a veggie version of that Guatemalan classic *pepián* (served with veggies, rice and *chuchito*).

Restaurante Casablanca EUROPEAN $$
(☎7762-1015; Calle Principal; mains Q55-96; ⏲11am-11pm) Easily spotted at the top end of Calle Santander by its magical mystery mural, this restaurant run by the German honorary consul features fondues, steaks and pastas of a Euro standard. There are airy dining rooms both upstairs and down, plus an excellent bar.

Atlantis SANDWICHES $$
(Calle Principal; mains Q40-60; ⏲7:30am-midnight; 📶) This cafe-bar serves excellent submarines (Q35) alongside more substantial meals. The back garden is the place to be on a balmy night.

Ristorante La Lanterna ITALIAN $$
(Calle Santander 4-72; mains Q80; ⏲7am-3pm & 6-10pm) Part of the Hotel Dos Mundos, this Italian restaurant makes its own pasta and stocks an impressive range of wines from the motherland. The adjacent cafe makes a mean espresso from Guatemala's prized beans. Bonus: you're welcome to use the hotel swimming pool if you eat here.

Chez Alex EUROPEAN $$$
(☎7762-2052; www.primaveraatitlan.com; Calle Santander, Hotel Primavera; mains Q100-200; ⏲lunch & dinner) Some of Pana's finest cuisine is served here, with plenty of European influence. After a meal of mussels in white wine sauce or rack of lamb, kick back with a Habana cigar.

Drinking & Entertainment

Crossroads Café CAFE
(☎5292-8439; www.crossroadscafepana.com; Calle del Campanario 0-27; ⏲9am-1pm & 2:30-6pm Tue-Sat) Bay area native Mike Roberts has made Panajachel a major crossroads for coffee aficionados. When he's not roasting beans or working the Cimbali at his hole-in-the-wall cafe near the center of town, Mike spends his time combing the highlands for small estate coffees to add to his roster, now starring the flavorful San Pedro volcanic.

Sunset Café BAR
(cnr Calles Santander & del Lago) This open-air lounge at the end of Calle Santander is the place to enjoy those phantasmagoric volcano sundowns. In high season, there's live music nightly.

Pana Rock Café LIVE MUSIC
(☎7762-2194; panarockcafe.com; Calle Santander) Like a Hard Rock by the lake, this lively little pub hosts plugged-in bands nightly from 9pm. It's big with Guatemala City youth, who settle in for the evening with a *cubetazo* (bucket of beer) or two.

Circus Bar LIVE MUSIC
(☎7762-2056; Av Los Árboles; ⏲noon-midnight) Behind the cowboy swinging doors, Circus Bar has a cabaret atmosphere, with live music nightly from 8:30pm to 11pm. Flamenco, folk or marimbas nicely complement the cozy atmosphere, as do the substantial list of imported liquors, Q10 cocktails and good pizza.

Salomon's Porch CLUB
(☎7762-6032; www.porchdesalomon.org; Centro Comercial El Dorado, Calle Principal; ⏲noon-10pm Tue-Sat; 📶) A coffee house inside a shopping center, Salomon's Porch hosts a variety of activities, from billiards to movies to live music, often by foreign visiting artists. And for something completely different, there's a 'worship gathering' every Sunday at 4pm (with free coffee).

Chapiteau CLUB
(Av Los Árboles; minimum Q20) If you've got your dancing legs on, check out this strobe-lit disco-bar in the middle of Pana's Zona Viva (nightlife zone).

El Aleph DJS
(Av Los Árboles) DJs keep the multitudes moving with a spirited mix of reggaetón, merengue, electronica and salsa. Beer is cheapest by the bucket.

Shopping

Stores and stalls along Pana's Calle Santander have some of the best prices for souvenirs in the country. Freelance vendors and artisans also set up tables or blankets, especially on weekends. Booths also adorn the beach end of Calle Rancho Grande.

Comerciales de Artesanías Típicas Tinamit Maya HANDICRAFTS
(⏲7am-7pm) One of Guatemala's most extensive handicrafts markets, this market sells traditional clothing, jade, leather items, wood carvings and more. You can get good deals if you're patient and bargain.

Oxlajuj B'atz' HANDICRAFTS
(Thirteen Threads; www.thirteenthreads.org; Calle 14 de Febrero) Supporting an NGO for the empowerment of indigenous women, this fair-trade shop features naturally dyed rugs, handbags, hand-woven goods and beaded jewelry.

La Señora de Cancuén CLOTHING
(☎7762-2602; Calle Santander) Displays the innovative clothing of Guatemalan designer Ana Kayax, produced by a cooperative of indigenous weavers.

The Book Store BOOKS
(Centro Comercial El Patio, Calle Santander) Eclectic selection of fiction and non-fiction run by a well-read gringo; also features a lending library.

Information

EMERGENCY

Proatur (Programa Asistencia al Turista; ☎5874-9450; proatur.solola@gmail.com; Calle Rancho Grande; ⏲9am-5pm)

MEDICAL SERVICES

The nearest hospital is at Sololá.

Pana Medic (☎4892-3499; drzulmashalom@hotmail.com; Calle Principal 0-72) Clinic run by an English-speaking doctor.

MONEY

The following banks have Visa/MasterCard ATMs.

Banco de América Central (Centro Comercial San Rafael, Calle Santander; ⏲9am-5pm Mon-Fri, 9am-1pm Sat) Visa, American Express and MasterCard cash advances, US cash exchanged.

Banco Industrial (Comercial Los Pinos, Calle Santander; ⏲9am-4pm Mon-Fri, 9am-1pm Sat)

POST

Post Office (cnr Calle Santander & Calle 15 de Febrero) About 200m from the lake.

Get Guated Out (☎tel/fax 7762-0595; gguated@yahoo.com; Comercial El Pueblito, Av Los Árboles) English-speaking outfit that can ship your important letters and parcels by air freight or international courier.

TOURIST INFORMATION

Inguat (☎2421-2953; info-pana@inguat.gob.gt; Calle Principal 0-87; ⏲9am-1pm & 2-7pm Tue-Sat) This tourist office is over the traffic-jammed intersection of Calle Principal and Av Los Árboles. The English-speaking director provides a wealth of information.

ℹ Getting There & Away

BOAT

Passenger **boats for Santiago Atitlán** (35 minutes) depart from the Playa Pública (public beach) at the foot of Calle Rancho Grande. All other departures leave from the **Embarcadero Tzanjuyú**, at the foot of Calle del Embarcadero. Frequent canopied *lanchas* (small motorboats) go counterclockwise around the lake, with direct and local service to San Pedro La Laguna. The latter stop in Santa Cruz La Laguna (15 minutes), Jaibalito, Tzununá, San Marcos La Laguna (30 minutes), San Juan La Laguna and San Pedro (45 minutes). The last boat departs around 7:30pm. To San Lucas Tolimán, there are five boats daily between 8:30am and 5:30pm.

One-way passage to San Pedro, Santiago or San Lucas costs Q25 (though local inhabitants are charged less). *Lanchas* are also available for private hire from the Playa Pública or Embarcadero Tzanjuyú: expect to pay around Q400 to San Pedro La Laguna.

BUS

The town's **main bus stop** is where Calle Santander and Calle Real meet, across from the Banco Agromercantil. Rébuli buses depart from the **Rébuli office** on Calle Real. For most destinations further afield, it's best to catch one of the many buses to Los Encuentros and find a connection there. To get to **Santa Catarina Palopó**, get a pickup (Q3, 20 minutes) at the corner of Calles Principal and El Amate.

Most departures are chicken buses, although there is one Pullman leaving at 11am daily for Antigua (Q45, 2½ hours), continuing on to Guatemala City.

SHUTTLE MINIBUS

Tourist shuttle buses take half the time of buses, for several times the price. You can book at a number of travel agencies on Calle Santander. The **Microbuses y Taxis San Francisco booth** (☎7762-0556; Calle Principal) also sells shuttle-bus seats. Typical one-way fares: Antigua Q120; Chichicastenango Q55; Guatemala City Q200; San Cristóbal de Las Casas, Mexico Q275; Quetzaltenango Q200.

Santiago Atitlán

POP 50,500 / ELEV 1606M

South across the lake from Panajachel, on the shore of a lagoon squeezed between the volcanoes of Tolimán and San Pedro, lies Santiago Atitlán, known to everybody as Santiago. It's the most workaday of the lake villages, home to Maximón (mah-shee-*mohn*; p127), who is paraded around during Semana Santa – a good excuse to head this way during Easter. The rest of the year, Maximón resides with a caretaker, receiving offerings. He changes house every year, but he's easy enough to find by asking around. If that's too much work, local children will take you to see him for a small tip.

Although the most visited village outside Panajachel, Santiago clings to the traditional lifestyle and clothing of the Tz'utujil Maya. The best days to visit are Friday and Sunday, the main market days, but any day will do.

Walking to and from San Pedro La Laguna is not recommended, unless the security situation improves, since this remote route has a robbery risk.

BUSES FROM PANAJACHEL

DESTINATION	COST (Q)	DURATION	DEPARTURES	FREQUENCY
Chichicastenango	20	1½ hr	7am-3pm	5 daily
Cocales	15	2½ hr	6:30am-5pm	4 daily
Guatemala City	35	3½ hr	5am-1pm	6 daily
Los Encuentros	6	35 min	6am-7pm	frequent
Quetzaltenango	25	2½ hr	7am-2pm	3 daily
Sololá	3	15 min	6am-7pm	frequent

WORTH A TRIP

VILLAGES & RUINS AROUND PANAJACHEL

Sololá

Nine steep kilometers uphill from Panajachel, Sololá's **market** (Tuesday, Friday and Sunday) – a local, rather than a tourist, affair – is one of the highlands' best. The plaza next to the cathedral comes ablaze with the colorful costumes from a dozen surrounding villages, and neatly arranged displays of meat, vegetables, fruit, housewares and clothing occupy every available space.

Every Sunday morning the *cofradías* (Maya religious brotherhoods) parade ceremoniously to the cathedral for their devotions. On other days, Sololá sleeps.

Santa Catarina Palopó

Four winding kilometers east of Panajachel lies Santa Catarina Palopó. Here, narrow streets paved in stone blocks run past adobe houses with roofs of thatch or corrugated tin, and the gleaming white church commands your attention. It's interesting to imagine that this is what all the lakeside villages would once have been like. If you really like it here, there are simple, inexpensive places to stay and eat. Most people drop in for the day, particularly looking to buy one of the luminescent indigo *huipiles* (long embroidered tunics) you see around Lago de Atitlán.

San Antonio Palopó

Continuing past Santa Catarina for 5km gets you to San Antonio Palopó, a larger but similar village where men and women in traditional clothing tend their terraced fields and clean mountains of scallions by the lakeshore. The **Hotel Terrazas del Lago** (☎7762-0157; www.hotelterrazasdellago.com; s/d/tr Q180/240/310;) is an attractive hotel with some great views.

Iximché

Off the Interamericana near the small town of Tecpán lie the ruins of **Iximché** (admission Q50; ⏲8am-4:30pm), capital of the Kaqchiquel Maya. Set on a flat promontory surrounded by cliffs and founded in the late 15th century, Iximché was easily defended against attack by the hostile K'iche' (Quiché) Maya. They had no such luck against the Spanish.

Entering the archaeological site, visit the museum (closed Monday) on the right, then continue to the four ceremonial plazas, which are surrounded by temple structures up to 10m high, and ball courts. Some structures have been uncovered: the original plaster coating is still in place on a few.

Any bus traveling on the Interamericana can drop you at the turnoff for Tecpán, from where it's about a 1km walk (or, if you're lucky, a short ride on an urban bus) to the center of town (Tecpán). 'Ruinas' microbuses to the site (Q2.50, 10 minutes) leave hourly from the plaza.

Sights

Iglesia Parroquial Santiago Apóstol CHURCH

At the top of the slope is the main square, flanked by the town office and a huge centuries-old church. Within are wooden statues of the saints, each of whom gets new handmade clothes every year.

On the carved pulpit, note the figures of corn (from which humans were formed, according to Maya religion), as well as a literate quetzal bird and Yum-Kax, the Maya god of corn. A similar carving is on the back of the priest's chair.

A memorial plaque at the back commemorates Father Stanley Francis Rother, a missionary priest from Oklahoma. Beloved by the local people, he was murdered in the church by ultraright-wing death squads in 1981.

Parque de Paz MEMORIAL

(Peace Park) During the civil war, Santiago became the first village in the country to succeed in expelling the army, following a notorious massacre of 13 villagers on December 2, 1990. The site of this massacre, where troops were encamped, is now the Parque de Paz (Peace Park), about 500m beyond Posada de Santiago.

Cojolya Association of Maya Women Weavers MUSEUM
(☎7721-7268; www.cojolya.org; Comercial Las Máscaras, 2nd floor, Calle Real; donation requested.; ⏲9am-5pm Mon-Fri, 9am-1pm Sat) FREE This is a small museum devoted to the art of backstrap loom weaving. The well-designed exhibit shows the history of the craft and the process from spinning the cotton fibers to the finished textile. There are also daily demonstrations of backstrap loom techniques, and a small shop.

Activities

There are many rewarding **day hikes** around Santiago. Unfortunately, owing to the security situation, it's highly advisable to go with a guide – ask in your hotel for a reputable one. You can climb any of the three **volcanoes**, the **Mirador de Tepepul** (a lookout about 4km south of Santiago), or the **Cerro de Oro**, some 8km northeast. Guides for all the above hikes charge around Q400 for two to five people.

Tours

Asotur TOUR
(Asociación guías de Turismo 'Aj tz'ikin jaay'; ☎5160-9805; asotur@hotmail.es; Playa Pública; ⏲8am-5pm Mon-Sat) This association of local, Inguat-authorized guides leads a variety of fascinating tours in and around Santiago Atitlán.

Cojolya Association of Maya Women Weavers CULTURAL TOUR
(☎7721-7268; www.cojolya.org) Here you can join a 'Meet the Weavers' tour (Q50, in Spanish). You'll visit three traditional homes where women demonstrate how to set up a backstrap loom, warp the threads and perform the *jaspe* technique, a form of Japanese tie-dye that reached Guatemala through indirect contact with Spain's Pacific trade routes.

Dolores Ratzan Pablo CULTURAL TOUR
(☎5730-4570; dolores_ratzan@yahoo.com) This English-speaking Tz'utujil woman can introduce you to the wonders of Maya birthing and healing, point out examples of Maya-Catholic syncretism at the church and *cofradías,* and describe the incidents that led to the massacre at Peace Park in 1990. Tours typically last two hours and cost Q235 per person.

Sleeping & Eating

There are plenty of cheap *comedores* above the market next to the plaza.

Hotel Ratzán HOTEL $
(☎7721-7840; www.hotelyposadaratzan.blogspot.nl; Calle a la Playa Pública; s/d Q100/150) Santiago's best budget option, near the centre of town, is a newish establishment with nice wood-beam ceilings and large, modern bathrooms. Only rooms 4 and 5 have exterior windows but considering it's just down the street from the giant new evangelical church, with raucous services nightly, maybe that's a good thing.

Hotel La Estrella HOTEL $$
(☎7721-7814; www.hotel-laestrella.blogspot.com; Calle Campo; s/d Q150/250; 📶) A short hike north of the ferry dock along the road to San Lucas is this newcomer, featuring modern, comfortable units with handsome wood ceilings and locally woven bedspreads. Room 13, adjacent to the top terrace, takes best advantage of the hotel's lakeside position looking straight across the inlet at San Pedro volcano.

Posada de Santiago LODGE $$
(☎7721-7366; www.posadadesantiago.com; s/d Q235/400, cottages s/d/tr Q475/600/675, ste from Q755; @📶❄) Striking a balance between rustic charm and luxury, the long-standing *posada* makes a nice retreat. Seven cottages and three suites are set around gardens stretching up from the lake. Some less expensive rooms are in a two-story building. The restaurant serves delicious, natural fare. The *posada* is 1.5km from the dock. Catch a tuk-tuk (Q5) or hire a *lancha* over to the hotel dock (Q70).

Restaurant El Gran Sol GUATEMALAN $
(☎7721-7157; mains Q55; ⏲7:30am-7:30pm) Two blocks up from the dock on the left, this family-run establishment is a good bet for breakfast, lunch or snacks, with a spiffy kitchen and a lovely thatched-roof terrace. The Mexican-born proprietor loves to cook – ask her to make one of her specials.

Information

You'll find a lot of fascinating information about Santiago at www.santiagoatitlan.com (in English).

There's a Cajero 5B ATM at **Banrural** (⏲8:30am-5pm Mon-Fri, 9am-1pm Sat), a block south of the plaza.

Getting There & Away

Boats leave hourly for San Pedro La Laguna (Q20, 30 minutes). Pickups to Cerro de Oro and San Lucas Tolimán depart from in front of the market. Buses to Guatemala City (Q40, 3½ hours) leave every half hour from 3am to 6am, then hourly until 3pm, from the main plaza.

San Pedro La Laguna

POP 11,500

It all comes down to what you're looking for – price wars between competing businesses keep San Pedro among the cheapest of the lakeside villages, and the beautiful setting attracts long-term visitors whose interests include (in no particular order): drinking, fire twirling, African drumming, Spanish classes, volcano hiking and hammock swinging.

While this scene unfolds at the lakefront, up the hill San Pedro follows more traditional rhythms. Clad in indigenous outfits, the predominantly indigenous *pedranos* (as the locals are called) congregate around the market zone. You'll see coffee being picked on the volcano's slopes and spread out to dry on wide platforms at the beginning of the dry season.

Activities

Kayaks are available for hire (Q15 per hour), turning right from the Pana dock. Hatha yoga sessions (Q30) are held Monday to Saturday at 9am in a circular garden along the path below the Buddha bar.

Hiking

Looming above the village, Volcán San Pedro (3020m) almost asks to be climbed by anyone with a bit of energy and adventurous spirit. The volcano has recently been placed within an ecological park to minimize environmental damage caused by hikers and also improve the security situation, which wasn't great before. **Excursion Big Foot** (☎7721-8203; 7a Av, Zona 2), 50m to the left at the first crossroads up from the Panajachel dock, has a track record of responsibility and departs at 3am when there are at least six people (Q100 each).

Another popular hike goes up the hill to the west of the village – referred to as **Indian Nose** – its skyline resembles the profile of an ancient Maya dignitary. **Asoantur** (☎4379-4545; asoantur21@gmail.com; ⏲7am-7pm), an association made up of 25 Tz'utujil guides from the local community, will lead a minimum of two people up there for around Q100 per person. It also offers cultural tours of San Pedro and nearby coffee plantations, horseback-riding tours, and kayak, bicycle and motorbike rentals. It operates from a hut on the lane up from the Pana dock.

Several **walks** between San Pedro and neighboring villages make terrific day trips, although armed muggings on the lonely roads between villages are not uncommon. You can walk west to San Juan La Laguna (30 minutes), San Pablo La Laguna (1½ hours), San Marcos La Laguna (three hours), Jaibalito (five hours) and finally, Santa Cruz (all day). From the last three you can easily hail a *lancha* back to San Pedro until around 3pm.

Swimming & Spas

Once you've watched the sunset, one of the best places to be is soaking in the solar-heated tubs at **Solar Pools** (7a Av 2-22), down a small path next to the Buddha bar. Book ahead so it has a pool already hot when you arrive.

If the lake hasn't swallowed it up by the time you read this, have a swim at **La Piscina** (adult/child Q20/10; ⏲11am-dusk Tue-Sun; 📶), by the Santiago dock, a global gathering place that revolves around a pool. Sundays are busiest with barbecues and Bocce ball.

Courses

The standard price for four hours of one-on-one Spanish-language classes, five days a week, is around Q800. Accommodations with a local family, with three meals daily (except Sunday) typically costs Q600 a week. Schools can also organize other sleeping options.

Cooperativa Spanish School LANGUAGE COURSE

(☎5398-6448; www.cooperativeschoolsanpedro.com) Run as a cooperative (therefore guaranteeing fair wages for teachers); a percentage of profits goes to needy families around the lake. After-school activities include videos, conferences, salsa classes, volunteer work, kayaking and hiking. This school comes highly recommended. The office is halfway along the path between the two docks.

Corazón Maya LANGUAGE COURSE

(☎7721-8160; www.corazonmaya.com) Well-established, family-run school with gorgeous lakeside setting, offering activities such as canoe trips, visits to local artists, and conferences on Guatemalan history and economics. Accommodation in on-site bungalows. Take the first left up from Santiago dock.

San Pedro Spanish School LANGUAGE COURSE
(☎5715-4604; www.sanpedrospanishschool.org; 7a Av 2-20) Well-organized school on the street between the two docks, with consistently good reviews. Classes are held under thatched-roof huts amidst an attractive garden setting. The school supports Niños del Lago, an organization that provides education, health care and nutrition for local Tz'utujil children.

Sleeping

★Hotel Gran Sueño HOTEL $
(☎7721-8110; 8a Calle 4-40, Zona 2; s/d Q75/125;) Beyond a plant-draped entryway and up a spiral staircase are bright rooms with colorful abstract designs and more style than elsewhere. Rooms 9 and 11 are fantastic lake-view perches. The hotel is up the street from the Pana dock to the left of Hotel Mansión del Lago.

Zoola HOSTEL $
(☎5847-4857; dm Q35, s/d Q100/125, without bathroom Q50/100) 'Laid-back' is the operable phrase at this Israeli-run establishment, a place to crash after a Middle Eastern feast at the adjoining restaurant. Reached down a long, jungly boardwalk opposite the Museo Tz'unun Ya,' it features eight brightly colored rooms around a peaceful garden. There's a two-night minimum stay.

Hotel Mansión del Lago HOTEL $
(☎7721-8124; www.hotelmansiondellago.com; cnr 3a Vía & 4a Av, Zona 2; s/d/tr Q100/150/225) Straight up from the Pana dock is this concrete monster. Large rooms are done up in a cloud motif, with wide balconies looking right at the Indian's Nose.

Hotel Nahual Maya HOTEL $
(☎7721-8158; 6 Av 8C-12; s/d Q75/100;) The forest of rooftop rebar somewhat mars the Mediterranean villa motif, but the rooms are sparkling clean and homey and have little balconies with hammocks out front.

Hotel Peneleu HOTEL $
(☎7721-8182; 5a Av 2-20, Zona 2; s/d Q30/60, without bathroom Q20/40;) The best of four budget options along a side street, this concrete tower offers well-maintained if modestly furnished rooms. It's all about the views; fly a kite from the amazing top terrace. Genial proprietor Don Alberto will gladly negotiate rates for longer stays. To find it, walk 500m up from the Santiago dock and turn left; or take a tuk-tuk up the steep approach.

Hotel Villa Cuba HOTEL $
(☎7959-5044; www.hotelvillacuba.com; Camino a la Finca, Zona 4; s/d Q60/120) A large, modern hotel on grounds that sweep down to the lake. The seven rooms are well furnished, swimming is good here, and it's only a tuk-tuk away from the bar and restaurant scene. To find it, take the first road to the left up from the Santiago dock and continue for 2km.

Hotel San Antonio HOTEL $
(☎5953-1917; s/d Q80/140;) Orange trumpet flowers cascade over the balconies of the San Antonio, last of the myriad lodgings east of the Pana dock. The cosy three-level structure has plenty of hammocks strung along the tiled corridors and a handy guest kitchen.

★Hotel Sak'cari El Amanecer HOTEL $$
(☎7721-8096; www.hotel-sakcari.com; 7a Av 2-12, Zona 2; s/d from Q125/225;) On the left just after Cooperativa Spanish School, the efficient Sak'cari has clean, tangerine-colored rooms with lots of shelves and wood paneling. Rooms at the rear are best, with big balconies overlooking a vast landscaped lawn.

Hotel Mikaso HOTEL $$
(☎7721-8232; www.mikasohotel.com; 4a Callejon A-88; dm/d/quad Q75/195/340;) The only real upmarket hotel in San Pedro, this prominent tower stands proudly by the lakefront. Big, colonially furnished rooms cooled by ceiling fans ring a garden bursting with birds-of-paradise. The rooftop bar/Spanish restaurant boasts fantastic lake views.

Eating

Prices are low in San Pedro La Laguna, but if you're hurting, there are a bunch of *comedores* up the hill in the main part of town.

★Ventana Blue FUSION $
(mains Q30-46; ⏲6-9:30pm Wed-Sun;) There are just four tables at this cozy bistro at a bend in the path between the docks. Created by lake native Santos Canel, the brief but exciting menu features an array of Asian and Guatemalan dishes, from Thai curries to *kaq-ik* (chicken and vegetables in a fiery

salsa). The Diosa Blue headlines the highly original cocktail selection.

Café La Puerta CAFE $
(☎4050-0500; 7a Av 2-20; breakfast Q25; ⏲7am-5pm Mon-Sat; ✉) It's not just the lakefront setting (just below Hotel Mikaso) that makes this such an appealing spot for breakfast and bird-watching, but also the abundant, natural fare. For lunch, it features Mexican burritos, tacos and quesadillas.

D'Noz INTERNATIONAL $
(☎7721-8078; 4a Av 8-18; mains Q36-45; ⏲9am-10pm Mon-Sat; ✉) Right up from the Pana dock, Dino's place sports a terrific deck for lake-view dining. The menu spans the globe from tempeh fajitas to Chinese tacos to Tecpán sausage. Offering movies, a lending library and a popular bar, it's San Pedro's closest thing to a cultural centre.

Hummus-Ya ISRAELI $
(felafel Q25; ⏲7:30am-9pm) *Sabich* (an Israeli sandwich lovingly stuffed with hard-boiled eggs, hummus, and fried eggplant) is just one highlight on the menu at this cheerful open-air eatery on the Pana dock side, near the connecting path. Saturday mornings there's *jachnun*, Yemeni bread rolls that sit in the oven overnight.

Shanti Shanti ISRAELI $
(8a Calle 3-93; mains Q20-25; ⏲7am-8pm; ✉) With terraced seating cascading down to the lakeside, this makes a pleasant perch for hippie staples like falafel, curried veggies and hearty soups.

Drinking & Nightlife

While many *pedranos* spend their evenings shouting the lord's praises at evangelical congregations, visitors tend to prowl San Pedro's hard-partying bar scene.

Café Las Cristalinas CAFE
(⏲7am-9pm; 📶) To savor a shot of the coffee grown on the surrounding slopes (and roasted here), head for this thatched-roof structure on the way up from the Pana dock to the center of town.

El Barrio PUB
(7a Av 2-07, Zona 2; ⏲5pm-1am) This boisterous pub on the path between the two docks has one of the most happening happy hours in town. Every night has a different theme but Fridays evenings the fun reaches a crescendo.

Alegre Pub PUB
(8a Calle 4-10) Near the Pana dock, the Alegre is a bit worse for wear but still a cheerful watering hole for San Pedro's cast of characters. Shoot pool with the locals (Tz'tujil rules) in the way-laid-back rooftop garden.

Buddha PUB
(☎4178-7979; 2a Av 2-24; ⏲noon-1am) The Buddha can be enjoyed on various levels – downstairs there's a boisterous bar with darts and rock concert videos; upstairs a restaurant doing convincing versions of Thai, Indian and Mideast fare; and up top a thatched-roof lounge for smoking, conversation and original cocktails.

Zoola ISRAELI
(⏲11am-midnight; 📶) Zoola remains San Pedro's premier global chillage venue. Travelers kick back on cushions around low tables, munching scrumptious Mideast fare, grooving on Manu, playing board games and generally unwinding. For serious DJ sessions, follow the cobblestone path to the sensational new lakefront lounge with swimming pool.

Getting There & Away

Passenger boats arrive here from and depart for Panajachel and Santiago Atitlán. Boats from San Pedro to Santiago (Q20, 30 minutes) run hourly from 6am to 4pm. Boats from San Pedro to Panajachel (Q25) run every half hour or so from 6am to 5pm. Some go direct; others make stops at San Juan, San Marcos (Q10) and Jaibalito/Santa Cruz (Q20) en route.

San Pedro is connected by paved roads to Santiago Atitlán (although this stretch is plagued by bandits) and to the Interamericana at Km 148 (about 20km west of Los Encuentros), the latter a hair-raising journey with spectacular lake vistas on the way up. A paved branch off the San Pedro–Interamericana road runs along the northwest side of the lake from Santa Clara to San Marcos La Laguna. Buses leave for Quetzaltenango (Q35, three hours) from San Pedro's Catholic church, up in the town center, roughly hourly from 5am to 10:30am.

San Marcos La Laguna

POP 4400

Without doubt this is the prettiest of the lakeside villages. The flat shoreline here has paths snaking though banana and coffee plantations, and avocado trees. The town has become something of a magnet for hippies-with-a-purpose, who believe the place has a particular spiritual energy, and is an

EXPLORE MORE OF LAGO DE ATITLÁN

Crowds of tourists getting to you? The lake still has a few untouched corners that are well worth checking out.

Jaibalito

Accessible only by boat or on foot, this little village between San Marcos and Santa Cruz hosts one of the country's most magical hotels, **La Casa del Mundo** (☎5218-5332; www.lacasadelmundo.com; r with/without bathroom Q550/288), with gorgeous gardens, swimming holes and a hot tub overhanging the lake. The nearby **Club Ven Acá** (☎5051-4520; sandwiches Q55-75, mains Q80-100), a bit to the east, offers a fusion menu, purple-basil mojitos, hot tub and infinity pool.

San Juan La Laguna

A 10-minute *tuk-tuk* ride (and another world away) from San Pedro, this little village is definitely still keeping it real, but with enough comforts for your average traveler, such as a couple of good budget hotels, some good places to eat, a weaving cooperative or two, and even a couple of Spanish schools.

excellent place to learn or practice meditation, holistic therapies, massage, reiki and other spiritually oriented activities.

Whatever you're into, it's definitely a great place to kick back and distance the everyday world for a spell. Lago de Atitlán is beautiful and clean here, with several little docks you can swim from.

There's a community information board in front of the San Marcos Holistic Center with postings on events and housing options. You'll find plenty of useful information and web links at www.atitlanresource.com. Get online at **Prolink** (per hr Q12; ⏲9am-7pm Mon-Sat, 10am-5pm Sun), across from the Paco Real hotel.

Sights & Activities

Las Pirámides Meditation Center MEDITATION
(☎5205-7302; www.laspiramidesdelka.com) The village's claim to fame, this retreat by the lake has been providing spiritual guidance for more than two decades. Most structures on the property are pyramidal in shape and oriented to the four cardinal points, including the two temples where sessions are held. A one-month personal development course begins every full moon (three sessions daily).

San Marcos Holistic Centre MEDITATION
(www.sanmholisticcentre.com; ⏲10am-5pm Mon-Sat) Run by various resident and visiting practitioners, the centre provides a range of massages, holistic therapies and training courses in kinesiology, EFT, reiki, shiatsu, massage and reflexology. The approach is relaxed and you're welcome to discuss possibilities before committing to anything. Most massages and therapies cost around Q250 per 90-minute session.

Cerro Tzankujil PARK
(admission Q15; ⏲8am-6pm) Completed in 2011, the nature reserve is on a sacred hill west of the village. Well-maintained pebbly trails lead to swimming areas with shelters by the bank and a diving platform. The water is crystal clear here. A branch off the main trail ascends to a Maya altar on the summit, while a lower spur reaches a volcano lookout.

Jovenes Maya Kaqchikeles HIKING
(☎5787-7728; atitlanresource.com/jovenesmayas_eng.htm; ⏲9am-5pm Mon-Sat) This group of bright, ecologically minded local lads, some of whom speak English, offer guided hikes to San Pedro La Laguna (2½ hours) and Santa Cruz La Laguna (four hours), each at Q100 per person, including the *lancha* back. Stop by the clubhouse, just above the Posada del Bosque Encantado, to discuss the possibilities.

Sleeping

Hotel La Paz HOSTEL $
(☎5061-5316; www.lakeatitlanlapaz.com; dm/r/bungalow Q50/150/250) Along a side path off the track behind Posada Schumann, the mellow La Paz has rambling grounds holding two doubles and five dormitory-style rooms. All are in bungalows of traditional *bajareque* with thatched roofs, and some have loft beds. The organic gardens and vegetarian restaurant, traditional Maya sauna

and morning yoga sessions (Q40) are additional attractions.

Hostel San Marcos HOSTEL $
(☎3009-5537; www.hostelsanmarcos.com; r incl breakfast Q75, without bathroom Q60) This newcomer features seven rustic cabins (three log, four stone) in two separate banks with large front windows (which unfortunately cannot be opened). The on-site restaurant/bar does wood-fired pizzas. From the dock, take the first left.

★Aaculaax HOTEL $$
(☎5287-0521; www.aaculaax.com; r Q100-515, ste from Q800; 📶) An artful, atmospheric hotel that looks like it grew out of the rock by itself, this place is constructed using recycled materials, such as old bottles. Each room is unique, and most have good lake views. There's a bar/chill-out area on the top floor with board games and comfy seating.

Posada del Bosque Encantado HOTEL $$
(☎5208-5334; www.hotelposadaencantado.com; s/d Q125/180) Set in jungle-like grounds that could well be an enchanted forest, the rooms here strike a good balance between rustic and stylish. Each room has a loft with a double bed and another bed downstairs. Walls are mud brick, beds are big and firm, and there are hammocks strewn around the place.

Eating

A couple of *comedores* around the plaza sell tasty, good-value Guatemalan standards.

Blind Lemon's BURGERS $
(www.blindlemons.com; mains Q35; ⏲noon-10pm; 📶) Named after one of owner Carlos's blues heroes, this hangout in a colonial-style mansion brings the Mississippi Delta to Atitlán, with weekly blues jams by Carlos and special guests. The menu features chicken platters, Cajun-blackened fish, pizza, burgers and other gringo comfort food. It's at the top of the western path.

Allala JAPANESE $
(mains Q35-45; ✎) This groovy little shack can be found by the creek east of the village. Japanese owner Seiko makes a mean miso soup, plus vegetarian sushi and tempura platters, and the plum wine is divine. All this, and complimentary cheesecake for dessert. Service can be slow, but the funky decor gives you something to look at.

Moonfish ORGANIC $
(sandwiches & burritos Q30; ⏲7am-6pm Wed-Mon; ✎) After a morning dive off the rocks, stroll up the path to Moonfish, with a lakeside terrace. Hippie-friendly fare includes tempeh sandwiches, tofu scrambles, and fresh salads with ingredients from the adjacent garden.

Comedor Susy GUATEMALAN $
(Comedor Mi Marquensita; Parque Central; set lunch Q30; ⏲7am-8pm) This 'mom and pop' store on the central plaza is where many expats go for a cheap, home-cooked meal, which might explain why tofu dishes pop up among the chicken and pork chops.

Getting There & Away

The last dependable boat back to Jaibalito, Santa Cruz and Panajachel usually leaves around 5pm.

A paved road runs east from San Marcos to Tzununá and west to San Pablo La Laguna and Santa Clara La Laguna, where it meets the road running from the Interamericana to San Pedro. You can travel between San Marcos and San Pedro by pickup, with a transfer at San Pablo.

Santa Cruz La Laguna

POP 1700

With the typically dual nature of the Atitlán villages, Santa Cruz comprises both a waterfront resort – home of the lake's scuba-diving outfit – and an indigenous Kaqchiquel village, about 600m uphill from the dock. The cobblestoned road up is a route villagers customarily take lugging sacks of avocados or firewood. The inaccessibility of the spot – it can only be reached by boat or on foot – may impede its development but also enhances its rugged beauty.

ATI Divers (☎5706-4117; www.atidivers.com) offers scuba courses. **Los Elementos** (☎5359-8328; www.kayakguatemala.com) rents kayaks and offers multiday kayak excursions.

Sleeping & Eating

★Hotel Isla Verde BUNGALOW $$
(☎5760-2648; www.islaverdeatitlan.com; s/d Q315/355, without bathroom Q235/275; 📶) A 10-minute walk west of the dock along the lakefront trail brings you to this lovely group of cabins dotted around the hillside. Decoration is simple, but pleasing, and the restaurant (featuring jaw-dropping views) serves excellent meals.

La Iguana Perdida LODGE $$
(☎5706-4117; www.laiguanaperdida.com; dm Q45, r from Q235, s/d without bathroom Q95/125; @) The first place you'll see coming off the dock offers a range of rooms, from primitive (electricity-free dorm in an A-frame cabin) to luxurious (new adobe structure with stylish furnishings, lake-view windows and balconies). Meals are served family-style, with everyone eating together. You always have a vegetarian choice, and everything here is on the honor system.

Café Sabor Cruceño GUATEMALAN $
(mains Q30-40; ⏲11am-3pm Mon-Fri) This innovative *comedor* is run by local students who are learning to make traditional Guatemalan dishes up to global tourism standards. Such Kaqchiquel fare as *subanik* (a tomato sauce of ground seeds and chilis accompanied by *tamalitos*) is prepared with locally grown herbs and veggies and served in the bay-view dining hall.

It's inside the CECAP training center, at the lower end of the Santa Cruz's central plaza.

Getting There & Away

Boats can stop here coming from either San Pedro or Panajachel. Make sure you tell the captain as you get on, though – it's not a regular stop. If you're going to Hotel Isla Verde, get dropped off at its dock to avoid the walk.

Chichicastenango

POP 72,000 / ELEV 2172M

Surrounded by valleys, with nearby mountains looming overhead, Chichicastenango seems isolated in time and space from the rest of Guatemala. When its narrow cobbled streets and red-tiled roofs are enveloped in mists, it's magical.

Chichi is a beautiful, interesting place with shamanistic and ceremonial undertones despite gaggles of camera-toting tour groups. *Masheños* (citizens of Chichicastenango) are famous for their adherence to pre-Christian religious beliefs and ceremonies. You can readily see versions of these old rites in and around the Iglesia de Santo Tomás and at the Pascual Abaj shrine on the outskirts of town.

Chichi has always been an important trading town, and its Sunday and Thursday markets remain fabulous. If you have a choice of days, come on Sunday, when the *cofradías* often hold processions.

History

Once called Chaviar, this was an important Kaqchiquel trading town long before the Spanish conquest. Just prior to the arrival of the conquistadors, the Kaqchiquel and the K'iche' (based at K'umarcaaj near present-day Santa Cruz del Quiché) went to war. The Kaqchiquel abandoned Chaviar and moved to Iximché, which was easier to defend. The conquistadors came and conquered K'umarcaaj, and many of its residents fled to Chaviar, which they renamed Chugüilá (Above the Nettles) and Tziguan Tinamit (Surrounded by Canyons).

These names are still used by the K'iche' Maya, although everyone else calls the place Chichicastenango, a foreign name given by the conquistadors' Mexican allies.

Sights & Activities

Mural PUBLIC ART
Make sure you check out the fascinating mural that runs alongside the wall of the **municipalidad** (Town Hall) on the east side of the plaza – it's dedicated to the victims of the civil war and tells the story of the war using symbology from the *Popol Vuh* (a book compiled by members of the Maya nobility soon after the Spanish Conquest).

Market MARKET
Maya traders from outlying villages come to Chichi on Wednesday and Saturday evenings in preparation for the indigenous market, one of Guatemala's largest. You'll see them carrying bundles of long poles up to the square, then laying down their loads and spreading out blankets to cook dinner and sleep in the arcades surrounding it.

Just after dawn on Sunday and Thursday, the poles are erected into stalls, which are hung with cloth, furnished with tables and piled with goods.

In general, the tourist-oriented stalls sell carved-wood masks, lengths of embroidered cloth and garments; these stalls are around the market's outer edges in the most visible areas. Behind them, the center of the square is devoted to locals' needs.

Most stalls are taken down by late afternoon. Prices are best just before the market breaks up, as traders would rather sell an item cheap than carry it back with them.

Arriving in town the day before the market in order to pin down a room is highly recommended. In this way, too, you'll be able to get up early for the action. Other-

Chichicastenango

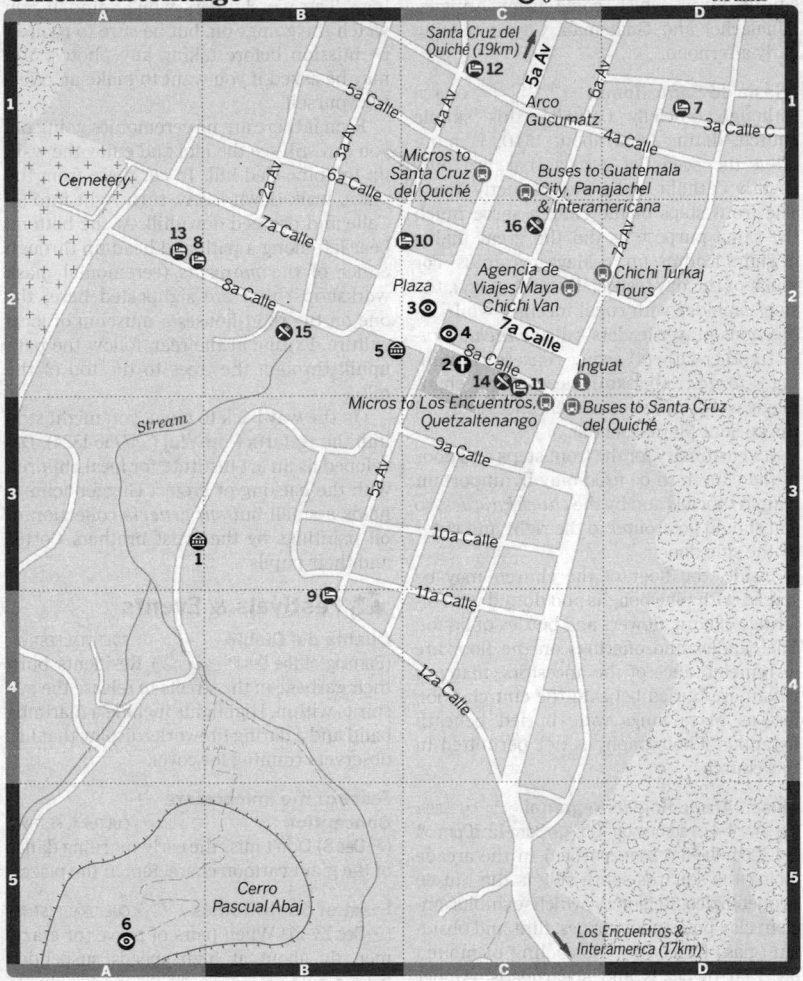

Chichicastenango

Sights

1 Galería Pop-Wuj A3
2 Iglesia de Santo Tomás C2
3 Market C2
4 Municipalidad C2
Mural ..... (see 4)
5 Museo Arqueológico Regional B2
6 Pascual Abaj A5

Sleeping

7 Chalet House D1
8 Hotel Mashito A2
9 Hotel San Jerónimo B4
10 Maya Lodge C2
11 Posada Conchita C2
12 Posada El Arco C1
13 Posada El Teléfono A2

Eating

14 Casa de San Juan C2
15 Mayan Inn B2
16 Tziguan Tinamit C2

wise, you can come by bus, or by market-day shuttle buses which come from Antigua, Panajachel and Guatemala City, returning early afternoon.

Iglesia de Santo Tomás CHURCH
Although officially Catholic, this simple church, dating from about 1540, is more often the scene of rituals that are only slightly Catholic and more distinctly Maya. The front steps of the church serve much the same purpose as did the great flights of stairs leading up to Maya pyramids. For much of the day (especially on Sunday), the steps smolder with copal incense, while indigenous prayer leaders called *chuchkajaues* (mother-fathers) swing censers containing *estoraque* (balsam) incense and chant magic words in honor of their ancestors and the ancient Maya calendar.

It's customary for the front steps and door of the church to be used only by important church officials and by the *chuchkajaues,* so you should go around to the right and enter by the side door.

Inside, the floor of the church may be spread with pine boughs and dotted with offerings of corn, flowers and bottles of liquor. The candles and offerings on the floor are in remembrance of the ancestors, many of whom are buried beneath the church floor, just as Maya kings were buried beneath pyramids. Photography is not permitted in this church.

Museo Arqueológico Regional MUSEUM
(5a Av 4-47; admission Q5; ⏲8am-12:30pm & 2-4:30pm Tue-Sat, 8am-2pm Sun) In the arcade facing the square's south side is the Museo Arqueológico Regional, which exhibits ancient clay pots and figurines, flint and obsidian (glass formed by the cooling of molten lava), arrowheads and spearheads, copper axe heads, *metates* (grindstones for maize) and a jade collection.

Pascual Abaj SHRINE
On a hilltop south of town, Pascual Abaj (Sacrifice Stone) is a shrine to the Maya earth god Huyup Tak'ah (Mountain Plain). A stone-faced idol stands amid a circle of squat stone crosses in a clearing. Said to be hundreds – perhaps thousands – of years old, it has suffered numerous indignities at the hands of outsiders, but local people still revere it.

Chuchkajaues come regularly to offer incense, food, cigarettes, flowers, liquor, and perhaps even a sacrificial chicken, in thanks and hope for the earth's continuing fertility. The area is littered with past offerings. The worshippers won't mind if you watch the goings on, but be sure to request permission before taking any photos. You may be asked if you want to make an offering yourself.

Even if there are no ceremonies going on, you can still see the idol and enjoy the walk up the pine-clad hill. To get there from the plaza, walk down 5a Av, turn right into 9a Calle and proceed downhill. At the bottom, bear left along a path and head up through either of the *morerías* (ceremonial mask workshops) that are signposted here; the one on the right houses a museum of local culture. Exiting at the rear, follow the path uphill through the trees to the top of the hill.

On the way back to town, you might stop into the **Galería Pop-Wuj** (☎7756-1324). Developed as an art institute for local children with the backing of Project Guggenheim, it holds a small but *sui generis* collection of oil paintings by the artist brothers Cortéz and their pupils.

Festivals & Events

Quema del Diablo CULTURAL FESTIVAL
(Burning of the Devil; ⏲Dec 7) Residents burn their garbage in the streets to release the evil spirits within. Highlights include a marimba band and a daring fireworks display that has observers running for cover.

Feast of the Immaculate Conception CULTURAL FESTIVAL
(⏲Dec 8) Don't miss the early-morning dance of the giant cartoon characters in the plaza.

Feast of Santo Tomás CULTURAL FESTIVAL
(⏲Dec 13–21) When pairs of brave (or crazy) men fly about at high speeds suspended from a pole.

Sleeping

Call in advance or arrive early on Wednesday or Saturday if you want to secure a room on market day.

★**Posada Conchita** GUESTHOUSE $
(☎5110-0866; posadaconchita@gua.net; 8a Calle 6-14; s/d Q100/150) Right beside Santo Tomás church stands this yellow colonial structure. Run by a friendly family, it has just four rooms, all done up in homey style with wood-beams overhead, fireplaces and paintings of the elders.

Hotel Mashito HOTEL $
(☎5168-7178; 8a Calle 1-72; s/d Q50/100, without bathroom Q40/80) Plain but comfortable rooms in a big family house.

Hotel San Jerónimo HOTEL $
(☎4929-1138; Final de 5a Av; s/d Q75/150, without bathroom Q50/100) Plain but spotless, with firm beds, fine window frames, and lovely balconies in some rooms.

Posada El Teléfono HOTEL $
(☎4624-5052; 8a Calle 1-64; s/d Q30/60) Not exactly luxury, but the rooms here are comfortable enough and good value for the price. The view of the town's technicolor cemetery from the rooftop is a draw in itself.

Chalet House GUESTHOUSE $$
(☎3084-5691; www.chalethotelguatemala.com; 3a Calle C 7-44; s/d incl breakfast Q265/290) A cozy option with good beds, homey touches and private hot-water bathrooms. Rooms get better the further upstairs you go – ask to see a few.

Posada El Arco GUESTHOUSE $$
(☎5883-3677; 4a Calle 4-36; s/d Q225/240) Near the Arco Gucumatz, this is one of Chichi's more original accommodations. Rooms are decorated with Maya weavings, colonial bedsteads and sparkly bathrooms, and the lovely garden has fine mountain views. Reservations recommended.

Maya Lodge HOTEL $$
(☎4258-8882; 6a Calle A 4-08; s/d Q200/245) Right on the plaza, this has a colonial atmosphere though it's a bit frayed at the edges. Adorned with woven rugs and Maya-style bedspreads, the 10 rooms are set alongside a patio dotted with rosebushes.

Eating

On Sunday and Thursday, eating at the cook shops in the center of the market is the cheapest way to go. Don't be deterred by the fried-food stalls crowding the fringe – dive into the center for wholesome fare. On other days, look for the little *comedores* near the post office on the road into town.

Tziguan Tinamit GUATEMALAN $
(Centro Comercial Chagüila, 6 Av; sandwiches Q30-45; ⏲6am-10pm) Popular with Guatemalan tourists, this is a clean, modern establishment with decorative nods to local culture and filling *típica* breakfasts. Service is on the clueless side.

Casa de San Juan GUATEMALAN $$
(☎7756-2086; 6a Av 7-28; mains Q60; ⏲9:30am-9:30pm Tue-Sun) The San Juan is one of the few eateries in town with style – art on the walls and the tables themselves, jugs of lilies, wrought-iron chairs – and its wide-ranging menu is great, too. Balcony tables overlook the market.

Mayan Inn GUATEMALAN $$
(☎5966 9127; 8a Calle A 1-91; mains Q70-90; ⏲7am-10pm) The three dining rooms at Chichi's classiest hotel feature colonial-style furnishings and canvases by Guatemala's most renowned painter, Humberto Garabito. Waiters wear costumes evolved from the dress of Spanish colonial farmers. The food is less traditional – steak platters, roast chicken, mixed grills – though lavishly presented and abundantly served.

Information

Most banks change US dollars and traveler's checks. Chichi's many banks all stay open on Sunday.

Banco Industrial (6a Calle 6-05) Has a Visa/MasterCard ATM.

Inguat (☎5966-1162; info-quiche@inguat.gob.gt; 7a Av 7-14; ⏲8am-4pm Sun-Thu, 8am-noon Fri) Authorized guides can be hired here for cultural tours of the town and up to Pascual Abaj.

BUSES FROM CHICHICASTENANGO

DESTINATION	DURATION	COST (Q)	DEPARTURES	FREQUENCY
Guatemala City	2½ hr	30	3am-5pm	every 30 min
Los Encuentros	30 min	6	daily	frequent
Panajachel	2 hr	15	6am, 9am, noon & 1pm	4 daily
Quetzaltenango	2 hr	20	7am-3pm	5 direct buses
Santa Cruz del Quiché	35 min	6	6am-11pm	frequent

Getting There & Away

Buses heading south to Panajachel, Quetzaltenango and all other points reached from the Interamericana arrive and depart from 5a Calle near the corner of 5a Av, one block uphill from the Arco Gucumatz. Northbound buses head up 7a Av, picking up passengers behind Santo Tomás church.

For buses to Antigua (3½ hours), take a bus heading for Guatemala City and change at Chimaltenango. For Panajachel or Quetzaltenango, take a direct bus or any southbound bus and change at Los Encuentros.

Chichi Turkaj Tours (☎5372-1349; 7a Av 5-41) offers shuttles to Guatemala City (Q200), Antigua (Q95), Panajachel (Q55) and Quetzaltenango (Q140) on Monday and Friday at 9am and Sunday and Thursday at 5pm. **Agencia de Viajes Maya Chichi Van** (☎5007-2051; 6a Calle 6-45) goes to the same destinations on Sunday and Thursday, at similar fares. In most cases they need at least five passengers. These agencies also run tours to K'umarcaaj near Santa Cruz del Quiché, Nebaj and elsewhere.

Santa Cruz del Quiché

POP 32,300 / ELEV 1979M

The capital of the Quiché department, Santa Cruz – which is usually called 'El Quiché' or simply 'Quiché' – is 19km north of Chichicastenango. This small, dusty town is quieter and more typical of the Guatemalan countryside than Chichicastenango. Saturday is the main market day, making things slightly more interesting and way more crowded.

Quiché's **tourist office** (☎7755-1106; turismoenquiche@gmail.com; ⏲8am-4:30pm Mon-Fri), inside the town hall, provides good information and a baroquely detailed map. Banco Agromercantil, at the plaza's north end, has a Cajero 5B ATM.

The best time to be here is mid-August during the **Fiestas Elenas** (www.fiestaselenas.com), a week of festivities and a proud display of indigenous traditions. It all leads up to the *convite feminino,* when El Quiché's women don masks and dance up a storm to marimba accompaniment.

Sights

K'umarcaaj ARCHAEOLOGICAL SITE

(Gumarkaaj | Utatlán; admission Q30; ⏲8am-4:30pm) The ruins of the ancient K'iche' Maya capital are 3km west of El Quiché. The kingdom of Quiché was established in late Postclassic times from a mixture of indigenous people and Mexican invaders. Around 1400, King Gucumatz founded his capital here at K'umarcaaj and conquered many neighboring cities. Eventually, the kingdom of Quiché extended its borders to Huehuetenango, Sacapulas, Rabinal and Cobán, even coming to influence the peoples of the Soconusco region in Mexico.

Once Pedro de Alvarado had defeated the K'iche', they invited him to visit their capital, where they secretly planned to kill him. Smelling a rat, Alvarado rallied his allies (including the anti-K'iche' Kaqchiquel), and together they captured the K'iche' leaders, burnt them alive and destroyed K'umarcaaj.

The history is more interesting than the ruined city, of which little remains but a few grass-covered mounds. Still, the site – shaded by tall trees and surrounded by defensive ravines – is a beautiful place for a picnic and is also still used by locals as a religious ritual site.

Gray 'Ruinas' microbuses depart for K'umarcaaj from in front of the cathedral in Santa Cruz every 20 minutes (Q1). The last one back is at 6:50pm.

Sleeping & Eating

The main hotel district is along 1a Av (Zona 5) north of the bus terminal, with at least five hotels within two blocks, and two more on either side along 9a Calle. As always, the area around the market is the prime hunting ground for budget grub.

Hotel Rey K'iche HOTEL $

(☎7755-0827; 8a Calle 0-39, Zona 5; s/d Q100/180; @) Between the bus station and plaza, the Rey K'iche' offers well-maintained, brick-walled rooms around a quiet interior. There's a decent cafe upstairs.

Posada Santa Cecilia HOTEL $$

(☎5332-8811; cnr 1a Av & 6a Calle; s/d Q125/200) Conveniently placed above an espresso vendor just south of the main plaza, this modern establishment offers a handful of bright, spiffy units with comfy beds and pretty quilts.

Café San Miguel BAKERY $

(☎7755-1488; 2 Av 4-42; sandwiches Q12; ⏲8am-8pm) Opposite the cathedral, this little bakery-cafe is a popular gathering place, with good coffee and freshly baked goods on offer.

Restaurant El Chalet STEAKHOUSE $$

(☎7755-0618; 1a Av 2-02, Zona 5; mains Q55-70; ⏲7am-9pm) The specialty here is grilled meats, served with homemade salsa. Dining is in pleasant gardens beneath an arbor. It's a few blocks east of the big clock tower.

Getting There & Away

El Quiché is the jumping-off point for the remote reaches of northern Quiché, which extend all the way to the Mexican border. The main bus terminal, a dusty lot in Zona 5, is located four blocks south and two blocks east of the plaza.

Microbuses to Chichicastenango depart from a parking lot off the southwest corner of the main plaza. Microbuses to Sacapulas depart from 1a Av off the northeast corner of the main plaza.

Nebaj

POP 42,400 / ELEV 2000M

Set deep in a bowl in the dramatic, largely untouched Cuchumatanes mountains, Nebaj's foreigner population consists of equal parts hard-core hikers and volunteers who work with the desperately poor communities in the surrounding countryside.

The locals, removed from modern influences, proudly preserve their ancient way of life. They make excellent handicrafts (mostly textiles) and the Nebaj women wear beautiful *huipiles*.

Nebaj's remote location has been a blessing and a curse. The Spaniards found it difficult to conquer and in more recent times, guerrilla forces made the area a base of operations, drawing strong measures from the army to dislodge them – particularly during the short, brutal reign of Ríos Montt. The few surviving inhabitants of these villages either fled across the border into Mexico or were herded into 'strategic hamlets' (settlements constructed to enable the army to keep inhabitants from having contact with the guerrillas). Refugees are still making their way back home here.

Sights & Activities

Centro Cultural Kumool MUSEUM

(5a Av 1-32; admission Q10; ⏲9am-noon & 1-6pm Mon-Fri, 8am-1pm Sat) Centro Cultural Kumool is a recently opened museum displaying a collection of mostly ceramic objects excavated in the Ixil region, all arranged by historical period.

Hiking

Las Cataratas, a series of waterfalls north of town, is easy enough to reach on your own: walk 1.25km past the Hotel Ileb'al Tenam along the Chajul road to a bridge over a small river. Immediately before the bridge, turn left (north) onto a gravel road and follow the river. Walking downriver for 6km, you'll pass several small waterfalls before reaching a larger waterfall about 25m high.

Pick up a copy of the *Guía de Senderismo Región Ixil* (Q50), with detailed descriptions and maps (in Spanish) for 20 treks in the Ixil region, and organize lodging and food on arrival in villages at *posadas comunitarias* – community-run lodges with wooden-board beds, drinking water and toilets. These humble accommodations operate at Xexocom, Chortiz and Parramos Grande, west of Nebaj, on a possible four-day hike route. The guidebook is sold at the tourist office in the Mercado de Artesanías.

Guías Ixiles HIKING

(☎5847-4747; www.nebaj.com; 3a Calle, El Descanso Bldg, Zona 1; ⏲8am-12:30pm & 2-5pm) Guias Ixiles offers half-day walks to Las Cataratas (Q55 for one person, plus Q25 for each extra person) or around town with visits to the sacred sites of the *costumbristas* (people who still practice non-Christian Maya rites). It also leads three-day treks over the Cuchumatanes to Todos Santos Cuchumatán and many destinations – see the website for details.

BUSES FROM SANTA CRUZ DEL QUICHÉ

DESTINATION	DURATION	COST (Q)	DEPARTURES	FREQUENCY
Chichicastenango	35 min	6	daily	frequent
Guatemala City	3 hr	35	3am-5pm	every 15 min
Huehuetenango	2 hr	25	5am-5:30pm	every 30 min
Nebaj	2 hr	20	9am-4:30pm	5 buses via Sacapulas
Sacapulas	1 hr	12	to 6:30pm	every 30 min
Uspantán	2 hr	25	5:30am-8:30pm	microbuses every 20 min

HIKING QUICHÉ

Nebaj is the jumping-off point for many picturesque hikes around Quiché. Here are just a few options:

- One of the worst hit of all villages during the civil war, **Cocop** is an easy four-hour hike from Nebaj.
- Stay in community-run lodges on a three-day loop through **Xeo**, **Cotzal** and **Ak'Txumbal**.
- Catch a bus or pickup to **Salquil Grande**, then take a gorgeous two-hour stroll past waterfalls to the village of **Parramos Grande**.

Courses

Nebaj Language School
(☎7756-0207; www.nebaj.com/nls.html; El Descanso Bldg, 3a Calle, Zona 1) Affiliated with El Descanso, this institute offers instruction in Spanish (Q600 for 20 hours per week). Combined with accommodation with a local family including two meals a day, two guided hikes to nearby villages and internet use, the fee is Q1300. Instruction in the indigenous Ixil language is another option.

You can also learn how to make regional dishes like *boxboles* (corn dough wrapped in squash leaves, served with a spicy peanut sauce) for Q50 per hour.

Festivals & Events

Nebaj's annual festival, coinciding with the Assumption of the Virgin Mary, runs for 10 days in mid-August.

Sleeping & Eating

Media Luna Medio Sol HOSTEL $
(☎5749-7450; www.nebaj.com/medialuna.html; 3a Calle 6-25; dm Q35, r per person Q45;) Nebaj's spiffiest hostel is around the corner from its parent organization, El Descanso, where you can check in. Two six-bed dorms and a few private rooms share clean toilets and showers. There's a sauna, TV lounge and kitchen facilities to keep you busy.

★Hotel Santa María HOTEL $$
(☎4212-7927; www.hotelsantamarianebaj.com; cnr 4a Av & 2a Calle; s/d Q125/200;) Scarlet woven bedspreads, carved wood headboards and other Ixil handicrafts decorate the bright, spotless rooms at this well-maintained property three blocks northwest of the main plaza.

Comedor El Si'm GUATEMALAN $
(3a Av; breakfast Q15; ⏲7am-9pm) This below-street-level place off the main plaza is great for a classic *desayuno*, here served with a bonus bowl of *mosh* and freshly baked cookie, and they refill your coffee cup. It's usually crammed with local characters by 8am.

El Descanso CAFE $
(3a Calle, Zona 1; mains Q25-30; ⏲breakfast, lunch & dinner) Sharing a property with the Nebaj Language School, this cozy restaurant features a bar, lounge areas and good music in Nebaj's most alternative ambience. It serves a range of snacks, salads and soups.

Asados El Pasabien STEAKHOUSE $
(cnr 5a Av & 9a Calle; mains Q35-45; ⏲noon-9pm) Steaks, chicken and shrimp are skillfully grilled and served up with heaping portions of halved potatoes, salad and nice homemade salsas at this locally popular dining hall.

Shopping

Mercado de Artesanías HANDICRAFTS
(Handicrafts Market; cnr 7a Calle & 2a Av, Zona 1; ⏲8am-6pm) You can buy a huge range of local textiles inside the Mercado de Artesanías.

Information

The **tourist office** (☎7755-8182; 7a Calle & 2a Av; ⏲8am-6pm), inside the Mercado de Artesanías, can answer any question as long as it's posed in Spanish.

Banrural, on the Parque Central, changes traveler's checks; the Cajero 5B **ATM** is in the town-hall building, opposite the Parque. The **post office** (5a Av 4-37) is one block north of the Parque.

Log on to www.nebaj.com for good information on hiking, volunteering and studying in the area.

Getting There & Away

Microbuses bound for Santa Cruz del Quiché (Q25, two hours), via Sacapulas, depart every half hour from 4am until 5pm from behind the church at the corner of 5a Av and 7a Calle. To head west to Huehuetenango, change at Sacapulas. To get to Uspantán and Cobán, get off at the Cunén junction (Q15) and hail any eastbound microbus.

The main bus terminal, behind the market, mainly serves outlying villages such as Tzalbal, Vicalama and Palop; a midnight bus travels all the way to Guatemala City (Q55, 5½ hours) via Chichicastenango.

Uspantán

Heading east out of Sacapulas, the road meanders up sadly deforested slopes before reaching the village of **Uspantán**. Rigoberta Menchú, the 1992 Nobel Peace Prize laureate, grew up in the Quiché area, a five-hour walk from Uspantán. Be aware that Menchú and her oft-controversial politics are not universally loved around here.

If you're headed to Cobán by bus (Q40, four hours), you may end up spending the night in Uspantán, as the last minibus leaves town at 4pm. It can get very cold here. **Hotel Don Gabriel** (☎7951-8540; hoteldongabriel@yahoo.es; 7a Av 6-22; s/d/tr Q75/150/210) provides excellent value and plenty of thick blankets. **Hotel Posada Doña Leonor** (☎7951-8041; caluti54@hotmail.com; 6a Calle 4-25, Zona 1; s/d/tr Q80/140/180; 📶) is about the best in town, offering firm beds, fresh paint, and huge spotless bathrooms with blasting-hot showers. Banrural, a block east of the church changes US dollars and has an ATM.

Quetzaltenango (Xela)

POP 167,200 / ELEV 2367M

Quetzaltenango – which the locals kindly shorten to Xela (*shell*-ah), itself an abbreviation of the original K'iche' Maya name, Xelajú – may well be the perfect Guatemalan town – not too big, not too small, enough foreigners to support a good range of hotels and restaurants, but not so many that it loses its national flavor. The Guatemalan 'layering' effect is at work in the downtown area here – once the Spanish moved out, the Germans moved in and their architecture gives the zone a somber, some would say Gothic, feel.

Xela attracts a more serious type of traveler – people who really want to learn Spanish, and then stay around and get involved in myriad volunteer projects on offer.

It also functions as a base for a range of spectacular hikes through the surrounding countryside – the constantly active Santiaguito and highest-point-in-Central-America Tajumulco volcanoes, and the picturesque, fascinating three-day trek to Lago de Atitlán to name a few.

History

Quetzaltenango came under the sway of the K'iche' Maya of K'umarcaaj in the 14th century. Before that it had been a Mam Maya town.

With the formation of the Federation of Central America in the mid-19th century, Quetzaltenango initially decided on federation with Chiapas and Mexico, instead of with Central America. Later, the city switched alliances and joined the Central American Federation, becoming an integral part of Guatemala in 1840. The late-19th-century coffee boom augmented Quetzaltenango's wealth. Plantation owners came to buy supplies, and coffee brokers opened warehouses. The city prospered until 1902, when a dual calamity – an earthquake and a volcanic eruption – brought mass destruction.

Still, Xela's position at the intersection of the roads to the Pacific Slope, Mexico and Guatemala City guaranteed it some degree of affluence. Today it's again busy with commerce.

Sights

Parque Centro América PLAZA

(Map p148) Most of Xela's impressive buildings crowd in and around the broad central plaza, known as the Parque Centro América.

At the southeast end of the plaza, the Casa de la Cultura holds the **Museo de Historia Natural** (Map p148; ☎7761-6427; 7a Calle; admission Q6; ⏲8am-noon & 2-6pm Mon-Fri, 9am-5pm Sat & Sun) which has exhibits on the Maya, the liberal revolution in Central American politics and the Estado de Los Altos, of which Quetzaltenango was the capital. Marimbas, weaving, taxidermy and other local lore also claim places here.

The once-crumbling **Iglesia del Espíritu Santo** (Map p148) has been rebuilt (well, its facade, anyway) in the last few decades. Up the block from the cathedral, the **Municipalidad** (Town Hall; Map p148) follows the grandiose neoclassical style so favored as a symbol of culture and refinement in this wild mountain country.

On the plaza's northwest side, the palatial **Pasaje Enríquez** (Map p148; btwn 4a & 5a Calles) was built to be lined with elegant shops, but now houses an assortment of travel agencies, language institutes, cafes and one major bar.

Quetzaltenango

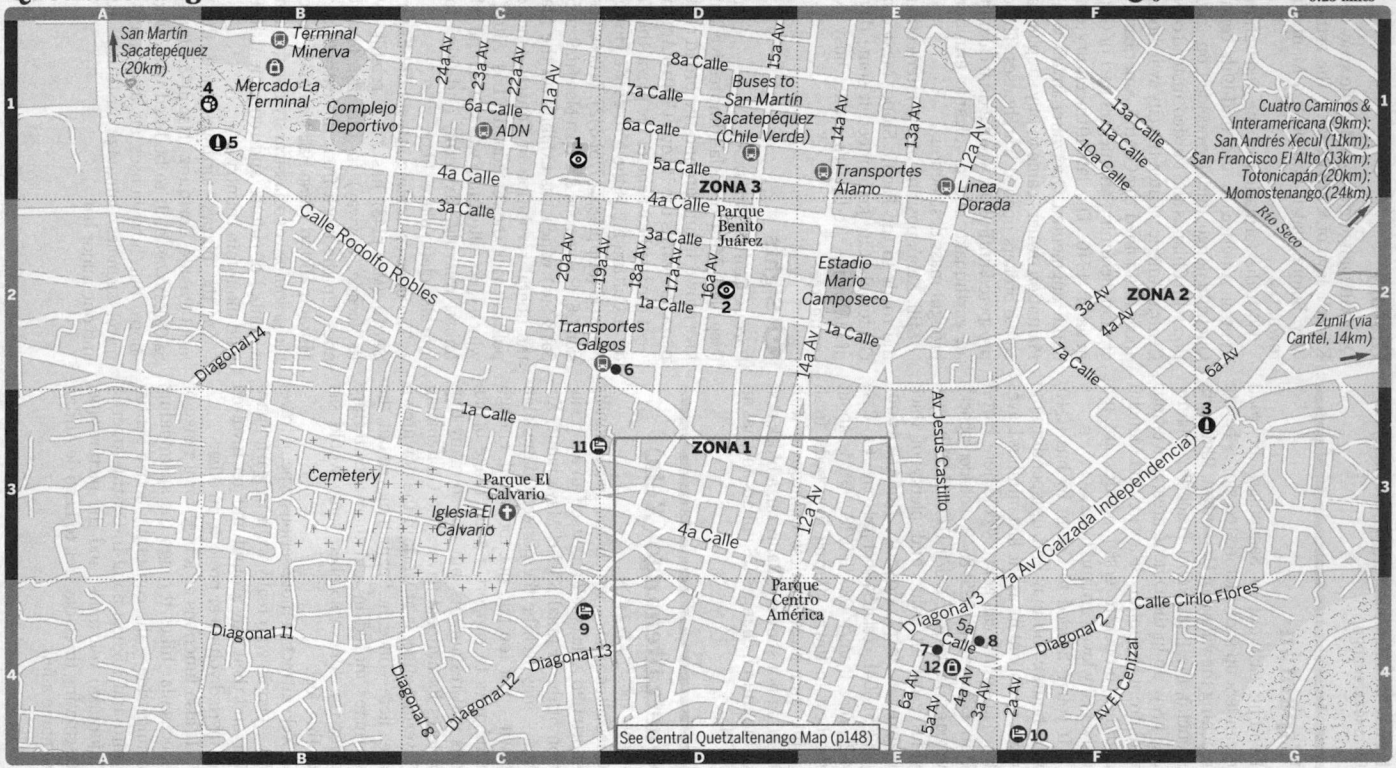

Quetzaltenango

Sights

1 Centro Intercultural de Quetzaltenango C1
2 Mercado La Democracia D2
3 Monumento a la Marimba G3
Museo de Arte ..... (see 1)
Museo del Ferrocarril de los Altos ..... (see 1)
Museo Ixkik' ..... (see 1)
4 Parque Zoológico Minerva B1
5 Templo de Minerva B1

Activities, Courses & Tours

6 Centro de Estudios de Español Pop Wuj D2
7 El Quetzal Spanish School E4
Maya Viva ..... (see 12)
8 Proyecto Lingüístico Quetzalteco de Español E4
Quetzaltrekkers ..... (see 9)

Sleeping

9 Casa Argentina C4
10 Casa San Bartolomé F4
11 Hostal 7 Orejas C3

Shopping

12 Manos Creativas E4

Mercado La Democracia MARKET
(Map p146; 1a Calle, Zona 3) Check out the Mercado La Democracia, 10 blocks north of Parque Centro América, for the hustle of a real Guatemalan city market.

Parque Zoológico Minerva ZOO
(Map p146; ☎7763-5637; Av Las Américas 0-50, Zona 3; ⏲9am-5pm Tue-Sun) About 3km northwest of Parque Centro América, near the Terminal Minerva bus station and another big market, is Parque Zoológico Minerva, a zoo-park with a few monkeys, coyotes, raccoons, deer and Barbary sheep.

Templo de Minerva MONUMENT
(Map p146) Outside the zoo on an island in the middle of 4a Calle stands the neoclassical Templo de Minerva, built by dictator Estrada Cabrera to honor the Roman goddess of education and to inspire Guatemalans to new heights of learning.

Centro Intercultural de Quetzaltenango CULTURAL CENTRE
(Map p146; 4a Calle & 19 Av, Zona 3) Quetzaltenango's old railroad station, 1km east of the Templo de Minerva along 4a Calle, served as a military base during the civil war, then lay dormant for years until the city converted it into the Centro Intercultural de Quetzaltenango. Inside is the **Museo Ixkik'** (Map p146; ☎7761-6472; 4a Calle & 19 Av, Zona 3; admission Q25; ⏲9am-1pm & 2-6pm), devoted to Maya weaving and traditional outfits, a **modern art museum** (Map p146; 4a Calle & 19 Av, Zona 3; admission Q6; ⏲8am-noon & 2-6pm) and the **Museo del Ferrocarril** (Map p146; 4a Calle & 19 Av, Zona 3; admission Q6; ⏲8am-noon & 2-6pm), which documents the ambitious and short-lived railroad that connected Xela with the Pacific coast for a few years.

Activities

Hiking

Volcán Tajumulco (4220m) is the highest point in Central America and a challenging two-day hike from Quetzaltenango. Volcán Santiaguito (2488m) and Volcán Santa María (3772m) can also be ascended.

Most tour companies charge around Q370 for a two-day trip to Tajumulco, Q150 for full-moon ascents of Santa María, Q650 for the three-day treks between Quetzaltenango and Lago de Atitlán, and Q1100 for the five-day Nebaj–Todos Santos Cuchumatán jaunt across the Cuchumatanes mountains.

Kaqchikel Tours HIKING
(Map p148; ☎5010-4465; www.kaqchikeltoursxela.com; 7a Calle 15-36, Zona 1) Does a challenging two-day hike right up close to the active Volcán Santiaguito (Q600).

Monte Verde Tours HIKING
(Map p148; ☎5729-6279; www.monte-verdetours.com; 13a Av 8-34, Zona 1) Does a variety of volcano hikes and offbeat tours around Xela.

Quetzaltrekkers HIKING
(Map p146; ☎7765-5895; www.quetzaltrekkers.com; Diagonal 12 8-37, Zona 1) Volunteer-run organization that supports a local school for kids from low-income families. It offers a range of trips – see its website for details.

Cycling

Cycling is a great way to explore the surrounding countryside or commute to Spanish class. Fuentes Georginas, San Andrés Xecul and the steam vents at Los Vahos are all attainable day trips.

Vrisa Books CYCLING
(Map p148; 15a Av 3-64, Zona 1) This place rents mountain and town bikes for Q40/100/200 per day/week/month; it also offers cycling tours.

Central Quetzaltenango

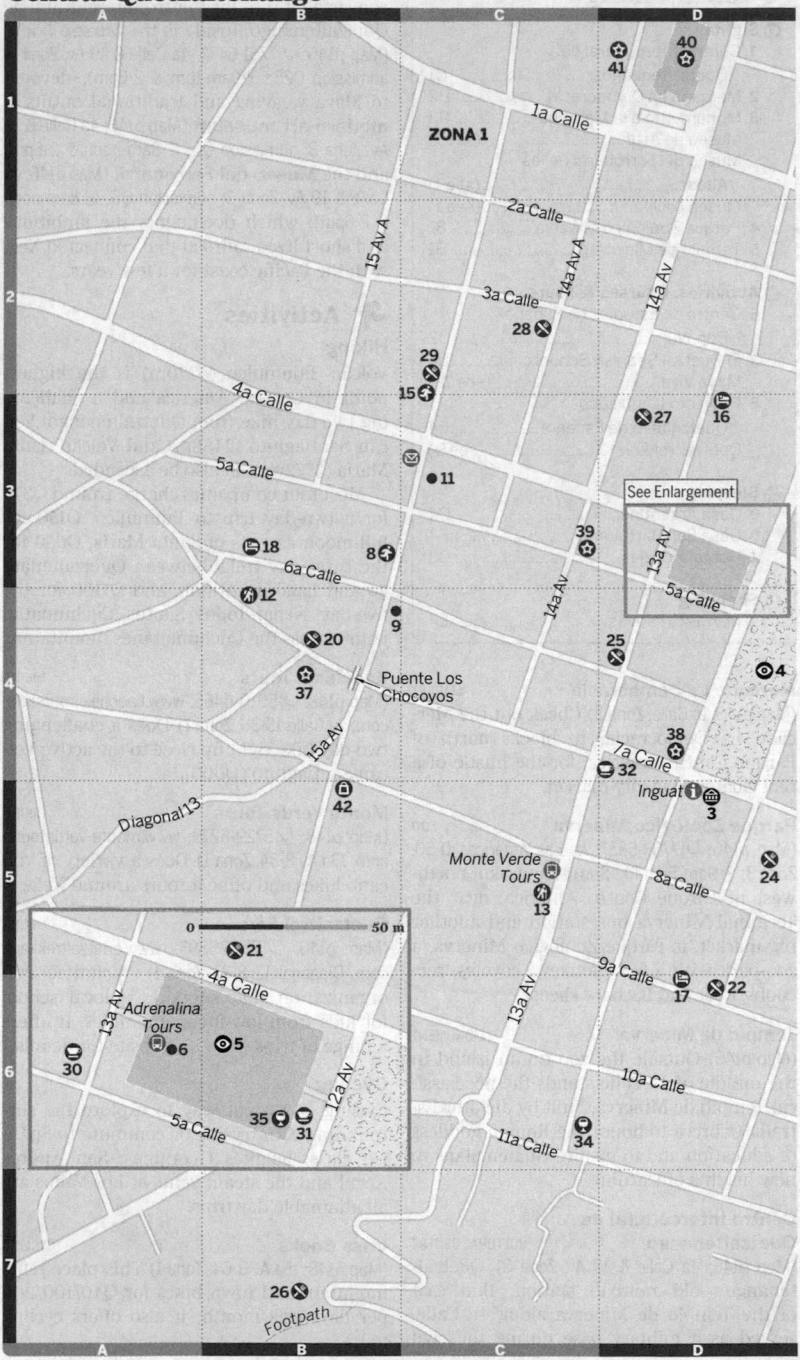

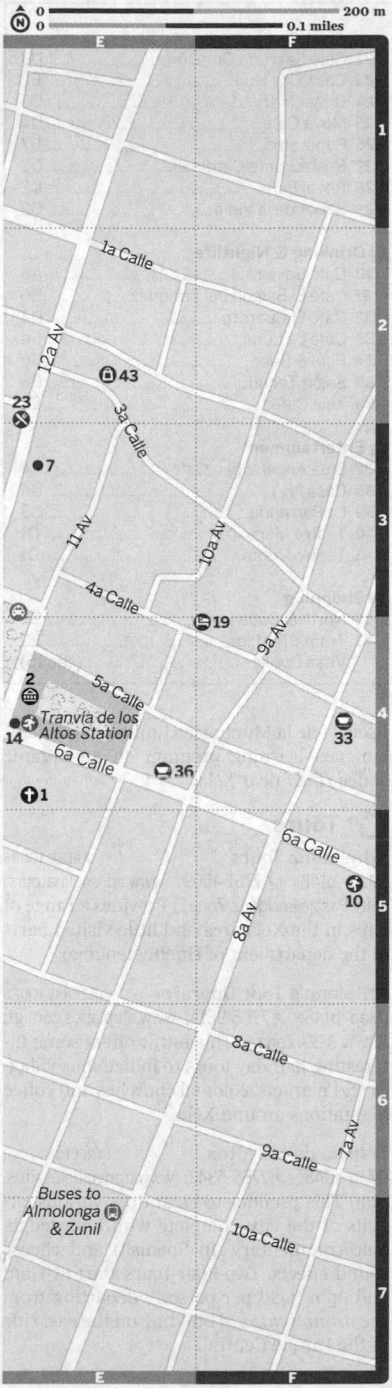

Bike House CYCLING
(Map p148; 15a Av 5-22) Street bikes or mountain bikes for Q40/80 per day.

Volunteering

EntreMundos VOLUNTEERING
(Map p148; ☎7761-2179; www.entremundos.org; 6a Calle 7-31, Zona 1; ⏲2-5pm Mon-Thu) EntreMundos is an excellent resource for volunteers seeking projects (and vice versa). The free searchable database on its website has details of hundreds of positions. If you'd like to drop in for more personalized service, it asks for a Q25 contribution. The organization also regularly seeks volunteers for capacity building workshops for NGOs and to produce its bimonthly newspaper.

Courses

In recent years, Xela has become well known for its Spanish-language schools. Unlike Antigua, Xela is not overrun with foreigners, but it does have a small student social scene.

Most of the city's Spanish schools participate in social-action programs with the local K'iche' people and provide students with an opportunity to get involved. The standard price is Q920/1050 per week for four/five hours of instruction per day, Monday to Friday. Add around Q330 for room and board with a local family. Some places charge up to 20% more for tuition from June to August, and many require nonrefundable registration fees, particularly when booking in advance from overseas. College students may be able to take classes for academic credit. The website www.xelapages.com has information about many of Xela's schools.

Manos Creativas (p153) and Trama Textiles (p153), both women's cooperatives, offer backstrap weaving classes and operate fairtrade fabric shops. Both places charge Q325 for 10 hours of instruction, in which learners produce a scarf, and Q650 for 20 hours and the chance to make an embroidered table runner. For a simple demonstration of techniques they charge Q35.

Celas Maya LANGUAGE COURSE
(Map p148; ☎7761-4342; www.celasmaya.edu.gt; 6a Calle 14-55, Zona 1) Busy, professional outfit with a good library and internet cafe. Official training and testing center for DELE (test of Spanish as a foreign language).

Central Quetzaltenango

Sights
1 Cathedral E4
2 Municipalidad E4
3 Museo de Historia Natural D5
4 Parque Centro América D4
5 Pasaje Enríquez B6

Activities, Courses & Tours
6 Adrenalina Tours A6
7 Altiplano's Tour Operator E3
8 Bike House B3
9 Celas Maya B4
10 EntreMundos F5
11 Inepas C3
12 Kaqchikel Tours B4
13 Monte Verde Tours C5
14 Tranvía de los Altos E4
15 Vrisa Books C2

Sleeping
16 Black Cat Hostel D3
17 Casa Renaissance D6
Guest House El Puente ..... (see 9)
18 Hostal Don Diego B3
19 Hostel Nim Sut F4

Eating
20 Artesano B4
21 Café El Árabe B5
22 Café Sagrado Corazón D6
23 Casa Ut'z Hua E2
24 Doña Cristy D5
25 Maya Café D4
26 Panorama B7
27 Restaurante Cardinali D3
28 Royal Paris C2
29 Sabor de la India C2

Drinking & Nightlife
30 Café Baviera A6
31 Café El Balcón del Enríquez B6
32 Café El Cuartito D4
33 Café La Luna F4
34 Pool & Beer C6
35 Salón Tecún B6
36 Xela Café E4

Entertainment
37 Blue Angel Video Café B4
38 Casa No'j D4
39 La Parranda C3
40 Teatro Municipal D1
41 Teatro Roma D1

Shopping
42 North & South B5
43 Trama Textiles E2
Vrisa Books ..... (see 15)

Centro de Estudios de Español Pop Wuj LANGUAGE COURSE
(Map p146; ☎7761-8286; www.pop-wuj.org; 1a Calle 17-72, Zona 1) Pop Wuj's profits go to development projects in nearby villages, in which students can participate. The school also offers medical and social-work language programs.

El Quetzal Spanish School LANGUAGE COURSE
(Map p146; ☎7761-2784; www.xelawho.com/elquetzal; 6a Calle 5-52 A, Zona 1) One of the few indigenous-run businesses in town, offering plenty of activities and a reading room.

Inepas LANGUAGE COURSE
(Instituto de Español y Participación en Ayuda Social; Map p148; ☎7765-1308; www.inepas.org; 15a Av 4-59) Students can participate in a variety of worthy projects, including a Unesco-recognized rural school. Offers a selection of inexpensive accommodations besides homestays.

Proyecto Lingüístico Quetzalteco de Español LANGUAGE COURSE
(Map p146; ☎7763-1061; www.plqe.org; 5a Calle 2-40, Zona 1) This collectively managed and politically minded institute also runs the Escuela de la Montaña, a limited-enrollment language-learning program on an organic coffee *finca* near Xela.

Tours

Adrenalina Tours GUIDED TOURS
(Map p148; ☎7761-4509; www.adrenalinatours.com; Pasaje Enríquez, Zona 1) Provides a range of trips in the Xela area and little-visited parts of the department of Huehuetenango.

Altiplano's Tour Operator CULTURAL TOURS
(Map p148; ☎7766-9614; www.altiplanos.com.gt; 12a Av 3-35, Zona 1) This outfit offers some interesting half-day tours to indigenous villages and markets, colonial churches and coffee plantations around Xela.

Tranvía de los Altos STREETCAR TOUR
(Map p148; ☎7765-5342; www.tranviadelosaltos.com) This pseudo-streetcar does various circuits of the city, complete with knowledgeable commentary (in Spanish) and cheesy sound effects. Two-hour tours start at 11am and 3pm (Q50 per person), departing from the *municipalidad* building on the east side of the Parque Central.

Maya Viva CULTURAL TOUR
(Map p146; ☎7761-6408; www.amaguate.org; cnr 5a Av & 6a Calle 6-17, Zona 1) This community tourism program is organized by the Asociación de Mujeres del Altiplano, a group that seeks to empower Maya women in the countryside. Visitors get to experience life in one of five rural communities near Quetzaltenango and learn about their customs, traditions and daily activities.

Festivals & Events

Xela Music Festival MUSIC FESTIVAL
Organized by the Alianza Francaise, this one- or two-day festival sees city streets blocked off as local musicians play on five or six stages around the downtown area.

Feria de la Virgen del Rosario CULTURAL FESTIVAL
(Feria Centroamericana de Independencia) Xela's big annual party. Residents kick up their heels at a fairground on the city's perimeter and there's plenty of entertainment at selected venues around town.

Sleeping

Zona 1 has the most options.

★Casa Renaissance HOTEL $
(Map p148; ☎3121-6315; www.casarenaissance.com; 9a Calle 11-26, Zona 1; r Q150, without bathroom Q110;) This colonial mansion has been reborn as a casual guesthouse, with five huge, beautifully restored rooms along a delightful patio. Managed by friendly, informative Dutch hosts, the place has a relaxed atmosphere: take drinks from the cooler, prepare your own meals in the kitchen or watch videos from the voluminous collection. Rates drop significantly by the week.

Black Cat Hostel HOSTEL $
(Map p148; ☎7756-8951; www.blackcathostels.net; 13a Av 3-33, Zona 1; dm incl breakfast Q60, r Q160;) A great place to stay if you're looking to meet up with other travelers, featuring a sunny courtyard, a bar-restaurant and lounge/TV area. Though sparsely furnished, the rooms are done in soothing colors with nice wood floors.

Hostel Nim Sut HOSTEL $
(Map p148; ☎7761-3083; www.hostelnimsutquetzaltenango.weebly.com; 4a Calle 9-42, Zona 1; dm Q62, s/d Q140/170, without bathroom Q95/115) Conveniently placed a block east of the Parque Centro América, this restored colonial relic has plenty of large rooms with basic bedding and clean parquet floors, some considerably brighter than others. The top terrace, with fine views over the town, is a good place to enjoy an espresso from the cafe downstairs.

Guest House El Puente HOSTEL $
(Map p148; ☎7761-4342; celasmaya@gmail.com; 15a Av 6-75, Zona 1; s/d 65/130, without bathroom Q50/100) The four rooms here surround a large garden; three share well-used bathroom facilities. Connected to the Celas Maya Spanish school, it's often occupied by language learners who congregate in the kitchen.

Casa Argentina HOSTEL $
(Map p146; ☎7763-2320; casargentina.xela@gmail.com; Diagonal 12 8-37, Zona 1; dm/s/d Q25/35/50) This sprawling guesthouse west of the center is a port of call for itinerant quetzal-pinchers, but steer clear of the outrageously overcrowded dorms and opt for the marginally pricier private rooms with cinderblock decor. Señora Argentina and daughter Leonor are eager to please.

Hostal Don Diego HOSTEL $
(Map p148; ☎7763-1000; www.hostaldondiegoxela.com; 6a Calle 15-12, Zona 1; dm Q45, s/d/tr from Q55/100/150;) Sparsely furnished rooms with good firm beds around a sunny courtyard. Reduced rates for weekly or monthly stays.

Casa San Bartolomé B&B $$
(Map p146; ☎7761-9511; www.casasanbartolome.com; 2a Av 7-17, Zona 1; s/d/tr incl breakfast Q205/287/350;) In the family for generations, this atmospheric old residence has been converted into a cozy B&B. There are six rooms, three apartments (with kitchens) and a cottage. All have beautiful furniture and modern art. An elaborate breakfast is served on the lovely rear terrace. Long-termers get substantial discounts.

Hostal 7 Orejas HOSTEL $$
(Map p146; ☎7768-3218; www.7orejas.com; 2a Calle 16-92, Zona 1; dm/s/d/tr Q75/160/265/320; @) A cordially managed, scrupulously maintained hostel on a quiet street northwest of the center. The spacious, fresh-smelling rooms each have three queen-sized beds and carved-wood chests for storage. Music, movies and cocktails keep guests occupied upstairs at the El Orejón lounge.

Eating

Quetzaltenango has a good selection of places to eat in all price ranges. Cheapest are the food stalls on the lower level of the central market, where snacks and main-course plates are sold for Q10 or less. One very popular breakfast locale is **Doña Cristy** (Map p148), serving *atol de elote* (a hot maize beverage), *empanadas* and *chuchitos*.

Casa Ut'z Hua GUATEMALAN $
(Map p148; ☎7768-3469; 12a Av 3-05; mains Q30-40; ⏲7am-8pm) Delicious, authentic Guatemalan and Quetzalteco dishes are the draw at this kitschily decorated country hut.

Artesano BAKERY $
(Map p148; 7a Calle 15-18; sandwiches Q30; ⏲8am-8pm Mon-Sat, noon-6pm Sun) A good place to stock up for that volcano climb, this craft bakery makes whole-wheat sandwiches (tofu, tempeh, eggplant, cheese), excellent cookies and granola.

Maya Café GUATEMALAN $
(Map p148; 13a Av 5-48; mains Q25-30; ⏲7am-6pm) Plenty of *típica* Xela fare on offer at this locally popular dining hall. Try the *quichom*, a spicy chicken concoction. Lunch comes with soup and a juice.

Café Sagrado Corazón GUATEMALAN $
(Map p148; 9a Calle 11-16; lunch combos Q20-30; ⏲8am-8pm; ✎) This hole-in-the-wall eatery is a good place to try Guatemalan home cooking, with regional specialties like *pepián* and *jocón*. Meals are truly filling, coming with soup, *tamalitos* (miniature tamales), rice, potatoes, avocado and salad.

★Sabor de la India INDIAN $$
(Map p148; ☎7765-2555; 15a Av 3-64; mains Q60-70; ⏲noon-10pm Tue-Sun; ✎) What is surely the most authentic Indian fare in the country is made here by a friendly fellow from Kerala. Servings are huge; the *thalis* – assortments of curried veggies – are recommended.

Panorama EUROPEAN $$
(Map p148; ☎7765-8580; www.restaurantepanorama.com; 13a Av A, D16-44; fondue Q80; ⏲noon-midnight Tue-Sun) This Swiss-owned restaurant (a 10-minute slog up the hill at the south end of town) does good set meals and Swiss Raclette cheese. The view is amazing and the setting is romantic.

Royal Paris FRENCH $$
(Map p148; ☎7761-1942; 14 Av A 3-06; salads Q50; ⏲noon-10pm Tue-Sun; 📶) Overseen by the French consul herself, this bistro ought to be authentic, and the *escargots*, baked Camembert and filet mignon approach Parisian standards. There's live folk and jazz Wednesday, Friday and Saturday nights (when reservations are a good idea).

Restaurante Cardinali ITALIAN $$
(Map p148; ☎7761-0924; 14a Av 3-25; pastas Q65-85; ⏲noon-10pm) Homemade pasta, good pizzas and an extensive wine list.

Café El Árabe MIDDLE EASTERN
(Map p148; 4a Calle 12-22, Zona 1; mains Q55; ⏲noon-midnight; ✎) Authentic Middle Eastern food, freshly made pitas and plenty of vegetarian choices.

Drinking & Nightlife

Coffee plays an important part in Xela's economy, and there's no shortage of places where you can grab a cup. Once nighttime rolls around, the preference turns towards beer.

★Café La Luna CAFE
(Map p148; ☎5174-6769; 8a Av 4-11; ⏲9am-9pm Mon-Sat; 📶) La Luna is a comfortable, relaxed place to hang out and eat a cake, salad or sandwich. The hot chocolate is the specialty – the coffee is so-so. Choose any of several rooms: decor is in a similar vein to Café Baviera but the music is classical instead of jazz.

Café Baviera CAFE
(Map p148; ☎7761-5018; 5a Calle 13-14; ⏲7am-8:30pm; 📶) This European-style cafe has good coffee, roasted on the premises, and is a decent place for breakfast or a snack (crepes, croissants, soups and salads, Q30 to Q40). The wooden walls are hung with countless photos and clippings on Xela and international themes.

Café El Cuartito CAFE
(Map p148; 13a Av 7-09; ⏲9am-11pm; 📶) Xela's hippest cafe does a good range of snacks and juices, and coffee just about any way you want it. Weekends it often has DJs spinning laid-back tracks, and there's always art on the walls by local contemporary artists.

Café El Balcón del Enríquez CAFE
(Map p148; 12 Av 4-40, Pasaje Enríquez; ⏲8am-10pm) The food and coffee at this outdoor,

upstairs cafe are only so-so, but the views are spectacular.

Salón Tecún PUB
(Map p148; Pasaje Enríquez; ⏲9:30am-12:30am) Busy all day and night with a healthy (but not *that* healthy) crowd of Guatemalans and foreigners; the Tecún claims to be the country's longest-running bar (since 1935). Good bar snacks and gringo comfort food, including probably the best burgers in town.

Pool & Beer PUB
(Map p148; 12a Av 10-21; ⏲6pm-1am Tue-Sun) The pool tables are worn and the cues crooked, but this slackers' clubhouse remains a friendly and refreshingly non-trendy spot. If the tables are occupied, you can be the DJ, choosing from the PC's 30,000 odd tracks.

☆ Entertainment

The live music scene is particularly strong in Xela. For details on what's on, pick up a copy of *XelaWho* or check www.xelawho.com. The most options can be found in Zona 1.

Though there's no proper movie house in the center of town, a number of venues run weekly film series, including Royal Paris and El Orejón, the lounge inside the Hostal 7 Orejas. In addition, the **Blue Angel Video Café** (Map p148; 7a Calle 15-79, Zona 1; admission Q10) shows Hollywood films nightly at 8pm, besides serving a nice range of vegetarian meals, herbal teas and hot chocolate. See *XelaWho* for schedules.

Casa No'j PERFORMING ARTS
(Map p148; ☎7768-3139; www.centroculturalcasanoj.blogspot.com; 7a Calle 12-12, Zona 1; ⏲8am-5pm Mon-Sat) The recently inaugurated Casa No'j, off the Parque's southwest corner, is Xela's premier cultural center. Besides staging photo and art exhibits, it also hosts film, theater and poetry festivals throughout the year. Check its blog for upcoming events.

Teatro Municipal THEATER
(Map p148; ☎7761-2218; 14a Av & 1a Calle) On 1a Calle is the impressive neoclassical Teatro Municipal, which stages regular performing arts productions, from international dance recitals to the crowning of La Señorita Quetzaltenango.

Teatro Roma THEATER
(Map p148; ☎3010-0100; 14a Av A-34) Facing Teatro Municipal; sometimes screens interesting movies.

La Parranda DANCE
(Map p148; 14a Av 4-47, Zona 1; cover Fri & Sat Q30; ⏲9pm-12:30am Wed-Sat) This glitzy, strobe-lit disco offers free salsa classes on Wednesday nights (basic and intermediate); other evenings have guest DJs and drinks giveaways.

Shopping

North & South BOOKS
(Map p148; cnr 8a Calle & 15a Av 13-77, Zona 1) Broad selection of titles on Latin America, politics, poetry and history. Also plenty of new and used guidebooks and Spanish student resources.

Manos Creativas HANDICRAFTS
(Map p146; ☎7761-6408; www.amaguate.org; cnr 6a Calle & 5 Av 6-17) Manos Creativas, a shop belonging to the women's empowerment association AMA, sells quality textiles and clothing produced by Maya weavers. **Trama Textiles** (Map p148; ☎7765-8564; 3a Calle 10-56, Zona 1), just uphill from the park, is a similar weaving cooperative, comprised of 400 Maya women.

Vrisa Books BOOKS
(Map p148; 15a Av 3-64) Excellent range of secondhand books in English and European languages, including Lonely Planet guides; plus a rental library (Q20 per book per week). It also rents out bikes for touring.

Information

EMERGENCY

Policía Municipal (☎7761-5805)
Proatur (☎4149-1104)

INTERNET RESOURCES

Xela Pages (www.xelapages.com) Packed with information about Xela and nearby attractions. Also a useful discussion forum.

MEDIA

The following English-language publications are available free in bars, restaurants and cafes around town.

EntreMundos (☎7761-2179; www.entremundos.org) Published every two months by the Quetzaltenango-based organization of the same name, this newspaper has plenty of information on political developments and volunteer projects in the region.

XelaWho (www.xelawho.com) Billing itself as 'Quetzaltenango's leading Culture & Nightlife Magazine,' this little monthly lists cultural events in the city, with some fairly irreverent takes on life in Guatemala in general.

MEDICAL SERVICES

Hospital Privado Quetzaltenango (☎7774-4700; Calle Rodolfo Robles 23-51) Usually has an English-speaking doctor on staff. 24-hour emergency service.

Hospital San Rafael (☎7761-4414; 9a Calle 10-41, Zona 1) 24-hour emergency service.

MONEY

Parque Centro América is the place to go for banks, but the ATMs are untrustworthy. **Banco Industrial** (⏲9am-6:30pm Mon-Fri, 9am-1pm Sat) has branches on the north and east sides of the plaza. Both change traveler's checks.

POST

Main post office (4a Calle 15-07, Zona 1)

TOURIST INFORMATION

Inguat (☎7761-4931; info-xela@inguat.gob.gt; 7a Calle; ⏲9am-5pm Mon-Fri, 9am-1pm Sat), at the southern end of Parque Centro América, is hit or miss, with staff attitudes ranging from helpful to clueless.

There's a plethora of tourist maps circulating; look for them at internet cafes, language schools and hotels. Although they're essentially advertising flyers, the better ones, such as **Xelamap** (www.xelamaponline.com) include plenty of useful information.

Getting There & Away

PULLMAN BUS

First-class bus companies heading for Guatemala City have their own terminals. They all charge around Q70 for the four- to five-hour trip.

ADN (☎6649-2089; www.adnautobusesdelnorte.com; 23a Av 5-06) Deluxe, non-stop buses at 6am and 3pm.

Linea Dorada (☎7767-5198; www.lineadorada.info; cnr 12 Av & 5 Calle) Deluxe, non-stop buses at 4am and 2:30pm. Also runs services to Huehuetenango (Q40) departing at 11:30am.

Transportes Álamo (☎7767-4582; 14 Av 5-15, Zona 3) Six departures from 4:30am to 2:30pm.

Transportes Galgos (☎7761-2248; Calle Rodolfo Robles 17-43, Zona 1) Pullmans at 4am and 12:30pm.

2ND-CLASS BUSES

For 2nd-class buses (see table, opposite), head out to the **Terminal Minerva** (7a Calle, Zona 3), a dusty, noisy, crowded yard in the west of town. Buses leave frequently for many highland destinations. Leaving or entering town, some buses make a stop east of the center at the *rotonda*, a traffic circle on Calz Independencia, marked by the **Monumento a la Marimba** (Map p146). Getting off here when you're coming into Xela saves the 10 or 15 minutes it will take your bus to cross town to Terminal Minerva.

2ND-CLASS BUSES FROM QUETZALTENANGO

DESTINATION	COST (Q)	DURATION	DEPARTURES	FREQUENCY
Almolonga	3	40 min	5:30am-5pm	every 15 min
Chichicastenango	25	3 hr	9am-3:30pm	hourly
Ciudad Tecún Umán (Mexican border)	40	3 hr	5am-6pm	hourly
Guatemala City	40	4 hr	6am-4pm	every 15 min
Huehuetenango	20	2 hr	5:30am-7pm	every 15 min
La Mesilla (Mexican border)	40	3½ hr	5am-4pm	hourly
Momostenango	9	1½ hr	5:45am-7pm	every 15 min
Panajachel	25	3 hr	10am-4:30pm	hourly
Retalhuleu	20	1½ hr	4:30am-7:30pm	every 10 min
San Andrés Xecul	4.50	40 min	6am-3pm	every 15 min
San Martín Sacatepéquez (Chile Verde)	5	1 hr	6am-3pm	every 15 min
San Pedro La Laguna	35	3 hr	10am-4pm	every 2 hr
Zunil	4.50	1 hr	6:30am-5:30pm	every 10 min

Buses for Almolonga and Zunil have an additional downtown stop at the corner of 8a Av and 10a Calle, southeast of Parque Centro América. Those for **San Martín Sacatepéquez** (Chile Verde) also stop at 6a Calle, two blocks north of Parque Benito Juárez.

To get to Antigua, catch any Guatemala City–bound bus passing Chimaltenango and change there. To get to the Mexican border at El Carmen/Talismán, take a bus to San Marcos (Q10, two hours, every 30 minutes), then another to Malacatán (Q15, two hours) and finally a collective taxi (Q5) or microbus to El Carmen (Q4).

SHUTTLE MINIBUS

Adrenalina Tours (☎7761-4509; www.adrenalinatours.com; Pasaje Enríquez, Zona 1) and **Monte Verde Tours** (☎7761-6105; www.monteverdetours.com; 13 Av 8-34, Zona 1) run shuttle minibuses to many destinations including Guatemala City (Q270), Antigua (Q230), Chichicastenango (Q150), Panajachel (Q150), and San Cristóbal de las Casas (Mexico; Q270).

ℹ Getting Around

Inguat (p154) has information on city bus routes. City buses charge Q1.25, doubling the fare after 7pm and on holidays. Frequent minibuses run between Terminal Minerva and the downtown area. The Rotonda bus stop on Calz Independencía is also served by 'Parque' microbuses running to the center.

Taxis wait at the stand on the north end of Parque Centro América. Bargain hard. Cab fare between Terminal Minerva and downtown is around Q30.

Around Quetzaltenango

The beautiful volcanic countryside around Quetzaltenango makes for exciting day trips and getting out there is as simple as hopping on one of the buses serving the traditional villages that pepper this region.

Market days in surrounding towns include Sunday in Momostenango, Monday in Zunil, Tuesday and Saturday in Totonicapán and Friday in San Francisco El Alto.

Fuentes Georginas

This is the prettiest natural **spa** (☎7763-0596; info@fuentesgeorginas.com; admission Q50; ⏲8am-5:30pm) in Guatemala. Here, pools of varying temperatures are fed by hot sulfur springs and framed by a high wall of tropical vegetation. Hurricane Agatha ripped through the spa in 2010, all but destroying the installations. Fortunately, it's been completely rebuilt and restored, though patches of the road in remain perilously damaged.

The site has a **restaurant** (meals Q60-75; ⏲8am-7pm), and three sheltered picnic tables with cooking grills (bring your own fuel). Down the valley are seven rustic **cottages** (per person Q95), each with a shower, a barbecue area and a fireplace to ward off the mountain chill at night. Included in the price of the cottages is access to the pools all day and night. Trails here lead to two nearby volcanoes: **Volcán Zunil** (three hours each way) and **Volcán Santo Tomás** (five hours each way). Guides (essential) are available for either trip. Ask at the restaurant.

Fuentes Georginas offers daily shuttles to the site (Q75 round trip, including entrance fee), leaving at 9am and 2pm from **Xela Café** (Map p148; 6a Calle 9-30) in Quetzaltenango. They return at 1pm and 6pm.

San Francisco El Alto

POP 42,100 / ELEV 2582M

High on a hilltop overlooking Quetzaltenango stands San Francisco El Alto, Guatemala's garment district. Every inch is jammed with vendors selling sweaters, socks, blankets, jeans and more. Bolts of cloth spill from overstuffed storefronts, and that is on the quiet days! On Friday the town explodes as the real **market** action kicks in. The large plaza, surrounded by the church and *municipalidad* and centered on a cupola-like *mirador* (lookout), is covered in goods. Stalls crowd into neighboring streets, and the press of traffic is so great that a special system of one-way roads is established. Vehicles entering the town on market day must pay a small fee.

This is regarded as the country's biggest, most authentic market, but it's not nearly as heavy with handicrafts as are the markets in Chichicastenango and Antigua. Beware of pickpockets and stay alert.

Around mid-morning when the clouds roll away, panoramic views can be had throughout town, especially from the church roof. The caretaker will let you up.

San Francisco's big party is the **Fiesta de San Francisco de Asís**, celebrated around October 4 with traditional dances such as La Danza de Conquista and La Danza de los Monos.

Hotel Vista Hermosa (☎7738-4010; cnr 2a Calle & 3a Av; s/d Q75/150, without bathroom Q35/70) does indeed have beautiful views from its big, comfortable rooms. Good *chuchitos* (small tamales), *chiles rellenos* and

EXPLORE MORE OF QUETZALTENANGO

Looking for more unpolished village life? Three places close to Xela are well worth the minimal effort required:

Los Vahos

The rough-and-ready sauna/steam baths of **Los Vahos** (The Vapors; admission Q10; ⏲8am-6pm), about 3.5km from downtown Xela, make for a good short hike. Take an Almolonga-bound bus and get off at the road to Los Vahos, which is marked with a small sign. From here it's a 2.3km uphill walk. **Altiplano's Tour Operator** (☎7766-9614; www.altiplanos.com.gt; 12a Av 3-35, Zona 1) organizes hikes up here. The views are remarkable.

San Andrés Xecul

Surrounded by fertile hills about 10km northwest of Xela, this small town boasts perhaps the most bizarre **church** anywhere – technicolor saints, angels, flowers and climbing vines share space with whimsical tigers and monkeys on its shocking-yellow facade. Regular buses (Q4.50, 40 minutes) run between Xela and San Andrés.

Zunil

This pretty agricultural market town is set in a lush valley and dominated by a towering volcano. The white colonial church gleams above the red-tiled and rusted-tin roofs of the low houses. The town has a particularly photogenic **church**, and is also home to the **Cooperativa Santa Ana** (⏲8am-6pm) handicrafts cooperative in which over 600 local women participate. Other draws include the weekly market held on Mondays and the image of **San Simón** (p127), an effigy of a local Maya hero venerated as a (non-Catholic) saint. The effigy is moved each year to a different house; ask anyone where to find San Simón. You'll be charged a few quetzals to visit him and take pictures. Buses running between Zunil and Xela (Q7, one hour) stop on the main road, beside the bridge.

other prepared foods are sold from stacks in the marketplace.

Banco Reformador (2a Calle 3-23; ⏲9am-4pm Mon-Fri, 9am-1pm Sat) changes traveler's checks and has a Visa ATM.

Buses to San Francisco leave Quetzaltenango (passing through Cuatro Caminos) frequently throughout the day (Q10, one hour). Arriving from Quetzaltenango on market day, get off on 4a Av at the top of the hill and walk towards the church.

San Miguel Totonicapán

POP 56,700 / ELEV 2500M

San Miguel Totonicapán is a pretty Guatemalan highland town known for its artisans. Shoemakers, weavers, tinsmiths, potters and woodworkers all make and sell their goods here. Market days are Tuesday and Saturday; it's a locals' **market**, not a tourist affair, and it winds down by late morning.

Flanking Totonicapán's 'parque' (as the plaza is called) are the requisite **colonial church** and a wonderful **municipal theater**, built in 1924 and restored in recent years.

Activities

Aventura Maya K'iche' TOUR

(☎5630-0554; kiche78@hotmail.com; 8a Av 2-17) The Casa de la Cultura Totonicapense, a short walk from the lower plaza, holds displays on indigenous culture and crafts. It also administers a wonderful 'Meet the Artisans' program that allows tourists to meet artisans and local families, observing how they live, work and play. A one-day program, requiring two weeks' advance booking, includes visits to various craft workshops (including potters, carvers of wooden masks and musical instruments, and weavers), a bit of sightseeing, a marimba concert and a traditional lunch in a private home. Rates are Q475 per person in groups of four or Q655 including a stay with a local family and two meals.

Sendero Ecológico El Aprisco NATURE RESERVE

(☎5355-0280; admission Q25; ⏲8am-4pm) Encompassing some 13 hectares of old-growth forest northeast of Totonicapán, the Sendero Ecológico El Aprisco makes for some delightful hiking. Well-marked trails traverse the community-run reserve. Pickup trucks head this way from the east end of 7a Calle. Alternatively, Aventura Maya K'iche' can organize trips to the reserve at Q175 per person.

Festivals & Events

Apparition of the Archangel Michael RELIGIOUS FESTIVAL
(May 8) Features fireworks and traditional dances.

Feria Titular de San Miguel Arcángel RELIGIOUS FESTIVAL
(Name-Day Festival of Archangel St Michael; Sep 24-30) Peaks on September 29.

Festival Tradicional de Danza CULTURAL FESTIVAL
(late Oct) Totonicapán keeps traditional masked dances very much alive with this festival.

Sleeping & Eating

Aventura Maya K'iche' can arrange stays with local families, including breakfast and dinner, at Q360/425/500 per person in groups of four/three/two, including dinner and breakfast.

Hospedaje Paco Centro HOTEL $
(7766-2810; 3a Calle 8-18, Zona 2; s/d Q65/130) Practically hidden inside a shopping center a couple blocks from the lower plaza, this sternly managed place has big, tidy rooms of three to four beds each.

Restaurante Bonanza RESTAURANT $$
(7a Calle 7-17, Zona 4; meals Q40-60; 7am-9pm;) Totonicapán's most conventional restaurant is a meat-and-tortillas sort of establishment, where bow-tied staff deliver heaping helpings of steak, chicken and seafood.

Getting There & Away

'Toto' buses from Quetzaltenango (Q6, one hour) depart every 20 minutes or so throughout the day from the Rotonda on Calz Independencia (passing through Cuatro Caminos). The last direct bus to Quetzaltenango leaves Toto at 6:30pm.

Momostenango

POP 51,800 / ELEV 2259M

Beyond San Francisco El Alto, and 35km from Quetzaltenango, Momostenango is Guatemala's famous center for *chamarras* (thick, heavy woolen blankets). The villagers also make ponchos and other woolen garments. As you enter the plaza, you'll see signs inviting you to watch blankets being made and purchase the finished products. The best time to do this is market day, Sunday; haggle like mad.

On market days, the streets will be thronged and so buses will often leave you on 3a Calle. It's about a five-minute walk to the plaza from here – follow the crowd or head toward the church spires.

Momostenango is also noted for its adherence to the ancient Maya calendar and traditional rites. Ceremonies coordinated with the important dates of the calendar take place in the hills about 2km west of the plaza. It's not easy for travelers to witness these rites, though try Takiliben May Wajshakib Batz (p157).

Activities

Takiliben May Wajshakib Batz CULTURAL TOUR
(7736-5537; www.alunajoy.com/wajshakib-batz.html; 3a Av A 6-85, Zona 3; 4-6pm Tue & Thu) This Maya Mission is dedicated to studying and teaching Maya culture and sacred traditions. Its director, Rigoberto Itzep Chanchavac, is a *chuchkajau* (Maya priest) responsible for advising the community on when special days of the Maya calendars fall. His full- or half-day workshops focus on customs that usually remain hidden from outsiders.

The mission also leads a tour of Momostenango, with visits to the sacred hill of Paclom and the ritual hot springs of Payashú (Q100, including a homestay with a local family).

Festivals & Events

Wajshakib Batz' (eight thread), marking the start of the ritual *tzolkin* calender, is considered the holiest day in the cycle, when Maya 'daykeepers' are ordained. During the ceremony, usually enacted atop sacred Paclom hill (accessed from the end of 5a Calle), the candidates for priesthood are presented with a 'sacred bundle' of red seeds and crystals, which they'll use for divination readings based on the ritual calendar, then they dance around the ceremonial fire holding their bundle. As it falls at the end of a 260-day cycle, the date varies from year to year. Contact Takiliben May to find out when it falls in the current year.

Sleeping & Eating

Accommodations are very basic.

Hotel Otoño HOTEL $
(☎7736-5078; gruvial.m@gmail.com; 3a Av A 1-48, Zona 2; r per person Q100) Momostenango's poshest lodging has 14 modern rooms with glossy tile floors and huge bathrooms. Some feature balconies or picture windows taking in the surrounding hills. The hotel restaurant serves all meals.

Information

Banco Reformador (1a Avenida 1-13, Zona 1; ⏲9am-5pm Mon-Fri, 8am-noon Sat) Changes traveler's checks and has a Cajero 5B ATM.

Getting There & Away

You can get buses to Momostenango from Quetzaltenango's Terminal Minerva (Q9, 1½ hours) or from San Francisco El Alto (45 minutes). Buses run about every 15 minutes, with the last one back to Quetzaltenango normally leaving Momostenango at 4:30pm.

Laguna Chicabal

This magical lake, at an elevation of 2712m, is nestled in the crater of Volcán Chicabal on the edge of a cloud forest. Considered a cosmic convergence point by the Mam and K'iche' Maya, it is a sacred place and a hotbed of ceremonial activity. There are Maya altars at each of the four cardinal points along its sandy shores, and Maya worshippers come from far and wide to perform ceremonies and make offerings here. Forty days after Easter Sunday is the observance of 13 Qanil, when faithful farmers flock here to pray for rain. By observing the level of the lagoon and seeing if the roots of surrounding trees are submerged, they can judge whether to plant. Because the lake and grounds have great ceremonial significance, campers and hikers are asked to treat them with the utmost respect.

Adding to the atmosphere of mystery, a veil of fog dances over the water, alternately revealing and hiding the lake's placid contours. Bird watchers might spot quetzals, horned guan and pink headed warblers.

Access to Laguna Chicabal is via the community of Toj Mech, southwest of the town of San Martín Sacatepéquez (also known as Chile Verde) along the road to Colomba. Microbuses from Xela depart every 20 minutes, Monday to Saturday, from 15a Av and 6a Calle in Zona 3 (Q5). These vehicles drop you at a parking lot in Toj Mech. From here, a cheerful fellow named Juan can take you up the steep, deeply rutted road to the park's **Visitor Center** (☎4349-6870; www.lagunadechicabal.com; admission Q15; ⏲7am-3pm) in his red pickup truck (Q60, 15 minutes). A trail leads another 3km uphill to the site. About two-thirds of the way up you'll reach a fork, where you can bear right to go directly to the lagoon, or left up to a *mirador* (observation post) and then a whopping 615 steep steps down to the edge of the lake. Start early for best visibility.

There are good accommodations at the Visitor Center managed by the local Mam community, including a pair of six-sided bungalows with four bunks each (Q40 per person) sharing a cold-water bath house, and a two-level log cabin with private bathrooms (doubles Q75 per person).

Huehuetenango

POP 155,500 / ELEV 1909M

Mostly a stopping-off point for more interesting places, Huehue (*way*-way) offers few charms of its own, but some people do love it for its true Guatemalan character. Either way, there are enough eating and sleeping options here to keep you happy, and the sight of the Cuchumatanes mountain range (the highest in Central America) in the background makes for some striking scenery.

The lively *indígena* (traditional) market is filled daily with traders who come down from surrounding villages. Surprisingly, the market area is about the only place you'll see traditional costumes in this town, as most of its citizens are *ladinos* wearing modern clothes. Coffee growing, mining, sheep raising, light manufacturing and agriculture are the region's main activities.

For travelers, Huehue is usually a leg on the journey to or from Mexico – the logical place to spend your first night in Guatemala. The town is also the perfect staging area for forays deeper into the Cuchumatanes or through the highlands on back roads.

Sights & Activities

Parque Central PLAZA
The main plaza is shaded by old trees and surrounded by imposing buildings: the *municipalidad* and the huge colonial **church**. The plaza has its own little **Mapa en Relieve** of Huehuetenango Department.

Huehuetenango

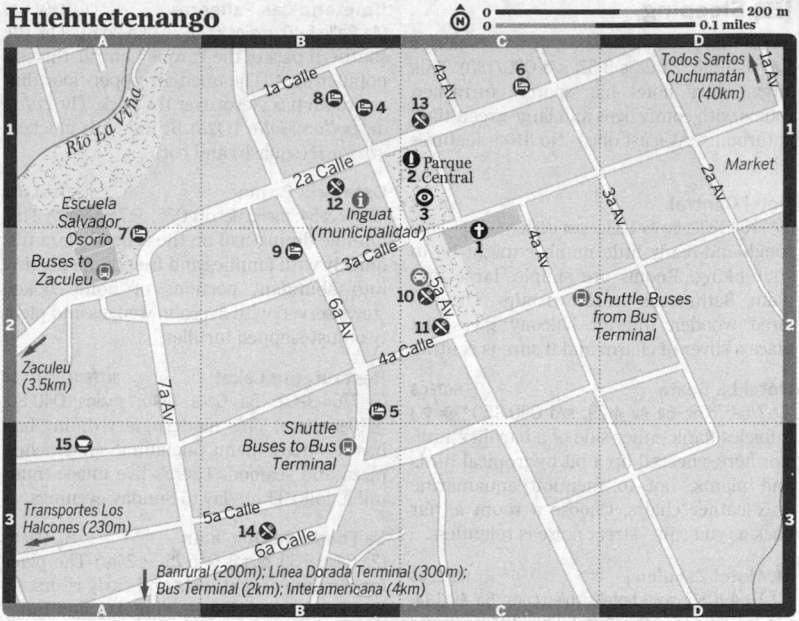

Zaculeu ARCHAEOLOGICAL SITE
(admission Q50; ⏲ 8am-4pm) With ravines on three sides, Zaculeu, a late Postclassic religious center, occupies a strategic defensive location that served its Mam Maya inhabitants well. It finally failed, however, in 1525, when Gonzalo de Alvarado (cousin of Pedro) and his conquistadors laid siege to the site for two months. It was starvation that ultimately defeated the Mam.

The parklike **archaeological zone**, of about 200 sq meters, is 4km west of Huehuetenango's main plaza. Cold soft drinks and snacks are available. A small **museum** at the site holds, among other things, skulls and items found in a tomb beneath Estructura 1, the tallest structure at the site.

Restoration by the United Fruit Company in the 1940s has left Zaculeu's pyramids, ball courts and ceremonial platforms covered by a thick coat of graying plaster. Many of the restoration methods were not authentic, but the work goes further than others in making the site look as it might have done to the Mam priests and worshipers when it was still an active religious center. All that's missing are the colorful frescoes that must have once covered the exterior. The buildings show a great deal of Mexican influence.

Huehuetenango

Sights
1 Church C2
2 Mapa en Relieve C1
3 Parque Central C1

Sleeping
4 Hotel Central B1
5 Hotel La Sexta B2
6 Hotel Mary C1
7 Hotel San Luis de la Sierra A2
8 Hotel Zaculeu B1
9 Royal Park Hotel B2

Eating
10 Cafetería Carilo C2
11 Cafetería Las Palmeras C2
12 La Fonda de Don Juan B1
13 Pastelería Monte Alto C1
14 Restaurante Lekaf B3

Drinking & Nightlife
15 Museo del Café A3

Buses to the site (Q2.50, 20 minutes) leave about every 30 minutes, 7:30am to 6pm, from in front of the school at the corner of 2a Calle and 7a Av. A taxi from the town center costs Q30 one way. One hour is plenty of time to look round the site and museum.

Sleeping

Hotel Mary HOTEL $
(☎7764-1618; 2a Calle 3-52; s/d Q80/130) This large, older hotel has sparely furnished rooms with comfy beds and large green-tiled bathrooms. At least one – No 310 – features a balcony.

Hotel Central HOTEL $
(☎7764-1202; 5a Av 1-33; r per person Q30) This rough-and-ready little number might be to your liking. Rooms are simple, large and plain. Bathrooms are downstairs. The pillared wooden interior balcony gives the place a sliver of charm and it sure is central.

Hotel La Sexta HOTEL $
(☎7764-7559; 6a Av 4-29; s/d Q90/150; @ 📶) Cubicles flank either side of a barnlike interior here, cheered up a bit by tropical birds and plants, not to mention aquamarine faux-leather chairs. Choose a room as far back as you can – street noise is relentless.

★Hotel Zaculeu HOTEL $$
(☎7764-1086; www.hotelzaculeu.com; 5a Av 1-14; s/d/tr Q150/275/290; @ 📶) This 125-year old hotel has oodles of character and 36 big rooms in two sections. Those in the 'new section' are a bit pricier but brighter and more stylish. There's a lovely patio and laid-back bar here, too.

Royal Park Hotel HOTEL $$
(☎7762-7774; hotelroyalpark1@gmail.com; 6a Av 2-34; s/d Q135/270; @ 📶) This business-class hotel is one of Huehue's poshest, with gold filigree bedspreads, padded headboards and jumbo flatscreen TVs. Rooms ending in -08 have mountain views.

Hotel San Luis de la Sierra HOTEL $$
(☎7764-9217; hsanluis@gmail.com; 2a Calle 7-00; s/d Q120/185) The simple, smallish rooms here have pine furniture and homey touches, and there's a decent restaurant on the premises. The real attraction, though, is the rambling rainforest garden out back, with paths for strolling.

Eating & Drinking

Pastelería Monte Alto CAFE $
(2a Calle 4-24; cakes & pastries Q8-15; ⏲9am-9pm) This old-fashioned establishment just off the plaza has a tempting array of cheesecake, eclairs, plum pie and other tantalizing pastries, plus all the essential espresso variations.

Cafetería Las Palmeras GUATEMALAN $
(4a Calle 5-10; mains Q25; ⏲7am-9pm) On the southern part of the Parque Central, this is a popular spot. The open-air upper-floor dining room has views over the park. The *caldo de pollo criollo* (Q25) brims with chicken, *güisquil* (squash) and corn.

Cafetería Carilo GUATEMALAN $
(5a Av 3-54; menú del día Q25; ⏲7am-9pm) This humble dining hall on the central plaza fills quickly with families and friends, all digging into abundant portions of home-cooked stews served with avocado wedges and plenty of just-slapped tortillas.

Restaurante Lekaf INTERNATIONAL $$
(☎7764-3202; 6a Calle 6-40; mains Q40-80; ⏲10am-11pm) This modern, airy dining hall has a varied menu, including sandwiches, pizza and seafood. There's live music (marimba, folk) Thursday to Sunday evenings.

La Fonda de Don Juan PIZZERIA $$
(2a Calle 5-35; pizzas Q45-75; ⏲24hr) The place for Huehue's night owls and early risers, La Fonda serves varied Guatemalan and international fare, including good-value pizzas.

Museo del Café CAFE
(www.cafemuseohuehue.com; 4a Calle 7-40; ⏲7am-9:30pm Mon-Sat; 📶) This 'museum' serves some of Huehue's best coffee, and that's saying something. More than just a place to get a well-prepared cup, it also provides some background on this bewitching bean that has so influenced Guatemala's history. The various salons and delightful patio buzz with java hounds from early morning till late evening.

After examining antique coffee-processing paraphernalia and some diagrams demonstrating coffee production techniques, you can roast your own for purchase. Owner Manrique López, son of a small-scale producer from Barrillas, also organizes coffee plantation tours.

Information

The town center is 4km northeast of the Interamericana. An **Inguat** (☎5768-7078; Parque Central; ⏲8am-noon & 2-5pm) office is reportedly inside the *municipalidad* though it seems seldom occupied.

Banco Industrial (6a Av 1-26), a block west of the main plaza, has a reliable ATM.

Getting There & Away

The bus terminal is in Zona 4, 2km southwest of the plaza along 6a Calle. A number of companies ply the same routes, though information is not posted in any coherent fashion. For 2nd-class bus schedules, see the table below. Microbuses leave from the south end of the station. Another stop, for microbuses to Cobán and Barrillas, via Soloma and San Mateo Ixtatán, is by a gas station at El Calvario, at the corner of 1a Av and 1a Calle, four blocks northeast of the Parque Central.

Two lines run Pullman buses to Guatemala City from their own private terminals: **Transportes Los Halcones** (☎7765-7986; www.transportesloshalcones.com; 10a Av 9-12, Zona 1) leaves at least five times a day (Q65), with deluxe service at 7am and 2pm; **Línea Dorada** (☎7768-1566; www.lineadorada.com.gt; 8a Calle 8-70) departs at 11pm (Q110).

The road from Huehuetenango to Cobán is rarely traveled and is often rugged, particularly since a major landslide buried a section of it, making a hair-raising detour necessary. Starting early and with several transfers, you can make the 150km trip in one day. It's well worth it for the views of highland life along the way.

Another option is to catch a Barrillas-bound bus, stay the night in one of the basic but doable hotels there, then head on to Playa Grande (Q50, four hours) in a pickup truck. From Playa Grande there are regular buses to Cobán (Q50, three hours).

Around Huehuetenango

Todos Santos Cuchumatán

POP 4100 / ELEV 2450M

Way up in the highlands, Todos Santos is as raw as Guatemalan village life gets – dramatic mountain scenery, mud streets, beans and tortillas, and everything shut by 9pm. There are a couple of language schools operating here and this is the end point for the spectacular hike from Nebaj. Hiking is also good in the local hills. Saturday is market day, with a smaller market on Wednesday. The notorious post-market inebriation ritual has faded into history since dry laws took over (the November 1 celebrations now being the only permissible time to get smashed).

The post office and Banrural are on the central plaza. The bank changes US dollars and traveler's checks. There is no ATM in town.

If you're coming to Todos Santos in winter, bring warm clothes.

Sights

Museo Balam MUSEUM

(admission Q5; ⏲8am-6pm) Todos Santos' museum is in a two-story house, along a sidestreet one block east of the plaza. The collection of outfits and masks, traditional kitchen implements, archaeological finds and musical instruments comes to life when Fortunato,

2ND-CLASS BUSES FROM HUEHUETENANGO

DESTINATION	COST (Q)	DURATION	DEPARTURES	FREQUENCY
Aguacatán	8	30 min	6am-7pm	every 20 min
Barrillas	50	7 hr	4:30am-2:30pm	hourly
Cobán	70	6 hr	1:40pm	one daily
Gracias a Dios (Mexican border)	30	4 hr	10am-4pm	4 daily
Guatemala City	60	5 hr	6am-4pm	every 30 min
La Mesilla (Mexican border)	20	2½ hr	3am-6pm	every 30 min
Quetzaltenango	20	2 hr	3am-6pm	every 15 min
Sacapulas	20	2 hr	11:30am & 12:45pm	2 daily
Santa Cruz del Quiché	25	2 hr	5am-5pm	every 15 min
Soloma	25	3 hr	4:30am-2:30pm	hourly
Todos Santos Cuchumatán	25	2 hr	4am-2:30pm	4 daily

its creator and a community leader, is there to provide commentary.

Activities

This is spectacular hiking country and there are many walks you don't need a guide for, the trailheads for which are either in town or a short bus ride away. Ask around for directions to **La Torre**, the highest non-volcanic point in Central America or **Las Cuevas**, a sacred cave where local Maya still perform rituals.

Rigoberto Pablo Cruz HIKING
(☎5206-0916; rigoguiadeturismo@yahoo.com) Knowledgeable, easygoing and English-speaking *todosantero* Rigoberto leads walks of the area, including a climb to the peak of La Torre followed by a descent to La Maceta. Another of Rigo's hikes reaches the isolated mountain community of San Juan Atitán, where the women wear dazzling *huipiles*, in about five hours, returning by bus to Todos Santos.

In addition, Rigoberto leads two-day treks to Nebaj (Q800 per person with minimum of two), including food and lodging in community dwellings. He also offers classes in both Spanish and Mam.

Festivals & Events

El Día de Todos los Santos
(⏲Nov 1) Todos Santos is famous for the annual horse races held on El Día de Todos los Santos, the culmination of a week of festivities and an all-night male dancing and *aguardiente* (sugarcane liquor) drinking spree on the eve of the races. Traditional foods are served throughout the day and there are mask dances.

Sleeping & Eating

Hotel Casa Familiar HOTEL $
(☎7783-0656; adelamendozaj@yahoo.es; s/d/tr without bath Q60/90/120) Undergoing major renovations at the time of writing, this central lodging has the town's coziest rooms, with hardwood floors, window frames, traditional textile bedspreads, good hot showers and plenty of blankets. New features include a common room with fireplace and a roof deck with a *chuj* (traditional Maya sauna).

Hotelito Todos Santos HOTEL $
(☎7783-0603; r Q125, s/d without bathroom Q45/90) Along a side street that goes off to the left a few meters up the hill beside the plaza. This budget option has small and bare, but well-scrubbed, rooms with tiled floors and firm beds.

Comedor Katy GUATEMALAN $
(meals Q22) Women in traditional garb attend to pots of *pepián* and chicken soup bubbling over glowing embers at this rustic cook shack just below the central plaza. Tables on the terrace overlook the market.

Comedor Evelín GUATEMALAN $
(⏲6am-8pm Mon-Sat) This often busy eatery features two dining halls; you'll find the menu scrawled on a styrofoam board at the back. Lunchtime it serves such classic traditional fare as *pepián de pollo* and *caldo de res*. It's 100m east of the plaza, turning uphill at the bookstore.

Getting There & Away

Buses and microbuses depart from the main street between the plaza and the church. About 10 buses leave for Huehuetenango (Q25, 2½ hours) between 4:30am and 2pm. Microbuses leave throughout the day, whenever they fill up. There are three buses northwest to Jacaltenango at 4:30am, 5am and 6am. The first goes all the way to the Mexican border at La Mesilla.

THE PACIFIC SLOPE

Divided from the highlands by a chain of volcanoes, the flatlands that run down to the Pacific are known universally as La Costa. It's a sultry region – hot and wet or hot and dry, depending on the time of year, with rich volcanic soil good for growing coffee at higher elevations, and palm-oil seeds and sugarcane lower down.

Archaeologically, the big draws here are Takalik Abaj and the sculptures left by pre-Olmec civilizations around Santa Lucía Cotzumalguapa

The culture is overwhelmingly *ladino*, and even the biggest towns are humble affairs, with low-rise wooden or concrete houses and the occasional palm-thatched roof.

Guatemalan beach tourism is seriously underdeveloped. Monterrico is the only real contender in this field, helped along by a nature reserve protecting mangroves and their inhabitants. Almost every town on the beach has places to stay, although more often than not they're very basic affairs. Sipacate gets the best waves and is slowly developing as a surf resort, although serious surfers find much more joy in Mexico or El Salvador.

Retalhuleu

POP 43,700

Arriving at the bus station in Retalhuleu or Reu (*ray*-oo) as it's known to most Guatemalans, you're pretty much guaranteed to be underwhelmed. The neighborhood in which the bus station is located is a tawdry affair, packed out with dilapidated wooden *cantinas* and street vendors.

The town center, just five blocks away, is like another world – a majestic, palm-filled plaza, surrounded by some fine old buildings. Even the city police get in on the act, hanging plants outside their headquarters. To find the plaza, look for the twin church towers and walk toward them.

On the outskirts are the homes of wealthy plantation owners, impressive weekend getaways and the gated communities that are springing up all over the country.

Sights

The main reason most people visit the town is for access to the Takalik Abaj site, but if you're up for some serious downtime, a couple of world-class fun parks, **Xocomil** (☎7772-9400; www.irtra.org.gt; Carretera CITO Km 180.5; adult/child Q100/50; ⏲9am-5pm Thu-Sun) and **Xetulul** (☎7722-9450; www.irtra.org.gt; Carretera CITO Km 180.5; adult/child Q100/50; ⏲10am-6pm Thu-Sun), are just down the road.

Museo de Arqueología y Etnología MUSEUM

(6a Av 5-68; admission Q15; ⏲8:30am-12:30pm & 2-5:30pm Mon-Fri, 9am-12:30pm Sat) The Museo de Arqueología y Etnología is a small museum with archaeological relics. Upstairs are historical photos and a mural showing the locations of 33 archaeological sites around Retalhuleu.

Sleeping

La Estancia HOTEL $

(☎7771-3053; 10a Calle 8-50, Zona 1; s/d Q100/180; ❄📶) The best budget deal in town with simple, clean rooms. A couple of blocks from the bus stop.

Hostal Casa Santa María HOTEL $

(☎7771-6136; www.hostalcasasantamaria.com; 4a Calle 4-23, Zona 1; s/d from Q160/250; ❄📶🏊) One of the more atmospheric options in Retalhuleu, this small hotel offers eight cool and spacious rooms with minimal but tasteful decorations. The small swimming pool in the courtyard is a good place for a dip.

Hotel Casa y Campo HOTEL $$

(☎7771-3289; 3a Calle 4-73, Zona 1; s/d Q125/250; ❄📶) Comfortable, good-value rooms a couple of blocks from the plaza. This one books up fast, so it's worth calling ahead.

AGROTOURISM AROUND RETALHULEU

With so many beautiful *fincas* (farms) in gorgeous rural settings, it was only a matter of time before agrotourism started to take hold in Guatemala. This is seriously low-impact tourism – often you can stay in the original farmhouse and tours basically consist of walking around the property. These are all working farms – if you're planning on staying, get in touch a few days in advance to let them know you're coming. See the websites for transportation details.

Aldea Loma Linda (☎4996-2110; www.asodill.org; r per person without bathroom volunteers/visitors Q25/50) A beautiful village nestled in the southern foothills of the Santa María volcano. Accommodations are basic but comfortable and volunteer work is available.

Finca Santa Elena (☎7772-5294; www.fincasantaelena.com; Carretera a Quetzaltenango Km 187; per person without bathroom Q125-140; 📶) One of the most easily accessible *fincas* in the region offering wonderfully informative tours. Accommodations are in the lovely wooden farmhouse.

Comunidad Nueva Alianza (☎5348-5290; www.comunidadnuevaalianza.org; dm/s/d without bathroom Q65/85/170; @) Set on a hillside overlooking the coast, this farm has gorgeous views and a great hike to a nearby waterfall. Short tours are information-packed and there are various short- and long-term volunteer positions available.

Eating

Reu seems to be slightly obsessed by pizza – 5a Av north of the plaza is almost wall-to-wall pizzerias.

Cafetería La Luna GUATEMALAN $
(cnr 8a Av & 5a Calle, Zona 1; mains Q25-60; ⏲8am-10pm) A block off the plaza this is a town favorite for simple but filling meals in a low-key environment.

Information

There is no official tourist office, but people in the **municipalidad** (Town Hall; 6a Av) facing the east side of the church, do their best to help.

Banco Agromercantil (5a Av) Facing the plaza, changes US dollars and traveler's checks and has a MasterCard ATM.

Banco Industrial (cnr 6a Calle & 5a Av) Changes US dollars and traveler's checks and has a Visa ATM.

Getting There & Away

Most buses traveling along the Carretera al Pacífico detour into Reu. The bus terminal is northeast of the plaza.

Shared taxis (Q7) are the best way to get to El Asintal (for Takalik Abaj). Look for station wagons with 'Asintal' painted on the windscreen around the bus stop and plaza.

Parque Arqueológico Takalik Abaj

The active archaeological dig at Takalik Abaj (tah-kah-*leek* ah-*bah,* K'iche' for 'standing stone') is 30km west of Retalhuleu. Large Olmecoid stone heads discovered here date the site as one of the earliest in the Maya realm. The **site** (admission Q50; ⏲7am-5pm) has yet to be restored and prettified, so don't expect a Chichén Itzá or Tikal. But if you want to see archaeology as it's done, pay a visit. This site is believed to be one of the few places where the Olmec and Maya lived together.

Set on the grounds of a working farm 2km past the entrance to the Takalik Abaj (and on top of a large, unexcavated section of it) **Takalik Maya Lodge** (☎2334-7693; www.takalik.com; bungalow/farmhouse Q490/330) is by far the most comfortable place to stay in the area. Accommodation options include the old farmhouse, or newly constructed 'Maya-style' houses set in the middle of the forest. Check the website for package deals including accommodation, meals and tours of the coffee, macadamia and rubber plantation as well as guided horseback tours of the waterfalls on the property and the archaeological site. Any pickup from El Asintal passing Takalik Abaj will drop you at the entrance.

To reach Takalik Abaj by public transportation, catch a shared taxi from Retalhuleu to El Asintal (Q7, 30 minutes), which is 12km northwest of Retalhuleu and 5km north of the Carretera al Pacífico. Less frequent buses leave from a bus station on 5a Av A, 800m southwest of Reu plaza, about every half hour from 6am to 6pm. Pickups at El Asintal provide transportation on to Takalik Abaj (Q5), 4km further by paved road. You'll be shown around by a volunteer guide, whom you will probably want to tip. You can also visit Takalik Abaj on tours from Quetzaltenango.

Champerico

The most accessible beach from Xela, Champerico isn't a bad place for a quick dip, although the rubbish-strewn sand and heavy undertow are definite turnoffs. It's a good place to avoid on weekends when the place packs out, but midweek is much mellower. A

BUSES FROM RETALHULEU

DESTINATION	COST (Q)	DURATION	DEPARTURES	FREQUENCY
El Asintal	Q5	30 min	6am-6pm	every 30 min
Champerico	10	1hr	6am-7pm	every few minutes
Tecún Umán (Mexican Border)	15	1½ hr	5am-10pm	every 20 min
Guatemala City	50-80	3hr	2am-8:30pm	every 15 min
Quetzaltenango	15	1hr	4am-6pm	every 30 min
Santa Lucía Cotzumalguapa	25	2hr		every 30 min

string of beachfront *comedores* serve good-value seafood dishes.

Beware of strong waves and an undertow if you go in the ocean, and stay in the main, central part of the beach. If you stray too far in either direction you put yourself at risk from impoverished, potentially desperate shack dwellers who live toward the ends of the beach; tourists have been victims of violent armed robberies here. Most beachgoers come on day trips, but there are several cheap hotels and restaurants. **Hotel Maza** (☎7773-7180; s/d Q150/250; ❄), on the beachfront, is the best bet. The last buses back to Quetzaltenango leave at about 6pm, a bit later for Retalhuleu.

Santa Lucía Cotzumalguapa

POP 111,700

A very ordinary coastal town, Santa Lucía stretches haphazardly over a couple of hills. The pace is sleepy and there's no real reason to be here, except to check out the remarkable archaeological sites outside of town, where huge, severe stone heads sit nestled among sugar plantations.

The local people of this area are descended from the Pipil, an indigenous culture known to have historical, linguistic and cultural links with the Nahuatl-speaking peoples of central Mexico. During the early Classic period, the Pipil grew cacao, the currency of the time. They were obsessed with the Maya-Aztec *juego de pelota* (ball game) – it's thought that the players had to try to keep a hard rubber ball airborne using any part of their body other than their hands, head or feet – and with the rites and mysteries of death.

Pipil art, unlike the flowery, almost romantic Maya style, is cold and severe, but it's finely done. Just how these 'Mexicans' ended up in the midst of Maya territory remains unexplained.

Sights

Taxi drivers in Santa Lucía's main square will take you around all three sites for about Q200 without too much haggling. In this hot and muggy climate, riding at least part of the way is a very good idea. If you do it all on foot and by bus, pack a lunch; the hilltop site at El Baúl is perfect for a picnic.

El Baúl Hilltop Site ARCHAEOLOGICAL SITE

This archaeological site has the additional fascination of being an active place of worship for locals. If you visit this hilltop site on a weekend, you may find worshippers here; people have been coming to pay homage to the idols for over 1400 years.

Of the two stones here, the great grotesque half-buried head is the more striking. The elaborate headdress, 'blind' eyes with big bags underneath, beaklike nose and smug grin seem at odds with the blackened face and its position, half-buried in the ancient soil. The head is stained with candle wax, liquor, and the smoke and ashes of incense fires – all part of worship. The other stone is a relief carving of a figure surrounded by circular motifs that may be date glyphs. A copy of this stone is in Santa Lucía's main square.

El Baúl is 4.2km northwest of El Calvario church. From the church (or the intersection just beyond it), go 2.7km to a fork in the road just beyond a bridge. The fork is marked by the entrance to the Ciudad España housing development – buses will go up to here. Take the right fork (an unpaved road). From the Los Tarros sign it's 1.5km to the point where a dirt track crosses the road; on your right is a tree-covered 'hill' in the midst of flat fields. It's actually a great, unrestored temple platform. Make your way across the field and around the hill's south side, following the track to the top. If you have a car, you can drive to within 50m of the top.

Museo El Baúl MUSEUM

(⏲8am-4pm Mon-Fri, 8am-noon Sat) FREE Museo El Baúl comprises a very fine open-air collection of Pipil stone sculpture collected from around Finca El Baúl's sugarcane fields. A large stone jaguar faces you at the entrance. Other figures include four humans or monkeys with arms folded across their chests, a grinning, blank-eyed head reminiscent of the one at the hilltop site and carvings of skulls.

From the hilltop site, backtrack 1.5km to the fork with the Los Tarros sign. Take the other fork this time, and follow the paved road 3km to the headquarters of Finca El Baúl. (If you're on foot, you can walk from the hilltop site back to the unpaved road and straight across it, continuing on the dirt track. This will eventually bring you to the asphalt road that leads to the *finca* headquarters. When you reach the road, turn right.) Buses trundle along this road every few hours, shuttling workers between the refinery and the town center.

Approaching the *finca* headquarters (6km from Santa Lucía's main square), cross a narrow bridge. Continue uphill and you will see the entrance on the left, marked by a machine-gun pillbox. Beyond, you pass workers' houses and a sugar refinery on the right, and finally come to the headquarters. Ask permission to visit the museum and a guard will unlock the gate.

Bilbao Stones ARCHAEOLOGICAL SITE
This ceremonial center flourished about AD 600. Plows have unearthed (and damaged) hundreds of carved stones during the last few centuries; thieves have carted off many others. In 1880 many of the best stones were removed to museums abroad.

Monumento 21, whose copy is in the Museo Cultura Cotzumalguapa, still stands with three other fine sculpted stones dotted about the Finca Bilbao cane fields to the northeast of El Calvario church, on the north edge of Santa Lucía town.

In the past, tourists have regularly visited these stones, often guided through the tall cane to Las Piedras (the Stones) by local boys, but this is an isolated area and assaults on tourists are not unknown – ask around to find out what the current safety situation is.

Museo Cultura Cotzumalguapa MUSEUM
(admission Q25; ⏲ 7am-1pm & 2-4pm Mon-Fri, 7am-1pm Sat) This indoor museum is very close to Bilbao – set in the *finca* that controls the Bilbao sugarcane fields – but, paradoxically, access is more difficult. Your reward is the chance to view hundreds of objects that have been collected from the fields over the centuries.

About 1.5km east of the town center on Carretera al Pacífico, shortly before the Tecún farm-supplies depot, take a side track 400m to the left (north) to find the museum.

Sleeping & Eating

Probably the nicest place to eat is **Robert's** (Carretera al Pacifico Km 89; mains Q50-150; ⏲ 11:30am-10pm), a steak house with leafy outdoor seating. Across the highway is **Beer House** (Carretera al Pacifico Km 89; mains Q40-80; ⏲ 1-11pm) which does good burgers and OK meals.

Hotel Internacional HOTEL $
(☎ 7882-5504; Callejón los Mormones; s/d Q110/160; ❄) Down a short signposted lane off Carretera al Pacífico is the best budget hotel in town. It has clean, good-sized rooms with a fan, cold showers and a TV. Air-conditioning costs Q70 extra. The attached restaurant serves meals (Q20 to Q40).

Hotel El Camino HOTEL $$
(☎ 7882-5316; Carretera al Pacífico, Km 90.5; s/d Q160/270; ❄ 📶) Hotel El Camino's rooms are almost ridiculously large, with a few sticks of furniture like clothes racks and writing tables. You could organize a game of five a side with the rest of the floor space, but don't tell management it was our idea. The attached restaurant serves meals (Q40 to Q80).

Information

Banco Industrial (cnr 4a Av & 4a Calle), a block north of the park, changes US dollars and traveler's checks and has a Visa ATM.

Getting There & Away

As Hwy 2 now bypasses Santa Lucía, a lot of buses along it do not come into town. Coming to Santa Lucía from the east, you will almost certainly need to change buses at Escuintla (Q11, 30

BEACH LIFE ALONG THE PACIFIC COAST

The coast is, logically, all about the beach. The two most popular beach spots for travelers happen to be the ones closest to Quetzaltenango and Antigua – Champerico and Monterrico. There are, however, plenty of little beach towns that are worth considering, where quite often you'll have the place to yourself:

➡ Literally a one-hotel village, **Tilapita** is a great place to get away from it all and take a couple of mangrove tours while you're at it.

➡ The coastline's gentle slope into the ocean makes **Tulate** one of Guatemala's best swimming beaches.

➡ A mellow little beach town that's way off the beaten track, **Chiquistepeque** has a community literacy program that is always looking for volunteers.

minutes). From the west you will probably have to change at Mazatenango (Q15, 1¼ hours). At Cocales, 23km west of Santa Lucía, a road down from Lago de Atitlán meets Hwy 2, providing a route to or from the highlands. Eight buses daily run from Cocales to Panajachel (Q28, 2½ hours, 70km, between about 6am and 2pm). Ask about the current situation, as there have been reports of robberies along this stretch of road in the past.

La Democracia

POP 17,500

A sleepy little village on the way to the beach, La Democracia makes it on the map for further investigation into the mysterious, ancient culture that carved the heads found around Santa Lucía.

At the **Monte Alto archaeological site**, on the outskirts of town, huge basalt heads have been found. Although cruder, the heads resemble those carved by the Olmec near Veracruz several thousand years ago. Today these heads are arranged around La Democracia's main plaza. As you come into town from the highway, follow signs to the *museo*, which will lead you left, then left again, and left yet again.

Facing the plaza, along with the church and the modest Palacio Municipal, is the small, modern **Museo Regional de Arqueologia** (☎7880-3650; admission Q30; ⏲8am-4pm Tue-Sat) which houses some fascinating archaeological finds. The star of the show is an exquisite jade mask. Smaller figures, 'yokes' used in the ball game, relief carvings and other objects make up the rest of this small but important collection.

Half a block from the plaza, **Guest House Paxil de Cayala** (☎7880-3129; s/d without bathroom Q50/100), the only place to stay, is OK for the night, with big, mosquito-proofed rooms. Just off the square, **Burger Chops** (mains Q25-45; ⏲8am-9pm) is as close as the town gets to a restaurant. The flour tortillas stuffed with meat from the little roadside stands around the plaza are delicious, and a bargain at Q20.

There is a 5B ATM on the main plaza.

The Chatía Gomerana company runs buses every half-hour from 6am to 4:30pm, from the Centra Sur terminal in Guatemala City to La Democracia (Q20, two hours) via Escuintla. From Santa Lucía Cotzumalguapa, catch a bus 8km east to Siquinalá (8km) and change there.

Sipacate

An hour and a half down the road from Santa Lucía is Guatemala's surf capital. Waves here average 6ft (2m), the best time being between December and April. The town is separated from the beach by the Canal de Chiquimulilla. Oddly unexploited, the beach here has only a couple of hotels, the budget choice being **El Paradon** (☎4994-1842; www.paredonsurf.com; campsite/dm Q30/80, s/d from Q240/320), a rustic little surf camp to the east of the village; see the website for directions. It's run by a couple of Guatemalan surfers, and board and kayak hire, surf lessons and good, simple meals (Q50 to Q80) are available. Book in advance.

Straight across the canal from Sipacate is **Rancho Carillo** (☎5517-1069; www.marmaya.com; r Q500, 6-person bungalow Q1000; ❄📶🏊), a short boat ride (Q10 return) from town. The only trouble you'll have sleeping is from the noise of crashing waves. Call ahead and you'll probably be able to get a better price. Surfboards are available for rent here. There are a couple of cheaper, basic *hospedajes* (singles/doubles Q60/100) in town, but remember you'll be paying for the boat ride every day. Buses from Guatemala City's Centra Sur terminal (Q32, 3½ hours) pass through La Democracia en route to Sipacate every two hours.

Escuintla

POP 166,800 / TRANSPORT HUB

Hot, noisy and crowded, Escuintla has good bus connections and very little else for the average traveler. Banks are located around the plaza. There's an ATM in the **Farmacia Herdez** (cnr 13a Calle & 4a Av), one block uphill from the bus terminal. Escuintla has some marginal hotels and restaurants. If stranded, try the **Hotel Costa Sur** (☎7888-1819; 12a Calle 4-13; s/d fan Q80/110, air-con Q110/130; ❄), a couple of doors from Banco Reformador, which has decent, cool rooms with TV and fan. Air-con costs an extra Q20. The **Hotel Sarita** (☎7888-1959; Av Centro América 15-32; s/d Q380/480; ❄📶🏊), behind the gloriously air-conditioned restaurant (mains Q40 to Q70) of the same name, provides more comfort.

All buses from the terminal pass along 1a Av, but if you really want to get a seat, head to the main bus station in the southern part of town, just off 4a Av. The station entrance is marked by a Scott 77 fuel station. Buses depart for Antigua (Q7, one hour) about every half-hour, from 5:30am to 4:30pm. Buses going to Guatemala City (Q20, 1½ hours) go about every 20 minutes from the street outside, from 5am to 6pm. Buses to Puerto San José (Q5 to Q10, 45 minutes), some continuing to Iztapa, have similar frequency. There are buses all the way through to Monterrico (Q25, one hour) at 12:50pm and 4:50pm; otherwise catch a bus to Puerto San José or Iztapa and make a connection there. Buses coming along the Carretera al Pacífico may drop you in the north of town, necessitating a sweaty walk through the hectic town center if you want to get to the main station.

Monterrico

A favorite for weekending Guatemalans (and Antigua-based language students), Monterrico is a relatively pretty town that is slowly developing into a coastal resort.

On the outskirts, particularly to the south, are some very opulent weekend houses owned by Guatemala City movers and shakers. Seeing these mansions next to simple thatched-roof huts is a stark reminder of the polarity of Guatemala's economic reality.

Swimming is good here, and there's occasionally a wave worth surfing. Take care, though – a vicious undertow claims victims every year.

Weekends can be hectic. Come on a weekday and you'll find a much mellower scene (with lower hotel prices). The village has a post office (on Calle Principal) but no bank. The Proyecto Lingüístico Monterrico is the best source of tourist information in town.

Behind the beach is a large network of mangrove swamps and canals, part of the 190km Canal de Chiquimulilla. Also in the area is a large wildlife reserve and a center for the hatching and release of sea turtles and caimans (crocodilians similar to alligators).

Sights & Activities

Biotopo Monterrico-Hawaii WILDLIFE RESERVE

A big attraction is the Biotopo Monterrico-Hawaii, a 20km-long nature reserve of coastal mangrove swamps filled with bird and aquatic life. The reserve is a breeding area for endangered leatherback and olive ridley turtles, who lay their eggs on the beach in many places along the coast.

Canals lace the swamps, connecting 25 lagoons hidden among the mangroves. **Boat tours** of the reserve, passing through the mangrove swamps and visiting several lagoons, take around 1½ to two hours and cost Q75 for one person, Q50 for additional people. Sunrise is the best time for wildlife. If you have binoculars, bring them for bird-watching, which is best in January and February. Locals will approach you on the street (some with very impressive-looking ID cards) offering tours, but the Cecon-run Tortugario Monterrico have the most environmentally knowledgeable guides. You can arrange a tour directly through them.

Tortugario Monterrico WILDLIFE CONSERVATION (admission Q50; ⏲ 7am-5pm) Tortugario Monterrico visitors center is just a short walk east down the beach and back a block from the Monterrico hotels (left, if you're facing the sea). Several endangered species of animals are raised here, including leatherback, olive ridley and green sea turtles, caimans and iguanas. There's an interesting **interpretative trail** and a little **museum** with pickled displays in bottles. The staff offer **lagoon trips** and **night walks** (Q50) from September to February to look for turtle eggs, and will accept volunteers.

Around sunset nightly from September to January on the beach in front of the *tortugario*, workers release baby turtles. For a Q10 donation you can 'buy' a turtle and release it. Despite what everybody else is doing, please refrain from using flash cameras and flashlights – the poor little things are probably already terrified and the flash may harm their eyes.

Parque Hawaii WILDLIFE RESERVE (☎ 4743-4655; www.arcasguatemala.com; ⏲ 8am-5pm) Parque Hawaii comprises a sea-turtle hatchery with some caimans 8km east along the beach from Monterrico. It is separate from and rivals Cecon's work in the same field. Volunteers are welcome year-round, but the real sea-turtle–nesting season is from June to November, with August and September being the peak months. Volunteers are charged Q580 a week for a room, with meals extra and homestay options. A bus (Q5, 30 minutes) leaves the Monterrico jetty every couple of hours during the week and every hour on weekends for the bumpy ride to the reserve. Pickups (Q30 per person) also operate on this route. Check out the Arcas website for more information.

Tours & Courses

Productos Mundiales BOAT TOUR
(Map p100; ☎2366-1026; www.productosmundiales.com; 11 Ave 10-13, Zona 10, Guatemala City) Guatemala City–based Productos Mundiales offers marine wildlife-watching tours (from Q1560 per person, six hours), leaving from nearby Puerto Iztapa. Throughout the year you stand a pretty good chance of seeing pilot whales, bottlenose dolphins, spinner dolphins, olive ridley turtles, leatherback turtles, giant manta rays and whale sharks. From December to May, humpback and sperm whales can also be seen. Reservations (five days in advance via bank account deposit) are essential – see its website for details.

Proyecto Lingüístico Monterrico LANGUAGE COURSE
(☎5475-1265; espanolmonterrico@yahoo.com; Calle Principal) Proyecto Lingüístico Monterrico is a recommended Spanish school based in central Monterrico. Twenty hours of tuition per week costs Q710; tuition with homestay (Q1100) or self-catering accommdations (Q1200) also available.

Sleeping & Eating

Many hotels are on the beach. To save a difficult, hot walk along the beach, take the last road to the left before you hit the sand. All these hotels, except for Hostel El Gecko, either front or back onto it. The majority have restaurants serving whatever is fresh from the sea that day. Many accommodations offer discounts for stays of three nights or more. Reserve for weekends if you want to avoid a long, hot walk while you cruise around asking for vacancies. Weekend prices are given here. Midweek, you'll have plenty more bargaining power.

There are many simple seafood restaurants on Calle Principal. For the best cheap eats, hit either of the two nameless *comedores* on the last road to the right before the beach, where you can pick up an excellent plate of garlic shrimp, rice tortillas, fries and salad for Q40.

Brisas del Mar HOTEL $
(☎5517-1142; r per person with fan/air-con Q100/150; ❄) Behind Johnny's, one block back from the beach, this popular newcomer offers good-sized rooms and a 2nd-floor dining hall with excellent sea views.

Johnny's Place HOTEL $
(☎5812-0409; www.johnnysplacehotel.com; dm Q45, s/d without bathroom Q70/140, r Q240-650, bungalows Q500-950;) The first place you come to turning left on the beach, Johnny's is one of the biggest operations in town. There's a huge variety of rooms on offer – truly something to suit every budget, and so attracts a good mix of backpackers and family groups.

Hostel El Gecko HOSTEL $
(☎5251-3522; dm Q50; @) Heading right from Calle Principal, the first place you'll come to is this very basic hostel run by a couple of young Guatemalans. There are very few frills here, but it's a backpackers' favorite, for the cheap beds and friendly atmosphere.

Hotel Pez de Oro BUNGALOW $$
(☎2368-3684; www.pezdeoro.com; s/d Q350/440;) This is the funkiest looking place in town, with comfortable little huts and bungalows scattered around a shady property. The color scheme is a cheery blue and yellow and the rooms have some tasteful decorations and big overhead fans. The excellent restaurant, with big sea views, serves great Italian cuisine and seafood dishes.

★**Taberna El Pelicano** ITALIAN, SEAFOOD $$
(mains Q40-110; ⏲12-2pm & 6-10pm Wed-Sun) By far the best place to eat in town, with the widest menu and most interesting food, such as seafood risotto (Q80), beef Carpaccio (Q75) and a range of jumbo shrimp dishes (Q140).

Drinking & Nightlife

Las Mañanitas BAR
(⏲12pm-late) On the beachfront at the end of the main street, this little beach bar is what Monterrico really needed – plenty of hammock chairs looking out over the beach, a good range of drinks and low-key music playing in the background.

Playa Club CLUB
This club, located at Johnny's Place, heats up on weekends, with plenty of reggaetón, house music and drinks specials keeping the crowd moving.

Getting There & Away

There are two ways to get to Monterrico: direct bus or shuttle bus to/from Guatemala City or Antigua, or via a bus to La Avellana then a car ferry or *lancha* to Monterrico.

BUS

Coming from Guatemala City or Antigua, it's most logical to catch a bus which, with the new bridge at Pueblo Viejo, goes right through to Monterrico. The Pueblo Viejo–Monterrico stretch makes for a pretty journey, revealing local life at a sane pace.

Shuttle buses also serve Monterrico. The most reliable leaves from outside the Proyecto Lingüístico Monterrico at 1pm and 4pm and charges Q70/150 to Antigua/Guatemala City. Book tickets and enquire for other destinations at the school.

BOAT

The other option is to head to La Avellana, where *lanchas* and car ferries depart for Monterrico. The Cubanita company runs a handful of direct buses to and from Guatemala City (Q40, four hours, 124km). Alternatively, you reach La Avellana by changing buses at Taxisco on Hwy 2. Buses operate half-hourly from 5am to 4pm between Guatemala City and Taxisco (Q35, 3½ hours) and roughly hourly from 7am to 4:30pm between Taxisco and La Avellana (Q5, 40 minutes), although taxi drivers will tell you that you've missed the last bus, regardless of what time you arrive. A taxi between Taxisco and La Avellana costs around Q70.

From La Avellana catch a *lancha* or car ferry to Monterrico. The collective *lanchas* charge Q5 per passenger for the half-hour trip along the Canal de Chiquimulilla, a long mangrove canal. They start at 4:30am and run more or less every half-hour or hour until late afternoon. You can always pay more and charter your own boat. The car ferry costs Q85 per vehicle.

CENTRAL GUATEMALA

This region holds some of the best, most rewarding opportunities for getting off the beaten track. While the tour buses are all whizzing between the capital and Tikal, independent travelers are finding a wealth of undiscovered gems.

Semuc Champey and Grutas de Lanquín are on everybody's must-visit list, but there are literally hundreds more caves, waterfalls and other natural attractions to check out, mostly scattered around the well-established travelers' hub of Cobán. Check www.cobanav.net for a little inspiration.

Salamá & Around

A wonderful introduction to Baja Verapaz's not-too-hot, not-too-cold climate, the area around Salamá hosts a wealth of attractions, both post-Colonial and indigenous.

The town itself is known for its ornate **church** (complete with grisly depiction of Jesus), bustling **Sunday market** and the photogenic ex-sugar-mill-turned-museum and impressive **stone aqueduct** in the neighboring town of San Jerónimo.

For caving, bird-watching, hiking, horseback riding and orchid trips, get in touch with **EcoVerapaz** (☎5722-9095; ecoverapaz@hotmail.com; 8a Av 7-12, Zona 1; 1-day tour per person Q350).

Salamá has some fine accommodation options, including the **Posada de Don Maco** (☎7940-0083; 3a Calle 8-26; s/d Q110/140) and the **Hotel Real Legendario** (☎7940-0501; 8a Av 3-57; s/d Q140/150;). There are restaurants and cafes around the plaza. The meat-stuffed flour tortillas at **Antojitos Zacapanecos** (cnr 6a Calle & 8a Av; mains Q20; ⏲10am-9pm) are not to be missed.

Buses leave Salama's downtown bus terminal frequently for Cobán (Q25, 1½ to two hours), Guatemala City (Q35 to Q50, three hours) and all the neighboring villages.

Salamá also marks the starting point for a back-roads route to Guatemala City, passing **Rabinal**, whose annual fiesta of San Pedro (January 19 to 25) is a beguiling mix of pre-Columbian and Catholic traditions, and **Cubulco**, where the *palo volador* tradition is still observed. There are basic, adequate hospedajes in both Rabinal and Cubulco.

From there it's 100km to Guatemala City, passing along the way the turn-off to **Mixco Viejo**, one of the least-visited and most spectacularly-situated Maya sites in the country. The former Poqomam capital, it lies wedged between deep ravines, with just one way in and one way out. The Poqomam further fortified the site by constructing impressive rock walls around the city. It took Pedro de Alvarado and his troops more than a month of concerted attacks to conquer it. When they finally succeeded, they furiously laid waste to this city, which scholars believe supported close to 10,000 people at its height. There are several temples and two ball courts here.

Biotopo del Quetzal

Along the main highway (CA-14), 34km north of the turnoff for Salamá, near the village of Purulhá (no services), is the Biotopo Mario Dary Rivera reserve, commonly called the **Biotopo del Quetzal** (Hwy 14, Km 161; admission Q40; ⏲7am-4pm). The ride along here is sobering: entire hillsides are deforested and covered in huge sheets of black plastic meant to optimize growing conditions for *xate,* a low-growing green palm exported for use in floral arrangements.

If you intend on seeing a quetzal, Guatemala's national bird, you'll likely be disappointed – the birds are rare and elusive, and their habitat is almost destroyed. The best time to see them is between February and September. However, it's still worth a visit to explore their lush, high-altitude cloud-forest habitat.

Two well-maintained trails wind through the reserve past several waterfalls, most of which cascade into swimmable pools. Deep in the forest is **Xiu Ua Li Che** (Grandfather Tree), some 450 years old, which was alive when the conquistadors fought the Rabinals in these mountains.

The reserve has a visitors center, a little shop for drinks and snacks, and a camping and barbecue area. The ruling on camping changes often. Check by contacting **Cecon** (Centro de Estudios Conservacionistas de la Universidad de San Carlos; ☎2331-0904; biotoposcecon@gmail.com; Av La Reforma 0-63, Zona 10, Guatemala City), which administers this and other *biotopos.* Trail guide maps in English and Spanish (Q5) are sometimes available at the visitors center. They contain a checklist of 87 birds commonly seen here. Other animals include spider monkeys and *tigrillos,* similar to ocelots. Good luck.

Sleeping

★Hotel Restaurant Ram Tzul HOTEL **$$**
(☎2355-1904; www.m-y-c.com.ar/ramtzul; Hwy 14 Km 158; s/d Q250/350;) Quite likely the most beautiful hotel in either of the Verapaces, this place features a restaurant/sitting area in a tall, thatched-roofed structure with fire pits and plenty of atmosphere. The rustic, upmarket theme extends to the rooms and bungalows, which are spacious and elegantly decorated. The hotel property includes waterfalls and swimming spots.

Ranchitos del Quetzal HOTEL **$**
(☎4494-3694; ranchitosdelquetzal@yahoo.com; Hwy 14 Km 160.5; r per person Q100) Carved out of the jungle on a hillside 200m away from the Biotopo del Quetzal entrance, this place has good-sized, simple rooms with warm (ie tepid) showers in the older wooden building and hot showers in the newer concrete one. Reasonably priced, simple meals (mains Q30) are served, and there are vegetarian options.

Getting There & Away

Any bus to/from Guatemala City will set you down at the park entrance. Heading in the other direction, it's best to flag down a bus or microbus to El Rancho and change there for your next destination. The road between the *biotopo* and Cobán is good – smooth and fast (although curvy). As you ascend into the evergreen forests, you'll still see tropical flowers here and there.

Cobán

POP 68,900 / ELEV 1320M

Not so much an attraction in itself, but an excellent jumping-off point for the natural wonders of Alta Verapaz, Cobán is a prosperous city with an upbeat air. Return visitors will marvel at how much (and how tastefully) the town has developed since their last visit.

This was once a stronghold of the Rabinal Maya. In the 19th century, German immigrants moved in, founding vast coffee and cardamom *fincas* and giving Cobán the look and feel of a German mountain town. The era of German cultural and economic domination ended during WWII, when the US prevailed upon the Guatemalan government to deport the powerful *finca* owners, many of whom supported the Nazis.

Guatemala's most impressive indigenous festival, the folkloric festival of **Rabin Ajau**, takes place in late July or early August.

Sights & Activities

Orquigonia GARDENS
(☎4740-2224; www.orquigonia.com; Hwy 14 Km 206; admission Q30; ⏲7am-4pm) Orchid lovers and even the orchid-curious should not miss the wonderfully informative guided tour of this orchid sanctuary just off the highway to Cobán. The 1½- to two-hour tour takes you through the history of orchid collecting, starting with the Maya, as you wend your way along a path in the forest.

To get here catch any bus from Cobán headed for Tontem and get off when you see the sign, about 200m up the dirt road off the highway.

Parque Nacional Las Victorias PARK
(3a Calle, Zona 1; admission Q10; ⏲8am-4:30pm, walking trails 9am-3pm) This forested 82-hectare national park, right in town, has ponds, a barbecue, picnic areas, campgrounds, children's play areas, a lookout point and extensive

Cobán

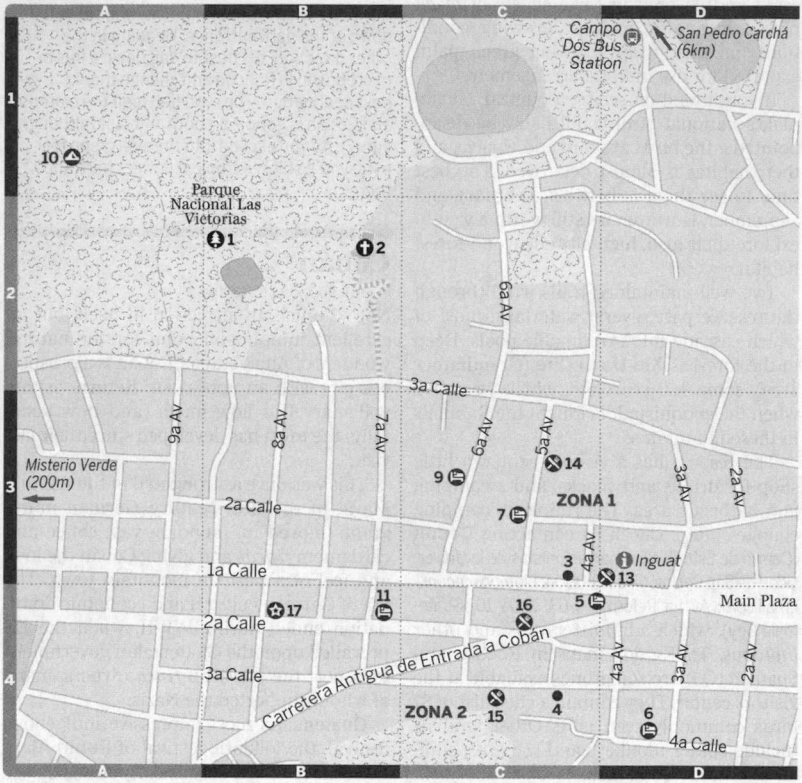

trails. The entrance is near the corner of 3a Calle and 9a Av, Zona 1. It's an isolated spot – consider hiking in a group.

Templo El Calvario CHURCH
(3a Calle, Zona 1) You'll get a fine view over town from this church atop a long flight of stairs at the north end of 7a Av, Zona 1. Indigenous people leave offerings at shrines and crosses in front of the church.

Tours

Aventuras Turísticas TOUR
(☎7951-2008; www.aventurasturisticas.com; 1a Calle 4-25, Zona 1) Leads tours to Laguna Lachuá, the caves of Lanquín, Semuc Champey, Tikal and Ceibal, and will customize itineraries. It employs French-, English- and Spanish-speaking guides.

Casa D'Acuña TOUR
(☎7951-0484; www.casadeacuna.com; 4a Calle 3-11, Zona 2) Located in the hotel of the same name, Casa D'Acuña offers tours to Semuc Champey, the Grutas de Lanquín and other places further afield. Its guides have been highly recommended.

Misterio Verde TOUR
(☎7952-1047; 2a Calle 14-36, Zona 1; ⏲8:30am-5:30pm) Acts as a booking agent for various community tourism projects in the area, including the Chicacnab cloud forests (near Cobán) and the subtropical rainforests of Rokjá Pomtilá (near the Laguna Lachua) in which participants stay in villages with a Q'eqchi' Maya family. For Q320 to Q400 you get a guide, lodging for two nights, and four meals.

Your guide will take you on hikes to interesting spots. The men of the family are the guides, providing them an alternative, sustainable way to make a living. Reservations are required at least one day in advance. It also rents boots, sleeping bags and binoculars at reasonable prices, so you need

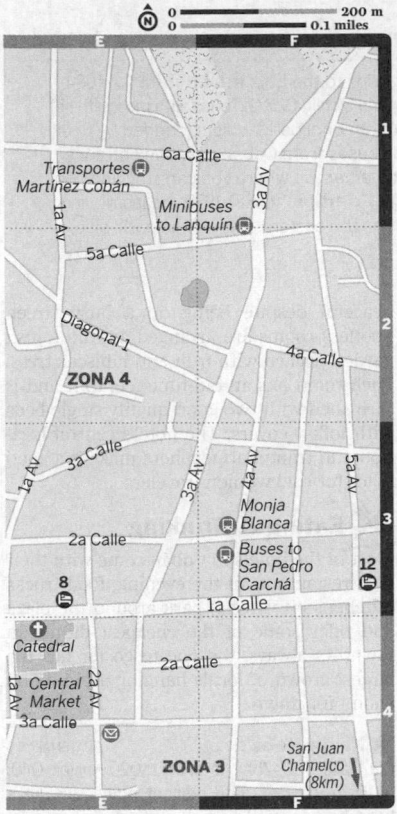

Cobán

Sights
1 Parque Nacional Las Victorias B2
2 Templo El Calvario B2

Activities, Courses & Tours
3 Aventuras Turísticas C3
Casa D'Acuña ..... (see 6)
4 Finca Santa Margarita C4

Sleeping
5 Casa Blanca Hostel C4
6 Casa D'Acuña D4
7 Casa Luna C3
8 Hotel Central E3
9 Hotel La Paz C3
10 Parque Nacional Las Victorias Camping A1
11 Pensión Monja Blanca B4
12 Posada de Don Antonio F3

Eating
13 Café Fantasia D3
El Bistro ..... (see 6)
14 El Peñascal C3
15 Kardamomuss C4
16 Xkape Koba'n C4

Entertainment
17 Bohemios B4

not worry if you haven't come prepared for such a rugged experience. Participants should speak at least a little Spanish. With a month's notice, this outfit also offers quetzal-viewing platforms; contact the office for full details.

Chicoj Cooperative COFFEE TOUR
(☎ 5524-1831; www.coffeetourchicoj.com; tours Q50) Just 15 minutes out of town by bus, this is a community-tourism initiative offering 2km, 45-minute tours of its coffee farm. Halfway through there's the standard stop for a canopy zip-line tour and the tour winds up with a cup of coffee made from beans grown and roasted at the farm.

Cobán tour operators offer this tour for Q160, but you can easily catch a bus from the stop near the police station on 1a Calle in town, which goes straight to the village of Chicoj.

Finca Santa Margarita COFFEE TOUR
(☎ 7952-1586; 3a Calle 4-12, Zona 2; admission Q30; ⏲ guided tours 8:30-11am & 2-4pm Mon-Fri, 8:30-11am Sat) This working coffee farm offers guided tours of its operation. From propagation and planting to roasting and exporting, the 45-minute tour will tell you all you ever wanted to know about these powerful beans. At tour's end, you're treated to a cup of coffee and can purchase beans straight from the roaster for Q25 to Q40 per 500g. The talented guide speaks English and Spanish.

Sleeping

Hotel Central HOTEL $
(☎ 7952-1442; 1a Calle 1-79, Zona 1; s/d Q120/170; 📶) Reasonable-sized rooms and lovely outdoor sitting areas make this a decent choice. Try for a room at the back for better ventilation and views out over the town.

Casa Luna HOSTEL $
(☎ 7951-3528; www.cobantravels.com/casaluna; 5a Av 2-28, Zona 1; dm/s/d without bathroom incl breakfast Q50/75/150; @📶) Modern rooms set around a pretty, grassy courtyard. Dorms have lockers and private rooms are well decorated. The shared bathrooms are spotless.

WORTH A TRIP

PARQUE NACIONAL LAGUNA LACHUÁ

You'll see many Cobán tour operators offering trips to the **Laguna Lachuá** (☎4084-1706; admission adult/child Q50/25, campsite per adult/child Q25/12, bunk with mosquito net Q70/35, tent hire Q15), a beautiful lagoon set in a national park and surrounded by thick jungle. It's not that hard to organize yourself as buses from Cobán pass the entrance to the park and there's a lovely lagoon-side, eco-*albergue* where you can stay and cook (bring food with you). The community of **Rocjá Pomtilá** (☎5381-1970; rocapon@yahoo.com; r for 2 nights incl guide & 4 meals Q320-400) on the eastern edge of the park, also offers homestays and tours of the area.

Casa D'Acuña HOTEL $
(☎7951-0482; www.casadeacuna.com; 4a Calle 3-11, Zona 2; dm/d without bathroom Q50/100;) This clean, very comfortable European-style hostel has four dormitories (each with four beds) and two private doubles, all with shared bathroom with good hot-water showers. Also here is a fabulous restaurant called El Bistro, a gift shop, laundry service and reasonably priced local tours.

Parque Nacional Las Victorias Camping CAMPGROUND $
(Parque Nacional Las Victorias; campsite per person Q40) Camping is available at Parque Nacional Las Victorias, right in town. Facilities include water and toilets, but no showers.

Hotel La Paz HOTEL $
(☎7952-1358; 6a Av 2-19, Zona 1; s/d Q45/75) This cheerful, clean hotel, 1½ blocks north and three blocks west of the plaza, is an excellent deal. It has many flowerbeds, and a good *cafetería* next door.

Casa Blanca Hostel
(☎4034-9291; 1a Calle 3-25, Zona 1; dm/s/d without bathroom Q35/50/100) This backpackers' favorite is a total winner in terms of location, and offers decent shared rooms, sleeping four in two bunks. The patio has a good simple cafe and the young staff are full of info and tips.

Posada de Don Antonio HOTEL $$
(☎7951-1792; www.hotelposadadedonantonio.com; 5a Av 1-51, Zona 4; s/d Q180/330;) This atmospheric two-story place provides some of the best value in town. Rooms are spacious with two (or even three!) double beds, high ceilings and loving attention to detail. Breakfast (Q30 to Q50) in the lush patio area is a great way to start the day.

Pensión Monja Blanca HOTEL $$
(☎7952-1712; 2a Calle 6-30, Zona 2; s/d Q170/225, without bathroom Q120/150) This place is peaceful despite being on a busy street. Spotless rooms are arranged around a lush garden packed with fruit and hibiscus trees. Each room has an old-time feel to it and is furnished with two good-quality single beds with folksy covers. The hotel's central location and tranqil atmosphere make it a good place for solo women travelers.

Eating & Drinking

Most of the hotels in Cobán come with their own restaurant. In the evening, food trucks (kitchens on wheels) park around the plaza and offer some of the cheapest dining in town. As always, the one to go for has the largest crowd of locals hanging around and chomping down.

★Xkape Koba'n GUATEMALAN $
(2a Calle 5-13, Zona 2; snacks Q20, mains Q40; ⏲10am-7pm) The perfect place to take a breather or while away a whole afternoon, this beautiful, artsy little cafe has a lush garden out back. Some interesting indigenous-inspired dishes including *b'ach-lancha* (spicy chicken stew) and *kaq-ik* (chicken and vegetables in a fiery salsa) are on the small menu. The cakes are homemade, the coffee delectable and there are some interesting handicrafts for sale.

Café Fantasia CAFE $
(1a Calle 3-13, Oficinas Profesionales Fray Bartolomé de Las Casas; breakfast Q20-30; ⏲8am-7pm Mon-Sat) Another good central cafe, this one offers several types of hot chocolate. It's a cozy little place in which to enjoy breakfasts, pastries and coffee or light meals, with a pleasant terrace away from the traffic.

El Bistro INTERNATIONAL $$
(4a Calle 3-11, Zona 2; mains Q60-120; ⏲7am-10pm) Casa D'Acuña's restaurant offers authentic Italian and other European-style dishes served in an attractive oasis of tranquility to background classical music. In addition

to protein-oriented mains, there is a range of pastas (Q40 to Q65), salads, homemade breads, cakes and outstanding desserts.

El Peñascal GUATEMALAN $$
(5a Av 2-61; mains Q55-90; ⏲11:30am-9pm) Probably Cobán's finest stand-alone restaurant, this one has plenty of regional specialties, Guatemalan classics, mixed meat platters, seafood and snacks in a relaxed, upmarket setting.

Kardamomuss FUSION $$
(3a Calle 5-34, Zona 2; mains Q40-90; ⏲8am-9pm; 📶) The widest menu in town is at this chic new place a few blocks from the plaza. Billing itself as 'fusion' food, it takes a pretty good stab at Indian, Chinese and Italian dishes, with locally-grown cardamom as the featured ingredient.

Bohemios CLUB
(cnr 8a Av & 2a Calle, Zona 2; admission Q10-25; ⏲Thu-Sat) A mega-disco with balcony seating and bow-tied staff.

Information

The Casa D'Acuña can also give you loads of information. There are plenty of card phones outside Telgua on the plaza.

Banco Industrial (cnr 1a Calle & 7a Av, Zona 1) Has a Visa ATM. Can change US dollars and traveler's checks.

Inguat (☎3176-7469; 1a Calle 3-13, Zona 1; ⏲8am-4pm Mon-Sat, 9am-1pm Sun)

Lavandería Econo Express (7a Av 2-32, Zona 1; ⏲7am-7pm Mon-Sat)

Post Office (crn 2a Av &3a Calle) A block southeast of the plaza.

Getting There & Away

The highway connecting Cobán with Guatemala City and the Carretera al Atlántico is the most traveled route between Cobán and the outside world. The road north through Chisec to Sayaxché and Flores is now paved all the way, providing much easier access to El Petén. The off-the-beaten-track routes west to Huehuetenango and northeast to Fray Bartolomé de Las Casas and Poptún are mostly unpaved and still provide a bit of an adventure (although the latter was being paved at time of research). Be aware that the road to Uspantan and Nebaj is prone to landslides – get the latest before setting out.

Buses leave from a variety of points around town, including the Campo Dos terminal. Minibuses, known as microbuses, are replacing, or are additional to, chicken buses on many routes. Always double-check bus departure times, especially for less frequently served destinations. Destinations not served by the Campo Dos terminal include the following:

Cahabón (Q30, 4½ hours, 85km) Catch any of the buses headed to Lanquín.

Guatemala City (Q50 to Q65, four to five hours, 213km) Transportes **Monja Blanca** (☎7951-3571; 2a Calle 3-77, Zona 4) has buses leaving for Guatemala City every 30 minutes from 2am to 6am, then hourly until 4pm.

Lanquín (Q25, 2½ to three hours, 61km) **Transportes Martínez** (6a Calle 2-40 , Zona 4) has departures throughout the day. **Minibuses** (cnr 5a Calle & 3a Av, Zona 4) also depart from the corner of 5a Calle and 3a Av, in Zona 4, from 7am to 4pm, some continuing to Semuc Champey. Check times, though, as they seem to be fluid.

San Pedro Carchá (Q3, 20 minutes, 6km) Buses every 10 minutes, from 6am to 7pm, from the lot in front of the Monja Blanca terminal.

Around Cobán

Lanquín

One of the best excursions to make from Cobán is to the pretty village of Lanquín, 61km to the east. People come for two reasons: to explore the wonderful cave system just out of town, and as a jumping-off point for visiting the natural rock pools at Semuc Champey.

The **Grutas de Lanquín** (admission Q30; ⏲8am-6pm) are a short distance northwest of the town and extend several kilometers into the earth. Aside from funky stalactites and stalagmites, these caves are crammed with bats; at sunset, they fly out of the mouth of the cave in dense, sky-obscuring formations. The river here gushes from the cave in clean, cool and delicious torrents; search out the hot pockets near the shore. The caves have lights, but bring a powerful flashlight anyway. You'll also need shoes with good traction, as it's slippery inside.

The sublimely located **El Retiro** (☎4513-6396; www.elretirolanquin.com; dm Q45, r with/without bathroom Q200/100, cabin without bathroom s/d Q150/180; @📶) is about 500m out of Lanquín town. Be warned – it's the sort of place you could lose yourself for months. *Palapas* look down over green fields to the beautiful wide river, the same one that flows out from the Lanquín caves. There's a very good bar-restaurant on the premises.

Another backpacker favorite, the **Zephyr Lodge** (☎5168-2441; www.zephyrlodgelanquin.

com; campsites per person Q30, dm Q40-50, r Q200-250) sits atop a hill nearer the center of town, giving it fantastic views. All sorts of gringo comfort food is available, as are tours and all the usual hostel amenities.

The large outdoor eatery, **Restaurante Champey** (mains Q20-50; ⏲8am-11pm), halfway between town and El Retiro, serves good-sized plates of steak, eggs and rice, and gets rowdy and beerish at night.

The Banrural on Lanquín's main square changes US dollars and traveler's checks, but at the time of writing did not have an ATM.

Buses operate several times daily between Cobán and Lanquín, continuing to Cahabón. There are eight buses to Cobán (Q30, three hours) between 6am and 5:30pm. Shuttles for Semuc Champey (Q30 return) leave at 9:30am (book at your hotel) and pickups (Q10 to Q15) leave whenever they are full, half a block from the main square.

Semuc Champey

Eleven kilometers south of Lanquín, along a rough, bumpy, slow road, is **Semuc Champey** (admission Q50; ⏲8am-6pm), famed for its great natural limestone 300m-long bridge, on top of which is a stepped series of pools of cool, flowing river water that's good for swimming.

The water is from the Río Cahabón, and much more of it passes underground, beneath the bridge. Although this bit of paradise is difficult to reach, the beauty of its setting and the perfection of the pools, which range from turquoise to emerald green, make it all worthwhile.

If you're visiting on a tour, some guides will take you down a rope ladder from the lowest pool to the river, which gushes out from the rocks below.

It's possible to camp (Q50 per tent) at Semuc Champey, but be sure to pitch a tent only in the upper areas, as flash floods are common. It's risky to leave anything unattended, as it might get stolen. The place now has 24-hour security which may reassure potential campers, but you need to bring everything with you. A simple restaurant at the parking area serves OK meals (including *cacki'ik*; Q40), but is a long way from the pools. It's a better idea to bring a picnic.

Just before the bridge leading to Semuc Champey, you'll see the turnoff to the right for the **Grutas K'anba** (admission Q50), a cave system which many find to be much more interesting than the Lanquín ones. Bring a flashlight for the two-hour tour of the caves, or you'll be stumbling around by candlelight. A half hour of river tubing is generally included in the price.

There are two very good places to stay near Semuc Champey: **Utopia** (☎3135-8329; www.utopiaecohotel.com; camping per person Q25, hammock/dm Q30/45, r with/without bathroom Q400/150; 📶) is located in the village of Semil, about 3km from Semuc Champey. It's set on a lovely riverbend and offers accommodation for all budgets. Call ahead for free pick up from Lanquín. **El Portal** (☎4091-7878; www.hostalelportaldechampey.com; dm Q40, r with/without bathroom Q200/100; 📶) is just 100m short of the entrance to Semuc Champey, and has well-spaced wooden huts

BUSES FROM COBÁN

Most buses will drop you out of town at the **Campo Dos bus terminal** (Campo Norte) north of town. It's a 15-minute walk (2km) or Q10 taxi ride to the plaza from there.

DESTINATION	COST (Q)	DURATION
Biotopo del Quetzal	12	1¼ hr
Chisec	20	2 hr
Fray Bartolomé de Las Casas	40	4 hr
Nebaj	60	5½-7 hr
Playa Grande (for Laguna Lachuá)	50	3 hr
Raxruhá	30	2½-3 hr
Salamá	25	1½ hr
Sayaxché	65	4 hr
Tactic	8	40 min
Uspantán	35	4½ hr

dotted around the bank sloping down to the river. There's no electricity, but meals and tours are available. Bookings are advised.

Fray Bartolomé de Las Casas

The Cobán to Poptún route via Fray Bartolomé de Las Casas used to be a desolate dirt road. Nowadays, plenty of buses and pickups ply the decent roads. This route is a great opportunity for you to get off the Gringo Trail and into the heart of Guatemala.

The hospitable town of Fray Bartolomé de Las Casas, often referred to as 'Fray' (pronounced 'fry'), is sizable for the middle of nowhere. You can't make it from Cobán to Poptún in one shot, so you'll be spending the night here. Banrural, just off the plaza, changes US dollars and traveler's checks and has an ATM. The post office and police station are nearby. The *municipalidad* is on the plaza.

The friendly **Hotel La Cabaña** (☎7952-0352; 2a Calle 1-92, Zona 3; s/d Q70/140, without bathroom Q35/75) has the best accommodations in town. Eating options are limited here – try **Comedor Jireh** and **Restaurante Doris** on the main street. Otherwise grab a steak (with tortillas and beans, Q20) at the informal barbecue shacks that open along the main street at night.

At least two daily buses depart from the plaza for Poptún (Q35, five hours). Buses for Cobán leave hourly between 4am and 4pm. Some go via Chisec (Q40, 3½ hours). Others take the slower route via San Pedro Carchá.

EASTERN GUATEMALA

In the hot, dry hill-studded flatlands that run down to the southern border, cowboy culture lives on in the Zacapa and Chiquimula departments. Packing a pistol is not uncommon here – indeed, it goes well with the big hat and boots. Most travelers use the area as a gateway to El Salvador and Honduras, but others come for the religious pilgrimage to Esquipulas or to check out the dinosaur museum at Estanzuela.

Capital of the department of the same name, Zacapa is just east of Hwy 10, a few kilometers south of Estanzuela. This town offers little to travelers, though the locals do make cheese, cigars and superb rum.

In Guatemala's far eastern corner, lush Izabal really packs in the attractions. The Río Dulce–Lago de Izabal area is gorgeous and largely untouched. The Garífuna enclave of Lívingston shows a whole other side to Guatemala and the little-visited ruins at Quiriguá have some of the finest carvings in the country.

Estanzuela

POP 10,700

Turning off the Carretera al Atlántico onto the CA-10, en route to Chiquimula, you enter the Río Motagua valley, a hot, 'dry tropic' area that once supported a great number and variety of dinosaurs. Three kilometers south of the Carretera al Atlántico you'll see a small monument on the right (west) side of the road commemorating the terrible earthquake of February 4, 1976.

Less than 2km south of the monument is the small town of Estanzuela, with its **Museo de Paleontología, Arqueología y Geología Ingeniero Roberto Woolfolk Sarvia** (Roberto Woolfolk Saravia Archeology & Paleontology Museum; Hwy 10, Estanzuela; ⏲8am-5pm Mon-Fri) **FREE**. This interesting museum holds bones of dinosaurs, a giant ground sloth some 30,000 years old and a prehistoric whale. Also on display are early Maya artifacts. To get here, go 1km west from the highway directly through town, following the small *museo* signs.

Chiquimula

POP 55,400

Capital of its namesake department, Chiquimula lies in a mining and tobacco-growing region on CA-10, 32km south of the Carretera al Atlántico. Although small, it's a major market town for eastern Guatemala. It's also a transportation point and overnight stop for those en route to Copán in Honduras (the reason most travelers stop here). Among other things, Chiquimula is known for its sweltering climate, decent budget hotels and the flower-packed central plaza.

Sleeping

Hotel Hernández HOTEL $

(☎7942-0708; 3a Calle 7-41, Zona 1; s/d with fan Q80/120, with air-con Q140/200, without bathroom Q50/90; ❄📶🏊) It's hard to beat the Hernández – it's been a favorite for years, and keeps going strong, with its central position, spacious, simple rooms and good-sized swimming pool.

Posada Perla de Oriente HOTEL $$
(☎7942-0014; 2a Calle 11-50, Zona 1; s/d with fan Q120/220, with air-con Q150/250; ❄📶🏊) Surprisingly tranquil for its location just around the corner from the bus terminal, with some of the best-value rooms in town. They're large and unadorned, but the grounds are quiet and leafy and the big swimming pool is a bonus.

Hostal Maria Teresa HOTEL $$
(☎7942-0177; 6a Calle 6-21, Zona 1; s/d Q190/350; ❄📶) Set around a gorgeous colonial courtyard with wide shady passageways. The single rooms are a bit poky, but the doubles are generous and all the comforts are here: cable TV, hot showers and air-conditioning.

Eating

There's a string of cheap *comedores* on 8a Av behind the market. At night, snack vendors and taco carts set up along 7a Av opposite the Parque Ismael Cerna, selling the cheapest eats in town.

Corner Coffee CAFE $
(6a Calle 6-70, Zona 1; bagels Q30, breakfast Q25-30; ⏲7am-10pm Mon-Sat, 3-10pm Sun) You could argue with the syntax, but this air-con haven right on the lovely Parque Calvario serves the best range of sandwiches, burgers and bagels in town.

Charli's INTERNATIONAL $$
(7a Av 5-55; mains Q50-100; ⏲8am-9pm) Chiquimula's 'fine dining' option (tablecloths!) has a wide menu, featuring pasta, pizza, seafood and steaks, all served amid chilly air-con, with relaxed and friendly service.

Parillada de Calero STEAKHOUSE $$
(7a Av 4-83; breakfast from Q30, mains Q50-100; ⏲8am-10pm) An open-air steakhouse, serving the juiciest flame-grilled cuts in town. This is also the breakfast hot spot – the Tropical Breakfast (pancakes with a mound of fresh fruit; Q40) goes down well in this climate.

Information

Banco G&T (7a Av 4-75, Zona 1; ⏲9am-8pm Mon-Fri, 10am-2pm Sat) Half a block south of the plaza, has a Visa and MasterCard ATM.

Post Office (10a Av, btwn 1a & 2a Calles) In an alley around the side of the building opposite the bus station.

Getting There & Away

Several companies operate buses and microbuses, arriving and departing from the bus station area on 11a Av, between 1a and 2a Calles. **Litegua** (☎7942-2064; 1a Calle, btwn 10a & 11a Avs), which operates buses to El Florido (the border crossing on the way to Copán) has its own bus station a half block north. For the Honduran border crossing at Agua Caliente, take a minibus to Esquipulas and change there. If you're headed to Jalapa, you'll need to go to Ipala to make the connection. For Río Dulce, take a Flores bus, or a Puerto Barrios bus to La Ruidosa junction and change there. If you're going to Esquipulas, sit on the left for the best views of the basilica.

Esquipulas

From Chiquimula, CA-10 goes south into the mountains, where it's cooler and a bit more comfortable. After an hour's ride through pretty country, the highway descends into a valley ringed by mountains. Halfway down

BUSES FROM CHIQUIMULA

DESTINATION	COST (Q)	DURATION	DEPARTURES	FREQUENCY
Anguiatú (Salvador border)	15	1 hr	5am-5:30pm	when full
El Florido (Honduras border)	25	1½ hr	5:30am-4:30pm	when full
Esquipulas	20	45 min	5am-9pm	every 20 min
Flores	100	7-8 hr	daily	2 daily
Guatemala City	40	3 hr	3am-3.30pm	every 30 min
Ipala	6	1½ hr	5am-7pm	hourly
Puerto Barrios	45	4½ hr	3:30am-4pm	every 30 min
Quiriguá	30	2 hr	3:30am-4pm	every 30 min
Río Hondo	15	35 min	5am-6pm	every 15 min

the slope, about 1km from town, a *mirador* provides a good view. As soon as you catch sight of the place, you'll see the reason for coming: the great Basílica de Esquipulas that towers above the town, its whiteness shining in the sun.

January 15 is the annual Cristo de Esquipulas festival, with mobs of devout pilgrims coming from all over the region to worship at the altar of the Black Christ (El Cristo Negro).

History

This town may have been a place of pilgrimage even before the conquest. Legend has it that Esquipulas takes its name from a Maya lord who ruled this region when the Spanish arrived.

With the arrival of the friars a church was built, and in 1595 an image of Christ carved from black wood was installed. It's known almost universally as the 'Black Christ'. The steady flow of pilgrims to Esquipulas became a flood after 1737, when Pedro Pardo de Figueroa, Archbishop of Guatemala, came here on pilgrimage and went away cured of a chronic ailment.

Delighted with this development, the prelate commissioned a huge new church to be built on the site. It was finished in 1758, and the pilgrimage trade has been the town's livelihood ever since.

Esquipulas is assured a place in modern history, too. Beginning here in 1986, President Marco Vinicio Cerezo Arévalo brokered agreements with the other Central American leaders on economic cooperation and conflict resolution. These became the seeds of the Guatemalan Peace Accords, which were finally signed in 1996.

Sights & Activities

Basílica de Esquipulas CHURCH

A massive pile of stones that has resisted earthquakes for almost 250 years, the basilica is approached through a pretty park and up a flight of steps. The impressive facade and towers are floodlit at night.

Inside, the devout approach **El Cristo Negro** (Black Christ) with extreme reverence, many on their knees. Incense, the murmur of prayers and the scuffle of sandaled feet fill the air. When throngs of pilgrims are here, you must enter the church from the side to get a close view of the famous Black Christ. Shuffling along quickly, you may get a good glimpse before being shoved onward by the press of the crowd. On Sundays, religious holidays and (especially) during the festival, the press of devotees is intense. Otherwise, you may have the place to yourself.

Centro Turístico Cueva de las Minas CAVE

(admission Q15; ⏲8am-4pm) The Centro Turístico Cueva de las Minas has a 50m-deep cave (bring your own flashlight), grassy picnic areas and the Río El Milagro, where people come for a dip and say it's miraculous. The cave and river are 500m from the entrance gate, which is behind the basilica's cemetery, 300m south of the turnoff into town on the road heading toward Honduras. Refreshments are available.

Parque Chatún AMUSEMENT PARK

(☎7873-0909; www.parquechatun.com; adult/child incl lunch from Q65/55; ⏲9am-6pm Tue-Sat) If you've got kids along (or even if you don't), Parque Chatún, a fun park 3km out of town, should provide some light relief from all the religious business. There are swimming pools, a climbing wall, campgrounds, a petting zoo, a canopy tour and a mini bungee jump. Entry includes the use of all these, except the canopy tour. If you don't have a vehicle, look for the minibus doing rounds of the town, or get your hotel to call it.

Sleeping

Esquipulas has an abundance of accommodations. On holidays and during the annual festival, every hotel in town is filled, whatever the price; weekends are busy as well, with prices substantially higher. On nonfestival weekdays, ask for a *descuento* (discount). For cheap rooms, look in the streets immediately north of the towering basilica.

Hotel Monte Cristo HOTEL $$

(☎7943-1453; 3a Av 9-12, Zona 1; s/d Q180/250, without bathroom Q80/100) Good-sized rooms with a bit of furniture and super-hot showers. A policy of not letting the upstairs rooms until the downstairs ones are full might see you on the ground floor.

Hotel La Favorita HOTEL $$

(☎7943-1175; 2a Av 10-15, Zona 1; r Q200, s/d without bathroom Q60/100) The real budget-watcher's choice, the rooms with shared bathroom here are a bit grim, but those with bathrooms are good enough.

Hotel Portal de la Fe HOTEL $$
(☎7943-4261; 11 Calle 1-70, Zona 1; s/d Q250/450; ❄@📶🏊) One of the few hotels with any real style in town. Subterranean rooms are predictably gloomy, but upstairs the situation improves considerably.

Hotel Mahanaim HOTEL $$
(☎7943-1131; 10a Calle 1-85, Zona 1; r Q350; ❄@📶🏊) This establishment is on three levels around a covered courtyard. Rooms are comfortable but plain. It wouldn't be such a good deal if it weren't for the big covered swimming pool out back.

Eating

Esquipulas' budget restaurants are clustered around the north end of the park, where hungry pilgrims can find them readily. Most eateries open from 6:30am until 9pm or 10pm.

The street running north opposite the church – 3a Av – has several eateries.

Restaurante Calle Real GUATEMALAN $
(3a Av; mains Q30-60; ⏲8am-10pm) Typical of many restaurants here, this big eating barn turns out cheap meals for the pilgrims. There's a wide menu, strip lighting and loud TV.

Restaurant El Angel CHINESE $$
(☎7943-1372; cnr 11a Calle & 2a Av; mains Q45-60; ⏲11am-10:30pm) This main-street Chinese eatery does all the standard dishes, plus steaks and a good range of *licuados* (milkshakes). Home delivery is available.

La Rotonda FAST FOOD $$
(11a Calle; mains Q50-100; ⏲8am-10pm) Opposite Rutas Orientales bus station, this is a round building with chairs arranged around a circular open-air counter under a big awning. It's a welcoming place, clean and fresh. There are plenty of selections to choose from, including pizza, pasta and burgers.

City Grill STEAKHOUSE $$
(cnr 2a Av & 10a Calle, Zona 1; mains Q40-120; ⏲8am-10pm) The best steakhouse in town also serves some decent seafood and pasta dishes. There's a cafe-bakery attached and the breakfasts (Q45) are a good (but slightly pricey) bet.

Information

The **post office** (6a Av 2-15) is about 10 blocks north of the center. **Telgua** (cnr 5a Av & 9a Calle) has plenty of card phones. **Banco Internacional** (3a Av 8-87, Zona 1) changes US dollars and traveler's checks and has a Visa ATM.

Getting There & Away

Buses to Guatemala City (Q50, four hours) arrive and depart hourly from 1:30am to 4:30pm from the **Rutas Orientales bus station** (☎7943-1366; cnr 11a Calle & 1a Av), near the entrance to town.

Minibuses to Agua Caliente (Honduran border; Q20, 30 minutes) arrive and depart across the street, leaving every half hour from 5am to 5pm; taxis also wait here, charging the same as the minibuses, once they have five passengers.

Minibuses to Chiquimula (Q15, 45 minutes, every 15 minutes from 5am to 6pm) depart from the east end of 11a Calle.

Transportes Guerra (cnr 5a Av & 10a Calle) goes to Anguiatú (Salvador border; Q15, one hour, every 30 minutes from 6am to 6pm).

There are three buses daily for Flores/Santa Elena (Q110, eight hours) from the **Transportes María Elena** (☎7943-0957; 11 Calle 0-54, Zona 1) office. They pass Quiriguá (Q45, two hours), Río Dulce (Q60, four hours) and Poptún (Q90, six hours).

Quiriguá

POP 4800

Quiriguá's archaeological zone is famed for its intricately carved stelae – gigantic sandstone monoliths up to 10.5m tall – that rise like ancient sentinels in a quiet tropical park. From the Río Hondo junction it's 68km along the Carretera al Atlántico to the village of Quiriguá.

History

Quiriguá's history parallels that of Copán, of which it was a dependency during much of the Classic period. The location lent itself to the carving of giant stelae. Beds of brown sandstone in the nearby Río Motagua had cleavage planes suitable for cutting large pieces. Although soft when first cut, the sandstone dried hard. With Copán's expert artisans nearby for guidance, Quiriguá's stone carvers were ready for greatness. All they needed was a leader to inspire them – and pay for the carving.

That leader was Cauac Sky (AD 725–84), who sought Quiriguá's independence from Copán. In a war with his former *suzerain*, Cauac Sky took Copán's King 18 Rabbit prisoner in 737 and beheaded him soon after. Independent at last, Cauac Sky called up the stonecutters and for the next 38 years they turned out giant stelae and zoomorphs dedicated to his glory.

In the early 20th century the United Fruit Company bought all the land around Quiriguá and turned it into banana groves. The company is gone, but the bananas and Quiriguá remain. In 1981, Unesco declared Quiriguá a World Heritage Site.

Sights

Quiriguá Archaeological Site ARCHAEOLOGICAL SITE
(admission Q80; ⏲8am-4:30pm) It's hot and there are mosquitoes everywhere, but the parklike archaeological zone is unforgettable. The giant stelae on the Great Plaza are awe-inspiring despite their worn condition.

Stelae A, C, D, E, F, H and J were built during the reign of Cauac Sky and carved with his image. **Stela E** is the largest Maya stela known, standing 8m above ground, with about another 3m buried in the earth. It weighs almost 60 tons. Note the elaborate head-dresses; the beards on some figures (an oddity in Maya art and life); the staffs of office held in the kings' hands; and the glyphs on the stelae's sides.

At the far end of the plaza is the **Acropolis**. At its base are several zoomorphs, blocks of stone carved to resemble real and mythic creatures; frogs, tortoises, jaguars and serpents were favorite subjects. The low zoomorphs can't compete with the towering stelae in impressiveness, but are superb as works of art, imagination and mythic significance.

A small museum just past the entrance has a few information displays and a model of how the site (much of it unexcavated) would have looked in its heyday. A *tienda* (small shop) near the entrance sells cold drinks and snacks.

Sleeping & Eating

Hotel y Restaurante Royal HOTEL $
(☎7947-3639; s/d Q100/150) The Hotel y Restaurante Royal is the pick of the very limited range of hotels in town, and also serves good, simple meals.

Getting There & Away

Buses running along the routes Guatemala City–Puerto Barrios, Guatemala City–Flores, Esquipulas–Flores or Chiquimula–Flores will stop at the turnoff to Quiriguá town. Drivers will drop you at the turnoff to the archaeological site if you ask.

The transportation center in this area is Morales, about 40km northeast of Quiriguá. It's not pretty, but it's where the bus for Río Dulce originates. If a seat isn't important, skip Morales and wait at the La Ruidosa junction for the Río Dulce bus.

Getting Around

From the turnoff on the highway (1.5km from Quiriguá town), it's 3.4km to the archaeological site. Buses and pickups provide transportation between the turnoff and the site for Q5 each way. If you don't see one, don't fret; it's a nice walk on a new road (complete with dedicated bicycle/tuk-tuk lane) through banana plantations to get there.

If you're staying in Quiriguá and walking to and from the archaeological site, take the shortcut along the railway line from the village through the banana fields, crossing the access road near the site entrance. A tuk-tuk from Quiriguá village to the site should cost around Q15.

To get to the village from the highway, walk down the main street, veering right at the first fork and then follow the road around to the left at the bend.

Lago de Izabal

Guatemala's largest lake is earning its place on travelers' radars. Many visitors stay at Río Dulce village, north of the bridge where Hwy CA-13, the road leading north to Flores and Tikal, crosses the lake. East of this bridge is the beautiful Río Dulce, which opens into El Golfete lake before flowing down into the Caribbean at Lívingston; a river trip is one of the highlights of a visit to eastern Guatemala.

Other lake highlights include El Castillo de San Felipe (an old Spanish fortress) and the Bocas del Polochic river delta. Many quiet and secluded spots in this area await your exploration.

Río Dulce

At the east end of the Lago de Izabal where it empties into the Río Dulce, this town still gets referred to as Fronteras. It's a hangover from the days when the only way across the river was by ferry, and this was the last piece of civilization before entering the wilds of El Petén.

Times have changed. A huge bridge now spans the water and the Petén roads are some of the best in the country. The town sees most tourist traffic from yachties – the

US coast guard says this is the safest place on the western Caribbean for boats during hurricane season. The rest of the foreigners here are either coming or going on the spectacular river trip down to Lívingston.

Tours

Ask around at any of the marinas for the latest on which sailboats are offering charter tours.

Aventuras Vacacionales SAILING
(☎7873-9221; www.sailing-diving-guatemala.com) Aventuras Vacacionales runs fun sailing trips on the sailboat *Las Sirenas* from Río Dulce to the Belize reefs and islands (from Q3200, seven days) and Lago Izabal (from Q1250, four days). The office is in Antigua but you can also hook up with this outfit in Río Dulce.

Sleeping

Places that are out of town on the water are the best places to be. You can call or radio them from Bruno's (p183) and they'll come and pick you up.

Most places – except for Hotel Backpacker's – are on the north side of the bridge. Get off near Río Bravo Restaurante. Otherwise you'll be walking the length of what may be Central America's longest bridge – a steamy 30-minute walk.

Hotel Backpackers HOSTEL $
(☎7930-5480; www.hotelbackpackers.com; dm Q30, s/d Q100/120, without bathroom from Q60/120; @) Across the bridge, this is an old (with the emphasis on old) backpacker favorite, set in a rickety building with very basic rooms. The bar kicks on here at night. If you're coming by *lancha* or bus, ask the driver to let you off here to spare yourself the walk across the bridge.

Hotel Vista al Río HOTEL $
(☎7930-5665; www.hotelvistario.com; dm Q40, r from Q160, without bathroom Q100;) Under the bridge just south of Bruno's, this little hotel/marina offers spacious, spotless rooms, some with river views. There's a good restaurant here, serving juicy steaks, Southern cooking and big breakfasts.

Casa Perico HOSTEL $
(☎7930-5666; dm Q45-50, bungalow s/d Q200/250, without bathroom from Q65/110; @) One of the more low-key options in the area, set on a little inlet about 200m from the main river. Cabins are well built and connected by boardwalks. The Swiss guys who run it offer river tours and put on an excellent buffet dinner (Q60), or you can choose from the menu (mains Q30 to Q40).

El Tortugal BUNGALOW $$
(☎7742-8847; www.tortugal.com; dm Q100, r without bathroom Q300, bungalow from Q300;) The best-looking bungalows on the river are located here, a five-minute *lancha* ride east from town. There are plenty of hammocks, seriously hot showers and free kayaks for guests.

Hacienda Tijax HOTEL $$
(☎7930-5505; www.tijax.com; s Q170-530, d Q230-590;) This 200-hectare hacienda, a two-minute boat ride across the cove from Bruno's, is a special place to stay. Activities include horseback riding, hiking, bird-

OFF THE BEATEN TRACK

CHAPÍN ABAJO

To get right off the beaten track, make your way to this charming little village on the southwest shore of Lago de Izabal. The **community tourism project** (☎4672-4773; www.turismocomunitarioguatemala.com/chapin_abajo.html) here offers accommodation in sweet wooden lakeside **bungalows** (☎4672-4773; s/d Q125/200, per person without bathroom Q75) with water views. Simple meals and boat tours (Q375, two hours) are available. The village is 25km west of Mariscos on an unpaved but passable road. It's tricky getting here by road – catch any bus heading along the Carretera al Atlántico and get off at Trincheras junction (Km 218) – the turnoff for Mariscos, where minibuses (Q10) make the run into town. Coming from Los Amates or Quiriguá, there are direct minibuses to Mariscos. From Mariscos, pickups (Q20, one hour) make the run to Chapín Abajo but peter out around 10am. Hitchhiking is common along this stretch, but carries the usual risks.

The easy way to get here is on one of the *lanchas* (Q15, 20 minutes) from El Estor across the lake. One leaves at midday every day and there may be additional departures.

IZABAL BEYOND RÍO DULCE

While Río Dulce town is OK, the best places to stay around here are much further afield. Here's a sampling:

Lagunita Creek (☎4113-0103; dm Q80) Heading northwest from Lívingston brings you to the small community of Lagunita Creek, where a community-tourism project offers lodging in a simple ecolodge. Simple meals (Q50 to Q65) are available here, or you can bring your own food to cook.

Included in the price is the use of kayaks to explore the beautiful, turquoise waters of the river and guided nature walks/bird-watching tours. Transport can be expensive – the only way to get here is by boat. *Lanchas* from Lívingston charge around Q1200 per boatload. Happy Fish Travel (p188) in Lívingston offers day/overnight tours here for Q280/480 but requires a minimum of six people.

Finca Tatin (☎4148-3332; www.fincatatin.com; dm Q50, s/d from Q140/180, without bathroom from Q75/120; 📶) About 10km upstream from Lívingston, this wonderful forest retreat offers accommodations in individually decorated wood-and-thatch cabins scattered through the jungle. There are plenty of walks and kayak tours to do in the area. *Lanchas* (small motorboats) traveling between Río Dulce and Lívingston (or vice versa) will drop you here. See the website for more transportation options.

Hotelito Perdido (☎5725-1576; www.hotelitoperdido.com; dm Q45, bungalow s/d from Q150/200, without bathroom Q120/150) Just across the river from the Finca Tatin, this beautiful new place is run by a couple of young travelers. The ambience is superb and the whole place is solar powered and constructed in such a way as to cause minimal impact on the environment. It's a small, intimate place, so it's a good idea to book ahead. Call to get picked up from Lívingston (Q40) or get dropped off by any boat going between there and Río Dulce.

Hotel Kangaroo (☎5363-6716, in English 4513-9602; www.hotelkangaroo.com; dm Q60, r Q150-180, cabin Q220; @📶) On the Río La Colocha, just across the water from El Castillo de San Felipe, this beautiful, simple Australian-run place is built up on stilts in the mangroves. Wildlife is particularly abundant around here, with blue warblers, pelicans, a 7ft iguana and turtles making the surrounds their home. Call from Río Dulce or San Felipe and they'll come and pick you up for free, even if you're just dropping in for lunch.

watching, sailboat trips, walking and canopy tours around the rubber plantation. Accommodation is in lovely little cabins connected by a boardwalk. Most cabins face the water and there's a very relaxing pool/bar area.

Bruno's HOTEL $$
(☎7930-5721; www.brunoshotel.com; dm Q50, s Q90-220, d Q125-300; ❄📶🏊) A path leads down from the northeast end of the bridge to this riverside hangout for yachties. The dorms are clean and spacious and the new building offers some of the most comfortable rooms in town, with air-con and balconies overlooking the river. They're well set up for families and sleep up to six.

Eating

Most hotels have restaurants. Bruno's (p183) serves good breakfasts, gringo comfort food and has a full bar. The Hacienda Tijax (p182) is a popular lunch spot – give them a call and they'll come pick you up.

★Sundog Café INTERNATIONAL $
(sandwiches Q30, meals from Q35; ⏲noon-9pm) Down a laneway opposite the Litegua bus office, this open-air riverfront bar-restaurant makes great sandwiches on homemade bread, a good selection of vegetarian dishes, tasty brick-oven pizzas and fresh juices. It's also the place to come for unbiased information about the area.

Information

Four banks in town, all on the main road, change cash or traveler's checks. **Banco Industrial** (⏲9am-5pm) has a Visa ATM. Banrural has Visa and MasterCard ATMs. The **Rio Dulce Chisme** (www.riodulcechisme.com; Rio Dulce) website has loads of information about Río Dulce.

Getting There & Away

BUS

Beginning at 9:30am, seven Fuente del Norte buses a day head north along a paved road to Poptún (Q35, two hours) and Flores (Q65, four hours). With good connections you can get to Tikal in a snappy six hours. There are also services to San Salvador (El Salvador; Q125) and San Pedro Sula (Honduras; Q135), both leaving at 10am.

At least 11 buses daily go to Guatemala City (Q65, six hours) with Fuente del Norte and Litegua. Línea Dorada has 1st-class buses departing at 1pm for Guatemala City (Q130) and 3pm for Flores (Q130). This shaves up to an hour off the journey times.

Minibuses leave for Puerto Barrios (Q25, two hours) when full, from the roadside in front of Hotel Las Brisas.

There's a daily shuttle to Lanquín (Q150, five hours), leaving from in front of the Sundog Café at 1:30pm.

Minibuses leave for El Estor (Q20, 1½ hours) from the San Felipe and El Estor turnoff in the middle of town, hourly from 7am to 6pm.

BOAT

Colectivo lanchas go down the Río Dulce (from the new dock) to Lívingston, usually requiring eight to 10 people, charging Q125/200 per person one-way/round-trip. The trip is a beautiful one, making a 'tour' of it, with several halts along the way. Boats usually leave from 9am to about 2pm. There are regular, scheduled departures at 9:30am and 1:30pm. Pretty much everyone in town can organize *lancha* service to Lívingston and most other places you'd care to go, but they charge more.

Río Dulce to Flores

Heading north from Río Dulce town is the road into El Petén, Guatemala's vast jungle province. It's 208km to Santa Elena and Flores, and another 71km to Tikal.

The entire stretch of road from the Carretera al Atlántico to Santa Elena has been paved, so it's a smooth ride all the way from Río Dulce to the Tikal ruins.

The forest here is disappearing at an alarming rate, falling to the machetes of subsistence farmers. As the UN's Food and Agriculture Organization has repeatedly reported, sections are felled and burned off, crops are grown for a few seasons until the fragile jungle soil is exhausted, then the farmer moves deeper into the forest to slash and burn anew. Cattle ranchers have contributed to the damage, as has the migration of Guatemalans from the cities to El Petén.

El Castillo de San Felipe

The fortress and **castle** (admission Q20; ⏲8am-5pm) of San Felipe de Lara, about 3km west of the bridge, was built in 1652 to keep pirates from looting the villages and commercial caravans of Izabal. Although it deterred the buccaneers a bit, a pirate force captured and burned the fortress in 1686. By the end of the next century, pirates had disappeared from the Caribbean and the fort's sturdy walls served as a prison. Eventually, the fortress was abandoned and became a ruin. The present fort was reconstructed in 1956.

Today, the castle is protected and is one of the lake's principal tourist attractions. In addition to the fort, the site has a large park, with barbecue/picnic areas, and you can swim in the lake.

Near the *castillo*, **Hotel Don Humberto** (☎7930-5051; s/d Q50/90) has basic rooms with big beds and good mosquito netting. It's nothing fancy, but more than adequate for a cheap sleep.

San Felipe is on the lakeshore, 3km west of Río Dulce. It's a beautiful 45-minute walk between the two, or minibuses provide transportation for Q10, running about every half hour. In Río Dulce they stop at the corner of the highway and the road to El Estor; in San Felipe they stop in front of Hotel Don Humberto, at the entrance to El Castillo.

Boats coming from Lívingston will drop you in San Felipe if you ask them. The Río Dulce boat trips usually cruise by El Castillo. Some will let you get out and visit the castle, or you can come over from Río Dulce by private launch.

Finca El Paraíso

On the lake's north side, between San Felipe and El Estor, the **Finca El Paraíso** (☎7949-7122; admission Q10, cabin with fan/air-con Q200/250) is a popular day trip from Río Dulce and other places around the lake. At the *finca,* which is a working ranch, you can walk to an incredibly beautiful spot in the jungle where a wide, hot waterfall drops about 12m into a clear, deep pool. You can bathe in the hot water, swim in the cool pool or duck under an overhanging promontory and enjoy a jungle-style sauna. Also on the *finca* are several interesting caves and good hiking. Next door to the farmhouse is the more humble but better-value **Brisas del Lago** (☎7958-0309; cabin per person Q100).

The *finca* is on the Río Dulce–El Estor bus route, about one hour (Q10) from Río Dulce and 30 minutes (Q7) from El Estor. To get to the waterfall, head north from the road. Head south for the farmhouse and lake. The last bus in either direction passes at around 4:30pm to 5pm.

El Estor

Gorgeously sited and rarely visited, this small town looks over the Lago de Izabal to the Sierra de las Minas. It's most often used as a staging point for visits to the **Refugio de Vida Silvestre Bocas del Polochic**, a highly biodiverse wildlife reserve at the west end of the lake, but is also a gateway for the difficult, but possible, back route to Lanquín and Cobán.

Sleeping & Eating

The best place to look for food is around the Parque Central, where **Café Portal** (5a Av 2-65; mains Q30-50; ⏲7am-9pm) serves a broad range of fare with some vegetarian options. On the other side of the park, **Restaurante del Lago** (mains Q40-80; ⏲8am-8pm), on the 2nd floor, catches some good breezes and a bit of a lake view – it has the widest menu in town.

Restaurante Típico Chaabil HOTEL $
(☎7949-7272; 3a Calle; r Q150) Although they go a bit heavy on the log-cabin feel, the rooms at this place, at the west end of 3a Calle, are the best deal in town. Get one upstairs for plenty of light and good views. The restaurant here, on a lovely lakeside terrace, cooks up delicious food, such as *tapado* (the Garífuna seafood and coconut stew; Q100). The water here is crystal clear and you can swim right off the hotel's dock.

Hotel Villela HOTEL $
(☎7949-7214; 6a Av 2-06; s/d Q75/150) The rooms are less attractive than the neat lawn and trees they're set around, but some are airier and brighter than others. All have fan and bathroom.

Hotel Vista al Lago HOTEL $$
(☎7949-7205; 6a Av 1-13; s/d Q150/200) Set in a classic, historic building down on the waterfront, this place has plenty of style, although the rooms themselves are fairly ordinary. Views from the upstairs balcony are superb.

Information

On the east side of Parque Central is **Café Portal** (5a Av 2-65; ⏲6:30am-10pm), which provides excellent information, tours and transportation. **Banrural** (cnr 3a Calle & 6a Av; ⏲8:30am-5pm Mon-Fri, 9am-1pm Sat) changes US dollars and American Express traveler's checks and has an ATM. The **municipal police** (cnr 1a Calle & 5a Av) are near the lakeshore. There are some excellent ecotourism options on offer in the nearby Bocas del Polochic wildlife reserve – contact the **Fundación Defensores de la Naturaleza** (☎7949-7130; www.defensores.org.gt; cnr 5a Av & 2a Calle) for details.

Getting There & Away

El Estor is easily reached from Río Dulce. Minibuses leave hourly to/from Río Dulce between 7am and 6pm.

The road west from El Estor via Panzós and Tucurú to Tactic, south of Cobán, once had a bad reputation for highway holdups and robberies, especially around Tucurú – ask around for current conditions. It's also prone to getting flooded out during the wet season – another reason to enquire. You can get to Lanquín by taking the truck that leaves El Estor's Parque Central at 10:30am for Cahabón (Q40, four to five hours), and then a bus or pickup straight on from Cahabón to Lanquín the same day. Coming the other way currently involves ungodly departure times and staying the night in Cahabón.

Puerto Barrios

POP 86,400

The country becomes even more lush, tropical and humid heading east from La Ruidosa junction toward Puerto Barrios. Port towns have always had a reputation for being slightly dodgy, and those acting as international borders doubly so. Perhaps the town council wants to pay homage to that here. Or perhaps the edgy, slightly sleazy feel is authentic. Either way, for foreign visitors, Puerto Barrios is mainly a jumping-off point for boats to Punta Gorda (Belize) or Lívingston, and you probably won't be hanging around.

The powerful United Fruit Company owned vast plantations in the Río Motagua valley. It built railways (whose tracks still run through the middle of town) to ship produce to the coast. Puerto Barrios was built early in the 20th century to put that produce onto ships sailing for New Orleans and New York. Laid out as a company town, Puerto Barrios has long, wide streets arranged neatly on a grid. Many of its Caribbean-style wood-frame houses are on stilts.

Sleeping

Hotel Europa HOTEL $
(☎7948-1292; 3a Av btwn Calles 11a and 12a; s/d with fan Q75/120, with air-con Q110/150; ❄📶) The best of the budget options in the port area, this hotel, just 1½ blocks from the Muelle Municipal, is run by a friendly family and has clean rooms with TV, arranged around a parking courtyard.

Hotel Ensenada HOTEL $
(☎7948-0861; hotelensenadapuertobarrios@hotmail.com; 4a Av btwn Calles 10 & 11; s/d Q110/150; ❄) Tidy little rooms with good bathrooms and OK beds. Get one upstairs to catch a breeze.

Hotel Lee HOTEL $
(☎7948-0685; 5a Av btwn Calles 9a and 10a; s/d with fan Q60/100, d with air-con Q160; ❄) This is a friendly, family-owned place close to the bus terminals. Typical of Puerto Barrios' budget hotels, it offers straightforward, vaguely clean rooms. The little balcony out front catches the odd breeze.

Hotel El Reformador HOTEL $$
(☎7948-0533; reformador@intelnet.net.gt; cnr 7a Av & 16a Calle; s/d with fan Q113/173, with air-con Q158/228; ❄📶) Like a little haven away from the hot, busy streets outside, the Reformador offers big, cool rooms set around leafy patios. Air-con rooms lead onto wide interior balconies. There is a restaurant (meals Q50 to Q80) here.

Hotel del Norte HOTEL $$
(☎7948-2116; 7a Calle; s/d with fan Q90/160, with air-con Q160/270; ❄@🏊) A large, classically tropical wooden construction with mosquito-screened corridors, the century-old Hotel del Norte is in a class by itself. Its weathered and warped frame is redolent of history and the floorboards go off at crazy angles. Pick a room carefully – some are little more than a wooden box, others have great ocean views and catch good breezes.

Eating

Kaffa CAFE $
(8a Av btwn Calles 7 & 8; sandwiches & breakfast Q30-50; ⏲8:30am-10pm) A hip coffee shop in Puerto Barrios? Well, why not? Let's see how long it lasts. The food's so-so, but the coffee and the breezy deck overlooking the park are both excellent.

La Habana Vieja CUBAN $$
(13 Calle btwn Avs 6a & 7a; mains Q40-80; ⏲11am-1pm) A good, wide selection of Cuban classics (including *ropa vieja* – a shredded beef stew) and some straightforward sandwiches. Also has a good bar if you're looking for a quiet drink.

Restaurante Safari SEAFOOD $$
(☎7948-0563; cnr 1a Calle & 5a Av; seafood Q60-120; ⏲10am-9pm) The town's most enjoyable restaurant is on a thatch-roofed, open-air platform right over the water about 1km north of the town center. Locals and visitors alike love to eat and catch the sea breezes here. Excellent seafood of all kinds including the specialty, *tapado* – that great Garífuna casserole (Q120).

Chicken and meat dishes are less expensive (Q50 to Q100). There's live music most nights. If the Safari is full, the Cangrejo Azul next door offers pretty much the same deal, in a more relaxed environment.

Orientation

Its spacious layout means you must walk or ride further in Puerto Barrios to get from place to place. It's 800m from the bus terminals in the town center to the Muelle Municipal (Municipal Boat Dock) at the end of 12a Calle, from which passenger boats depart. **El Muñecón** (intersection 8a Av, 14a Calle & Calz Justo Rufino Barrios) is a statue of a dock worker; it's a favorite landmark and monument in the town.

Information

Banco Industrial (7a Av; ⏲9am-5pm Mon-Fri, 9am-1pm Sat) Changes US dollars and traveler's checks, and has a Visa ATM.

Immigration Office (cnr 12a Calle & 3a Av; ⏲24hr) A block from the Muelle Municipal. Come here for your entry or exit stamp if you're arriving from or leaving for Belize. If you're heading to Honduras, you get your exit stamp at another immigration office on the road to the border.

Getting There & Around

BOAT

Boats depart from the Muelle Municipal at the end of 12a Calle.

Regular *lanchas* depart for Lívingston (Q35, 30 minutes) five times daily between 6:30am and 5pm. Buy your ticket as early as you can on the day (you can't book before your day of departure) – spaces are limited and sometimes sell out.

Outside of these regular times, *lanchas* depart whenever they have six people ready to go and cost Q50.

Most of the movement from Lívingston to Puerto Barrios is in the morning, returning in the afternoon. From Lívingston, your last chance of the day may be the 5pm *lancha*, especially during the low season when fewer travelers are shuttling back and forth.

Lanchas also depart from the Muelle Municipal three times daily for Punta Gorda, Belize (Q200, one hour). The 10am departure arrives in time for the noon bus from Punta Gorda to Belize City. Tickets are sold at the dock. Before boarding you also need to get your exit stamp at the nearby immigration office.

BUS & MINIBUS

Transportes Litegua (☎7948-1172; cnr 6a Av & 9a Calle) leaves for Guatemala City (Q65 to Q100, five to six hours), via Quiriguá and Río Hondo, frequently between 1am and 4pm. *Directo* services avoid a half-hour detour into Morales.

Minibuses for Chiquimula (Q45, 4½ hours), also via Quiriguá, leave every half-hour, from 3am to 3pm, from the corner of 6a Av and 9a Calle. Minibuses to Río Dulce (Q20, two hours) leave from the same location.

TAXI

Most cabs charge around Q20 for longish rides around town.

Punta de Manabique

This promontory to the north of Puerto Barrios is being slowly and carefully developed for ecotourism. As well as sporting Guatemala's best Caribbean beaches, the area offers endless bird-watching, hiking, sportfishing and other nature-based activities. The community of **Estero Lagarto** (☎5303-9822; www.turismocomunitarioguatemala.com/estero_lagarto_turismo.html) offers accommodations in its ecolodge where good, simple meals are available. You can arrange tours of the area from here. For transportation information and to make reservations, contact **Fundary** (Fundación Mario Dary; ☎7948-0944; www.fundary.org; 17a Calle).

Lívingston

POP 26,300

Quite unlike anywhere else in Guatemala, this largely Garífuna town is fascinating in itself, but also an attraction for its couple of good beaches, and its location at the end of the river journey from Río Dulce.

Unconnected by road from the rest of the country (the town is called 'Buga' – mouth – in Garífuna, for its position at the river mouth), boat transportation is (logically) quite good here, and you can get to Belize, the cays, Honduras and Puerto Barrios with a minimum of fuss.

The Garífuna (Garinagu, or Black Carib) people of Lívingston and southern Belize are the descendants of Africans brought to the New World as slaves. They trace their roots to the Honduran island of Roatán, where they were forcibly settled by the British after the Garífuna revolt on the Caribbean island of St Vincent in 1795. From Roatán, the Garífuna people spread out along the Caribbean Coast, from Belize to Nicaragua. Intermarrying with the Carib people, as well as with Maya and shipwrecked sailors of other races, they've developed a distinct culture and language incorporating African, *indígena* and European elements.

Town beaches are largely disappointing, as the jungle comes to the water's edge. Those beaches that do exist are often clogged with vegetation and unsafe for swimming, thanks to contaminated water. Safe swimming is possible at Los Siete Altares and Playa Blanca.

Sights & Activities

The best beaches in the area are **Playa Quehueche** – reachable by taxi (Q20) in about 10 minutes and **Playa Blanca** (admission Q10), around 12km from Lívingston. This is privately owned and you need a boat to get there.

Use mosquito repellent and take other precautions, especially in the jungle; mosquitoes near the coast carry malaria and dengue fever.

Los Siete Altares WATERFALL

(The Seven Altars; admission Q20) The 'Seven Altars' is a series of freshwater falls and pools about 5km (1½-hours' walk) northwest of Lívingston along the shore of Bahía de Amatique. It's a pleasant goal for a beach walk and a good place for a picnic and swim. Follow the shore northward to the river mouth and walk along the beach until it meets the path into the woods (about 30 minutes). Follow this path all the way to the falls.

Boat trips go to the Seven Altars, but locals say it's better to walk there to experience the natural beauty and the Garífuna people along the way. About halfway along, just past the swinging bridge is Hotel Salvador

Gaviota, whose attached **restaurant** (mains Q40-80; ⏲breakfast, lunch & dinner) serves decent food, ice-cold beers and soft drinks.

Tours

A few outfits in Lívingston offer tours that let you get out and experience the natural wonders of the area. **Exotic Travel** (☎7947-0133; www.bluecaribbeanbay.com; Restaurante Bahía Azul, Calle Principal) and **Happy Fish Travel** (☎7947-0661; www.happyfishtravel.com; Restaurante Happy Fish, Calle Principal) are both well-organized operations. Happy Fish gets extra points for supporting community tourism initiatives in the area and its willingness to share information on how you can visit many of the local attractions without a guide.

Offered by both companies, the popular Ecological Tour/Jungle Trip (Q90 including lunch) takes you for a walk through town, out west up to a lookout spot and on to the Río Quehueche, where you take a half-hour canoe trip down the river to Playa Quehueche. Then you walk through the jungle to Los Siete Altares, hang out there for a while, and walk back down the beach to Lívingston.

The Playa Blanca tour goes by boat first to Los Siete Altares and then on to Playa Blanca for two or three hours at the best beach in the area. This trip goes with a minimum of two people and costs Q100 per person.

Happy Fish offers a return boat trip (Q200) just along the canyon section of Río Dulce (the most interesting and picturesque part), and transport to the community tourism projects at Cueva del Tigre (Q160 for a tour, or they'll tell you how to get there on your own) and Lagunita Creek (p183).

Also popular are day/overnight trips to the Cayos Sapodillas (or Zapotillas), well off the coast of southern Belize, where there is great snorkeling (Q400/1000 for one/two days). A minimum of eight people is required and exit taxes and national park fees (Q160 in total) are separate.

Courses

Rasta Mesa CULTURAL BUILDING
(☎4459-6106; Barrio Nevago; ⏲10am-2pm & 7-10pm) Offers classes in Garífuna cooking (per person Q50) and drumming (per person Q100), as well as massages (Q150) and can hook you up with volunteer work in the area.

Festivals & Events

Semana Santa RELIGIOUS FESTIVAL
(⏲Easter week) Packs Lívingston with merrymakers.

Garifuna National Day CULTURAL FESTIVAL
(⏲Nov 26) Celebrated with a variety of cultural events.

Sleeping

Prices in Lívingston hit their peak from July to December – outside of these months many midrange and top-end places halve their rates.

Casa de la Iguana HOSTEL $
(☎7947-0064; www.casadelaiguana.com; Calle Marcos Sánchez Díaz; hammock/dm Q20/45, cabin with/without bathroom Q160/110; 📶) Five minutes' walk from the main dock, this party hostel offers good-value cabins. They're clean, wooden affairs, with simple but elegant decoration. Happy hour here rocks on and you can camp or crash in a hammock for Q20 per person.

Flowas BUNGALOW $
(☎7947-0376; infoflowas@gmail.com; per person Q100) An extremely laidback little backpacker enclave, this place offers rustic wood-and-bamboo cabins set up on the 2nd floor (catching the odd breeze) right on the beachfront. The atmosphere is relaxed and there's good, cheap food available. A taxi (Q15 from the dock) will drop you within 150m of the front gate.

Hotel Ríos Tropicales HOTEL $$
(☎5755-7571; www.mctropic.webs.com; Calle Principal; s/d Q150/200, without bathroom from Q60/120; 📶) The Ríos Tropicales has a variety of big, well-screened rooms facing a central patio with plenty of hammocks and chill-out space. Rooms with shared bathroom are bigger, but others are better decorated.

Hotel Salvador Gaviota BUNGALOW $$
(☎7947-0874; www.hotelsalvadorgaviota.com; Playa Quehueche; per person with/without bathroom Q140/70; @) Beautiful, simple wood-and-bamboo rooms set back a couple of hundred meters from a reasonably clean beach. Day trippers going to and from Los Siete Altars drop in for meals (Q40 to Q80) and drinks here – otherwise you may have the place to yourself. It's 500m from the swing bridge where the road ends – a taxi will charge about Q15 to get you there.

Vecchia Toscana HOTEL $$
(☎7947-0884; www.vecchiatoscana-livingston.com; Barrio Paris; s/d from Q341/488; ❄@📶🏊) This beautiful Italian-run place down on the beach has some of the best rooms in town. There are a variety of rooms on offer, going up to apartments that sleep eight comfortably. The grounds and common areas are immaculate and there's a good Italian restaurant with sea views out the front.

A taxi here from the dock will cost around Q10.

Eating

Food in Lívingston is relatively expensive because most of it (except fish and coconuts) must be brought in by boat. There's fine seafood here and some unusual flavors for Guatemala, including coconut and also curry. *Tapado,* a rich stew made from fish, shrimp, shellfish, coconut milk and plantain, spiced with coriander, is the delicious local specialty. Calle Principal is dotted with many open-air eateries.

Restaurante Gaby GUATEMALAN $
(Calle Marcos Sánchez Díaz; mains Q30-50; ⏲8am-9pm) For a good honest feed in humble surrounds, you can't go past Gaby's. She serves the good stuff: lobster, *tapado,* rice and beans, and good breakfasts at reasonable prices. The *telenovelas* (soap operas) come free.

Antojitos Yoli's BAKERY $
(Calle Principal; baked goods Q10-30; ⏲8am-5pm) This is the place to come for baked goods. Especially recommended are the coconut bread and pineapple pie.

Happy Fish SEAFOOD $$
(Calle Principal; mains Q40-100; ⏲7am-10pm; 📶) This bustling and breezy main street eatery is always busy with locals and tourists, keeping the food fresh and the service snappy. The requisite *tapado* is here, plus a good range of other options.

Restaurante Buga Mama SEAFOOD $$
(Calle Marcos Sánchez Díaz; mains Q60-100; ⏲8am-9pm; 📶) This place enjoys the best location of any restaurant in town, and profits go to the Asociación Ak' Tenamit (p190). There's a wide range of seafood, homemade pasta, curries and other dishes on the menu, including a very good *tapado* (Q100). Most of the waiters here are trainees in a community sustainable-tourism development scheme, so service can be sketchy, but forgivable.

Drinking

Adventurous drinkers should try *guifiti,* a local concoction made from coconut rum, often infused with herbs. It's said to have medicinal as well as recreational properties.

A handful of bars down on the beach to the left of the end of Calle Principal pull in travelers and locals at night (after about 10pm or 11pm). It's very dark down here, so take care. The bars are within five minutes' walk from each other, so you should go for a wander and see what's happening. Music ranges from *punta* to salsa, merengue and electronica. On Fridays things warm up but Saturday is party night – often going till 5am or 6am.

Happy hour is pretty much an institution along the main street, with every restaurant getting in on the act. One of the best is at Casa de la Iguana (p188).

Entertainment

A traditional Garífuna band is composed of three large drums, a turtle shell, some maracas and a big conch shell, producing throbbing, haunting rhythms and melodies. The chanted words are like a litany, with responses often taken up by the audience. *Punta* is the Garífuna dance; it's got a lot of gyrating hip movements.

Quite often a roaming band will play a few songs for diners along the Calle Principal around dinnertime. If you like the music, make sure to sling them a few bucks. Several places around town have live Garífuna music, although schedules are unpredictable.

Café-Bar Ubafu LIVE MUSIC
(Calle al Cementerio; ⏲6pm-late) Probably the most dependable. Supposedly has music and dancing nightly, but is liveliest on weekends.

Hotel Villa Caribe LIVE MUSIC
(www.hotelvillacaribeguatemala.com; Calle Principal) Diners can enjoy a Garífuna show each evening at 7pm.

Information

After half an hour you'll know where everything is. For more on Lívingston, check out its community website, www.livingston.com.gt.

WORTH A TRIP

RÍO DULCE CRUISES

Tour agencies in town offer day trips up the Río Dulce to Río Dulce town, as do most local boatmen at the Lívingston dock. Many travelers use these tours as one-way transportation to Río Dulce, paying Q125/180 one way/round trip. It's a beautiful ride through tropical jungle scenery, with several places to stop on the way. At the time of writing both departures (9:30am and 2:30pm) were doing the tour.

While a boat ride on the Río Dulce is not to be missed, if you're coming from Guatemala City or Puerto Barrios it makes much more sense to catch a boat from Puerto Barrios to Lívingston and do the tour on your way out.

Shortly after you leave Lívingston, you pass the tributary Río Tatin on the right, then will probably stop at an **indigenous arts museum** set up by Asociación Ak' Tenamit, an NGO working to improve conditions for the Q'eqchi' Maya population of the area. The river enters a gorge called **La Cueva de la Vaca**, its walls hung with great tangles of jungle foliage and the humid air noisy with the cries of tropical birds. Just beyond that is **La Pintada**, a rock escarpment covered with graffiti. Further on, a **thermal spring** forces sulfurous water out of the base of the cliff, providing a chance for a warm swim. The river widens into **El Golfete**, a lake-like body of water that presages the even vaster expanse of Lago de Izabal further upstream.

On the northern shore of El Golfete is the **Biotopo Chocón Machacas**, a 72-sq-km reserve established within the Parque Nacional Río Dulce to protect the beautiful river landscape, the valuable forests and mangrove swamps, and their wildlife, which includes such rare creatures as the tapir and the manatee. A network of 'water trails' (boat routes around several jungle lagoons) provide ways to see other bird, animal and plant life of the reserve. You can stay here, at the **community-run hotel** (☎5992-1853; www.lagunitasalvador.com; r Q185, bungalow Q350) in Lagunita Salvador, but you will have to arrange transportation separately.

Boats will probably visit the **Islas de Pájaros**, a pair of islands where thousands of waterbirds live, in the middle of El Golfete. From El Golfete you continue upriver, passing increasing numbers of expensive villas and boathouses, to the town of Río Dulce, where the soaring Hwy 13 road bridge crosses the river, and on to **El Castillo de San Felipe** on Lago de Izabal.

You can also do this trip starting from Río Dulce.

DANGERS & ANNOYANCES

Lívingston has its edgy aspects and a few hustlers operate here – exercise normal precautions. Use mosquito repellent and other sensible precautions here, especially if you go out into the jungle; mosquitoes here carry both malaria and dengue fever.

IMMIGRATION

Immigration Office (Calle Principal; ⏲6am-7pm) Issues entry and exit stamps for travelers arriving directly from or going directly to Belize or Honduras. Outside its normal hours, you can knock at any time.

MONEY

Banrural (Calle Principal; ⏲9am-5pm Mon-Fri, 9am-1pm Sat) Changes US dollars and traveler's checks and has an ATM.

Getting There & Away

Frequent boats come downriver from Río Dulce and across the bay from Puerto Barrios. There are also international boats from Honduras and Belize.

Happy Fish (p188) and Exotic Travel (p188) operate combined boat-and-bus shuttles to La Ceiba (the cheapest gateway to Honduras' Bay Islands) for around Q450 per person, with a minimum of four people. Leaving Lívingston at 6am or earlier will get you to La Ceiba in time for the boat to the islands, making it a one-day trip, which is nearly impossible to do independently.

There's also a boat that goes direct to Punta Gorda daily at 7am (Q200, 1½ hours), leaving from the public dock in Lívingston. In Punta Gorda, the boat then connects with a bus to Placencia and Belize City. The boat waits for this bus to arrive from Placencia before it sets off back for Lívingston from Punta Gorda at about 10:30am.

If you are taking one of these early international departures, get your exit stamp from immigration in Lívingston the day before.

EL PETÉN

Once synonymous with bad roads and impassible jungle, this region has been tamed over the years. Ever since the Maya exodus in the 9th century AD, this has been Guatemala's least-populated region, but continued government efforts to populate it have been hugely successful. In 1950 barely 15,000 people lived here. Now the number is well over 500,000. It's no surprise that most people you meet here were born elsewhere.

The regional superstar is, of course, Tikal, but many visitors are far more blown away by 'lesser' ruins such as Yaxhá and the massive, largely unexcavated sites at El Mirador.

In 1990 the Guatemalan government established the one-million-hectare Maya Biosphere Reserve, which includes most of northern El Petén. The Guatemalan reserve adjoins the vast Calakmul Biosphere Reserve in Mexico and the Río Bravo Conservation Area in Belize, forming a reserve of over two million hectares.

Many visitors linger in Poptún, a small town 113km southeast of Santa Elena that has been a popular backpacker layover for years. For easy access to Tikal, most people opt for the quaint island town of Flores, the tranquil lakeside village of El Remate or staying in the park itself.

Getting There & Around

The roads leading into El Petén have now all been paved, so travel is fast and smooth. Unfortunately, improved access has encouraged the migration of farmers and ranchers from other areas, increasing the pressure on resources and leading to further deforestation in a region where forests were already disappearing at an alarming rate.

The Guatemalan government has developed the adjoining towns of Flores, Santa Elena and San Benito, on the shores of Lago de Petén Itzá, into the region's tourism base. Here you'll find an airport, hotels and other services. A few small hotels and restaurants are at Tikal, but other services there are limited.

Sayaxché

Sayaxché, on the south bank of the Río de la Pasión, 61km southwest of Flores, is the closest town to nine or 10 scattered Maya archaeological sites, including Ceibal, Aguateca, Dos Pilas, Tamarindito and Altar de Sacrificios. Otherwise, for travelers it's little more than a transportation halt between Flores and Cobán.

East of the center is **Hospedaje Yaxkín** (☎4053-3484; bungalow per person Q50, without bathroom Q30), with 15 cheery bungalows amidst an impressive variety of plants and trees. A big open-air restaurant serves pastas, tacos and river fish (Q50). It's four blocks east and a block south of the church. Gregarious host Rosendo will pick you up at the dock if you phone ahead.

About the best bet for grub is **Café Maya** (Calle del Ferry; mains Q40-60; ⏲6:30am-9pm), a casual, open-air hall that is a popular gathering place both morning and evening. Aside from the usual fried chicken and grilled steak, there's river fish served with abundant portions of salad, beans and rice, and fries.

Banrural (⏲7:30am-4:30pm Mon-Fri, 7:30am-1pm Sat), just up the main street from Hotel Guayacán, has an ATM and changes euros and American Express travelers checks.

Minibuses and buses from Santa Elena stop on the north bank of the Río de la Pasión. Frequent ferries carry you across to the town. Southbound from Sayaxché, four microbuses head for Cobán (Q60, four hours) between 5am and 3pm. Every 25 minutes or so, Raxrujá-bound micros go to the San Antonio junction (Q30, 1½ hours), from where there are frequent departures for Cobán. Vehicles depart from a lot behind the Hotel Guayacán. From the north side, micros leave for Santa Elena every 15 minutes, from 5:45am to 6pm (Q23, 1½ hours).

Ceibal

Unimportant during the Classic period, Ceibal grew rapidly thereafter, attaining a population of perhaps 10,000 by AD 900. Much of the growth might have been due to immigration from what is now Chiapas, in Mexico, because the art and culture of Ceibal seems to have changed markedly during this period. The Postclassic period saw the decline of Ceibal, after which its low ruined temples were quickly covered by thick jungle.

Ceibal is not one of the most impressive Maya sites, but the journey to Ceibal is among the most memorable. A two-hour voyage on the jungle-bound Río de la Pasión brings you to a primitive dock. After landing you clamber up a rocky path beneath

El Petén

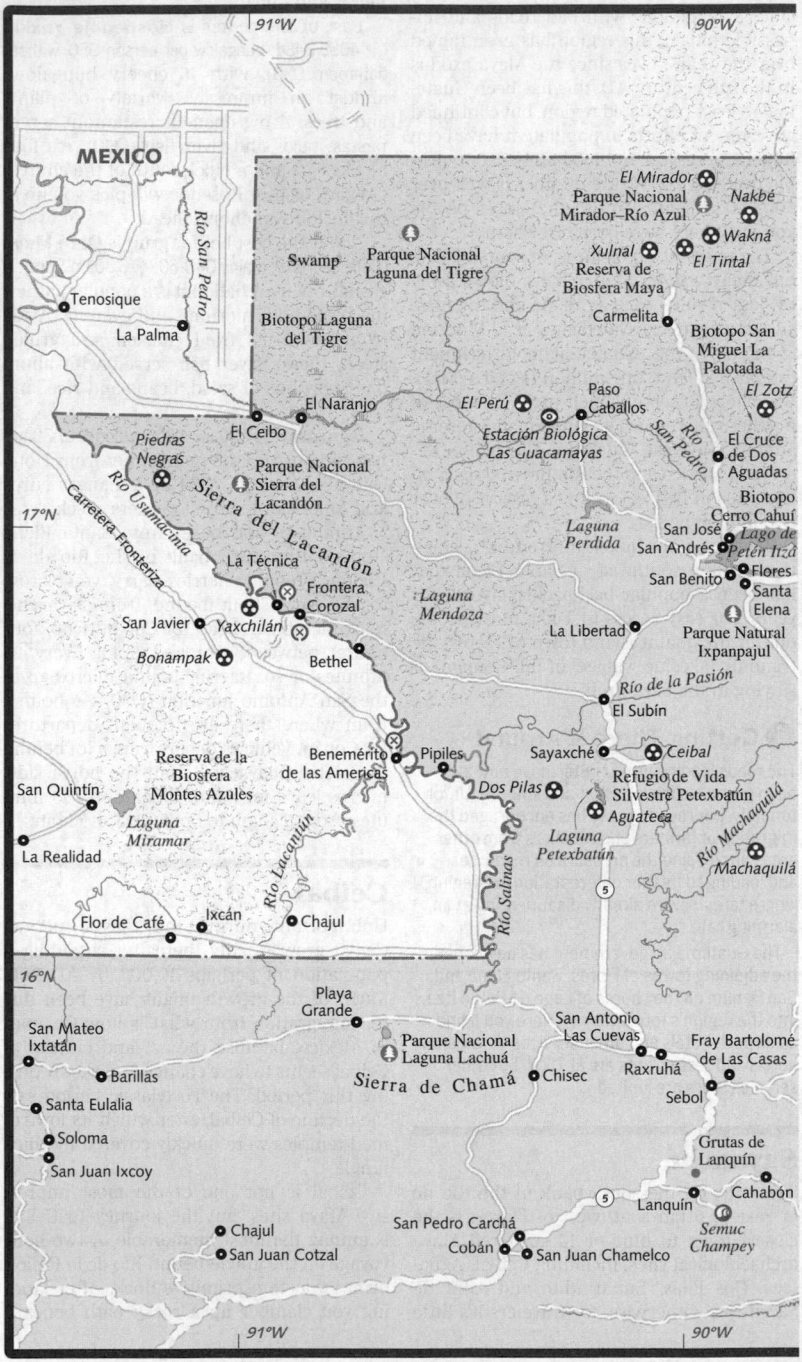
91°W
90°W
MEXICO
Río San Pedro
Tenosique
La Palma
Swamp
Parque Nacional Laguna del Tigre
Biotopo Laguna del Tigre
El Mirador
Parque Nacional Mirador–Río Azul
Nakbé
Wakná
Xulnal
Reserva de Biosfera Maya
El Tintal
Carmelita
Biotopo San Miguel La Palotada
El Zotz
El Naranjo
El Ceibo
El Perú
Paso Caballos
Estación Biológica Las Guacamayas
Río San Pedro
El Cruce de Dos Aguadas
Piedras Negras
Parque Nacional Sierra del Lacandón
Río Usumacinta
Sierra del Lacandón
Carretera Fronteriza
17°N
Laguna Perdida
Biotopo Cerro Cahuí
San José
San Andrés
Lago de Petén Itzá
Flores
San Benito
Santa Elena
La Técnica
Frontera Corozal
Laguna Mendoza
San Javier
Yaxchilán
Bonampak
Bethel
La Libertad
Parque Natural Ixpanpajul
Río de la Pasión
El Subín
Reserva de la Biosfera Montes Azules
Benemérito de las Americas
Pipiles
Sayaxché
Ceibal
San Quintín
Dos Pilas
Refugio de Vida Silvestre Petexbatún
Aguateca
Laguna Miramar
Laguna Petexbatún
Río Machaquilá
Machaquilá
La Realidad
Río Lacantún
Río Salinas
5
Flor de Café
Ixcán
Chajul
16°N
Playa Grande
San Mateo Ixtatán
Parque Nacional Laguna Lachuá
San Antonio Las Cuevas
Fray Bartolomé de Las Casas
Barillas
Sierra de Chamá
Chisec
Raxruhá
Sebol
Santa Eulalia
Soloma
San Juan Ixcoy
Grutas de Lanquín
Cahabón
Lanquín
Semuc Champey
Chajul
San Pedro Carchá
San Juan Cotzal
Cobán
San Juan Chamelco
91°W
90°W

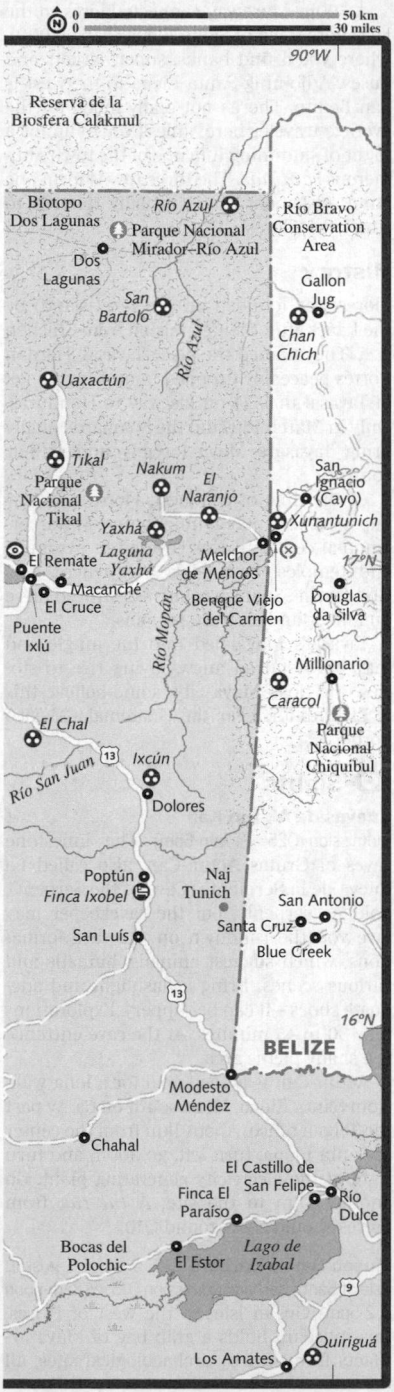

gigantic trees and vines to reach the archaeological zone.

Smallish temples, many still (or again) covered with jungle, surround two principal plazas. In front of a few temples, and standing seemingly alone on jungle paths, are magnificent, intact stelae. Exploring the site takes about two hours.

Travel agents offer tours to Ceibal from Flores. From Sayaxché, **Café del Río** (Calle del Ferry; ⏲ 6:30am-9pm), runs *lanchas* (Q470 for up to three people). **Viajes Don Pedro** (✎ 4580-9389; servlanchasdonpedro@hotmail.com) charges Q500 for up to five passengers. The fee should include a guide to the site, who may be the boatman. In high season, ask the *lancheros* about joining a tour group.

If you wish, you can get to Ceibal cheaper by land: get any bus, minibus or pickup heading south from Sayaxché on Hwy 5 (toward Raxruhá and Chisec) and get off after 9km at Paraíso, from which a dirt track leads 8km east to Ceibal. You may have to walk this last 8km. In the rainy season check first that this stretch is passable.

Finca Ixobel

This friendly, relaxed 160-hectare **farm** (✎ 5410-4307; www.fincaixobel.com; @) midway between Río Dulce and Flores offers tent sites (per person Q30), *palapas*, bungalows (single/double Q175/300) and 'tree houses' (single/double Q80/120) and good homemade meals with veggie options galore. Swimming, horseback riding, camping trips, inner-tubing on the river and a famous, thrilling cave trip (which even includes bodysurfing rapids) are all organized on a daily basis, for a reasonable charge.

Meals here are excellent, including the all-you-can-eat buffet dinner. After 9pm many people move on to the pool bar, where reasonably priced cocktails and other drinks are served. Volunteer opportunities exist for bilingual English-Spanish speakers; volunteers get free room and board.

Getting There & Away

The *finca* is 5km south of the regional commercial center of Poptún. The turnoff for the *finca* is marked on Hwy 13. In the daytime ask the bus or minibus driver to let you off there; it's a 15-minute walk to the *finca*. After hours, or to skip the hike in, get off the bus in Poptún and take a taxi (Q30) or *tuk-tuk* (Q20). When leaving Finca Ixobel, most buses will stop on the

OFF THE BEATEN TRACK

VILLAGES & RUINS AROUND EL PETÉN

El Petén isn't all about Tikal or Flores – there are some sweet little villages out there, just waiting to be explored.

➡ The towns of **San José** and **San Andrés**, on the western edge of Lago de Petén Itzá both have good budget hotels, Spanish schools and volunteer opportunities. San José has a lakefront waterslide park, too. Boats and buses run from Flores/Santa Elena to both these villages.

➡ The **Museo Regional del Sureste de Petén** (⏲8am-5pm) at Dolores, 25km north of Poptún, is reason enough to go there – it displays some of the most significant finds from the southern Petén sites. An hour's walk to the north is the site of **Ixcún** (admission Q30; ⏲8am-5pm), housing the second-largest stela in the Maya world.

highway to pick you up, but not after dark. The *finca* also offers shuttles to/from Flores for Q50. Shuttles coming from Flores should drop you at the gate, but check first. Bus departures from Poptún include the following:

Flores/Santa Elena (two hours, 113km) Línea Dorada offers 1st-class service at 4am, 4:30am and 5pm among the sleepy passengers coming from Guatemala City. The best option is to take a minibus (Q30, every 10 minutes, 6am to 6pm).

Guatemala City (seven hours, 387km) First-class buses by Línea Dorada (Q150 to Q190) depart at 11:30am and 11pm. Fuente del Norte buses (Q80) pass through approximately every hour from 5:30am to midnight.

Río Dulce (Q50, two hours, 99km) All Guatemala City–bound buses make a stop in Río Dulce.

Flores & Santa Elena

Flores (pop 30,700) is spectacularly located on an island in Lago de Petén Itzá. Small hotels and restaurants line the lakeside streets, meaning you don't have to shell out the big bucks to get a room with some awesome views. It does have a slightly twee, built-up edge to it, though, and many Tikal-bound shoestringers opt for the natural surrounds and tranquillity of El Remate, just down the road.

A 500m causeway connects Flores to the lakeshore town of Santa Elena (pop 29,000), where you'll find banks, supermarkets and buses. Adjoining Santa Elena to the west is San Benito. There's not really much for the average traveler here, unless you're up for a night of slumming it in one of the town's numerous *cantinas*. The three towns form one large settlement that is usually referred to simply as 'Flores'.

History

Flores was founded on a *petén* (island) by the Itzáes after their expulsion from Chichén Itzá. They named the place Tayasal. Hernán Cortés peaceably dropped in on King Canek of Tayasal in 1524 on his way to Honduras. Only in March 1697 did the Spaniards finally bring Tayasal's Maya forcibly under their control.

At the time of conquest, Flores was perhaps the last major functioning Maya ceremonial center; it was covered in pyramids and temples, with idols everywhere. The God-fearing Spanish soldiers destroyed these buildings, and no trace remains.

Tayasal's Maya fled into the jungle and may have started anew, giving rise to stories of a 'lost' Maya city; some believe this is El Mirador, near the Guatemala–Mexico border.

Sights

Cuevas de Ak'tun Kan CAVE

(admission Q25; ⏲7am-6pm) The limestone caves of Grutas Actun-Can, also called La Cueva de la Serpiente (Cave of the Serpent), hold no serpents, but the cavekeeper may give you the rundown on the cave formations, which suggest animals, humans and various scenes. Bring a flashlight and adequate shoes – it can be slippery. Explorations take 30 to 45 minutes. At the cave entrance is a shady picnic area.

Actun-Can is a good goal for a long walk from Santa Elena. Head south on 6a Av past the Telgua office. About 1km from the center of Santa Elena, turn left, go 300m and turn right at the electricity generating plant. Go another 1km to the site. A *tuk-tuk* from Flores should cost around Q10.

Museo Santa Bárbara MUSEUM

(Isle of Santa Bárbara; admission Q15; ⏲8am-noon & 2-5pm) On an islet to the west of Flores, this museum holds a grab bag of Maya artifacts from nearby archaeological sites, all

Flores

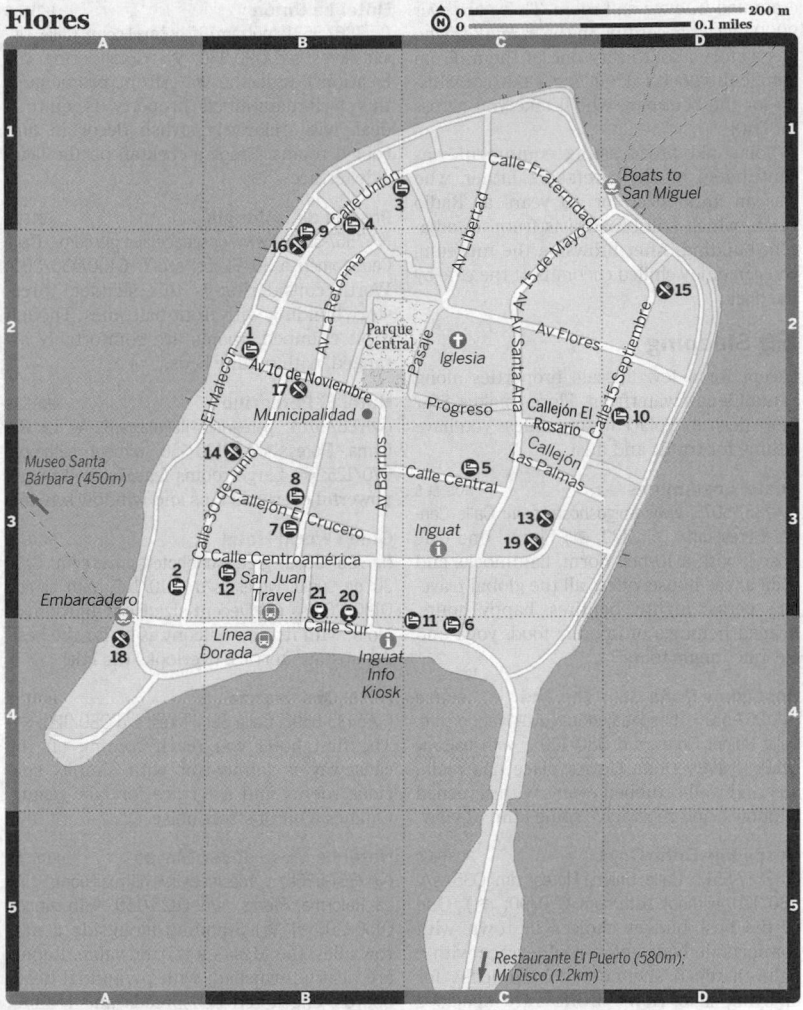

Flores

Sleeping

1 Casa Amelia B2
2 Green World Hotel A3
3 Hospedaje Doña Goya B1
4 Hospedaje Doña Goya the 2nd B1
5 Hostel Los Amigos C3
6 Hotel Casablanca C4
7 Hotel El Peregrino B3
8 Hotel La Mesa de los Mayas B3
9 Hotel La Unión B2
10 Hotel Mirador del Lago D2
11 Hotel Petenchel C4
12 Posada de la Jungla B3

Eating

13 Café Arqueológico Yax-ha C3
14 Capitán Tortuga B3
15 Cool Beans D2
16 Il Terrazo B2
17 La Luna B2
18 Raíces A4
19 Restaurante & Pizzería Picasso C3
Restaurante El Peregrino ..... (see 7)

Drinking & Nightlife

20 Casa de Palmas B3
21 El Trópico B3

crammed into a small room. There are over 9000 pieces, according to the caretaker who has a story about every one of them. From San Benito dock, call (☎7926-0660) or whistle for the boatman, who'll take you across for Q10.

Some old broadcasting equipment was contributed by the caretaker's father, who was an announcer for 40 years at Radio Petén, which still broadcasts from an adjacent building. After browsing the museum, you can enjoy chilled coconuts at the cafe by the dock.

Sleeping

Except for a few upscale properties along Santa Elena's waterfront, Flores makes a far more desirable place to stay, unless you have a thing for traffic and dust.

Hostel Los Amigos HOSTEL $
(☎7867-5075; www.amigoshostel.com; Calle Central, Flores; dm/r Q55/120; @) Flores' one true hostel, with a 10-bed dorm, hammocks and even a tree house, offers all the global traveler's perks: nightly bonfires, happy hours, heaped helpings of organic food, yoga and cut-rate jungle tours.

Hospedaje Doña Goya the 2nd HOTEL $
(☎7867-5516; hospedajedonagoya@yahoo.com; Calle Unión, Flores; s/d Q80/120, r with balcony Q160; ❄@📶) Doña Goya's place has plain, airy and well-scrubbed rooms with screened windows, and most have some kind of view.

Hospedaje Doña Goya HOSTEL $
(☎7867-5513; Calle Unión, Flores; dm Q35, s/d Q80/120, without bathroom Q70/90; 📶) One of the best budget choices in town with comfortable beds and a roof terrace with a palm-thatched shelter and hammocks for enjoying lake views. Dorms are spacious and spotless.

Hotel Mirador del Lago HOTEL $
(☎7867-5409; Calle 15 de Septiembre, Flores; s/d Q60/90, r with rear view Q130/150; @📶) Though minimally maintained, this hotel holds a good position just up from the causeway, with a terrace facing the lake. Upstairs units catch good afternoon breezes.

Hotel Petenchel HOTEL $
(☎7867-5450; Calle Sur, Flores; s/d Q100/120, with air-con Q150/170; ❄) Eight spacious rooms, with firm beds and high-arched ceilings, set around a lush courtyard.

Hotel La Unión HOTEL $
(☎7867-5531; gulzam75@hotmail.com; Calle Unión, Flores; s/d Q90/130; 📶) Considering the location beside the waterfront promenade, this well-maintained property is quite a deal, with relatively stylish decor in fan-cooled rooms. Enjoy a cocktail on the lakeside terrace.

Posada de la Jungla HOTEL $
(☎7867-5185; www.posadadelajungla.com; Calle Centroamérica 30, Flores; s/d/tr Q100/150/200) Worth considering is this slender, three-story building with front balconies. Though a bit cramped, rooms are comfortably arranged, with quality beds.

Hotel El Peregrino HOTEL $
(☎7867-5701; peregrino@itelgua.com; Av La Reforma, Flores; s/d Q120/150, without bathroom Q70/125; ❄) Large rooms feature tiled floors, powerful overhead fans and window screens.

Green World Hotel HOTEL $
(☎7867-5662; greenworldhotel@gmail.com; Calle 30 de Junio, Flores; s/d Q110/160, with air-con Q190/260; ❄@) Decent-sized, low-lit rooms – No 8, with its rear balcony, is by far the best. An upstairs terrace overlooks the lake.

Hotel Casablanca HOTEL $
(☎5435-6592; Calle Sur, Flores; s/d Q80/120; 📶) The first hotel you reach coming off the causeway is family-run with simple, spacious rooms and a terrace for lake-gazing. Catches a bit of street noise.

Hotel La Mesa de los Mayas HOTEL $$
(☎7867-5268; mesamayas@hotmail.com; Av La Reforma, Flores; s/d Q125/150, with air-con Q150/200; ❄📶) Standing alongside a narrow alley, the Mesa's a terrific value. Rooms are neatly furnished, with pyramidal headboards, checkered bedspreads and reading lamps; some feature plant-laden balconies.

Casa Amelia BOUTIQUE HOTEL $$
(☎7867-5430; www.hotelcasamelia.com; Calle Unión, Flores; s/d Q220/340; ❄@📶) Bright, stylish chambers with excellent lake views. There are good views from the roof terrace.

Eating

As might be expected, Flores is rife with tourist-oriented joints pitching a bland melange of 'international' fare to the package crowd. Nevertheless, a few local gems rise above the pack.

On the menu at many places is a variety of local game, including *tepezcuintle* (paca, a rabbit-sized jungle rodent), *venado* (venison), armadillo, *pavo silvestre* (wild turkey) and *pescado blanco* (white fish). You may want to avoid dishes that might soon jump from the menu to the endangered species list.

Cool Beans CAFE $
(Calle 15 de Septiembre, Flores; coffee & snacks Q8-25; ⏲7am-10pm Mon-Sat; 📶) Also known as Café Chilero, this laid-back locale features salons for chatting, watching videos or laptop browsing. The lush garden with glimpses of the lake makes a *tranquilo* spot for breakfast or veggie burgers. Be warned – the kitchen closes at 9:01pm sharp.

★Il Terrazo ITALIAN $$
(Calle Unión, Flores; pasta Q65-75; ⏲8am-10pm Mon-Sat) An Italian gourmet restaurant set on a rooftop terrace underneath a thatched canopy. The fettuccine, tortellini and taglioni are all produced in house, and they'll prepare panini to go. The fruit smoothies are unbelievable.

Café Arqueológico Yax-ha CAFE $$
(www.cafeyaxha.com; Calle 15 de Septiembre, Flores; mains Q35-65; ⏲6:30am-10pm) Wallpapered with photos and articles relating to local Maya sites, this cafe-restaurant is home base for an archaeological tour outfit. What's special here is the pre-Hispanic and Itzá items featured on the menu – pancakes with ramón seeds, yucca scrambled with mora herbs, chicken in *chaya* (a spinach-like leafy vegetable) sauce.

Restaurante & Pizzería Picasso PIZZERIA $$
(Calle 15 de Septiembre, Flores; pizza Q35-120; ⏲2:30-10:30pm Sun-Fri) This long-standing, Italian-owned joint does primo wood-fired pizzas, with room to lounge in the courtyard.

Restaurante El Peregrino GUATEMALAN $$
(☎7867-5115; Av La Reforma, Flores; mains Q40-60; ⏲7am-10pm) Serving generous helpings of home-cooked fare, such as pork-belly stew and breaded tongue. Daily lunch specials (Q20) are a bargain.

Capitán Tortuga INTERNATIONAL $$
(Calle 30 de Junio, Flores; pizzas Q45-100; ⏲8am-10:30pm) A barnlike locale with a pair of lakeside terraces serving heapings of comfort food – especially pizzas – at medium prices. Beer-quaffing groups should opt for the *cubetazos* – five bottles in a bucket for Q75.

La Luna MEDITERRANEAN $$
(cnr Calle 30 de Junio & Av 10 de Noviembre, Flores; mains Q60-120; ⏲noon-11pm Mon-Sat; ✎) In a class by itself, this popular restaurant cultivates a classic tropical ambience, with innovative chicken, fish and beef dishes surpassing similar dishes anywhere else in Guatemala. There are also good pasta and vegetarian options.

Raíces STEAKHOUSE $$
(Calle Sur, Flores; mains Q80-110; ⏲4-10pm Sun-Thu, 4pm-1am Fri & Sat) A broad deck and a flaming grill are the main ingredients at this stylish lakefront restaurant/bar. Chargrilled meats and seafood are the specialty, and you can choose your grills by the pound or half-pound.

Restaurante El Puerto SEAFOOD $$
(1a Calle 2-15, Santa Elena; mains Q100; ⏲11am-11pm) Seafood is the star attraction at this breezy, open-air hall by the lakefront in Santa Elena, with a well-stocked bar at the front. It's an ideal setting to enjoy shellfish stews, *ceviches* or the famous *pescado blanco* – whitefish from the lake.

Drinking & Entertainment

Flores doesn't exactly jive at night but there are a couple of places to hang out. Flores' little Zona Viva is a strip of bars along Playa Sur, and nearly all the lakeside restaurants in Santa Elena have afternoon happy hours – a great way to unwind and watch the sunset.

Locals gather in the cool of the evening for long drinks, snacks and relaxation in the Parque Central, where a marimba ensemble plays some nights.

El Trópico BAR
(Calle Sur, Flores; ⏲4:30pm-1am Mon-Sat) This is a nice spot to start the night: the candlelit terrace is good for gazing at the lights of Santa Elena reflected across the lake while enjoying an icy *cerveza* (beer).

Casa de Palmas BAR
(Calle Sur, Flores) Aside from drinking and conversing at the terrace tables, there's nonstop dancing on the crowded dance floor. It's a mostly middle-class Guatemalan scene.

Mi Disco DISCO
(cnr Calle Central & Av Santa Ana, Santa Elena; ⏲Mon-Sat) 'El Mi' is Santa Elena's major disco, a cavernous hall with a big stage for salsa combos. If you'd rather croon than

dance, Monday to Wednesday evenings are reserved for karaoke.

Orientation

The airport is on the eastern outskirts of Santa Elena, 2km from the causeway connecting Santa Elena and Flores. Most buses arrive and depart from the new bus terminal 1km south of the causeway.

Information

EMERGENCY

Proatur (Tourist Police; ☎5414-3594)

Hospital Privado de Petén (☎7926-1140; 3a Av 4-29, Zona 2, Santa Elena)

MONEY

Banrural (Av Flores, Flores), off the Parque Central in Flores, changes dollars and euros, cash or traveler's checks. There's a handy Banco Industrial **ATM** (Calle 30 de Junio, Flores) at the Fotomart convenience store, opposite Capitán Tortuga on Calle 30 de Junio.

There are plenty of other banks with ATMs along 4a Calle in Santa Elena.

Many travel agencies and places to stay will change cash US dollars, and sometimes traveler's checks, though at poorer rates.

POST

There's a **post office** (4a Calle & 4a Av, inside Centro Comercial Karossi, Santa Elena) in Santa Elena

TOURIST INFORMATION

Inguat (☎7867-5365; info-mundomaya@inguat.gob.gt; Calle Centroamérica; ⏲8am-4pm Mon-Fri) The official Inguat office is more of a business center than info provider; the kiosk on Calle Sur (☎4210-9992; info-mundomaya@inguat.gob.gt; Calle Sur, Flores; ⏲9:30am-5:30pm) is a better bet. There's another info kiosk (☎7926-0533) at the Aeropuerto Internacional Mundo Maya.

TRAVEL AGENCIES

Several travel agencies in Flores and Santa Elena offer trips to archaeological sites, shuttle minibuses and other services.

Aventuras Turísticas (☎4034-9291; www.aventurasturisticas.com; Av Barrios, Flores) Shuttles to Cobán, tours to Tikal, bicycle rentals.

Martsam Travel (☎7867-5093; www.martsam.com; Calle 30 de Junio, Flores) Central America–wide operator specializing in custom-designed tours; supports ecotourism initiatives and community involvement.

Getting There & Away

AIR

Aeropuerto Internacional Mundo Maya, sometimes called Petén International Airport, is just east of Santa Elena. **Grupo TACA** (www.taca.com) has at least three flights daily between here and the capital (Q1255/2165 one way/round trip). The Belizean airline **Tropic Air** (☎7926-0348; www.tropicair.com) flies twice a day from and to Belize City, charging Q1015 each way for the one-hour trip.

BUS & MINIBUS

The Terminal Nuevo de Autobuses is on 6a Ave in Santa Elena, about 1km south of the causeway to Flores. The following lines use the terminal: **Autobuses del Norte** (☎7924-8131; www.adnautobusesdelnorte.com); **Fuente del Norte** (☎7926-2999); and **Línea Dorada** (☎7924-8535).

Santa Elena's terminal is also used by a slew of microbuses, with frequent service to numerous destinations. The cooperative **ACTEP** (☎7924-8215), with an office on the left side of the terminal, runs micros to Poptún, Melchor de Mencos, San Andrés, Bethel–La Técnica, Paso Caballos and elsewhere, while others offer service to Sayaxché, El Remate and Tikal.

Going to Belize City, it's cheaper but slower to take microbuses to the border and on from there. Going to Cobán, it's cheaper to catch a bus to Sayaxché, from where connecting micros leave for Cobán at 11am and 3pm. To get to Puerto Barrios, take a Guatemala City–bound Fuente del Norte bus and change at La Ruidosa junction, south of Río Dulce.

Schedules are changeable and should be confirmed before heading out.

SHUTTLE MINIBUS

Aventuras Turísticas (p198) offers daily shuttles to Cobán (Q125, four hours), Lanquín, Semuc Champey and Antigua. **San Juan Travel** (☎5461-6010; Calle Playa Sur) operates shuttle minibuses to Tikal (Q60, 1¼ hours each way). They leave hourly from 5am to 10am. Most hotels and travel agencies can book these shuttles and they will pick you up where you're staying. Returns leave Tikal at 12:30pm, 2pm, 3pm, 4pm and 5pm. If you know which round trip you plan to be on, ask your driver to hold a seat for you or arrange one in another minibus. If you stay overnight in Tikal and want to return to Flores by minibus, it's a good idea to reserve a seat with a driver when they arrive in the morning.

Getting Around

A taxi from the airport to Santa Elena or Flores costs Q20. *Tuk-tuks* will take you anywhere between or within Flores and Santa Elena for

Q5. Aventuras Turísticas (p198) rents mountain bikes for Q30 per day.

El Remate

This idyllic spot at the eastern end of Lago de Petén Itzá makes a good alternative base for Tikal-bound travelers – it's more relaxed than Flores, and closer to the site. Just two roads, really, El Remate has a ramshackle charm all of its own.

El Remate begins 1km north of Puente Ixlú, where the road to the Belize border diverges from the Tikal road. The village strings along the Tikal road for 1km to another junction, where a branch heads west along the north shore of the lake.

El Remate is known for its wood carving. Some fine examples of the craft are sold from stalls along the main road.

Sights & Activities

Most El Remate accommodations can book two-hour boat trips for bird-watching or nocturnal crocodile-spotting (each Q100 per person). Try Casa de Ernesto (p200) or Hotel Mon Ami (p200); the latter also offers sunset lake tours with detours up the Ixlú and Ixpop rivers (Q150 per person).

Ascunción, found by the second speed bump from the north shore junction, rents kayaks (Q35 per hour), bicycles (per hour/day Q10/70) and horses (Q150 per person, 2½ hours).

Biotopo Cerro Cahuí NATURE RESERVE

(admission Q40; ⏲7am-4pm) At the northeast end of Lago de Petén Itzá, about 3km from the Flores–Tikal road, the Biotopo Cerro Cahuí covers 651 hectares of subtropical forest. Within are mahogany, cedar, ramón, broom, sapodilla and cohune palm trees, as well as many species of lianas and epiphytes, these last including bromeliads, ferns and orchids. The hard wood of the sapodilla was used in Maya temple-door lintels, some of which have survived from the Classic period to our own time. Chicle is still sapped from the trees' innards.

Among the many animals within the reserve are spider and howler monkeys, ocelots, white-tailed deer, raccoons, armadillos, numerous species of fish, turtle and snake, and the Petén crocodile. Depending upon the season and migration patterns, you might see kingfishers, ducks, herons, hawks, parrots, toucans, woodpeckers and the beautiful ocellated (Petén) turkey, which resembles a peacock.

A network of loop trails starts at the road and goes uphill, affording a view of Lago de Petén Itzá and Lagunas Salpetén and Petenchel. A trail map is at the entrance.

The admission fee includes the right to camp or sling your hammock under small thatched shelters inside the entrance. There are toilets and showers.

The dock opposite the entrance is the best place to swim along the generally muddy shore of the lake.

BUSES FROM FLORES & SANTA ELENA

DESTINATION	COST (Q)	DURATION	DEPARTURES	FREQUENCY
Belize City	160	4-5 hr	7am	daily
Bethel (Mexican border)	35	4½ hr	11am-4pm	5 daily
El Ceibo/La Palma (Mexican border)	35	4 hr	4:40am-6pm	every 20 min
El Remate	20	40 min	5am-6pm	every 30 min
Esquipulas	110	8 hr	6am-2pm	every 4 hr
Guatemala City	from 110	8-9 hr	3am-11pm	hourly
Melchor de Mencos (Belizean border)	25	2 hr	5:45am-6pm	hourly
Poptún	25	1¾ hr	5am-6:30pm	every 10 min
Río Dulce	from 60	4 hr	3am-11pm	hourly
Sayaxché	20	1½ hr	5:45am-6pm	every 15 min
Tikal	50	1¼ hr	5am-1pm	every 2 hr

Sleeping & Eating

Most hotels have their own restaurants and there are simple *comedores* scattered along the main road.

Casa de Ernesto BUNGALOW $

(☎4915-8309; hotelcasadernesto@gmail.com; Jobompiche Rd; s/d Q100/150, without bathroom Q40/80; ❄) Ernesto and his clan offer cool and comfortable adobe huts in the woods with thatched roofs, tiled floors, and good rustic-style beds. Add Q50 for air-con. Canoe rentals, horseback riding to Laguna Salpetén and expeditions for the great white fish are among the activities offered.

★Posada del Cerro BUNGALOW $$

(☎5376-8722; www.posadadelcerro.com; s/d Q220/330; 📶) This ecologically sound option blends brilliantly into its jungle setting, close enough to the Cerro Cahui nature reserve to hear the monkeys howl the evening in. Ten thoughfully furnished rooms occupy stone-and-hardwood houses and solitary huts scattered over the hillside; one is open to the woods with its own lake-view deck.

Herbs from the forest are stirred into local recipes in the neat, thatched-roof restaurant.

Hotel Mon Ami HOTEL $$

(☎7928-8413; www.hotelmonami.com; Jobompiche Rd; dm/s/d Q50/150/200; 📶) A 15-minute walk from the Tikal road and a stone's throw from the Biotopo Cerro Cahui, this maintains a good balance between jungle wildness and Euro sophistication. Quirkily furnished cabins and dorms with hammocks are reached along candlelit paths through gardens bursting with local plant life, though the bathhouse needs a feng-shui overhaul. Fans of French cuisine will appreciate the open-air restaurant (mains Q75 to Q115; open for breakfast, lunch and dinner).

Hostal Hermano Pedro HOSTEL $$

(☎4326-6253; www.hhpedro.com; dm/s/d Q96/152/208; 📶) Set in a two-story wood-and-stone house, 20m off to the right from the main road, the spacious rooms are refreshingly simple and comfortable, with a few frills like lacy curtains, big fans and balcony porches. Guests can use the kitchen or grab a hammock in the common room.

Las Orquideas ITALIAN $$

(☎5819-7232; Jobompiche Rd; pastas Q55-80; ⏲noon-9pm Tue-Sun) Las Orquideas has a genial Italian owner-chef cooking up genuine Mediterranean fare, with tempting desserts too.

Information

You can change US dollars and euros, or check your email, at **Horizontes Mayas** (☎7928-8471; www.horizontesmayas.com), adjacent to Hotel Las Gardenias.

Getting There & Around

El Remate is linked to Flores by a frequent microbus service (Q20).

For Tikal, collective shuttles leave El Remate at 5:30am, starting back at 2pm (Q50 round trip). Any El Remate accommodations can make reservations. You can also catch one of the hourly shuttles (Q30 to Q50) passing through from Santa Elena to Tikal.

For Melchor de Mencos on the Belizean border, get a minibus or bus from Puente Ixlú, 2km south of El Remate.

Tikal

Towering pyramids poke above the jungle's green canopy to catch the sun. Howler monkeys swing noisily through the branches of ancient trees as brightly colored parrots and toucans dart from perch to perch in a cacophony of squawks. When the complex warbling song of some mysterious jungle bird tapers off, the buzz of tree frogs fills the background and it will dawn on you that this is, indeed, hallowed ground.

Certainly the most striking feature of **Tikal** (☎2367-2837; www.parque-tikal.com; admission Q150; ⏲6am-6pm) is its steep-sided temples, rising to heights of more than 61m. But Tikal is different from Copán, Chichén Itzá, Uxmal and most other great Maya sites because it is deep in the jungle. Its many plazas have been cleared of trees and vines, its temples uncovered and partially restored, but as you walk from one building to another you pass beneath the dense rainforest canopy. Rich, loamy smells of earth and vegetation, a peaceful air and animal noises all contribute to an experience not offered by other Maya sites.

You can, if you wish, visit Tikal in a day trip from Flores or El Remate. But you'll get more out of Tikal if you spend a night here, enabling you to visit the ruins twice and to be here in the late afternoon and early morning, when other tourists are rare and wildlife more active.

History

Tikal is set on a low hill above the surrounding swampy ground – which might be why the Maya settled here around 700 BC. Another reason was the abundance of flint, used to make clubs, spearheads, arrowheads and knives. Flint could also be exported in exchange for other goods. Within 200 years, the Maya of Tikal had begun to build stone ceremonial structures, and by 200 BC a complex of buildings stood on the site of the North Acropolis.

Classic Period

The Great Plaza was beginning to assume its present shape and extent 2000 years ago. By the dawn of the early Classic period, about AD 250, Tikal had become an important, heavily populated religious, cultural and commercial city. King Yax Ehb' Xooc, whose reign began around AD 230, founded the ruling dynasty.

Under Chak Tok Ich'aak I (King Great Jaguar Paw), who ruled in the mid-4th century, Tikal adopted a new, brutal method of warfare used by the rulers of Teotihuacán in central Mexico. Rather than meeting their adversaries in hand-to-hand combat, the army of Tikal encircled their enemy and killed them by throwing spears. This first use of 'air power' among the Maya of Petén enabled Tikal to conquer Uaxactún and become the dominant kingdom in the region.

By the middle of the Classic period, during the mid-6th century, Tikal sprawled over 30 sq km and had a population of perhaps 100,000. In 553 Yajaw Te' K'inich II (Lord Water) ascended to the throne of Caracol (in southwestern Belize), and by 562, using the same warfare methods learned from Tikal, conquered and sacrificed Tikal's king. Tikal and other Petén kingdoms suffered under Caracol's rule until the late 7th century.

Tikal's Renaissance

Around 700 a powerful king named Jasaw Chan K'awiil I (682–734, also called Ah Cacao or Moon Double Comb), 26th successor of Yax Ehb' Xooc, ascended Tikal's throne. He restored not only its military strength, but also its primacy as the Maya world's most resplendent city. He and his successors were responsible for building most of the surviving temples around the Great Plaza. He was buried beneath the staggering height of Temple I.

Tikal's greatness waned around 900, part of the mysterious general collapse of lowland Maya civilization.

No doubt the Itzáes, who occupied Tayasal (now Flores), knew of Tikal in the late Postclassic period (1200–1530). Perhaps they even came to worship at the shrines of their old gods. Spanish missionary friars left brief references to these jungle-covered structures, but these writings moldered in libraries for centuries.

Rediscovery

It wasn't until 1848 that the Guatemalan government sent an expedition, under Modesto Méndez and Ambrosio Tut, to visit the site. In 1877 Dr Gustav Bernoulli of Switzerland visited Tikal and removed lintels from Temples I and IV to Basel, where they are still on view in the Museum für Völkerkunde.

Scientific exploration at Tikal began with the arrival of English archaeologist Alfred P Maudslay in 1881; others who continued his work include Teobert Maler, Alfred M Tozzer and RE Merwin. Tozzer worked at Tikal from the beginning of the century until his death in 1954. Tikal's inscriptions were studied and deciphered by Sylvanus G Morley.

Since 1956 archaeological research and restoration has been carried out by the University of Pennsylvania and the Guatemalan Instituto de Antropología e Historia. In the mid-1950s an airstrip was built to make access easier. In the early 1980s the road between Tikal and Flores was paved, and direct flights abandoned. Tikal National Park was declared a Unesco World Heritage Site in 1979.

Sights

Gran Plaza

Follow the signs to reach the Gran Plaza. The path enters the plaza around **Temple I**, the Temple of the Grand Jaguar, built for Jasaw Chan K'awiil I (King Moon Double Comb). The king might have worked out the plans himself, but it was erected above his tomb by his son, who succeeded him to the throne in 734. Burial goods included 180 beautiful jade objects, 90 pieces of bone carved with hieroglyphs, and pearls and stingray spines, used for ritual bloodletting. At the top of the 44m-high temple is a small enclosure of three rooms covered by a corbeled arch. The lofty roof comb was originally adorned with reliefs and bright paint, perhaps symbolizing the 13 realms of the Maya heaven.

Tikal

SURVEYING THE CLASSIC MAYA KINGDOM

Constructed in successive waves over a period of at least 800 years, Tikal is a vast, complicated site with hundreds of temples, pyramids and stelae. There's no way you'll get to it all in a day, but by following this itinerary you'll see many of the highlights. Before setting out be sure to stop by the visitor center and examine the scale model of the site, then admire the wealth of kings at the small **Museo Tikal** 1. Present your ticket at the nearby control booth and when you reach the posted map, take a left. It's a 20-minute walk to the solitary **Templo VI** 2. From here it's a blissful stroll up the broad Méndez causeway to the **Gran Plaza** 3, Tikal's ceremonial core, where you may examine the ancient precinct of the **North Acropolis** 4. Exit the plaza west, and take the first left, along a winding path, to **Templo V** 5. Round the rear to the right, a trail encircles the largely unexcavated South Acropolis to the **Plaza de los Siete Templos** 6. Immediately west stands the great pyramid of the **Mundo Perdido** 7. From here it's a quick stroll and a rather strenuous climb to the summit of **Temple IV** 8, Tikal's tallest structure.

TOP TIPS

» Bring food and water.

» If you enter after 4pm, your ticket is good for the next day.

» Stay at one of the onsite hotels to catch the sunset/sunrise.

» To watch the sunset/sunrise from Temple IV, you'll need to purchase an additional ticket (Q100).

» Bring mosquito repellent.

DANIEL SCHECHTER

Templo IV
Arrive in the late afternoon to get magically tinted photos of Temples I, II and III poking through the jungle canopy. If you're lucky you might also get a glimpse of an orange-crested falcon swooping around the treetops.

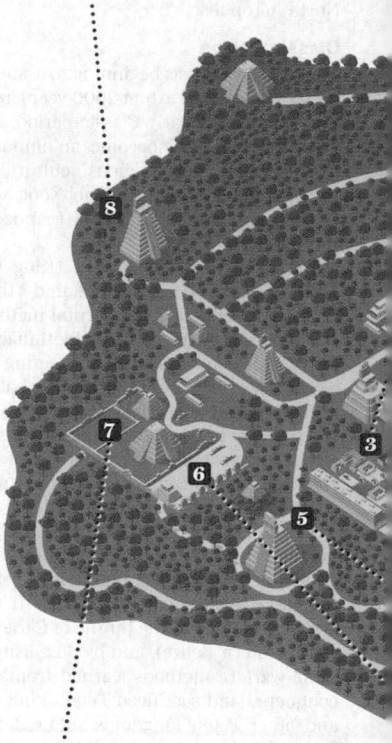

Mundo Perdido
The smaller temple to the west of the great pyramid may look familiar to those who've visited Teotihuacán near Mexico City, with its elegant stepped *talud-tablero* design, a vivid reminder of that distant kingdom's influence.

DAVID CHEREPUSCHAK/ALAMY ©

DANIEL SCHECHTER

Gran Plaza

Though the surreally tall Templo I, a mausoleum to the Late Classic ruler Ah Cacao, is off-limits to climbers, you're welcome to ascend the almost-as-tall Templo II across the plaza.

North Acropolis

Amid the stack of smaller and much older temples that rise up the hillside north of the plaza, take a peek beneath the two thatched shelters on a ledge to find a pair of fearsome masks.

Museo Tikal

Volumes have been written about the remarkably preserved Stela 31, a portrait of the ruler Stormy Sky crowning himself, flanked by spear-toting warriors in the attire of (ally or overlord?) Teotihuacán.

DANIEL SCHECHTER

Ticket Booth

1

Posted Map

Visitor Centre

4

2

Templo VI

The secluded temple has a lengthy set of glyphs inscribed on the back of its lofty roof comb, recording the lineage of successive kingdoms. Be patient: the contents of the weathered slab may take some effort to discern.

Plaza de los Siete Templos

Seven miniature temples line up along the east side of this grassy courtyard. Climb the larger 'palace' at the south end to get a sightline along the septet.

DANIEL SCHECHTER

Templo V

As steep as it is massive, Tikal's second tallest temple has unusual rounded corners. Don't try climbing the broad front staircase but instead scale the almost vertical wooden ladder on the left.

DANIEL SCHECHTER

Since at least two people tumbled to their deaths, the stairs up Temple I have been closed. Don't fret: the views from **Temple II** just across the way are nearly as awe-inspiring. Temple II was once almost as high as Temple I, but now measures 38m without its roof comb.

The **North Acropolis** (Acrópolis del Norte), while not as impressive as the twin temples, is of great significance. Archaeologists have uncovered about 100 structures dating as far back as 400 BC. The Maya rebuilt on top of older structures, and the many layers, combined with the elaborate burials, added sanctity and power to their temples. Look for the two huge, powerful wall masks, uncovered from an earlier structure. The final version of the Acropolis, as it was around AD 800, had more than 12 temples atop a vast platform, many of them the work of Jasaw Chan K'awiil I (King Moon Double Comb).

On the plaza side of the North Acropolis are two rows of **stelae**. Although hardly as impressive as those at Copán or Quiriguá, these served the same purpose: to record the great deeds of the kings of Tikal, to sanctify their memory and to add 'power' to the surrounding structures.

Acrópolis Central

On the south side of the Great Plaza, the **Acrópolis Central** (Central Acropolis) is made up of a maze of courtyards, little rooms and small temples. It is thought by some to have been a residential palace for Tikal's nobility. Others believe the tiny rooms might have been used for sacred rites, as graffiti found within suggests. Over the centuries the room configuration was repeatedly changed, indicating perhaps that this 'palace' was in fact a residence changed to accommodate different groups of relatives. A century ago, one part of the acropolis, called **Maler's Palace**, provided lodgings for archaeologist Teobert Maler when he worked at Tikal.

Templo III & Plaza Oeste

The **Plaza Oeste** (West Plaza) is north of Temple II. On its north side is a large late-Classic temple. To the south, across the Calzada Tozzer (Tozzer Causeway), is **Temple III**, 55m high. Yet to be uncovered, it allows you to see a temple the way the last Tikal Maya and first explorers saw them. The causeway leading to **Temple IV** was one of several sacred ways built among the complexes, no doubt for astronomical as well as aesthetic reasons.

Templo V & Acrópolis del Sur

Due south of the Gran Plaza is the **Acrópolis del Sur** (South Acropolis). Excavation has just begun on this 2-hectare mass of masonry. The palaces on top are from late-Classic times, but earlier constructions probably go back 1000 years.

Temple V, just east of the Acrópolis del Sur, is 58m high and was built around AD 700. Unlike the other great temples, this one has rounded corners and one tiny room at the top. The room is less than a meter deep, but its walls are up to 4.5m thick. Restoration of this temple started in 1991.

Plaza de los Siete Templos

This plaza is on the other side of the South Acropolis. The little temples, clustered together, were built in late-Classic times, though the structures beneath go back at least a millennium. Note the skull and crossbones on the central temple (the one with the stela and altar in front). On the plaza's north side is an unusual **triple ball court**; another, larger version of the same design stands just south of Temple I.

El Mundo Perdido

About 400m southwest of the Great Plaza is **El Mundo Perdido** (The Lost World), a complex of 38 structures surrounding a huge pyramid. Unlike the rest of Tikal, where late-Classic construction overlays earlier work, El Mundo Perdido holds buildings of many different periods. The **large pyramid** is thought to be Preclassic with some later repairs and renovations, the **Templo del Talud-Tablero** (Temple of the Three Rooms) is an early Classic structure, and the **Templo de las Calaveras** (Temple of the Skulls) is late-Classic.

The pyramid, 32m high and 80m along its base, had huge masks flanking each stairway but no temple structure at the top. Each side displays a slightly different architectural style. Tunnels dug by archaeologists reveal four similar pyramids beneath the outer face; the earliest (Structure 5C-54 Sub 2B) dates from 700 BC, making the pyramid the oldest Maya structure in Tikal.

Templo IV & Complejo N

Complejo N, near Temple IV, is an example of the '**twin-temple**' complexes popular during the late-Classic period. These complexes are thought to have commemorated the completion of a katun, or 20-year cycle in the Maya calendar. This one was built in 711 by Jasaw Chan K'awiil I to mark the 14th katun of baktun 9. (A baktun is about 394 years.) The king is portrayed on **Stela 16**, one of Tikal's finest.

Temple IV, at 64m, is Tikal's highest building. It was completed about 741, in the reign of Jasaw Chan K'awiil I's son. A series of steep wooden steps and ladders takes you to the top.

Templo de las Inscripciones (Templo VI)

Compared to Copán or Quiriguá, Tikal sports relatively few inscriptions. The exception is **Templo de las Inscripciones** (Templo VI), 1.2km southeast of the Great Plaza. On the rear of the 12m-high roof comb is a long inscription; the sides and cornice of the roof comb bear glyphs as well. The inscriptions give us the date AD 766. Stela 21 and Altar 9, standing before the temple, date from 736. Badly damaged, the stela has now been repaired.

Northern Complexes

About 1km north of the Great Plaza is **Complejo P**. Like Complejo N, it's a late-Classic twin-temple complex that probably commemorated the end of a katun. **Complejo M**, next to it, was partially torn down by late-Classic Maya to provide material for the causeway – now named after Alfred Maudslay, who is most widely known for his photographs of Central American ruins – that runs southwest to Temple IV.

Complejo Q and **Complejo R**, about 300m due north of the Great Plaza, are late-Classic twin-pyramid complexes. Complejo Q is perhaps the best example of the twin-temple type, as it has been mostly restored. **Stela 22** and **Altar 10** are excellent examples of late-Classic Tikal relief carving, dated 771.

Complejo O, due west of these complexes on the west side of the Calzada Maler (Maler Causeway), has an uncarved stela and altar in its north enclosure. The point of stelae was to record happenings – why did this one remain uncarved?

Museums

Museo Lítico MUSEUM

(Stone Museum; admission Q10, also valid for Museo Tikal; ⏲9am-noon & 1-4:30pm) The larger of Tikal's two museums is in the visitors center. It houses a number of stelae and carved stones from the ruins. Outside is a large model showing how Tikal looked around AD 800. The photographs taken by Alfred P Maudslay and Teobert Maler of the jungle-covered temples in various stages of discovery in the late 19th century are particularly striking.

Museo Tikal MUSEUM

(free with ticket from Museo Lítico; ⏲9am-5pm Mon-Fri, 9am-4pm Sat & Sun) The Museo Tikal or Museo Cerámico has some fascinating exhibits, including the burial goods of Jasaw Chan K'awiil I (King Moon Double Comb), carved jade, inscribed bones, shells, stelae, ceramics and other items recovered from the excavations.

Activities

Bird-Watching

Around 300 bird species (migratory and endemic) have been recorded at Tikal. Early morning is the best time to go bird-watching; even amateurs will have their share of sightings. Ask at the visitors center about early-morning and late-afternoon tours. Bring binoculars, tread quietly and be patient and you'll probably see some of the following birds:

- Tody motmots, four trogon species and royal flycatchers around the Templo de las Inscripciones.
- Two oriole species, collared aracaris, and keel-billed toucans in El Mundo Perdido.
- Great curassows, three species of woodpecker, crested guans, plain chachalacas and three species of tanager around Complejo P.
- Three kingfisher species, jacanas, blue herons, two sandpiper species and great kiskadees at the Tikal Reservoir near the entrance.
- Tiger herons in the huge ceiba tree along the entrance path.
- Red-capped and white-collared manakins near Complejo Q; emerald toucanets near Complejo R.

Dedicated birding tours of the site are offered by **Roxy Ortíz** (☎5197-5173; tikalroxy.blogspot.com), an English-speaking naturalist who has studied wildlife at Tikal for a number of years.

Hiking

The Sendero Benilj'a'a, a 3km trail with three sections, begins in front of the Jungle Lodge. Ruta Monte Medio and Ruta Monte Medio Alto (both one hour) are accessible year-round. Ruta Monte Bajo (35 minutes) is accessible only in summer. A short interpretive trail called El Misterio de la Vida Maya (The Mystery of Maya Life) leads to the Great Plaza.

Tours

All the hotels can arrange guided tours of the ruins, as well as tours to other places in the region. Day tours from Flores/Santa Elena can be arranged through Martsam Travel (p198).

Tikal Canopy CANOPY TOUR
(☎5819-7766; www.canopytikal.com; tour Q248; ⏲7am-5pm) At the national park entrance, you can take a fairly expensive one-hour treetop tour through the forest by harness attached to a series of cables linking trees up to 300m apart. The fee includes transport to and from Tikal.

Sleeping & Eating

The days of bribing a guard and sleeping on top of Templo IV are long gone – if you are caught in the ruins after hours you'll be escorted out, for security reasons. Nowadays, the best way to catch solitude and get an early glimpse of the wildlife is to camp at the entrance.

Other than camping, there are a few places to stay at Tikal. Most get booked up by tour groups.

On the other hand, staying at Tikal enables you to relax and savor the dawn and dusk, when most of the jungle fauna can be observed.

As you arrive in Tikal, look on the right-hand side of the road to find the little *comedores* offering dining in rustic surroundings with generally unimaginative fare like grilled chicken or grilled steak (Q40 to Q50); some serve veggie plates consisting of boiled *güisquil* (squash), carrots, beans and plantains. All are open from 5am to 9pm daily.

In the visitors center, **Restaurante Café Tikal** has a more upmarket attitude, though prices are only slightly higher than at the *comedores*, with pastas and hamburgers among the offerings. Among the hotel restaurants the Jungle Lodge is best.

Picnic tables beneath shelters are located just off Tikal's Gran Plaza, with soft-drink and water vendors standing by, but no food is sold. If you want to spend all day at the ruins without having to make the 20- to 30-minute walk back to the *comedores*, carry food and water with you.

Campground CAMPGROUND $
(campsite per person Q50, hammock with mosquito net Q85) There's no need to make reservations if you want to stay at Tikal's campground behind the new research center. This is a large, grassy area with a clean bathroom block, plenty of space for tents and *palapa* shelters for hanging hammocks.

Jaguar Inn HOTEL $$$
(☎7926-0002; www.jaguartikal.com; campsite per person Q25, with tent Q80, s/d Q395/590; ❄ @ 📶) The inn of choice for youthful, independent travelers has duplex and quad bungalows with thatched roofs, and hammocks on the porches, plus a smart little restaurant with a popular terrace out front. For those on a tight budget there are tents for rent on a platform.

Jungle Lodge HOTEL $$$
(☎2477-0570;www.junglelodgetikal.com;s/dQ622/772, without bathroom Q298/338; @ 🏊) Nearest of the hotels to the site entrance, this was originally built to house archaeologists working at Tikal. Self-contained bungalows, plus a bank of cheaper units, are well spaced throughout rambling, jungly grounds. The restaurant-bar serves veggie pastas, crepes, pepper steak and other international dishes in a tropical ambience (main dishes Q80 to Q100).

Orientation

The 550-sq-km Parque Nacional Tikal contains thousands of separate ruined structures. The central area of the city occupied about 16 sq km, with more than 4000 structures. The road from Flores enters the national park 17km south of the ruins.

From the parking lot at the site, it's a short walk back to the junction where there's an information kiosk. Immediately south of this junction, a visitor center sells books, maps, souvenirs, hats, insect repellent, sun block and other necessities; it also houses a restaurant and museum. Near the visitor center are Tikal's hotels, a camping area, a few small *comedores* and a second museum.

From the visitors center it's a 1.5km walk (20 to 30 minutes) southwest to the Gran Plaza. To visit all the major building complexes, you must walk at least 10km, so wear comfortable shoes.

Information

The gate opens at 6am. Tickets purchased after 4pm are valid for the whole next day. Everyone must purchase a ticket at the entry gate on the road in. Those staying more than one day can purchase additional tickets at the ticket control booth along the path to the site entrance. Seeing the sunrise from Templo IV at the west end of the main site is possible from about October to March, but to enter the park before or after visiting hours you must purchase an additional ticket for Q100, presumably to pay the guide who must accompany you.

It's a good idea to wear shoes with good rubber treads that grip well. The ruins here can be very slick from rain and organic material, especially during the wet season. Bring plenty of water, as dehydration is a real danger when you're walking around in the heat. Please don't feed the *pisotes* (coatis; a tropical mammal related to a raccoon) that wander about the site.

The Jaguar Inn will exchange US dollars and traveler's checks at a poor rate and offers internet access for a cool Q50 per hour.

GUIDES

Multilingual guides are available at the information kiosk. These authorized guides display their accreditation carnet, listing the languages they speak. Before 7am, the charge for a half-day tour is Q100 per person. After that you pay Q300 for a group of up to four people, plus Q40 for each additional person.

RESOURCES

For more complete information on the monuments at Tikal, pick up a copy of *Tikal – A Handbook of the Ancient Maya Ruins*, by William R Coe, which is available in Flores and at Tikal. A book you're best off finding before you come is *The Lords of Tikal*, by Peter D Harrison, a vivid, cogent summary of the city's history. Guards at the ticket booth sell you an 'official' site map (Q10) which is identical to the one posted at the site entrance. A better map, available at the visitor center shops, is published by Mapas de Guatemala (Q20).

Getting There & Away

Four microbuses by **Asociación de Transportistas Imperio Maya** (ATIM; ☎4478-5996) depart Flores between 6am and 3pm (Q30, 1½ hours), the last returning at 5pm. They return from Tikal at noon, 1:30pm, 3pm and 6pm. You could also take the Uaxactún-bound bus from Flores at 2pm, which goes a bit slower, or one of the many shuttle buses run by Aventuras Turísticas (p198). Autobuses del Norte (p198) provides Pullman service to Tikal at 6am and 8am (Q80).

From El Remate a collective shuttle departs at 5:30am for Tikal, starting back at 2pm (Q30/50 one way/round trip). Any El Remate accommodations can make reservations.

If traveling from Belize, get a Santa Elena–bound microbus to Puente Ixlú, sometimes called El Cruce, and switch there to a northbound microbus for the remaining 36km to Tikal. But note that there is little northbound traffic after 11am. Heading from Tikal to Belize, start early and get off at Puente Ixlú to catch a bus or microbus eastward. Be wary of shuttles to Belize advertised at Tikal: these have been known to detour to Flores to pick up passengers!

It is possible to fly to Tikal from Guatemala City for a whistle-stop visit using the airport at Santa Elena. Grupo TACA has at least three flights daily (Q1255/2165 one way/round trip).

Uaxactún

POP 960

Uaxactún (wah-shahk-*toon*), 23km north of Tikal along an unpaved road through the jungle, was Tikal's political and military rival in late Preclassic times. It was eventually conquered by Tikal's Chak Tok Ich'aak I (King Great Jaguar Paw) in the mid-4th century, and was subservient to its great southern sister for centuries thereafter.

Villagers in Uaxactún live in houses lined up along the airstrip. They make a living by collecting chicle, *pimienta* (allspice) and *xate* (*sha*-tay; a frond exported for floral arrangements) from the surrounding forest.

Sights

The pyramids at Uaxactún were uncovered and stabilized to prevent further deterioration; they were not restored. White mortar is the mark of the repair crews, who patched cracks to keep out water and roots.

The fee of Q50 is collected at the gate to Tikal National Park, though there is no ticket control at the site itself.

Tours to Uaxactún can be arranged in Flores or at the hotels in El Remate and Tikal. Both of the hotels in the village offer tours to more remote Maya sites such as El Mirador, El Zotz, Río Azul, Xultún, Nakbé and San Bartolo.

Grupos E & H

Turn right from the airstrip to reach **Grupos E and H**, a 15-minute walk. Perhaps the most significant temple here is **E-VII-Sub**, among the earliest intact temples excavated, with foundations going back perhaps to 2000 BC. It lay beneath much larger structures, which have been stripped away. On its flat top are sockets for poles that would have supported a wood-and-thatch temple.

Grupos A & B

About 20 minutes' walk to the northwest of the runway you'll find **Grupos A and B**. At Grupo A early excavators, sponsored by Andrew Carnegie, cut into the temple sides indiscriminately, looking for graves, occasionally using dynamite. This process destroyed many temples, which are now being reconstructed.

Sleeping & Eating

To reach anyone in Uaxactún call ☎7783-3931, then wait a few minutes for them to fetch your party. There is currently no cell phone coverage, though that may well have changed by the time you read this.

A few basic *comedores* also provide food, including Comedor Uaxactún and Comedor Imperial Okan Arin.

Aldana's Lodge HUT $

(campsite per person Q20, r per person Q25) To the right off the street leading to Grupos B and A, the Aldana family offers half a dozen clapboard cabins, with thin mattresses on pallets. Father and son Alfido and Hector Aldaña lead tours to jungle sites, and Amparo prepares good meals. Camping using Aldana's equipment costs Q20 per person.

Campamento, Hotel & Restaurante El Chiclero HOTEL $

(☎7926-1095; campamentochiclero@gmail.com; campsites per person Q25, r per person Q50) On the north side of the airstrip, El Chiclero has 10 spartan, institutional green rooms underneath a thatched roof, with decent mattresses and mosquito-netted ceilings and windows. Clean showers and toilets are in an adjacent outbuilding; lights out at 9pm. Perky owner Neria does the best food in town (Q50 for soup and a main course with rice). Accommodations prices are very negotiable.

Getting There & Away

A Pinita bus leaves Santa Elena for Uaxactún (Q35) at 2pm, passing through El Remate around 3pm and Tikal by 4pm, and starting back for Santa Elena from Uaxactún at 6am the following day. This means you'll need to spend two nights in Uaxactún to see the ruins. Otherwise, shuttles from El Remate to Uaxactún and back by **La Casa de Don David** (☎5306-2190; www.lacasadedondavid.com; Jobompiche Rd; s/d incl breakfast from Q235/360; restaurant 6:30am-9pm;) cost Q624 for up to five persons.

Remote Maya Sites

Several of the country's sites of interest to archaeology buffs and adventurous travelers are open for limited tourism. Outfits like Martsam Travel (p198) and Aventuras Turísticas (p198) work with the local Comités Comunitarios de Ecoturismo (Community Ecotourism Committees) in the remote villages that serve as starting points for these treks. By choosing them, you'll be participating in a considered program of low-impact, sustainable tourism and you will have a guide who is highly knowledgeable about local conditions.

Few of these tours offer anything approaching comfort, and you should be prepared for buggy, basic conditions. For some good descriptions on how to get to these and other remote sites, have a look at www.mostlymaya.com.

Yaxhá

The ceremonial site of **Yaxhá** (☎5204-1851; admission Q80; 6am-5pm), on the lake of the same name, is about 48km east of El Remate. Scholars believe it may have been a vacation spot for Maya nobility during the Classic period. The ruins here include a large plaza and two temples. A ruined observatory sits on Topoxté island in the middle of the lake.

El Zotz

El Zotz is about 25km west of Tikal. Zotz means 'bat,' and you'll encounter plenty on a trek here. Among the many unexcavated mounds and ruins is **Devil's Pyramid**, which is so tall that you can see the temples of Tikal from its summit. Trips to El Zotz can be extended to include a trek to Tikal.

El Perú & Parque Nacional Laguna del Tigre

El Perú, 62km northwest from Flores in the Parque Nacional Laguna del Tigre, lies along the Scarlet Macaw Trail. The trek starts in Paso Caballos and continues by boat along the Río San Pedro. Several important structures here have been dated to between AD 300 and 900. Archaeologists believe El Perú was an important commercial center.

Another destination in Parque Nacional Laguna del Tigre that is sometimes combined with El Perú trips is the **Estación**

Biológica Las Guacamayas (☎4890-9797; www.lasguacamayas.org) on the Río San Juan. This is a scientific station surrounded by rainforest, where among other things scarlet macaws and white tortoises are observed.

El Mirador

El Mirador (www.miradorbasin.com) is buried within the furthest reaches of El Petén's jungle, just 7km from the Mexican border. A trip here involves an arduous 60km trek in primitive conditions. The metropolis at El Mirador flourished between 150 BC and AD 150, when it was abandoned for mysterious reasons. The site holds the tallest pyramid ever built in the Maya world: **El Tigre** is over 60m high, and its base covers 18,000 sq meters. Its twin, **La Danta** (Tapir), although technically smaller, soars higher because it's built on a rise. There are hundreds of buildings at El Mirador, but almost everything is still hidden beneath the jungle.

This trip is not for the faint of heart, but if expense is not a concern, you can go the easy way: by helicopter. **Mirador Park** (www.miradorpark.com) offers one- and two-day 'heli-tours' to El Mirador from Flores, arriving in just half an hour at the site.

UNDERSTAND GUATEMALA

Guatemala Today

In mid-January 2012, Otto Fernando Perez Molina was sworn in as Guatemala's president. Molina is a former army general who served during Efraín Ríos Montt's dictatorship and was stationed in the Ixíl region, where many of the worst human-rights abuses and massacres of the civil war took place.

Molina's successful campaign was simple – he offered Guatemalans the two things that polls consistently say they want – security and jobs. One of Molina's first moves was to announce a plan that would put 7000 soldiers on the streets in the country's most dangerous and criminally active areas. While arrest rates skyrocketed, crime rates remained steady.

Recent years have shown that often the worst criminal excesses are committed by security forces. In just one month in early 2012, four police officers were charged with assault, conspiracy and unlawful association while various members of the Secret Service were accused of being members of a countrywide kidnapping gang.

Molina's own anti-corruption credentials were called into question as he came under fire for defending three members of his government who had each racked up over Q800,000 (over US$100,000) in travel expenses in a three month period. The trips were defended by Molina as being necessary, to avoid becoming 'isolated'. Meanwhile Congress opened up the way to grant themselves whatever pay rises they feel like, whenever.

Far from being happy with more soldiers on the streets, many Guatemalans took it to be a bad sign. One very touchy subject in rural Guatemala has to do with large (often foreign-administered) projects such as hydroelectric dams and mineral mines. Opponents to Molina's mobilization of troops claim that the security argument is a smokescreen and what the soldiers are really there for is to protect the interests of these projects. As if to prove them right, troops were sent in to 'restore order' at various anti-mining and anti-dam protests around the country. In late 2012 soldiers shot into crowds at a protest outside of Totonicapán, killing seven and wounding 40, a result characterized by Foreign Minister Harold Caballeros to international media as 'not a big deal'.

Guatemala is on the slow road to recovery from its civil war wounds. While this is in part due to the passing of generations who lived through the war, official recognition of some atrocities has been an important step in the recovery process. Though President Molina has gone on record as saying he does not believe the killings amounted to genocide, a campaign is underway to exhume clandestine cemeteries used by the military to bury 'disappeared' dissidents and the legal processes have at last begun, with some war criminals being brought to justice. So far the heftiest penalty to be handed down was to ex-Military Commissioner Lucas Tecún, who was sentenced to 7710 years in prison.

In March 2012, in a move that shocked many hardened cynics, a Guatemalan judge removed the final obstacle barring former dictator Efraín Ríos Montt from facing trial on charges of genocide. It will be the first time that a former Latin American head of state has faced such charges in a national court.

History

Earliest estimates put humans in what is now Guatemala as far back as 11,000 BC. The prevailing theory is that they got here by walking across an ice bridge from Siberia. The development of agriculture and resulting improvement in the stability of the food supply led to population growth, the development of early art forms and a language that is traceable to what many Maya speak today.

Rise & Fall of the Maya

Further developments in agriculture and increases in population gave these early civilizations time and resources to develop artistic and architectural techniques.

Between 800 BC and AD 100 population centers such as El Mirador and Kaminaljuyú grew with trade and conquest and hundreds (if not thousands – many are yet to be uncovered) of temples and ceremonial centers were built. Guatemala's most famous Maya site, Tikal, came into its own around the start of the Classic period – AD 250.

The history of these – and many other – city states was troubled at best, characterized by broken military alliances, food shortages and droughts.

By the early 16th century, Maya civilization was already in trouble. Some centers, such as El Mirador, had already been abandoned and others, such as Tikal and Quiriguá, had shrunk to the size of minor towns. Theories suggest that many abandoned El Petén in favor of the highlands, setting up capitals in K'umarcaaj, Iximché, Zaculeu and Mixco Viejo.

Relocation didn't bring peace, though – soon Toltec tribes, having abandoned the Yucatán, moved in and began to take control. Infighting among tribes, overpopulation and the resulting strain on the food supply combined to make conditions very favorable to the Spanish when they arrived in 1523.

Conquest & Colonization

The Spanish didn't just walk on in, as many think. Spirited resistance was met, most notably from the K'iche' (in a famous battle led by Tecún Umán, near present-day Quetzaltenango). Neighboring Kaqchiquel not only refused to join forces with the K'iche', they joined the Spanish and fought against them.

It didn't take long for the Spanish to turn on the Kaqchiquel, though, and pretty soon most of the Maya were under Spanish control, the exceptions being the Rabinal (who have largely maintained their culture) and the Itzáes, who, hidden out on the island of Flores in El Petén were unconquered until 1697.

Independence & the 19th Century

By the time thoughts of independence from Spain began stirring among Guatemalans, society was already rigidly stratified. Angered at being repeatedly passed over for advancement, Guatemalan criollos (Guatemalan-born Spaniards) successfully rose in revolt in 1821. Independence changed little for Guatemala's indigenous communities, who remained under the control of the church and the landowning elite.

During the short existence of the United Provinces of Central America, liberal president Francisco Morazán (1830–39) instituted reforms aimed at correcting three persistent problems: the overwhelming power of the church; the division of society into a Hispanic upper class and an indigenous lower class; and the region's impotence in world markets.

But unpopular economic policies, heavy taxes and an 1837 cholera epidemic led to an indigenous uprising that brought conservative Rafael Carrera to power. Carrera ruled until 1865 and undid many of Morazán's achievements.

The liberals regained power in the 1870s under president Justo Rufino Barrios, a coffee-plantation owner who embarked on a program of modernization – constructing roads, railways, schools and a modern banking system – and did everything possible to encourage coffee production, including promoting forced relocation and labor. Succeeding governments generally pursued the same policies, maintaining control by a wealthy minority and repression of the opposition.

The Early 20th Century

From 1898 to 1920, Manuel Estrada Cabrera ruled as a dictator, bringing progress in technical matters but placing a heavy burden on all but the ruling oligarchy. He fancied himself a bringer of light and culture to a backward land, styling himself the 'Teacher and Protector of Guatemalan Youth'.

When Estrada Cabrera was overthrown, Guatemala entered a period of instability that ended in 1931 with the election of General Jorge Ubico, who modernized the country's health and social welfare infrastructure but was forced into exile in 1944.

Philosopher Juan José Arévalo came to power in 1945, establishing the nation's social security system, a bureau of indigenous affairs, a modern public health system and liberal labor laws. His six years as president saw 25 coup attempts by conservative military forces.

Arévalo was succeeded in 1951 by Colonel Jacobo Arbenz Guzmán, who looked to break up estates and foster high productivity on small farms. But in 1954 (in one of the first documented covert CIA operations) the US government orchestrated an invasion from Honduras led by two exiled Guatemalan military officers.

Arbenz was forced to step down and land reform never took place. Violence, oppression and disenfranchisement ensued, fueling the formation of left-wing guerilla groups.

Civil War

During the 1960s and '70s, economic inequality and the developing union movement forced oppression to new heights. Amnesty International estimates that 50,000 to 60,000 Guatemalans were killed during the political violence of the 1970s. In 1976 an earthquake killed about 22,000 people and left about a million homeless.

In 1982 General José Efraín Ríos Montt initiated a 'scorched earth' policy in Guatemala. Huge numbers of people – mainly indigenous men – from more than 400 villages were murdered in the name of anti-insurgency, stabilization and anticommunism. An estimated 15,000 civilians were tortured and massacred; 100,000 refugees fled across the border to Mexico. In response, four guerrilla organizations united to form the URNG (Guatemalan National Revolutionary Unity).

In August 1983 Ríos Montt was deposed in a coup led by General Oscar Humberto Mejía Victores, but human-rights abuses continued. The US suspended military aid, and 1985 saw the election of civilian Christian Democrat Marco Vinicio Cerezo Arévalo – but the military had secured immunity from prosecution and armed conflict festered in remote areas.

The Signing of Peace Accords

In 1996 Álvaro Enrique Arzú Irigoyen of the middle-right PAN (Partido de Avanzada Nacional) was elected. In December he and the URNG signed peace accords ending the 36-year civil war – a war in which an estimated 200,000 Guatemalans were killed, a million were left homeless and untold thousands 'disappeared'.

The accords called for accountability for the armed forces' human-rights violations and resettlement of one million refugees. They also addressed the identity and rights of indigenous peoples, health care, education and other basic social services, women's rights, the abolition of compulsory military service and the incorporation of the ex-guerrillas into civilian life.

It's been a rocky road since the war's end. The greatest challenge to peace stems from inequities in the power structure. It's estimated that 70% of the country's arable land is owned by less than 3% of the population. According to a UN report, the top 20% of the population has an income 30 times greater than the bottom 20%. Or, as many Guatemalans will tell you, there are seven families who 'own' Guatemala.

Guatemala in the 21st Century

Any hopes for a truly just and democratic society have looked increasingly frayed in the years since 1996. International organizations regularly criticize the state of human rights in the country and Guatemalan human-rights campaigners are threatened or simply disappear on a regular basis. The major problems – poverty, illiteracy, lack of education and poor medical facilities (all much more common in rural areas, where the Maya population is concentrated) – remain a long way from being solved.

The 1999 presidential elections brought Alfonso Portillo of the conservative Frente Republicano Guatemalteco (FRG) to power. Portillo was seen as a front man for FRG leader, ex-president General Efraín Ríos Montt. Portillo fled the country at the end of his presidency in the face of allegations that he had diverted US$500 million from the treasury to personal and family bank accounts. Having evaded prosecution for years, Portillo was charged by the United States for laundering money using US banks, and looks set to be extradited and put on trial there.

Ríos Montt was granted permission by Guatemala's constitutional court to stand in the 2003 elections, despite the fact that the constitution banned presidents who had taken power by coup in the past, as Ríos Montt had in 1982.

In the end Guatemala's voters dealt Ríos Montt a resounding defeat, electing Oscar Berger of the moderately conservative Gran Alianza Nacional as president. Berger managed to stay relatively untouched by political scandal, critics saying this was because he didn't really do *anything,* let alone anything bad.

The Central America Free Trade Agreement (CAFTA; TLC or Tratado de Libre Comercio) was ratified by Guatemala in 2006. Supporters claim it frees the country up for greater participation in foreign markets, while detractors state that the agreement is a bad deal for the already disenfranchised rural poor.

In late 2007, a round of elections brought Álvaro Colom of the center-leftist Unidad Nacional de la Esperanza to power. Colom followed from Berger's example of steady, minimalist governance and spearheaded some much needed improvements to the country's infrastructure. However, his entire presidency was dogged by corruption claims, from straight-out vote buying to back-room deals granting contracts to companies who had contributed to his campaign fund.

But probably the most bizarre twist of the Colom presidency happened as he was leaving office. The Guatemalan constitution prohibits members of the president's family from running for the subsequent presidency (supposedly an anti-dictatorship measure), so Colom and his wife filed for divorce in the lead-up to the 2011 elections in an attempt to make her a valid candidate. The Constitutional Court banned her candidature anyway, leaving the door open for ex-civil war general Otto Pérez Molina to take office in early 2012.

The Culture

The National Psyche

You'll be amazed when you first reach Guatemala just how helpful, polite and unhurried Guatemalans are. Everyone has time to stop and chat and explain what you want to know. Most Guatemalans like to get to know other people without haste; feeling for common ground and things to agree on.

What goes on behind this outward politeness is harder to encapsulate. Few Guatemalans exhibit the stress, worry and hurry of the 'developed' nations, but this obviously isn't because they don't have to worry about money or employment. They're a long-suffering people who don't expect wealth or good government but make the best of what comes their way – friendship, their family, a good meal, a bit of good company.

Outwardly, it appears that family ties are strong, but beneath the surface you may find that the real reason that three generations live together in one house has more to do with economics than affection.

Guatemalans are a religious bunch – agnostics and atheists are very thin on the ground. People will often ask what religion you are quite early in a conversation. Unless you really want to get into it, saying 'Christian' generally satisfies. Orthodox Catholicism is gradually giving way to evangelical Protestantism among the *ladinos* (persons of mixed indigenous and European race), with the animist-Catholic syncretism of the traditional Maya always present.

Some say that Guatemala has no middle class, just a ruling class and an exploited class. It's true that Guatemala has a small, rich, *ladino* ruling elite; it also has an indigenous Maya population, which tends to be poor, poorly educated and poorly provided for.

But as well as these two groups, there's a large group of poor and middle-class *ladinos,* with aspirations influenced by education, TV, international popular music and North America (of which many Guatemalans have direct experience as migrant workers) – and maybe by liberal ideas of equality and social tolerance. This segment of society has its bohemian/student/artist circles whose overlap with educated, forward-looking Maya may hold the greatest hope for progress toward an equitable society.

Lifestyle

The majority of Guatemalans live in one-room brick or concrete houses, or traditional *bajareque*, with roofs of tin, tiles or thatch. They have earth floors, a stove/fireplace and minimal possessions – often just a couple of bare beds and a few pots. Thus live most of Guatemala's Maya majority, in the countryside, in villages and in towns.

The few wealthier Maya and most *ladino* families have larger houses in towns and the bigger villages, but their homes may still not be much more than one or two bedrooms and a kitchen that also serves as a living area. Middle-class families in the wealthier suburbs of Guatemala City live in good-sized one- or two-story houses with gardens. The elite few possess rural as well as urban properties – for example a comfortable farmhouse on the Pacific Slope, or a seaside villa on the coast.

Despite modernizing influences, traditional family ties remain strong. Extended-family groups gather for weekend meals and vacations. Old-fashioned gender roles are strong too: many women have jobs to increase the family income but few have positions of power. Homosexuality barely raises its head above the parapet: only in Guatemala City is there anything approaching an open gay scene, and that is pretty much for men only.

The CIA's World Factbook states that more than half of all Guatemalans live in poverty. The official national minimum wage is only Q56 (about US$7) per day – and not everyone is entitled even to this. An established school teacher can earn around Q1800 (about US$225) per month. Poverty is most prevalent in rural, indigenous areas, especially the highlands. Wealth, industry and commerce are concentrated overwhelmingly in sprawling, polluted Guatemala City.

People

The great majority of Guatemala's 16 million people live in the highland strip from Guatemala City to Quetzaltenango, the country's two biggest cities. Many towns and large villages are dotted around this region. Some 49% of the population lives in towns and cities, and nearly half are aged under 19.

Some 41% of Guatemalans are indigenous, but this line is blurred as many people have indigenous blood, but some choose not to describe themselves as such. Nearly all of this indigenous population is Maya, although there is a very small population of non-Maya indigenous people called the Chinka' (Xinca) in the southeastern corner of the country. The four biggest Maya groups – the K'iche' (Quiché), Mam, Q'eqchi' (Kekchí) and Kaqchiquel – are most densely concentrated in the highlands. The rest of Guatemala's population is nearly all *ladinos* – descended from both the Maya and European (mostly Spanish) settlers. There are also a few thousand Garífuna (descended from Caribbean islanders and shipwrecked African slaves) around the Caribbean town of Lívingston.

Maya languages are still the way many Maya communicate, with over 20 separate (and often mutually unintelligible) Maya languages spoken in different regions of the country. It's language that primarily defines which Maya people someone belongs to. Though many Maya speak some Spanish, it's always a second language – and there are many who don't speak any Spanish at all.

Religion

Roman Catholicism is the predominant religion in Guatemala, but it is not the only religion. Since the 1980s evangelical Protestant sects, around 58% of them Pentecostal, have surged in popularity, and it is estimated that 30% to 40% of Guatemalans are now evangelicals. These numbers continue to grow as evangelical churches compete hard for further souls.

Catholicism's fall can also be attributed in part to the civil war. Catholic priests were (and still are) outspoken defenders of human rights, and attracted persecution from dictators at the time, especially from Ríos Montt. As a result, many Catholic churches in rural areas simply closed down during this time and evangelical ones moved in to fill the vacuum.

The number of new evangelical churches in some towns and villages, especially indigenous Maya villages, is astonishing. You will undoubtedly hear loud Guatemalan versions of gospel music pouring out of some of them as you walk around, and in some places loudspeakers broadcast the music and its accompanying preaching across entire towns.

Catholicism in the Maya areas has never been exactly orthodox. The missionaries who brought Catholicism to the Maya in the 16th century permitted aspects of the existing animistic, shamanistic Maya religion to continue alongside Christian rites and beliefs. Syncretism was aided by the identification of certain Maya deities with certain Christian saints and survives to this day. A bizarre example is the deity known, among other things, as Maximón (p127).

The Maya still worship at a number of places sacred since ancient times, bringing offerings and sacrificing chickens to gods who predate the arrival of the Spanish. Each place has its own different set of gods – or at least different names for similar gods.

Visitors might also be able to observe traditional Maya ceremonies in places such as the Pascual Abaj shrine (p140) at Chichicastenango, the altars on Laguna Chicabal (p158) outside Quetzaltenango, or El Baúl (p165) near Santa Lucía Cotzumalguapa, but a lot of traditional rites are off-limits to foreigners.

Arts

Literature

Guatemalan writer Miguel Ángel Asturias (1899–1974) won the Nobel Prize for Literature in 1967. Best known for his thinly veiled vilification of Latin American dictators in *El señor presidente,* Asturias also wrote poetry (collected in *Sien de alondra,* published in English as *Temple of the Lark*). Other celebrated Guatemalan writers include poet Luis Cardoza y Aragón (1901–92) and short-story master Augusto Monterroso (1921–2003). Gaspar Pedro Gonzáles' *A Mayan Life* is claimed to be the first novel written by a Maya author.

Music

Music is a very important part of Guatemalan society, and a source of pride is that the marimba (xylophone) may have been invented here (although some claim it was brought from Africa by slaves). The Maya also play traditional instruments including the *chirimía* (of Arabic origin and related to the oboe) and reed flute.

Guatemalan tastes in pop music are greatly influenced by the products of other Latin American countries. Reggaetón is huge – current favorites being Pitbull, Wisin & Yandel and Daddy Yankee. The only record label seriously promoting new Guatemalan artists (mostly in the urban/hip-hop vein) is Guatemala City–based **UnOrthodox Productions** (www.uoproductions.com).

Guatemalan rock went through its golden age in the '80s and early '90s. Bands from this era such as Razones de Cambio, Bohemia Suburbana and Viernes Verde still have their diehard fans. The most famous Guatemalan-born musician is Ricardo Arjona, who has lived in Mexico since the '90s.

Weaving

Guatemalans make many traditional *artesanías* (handicrafts), both for everyday use and to sell. Crafts include basketry, ceramics and wood carving, but the most prominent are weaving, embroidery and other textile arts practiced by Maya women.

The *huipil* (a long, sleeveless tunic) is one of several types of garment that have been worn since pre-Hispanic times. Other colorful types include: the *tocoyal,* a woven head-covering often decorated with bright tassels; the *corte,* a piece of material 7m or 10m long that is used as a wraparound skirt; and the *faja,* a long, woven waist sash that can be folded to hold what otherwise might be put in pockets.

Colorful traditional dress is still predominant, generally in the heavily Maya-populated highlands, but you'll see it in all parts of the country. The variety of techniques, materials, styles and designs is bewildering to the newcomer, but you'll see some of the most colorful, intricate, eye-catching and widely worn designs in Sololá and Santiago Atitlán, near the Lago de Atitlán; Nebaj in the Ixil Triangle; Zunil near Quetzaltenango; and Todos Santos and San Mateo Ixtatán in the Cuchumatanes mountains.

Landscape & Wildlife

The Land

Consisting primarily of mountainous forest highlands and jungle plains, Guatemala covers an area of 109,000 sq km. The western highlands hold 30 volcanoes, reaching heights of more than 4200m southwest of Huehuetenango. In the Cuchumatanes range, land not cleared for Maya *milpas* (cornfields) is covered in pine forests, although these are dwindling rapidly.

The Pacific Slope holds rich coffee, cacao, fruit and sugar plantations. Down along the shore the volcanic slope meets the sea, yielding vast, sweltering beaches of black volcanic sand.

Guatemala City lies at an altitude of around 1500m. To the north, the Alta Verapaz highlands gradually give way to El Petén, whose climate and topography is similar to the Yucatán: hot and humid or hot and dry. Southeast of El Petén is the banana-rich valley of the Río Motagua, dry in some areas, moist in others.

Guatemala is at the confluence of three tectonic plates, resulting in earthquakes and volcanic eruptions. Major quakes struck in 1773, 1917 and 1976. Its dynamic geology includes a tremendous system of surface-level and subterranean caves. This karst terrain riddles the Verapaces region and has made Guatemala a popular spelunking destination. Surface-level caves have been used for Maya ceremonies since ancient times.

Animals

The country's abundance of animals includes 250 species of mammal, 600 bird species, 200 species of reptile and amphibian, and numerous butterflies and other insects.

The national bird, the resplendent quetzal, is often used to symbolize Central America. Though small, the quetzal is exceptionally beautiful. The males sport a bright red breast, brilliant blue-green across the rest of the body and a spot of bright white on the underside of the long tail.

Other colorful birds include toucans, macaws and parrots. Boasting the ocellated turkey (or 'Petén turkey') – a large, impressive, multicolored bird reminiscent of a peacock – Tikal is a bird-watching hot spot, with some 300 tropical and migratory species sighted to date. Several woodpecker species, nine types of hummingbirds and four trogon species are just the beginning of the list. Also in the area are large white herons, hawks, warblers, kingfishers, harpy eagles (rare) and many others.

Although Guatemala's forests host several mammal and reptile species, many remain difficult to observe. Still, visitors to Tikal can enjoy the antics of the omnipresent *pizotes* (coatis, a tropical mammal related to raccoons) and might spy howler and spider monkeys.

Other mammals deeper in the forest include jaguars, ocelots, pumas, peccaries, agoutis, opossums, tapirs, kinkajous (nocturnal arboreal mammals), *tepezcuintles* (pacas, white-spotted brownish rodents), white-tailed and red brocket deer, armadillos and very large rattlesnakes. Reptiles and amphibians in the rest of Guatemala include at least three species of sea turtle (leatherback, *tortuga negra* and olive ridley) and two species of crocodile (one found in El Petén, the other in the Río Dulce). Manatees have also been found to frequent the waters around Río Dulce.

Plants

Guatemala has over 8000 plant species in 19 different ecosystems, ranging from coastal mangrove forests to mountainous interior pine forests to high cloud forests. El Petén supports a variety of trees, including mahogany, cedar, ramón and sapodilla.

The national flower, the *monja blanca* (white nun orchid), is said to have been picked so much that it's now rare in the wild. Nevertheless, the country has around 600 species of orchid, a third of which are endemic.

Guatemala also has the perfect climate for *xate* (*sha*-tay), a low-growing palm that thrives in El Petén and is prized in the developed world as a flower-arrangement filler.

National Parks & Reserves

Guatemala has 92 protected areas, including biosphere reserves, national parks, protected biotopes, wildlife refuges and private nature reserves. Even though some areas are contained within other, larger ones, they amount to 28% of the national territory.

Many of the protected areas are remote and hard to access by the independent traveler; the list below outlines those that are easiest to reach and/or most interesting to visitors, but excludes the volcanoes, nearly all of which are protected, and areas of mainly archaeological interest.

➡ **Parque Nacional Tikal** Diverse jungle wildlife among Guatemala's most magnificent Maya ruins (p200).

➡ **Parque Nacional Laguna del Tigre** A remote, large park within the Reserva Maya, featuring freshwater wetlands. Wildlife includes scarlet macaws, monkeys and crocodiles (p208).

➡ **Parque Nacional Mirador-Río Azul** A national park within the Reserva Maya containing the El Mirador archaeological site (p208).

➡ **Parque Nacional Río Dulce** The beautiful jungle-lined lower Río Dulce between Lago de Izabal and Caribbean serves as a manatee refuge (p181).

➡ **Parque Nacional Grutas de Lanquín** A large, bat-infested cave system 61km east of Cobán (p175).

➡ **Biotopo del Quetzal** An easily-accessible cloud-forest reserve sheltering howler monkeys and birds – and possibly a quetzal (p170).

➡ **Biotopo Cerro Cahuí** A forest reserve beside Lago de Petén Itzá offering abundant wildlife spotting and good walking trails (p199).

➡ **Refugio de Vida Silvestre Bocas del Polochic** Guatemala's second-largest freshwater wetlands, at the western end of Lago de Izabal (p185). Abundant bird-watching (more than 300 species).

➡ **Reserva Natural Monterrico-Hawaii** Covers beach and wetlands, protecting birdlife and marine turtles (p168).

Environmental Issues

Environmental consciousness is not largely developed in Guatemala, as vast amounts of garbage strewn across the country will quickly tell you.

Despite the impressive list of parks and protected areas, genuine protection for those areas is harder to achieve, partly because of official collusion to ignore the regulations and partly because of pressure from poor Guatemalans in need of land.

Deforestation is a problem in many areas of Guatemala, especially El Petén, where jungle is being felled at an alarming rate not just for timber but also to make way for cattle ranches, oil pipelines, clandestine airstrips, new settlements and new maize fields cleared by the slash-and-burn method.

On the more populous Pacific side of the country, the land is mostly agricultural or given over to industry.

The remaining forests in the Pacific coastal and highland areas are not long for this world, as local communities cut down the remaining trees for heating and cooking fuels.

Nevertheless, a number of Guatemalan organizations are doing valiant work to protect their country's environment and biodiversity. NGOs can be good resources for finding out more about Guatemala's natural parks and protected areas.

SURVIVAL GUIDE

Directory A–Z

ACCOMMODATIONS

Guatemalan accommodations range from luxury hotels to budget hotels to ultrabudget guesthouses called *hospedajes, casas de huéspedes* or *pensiones*.

Places at the lower end of the budget range are generally small, dark and not particularly clean. Security may not be the best in such places. At the upper end you should expect a clean, sizable and airy room, with a bathroom, TV and, in hot parts of the country, a fan (and possibly air-con).

Midrange rooms are almost always comfortable: private hot-water bathroom, TV, decent beds, fan and/or air-con are standard. Good midrange hotels have attractive public areas such as dining rooms, bars and swimming pools.

Top-end accommodation in Guatemala mainly consists of Guatemala City's international-class business-oriented hotels, Antigua's very finest hostelries, and a few resort hotels elsewhere. These places offer all the comforts (and many more) that you would expect for the price.

Room rates often go up in places popular with tourists during Semana Santa (the week leading up to Easter Sunday), Christmas–New Year and July and August. Semana Santa is the major Guatemalan holiday period, and prices can rise by anything from 30% to 100% on the coast and in the countryside – anywhere Guatemalans go to relax. At this time advance reservations are a very good idea.

Regardless of your budget, if you're planning on staying for longer than a few days, it's worth asking for a discount.

Be aware that room rates are subject to two large taxes – 12% IVA (value-added tax) and 10% to pay for the activities of the Guatemalan Tourism Institute (Inguat), although there is discussion about eliminating this second tax. All prices listed include both taxes. Some of the more expensive hotels forget to include them when they quote their prices.

ACTIVITIES

Caving

Guatemala attracts cavers from all over the world. The limestone area around Cobán is particularly riddled with cave systems whose true extents are far from known. The caves near Lanquín (p175) are open for tourist visits and there are others near Finca Ixobel (p193) and Flores (p194).

Climbing & Hiking

Guatemala's volcanoes are irresistible challenges, and many of them can be climbed in one day from Antigua (p113) or Quetzaltenango (p147). There's further great hill country in the Ixil Triangle and the Cuchumatanes mountains north of Huehuetenango, especially around Nebaj (p143) and Todos Santos (p162).

The Lago de Atitlán is surrounded by spectacular trails, although robberies here have made some routes inadvisable. Hikes of several days are perfectly feasible, and agencies in Antigua, Quetzaltenango and Nebaj can guide you. In the Petén jungles, hikes to remote archaeological sites such as El Mirador and El Perú (p208) offer an exciting challenge.

Cycling

There's probably no better way to experience the highlands than by bicycle. Panajachel (p123), Quetzaltenango (p147) and Antigua (p113) in particular, are the best launch points, with agencies offering trips and/or equipment.

Horseback Riding

You can organize riding trips of varying lengths outside of Antigua (p113) and in El Remate and San Pedro La Laguna.

Water Sports

You can dive inside a volcanic caldera at Lago de Atitlán; raft the white-water of the Río Cahabón near Lanquín; sail from the yachtie haven of Río Dulce; and canoe or kayak the waterways of Monterrico, Lívingston, the Bocas del Polochic or Punta de Manabique. Surfing is a relatively young sport in Guatemala, but there are a couple of places where you might catch a wave, the best-established being Sipacate.

CHILDREN

For general information on traveling with children, have a look at Lonely Planet's *Travel with Children*.

Facilities such as safety seats in hired cars are rare but nearly every restaurant can rustle up something resembling a high chair. If you are particular about brands of diapers and creams, bring what you can with you and stock up in supermarkets. Fresh milk is rare and may not be pasteurized – again, supermarkets are your best bet. Packet UHT milk and milk powder are much more common. If your child has to have some particular tinned or packaged food, bring supplies with you. Public breastfeeding is not common among urban, non-indigenous women and, when done, is done discreetly.

CUSTOMS REGULATIONS

Normally customs officers won't look seriously in your luggage and may not look at all. Guatemala restricts import/export of pretty much the same things as everybody else (weapons, drugs, large amounts of cash, etc).

EMBASSIES & CONSULATES

New Zealand and Australia do not have embassies in Guatemala. The Canadian embassy can be of some assistance, but otherwise you'll have to go to Mexico City.

Belizean Embassy (☎2367-3883; www.embajadadebelize.org; 5a Av 5-55, Europlaza 2, Office 1502, Zona 14, Guatemala City)

Canadian Embassy (☎2363-4348; www.guatemala.gc.ca; 13a Calle 8-44, 8th fl, Edificio Edyma Plaza, Zona 10, Guatemala City)

French Embassy (☎2421-7370; www.ambafrance-gt.org/; 5a Av 8-59, Zona 14, Guatemala City)

German Embassy (☎2364-6700; www.guatemala.diplo.de; Edificio Reforma 10, 10th fl, Av La Reforma 9-55, Zona 10, Guatemala City)

Honduran Embassy (☎2366-5640; embhond@intelnet.net.gt; 19a Av A 20-19, Zona 10, Guatemala City)

Irish Honorary Consulate (☎2384-9442; irelandgua@gmail.com; Edificio La Galería, Office 15A, 7a Av 14-44, Zona 9, Guatemala City)

Mexican Embassy (☎2420-3400; www.sre.gob.mx/guatemala/; 2a Av 7-57, Zona 10, Guatemala City)

Netherlands Embassy (☎2381-4300; www.embajadadeholanda-gua.org; 16a Calle 0-55, 13th fl, Torre Internacional, Zona 10, Guatemala City)

Salvadoran Embassy (☎2245-7272; EmbajadaGuatemala@rree.gob.sv; Av Las Américas 16-40, Zona 13, Guatemala City)

UK Embassy (☎2380-7300; www.ukinguatemala.fco.gov.uk; 11th fl, Torre Internacional, 16a Calle 0-55, Zona 10, Guatemala City)

US Embassy (☎2326-4501; http://guatemala.usembassy.gov; Av La Reforma 7-01, Zona 10, Guatemala City)

FOOD & DRINK

Food

Desayuno chapín, or Guatemalan breakfast, is a large affair involving eggs, beans, fried plan-

SLEEPING PRICE RANGES

The following price ranges refer to a double room with bathroom in high (but not absolute peak) season. Unless otherwise stated, taxes of 22% are included in the price. Most accommodations in this chapter are in the $ to $$ range.

$	Less than Q180
$$	Q180–500
$$$	More than Q500

PRACTICALITIES

- Guatemalans use the metric system for weights and measures, except that they pump gasoline by the *galón* (US gallon) and occasionally weigh things such as laundry and coffee in pounds.
- Videos and DVDs on sale use the NTSC image registration system.
- Electrical current is 115V to 125V, 60Hz, and plugs are two flat prongs, all the same as in the US and Canada.
- The most respected of Guatemala's many newspapers are **La Prensa Libre** (www.prensalibre.com), **Siglo Veintiuno** (www.sigloxxi.com), **La Hora** (www.lahora.com.gt) and **El Periódico** (www.elperiodico.com.gt). Some of the best investigative journalism in the country can be found in the magazine **Revista ...Y Qué?** (www.revistayque.com).
- For Guatemala-related articles from around the world and Guatemala in English, check the **Guatemala Times** (www.guatemala-times.com). **The Revue** (www.revuemag.com) is Guatemala's free, widely distributed, monthly English-language magazine – a lot of ads, a few interesting articles.
- Almost every TV is cable, which ensures reception and brings a number of US stations to hotel TVs.

tains, tortillas and coffee. Breakfast is usually eaten between 6am and 10am.

Lunch is the biggest meal of the day and is eaten between about noon and 2pm. Eateries usually offer a fixed-price meal (*almuerzo* or *menú del día*) – consisting of soup and a main course featuring meat with rice or potatoes and a little salad or vegetables – or just a *plato típico:* meat or chicken, rice, beans, cheese, salad and tortillas.

La cena (dinner) is, for Guatemalans, a lighter version of lunch, usually eaten between about 7pm and 9pm. Even in cities, few restaurants will serve much after 10pm. In rural areas, sit down no later than 8pm to avoid disappointment.

On the coast, seafood is the go. In Lívingston try the delicious coconut and seafood stew called *tapado*. Elsewhere, your fish or shrimp is generally fried, but can also be cooked *con ajo* (with garlic). These plates generally come with salad, fries and tortillas. Also good is *caldo de mariscos*, a seafood stew with fish, shrimp and mussels.

You can expect the average cost of a main dish to be anything from Q20 in a small *comedor* to Q70 in a decent restaurant.

Drinks

Ron (rum) is one of Guatemala's favorite strong drinks, and though most is cheap in price and taste, some local products are exceptionally fine. It should be sipped slowly, like fine cognac. Cheaper rums are often mixed with soft drinks. *Aguardiente* is a sugarcane firewater that flows in *cantinas* and on the streets, and gets you drunk hard and fast.

Jugos (fresh fruit and vegetable juices), *licuados* (milkshakes) and *aguas de frutas* (long, cool, fruit-flavored water drinks) are wildly popular and with good reason. Many eateries offer them, and almost every village market and bus terminal has a stand with a battalion of blenders. The basic *licuado* is a blend of fruit or juice with water and sugar. A *licuado con leche* uses milk instead of water. Soft drinks as a whole are known as *aguas* (waters). If you want straight, unflavored water, say *'agua pura.'*

On the coast, the most refreshing nonalcoholic option is a green coconut – you'll see them piled up roadside. The vendor simply slices the top off with a machete and sticks a straw in.

GAY & LESBIAN TRAVELERS

Few places in Latin America are outwardly gay-friendly, and Guatemala is no different. Technically, homosexuality is legal for persons 18 years and older, but the reality can be another story, with harassment and violence against gays too often the norm. Guatemala City and Quetzaltenango have a small community of transvestite streetwalkers who are often the victims of violent assault. Don't even consider testing the tolerance for homosexual public displays of affection here.

Although Antigua has a palatable – if subdued – scene, affection and action are still kept behind closed doors; the chief exception is the gay-friendly club La Casbah (p118). In Guatemala City, Genetic (p103) and the Black & White Lounge (p103) are the current faves. Mostly, though, gays traveling in Guatemala will find themselves keeping it low-key and pushing the twin beds together.

The **Gully** (www.thegully.com) usually has some articles and information relevant to Guatemala. The best site, **Gay Guatemala** (www.gayguatemala.com), is in Spanish.

INSURANCE

Getting travel insurance to cover theft, loss and medical problems is recommended. Some policies specifically exclude dangerous activities, which can include scuba diving, motorcycling, and even trekking.

You may prefer a policy that pays doctors or hospitals directly, rather than your having to pay on the spot and claim later. If you have to claim later, ensure you keep all documentation.

Check that the policy covers ambulances or an emergency flight home.

Worldwide travel insurance is available at www.lonelyplanet.com/travel_services. You can buy, extend and claim online anytime – even if you're already on the road.

INTERNET ACCESS

Most travelers make constant use of internet cafes and free web-based email. Most towns have cybercafes with fairly reliable connections. Internet cafes typically charge between Q5 and Q10 an hour.

Wi-fi is becoming readily available across the country, but can only really be counted on in large and/or tourist towns. Most (but not all) hostels offer wi-fi, as do many hotels in the mid-range and up category. The best reliable source of wi-fi around the country is at Pollo Campero restaurants – they're in pretty much every town of any size and all offer free, unsecured access.

LANGUAGE COURSES

Guatemala is celebrated for its many language schools. A spot of study here is a great way not only to learn Spanish but also to meet locals and get an inside angle on the culture. Many travelers heading south through Central America to South America make Guatemala an early stop so they can pick up the Spanish skills they need for their trip.

Guatemalan language schools are some of the cheapest in the world, but few people go away disappointed. There are so many schools to choose from that it's essential to check out a few before deciding.

You can start any day at most schools, and study for as long as you like. If you're coming in peak season and hoping to get into one of the more popular schools, it's a good idea to book ahead, although many schools charge around Q300 for phone or internet reservations. All decent schools offer a variety of elective activities from salsa classes to movies to volcano hikes. Many schools offer classes in Maya languages as well as Spanish.

Where to Study

Antigua is the most popular place to study. Quetzaltenango is second, perhaps attracting a more serious type of student; Antigua has a livelier students' and travelers' social scene. Outside of those areas, there are Spanish schools scattered across the country. On average, schools charge Q900 to Q1200 for four hours of one-on-one classes five days a week and accommodation with a local family.

Studying in a small town has its pros and cons. On the upside, you may be the only foreigner around, so you won't be speaking any English. On the downside, Spanish may be the second language of the inhabitants of the village (including your teacher), meaning that you could pick up all sorts of bad habits.

Choosing a School

Choosing between the mass of Spanish schools in Guatemala can be tough. Many schools don't have in-house teacher training programs, so there aren't so many 'good schools' as there are 'good teachers'. It's best to pay for as little time as possible (a week, usually) so you can change if you're really unhappy. You should be completely up-front about what your goals (conversation, grammar, vocabulary etc) are when starting, as well as any specialized interests that you have (politics, medical, legal etc) so the school can design a curriculum and assign you a teacher to best suit your needs. If you end up liking like the school, but not the teacher, ask for a new teacher as soon as possible – personality conflicts occur, and four or five hours of one-on-one with someone you don't like can soon turn into hard work.

Here are some questions to think about when you're looking at schools. Some you can find out just by turning up, some you should ask the school, others you'll have to talk to current and ex-students to get a feel for.

- Where do the classes take place – on a quiet, shaded patio or in hot classrooms with buses roaring along the street outside?
- What experience and qualifications do the teachers have in teaching as a second language?
- Is Spanish your teacher's first language?
- What afternoon and evening activities are available?
- Many schools offer gimmicks to get you in, like a half hour of free internet per day, which ends up saving you around Q2.50 per day – should these little perks really sway your judgment?

EATING PRICE RANGES

The following price ranges, used throughout this chapter, refer to a standard main course, including taxes but not including tip.

$	Less than Q40
$$	Q40–130
$$$	More than Q130

➡ What is the general atmosphere of the school? Serious students probably won't fit in at a school whose activities include all-night bar crawls, and party animals may feel out of place at schools with names like the Christian Spanish Academy.

➡ Does the school offer opportunities for voluntary work – for example, visiting hospitals?

➡ If the school claims to be involved in social/community projects, is it a serious commitment, or just a marketing ploy?

For (completely unverified) reviews of some of Guatemala's Spanish schools by ex-students, check out www.guatemala365.com.

LEGAL MATTERS

Police officers in Guatemala are sometimes part of the problem rather than the solution. The less you have to do with the law, the better.

Whatever you do, don't get involved in any way with illegal drugs: don't buy or sell, use or carry, or associate with people who do – even if the locals seem to do so freely. As a foreigner you are at a distinct disadvantage, and you may be set up by others. Drug laws in Guatemala are strict and, although enforcement may be uneven, penalties are severe.

MONEY

Guatemala's currency, the quetzal (ket-*sahl*, abbreviated to Q), is fairly stable, hovering somewhere between Q7.5 and Q8 to the US dollar. The quetzal is divided into 100 centavos.

Cash

Cash is king in Guatemala, although carrying too much of it makes getting robbed a bigger pain than it would otherwise be. Some towns suffer from change shortages: always try to carry a stash of small bills. Keep a small supply of low-denomination US dollars (which are accepted pretty much anywhere, at various rates of exchange) as an emergency fund.

Currencies other than the US dollar are virtually useless, although a small handful of places now change cash euros.

ATMs

You'll find ATMs (cash machines, *cajeros automáticos*) for Visa/Plus System cards in all but the smallest towns, and there are MasterCard/Cirrus ATMs in many places too, so one of these cards is the best basis for your supply of cash in Guatemala. The 5B network is widespread and particularly useful, as it works with both Visa and MasterCard cards.

Be aware that card skimming is as rife in Guatemala as it is in the rest of the world. Avoid ATMs that are left unguarded at night (ie, those in the little room out front of the bank) and look for one that is in a secure environment (such as those inside supermarkets, shopping malls, etc). Failing that, keep your hand covered when entering your PIN and check your balance online.

Tipping

A 10% tip is expected at restaurants and automatically added to your bill in places such as Antigua – a practice that is spreading to other tourist towns as well. In small *comedores* (basic, cheap eateries) tipping is optional, but follow local practice and leave some spare change. Tour guides are generally tipped, around 10%, especially on longer trips.

Travelers Checks

If you're not packing plastic, a combination of Amex US-dollar traveler's checks and some cash US dollars is the way to go. Take some of these as a backup even if you do have a card. Many banks change US-dollar traveler's checks, and tend to give the best rates. Amex is easily the most recognized traveler's check brand. Few businesses will accept traveler's checks as payment or change them for cash.

OPENING HOURS

Guatemalan shops and businesses are generally open from 8am to noon and 2pm to 6pm Monday to Saturday, but there are many variations. Banks typically open 9am to 5pm Monday to Friday (again with variations), and 9am to 1pm on Saturday. Government offices usually open 8am to 4pm Monday to Friday. Official business is always better conducted in the morning.

Restaurant hours are typically 7am to 9pm, but can vary by up to two hours either way. Most bars open from 11am to midnight. The *Ley Seca* (dry law) stipulates that bars and *discotecas* must close by 1am, except on nights before public holidays. It is rigidly adhered to in large cities and universally laughed at in smaller towns and villages.

¿QUÉ ONDA VOS?

Guatemala has some great slang, and various books have been written on the subject (the best being *¿Qué onda vos?* by Juan Carlos Martínez). Here's a small selection to get you started:

canche – blonde or light-skinned person

chapín – Guatemalan

chavo/a – guy/girl

de huevos – cool

papichulo/mamichula – attractive man/woman

pisto – money

If restaurants or bars have a closing day, it's usually Sunday. Typical shopping hours are 8am to noon and 2pm to 6pm Monday to Saturday.

PHOTOGRAPHY

Ubiquitous film stores and pharmacies sell film, though you may not find the brand you like without a hunt. There are quick processing labs in the main cities. Most internet cafes have card readers *(lectores de tarjeta)*, so you can upload your digital photos or burn them onto CD. For tips on taking professional-grade travel pics, hunt down a copy of Lonely Planet's *Travel Photography*.

Photographing People

Photography is a sensitive subject in Guatemala. Always ask permission before taking portraits, especially of Maya women and children. Don't be surprised if your request is denied. Children often request payment (usually Q1) in return for posing. In certain places such as the church of Santo Tomás in Chichicastenango, photography is forbidden. Maya ceremonies (should you be so lucky to witness one) are off-limits for photography unless you are given explicit permission to take pictures. If local people make any sign of being offended, put your camera away and apologize immediately, both out of decency and for your own safety. Never take photos of army installations, men with guns or other sensitive military subjects.

POST

The Guatemalan postal service was privatized in 1999. Generally, letters and parcels take eight to 10 days to travel to the US and Canada and 10 to 12 days to reach Europe. Almost all cities and towns (but not villages) have a post office where you can buy stamps and send mail. If you want to get a package couriered to you, make sure the courier company has an office in the town where you are staying; otherwise you will be charged some hefty 'handling fees'.

PUBLIC HOLIDAYS

The main Guatemalan holiday periods are Semana Santa (Easter), Christmas–New Year and July and August. During Semana Santa room prices rise in many places and it's advisable to book accommodations and transportation in advance.

Guatemalan public holidays:

New Year's Day January 1
Easter (Holy Thursday to Easter Sunday inclusive) March/April
Labor Day May 1
Army Day June 30
Assumption Day (Día de la Asunción) August 15
Independence Day September 15
Revolution Day October 20
All Saints' Day November 1
Christmas Eve afternoon December 24
Christmas Day December 25
New Year's Eve afternoon December 31

SAFE TRAVEL

Drunk, alone, lost, late at night and loaded with cash is the stupidest way to walk around Guatemala. And pretty much any combination of the above is kind of stupid. A lot of people do things here they would never do back home. Sometimes they get away with it. Sometimes it backfires. Use your intuition and chances are you'll stay out of trouble.

The days of robbers targeting buses and tourist shuttles out on the open highway, thankfully, seem to be in the past, although some tourists in rental cars have been targeted. This information is incredibly fluid – if you're planning on driving yourself around, check with Proatur (p104) for the latest.

It's best to travel and arrive in daylight hours. If that's not possible, travel at night using 1st-class buses and catch a taxi to your hotel once you arrive.

These days the most frequently reported type of nasty incident involves robbery on walking trails.

The crime travelers are most likely to become a victim of involves pickpocketing, bag-snatching, bag-slitting and the like in crowded bus stations, buses, streets and markets, but also in empty, dark city streets.

Hiking on active volcanoes obviously has an element of risk. Get the latest story before you head out. In the wet season, hike in the morning before rain and possible thunderstorms set in.

Be careful, especially in rural areas, when talking to small children, always ask permission to take photographs and generally try not to put yourself in any situation that might be misinterpreted.

Safety Tips

Use your street smarts and you should stay out of trouble. Some other tips:

- Only carry the money, cards, checks and valuables that you need. Leave the rest in a sealed, signed envelope in your hotel's safe, and obtain a receipt for the envelope. If your hotel doesn't have a safe, it is usually safer to secrete your money and valuables in three or four different stashes among your locked luggage in your room than to carry them with you.
- Don't flaunt jewelry, cameras or valuable-looking watches. Keep your wallet or purse out of view.
- On buses keep your important valuables with you, and keep a tight hold on them.
- Use normal precautions when using ATMs (and be aware that card skimming is a reality here).

- Hiking in large groups and/or with a police escort reduces the risk of robbery.
- Resisting or trying to flee from robbers usually makes the situation worse.

Scams

One common scenario is for someone to spray some sticky liquid like ketchup on your clothes. An accomplice then appears to help you clean up the mess and robs you in the process. Other methods of distraction, such as dropping a purse or coins, or someone appearing to faint, are also used by pickpockets and bag-snatchers.

Regrettably, ATM-card cloners have moved into Guatemala, targeting locals and foreigners alike. They operate by attaching a card-reading device to the ATM (often inside the slot) and once they have your data, proceed to drain your account. There have been reports of card cloning in all the major tourist destinations. The only way to avoid it is to use ATMs that cannot be tampered with easily (inside supermarkets or malls) or by going into the bank and getting a cash advance there. The ATMs most prone to tampering are the ones in the little unlocked room at the front of a bank.

You should *never* have to enter your PIN number to gain access to an ATM room.

Government Travel Advice

The following government websites offer travel advisories and information on current hot spots. Please bear in mind that these sites are updated occasionally and are obliged to err on the safe side – many, many travelers visit Guatemala and don't experience any of these problems.

- **Australian Department of Foreign Affairs** (www.smartraveller.gov.au)
- **British Foreign Office** (www.fco.gov.uk)
- **Canadian Department of Foreign Affairs** (www.dfait-maeci.gc.ca)
- **US State Department** (http://travel.state.gov/)

TELEPHONE

Guatemala has no area or city codes. Calling from other countries, you just dial the international access code (00 in most countries), then the Guatemala country code (502), then the eight-digit local number. Calling within Guatemala, just dial the eight-digit local number. The international access code from Guatemala is 00.

Many towns and cities frequented by tourists have privately run call offices where you can make international calls for reasonable rates.

Many travelers use an account such as Skype. If an internet cafe does not have Skype installed, it can usually be downloaded in a matter of minutes. Headphone and microphone equipment in Guatemala is of varying quality, if it exists at all – if you're planning on using internet cafe computers to make calls, buy earbuds with a microphone attached before you leave – they take up very little room in your pack and you can plug them into the front of most computers in the country.

The most common street phones are those of Telgua, for which you need to buy a Telgua phone card *(tarjeta telefónica de Telgua)* from shops, kiosks and the like. Card sales points may advertise the fact with red signs saying '*Ladatel de Venta Aquí*.' The cards come in denominations of Q20, Q30 and Q50: you slot them into a Telgua phone, dial your number, and the display will tell you how much time you have left.

Unless it's an emergency, don't use the black phones placed strategically in tourist towns that say 'Press 2 to call the United States free!' This is a bait and switch scam; you put the call on your credit card and return home to find you have paid between US$8 and US$20 per minute.

Telgua street phones bear instructions to dial 147110 for domestic collect calls and 147120 for international collect calls.

Cell Phones

Cell phones are widely used. It's possible to bring your cell phone from home, have it 'unlocked' for use in Guatemala (this costs around Q50 in Guatemala), then substitute your SIM card for a local one. This works on some phones and not others and there doesn't appear to be a logic behind it. Guatemalan phone companies work on either 850, 900 or 1900 MHz frequencies – if you have a tri- or quad-band phone you should be OK. Compatibility issues, and the possibility of theft (cell phones are a pickpocket's delight) makes buying a cheap prepaid phone on arrival the most popular option.

Prepaid phones are available pretty much everywhere and cost around Q100 to Q150, often coming with Q100 or so in free calls. Cards to restock the credit on your phone are sold in nearly every corner store. Calls cost Q1.50 per minute anywhere in the country, the same for the US (depending on the company you're with) and up to five times that for the rest of the world.

At the time of writing, Movistar had the cheapest rates (with coverage limited not much further than major cities) and Tigo and Claro had the best coverage.

TIME

Guatemala runs on North American Central Standard Time (GMT/UTC minus six hours). The 24-hour clock is often used, so 1pm may be written as 13 or 1300. When it's noon in Guatemala, it's 1pm in New York, 6pm in London, 10am in San Francisco and 4am the next day in Sydney. For more time conversions, see www.timeanddate.com/worldclock.

TOILETS

You cannot throw *anything* into Guatemalan toilets, including toilet paper. Bathrooms are equipped with some sort of receptacle (usually a small wastebasket) for soiled paper. Toilet paper is not always provided, so always carry some. If you don't have any and need some, asking a restaurant worker for *un rollo de papel* (a roll of paper), accompanied by a panicked facial expression, usually produces fast results.

Public toilets are rare. Use the ones at cafes, restaurants, your hotel and archaeological sites. Buses rarely have toilets on board and if they do, don't count on them working.

TOURIST INFORMATION

Guatemala's national tourism institute, **Inguat** (www.visitguatemala.com), has information offices in major tourist areas. A few towns have departmental, municipal or private-enterprise tourist information offices. **Proatur** (☎ in English 1500), a joint private-government initiative, operates a 24-hour toll-free advice and assistance hotline.

TRAVELERS WITH DISABILITIES

Guatemala is not the easiest country to negotiate with a disability. Although many sidewalks in Antigua have ramps and cute little inlaid tiles depicting a wheelchair, the streets are cobblestone, so the ramps are anything but smooth and the streets worse!

Many hotels in Guatemala are old, converted houses with rooms around a courtyard; such rooms are wheelchair accessible, but the bathrooms may not be. The most expensive hotels have facilities such as ramps, elevators and accessible toilets. Transportation is the biggest hurdle for travelers with limited mobility: travelers in a wheelchair may consider renting a car and driver as the buses will prove especially challenging due to lack of space.

Mobility International USA (www.miusa.org) advises travelers with disabilities on mobility issues, runs exchange programs (including in Guatemala) and publishes some useful books. Also worth consulting are **Access-Able Travel Source** (www.access-able.com) and **Accessible Journeys** (www.disabilitytravel.com).

Antigua-based **Transitions** (www.transitionsfoundation.org) is an organization aiming to increase awareness and access for disabled persons in Guatemala.

VISAS & DOCUMENTS

Citizens of the US, Canada, EU countries, Norway, Switzerland, Australia, New Zealand, Israel and Japan are among those who do not need a visa for tourist visits to Guatemala. On entry into Guatemala you will normally be given a 90-day stay. (The number 90 will be written in the stamp in your passport.)

In August of 2006 Guatemala joined the Centro America 4 (CA-4), a trading agreement with Nicaragua, Honduras and El Salvador. Designed to facilitate the movement of people and goods around the region, it has one major effect on foreign visitors – upon entry to the CA-4 region, travelers are given a 90-day stay *for the entire region*. You can get this extended once, for an additional 90 days, for around Q120. The exact requirements change with each government, but just for kicks, here's how it was working at the time of writing: you needed to go to the **Departamento de Extranjería** (Foreigners' Office; ☎ 2411-2411; 6a Av 3-11, Zona 4, Guatemala City; ⏲ 8am-2:30pm Mon-Fri), with *all* of the following:

- One black and white passport-sized photo on matte paper
- A valid passport
- Two photocopies of the first page of your passport and one of the page where your entry visa was stamped
- A credit card with a photocopy of both of its sides (or photocopy of US$400 worth of travelers' checks)
- A ticket out of the country or proof of flight reservation (on Travel Agency letterhead, signed and sealed by a Travel Agent)

Extensions can take up to a week to process, but this period is also very flexible – it's worth asking about before you start the process.

Citizens of some Eastern European countries are among those who do need visas to visit Guatemala. Enquire at a Guatemalan embassy well in advance of travel.

Visa regulations are subject to change – it's always worth checking with a Guatemalan embassy before you go.

If you have been in the CA-4 for your original 90 days and a 90-day extension, you must leave the region for 72 hours (Belize and Mexico are the most obvious, easiest options), after which you can return to the region to start all over again. Some foreigners have been repeating this cycle for years.

VOLUNTEERING

If you really want to get to the heart of Guatemalan matters and you have altruistic leanings, consider volunteer work. It's rewarding and exposes foreigners to the local culture typically out of reach for the average traveler. Opportunities abound, from caring for abandoned animals to writing grant applications to tending fields. Travelers with specific skills such as nurses, doctors, teachers and website designers are particularly encouraged to investigate volunteering in Guatemala.

Most volunteer posts require basic or better Spanish skills and a minimum time commitment. Depending on the organization, you may have to pay for room and board for the duration of your stay. Before making a commitment, you may want to talk to past volunteers and read the fine print associated with the position.

Two excellent sources of information on volunteer opportunities is Quetzaltenango-based EntreMundos (p149). You only have to visit their website to see the huge range of volunteer opportunities that exists. Many language schools have close links to volunteer projects and can introduce you to the world of volunteering. The best worldwide site for volunteer positions (with many Guatemala listings) is www.idealist.org.

WOMEN TRAVELERS

Women should encounter no special problems traveling in Guatemala. The primary thing you can do to make it easy for yourself while traveling here is to dress modestly. Modesty in dress is highly regarded, and if you practice it, you will usually be treated with respect.

Specifically, shorts should be worn only at the beach, not in town, and especially not in the highlands. Skirts should be at or below the knee. Wear a bra, as going braless is considered provocative. Many local women swim with T-shirts over their swimsuits – you may want to follow suit.

Women traveling alone can expect plenty of attention from talkative men. Often they're just curious and not out for a foreign conquest. It is, of course, up to you how to respond, but there's no need to be intimidated. Consider the situation and circumstances (on a bus is one thing, on a barstool another) and stay confident. Try to sit next to women or children on the bus. Local women rarely initiate conversations, but usually have lots of interesting things to say once the ball is rolling.

While there's no need to be paranoid, the possibility of rape and assault does exist. Use your normal traveler's caution – avoid walking alone in isolated places or through city streets late at night, and skip hitchhiking.

WORKING

Some travelers find work in bars, restaurants and places to stay in Antigua, Panajachel or Quetzaltenango, but the wages are just survival pay. Río Dulce is the place to go if you're looking to crew on a boat around the Caribbean or north to the US.

If you are considering working here, bear in mind that the job you take could probably go to a Guatemalan.

Getting There & Away

AIR

Guatemala's two major international airports are Aeropuerto Internacional La Aurora (p104), in Guatemala City, and Aeropuerto Internacional Mundo Maya, near Flores and Santa Elena.

Destinations include Atlanta, Belize City, Cancún, Havana, Houston, Los Angeles, Madrid, Managua, Mexico City, Miami, Newark, Panama City, San José (Costa Rica) and San Salvador.

Airlines serving Guatemala have offices in Guatemala City. Many also have offices in Aeropuerto Internacional La Aurora.

BORDER CROSSINGS

Guatemala is linked to Chiapas (Mexico) by two official highway routes; to Belize by one road route; and to Honduras and El Salvador by numerous overland routes.

The most popular and easily accessible entry points to Guatemala from Mexico are at Tecún Umán–Ciudad Hidalgo, and at La Mesilla–Ciudad Cuauhtémoc. More adventurous routes take you by country bus and riverboat from Yaxchilán in Chiapas via the Río Usumacinta or the Río de la Pasión to El Petén.

Direct international bus routes from Guatemala City include: Belize City, Managua (Nicaragua), San Salvador (El Salvador), Tapachula (Mexico), Tegucigalpa and other Honduran destinations.

El Salvador

To Santa Ana via Anguiatú Thirty-five kilometers from Chiquimula and 14km from Esquipulas, Padre Miguel junction is the turnoff for Anguiatú, the border of El Salvador, which is 19km (one hour) away. Minibuses pass frequently, coming from Chiquimula, Quezaltepeque and Esquipulas.

The border at Anguiatú is open 24 hours. Plenty of trucks cross here. From Angiatú, microbuses run every half hour to Metapan where you'll find onward connections to Santa Ana and other Salvadoran destinations.

To Santa Ana via San Cristóbal Hourly buses connect El Progreso on the Guatemalan side with the border crossing at San Cristóbal.

To Las Chinamas Frequent minibuses connect Guatemala City, Cuilapa and Valle Nuevo (the border crossing for Las Chinamas in El Salvador). Note that there's nowhere you'd want to stay between Cuilapa and the border.

Honduras

To Copán Ruinas Frequent buses depart Chiquimula for the border town of El Florido, where you'll have to walk across the border and get a minibus for the remaining 12km to Copán Ruinas. Hedman Alas (p105) runs luxury non-stop buses from Guatemala City direct to Copán, and many Antigua travel agents offer that run as well.

To Corinto Minibuses leave Puerto Barrios for the Honduran border (Q25, 1¼ hours) every 20 minutes, from 5am to 5pm, from 6a Av outside the market. The road to the border turns off the CA-9 at Entre Ríos, 13km south of Puerto Barrios. Buses and minibuses going in all directions wait for passengers at Entre Ríos, making the trip from the border fairly easily, whichever direction you are traveling in. Minibuses from Puerto Barrios stop en route to the border at Guatemalan immigration, where you might have to pay Q10 for an exit stamp. Think of it as one last tip to Guatemalan officialdom.

Belize

To San Ignacio It's 100km from Flores to Melchor de Mencos, the Guatemalan town on the border with Belize. There are bus services to the border, as well as more expensive services going right through to Belize City and Chetumal, Mexico.

The road to the border diverges from the Flores–Tikal road at Puente Ixlú (also called El Cruce), 27km from Flores. It continues paved until about 25km short of the border.

There should be no fees at the border for entering or leaving Guatemala, and none for entering Belize. There are moneychangers at the border with whom you can change sufficient funds for immediate needs.

To Punta Gorda *Lanchas* (small motorboats) depart from the Muelle Municipal in Puerto Barrios three times daily for Punta Gorda (Q200, one hour). The 10am departure arrives in time for the noon bus from Punta Gorda to Belize City.

There are also boat departures for Punta Gorda from Lívingston. Before boarding you need to get your exit stamp at the immigration office.

Mexico

To Ciudad Cuauhtémoc Four kilometers separate the Mexican and Guatemalan immigration posts at La Mesilla and Ciudad Cuauhtémoc, and you'll have to drive, walk, hitch or take a *tuk-tuk* (Q5) between them. The strip in La Mesilla leading to the border post has a variety of services, including a police station, post office and a Banrural.

Moneychangers at the border give a good rate if you exchange your dollars for their pesos or quetzals, a terrible one if you want dollars for your pesos or quetzals.

If you get marooned in La Mesilla, try the very basic **Hotel Mily's** (☎7773-8665; s/d Q120/160; ❄). Bargaining may be in order. Onward connections are available from the border post northwest to Comitán (Mexico).

To Frontera Corozal The only river route with regular transportation connections to Mexico is via Bethel or La Técnica on the eastern (Guatemalan) bank of the Río Usumacinta in El Petén, and Frontera Corozal on the Mexican bank. There are bus services to and from Bethel and La Técnica, and shuttle minibus services all the way through to Palenque. Guatemalan immigration is in Bethel; bus drivers to La Técnica will normally stop and wait for you to do the formalities in Bethel.

> **DEPARTURE TAX**
>
> A US$30 departure tax is charged on all international flights leaving Guatemala. The departure tax is usually (but not always) included in the price of your ticket. All passengers on domestic flights are charged a Q10 departure tax, payable at the airport.

It's cheaper and quicker from La Técnica than from Bethel, but crossing at La Técnica means a longer bus journey on the Guatemalan side.

To Tenosique and Palenque You can also cross the border at a new crossing from the Mexican state of Tabasco to El Ceibo, a village on the Río San Pedro. There is also a microbus service from Flores. Immigration posts operate on both sides of the border from 9am to 5pm. From the Mexican side, vans and buses proceed to Tenosique, Tabasco, from where minibuses leave for Palenque up to 7pm.

Getting Around

AIR

There are various domestic airports around the country, but the only *scheduled* domestic flights operating at the time of research were between Guatemala City and Flores, run by Grupo TACA (p104) and TAG (p104).

BICYCLE

Cycling is coming into its own in Guatemala. You can join biking tours or take to the hills independently. Bicycles can be rented in Antigua, Flores, Panajachel and Quetzaltenango. Remember that size matters on Guatemalan roads and as a cyclist nobody will be yielding to you.

BOAT

Speedy *lanchas* (small motorboats) are becoming the norm for transportation on Lago de Atitlán and between Puerto Barrios, Lívingston and Río Dulce, replacing bigger, cheaper ferries.

A few of Guatemala's natural reserves and archaeological sites are accessible only – or preferably – by water.

BUS

Buses go just about everywhere in Guatemala, and where they don't, you'll find minivans and trucks picking up the slack. Fares are generally cheap (around Q15 per hour or less), although comfort levels vary. If you can't bear another jaunt on a 'chicken bus', ask if there is a Pullman service available. These larger, coach-style buses are way more comfortable, run between major destinations and only cost slightly more than the 2nd-class buses.

WARNING

While bus travel at night in Guatemala is rarely a good idea for anybody, it is strongly advised that solo female travelers not catch buses – Pullman or 'chicken' – at night time, the exceptions being the overnight buses traveling between Guatemala City and Flores. There have been no incident reports regarding those services.

Basically, what you want to avoid is being the last person on the bus when it arrives, if it's going to arrive at night.

If you're traveling light, keep your luggage with you inside the bus. Otherwise, heave it onto the roof or stuff it into the luggage compartment and keep your eye on it.

Long-distance buses rarely have working toilets, but usually stop for 20-minute meal and relief breaks at appropriate times. If not, drivers will stop to let you fertilize the roadside.

CAR & MOTORCYCLE

Although few people do, it's possible to hire a car in Guatemala City (at the airport), Antigua, Cobán, Flores and Quetzaltenango. You can hire motorcycles in Antigua and San Pedro La Laguna.

HITCHHIKING

Hitchhiking in the Western sense of the word is not practiced in Guatemala because it is not safe. However, where the bus service is sporadic or nonexistent, pickup trucks and other vehicles serve as public transportation. Stand by the side of the road, hold your arm out and someone will stop. You are expected to pay the driver as if it were a bus, and the fare will be similar. This is a safe and reliable system used by locals and travelers; get used to severe overcrowding.

LOCAL TRANSPORTATION

Local buses (available only in larger cities) are crowded and cheap. Few Guatemalan taxis are metered, and fares can be exorbitant. If you don't like the price quoted, walk away. Then go back and bargain. Then walk away again. Repeat process until a reasonable price is established.

Also whizzing around streets are *tuk-tuks*, three-wheeled motor taxis that visitors to Asia will be familiar with. Rides in these are generally cheap (under Q10 per person) and can be hair-raising, particularly if your driver has not yet entered puberty.

Belize

501 / POP 312,700

Includes

Belize City 228
Caye Caulker 235
Ambergris Caye & San Pedro 240
Altun Ha 245
Lamanai 246
Corozal 248
Belmopan 253
San Ignacio (Cayo) 254
Mountain Pine Ridge Area 259
Dangriga 263
Villages of Toledo 272

Best Places to Eat

- Rumfish (p268)
- Nahil Mayab (p247)
- Benny's Kitchen (p260)
- Ko-Ox Han-Nah (p257)
- Habaneros (p239)

Best Places to Stay

- Coconut Row Guesthouse (p265)
- Cool M Farm (p259)
- Sea Dreams Hotel (p237)
- Howler Monkey Resort (p245)

Why Go?

Sitting smack dab between Spanish-speaking Central America and the Caribbean (geographically and culturally), Central America's youngest nation definitely dances to its own beat. Belize's 240 miles of coastline and uncountable islands offer amazing swimming and beachcombing, and its barrier reef (the northern hemisphere's largest) is a diver's paradise. Belize's jungles are dotted with ancient structures built in the days when Belize was but a small part of the greater Maya kingdom, offering much for the intrepid to explore.

Culturally, Belize is surprisingly diverse. Though officially an English-speaking nation, expect to hear Spanish, Kriol, Garifuna and Maya, with perhaps a bit of Cantonese and Mennonite German thrown in for good measure.

Though among the pricier destinations in Central America, for cuisine, diversity and culture, Belize still offers more than enough bang for your buck to make it worth the trip. So what's not to love?

When to Go

Belize City

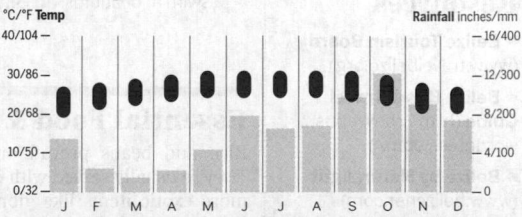

Mid-Dec–Apr Higher prices and drier weather; ideal for beachside days, diving and wildlife spotting.

May–Nov Discounts abound for those willing to brave the heat and heavy rains.

Sep National holidays spark two festive weeks of music, dancing and parades.

AT A GLANCE

Currency Belize dollars (BZ$); US dollars (US$) accepted everywhere

Languages English, Spanish, Kriol, Garifuna

Money ATMs are widely available

Visas Generally not required for stays of less than 30 days

Time GMT minus six hours

Fast Facts

- **Area** 8875 sq miles (22,966 sq km) – slightly larger than Wales or the US state of Massachusetts
- **Capital** Belmopan
- **Emergency** ☎ 911

Set Your Budget

- **Budget hotel** in Belize City US$25
- **Bottle of beer** US$2
- **Set lunch** US$5
- **Three-hour bus ride** US$6

Resources

- **Belize Tourism Board** (www.travelbelize.org)
- **Belize Bus & Travel Guide** (http://belizebus.wordpress.com/)
- **Belize by Naturalight** (www.belizenet.com)

Connections

The Mexican border town of Chetumal has good connections into Belize, both overland into Corozal and by boat to Ambergris and Caye Caulker. The other popular entry point is Benque Viejo del Carmen on the Guatemalan border on the road from Tikal. A southern road from the Toledo district into Guatemala is currently being built and may be finished in 2014. For more info, see Survival Guide on p281.

FIRST TIME IN BELIZE

One Week

Starting from Belmopan or Belize City, make a beeline for **San Ignacio** on the western border. Start by visiting the ruins of **Xunantunich**, then explore more of the Cayo region; jungle activities abound. With a few days left, head to **Caye Caulker** (perhaps with a quick trip to the always-worth-it Belize Zoo) to spend a few days swimming, snorkeling, eating great seafood or just lazing in a hammock.

Two Weeks

From Caye Caulker, travel to **Corozal** to discover some of the town's subtler charms, before heading deeper into nature. If birds are your thing, head to **Crooked Tree**; if it's a deeper jungle experience you're after, check out the **Community Baboon Sanctuary**. Stop at Marie Sharp's Factory for a quick hot-sauce tour before heading to **Dangriga** for a taste of genuine Garifuna culture.

Dangriga is the jump-off point for Belize's central Cayes, including **South Water**, **Tobacco** and **Glover's Reef**. If you want to keep on the terrestrial tip, continue south to **Hopkins** or **Placencia** for a few days on the beach.

When you're fully chilled out, make the trek south to **Punta Gorda** to get the latest information on Maya village homestays and guesthouses. If drumming interests you, visit Emmeth Young's Maroon Creole Drum School. Next, head to **San Pedro Columbia** and use it as a base to explore nearby Lubaantun, then head further still to the small Maya villages of the region, stopping for a hike and a swim at beautiful **Río Blanco National Park**.

Essential Food & Drink

Rice and beans prevail on Belizean menus and plates. They're usually served with chicken or beef (and sometimes more exotic items like gibnut; a type of rodent found in South and Central America) – plus some spices and condiments, such as coconut milk.

Seafood abounds everywhere on the coast. Lobster – in season (June to February) – is always excellent, and conch fritters are a must-try. And of course, no visit to Dangriga or Hopkins would be complete without tasting Hudut, a beloved Garifuna dish.

BELIZE CITY

POP 65,000

While no longer the capital, Belize City retains its importance. It's got the shops, the schools and the population. And there's a buzz on the streets that the actual capital (Belmopan) can only dream about.

Sitting right on the coast and straddling the Haulover Creek, the city is mildly picturesque, though most travelers tend to spend their time elsewhere in the country.

Sights

In just a few hours it's possible to take in many of the city's major sights and sounds by foot.

Regent St is one block inland from the shore. Albert St is the city's main commercial thoroughfare. Note the unlikely little **Hindu temple** between South and Dean Sts.

Court House HISTORIC BUILDING
(Map p234) You can't miss the prominent Court House on Regent St, built in 1926 as the headquarters for Belize's colonial administrators. It still serves administrative and judicial functions.

Battlefield Park PARK
(Map p234) Battlefield Park sits off Regent St, just behind the city's Court House. Always busy with vendors, loungers, con artists and other slice-of-life segments of Belize City society, the park offers welcome shade in the midday heat.

Bliss Institute CULTURAL BUILDING
(Map p234; www.nichbelize.org) Belize City's prime cultural institution is home to the National Institute for Culture and History, which stages periodic exhibits, concerts and theatrical works.

St John's Cathedral CHURCH
(Map p234; Albert St; ⏲6am-6pm) The oldest Anglican church in Central America, dating from 1847.

Yarborough Cemetery CEMETERY
(Map p232) A block southwest of St John's Cathedral is Yarborough Cemetery, whose gravestones outline the turbulent history of Belize going back to 1781.

Sleeping

Budget accommodations are mainly clustered within a few blocks of the Swing Bridge, though there's one good guesthouse in a more sedate area to the north.

Bayview Guest House GUESTHOUSE $
(Map p232; ☎223-4179; www.belize-guesthouse-hotel.com; 58 Baymen Ave; s with/without bathroom BZ$35/50, d with/without bathroom BZ$50/65; ❄📶) At the Bayview Guest House you'll find clean and simply furnished rooms with double beds and cable TV in a secure part of town.

The large, gated yard, filled with fruit trees, is a great place to decompress after a day hanging out in the city.

Sea Breeze Guesthouse GUESTHOUSE $
(Map p234; ☎203-0043; info@seabreeze-belize.com; 18 Gabourel Lane; s/d without bathroom BZ$45/50, r with bathroom BZ$55-80; ❄📶) A budget traveler's dream, though the razor wire is a bit daunting. The nine rooms are super clean and comfortable for the price and the Kalam family offers low-key but accommodating service.

Belcove Hotel HOTEL $
(Map p234; ☎227-3054; www.belcove.com; 9 Regent St; s/d with/without bathroom BZ$55/69, s/d with bathroom BZ$65/80, deluxe rooms d/tr BZ$104/115; ❄📶) This place is freshly painted and impeccably clean throughout, with courteous and accommodating staff. The creekside setting is atmospheric, and the next door Marlin's restaurant serves excellent seafood.

Ma Ma Chen Guesthouse GUESTHOUSE $
(Map p234; ☎223-4568; 7 Eve St; r BZ$60; ❄) Rooms are small and cell-like at this Taiwanese-owned budget guesthouse north of the Swing Bridge. On the bright side, the Chen family run a great vegetarian cafe in the same building.

Chateau Caribbean Hotel HOTEL $$
(Map p234; ☎223-0800; www.chateaucaribbean.com; 6 Marine Parade Blvd; s/d/tr/ste BZ$158/178/198/218; P❄📶) This converted colonial mansion in the Fort George district of Belize City offers a spacious lobby, bar and dining room, as well as gracefully appointed rooms with big beds, large windows with white curtains and Caribbean views. Gin and tonic, anyone?

Coningsby Inn GUESTHOUSE $$
(Map p234; ☎227-1566; coningsby_inn@btl.net; 76 Regent St; d/tr BZ$119/131; ❄@📶) Clean, secure and well positioned for a midpriced Belize City stay. The restaurant serves tasty and economical meals.

Belize Highlights

1. Enjoy inexpensive accommodations, great food and nautical pleasures galore in **Caye Caulker** (p236)
2. Soak up the low-key, beachside vibe of **Hopkins** (p264)
3. Explore the once-difficult-to-access ancient city of **Caracol** (p258), Tikal's crowd-free rival
4. Go underground at **Actun Tunichil Muknal** (p258) cave in Cayo
5. Take a crash course in chocolate making at **Cyrila's Maya Belizean Chocolate** (p273)

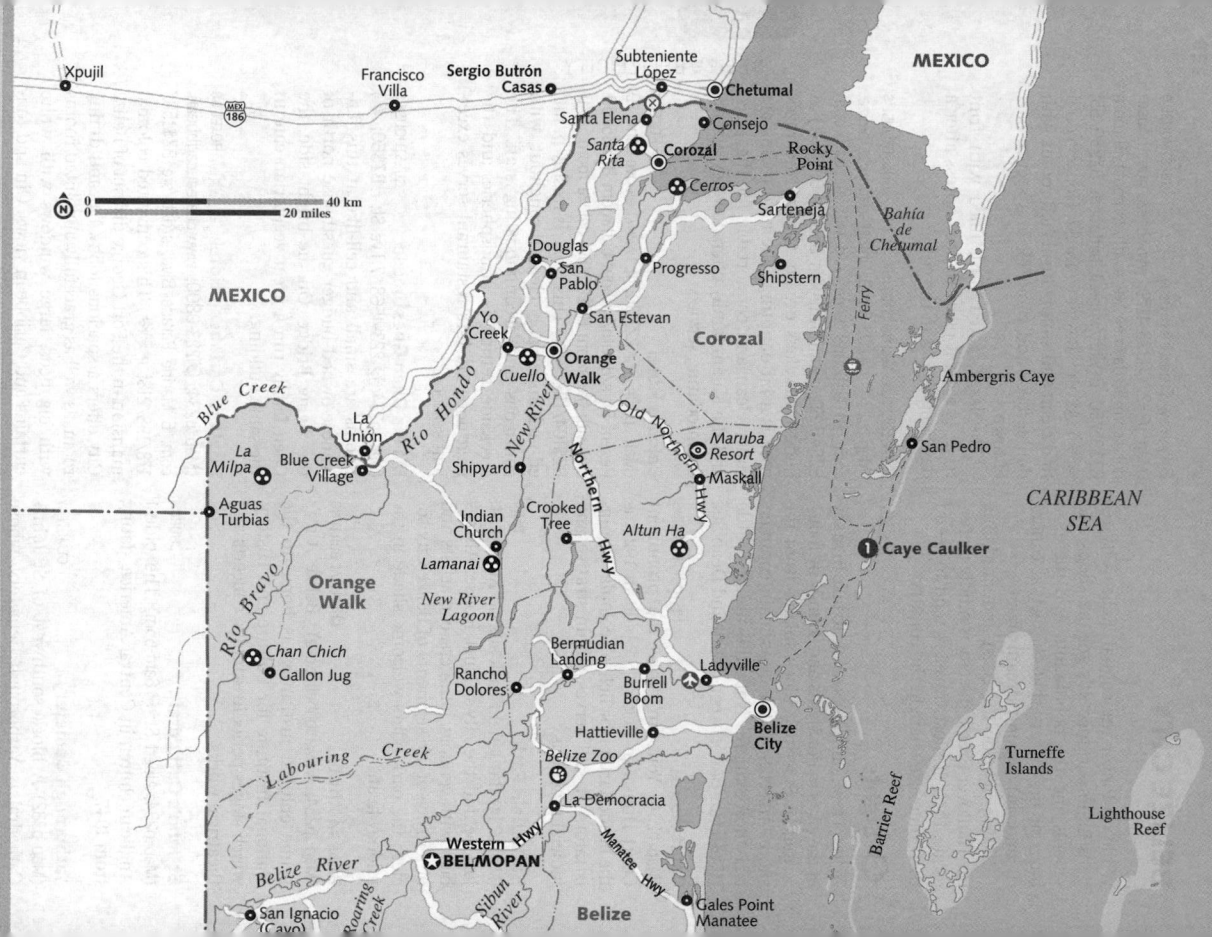

6 Get a taste of Belize's diverse culture in the remote **Maya** and **Garífuna villages** of southern Belize's Toledo district (p272)

Belize City

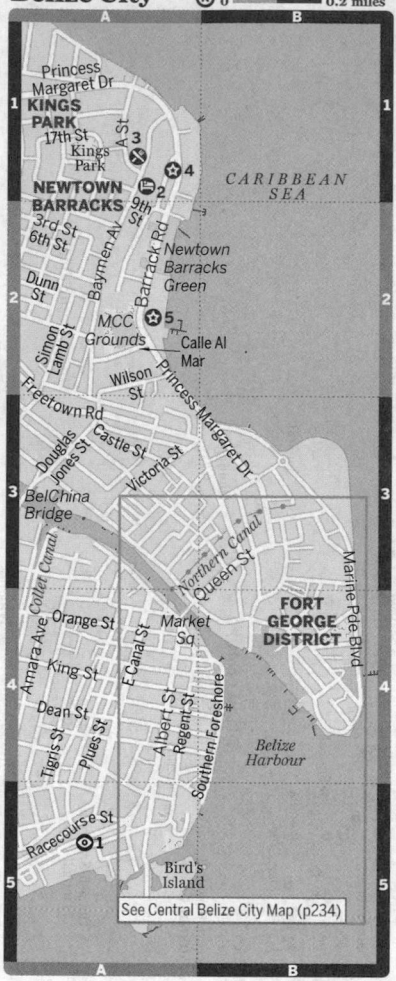

Belize City

Sights
1 Yarborough Cemetery A5

Sleeping
2 Bayview Guest House A1

Eating
3 Sumathi Indian Restaurant..... A1

Drinking & Nightlife
Vogue Bar & Lounge .....(see 5)

Entertainment
4 Caesar's Palace A1
5 Princess Hotel & Casino A2

Eating

Belize City's restaurants present a well-rounded introduction to Belizean cuisine. Street food – usually sold from carts around Market Sq – is surprisingly good.

Cenie's Deli CAFETERIA $
(Map p234; Commercial Center, Regent St; pastries BZ$3, lunch BZ$8-10; breakfast & lunch) Lunch is served cafeteria-style from 11am and lasts until the food is gone. Still one of the cheaper places in town; head upstairs for river views.

Marlin's Seafood SEAFOOD $
(Map p234; Regent St; mains BZ$7-10; breakfast, lunch & dinner Mon-Sat) Choose one of the seafood specials listed on the chalkboard – such as chimole, fish or conch soup – then take a seat at a picnic table, which comes complete with river views.

Dit's Restaurant DINER, BAKERY $
(Map p234; 50 King St; snacks BZ$3, mains BZ$6-12; breakfast & lunch) Dit's is a local favorite, a fine place to get rice-and-bean Belizean standards, sandwiches and Mexican dishes such as *panades* and *salbutes* (variations on the tortilla). Especially good are the desserts, coconut and lemon pies, milkshakes and juices.

Le Petit Café BAKERY $
(Map p234; Cork St; pastries BZ$1-5, sandwiches BZ$11-14; breakfast, lunch & dinner;) For muffins, croissants, cookies and a wide variety of coffee drinks, stop in at this excellent little cafe and bakery run by the Radisson.

Moon Clusters Coffee House CAFE $
(Map p234; 203-0139; 25 Daly St; breakfast & lunch Mon-Sat) The coolest cafe in town, serving up six types of espresso, frappuccino and donuts and pastries.

Ma Ma Chen Restaurant TAIWANESE, VEGETARIAN $
(Map p234; 7 Eve St; mains from BZ$5; breakfast, lunch & dinner;) Serves excellent vegetarian cuisine with a definite Taiwanese flair.

Sumathi Indian Restaurant INDIAN $$
(Map p232; 223-1172; 19 Baymen Ave; dishes BZ$18-38; 11am-11pm Tue-Sun;) Curries, tandooris and *biryanis* (spicy rice and meat-or-vegetable dishes), with plenty of vegetarian options, all in generous quantities.

★Celebrity Restaurant INTERNATIONAL $$
(Map p234; ☎223-7272; www.celebritybelize.com; cnr Marine Parade Blvd & Goal Lane; mains BZ$20-30; ⏲11am-11pm) Steaks and seafood, fajitas and quesadillas, pasta dishes and Mediterranean surprises like hummus and kebabs. A happening bar complements the casual ambience and sea views.

Drinking & Entertainment

Weekends are your best bet to party in Belize City. There are a few places to have a beer in the center, but the real action takes place 1.2 miles (2km) north, about a BZ$6 taxi ride.

Bird's Isle Restaurant BAR
(Map p234; Bird's Island; ⏲10:30am-2:30pm & 5:30pm-late Mon-Fri, 10:30am-10pm Sat) Locals and tourists alike flock to the open-air *palapa* (thatched palm-leaf shelter) to partake of sea breezes, freshly squeezed juice, good food and cold beers. Thursdays from 8:30pm to 1am is karaoke night; the bar also has live music occasionally.

Vogue Bar & Lounge LOUNGE
(Map p232; www.princessbelize.com; Newton Barracks, Kings Park, Princess Hotel & Casino; ⏲noon-midnight Sun-Wed, noon-2am Thu-Sat) The lounge at the Princess gets lively on Friday nights when a mixed young crowd launches a new weekend. A DJ helps to get things moving from 9pm Thursday to Saturday.

Caesar's Palace CLUB
(Map p232; ☎223-7624; 190 Barrack Rd; cover men BZ$5, women free; ⏲10pm-4am Fri & Sat) Catch Latino-flavored music and all the action on a small dance floor. The crowd starts turning up at about 10:30pm.

Princess Hotel & Casino CINEMA, CASINO
(Map p232; Newtown Barracks, Kings Park; ⏲noon-4am) This is the only cinema in Belize City; check daily papers for what's showing. Also here are a bowling alley, video arcade, a couple of upmarket bars and, of course, the casino.

Shopping

Image Factory ART GALLERY
(Map p234; 91 N Front St; ⏲9am-5pm Mon-Fri) This art gallery has the country's best range of books, including international literature, and titles on Belizean and Caribbean society and history. There is also one room that is packed with paintings and other local art.

Orientation

Haulover Creek, a branch of the Belize River, runs through the middle of the city, separating the commercial center (bounded by Albert, Regent, King and Orange Sts) from the slightly more genteel residential district of Fort George to the northeast. Just south of the Swing Bridge and Haulover Creek is the old part of town, which can be slightly seedy and best explored during the day. At the bridge's northern end is the Belize Marine Terminal, which is used by motor launches traveling to Caye Caulker and Ambergris Caye.

Information

DANGERS & ANNOYANCES

Yes, there is petty crime in Belize City, but it's not as bad as some doomsayers will tell you. Take the same commonsense precautions for avoiding theft that you would in any major city. It's always better to walk in pairs or groups and to stick to major streets in the city center, Fort George and King's Park. Especially avoid walking along Front St south and east of the Swing Bridge; this is a favorite area for muggers.

EMERGENCY

Ambulance (☎90, private ambulance 223-3292)
General Emergency/Police (☎911)
Tourist Police (☎227-6082, 1-800-898-000)

INTERNET ACCESS

KGS Internet Café (29 King St; per hr BZ$3; ⏲9am-6pm)
Turton Library (156 N Front St; per hr BZ$4; ⏲9am-5pm Mon-Fri, 9am-noon Sat) Cheapest internet access in town, fast connections and air-con.

GETTING INTO TOWN

From the Airport
The taxi fare to or from the international airport is BZ$50. It's a half-hour, 1.8-mile (3km) walk from the air terminal out along the access road to the Northern Hwy, where one can usually catch a bus going either north or south.

From the Bus Station
The bus station is on the west bank of the canal, about five-minutes' walk from the Swing Bridge. As you exit the terminal, turn left, then take the first right along Orange St. This is a dodgy area – if you arrive at night, take a taxi to your hotel.

Central Belize City

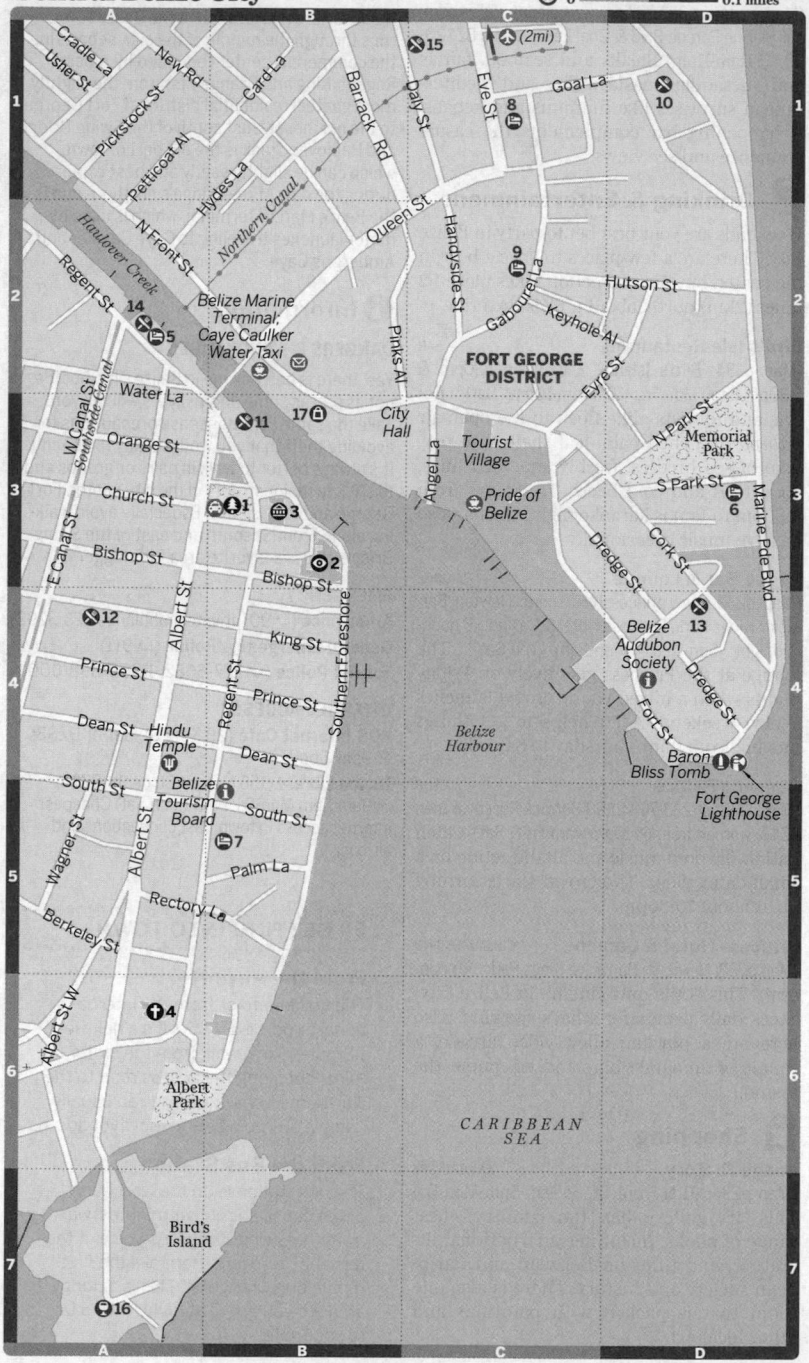

Central Belize City

Sights
1 Battlefield Park B3
2 Bliss Institute B3
3 Court House B3
4 St John's Cathedral A6

Sleeping
5 Belcove Hotel A2
6 Chateau Caribbean Hotel D3
7 Coningsby Inn B5
8 Ma Ma Chen Guesthouse C1
9 Sea Breeze Guesthouse C2

Eating
10 Celebrity Restaurant D1
11 Cenie's Deli B3
12 Dit's Restaurant A4
13 Le Petit Café D4
Ma Ma Chen Restaurant ..... (see 8)
14 Marlin's Seafood A2
15 Moon Clusters Coffee House C1

Drinking & Nightlife
16 Bird's Isle Restaurant A7

Shopping
17 Image Factory B3

LAUNDRY

G's Laundromat (22 Dean St; wash per load BZ$10; ⏲7:30am-5:30pm)

North Front Street Laundry (22 N Front St)

MEDICAL SERVICES

Karl Heusner Memorial Hospital (☎223-1548, 223-1564; Princess Margaret Dr; ⏲24hr emergency services) A public hospital in the north of town.

MONEY

There are several international ATMs throughout the city, including one next to the Marine Terminal building.

Belize Bank (60 Market Sq; ⏲8am-1:30pm Mon-Thu, 8am-4:30pm Fri)

Scotia Bank (cnr Albert & Bishop Sts; ⏲8am-1:30pm Mon-Thu, 8am-4:30pm Fri)

First Caribbean International Bank (21 Albert St; ⏲8am-1:30pm Mon-Thu, 8am-4:30pm Fri)

POST

Post Office (N Front St; ⏲8am-noon & 1-5pm Mon-Sat) Facing the Marine Terminal building.

TELEPHONE

BTL (☎227-7085; 1 Church St; ⏲8am-6pm Mon-Fri) Sells phone cards and has private cabins with air-con where you can make local and international calls.

TOURIST INFORMATION

Belize Audubon Society (☎223-5004; www.belizeaudubon.org; 12 Fort St) Offers information on national parks and wildlife reserves throughout the country.

Belize Tourism Board (BTB; ☎227-2417, 227-2420; www.travelbelize.org; 64 Regent St; ⏲8am-5pm Mon-Thu, 8am-4pm Fri) Pick up maps, magazines and all sorts of information relating to travel around Belize. This is also where you will find the cruiseship schedule which is published and distributed on a biannual basis.

Getting There & Away

AIR

Belize City's Municipal Airport (TZA) is 1.5 miles (2.5km) north of the city center, on the shore. You can take domestic flights from the international terminal, but it's always cheaper to depart from the Municipal Airport.

Local Belizean airlines are **Maya Island Air** (☎223-1140, 223-1362; www.mayaairways.com) and **Tropic Air** (☎226-2012; www.tropicair.com).

BOAT

Fast motor launches run by **Caye Caulker Water Taxi** (☎223-5752; www.cayecaulkerwatertaxi.com)

BUSES FROM BELIZE CITY

DESTINATION	DURATION (HR)	COST (BZ$)	FREQUENCY
Belmopan	1-1¼	local/express 5/10	half-hrly
Benque Viejo del Carmen	3	local/express 8/12	half-hrly
Chetumal (Mexico)	3	16	3 daily
Corozal	2-3	local/express 10/15	hrly
Dangriga	3-4	local/express 10/15	regular
Orange Walk	2	local/express 5/7	hrly
Placencia	4	local/express 20/26	regular
Punta Gorda	6-7	local/express 24/28	regular
San Ignacio	2-3	local/express 7/11	half-hrly

zoom between Belize City, Caye Caulker and Ambergris Caye frequently every day, and there's now a weekly boat to Guatemala as well.

The Belize Marine Terminal, at the north end of the Swing Bridge, is the main dock for boats to the northern cayes.

BUS

All roads lead to Belize City, and nearly all buses now stop at the main terminal, regardless of company. Easy to find, it's the large building painted Rasta red, gold and green. Authorities have recently been discouraging bus drivers from overloading their buses, so it's easier to get a ride from the terminal than the highway.

Getting Around

Trips by taxi within Belize City (including to/from Municipal Airport) cost BZ$10 for one or two people. Prices go up at night, and haggling is possible.

THE NORTHERN CAYES

Belize's go-to place for water-based fun are two tiny cayes to the northeast of Belize City. Diving, snorkeling, windsurfing, sailing – it's all here. Protected sea grass along the shoreline doesn't really encourage swimmers, and most people swim off docks that jut into deeper water. If you just want to laze around on the beach, southern towns such as Hopkins or Placencia might be a better bet.

Caye Caulker

POP 1300

A short hop from Belize City, Caye Caulker remains a backpacker favorite. A tiny place, you could make a tour of it in less than two hours. Travelers with cash head to Caulker for a couple of days before heading to more developed Ambergris; those on budgets are advised not to hit Ambergris at all.

Caulker is actually two islands, since Hurricane Hattie split the island just north of the village. The split is called, simply, the Split (or the Cut). It has a tiny beach, with swift currents running through it. North of the split is mostly undeveloped land, and part of it has been declared a nature reserve.

The water is good for swimming here, though there is lots of sea grass. The spot to see and be seen is by the dock by the Split.

Activities

The surf breaks on the barrier reef, easily visible from the eastern shore of Caye Caulker. However, don't attempt to swim out to it – the local boaters are completely heedless of swimmers. Swim only in protected areas.

A short boat ride takes you out to the reef to enjoy some of the world's most exciting **snorkeling**, **diving** (including the shark-filled Blue Hole) and **fishing**. With their calm waters protected by the reef, near constant onshore winds and sweet water temperature, the cayes are also making a name for themselves as a **kitesurfing** location.

Several places in town rent water-sports equipment. Snorkeling gear and beach floats each cost around BZ$10 per day and sea kayaks are BZ$15 per hour.

Kitexplorer KITESURFING

(☎626-4613; www.kitexplorer.com; Front St) Kitexplorer offers introductory, refresher and advanced courses, as well as renting equipment to licensed, experienced kitesurfers. Courses start from BZ$260.

Belize Diving Services DIVING

(☎226-0143; http://belizedivingservices.net) Belize Diving Services does certification and leads dive tours to Turniffe Atoll and the local reef.

Tours

A variety of inland and sea trips can be arranged from Caulker.

Anda De Wata Tours ADVENTURE

(☎666-7374; Luciano Reyes St) Does floating on an inner tube pulled behind a slow-moving boat sound like a dream come true? Anda De Wata's 90 minute boat-and-float tour (BZ$50) may be your own personal paradise! It also offers a variety of interesting snorkeling tours around local reefs.

Raggamuffin Tours BOAT

(☎226-0348; www.raggamuffintours.com; Front St) Offers a three-day, two-night sailing trip (BZ$600), camping on Tobacco and Rendezvous cayes. There are plenty of opportunities for snorkeling and fishing along the way to Placencia.

Reef Watersports WATER SPORTS

(☎635-7219; www.reefwatersports.com; Av Hicaco) This newly opened shop is located right at the Split and offers jet-ski rentals (BZ$140 per half-hour). It also does various packages including wake boarding and waterskiing. Check the website for package details.

Tsunami Adventures ADVENTURE
(☎226-0462; www.tsunamiadventures.com; Front St) A great one-stop tour shop that pretty much does everything. Among the tours it arranges are three-hour night snorkeling trips (BZ$65), one-day trips to Turniffe Atoll (BZ$140) and two-hour boat tours of Caulker (BZ$50). All prices are per person. Tsunami also rents snorkels (BZ$10) and canoes (BZ$50) by the day.

Sleeping

Dirty McNasty's Hostel HOSTEL $
(☎636-7512; Crocodile St; dm BZ$28, d $BZ66) What backpacker could resist a place called Dirty McNasty's? Despite the name, this newly opened hostel is neither especially unhygienic nor foul, though there is a certain raffish pirate-ship quality about the place. Dorms and double rooms are clean enough, though obviously hostel-basic, and all rooms are equipped with hot showers for when things get too dirty and/or nasty.

Yuma's House Belize HOSTEL $
(☎206-0019; www.yumashousebelize.com; Front St; dm/s/d BZ$27/55/62;) Yuma's takes full advantage of the beachfront property, reserving a dock for guests and stringing up hammocks in the leafy garden. Crowded dorm rooms have fresh paint and new beds and mattresses. Shared facilities include two fully equipped kitchens, games and cold-water showers.

Bella's Hostel HOSTEL $
(☎226-0360; bellas.hostel@yahoo.com; dm/d BZ$20/50, campsite per person BZ$15;) On the back side of the island, Bella's is a hideaway for the backpacker set, who can camp on the shady grounds or snag a bed in the lofty bunkhouse. You are likely to see travelers sharing a meal in the kitchen, playing cards on the balcony and taking advantage of free stuff such as canoes and bikes.

Ignacio Beach Cabins CABINS $
(☎226-0175; http://aguallos.com/ignaciobeach; d BZ$30-45, ste BZ$110;) Simple waterfront lodging in weathered cabins on stilts. There is little foot traffic this far south, so it feels private and pristine. The cold-shower cabins all have easy access to the beach, but the pricier ones are at the water's edge.

Daisy's Hotel HOTEL $
(☎226-0150; s/d/tr BZ$25/38/48) Some of the cheapest rooms on the island, and not a bad deal, either – spacious and airy, but basic. Get one upstairs where the ventilation's better.

Tropical Oasis HOSTEL $
(☎629-0511; karianne_mokkelbost@hotmail.com; La Posa St; dm BZ$25, cottage BZ$50) This colorful ramshackle set of shacks, cottages, and even a trailer, is among the most budget options in Caye Caulker. The Oasis has an eight-bed dorm, a four-bed dorm and two small cottages that sleep two. There's also a communal kitchen.

★Sea Dreams Hotel B&B $$
(☎226-0602; www.seadreamshotel.com; r BZ$210, apt BZ$310-410;) A lovely guesthouse just west of the Split, Sea Dreams offers a rare combination of easy access and sweet tranquility. Spend the day lounging around the split, then retreat to the cozy accommodation just a few steps away. Guests are invited to enjoy glorious sunset views from the private dock or over drinks at the rooftop lounge. Breakfast, bike and canoe use is included.

Costa Maya Beach Cabanas CABINS $$
(☎226-0432; www.tsunamiadventures.com; Front St; d BZ$110-130, apt BZ$150;) Six two-story beachfront hexagon-shaped *cabañas* are clustered around a sandy courtyard. The pricier beachfront units are fitted with kitchenettes, cable TV, air-con and private patios with wonderful views. Guests enjoy complimentary bicycles, beach chairs, swimming dock and canoes, as well as discounts on tours at Tsunami Adventures.

Colinda Cabanas CABAÑA $$
(☎226-0383; www.colindacabanas.com; Playa Ascension; r from BZ$98-278;) It's hard to miss Colin and Linda's brightly colored yellow-and-blue property, which sits south of the cemetery. The five *cabañas* and five suites are all nicely appointed with mini-fridges, coffee makers, hot showers and comfy beds. Balconies with hammocks provide plenty of spots for lounging.

Barefoot Beach Belize GUESTHOUSE $$
(☎226-0205; www.barefootbeachbelize.com; r BZ$138-158, ste BZ$258, cottages BZ$258;) This pretty little pink-and-turquoise beachfront hotel has rooms with king- or queen-sized beds, fridges, air-con and private patios. Suites have full kitchens. Cottages are stand-alone houses that fit a family of four.

Caye Caulker

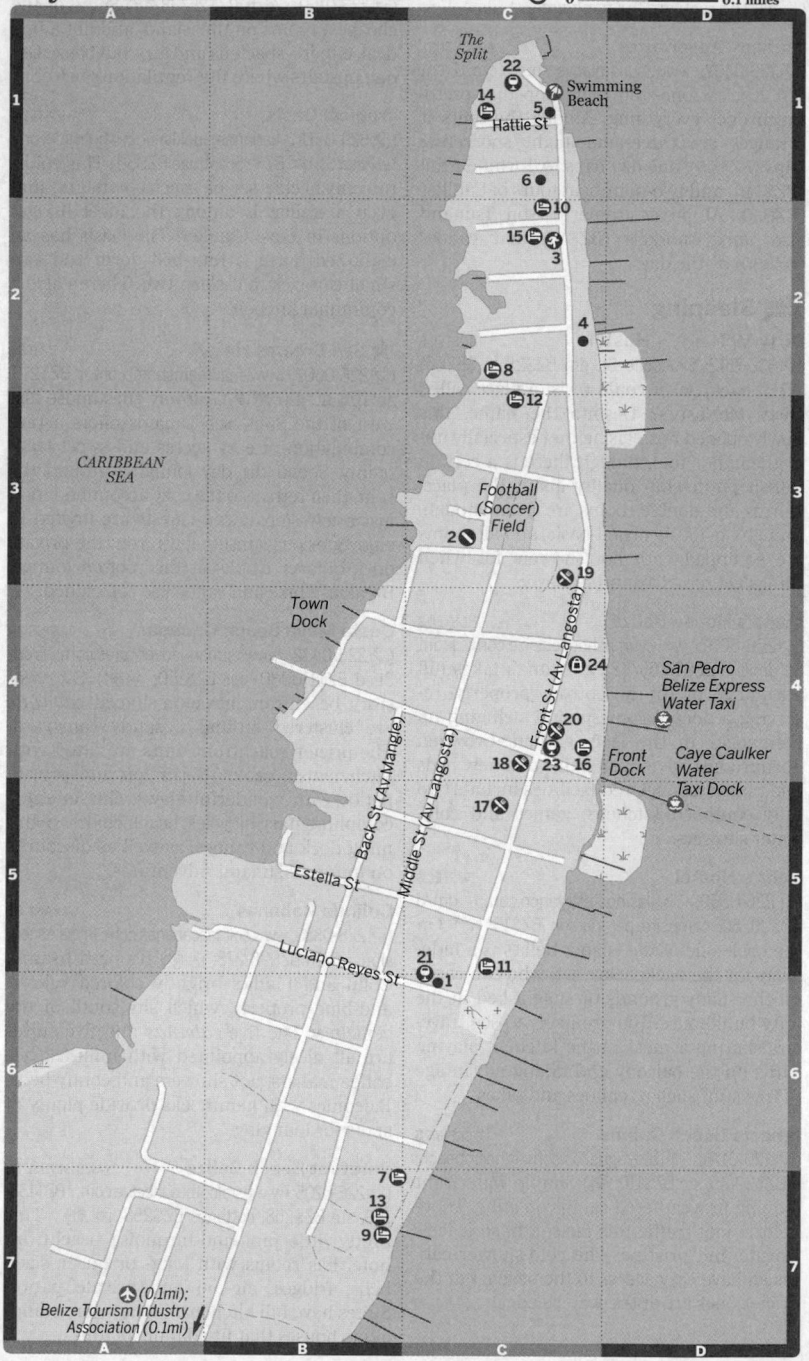

Caye Caulker

Activities, Courses & Tours
1 Anda De Wata Tours C6
2 Belize Diving Services C3
3 Kitexplorer C2
4 Raggamuffin Tours C2
5 Reef Watersports C1
6 Tsunami Adventures C1

Sleeping
7 Barefoot Beach Belize B7
8 Bella's Hostel C2
9 Colinda Cabanas B7
10 Costa Maya Beach Cabanas C2
11 Daisy's Hotel C5
12 Dirty McNasty's Hostel C3
13 Ignacio Beach Cabins B7
14 Sea Dreams Hotel C1
15 Tropical Oasis C2
16 Yuma's House Belize C4

Eating
17 Amor Y Café C5
18 Habaneros C4
19 Happy Lobster C3
20 La Cubana C4

Drinking & Nightlife
21 I&I Reggae Bar C5
22 Lazy Lizard C1
23 Sand Box C4

Shopping
24 Caribbean Colors C4

Eating

On any given evening you'll find half a dozen or so small grill and picnic table setups along the beach, along with folks selling pasties and Belizean items like conch and lobster fritters (in season) out of bicycle carts. These ad-hoc eateries range from good to excellent, and are generally a great value.

La Cubana CUBAN $
(Front St; mains from BZ$12; breakfast, lunch & dinner;) La Cubana serves seafood, chicken and even a range of vegetarian dishes. But what brings people here nightly is the roast pork. Best deal is the all-you-can-eat buffet (BZ$28), an awesome spread with a variety of veggie dishes, meat dishes, desserts and, of course, dead piglet.

Amor Y Café BREAKFAST $
(Front St; mains BZ$8-12; breakfast & lunch;) Take your pick from fresh-squeezed juices, scrambled eggs or homemade yogurt topped with fruit, and don't miss out on the fresh-brewed coffee. If you have to pack a lunch, sandwiches are available to go.

Little Kitchen Restaurant BELIZEAN $$
(667-2178; Marvin Gainy St; meals from BZ$6-20; lunch & dinner) This 3rd-floor open-air restaurant serves traditional Belizean dishes like curry shrimp, coconut red snapper, stews and excellent conch fritters. It's also a great spot to watch the sun go down with a cocktail made with local Belizean rum, ginger wine or a fresh juice. Located in a more residential part of Caye Caulker, Little Kitchen is a bit tricky to find. Head to the east–west street just north of the airstrip, then head west and look for the signs or just ask a local.

Happy Lobster SEAFOOD $$
(Front St; mains BZ$18-30; breakfast, lunch & dinner Wed-Mon;) A Caulker institution, Happy Lobster has lots of fish, meat and vegetarian options. The breakfast menu is especially popular, and the front porch is a pleasant place to catch the breeze off the ocean and watch the activity on Front St.

★ Habaneros INTERNATIONAL $$$
(620-4911; habanerosdream@gmail.com; cnr Front St & 'The Dock Street'; mains BZ$25-50; dinner Fri-Wed) Habaneros serves up gourmet international food, combining fresh seafood, meat and vegetables with insanely delicious sauces and flavors. Sit in the funky bar and sip a fruity cocktail, wine or sangria, or eat by candlelight on the verandah. Reservations are recommended.

Drinking & Nightlife

Much of the nightlife on Caye Caulker happens in an ad-hoc fashion on the beach and up by the split.

Sand Box BAR
(Front St; 8am-late) With outdoor seating facing the dock, and a happy hour from 3pm to 6pm, the Sand Box is an island institution. Locals and expats gather to socialize and catch up on gossip. If you can't check into your hotel straight away, make this your first stop coming off the water taxi.

Lazy Lizard BEACH BAR
(The Split; 10am-midnight) A 'sunny place for shady people' – and there is no shortage of the latter hanging about. The in-place to see and be seen on the Split.

DIVING THE BLUE HOLE

If you've ever seen a tourism poster for Belize, you probably know what the Blue Hole looks like – a lot of people come to Belize just to dive it. Situated in the middle of Lighthouse Reef, it's a sinkhole of startling blue water about 400ft (122m) deep and 1000ft (305m) wide.

After a fast descent to 130ft (40m), you swim beneath a stalactite-laden overhang and among a variety of reef sharks (black tips, bulls, lemons and maybe hammerheads or tiger sharks).

The dive can be undertaken with an open-water diving license, and can be arranged with nearly every dive shop on the cayes. Prices are around BZ$380 for a day trip (which involves three dives).

I&I Reggae Bar BAR
(⏲6pm-midnight) On the south end of town, I&I Bar is the happening reggae spot.

Shopping

Caribbean Colors ART
(www.caribbean-colors.com; Front St; ⏲7am-9pm; 📶) This 2nd-floor shop owned by local artist Lee Vanderwalker displays both her work and that of about a dozen other Belizean artists. While you browse you can treat yourself to a hot espresso or a cool smoothie.

Information

South of the village is the **Belize Tourism Industry Association** (☎226-2251) where you can get information on what to see and do on the island. Cash is available at **Atlantic Bank** (Middle St; ⏲8am-2pm Mon-Fri, 8:30am-noon Sat), though the machine is temperamental, and you can check your email at **Cayeboard Connection** (Front St; per hr BZ$12; ⏲8am-9pm). Caye Caulker's website (www.gocayecaulker.com) is a great source for pre-trip information.

Getting There & Away

Caye Caulker is serviced by regular flights between Belize City and Ambergris by **Maya Island Air** (☎226-0012; www.mayaairways.com) and **Tropic Air** (☎226-0040; www.tropicair.com). Caulker is also the midpoint for the **Caye Caulker Water Taxi** (☎226-0992; www.cayecaulkerwatertaxi.com) and San Pedro Belize Express (p244) water taxis between Belize City and Ambergris.

Getting Around

Caulker is so small that most people walk. If need be, you can rent a bicycle (BZ$20 per day) or golf cart (BZ$100 per day) or use the golf-cart taxi service, which costs around BZ$5 for a one-way trip anywhere on the island.

Ambergris Caye & San Pedro

POP 8500

Less laid-back than Caye Caulker, more developed than Placencia, Ambergris is Belize's most upscale tourist beach spot. Crowded with cars, golf carts and tourists, San Pedro is a miniature Cancun, though sandy streets and beachside bars maintain the impression of a tropical paradise. Most of the budget establishments are downtown.

Outside of town, especially to the south and directly to the north, large resorts and gated retirement villages are springing up with frightening regularity.

Most of the island's population lives in the town of San Pedro, near the southern tip. The barrier reef is only a half mile (800m) east of San Pedro.

Activities

Ambergris is good for all water sports: scuba diving, snorkeling, sailboarding, kitesurfing, boating, surfing, parasailing, swimming, deep-sea fishing and sunbathing. Many island hotels have their own dive shops, which rent equipment, provide instruction and organize diving excursions. In fact, just about any local can put you in touch with someone organizing water-sports trips.

All beaches are public, and most waterside hotels and resorts are generous with their lounge chairs on slow days. While sandy beaches are plentiful, protected sea grass at the waterline makes entry from the shore not terribly pleasant, so you'll be swimming from piers. The beaches north of San Pedro tend to be the quietest. To access them, head to where the river passes at the end of Pescador Dr where you'll cross a small metal bridge (a BZ$2 toll is sometimes asked for). From there, a single dirt road runs north for close to 15 miles (25km). Pass through the condos and new developments just over the bridge; you'll find some outstanding beaches, as well as several laid-back eating and drinking venues.

Sailsports Belize WATER SPORTS
(☎226-4488; www.sailsportsbelize.com) Hourly sailboat rentals from BZ$44 to BZ$98 and sailboards from BZ$44 hourly. Also teaches sailing, sailboarding and kite surfing. Sailsports is located ¾ mile south of town on the beach in front of Caribbean Villas Hotel.

Tours

The *Reef Runner* glass-bottom boat, found on Barrier Reef Dr, makes daily reef trips for BZ$70 per person. The aptly named *Rum Punch II,* a wooden sailboat, runs sunset cocktail cruises for BZ$50 (book at tour agents in town). *La Gaviota* is a sailing boat; go to Lily's Hotel (Barrier Reef Dr) across from Belize Bank.

Tours are available to the Maya ruins at Altun Ha (BZ$180) and Lamanai (BZ$310) or beyond to the Belize Zoo, Xunantunich, Crooked Tree Wildlife Sanctuary, the Community Baboon Sanctuary, Mountain Pine Ridge and Tikal (Guatemala). Any hotel, travel agency or dive shop can fill you in on tours, or contact **Seaduced by Belize** (☎226-2254; www.seaducedbybelize.com; Vilma Linda Plaza, Tarpon St) or **Bottom Time Dive Shop** (☎893-3825; www.sanpedroholiday.com) at Banyan Bay Resort.

Sleeping

Pedro's Hotel HOSTEL, HOTEL $
(☎226-3825, 206-2198, mobile 610-5526; www.pedroshotel.com; Sea Grape Dr; s/d without bathroom BZ$30/50, r with bathroom & air-con BZ$120, deluxe rooms BZ$130; ❄ 📶 🏊) Pedro's is a long-time San Pedro party hotel favorite. The best deal at Pedro's is the brand-spanking new deluxe annex, which has 12 rooms featuring flat-screen TVs with 110-plus channels, air-con and en-suite bathrooms with hot showers. The slightly older hotel is a bargain, offering affordable wood-paneled rooms with air-con and hot water. The original 'hostel' has cell-like rooms with thin walls and shared (cold-water) bathrooms.

Ruby's Beachfront HOTEL $
(☎226-2063; www.ambergriscaye.com/rubys; Barrier Reef Dr; d with/without bathroom BZ$80/50; 📶) The most attractive feature of this long-standing backpacker fave is the downstairs cafe, which guarantees a delicious breakfast every morning. Fan-cooled rooms themselves are pretty tired – but not bad value considering the price and location.

Hotel San Pedrano GUESTHOUSE $
(☎226-2054; sanpedrano@btl.net; Barrier Reef Dr; s/d/tr BZ$76/87/87, with air-con BZ$96/107/107; ❄) There are no views from this 2nd-story, streetside hostelry, but you might catch the breeze from the balcony. Relatively spacious rooms have two or three beds.

Thomas Hotel GUESTHOUSE $
(☎226-2061; Barrier Reef Dr; s/d with fan BZ$65/85, d with air-con BZ$93; ❄ 📶) Large clean rooms with refrigerator, TV and private bath. A good deal for the middle of San Pedro.

Conch Shell Inn HOTEL $$
(☎627-5202, 226-2062; www.ambergriscaye.com/conchshell; 11 Foreshore St; r downstairs/upstairs BZ$130/152; ❄ 📶) Recently revamped, the 10 brightly tiled rooms are now equipped with new beds, kitchenettes, and hammocks hanging on the shared balcony. The downstairs rooms do not have the kitchen area, but they do have direct access to the sweet sandy beach, lovingly furnished with lounge chairs and palm trees.

Ak'bol Yoga Retreat RESORT $$
(☎226-2073; www.akbol.com; s/d BZ$70/100, cabaña BZ$290-330; 🏊) Ak'bol's seven colorful *cabañas* have delightful details, like handcrafted hardwood furniture and mosaic sinks with conch shell faucets. Alternatively, save your cash and sleep in the rustic yoga barracks with shared bathrooms. Either way, indulge in good food at the breezy beach bar and daily yoga classes in the studio surrounded by sea. Kids' camp available (which includes children's yoga).

Tio Pil's Hotel GUESTHOUSE $$
(☎226-2059; www.tiopilshotel.com; cnr Barrier Reef Dr & Caribeña St; s BZ$110-130, d BZ$130-150; ❄ 📶) This long-standing favorite has a prime beach location and a long wooden balcony offering views of it all. Rooms are spacious and simple, with a modicum of style; if you get one facing the sea, the big, breeze-inducing windows are all you need.

Changes in Latitude B&B $$
(☎226-2986, in USA 317-536-5160; www.ambergriscaye.com/latitudes; 36 Coconut Dr; d BZ$230; ❄ 📶 🏊) This charming little gay-friendly bed and breakfast in the south side of town features individually themed rooms.

San Pedro (Ambergris Caye)

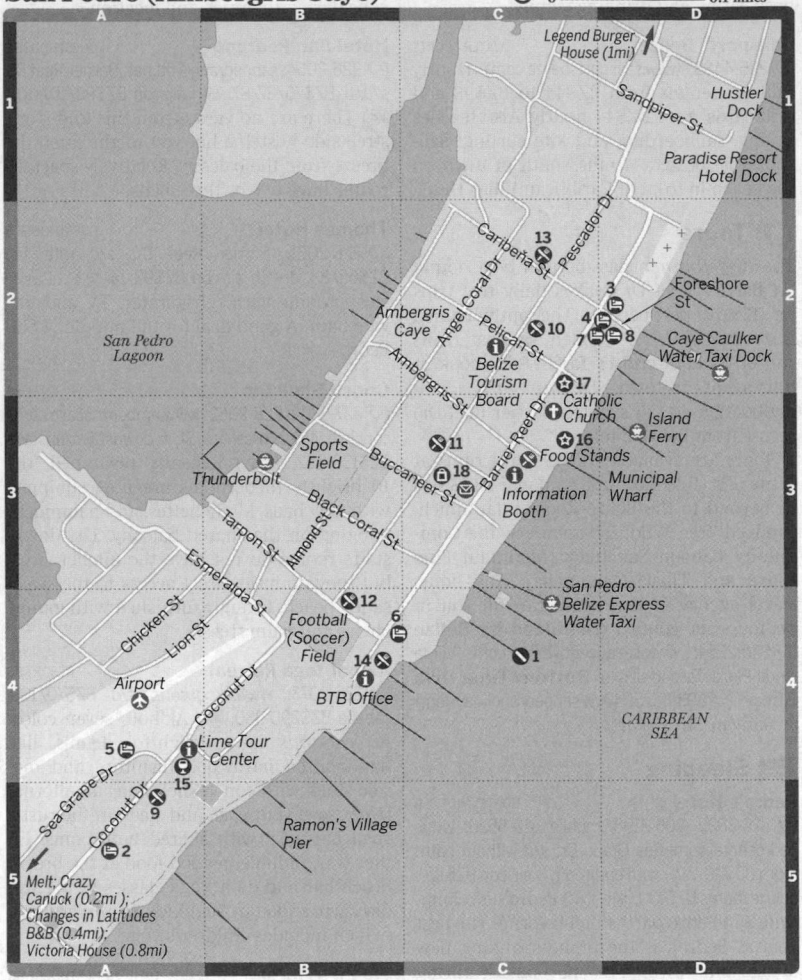

Sun Breeze Hotel HOTEL **$$$**
(☎226-2191; www.sunbreezehotel.com; 8 Coconut Dr; d standard/deluxe/premier BZ$280/330/390; ❄📶) Sun Breeze has lovely, clean and comfortable rooms featuring two double beds, air conditioning and hot showers. Deluxe rooms have spa tubs and flat-screen TVs. All have full cable channels and views ranging from nice to downright lovely.

★Victoria House RESORT **$$$**
(☎226-2067, in USA 800-247-5159; www.victoriahouse.com; Sea Grape Dr; r from BZ$370, casitas BZ$596, villas BZ$1190-1810; ❄📶🏊) Splurge at this elegant beach resort offering rooms in thatched-roof *casitas* with colorful Caribbean themes and colonial-style 'plantation' houses that ooze luxury. Villas are fully furnished with flat-screen TVs, cable and a huge array of luxurious mod-cons. Victoria House is on the far southern end of the island, but complimentary bicycles and four daily shuttles will help get you into town. Considering the beautifully landscaped gardens, smooth sandy beaches and several highly touted restaurants, you might never leave the resort!

San Pedro (Ambergris Caye)

Activities, Courses & Tours
1 Bottom Time Dive Shop C4

Sleeping
2 Changes in Latitude A5
3 Conch Shell Inn D2
4 Hotel San Pedrano D2
5 Pedro's Hotel A4
6 Ruby's Beachfront B4
7 Thomas Hotel C2
8 Tio Pil's Hotel D2

Eating
9 Ali Baba A5
10 Dande's C2
11 Elvi's Kitchen C3
12 Hummingbird Cafe B4
13 My Secret Deli C2
14 Wild Mango's B4

Drinking & Nightlife
15 Lime Bar & Grill A4

Entertainment
16 Big Daddy's Disco C3
17 Fido's C2

Shopping
18 Rum, Cigar & Coffee House C3

Eating

Several small cafes in the center of town serve cheap, simple meals. The best places for low-budget feasting are the stands in front of Central Park, where you can pick up a plate of stewed chicken with beans and rice, barbecue and other delicacies for about BZ$6. Budget snackers take note: a small home-front stand on Ambergris St, between Pescador and the lagoon, serves up freshly cut fruit, nuts and baked goods daily.

My Secret Deli BELIZEAN $
(Caribeña St; meals BZ$8-12; breakfast & lunch) This is one secret too good to keep, especially for the budget-conscious traveler looking for good bargain eats. This family-run eatery serves filling Belize favorites like stewed chicken, steak and rice and chunky chicken vegetable soups. Save room for the great desserts, including lemon pie and *tres leches* cakes.

Hummingbird Cafe CAFE $
(Vilma Linda Plaza, Tarpon St; burgers BZ$8) Formerly Tabu, this hip little cafe serves up healthy breakfasts, bagels and burgers. There's a mouthwatering selection of home-made cakes and excellent coffee.

Dande's ICE CREAM $
(Pescador Dr) San Pedro's only premium ice cream, custard and sorbet.

Melt SANDWICHES $
(633-6831; Exotic Caye Beach Resort; meals from BZ$12; lunch & dinner;) San Pedro's newest eatery specializes in artisan grilled cheese sandwiches, made with locally baked breads. Also on offer at this charming cafe are morning smoothies, locally sourced coffee, fresh lemonade and ice tea, green or grain salads and – yes – gluten-free bread. Check the board for daily chef's specials.

Ali Baba MIDDLE EASTERN $$
(226-4042; Coconut Dr; mains BZ$20-30; lunch & dinner) Ali Baba serves some good Middle Eastern and Mediterranean food, and even has Egyptian-style *shisha* pipes (BZ$20).

Wild Mango's INTERNATIONAL $$$
(226-2859; 42 Barrier Reef Dr; mains BZ$30-50; lunch & dinner;) Offers creative, carefully prepared food by an award-winning chef. Lunches are gourmet sandwiches, dinner features international fare such as Argentine steaks and Guatemalan chicken and a range of seafood dishes.

Elvi's Kitchen BELIZEAN $$$
(226-2176; Pescador Dr; mains BZ$20-50; lunch & dinner;) A long-standing San Pedro favorite, Elvi's all you can eat Grand Maya buffet dinner (Friday; BZ$50) may be the best meal splurge on the island.

Drinking & Nightlife

Legends Burger House BAR
(www.legendsburgerhouse.com; Tres Cocos; noon-midnight;) There's a lot going on at Legends, even besides the burgers, including live music two nights a week (Tuesday at 7pm, Saturday at 8pm). Ice-cold beers, wacky cocktails and sometimes even free jello shots complete the scene.

Crazy Canuck's BEACH BAR
(www.belizeisfun.com; Exotic Caye Beach Resort, Coconut Dr) Open to the cooling sea breezes; staff are friendly and regular patrons welcoming.

Sunday is the big day, with horseshoe tournies in the afternoon and crowd-drawing live music in the evening. There's also live punta music on Monday nights and pulled pork and live band karaoke on Tuesdays.

Lime Bar & Grill BAR
(☎226-4152; Coconut Dr; drinks from BZ$5; 📶) This relative newcomer to the San Pedro scene has a full bar, kitchen and free wi-fi.

Fido's CLUB
(www.fidosbelize.com; 18 Barrier Reef Dr; ⏲11am-midnight) This bar, near Pelican St, is the landlubbers' favorite, with live music most nights.

Big Daddy's Disco CLUB
(Barrier Reef Dr) Right next to San Pedro's church, this is a hot nightspot, often featuring live reggae, especially during winter.

Shopping

Rum, Cigar & Coffee House FOOD
(☎226-2020; saul.rums@gmail.com; Pescador Dr; ⏲9am-9pm; 📶) The three staples of a great Belize vacation. Come in for coffee and rum samples, or to enjoy a cup of great coffee and wi-fi in a cool setting.

Belizean Arts HANDICRAFTS
(☎226-3019; Fido's Courtyard, 18 Barrier Reef Dr; ⏲9am-10pm Mon-Sat) One of the best shopping spots, it sells ceramics, woodcarvings and paintings alongside affordable and tasteful knickknacks.

Orientation

San Pedro has three main north–south streets: Front St (to the east), Middle St and Back St (to the west). Now these streets have tourist names – Barrier Reef Dr, Pescador Dr and Angel Coral Dr – but some islanders still use the old names.

Information

Various private roadside **tourist kiosks** (⏲10am-9pm) are scattered around town. Tourist information is also available on the caye's own website (www.ambergriscaye.com). **Lime Tour Center** (☎226-4152; www.limetours.com; opposite Tropic Air) is also a convenient spot for information and meeting other travelers and locals.

Caribbean Connection (cnr Barrier Reef Dr & Black Coral St; per hr BZ$10; ⏲7am-10pm) and **Pelican Internet** (Barrier Reef Dr; per hr BZ$12) all offer internet, coffee and fresh juices. Several laundromats lie at the southern end of Pescador Dr, among them **Nellie's Laundromat** (Pescador Dr; ⏲7am-9pm Mon-Sat).

You can change money easily in San Pedro, and US dollars and traveler's checks are accepted in most establishments. **Atlantic Bank** (Barrier Reef Dr; ⏲8am-2pm Mon-Fri, 8:30am-noon Sat) and **Belize Bank** (Barrier Reef Dr; ⏲8am-3pm Mon-Thu, to 4:30pm Fri) have 24-hour ATMs.

For medical services, head to the **Lion's Club Medical Clinic** (☎600-9071, 226-4052; Lion St), located across the street from the Maya Island Air terminal at the airport. **San Carlos Medical Clinic** (☎226-2918, emergencies 614-9251; 28 Pescador Dr) treats ailments and does blood tests. There is also a pharmacy and pathology lab onsite. There's also a **Hyperbaric Chamber** (☎684-8111, 226-2851; Lion St; ⏲24hr) for diving accidents.

Getting There & Away

Maya Island Air (☎226-2435; www.mayaairways.com) and **Tropic Air** (☎226-2338; www.tropicair.com) offer several flights daily between San Pedro and the Belize City airports, and flights to Corozal.

The **Caye Caulker Water Taxi** (☎226-4646; www.cayecaulkerwatertaxi.com; Caribeña St) and **San Pedro Belize Express Water Taxi** (☎223-2225; www.belizewatertaxi.com; Black Coral St, reef side) run regular boats from Ambergris to Belize City via Caye Caulker. There's also a daily **Thunderbolt** (☎422-0026; www.ambergriscaye.com/thunderbolt; Buccaneer St, lagoon side) boat service from Ambergris to Corozal that will stop in Sarteneja if requested. SPBE also operates a daily boat between San Pedro and Chetumal, Mexico.

Getting Around

You can walk to town from the airport in 10 minutes or less, and the walk from the boat docks is even shorter. A taxi from the airport costs BZ$5 to any place in town or BZ$10 to the hotels south of town. Nearly all hotels have bicycles for rent.

Joe's Bicycle Rental (☎226-5371; cnr Pescador Dr & Caribeña St; ⏲8am-6pm) rents bikes for BZ$20/80 per day/week.

Polo's Golf Carts (☎226-3542; Barrier Reef Dr) rents carts for BZ$130/500 per day/week. You'll need a valid driver's license.

For something a little different, **Segway of Belize** (☎226-3344; http://www.segwayofbelize.com; Fairdale Plaza, Coconut Dr) rents all-terrain Segways by the hour (BZ$56 per hour). It also does Segway island tours (BZ$150 and up).

Minivan taxis cost BZ$5 for a one-way trip anywhere, but prices go way up if the taxi has to cross the river to the north end of the island (so you're better off taking a water taxi).

The **Island Ferry** (☎226-3231) operates an Ambergris-only water-taxi service from Fido's Dock every two hours from 7am to 5pm and hourly from 6pm to 10pm, stopping at the north-end resorts. The ferry also runs south to Fido's Sandbar (just south of Victoria House) four times a day.

NORTHERN BELIZE

Much more Latino than the rest of the country, you'll find whatever Spanish you have useful here. The landscape is flat and lush, mostly given over to farming, although there are a couple of interesting and easily accessible wildlife reserves.

Some important Maya sites can be found here, too. The most popular, Lamanai, is reached by a riverboat ride that is a joy in itself, and Altun Ha (whose image has been immortalized on banknotes and beer-bottle labels) is something of a 'symbol of Belize.'

Bermudian Landing

In 1985 local farmers organized to help preserve the endangered black howler monkey and its habitat. Care is taken to maintain the forests along the banks of the Belize River, where the black howler, found only in Belize, feeds, sleeps and howls. While we can't promise you'll spot the howlers on your trip, if you stick around long enough you'll definitely hear them (generally between dusk and dawn). Their mating growls are loud and unmistakable.

Activities

Community Baboon Sanctuary WILDLIFE RESERVE

(CBS; www.howlermonkeys.org; admission $BZ10; ⏲8am-5pm) At the Community Baboon Sanctuary you'll learn about the black howler monkey, whose surreal growls fill the night air, as well as the 200-odd other species of wildlife found in the reserve. A one-hour guided nature walk is included with your admission, arranged at the visitors center. Horseback riding is available for BZ$50, as are three-hour canoe trips (BZ$56) and 1½-hour night hikes (BZ$24). Crocodile-viewing night tours are BZ$110.

Sleeping & Eating

Rustic accommodations are available at the reserve but are best arranged in advance. **Village homestays** (d with half board BZ$50) can be arranged at the visitors center or through the Howler Monkey Resort.

★**Howler Monkey Resort** JUNGLE LODGE **$$**

(☎607-1571; www.howlermonkeyresort.bz; cabins from BZ$120-170; P ❄ 📶 🏊) Come to Ed and Melissa Turton's rustic resort to hear howler monkeys roar at night and watch birds, agouti, iguana and even the occasional crocodile roam during the day. Ed and Mel are excellent wildlife guides (and chefs), and their resort has trails to explore, canoes to rent (BZ$80 per day) and a small swimming pool. Prices are per cabin (so one split between four or six people becomes quite cheap indeed) and include breakfast and dinner for two at the on-site dining room, with additional meals available for around BZ$16.

Getting There & Away

Bermudian Landing is 26 miles (42km) west of Belize City – an easy day trip from Belize City or the cayes.

If you're driving, turn west off the Northern Hwy at the Burrell Boom turnoff (Mile 13). From there it's another 12 miles (20km) of dirt road to the sanctuary. Buses from Belize City leave from the corner of Amara Ave and Orange St from Monday to Saturday at noon, 12:20pm, 3:30pm, 4pm, 4:30pm, 5pm and 5:30pm, with return buses throughout the day.

Altun Ha

Northern Belize's most famous Maya ruin is **Altun Ha** (www.nichbelize.org; admission BZ$10, children under 5 free; ⏲7am-5pm), 34 miles (55km) north of Belize City along the Old Northern Hwy. The site is near Rockstone Pond village, south of Maskall.

Altun Ha (Maya for 'Rockstone Pond') was undoubtedly a small but rich and important Maya trading town, with agriculture also playing an essential role in its economy. Altun Ha had formed as a community by at least 600 BC, perhaps several centuries earlier, and the town flourished until the mysterious collapse of Classic Maya civilization around AD 900.

Highlights of the grass-covered temples arranged around the two plazas are the **Temple of the Masonry Altars** (Structure B-4) in Plaza B and the **Temple of the Green Tomb** in Plaza A.

Modern toilets and a drinks shop are on site.

Sleeping & Eating

Camping, though not strictly legal, is sometimes permitted; ask at the site.

Mayan Wells CABIN

(☎225-5505; www.mayanwells.com; cabins BZ$50, campsites per person BZ$10) About 1.25 miles (2km) before reaching Altun Ha, this is a popular stop for lunch or refreshments. The one cabin is simple but adequate and camping is allowed on the premises; bathroom and shower facilities are available.

Getting There & Away

The easiest way to visit Altun Ha is on one of the many tours running daily from Belize City (BZ$80, half day including admission); most travel agents can line you up with one. Getting to Altun Ha by public transportation is difficult, though you could take a bus to Maskall and hitch the rest of the way (see Hitchhiking Safety, p282).

Lamanai

By far the most impressive site in this part of the country is Lamanai, in its own archaeological reserve on the New River Lagoon near the settlement of Indian Church. Though much of the site remains unexcavated and unrestored, the trip to Lamanai, by motorboat up the New River, is an adventure in itself.

Take along a sun hat, sunblock, insect repellent, shoes (rather than sandals); if you're not going with a tour operator, take along lunch and water.

As with most sites in northern Belize, Lamanai ('Submerged Crocodile,' the original Maya name) was occupied as early as 1500 BC, with the first stone buildings appearing between 800 and 600 BC. Lamanai flourished in late Preclassic times, growing into a major ceremonial center with immense temples long before most other Maya sites.

Most visitors opt to reach Lamanai by taking a spectacular boat ride up the New River from the Tower Hill toll bridge south of Orange Walk. River trips to Lamanai cost around BZ$90 per person for a tour including lunch, guide, fruit and admission fees. Any hotel in Orange Walk can connect you with a reputable guide.

Though the river voyage is much more convenient and enjoyable, Lamanai can be reached by road (36 miles/58km) from Orange Walk via Yo Creek and San Felipe. A bus service from Orange Walk is available but limited, making a day trip impossible. Hitching a ride with farmers is always an option.

Orange Walk

POP 13,400

Nestled on a bend in the New River, Orange Walk is a medium-sized Belizean town best known as a place where farmers from the

WORTH A TRIP

CROOKED TREE WILDLIFE SANCTUARY

Midway between Belize City and Orange Walk, 3.5 miles (5.5km) west of the Northern Hwy, lies the fishing and farming village of Crooked Tree. In 1984 the Belize Audubon Society succeeded in having 5 sq miles around the village declared a **wildlife sanctuary** (admission BZ$8; ⏲8am-4pm) principally because of the area's wealth of birdlife. The best time of year for wildlife watching is from January to mid-May, when the water in the lagoon drops to its lowest level and the animals must come further out into the open to reach their food.

Day trips to Crooked Tree are possible, but it's best to stay the night so you can be here at dawn, when the birds are most active. A guided tour costs BZ$160 for groups of four (less per person for larger groups). Arrangements can be made through the visitors center or the Belize Audubon Society (p235).

There are a number of guesthouses in Crooked Tree. One place is **Tillett's Village Lodge** (☎245-7016, 607-3871; www.tillettvillage.com; r from BZ$70, lakeside cabin BZ$200; P ❄), which has five simple rooms (two with air-con, the rest fan-cooled) with comfortable beds, hot showers and an assortment of original artwork featuring the local birdlife. The lodge is on the main street, 500yd north of the 'Welcome to Crooked Tree' sign. There are a few small eateries as well.

The village is 3½ miles (5km) west of the Northern Hwy. Jex Bus offers daily services departing from Belize City at Regent St West for Crooked Tree village at 10:50am daily; return trips leave Crooked Tree at 6:00am and 6:50am. If you start early from Belize City or Corozal, you can bus to Crooked Tree Junction and walk or hitch the 3½ miles (5.5km) to the village.

surrounding district come to trade and socialize. The country's biggest rum distillery is here, and the town itself can get pretty lively in the evenings. Most tourists use the town as a base for boat trips to the ruins at Lamanai and other trips into the jungles of the Orange Walk district.

The Northern Hwy, called Queen Victoria Ave in town, serves as the main road. The center of town is shady Central Park, on the east side of Queen Victoria Ave.

Sleeping

Orchid Palm Inn INN $

(☎322-0719; www.orchidpalminn.com; 22 Queen Victoria Ave; basic s/d BZ$65/80, deluxe d BZ$110; P ❄ @) Set on a busy corner in the center of all the action, the little Orchid Palm Inn is a tiny island of tranquility. It has eight well-furnished and nicely decorated rooms that come in a variety of configurations, from singles to doubles with kitchenettes. Air-con is an additional BZ$10.

Akihito Hotel HOSTEL, HOTEL $

(☎302-0185; cnr Queen Victoria Ave & Gravel Lane; dm BZ$15, d with/without bathroom BZ$45/30; ❄ @) The cheapest of the bunch, the Akihito has the goods for budget travelers. That means rooms are very plain but very clean. The family who runs the Akihito are a treasure trove of local information – the teenage son's handmade map of Orange Walk will prove an invaluable tool for those who like to wander.

St Christopher's Hotel HOTEL $

(☎302-1064; www.stchristophershotelbze.com; 10 Main St; r with fan/air-con BZ$66/98; P ❄ @) The flowering gardens and riverside setting make this otherwise nondescript hotel an attractive place to stay. The rooms themselves are spacious but plain, although you might appreciate the colorful artwork and stenciled walls that adorn the pricier quarters.

Lamanai Riverside Retreat GUESTHOUSE $

(☎302-3955; Lamanai Alley; r BZ$80; P ❄ @) Offers three rustic wooden rooms with breezy balconies and mosquito-netted beds. Adjoining the retreat is one of Orange Walk's more picturesque eating and drinking spots, so come for a beer, even if the rooms are booked.

Hotel de la Fuente HOTEL $$

(☎322-2290; www.hoteldelafuente.com; 14 Main St; r BZ$70-110, ste BZ$150; P ❄ @) This family-run hotel is smack dab in the center of Orange Walk, but most of the rooms are in a brand new building set back from the hustle and bustle (and noise) on the road. The clean, cozy rooms – all equipped with fridge and coffee maker – are probably the best in town, while the suite has a full kitchen.

Eating & Drinking

Street food rules in Orange Walk, where snack stalls, fruit stands and pushcarts offer a veritable smorgasbord of northern Belizean and Mexican foods. Everything is super cheap, between BZ$1 and BZ$5, and hygiene standards are generally pretty good.

Natural Balance CAFE $

(San Antonio Rd; coffee & tea from BZ$5; ⏲9am-5:30pm;) This Taiwanese-owned cafe serves fresh brewed coffee drinks (iced and hot), as well as the ever-popular in Asia (but almost unknown in Belize) bubble milk tea. Light vegetarian snacks are also available.

Panificadora La Popular BAKERY $

(Beytias La; pastries BZ$2-8; ⏲6:30am-8pm Mon-Sat, 7:30am-noon & 3-6pm Sun) The best bakery in Belize. Trust us on this one.

★Nahil Mayab BELIZEAN, MEXICAN $$

(www.nahilmayab.com; cnr Santa Ana & Guadalupe Sts; lunch BZ$8-20, dinner BZ$20-30; ⏲lunch only Mon, lunch & dinner Tue-Sat;) Decked in exotic greenery and faux Maya carvings, the dining room evokes the district's surrounding jungles, as does the pleasantly shaded patio. It's a fun, kitschy atmosphere in which to sample some Yucatan-inspired food like Ke'Ken (salted pork in tomato sauce) or Cham Cham (empanadas). Less adventurous eaters will appreciate the sandwiches, burritos and good old-fashioned rice and beans.

Paniscea Restaurant & Lounge CONTINENTAL $$

(meals BZ$12-40; ⏲11am-2pm & 5pm-2am Wed-Mon; P) Local favorites like shrimp *ceviche* (BZ$12) share a menu with grilled imported steaks (BZ$24 to BZ$40). Other dishes include smoked pork chop (BZ$24). There's also a full bar with two flat-screen TVs.

Lamanai Riverside Retreat BAR

(Lamanai Alley; mains BZ$12-25; ⏲8am-10pm) With its breezy deck and tables with lovely river views, this restaurant-bar gets crowded on weekends. The menu is pretty extensive, but the place is recommended mainly for drinking and socializing.

Information

The town hospital is in the northern outskirts, readily visible on the west side of Northern Hwy. There is a **Scotia Bank** (cnr Park & Main Sts) on Main St, one block east of Central Park. You can check your email at **Cyberwalk** (☎322-3024; 115 Otro Benque; internet per hr BZ$4; ⏲8am-9pm Mon-Sat, 8am-5pm Sun) at the north end of town, and clean jungle-dirty clothes at **Mary's Laundry.** (☎322-3454; Progresso St; per pound BZ$1)

Getting There & Away

Buses run hourly for Belize City (BZ$5, two hours) and Corozal (BZ$4, one hour), and points in between, with additional southbound runs in the early morning and northbound runs in the late afternoon to accommodate work and school schedules. Some services stop in the town square (by the main market), while others stop at a temporary lot set up just west of the cemetery.

Corozal

POP 9900

This gateway to Mexico (and the northern cayes) is far enough from the border to have the best of both worlds – that fascinating mix of cultures that border towns have, without the associated sleaze and hassle.

Corozal is a pretty place, with many parks and a seaside promenade offering a good selection of restaurants. Arranged around a town square in the Mexican style, the town has a number of beautiful homes (in various states, from crumbling to fully restored) with a lovely Spanish Colonial feel, and even the remains of the Maya temple of Santa Rita just north on the main highway.

Sights

Cerros Archaeological Site RUIN

(admission BZ$10; ⏲8am-5pm) Cerros flourished as a coastal trading center in late Preclassic times. Unlike at other Maya sites, little subsequent construction from the Classic and Postclassic periods covers the original structures here because, at around AD 150, Cerros reverted rapidly to a small, unimportant village. Thus the site has given archaeologists important insights into Maya Preclassic architecture. Climb **Structure 4**, a temple more than 65ft (20m) high, for stunning panoramic views.

This small site is located on a peninsula 3.5 miles (5.6km) south of Corozal across the bay. Most people catch a boat to the site, but you can drive there on a rough dirt road. Tours (approximately BZ$50 per person including guide) can be arranged through your hotel.

Sleeping

★Sea Breeze Hotel GUESTHOUSE $

(☎front desk 422-3051, mobile 661-9453; www.theseabreezehotel.com; 23 1st Ave; r BZ$40-70; P ❄ @ 📶) Reminiscent of the kind of cheap and pleasant Key West hotel where Ernest Hemingway might have spent his last years, this hotel has plain but comfortable rooms, each with a queen-sized bed, desk and chair, and en suite with hot shower. The feature that would have appealed most to Papa Hemingway might well have been the usually lively and always fully stocked bar on the 2nd floor, complete with indoor and outdoor seating and a stunning view of Corozal Bay. Good food and strong coffee available on request, and the Sea Breeze's breakfasts are the stuff of legend.

Maya World Guest House GUESTHOUSE $

(☎666-3577; www.aguallos.com/mayaworld; 16 2nd St North; s/d BZ$45/55; @) An offbeat and artistically decorated guesthouse run by Mr and Mrs Byron Chu, Maya World consists of two houses and an enclosed garden-filled courtyard. The front house, a restored two-story colonial home with a wraparound veranda complete with hammock, is where guests stay, while the rear house is home to your gracious hosts.

Hotel Maya & Apartments HOTEL $

(☎422-2082; www.hotelmaya.net; 7th Ave, South End; s/d/tr/q BZ$68/75/89/89, with air-con BZ$89/100/100/126; ❄ 📶) Run by the very friendly Rosita May, the Hotel Maya is a longtime favorite of budget-conscious travelers. Rooms are clean, and enlivened by colorful bedspreads and paintings by local artists.

Corozal Bay Inn RESORT $$

(☎422-2691; www.corozalbayinn.biz; Almond Dr; cabañas BZ$110; P ❄ 📶 🏊) Ten cozy, colorful *cabañas* are set around a broad sandy area that faces the sea at the far southern end of town. Tucked in under thatched roofs, the *cabañas* are fully equipped (mosquito-netted beds, fridge, coffee maker) and nicely decorated (tile floors, bamboo furnishings).

Corozal Town

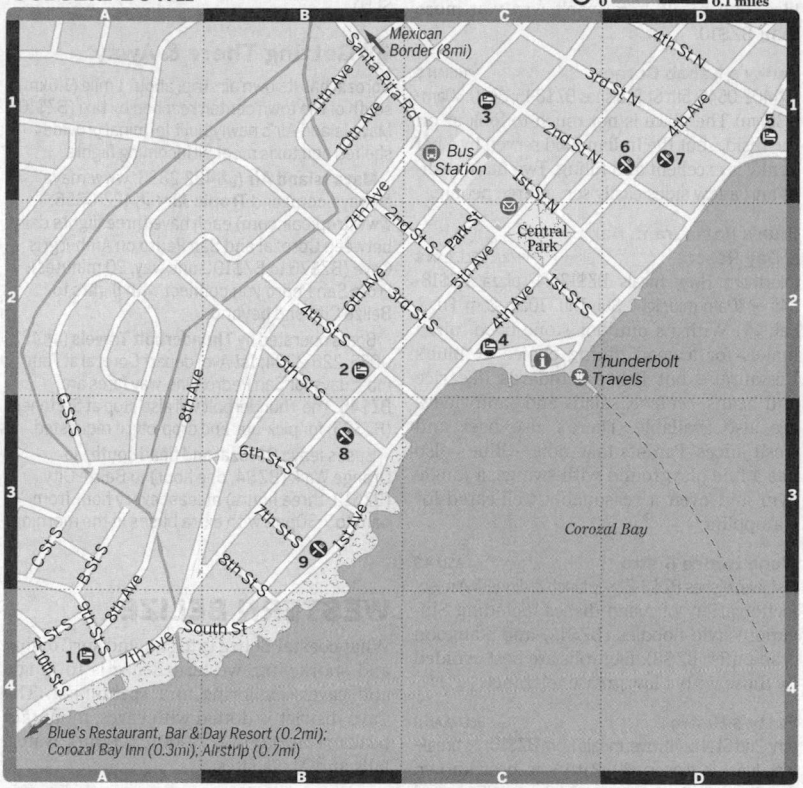

The best deal are the four fan-cooled budget *cabañas* (BZ$50).

Mirador Hotel HOTEL $$

(☎422-0189; www.mirador.bz; cnr 4th Ave & 3rd St S; s/d/tr BZ$70/90/110, with air-con BZ$100/120/150; ❄@📶) The 20 rooms of the four-story Mirador Hotel are all clean and nicely arranged, with pastel-colored walls and tile floors, and most rooms are enhanced by lovely ocean views. The rooftop patio is a welcoming respite; on good days it offers hammocks, lounge chairs and views clear out to Mexico.

Las Palmas Hotel HOTEL $$

(☎602-5186, 422-0196; www.laspalmashotelbelize.com; 123 5th Ave; d/tw/tr from BZ$90/140/160; P❄📶) Thanks to the hard work of owner Charles Rublee, this newly renovated hotel has rooms with a crisp, minimalist feel, white stucco walls, wooden furniture and a southwestern motif. Two resident cats and a wrought-iron gate ensure good security.

Corozal Town

Sleeping

1 Hotel Maya & Apartments A4
2 Las Palmas Hotel B2
3 Maya World Guest House C1
4 Mirador Hotel C2
5 Sea Breeze Hotel D1

Eating

6 Patty's Bistro D1
7 Purple Toucan D1
8 Venky's Kabab Corner B3
9 Wood House Bistro B3

Eating

Corozal Market MARKET $

(⏲6:30am-5:30pm Mon-Sat, to 3pm Sun) Though Corozal isn't a street-food mecca like Orange Walk, the Corozal market is a good place to get cheap Mexican snacks and fresh vegetables. Full meals here won't cost you more than BZ$10.

Venky's Kabab Corner INDIAN $
(☎ 402-0546; 5th St S; dishes BZ$8-15; ⏲ 10:30am-9:30pm) The place is not much to look at on the inside, but the Indian food served by Chef Venky is excellent and filling. Two main dishes and a few sides easily serve three people.

Blue's Restaurant, Bar & Day Resort PIZZA, BELIZEAN $
(Northern Hwy; meals BZ$12-24, pizza BZ$18-24; ⏲ 10am-midnight Sun-Thu, 10am-2am Fri & Sat; ✎) With its outdoor stone oven, pizza makes for a good dining choice at Blue's Restaurant, but Belize standards like rice and beans, *ceviche*, salads and sandwiches are also available. There's also beer and fresh juices. Parents take note – Blue's also has a fine playground with swings, a jungle gym and even a reasonably well-cared-for trampoline!

Wood House Bistro ASIAN $
(1st Ave; dishes BZ$8-22; ⏲ lunch & dinner) An eclectic variety of Asian dishes including Singapore-style noodles (BZ$12) and Rangoon crab puffs (BZ$8). Egg rolls are best avoided by those with a low grease tolerance.

Patty's Bistro BELIZEAN $
(cnr 2nd St N & 4th Ave; meals from BZ$10; ⏲ breakfast, lunch & dinner; ❄) Patty's is best known for its conch soup, a thick potato-based chowder with vegetables, rice and chunks of conch meat, but more-adventurous diners may want to go for the cow-foot soup. You'll also find more Mexican and Belizean fare on the menu, not to mention burgers, sandwiches and other standards.

★ Purple Toucan MEXICAN, MAYA $$
(☎ 622-9329; 52 4th Ave; meals BZ$15-30; ⏲ 11am-3:30pm & 6:30-11pm) Joe and Yolanda's Purple Toucan serves some of the best food in Corozal, from Mayan *pork choc* (a grilled pork dish with onions, tomato and a delightfully savory sauce) to garlic shrimp to fish filet stuffed with shrimp. While some meals are pricier, you can eat for under BZ$10 if you stick to the superb tacos.

Information

Corozal boasts the usual banking trifurcate of **Belize Bank** (cnr 5th Ave & 1st St N), **Scotia Bank** (4th Ave) and **Atlantic Bank** (cnr 4th Ave & 3rd St N). Internet services are provided at **Gamma Computer Center** (cnr 4th Ave & 4th St N).

Getting There & Away

Corozal has its own airstrip, about 1 mile (1.6km) south of the town center, reached by taxi (BZ$10). Maya Island Air's newly built terminal provides shelter, and taxis meet all incoming flights.

Maya Island Air (☎ 422-2333; www.mayaairways.com) and **Tropic Air** (☎ 422-0356; www.tropicair.com) each have three flights daily between Corozal and San Pedro on Ambergris Caye (BZ$76 to BZ$100 one way, 20 minutes). From San Pedro you connect with flights to Belize City and beyond.

Boats operated by **Thunderbolt Travels** (☎ 422-0026, 226-2904; 1st Ave) depart Corozal at 7am most days for San Pedro. One-way fares are BZ$45. The Thunderbolt will also stop at Sarteneja (BZ$25) for pick-ups and drop-offs if requested.

Buses leave Corozal and head south via Orange Walk (BZ$4, one hour) to Belize City (BZ$12, three hours) at least every hour from 4am to 7:30pm, with extra buses in the morning.

WESTERN BELIZE

What coastal Belize is to sun and surf, diving and snorkeling, western Belize is to jungle and caves, exploring and spelunking. The Cayo district is dotted with caves, mountain peaks rising to over 3000ft (900m), waterfalls and Maya sites.

Starting West on the Western Highway

Heading west from Belize City along Cemetery Rd, you'll pass right through Lords Ridge Cemetery and soon find yourself on the Western Hwy. In 15 miles (25km) you'll pass Hattieville, founded in 1961 after Hurricane Hattie wreaked destruction on Belize City, and in another 13 miles (21km) you'll come to the Belize Zoo. Buses run at least hourly along the Western Hwy and upon request will drop you anywhere between Belize City and Belmopan.

Sights & Activities

★ Belize Zoo & Tropical Education Center ZOO
(☎ 220-8004; www.belizezoo.org; Western Hwy Mile 29; adult/child BZ$20/10; ⏲ 8:30am-5pm, closed major holidays) 'A zoo for people who don't like zoos' is what some call the Belize Zoo, the

inhabitants of which are nearly all animals rescued from unscrupulous collectors. On a self-guided tour (45 to 60 minutes) you'll see over 125 native animals, including jaguars, ocelots, howler monkeys, peccaries, vultures, storks, crocodiles, tapirs and *gibnuts*. The zoo also offers night tours, a rare treat as many of the occupants are nocturnal. To arrange a night tour, call or contact the zoo before closing time.

Competing for customers just west of the zoo on the Western Hwy are Cheers and Amigo's, both at Mile 31 of the Western Hwy. Each serves Belizean, Mexican and American dishes accompanied by ice-cold Belikins, all at moderate prices.

Monkey Bay Wildlife Sanctuary WILDLIFE RESERVE
(☎822-8032; www.belizestudyabroad.net; Western Hwy Mile 31½) Offers lodging and activities as well as the opportunity to do an internship with the organization for those with a more long-term interest in Belize. Casual visitors should contact the sanctuary in advance to find out what activities will be available at the time of their visit. Possibilities include canoe and caving trips (per person BZ$70) and dry-season trips to Cox Lagoon, about 12 miles (19km) north, which is home to jabiru storks, deer, tapirs, black howlers and lots of crocodiles. The sanctuary offers accomodations including camping (per person BZ$15), bunkhouse beds (per person BZ$35) and even double cabins (BZ$90).

Guanacaste National Park PARK
(admission BZ$5; ⏲8am-4:30pm) Further west down the highway, at the junction with Hummingbird Hwy, is Guanacaste National Park, a small 52-acre (21-hectare) nature reserve at the confluence of Roaring Creek and the Belize River.

A hike along the park's 2 miles (3km) of trails will introduce you to the abundant and colorful local birdlife. After your hike, you can head down to the Belize River for a dip in the park's good, deep swimming hole.

Belmopan

POP 16,400

Travelers arriving in Belize's capital are faced with an existential question: what am I doing here? Thankfully, the town provides a ready answer: changing buses (or getting a visa extension). There are embassies, government buildings and, if you do get stuck, enough services to satisfy your basic needs.

Sleeping & Eating

A town geared for bureaucrats and diplomats, Belmopan offers little in the way of value-for-money for the budget traveler.

El-Rey Inn HOTEL $
(☎822-3438; www.belmopanhotels.com; 23 Moho St; r BZ$65-85; P ❄ 📶) An affordable option for budget travelers, this place is just outside the ring road, northeast of the green. Named after the affable owner, 'Elroy' Garbutt, the El-Rey has 12 plain, clean rooms equipped

OFF THE BEATEN TRACK

SARTENEJA

Sarteneja (sar-ten-*eh*-ha) is a fishing village near the northeast tip of the Belizean mainland, and a hidden gem for those looking for a beautiful and inexpensive place from which to explore both the nautical and jungle treasures of the region.

The village spreads just a few blocks back from its long, grassy seafront, and it's from this lovely seaside setting that visitors can head out to the **Shipstern Nature Reserve** and take bird-watching, snorkeling, fishing and manatee-watching trips all along the fabulous coast of northern Belize.

Sarteneja is also where you'll find **Backpackers Paradise** (☎423 2016; http://backpackers.bluegreenbelize.com/; Bandera Rd, Sarteneja; camping BZ$7, cabañas with/without bathroom BZ$48/28, little/family house BZ$66/88, breakfast BZ$4-8, lunch & dinner BZ$10-18; 📶) an idyllic 27-acre (11-hectare) patch of unspoiled jungle and tropical farmland where you can spend days exploring the jungle, eating tropical fruit and swimming in the nearby ocean. *Cabañas* are screened-in huts with thatched roofs and king-sized beds, and there's a communal kitchen, a screened-in chill-out spot, and a small onsite restaurant serving a number of French and Belizean favorites. Horses and bicycles are available for rent.

Western Belize

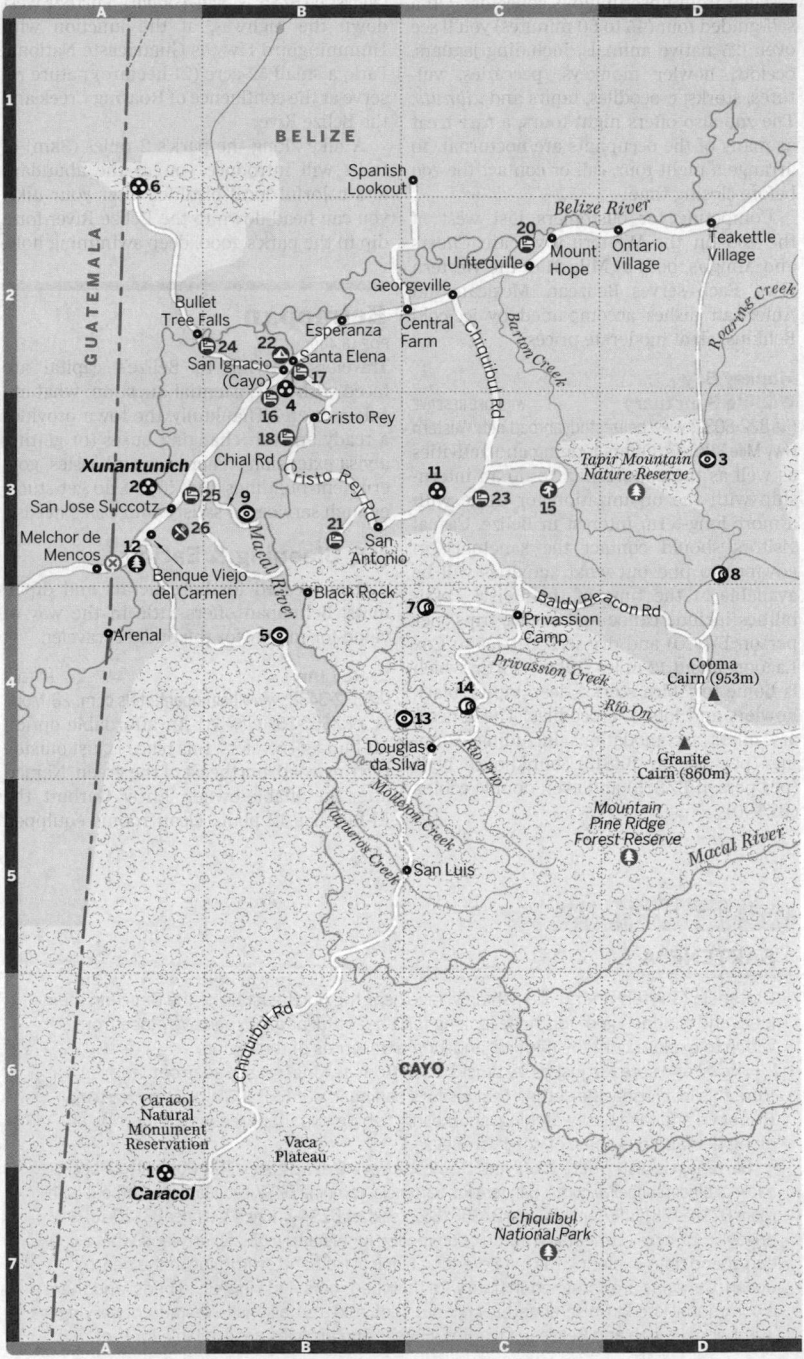

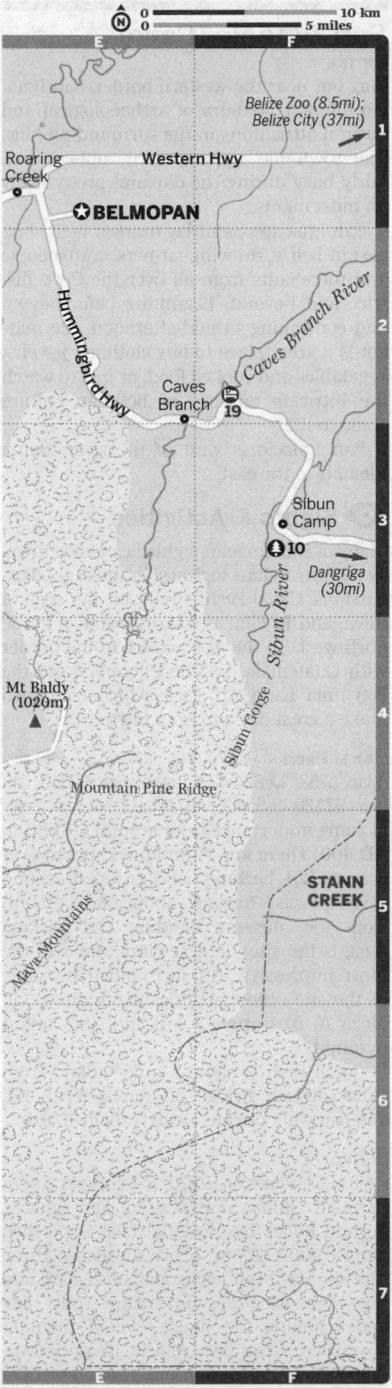

Western Belize

Top Sights

1 Caracol A7
2 Xunantunich A3

Sights

3 Actun Tunichil Muknal D3
4 Cahal Pech B2
5 Che Chem Ha B4
6 El Pilar A1
7 Five Sisters Falls C4
8 Hidden Valley (Thousand Foot) Falls D3
9 Ix Chel Farms B3
10 National Park F3
11 Pacbitun C3
12 Poustinia Land Art Park A3
13 Río Frio Cave C4
14 Río On Pools C4

Activities, Courses & Tours

15 Barton Creek Cave C3
Rainforest Medicine Trail ..... (see 9)

Sleeping

16 Cahal Pech Village Resort B3
17 Cool M Farm B2
18 Crystal Paradise Resort B3
19 Ian Anderson's Caves Branch Jungle Lodge F2
20 Lower Dover Field Station & Eco Lodge C2
21 Macaw Bank Jungle Lodge B3
22 Mana Kai Camp & Cabins B2
23 Mountain Equestrian Trails C3
24 Parrot Nest Jungle Lodge B2
25 Trek Stop A3

Eating

26 Benny's Kitchen A3

with private bathrooms and fans. More expensive rooms have air-con.

Bull Frog Inn HOTEL **$$**

(☎822-2111; www.bullfroginn.com; 25 Half Moon Ave; s/d BZ$140/170; P ❄ @) On the edge of the village green, just inside the ring road, the Bull Frog is a cheerful, civilized sort of place. The 25 rooms are void of any special atmosphere, but they are spacious and comfortable, complete with telephones and cable TV, while big bathrooms have strong, hot showers.

Hibiscus Hotel HOTEL **$$**

(☎822-0400, 610-0400; www.hibiscusbelize.com; Market Sq; s/d BZ$110/120; P ❄) Adjacent to the bus station, Hibiscus isn't a bad place to spend an evening stuck in Belmopan. Upgrades include new king- and twin-sized beds, flat-screen cable TV and tea and coffee facilities in every room.

Food Stalls STREET FOOD $
(Market Sq) Another option for food is the market food stalls, which feature plenty of snack carts selling tasty, low-cost munchies.

Veggie Garden VEGETARIAN $
(43 Forest Dr; meals from BZ$7; ⏲lunch & dinner Mon-Sat; ❄✎) This Taiwanese vegetarian restaurant serves excellent meat-free dishes and fresh juices. The owners also run a small shop selling Chinese health and beauty products.

Moon Clusters Coffee Shop CAFE $
(4 Shopping Center, E Ring Rd; coffee & drinks BZ$3.30-11; ⏲11:30am-7pm Mon-Sat; ❄) The Aguilar family's excellent little coffee shop serves some of the best Java in Belize. There's also a variety of smoothies and ice-cream drinks, and a few snack items on the menu.

Corkers BRITISH $$
(✎822-0400; Hibiscus Plaza, Melhado Pde; mains BZ$15-40; ⏲11am-8pm Mon-Wed, 11am-late Thu-Sat; 📶✎) Corkers offers a melange of seafood, meat and pasta dishes, as well as a few less-expensive snack items and burgers. There's also a fully stocked bar.

Information

The regional bus lines all stop at Market Sq, which is near the post office, police station, market, **Belize Bank** (Constitution Dr), **Scotia Bank** (Constitution Dr) and the **BTL telephone office** (Bliss Pde).

Being the capital, Belmopan naturally has the usual array of banking facilities, and an **internet cafe** (per hr BZ$5; ⏲8am-8pm) inside the bus station is as good a place as any to while away your time.

Getting There & Away

In Belize, all roads lead through Belmopan, and buses to all points south, west and east leave regularly throughout the day. You shouldn't have to wait more than an hour for a bus to leave Belmopan during daylight hours.

DESTINATION	DURATION	COST (BZ$)
Belize City	1¼hr	6
Benque Viejo del Carmen	1½hr	6
Dangriga	2hr	6
Punta Gorda	5-6hr	local/express 20/24
San Ignacio	1hr	5

San Ignacio (Cayo)

POP 16,677

Way out near the western border, San Ignacio offers a plethora of archaeological and natural attractions in the surrounding hills. The town has a prosperous, upbeat feel, fairly busy during the day and pretty lively on most nights.

San Ignacio's Saturday **market** is the biggest in Belize, drawing farmers, craftspeople and merchants from all over the Cayo district and beyond. Beginning before dawn and continuing to mid-afternoon, the market is a great place to buy clothing, jewelry, vegetables and cooked food, or just to watch the intricate tapestry of Belizean culture come to life.

San Ignacio is west of the river; Santa Elena is to the east.

Sights & Activities

Many of San Ignacio's sights lie outside town. Two Maya archaeological sites make good excursions. Cahal Pech is right on the edge of town, and El Pilar is a short distance to the northwest. To the west, closer to the border with Guatemala, lie Che Chem Ha and the Poustinia Land Art Park, which combined make a great day trip from town.

Cahal Pech RUIN
(Map p252; ✎824-4236; admission BZ$10, 2hr tours BZ$20; ⏲6am-6pm) Cahal Pech was a city of some importance from around 900 BC to AD 800. There are 34 buildings spread over 6 acres (2.4 hectares) and grouped around seven plazas. **Plaza B**, about 500ft (150m) from the museum building and parking area, is the site's largest plaza and also the most impressive. It's surrounded by some of the site's most significant buildings. Off Plaza A, **Structure A-1** is the site's tallest pyramid.

Cahal Pech is about a mile (1.6km) from Hawkesworth Bridge off Buena Vista Rd. You can walk or catch a taxi (about BZ$6).

El Pilar RUIN
(Map p252; admission BZ$20; ⏲8am-4pm) About 12 miles (19km) northwest of San Ignacio, beyond Bullet Tree Falls, El Pilar is perched almost 900ft (275m) above the Belize River. The site has been left largely uncleared, and five archaeological and nature trails meander among the jungle-covered mounds. If you have your own vehicle, it's an incredible, remote and rewarding place to wander

San Ignacio

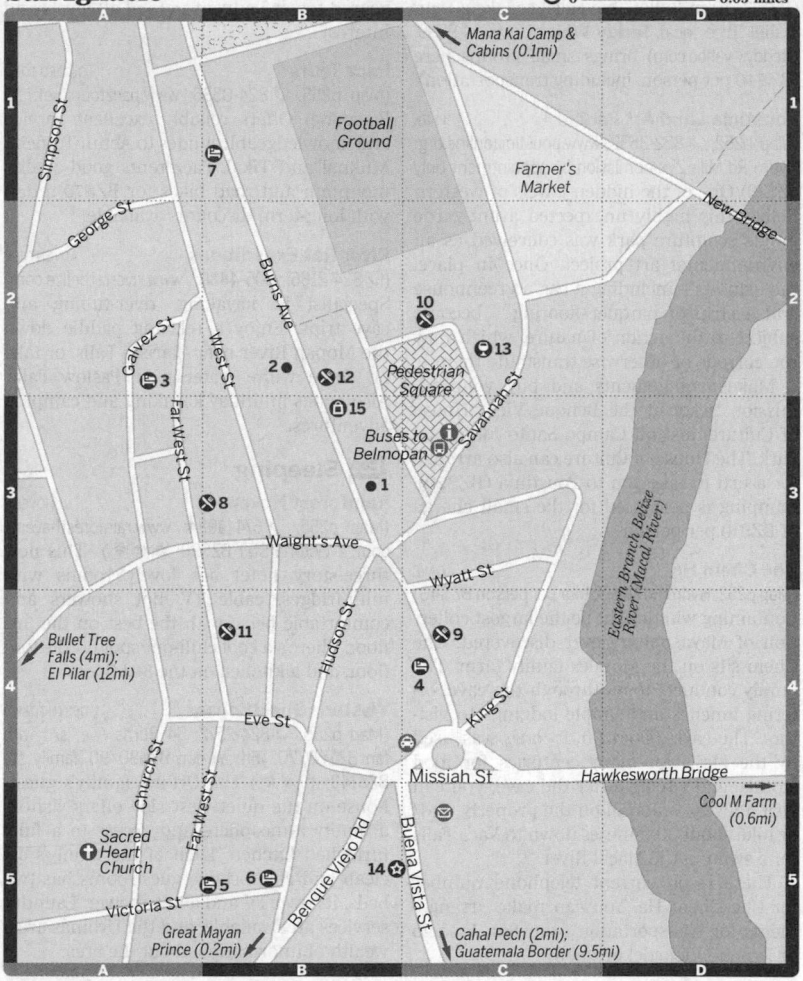

San Ignacio

Activities, Courses & Tours
1 Mayawalk Tours B3
2 Pacz Tours B2

Sleeping
3 Bella's Backpacker's A2
4 Casa Blanca Guest House C4
5 J&R's Guest House B5
6 Rainforest Haven Inn B5
7 Western Guesthouse B1

Eating
8 Erva's B3
9 Ko-Ox Han-nah C4
10 New French Bakery C2
11 Pop's Restaurant B4
12 Serendib B2

Drinking & Nightlife
13 Bamboo Bar C2

Entertainment
14 Soul Project Space for the Creative Arts B5

Shopping
15 JNC Mall B3

on your own. Otherwise, you can hire a taxi (BZ$50 from Bullet Tree Falls) or take a tour. Bullet Tree local **Teddy Waight** (☎664-9599; vlteddy@yahoo.com) brings small groups here (BZ$40 per person, including transportation).

Poustinia Land Art Park PARK
(Map p252; ☎822-3532; www.poustiniaonline.org; Hydro Rd Mile 2½; admission by appointment only BZ$20) One of the hidden jewels of western Belize, this highly unexpected avant-garde jungle sculpture park was conceived as an environmental art project. Once in place, the exhibits – including a car, a greenhouse and a strip of parquet flooring – become subject to the action of nature, which may rot, corrode or otherwise transmute them.

Make arrangements and buy your admission ticket at the Benque Viejo House of Culture, just off Campo Santo Memorial Park. The House of Culture can also arrange for a taxi to take you to Poustinia (BZ$20). Camping is permitted for the small charge of BZ$10 per person.

Che Chem Ha CAVE
(Map p252; Hydro Rd Mile 8; tour per person BZ$40) Containing what might be the largest collection of Maya pottery ever discovered, Che Chem sits on the Morales family farm. The family conducts tours through the cave, offering lunches and simple lodgings to visitors. The cave, about 800ft long, was used by the Maya for many centuries for food storage and rituals. After the cave, you can visit a lovely waterfall on the property and/or hike about 30 minutes down to Vaca Falls for a swim in the Macal River.

There is no current telephone number for Che Chem Ha. You can make arrangements for transportation from San Ignacio or Benque Viejo del Carmen.

Tours

Several operators offer a range of tours in the surrounding area and as far afield as the cayes and Tikal, Guatemala.

Carlos Panti CAVING
(☎669-5552; carlos.caveguide@yahoo.com) Cayo native Carlos Panti specializes in small-group spiritually themed journeys into the Actun Tunichil Muknal cave for BZ$150 per person.

Mayawalk Tours ADVENTURE
(Map p255; ☎824-3070, 610-1129; www.mayawalk.com; 19 Burns Ave) Does trips to Caracol and Actun Tunichil Muknal (see p258), Tikal (Guatemala) and many other tours geared toward adventurers of all levels and interests.

Pacz Tours GUIDED TOUR
(Map p255; ☎824-0536; www.pacztours.net; 30 Burns Ave) Offers reliably excellent service and knowledgeable guides to Actun Tunichil Muknal and Tikal. Pacz rents good-quality mountain and road bikes for BZ$70 a day, with long-term discounts available.

River Rat Expeditions ADVENTURE
(☎824-2166, 605-4480; www.riverratbelize.com) Specialist in kayaking, river-tubing and cave trips. Enjoy a relaxing paddle down the Mopan River near Clarissa Falls, or take on some white water near Paslow Falls. Also books multiday kayaking and camping adventures.

Sleeping

Rainforest Haven Inn HOTEL $
(Map p255; ☎674 1984; www.rainforesthavens.com; 2 Victoria St; r BZ$90; ❄ @ 📶) This new three-story hotel has lovely rooms with mini-fridges, cable TV, hot showers and comfortable beds, with the best on the 3rd floor. There's a cool chill-out spot on the 2nd floor, and a kitchen on the 3rd floor.

Western Guesthouse GUESTHOUSE $
(Map p255; ☎824-2572; 54 Burns Ave; s/d with fan BZ$60/70, with air-con BZ$80/90, family ste BZ$140; P ❄ 📶) The Urbina family's guesthouse on the quiet west side offers visitors a family atmosphere and access to a fully furnished kitchen. Each of the family's six clean and comfortable guestrooms has two beds, its own TV and a hot shower. Laundry services are available, and the Urbinas are a wealth of information about the area.

J&R's Guest House GUESTHOUSE $
(Map p255; ☎626-3604; 20 Far West St; s/d/tr BZ$25/30/35) This is a modern home up the hill from the main drag, with a family atmosphere, and a porch out front that is a great place for breakfast (complimentary) and to watch the hummingbirds flit.

Bella's Backpacker's HOSTEL $
(Map p255; ☎671-2248, 824-2248; bellabackpackers@yahoo.com; 4 Galvez St; dm BZ$15, r per person BZ$25; 📶) Bella's has two well-laid-out multistory dorm areas with new bunk beds and bathrooms with showers. Private rooms are fan cooled with big screened-in windows and a rock-motif bathroom. There's a 1st-

floor communal kitchen, as well as a breezy top-floor communal chill-out spot with hammocks and comfy couches.

Casa Blanca Guest House GUESTHOUSE $
(Map p255; ☎824-2080; www.casablancaguesthouse.com; 10 Burns Ave; s/d with fan BZ$45/55, with air-con BZ$75/95; ❄) Set in a family-style home, the rooms at Casa Blanca are well appointed and very homey.

Mana Kai Camp & Cabins CAMPGROUND $
(Map p252; ☎624-6538, 824-2317; Branch Mouth Rd; s/d BZ$35/45, camping per person BZ$10; 📶) Simple cabins are basic and clean, with hot-water showers and private bathrooms.

Cahal Pech Village Resort RESORT $$
(Map p252; ☎824-3740; www.cahalpech.com; Cahal Pech Hill; d/family stes BZ$158/198; P ❄ @ 📶 🏊) Atop Cahal Pech hill, half a mile up from the town center, you can enjoy splendid views from this upscale resort offering 21 bright, tiled rooms, nine full-sized suites and 27 comfortable *cabañas* with thatched roofs. The on-site restaurant serves good international, Belizean and Maya food (mains BZ$12 to BZ$20), so you don't need to trek into town for dinner.

Eating

Pop's Restaurant DINER $
(Map p255; West St; breakfast BZ$8-10; ⏲breakfast, lunch & dinner) Friendly and clean six-booth, old-school style hole-in-the-wall diner run by an older gentleman with a bushy white beard called – you guessed it – 'Pops'. All-day breakfasts and bottomless cups of coffee. What more could you ask for?

Great Mayan Prince BELIZEAN $
(☎824-2588; 28 Benque Viejo Rd; breakfast & lunch BZ$8-10; ⏲7am-9pm Mon-Thu, 7am-10pm Fri & Sat, 7am-3pm Sun; 📶 ✎) Off the main tourist drag, the Great Mayan Prince is worth the short hike. Besides serving the best breakfast burrito in town, the restaurant also has a sweeping view of Cayo out to Guatemala. Their Sunday breakfast buffet (BZ$15) is excellent as well.

New French Bakery BAKERY $
(Map p255; Market Sq; baked goods from BZ$2; ⏲6:30am-6:30pm Mon-Sat) With a new location but the same owners, this place serves excellent sticky buns, breads, coffee and even goat cheese.

★Ko-Ox Han-nah MAYA $$
(Map p255; ☎824-3014; 5 Burns Ave; breakfast BZ$8-12, Belizean dishes BZ$10-12, Indian dishes BZ$15-20; ⏲6am-9pm; ✎) Han-nah's (as it's called) is the most popular spot in town any time of day. All food served comes from the owner's farm in nearby Calla Creek, including the lamb, pork and chicken. Breakfasts are excellent, and dinners unbeatable, with plenty of meatless options for vegetarians.

Serendib SRI LANKAN $$
(Map p255; Burns Ave; mains from BZ$15; ⏲lunch & dinner) San Ignacio's only Sri Lankan restaurant serves excellent curries, spicy chicken tandoori, and all manner of other delicacies from the Indian subcontinent. Friendly owners, sensational food and a peaceful courtyard dining area are bound to promote serendipity.

Erva's SEAFOOD, BELIZEAN $$
(Map p255; ☎824-2821; 9 Far West St; mains BZ$10-25; ⏲8am-10pm, closed Sundays; ✎) This longtime Cayo favorite has a snazzy new menu featuring a wide variety of seafood dishes (Creole conch and lobster tail in their respective seasons), as well as Belizean favorites, sandwiches and a good variety of fresh juices. The Pitaya – bright magenta dragon-fruit juice is particularly refreshing.

Drinking & Entertainment

Bamboo Bar BAR
(Map p255; South Side, Pedestrian Sq; ⏲9am-midnight) On the east side of the new tourist plaza, Bamboo Bar is Cayo's newest spot for socializing, music, information and libation. Bamboo Bar has seating for 50, beer on tap, and all the hard spirits anyone who knows Belize has come to respect.

Soul Project Space for the Creative Arts ARTS CAFE
(Map p255; ☎653-1855; guanamon@yahoo.com; Buena Vista Rd, across from Police Station; ⏲11am-11pm; 📶) Art space, restaurant, cafe and bar, Soul Project is housed inside a distinctly New Orleansesque building on San Ignacio's less-trammeled east side. As well as being a cafe serving excellent and healthy Belizean and international cuisine, Soul Project is also a venue for local artists and musicians. There's also a bar featuring beer, wine, smoothies and coffee.

Information

Belize Bank (16 Burns Ave) and **Atlantic Bank** both have 24-hour ATMs. The **post office** (Missiah St) is on the upper floor of Government House, near the bridge.

Trade Winds Internet (☎824-2396; West Street; per hr BZ$5) offers internet access on new computers.

The basic San Ignacio Hospital is up the hill off Waight's Ave, west of the center. Across the river in Santa Elena is Hospital La Loma Luz.

Getting There & Away

Buses from San Ignacio's Market Sq run to and from Belize City (local/express BZ$10/14, two/three hours) and Belmopan (local/express BZ$4/6, 1½ hours/45 minutes) nearly every half hour. From here you can travel to Benque Viejo del Carmen and onwards to Guatemala.

The taxi stand is located on the traffic circle opposite Government House. Rates can be surprisingly high for short trips (a trip of a few miles can easily cost BZ$10 to BZ$20).

Mountain Pine Ridge Area

South of the Western Hwy, between Belmopan and the Guatemalan border, the land begins to climb toward the heights of the Maya Mountains, which separate the Cayo district from the Stann Creek district to the east and the Toledo district to the south.

In the heart of this highland area – a land of macaws, mahogany, mangoes and jaguars – over 300 sq miles (777 sq km) of tropical pine forest has been set aside as the Mountain Pine Ridge Forest Reserve. The reserve and its surrounding area are full of rivers, pools, waterfalls and caves to explore.

Sights & Activities

The highlands here hold two Maya ruins of interest, one small and one huge – Pacbitun and Caracol. If you want to visit any of the area's caves, you'll have to join a tour. Ask at your hotel or check out some of the suggested Cayo guides.

Actun Tunichil Muknal — CAVE

(Map p252) One of the most unforgettable and adventurous tours you can make in Belize, the trip into ATM takes you deep into the underworld that the ancient Maya knew as Xibalba. The entrance to the three-mile-long cave lies in the northern foothills of the Maya Mountains. Prepare for a fairly strenuous hike!

At the wide, hourglass-shaped entrance to the cave, you'll don your helmet, complete with headlamp. To reach the cave entrance, you'll start with a frosty swim across a deep pool (about 15ft across), so you must be a reasonably good swimmer. From here, you will follow your guide, walking, climbing, twisting and turning your way through the blackness of the cave for about an hour before reaching the cave's main chamber, where you will be required to remove your shoes. Make sure you wear socks – not only to protect your feet from sharp rocks, but also to protect the artifacts from the oils on your skin.

The trip takes about 10 hours from San Ignacio, including a one-hour drive each way. A number of San Ignacio-based tour companies do the trip for around BZ$160 per person, including admission, lunch and equipment. You must be accompanied by a licensed guide.

★Caracol — ARCHAEOLOGICAL SITE

(Map p252; admission BZ$30; ⏲8am-4pm) Once one of the most powerful cities in the entire Maya world, Caracol now lies enshrouded by thick jungle near the Guatemalan border, a 52-mile, two-hour drive from San Ignacio. Sitting high on the Vaca Plateau, 1650ft above sea level, this is the largest Maya site in Belize, having stretched over possibly 70 sq miles at its peak around AD 650. Nearly 40 miles of internal causeways radiate from the center to large outlying plazas and residential areas, and connect parts of the city. At its height, the city's population may have approached 150,000, more than twice as many people as Belize City has today.

At the ticket office, a small visitors center outlines Caracol's history and has a helpful scale model. There are toilets, picnic tables and a small gift shop. Be sure to bring food, water and, if you're driving, a spare tire. Overnight stays are not permitted.

Ix Chel Farms — MEDICINAL FARM

(Map p252; admission BZ$10; ⏲8am-noon & 1-5pm) This herbal-cure research center is located 8 miles (13km) southwest of San Ignacio up Chial Rd.

Dr Eligio Pantí, who died in 1996 at age 103, was a healer in San Antonio village who used traditional Maya herb cures. Dr Rosita Arvigo, an American, studied medicinal plants with Dr Pantí, then began several projects to spread the wisdom of traditional healing methods and to preserve the rain-

GET OUTTA TOWN!

Just outside of San Ignacio are a number of beautiful and low-key campsites, ecoresorts and family homestays.

Cool M Farm (Map p252; ☎824-2276; cool.m.farm@gmail.com; Cristo Rey Rd ¼ mile; cabañas d BZ$100, per extra person BZ$10) Spend a few days in a genuine Mennonite farm atmosphere at the Löhr family's 75-acre garden-filled dairy farm. The farm has two lovely fan-cooled *cabañas* equipped with comfortable double beds, desks, modern bathrooms with hot showers and a sun porch overlooking the valley, meadows and (of course) the farm. Breakfast for two of organic eggs, yogurt, granola and bread (all from the farm) is included in the price.

Lower Dover Field Station & Eco Lodge (Map p252; ☎834-4200; www.lowerdoverbelize.com; Western Hwy Mile 59; camping per tent BZ$20, bunk house per person BZ$30, cabins with/without bathroom incl breakfast BZ$140/100, luxury air-con cabin BZ$200; P ❄ 📶) Home to 99 acres of prime jungle bush containing sparkling clear creeks with swimming holes and extensive and largely unexcavated Maya ruins. The bunkhouse sleeps six, and beautifully furnished cabins sleep three. Among the activities at Lower Dover are canoeing on the Belize River, swimming in one of the seven river-fed swimming holes, fishing and bird-watching.

Parrot Nest Jungle Lodge (Map p252; ☎669-6068, 660-6336; www.parrot-nest.com; treehouse or cabin without bathroom BZ$90, q cabins with hot showers & bathrooms BZ$105, breakfast BZ$8-12, dinner BZ$24; P 📶) Nine cabins – some on stilts, some in trees – all have sturdy wood construction, tin roofs and shared bathrooms; four larger cabins have private bathrooms and inviting verandahs. Kids will love playing on the jungle-y grounds, a haven for wildlife watching, river swimming and hammock swinging. Guests enjoy free use of kayaks, tubes and bicycles.

forest habitats, which harbor an incredible 4000 plant species.

One of her projects was the establishment of the **Rainforest Medicine Trail** (Map p252; ⏲tours hourly 8am-5pm), a self-guiding path among the jungle's natural cures. Guided tours are available for BZ$10.

Río On Pools — WATERFALL

(Map p252) At Río On Pools, small waterfalls connect a series of pools that the river has carved out of granite boulders. Some of the falls double as water slides.

Río Frio Cave — CAVE

(Map p252) The Río Frio Caves are the region's most-visited and famous caverns. The river gurgles through the sizeable cave, keeping it cool while you go off and explore.

Five Sisters Falls — WATERFALL

(Map p252) The pools at tranquil Five Sisters Falls, accessible by an outdoor-elevator ride (small charge, usually BZ$5) at Five Sisters Lodge, are connected by five falls cascading over a short drop-off.

Hidden Valley (Thousand Foot) Falls — WATERFALL

(Map p252) The region's aquatic highlight is Hidden Valley (Thousand Foot) Falls, southeast of San Antonio. Hiking trails surround the falls and a viewing platform at the top of the cascade is a great spot for catching a Mountain Pine Ridge vista. The falls actually are around 1500ft (450m) high, but they aren't spectacular in the dry season.

Pacbitun — ARCHAEOLOGICAL SITE

(Map p252) Pacbitun, a small site 12 miles (19km) south of San Ignacio via Cristo Rey Rd near San Antonio, seems to have been occupied continuously through most of Maya history, from 900 BC to AD 900. Today only lofty **Plaza A** has been uncovered and partially consolidated. **Structures 1** and **2**, on the east and west sides of the plaza, respectively, are worth a look.

Barton Creek Cave — CAVE

(Map p252) One of the more popular day trips offered out of San Ignacio, the cave holds spooky skulls and bones, and pottery shards from the ancient Maya. To see them you'll have to negotiate some very narrow passages. Full-day tours are around BZ$130 per person, including meals.

Sleeping

The forests and mountains of the greater Mountain Pine Ridge area are dotted with small inns, lodges and ranches offering accommodations, meals, hiking, horseback trips, caving, swimming, bird-watching and similar outdoor activities.

Crystal Paradise Resort RESORT $$
(Map p252; ☎820-4014, 834-4016; www.crystalparadise.com; Cristo Rey Rd; standard s/d/tr BZ$150/210/270, garden/garden loft/valley-view cabañas s/d/tr BZ$190/250/310; P @) The Tut family's resort is spread out over well-tended gardens just above the Macal River, and offers utilitarian but comfortable *cabañas*. Most guests come here on packages that incorporate preplanned tours, including horseback riding, canoeing, trips to Maya ruins and other activities. Breakfast and dinner are included.

Macaw Bank Jungle Lodge LODGE $$$
(Map p252; ☎603-4825; www.macawbankjunglelodge.com; off Cristo Rey Rd; small/large cabañas BZ$220/290; P) A wildlife wonderland, teeming with birds and other animals. Hike the network of trails, meditate beneath a 900-year-old bullet tree, explore an unexcavated Maya site or float down the river in a tube, then retire to your rustic, kerosene-lit cabin (though there is now basic solar-powered electricity) decorated with hand-hewn furniture, beautiful mosaic-tile floors and woven tapestries. A restaurant serving locally grown and sourced fruits, vegetables and meats is on site, but meals must be ordered in advance.

Mountain Equestrian Trails RESORT $$$
(Map p252; ☎669-1124, in USA 800-838-3918; www.metbelize.com; s/d/tr/q BZ$220/264/308/352, breakfast/lunch/dinner BZ$16/22/40; P) After a day of horseback riding, rest your weary body in one of the 10 spacious thatched-roof *cabañas*, decorated with beautiful Maya tapestries and boasting lovely forest views. Kerosene lamps light the way (as there is no electricity), making for a particularly romantic atmosphere. Good home-style meals are served in the *cantina*. Multiday packages including horseback riding, tours and accommodations, and transfers are also available.

West to Guatemala

From San Ignacio it's another 10 miles (16km) southwest down Western Hwy to the Guatemalan border.

San Jose Succotz

This small town sits on the Mopan River at the crossing point to Xunantunich. The town comes alive every year during the annual **Succotz festival** for a three-day celebration featuring dances, football, greasy-pole climbs, greased-pigs chasing, marimba music, and of course, local food. The festival takes place on the weekend following Easter.

Sleeping & Eating

★Trek Stop LODGE, CAMPGROUND $
(Map p252; ☎823-2265; www.thetrekstop.com; Western Hwy Mile 71; camping per person BZ$10, d/tr/q with bathroom BZ$83/109/131, s/d/tr/q without bathroom BZ$33/52/83/96, breakfast BZ$7-12, mains BZ$10-15; ⏲restaurant 7am-8pm; P @) The Trek Stop offers a unique combination of ecolodge and backpackers' outpost, perfectly located to provide a remote jungle setting and easy access to all the local sites. Hand-hewn cabins have simple wood furnishings and private verandahs. There is plenty of hang-out space, including a shady hammock lounge, a self-catering kitchen and an affordable restaurant. Its 22 acres extend back into the wilds, where you can enjoy Frisbee, golf, nature trails and other jungle activities.

Benny's Kitchen RESTAURANT $$
(Map p252; ☎823-2541; Western Hwy Mile 72; meals BZ$10-20; ⏲7am-10pm Sun-Thu, to midnight Fri & Sat) This local institution serves local specialties like tangy *escabeche* (spicy chicken with lime and onions), fiery barbecue, cow-foot soup and more. Visit on the weekend for a chance to sample more exotic rotating specials like *gibnut* stew and venison steak. A wide selection of beer and libations are available. Benny's also has a small store, children's playground and an air-conditioned internet cafe (open 10am to 9pm).

Xunantunich

Belize's most accessible Maya site of significance, **Xunantunich** (Map p252; admission BZ$10; ⏲7:30am-4pm), pronounced soo-*nahn*-too-neech, is reached via a free ferry crossing at San Jose Succotz, about 7 miles

(12km) west of San Ignacio. From the ferry it's a 1-mile walk (2km) uphill to the ruins.

The site's dominant structure, **El Castillo** (Structure A-6), rises 130ft (40m) above the jungle floor. The stairway on its northern side – the side you approach from the courtyard – goes only as far as the temple building. To climb to the **roof comb** you must go around to the southern side and use a separate set of steps. On the temple's east side, a few of the masks that once surrounded the structure have been restored. Structure A-11 and Plaza A-3, formed a residential 'palace' area for the ruling family.

Buses on their way between San Ignacio and Benque Viejo del Carmen will drop you at the ferry, which runs from 8am to 5pm; crossing is on demand and free for both foot passengers and cars.

SOUTHERN BELIZE

Less trammelled by travelers, southern Belize is well worth the trip. For Garifuna culture, check out the towns of Dangriga and Hopkins. For a budget-friendly island experience, visit Tobacco Caye and Glover's Reef (both good for diving and snorkeling). Placencia remains low-key in all but absolute peak season, and Punta Gorda is the jumping-off point for the Toledo district, home of unrestored ruins, natural wonders and traditional villages.

Hummingbird Highway

Heading southeast from Belmopan, the Hummingbird Hwy stretches 49 miles (79km) to the junction of the Southern Hwy and the turnoff to Dangriga. Though easily one of the most beautiful stretches of road in Belize, keep in mind that to most Belizeans it's just another road to be driven as fast (and often recklessly) as possible.

Blue Hole National Park

The **Blue Hole** – focus of the like-named **national park** (Map p252; admission US$4; ⏲8am-4pm) – is a cenote (se-*noh*-tay; water-filled limestone sinkhole) some 328ft (100m) in diameter and 108ft (33m) deep. Fed by underground tributaries of the Sibun River, it's deliciously cool on the hottest days and makes an excellent swimming hole.

The park visitors center is about 11 miles (18km) south of Belmopan on Hummingbird Hwy. At the center is the trailhead to **St Herman's Cave**, a large cavern once used by the Maya during the Classic period. This is one of the few caves in Belize you can visit independently, although a guide is required if you wish to venture in further than 150yd. Also here are a series of nature trails and an observation tower.

Sleeping & Eating

Ian Anderson's Caves Branch Jungle Lodge LODGE **$$$**

(Map p252; ☎in Belize 610-3452, toll free from USA & Canada 866-357-2698; www.cavesbranch.com; Hummingbird Hwy Mile 41½; d cabaña & bungalow BZ$338-$492, d ste & treehouse BZ$588-$1182, breakfast/lunch/dinner BZ$16/24/32; P📶🏊)

Looking for a jungle splurge? This 90-sq-mile private jungle estate acts as both starting point and nerve center for a variety of jungle activities, including horseback riding, cave-tubing, nocturnal jungle walks, and day, night and overnight cave expeditions, as well as jungle and kayak expeditions. Check the website for a full description of what's on offer at the lodge. Accommodations are jungle-chic, and the restaurant serves excellent Belizean, Caribbean and international cuisine.

Dangriga

POP 9100

Dangriga is the largest town in southern Belize. Much smaller than Belize City, it's friendlier and quieter and a great place to get amid the Garífuna culture. November 19 is **Garífuna Settlement Day**, a frenzy of dancing, drinking and celebration of the Garífuna's heritage. For the rest of the year you'll find the folks here a bit more laid-back, but equally welcoming.

Sights

Marie Sharp's Factory LANDMARK

(☎532-2087; www.mariesharps-bz.com; ⏲7am-4pm Mon-Fri) Eight miles (13km) northwest of town on Melinda Rd is Marie Sharp's Factory, the source of Belize's beloved hot sauce. Casual tours, often led by Marie herself, are offered during business hours. There is also a gift shop. Due to an assault in the past, the Sharp family advises against walking the road from the main highway, and offers transportation with advanced notice.

Dangriga

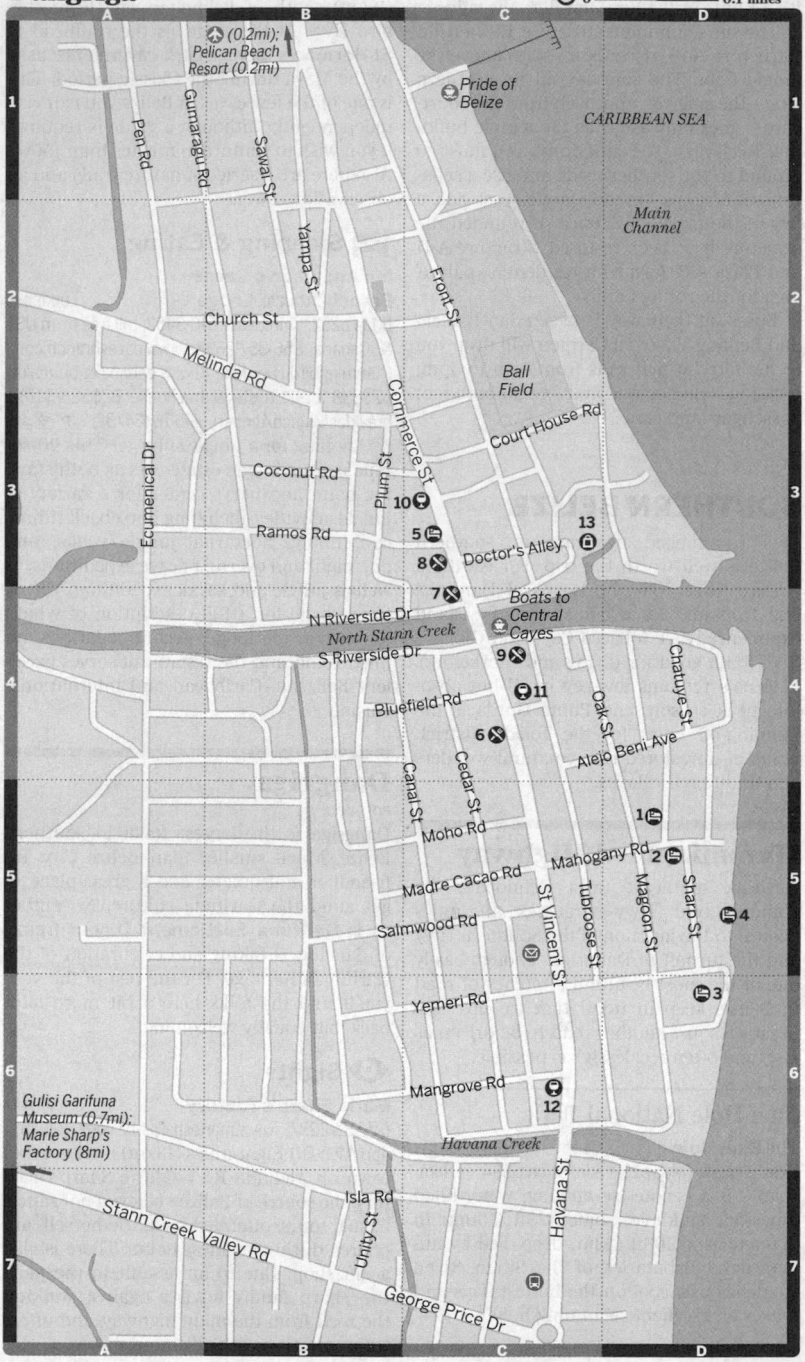
0 200 m
0 0.1 miles
(0.2mi); Pelican Beach Resort (0.2mi)
Pride of Belize
CARIBBEAN SEA
Main Channel
Pen Rd
Gumaragu Rd
Sawai St
Yampa St
Front St
Church St
Melinda Rd
Ball Field
Commerce St
Court House Rd
Coconut Rd
Plum St
Ecumenical Dr
Ramos Rd
Doctor's Alley
Boats to Central Cayes
N Riverside Dr
North Stann Creek
S Riverside Dr
Chatuye St
Bluefield Rd
Oak St
Alejo Beni Ave
Canal St
Cedar St
Moho Rd
Mahogany Rd
Madre Cacao Rd
Tubroose St
Magoon St
Sharp St
Salmwood Rd
St Vincent St
Yemeri Rd
Mangrove Rd
Gulisi Garifuna Museum (0.7mi); Marie Sharp's Factory (8mi)
Havana Creek
Isla Rd
Havana St
Stann Creek Valley Rd
Unity St
George Price Dr
1
2
3
4
5
6
7
8
9
10
11
12
13

Dangriga

Sleeping
1 Chaleanor Hotel D5
2 D's Backpacker Hostel D5
3 Ruthie's Cabanas D6
4 Sea Breeze Inn D5
5 Wayohan C3

Eating
6 Family Restaurant C4
7 King Burger C4
8 Pomce C3
9 Riverside Café C4

Drinking & Nightlife
10 Local Motion Bar & Pool C3
11 Riverside Tavern C4
12 Wadini Shed C6

Shopping
13 Dangriga Central Market C3

Gulisi Garifuna Museum MUSEUM
(☎669-0639; www.ngcbelize.org; Stann Creek Valley Rd, Chuluhadiwa Park; admission BZ$10; ⏲10am-5pm Mon-Fri, 8am-noon Sat) The Gulisi Garífuna Museum provides an excellent overview of the vibrant Garífuna culture in photographs, film and music. Workshops and language courses are held here. It's about 1.2 miles inland from the bus station – any bus leaving town can drop you here.

Sleeping

D's Backpacker Hostel HOSTEL $
(☎502-3324; valsbackpackerhostel.com; cnr Mahogany Rd & Sharp St; dm BZ$25; @ 📶) Formerly known as Val's, Dangriga's one and only hostel is a local institution, offering three fan-cooled dorm rooms with separate hot-shower bathrooms, a communal kitchen with movies, wi-fi and luggage lockers for guests. Dangriga native Dana (she's the D) is a great source of local information. D's also has bicycle rental (BZ$10 per day), a book exchange, freshly brewed coffee and more.

Ruthie's Cabanas GUESTHOUSE $
(☎502-3184; 31 Southern Foreshore; s cabañas BZ$54, additional person BZ$10) Ruthie's comprises four pleasant, seaside, thatched-roof huts on the north side of Havana Creek. It offers hot and cold showers, plenty of coconut-tree shade and a chilled and cheap place to stay in 'Griga. Ruthie also serves home-cooked meals for an additional charge.

Wayohan HOTEL $
(☎522-2278; 105 Commerce St; s/d with fan BZ$50/65, with air-con BZ$70/90; ❄) This hotel offers antiseptic rooms, hot showers, TVs and little in the way of charm. Not a bad choice for travelers on the cheap.

Chaleanor Hotel HOTEL $$
(☎522-2587; www.toucantrail.com/chaleanor-hotel.html; 35 Magoon St; s/d/tr with bathroom BZ$76/121/150, without bathroom BZ$27/44/57, with air-con add BZ$30; P ❄ 📶) Rooms in this family-run hotel are clean and comfortable, with the ones upstairs having the best views. The cheaper units on the side of the hotel are fairly run-down and best suited to those placing budget above comfort. The owners will also be glad to help you arrange any trips or boat charters.

Sea Breeze Inn HOTEL $$
(☎522-3766; Southern Foreshore; d with air-con BZ$90-130, with fan BZ$75; ❄ 📶) The family-run Sea Breeze offers clean and cheery rooms with balconies and double beds, all with bathrooms and showers. There's also an on-site restaurant with rotating daily specials (BZ$7 to BZ$15), as well as a fully stocked bar.

Eating

Pomce MEXICAN, BELIZEAN $
(Commerce St; dishes from BZ$1; ⏲lunch & dinner) Serving excellent burritos, *salbutes* and *garnaches* (local variations of tortilla), and tacos on the cheap, a meal here will fill your belly with nary a dent on the wallet. There's no sign on this local favorite, so look for a pink-and-yellow shack with three picnic tables across from a grocery store called Best Buy.

King Burger BELIZEAN $
(Commerce St; dishes BZ$4-15; ⏲breakfast, lunch & dinner Mon-Sat) Reliably fresh breakfasts of eggs, beans and fry-jacks for BZ$6.50, as well as hamburgers and plates of fried shrimp. Coffee is instant, but juices are fresh.

Family Restaurant CHINESE $$
(Commerce St; mains BZ$8-20; ⏲10am-11pm) A clean, fun (check out the swinging tables and chairs in the back) and well-run Chinese restaurant that serves both Sino–Belizean fare and dishes to cater to the tastes of local Chinese who still remember what Chinese food is supposed to taste like. Best of the authentic Chinese menu items is Family's spicy Zhe Jiang beef (BZ$17.50), a taste of Sichuan in the Caribbean.

Riverside Café SEAFOOD $$
(S Riverside Dr; mains BZ$10-25; ⏲ breakfast, lunch & dinner) Just east of the North Stann Creek Bridge, this long-time favorite cafe serves tasty meals at budget to moderate prices. Right on the river, this is a good place to ask about fishing and snorkeling trips out to the cayes or treks inland.

Drinking

Wadini Shed BAR
(St Vincent St; ⏲ 4pm-midnight) One thatched roof, no walls and a mainly local clientele make this a great spot to have a stout and get down with Dangriga culture. During the week of Garifuna Settlement Day (November 19), the place explodes with music and dancing.

Local Motion Bar & Pool BAR
(Commerce St) Loud music, cold beer, dodgy characters...what more could you want?

Riverside Tavern CLUB
(St Vincent St) Just south of the bridge, this club (known locally as 'the club') gets a bit of a crowd for midweek karaoke sessions, but things really start jumping on the weekends.

Pelican Beach Resort BAR
(www.pelicanbeachbelize.com; 1st St) The Friday happy hour at this beachfront resort bar from 6pm to 8pm usually pulls in a crowd.

Information

Belize Bank (St Vincent St) and **Scotia Bank** (St Vincent St) are both on the main drag south of the creek.

You can get your clothes washed and check your email at the same time at **Val's Laundry** (cnr Mahogany Rd & Sharp St; internet per hr BZ$4, laundry wash & dry per lb BZ$2; ⏲ 7:30am-7pm; 📶).

Getting There & Away

Maya Island Air (☎ 522-2659) and **Tropic Air** (☎ 226-2012) serve Dangriga on flights also stopping at Placencia, Punta Gorda and Belize City. The airstrip is a mile (2km) north of the center.

Boats to the southern cayes can be chartered in front of the Riverside Cafe. It is possible to catch a boat from Dangriga to Honduras with **Pride of Belize** (see p281).

Buses to Belize City (local/express BZ$10/14, three to four hours) leave regularly from 5am to 7pm and pass through Belmopan, from which transfer to Cayo is available. Buses to Punta Gorda (local/express BZ$10/13, 4½ hours) leave from 5:30am to 6:15pm. There are currently three buses per day to Hopkins (BZ$5, 45 minutes) at 11:30am, 12:30pm and 6:15pm, and five per day to Placencia (BZ$10, 2½ hours) beginning at 9am and running until 6pm. The bus station is at the southern end of Havana St.

Southern Highway

South of Dangriga are some great opportunities for experiencing off-the-beaten-track Belize.

Hopkins

POP 1800

Beaches as nice (nicer, some say) as those found in Placencia, more Garifuna culture than you can shake your booty at, good food and plenty of mid-range (and even a few good budget) accommodations – is there any reason not to visit Hopkins?

Tours

Closer to the Barrier Reef than Placencia by 10 miles (16km), Hopkins is a good place to be based for the budget-minded ocean voyager. **See More Adventures** (☎ 667-6626; seemoreadventures@gmail.com) and **Bullfrog Tours** (☎ 669-0046; issymcm@yahoo.com) are both independent tour operators based in town that do land and sea trips around the region.

Motorbike Rentals & Alternate Adventures ADVENTURE
(☎ 665-6292; info@alternateadventures.com; South Side) Rents motorcycles for BZ$118 per day, helmets, cellphone and maps included. Also rents camping gear, snorkeling equipment, underwater cameras and electric golf carts, as well as offering other specialty tours.

Sleeping

Lebeha CABINS $
(☎ 665-9305; North Side; dm BZ$20, s/d cabañas BZ$30/50, cabins from BZ$124; 📶) On the north end of town, the Garifuna drumming school set up by local drummer Jabbar Lambey and his wife Dorothy also has a dorm room, two beachfront cabins and three *cabañas* for rent. Lebeha also rents two beachfront houses with queen and single beds, hot-water showers and screened-in porches with hammocks.

Funky Dodo HOSTEL $
(☎ 667-0558; www.thefunkydodo.com; South Side; dm BZ$15, d/tr/q BZ$38/51/68; 📶) The cen-

trally located Funky Dodo has 24 beds in a rough and rustic screened-in wooden bunkhouse and four private rooms that sleep two to four each. Beds are comfortable, sheets clean, blankets colorful, and there's a communal kitchen as well. A short wooden boardwalk leads to shared bathrooms with cold-water showers, and a thatched-roof bamboo patio provides a fine spot to hang out and watch Hopkins go by.

★All Seasons Guest House GUESTHOUSE **$$**
(523-7209; www.allseasonsbelize.com; South Side; r BZ$86-150, family cabins BZ$196; P ❄ 📶) With its octagonal, thatch-covered upstairs porch and its four uniquely decorated rooms with big private bathrooms, All Seasons may just be the prettiest guesthouse in town. All rooms have air-con, coffee makers and hot showers, and there's a great patio out front with a massive grill and picnic area. There's also a little shop in front of All Seasons that serves healthy breakfasts (BZ$14) and smoothies.

★Coconut Row Guesthouse GUESTHOUSE **$$**
(670-3000, in USA 518-223-9775; www.coconutrowbelize.com; Beachside, south of King Cassava; d BZ$198, apartments BZ$250-290; P ❄ 📶) This colorful hotel offers five rooms, two of which are full two-bedroom apartments, two rooms with two double beds and one with two queen-sized beds. Beds have hand-carved headboards, ceramic sinks have bright mosaic patterns, and local art adorns the walls.

Tipple Tree Beya HOTEL **$$**
(533-7006; www.tippletree.com; South Side; r BZ$70-110; 📶) This sturdy wooden beachside hotel has three cozy, clean, fan-cooled rooms sharing a sociable verandah beneath the owner's quarters upstairs. Two rooms have private hot-water bathrooms, while the cheapest one has a cold-water shower. All have coffee makers and seafront views.

Eating

Most restaurants serve good, inexpensive seafood and Belizean dishes, including *gibnut* from around BZ$12.

Sandy Beach Women's Cooperative Restaurant GARIFUNA **$**
(sandybeachhopkins@gmail.com; South Side beachfront; meals BZ$10-15; ⏲ 11am-9pm Mon-Sat, 10am-3pm Sun) The colorfully dressed ladies of the Sandy Beach Women's Cooperative serve up daily Garifuna specials like *hudut* (a creamy fish stew served with mashed plantain) with distinctive local flair. The newly opened restaurant also promises to soon have a full menu of local cuisine including plantain chips, sandwiches, quesadillas and burritos.

WORTH A TRIP

CAYES OF SOUTHERN BELIZE

Tobacco Caye, South Water Caye and the resorts of Glover's Reef are all accessed by boat from Dangriga, Hopkins and Sittee River. Their distance from Belize City has kept casual visitors away, protecting the reef from much human impact. Dolphins, manta rays and manatees are commonly sighted, and the quantity and variety of coral that is on display is incredible. Good snorkeling and diving can be had right off the shore from the cayes.

Tobacco Caye is a 5-acre (2-hectare) island catering to travelers on a low-to-moderate budget. Diving, fishing, snorkeling and hammocking are the favorite pastimes here. Lodging possibilities include **Lana's** (520-5036; s & d per person incl meals BZ$70). Passage to Tobacco Caye can be arranged along the river near the Riverside Café in Dangriga. The cost is around BZ$50 one way.

Probably the best deal for the money is **Glover's Atoll Resort** (520-5016; www.glovers.com.bz; per person per week camping BZ$198, dm & on-site tents BZ$298, cabins BZ$498-598; 📶). Located on Glover Reef's Northeast Caye, the resort offers budget accommodations on a 9-acre (3.6-hectare) atoll about 20 miles (32km) from the mainland. Facilities at the resort are rustic, but the 360-degree Caribbean view can't be beat. It's a great deal for budget travelers, especially if you plan ahead and bring your own water, food and other supplies (though meals are available at the resort for between BZ$18 and BZ$24). The folks who run the resort offer all sorts of activities, from snorkeling to sailing to dive training. Check the website for more details.

King Cassava BELIZEAN $$
(South Side; mains BZ$8-20; ⏲11am-midnight) Excellent meat and seafood dishes, and naturally, there's no shortage of Belizean standards such as stewed chicken, fried fish, and rice and beans.

Yugadah Café BELIZEAN $$
(South Side; mains BZ$8-25; ⏲breakfast, lunch & dinner) Serves Belizean fare, burgers and burritos and a variety of world-class homemade sauces.

Thongs Café CAFE $$
(South Side; mains BZ$8-23; ⏲8am-2pm Wed-Sun, 6-9pm Fri & Sat; 📶) This colorful cafe serves up an esoteric variety of moderately priced meals, not to mention hands-down the finest coffee in town. Bonus: free wireless!

Information

At the junction of Hopkins Rd and the village sits a privately run information booth, a grocery store and an ATM.

Getting There & Away

Buses from Dangriga to Hopkins (BZ$5, one hour) run Monday through Saturday at 10:30 am and 5:15pm, with a 5:15pm bus on Sunday.

Dangriga-bound buses depart Hopkins Monday through Saturday at 7am and 2pm and Sunday at 2pm.

Any bus on the Southern Hwy will drop you at the Hopkins turnoff, from where you can usually hitch a ride.

Placencia

POP 1200

Perched at the southern tip of a long, narrow, sandy peninsula, Placencia is known as 'the caye you can drive to.' Not too long ago, the only practical way to get here was by boat from the mainland. Now a road runs all the way down the peninsula and an airstrip lies just north of town. The palm-lined beaches on its east side attract an international crowd looking for sun and sand, and they make low-key pastimes such as swimming, sunbathing and lazing about the preferred 'activities' for many visitors.

High season in Placencia begins the week before Christmas and lasts until late April. During the full moons of May and June the town hops as whale sharks come to spawn in the waters off Placencia. Bargain hunters should be able to get discounted rates during the low season.

Tours

Vying to sign up customers for tours of the region are **Ocean Motion Guide Service** (☎512-3363, 523-3162) and **Nite Wind Guide Service** (☎609-6845, 523-3487), both operating out of small offices near the wharf.

Trip & Travel (☎523-3205; ⏲Mon-Sat) operates out of Placencia Office Supply and mainly focuses on fly-fishing tours up Monkey River. Egbert Cabral, owner of **Permit Angling** (☎523-3132; permit@btl.net), also runs fishing tours off his motor boat for BZ$600.

On a pier in the main part of the village is **Sea Horse Dive Shop** (☎523-3166; www.belizescuba.com), which runs certification courses and dives for certified divers.

★**Splash Dive Center** DIVING, TOURS
(☎523-3058; www.splashbelize.com) There are a number of dive shops in the village, but the one enjoying the best reputation (indeed, they taught our lifelong aquaphobic writer to dive) is this place. Patty Ramirez's Splash teaches PADI courses to divers of all levels, as well as offering diving and snorkeling tours to islands and reefs throughout the area. Her husband Ralph also leads tours inland, including trips to ruins, jungles and other spots around the country.

Festivals & Events

The three big events in Placencia are **Lobsterfest**, on the last weekend of June, the **Mistletoe Ball**, in mid-December, and the **Placencia Arts Festival** in February. Try to time your trip to hit one of these. Check www.placencia.com for more details.

Sleeping

Most lodgings in Placencia village are mid-budget, with a few cheaper options here and there. The fancy resorts are all north of the village.

Manatee Inn HOTEL $
(☎523-4083; www.manateeinn.com; s/d/tr BZ$70/80/90; P📶) This classical wooden hotel wins 'best in show' for the budget category. Set back a bit from the noisy center of town, the Manatee puts you close enough to the beach to feel a constant breeze. Amenities are as good (if not better) than some of Placencia's pricier hotels. Rooms are especially airy, with high ceilings, hardwood floors, refrigerators and private bathrooms with hot-water showers.

Placencia

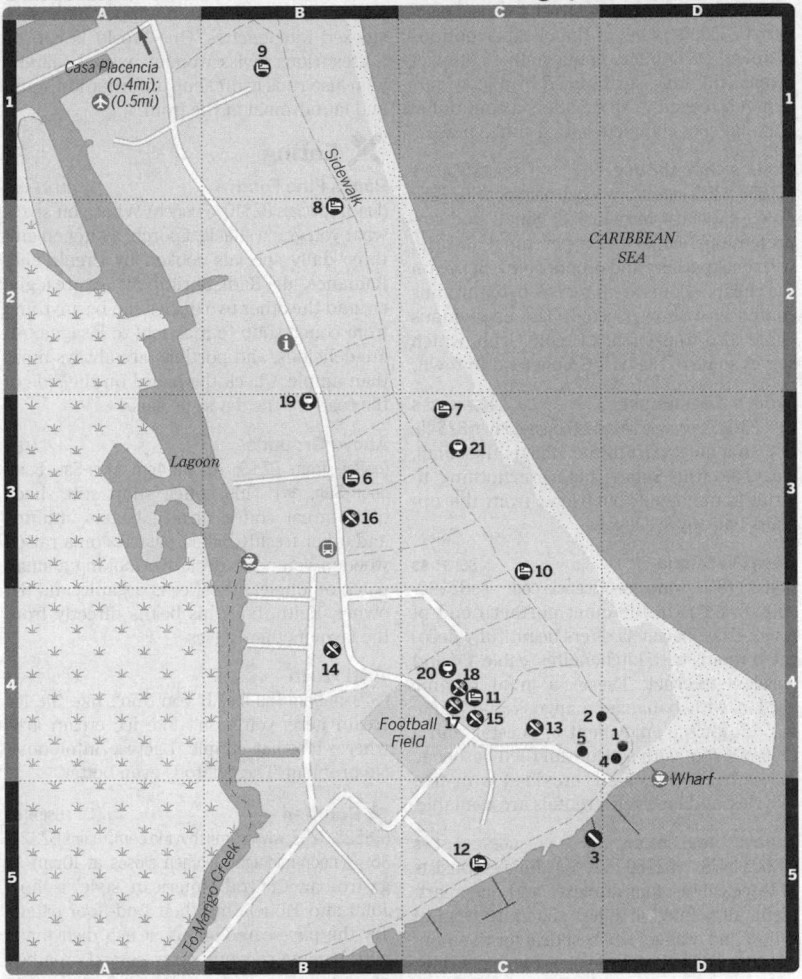

Placencia

Activities, Courses & Tours

1 Nite Wind Guide Service D4
2 Ocean Motion Guide Service C4
3 Sea Horse Dive Shop C5
4 Splash Dive Center D4
5 Trip & Travel C4

Sleeping

6 Deb & Dave's Last Resort B3
7 Julia's Guesthouse C3
8 Lydia's Guesthouse B2
9 Manatee Inn B1
10 Omar's Guesthouse C3
11 One World Rentals C4
12 Sea Glass Inn C5

Eating

13 Above Grounds C4
14 Omar's Creole Grub B4
15 Purple Space Monkey Bar & Grill C4
16 Radi's Fine Food B3
17 Rumfish C4
18 Tutti Frutti C4

Drinking & Nightlife

19 Barefoot Bar B3
20 Pickled Parrot C4
21 Tipsy Tuna Sports Bar C3

Deb & Dave's Last Resort GUESTHOUSE $
(☎523-3207; debanddave@btl.net; r without bathroom BZ$50;) One of the cheaper options in town, D&D offers comfortable, compact rooms with fans, surrounded by a leafy garden. A screened-in space offers a communal chill-out spot complete with a coffee maker.

Omar's Guesthouse GUESTHOUSE $
(☎634-4350; dm/s/d without bathroom BZ$25/40/45, d with bathroom BZ$55) Small and unpretentious, Omar's is a perennial favorite with backpackers and others doing Belize on the cheap. Rooms are fan-cooled, bathrooms shared and showers cold. The eponymous Omar also runs Omar's Creole Grub, which serves some of the best Creole food in town.

Lydia's Guesthouse GUESTHOUSE $
(☎523-3117; www.lydiasguesthouse.com; r BZ$45;) In a quiet part of the village, the small, clean, no-frills rooms here are nothing to write home about, but views from the upstairs balcony are lovely.

Casa Placencia SUITES $$
(☎630-7811; www.casaplacencia.com; r BZ$90-230; P) On the quiet northern end of town, Casa Placencia offers beautifully decorated rooms with kitchenettes, cable TV and wireless internet. There's a great organic garden with bananas, mangoes and papayas (all for the enjoyment of guests), and a chill-out spot with a beautiful tiled barbecue in the back. Guests are provided with free bicycles, and long-term rentals are available.

Julia's Guesthouse GUESTHOUSE $$
(☎503-3478; r BZ$80-150;) Julia's consists of three cabins, four duplexes and one apartment, all painted in Julia's signature tropical yellow and orange. The best deal for the money is the apartment, which has two bedrooms, a living and dining room, and a small kitchen.

Sea Glass Inn HOTEL $$
(☎523-3098; www.seaglassinnbelize.com; s/d/tr BZ$158/158/188, per additional person BZ$20; @) The newly renovated Sea Glass Inn offers unobstructed ocean views and endless sea breezes thanks to its position a stone's throw from Placencia's southern shore. Rooms are newly renovated, and all have coffee makers, microwaves and refrigerators. The wide, wood-floored verandah has chairs and hammocks for long-term lounging.

One World Rentals HOTEL $$
(☎620-9975, 523-3103; studio apartments BZ$98; P) On the south side of town, these clean, meticulously managed studios come well furnished and fully equipped with well-stocked kitchenettes. One World is run by a gregarious Swiss woman named Claudia who also runs a gift shop, information stand and laundromat at the front.

Eating

Radi's Fine Food BELIZEAN $
(lunch specials BZ$10; lunch) What you see is what you get: a shack, a porch, a kitchen and three daily specials cooked by Creole chef Radiance, aka Radi. Shrimp dishes are a given, and the other two dishes can be anything from conch soup to meatloaf to lasagna. All are delicious, and portions are always more than ample. Check the board on the side of the road for the day's specials.

Above Grounds CAFE $
(coffee from BZ$3; 7am-4pm Mon-Sat, 8am-noon Sun;) This coffee shop stilt shack offers great coffee drinks, bagels, muffins and other freshly baked pastries on a raised wooden verandah deck overlooking a small patch of jungle. All coffee is organic, and the owner, Keith, buys his beans directly from the farmers themselves.

Tutti Frutti ICE CREAM $
(9am-9pm Thu-Tue) If you don't like the ice cream here, you won't like ice cream anywhere. It's that simple. Lactose intolerant? No problem. The gelato is even better.

★ Rumfish FUSION $$
(☎523-3293; www.rumfishyvino.com; mains BZ$22-36; noon-midnight, kitchen closes at 10pm) 'A gastro-bar, Central American style' is how John and Pamela bill their 2nd-floor eatery. Try the pan-seared snook, a fish dish made with banana coconut curry, served on a bed of sauteed vegetables with potato latkes. At BZ$7 a pop, travelers on a budget should try the rumfish tacos: beer-battered fillets served with shredded cabbage and *pico de gallo* (fresh salsa). For dessert, try the chocolate habenero canoli (BZ$12), sweet on the front with a little kick on the back end.

Omar's Creole Grub SEAFOOD $$
(mains BZ$16-22; breakfast, lunch & dinner, closed Fri night & lunch Sat) How does Omar serve both the freshest and cheapest seafood in Placencia? By cutting out the middleman and catching it all himself. Crab, lobster, conch, shrimp and fish of all description, all trapped, speared or otherwise caught by

Omar and grilled to perfection. The only way to get it fresher would be to catch it yourself.

Purple Space Monkey Bar & Grill FUSION $$
(☎523-3169; ⏲11am-midnight; 📶☎) Under new management since our last visit, this Placencia landmark's latest incarnation has a decidely more international flair than its predecessors. The menu offers dishes from around the world, including baked lobster tail (BZ$42), five-spice chicken breast (BZ$24) and honest-to-god sushi rolls (BZ$12). With a full bar, the Monkey occasionally hosts live-music acts.

Drinking

Though not quite as openly alcoholic as Ambergris, Placencia definitely caters to the drinking crowd. You'll have no problem getting your drink on here!

Barefoot Bar BAR
(⏲11am-midnight; 📶) Placencia's most happening spot for drinking and entertainment has live music five nights a week, full-moon parties and more. Happy hours are from 5pm to 6pm, with bitters and cheap rum.

Pickled Parrot BAR
(www.pickledparrotbelize.com; ⏲noon-midnight or later) A popular spot for locals and tourists alike. Beer is cheap (BZ$4) and their food – including amazing wings, ham and cabbage plates and Philly-cheese steaks – is excellent as well!

Tipsy Tuna Sports Bar BAR
(⏲7pm-midnight Sun-Wed, to 2am Thu-Sat) The Tipsy Tuna, a towering 'sports bar' with occasional live music and a happening little beachfront bar, is usually more hit than miss.

Orientation

The village's main north–south 'street' is actually a narrow concrete footpath that threads its way among simple wood-frame houses (some on stilts) and beachfront lodges. The paved road to the west is where most of the restaurants are. An easy walk takes you anywhere in town. The airstrip is about half a mile (0.8km) from the start of the village.

Information

Placencia has three banks with ATMs accepting most cards. **Placencia Office Supply** (☎523-3205; internet per hr BZ$10; ⏲8:30am-7pm) has high-speed internet, CD burning and digital-card readers.

Getting There & Around

Ritchie's (☎523-3806; www.ritchiesbusservice.com) has three daily buses between Placencia and Dangriga (BZ$10, two hours). From Placencia, buses leave from the main street by the Hokey Pokey Water Taxi at 6:20am, 7:00am and 1pm. From Dangriga station, buses leave at 11am, 2pm and 4:30pm. On Sundays the earliest buses do not run.

Maya Island Air (☎523-3475; www.mayaairways.com) and **Tropic Air** (☎523-3410; www.tropicair.com) offer daily flights linking Placencia with Belize City and Dangriga to the north and Punta Gorda to the south. Taxis meet most flights and will bring you anywhere in town for BZ$5.

The quickest way out of town is on the **Hokey Pokey Water Taxi** (☎665-7242), which departs Placencia five times between 10am and 6pm for Mango Creek. At Mango Creek, walk five minutes up the main street, turn left at the gas station and wait in front of Sherl's Restaurant. Buses to Punta Gorda (BZ$10, two hours) and Belize City (BZ$20, 4½ hours) roll in every hour or so.

Punta Gorda

POP 5200

The southern seafront town of Punta Gorda is so laid back that most people don't even call it by its full name – all over Belize it's known simply as PG. But PG's days as a quiet backwater may be coming to an end thanks to the extension of the Southern Hwy into Guatemala. We suggest you check it out now while it's still quiet.

Rainfall and humidity are at their highest, and the jungle at its lushest, here in the Toledo district. Prepare yourself for at least a short downpour almost daily and some sultry weather in-between.

PG was founded for the Garífuna who emigrated from Honduras in 1832. Though it's still predominantly Garífuna, it's also home to the usual bewildering variety of Belizean citizenry: Creoles, Q'eqchi' Maya, expat Americans, Brits, Canadians, Chinese and people from eastern India.

Courses

Maroon Creole Drum School MUSIC
(☎632-7841, 668-7733; methos_drums@hotmail.com; Joe Taylor Creek) When he's not touring the country performing, Emmeth Young (easily one of Belize's most respected Creole drummers) hosts drum-making workshops and group presentations at his new place off Joe Taylor Creek, a quarter mile out of PG. Prices vary, but for around BZ$250 students can spend a few days learning both

Punta Gorda

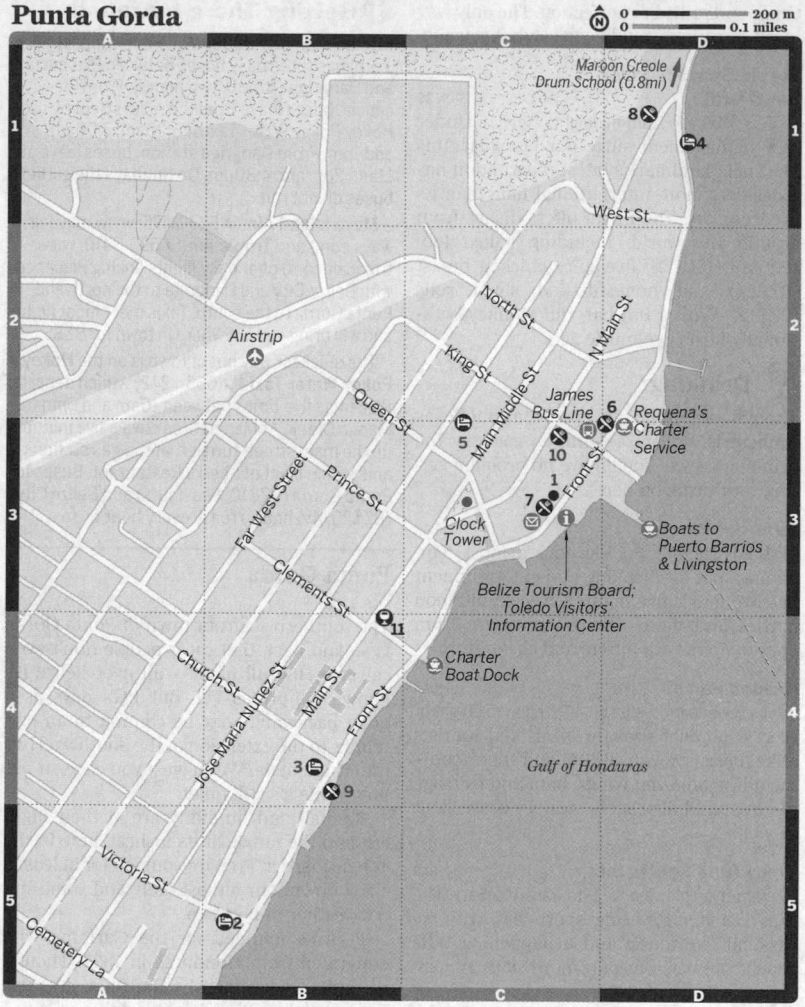

Punta Gorda

Activities, Courses & Tours

1 Tide Tours C3

Sleeping

2 Blue Belize Guest House B5
3 Nature's Way Guest House B4
4 Sea Front Inn D1
5 Tate's Guest House C3

Eating

6 Driftwood Cafe D3
7 Fajina Maya Food C3
8 Gomiers D1
9 Marian's Bayview Restaurant B4
10 Snack Shack C3

Drinking & Nightlife

11 Olympic Bar & Grill B4

drumming and drum making, leaving with their own hand-crafted drum. Camping at the school is available for BZ$10.

Tours

Tide Tours GUIDED TOUR
(☎ 722-2129; www.tidetours.org; 41 Front St) Always ecofriendly, Tide does tours throughout the Toledo area.

Sleeping

Tate's Guest House GUESTHOUSE $
(☎ 722-0147; tatesguesthouse@yahoo.com; 34 Jose Maria Nunez St; s/d BZ$38/76, additional person BZ$11; ❄ @ 📶) Clean rooms in the Tate family's quiet, lilac-colored guesthouse are all are equipped with cable TV and hot showers. The pricier rooms have air-con and kitchenettes; the cheaper ones are fan-cooled. Long-term rental discounts are available.

Nature's Way Guest House GUESTHOUSE $
(☎ 702-2119; natureswayguesthouse@hotmail.com; 82 Front St; s/d/tr/q BZ$28/38/48/58) This family guesthouse has been a long-standing favorite of backpackers and students for years (group rates are available). Simple, screened-in, ocean-breeze-cooled wooden rooms are upstairs, and a large airy communal area with TV, music and internet below. There's also a big communal sleeping area where there are bunks with mosquito netting. Nature's Way also rents kayaks (BZ$15 per day).

Blue Belize Guest House B&B $$
(☎ 722-2678; www.bluebelize.com; 139 Front St; ste BZ$150, honeymoon ste BZ$190, 2-bed ste BZ$270; @ 📶 ❄) BB's six breezy and beautifully decorated suites are more like serviced apartments than hotel rooms, offering well-furnished living rooms and kitchenettes. Suites in the newly built north wing include flat-screen TVs. The north wing also has an amazing verandah for stargazing.

Sea Front Inn HOTEL $$
(☎ 722-2300; www.seafrontinn.com; 4 Front St; s/d BZ$130/160; P ❄ 📶) A strong contender for the quirkiest-looking hotel in Belize, this four-story gabled stone, wood and concrete construction offers good-sized, air-con rooms (some boasting their own balconies), each with a different animal theme. The rear building – no less unusual looking – houses three apartments for medium and long-term visitors.

Eating & Drinking

Punta Gorda has a number of stalls and restaurants serving traditional Belizean fare. You'll find most of these along the main street on either side of the town square. Best bet for lunch is easily one of the sidewalk stands serving grilled chicken, beans and slaw for around BZ$5. Saturday is market day, when area villagers come to town to buy, sell and barbecue.

Gomiers VEGETARIAN $
(5 Alejandro Vernon St; meals BZ$6-16; ⏲ 11am-2pm & 5:30-10pm; ✎) In a town where coleslaw constitutes a vegetable and shacks serving fried fish and stewed chicken mark the culinary landscape, Gomier's consciously crafted vegetarian dishes, herbal tonics and seaweed-based energy shakes stand out like a Rastafarian at a Mitt Romney fundraiser.

Marian's Bayview Restaurant CARIBBEAN $
(76 Front St; mains BZ$8-14; ⏲ lunch & dinner) A 3rd-floor outdoor eatery with an amazing view over the Gulf of Honduras, this place is worth visiting for the ambience alone. Marian serves excellent East Indian cuisine along with some of the wickedest homemade hot sauce south of the Rio Grande. Lunch and dinner are served buffet style.

Fajina Maya Food MAYA $
(Front St; mains BZ$5; ⏲ 6am-9pm Mon-Sat) This small, 2nd-floor restaurant serves interesting Maya soups and stews with vegetables and poultry from farms in the outlying communities. The specialty of the house is *caldo*, a chicken soup colored red with annatto, a local vegetable. Lack of ambience is more than made up for by the sea breeze and ocean view.

Driftwood Cafe CAFE $
(☎ 632-7841; 9 Front St; meals from BZ$8; ⏲ 7am-4pm; ✎) The Driftwood serves a unique variety of dishes drawing on local ingredients and inspiration from North American culinary traditions. Specialties of the house include the 100% vegan chocolate chili, the green fruit freeze (orange juice and callalo, a local ameranth green), milkshakes made with local cacao, coffee drinks made with local Belizean coffee and tamales and quesadillas.

Snack Shack CAFE $
(Main St; mains BZ$10-20; ⏲ 7am-3pm Mon-Sat) This popular eatery with an outdoor wooden

porch serves Belizean breakfasts and generally healthy lunch items like shrimp salads and sandwiches all day. For something really unique, try a soursop slushie (BZ$3.50).

Olympic Bar & Grill BAR
(cnr Main & Clements Sts; ⏲7am-11pm) The latest hotspot with the PG expat crowd serves ice-cold beers, spicy-hot wings, homemade ice cream, and snacks galore. Alvan and Yvette Vernon also do catering for group functions, including snacks, pastries and local delicacies.

ℹ Information

The **Belize Tourism Board** (☎227-2420; Front St; ⏲8am-noon & 1-5pm Mon-Fri, to noon Sat) and **Toledo Visitors' Information Center** (☎722-2531; ⏲8am-noon & 1-5pm Tue-Fri, 8am-noon Sat) share office space.

Belize Bank (30 Main St) and **Scotia Bank** (1 Main St) both have ATMs.

Wash your clothes at the **Punta Gorda Laundry Service** (wash & dry per lb BZ$2; ⏲8:30am-5pm Mon-Sat) and while you wait, access the internet at **V-Comp** (29 Main St; per hr BZ$8; ⏲8am-8pm Mon-Sat).

ℹ Getting There & Away

Punta Gorda is served daily by **Maya Island Air** (☎722-2856; www.mayaairways.com) and **Tropic Air** (☎722-2008; www.tropicair.com). Ticket offices are located at the airport. Flights to Belize City are between BZ$164 and BZ$204.

Requena's Charter Services (☎722-2070; 12 Front St) and **Memos boat service** (☎630-5889, in Guatemala 00502-4896-9215; memosboatservicandtours@yahoo.com; Front St) both do the Punta Gorda–Puerto Barrios (Guatemala) run daily for BZ$50 one way, departing at 10am and 12:45pm. A few other services offer regular and chartered services to Lívingston (Guatemala). Check the Belize Tourism Industry Association (BTIA) office for more information.

James Bus Line (☎702-2049, 722-2625; King St) operates buses to Belize City (local/express BZ$20/22, six/seven hours), stopping in Independence (from where a quick taxi and boat will take you to Placencia), Dangriga and Belmopan (for all points west).

Local village buses run daily between PG and villages throughout the Toledo district. Buses leave from around the town square, and schedules can be obtained through TEA, the Toledo Visitor's Information Center or online (www.guidetobelize.info; go to the Travel page and click on the Bus link).

Villages of Toledo

San Pedro Columbia

Around 20 miles (32km) northwest of Punta Gorda is the village of San Pedro Columbia, the largest Q'eqchi' Maya community outside of Guatemala. In addition to having a few stores and restaurants, the village is close to the source of the Columbia branch of the Río Grande, a lovely river great for swimming and tubing. Behind the village, up into the hills, you'll find the **Columbia Forest Reserve**, which has thousands of acres of forest, sinkholes, caves and ruins hidden in the valleys.

Maya Mountain Research Farm (www.mmrfbz.org) is just a few miles upriver from the village. The 70-acre organic farm and registered NGO in Toledo offers internships for those interested in learning about organic farming, biodiversity and alternative energy. Interns pay BZ$400 for the week, or BZ$1200 for the month, which includes everything.

Columbia is also close to Lubaantun and 20 minutes by bus from Nim Li Punit, making the village an ideal place from which to explore two of the area's most complex and amazing ruins.

San Miguel

This Q'eqchi' village of 400 people is on the road close to the Lubaantun ruins and the Southern Hwy. You can walk to Lubaantun or make a little expedition to **Tiger Cave**, 1½ hours' walk away, returning by canoe along the Río Grande.

Laguna

About 13 miles (21km) northwest of Punta Gorda, Laguna is just 2 miles (3km) off the Southern Hwy and quick and easy to get to. It's home to about 300 Q'eqchi' Maya villagers. The lagoon the village is named for, about a two-hour walk away, is at the heart of the 8.6-sq-mile (22-sq-km) **Aguacaliente Wildlife Sanctuary**, an extensive wetland area.

San Antonio

The largest Mopan Maya community in Belize (population about 2500), San Antonio is home to a beautiful **stone church**

DON'T MISS

CYRILA'S MAYA BELIZEAN CHOCOLATE

Love chocolate? Visit **Cyrila's Maya Belizean Chocolate** (http://www.cyrilaschocolate.org/; San Felipe village; ⏲9am-5pm), Juan and Abelina's beautiful cacao farm and chocolate factory in the Maya village of San Felipe, where the gregarious Juan will walk you through the traditional chocolate-making process – from harvest and fermentation to drying and roasting to deshalling and grinding.

Tours are held daily, and the couple will also cook traditional Maya lunches of corn tortilla, vegetable rice, chocolate chicken, salads made from organic vegetables from the farm and, yes, hot chocolate. Day tours are BZ$60, and include lunch, choclate making and more. Drop-in visitors are welcome, and can experience just the chocolate making for BZ$20, with lunches available for a separate charge of BZ$10.

If you want to stay, Juan and Abelina have a small homestay bunkhouse next to the factory with two double rooms and two sets of single bunk beds for BZ$40 (which includes breakfast and dinner).

with wonderful stained-glass windows. The **Feast of San Luis**, a harvest festival where the famous Deer Dance is performed, is celebrated in town from about August 15 to 25.

Santa Elena

Santa Elena is another Mopan village, 6 miles (10km) west of San Antonio, with about 300 people. Just east is the little **Río Blanco National Park**, containing the spectacular **Río Blanco Falls** and one of the country's best swimming holes.

Pueblo Viejo

Three miles (5km) beyond Santa Elena, the name Pueblo Viejo is Spanish for 'Old Town,' which is appropriate as this was the first settled Mopan village in Belize. Today it is home to about 550 people. It's still an isolated place, without electricity. There are beautiful **waterfalls** close by and you can take **jungle hikes** or go **horseback riding**.

San Jose

Also known as Hawaii (a Mopan word, pronounced ha-wee-ah), this Mopan village of 700, known for practising organic farming, is located in the foothills of the Maya Mountains. The rainforest surrounding it is among the most pristine in Toledo. You can make jungle hikes to **Gibnut Cave** and a 200ft **sinkhole**. The village honors its patron saint with three days of eating and dancing to marimba and harp music around March 19.

Blue Creek

This village of some 250 people, part Q'eqchi' and part Mopan, does indeed have a pretty, blue-tinted river running through the middle. Howler monkeys inhabit the surrounding hilly jungles, otters live along the creek and green iguanas are plentiful. Blue Creek is a tourist stop for the **Blue Creek Cave** (Hokeb Ha Cave; admission BZ$2) and some excellent hiking around a hill known as **Jungle Height**.

Barranco

An anomaly, Barranco is a Garífuna community surrounded by Maya villages. It is a major spiritual homeland of the Garífuna, and a great base from which to explore **Temash-Sarstoon National Park**, an amazing and remote 64-sq-mile (166-sq-km) protected reserve of rainforest, wetlands, estuaries and rivers lined by towering mangroves and stretching all the way to Guatemala. Other activities available at Barranco include **drumming** and **dory building** (a dory is a traditional Belizean canoe).

Maya Ruins of Toledo

The Toledo district boasts two major Maya ruins. **Lubaantun** (admission BZ$20; ⏲8am-5pm), 1 mile (1.6km) northwest of the village of San Pedro Columbia has been excavated to some extent but not restored. The many temples are still mostly covered with jungle, so you will have to use your imagination to envisage the great city that once thrived here.

Somewhat more restored is **Nim Li Punit** (admission BZ$20; ⏲8am-5pm). Named after the headgear worn by the richly clad figure on Stela 14, Nim Li Punit may have been a tributary city to the larger, more powerful Lubaantun.

Both ruins are an easy trip from Punta Gorda, and can be seen together in a day.

UNDERSTAND BELIZE

Belize Today

Laid-back Belize lacks the headline-grabbing riots and military coups of its Central American neighbors. Current topics in Belizean newspapers concern a steady stream of crime stories ranging from armed robberies to pedophilia to murder. The big story in 2012 concerned software developer turned fugitive John McAffee's strange adventures on the run from local law enforcement; 2013's big story concerns ongoing tensions with neighboring Guatemala, which still claims wide swaths of Belize south of the Hummingbird Hwy as its own.

Distribution of oil revenue is also a hot topic: Belize is a small-scale oil producer, and debate is pretty fierce over whether the potential benefits of exploration and shipment are worth the risks of environmental damage. The debate is made even more heated by the fact that oil revenue is largely concentrated in a few hands, whereas the consequences of environmental damage will almost certainly damage the country as a whole.

Drugs are still an issue: Belize is a transshipment point for the northbound drug trade, and drug-related crime, though usually not directed towards tourists, is common.

History

Belize before Columbus

Belize certainly earns its place on the Ruta Maya – ruins are everywhere and the Maya population is still thriving, particularly in the southwest. The Maya have been in Belize since the first human habitation. One of the earliest settlements in the Maya world, Cuello, was near present-day Orange Walk. Maya trade routes ran all through the country, and the New River, Río Hondo and Belize River all played an important role in early trade and commerce. Important archaeological sites such as Cahal Pech, near San Ignacio and Lamanai, date from this period.

Pirate's Paradise

Lack of effective government and the onshore safety afforded by the barrier reef attracted English and Scottish pirates to Belizean waters during the 17th century. They operated freely, capturing booty-laden Spanish galleons. In 1670, however, Spain convinced the British government to clamp down on the pirates' activities. Most of the unemployed pirates went into the logwood business.

During the 1780s the British actively protected the loggers' interests, at the same time assuring Spain that Belize was indeed a Spanish possession. But this was a fiction. By this time, Belize was already British by tradition and sympathy, and it was with relief and jubilation that Belizeans received the news, on September 10, 1798, that a British force had defeated the Spanish armada off St George's Caye.

Into the 19th Century

With the diminishing importance of logging, Belize's next trade boom was in arms, ammunition and other supplies sold to the Maya rebels in the Yucatán who fought the War of the Castes during the mid-19th century. The war also brought a flood of refugees from both sides to Belize.

In 1859 Britain and Guatemala signed a treaty that gave Britain rights to the land provided that the British built a road from Guatemala to the Caribbean coast. The treaty still stands, and the road, long ignored, is only now being constructed. Many Guatemalan-made maps show most of Belize south of the Hummingbird Hwy as being part of Guatemala.

Independence & Beyond

The country's first general election was held in 1954, and the People's United Party (PUP) won handsomely on leader George Price's pro-independence platform. On September 21, 1981, the colony of British Honduras officially became the independent nation of Belize.

Since independence, the political landscape has been one of one-term governments (the United Democratic Party, or UDP, being the other player there), corruption scandals, power struggles and broken electoral promises. In 2003 PUP won an unprecedented second term. In 2007, the UDP again took the reigns of power after a campaign promising hope and change, winning again in 2012 in the face of a slowing economy.

The Culture

The National Psyche

Rule number one in Belize: give respect and you'll get respect. Belizeans are friendly and curious by nature, but often wait to see what you're like before deciding how they're going to be. Treat them well, they're bound to do the same for you.

Belize's long association with the UK has left some odd legacies. Perhaps because of this (and the language thing), the country is more closely aligned with the USA than with other Central American countries.

Many Belizeans identify more closely with the Caribbean than they do with Central American culture. For this reason, your bus driver is more likely to be blasting reggae than Latino music, even if the route you're on is going through Maya villages on the Guatemalan border in the Toledo district and there's nary a dreadlock in sight.

People

But don't let the prevalence of reggae music fool you into thinking that Belize's cultural mix is solely Caribbean. While Creoles – descendants of the African slaves and British pirates – make up the country's largest ethnic group, a full one-third of Belize's people are *mestizos* (persons of mixed European and Central American indigenous ancestry), some of whose ancestors immigrated from the Yucatán during the 19th century.

The Maya people of Belize make up about 10% of the population and are divided into three linguistic groups. The Yucatec live in the north near the Yucatán border, the Mopan live in western Belize around the border town of Benque Viejo del Carmen, and the Q'eqchi' inhabit far southern Belize in and around Punta Gorda. In recent years, political refugees coming in from Guatemala and El Salvador have added to Belize's Maya population.

Southern Belize is the home of the Garífuna (or Garinagus, also called Black Caribs). The Garífuna are of South American indigenous and African descent. They look more African, but they speak a language that's much more indigenous and their unique culture combines aspects of both peoples.

Other ethnic groups in Belize include small populations of Europeans, North Americans and East Indians. Though small in percentage, Belize's Mennonite community is considered the backbone of the country's agricultural sector, and much of the dairy and produce you're likely to consume on your travels will have come from a Mennonite farm. Immigration from Taiwan and China is also on the rise.

Arts

Music

Music is by far the most popular art form in Belize, from the reggae-soaked cayes to the ribcage-rattling tunes pumped out on every bus in the country. Styles are much more Caribbean than Latin – after a few weeks you'll be an expert on calypso, soca, steel drums and, quite possibly, reggae.

Punta rock is the official musical style of Belize. Its origins are from the music of the Garífuna – drum heavy with plenty of call and response. This music is designed to get your hips moving. Probably the most famous *punta* rocker is Pen Cayetano (who has collaborated with various artists), who plays in Belize regularly when not touring internationally.

The blending of Garífuna rhythms with reggae dance hall and soca has produced a new generation of *punta* rockers who often rely on electronic accompaniment instead of live musicians. If you want to catch one of these lively shows, keep an eye out for Super G and the Griga Boyz or Poots 'Titiman' Flores.

The *parranda* style, which owes its roots to more traditional Garífuna arrangements with acoustic guitar, drums and shakers is most widely associated with artists such as Paul Nabor and the late Andy Palacio.

Brukdown, another Belizean style, was developed by Creoles working in logging camps during the 18th and 19th centuries. It involves an accordion, banjo, harmonica and a percussion instrument – traditionally a pig's jawbone is used, the teeth rattled with a stick. Wilfred Peters' Boom and Chime band is perhaps the best known of the *brukdown* artists.

The Maya of Belize are off on their own tangent when it comes to music. Most notable here is the flute music of Pablo Collado and the traditional marimba (played with large wooden xylophones, double bass and drum kit) of Alma Beliceña.

Landscape & Wildlife

The Land

Belize is mostly tropical lowland, typically hot and humid for most of the year. Rainfall is lightest in the north, heaviest in the south. The southern rainforests receive almost 4m of precipitation annually, making the south the country's most humid region.

An exception to Belize's low-lying topography and hot, sticky climate can be found in the Maya Mountains, which traverse western and southern Belize at elevations approaching 1000m. The mountains enjoy a more pleasant climate than the lowlands – comfortably warm during the day, cooling off a bit at night.

The country's coastline and northern coastal plain are largely covered in mangrove swamp, which indistinctly defines the line between land and sea. Offshore, the limestone bedrock extends eastward into the Caribbean for several kilometers at a depth of about 16.5ft (5m). At the eastern extent of this shelf is the second-longest barrier reef in the world (after Australia's Great Barrier Reef).

Wildlife

The lush tropical forests contain huge ceiba trees as well as mahogany, guanacaste and cohune palms, all festooned with orchids, bromeliads and other epiphytes and liana vines. Much of the shorelines of both the mainland and the islands are cloaked in dense mangrove.

Baird's tapir is Belize's national animal. The *gibnut* or *tepezcuintle* (paca), a rabbit-size burrowing rodent, is abundant. Other tropical animals include the jaguar, ocelot, howler monkey, spider monkey, peccary, vulture, stork and anteater.

There are 60 species of snake in the forests and waters of Belize, but only a handful are poisonous: the fer-de-lance, the coral snake and the tropical rattlesnake are especially dangerous.

Two types of crocodile call Belize home – the American crocodile, which lives in fresh- and saltwater, and Morelet's croc, which only lives in freshwater and doesn't eat people.

Birdlife is varied and abundant, with hummingbirds, keel-billed toucans, woodpeckers and many kinds of parrots and macaws.

In the seas live turtles, lobsters, manatees and a great variety of fish.

National Parks & Protected Areas

Nearly 40% of land in Belize is protected, either by national organizations or private trusts. Much of the Maya Mountain forest south of San Ignacio is protected as the Mountain Pine Ridge Forest Reserve and Chiquibul National Park. There are smaller parks and reserves, including marine reserves, throughout the country.

Environmental Issues

Belize takes environmental issues quite seriously, and much has been done to protect the endangered species that live within its borders. Species under threat include the hawksbill, green and leatherback sea turtles, the Morelet's and American crocodiles, the scarlet macaw, the jabiru stork and the manatee.

Deforestation for farmland is becoming an issue, leading to loss of habitat, soil erosion and salination of waterways.

Continuing oil drilling in the Cayo district, as well as new exploration in other parts of the country, is also an environmental concern.

SLEEPING PRICE RANGES

The following price ranges refer to a double room with bathroom in high season.

$	Less than BZ$90
$$	BZ$90–BZ$240
$$$	More than BZ$240

SURVIVAL GUIDE

Directory A–Z

ACCOMMODATIONS

Lodgings in Belize vary from very basic to charming to downright decadent. There are plenty of beachfront *cabañas* on the cayes and in seafront towns, jungle huts down south, and hotels ranging from grim to opulent in towns.

Some lodgings offer separate prices for rooms with or without air-con; these are generally the same rooms, but the extra BZ$15 to BZ$30 gets you the air-con remote. Hotels without air-con options are noted in text. Nearly all hotels discourage in-room smoking.

The HI (Hostelling International) is nonexistent in Belize, but there are a few places around offering dorm-style accommodations costing from around BZ$25. This is a good way to save money and meet people.

During the peak seasons (mid-December to April, and June to August) prices can be higher and lodging is harder to find. However, during low season, bargaining is possible.

ACTIVITIES

Snorkeling and diving are best on the cayes. Boats depart Ambergris and Caulker cayes on day and overnight voyages to the best spots.

Inland, horseback riding, canoeing and kayaking, cave-tubing, hiking, bird-watching and archaeology are all possibilities.

BOOKS

Belizean historian Assad Shoman's *13 Chapters in the History of Belize* is a detailed account of the history of the country and tends not to glamorize the colonial past as some other studies do.

Warlords and Maize Men: A Guide to the Maya Sites of Belize, by Byron Foster, is recommended for its descriptions of the lives of the Maya.

Snapshots of Belize: An Anthology of Short Fiction, published in Belize by Cubola Productions, features short stories of past and present Belize.

CLIMATE

Busy season is winter from mid-December to April, with a second peak from June to August. The dry season (November to May) is the best time to travel (although prices can be higher and lodging harder to find). If you do visit in summer (July to November), be aware this is hurricane season. Belize City was badly damaged by hurricanes, with heavy loss of life, in 1931, 1961 and 1978.

EMBASSIES & CONSULATES

Canadian Consulate (☎223-1060; cdncon.bze@btl.net; 80 Princess Margaret Dr, Belize City)

EATING PRICE RANGES

The following price ranges refer to a standard main course.

$	Less than BZ$15
$$	BZ $15–35
$$$	More than BZ$35

German Honorary Consulate (☎222-4369; seni@cisco.com.bz; Western Hwy Mile 3½, Belize City)

Guatemala Embassy (☎223-3150; embbelice@minex.gob.gt; 8 A St, Belize City; ⏲8:30am-12:30pm Mon-Fri)

Honduran Consulate (☎224-5889; 114 Bella Vista, Belize City)

Mexican Consulate (☎223-0193; cnr Wilson St & Newtown Barracks Rd, Belize City)

Netherlands Honorary Consulate (☎223-2953; mchulseca@btl.net; cnr Baymen Av & Calle Al Mar, Belize City)

UK High Commission (☎822-2146; http://ukinbelize.fco.gov.uk; Embassy Sq, Belmopan; ⏲8am-noon & 1-4pm Mon-Thu, 8am-2pm Fri)

US Embassy (☎822-4011; http://belize.usembassy.gov; Floral Park Rd, Belmopan; ⏲8am-noon & 1-5pm Mon-Fri)

GAY & LESBIAN TRAVELERS

Unfortunately, the rules for gay and lesbian travelers in Belize seem to be the same as those in most Central American countries – keep it low key, and look but don't touch. While it's an incredibly tolerant society, underlying Latino machismo and traditional religious beliefs combine to make public displays of same-sex affection a pretty bad idea.

INTERNET ACCESS

All but the smallest of towns have cybercafes, and nowadays even many budget hotels boast wireless access. Expect to pay between BZ$4 to BZ$10 for internet access. Note that Belize is one of a handful of countries that not only blocks Skype, but also several other text-chat programs as well.

INTERNET RESOURCES

Belize Bus & Travel Guide (http://belizebus.wordpress.com/) A regularly updated information site about transportation pertaining to Belize. Very useful!

Belize by Naturalight (www.belizenet.com) Covers just about everything visitors might want to know.

Belize First Magazine (www.belizefirst.com) Information of interest to travelers and expats. Especially helpful are reader recommendations on lodgings, restaurants and tours.

Belize Forums (www.belizeforum.com/cgi-bin/ultimatebb.cgi) An excellent bulletin board with mostly reliable information.

Belize Tourism Board (BTB; www.travelbelize.org) Has comprehensive tourist information.

LANGUAGE

Belize is officially English speaking, and most of its citizens, with the exception of new arrivals from Guatemala, Honduras and Mexico, read and speak English fluently. Creole people speak their own colorful dialect as well as standard English, flavored with the Caribbean's musical lilt. You'll hear Garífuna in the south. Spanish is the first language in the north and in some towns in the west. Other languages in the mix are Maya, Chinese, Mennonite German and Hindi.

MAPS

If you're driving, pick up a copy of Emory King's annual *Driver's Guide to Beautiful Belize,* sold in bookstores and gift shops in Belize City. The guide has basic maps and detailed route descriptions – which is helpful since road markers in Belize are few and far between.

For more detail, the 1:350,000 *Belize,* published by International Travel Maps and Books of Vancouver is widely available throughout the country.

MEDIA

Newspapers & Magazines

Most Belizean newspapers are supported by one political party or another, and as a consequence, much space is devoted to political diatribe. The left-leaning **Amandala** (www.amandala.com.bz) has the largest circulation in the country. The **Belize Times** (www.belizetimes.bz) represents the PUP perspective, while the **Guardian** (www.guardian.bz) goes in to bat for the UDP. The **Reporter** (www.reporter.bz) appears to present the most neutral coverage.

Belize News (www.belizenews.com) has links to most of the country's media. Run out of San Ignacio, **The Review** (www.aguallos.com) is a bimonthly directory for tourism and promotional news widely available throughout the country.

THE TOLEDO HOWLER

The *Howler* is a community-based newspaper with calendars of events, current affairs, restaurant guides, maps, and plenty of other useful information for traveling around the deep south. Best of all, the *Howler* is available in print and in downloadable pdf format at http://belizenews.com/howler.

Radio

LOVE-FM (www.lovefm.com) is the most widely broadcast radio station in Belize, with spots at 95.1 and 98.1 on the dial. It's a beguiling mix of local news, public-service announcements ('Belizeans! Be kind to tourists!') and the world's best (and worst) love songs. KREM at 96.5 plays a more modern selection of music.

MONEY

The Belizean dollar (BZ$) is divided into 100 cents. Coins come in denominations of one, five, 10, 25 and 50 cents, and one dollar; bills (notes) are all of the same size but differ in color and come in denominations of two, five, 10, 20, 50 and 100 dollars. Be sure to carry small denominations if you're heading off the tourist trail.

Prices in the country are generally quoted in Belizean dollars, written as '$30 BZ,' though you will also occasionally see '$15 US.' To avoid surprises, be sure to confirm with service providers whether they are quoting prices in US or Belizean dollars.

ATMs

Belize Bank, Scotia Bank and Atlantic Bank have the most reliable ATMs, nearly all of which accept international cards and are open 24/7. Corozal, Orange Walk, Belize City, Belmopan, San Ignacio, Dangriga, Placencia and Punta Gorda all have banks with ATMs, and there's a Belize Bank kiosk in Hopkins.

Credit Cards

Credit cards are useful, particularly when buying cash from a bank. Visa and MasterCard are the most widely accepted. Some tour operators and many midrange and high-end hotels and restaurants accept cards.

Exchanging Money

Most businesses accept US currency in cash without question. They usually give change in Belizean dollars, though they may return US change if you ask for it. Many also accept US-dollar traveler's checks.

Canadian dollars and UK pounds sterling are exchangeable at any bank, although non-US-dollar traveler's checks are not consistently accepted by Belizean banks. It is difficult, if not impossible, to exchange other foreign currencies in Belize.

Money changers at border-crossing points will change your US cash for Belizean dollars legally at the standard rate of BZ$2 for US$1. If you change money or traveler's checks at a bank, you may get only BZ$1.97 for US$1; they may also charge a fee of BZ$5 (US$2.50) to change a traveler's check.

International Transfers

The fastest way to have money transferred from abroad is with Western Union. It has offices all over the country and charges US$85 for a US$1000 transfer.

OPENING HOURS

Most restaurants in Belize are open from around 8am until 8pm, though some stay open well into the night. Some restaurants cater mostly to workers, and will thus open earlier for breakfast and lunch only. Exceptions – those only open for breakfast and lunch, for example – are noted. Most banks are open 8am to 1:30pm Monday to Thursday and 8am to 4:30pm Friday. Most banks and many businesses and shops close on Wednesday afternoon. Shops are usually open 8am to noon Monday to Saturday and 1pm to 4pm Monday, Tuesday, Thursday and Friday. Some shops have evening hours from 7pm to 9pm on those days as well.

Most businesses, offices and many restaurants close on Sunday.

POST

A postcard sent by airmail to Canada or the US costs BZ$0.30; a letter BZ$0.60. To Europe it's BZ$0.40 for a postcard and BZ$0.80 for a letter. Address poste restante (general delivery) mail to: (name), c/o General Delivery, (town), (district), Belize, Central America. To claim poste restante mail, present a passport or other identification; there's no charge.

Post offices in Belize are open from 8am until 5pm Monday to Friday, and from 8am until 1pm on Saturday. Most branches close for lunch between noon and 1pm.

RESPONSIBLE TRAVEL

Many people come to Belize to appreciate the natural beauty of the country. Belizeans are quite conscientious about maintaining their environment, and visitors should show the same respect.

Don't remove coral or shells from the sea, and mind your fins when snorkeling or diving; coral is fragile and endangered. Avoid buying items made from turtle shell or coral. Don't swim with manatees or attempt to piggyback a sea turtle. You may like it, but they find it very stressful.

Don't take or buy Maya artifacts – it's illegal, and some say you'll be hexed!

Use air-con sparingly. It's expensive and places an enormous strain on local energy reserves. Instead, move more slowly than normal and use fans (or hang out in the lobby of fancy hotels); you'll find that you adjust to the heat after a few days.

When in the jungle, stay on trails to avoid trampling plants. Appreciate wildlife from a distance. Never feed wild animals, including those in the sea.

SAFE TRAVEL

Petty theft is the greatest danger (and annoyance) to travelers in Belize. Take care not to show obvious signs of wealth. Keep a close eye on camera equipment, don't leave valuables in plain view in cars and try to watch your bags when you're on a bus. Belize City has a bad reputation, mostly a hangover from the past, but you should still exercise normal precautions.

Assaults have been known to happen and it is strongly advised that single travelers avoid walking on secondary roads.

If you're driving, be careful – road accidents are a fact of life in Belize, where highways are little more than two-lane roads lacking paved shoulders or dividing lines. Take extra caution when driving in Belize; wear your seat belt, be aware of what's going on in front and behind you, and avoid driving at night if possible. For safety information on hitchhiking, see p282.

STUDYING

Educational opportunities in Belize are as varied and laid-back as the Belizean people themselves. Head to Gales Point Manatee (a charming little village 1½ hours south of Belize City) to learn both Creole drumming and drum making at the Maroon Creole Drum School (p269).

If getting your hands dirty learning sustainable agriculture and solar engineering are more your thing, medium and long-term live-work opportunities are offered at the breathtakingly beautiful Maya Mountain Research Farm (p272) in the mountains west of San Pedro Colombia in the Toledo district.

And down in Punta Gorda, master vegetarian chef Gomier (p271) teaches tofu-making and vegetarian cooking classes at his restaurant on the north end of town.

TELEPHONE

Formerly privately owned, the country's telephone system **Belize Telemedia Ltd** (www.belizetelemedia.net/; BTL) was nationalized in 2009, and is now controlled by the Belizean government. BTL has offices in major cities. Telephones are generally very reliable (and inexpensive) when calling within the country. International calls are sometimes a different story. BTL has an online directory.

Local calls cost BZ$0.25 (US$0.13). Telephone debit cards are sold in denominations of BZ$10, BZ$20 and BZ$50. In some stores you can choose your amount and they just print out a docket with your pin number on it.

Travelers with cell phones can purchase stored-value SIM cards with local numbers for BZ$50 from any BTL shop. This will allow you to make and receive calls, as well as send text messages within Belize. Stored-value phones can be recharged at nearly any shop.

Users of Skype should note that Belize is one of a handful of countries that block this and most other voice-over-internet software. Some internet cafes get around this by using a non-Belize-based satellite provider.

TOURIST INFORMATION

The government-run Belize Tourism Board (p278) maintains tourist offices in Belize City, Punta Gorda and Corozal. They're generally underfunded, but staffed by friendly folks who usually do what they can to answer your questions.

TOURS

A variety of companies offer tailored and themed travel packages for individuals and groups.

Vitalino Reyes (☎602-8975, 832-2640; http://cavetubing.bz; per person BZ$65-100, depending on group size) Both a cave-tubing pioneer and tour guide specializing in package tours combining popular destinations such as Tikal, Altun Ha and the Belize Zoo with cave-tubing expeditions. His tours range throughout the country, and are a great way to get from one end of Belize to the other.

Programme for Belize (PFB; ☎227-1020, 227-5616; www.pfbelize.org; 1 Eyre St, Belize City; ⏲8am-5pm Mon-Fri) The creed of ecotourism has always been to leave nothing but footprints (and light ones at that) and take away nothing but photos and memories. Established in 1988, Programme for Belize is a Belizean nonprofit organization that works with individual conservationists, private landowners and the Belizean government to demonstrate that the long-term benefits of land preservation outweigh the short-term profits of resource exploitation. PFB organizes trips to a number of sites deep within Belize's difficult to reach interior. Check its website for full details.

TRAVELERS WITH DISABILITIES

Unfortunately, Belize's infrastructure for travelers with a disability is virtually nonexistent.

VISAS & DOCUMENTS

Citizens of the EU and many countries (among them Australia, Canada, Mexico, New Zealand, the USA and many Caribbean nations) do not need to obtain a Belizean visa in advance, provided you have a valid passport and an onward or round-trip airline ticket (with a departure from Belize, or any other country in the region). A visitor's permit valid for 30 days will be stamped in your passport at a border crossing or at the airport. One-month extensions are easily obtainable from immigration offices in Belize City, Corozal, Orange Walk, Dangriga, Belmopan, Independence and Punta Gorda. Visa offices are open from 8am until noon and 1pm to 5pm Monday to Friday. The price of an extension is BZ$50; after six months, the price increases to BZ$100.

Also check out the Belizean government website (www.belize.gov.bz) for up-to-date visa information.

VOLUNTEERING

Belize is full of volunteer opportunities; not surprisingly, many of them are environmentally based. Most programs expect volunteers to pay, and costs can vary wildly.

Belize Wildlife & Referral Clinic (www.belizewildlifeclinic.org) Offers short-term internships in wildlife medicine ranging from two to six weeks for veterinary and non-veterinary students for between BZ$1500 and BZ$2000 per week (including lodging, breakfasts and airport transfers). Various scholarships and work exchanges are available for students with sincere interests and skills, and the clinic is flexible and always interested in speaking with sincere potential interns and long-term volunteers.

Help for Progress (www.helpforprogress.interconnection.org) Belizean NGO that works with grass-roots organizations in fields such as education, gender issues, citizen participation and environment.

Plenty International (www.plenty.org) Has opportunities to work with community groups and cooperatives in the Toledo district.

Teachers for a Better Belize (www.tfabb.org) US-based organization that sends volunteers to schools in the Toledo district to train local teachers.

WOMEN TRAVELERS

Men in Belize can be forward and at times aggressive with comments about women's appearance. This can be uncomfortable and embarrassing, but shouldn't be considered threatening. The more modestly you're dressed, the less attention you'll receive.

WORK

Officially you need a resident's visa to get a job in Belize. You might, however, pick up some work on the cayes or in Placencia working in bars, but you'll want to get your paperwork in order if it's anything other than a short-term thing.

Getting There & Away

AIR

Belize City has two airports. All international flights use Philip SW Goldson International Airport (BZE), 9 miles (16km) northwest of the city center.

Major airlines serving Belize include American (from Miami and Dallas), Continental (from Houston), Delta (from Atlanta) and Grupo TACA (from Los Angeles). Most international air routes to Belize City go via these gateways. Grupo TACA also offers direct flights between Belize City and Guatemala City (Guatemala), San Salvador (El

Salvador), and San Pedro Sula (Honduras), as well as connecting flights from Nicaragua, Costa Rica and Panama.

Belize's two national airlines are **Maya Island Air** (www.mayaairways.com) and **Tropic Air** (☎ 226-2012; www.tropicair.com). Though primarily domestic airlines, both also run flights to Belize City, Tikal, and occasionally Guatemala City. Though Tropic Air's Belize City–Cancun flight isn't yet running, the airline claims it will be by mid-2013.

Many travelers save money by flying into Cancún and taking an ADO bus south to Chetumal, crossing into Corozal by land or San Pedro by sea.

BORDER CROSSINGS

Guatemala

Buses run from San Ignacio (Cayo) to Benque Viejo del Carmen, the border town for crossing into Guatemala, nearly every half hour. From the bus station, it's another 3km to the border. A taxi will cost BZ$10.

Two **ADO** (www.ado.com.mx) buses run from Belize City from the water-taxi terminal to Flores, Tikal, El Remate and other points in Guatemala. The morning bus leaves at 9:30am, and the afternoon bus leaves at 2:30pm.

Cross early in the morning to have the best chance of catching buses onward. Get your passport (and, if applicable, your car papers) stamped at the Belizean station, then cross Into Guatemala. The border station is supposedly open 24 hours a day, but try to cross during daylight hours. If you need a Guatemalan visa or tourist card, obtain it before you reach the border.

A bank at either side of the border changes money, but the itinerant money changers often give you a better deal – for US cash. The rates for exchanging Belizean dollars to Guatemalan quetzals and vice versa are sometimes poor.

Both Transportes Pinita and Transportes Rosalita buses westward to Santa Elena–Flores (Guatemala) depart town the Guatemalan side early in the morning. More comfortable minibuses are sometimes available for BZ$12 per person.

To go on to Tikal, get off the bus at El Cruce (Puente Ixlú), 22 miles (36km) east of Flores, and wait for another bus, minibus or obliging car or truck to take you the final 21 miles (35km) north to Tikal.

Several companies operate scheduled and chartered passenger boats between Punta Gorda in southern Belize and Lívingston and Puerto Barrios in eastern Guatemala; see p272 for details.

Honduras

The weekly **Pride of Belize** (☎ 607-9837; http://www.prideofbelize.com/; Caye Caulker Water Taxi Terminal; one-way BZ$145) departs Belize City at 9am each Saturday, reaches Dangriga at 10:30am and Puerto Cortes (Honduras) at 2:30pm. The return trip departs Puerto Cortes on Monday at 10:30am, reaches Dangriga at 3pm and Belize City at 4:30pm.

The **Gulf Cruza** (☎ 523-4045; one-way BZ$120) operates a Friday boat between Placencia and Honduras, leaving Placencia at 9:30am and arriving at Puerto Cortés at 2pm.

Mexico

Corozal is 8 miles (13km) south of the border crossing at Santa Elena–Subteniente López. Most of the frequent buses that travel between Chetumal (Mexico) and Belize City stop at Corozal. Otherwise, hitch a ride or hire a taxi (BZ$20) to get to Santa Elena. Buses running between Corozal and Chetumal will wait for you to complete border formalities.

The daily **San Pedro Belize Express Water Taxi** (☎ 223-2225; www.belizewatertaxi.com) operates one daily boat to Chetumal, Mexico, (one-way/round trip BZ$80/140) departing Caulker at 7:00am, San Pedro at 7:30am and reaching Chetumal around 11am; it returns at 3:30pm.

ℹ Getting Around

Belize is a relatively small country, and all main highways are now fully paved. Bus is the mode of transportation for most Belizeans, so departures are frequent – there's no real need to book ahead, apart from around public holidays. Bus lines are now discouraged from overpacking their buses, so if you don't show up early enough to snag a seat you may be forced to wait for the next bus.

DEPARTURE TAX

Departure taxes and airport fees of BZ$60 (US$30) are levied on non-Belizean travelers departing Goldson International Airport in Belize City for foreign destinations. The departure tax at Belizean land border-crossing points is BZ$30 (US$15). Exit fees by water are the same.

Regardless of how you leave Belize, you'll be required to pay an additional BZ$7.50 (US$3.75), which is the PACT (Protected Areas Conservation Tax). Funds from this tax help to maintain the country's impressive tracts of protected natural areas. For more information, see www.pactbelize.org.

BELIZE BY BOAT

Caye Caulker Water Taxi Association (☎226-0992; www.cayecaulkerwater taxi.com) and **San Pedro Water Taxi** (☎226-2194; www.sanpedrowater-taxi.com) both run boats between Belize City and San Pedro with a stop at Caye Caulker. Boats run more or less hourly from Belize City to Caulker (BZ$24, 40 minutes) then San Pedro (BZ$35, 45 minutes) from 8am to 5:30pm. Boats between Caye Caulker and San Pedro (BZ$20, 45 minutes) run on a similar schedule.

Thunderbolt Travels (☎422-0026, 226-2904) has boats that depart San Pedro at 3pm (most days) for Corozal.

AIR

Belize's two domestic airlines are Maya Island Air (p280) and Tropic Air (p235). Both airlines service two principal domestic air routes: Belize City–Caye Caulker–San Pedro–Corozal; and Belize City–Dangriga–Placencia–Punta Gorda, and both have offices in each municipal airport. Tickets for both airlines can be booked through hotels, tour agencies, or through the local airline offices themselves.

When flying into Belize City, remember to confirm whether you're flying into the municipal or international airport. Unless you've got to catch an onward international flight, the municipal airport is generally cheaper.

The following are the current one-way prices and flight times for Tropic Air to and from Belize Municipal Airport. Both Tropic and Maya Air offer occasional discounts that can reduce the cost of flying in Belize.

Caye Caulker (BZ$95, 20 minutes)
Corozal (BZ$195, 45 minutes flying time, connect through San Pedro)
Dangriga (BZ$107, 15 minutes)
Placencia (BZ$197, 35 minutes)
Punta Gorda (BZ$260, one hour)
San Pedro (BZ$95, 20 minutes)

BOAT

Fast motor launches zoom between Belize City, Caye Caulker and Ambergris Caye frequently every day. Even faster boats run between Corozal and Ambergris Caye, and a handy ferry service runs between Placencia and Mango Creek.

BUS

First the bad news: the dizzying array of companies offering bus services throughout Belize can be intimidating to those used to consistent scheduling. Now the good news: most Belizeans get around by bus, and though it may seem chaotic, getting around in Belize by bus is fairly simple. Most of the bus companies often congregate around central terminals or market areas. A great website keeping tabs on the ever-changing companies, schedules and bus stops (and more) in Belize is http://www.guidetobelize.info.

Outside Belize City, bus drivers will sometimes pick up and drop off passengers at undesignated stops – either tell the driver's helper where you want to get off or flag them down on the roadside to get on. Express buses generally only stop at designated stops.

CAR & MOTORCYCLE

If you plan to drive in Belize, you'll need to bring a valid driver's license from your home country. There are an increasing number of car-rental places in Belize. You must be 25 years or older and pay with a credit card. Depending on the season, rental rates can hit US$80 per day, though long-term discounts are available. See p279 for info about safety on the roads.

HITCHHIKING

Hitching is never entirely safe, and we don't recommend it. Travellers who hitch should understand that they are taking a small but potentially serious risk. That said, it is a common means of getting around for Belizeans, especially in areas with limited bus service. If you chose to hitchhike in Belize, travel in pairs and don't hitch at night. Single female travelers should avoid hitching.

TAXI

Except for in Belize City, you're never really going to need a taxi inside of towns. In Belize City, the fixed fare is BZ$10 in the daytime, within the city. At night, the price gets a bit more flexible (in an upwards direction).

El Salvador

☎503 / POP 6.3 MILLION

Includes ➡

San Salvador.....285
La Costa del Bálsamo.....305
Parque Nacional Los Volcanes.....308
Santa Ana.....309
Ruinas de Tazumal.....314
Ruta de las Flores.....316
Parque Nacional El Imposible.....321
San Miguel.....327
La Unión.....330
Golfo De Fonseca Islands.....332
Suchitoto.....336
La Palma.....341

Best Places to Eat

- ➡ Beto's (p297)
- ➡ R&R (p318)
- ➡ Balompie Cafe (p313)
- ➡ Danilo's (p304)

Best Places to Stay

- ➡ La Tortuga Verde (p333)
- ➡ Hotel Mopelia (p306)
- ➡ Los Almendros de San Lorenzo (p338)
- ➡ Casa ILB (p293)

Why Go?

El Salvador is that little dynamo in Central America that past visitors just keep going on and on about. Glimpses of tropical paradise, lush tracts of pre-industrial national park, colonial splendor astride pristine volcanic lakes, searing colors and a fierce creative vision sit quietly in the shadows of an indomitable local pride. Here you'll find a glorious coastline with world-class waves, a culture-clad capital famed for its nightlife, hard-core war tourism and small-town charm by the plaza-load.

Salvadorans themselves are genuinely hospitable. Once departing en masse, many are now content to return home, the once enviable rite of passage now cut short by global economics and a growing sentiment that home might just be where the fresh start is.

When to Go

San Salvador

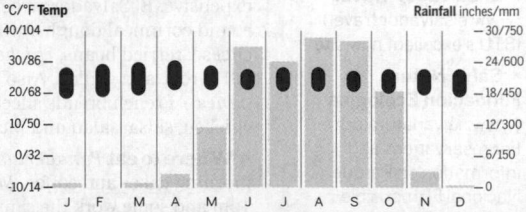

Dec & Jan End of the rain, bright green landscapes, perfect weather. Friendly, relaxed scene.

May–Aug Surf is up (so high you need to know what you're doing).

Jul–Nov Turtle nesting season! Chaperone baby sea turtles to their new homes among the waves.

AT A GLANCE

Currency US dollar (US$)

Languages Spanish, Nahuat

Money US$30 to US$35 per day

Visas US$10 tourist card for citizens of most countries

Time GMT minus six hours

Fast Facts

- **Area** 21,040 sq km (smallest in Central America)
- **Capital** San Salvador
- **Emergency** ☎ 911

Set Your Budget

- **Budget hotel** US$15
- **Bottle of beer** US$1.50
- **Three-hour bus ride** US$1.70
- **Bean-and-cheese pupusa** US$0.40
- **Surfboard rental per day** US$10

Resources

- **El Salvador Travel** (www.elsalvador.travel) ISTU's excellent new site.
- **Salva Natura Fundacion Ecologica** (www.salvanatura.org) For reservations and information on Parque Nacional El Imposible and Parque Nacional Los Volcanes.
- **Search Beat** (www.search-beat.com/elsalvador.htm) Topic-based lists of Salvadoran websites.

Connections

From Guatemala, enter through Anguiatú, San Cristóbal or La Hachadura. From Honduras, El Poy or El Amatillo are your two official options.

Many operators are now offering boat transfers from La Union, El Salvador to Potosi, Nicaragua. The best of these are La Tortuga Verde in El Cuco and Suchitoto Outfitters in Suchitoto. This is a both a time- and cost-effective way to continue your travels through Central America. For more detailed information, see Survival Guide on p352.

FIRST TIME IN EL SALVADOR

El Salvador is small so you don't need a lot of time to see a lot of the country; this itinerary can be done in a week. Start in the capital, **San Salvador**, to get your head around recent history in the excellent museums and galleries. If it's a weekend, party in **Zona Rosa** and **Colonia Escalon**.

Shake off the smog for a night or two in **Suchitoto** then veer west to **Lago Coatapeque** for a dip in the volcano lake. Next scoot along the **Ruta de las Flores**, ducking in and out of coffee plantations and waterfalls. Stay in either **Juayúa** or **Ataco**.

Reach an endpoint in **Tacuba** before braving **Parque Nacional El Imposible** all the way to the Pacific Coast at Barra de Santiago. Cruise along the **Costa del Balsamo**, stopping for a night or two in **Playa El Tunco**, then punch east along the highway to **El Cuco**, where you can arrange your boat to Nicaragua.

Essential Food & Drink

- **What to eat** A typical breakfast includes eggs, beans or *casamiento* (rice and beans mixed together), fried plantains, cheese, tortillas and coffee or juice. *Almuerzo* (lunch) is the largest meal of the day and often the most expensive. El Salvador street food is all about *pupusas*: round cornmeal dough stuffed with a combination of cheese, refried beans, *chicharrón* (pork rinds), or *revuelta* (all three), and grilled. Also popular in the evening are *panes* – French breads sliced open and stuffed with chicken, salsa, salad and pickled vegetables.
- **Where to eat** *Panaderías* usually offer a selection of morning cakes and coffee. Most *pupuserías* open at around 4pm and some work the same sidewalk space for years.
- **What to drink** *Licuados* (fruit drinks made with water or milk); *horchata* (rice milk and cinnamon); and *refresco de ensalada* – a mixed fruit juice served with a spoon for the fruit salad floating on top, sangria style. Note that *refresco,* which means soft drink in many countries, here means lemonade.

SAN SALVADOR

POP 1.8 MILLION (METROPOLITAN AREA)

At first glance San Salvador feels like any midsized American city, with its wide boulevards prey to chain stores, gas-guzzling 4WDs and endless fast-food joints. But lift your head above the consumerist, smog-filled haze, and you'll find a lush volcanic skyline, the finest nightlife in Central America, a vibrant arts scene leaning hard left, and a *centro* crackling with friendly, market-driven chaos.

Delaying your jaunt to the countryside will ensure encounters by the barload with straight-talking, hard-working locals who practice a unique blend of reconciliation, resilience and civic pride. This is an open-hearted city: the taxi driver talks of his two decades in Melbourne; the guerrilla-turned-barber is obsessed with *telenovelas;* the poets, painters and engineers dance all night to heavy metal, reggaetón and *cumbia*, and gossip all morning in a tree-lined city park, fine museum, mall or restaurant. There's enough going on here to extend a trip a day or two – like day trips to the festive Pipil neighborhood of Panchimalco or to El Boqueron – especially if you befriend a few *guanacos* (a nickname for Salvadorans).

Known as *la ciudad de las dos caras de la moneda* (the city of two sides of the coin), San Salvador's huge wealth gap means that crime is a reality. But the hard-core violence is limited to a few neighborhoods east of town, like Soyopango, which is of no interest to most travelers. Follow the lead of locals and move with purpose, which won't be hard when your next brightly painted microbus whizzes around the corner at full throttle.

History

San Salvador was founded in 1525 by the Spanish conqueror Pedro de Alvarado, about 30km northeast of where it now stands, near Suchitoto. It was moved to its present site three years later, and declared a city in 1546. It was here in San Salvador in 1811 that Father José Matías Delgado first called for Central American independence. Once this was achieved, San Salvador became the capital of the united Provinces of Central America from 1834 to 1839 when El Salvador gained its own independence. It has since been the capital of El Salvador.

Natural disasters have beleaguered the city, including more than a dozen major earthquakes (and hundreds of smaller ones). San Salvador was destroyed by tremors in 1854 and 1873, by the eruption of Volcán San Salvador in 1917 and yet again by floods in 1934. The earthquake of October 10, 1986 caused considerable damage, and the most recent on January 13, 2001 also contributed its share.

From assassinations to student protests, San Salvador served as a flashpoint in El Salvador's long civil war. In November 1989, the FMLN's 'final offensive' brought bitter fighting into the city streets. To quell the attack, government forces bombed neighborhoods thought to harbor guerrillas and their supporters. Hundreds of civilians and soldiers on both sides died. After a 26-month stalemate, peace accords were signed in 1992.

Today over a quarter of the population of El Salvador inhabits the metropolitan area of the capital. Though San Salvador produces nearly 65% of the national GDP, unemployment is high and people do whatever they can to get by – vendors of all ages ply the streets and major intersections, selling everything from candy to cell-phone chargers. On buses, vitamins and other supplements are marketed with vigor and creativity.

Sights

City Center

El centro overloads the senses with blaring beats, sputtering traffic and crowds squeezing through the artery of busy markets. The main plaza is **Plaza Barrios**, where local protests – if anticipated – usually begin or end. Two blocks east is **Parque Libertad**, where a winged statue of Liberty holds court.

Catedral Metropolitana CATHEDRAL
(Map p296) The blue-and-yellow-checked dome faces Plaza Barrios and marks the center of the city's street grid. It was damaged by fire in 1956; the renovation was officially completed in 1999 and it is the resting place of Archbishop Oscar A Romero.

★**Iglesia El Rosario** CHURCH
(Map p296; 4a Calle Oriente) If you only see one church in El Salvador – and there are *plenty* to choose from – check out this rare non-colonial structure with a rainbow of colored glass across its belly. The soaring arched roof covers a unique interior adorned with scrap-metal figures. More stone and metal statues

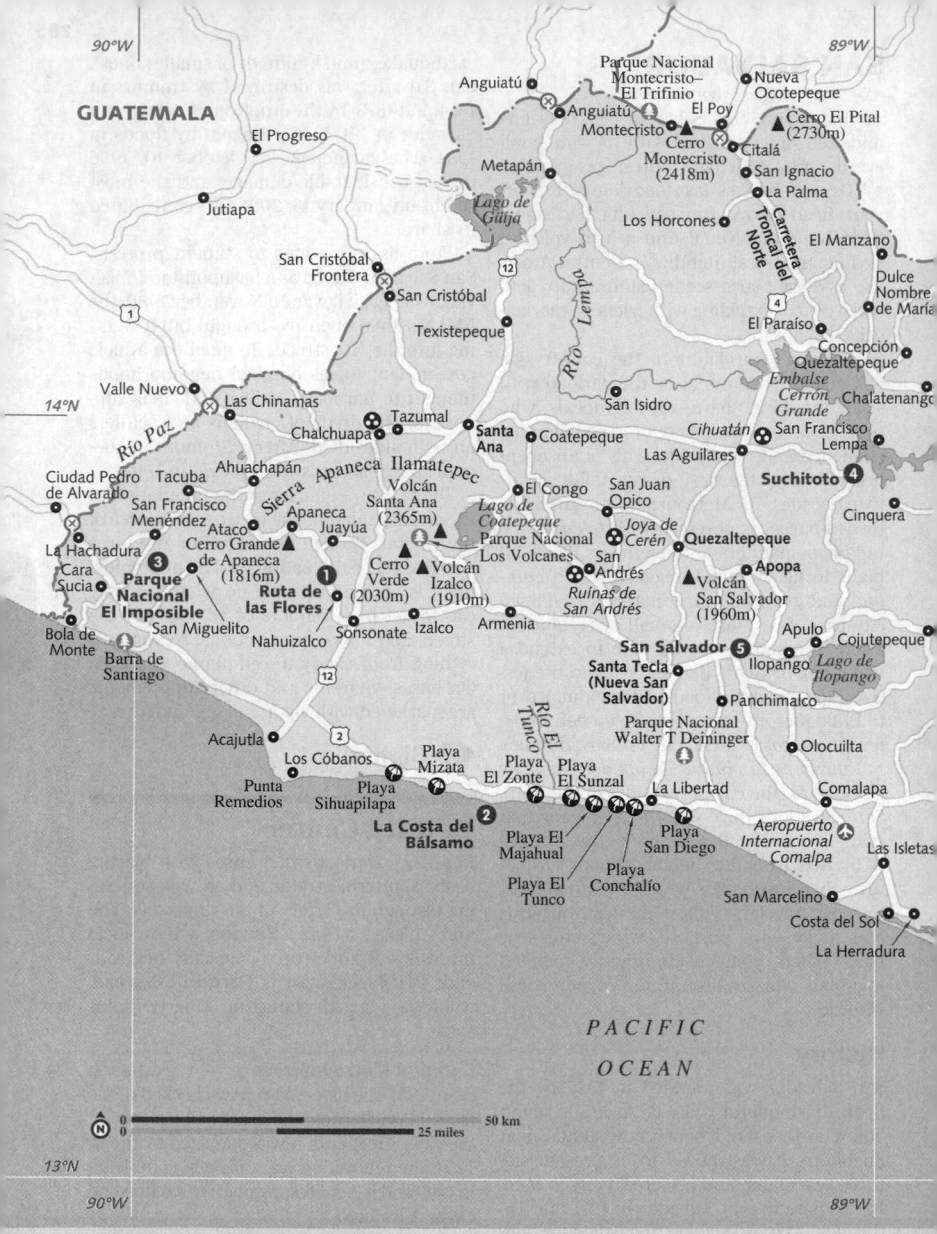

El Salvador Highlights

1 Charge the western highlands on the **Ruta de las Flores** (p316), hiking *fincas* (plantations), stepping into hot springs and chowing at the weekend food fairs.

2 Ride great breaks, string a hammock under the palms and soak up the relaxed atmosphere of **La Costa del Bálsamo** (p305).

3 Steal stunning ridgetop views and splash in river pools, while hiking from the remote backdoor of **Parque Nacional El Imposible** (p316).

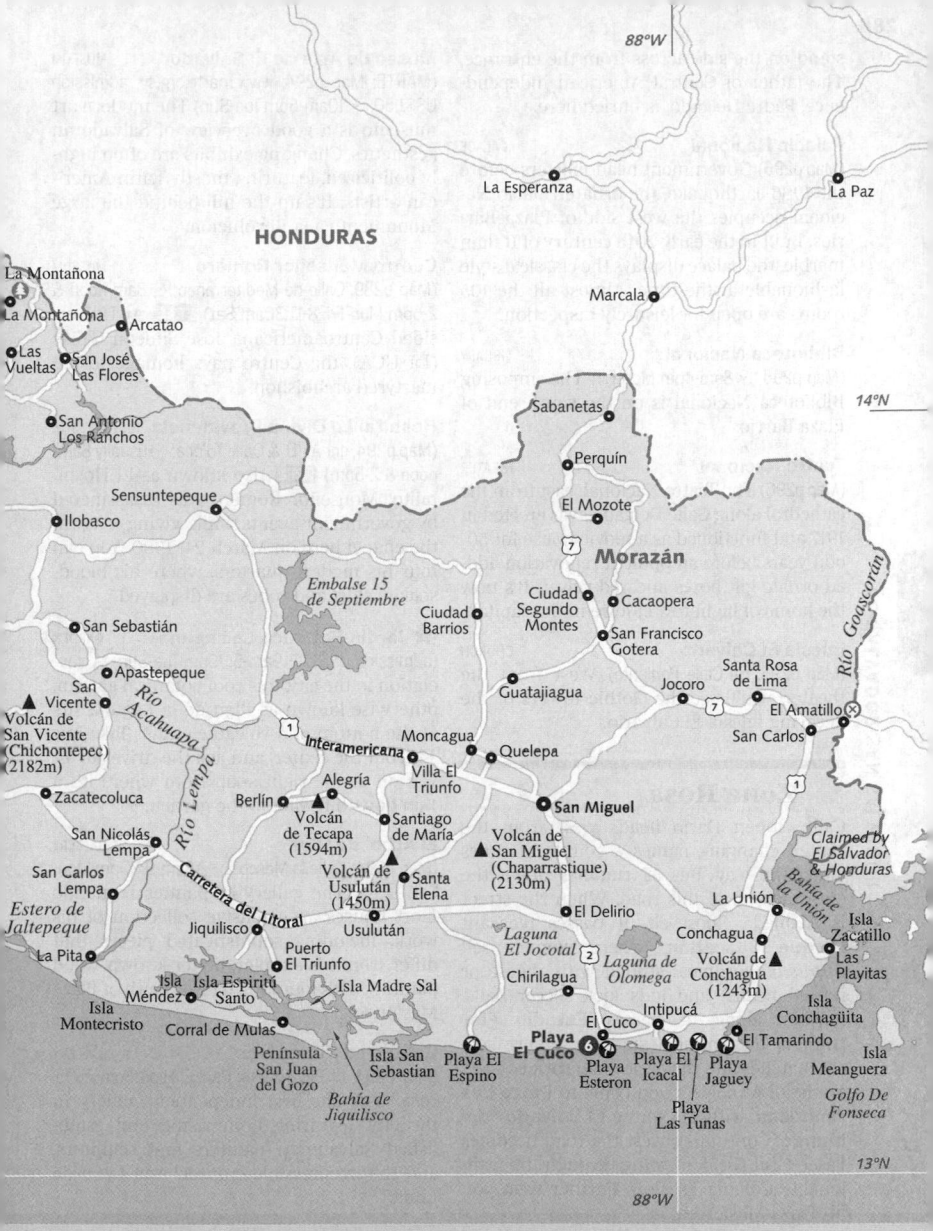

4 Scope the weekend arts scene with the hip *capitalinos* in **Suchitoto** (p336), El Salvador's unofficial cultural capital.

5 Put your hands up in the air for Central America's finest nightlife and museums in **San Salvador** (p285).

6 Take a boat from **Playa El Cuco** near famed Las Flores to the remote islands off Nicaragua (p332).

stand on the side across from the entrance. The father of Central American independence, Padre Delgado, is buried here.

Palacio Nacional PALACE
(Map p296) Government headquarters before the 1986 earthquake, the ornate Palacio Nacional occupies the west side of Plaza Barrios. Built in the early 20th century of Italian marble, the palace displays the classical style fashionable at the time. Almost all the 105 rooms are open for leisurely inspection.

Biblioteca Nacional LIBRARY
(Map p296; ⏲8am-4pm Mon-Fri) The imposing Biblioteca Nacional is on the south end of Plaza Barrios.

Teatro Nacional THEATER
(Map p296) The Teatro Nacional, east from the cathedral along Calle Delgado, was erected in 1917 and functioned as a movie house for 50-odd years before an opulent renovation added ornate gilt boxes and red velvet. It's now the home of highbrow culture in the capital.

Iglesia El Calvario CHURCH
(Map p296; 6a Calle Poniente) West from the theater, you'll see the Gothic towers of the decaying Iglesia El Calvario.

Zona Rosa

Calle Rubén Darío heads west from the center, changing names a couple of times along the way. Bus 52 rumbles down the entire length of this road. When the street is Alameda Roosevelt, it passes pleasant **Parque Cuscatlán**, where women sell *pupusas* (cornmeal stuffed with cheese or refried beans) and kids kick soccer balls. Further along, it passes **Estadio Flor Blanca**, the national stadium, where soccer matches and the occasional rock concert are held. At 65a Av, you come to **Plaza Las Américas**, with the statue **El Salvador del Mundo**. Continuing west the road becomes Paseo Gral Escalón, going through the fashionable Colonia Escalón. Further west you hit Plaza Masferrer.

Museo Nacional de Antropología David J Guzmán MUSEUM
(Map p294; Av La Revolución; admission US$3; ⏲9:30am-5pm Tue-Sun) This outstanding anthropology museum has two floors of well-presented exhibits on the Maya and Salvadoran history, arts and economy. All explanations are in Spanish.

Museo de Arte de El Salvador MUSEUM
(MARTE; Map p294; www.marte.org.sv; admission US$1.50; ⏲10am-6pm Tue-Sun) The modern art museum is a good overview of Salvadoran aesthetics. Changing exhibits are often highly politicized, featuring mostly Latin American artists. It's up the hill behind the large Monumento a la Revolución.

Centro Monseñor Romero MUSEUM
(Map p289, Calle de Mediterraneo; ⏲8am-noon & 2-6pm Mon-Fri, 8-11:30am Sat) FREE At Universidad Centroamericana José Simeón Cañas (La UCA), the Centro pays homage to the martyred archbishop.

Hospital La Divina Providencia HISTORIC SITE
(Map p294; cnr Av 'B' & Calle Toluca; ⏲usually 8am-noon & 2-5pm) FREE Also known as El Hospitalito. Monseñor Romero was assassinated by government agents while giving mass in the chapel here on March 24, 1980. You can tour his modest quarters, where his blood-soaked shirt and robes are displayed.

★ **Jardín Botánico La Laguna** GARDEN
(admission US$1; ⏲9am-5:30pm Tue-Sun) A revelation in the city, this cool botanical garden, otherwise known as Plan de la Laguna sits at the bottom of a volcanic crater. Take bus 44 from the center, and ask the driver to let you off at the right spot, from where it's a 1km downhill walk to the garden.

El Arbol de Dios GALLERY
(Map p294; Calle la Mascota; ⏲9am-9:30pm Mon-Sat) FREE The gallery of painter Fernando Llort houses an extensive collection of his work, including sophisticated pieces that differ from his simpler, better-known wood paintings. It's four long blocks south of Plaza Masferrer.

Galería La Pinacoteca GALLERY
(Map p294; ☎2223-2808; Blvd El Hipódromo 305, Zona Rosa) The best independent gallery in the city, featuring both rising and established Salvadoran painters and sculptors, and the irrepressible curator, Ana Lynn de Lima.

Boulevard de los Héroes

Museo de La Palabra y La Imagen MUSEUM
(Map p294; www.museo.com.sv; 27 Av Norte 1140; admission US$1; ⏲8am-noon & 2-5pm Mon-Fri, 8am-noon Sat) Left-wing activism is documented in black-and-white photographs and

San Salvador

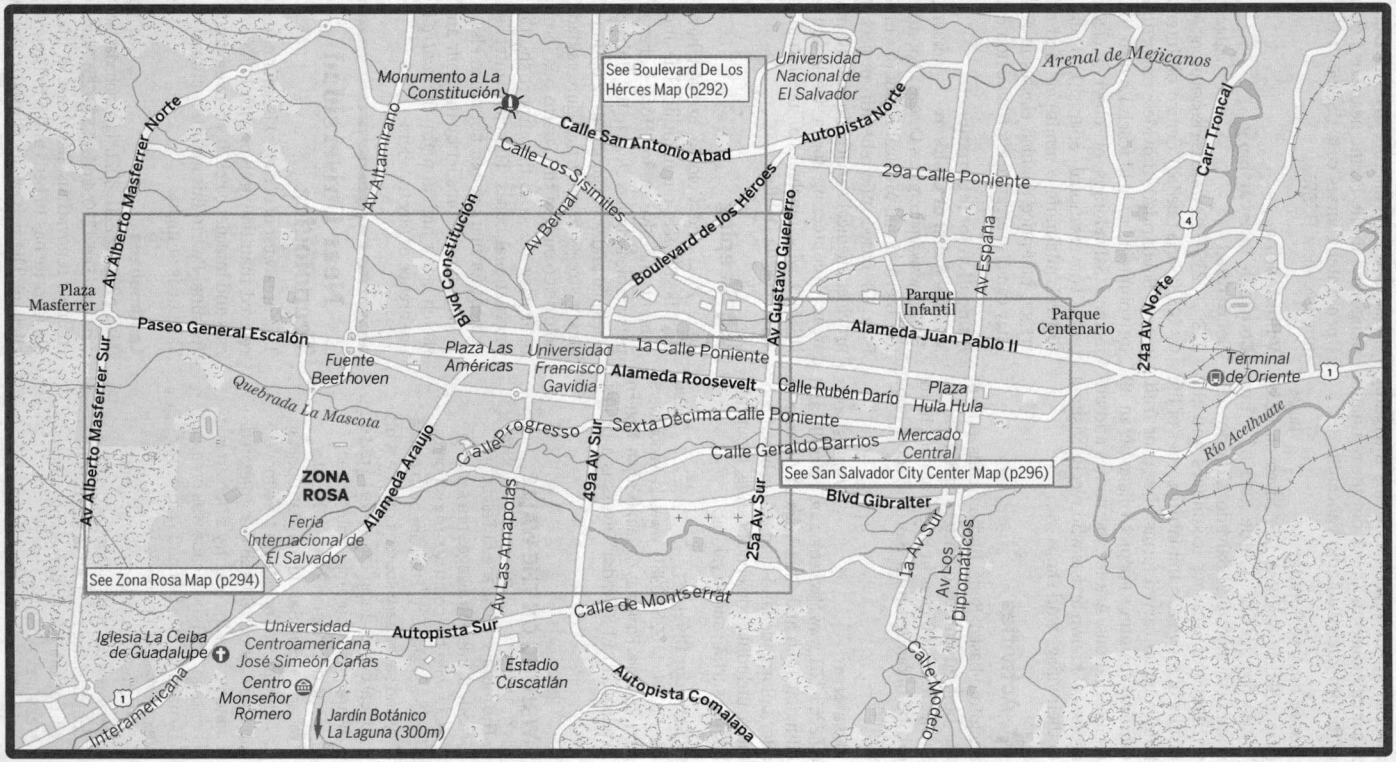

modern art installations at this intriguing inner city museum. Check out the remnants of the pro-guerrilla Radio Venceremos.

Museo de Arte Popular MUSEUM
(Map p292; Av San José 125; admission US$2; ⏲10am-5pm Tue-Sat) A little gem of a museum dedicated to El Salvador's quirky folk art. Discover weaving techniques and the history of *sorpresas,* miniature scenes of life hidden under carved forms of eggs or fruit. *Cuadros* (paintings) depict village life in all its incarnations. Ask for the names and addresses of known artists who receive visitors to their village workshops.

Activities

Suchitoto-based René Barbon runs one of the best adventure outfitters (p337) in El Salvador. His office is in Suchitoto but tours can be organized from San Salvador; book online.

Akwaterra ADVENTURE SPORTS
(☎2263-2211; www.akwaterra.com) Friendly and bilingual Julio and Gabi Vega of Akwaterra offer tailormade land- and water-based ecotours, including horseback riding, mountain biking, surfing and kayaking.

El Salvador Divers DIVING
(Map p294; ☎2264-0961; www.elsalvadordivers.com; 3a Calle Poniente; ⏲9am-6.30pm Mon-Fri, 9am-1pm Sat) El Salvador Divers is a professional dive shop offering dives in Lago Ilopango and in the Pacific near Los Cóbanos. Open-water courses cost US$365, two-tank fun dives cost US$75.

Volunteering

Centro de Intercambio y Solidaridad VOLUNTEERING
(CIS; ☎2235-1330; www.cis-elsalvador.org; Av Bolivar 103, Colonia Libertad) Centro de Intercambio y Solidaridad provides opportunities for volunteers to help teach English to low-income Salvadorans or observe elections (with conversational Spanish). There's a 10-week minimum commitment and teachers get half-price Spanish classes in return. They can also arrange affordable homestays.

Foundation for International Medical Relief of Children VOLUNTEERING
(FIMRC; www.fimrc.org; Las Delicias) Foundation for International Medical Relief of Children is a US-based micro-health project that provides medical services in disadvantaged areas. Volunteering for a week starts at US$500, which includes all meals and lodging at Posada Del Rey I.

Sleeping

Zona Rosa and Colonia Escalón have the city's best hotels and nightlife. Safe and convenient, the Blvd de los Héroes area offers reasonable lodgings close to the Universidad Nacional and some good eating options. The shady streets around the Universidad Tecnológica (south of the Puerto bus terminal) offer easy access to the airport shuttle and international buses. The city center is convenient for markets but not much else.

With most rooms let by the hour and the sketch factor high at night, the *centro* is the preference of few travelers.

WRITING ON THE WALL?

The murals that grace El Salvador's many towns and villages are synonymous with the country's transition to post-war stability. They are both primary and secondary sources of recent historical events and often serve to raise awareness of current social issues.

The destruction in late 2012 of a facade at San Salvador's Metropolitan Cathedral was an unexpected move by the Catholic Church that triggered concerns for the country's rich artistic heritage. That the facade was created by national icon Fernando Llort only exacerbated the shock.

Protests have fallen silent since the event but artists from across the country have resolved to stop political posturing from damaging national treasures.

Near Universidad Tecnológica

This area west of *el centro* is safer and more relaxed than downtown, with lots of cheap eats and internet cafes. It's convenient to the Terminal Puerto Bus for international buses. Take taxis at night.

La Almohada BOUTIQUE $
(Map p292; ☎2211 8021; la-almohada@hotmail.com; Calle Berlín 220; dm/d US$10/25) New owners, new renovations, new lease of life. This old favorite has 16 beds and a fully equipped kitchen. There is a big dining room with

long wood tables and a comfy common TV room, both excellent places for socializing with fellow travelers. Cleanliness is just OK (wear flip flops in the bathrooms) but you can take hot showers and the beds are good. Service is spotty.

Hotel Pasadena II HOTEL $
(Map p296; ☎2221-4786; 3a Calle Poniente 1037; s/d US$13/19) Pasadena II is an affordable choice with friendly service and an array of abodes ranging from cramped and noisy to spacious and quiet. Look around for the better rooms. There's a reasonable restaurant facing the street.

★Hotel Villa Florencia Centro Historico HOTEL $
(Map p296; ☎2221-1706; www.hotelvillaflorencia.com; 3a Calle Poniente 1023; s/d/tr US$14/20/25) The more central of the two Florencia colonial hotels (the other is in Zona Rosa) features terracotta tiles and a sunny courtyard decked with antique bits and bobs. The restaurant next door serves cheap meals (*carne asada*, roasted beef, is US$2) and plays the evening *telenovelas*. There is no hot water in the small, clean rooms but staff are a delight.

Arbol de Fuego HOTEL $$
(Map p296; ☎2275-7065; www.arboldefuego.com; Av Antiguo Cuscatlan, Colonia La Sultana; incl breakfast s US$50-60, d US$60-70; ❄ @) The 20-odd rooms at the eco-conscious 'Fire Tree' are daubed with the full pastel palette and include locally sourced linens, artwork and fresh flowers. There is an impressive urban garden where guests take the yummy breakfasts. It's very popular with long-term visitors to the university.

Boulevard de los Héroes

You can easily walk to bars and restaurants on Calle San Antonio Abad or Blvd Universitario, or down to Metrocentro mall. Buses to the bus terminals, Zona Rosa and the center (and from there, the airport) all pass here.

La Estancia BOUTIQUE $
(Map p292; ☎2275-3381; Av Cortés 216; dm/d US$12/30; @) This unmarked lilac-trim house is known by locals and inveterate shoestringers as an easy choice in a sound neighborhood. The private rooms with TV, bathroom and faux-wood paneling are excellent value: number 5 located on the corner is the pick. Dorms are not the best in town but the communal facilities are very decent.

OFF THE BEATEN TRACK

COSTA DEL SOL

If you fly into San Salvador airport, an alternative to staying in the city is to take a taxi to the boating playground at **Costa del Sol**. Here you'll find empty beaches and some tacky resorts and fish restaurants. Still, it's only 25km from the airport and can make a more peaceful entry to the country than downtown San Sal.

International Guest House HOTEL $
(Map p292; ☎2226-7343; i_guesthouse@hotmail.com; 35a Av Norte 9 Bis; s/d US$18/25; @ ☎) In a street with a few reasonable cheap sleeps, the International is run by the cheerier family and boasts the strongest wi-fi. If it's full, go next door or across the road.

Ximena's Guest House HOSTEL $
(Map p292; ☎260-2481; www.ximenasguesthouse.com; Calle San Salvador 202; dm US$10-12, d US$35; @) Fairly comprehensive renovations may resusciate this cranky old beast from its hazy-gringo trail memories. Regardless, location is excellent and the owners are connected to the travel scene.

Casa de Huéspedes Tazumal HOTEL $$
(Map p292; ☎2235-0156; www.hoteltazumalhouse.com; 35a Av Norte 3; s/d without bathroom US$25/32, with air-con US$27/35, with bathroom US$28/33, with bathroom & air-con US$35/45; @) Tazumal is the pick of a string of small hotels in a quiet suburban street. The friendly managers are astute at handling drop-in guests and the beds are pulled tight with fine linen. Free internet, bottled water and courtyard banter make the price a little fairer.

El Torogoz Casa de Huéspedes HOTEL $$
(Map p292; ☎2235-4172; eltorogoz@telsal.net; 35a Av Norte 7B; s/d incl breakfast US$28/45; @ ❄) Relaxed family hotel with a steady flow of business travelers.

Hostal San José HOSTEL $$
(Map p292; ☎2235-0156; www.sanjosehostal.com; Blvd Universitario 2212; s/d US$35/45; @) The Hostal San José is a no-fuss mainstay of the independent travel scene in San Sal that is tiring a little but still provides sincere

Boulevard De Los Héroes

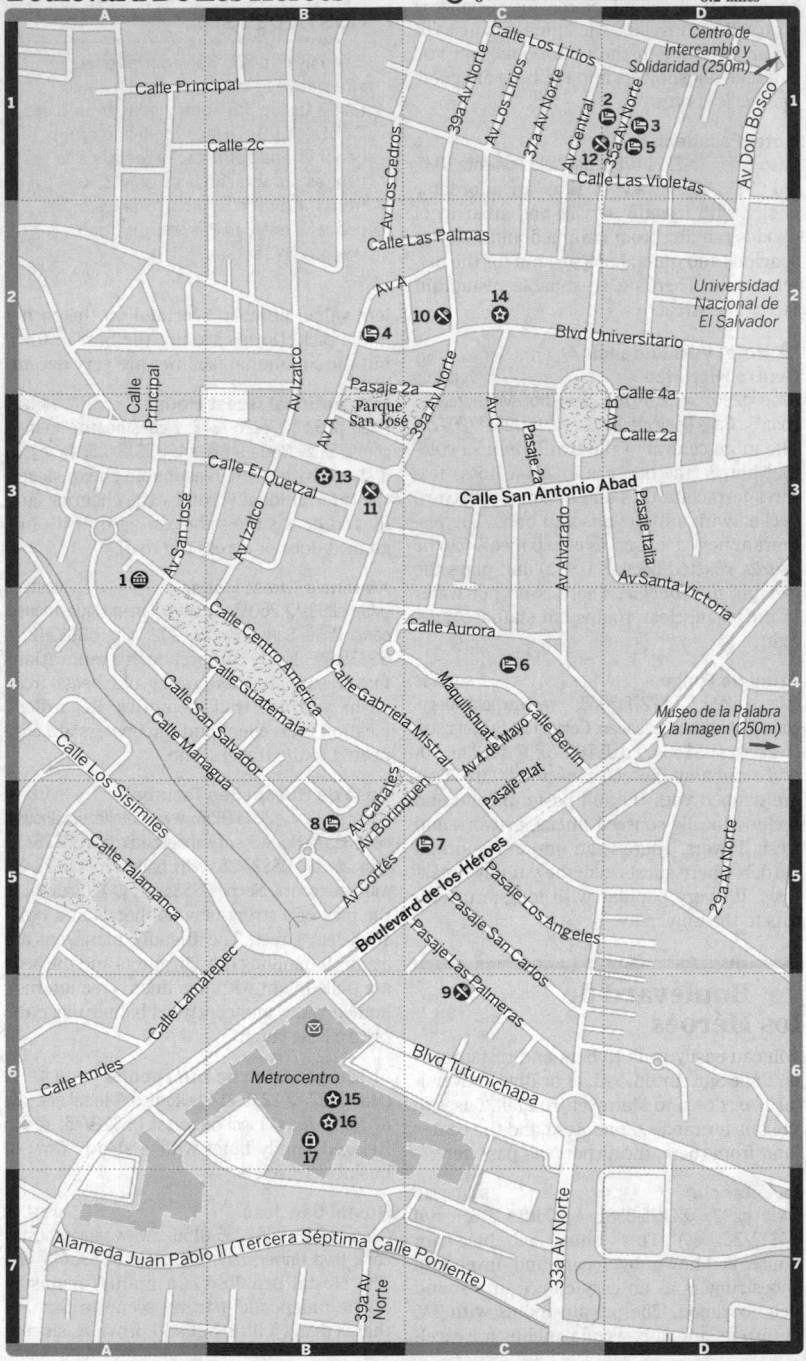

Boulevard De Los Héroes

Sights
1 Museo de Arte Popular A3

Sleeping
2 Casa de Huéspedes Tazumal D1
3 El Torogoz Casa de Huéspedes D1
4 Hostal San José B2
5 International Guest House D1
6 La Almohada C4
7 La Estancia C5
8 Ximena's Guest House B5

Eating
9 El Sopón Típico C6
10 Las Fajitas C2
11 Pupusería La Ceiba B3
12 Salvatore's C1

Entertainment
13 Café La 'T' B3
14 Cine Reforma C2
15 CineMark B6
16 Teatro Luis Poma B6

Shopping
17 La Ceiba Libros B6

family service. The bathrooms are spotless, breakfast is delicious and there's a free bus pick-up service.

Zona Rosa & Colonia Escalón

Hostal Cumbres del Volcan HOSTEL **$$**
(☎2207-3705; www.cumbresdelvolcan.com; 85 Av Norte 637; r US$35-40; ❄ 📶) This super little addition to the Escalón neighborhood is run by an erstwhile Californian chap. The five rooms are well spaced, comfortable and private. There's free wi-fi, plenty of security and anything from the kitchen will do.

★Hotel Villa del Angel BOUTIQUE HOTEL **$$**
(☎2223 7171; www.villadelangelhotel.com; 71 Av Norte 219, Colonia Escalón; d incl breakfast US$63-69) In a quiet street near one of the city's better shopping malls, this is one of the best-value midrange places in San Salvador. Rooms are huge for the price and the English-speaking hosts are very hospitable.

★Casa ILB LUXURY HOTEL **$$$**
(Map p294; ☎2528-4200; www.casailb.com; Boulevard del Hipódromo 605, Colonia San Benito; ste from US$108; P ❄ 📶) If the grotty trail gets too much and you just need to sort your life out a bit, then please stay at Casa ILB. It will make you cancel those ridiculous plans to swim in volcanic lakes with feral strangers and move back to that empty loft apartment and get on with things. The five finest suites in San Salvador (pick 1, 2 or 3) are complemented by a world-class gin bar, restaurant and hip artwork dripping off the walls.

Hotel Villa Florencia Zona Rosa BOUTIQUE HOTEL **$$**
(Map p294; ☎2257-0236; www.hotelvillaflorencia.com; Av La Revolución; s/d/tr incl breakfast US$43/55/75; P ❄ @) Top location around the corner from the Zona Rosa posh shops, this Villa Florencia is earnest and faux-gold and the rooms are too small, but the writing desks give the tightness a sense of purpose. The stone courtyard is sweet for breakfast.

Hotel Morrison HOTEL **$$**
(Map p294; ☎2223-7111; www.hoteldelaescalon.com; 1 Calle Nueva 3999; r from US$45; P ❄ 📶 ≋) The Morrison is a very welcoming cross between bed and breakfast and business hotel. The owner has extensive experience living out of a suitcase and appreciates the value of unruffled hospitality and affordability. The rooms feel a bit like your auntie's spare bedroom but that's not a bad thing. Breakfast is divine and the location is suitable for short walks.

La Posada del Rey I HOTEL **$$**
(☎2264-5245; www.posadadelreyprimero.com; Pasaje Dordelly, Colonia Escalón; s/d/tr US$47/70/93; ❄ @ ≋) The proprieteress is a delight at this smart hotel in a pleasant area for walking. Rooms are busy with carved furniture, blue-washed walls and ornate, comfortable bedding. The pretty courtyard restaurant is better suited to tour groups but you can do bombs in the tiny pool while you wait for breakfast.

Suites Las Palmas APARTMENTS **$$**
(Map p294; ☎2250-0800; www.hotelsuiteslaspalmas.com.sv; Blvd El Hipódromo, Colonia San Benito; r/ste incl breakfast US$55/75; ❄ @ ≋) Apartment living in the heart of Zona Rosa is a great option for a small group, especially if you plan to hit the excellent nightlife across the road. The best have king-sized beds, plus a generous living area with fold-out sofas and flashy bathrooms. Views from the rooftop pool are outstanding.

Zona Rosa

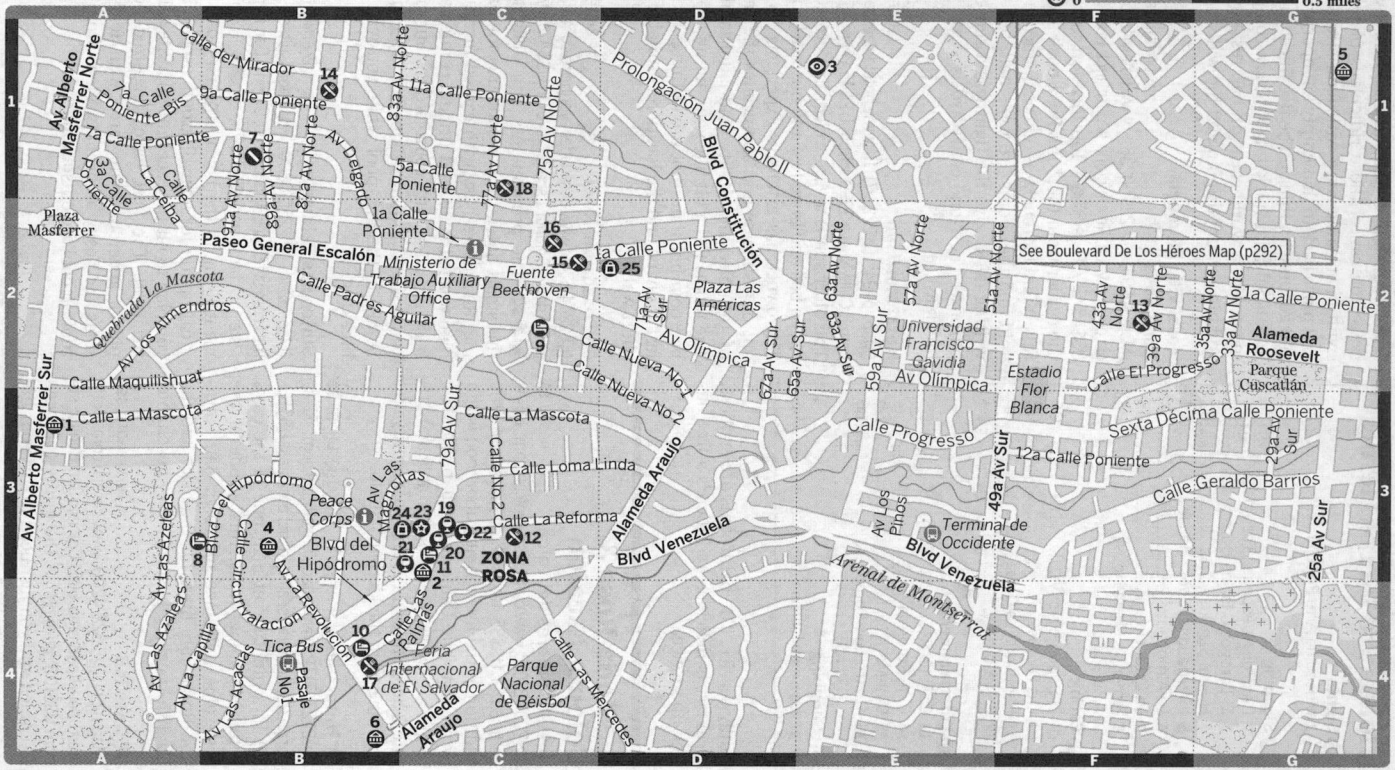
0 1 km
0 0.5 miles
See Boulevard De Los Héroes Map (p292)
Av Alberto Masferrer Norte
Av Alberto Masferrer Sur
Calle del Mirador
7a Calle Poniente Bis
9a Calle Poniente
7a Calle Poniente
3a Calle Poniente
Calle La Ceiba
Plaza Masferrer
Paseo General Escalón
Quebrada La Mascota
Av Los Almendros
Calle Maquilishuat
Calle La Mascota
91a Av Norte
89a Av Norte
87a Av Norte
Av Delgado
83a Av Norte
11a Calle Poniente
5a Calle Poniente
1a Calle Poniente
Ministerio de Trabajo Auxiliary Office
Calle Padres Aguilar
Fuente Beethoven
77a Av Norte
75a Av Norte
Prolongación Juan Pablo II
Blvd Constitución
1a Calle Poniente
Plaza Las Américas
71a Av Sur
Av Olímpica
Calle Nueva No 1
Calle Nueva No 2
63a Av Norte
63a Av Sur
67a Av Sur
65a Av Sur
57a Av Norte
59a Av Sur
51a Av Norte
Universidad Francisco Gavidia
Av Olímpica
Estadio Flor Blanca
43a Av Norte
39a Av Norte
35a Av Norte
33a Av Norte
1a Calle Poniente
Alameda Roosevelt
Parque Cuscatlán
Calle El Progresso
Sexta Décima Calle Poniente
29a Av Sur
Calle Progresso
12a Calle Poniente
49a Av Sur
Calle Geraldo Barrios
25a Av Sur
73a Av Sur
Calle La Mascota
Calle Loma Linda
Calle No 2
Calle La Reforma
Alameda Araujo
Blvd Venezuela
Av Los Pinos
Terminal de Occidente
Arenal de Montserrat
Av Las Magnolias
Peace Corps
Blvd del Hipódromo
Av Las Azaleas
Calle Circunvalación
Av La Revolución
Av La Capilla
Av Las Palmas
Calle Las Palmas
Tica Bus
Pasaje No 1
Feria Internacional de El Salvador
Parque Nacional de Béisbol
Calle Las Mercedes
ZONA ROSA
1
2
3
4
5
6
7
8
9
10
11
12
13
14
15
16
17
18
19
20
21
22
23
24
25

Zona Rosa

Sights
1 El Arbol de Dios A3
2 Galería La Pinacoteca C3
3 Hospital La Divina Providencia E1
4 Museo de Arte de El Salvador B3
5 Museo de La Palabra y La Imagen G1
6 Museo Nacional de Antropología David J Guzmán B4

Activities, Courses & Tours
7 El Salvador Divers B1

Sleeping
8 Casa ILB A3
9 Hotel Morrison C2
10 Hotel Villa Florencia Zona Rosa B4
11 Suites Las Palmas C3

Eating
12 Citron C3
13 El Cafe de Don Pedro F2
14 Las Cofradías B1
15 Le Croissant C2
16 Rustico Bistro C2
17 Shen Zhuan B4
18 Típicos Margoth C1

Drinking & Nightlife
19 Caminito Chocos C3
20 Jungle C3
21 Los Rinconcitos C3
22 Republik C3

Entertainment
23 Zanzibar C3

Shopping
24 Bookmarks C3
25 Galerías Escalón D2

Eating

City Center & Around

The center has plenty of eateries but few standouts.

Sidewalk Comedores SALVADORAN $
(Map p296; mains US$1-3) For a quick bite check out the sidewalk *comedores* a block west of Plaza Barrios, dishing up *panes de pollo* (big chicken sandwiches) and *bistec encebollada* (onion grilled beef).

Le Croissant PATISSERIE $
(Map p294; 1a Calle Poniente 3883, Colonia Escalón; pastries US$1-3; ⏲7:30am-6:30pm) Chain patisserie worth following.

Café Maquilishuat TÍPICA $
(Map p296; Simáu Centro, 1st fl; mains US$2-6; ⏲7:30am-7pm) The pick of the inner-city eateries is this super-busy, pristine *típica* joint with a steady flow of diners enjoying daily meat and dessert specials and huge glasses of *horchata* (malted milk) and *atole* (cinnamon rice milk).

Típicos Margoth TÍPICA $$
(Map p294; ☎2263-3340; 77a Av Norte, Colonia Escalon; mains US$5-8; ⏲7am-9.30pm) Four locations across the city are always packed at this classic Salvadoran family restaurant that offers a fun way to initiate yourself in Salvadoran cuisine. Try *lorocas, pupusas y arroz, ayote* and the famous *pan con pavo* (turkey sandwich).

El Cafe de Don Pedro SALVADORAN $$
(Map p294; ☎2260-2011; 39 Av Norte y 2 Calle Oriente; mains US$4-8; ⏲7am-4pm) The Roosevelt branch of this family restaurant is impeccable. Homemade dishes like *libra de lomo rollizo* (barbecued ribs) or delicious *pinchos* (skewered meat and vegetables) are served promptly and with loads of sides. For breakfast specials, try the bacon-covered Aztec or the gooey Holandes. You can finish off with a glass of beer or choose from the sweet trolley.

Las Cofradías SALVADORAN $$
(Map p294; ☎2264-6148; Calle de Mirador, Colonia Escalón; buffet US$8; ⏲dinner) *Tradición del campo* and other Salvadoran specialties.

Shen Zhuan VEGETARIAN $$
(Map p294; ☎2243-0424; 5 Av La Revolucion; mains US$5-10; ⏲11am-10pm Tue-Sun; ✎) Lots of lotus root and mock meat dishes are served by a charming elderly Taiwanese couple who specialise in vegan fare (though egg is available). Prices are very reasonable.

Restaurante Hong Kong CHINESE $$
(Map p296; 9a Av Sur; mains US$4-9; ⏲lunch & dinner) Negotiate the sticky floor and the 100-capacity seating plan to find 10 bored waitresses, blaring televisions and a long tradition of no-fuss universal Chinese food. The vegetable chow mein (US$5) is pretty good, as are the *licuados* (fruit shakes).

Boulevard de los Héroes

Calle San Antonio Abad has the best dining options but the many spots in and around the Metrocentro mall are clean and convenient.

San Salvador City Center

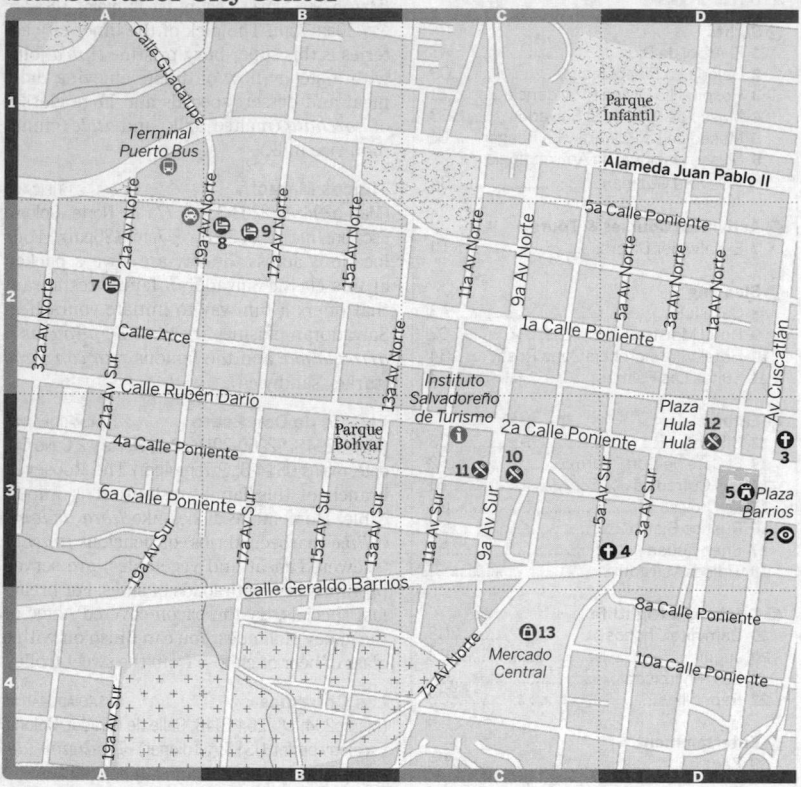

Pupusería La Ceiba PUPUSAS $

(Map p292; Calle San Antonio Abad; mains US$1-3; ⏲Mon-Sat) Whether you're grabbing a dollar breakfast of tamales, coffee and eggs or downing a few hot *pupusas,* this corner cafe is a bargain.

El Sopón Típico SALVADORAN $$

(Map p292; cnr Pasajes las Palmeras & los Almendros; mains US$5; ⏲10:30am-9pm) Soups and *antojitos* (appetizers) are the reasons to frequent this bustling corner restaurant. Gather around the grill with local families and watch the traffic go by.

Las Fajitas MEXICAN $$

(Map p292; Blvd Universitario; mains US$4-8; ⏲lunch & dinner) Popular Tex-Mex with an open kitchen.

Salvatore's ITALIAN $$

(Map p292; 35a Av Norte; mains US$4-7; ⏲lunch & dinner) Quality pizza and pasta.

Rustico Bistro BURGERS $$

(Map p294; ☎2224-5656; 3 Calle Poniente; burgers US$10-12) The capital has a hot new burger haunt that takes its inspiration from further north. The pulled-pork sandwiches with tamarindo sauce almost trump the massive burger list. Almost. Stick around for dessert.

Caminito Chocos ARGENTINE $$

(Map p294; ☎2223-6807; Calle La Reforma; mains US$7-9) This rowdy boutique beer hall heaves with drinkers and serves huge Argentine meat sandwiches and greasy, barbecued varietals.

La Tour FRENCH FUSION $$

(☎2101-9292; www.latour-bistro.com; Centro Comercial 13G Mascota, Calle La Mascota, Colonia Escalón; mains US$8-15) This understated French bistro was the pride of the many locals who swore by its food and service. When we visited we thanked them in the crepes, we bless-

San Salvador City Center

Top Sights
1 Iglesia El Rosario E3

Sights
2 Biblioteca Nacional D3
3 Catedral Metropolitana D3
4 Iglesia El Calvario D3
5 Palacio Nacional D3
6 Teatro Nacional E3

Sleeping
7 Arbol de Fuego A2
8 Hotel Pasadena II B2
9 Hotel Villa Florencia Centro Historico B2

Eating
10 Café Maquilishuat C3
11 Restaurante Hong Kong C3
12 Sidewalk Comedores D3

Shopping
13 Mercado Central C4
14 Mercado Ex-Cuartel F3

ed them in the *viandes* and we chugged to their health from a carafe of house plonk.

★Beto's SEAFOOD $$
(85 Av Norte Pasaje Dordello No 4407, Colonia Escalón; mains US$7-18) This new Escalón franchise of the country's most affordably posh seafood restaurant is great for watching people eat the heads off miniature fish and sip beer like it's some far more exotic and expensive cocktail.

Citron FUSION $$$
(Map p294; ☎2208-4000; Calle La Reforma 220, Zona Rosa; mains US$15-20) If you've got a special occasion to celebrate while on the road then throw some bills down at this converted Zona Rosa home and treat yourselves to citrus-inspired cocktails, seafood and original chef creations. Much of the produce comes from the garden out back.

Drinking & Nightlife

Republik BAR
(Map p294; ⏲3pm-1am Wed-Sun) The hottest bar when we visited was easily Republik. Brass knobs and faux-oak panels are scratched up in time to the sexy basslines and soulful live sets in the back half of the week. Good *mojitos* (US$5) too.

La Ventana BAR
(☎2264-4885; 83 Av Norte 510; mains US$5-12; ⏲noon-midnight Mon-Thu, noon-1am Fri & Sat, 8am-10pm Sun) An unpretentious bar-restaurant that works just as well for an evening of European ales or a smart dinner of soups, crepes and other international fare. The modern sculpture and crowd are equally unpredictable.

Los Rinconcitos BAR
(Map p294; Blvd del Hipódromo 310; ⏲6pm-1am Wed-Sat) A sophisticated party-set lingers over stiff drinks and tapas at this former karaoke bar that sees Latin rock steal the stage on weekends. Head out back for some intimate outdoor entertainment.

Jungle NIGHTCLUB
(Map p294; ☎2124-7341; Blvd del Hipódromo; ⏲10pm-7am Thu-Sat) When only the most raucous nightclub will do. It opens late and closes in time for *desayuno* (breakfast).

A DAY IN THE ART OF A CITY

Aside from the usual museums and galleries, visit the cathedral downtown for the image of the Madre del Salvador, a 17th-century polychrome wooden sculpture that was a gift of Queen Sofia of Spain, and an extraordinary tabernacle with images taken from the first engravings done in America. If you visit the Jardín Botánico La Laguna in Antiguo Cuscatlán you can walk up to the charming town plaza, which has a nice church and famous *pupuserías*. The **Sala Nacional de Arte** is at Parque Cuscatlán – it always has interesting exhibitions. Finally, if you're a bit adventurous, then visit sculptor **Guillermo Perdomo's studio** in the artist enclave of Panchimalco, just outside the city on the slopes of Cerro Chulo. Here you will also find Casa Taller Encuentros, home to painter Miguel Angel Ramirez.

La Cueva BAR
(☎2243-7155; Multiplaza, Calle El Pedregal; ⏲7pm-late) Tiny bar with live music on weekends, intimate seating arrangements and a buzzing outdoor section.

Scape & Milenio BAR
(Condominios Juan Pablo II; ⏲9:30pm-1am Thu-Sat) Two gay bar-discos in the same building. On Prolongación Juan Pablo II.

Café La 'T' CAFE
(Map p292; Calle San Antonio Abad 2233; ⏲10am-9:30pm Mon-Wed, 10am-11pm Thu-Sat) This is a little lefty cafe with live music (jazz or folk) on some Fridays (US$2) and free films on Wednesday and Thursday at 7:30pm. There's light food, beer and wine, and fine coffee.

Zanzibar LIVE MUSIC
(Map p294; ☎2279-0833; Centro Commercial Basilea; ⏲11am-1am) Latin fusion, mostly.

Entertainment

Check out the weekly concert and event listings in *Diario de Hoy*, El Salvador's most popular newspaper.

Hollywood films with Spanish subtitles dominate the theaters, while some bars have alternative movie nights. Major newspapers have schedules, as does www.multicinema.com.sv.

Cine Reforma CINEMA
(Map p292; ☎2225-9588; Blvd Universitario) Discounts on random Tuesdays.

CineMark CINEMA
(Map p292; ☎2261-2001; Blvd de los Héroes, Metrocentro, 3rd fl; admission US$3) The best place to catch a movie.

Teatro Luis Poma THEATER
(Map p292; ☎2261-1029; Metrocentro; admission US$5) A modern playhouse with great offerings, strangely set at the mall.

Shopping

Mercado Ex-Cuartel MARKET
(Map p296; Calle Delgado; ⏲7:30am-6pm Mon-Sat, 7:30am-2pm Sun) The former army barracks is now the Mercado Ex-Cuartel where *artesaños* from across the country hawk their wares – hammocks and embroidered fabrics are the go.

Mercado Central MARKET
(Map p296; Calle Delgado; ⏲7:30am-6pm Mon-Sat, 7:30am-2pm Sun) The Mercado Central is the locals' favorite for clothes and electronics.

Galerías Escalón SHOPPING CENTER
(Map p294; Paseo General Escalón; ⏲8am-8pm) Galerías Escalón boasts three air-conditioned levels of upscale clothing and jewelry stores, electronics stores, cell-phone offices and banks. Grab some sushi at the swish food court then catch a movie at the Cinépolis mega-cinema.

La Gran Vía MALL
A very pleasant mall experience, with good nightclubs and restaurants.

Bookmarks BOOKS
(Map p294; www.bookmarks.com.sv; Blvd del Hipódromo, Centro Commercial Basilea) Good range of English-language fiction and guidebooks (including Lonely Planet).

Centro de Intercambio y Solidaridad BOOKS
(CIS; Av Bolivar No 103, Colonia Libertad) This center for peace and social justice has a good library for students and volunteers. Can also arrange homestays and Spanish classes.

La Ceiba Libros BOOKS
(Map p292; Blvd de los Héroes, Metrocentro, 1st fl) Stock up on Salvadoran history and literature in Spanish here.

Orientation

San Salvador follows the same grid pattern as most Central American cities. Unfortunately, signage is sparse in the central area (check for names on the street curbs). From the zero point at the cathedral, Av España goes north and Av Cuscatlán south; Calle Arce runs to the west and Calle Delgado to the east.

Avenidas (avenues) run north–south, and change from Sur (South) to Norte (North) when they cross the major east–west artery (Calles Arce and Delgado). Likewise, avenues are odd- or even-numbered depending on whether they are east or west of the north–south artery (Avs Cuscatlán and España).

So, 5a Av Sur is south of Calle Arce and west of Av Cuscatlán (because it's odd-numbered). Calles (streets) are similarly ordered, only using Oriente (East; abbreviated 'Ote') and Poniente (West; abbreviated 'Pun' or 'Pte').

It's confusing to the visitor at first, but you'll quickly learn the orderliness of it. The odd/even thing can be tricky, ie 25a Av is one block from 27a Av, but it is more than 25 blocks from 26a Av!

From the city center, 1a Calle Poniente and Calle Rubén Darío, to the north and south of Arce respectively, are the main roads to the wealthier west.

Information

DANGERS & ANNOYANCES

Crime is still a serious problem in San Salvador. Travel light, avoid wearing flashy jewelry and watches, and stay aware of your belongings, especially on buses, in market areas and among street crowds. If you are robbed, just hand over the goods.

Always take taxis after 8pm. The center is off-limits for walking around at night, along with Parque Cuscatlán. Ample nightlife lines Calle San Antonio Abad and Blvd de los Héroes, but take a cab to get to your hotel, even if it's just around the corner.

Pollution is a consistent pest, seemingly set in place by the surrounding mountains. Thick vehicle exhaust, especially from buses, can leave you with runny eyes and a sore throat.

Accidents between cars and pedestrians are frequent and frightening. Be extra careful crossing the street. Pedestrians don't have the right of way and no car will chivalrously cede it to you.

EMERGENCY

Police (☎2261-0630; Calle Berlin; ⏲24hr)

IMMIGRATION

Immigration Office (Direccíon General de Migracíon y Extranjería; ☎2202-9650, 2221-2111; Paseo General Escalón; ⏲9am-5pm Mon-Fri, 9am-1pm Sat) For visa renewal and other immigration matters.

INTERNET ACCESS

Internet cafes are plentiful along Calle Arce, near the Universidad Tecnológica. Around Blvd de los Héroes also check out **PC Station**.

Ciber Snack (cnr 2a Av Sur & 4a Calle Oriente; per hr US$1; ⏲7:30am-6:30pm Mon-Sat) The smoothest operator by a long way; it's not every day you can enjoy a tropical banana *licuado* while you check your email.

Cybercafé Genus (Av Izalco 102A; per hr US$1; ⏲9am-11pm Mon-Fri, 10am-8pm Sat & Sun) One of the only internet cafes in town that stays open late. CD burning available.

LAUNDRY

Lavapronto (Calle Los Sisimiles 2944; ⏲7am-6pm Mon-Fri, 7am-5pm Sat) Same-day laundry service available.

MEDICAL SERVICES

Hospital Bloom (☎2225-4114; cnr Blvd de los Héroes & Av Gustavo Guerrero) Public hospital with long lines. Specializes in children.

Hospital Diagnóstico Escalón (☎2264-4422; 3a Calle Poniente) Recommended by the US embassy.

MONEY

Banks and 24-hour ATMs are found throughout the capital, issuing US dollars.

Banco Credomatic Branches located in the *centro* and next to the Super Selectos supermarket, in the Centro Comercial San Luis, off Calle San Antonio Abad. Changes traveler's checks or gives cash advances on MasterCard.

DON'T MISS

SANTA TECLA

Also known as New San Salvador, Santa Tecla is effectively a satellite town roughly 15km from the capital. Inspired development, however, has led to a surge of domestic visitors to the area primarily around **Paseo El Carmen**, a restored colonial street filled with classy bars, restaurants, cafes and antique stores. San Salvador can feel a little overwhelming at times with the threat of crime and shopping malls and urban sprawl killing a good night out. In Santa Tecla, it feels like the residents have taken back their streets. And it's a wonderful feeling. Taxis cost around US$15 one way.

LOCAL KNOWLEDGE

MUSIC IN THE CITY

Live music in San Salvador rocks! Right now the coolest bands in the country are Shaka & Dres (hip-hop), Friguey (pop), Esquina Opuesta (progressive rock), Lavanda (indie rock), Anastacio y los de monte (reggae) and Adhesivo (new wave ska).

Letty, San Salvador

Citibank ATMs that accept all cards are located in Metrocentro Mall and Galerías Mall. Branches change traveler's checks and can give cash advances on Visa cards.

Dispensa de Don Juan Near Plaza Barrios, has several ATMs and is probably the most secure place to withdraw money in the *centro*.

POST

Correos Central (Centro Gobierno; ⏲7:30am-5pm Mon-Fri, 8am-noon Sat) A smaller branch is in Metrocentro by the Blvd de los Héroes entrance.

TOURIST INFORMATION

Corporación Salvadoreña de Turismo (Corsatur; ☎2243-7835; www.elsalvador.travel; Blvd Santa Elena; ⏲8am-12:30pm & 1:30-5:30pm) Inconveniently located outside the city; luckily it has an excellent website.

Instituto Salvadoreño de Turismo (ISTU; ☎2222-8000; istu@mh.gob.sv; Calle Rubén Darío 619; ⏲8:30am-noon & 1-4pm Mon-Sat) General information about El Salvador's national parks and *turicentros*.

Ministerio de Trabajo Auxiliary Office (☎2209-3700; Paseo General Escalón 19; ⏲8am-12:30pm & 1:30-4pm Mon-Fri) Issues permits to stay at the four government-run workers' vacation centers in Lago de Coatepeque, El Tamarindo, La Palma and La Libertad. Plan your stay between Wednesday and Saturday (the centers are closed other days), and workers get weekend preference.

Peace Corps (☎2208-2911; www.peacecorps.gov; Calle Las Dalias 3; ⏲9am-4.30pm Mon-Fri) If you want to get off the beaten track, this US-based organization may be a good resource. Volunteers are very receptive to visitors.

SalvaNatura (☎2279-1515; www.salvanatura.org; 33 Av Sur 640; ⏲8am-12:30pm & 2-5:30pm Mon-Fri) Friendly and helpful staff manage Parque Nacional El Imposible and Parque Nacional los Volcanes. Call before visiting either park.

Tourist Police (☎2298-9983)

Getting There & Away

AIR

Aeropuerto Internacional Comalpa (☎2339-8264) Located 50km southeast of San Salvador, a major Central American hub.

American Airlines (☎2298-0777; Edificio La Centroamericana, Alameda Roosevelt)

Continental Airlines (☎2207-2040; Metrocentro, 2nd fl)

Copa Airlines (☎2209-2672; World Trade Center I, cnr 89a Av Norte & Calle del Mirador)

Delta Airlines (☎2275-9292; World Trade Center I, cnr 89a Av Norte & Calle del Mirador)

TACA (☎2267-8222; Galerías Escalón, street level)

United Airlines (☎2279-3900; Galerías Escalón, street level)

BUS

International buses leave from **Terminal Puerto Bus** (cnr Alameda Juan Pablo II & 19a Av Norte). Take city bus 29, 101D, 7C or 52 to get there.

King Quality (☎2271-1361; www.king-quality-ca.com) offers deluxe service to Guatemala City from the Terminal Puerto Bus, featuring air-con, movies and a meal (US$40 one way, five hours), departing at 6:30am and 3:30pm. It also has daily services to San José (US$67, 18 hours) leaving at 3am. For Honduras, air-conditioned buses leave every day for Tegucigalpa at 5.30am (US$40, six hours) and San Pedro Sula at 7am (US$46, six hours).

Tica Bus (☎2222-4808; www.ticabus.com; ⏲8am-4:30pm) has service to Guatemala City at 6am and 2pm (US$18, five hours) from the Hotel San Carlos. Reserve one to two days in advance and arrive at the San Carlos a half-hour early. Tica Bus is inside the hotel. From Guatemala City it continues to the Mexican border at Tapachula, Chiapas. From San Salvador, the trip takes 12 hours and costs US$37.

Tica Bus leaves the Hotel San Carlos at 5am and arrives in Managua, Nicaragua, at 3:30pm (US$30). The bus arrives in San José, Costa Rica, between 3pm and 4pm (US$56 one way from San Salvador). It then leaves at 10pm for Panama (US$96 one way from San Salvador), where you arrive between 3pm and 4pm on the third day.

San Salvador has three main terminals for national long-distance buses.

Getting Around

BUS

San Salvador's bus network is extensive, from large smoke-spewing monsters to zippy microbuses. Fares are US$0.20 to US$0.30.

Buses run frequently from 5am to 7:30pm daily; fewer buses run on Sunday. Services stop between 7:30pm and 8:30pm; microbuses run later, until around 9pm. After 9pm you'll have to take a taxi.

In the center, it is fastest to walk a few blocks away from Plaza Barrios to catch your bus. Key routes include the following:

Bus 9 Goes down 29a Av Norte alongside the Universidad de El Salvador. Then it turns east toward the city center, heading past the cathedral and up Independencia past Terminal de Oriente.

Bus 26 Passes Plaza Barrios and Parque Zoológico on its way to Terminal del Sur.

BUSES FROM SAN SALVADOR

Buses serving all points east and a few northern destinations arrive and depart from the **Terminal de Oriente** (Alameda Juan Pablo II). To get to the terminal, take bus 9, 29 or 34 east from the city center; bus 29 or 52 from Blvd de los Héroes; bus 7C or 34 from Terminal de Occidente; or bus 21 from Terminal de Sur. Frequent departures are as follows; note that faster *especial* services are available for La Unión and San Miguel.

DESTINATION	BUS	COST (US$)	DURATION
Chalatenango	125	1.10	2hr
El Poy (Honduran border)	119	1.75	3hr
Ilobasco	111	0.75	1½hr
La Palma	119	1.70	2¾hr
La Unión	304	3.25	4hr
San Miguel	301	1.25-2.50	3hr
San Vicente	116	0.95	1½hr
Suchitoto	129	0.90	1½hr

Buses serving all points west, including the Guatemalan border, arrive and depart from the **Terminal de Occidente** (Blvd Venezuela, near 49a Av Sur). To get here, take bus 34 from the city center; bus 44 from Blvd de los Héroes (get off at Blvd Venezuela and walk a few blocks west to the terminal); or bus 7C or 34 from Terminal de Oriente. Frequent departures include:

DESTINATION	BUS	COST (US$)	DURATION
Ahuachapá	202	1	2¼hr
Cerro Verde	Santa Ana to El Congo, then 246	0.90	40min
Joya de Cerén	108 to San Juan Opico	0.65	1¾hr
La Hachadura	205 to Sonsonate then 259	1.55	3½hr
La Libertad	102	0.70	1hr
Lago de Coatepeque	Santa Ana to El Congo then 248	0.90	40min
Las Chinamas	202 to Ahuachapán then 263	1.60	2½hr
Los Cóbanos	205 to Sonsonate then 257	1.30	2½hr
Metapán	201A	2.50	1¾hr
Ruinas de San Andrés	Santa Ana bus 201	0.80	40min
San Cristóbal	498	1.30	3hr
Santa Ana	201	0.90	1¼hr
Sonsonate	205	1	1¼hr

Terminal de Sur (Autopista a Comalapa), also called Terminal San Marcos, serves the south and southeast. To get here take bus 26 or microbus 11B from the center; or bus 21 from Terminal de Oriente. Departures as follows; note that a faster *especial* service is available for Usulután.

DESTINATION	BUS	COST (US$)	DURATION
Costa del Sol	495	1.25	2½hr
Puerto El Triunfo	185	1.60	2hr
Usulután	302	1.70	2½hr

GETTING INTO TOWN FROM THE AIRPORT

Shuttles operated by **Taxis Acacya** (☎ airport 2339-9282, in town 2271-4937; cnr 19a Av Norte & 3a Calle Poniente) offer the best way to/from the airport. The trip costs around US$5 and takes 45 minutes. In San Salvador, shuttles leave from Taxis Acacya behind the Puerto bus terminal, at 6am, 7am, 10am and 2pm. From the airport, they depart at 9am, 1pm and 5:30pm.

Microbus 138 (US$0.60, 45 minutes to one hour, every 10 minutes) passes the airport – if you remind the driver – traveling to and from the city center. Pick it up just south of Plaza Barrios in town. If heading into town, cut through the parking lot to reach the highway (a 75m walk) and a bus shelter. Once downtown, a taxi costs US$5 to US$8. Bus 30 goes to Metrocentro and Blvd de los Héroes (from Plaza Barrios walk two blocks north, turn right one block to Parque Libertad).

You can also go directly from the airport to La Libertad – it's about the same distance as San Salvador. Take bus 133 to the *puente a Comalapa* (Comalapa overpass) a few minutes away. A path leads up onto the intersecting road; from there it's 100m to the town of Comalapa, where bus 187 or 495 goes every 20 minutes to La Libertad (US$0.40).

A taxi between San Salvador or La Libertad and the airport costs US$25 to US$30.

Bus 29 Goes to Terminal de Oriente via the center. Buses stop between Metrocentro and MetroSur.

Bus 30 Heads downtown and is the best way to get to and from bus 138 to the airport. Pick it up on behind Metrocentro or at Parque Libertad in the center.

Bus 30B A very useful route, especially from Blvd de los Héroes. The bus goes east on Blvd Universitario, then southwest down Blvd de los Héroes to Metrocentro. From there, it goes west along Alameda Roosevelt. It then turns south at 79a Av and continues along Blvd del Hipódromo to Av Revolución, then returns on Alameda Araujo, Roosevelt, and 49a Av Sur back to Metrocentro.

Bus 34 Runs from Terminal de Oriente to Metrocentro then down to the Zona Rosa, turning around right in front of MARTE art museum. Passes Terminal de Occidente on return.

Bus 42 The bus goes west along Calle Arce from the cathedral and continues along Alameda Roosevelt. At El Salvador del Mundo, it heads southwest along Alameda Araujo, passing the Mercado de Artesanías and Museo Nacional de Antropología David J Guzmán, and continues down the Carretera Interamericana, passing La Ceiba de Guadalupe.

Bus 101 Goes from Plaza Barrios in the center, past Metro Sur, the anthropology museum, La Ceiba de Guadalupe and on to Santa Tecla.

CAR & MOTORCYCLE

Avoid driving through the city center. The traffic gets snarled in daytime and the area is unsafe at night. It's quickest to take major thoroughfares. One-way streets have an arrow painted on the pavement or signage.

TAXI

Taxis are plentiful but unmetered so negotiate a price in advance. A ride in town should cost between US$5 and US$10 during daytime. Rates go up a few dollars late at night. License plates beginning with 'A' indicate a registered taxi; in theory they can be held accountable for problems. If you don't spot a passing taxi, call **Taxis Acacya** (☎ 2271-4937) or **Acontaxis** (☎ 2270-1176).

AROUND SAN SALVADOR

San Salvador's perimeter is a profane mix of shantytowns and ancient ruins. Further out, cool volcano-top towns offer respite from the heat, while La Libertad is the gritty gateway to the Western Pacific coast and a plethora of world-class surfing options.

Cihuatán

The modest ruins of **Cihuatán** (admission US$3; ⏲ 9am-4pm Tue-Sun) were once an immense urban area alongside the Río Guazapa, possibly the largest pre-Columbian city between Guatemala and Peru. The city thrived for 100 years before being sacked and burned by unknown invaders in the 10th century AD. It was likely occupied by Maya, Lenca and other groups joined together for commerce during an unstable period.

From San Salvador's Terminal de Oriente, take bus 119 toward Chalatenango and get off about 4km beyond Las Aguilares; ask the driver to let you off at the ruins. It's a 900m walk to the site.

El Boquerón

Quezaltepeque (Volcán San Salvador) has two peaks. The higher peak, at 1960m, is called Picacho. The other, Boquerón (Big Mouth), is 1893m high and has a second cone within its crater – 45m high and perfectly symmetrical – formed in 1917. A paved road to the top affords an easy climb with unbelievable views as your reward. Bring a bag to pick up litter if you're so inspired. **El Boquerón Canopy Tours** (☎2508-0398; canopy ride US$27; ⏲9am-5pm) can provide a not-so-cheap thrill.

Get an early start as buses from San Salvador take a couple of hours. From Parque Cuscatlán, take bus 101A or B to Santa Tecla. From there, bus 103 departs from 6a Av Sur to the village of Boquerón. The bus comes sporadically, but pickups depart from the same place. The summit is 1km beyond the village.

Ruinas de San Andrés

In 1977 a step pyramid and a large courtyard with a subterranean section were unearthed at this **site** (admission US$3; ⏲9am-5pm Tue-Sun), inhabited by Maya between AD 600 and AD 900. Experts believe that up to 12,000 people lived here. The city once dominated the Valle de Zapotitán and possibly the neighboring Valle de las Hamacas, where San Salvador is now situated.

The peaceful ruins are 300m north of the highway and 33km west of San Salvador in the Valle de Zapotitán. Take the Santa Ana bus 201 from San Salvador's Terminal de Occidente and get off at Km 33, at a small black sign for the ruins. If combining this with a visit to Joya de Cerén, visit Joya de Cerén first, then catch any bus on the highway for the short distance to San Andrés.

Joya de Cerén

Called the Pompeii of America, Unesco World Heritage Site **Joya de Cerén** (www.cihuatan.org; admission US$3; ⏲9am-5pm Tue-Sun) was a small Maya settlement buried under volcanic ash when the Laguna Caldera Volcano erupted in AD 595. Fleeing residents left behind a wealth of everyday items that provide clues into ancient planting, home building and food storage.

The remodeled museum offers a good collection of artifacts and models of the villages. One compelling piece is a small dish showing fingerprints smeared in the remains of an interrupted meal.

The site is 36km west of San Salvador – take bus 108 from Terminal de Occidente and get off after crossing the bridge over the Río Sucio.

Los Planes de Renderos

This hillside district, 12km to the south of San Salvador, is famous for **Puerta del Diablo** (Devil's Door). Two towering boulders, reputedly one single stone split in two, form a lookout with fantastic views (minus those of garbage strewn about). During the war this place was an execution point, the cliffs offering easy disposal of the bodies.

The boulders are 2km past the family-friendly **Parque Balboa** (admission US$0.80). Take bus 12 'Mil Cumbres' from the east side of the Mercado Central, at 12a Calle Poniente. If you're driving, head down Av Cuscatlán until you see the signs.

Panchimalco

Set on the green slopes of Cerro Chulo, Panchimalco is a small town renowned for its religious festivals, particularly Palm Sunday, when residents march through the streets bearing decorated palm fronds. Early May's **Fería de Cultura de las Flores y las Palmas** features palm artistry, folk dancing and fireworks. Inhabited by descendants of the Pipils, Panchimalco has reinvented itself as an artist enclave.

Bus 17 departs for Panchimalco from Av 29 de Agosto on the south side of the Mercado Central in San Salvador.

La Libertad

POP 20,100

El Salvador's most infamous port still sports an uneasy mix of drugs, crime and surfing, but there is change in the salty air. From the fabulous, sticky fish market on the pier to the sunset barrels on famed Punta Roca point, local authorities have poured money into gentrifying an otherwise sketchy patch of prime coastal real estate. Police abound; cool cafes, bars and restaurants hawk for passing custom; and an amphitheatre, skate park and convention center invite corporate and community events.

Off the beach La Libertad is still a stinking-hot, working-class city with far more energy, souped-up buses and loud-mouthed touting than you'd expect for a town of such modest proportions. Most travelers bypass it for the more chilled-out beaches to the west, but it's an ideal stop for banks and other amenities, or for a steady dose of seaside grit.

Sights & Activities

Beaches

La Libertad fills up with city dwellers on weekends. The beach is rocky and covered with large black boulders, and the riptide, along with sewage, makes the water uninviting in the rainy season (May to October). If you just want to frolic in waves, hit the Costa del Bálsamo or go 4km east to sandy Playa San Diego.

Surfing

You'll find world-class surfing at **Punta Roca**, a lively right-hand break smack in front of town. Scenes from classic surf flick *Big Wednesday* were filmed here. Beginners launch at Playa La Paz (November to February), El Zonte or El Sunzal. Top surf spots with accommodation are found on the Costa Bálsamo.

Surf Doctor Saul has expanded **Hospital de Tablas de Surf** (☎2335-3214; 3a Av Norte 28-7) into the neighboring premises, so there's even more space for repairing, renting and selling boards, in addition to offering surfing lessons. Just knock if it appears closed.

Wildlife-Watching

About 4km north of La Libertad, along the Comalapa road, **Parque Nacional Walter T Deininger** (admission US$1, guide US$12; ⏲7am-noon & 1-5pm) is named for the German settler who donated the land. It includes two types of forest: *caducifolio,* which sheds its leaves in summer, and *galería,* which retains its foliage year-round. A well-maintained 18km trail skirts the park; you must be accompanied by a ranger. Signs mark trails to Río Amayo, 'the Mystery Cave' and a lookout showing the forest cascading to the sea. Deer, raccoon and the endangered *tepezcuintle* (paca) can be spotted, in addition to many bird species, including the *torogoz* (blue-crowned motmot), El Salvador's national bird.

To visit Parque Deininger, you supposedly must obtain a permit from ISTU (p300) in San Salvador five days prior to arrival. You might just try showing up and talking with the guard. It's a 15-minute ride from La Libertad – catch bus 187.

Sleeping

Hotel Renacer HOTEL $

(☎7027-2899; Calle 4a Poniente 3 Av Sur; per person with/without air-con US$15/20) This new hotel in the heart of the La Libertad action has seven rooms with private bathrooms and a cheap restaurant. It's miles above the competition for value and service.

Hotel Rick HOTEL $

(☎2335-3542; 5a Av Sur; d US$28; ❄) Bright orange Rick has been running for nearly three decades and has still barely gentrified. Go for the 2nd floor where the rooms get more sunlight and the bathrooms have been remodeled.

Sol Bohemio HOSTEL $$

(☎7262-0497; www.solbohemio.com; Playa San Blas; s/d US$25/40; ❄) Between La Libertad and El Tunco is tiny Playa San Blas where you'll find a handful of restaurants and this fine guesthouse, which has four cute rooms with private bathrooms. The pool and restaurant are open for day guests.

La Hacienda de Don Lito HOTEL $$

(☎2335-3166; 5a Av Sur; r US$42-57; ❄) New management but still the same big, breezy rooms, a huge 2nd-floor balcony, a compact swimming pool facing the beach and a neat bar.

Eating

Los Asados JC SALVADORAN/MEXICAN $

(3a Av Norte, btwn Calle El Calvario & 2a Calle Poniente; mains US$3-4; ⏲5-9:30pm) Vibrant surfer decor and El Sal-Mex. The beef is morish, served in or around *pupusas* and wonderfully sloppy tacos.

Punta Roca SEAFOOD $$

(cnr 5a Av Sur & 4a Calle Poniente; mains US$4-10; ⏲8am-8pm, later on weekends) This is a local institution, with an expat surf family at the helm. The cook serves up superb *mariscadas* (seafood soup) and shrimp cocktails on the beachfront. Stay for at least one sunset beverage.

★Danilo's Bar & Restaurant SEAFOOD FUSION $$

(Malecon; mains US$6-18) Former big-city chef Daniel has made a sea-change for the better in his hip little seafood diner in the heart of the new waterside development, Malecon. We gorged on fresh sashimi and killer ceviches. As the sun set we got lost in his signature Pisco Sour, made with a local spirit.

Nuevo Altamar SEAFOOD **$$**
(4a Calle Poniente; mains US$6-16; ⏲11am-11pm) A team of brisk, old-school waiters serves highly recommended *cazuela* (seafood soup) and other pescatarian delights to in-the-know locals at the pick of the restaurants in the strip towards Punta Roca.

La Dolce Vita ITALIAN **$$**
(☎2335-3592; Calle San Diego; mains US$9-12; ⏲9am-10pm) The pick of the two Italian chain restaurants is at the turnoff to Playa San Diego. Here you will find pretty authentic pizza and pasta dishes.

Super Selectos SUPERMARKET
(El Faro Mall; ⏲7:30am-8pm) Self-caterers can stock up at Super Selectos.

ℹ Information

Banco Agrícola Branches are located east of the market in Barrios or in El Faro mall. Changes traveler's checks; there's a new 24-hour ATM at El Faro mall.

Cyber Fenix (2a Calle Poniente; per hr US$1; ⏲8am-8pm)

Post Office (2a Calle Oriente) Near 2a Av Norte.

DANGERS & ANNOYANCES

La Libertad has a dangerous reputation thanks to its long-standing drug trade, though the local government is taking steps to rectify the problems. Still, best to avoid the area southeast of the plaza at night (there's better nightlife on the Malecon).

Strong rip currents proliferate throughout the coast. Lifeguards only work weekends in La Libertad and Playa San Diego. Avoid eating the black clams if you want to keep catching waves.

ℹ Getting There & Away

There is no bus terminal. Bus 102 goes to and from San Salvador (US$0.60, one hour). In San Salvador, catch it at its terminal behind Parque Bolivar or at Terminal de Occidente. In La Libertad, buses leave from the corner of 4a Av Norte and Calle Gerardo Barros.

To Sonsonate, take bus 287 (US$1.25, 2½ hours, 1:45pm only) from the bus stop at 2a Calle Poniente or bus 192 to Playa Mizata and change.

MALECON

Part of the city's attempts to fight back against crime has been the heavy investment in the gentrification of Libertad's long waterfront. Only 40 minutes from the capital, Malecon has transformed into a seaside playground with fine restaurants, the famous fish market, late-night bars and cafes and two protected swimming areas. Painting and sculpture line the pathways, while parking is secure and gated.

Salvadorans have responded en masse; it's a far cry from the seagulls, drunks and thieves who used to roam unchecked along this 1km-long stretch of prime ocean real estate.

ℹ Getting Around

Surfers can take boards on all buses. Bus 80 goes west from La Libertad to Playa El Tunco and Playa El Sunzal (US$0.25, every 15 minutes 4:30am to 6pm) or east to Playa San Diego (US$0.30, every 15 minutes 5:40am to 6pm). Buses leave from 4a Av Norte at 2a Calle Oriente.

For Playa El Zonte or Playa Mizata take bus 192 (US$0.50, every 30 minutes 7am to 5:30pm).

La Costa del Bálsamo

This spectacular coast stretches from La Libertad westward to Sihuapilapa. The region takes its name from the valuable aromatic oil extracted here by burning the bark of live balsam trees. Today only a handful of trees remain.

From La Libertad, the road west twists around rocky headlands, giving glimpses of sheltered coves and sandy beaches (mostly private). The western sections of this route are especially raw and beautiful. Skip the weekend hordes and parking lots at Playas Conchalío and El Majahual and press on for a whole 50km of uninterrupted beaches.

Bus 80 goes as far as Playa El Sunzal. Beyond that, take the less frequent bus 192.

Playa El Tunco

El Tunco's popularity is creeping up on the world pretty quickly, so tread carefully in this tiny beach party hamlet.

Sleeping

Sombra HOSTEL $
(☎ 7729-5628; www.surflibre.com; dm/d US$6/14, dm/d/tr with bathroom US$7/14/21;) Salvador pro Jose goes overboard to get his guests barrelled and rested, preferably in that order. There's free Zona Rosa bus pick-up in San Salvador, a small pool with outdoor shower and a guarantee of finding at least one gnarly grommet bleeding on the deck.

Papaya's Lodge HOSTEL $
(☎ 2389-6231; www.papayalodge.com; r with/without bathroom US$22/15) Local surf deity Jamie Delgado has cobbled together the premier budget option in Tunco. Eight cement block rooms, some with private bathrooms, face a shady river deck backed by mangroves. It's intimate and wholly friendly. The surf shop offers repairs and lessons.

Hotel Mopelia BOUTIQUE HOTEL $
★ (☎ 2389-6225; www.hotelmopelia-salvador.com; dm US$10, r with/without air-con US$30/15;) Mopelia has overtaken some fancier rivals thanks to its eight splendid rooms spread over a larger than average property. There's a popular pizza joint, Tunco Veloz, and an underrated bar serving microbrew. Weekly ping-pong tournaments draw the crowd and the multilingual owner is a delight.

Eco Del Mar BOUTIQUE HOTEL $$
(☎ 7852-2124; www.ecosurfelsalvador.com; r US$50-55, with air-con US$60-65;) These five sustainably designed apartments have increased in price due mostly to their popularity and relatively peaceful outlook.

Roca Sunzal SURF RESORT $$
(☎ 2389-6126; www.rocasunzal.com; s/d US$30/60; P) With a prime location and attention to customer needs befitting a hotel of much higher class, Roza Sunzal is very popular with both domestic and international visitors. The pool is excellent, the food is worth the expense and the rooms are spacious and stylish. Check for standby rates.

Tekuani Kal BOUTIQUE HOTEL $$
(☎ 2389-6388; www.tekuanikal.com; s/d incl breakfast US$50/65;) Ultra stylish, with a faux-indigenous vibe.

La Guitarra BOUTIQUE HOTEL $$
(☎ 2389-6388; www.surfingeltunco.com; r US$35-45, with air-con US$65-75; @) The standards have slipped a little at this rock'n'roll-themed high-end hostel with a prime position and a reliable beachside bar. The thatched rooms, each with private bathroom and firm beds, face into a grassy thoroughfare and the hang-out area by reception is kitted out with political pop art, a big pool table and TV lounge.

Eating & Drinking

Take a Wok NOODLES $
(mains US$6-8) Take a stool at the counter, pick your combination of sauce/noodle/protein and watch the bloke with the fire and oil sizzle your heart out. Properly delicious and always packed.

Dare Dare Cafe CAFE
(☎ 7080-0263; sandwiches $5-7) Killer chai lattes (among other exotic blends), American breakfasts and house smoothies in a smartly decorated deli with full magazine racks and a hammock-strewn gazebo on the river mouth.

La Bocana SEAFOOD $$
(mains $6-16) This reliable seafood restaurant turns into a popular nightspot.

Comedor La Esquina SALVADORAN $
(mains US$4-6) A local favorite right on 'the corner'. Massive plates of burritos and *típico* are incredible value and come served hot and fast.

Soya Nutribar JUICE BAR $
(☎ 7887-1596; ⏲ 8.30am-3pm) Super juices, organic muesli and photonutritious combinations, mostly in liquid form, are found at this tiny, well-signed place up a short flight of stairs.

D'Rocas NIGHTCLUB
(☎ 2389-6313; ⏲ noon-2am Fri & Sat) The most happening summer nightspot in the whole country is now in El Tunco. On weekends if you want to dance to quality house and Latin music with hordes of locals and foreigners then get to D'Rocas, a surprisingly stylish outdoor venue with indigenous flavour and gorgeous staff. Before the carnage begins there's excellent food and a laidback pool scene.

Brew Revolution MICROBREWERY
(⏲ noon-6pm) The Brew Revolution has started in Tunco at the Brew Bar. This little caravan on the main street is the unofficial home of El Salvador's craft beer industry. Flavorsome ales are making their way around the country and you'll soon be smashing that watery Golden on the floor and demanding a tastier beverage.

Playa El Sunzal

This relaxed surf spot is just down the beach from El Tunco.

Sunzal Point Surf Lodge SURF LODGE $
(☎2389-6070; www.surfsunzal.com; Carretera Litoral Km 44; dm US$7, d with/without air-con US$30/18; ❄ @) El Salvador's original early-'60s surf retreat has been reinvigorated in recent years by three ex-backpackers who fell in love with the famed Sunzal break. The grounds are spacious, the shared bathrooms are brand new and there's full use of kitchen facilities. Nonsurfers can choose from a range of land-based tours.

El Balsamo HOSTEL $
(☎7404-8117, 2389-6140; www.elbalsamo.com; dm US$5, s/d without bathroom US$7/14, with bathroom US$20/25) Veronica and Gijs maintain a secluded little property with spotless double and dorm rooms surrounded by green foliage. The tiled floors and tasteful furniture make you feel less guilty for staying indoors. For the radical, there's even a skate ramp.

Hostal Los Almendros HOSTEL $$
(☎7727-3194; d from US$25) An old mansion converted into a surf retreat. Highly recommended by locals.

Sharky's TEX-MEX $
(mains US$3-6; ⏲7am-3pm) Perfect post-surf gringo food courtesy of Richard, an ex-TACA pilot and local identity. The salads and hot dogs are a particular success. By the time this is published, expect the hostel to be opened in a spectacular style.

Playa El Zonte & Beyond

The ultimate *playa* for chilling – and learning to surf – on the Costa del Bálsamo. Life has changed sharply for this tiny community; show respect by traveling sustainably.

Canegue Hostal HOSTEL $
(☎7599-4080; www.caneguehostal.com; Playa El Zonte; r US$10, hammocks/camping US$5) The most basic of El Zonte's sleeping options is run by a friendly Canadian-Salvadoran couple who surf hard and play fair. It's a staple of the surfing scene and the bar gets pretty loose.

Casa Garrobo HOSTEL $
(www.casagarrobo.com; Los Cobanos; s/d US$20/30; P ❄ 🏊) One of the few fully-functioning guesthouses in Los Cobanos visited by foreigners, the Garrobo is actually three separate beach houses that you can book by the room (or by house if you so desire). You have to book via the website as the owners come and go. The Caracol was our favorite but all three have fairly weatherbeaten exteriors, a small pool, spacious landing with hammocks and dark wooden furniture and excellent bedrooms with firm beds and quality linens.

Horizonte Surf Resort HOSTEL $
(☎2355-7337; www.horizontesurfresort.com; Playa El Zonte; dm US$12, d US$20-40; P ❄ 🏊) The home of Paco the iguana has comfortable rooms (the best are upstairs), a manicured garden and two pools to choose from. It also runs a decent restaurant, but guests can use the clean kitchen if they prefer. Surf lessons are available.

Esencia Nativa BOUTIQUE HOTEL $$
(☎7737-8879; www.esencianativa.com; s/d/tr US$15/25/30, r with bathroom & air-con US$35; P ❄ 🏊) Alex is still the man at this upscale backpacker retreat and soul of El Zonte. New double rooms have been built upstairs and are the best to be had on the small Zonte strip. Bathrooms are impeccable. The real attraction at this boutique hotel though is the social scene by the pool and the superb munchie shack with lofty views of the main break.

El Dorado BOUTIQUE HOTEL $$
(☎7226-6166; www.surfeldrado.com; dm/s/d US$16/35/58; P ❄ 🏊) The pick of the hotels across the river is El Dorado, a French-Canadian surf venture with beautiful, breezy rooms fitted with bamboo art.

WESTERN EL SALVADOR

El Salvador's coffee stronghold offers a heady blend of adventure and old money, gastronomy and lush national parks. It's here that the Ruta de las Flores winds its charms through cobblestone villages, where stumbling across running waterfalls and bubbling hot springs is as easy as finding a good espresso and a thriving marketplace. Meanwhile Santa Ana, the provincial capital, is a confident, colonial town with a mesmerizing lake at its doorstep and some grand ruins out back. But western El Salvador is also an exercise in inequality. On baking-hot, volcanic precipices, *campesinos* (agricultural workers) struggle to subsist, stuck deep beneath the poverty line as coffee dynasties hold on to the good life. When El Salvador finally enjoys the destination status of its neighbors, you'll see its impact here first.

Parque Nacional Los Volcanes

This **park** (admission US$1; ⏲8am-5pm) is a natural treasure, encompassing three major volcanoes (Cerro Verde, Volcán Santa Ana and Volcán Izalco) and thousands of hectares. It's a major bird sanctuary, with many migratory species passing through, including emerald toucanets, jays, woodpeckers, motmots and 17 species of hummingbird.

Active Volcán Izalco is the youngest in the group. Its cone began forming in 1770 from a belching hole of sulfuric smoke and today stands 1910m high. Izalco erupted throughout the 20th century, spewing smoke, boulders and flames and earning its reputation as 'the lighthouse of the Pacific.' Today, this bare, perfect cone stands devoid of life in an otherwise fertile land.

Without Izalco's stark drama but 400m higher, Santa Ana (also known as Ilamatepec) is El Salvador's third-highest point. Its eruption in October 2005 triggered landslides that killed two coffee pickers and forced the evacuation of thousands. The barren and windy summit affords spectacular views of a steep drop into the crater on one side and Lago de Coatepeque on the other.

Tourist police are posted along the trails and at the summits. Crime has dropped dramatically in recent years, but you should not hike solo.

Four-hour guided hikes to either volcano (Izalco US$1; Santa Ana US$2) begin at 11am *only*, so don't arrive late! This also means you can't do both in one day. Wear sturdy shoes. A short alternative is a 40-minute nature trail which offers views of the lake and Volcán Santa Ana. All hikes start from the carpark, near the park entrance.

Sleeping & Eating

San Blas has two camping complexes in the shadow of Volcán Santa Ana.

Campo Bello CABIN **$$**
(☎2271-0853; US$25-60) Campo Bello offers round cement dwellings that sleep four.

Casa de Cristal CABIN **$$**
(☎2483-4713; US$12-18) Casa de Cristalhas rustic *cabañas*. Call ahead for prices, camping possibilities and availability.

Campground CAMPGROUND **$$**
(☎2483-4713, 2483-4679; 2 adults US$35) A local cooperative manages a rustic campground, 13km from San Blas heading toward Los Andes. Los Andes has a ranger who can also guide Santa Ana hikes. For information, contact SalvaNatura (p300) in San Salvador.

Getting There & Away

Arrive by 11am since the guided hikes leave just once a day. The easiest, surest route is to come from Santa Ana, where bus 248 goes all the way to the entrance. The last bus leaves the park at 5pm but verify times with the driver who drops you off.

Leave early from San Salvador to make connections. Take any bus to Santa Ana and disembark at El Congo on the Carretera Panamericana; walk uphill to the overpass and catch bus 248. Ask to be sure you're in the right place.

If you're driving, Parque Nacional Los Volcanes is 67km from San Salvador via Sonsonate or 77km by the more scenic route toward Santa Ana.

Lago de Coatepeque

Unlike more famous lakes in Central America (hint, hint, Guatemala) you can happily swim in this 6km-wide sparkling blue volcanic puddle while above you broods the dramatic peaks of Cerro Verde, Izalco and Santa Ana. Ah, El Salvador!

A handful of cheap hotels dot the lake's edge, but most accommodation is the preserve of San Salvador's elite – one ex-president even owns an island here. For around US$5 you can relax and enjoy lake access at one of the hotels on the northeast shore. For US$20 you can rent a boat for a couple of hours.

Sleeping & Eating

Hostal Amacuilco HOSTEL **$**
(☎2441-6239; amacuilcohostal@gmail.com; dm/s/d US$9/12/24; ❄ @ ≋) Here's a place to chuck out the itinerary. The five well-presented rooms and elevated dorm are brightly decorated and have varying views of the lake. There's a good-quality book exchange, a small pool and sauna, kayak and canoe rental, plus a yummy lakeside restaurant. You can even take a Spanish lesson in the lovely gardens.

El Gran Mirador HOTEL $$
(☎7822-4251; r incl breakfast US$25) Eat fresh *mojarro* fish from the lake at the slick upstairs seafood restaurant then sleep in one of three small, cement rooms with the lake in your lap. It's on your left, about halfway down the road from Santa Ana.

Hostal Nantal HOSTEL $$
(☎2319-6792; Carretera al Cerro Verde Km 53.5; d incl breakfast US$30; ❄ @) A smart option for exploring Cerro Verde, this garden retreat has recently reopened its four rooms with private bathrooms (some with lake views). The friendly owner Claudia can arrange tours. To get here take the Parque Nacional de los Volcanes bus from Santa Ana.

Rancho Alegre HOTEL $$
(☎7888-0223; Carretera al Cerro Verde Km 53.5; US$40 for 4 people; ❄) Great place for a lakeside party. A younger crowd tucks into *mojara rellena de camarrones* (local fish stuffed with prawns) while bands and house DJs bang tunes across the clear blue water. Set back from the scene are neat bungalows should you get a bit heavy on the Pilsener.

Los Trozos Coatapeque LUXURY HOTEL $$$
(☎2415-9879; www.lostrozos.com.sv; d US$140-300) On the western side of the lake is a new luxury hotel relocated (well, reopened really) from a previous venue in the hills of Sonsonate. This red-tile roof and whitewashed property is very unassuming and has five rooms decorated in classical Salvadoran aristocratic style. The pool by the lake's entrance is glorious and guests can indulge in all manner of water activity.

Comedor Patricar SALVADORAN $
(mains US$2-5; ⏲7:30am-8pm) Enjoy the no-frills *típica* and seafood.

Getting There & Away

Buses 220 and 242 depart Santa Ana for the lake every half-hour. They pass El Congo and descend to the shoreline, passing the Centro de Obreros, Amacuilco and Hotel Torremolinos in that order. The last return bus to Santa Ana leaves at 6pm.

Santa Ana

POP 178,600

Hints of a wealthy yesteryear linger in the colonial backstreets of Santa Ana, a socially conservative major city, and long home to the country's largest coffee plantations. Santa Ana is also the closest thing to a university town outside San Salvador, reflected in the lively nightlife and proud entrepreneurial spirit. The plaza is among the grandest in El Salvador, making it more than a handy departure point for Lago de Coatepeque, the Maya ruins at Tazumal or the Ruta de las Flores.

Sights

Santa Ana's biggest attraction is its large neo-Gothic **cathedral**. Ornate moldings cover the front, and interior archways and pillars are painted in slate and pink stripes (consider it preppy-neo-Gothic). On the square west of the cathedral is the **Teatro de Santa Ana**, with an impressive, ornate interior.

Sleeping

Casa Frolaz B&B $
(☎2440-5302; 29a Calle Poniente; per person US$9) The dorm rooms and doubles in the shared home are huge and dust-free, each with a private balcony for guests. You can use the bright kitchen and living area, or just doss in the garden of a real life *salvadoreño*. There's plenty of street parking.

Hotel Livingston HOTEL $
(☎2441-1801; 10a Av Sur; d US$10, with cable TV US$15; ❄) A cement-block complex off the street, Livingston offers well-kept, cavernous rooms. Beds have mirrored headboards and the hodgepodge of sofas and chairs pass for decor. A good choice for quick access to the bus terminals.

★**Casa Verde** HOSTEL $
(☎7540-4896; hostalverde.wordpress.com; 7a Calle Poniente; s/d/tr incl breakfast US$10/18/25; ❄ @) Green House offers an unobtrusive and often unforgettable hostel experience near the historic district of Santa Ana. The seven-bed dorm could fit 12 and the double rooms are a colorful bargain. The kitchen and relaxation areas exude domestic bliss. Call if unattended as Carlos works across the road in the hardware store. When you do get in just shout for joy from the rooftop landing.

Villa Napoli B&B
(☎7808-0831; www.villanapoli.hostel.com; Quinta del Moral Km 62-63; d US$20-30) Run by Rosa, whose husband Franklin runs the iconic Cafe Expresiones in town, the Napoli is a very welcoming guesthouse en route to Lago de Coatapeque. Manicured gardens, a cozy living room and access to a real kitchen

Santa Ana

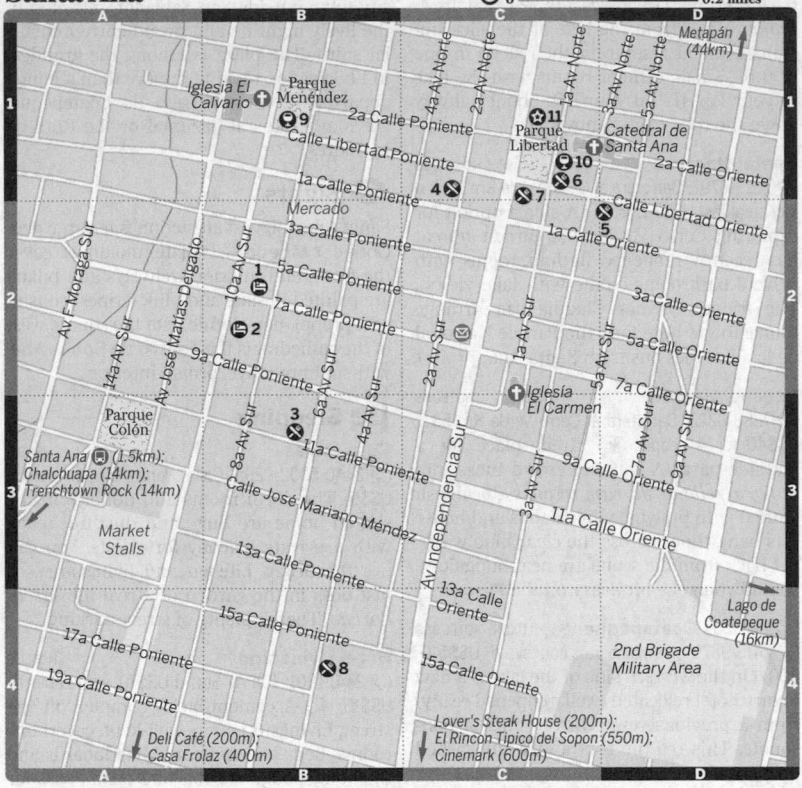

make this a preference for long-term travellers. Guests can be picked up at Cafe Expresiones. All kinds of tours and courtesy services are offered in exchange for your company.

Eating

El Sin Rival ICE CREAM $

(Av Independencia Sur; cones US$0.50-1; ⏲9am-9pm) This popular chain makes natural sorbets so good it's outrageous. Try the tart *arrayán* (a bittersweet local fruit) or *mora* (blackberry).

Deli Café CAFE $

(cnr 10a Av Sur & 25a Calle Poniente; smoothies US$1-2; ⏲9am-6:30pm) Green picnic tables and floral arrangements mask the true intention of this excellent deli: award-worthy smoothies, juices and cakes. It's between the market and Casa Frolaz.

Pastelería Ban Ban PATISSERIE $

(Av Independencia Sur; pastries US$0.50-2.50; ⏲8am-7pm) One of Santa Ana's charms is that the whole population breaks for coffee and cake mid-afternoon. It's likely that you'll find them here enjoying simple sandwiches and pastries in an air-conditioned setting.

Food Stands FAST FOOD $

(1a Av Norte; US$1-2) Hit the row of food stands on the plaza for enormous chicken sandwiches in soft bread, burgers and greasy fries.

★Café Expresiones CAFE $

(Calle 11 Poniente, btwn 6a & 8a Av Sur; meals US$3-6; ⏲Mon-Sat) Santa Ana's favorite, mind-bending cafe sells books, small sandwiches, big breakfasts and *objets d'art* to restless youth and curious tourists. The owner is an an intellect who forbids smoking and drinking on the premises. The cafe somehow expands at every turn to reveal another lost

Santa Ana

Sleeping
1 Casa Verde B2
2 Hotel Livingston B2

Eating
3 Café Expresiones B3
4 Cafe Santaneco C1
5 El Sin Rival D2
6 Food Stands C1
7 Pastelería Ban Ban C1
8 Taberna de Capitan B4

Drinking & Nightlife
9 Los Cuñados B1
10 Los Horcones C1

Entertainment
11 Teatro de Santa Ana C1

soul pondering the meaning of coffee. Cosmopolitan hookers work the street outside.

El Rincon Tipico del Sopon TÍPICA $
(☎2440-5697; 3a Av Sur; mains US$3-5) Lively restaurant in town with killer marimba xylophone on weekends. The soups are the specialty but we loved the salads and massive homemade soft drinks. Popular with families.

Cafe Santaneco SALVADORAN $
(☎2447-8431; Calle Libertad Poniente; mains US$2-4; ⏲breakfast & lunch) Cheap and particularly cheerful city eatery with green and yellow walls and a knowing clientele enjoying fresh *comida a la vista*.

Lover's Steak House STEAKHOUSE $$
(☎2484-7511; www.loverssteakhouse.com; 21a Calle Oriente, Barrio San Miguelito; mains US$8-20) Santa Ana's date-place serves seafood, steak and whopping plates of Chinese food in a tiki torch-lit setting. The music can get pretty loud at night.

Taberna de Capitan SEAFOOD $$
(cnr 4 Av Sur & 17a Calle Poniente; mains US$8-14) In an area with a couple of good restaurants, this one stands out for its thumping post-seafood party anthems. Go easy on the squid before you hit the dancefloor.

Drinking & Nightlife

Trenchtown Rock CLUB
(Carretera Panamericana desvío a Chalchuapa; ⏲7pm-late Wed-Sat) Test your capacity for spontaneous fits of joy in this electric roadside Rasta club, opposite the new Santa Ana bus terminal.

Los Horcones BAR
(☎2484-7511; 1a Av Norte; ⏲10am-2am) For the perfect place to tipple a beer, consider this offbeat open-air spot overlooking the cathedral. Tree-trunk pillars and hand-hewn benches provide a rustic setting.

Los Cuñados BAR
(cnr Calle Libertad Poniente & 10 Av Sur 25; mains US$2-10; ⏲8am-9:30pm) Drink tall glasses of freezing beer at this downtown watering hole with sticky floors and big-screen TVs.

Entertainment

Teatro de Santa Ana THEATER
(☎2447-6268; 2a Calle Poniente) Stop by for the current program of concerts, plays and dance performances.

Cinemark CINEMA
(cnr Av Independencia & 35a Av Poniente; admission US$3) For Hollywood action flicks and the occasional tear-jerker.

Information

Ciberworld (Av Independencia Sur, btwn 9a & 11a Calle Poniente; per hr US$1; ⏲8am-7:30pm Mon-Sat, 9am-6pm Sun) Friendly service.

Citibank (cnr Independencia Sur & 3a Calle Oriente) Has an ATM.

Red Cross (☎447-7213, 441-2645; cnr 1a Av Sur & 3a Calle Oriente; ⏲24hr)

Virtu@l Center (cnr 3a Av Sur & 7a Calle Oriente; per hr US$0.60; ⏲8am-7pm Mon-Fri, 8:30am-6pm Sat, 9am-1pm Sun) Internet access.

Getting There & Away

Several destinations are now served by Santa Ana's new bus terminal (see box, p312). For Las Chinamas (Guatemalan border) take any Ahuachapán bus and transfer.

LOCAL KNOWLEDGE

TRENCHTOWN ROCK

The best party in El Salvador is in Chalchuapa! Trenchtown Rock (this page) is a mystical place where you can kick your shoes off and dance the night away, feel the 'riddim' of El Salvador's best reggae and ska bands, enjoy fancy fire and drumming, or even perform your own show. You can't miss the baked potatoes and the positive vibrations. *Ja! Ja! Ja!*

Rasta Maya Jorge, Chalchuapa

BUSES FROM SANTA ANA

DESTINATION	BUS	COST (US$)	DURATION
Ahuachapán	210	0.45	1¼hr
Lago de Coatepeque	220, 242	0.40	1¼hr
San Cristóbal (Guatemalan border)	236	0.50	1hr
San Salvador *directo*	201	0.80	1½hr
San Salvador *especial*	–	1.25	1¼hr
Sonsonate	209	0.55	1½hr
Tazumal, Chalchuapa	218	0.25	30min

Destinations served from other locations in town include Sonsonate (bus 216; departs from La Vencedora terminal, one block west of Parque Colón) and Metapán (bus 235, US$0.90, 1½ hours; departs from the corner of Av F Moraga Sur and 13a Calle Poniente). For Anguiatú (Guatemalan border) take bus 235 to Metapán and transfer.

Bus 248 to Parque Nacional los Volcanes (Cerro Verde; US$0.90; 1¾ hours) departs from La Vencedora Terminal one block west of Parque Colón at 7am, 8am, 10:15am, 11:20am, 12:20pm, 1:40pm and 3:30pm. Last bus returns at 5pm. Confirm departure times.

Metapán

POP 18,500

Metapán is the gateway to Parque Nacional Montecristo–El Trifinio, the country's most inaccessible and perhaps most beautiful national park. It's closed from May to November to let the wildlife breed in peace. When it is open you need a 4WD vehicle to get there. While Metapán is mostly what a border town should be – hot, hectic and dead after dark – the town square (10 blocks off the main drag) has been thoughtfully renovated and the old town is still largely intact.

Sights & Activities

On the El Salvador–Guatemala border, Lago de Güija is a beautiful fishing and bird-watching wetland. In the dry season you can hike to archaeological sites and find rock carvings along the shore. Swimming is dependent on the extent of the blue-green algae, but boat trips can be arranged from local operators including **La Perla de Azacualpa** (☎2415-6490; incl lunch US$35), which makes it to a Guatemalan village. It's several kilometers south of Metapán and 30km north of Santa Ana along CA12. To get there, take a Santa Ana–bound bus and get dropped off at the junction to the lake. It is a 2km walk from there.

Apuzunga Water Park RAFTING
(☎2483-8952; www.apuzunga.com; entry US$3, rafting trips per person US$50) This friendly operation offers a good-value rafting/canopy package at Apuzunga Water Park outside Metapán. Its main office is at Metrocentro in Santa Ana.

Sleeping & Eating

The town plaza, with regulation church, hall, grassy patch and market stalls, also features a string of bright cafes in beautiful old facades.

Hotel Christina HOTEL $
(☎2442-0044; 4a Av Sur, btwn Calle 15 de Septiembre & 2a Calle; s/d US$12/15, with air-con US$18/23; ❄) For those who want to stay 'in town', Hotel Christina is downhill from the terminal. The upstairs terrace is great for people-watching and there's a handy general store downstairs.

Hostal de Metapan HOSTEL $$
(☎2402-2382; d inc breakfast US$20; P ❄ 📶) This new choice in the town proper has shiny, fake-marble interiors and a sandy coloured exterior. Well-maintained rooms have flat-screen TVs and lumpy beds. The price is very fair and the staff are only too pleased to accommodate.

Hostal Villa Lemon ECO-HOSTEL $$
(☎2442-0149; cottages US$55) Located 4km north of Metapán on a pretty dodgy road is Reserva Ecologica El Limo. On the way to the waterfall is this gorgeous series of three cottages, each of which can sleep four guests comfortably. Views will quicken then slow your pulse.

★Balompie Cafe CAFE $
(☎2402-3567; 3 Av Norte 17; pupusas US$1-2; ⏲10am-1pm Wed-Sun) Amadeo Gonzalez enjoys enormous success with a *pupusa* joint in San Francisco and brought the love back to his native country. The colonial-style entrance to the best restaurant in town bares no hint that the soccer stadium lies at the rear. Enjoy gourmet street food and a drink while *Los Caleros* tackle the boys from the city.

Kikes Coffee CAFE $
(Parque Central; iced coffee US$1) Kikes Coffee is the best of the cafes at the town plaza.

ℹ Information

Fusión Ciber Café (2 Av Sur at 15 de Septiembre; per hr US$0.60)

Scotiabank (Av Ignacio Gómez) Exchanges traveler's checks and has a 24-hour ATM.

ℹ Getting There & Away

The bus terminal sits on the highway facing the entrance to town. For Santa Ana, take bus 235 (US$0.90, 1½ hours) or a *directo* (US$2.50, one hour). San Salvador bus 201A (US$2.50, 1¾ hours) departs seven times daily. Bus 235 and microbuses go to the Guatemalan border at Anguiatú (US$0.50, 30 minutes); the last leaves at 6:30pm. Bus 463 departs 5:30am and noon daily for the gorgeous and also hair-raising haul over the mountains to Citalá (US$2, three hours), close to the Honduran border crossing at El Poy.

Parque Nacional Montecristo–El Trifinio

Isolated and pristine, this borderland park boasts thick cloud-forest canopy, exotic orchids and abundant wildlife. The borders of El Salvador, Honduras and Guatemala converge at the highest point (2418m), referred to as El Trifinio. Oak and laurel trees grow to 30m, and leaves intertwine to form a canopy impenetrable to sunlight. The forest floor provides a habitat for abundant exotic plant life including mushrooms, lichens and mosses, and tree ferns up to 8m tall. The temperature averages between 10°C (50°F) and 15°C (59°F). This is the most humid region in the country, with 2000mm annual precipitation and 100% average relative humidity.

Animals seen (albeit rarely) include spider monkeys, two-fingered anteaters, porcupines, spotted and hooded skunks, pumas, red and gray squirrels, wild pigs, opossums, coyotes and agoutis (cat-sized rodents). The forest is also home to at least 87 bird species, including quetzals, green toucans, woodpeckers, hummingbirds, nightingales, white-faced quails and striped owls.

There is no place to stay here – you must camp. Ask trail directions from the owner of the small shop here. You have a few options but none of the trails are well marked. Several hiking trails begin from Los Planes (about 1900m), a grassy clearing in a bowl at the foot of Cerro Montecristo. Two trails lead about 1km each to wooden observation towers with views of the park and surrounding area. The trail you are probably looking for is the one to the top. The park highlight, the trail is a tough 7km climb through dense, misty cloud forest. At the summit a plaque marks the borders of the three countries. The views and the photo opportunities are outstanding.

ℹ Information

The area above Los Planes is closed from May to November, the breeding season of the local fauna. To take full advantage of the park, you'll need to spend the night. Camping is free at Los Planes – bring all your own equipment, food and water. Get advance permission from the National Parks and Wildlife Service at the **Ministerio de Medio Ambiente** (☎2267-6276, 2267-6259; www.marn.gov.sv; Alameda Araujo/Carretera Santa Tecla Km 5.5; ⏲7:30am-4:30pm Mon-Fri) in San Salvador. Admission is US$6 per day for foreigners plus US$1.15 per vehicle, required for taxis as well.

ℹ Getting There & Away

Getting to Los Planes is a challenge, and not a cheap one. If you have a 4WD, you can drive there (22km from Metapán). **Francisco Monterrosa** (☎2402-2805) charges US$55 for day trips or US$95 to drop you off and return a day or two later. If he isn't available, look for other drivers in Metapán near the park turnoff.

If you wait at the road in early morning, you may be able to catch a ride with the rangers or residents of a small village in the park; but there are no guarantees and the trip back remains unresolved. You can walk to the gate (5km), but you can't walk beyond that without a private vehicle – that's the rule.

WORTH A TRIP

CHALCHUAPA

Most visitors leave Chalchuapa after an hour at the town's ruins of Tazumal (p314) – what a shame! This pre-Columbian settlement is a great snapshot of everyday Salvadoran life.

Laguna Cuzcachapa is a natural sulfur pond located in the suburbs, a very mystical place of great significance in Maya culture. Locals suggest coming here when faced with difficult decisions, but beware the *siguanaba* (a mythical creature that poses as a beautiful woman to lure solo male travelers)! You can swim in natural spring-water pools at **El Trapiche** (location of the first Maya settlement in 2000 BC) or jump into a waterfall in **Salto El Espino**.

Art lovers can check out **Maya Contemporaneo**, opposite the entrance to Tazumal, or **Arte en Las Manos**, opposite La Rinconchita.

Chalchuapa's beautiful young things cram into the new corner bar-restaurant **La Rinconchita** (Av 2 de Abril y 6a Calle Poniente; ⏲ noon-10pm Sat, noon-6pm Sun) for cocktails and spicy *ceviches* and to celebrate with a mix of *fin-de-siecle* gusto and ennui. For a more intimate dinner with acoustic tunes, try the highly recommended **Los Aldabones.** (☎ 7730-1374; 6a Av Norte; ⏲ noon-late Wed-Sun)

The yummiest *chilate,* a nourishing drink made of corn served with *camote* (sweet potato) and sugary *buñuelos* (cassava), is found at **Chilate & Crafts** (5 Av Sur 6). Opposite Tazumal is a famous *yuqateria* serving *yuka* (yam) with roasted pork – a national delicacy. You can find beautiful, cheap jade and quartz jewelry nearby too.

If you decide to stay there's a good guesthouse, **Hostal Las Flores** (☎ 2408-1098; Av 2 de Abril; r US$25; ❄).

Ruinas de Tazumal

The Maya ruins of **Tazumal** (admission US$3; ⏲ 9am-5pm Tue-Sun), the most important and impressive in El Salvador, are in the pre-Columbian town of **Chalchuapa**, 13km west of Santa Ana on the way to Ahuachapán. In the K'iche' language Tazumal means 'pyramid where the victims were burned.'

Archaeologists estimate that the area was first settled around 5000 BC. Part of a 10-sq-km zone, much is still buried under Chalchuapa's more basic housing. Theft of the ruins – and the resale of precious artifacts – is an ongoing concern. The excavated areas span a period of over 1000 years. While these ruins are very important for El Salvador, they pale in comparison to those in neighboring countries. The latest restoration, inaugurated in December 2006, restored the original stone-and-mortar construction in much of the ruins. Don't expect to get too close – a chain-link enclosure prevents visitors walking on the pyramids.

The **museum** displays artifacts showing active trade as far away as Panama and Mexico, with explanations in detailed English. Other finds, including the Estela de Tazumal, a 2.65m-high basalt monolith inscribed with hieroglyphics, are at the Museo Nacional de Antropología David J Guzmán in San Salvador. Across the highway is **Casa Blanca** (admission US$3; ⏲ 9am-5pm Tue-Sun), home to some Preclassic ruins and an indigo workshop where you can dye your own fabrics.

Bus 218 comes from Santa Ana, 14km (45 minutes) away. A sign on the main road through Chalchuapa points toward the ruins, about a five-minute walk from the highway. If driving from Santa Ana, stay right at the fork in the road, continuing toward Ahuachapán, then turn left at the Texaco station in Chalchuapa. The ruins are at the end of the road.

Ahuachapán

POP 38,630

Regardless of how you tackle the Ruta de las Flores, you'll probably pass through Ahuachapán, an elevated regional center 16km short of Guatemala. As a commercial hub for coffee, you'd expect a bit more, well, perk, but the real action in Ahuachapán bubbles deep underground – its geothermal energy supplies over 15% of the country's electrical power.

The hubs of Plaza Concordia and Parque Menéndez are five blocks apart, connected by the busy commercial street Av Menéndez, which runs north–south. The road to Tacuba is poorly marked; ask a local.

Sights & Activities

Ahuachapán bubbles with geothermal activity, evidenced in the steaming mud pits found about. To visit **Los Ausoles**, aka *los infernillos* (the little hells), contact guide **Carlos Alvarado Martínez** (☎2413-3360).

Plaza Concordia PLAZA
Green gardens and palms make Plaza Concordia an agreeable stop to catch a breeze. The kiosk occasionally holds concerts and free events.

Nuestra Señora de Asunción CHURCH
East of the plaza is Nuestra Señora de Asunción, with pretty *azuelo* floors and a stained-glass Virgin.

Sleeping

Budget hotels here have all but disappeared. Head for Tacuba or the Ruta de las Flores for a cheap bed.

La Casa de Mamapan B&B $$
(☎2413-2507; www.lacasademamapan.com; 2a Ave Sur y Pasaje La Concordia; s/d US$26/52; P ❄ 📶) This fine boutique hotel across from the popular Parque de Concordia is owned by the charming Claudia and Roberto and lends a hint of much-needed elegance to the small-town tourist scene. Rooms are classically decorated and the lobby and hallways feature interesting Salvadoran antiques and artwork. Large groups occasionally book out the premises for functions.

Hotel Casa Blanca HOTEL $$
(☎2443-1505; cnr 2a Av Norte & Calle Barrios; s/d with fan US$24/34, with air-con US$35/63; P ❄ @ 🏊) Set in a lovely period street is this doll house-hotel managed by a gracious woman who is adept at handling fussy guests. The rooms are a little busy for some but rightfully decadent for others. The bathrooms are a highlight.

Termales de Santa Teresa HOT SPRINGS RESORT $
(☎2423-8041; www.termalesdesantateresa.com; Beneficio Bendix, Carretera Hacia Ataco, frente a Ciudadela; Spanish/French/Japanese-themed quarters US$25/45/50) Stay in the Spanish-, French- or Japanese-themed quarters at this charming hot springs resort outside Ataco. Coffee plantation tours and locally sourced cuisine round out the experience.

Eating

La Estancia SALVADORAN $
(1a Av Sur btwn Calle Barrios & 1a Calle Oriente; mains US$2-4; ⏲7am-6pm Mon-Sat) The old colonial Villa Carmen is residence to the town's finest restaurant. It's busy with the work crowd, but the menu is quite humble, serving buffet-style *típica* throughout the day.

Restaurant Mixta 'S' SALVADORAN $
(cnr 2a Av Sur & 1a Calle Poniente; mains US$4-5; ⏲8am-9pm) Definitely stop at this shiny, happy diner if you're after fresh *mixtas* – pitas stuffed with pickled veggies, salsa and meat or cheese. Add an extra straw to your overflowing *licuado* for the full date experience.

Information

Most services and restaurants are near Plaza Concordia.

Ciber Café Cetcomp (cnr 2a Av Sur & 1a Calle Poniente; per hr US$0.60; ⏲9am-8pm Mon-Fri, 9:30am-8:30pm Sat, 10am-9pm Sun)

Scotiabank (cnr 2a Av Sur & 1a Calle Poniente) Changes Amex and Visa traveler's checks.

BUSES FROM AHUACHAPÁN

DESTINATION	BUS	COST (US$)	DURATION
Las Chinamas	63 or Ruta 11	0.60	40min
San Salvador	202	1.20	2½hr
San Salvador *especial*	–	2	1¼hr
Santa Ana	210	0.60	1hr
Sonsonate via Apaneca & Juayúa	249	0.90	2hr
Sonsonate *directo*	23	1.25	1½hr
Tacuba or Ruta	264 or Ruta 15	0.70	40min

Getting There & Away

Buses line the market-choked Av Menéndez at 10a Calle Oriente, one block north of the Parque Central. Buses for the Guatemalan border at Las Chinamas leave from 8a Calle Poniente, at the northwest corner of Parque Menéndez. The following buses travel to and from Ahuachapán (note that for Santa Ana you can also take the faster San Salvador bus, get off at Metrocentro and catch a local bus into town).

Tacuba

The Americas' first communist revolution took place here in 1932, but time – and government – has long forgotten this poor mountain outpost on the back doorstep of spectacular Parque Nacional El Imposible. A freshly paved road has increased Tacuba's fee-paying adventurers from a trickle to a steady flow. Sustainable tourism is almost assured here, and Tacuba's end-of-the-road location means that your small effort still brings a large reward.

Sights & Activities

Parque Nacional El Imposible – Northern Entrance NATIONAL PARK

Parque Nacional El Imposible is a tropical treasure edging Guatemala and oddly absent from most itineraries. The mostly primary forest here runs deep with rivers and beautiful waterfalls.

Patient wildlife spotters can eye pumas and black-crested eagles, but it's the misty peaks and gleaming Pacific Ocean vistas that capture the attention of most visitors.

It's safe to go it alone in Parque Nacional El Imposible – you can either enter the park from this northern entrance and end at the visitor center, or start at the center in the south. See p321 for more information about the park's attractions.

The park is run by **SalvaNatura** (☎2279-1515; www.salvanatura.org; admission US$6).

Imposible Tours TOURS

(☎2417-4268; www.imposibletours.com; Hostal de Mamá y Papá; waterfall tour US$30, Barria de Santiago 2-day tour incl food & drink US$65, Termas Santa Teresa US$20) If you get to Tacuba, you must take an Imposible Tour. Manolo is an extremely dedicated and knowledgeable guide whose passion for his surrounds rubs off on clients. His hugely popular waterfall tour is an ever-growing series of plunges (or assisted abseils) into icy pools. Among other tours is a mountain-bike ride to the Pacific Ocean, camping at the highest point of the park, Cerro Ceballo, and three-day missions up to Rio Paz on the Guatemalan border. More gentle tours include a hike to the seven hot pools at Termas Santa Teresa.

Sleeping & Eating

Hostal de Mamá y Papá HOSTEL $

(☎2417-4268; www.imposibletours.com; dm/d US$7/14, meals US$4) The mainstay of Tacuba's travel community is a peaceful family home criss-crossed by lush garden. Mama feeds her guests like they are her children's children while Papa tinkers and charms. Rooms are basic but very clean and intimate. Bathrooms are serviceable. English-speaking Manolo, the country's most energetic guide, will need no introduction by the time you check in.

The ground-floor rooms are spacious and include private hot showers, while those beyond the bird-filled garden are more secluded. The upstairs chill-out area has great views. Call ahead for directions. Ask about the new medical volunteer project.

La Cabaña CABIN $$

(☎2417-4332; r US$30; ❄) Big grounds; downhill from the square.

Sol de Media Noche VEGETARIAN $

(mains US$2-4; ⏲6:30am-5pm Mon-Sat; ✎) Soy lasagna, leafy salads and carrot *tortas* were on offer when we visited this informal vegetarian cafe run by a Salvadoran Hindu sect. Menu changes daily. It's two blocks past the plaza.

Getting There & Away

Bus 264 and Ruta 15 (US$0.60, 40 minutes, 5:30am to 7pm) go to Ahuachapán from the main plaza.

Ruta de las Flores

The wildflower of Salvadoran tourism is a 36km-long winding trip through brightly colored colonial towns famed for lazy weekends of gastronomy and gallery-hopping, as well as more adventurous pursuits like mountain biking, horseback riding and hiking to hidden waterfalls scattered throughout the glorious Cordillera Apaneca. Home to the country's first coffee plantations, some of its finest indigenous artisans and a world-famous weekly food festival, the

'Flower Route' anticipates El Salvador's return to the traveler's map.

Bus 249 runs frequently between Sonsonate and Ahuachapán, stopping in all the towns along the way, including Juayúa, Apaneca and Ataco.

Juayúa

POP 10,100

'Why-*ooh*-ah' is famed for its weekend **fería gastronómica** (food fair) where crowds from across the country sample the region's best cuisine and dance to live music on the plaza. Barbecued iguana, guinea pig and frog skewers headline an ambitious menu; less risky fare includes *riguas de coco* (fried coconut and cornmeal) and *elote loco* (crazy corn) lathered with parmesan cheese and mustard.

During the week, Juayúa returns to its relaxed roots, as travelers stroll the warm, cobblestone streets, venture into the surrounding hills to explore hot springs and waterfalls, or just catch their breath by **Cristo Negro**, an important religious statue carved by Quirio Cataño in the late 16th century and housed in the church.

Ideal for wandering, Juayúa is small and its streets follow a standard grid. The church is on the west side of the plaza and behind it is the market.

Juayúa has a tumultuous past. Indigenous uprisings in the region ignited the revolutionary movement of 1932. Backed by the coffee elite, government forces brutally quelled the ill-organized insurrection.

Activities

A recommended hike and swim is to **Los Chorros de Calera**, a series of falls spewing from fractured cliffs to form large, cold pools. The **Ruta de las Seite Cascadas** follows the Río Bebedero over seven scenic drops. Consult Hotel Anáhuac or Casa Mazeta for directions or guides. Occasional thefts mean that certain activities are better undertaken with guides. Other guided excursions include lake visits, coffee tours and waterfall rappels.

Sleeping

Hotel Anáhuac HOSTEL $

(☎2469-2401; www.tikal.dk/elsalvador; dm/s/d US$9/17/25; @) Owner César has nothing but love for the itinerant out-of-towner. The Anáhuac is an institution on the Ruta de las Flores and return travellers swear by the great-value double rooms featuring the works of national artists. There's a lovely green courtyard out back and a real sense of calm and respect. Among the many tours is a new venture following world-class coffee from farm to cup.

Casa Mazeta Hostal HOSTEL $

(☎2406-3403; www.casamazeta.com; 1 Calle Poniente No 22; dm/s/d US$9/20/25; @) This old home has been converted into one of the country's best cheap sleeps. New owners Darren and Carlos present a beautiful premises with eclectic touches throughout. The dorms are fit for slacker princes and there's enough storage to swing a banjo-strapped backpack. Light pours across the tiled floors to give a fairytale feel. Tours are highly recommended.

Portezuelo Park ADVENTURE LODGE $$

(☎2265-1111; www.akwaterra.com; Cantón San Juan de Dios; r/ste sleeping 4 US$55/65, raised tent d US$35, campsite US$5) Managed by the adventurous travel team, Akwaterra, in the capital city, this outdoor playground is a cool place to stay. Loads of activities are on offer including hiking, ropes course, mountain biking and horse riding, but we really loved the tutti-frutti interiors of both the cabins and the kick-ass raised tents. This is hipster camping 6km from Juayúa proper.

Hotel-Posada y Restaurante El Mirador HOTEL $$

(☎2452 2432; 4a Calle Pte 4-4; r US$25-30) A huge mural near the main plaza welcomes guests to this odd assemblage of standard rooms over two floors. Hot water is available at a small charge, the beds are firm and cable TV keeps you company. The rooftop restaurant has a great view of Juayúa and the volcanoes.

Eating & Drinking

Tienda San José FAST FOOD $

(main plaza; mains US$2-7; ⏲8:30am-11pm) One part mini-mart, one part late-night rice and beans and booze joint. Lots of fun on the park square.

Taquería la Guadalupana MEXICAN $

(2a Calle Oriente; mains US$2-7; ⏲lunch & dinner Tue-Sun) Pretty rock solid Mexican food, especially the sloppy tortilla soups and *nopal* (cactus) salads. Young crowd hangs in the courtyard.

R&R SALVADORAN FUSION **$$**
★(Calle Mercedes Caceres 1-4 Poniente; mains US$7-17; ⏲lunch & dinner Tue-Sun) English-speaking Carlos has set up a Yankee-*guanaco* hybrid eatery that stuns diners who find themselves hungry in mountains. Steak in all its salivating incarnations is your best bet, but we still love the *revolotijo vegetariano*, salads and desserts. Service in the art-filled courtyard is superb.

El Cadejo BAR
(3a Av Norte; mains US$4-10; ⏲11am-late Wed-Sat) The center of Juayúa's nightlife, high-life and lowlife hosts acoustic music nights and revolving art shows by local artist and owner Capitan Roca. The award-winning barista Alejandro gets the beans just right and locals line up to try it. The menu is fairly standard Western fare.

Tostaduria de Cafe de Juayua COFFEE
Over by the stadium is this brand new coffee emporium care of the Hotel Anáhuac crowd. Get your green beans roasted or sample various batches from across the country.

Shopping

Canchis Canchis CRAFTS
(☎2469-2730; main plaza) The pick of the town's *tiendas* is this colorful shop run by artists Jorge and Veronica who make or sell everything from handpainted coasters to wooden fish and pencil drawings.

Information

Cyber & Equipment (1a Av Norte; per hr US$0.75; ⏲8:30am-9pm) Internet access. Located half a block north of the plaza; sometimes open until 11pm.

Juayutur (⏲9am-5pm Sat & Sun) Juayúa's tourist agency dispenses information about the town and area excursions at its kiosk on the east side of the plaza.

Scotiabank (Calle Monseñor Óscar Romero) Exchanges traveler's checks, gives Visa cash advances and is adding an ATM.

Getting There & Away

Bus 249 has services northwest to Apaneca (US$0.60, 20 minutes), Ataco (US$0.70, 30 minutes) and Ahuachapán (US$0.90, one hour) and also south to Sonsonate (US$0.80, 45 minutes) during daylight. Buses leave every 15 minutes from the park, or from four blocks west on weekends. For Santa Ana, bus 238 (US$0.75, 40 minutes) goes direct, leaving a few blocks west of Parque Central six times daily.

Apaneca

POP 8600

There's a slight chill in the air in this unearthly, quiet mountain town – at 1450m, Apaneca is the second-highest town in El Salvador, which largely explains why its coffee is so highly sought after. Cruising the cobblestone streets and the odd nursery aside, there's not much happening in town. Hunt out some locally crafted furniture, or do what the active travelers do, and use it as a base for more high-octane pursuits in the surrounding Sierra Apaneca Ilamatepec.

The beautiful **Iglesia San Andres** was one of the oldest churches in the country until the 2001 earthquake reduced it to rubble. Restorations are near completion.

Sights & Activities

The crater lakes **Laguna de las Ninfas** and **Laguna Verde**, north and northeast of town, are within hiking distance. The former is swampy, reedy and rife with lily pads; the latter is deep and cold. You can camp at **Chichicastepeque** (aka Cerro Grande), which at 1816m affords outstanding views of the region, although the antennae make it look a lot less wild. For directions or a guide stop by the tourist kiosk.

Vivero (nursery) tours make for a relaxed afternoon of strawberries, strong coffee and rare plants. **Vivero Alejandra** (⏲7am-4pm Wed-Sun) is a short walk from the center (toward Juayúa). Other *viveros* include **Vivero Santa Clara**, across from Alejandra.

Apaneca Canopy Tours TOURS
(☎2433-0554; US$30) Apaneca Canopy Tours offers a 2.5km zip-line ride through mountain forest. Tours leave daily at 9:30am, 11:30am, 2pm and 4pm.

Apaneca Aventura TOURS
(☎2433-0470, 7136-5851; www.apanecaaventura.com; 4a Avenida Norte; 2hr tour for 2 people US$65) A convoy of dirt buggies now leaves Apaneca Aventura daily for Laguna Verde. It's a novel way of getting around and getting dirty.

Finca Santa Leticia FARM
(☎2433-0357; www.hotelsantaleticia.com; Km 86.5; d incl breakfast US$150) Finca Santa Leticia restaurant and coffee farm is just south of Apaneca. The highlight of the small onsite **archaeological park** (admission US$5) is two pot-bellied figures carved from huge basalt boulders, weighing between 6350kg and 11,000kg. Experts speculate that these

2000-year-old chubbies were created by early Maya in deference to their rulers. The hotel is overpriced but may suit families or groups.

Sleeping & Eating

For more options, check out resort lodges near Apaneca on the highway. Their upmarket restaurants offer the inevitable *buena vista* and a relaxed atmosphere to dally in.

Laguna Verde Guest House CHALET $
(☎7859-2865, 2102-8575; gpssal@intercom.com.sv; dm/d $15/35) About 3km from Apaneca on the edge of the Cuyanausal Range is this peaceful guesthouse more or less on the rim of a volcano. There are two buildings to choose from: one with dormitory-style bedding and the other a more comfortable Swiss-style chalet with four spacious rooms. Self-catering facilities are excellent but you'll have to lug your supplies from town. Call ahead for pick-ups.

Hostal la Magaña B&B $
(☎2433-0268; Av Central btwn 4 & 6 Calles Sur; s/d US$12/24) Quiet and hospitable, this home has two large rooms steeped in burgundy and varnish, as well as impeccable bathrooms. Guests can cook, or relax on the billowy living-room sofas.

Hostal Colonial HOSTEL $$
(☎2433-0662; hostalcolonial_apaneca@hotmail.com; cnr 1a Av Sur & 6a Calle Poniente; r US$20-30) Colorful rooms face onto a peaceful courtyard. The owners are very private.

El Jardin de Celeste CABIN $$
(☎2433-0281; www.eljardindeceleste.com; cabins US$30-50; P ❄ 📶) Roughly 2km from the turnoff to Apaneca (on the way to Ataco) is this beautiful nursery complex with affordable log cabins and a fine restaurant. The neighbouring **Las Flores de Eloisa** is a gorgeous cafe run by the same family.

Mercado Saludable MARKET $
(mains US$2-3; ⏲6:30am-8pm) Cheap eats deluxe, this market facing the park offers good little eateries serving ham, eggs and beans, and *atole* as well as chicken dishes and *pupusas*.

Information

A tourist information booth operates on the plaza on weekends. There are no banks.

Cybercafé Apaneca (3a Av Sur; per hr US$0.75; ⏲8am-11pm) Behind the former church.

Getting There & Away

Buses drop off and pick up on the main street, right in front of the market. Bus 249 plies the route between Ahuachapán and Sonsonate, stopping in Apaneca every half-hour. The last bus runs between 7pm and 8pm. Ask a local to be sure.

Ataco

With a small indigenous presence, and many locals involved in the town's thriving textile trade, pastel-colored Ataco is earmarked for bigger crowds. More intimate than Juayúa, it has seen a surge in sleeping and dining options. The town seems commited to keeping its colonial charms intact – though it could keep an eye on protecting its water source – and recent excavations have revealed good ruins nearby.

The **tourist information kiosk** (⏲7am-7pm Sat & Sun) sits at the entrance to town. You can pick up a handy street map here. Ask about guide services (US$5 to US$10 per person). Options to explore include **Salto de Chacala**, a 50m waterfall on the Río Matala, and **Chorros del Limo**, a spring which forms a broad pool ideal for a dip.

Diconte-Axul (cnr 2a Av Sur & Calle Central; ⏲8am-6pm) is popular for its homemade textiles, tie-dyes and hand-painted objects. The rambling **market** (2a Av Sur) makes for a fascinating walkabout.

Founded by the pre-Columbian Pipils, the next town along is **Salcoatitán**, which has lots of tiny art galleries down cobblestone streets.

Sleeping

Villa Santo Domingo HOTEL $
(☎2450-5442; r US$25; @) Beautiful gardens and a spread of local antiques and artworks round out a very pleasant hotel experience hidden inside this red-brick building.

Segen Hostel HOSTEL $$
(☎2450-5832; alicanteapaneca@hotmail.com; Calle Poniente 3; s/d US$15/30) A block and a bit north of the town square is this laid-back little hostel with an attractive internal courtyard and rooftop balcony where travelers plan their next coffee-fuelled assault. The

WORTH A TRIP

LA COCOTERA

La Cocotera (☎2245-3691; www.lacocoteraresort.com; Barra de Santiago; d per person incl meals from US$128; @) is one of few luxury resorts in the country and the only one on the wild Barra de Santiago. The 'eco' tag here is no buzz moniker; only natural materials are used in the furnishings – palm fronds, handwoven fabrics, plant vines – that are sourced locally and crafted with local hands. Six oceanfront rooms with king-sized beds open onto a long, empty beach surrounded by coconut and mango trees. Estuary and nature tours are first class, as are the inclusive meals and gigantic swimming pool. Decompress with Guatemala in the background.

showers are hot and the beer is cold though the beds were a little dated when we visited.

El Carmen Estate BOUTIQUE HOTEL $$
(☎2243-0304; www.elcarmenestate.com; r sleeping 4 incl breakfast from US$70; P) While driving through coffee country you may feel a pressing desire to sleep among the beans. This *finca* is great value for small groups or couples who want to get off the trail for a few nights. Rooms are busy with furniture but immaculately presented and the food and service are excellent.

Eating

La Caretta TÍPICA $
(☎2450-5369; cnr Av Central & 4a Calle Poniente; mains $3-9) A fine *comida típica* place that also trades in colorful *artesanías*. The *gallo en chicha* (rooster in corn liquor) is the best in town.

House of Coffee CAFE $$
(☎2450-5353; Av Central; meals US$2-10; ⏲9am-7pm Mon-Fri, 9am-10pm Sat & Sun) From plantation to cup in no time at Ataco's sharpest coffee shop, where families and hip city couples scoff cheesecake and hearty soups on dark wooden benches.

Café Tayua CAFE $$
(1a Calle Poniente; meals US$5-12) Known as 'the night' in Nahuatl, Tayua is a longstanding bar cafe that acts as an informal gallery and unofficial information booth. Try the cinnamon rolls (US$1) or the paninis (US$5).

Getting There & Away

Bus 249 stops on the corner of 2a Calle Oriente and 4a Av Sur. One heads north to Ahuachapán (US$0.35, 15 minutes), and south to Apaneca (US$0.25, 10 minutes), Juayúa (US$0.45, 30 minutes) and Sonsonate (US$0.70, one hour). Frequency is every 15 minutes.

Sonsonate

POP 65,100

The southern end of the flower route is a bustling, sweaty commercial town nicknamed 'Cincinnati.' Home to some of El Salvador's most notorious gangs, it mostly makes a living from coffee and cattle. It's also an important transport hub, so chances are you'll find yourself at the swanky new bus terminal. One thing Sonsonate does well is party – the city's vivid **Semana Santa** celebration is a national highlight.

Sights & Activities

The artisan village of Izalco, 8km northeast of Sonsonate at the foot of Volcán Izalco, was the site of a major indigenous revolt in 1932. Nearby is Atecozol, a *turicentro* with swimming holes, kiosks and gardens. The grounds feature stone sculptures by Agustín Estrada – one commemorates Atonatl, a feisty indigenous warrior who pegged conquistador Pedro de Alvarado with an arrow in 1524.

There's easy access to the coastal points of Los Cóbanos, a prime Pacific Ocean diving destination, and Barra de Santiago, a protected mangrove forest reserve where you can swim with cayman crocodiles, canoe with local fishers and fossick for ancient ruins in the muddy shores. It is possible to stay on the huge, unspoilt ocean beach; contact Ximena's Guest House (p291) in San Salvador or Hostal de Mamá y Papá (p316) in Tacuba.

Sleeping & Eating

Dirt-cheap hotels are in the rough area by the old bus terminal – 'dirt' being the operative word here. Better options are in town.

Hotel Orbe HOTEL $
(☎2451-1517; cnr 4a Calle Oriente & 2a Av Flavian Muchi; s/d US$14/18, with air-con US$20/24;)

The long-standing Orbe is still the best-value pick in the center. Service is good, and it's close to amenities.

Hotel Plaza HOTEL **$$**
(☎ 2451-6626; cnr 9a Calle Oriente & 8a Av Norte; s/d US$40/50; P ❄ 📶) So what if it's stuck in the '80s? The Plaza's rooms are Alaska-cool with firm beds and cable TV. You can rest your traveling bones by the pool, and the restaurant is worth trying too.

La Casona PUPUSAS **$**
(3 Calle Poniente btwn 1 & 3 Av Norte; mains US$1.50-4; ⏲ breakfast & lunch Mon-Sat) *Comida a la vista* is dished up fresh and *pupusas* sizzle and steam in the city's best bargain restaurant, located in an antiquated building.

Food Stands FAST FOOD **$**
(cnr 7a Calle Oriente & 10a Av Norte; ⏲ 5-10pm) For junk-food feasting, try the food stands where you can grab burgers, sandwiches, fries and *pupusas*.

ℹ Orientation

The main north–south street is Av Morazán/Av Rafael Campos. To orient yourself in town, the church is on the east side of the Parque Central.

ℹ Information

Citibank (cnr Calle Marroquín & 4a Av Norte) Has a 24-hour ATM.

Post Office (1a Av Norte, btwn 1 & 3 Calles Poniente)

ℹ Getting There & Away

Take a taxi or bus 53C from the central park to the bus station, 2km east of the city center. Buses to San Salvador leave from outside the terminal.

The terminal also serves Izalco (bus 53A), Nahuizalco (bus 53D) and Acajutla (bus 252). For Parque Nacional El Imposible take any La Hachadura bus to Puente Ahuachapío or Cara Sucia (US$0.45, 30 minutes). An alternative for Barra de Santiago is to take bus 259 to the turnoff and catch a pickup.

Parque Nacional El Imposible

Tropical mountain forest Parque Nacional El Imposible was named for the perilous gorge that claimed the lives of farmers and pack mules transporting coffee to the Pacific port. Decreed a national park in 1989, it sits in the Apaneca Ilamatepec mountain range between 300m and 1450m above sea level, and includes eight rivers which feed the watershed for Barra de Santiago and the mangrove forests along the coast.

This original forest – the remains of a threatened ecosystem – is still home to an extraordinary variety of plant and animal life, including pumas, tigrillos, wild boars, king hawks and black-crested eagles. Hiking can get muddy and steep but offers grand vistas of misty peaks and the gleaming Pacific Ocean.

The main San Benito entrance is on the southeast side, beyond the hamlet of San Miguelito. The park is run by **SalvaNatura** (☎ 2279-1515; www.salvanatura.org; entry US$6); in theory you need to visit the San Salvador office to pay the entry fee and arrange for guide service (there is no guide fee but a US$5 tip is customary). The best time to visit is October to February, as the rainy season hinders travel.

The solar-powered visitor center has a modest museum and lookout tower with ocean views.

BUSES FROM SONSONATE

DESTINATION	BUS	COST (US$)	DURATION
Ahuachapán via Juayúa, Apaneca & Ataco	249	0.95	2hr
Barra de Santiago	285	1	1¼hr, leaves 10:30am & 4:30pm
La Hachadura	259	0.85	1¾hr
La Libertad	287	1.25	2½hr
La Perla	261	0.80	1½hr
Los Cóbanos	257	0.50	40min
San Salvador *directo*	205	0.80	1½ hr
San Salvador *especial*	205	1.50	1½hr
Santa Ana	216	0.65	1¼hr

Sleeping & Eating

Three large camping areas with toilets and grills are within walking distance of the visitor center; the furthest one (20-minute walk) is the least crowded. Camp free with your entrance fee; the visitors center rents gear (tents US$5 to US$7, bring bedding). Small fires are allowed and potable water is available.

Hostal El Imposible HOTEL **$$**
(☎2411-5484; d US$30, extra person US$10; ❄)
About 1km from the park entrance is this smart eco-resort featuring five A-frame cabins. The views from the patios are gorgeous, plus there's the delicious organic Restaurant Ixcanal to recharge on local dishes.

Activities

There are three major hikes in the park.

Cerro El Leon HIKE
A tough 8km circuit topping out on one of the park's highest peaks (1113m), starting in a lush, humid gorge and climbing through dense forest. This trail offers terrific panoramic views. From the visitor center the trail descends steeply 1km to the Río Ixcanal. Crossing the river you climb the other side, known as Montaña de los Águilares, to the summit. Return by a different route, along the narrow ridge between the Ixcanal and Guyapa river valleys. Allow several hours and bring plenty of water.

OFF THE BEATEN TRACK

INDIGENOUS WESTERN EL SALVADOR

If you've a sense of adventure and an interest in how indigenous forms have transformed through time, Here are a couple of options.

➡ View local artisans crafting basketry and furniture in **Nahuizalco**, but the real trip is to the night market, with indigenous treats such as grilled *garrobo* (lizard) and rabbit tacos. There's no lodging. Take bus 249 from Juayúa (to the highway turnoff, 500m away) or bus 53D from Sonsonate.

➡ The ancient Nahual community of **Izalco** has famed religious wood carvings parading in both Catholic and indigenous rites. Access via Sonsonate bus 53A.

Los Enganches HIKE
An ideal picnic spot, this big swimming hole is reached by a trail (3.5km one way), which passes Mirador El Mulo and descends steeply. Along the way you'll pass Mirador Madre Cacao, with views of the southeastern part of the park. Look for agoutis and coatis.

Piedra Sellada HIKE
A 4km trail to a swimming spot and a stone etched with Maya writings. Take the Los Enganches trail; just before the end another trail cuts upriver 1km to Piedra Sellada.

Getting There & Away

From Sonsonate catch bus 259 toward La Hachadura and get off at Cara Sucia. From there, a bus leaves at 11am and a pickup at 2pm (both US$2, one hour) for the main entrance. The trucks return to Cara Sucia every morning at 5:30am and 7:30am. If you think you might miss the pickups in Cara Sucia, you may be able to cut them off at Puente Ahuachapío (bridge), a few kilometers short of Cara Sucia. If the pickups have already passed, you may be able to hitch a ride (13.5km).

You can also visit the park from the northern side via Tacuba (p316).

EASTERN EL SALVADOR

Eastern El Salvador may not possess the star attractions of elsewhere in the country, but with timeless mountain villages such as Alegría, the visceral war history around Morazán, and the long, deserted beaches near El Cuco, even the most worldly traveler will find reason to explore.

Prior to the war, subsistence farming was long the primary means of survival here. The inevitable demand for nationwide land reform resonated throughout the poorer communities, and the northeast in particular became a fierce guerrilla stronghold. Far from the capital, these mountainous areas witnessed horrific atrocities – none worse than El Mozote – but barely a village was spared from the fighting, and the resilience of the locals will stir visitors for generations to come.

Remittances continue to pour in from relatives working abroad – whether this is a long-term economic solution is still to be seen, but new money is nonetheless providing opportunities to a generation bristling with positive intent. However, stalled construction of a deluxe port at La Unión is a

OFF THE BEATEN TRACK

EAST ALONG THE INTERAMERICANA

The Carretera Interamericana goes east from San Salvador to San Miguel, on to La Unión and up again to the El Salvador–Honduras border at El Amatillo.

A few towns of interest lie between San Salvador and San Vicente on the Interamericana. **Cojutepeque**, 32km east of San Salvador, is a small town best known for the Cerro las Pavas (Hill of the Turkeys), featuring an outdoor shrine to the Virgen de Fátima, brought here from Portugal in 1949. Religious pilgrims come on Sunday and on May 13, **El Día de la Virgen**. In San Salvador, catch bus 113 from the Reloj de Flores, just west of the Terminal de Oriente; it's about a 45-minute ride.

Further along the highway (54km from San Salvador or 22km from Cojutepeque) is the turnoff to **Ilobasco**, a town famous for ceramics known as *sorpresas*. Upon entering the town a string of *artesanía* shops lines Av Carlo Bonilla. The annual **crafts fair** runs September 24 to 29. Take bus 111 or 142 from the Terminal de Oriente or from Cojutepeque.

Another 8.5km heading east along the Interamericana is the road to **San Sebastián**, known for woven hammocks and textiles, and unique in that most of the weavers are male. The fair takes place at the end of January. Take bus 111 or catch a bus in Cojutepeque.

reminder that development takes time in the 'Wild East.'

Further south there are beautiful sand beaches, especially around El Cuco and Las Flores. They only see fleeting traffic from nearby cities such as San Miguel, the working-class capital with a distinctly cavalier attitude. Real off-the-beaten-track coastal adventure is found at Golfo de Fonseca and Bahía de Jiquilisco, where tiny fishing villages pay little attention to the outside world.

There are two ways to travel east – along the Carretera Interamericana or along the Carreteradel Litoral (CA2); the latter accesses the beaches, and the former the northern reaches. The Ruta de La Paz (peace route) runs north from San Miguel.

San Vicente

POP 34,600

San Vicente is dwarfed by pointy Volcán Chichontepec in the Jiboa Valley. Look out for the equally dramatic behemoth of Torre Kiosko, an otherwordly clock tower that juts from the farmland like some Disneyland ride gone haywire. Home to many musicians, San Vicente is also very gay-friendly – the annual Miss Gay San Vicente draws quite the crowd (and the contestants!).

El Pilar, a beautiful colonial church built in the 1760s, was badly damaged by an earthquake; despite renovations, it remains closed.

Activities

The double-peaked **Chichontepec** (also known as Volcán San Vicente) offers a moderate climb through coffee plantations. This eight-hour round trip is relatively safe but it's best to go in a group or get a police escort from Nuevo Tepetitán or San Vicente. Wear sturdy boots and bring a sweater, lots of water and food for you and your escorts. Take bus 191 (US$0.30, 20 minutes) to Nuevo Tepetitán, where the trail begins. Buses leave from the corner of Calle Alvaro Quiñonez de Osorio and 9a Av every half-hour from 6:30am; last return bus is at 7:15pm.

Sleeping & Eating

Hotel Central Park HOTEL $

(☎2393-0383; r with fan/air-con US$10/15; ❄) Come for the 2nd-floor terrace, stay for a bed if you really must – only the sheets resemble anything fresh or clean – but unfortunately it's the only place we could find to stay. The small bar is popular among the gay community, and the restaurant (open 6:30am to 10pm) below the hotel serves decent *típica*. Doors are locked at 8pm.

Comedor Rivolí SALVADORAN $

(1 Av Sur; mains US$2-4; ⏲7am-8:30pm) The most popular place in town, and justly so with fresh and homemade dishes. This *comida a la vista* is served in a spotless dining room alongside rose gardens. Don't miss the delicious dollar *licuados*.

BUSES FROM SAN VICENTE

DESTINATION	BUS	COST (US$)	DURATION	DEPARTURES
Ilobasco	530	0.60	1hr	6:50am, 11am, 4pm
San Miguel	301 from the turnoff at the hwy	1.50	1½hr	last bus 6pm
San Salvador	116	0.85	1½hr	last bus 6pm
Zacatecoluca	177	0.60	50min	–

EcoRestaurant TRADITIONAL $
(mains US$3-6) Food straight from the farm to your table (via the kitchen we hope).

Information

Citibank (2a Av Sur) Cashes traveler's checks and has a 24-hour ATM.

Fast Line Ciber Café (2a Calle Oriente; per hr US$1; 9am-9pm)

Police (2303-7300, 2396-3353; cnr 1a Av Norte & 3a Calle Poniente) Can arrange for an escort up the volcano.

Getting There & Away

All buses pass by the Parque Central after leaving the terminal uphill on 6a Calle and 15 Av. Beat the crowds at the park without hoofing it to the terminal by catching buses at 6a Calle and 2a Av. For Alegría, catch an eastward bus from the Carretera Interamericana and transfer at Villa El Triunfo.

Alegría

Alegría is a beautiful mountain town enjoying a renaissance with domestic visitors. Its lofty location, near-spotless streets and windowsills overflowing with rose bushes, sunflowers and orchids give it a fairytale feel quite unlike the rest of El Salvador. Young artists and new businesses are infusing energy here. A few lazy days and nights hiking by the lake and promenading the town square could well prove a highlight of your travels.

The friendly **tourist agency** (2628-1087; 1a Av Norte at 1a Calle Poniente) has a municipal office and a booth on the Parque Central. It also offers some worthy guided hikes (US$10 to US$15 per half day) to coffee plantations, geothermal plants and sites related to philosopher and native Alegrían, Alberto Masferrer.

The scenic crater lake **La Laguna de Alegría** (admission US$0.25) is a 2km downhill walk from town. Its icy waters are said to be medicinal. Don't miss the beautiful view from the **Mirador de las Cien Grados** – a vista point at the top of 100 steps. You can also take the road toward **Berlín**, another pretty mountain village.

Sleeping

Casa de Huéspedes la Palma B&B $
(2628-1131; 1a Av Norte, near Calle Alberto Masferrer; dm US$10; @) Search beyond the flowerpots for this friendly old family home. Inside you'll find a curious clutter of photos, carvings and religious dioramas, plus an onsite internet cafe serving coffee on the plaza. Rooms are tiled and scrappy but cheap.

Cabanas La Estancia de Daniel CABIN $
(2628-2030; per person US$10) These cabins out the back of the owner's house are great value. Each has two beds and a detached bathroom. The communal area has a few slung hammocks and random furniture. The property is located a block south of the plaza.

Entre Piedras Hotel HOTEL $$
(2313-2812; entrepiedras.alegria@hotmail.com; Av Camilo Campus; s/d US$16/32; ❄ @) By far the most stylish hotel in Alegría boasts original stone foundations and breezy rooms with wooden paneling throughout. Firm beds have high-quality linens and there's a charming courtyard cafe (paninis US$5). Chocolate is made on premises and the owners can give valuable information about hiking in the area. Book ahead on weekends.

La Casa Mia HOTEL $$
(2634-0608; www.berlinlacasamia.com; 2a Av Norte, Berlín; d US$33) Nearby Berlín is a copycat cute village. If Alegría is full, or you just want some real mountain beauty, stay at this intimate family hotel that opened more than 70 years ago.

Eating & Drinking

El Portal CAFE
(11am-9pm) The pick of the park cafes for an evening beer (US$1).

Merendero Mi Pueblito SALVADORAN $
(mains US$1-5; ⏲7am-7pm) Alegría's best-value food is at this worn cafe where beans simmer in cast-iron pots over an open flame and the whole family chips in. It's south of the park.

Getting There & Away

Alegría sits between the Interamericana and Litoral highways and is accessible from either side. From Carretera Interamericana, catch a minibus from Villa El Triunfo to Santiago de María (US$0.30, 15 minutes), where buses leave hourly for Alegría (US$0.60, 45 minutes).

Carretera del Litoral

The Carretera del Litoral (Hwy CA2) runs from San Salvador southeast through Zacatecoluca and Usulután, eventually coming to a crossroads with routes heading north to San Miguel and south to the Pacific coast.

The first town of any size southeast of San Salvador is **Zacatecoluca** (57km), near *turicentro* Ichanmichen. From there, the Litoral is a well-marked four-lane highway with shoulders, until you get to the Río Lempa. Beyond the bridge, the road narrows but maintains decent shape. Another 27km to the east is the departmental capital of Usulután.

The highway then skirts a rugged range to the south. The turnoff for one of El Salvador's best beaches, **Playa El Espino**, is just past El Tránsito, 10km east of Usulután. The newly paved road has cut the trip to 20 minutes. Further east, **Laguna El Jocotal** is an important migratory bird sanctuary, sadly littered with trash. Your best bet is to tour the lagoon via canoe with a local.

The road then winds up into lava hills until the roundabout at El Delirio. From there, it's a straight shot north to San Miguel or south to Playa El Cuco and the eastern beaches.

Isla Montecristo

A steamy, pristine sanctuary for hundreds of pelicans and egrets, this island and estuary sit where the Río Lempa meets the Pacific Ocean. During the war, the island and its cashew plantation were abandoned and taken over by the FMLN. After 1992, it was resettled by local farmers taking advantage of the postwar land transfer program. These days there are about 25 families growing organic cashews as an export crop.

★**Hostal Lempa Mar** (☎2310-9901; www.gbajolempa.net; La Pita; r US$25), operated by a local development group, is highly recommended. Simple cabins offer basic rooms with shared bathrooms and a comfortable terrace, and there are meals available in the restaurant. **Boat tours** travel through narrow corridors in the mangroves; some visit the cashew plantations as well. A fishing cooperative in Estero Jaltepeque can arrange fishing trips or the rental of traditional canoes.

La Pita and Montecristo are at the end of a 22km road which connects the Carretera Litoral to the coast. The road can be rough in rainy season. Take bus 155 (US$0.70, 40 minutes) or a pickup from the Texaco in San Nicolas Lempa, with departures between 6am and 5:30pm.

From La Pita, *lanchas* (small motorboats; US$20 round trip) or canoes (US$4 one way) can take you out to the island.

Usulután

POP 45,300

Tented market stands choke the streets of this chaotic departmental capital at the foot of 1450m Volcán de Usulután. Middle Eastern immigrants exert a strong influence over the town's commerce. For travelers Usulután will probably serve as a way station to Bahía de Jiquilisco and the lovely **Playa El Espino**.

BUSES FROM USULUTÁN

DESTINATION	BUS	COST (US$)	DURATION
Alegría	348	1	1hr
Playa El Cuco	373	0.80	2hr
Puerto Parada	350	0.30	30min
San Salvador *directo*	302	1.50	2½hr
San Salvador *especial*	302	2	1½hr
Zacatecoluca	302	0.70	1½hr

You can also reach the mountain hamlet of Alegría from here.

Sleeping & Eating

La Posada de Don Quijote HOTEL $
(☎2635-9792; cnr 1a Calle Poniente & 1a Av Sur; s/d US$12/24; ❄) This hotel, inside a small shopping complex, has spacious rooms with freshly unpacked mattresses, piping-hot showers and a pleasant 1st-floor terrace.

Hotel Sevilla HOTEL $$
(☎2633-8500; Caretera Litoral 114; r US$60; P❄📶🏊) This shiny new three-star business hotel has boxlike rooms that are nonetheless very comfortable. Staff are friendly but speak no English. The restaurant is so quiet you can hear yourself chew and there's a neat outdoor pool.

Pastelería Trigo Puro PATISSERIE $
(Calle Dr Penado; mains US$2-3; ⏲7am-5pm Mon-Sat) Fat cinnamon rolls, doughnuts and coconut cookies beckon from the glass case of this popular bakery, also serving cafeteria-style *típico*. It's one block west of the park.

L'Azteca MEXICAN $
(cnr Calle Dr Federíco Penado & 1a Av Norte; mains US$2-3; ⏲10am-8pm) Large Mexican place with open windows, long wooden benches and a sizzling barbecue. The *tortas* cooked out front are delicious, as are the sizable tacos and the icy cold *licuados*.

Mercado Central STREET FOOD $
(4a Av Norte btwn 2a & 4a Avs Norte) The Mercado Central is a hit with street-food aficionados.

Information

Citibank (2a Calle Oriente, near Av Dr Guandiquil) On the Parque Central, it cashes traveler's checks and has a 24-hour ATM.

Cyber Planet (4a Calle Oriente, btwn 2a & 4a Avs Norte; per hr US$0.50; ⏲8:30am-6pm Mon-Sat, 8:30am-noon Sun) Internet access.

Getting There & Away

Usulután's main bus terminal is 1.5km east of the Parque Central (taxi US$2). The San Miguel terminal is west of town, but passengers can board along 1a Calle Oriente, a block south of the Parque Central. The San Miguel bus is number 373 (US$0.80, 1½ hours); take it to connect to La Unión.

Buses to Alegría, Puerto Triunfo and San Salvador all take 4a Calle west through the center of town. Since most buses travel this way through town you don't necessarily have to go to the terminal (unless you want a seat).

For Playa El Espino, buses 351 & 358 (US$1.20, 1½ hours leave from a small lot 100m west of main terminal, across from a supermarket. For Puerto El Triunfo take bus 363 (US$0.50, one hour) from a lot along the highway.

Bahía de Jiquilisco

With kilometer after kilometer of white sand pounded by surf, and inland mangroves facing the volcanoes, the Península San Juan del Gozo beckons. The inland sector is a habitat for gray egrets, pelicans and other waterbirds. Fishing towns include **Corral de Mulas** and **Isla Méndez**. Other less accessible beaches are at **Punta San Juan** on the peninsula's east end and **Isla Madre Sal**. Also called Isla Jobal, **Isla Espíritu Santo** has endless coconut groves and a coconut-oil processing plant, but the beaches are no big deal. The Pacific side has strong and powerful surf, so be careful.

The gateway to Bahía de Jiquilisco, seedy **Puerto El Triunfo**, is best sped through. If you're desperate, Hotel El Jardín has doubles for US$12. The pier eateries overlooking the bay offer fresh fish, *pupusas* and *licuados*.

Isla San Sebastian

Isla San Sebastian is the largest island on the Bahía de Jiquilisco. To get here, take the 350 bus to Puerto Parada from Usulután. The road ends at an estuary; there are a couple of cheap fish restaurants here and a few boats bobbing about (US$25 round trip). If the empty beaches convince you to stay in the pretty little archipelago, ask for **La Familia Flores** (r US$15) and you'll be shown to a unique family home made entirely from coconut husks, a potentially lucrative building material. You might just be the second foreigner to stay here!

Corral de Mulas & Isla Méndez

Passenger boats to **Corral de Mulas** (US$2) leave in the early morning from the dock at Puerto El Triunfo. *El Icaco* is a better option to *Corral II*. Once there, cut through town on sandy – sometimes flooded – roads to the beach (30 minutes). The last boat back is at 4pm; if you miss it, ask for a lodging recommendation at the *alcaldía*.

Isla Méndez offers a bay beach with calm, shallow waters and a palm-frocked

WORTH A TRIP

PUERTO BARILLAS

A visit to the remote and spectacular Bahía de Jiquilisco may well be a highlight of your visit to El Salvador. This UNESCO-designated Biosphere Reserve contains the largest estuary in El Salvador and includes numerous bays, canals and sandy beaches with perilous swells. Dotted throughout are tiny fishing villages where life has changed little in decades.

Puerto Barillas (☎ San Salvador head office 2263-3620; www.puertobarillas.com; tree house $118, apartment $236, half price for members paying $600 annual fee) is a revamped marine club that offers a wonderful opportunity to experience this unique biosphere and perhaps even visit the country from a more solitary base. Accommodation includes a choice of posh treehouse or luxury apartment that can sleep four.

The hotel works closely with environmental groups to protect hawksbill turtle nesting sites and monitor the remarkable influx of migratory birds. Guests can visit a cacao plantation and hang with mobs of spider monkeys (who escaped from a zoo) and take boat tours past curious alligators. Visiting the ramshackle **Hacienda San Jose de La Carrera**, which feels like entering a Central American version of *Great Expectations*.

A host of dignitaries have choppered in or arrived by boat and there is even an immigration post should you wish to join the international jetset. The marine club will pick up from San Salvador hotels or the airport (U$S35/25). If arriving by car, exit the Carera Litoral (CA2) at 108.5km. If arriving by bus, change at Usulutan or pick up a minibus or taxi at the turnoff (US$0.50/5).

ocean beach with crashing surf. Due to bus schedules, travelers are obliged to stay the night. It could be interesting, however. Local community development group **Adesco** (☎ 7727-3453) can arrange US$10 overnight family homestays. It also arranges boat trips around the bay (US$35 per group) that travel through mangroves and Palacio de las Aves, home to hundreds of waterfowl.

Bus 368 (US$1, 1¼ hours) goes to Isla Méndez from San Marcos Lempa (30km away on the Carretera Litoral) at 1pm and 2pm, returning at 5:30am and 6:30am. From San Marcos Lempa buses go to Puerto El Triunfo (11km) frequently.

The last bus to Puerto El Triunfo is at 4:40pm, the last one back to Usulután is at 5:30pm. From the highway turnoff, take bus 377 to San Miguel (US$1.35, 2½ hours, last bus 2:50pm) or bus 185 to San Salvador (US$1.55, two hours, every 30 minutes, last bus 2:50pm).

San Miguel

POP 218,400

San Miguel is an intense working-class city, its sticky heat rising up from calamitous streets. It's also a brashly confident place with a commercial energy to rival the capital and its locals relish the seedy, sexy nightlife.

San Miguel was founded in 1530, and organised crime has long been at loggerheads with the law here. It's hoped the new government will draw vigilantes into the fold, but with remittances still pouring in – and unemployment still high – it's as likely to change face as iconic Volcano Chaparrastique is to erupt anytime soon.

Parque David J Guzmán is Parque Central, with the cathedral to the east. The area is choked with traffic by day and dodgy by night. The area west of central park is quieter and more secure. Av Roosevelt (Carretera Interamericana) skirts the southwestern edge of town, where you'll find the majority of nightclubs and a large Metrocentro mall.

Sights & Activities

Catedral Nuestra Señora de la Paz CATHEDRAL

Facing Parque David J Guzmán, San Miguel's cathedral dates from the 18th century.

Antiguo Teatro Nacional THEATER

(2a Calle Oriente) A neoclassical gem which functioned as a cinema during the silent-film era and later as the Telecom headquarters and a public hospital.

Museo Regional del Oriente MUSEUM

(2a Calle Oriente) FREE The Museo Regional del Oriente is in the same building as the Antiguo Teatro Nacional on the 2nd floor.

San Miguel

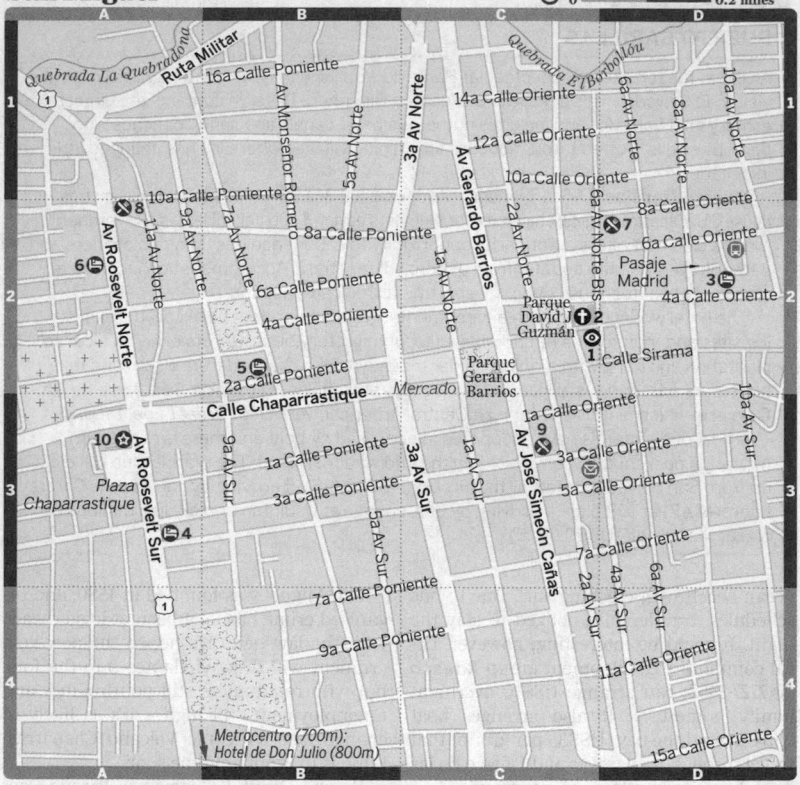

San Miguel

Sights
1 Antiguo Teatro Nacional C2
2 Catedral Nuestra Señora de la Paz C2
Museo Regional del Oriente ..... (see 1)

Sleeping
3 Hotel Inn El Guanaco D2
4 Hotel Plaza Floresta A3
5 Hotel Posada Real B2
6 Villa San Miguel A2

Eating
7 Comedor Chilita D2
8 Don Taco A2
9 Pastelería Lorena C3

Entertainment
10 Melodia A3

The collection of pottery and photos is meager but it's free.

Ruinas de Quelepa ARCHAEOLOGICAL SITE

Archaeology buffs will appreciate the Ruinas de Quelepa, grassy mounds covering 40 terraced ceremonial platforms, largely unexcavated. Lenca inhabited the site between the 2nd and 7th centuries AD, trading with Copán in Honduras as well as Mexico. Stone sculptures uncovered here are on display in the Museo Regional del Oriente. The ruins are 8km west of San Miguel off the Interamericana. From the cathedral, bus 90 to Moncagua (US$0.50, 30 minutes) passes them.

Volcano Chaparrastique HIKE

If you're game for a steep nine-hour slog, consider climbing 2130m Volcano Chaparrastique, aka Volcán de San Miguel, a towering cone southwest of San Miguel.

Arrange police escorts by contacting the **Chinameca Police Station** (☎2665-0074; fax 2665-1014). Request with two weeks' notice, if possible. The top affords gaping views of the coast and a patchwork of rolling farmland. The crater is hundreds of meters deep, with a jumble of boulders and Virgins at the bottom.

Get there with a rental car or take the Placitas bus from San Miguel at the corner of Calle Chaparrastique and 7a Av Sur and then arrange a taxi.

Festivals & Events

Every November San Miguel honors the Virgen de la Paz with **Fiestas Patronales**, marking the occasion with holy processions and enormous, colorful sawdust carpets. Save yourself for its blowout finale, **Carnaval**, a citywide party held the last Saturday of November.

Sleeping

The cheapest places to stay are by the bus terminal, a gritty area unsafe after dark.

Hotel de Don Julio HOTEL $$
(☎2661-4113; 14 Calle Elizabeth; d US$25; P ❄ @) Modern hotel with clean rooms. Extras include cable TV, minibar, small gym and internet cafe. It's in one of San Miguel's better neighborhoods.

Hotel Inn El Guanaco HOTEL $$
(☎2261-5029; cnr 8a Av Norte & Pasaje Madrid; s/d US$20/30; ❄) Small and welcoming, El Guanaco has enormous spotless rooms with hot-water bathrooms and cable TV. For something quiet and removed, choose the 3rd floor. There's a pool table and promising smells wafting up from its ground-level restaurant.

Hotel Posada Real HOTEL $$
(☎2261-7174; cnr 7a Av & 2a Calle Poniente; s/d US$23/30; ❄) In the safer and subdued neighborhood west of the market, this well-kept pink two-story hotel offers bland but amenable rooms, with good beds, air-con and TV. Take an upstairs room; those downstairs smell of mildew.

Hotel Plaza Floresta B&B $$
(☎2640-1549; Av Roosevelt 704; s/d $25/50; P ❄ 📶 🏊) The Ignacio Cordova family presides over this lovely small hotel on Alameda Roosevelt. The tiled lobby is cool and inviting and gives way to a spacious courtyard and a series of attractive rooms on two floors. There's a small pool and a well-tended standing garden that offer respite from the noise outside.

Villa San Miguel HOTEL $$
(☎2669-6969; www.hotelvillasanmiguel.com; Av Roosevelt 407; s/d $30/60; P ❄ 📶 🏊) The city has been crying out for this kind of hotel: modern, stylish, affordable and with an emphasis on customer service. The quiet, cool rooms at Villa San Miguel have excellent beds and piping-hot showers. Room service is very reasonably priced and breakfast is included. There's also a gym to iron out your bus neck.

Eating

The best value is *comida a la vista* for breakfast and lunch at a *comedor;* show up early when the trays are full and the food is fresh.

Pastelería Lorena PASTELERIA $
(3a Calle Poniente 21; cakes US$0.20-3; ⏲7am-7pm) El Salvador's most famous bakery started here. A glass of *horchata* and a slice of *Maria Luisa* (jam cake) are the business.

Comedor Chilita CAFE $
(cnr 8a Calle Oriente & 6a Av Norte Bis; mains US$2-3; ⏲7am-10pm) This buzzing cafeteria spoons up a happy, huge variety that includes steamed veggies, spaghetti and roasted pepper chicken. After 4pm, it's all *pupusas* – use the side entrance on 8a Calle Oriente.

Don Taco MEXICAN $
(Av Roosevelt Norte 320; mains US$2-3; ⏲noon-10pm) Good, cheap Mexican is found atDon Taco.

La Pema SALVADORAN $$
(mains US$7-15; ⏲10:30am-4:30pm) This church-like structure is home to one of the country's most enjoyable gastronomic experiences. Located 5km out of town on the road to Playa El Cuco, La Pema is famous for its creamy soups and long lunches. Don't miss the *mariscada* (creamy seafood soup), served up with thick cheese tortillas. The service is earnest and quick and the crowd comes in from afar. Taxis know where to go.

Drinking & Nightlife

The notorious party district *el triángulo* (intersection of Av Roosevelt and the highway) doesn't get going until 11pm, when the mariachis congregate at the intersection ga station to await a prized gig. Be sure to ask your taxi driver for a *discoteca*, and not a 'nightclub,' unless of course you're looking for strippers. Robberies have been committed by men posing as taxi drivers outside nightspots.

Melodia CLUB
(Av Roosevelt Sur, Plaza Chaparrastique) They should make all *discotecas* like this – booming, cheesy, high-heeled and high-octane Latin pop paradise where large contingents of well-heeled students compete for each other's attention. Drinks are cheapest before midnight, but it's empty till 1am.

Information

Banco Cuscatlán (cnr 4a Calle Oriente & Av Barrios) Exchanges traveler's checks and foreign currency and has a 24-hour ATM.

Banco Salvadoreño (cnr Av Barrios & 2a Calle Poniente) Cashes traveler's checks, does Visa cash advances and has a 24-hour ATM.

Immigration Office (Migración; ☎2660-0957; cnr 15a Calle Oriente & 8a Av Sur; ⏲8am-4pm Mon-Fri)

Post Office (cnr 4a Av Sur & 3a Calle Oriente)

DANGERS & ANNOYANCES

Although gang violence has quietened with new security measures, the city center is still the wrong place to be once the sun sets.

Getting There & Away

BUS

San Miguel's **Bus Terminal** has clearly marked bus lanes but ask around for schedules. Taxi to your hotel if you arrive at night.

For the Honduran border, the El Amatillo bus 330 (US$1.90, 1½ hours) leaves at 10-minute intervals from 4am to 6pm. For Perquín, bus 332 (US$1.35, three hours) leaves at 6:20am, 9:50am, 10:20am, 12:40pm and 3:20pm. Alternately, take 328 to San Francisco Gotera and transfer to a pickup. See table, below, for more departures.

CAR

Hire a car through **Uno Rent A Car** (☎2661-0344; Av Roosevelt Sur).

La Unión

POP 23,600

While some pockets retain a salt-crusted colonial charm, La Unión is the kind of town even the saltiest sea dogs are keen to avoid. It's hot and downright dirty, with little to keep you here but an overdue boat headed for the horizon. The heat is brutal; even dogs whimper at noon. Locals hope that the new deep-sea port will generate more prospects, but two years on from construction it still sits ominously quiet, awaiting clearance from the captains of industry. Till then, chow down on dried squid and ready your beach bum for the remote islands in the Golfo de Fonseca.

Playa Las Tunas and Playa Jaguey are good beaches on the coast west of La Unión, while beaches near Playa El Cuco and El Tamarindo are excellent.

For some respite from the heat, and views of the gulf, head to **Conchagua**, at the base of the imposing volcano of the same name.

Sleeping & Eating

For seafood dining check out the waterfront east of the center.

Hotel San Francisco HOTEL $$
(☎2604-4159; Calle San Carlos, btwn 9a & 11a Avs Sur; s/d US$32/40; ❄) Fernando is the eccentric barefooted owner of this colonial structure that is more impressive from the outside. Rooms are pricey given the old beds and leaky bathrooms, but it's located in a decent street and guests can store their belongings if headed for the islands.

BUSES FROM SAN MIGUEL

DESTINATION	BUS	COST (US$)	DURATION
El Cuco	320	1	1½hr
La Unión	324	1	1¼hr
Marcala, Honduras	426	3.50	5½hr
Puerto El Triunfo	377	1.60	2hr
San Salvador	301	2.20	3hr
San Salvador *especial*	301	US$3.20	2hr
Usulután	373	1	1½hr

La Unión

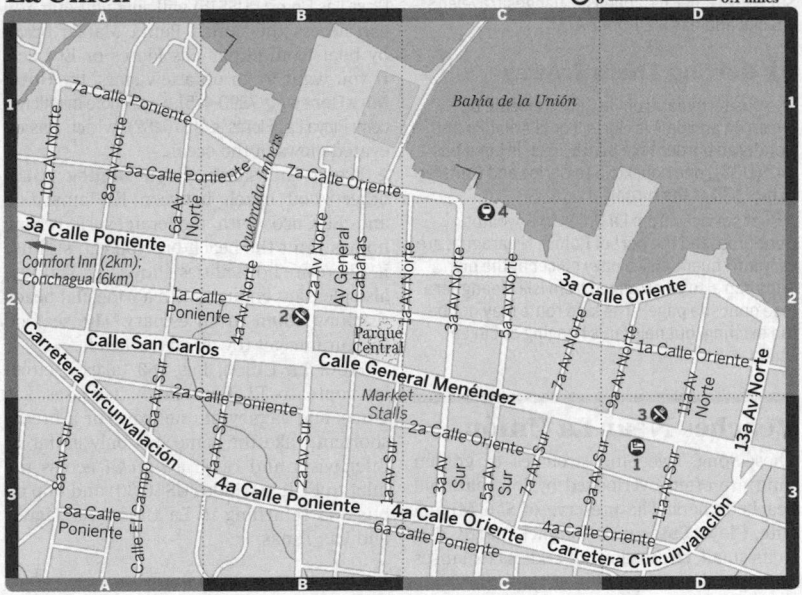

Comfort Inn

MOTEL **$$$**

(☎2665-6565; Km 2.8 Calle a Playitas Carretera Panamericana; r US$75; ❄@🏊) It's a pretty sad state of affairs when the best hotel in town, regardless of criteria, is from the good ol' Comfort Inn chain. The rooms are very comfortable though and the swimming pool is big enough to cut laps while you plan your trip to the islands. Breakfast is spot on. Best of all you can sleep four people for the one room price.

Pupusería Mayra

PUPUSAS **$**

(Calle San Carlos; mains US$1-2; ⏲5-10pm) Across the road from San Francisco, and heaving with a post-gospel crowd, this local insitution is the best bet for *panes de pollo* (chicken sandwiches) and fresh *pupusas*. Get in quick or they'll run out.

Cappucino's

CAFE **$**

(1a Calle Poniente 2-2; coffee US$2, snacks US$2-5; ⏲8am-7pm) Like a mirage in a desert of dodgy street food, Cappucino's is a flash cafe with ice-cold air-con and plush vinyl lounges. The coffee is clearly the star, but try the breakfast sandwiches (US$4).

Oasis Luna

BAR

(3a Av Norte, Playa Los Coquitos; ⏲2pm-2am) Las Lunas offers nightlife in the form of karaoke and occasional concerts under a thatched bar. There's a new restaurant overlooking the water.

La Unión

Sleeping

1 Hotel San Francisco D3

Eating

2 Cappucino's B2
3 Pupusería Mayra D3

Drinking & Nightlife

4 Oasis Luna C2

Information

Cyber Café (3a Av Norte, btwn 3a & 7a Calles Oriente; per hr US$0.70) High speeds and newish computers.

Immigration Office (☎2604-4375; cnr Av General Cabañas & 7a Calle Poniente; ⏲6am-10pm Mon-Sat) Next door to the post office; the sign says *Control Migración*. You must stop by here if you're arriving or departing by boat from Nicaragua or Honduras.

Plaza Médica Vida (☎2604-2065; Calle General Menéndez btwn 7a & 9a Avs Sur; ⏲24hr) A decent hospital near the center.

Scotiabank (3a Calle Oriente btwn 1a Calle Sur & Av General Cabañas) Changes traveler's checks and has a 24-hour ATM.

Getting There & Away

The bus terminal is on 3a Calle Poniente between 4a and 6a Avs Norte. For El Amatillo at the Honduran border take Santa Rosa de Lima bus 342 (US$1, one hour) to San Carlos and transfer to bus 330 at the turnoff.

Boat services from La Unión to Coyolitos, Honduras, and the port of Potosí, Nicaragua, are very infrequent. Ask a navy officer at the pier. Trips can also be arranged from Isla Meanguera (see opposite page). The land route may not be too exciting, but neither is hanging out in La Unión.

Beaches Near La Unión

These long, sweeping stretches of golden sand are often overlooked by international beachcombers. The preserve of San Miguel elite, **Playa Esteron** is the pick, partly due to its small, clean surf and endless expanses of empty shore.

About 3km west of Esteron is the more prominent **Playa El Cuco**, which is overrun with weekenders from San Miguel. Be aware of potential jellyfish and manta rays – shuffle while walking out. There are plenty of good, cheap seafood restaurants in the sandy town square. **Azul Surf Club** (☎2612-6820; www.azulsurfclub.com; Playa El Cuco; s/d US$75/85; ❄ @ 🏊) is a beautiful new high-end surf resort that runs admirable service projects in the area. It specialises in package stays; passing travelers can get a pretty good deal too.

Further west, **Las Flores** is a prime surfing point suitable for beginners from December to February. The rest of the time it's best left to pros. Mama Cata at **Familia Segovia** (☎2619-9173; casacata1@hotmail.com; Playa Las Flores; r US$15) will sort you out. You can access the famed Punta Mango break by boat from either Las Flores or El Cuco. If you want to go up a few stars, try **Hotel Miraflores** (☎7890-4751; www.elhotelmiraflores.com; Playa Las Flores; s/d $70/82), which has elevated views of the ocean.

Broad and sandy **Playa Jaguey** is another good beach between El Tamarindo and El Cuco, with moderate surf. Private homes front the beach but you can still use it. There are no facilities. **Playa Las Tunas** is also pleasant enough, with a wide, flat beach reaching 100m to an estuary. The seafood restaurants get rowdy on weekends.

From La Unión, bus 383 takes a circular route to El Tamarindo; it passes Las Tunas and Jaguey on the way. For a breezy shortcut, take the same bus only as far as Buenavista and catch a *lancha* across the inlet to El Tamarindo (US$0.30) and hop on bus 383 returning to La Unión via Jaguey and Las Tunas.

Golfo De Fonseca Islands

About as remote as it gets in tiny El Salvador, these lush, volcanic gulf islands are not quite tourist-brochure material. Once the playground of 17th-century pirates, they now feature isolated fishing villages, bored locals, and trash-strewn black-sand beaches that jar against cinematic bird sanctuaries, pretty pepper-colored coves and warm, abundant waters.

The nearest island, **Isla Zacatillo**, has the largest commuity, and numerous coves with sandy beaches can be explored here. The principal village has a few stores and lodgings in a wooden shack over the bay. For solitary beaches, head for **Isla Martín Pérez**, just south of Zacatillo. More mountainous

BUSES FROM LA UNIÓN

DESTINATION	BUS	COST (US$)	DURATION
Conchagua	382A	0.25	15min
El Tamarindo	383	1.05	1¾hr
Las Playitas	418	1	1hr
San Miguel	324	1	1¼hr
San Miguel especial	324	1.20	1hr
San Salvador	304	3	4hr
San Salvador especial	304	5	3hr
Santa Rosa de Lima	342	0.90	1½hr

WORTH A TRIP

LA TORTUGA VERDE

The **Green Turtle** (☎ 7774-4845; www.latortugaverde.com; Playa Esteron; dm/s/d US$10/25/50, house US$150; ❄ 🏊) is our favourite place in El Salvador, both as a eco-destination in its own right and a straight-up fun place to stay. This collection of coconut plantations on empty beachfront is overseen by ex-New Yorker Tom Pollack, veteran big-wave surfer, environmentalist and, most recently, a national TV personality.

On the main property, superlative beachfront rooms are constructed from recycled wood and found stone. Old cheese presses and canoe paddles lead to a landscaped garden and swimming pool.

Dorm rooms are within ear-reach of the ocean. Guests can use a fully-functioning kitchen or opt to eat with staff (US$7 per person for breakfast and lunch) and practise their Spanish. Next door to the main property is a beachside day club (US$2 entry) and two multi-bedroom holiday houses. A day spa offers hour-long facials (US$10) and a yoga studio faces the setting sun.

The restaurant (mains US$5 to US$15) by the sand serves huge plates of fresh, healthy local seafood, special traveller 'requests' and loads of vegetarian options.

All-day ocean adventures to the Golfo do Fonseca are offered (US$30 per person). For those making the passage to Nicaragua, the hotel guarantees your same-day crossing by boat or you stay at the hotel free until they do so.

La Tortuga Verde is 3km east of Playa El Cuco. Once you reach El Cuco, turn left and follow the gravel road for roughly 3km. La Tortuga Verde is on the right.

Isla Conchagüita offers hiking opportunities. Fishing boats are neatly lined up under *enramadas* (arbors or protective awnings, typically made of wood or branches) along the beachfront of the main village. Locals say there are prehistoric rock carvings on the way out to Playa Brava, a black-sand beach an hour's walk from the village.

The pick of the islands is the furthest from the mainland. **Isla Meanguera** was long the subject of territorial disputes with Honduras and Nicaragua, until an international court declared it part of El Salvador in 1992. Aside from a small, friendly village, the island boasts **Playa Majahual**, a spectacular beach when clean. It's a 45-minute walk from the ferry landing; shuttles (US$1) depend on availability.

Hotel La Joya del Golfo (☎ 2648-0072; www.hotellajoyadelgolfo.com; Isla Meanguera; d US$79-89, extra person US$10; ❄ @) is a gorgeous boutique hotel nestled in a picturesque bay. The rooms are large, with gilt-edged bathrooms, cable TV and clear views of 'Bird Island.' Rina, the friendly owner, is also a tremendous chef, while partner Richard is a keen fisherman who can arrange excellent trips. Call before arriving or to arrange pick-up.

Getting There & Away

La Unión has services to Zacatillo (US$2, 20 minutes) and Meanguera (US$2.50, 1½ hours) from the pier. Departure times vary, but are generally from 10:30am, returning at 5am the next day. Day trippers have to arrange a private pick-up.

A private 'express' lancha costs US$60 round trip to Meanguera. Agree on a price before the journey starts, and pay only half up front to ensure your return trip. Ferries for the islands also depart from Las Playitas further down the coast.

It is possible to get to Coyolitos, Honduras, and the port of Potosí, Nicaragua, from the Golfo De Fonseca Islands but services are very infrequent. Try calling Hotel La Joya del Golfo on Isla Meanguera to see if it has a trip planned. Prices vary widely.

Morazán

The rugged northeastern Morazán Department is a predominantly poor farming region that is generating a quiet buzz for its sustainable, community-based nature and war tourism. The museum in Perquín and a memorial in El Mozote are powerful displays of reconciliation and remembrance. The cool climate attracts an increasing number of city-slicker nationals, as does the country's cleanest river, the Río Sapo, and the countless hikes to waterfalls and war hideouts.

Indigenous traditions survive in villages around San Francisco Gotera, the department capital. The village of **Cacaopera** (bus 337 from San Francisco Gotera) has a small ethnographic **museum** (admission US$1; ⏲9am-noon & 2-5pm Mon-Fri) with photo exhibits and artifacts from the local Kakawira indigenous community. Miguel Ayala of the museum is a good contact.

Through the museum you can also arrange guided hikes in the dry season (December to April) to pre-Columbian petroglyphs (US$15 per group). The museum maintains a rustic **hostel** (☎2651-0251; dm US$5), without electricity or running water. You can bathe in the nearby Río Torola and cook on the wood-burning stove. Sure, it's roughing it, but the experience is undoubtedly unique.

The community at **Guatajiagua** produces quality black pottery in the Lenca tradition. Visit craft shop **Cedart** (Calle Principal; ⏲8am-5pm Mon-Fri, 8am-noon Sat) or ask the clerk to point you in the direction of local artist workshops.

Perquín

POP 5500

A visit to the former FMLN headquarters in the mountain town of Perquín is paramount to understanding El Salvador's brutal civil war. It was in these hills that the opposition garnered its most loyal support, and despite vigorous bombing campaigns, the military was unable to dislodge the guerrilla forces. The town itself isn't beautiful but the cool mountain climate and excellent war museum make a trip here the highlight of El Salvador for many visitors.

Sights

Museo de la Revolución Salvadoreña MUSEUM

(Calle Los Héroes; admission US$1.20; ⏲8:30am-4:30pm Tue-Sun) A few blocks north of the park, the Museo de la Revolución Salvadoreña charts the causes and progress of the armed struggle. Highlights include the collection of anti-war posters from throughout the world, the stark color photos of life inside guerrilla camps, the incredible assortment of Soviet weapons and some histories of those who died in action. It's a somber, stirring visit.

El Campamento Guerrillero Simulado MUSEUM

(Calle Los Héroes; admission US$0.50, guided trip per group US$20; ⏲8:30am-4:30pm Tue-Sun) El Campamento Guerrillero Simulado is a reconstructed guerrilla camp connected by swing bridges and dirt tracks in a patch of partially cleared woodland. Sites include the remains of the downed helicopter that carried Lieutenant Colonel Domingo Monterrosa, head of the notorious Atlacatl Battalion, to his death. You'll see the studios of the FMLN's clandestine station Radio Venceremos ('We Will Win Radio'), part of an elaborate hoax that used a radio transmitter rigged with explosives to bring Monterrosa's helicopter down.

The museum is also the contact point for ex-guerrilla guides who can take visitors on fascinating **guided trips** throughout the war zone. The most popular destination is El Mozote.

OFF THE BEATEN TRACK

AROUND MORAZÁN

Morazán is opening itself up to community-based tourism. Former Peace Corps volunteer Ari Borinsky has some cool suggestions for getting out and about in his designated patch:

➡ Visit the **aguas termales** (hot springs) in Canton El Progreso, where you can bathe in a beautiful *pila* (bath) perfectly made for two. It's an hour-long bus ride from Perquín, then a one-hour hike to the Río Araute. Pass the small school (wave to the students) then follow an old sign pointing the way.

➡ **El Salto** waterfall is only for the true *aventureros*. To get here you must walk along the slippery banks of the Río Araute. Local guides and brothers, **Edwin and Carlos** (☎7490-8082, 7219-5750; tours US$10-20), can happily assist.

➡ Near San Fernando, **La Cascada del Chorreron** is the most impressive and most accessible waterfall in the region. The water comes from a permanent, natural spring and saw one of the bloodiest battles of the civil war, La Batalla del Moscardon. From San Fernando, you can hike for 2km through a *reserva natural* along smooth terrain. The 40m-high waterfall streams into a beautiful crater which is perfect for swimming.

Activities

Mountainous Perquín offers excellent hiking and river swimming. An abundance of orchids and butterflies make it a prime birdwatching zone – 12 varieties of oriole have been spotted along with the rare chestnut-headed oropendola. The **Río Sapo** is one of three rivers cutting through the forest – you can swim or camp here after visiting El Mozote. It's about a 45-minute walk and well worth the effort. The beautiful upper watershed has lots of friendly communities such as **Cumaro**. Ask around for local guide Don Santos, who can arrange visits to the local swimming hole and extremely welcome guest appearances at the local school. Likewise local farmers will show you a day on the pick in coffee, corn and sugar plantations. You can stay at Cabaña las Veraneras (p335).

Quebrada de Perquín is a smaller, craggier creek, also good for swimming. **Cerro de Perquín** is a 10-minute hike from town, while **Cerro el Pericón** is a longer haul. Both offer gorgeous views. For guides consult Prodetur or the museum.

Tours Ciclista de Montaña is a major cycling race held in November, while **Festival de Montaña** is a new weeklong cultural festival in late December.

Sleeping & Eating

Cabaña las Veraneras CABIN $
(☎7733-4493; Caserio Cumaro; campsites/r per person US$2/6, meals US$1.50) Guests of Niña Nilda become one more member of the family. You can also contact the Prodetur office in Perquín for reservations.

La Posada de Don Manuel B&B $
(☎2680-4037; s/d US$9/18;) The best budget choice by far is this converted lumber mill tucked away 500m to the left of town as you enter. The concrete rooms are cool in summer and the hot water and wi-fi are strong. Manuel is an indefatigable guide and his wife Corina cooks up a storm.

Hostal Perquín Real HOSTEL $
(☎2680 4158; s/d US$8/16) One of the better restaurants in town, Cocina de Mama Toya y Mama Juana, also has a six large double rooms. The shared bathrooms have been spruced up nicely but you will share them with diners. It's located at the south entrance of town.

Eco Albergue Río Sapo CABIN $
(☎2680-4087, 2680-4086; campsites/dm per person US$4/7) Access to a swimming hole and a dozen hikes is the best reason for staying at these rustic dorm-style cabins at Area Natural Protegida Río Sapo. There's no electricity and limited water; bring your own food and flashlights. You can rent a tent (US$3) or sleeping bag (US$1) if you don't have your own. It's operated by Prodetur.

★Hotel Perkin Lenca HOTEL $$
(☎2680-4046; www.perkinlenca.com; r per person incl breakfast US$25, cabins sleeping 1-4 incl breakfast US$50-74) Perkin Lenca has been handcrafted from pine and oak by American bulider Robert Brennerman and the thoughtful upkeep has made it one of the more comfortable hotels in the country. The cabins are perfect for families, and the double rooms are great value, all with hot water. Tours are readily available.

La Cocina de Ma'Anita SALVADORAN $
(Hotel Perkin Lenca; mains $5-10; breakfast, lunch & dinner) The huge A-frame dining area is more ski-lodge than mountain bistro, but the tables along the front windows get nice morning light and have overhead lamps for night-time. The produce is mostly organic and always delicious. Try the preserves, ice creams and meat dishes. Afterward, head up to the much cozier bar for drinks.

La Cocina de la Abuela SALVADORAN $
(mains US$2-4) The pick of the cheap *comedores* on the town square.

Information

Cyberspace (per hr US$1; 8am-9pm Sat-Thu, 8am-6pm Fri) Internet access.

Prodetur (☎2680-4086; Parque Central; 8am-5pm Mon-Fri, 8am-2pm Sat) Perquín's helpful tour office organizes guided tours and hikes (US$15) with a few days' notice. Early August commemorates the signing of the peace accords with various guided trips available.

Getting There & Away

The CA7 north of San Miguel to the Honduran border is in good shape. Bus 332 runs from San Miguel to Perquín (US$1.50, 2½ hours) at 6am, 7am, 9:50am and 12:40pm. Alternatively, there's the more frequent bus 328 to San Francisco Gotera (US$0.70, 1½ hours) from where pickups go on to Perquín (US$0.50, one hour). The last bus back to San Miguel is at 4pm; the last pickup to Gotera leaves at 5:40pm, but you have to catch the 5pm to make the last Gotera–San Miguel bus.

El Mozote

On December 11, 1981, government soldiers terrorized and executed the residents of this northern hill village. It's estimated that 757 people died: of the 143 victims uncovered, 131 were children. El Mozote is now a destination for those paying homage to the massacre. A tribute includes bright murals painted on the church, depicting the town as it was back then and as its children hope it to some day be again. There is also a plaque with the names of those who died and a rose garden planted over the collective grave of the massacred children. This modest village has no lodgings and few services.

It's important to remain sensitive to the seriousness of the site. Locals are accustomed to an international presence; they've even set up snack bars and children tag behind visitors asking for handouts. As tempting as it is to give, it's best if you donate directly to the box inside the tour office.

From Perquín, walk or take a pickup 3km south to a fork in the highway. El Mozote is 10km from the paved road; Jateca-bound buses pass here at 8am. On the way you'll pass Arambala, once decimated by air raids. The same bus returns from El Mozote at 12:45pm and can drop you at the turnoff. Combine this trip with a visit to Río Sapo, a 30-minute walk from El Mozote.

Prodetur and the Museo de la Revolución Salvadoreña in Perquín can do trips here, but show respect by using local Spanish-speaking El Mozote guides once in the village.

THIRTY YEARS ON

Official recogniton of the El Mozote massacre has been a long time coming, but after three decades of political resistance an international ceremony was held in the small mountain village in late 2011. New roads welcomed visiting dignitaries, and relatives of victims spoke of the impact the event has had on their lives.

A striking **monument** was also constructed to honor those killed in the conflict. It features silhouettes of children and is surrounded by great figures in peaceful resistance from around the world. It's about 1km past the town itself and adds an element of closure for locals and insight for those who make the effort to pay their respects.

NORTHERN EL SALVADOR

Timeless, charming Suchitoto – an immaculate colonial town just 47km from the capital – is the star of northern El Salvador, a mostly mountainous farming region enjoyed by trekkers. Travelers en route to Honduras will find themselves high above the world here, slowly traversing craggy hills and pine forests, with time no longer of the essence and other travelers a whole countryside away.

Detours too are well rewarded. La Palma is a unique artist hangout where *arte naif* continues to capture the world's imagination. Hiking trips from San Ignacio and Miramundo are the equal of any in Central America. The commercial hub of Chalatenango – now the center of El Salvador's safest province – is set to enjoy stronger economic prospects if a new national highway development goes ahead as planned.

The Chalatenango district bore the brunt of the military's *tierra arrasada* (scorched land) tactics, which burned fields and killed livestock as a form of combat. The main provider of water and hydroelectric power for El Salvador, the district faces a serious deforestation problem.

Suchitoto

Seemingly lifted from a magical realist novel, Suchitoto has held firm – nay, prospered – against the weight of history just as its weekend arts fest turns the quintessential town square into one giant production of *guanaco* pride. None of this is new, however; when indigo ruled the marketplace and the beautiful Spanish church was packed daily, Suchitoto was the country's unabashed cultural capital. It retains its title with ease.

For those not fussed by the gallery and bar scene – much of it not open during the week – there are countless hikes to waterfalls, caves and beautiful Lago Suchitlán that begin and end just meters from town. Suchitoto is also a bird migration zone with over 200 species. Thousands of hawks and falcons fill the skies as the seasons change, and birds of all sorts nest in the relative safety of the lake islands.

It is presumed that Yaquis and Pipil peoples settled in the area some 1000 years ago. El Salvador's capital was established near here in the early 16th century. More recently, some of the earliest fighting of the civil war began in Suchitoto, accompanied by much destruction and emigration. Today the town has rebounded to become the highland seat of national tourism.

Sights & Activities

Geologic oddity **Cascada los Tercios** tumbles over a cliff of tightly packed hexagonal stone spires. The waterfall underwhelms when water is low (often), but the rock formation and the trip there are interesting enough.

It's 1.5km to the west on the main road, but don't hike solo as some robberies have been reported; book a trip through El Gringo (p338) hostel.

It's a 1½-hour hike to **Salto El Cubo**, a 15m waterfall cascading into a pair of pools. You can climb from the lower one to the upper, hemmed in by rocks with the water crashing down from above. To get there, take Calle Francisco Morazán west out of town to a rocky trailhead, a narrow path descending steeply to the falls.

Southwest of town, the former FMLN hideout of Volcán Guazapa is a popular **horseback riding** (six-hour trip US$30) destination operated by an independent cooperative. Visitors can check out *tatús,* clever dugout hideouts, as well as craters and bomb shells. Book trips through the tourism office.

The tourism office arranges city tours that include some 30 historic buildings. Browsing the **art galleries** can also make an agreeable afternoon. Check out **Casa del Escultor** (☎2335-1836; www.miguelmartino.com; 2a Av Sur; ⏲Sat & Sun), the studio of acclaimed Argentine sculptor Miguel Martino, and **Shanay** (☎2335-1836; www.miguelmartino.com; 3a Av Norte; ⏲Sat & Sun), home of Víctor Manuel Sanabria.

Centro Arte para la Paz CULTURAL CENTER
(☎2335-1080; www.capsuchitoto.org; 2a Calle Poniente 5) The Centro Arte para la Paz organises a range of cultural activities from its premises in an old Dominican convent. Free films are screened on Friday at 5pm.

★**Suchitoto Adventure Outfitters** TOURS
(☎2250-0113, 2250-0800; www.suchitotooutfitters.com) René Barbon is your man for adventurous and informed travel in El Salvador. Brilliant tailormade tours include the usual Suchitoto and El Salvador routes, plus more obscure adventures such as kayaking trips to the Pacific Ocean, moving tours to nearby Cinquera and unforgettable missions to Nicaragua.

IPES VOLUNTEERING
(☎2335-1891; www.permacultura.com.sv; 2a Av Sur 38, Barrio El Cavario) Highly recommended opportunity to volunteer in grassroots permaculture projects on a purpose-built site 15km outside Suchitoto where local farmers complete formal studies in sustainable farming. For US$400 a month volunteers receive lodging onsite, immersion in the local community and access to experienced instructors.

El Tejado SWIMMING
(☎2335-1769; 3a Av Norte 58) To escape the heat, swim for US$3 in the huge pool with a view at this hotel (d US$65), owned by an evangelical church. It's also a good spot for a beer.

Courses

Pajaro Flor Spanish School LANGUAGE
(☎2335-1509; www.pajaroflor.com; 4a Calle Poniente 22) Pajaro Flor Spanish School offers 20 hours of accomplished private instruction for US$160; homestays can be arranged for U$4 to US$10 per day.

Global Platform LANGUAGE
(☎7655-8997; www.globalplatform.org.sv; 2a Calle Poniente 9) Global Platform is a Danish NGO that offers Spanish lessons in conjunction with grassroots development projects around Suchitoto. Non-Danes are welcome to apply; a month costs roughly US$400, which includes basic lodging, food and various excursions.

Sleeping

On weekends food vendors fill the plaza selling *riguas* (sweet buttery corn tortillas wrapped in a corn husk) and *fogonazo* (sugarcane juice), spiked with the strong stuff on request. The two top hotels, **La Posada Suchitatlan** (☎2335-1064; Barrio San José) and **Los Almendros de San Lorenzo**, are busy with weekend diners.

Blanca Luna HOSTEL $
(☎2335-1661; 1a Calle Oriente; r per person US$7) This friendly budget choice has a huge communal balcony and an appealing position behind the church. The six rooms are tasteful for the price and the sunny courtyard is ideal for meeting fellow travellers.

OFF THE BEATEN TRACK

CINQUERA

This former FMLN stronghold has transformed itself into a successful example of grassroots tourism. The friendly community has initiated a series of projects that have helped it to rebound from the horrors for the civil war. Ex-guerillas share firsthand accounts of the conflict at a new **war museum**. A terrific little **rainforest park** is great for a short hike and waterfall swim and there's a new sustainable **iguana farm** for the herpophiles.

An excellent **hostel** (☎2389-5732; ardmcqr@yahoo.es; cabins US$30), run by the Association for Reconstruction and Municipal Development (ARDM), is seeking volunteers for community and ecotourism projects. Call the hostel for details.

El Gringo HOSTEL $

(☎2327-2351; www.elgringosuchitoto.com; Calle Francisco Morazan 27; s/d US$12/18, dm US$7; P ❄ 📶) Long-term expat and tour operator Robert Broz Morán and his charming wife run this bright pink travel hang-out a short walk west of the square. The two small rooms are bright and comfortable; the five-bed dorm is very basic but the mattresses are firm and new. The real highlight is the delicious Tex-Mex restaurant open 24 hours.

Hostal Vista Lago HOSTEL $

(☎2335-1357; 2a Av Norte 18; r per person US$8) Located on the slope towards the lake, this eccentric hostel has one of the best views in town. The small colorful rooms are a little claustrophobic for some but the sweet service and adventurous clientele make for a fun stay.

Las Puertas HOTEL $$$

(☎2393-9200; www.laspuertassuchitoto.com; cnr 2a Av Norte & Av 15 de Septiembre; r US$75-95; ❄ @) Situated on the town square opposite the church, Las Puertas is a good-value high-end hotel with large rooms and an unpretentious old world feel. Handcrafted artworks abound in lavish rooms with views in two directions – the mob below or the mountains above. The convivial downstairs bar feels like a Central American film noir set.

★**Los Almendros de San Lorenzo** BOUTIQUE HOTEL $$$

(☎2335-1200; www.hotelsalvador.com; 4a Calle Poniente; d/ste US$120/150; ❄ @ 🏊) Without a doubt this is one of the best places to stay in El Salvador. A posh boutique hotel set in a restored 200-year old home, high-end Salvadoran art, antique and modern furnishings, custom-made doors and several gurgling fountains set the scene for six immaculate rooms. All have high ceilings, large tile bathrooms and classy, simple decor. The suites – one with its own fountain, the other distributed over two floors – are worth every extra cent.

In addition to rooms that are hard to leave, guests can lounge in a luxurious library, at the well-tended pool, or in the lush garden. A fine restaurant and hip lounge bar only complete the experience.

Eating

★**La Lupita del Portal** CONTEMPORARY $

(☎2335-1429; mains US$3-8) Lovely Lorena and her friendly team oversee the best-value restaurant in town, situated on the south side of the square. Service is brisk and smiley, and meat and vegetarian dishes are accompanied by fresh salads, sandwiches and gigantic juices.

Xela's Pizza PIZZERIA $

(☎2335-1397; pizza US$6-10) Delicious pizza under the trees. Follow the signs from the plaza.

Drinking & Nightlife

El Necio BAR

(4a Calle Oriente No 9; ⏲6pm-1am) Revolutionary flags drape across the tables at this leftist bolthole that opens intermittently. Run by Jerry, an amiable ex-guerrilla; the revolutionary spirit is as strong as the drinks.

Harlequín BAR

(⏲7pm-1am Fri-Sun) Harlequín plays eclectic tunes in a trellised garden with twinkling lights. There are occasional film nights and a steady expat crowd.

Orientation

La Iglesia Santa Lucía stands on the east side of the Parque Centenario, the town center. Signs to the lake lead you a block east of the park, left onto 3a Av Sur, then down steeply to the water (about 1km). You can also follow the street that forms the park's western edge (Av 15 de Septiembre); it merges with 3a Av Sur several blocks down. Parque San Martin is two blocks west and two blocks north of the town center.

Information

A 24-hour **HSBC ATM** is found on the town square; **Banco ProCredit** (cnr 2a Av Norte & 2a Calle Poniente) can change some foreign currency and cash travelers' checks.

Internet cafes abound; try **X-Streme Speed Cyber Cafe** (2235-1722; 1a Calle Poniente; per hr US$1; 8am-8pm).

Suchitoto's **tourism office** (2335-1739; www.gaesuchitoto.com; Calle San Martin 2; 8am-4pm) rents bikes (per hour US$1) and informs about hikes, activities and cultural events. For more up-to-date information, visit www.gaesuchitoto.com or the restaurant at El Gringo (p338).

Getting There & Away

From San Salvador's Terminal de Oriente take bus 129. To return, the same bus departs from the corner of 1a Calle Poniente and 4a Av Sur, a block west of Parque Centenario. By car, go toward Cojutepeque on the Interamericana. When you get to San Martín, turn left at the Texaco sign.

If you're headed north, catch bus 163 to Las Aguilares (US$0.80, one hour), where buses pass for Chalatenango, Las Palmas and the El Salvador–Honduras border. A slower but more scenic option is to take a boat (per person US$6, 20 minutes) or car ferry (per person US$1, per car US$4) across Lago de Suchitlán to San Francisco Lempa and from there catch a bus to Chalatenango. The last one leaves at 3pm.

Chalatenango

POP 16,200

The sleepy Chalatenango province comes momentarily to life each morning in the capital, 'Chalate,' the business headquarters of northern El Salvador. Honking trucks navigate the narrow streets, overflowing with pineapples, sugarcane, indigo and coffee, while colorful buses are stacked with friendly locals selling DVDs, toiletries and glittery sequined dresses. As the commercial center for small rural mountain villages, there's a real contrast between the ambitious, city-bound youth and a generation of leather-skinned subsistence farmers recounting tales of FMLN might. The large military garrison on the plaza was built during wartime to rein in revolutionary activity in this FMLN stronghold.

Sights

Iglesia de Chalatenango CHURCH

The Iglesia de Chalatenango, with its squat bell tower and bright chalky facade, sits on the east side of the Parque Central, a stone's throw from the military garrison.

Turicentro Agua Fría PARK

(admission US$0.80; 8am-5pm) A 20-minute walk from the Parque Central, Turicentro Agua Fría has a lush park with picnic tables, but the main draw is the pools set with an artificial rock island topped by a waterslide. Dry season means water shortages – expect an overdose of chlorine. A cafeteria serves beer and meals. To get here, go up Calle Morazán (east) about 400m, and turn left at the big sign.

Cerro La Peña HIKE

For panoramic views of the Cerrón Grande reservoir, climb Cerro La Peña, a 1½-hour hike starting at a trailhead before the *turicentro*. A number of roads and paths reach the top; ask passersby for directions.

Sleeping & Eating

La Posada del Jefe HOTEL $

(2335-2450; Calle el Instituto, Barrio El Calvario; s/d US$16/25;) Up the hill 10 blocks to the east you'll find this decent place, with bone-white concrete rooms filled with ex-office furniture. There's a little convenience store out front. To get here take a little red moto-taxi (US$1). It's kind of fun.

La Posada de Don Santana HOTEL $$

(2278-7783; www.laposadadedonsantana.com; Calle La Vega 33; s/d from $38/48;) Don Santana is a small mountain hotel with five rooms facing into an attractive courtyard. It's the kind of crisp, quiet retreat for wearing out a hammock or finishing the final chapters in your novel.

Cafe Colombia CAFE $

(4a Calle Poniente; coffee US$1) Cruisy locals play chess beneath a ceiling made from continental coffee bags. Aerobics and techno blare through the open gym window. Tasty ham sandwiches are served by bored women.

Comedor Carmary TÍPICA $

(3a Av; mains US$2-3; 7am-2pm Mon-Sat) This tidy cafeteria packed with bus-stop patrons serves tasty *comida a la vista,* which might include stewed chicken in tomatoes, plantains and the ubiquitous beans and rice, alongside tall glasses of fresh juice.

Market MARKET $
(⏲5am-1pm) The open-air market offers a visual feast of veggies, fruits and grains, as well as stock to replenish your toiletries. It's just east of Av Fajardo. A cacophanous market is also held on Tuesday and Sunday in the town center.

Orientation

The Parque Central is divided by 3a Av, with the church on the east (uphill) side and the main park on the west (downhill) side. The market extends up the main east–west street, Calle San Martín-Calle Morazán. A huge army barracks stands north of the main park; most buses pick up and drop off on 3a Av, south of the park. Exceptions are the buses to Arcatao and Las Vueltas, which leave at the top of Calle Morazán, near the turnoff to the *turicentro*.

Information

There's a 24-hour ATM at **Citibank** (4a Calle Poniente, near 6a Av Sur), and it also changes traveler's checks. Try **Cibercafé@halate Online** (1a Calle Oriente at 5a Av Norte; per hr US$0.80; ⏲8am-9:30pm Mon-Sat, 9am-1pm Sun) for internet access.

Getting There & Away

Bus 125 runs regularly from San Salvador (US$0.90, two hours) and terminates on 3a Av Sur, a few blocks south of the church. To La Palma and El Poy, take bus 125 toward El Amayo (the highway intersection) and transfer to bus 119 (1½ hours) heading north.

Around Chalatenango

The countryside around Chalate climbs into dry forest studded with toothy peaks and rugged tawny hills. The small villages in this remote area have stunning landscapes and interesting histories.

Beyond the Río Sumpul, **Arcatao** is a beautiful village in the mountains bordering Honduras. Ask in the municipal office about tours of the *tatus* (cave hideouts), which attest to Arcatao's former role as an FMLN stronghold. The local **Jesuit order** (☎2354-8009; bartolome2408@yahoo.com) receives guests and can set up guided tours of the area. Call ahead.

Northwest of Chalate, **Concepción Quezaltepeque** is a hammock-making center. You'll see women threading them along the side of the road. Prices range from US$30 to US$150, depending on size, length, thickness and material. Shops line the main street; browse a few first to compare quality.

La Montañona is a pine-forest reserve at 1600m with prime views and pre-Columbian rock carvings. The civil war left several *tatus,* including one used by clandestine guerrilla radio station Radio Farabundo, as well as an underground guerrilla hospital. You can stay in the small village – a rustic cabin has beds and shared bathroom (US$5 per night). Teresa Avilar cooks up basic meals. Call **Cesar Alas** (☎7723-6283) before going; he oversees the lodging and acts as a guide to the area.

A strenuous climb passing Dulce Nombre de María travels cobbled roads through pastel villages. Enjoy views of flat valleys sprung with volcanoes and the mountainous Honduran border beyond. North is **El Manzano**, a cooperative of ex-FMLN combatants. Its trails cross forest and coffee farms, and destinations include historic war sites and waterfalls. The top of El Pilón offers more incredible views. The *tienda* in the middle of town has information on lodging, meals and guides.

Getting There & Around

The following bus departures originate in Chalatenango:

Aracatao Bus 508 (US$1.15, two hours) departs hourly from 7am to 5:30pm from the top of Calle Morazán.

Concepción Quezaltepeque Catch bus 300B (US$0.35, 20 minutes) at 3a Av Sur terminal in Chalate.

El Manzano No direct service. Take 125 to the *desvío* (turnoff) for Dulce Nombre de María to pick up bus 124 from San Salvador to Dulce Nombre de María. Take a pick-up to El Manzano.

La Montañona Buses 295 or 542 (US$1, two hours) pass by the turnoff to Montañona, departing at 11:15am and 12:15am from 3a Av Sur between 1a and 3a Calles Poniente. From the turnoff it's a steep 6km climb to the village – pickups often make the trip.

La Palma

A collective exercise in street art en masse, La Palma must have more public murals per capita than anywhere else on earth. This cool mountain village 84km north of San

Salvador is literally splashed with loud, tutti-frutti tones. Everything from street signs to market stalls gives off an inner-child vibe, á la *Sesame Street* in the '70s. Hikers will enjoy the contrast between the surrounding verdant, challenging peaks and the apricot, mauve and lemon-colored homes. Locals are adept at handling tourists.

Painter Fernando Llort moved here in 1972, founding Naïve Art, a trend that still represents El Salvador around the world. These bright, primitive images of mountain villages, *campesinos* or Christ are synonomous with the modern Salvadoran art movement. Llort taught local residents how to create the same images and started a successful cooperative. Today 75% of the village makes a living by mass-producing these bright motifs.

Hikers often prefer lodging in the neighboring village of **San Ignacio** as it's closer to the trails.

Sights

Visitors are welcome to peek into workshops to see families painting away.

La Semilla de Dios WORKSHOP
(cnr 3a Calle Poniente & 5a Av Norte) Local cooperative La Semilla de Dios, founded in 1977 by Fernando Llort himself, crafts quality products in workshops behind the store. If you ask permission you can wander through the workshops and watch the painters and woodworkers at work.

Copapase WORKSHOP
(☎2305-9376; ⏲8am-5pm Mon-Fri, 8am-noon Sat & Sun) Copapase is the most established cooperative in the area – it even has a small museum.

Activities

Cerro El Pital (2730m) is the highest peak in El Salvador, but thanks to an access road it is also one of the easiest to hike. From nearby San Ignacio catch bus 509 to Las Pilas, which leaves you at Río Chiquito near the trail. It's about 1½ hours to the top of El Pital, where spectacular views await. You will know you've reached the summit when you find the cement block marking it. It is private property, so bring US$2 to cover admission.

Once there, ask for directions to **Piedra Rajada**, a huge cloven rock a half-hour walk from the summit, accessed by a nerve-wracking log bridge spanning a 25m drop. Don't try this one in wet weather.

The pinnacle of awesome forest views is in **Miramundo**, a small, aptly named community perched on a steep hillside. Back at Río Chiquito, follow the right-hand fork for about an hour to Miramundo. Right on the trail is the ridgetop Hostal Miramundo (see below).

San Ignacio is a great base for hard-core hiking enthusiasts. For a guide, contact José Samuel Hernández, the owner of **Comedor y Artesanías El Manzana** (☎2305-8379; Carretera La Palma–El Poy km 85), outside La Palma, or **Humberto Regalado** (☎2352-9138), who owns and maintains the trail to Peña Cayaguanca.

Buses to Las Pilas, passing through Río Chiquito, leave San Ignacio at 7am, 9:30am, 12:30pm, 2:30pm and 4:30pm and return at the same times.

Sleeping

Five kilometers south of town, **Centro Obrero Dr Mario Zamora Rivas** offers 15 remodeled cabins and a couple of pools, and is free with permission from the Ministerio de Trabajo (p300) in San Salvador. Trails crisscross the forested grounds.

Hotel Posada Real HOTEL $
(☎2335-9009; r per person US$9) A nice location and a cute little snack bar, but there's not much character in these cinderblock rooms. The price is good though, plus they have hot water.

Hotel La Palma HOTEL $
(☎2305-9344; www.hotellapalma.com.sv; r per person US$14; @❄) The older mountain getaway bordered by the Río La Palma has 40 rooms of various quality and a great restaurant for sampling local dishes. Mosquitoes can be a problem. It's a short taxi ride from San Ignacio.

Hotel de Montaña El Pital HOTEL $$
(☎2335-9344; r per person with bathroom US$25-35; ❄❄) Renovations have held strong at this L-shaped city hotel and the newer rooms are still the best in town. Grab one by the huge pool with mountain views. The restaurant caters to groups.

Hostal Miramundo HOTEL $$
(☎2230-0437; www.hotelmiramundo.com; Miramundo; 4-person cabins US$50) This ridgetop place has cosy new cabins, with nice wooden touches and great beds. Highly recommended

tours are available, including a horseback ride to Casa Grande.

Entre Pinos HOTEL $$$
(☎2335-9312; www.entrepinosresortandspa.com.sv; Km 87.5 Troncal de Norte; d $75-95, cabin $130) This large family-style resort spread over 100 acres of mountainside glory has three restaurants, two pools and a health club to offer guests. The plain, small rooms are not the reason to stay here; the friendly English-speaking staff and numerous opportunities to explore the area from a peaceful base more than compensate for a star below the advertised number.

Eating

Cafe de Cafe CAFE $
(☎2335-9190; Calle El Principal; 📶) The closest thing to a city cafe, with leather lounges, fine coffee (US$1) and *licuados* (US$1.50 to US$2), and free wi-fi. It's popular with teenagers.

Restaurante del Pueblo SALVADORAN $
(mains US$1-5; ⏲7am-9pm) Behind the town's wildest mural lies chunky beef sandwiches outdone only by a sausage and steak-laden *plato típico* (grilled meat, bananas, beans, cheese and cream).

Cartagena Pizza PIZZERIA $
(☎2305-9475; Barrio el Centro; pizzas US$3-12) These delicious thin-based pizzas make a welcome change from the standard Central American fare.

Information

Citibank (cnr Calle Barrios & 1a Calle Poniente) 24-hour ATM on the northeast corner of Parque Centro.

Palma City Online (Calle Principal; per hr US$0.80; ⏲8am-7pm)

Tourist Office (☎2335-9076; Parque Municipal; ⏲8am-4pm Mon-Fri, 9am-1pm Sat & Sun) Very helpful. Spanish only.

Getting There & Away

Bus 119 runs every half-hour from San Salvador's Terminal de Oriente to the El Salvador–Honduras border at El Poy, stopping at La Palma (US$1.60, 2¾ hours). Some enter San Ignacio, 3km to the north, others drop you off at the entrance.

A shuttle bus runs half-hourly between La Palma and San Ignacio (10 mins, US$0.25). From San Ignacio you can catch the bus to El Pital and its environs.

UNDERSTAND EL SALVADOR

El Salvador Today

Political change hit El Salvador in March 2009 when the left-wing Frente Farabundo Martí para la Liberación Nacional (FMLN) party – led by former TV journalist Mauricio Funes – rose to power for the first time since its inception as a guerrilla resistance movement. This represented a major victory for democratic process and reconciliation in the country. A January 2010 formal apology for the government's role in past atrocities – and full compliance in external investigations – was a bright beginning to the five-year term. Other positive moves include an apparently 'secret' deal between government and leading gang figures which has led to a marked reduction in crime rates.

The economy is still too reliant on remittances from abroad (one fifth of the national economy) – rising interest rates have made it more difficult for the American dream to be replicated further south. Microfinance institutions are set to play a bigger role in enabling Salvadorans to better invest their hard-earned overseas capital. Meanwhile the increasing privatization of state assets is making El Salvador more compliant – some would argue more vulnerable – with North American economic policy.

Since 2012, the most publicized issues in El Salvador have included the usual staple of gang truces, rural development, left-right politics, football, a Latin American pope and the continuing pursuit of justice for past military indiscretions.

History

Traders & Raiders

Paleo-Indian peoples populated El Salvador as early as 10,000 years ago, literally leaving their mark with cave paintings in modern Morazán. Around 2000 BC the Olmecs followed, leaving as their legacy the Olmec Boulder, a giant head sculpture similar to those from Mexico, found near Casa Blanca.

El Salvador was once a key regional trading center. Archaeological remains reveal diverse influences, from Pipil, Teotihuacan and Maya in the west to Lenca, Chorti and Pok'omama in the east. The step pyramid ruins at Tazumal, San Andrés and Casa Blanca show 3000 years of nearly constant pre-Hispanic habitation.

When Spanish conquistador Pedro de Alvarado arrived in 1524, he saw a country dominated by Pipils, descendants of Toltecs and Aztecs. These northern peoples (from modern-day Mexico) dubbed their home Cuscatlán, 'Land of Jewels.' Their maize-based farming economy flourished enough to support several cities and a sophisticated culture with pursuits that included hieroglyphics, astronomy and mathematics. Their dialect is related to modern Nahuat.

From Indigo to Independence

Spanish rule started with a year-long struggle against the Pipil. The Spaniards prevailed and laid claim to the land, transforming it into plantations of cotton, balsam and indigo. Agriculture boomed throughout the 1700s, with indigo the number-one export. A small group of Europeans, known as the 'fourteen families,' controlled virtually all of the colony's wealth and agriculture, enslaving indigenous peoples and Africans to work the land.

Conflict simmered under this gross imbalance of power. A revolt against Spain in 1811 was led by Padre (Father) José Delgado. While it failed, it planted a seed of discontent. Independence was gained 10 years later, on September 15, 1821, when El Salvador became part of the Central American Federation.

Pushing for land reform, Anastasio Aquino led an indigenous rebellion in 1883. Though it was subdued and Aquino was executed, he became a national hero. El Salvador withdrew from the Central American Federation in 1841, but Independence Day continues to be celebrated on September 15.

In Comes Coffee

In the late 19th century, synthetic dyes undermined the indigo market, and coffee took the main stage. A handful of wealthy landowners expanded their properties, displacing more indigenous people. Coffee became the most important cash crop and *cafetaleros* (coffee growers) earned purses full of money that was neither taxed nor redistributed at reasonable wages to the workers. By the 20th century, 95% of El Salvador's income derived from coffee exports, but only 2% of Salvadorans controlled that wealth.

The 20th Century

The government vigorously eradicated union activity in the coffee industry during the 1920s. In January 1932, Augustín Farabundo Martí, a founder of the Central American Socialist Party, led an uprising of peasants and indigenous people. The military responded brutally by systematically killing anyone who looked indigenous or supported the uprising. La Matanza (the Massacre) resulted in the death of 30,000 individuals, including Martí, who was killed by firing squad. The FMLN (Frente Farabundo Martí para la Liberación Nacional) revolutionary army would later take up his name in his honor.

Over the course of the 1970s, landlessness, poverty, unemployment and overpopulation became serious problems. In government, the polarized left and right tangled for power through coups and electoral fraud. In 1972, José Napoleon Duarte, cofounder of the Christian Democrat Party (Partido Democrático Cristiano; PDC), ran for president supported by a broad coalition of reform groups. When his victory was denied amid allegations of fraud, protests followed. The military averted an attempted coup, and the right responded to increasing guerrilla activity by creating 'death squads.' Thousands of Salvadorans were kidnapped, tortured and murdered.

In 1979 a junta of military and civilians overthrew President Carlos Humberto Romero and promised reforms. When promises were not met, opposition parties banded together as the Frente Democrático Revolucionario (FDR) and allied with the FMLN, a revolutionary army composed of five guerrilla groups for whom armed struggle appeared to be the only means of change. The successful revolution in Nicaragua in 1979 had encouraged many Salvadorans to demand reforms. One of them was Monsignor Oscar Romero, a formerly conservative priest who took up the cause of the people.

On March 24, 1980, outspoken Archbishop Romero was assassinated while saying Mass in the chapel of the San Salvador Divine Providence Cancer Hospital. His murder ignited an armed insurrection that same year that was to turn into a civil war.

Civil War

The rape and murder in late 1980 of four US nuns performing relief work in El Salvador prompted the Carter administration to suspend military aid. But in 1981, the newly elected Reagan administration, bristling from the threat of Nicaragua's socialist revolution, pumped huge sums into the moribund Salvadoran military. Uncle Sam's support would effectively prolong the conflict. When guerrillas gained control of areas in the north and east, the Salvadoran military retaliated by decimating villages. In 1981, the US-trained elite Atlacatl Battalion killed more than 700 men, women and children in El Mozote, Morazán. As many as 300,000 citizens fled the country.

In 1982 Major Roberto D'Aubisson, founder of the extreme-right Arena party, became president of the legislative assembly and enacted a law granting the legislative body power over the president. D'Aubisson created death squads targeting, among others, trade unionists and agrarian reformers. In response, the FMLN offensive blew up bridges, cut power lines and destroyed coffee plantations and livestock – anything to stifle the economy. When the government ignored an FMLN peace proposal, the rebels refused to participate in the 1984 presidential elections, in which Duarte won over D'Aubisson. For the next few years the PDC and FMLN engaged in peace talks unsuccessfully. Death squads continued pillaging, and the guerrillas continued to undermine the military powers and jeopardize municipal elections.

THE SEARCH GOES ON

When government forces razed villages during the civil war, they didn't always kill everyone. Some children, taken from their mothers' arms or found helpless on the killing field were spared. Those survivors were given up for adoption and displaced.

The organization Pro-Búsqueda was formed to find displaced children and reconnect them to their original families. Through a combination of DNA tests, family accounts, adoption files and newspaper reports, Pro-Búsqueda has managed to reunite hundreds of families. An estimated 5000 children were displaced by the war, hence Pro-Búsqueda has many cases still pending.

For more information, contact **Pro-Búsqueda** (☎ 2235-1039; www.probusqueda.org.sv).

The Price of Peace

Hope for peace neared in 1989, when the FMLN offered to participate in elections if the government agreed to a postponement to ensure democratic polls. Its calls were ignored and Alfredo Cristiani, a wealthy Arena businessman, was elected president. The FMLN's response was a major attack on the capital. In retaliation, the military killed an estimated 4000 'leftist sympathizers.'

UN-mediated negotiations began between the government and FMLN in April 1990. Among the first agreements was a human-rights accord signed by both parties. Yet violent deaths actually increased in 1991 when a UN mission arrived to monitor human rights.

On January 16, 1992, a compromise was finally signed. The FMLN became an opposition party, and the government agreed to various reforms, including dismantling paramilitary groups and death squads, replacing them with a national civil police force. Land was to be distributed to citizens and human-rights violations to be investigated. But instead, the government gave amnesty to human-rights abusers.

During the course of the 12-year war, an estimated 75,000 people were killed.

Modern Currents

The FMLN has mostly proven to be a model example of a former guerrilla organization transitioning to mainstream politics. Sceptics argued that Salvadorans would always prefer conservatives. However this all changed in 2009 when Mauricio Funes led the FMLN to power in a popular victory.

An ongoing issue for the Funes administration has been dealing with the actions of the Mara Salvatrucha (*mara* means 'gang', *trucha* means 'clever trout'). Also known as M-13 and M-18, these gangs of roughly 100,000 across Central America were formed in the US in response to orchestrated attacks by Mexicans. Deported en masse between 2000 and 2004, the *maras* became heavily involved in drug cartels, guns, the sex trade and illegal immigration.

Despite countless arrests, the previous government's policies failed to have a lasting impact, which led to the Funes government ceding the majority of seats to the right-wing Arean party in a 2012 legislative election. This occurred even though a truce was signed between rival gangs and some evidence exists to suggest violence is decreasing.

In 2012, the US government declared the gangs 'international criminal groups', thereby widening the powers of law enforcement agencies to curtail suspected activities on American soil.

The Culture

The National Psyche

Most travelers who have been to El Salvador rate its people as the best part of traveling here. Straight-talking, strong-minded and hard-working, Salvadorans are also extremely helpful and almost universally friendly (even gang members can rustle up charm when interviewed).

Salvadorans have a powerful sense of justice and freely express their opinion. The civil war still looms large in the national psyche, as it must – not only are the memories too searing to forget, but many ex-combatants (and their disciples) remain in positions of power. At the same time, Salvadorans are genuinely dismayed to learn that many foreigners know little about El Salvador beyond the war. They will eagerly volunteer information and assistance.

Lifestyle

With a strong work ethic, Salvadorans have quickly raised their country from the wreckage of civil war to nearly the top of Central America's economic ladder. Remittances sent home from Salvadorans living abroad, which annually total US$3 billion (20% of national GDP), provide a significant boost and, despite a downturn sparked by the weakened US economy, has changed the way Salvadorans live and work. Poverty and unemployment persist, with 30% of the population below the poverty line, mostly in rural areas. That said, El Salvador enjoys the highest minimum wage in Central America (about US$150 per week) and is notably more prosperous than neighboring countries.

People

Salvadorans show more European physical traits than other Central Americans, due largely to the brutal repression of indigenous people and minor Afro-Caribbean influence. Roughly 94% of the population is *mestizo* (a mixture of Spanish and indigenous) but fair features are not uncommon. Indigenous people are descended from the Pipils, with Toltec and Aztec roots. Government brutality against them has taken its toll, and they now represent only 1% to 2% of the population. Few speak Nahuat or wear traditional dress.

Religion

El Salvador, like the rest of Latin America, is experiencing an explosive growth of evangelical churches. Their fiery services seem to have brought fresh energy to faith. Town-square services with booming speakers are becoming an all-too-typical way of spreading 'the word.' Protestant churches now account for 50% of believers, which speaks of frustration with the traditional Catholic church. Before and during the war, priests and missionaries were often outspoken critics of government repression – many, such as Archbishop Oscar Romero, were killed for their stands.

Arts

El Salvador's artisan products can be innovative and high quality. Fernando Llort's Naïve Art inspired an industry of brightly painted crafts in childlike motifs in the community of La Palma. Guatajiagua in Morazán produces unique black pottery with a Lenca influence and Ilobasco is known for its *sorpresas,* intricate miniatures hidden in ceramic shells.

Poetry is beloved in El Salvador. Iconoclast poet Roque Dalton was exiled for radical politics. He eventually returned home to aid the guerrilla cause but was executed by his own side under suspicion that he was a CIA operative. Notable works include *Taberna y otros lugares* (1969), a political vision in verse, and *Miguel Marmol.* Progressive poet Claudia Lars wrote spare, bold erotic poetry and is considered one of the country's foremost writers.

Using the pen name Salarrué, lauded writer Salvador Efraín Salazar Arrué's *Cuentos de barro* (Tales of Mud), published in 1933, marks the beginning of Central America's modern short-story genre.

Likewise Manlio Argueta's *One Day of Life* (1980), a tale of a rural famly in the backdrop of the civil war, is considered a modern classic. Matilde Elena Lopez is a

BEHIND THE SCENES OF NAÏVE ART

Holy scenes, strange birds, unabashed rainbow colors: the childlike images of Fernando Llort have come to symbolize hope in a war-torn Central America. Compared to Miró and Picasso, Llort differs with earnest iconography and flat tropical hues in a style dubbed as primitive modern.

Ironically, this strong Latin American identity was forged when Llort went to France to study architecture and then theology. Religious symbols are recurring motifs in his artwork. He prefers the rough and everyday to the exalted.

When Llort returned to El Salvador in the early 1970s, he arrived to the tensions and violence leading up to the civil war. Llort moved to La Palma, a distant mountain town in the north, to take refuge. The apparent simplicity of a life in harmony with nature further informed his style. He started La Semilla de Dios (God's Seed), a workshop to teach others his craft and professionalize local artisans.

Llort has since lived in San Salvador and abroad, but the workshop is still going strong in his former studio. You can find his work on the face of the Catedral Metropolitana in San Salvador as well as in the White House, MoMA and the Vatican.

playwright who wrote a compelling 1978 play based on the life of indigenous leader Anastasio Aquino.

One of the more interesting contemporary Salvadoran novelists is Horacio Castellanos Moya. His recently translated *Senselessness* (2004) is a burning black comedy about government-sponsored violence. For further information about these and other modern writers, see **Concultura** (www.dpi.gob.sv), the country's official arts and culture board, which has a bibliography of Salvadoran authors.

Films *Romero,* produced by Ellwood Kieser in 1988, and *Salvador,* directed by Oliver Stone, offer Hollywood versions of the civil war.

Books

Major Salvadoran authors are available in translation. Joan Didion's *Salvador* is a moving account of the early days of the war. Nonfiction about the civil war includes *Massacre at El Mozote* by Mark Danner and *Rebel Radio,* a fascinating, firsthand account of clandestine radio stations operated by FMLN guerrillas.

Óscar Romero: Memories in Mosaic by María López Vigil, is a recommended account of the clergyman's life and political conversion told by those who knew him. *When the Dogs Ate Candles,* by Bill Hutchinson, is an anecdotal history of the conflict based on interviews with refugees. Archaeology buffs can read about Central America's Pompeii in *Before the Volcano Erupted: The Ancient Ceréen Village in Central America* by Payton Sheets.

Landscape & Wildlife

The Land

The Land of Volcanoes, El Salvador has two volcanic ranges spanning east to west, spicing the views, as well as daily life, with a little drama. Much of the land is deforested but mountains in the far north are blanketed in pine and oak, jagged rock formations and cloud forests. The Río Lempa bisects the country with a fertile swath of land. While El Salvador is the only Central American country not to have a Caribbean coast, there is over 300km of Pacific coastline bordering mangroves, estuaries and tropical dry forest. Lakes and freshwater lagoons provide drinking water and recreation.

Wildlife

El Salvador was drastically deforested over the 20th century. As a result, many species of plants and animals ceased to exist in the country. However, national parks and protected lands still maintain good biodiversity.

The country has over 800 animal species. Almost half are butterflies, with bird species second in number, with about 330 resident species (and 170 migratory), including quetzals, toucans, herons, kingfishers, brown pelicans, egrets, parakeets and sandpipers. The remaining mammal species number around 200 and can be seen mostly in reserves. They include opossums, anteaters, porcupines, agoutis, ocelots, spider monkeys and white-tailed deers. In all, about 90 species are in danger of extinction, including marine turtles, armadillos and over 15 types of hummingbird.

With so much of the land cultivated, few original plants still exist. Small stands of balsam trees survive along the western Pacific coast (dubbed the Costa del Bálsamo) and mangroves line many estuaries. Bosque Montecristo and El Imposible offer the widest variety of indigenous plants, and Parque Nacional los Volcanes offers good vegetation. Plants in these areas include mountain pines, oaks, figs, magueys, ferns and orchids.

National Parks & Reserves

El Salvador has only four official national parks, but there are a number of locally or privately administered reserves.

Barra de Santiago A remote bar of mangrove-fringed estuaries and beaches on the Pacific coast (p320).

Cerro El Pital El Salvador's highest peak. *Torogoz* (blue-crowned motmots) and quetzals can be observed on its piney slopes (p340).

Laguna de Alegría (p324) An emerald-green lake fed by hot springs, in the crater of dormant Volcán de Tecapa. Ocelots and coatis are among wildlife inhabiting primary growth forest surrounding the lake.

Laguna El Jocotal This freshwater lagoon east of Usulután is an important sanctuary for migratory birds from October to March.

Parque Nacional El Imposible Near El Salvador's western limit; one of the last remnants of original tropical forest with waterfalls, views and numerous endangered plant and animal species (p321).

Parque Nacional Los Volcanes (Cerro Verde; p308) A volcano-crater forest with amazing views of nearby Izalco and Santa Ana volcanoes. Highlights include emerald toucanets, motmots and hummingbirds.

Parque Nacional Montecristo–El Trifinio (p313) A mountainous cloud-forest reserve at the borders of El Salvador, Honduras and Guatemala. Wildlife includes pumas, spider monkeys and agoutis. Giant ferns, orchids and bromeliads are abundant.

Parque Nacional Walter T Deininger (p304) This dry tropical forest on the Pacific coast is the habitat for 87 bird species, deer and pacas.

Environmental Issues

Overpopulation and the exploitation of the land for export agricultural crops (such as coffee, sugar and cotton) continue to propel El Salvador's massive deforestation. High population density remains the principal obstacle to the regeneration of ecosystems. Today, a mere 14% of the country is forested, with only a minuscule 2% to 5% of that primary forest. As a result, many native species have become endangered or extinct.

Deforestation and unplanned urban sprawl intensify the effects of natural disasters. In recent years El Salvador has been pummeled by Mother Nature, producing a laundry list of disasters. Earthquakes in 2001 brought on landslides and destroyed buildings, killing 1159 people and destroying or damaging almost 300,000 homes.

The eruption of Santa Ana volcano in October 2005, coupled with Hurricane Stan's torrential rains, unleashed scores of landslides, with the largest loss of life in poor areas built on steep slopes or riverbeds. In 2009, massive floods killed 200 people and devastated large tracts of land and housing within 50km of the capital.

Río Lempa, a crucial watershed for the country, suffers from pollution due to decades of pesticide use and the destabilising effects of global warming. In recent years local community leaders have labelled damage to the protected biosphere around Bahía de Jiquilisco an environmental emergency

¿TÍPICA OR PÍCARA?

Sorpresas (surprises) are little scenes and figures hidden in egg-sized shells, pioneered by folk artist Dominga Herrera of Ilobasco. Underneath a bulbous papaya or white chapel you'll find a charming microsized scene of village life – usually. One local artist got sassy and sculpted a couple in the giddy throes of sex. The illicit art was condemned by the town priest and briefly removed from stores. But prosperity may have beat out piety. '*Pícara*' (sinful) *sorpresas*, now available as matchbox copulation scenes, continue selling strong. Expect yours to come discreetly wrapped.

and a government response is being closely monitored by climate-change watchdogs.

In 2012, major volcanic activity off the Pacific coast reminded the country of the volatile nature of life on the Rim of Fire.

SURVIVAL GUIDE

Directory A–Z

ACCOMMODATIONS

El Salvador has a decent selection of hotels and improved backpacker infrastructure. The cheapest places are often in seedy areas near bus terminals; paying a bit more is worthwhile for personal security. We attempt to include the safest and most secure options for travelers here.

Camping and *eco-albergues* (eco-hostels; basic shared cabins, some with modest kitchen facilities) are appearing around popular outdoor destinations. Bring your own camping equipment, as the selection is scant.

You can stay for free at *centros de obreros* (government workers' centers), which are huge compounds designed to give workers and their families a place to relax on the weekend. The main locations are Lago de Coatepeque, El Tamarindo, La Palma and outside La Libertad. You must reserve them in advance at the appropriate office in San Salvador.

Room rates are stable season to season, except during the summer holidays (first week of August), when hotels in popular towns fill up fast. The average rate for dorms is around US$10, and for doubles US$25.

ACTIVITIES

Diving

Diving in El Salvador is more expensive and admittedly inferior to nearby Honduras or Belize. That said, it does offer one of the few coral reefs on the American side of the Pacific, as well as a chance to dive in crater lakes. The best time for diving is from October to February, especially December and January. One five-star operator is El Salvador Divers (p290), offering open-water and advanced certification courses for around US$350.

Hiking

El Salvador has some excellent hiking, in spite of serious deforestation. Parque Nacional El Imposible, near the border with Guatemala, offers the best combination of easy access and rewarding primary-forest hikes. The Ruta de las Flores offers waterfall and hot-springs hikes; find guides for hire in Juayúa. Further north, the pristinely beautiful Parque Nacional Montecristo–El Trifinio is renowned for wildlife. Access is difficult and it's closed during the May-to-November mating season. Parque Nacional los Volcanes, with two climbable volcanoes, is a beautiful, if sometimes crowded, destination. Hikes from the northwestern towns of La Palma and San Ignacio offer stunning vistas. You can access El Salvador's highest peak (Cerro El Pital, 2730m) from here. The northeastern state of Morazán, in particular Perquín, has a cool climate and fine hiking. As a longtime stronghold of the FMLN, it also has interesting and sobering sites related to the civil war.

Surfing

El Salvador is a world-class surf destination, with kilometers of empty right-hand breaks. Punta Roca, the country's most notorious wave, is at the scruffy port of La Libertad, which is readily accessible from the capital. Several beaches west of here also have excellent waves and all-service surf lodges. Your best bets for lessons are at Esencia Nativa in Playa El Zonte, or a number of places in Playa El Tunco. Further east are less crowded breaks at Las Flores and El Cuco. Peak season is March to December.

CLIMATE

The *invierno* (wet season) is from May to October, and the *verano* (dry season) is from November to April. During the rainy season, it usually only rains at night.

In San Salvador, the maximum temperature varies from 27°C (80°F) in November to 30°C (86°F) in March and April; the minimum temperatures range from 16°C (61°F) in January and February to 20°C (68°F) in March. The coastal lowlands are the hottest region.

CUSTOMS

Salvadoran border officials are among the most scrutinizing in the region. They check for previous entry and exit stamps. If you're entering on an international bus, your bags may well be searched. Carry your passport with you in all border regions, regardless of whether you're leaving the country, since there are a lot of police checkpoints (mostly searching for drugs).

SLEEPING PRICE RANGES

Price ranges denote the cost of a double room with private bathroom unless stated otherwise.

$	Less than US$25
$$	US$25-70
$$$	More than US$70

EL SALVADOR'S TOP FIVE SURF SPOTS

With 16 right-hand point breaks and 28°C (82°F) water swarming with sea turtles, what's not to love? Bad luck for lovers of the left-hand – Playa El Tunco is pretty much your only bet. Our favorites:

Punta Roca Iconic for a reason. Central America's best wave is often compared to South Africa's J Bay. A rocky bottom makes it fast and strong. Bring just your board – theft is common on the walk to the point.

Las Flores A fast sandy point break best at low tide. Picture a hollow take-off ending on a black sand beach. A 300m ride is possible – welcome to the Wild East.

Punta Mango Short, strong and vertical, this aggressive Indo-men Hawaiian-style break is best reached by boat from Las Flores beach or via bus from El Cuco. A pretty tightly held wave, so don't drop in!

Playa El Sunzal The most popular wave in El Salvador; fun, consistently big right-hander with a seasoned surf crowd of friendly locals and fly-ins.

'Secret Spot' Surfers love their secrets, however poorly kept. Temperamental at times, but fast and hollow when cranking, it's named after a distance between Km 58 and Km 60...

DANGERS & ANNOYANCES

Crime shouldn't deter travelers from El Salvador any more than it does from the rest of Central America. Despite the country's reputation for violence, attacks on tourists are rare.

Take commonsense precautions: carry as little as possible on day trips, be aware of your bags on buses, and avoid toting expensive items. Before traveling, make copies of your credit cards and important documents; carry a copy with you and leave one with someone at home who could fax them to you in a pinch. After dark it's best to take a taxi, even if the rates can be a little steep. This is particularly important in San Salvador, San Miguel, Sonsonate, La Unión and La Libertad.

Most volcano climbs are best done with a police escort, partly for your safety and partly so you won't get lost on unmarked and intersecting trails. The service is free, but you must request it by phone or in person a day in advance (and preferably more). Officers are friendly and trustworthy.

Of course, violence does occur. Two major *maras* (gangs) operate in the country. Travelers are unlikely to have encounters with a gang member as groups concentrate in neighborhoods with no outside appeal, and also because the police control most tourist areas. Still, visitors should avoid traveling at night. Weapons are widespread, so never resist a robbery – it's not worth it.

EMBASSIES & CONSULATES

Australia, New Zealand and the UK do not have consular representation in El Salvador. Australians can get assistance at the Canadian embassy. Except for the US embassy, the following embassies are in San Salvador.

Canadian Embassy (☎2279-4655; 63a Av Sur, Alameda Roosevelt, Torre A)

French Embassy (☎2279-4016; www.embafrancia.com.sv; 1a Calle Poniente 3718)

German Embassy (☎2247-0000; www.san-salvador.diplo.de; 7a Calle 3972)

Guatemalan Embassy (☎2271-2225; 15a Av Norte, btwn Calles Arce & 1a Calle Poniente, Colonia Escalón)

Honduran Embassy (☎2263-2808; 89a Av Norte, btwn 7a & 9a Calle Poniente, Colonia Escalón)

Mexican Embassy (☎2243-0445; cnr Calle Circunvalación & Pasaje 12, Colonia San Benito)

Nicaraguan Embassy (☎2263-8789; Calle El Mirador, btwn 93a & 95a Av Norte, Colonia Escalón)

US Embassy (☎2278-4444, ext 2628; www.sansalvador.usembassy.gov; Blvd Santa Elena Final, Antiguo Cuscatlán, La Libertad)

FESTIVALS & EVENTS

Fería Gastronómica A wonderful food fair held every weekend in Juayúa.

Festival de El Salvador Celebrates El Salvador's patron saint on August 1 to 6; all cities have festivities with San Salvador's the biggest.

Festival del Invierno Perquín's art and music festival is held in August and is popular with the boho crowd and college students.

Festival de Maíz Suchitoto's corn harvest festival in August has religious processions and street parties.

PEOPLE PACKING HEAT

Enter El Salvador and you'll wonder if you've stumbled onto an National Rifle Association convention. Banks, hotels and even bikini boutiques are patrolled by clean-shaven guards packing M16s and 9mm pistols. While the war is long over, this security-obsessed country employs over 18,000 security guards. In addition, there are countless private citizens accessorizing with arms, easily purchased in gun shops at the mall among the boutiques.

Of the estimated 500,000 firearms in El Salvador, 60% are illegal. The stricter measures of former president Saca's Super Mano Dura (Super Hard Hand) policy created more arrests but few convictions. His successor Mauricio Funes adopted a more progressive strategy, such as a nationwide amnesty on illegal weapons.

A late 2012 ceasefire between rival gangs has led onlookers to suggest some form of deal was mediated by government and church officials – one of the first of its kind in the region.

Bolas de Fuego To commemorate an eruption of Volcán San Salvador that destroyed the original town, Nejapa residents spar by throwing balls of fire then dance till dawn around street bonfires on August 31.

Festival de Hamacas Hammocks fill the streets of Concepción Quezaltepeque during this street fair in mid-November.

GAY & LESBIAN TRAVELERS

Gay people receive little tolerance. Some hotels refuse to rent a room with one bed to two men; women will encounter less scrutiny. In San Salvador, the area around Blvd de los Héroes has cultural centers and clubs that, being more bohemian, are also more gay-friendly. Gay organization **Entre Amigos** (☎2225-4213; entreamigos@salnet.net; Av Santa Victoria No 50, near Blvd de los Héroes) is the most established in the country, dedicated mostly to HIV/AIDS outreach.

INTERNET ACCESS

The internet is easy to access at internet cafes across the country, though speeds vary considerably. Expect to pay between US$0.50 to $1 per hour.

LANGUAGE

Spanish is the national language. In a few indigenous villages only a handful of people still speak the Nahuat language of the Pipil, but there is academic interest in preserving it. Many Salvadorans pick up some English working in the USA, Australia and elsewhere, and English speakers pop up in the unlikeliest places.

LANGUAGE COURSES

Options are few but some English institutes offer Spanish classes. The best is the **Centro de Intercambio y Solidaridad** (CIS; ☎2226-2623; www.cis-elsalvador.org), which offers Spanish classes with progressive sensibilities. Homestays are available. Suchitoto has two excellent new schools.

LEGAL MATTERS

Law enforcement is strict and effective, from beat cops to border officials. Police are entitled to stop buses and search people and bags, and do so with some frequency, often helped by army soldiers.

Bribes are generally not expected in El Salvador, though can assist in minor indiscretions. If arrested, cooperate and call your embassy, although if you have committed a crime there's little your embassy can do. Even minor offences require jail time.

MAPS

Corsatur and the Ministry of Tourism offer glossy maps of El Salvador and the capital, available at some hotels and tour offices.

Map addicts should hit the **Centro Nacional de Registros** (IGN; www.cnr.gob.sv; 1a Calle Poniente, 2nd fl; ⏲8am-12:30pm & 2-5pm Mon-Fri), behind MetroSur in San Salvador, for high-quality city and country maps. Simple maps of hiking trails are sometimes available at visitor centers.

MEDIA

San Salvador's main newspapers are *La Prensa Gráfica* and the conservative *El Diario de Hoy;* check them for domestic and international news, plus entertainment listings. *El Mundo* and *El Latino* are thinner afternoon papers.

MONEY

On January 2001, El Salvador adopted the US dollar as its official currency. The previous currency (the colón) technically still exists, but you'll probably never see one though you may find some rare US$2 notes.

ATMs

ATMs are found in most cities and towns, with the exception of Perquín. Citibank, Scotiabank and Banco Atlántida have the largest network of ATMs. Plus/Visa and Cirrus/MasterCard cards generally work well. Look for safer locking cabins to withdraw money, and avoid taking out cash at night.

Bargaining & Tipping

Bargaining is less common here than in other Central American countries. A little back-and-forth is common with taxi drivers and market shopkeepers, but hard bargaining can seem a bit rude. Tip 10% in restaurants; it is not customary to tip taxi drivers, though rounding up the amount is appreciated.

Cash

Bring US dollars, preferably in US$20 bills and smaller. There is no need to buy, carry or use the old currency as ATMs have dollars. Only Banco Cuscatlán exchanges non-US currency. The border crossings have moneychangers.

Credit Cards

Credit cards are accepted in modern malls, high-end hotels and upmarket stores. Smaller establishments add a 6% to 12% surcharge. Visa cards encounter the least resistance. MasterCard is becoming more widely accepted while American Express is less common.

Travelers Checks

Most Citibank, Scotiabank and Banco Atlántida branches change travelers checks (passport and purchase receipt required). American Express checks are best. There are also Western Union offices in most towns.

OPENING HOURS

Businesses generally operate 9am to 6pm weekdays, while government offices are open 8am to 4pm. Some offices and stores close at lunchtime, between noon and 2pm, but this practice is fading. Banks are open 8am to 4pm or 5pm weekdays, and most open Saturday morning as well. Restaurants serve dinner early, and 4pm is *pupusa* hour.

POST

There are two rates for sending international mail: airmail and express mail. Letters sent by airmail to the USA should arrive in 10 days (US$0.50), to Europe and Asia up to 15 days (US$0.65). Letters sent express to the USA should take five days (US$1), to Europe and Australia 10 days (US$1.20). FedEx and DHL have offices in large cities.

RESPONSIBLE TRAVEL

Many travelers come to El Salvador with a notion of which 'side' they supported in the civil war (usually the FMLN). In fact, both sides committed terrible atrocities and in 12 years of war, neither came to fully represent (or betray) the ideals of the majority of Salvadorans. Visitors should not be hesitant to discuss the war, but should honor the personal experiences of everyday Salvadorans.

Tourism is starting to make itself felt but Salvadorans remain relatively unjaded toward backpackers. Hard bargaining, whether in taxis or in markets, is rare. It may be too late to reverse the unpleasant wheeling and dealing of Guatemala and elsewhere, but in El Salvador, an honest price and a friendly transaction are still the norm.

TELEPHONE

The country code when calling El Salvador from abroad is ☎ 503. Phone numbers usually have eight digits; there are no internal area codes. Telecom and Telefónica payphones accept their respective phone cards. Buy prepaid phone cards (in US$3, US$5 and US$10 denominations) at pharmacies and corner stores. Phone booths post local and international dialing instructions in English and Spanish. Some internet cafes offer web-based calling.

TOURIST INFORMATION

El Salvador has few tourist information offices, and even fewer that provide more than fluff. Offices with friendly and informed staff include those in Perquín and Suchitoto. Juayúa and Apaneca have information kiosks open on weekends. Friendly hotel owners can be very helpful resources. In the capital you'll find the office of Corporación Salvadoreña de Turismo (p300), offering brochures and fliers. The Instituto Salvadoreño de Turismo (p300) has very general information about El Salvador's national parks and *turicentros*.

TRAVELERS WITH DISABILITIES

There are many disabled people in El Salvador – most victims of war-related violence – but there are still limited services or amenities to make their lives easier. There are few well-

EATING PRICE RANGES

The price ranges used throughout this chapter refer to a standard main course, including taxes but not including tip.

$	Less than US$5
$$	US$5-12
$$$	More than US$12

maintained ramps and handrails or services for the visually and hearing impaired. However, disabled travelers (and all travelers) will find Salvadorans extremely friendly and eager to help.

VISAS & DOCUMENTS

Citizens of the USA, Canada, Australia, New Zealand, South Africa, Switzerland, Norway, Japan, Taiwan, Brazil, Argentina, Mexico, other Central American countries, Israel and EU member countries do not need a visa, but must purchase a single-entry tourist card for US$10 when entering the country. For those who do need a prearranged visa, the cost is US$30. The standard length of stay is 30 days, but you can request up to 90 days – do so quickly before the official stamps your passport! If you leave and return within the allotted time, you can use the same tourist card.

The Central America-4 agreement allows for travel between the borders of Guatemala, Honduras, El Salvador and Nicaragua with one entry fee and one passport stamp (in this case, be sure you ask for the 90-day option). If you are traveling overland, please note the change; it's possible you will have to 'remind' some border guards about the agreement.

For up-to-date visa information visit http://www.lonelyplanet.com/el-salvador/practical-information/visas.

No vaccinations are required unless you are coming from an area infected by yellow fever (some are recommended, however).

VOLUNTEERING

In San Salvador's Blvd de los Héroes area, Centro de Intercambio y Solidaridad (p290) offers Spanish classes to tourists and English classes to low-income and activist Salvadorans, always with a strong emphasis on progressive politics. A friendly place to visit, the CIS has positions for volunteer English teachers (10-week minimum), and information about NGOs working on various issues, including community development, gang intervention, the environment and more. CIS cannot arrange an actual volunteer position, but can point you in the right direction. During national elections, you can volunteer with CIS's well-respected international election-observer mission.

Global Platform (p337) is a Danish NGO based in Suchitoto that offers Spanish lessons and lodging in return for assistance on community projects in the surrounding area. A month costs roughly US$400 all-inclusive.

WOMEN TRAVELERS

Foreign women spark interest, there is no doubt. Men will hiss or catcall but for many it's harmless hormonal babble, as much about male bonding as the female passerby. Nearly all the men you actually meet are extremely courteous and polite. Solo women are unlikely to encounter dangerous situations if they take ordinary precautions. On long bus rides, sitting next to a woman or kids avoids painful, 'Do you have a boyfriend?' conversations.

ENTRY & DEPARTURE TAXES

US citizens and some other nationalities are required to pay for a US$10 tourist card upon arrival to El Salvador's airport. The Central America-4 agreement allows for travel between the borders of Guatemala, Honduras, El Salvador and Nicaragua with one entry fee.

Getting There & Away

El Salvador's discerning immigration officials scrutinize entry and exit stamps, so avoid cutting corners. Request a 90-day tourist card in advance if you'd like one, otherwise you may be given less time.

AIR

The Aeropuerto Internacional Comalpa (p300) is located 44km south of San Salvador. A major Latin American hub, it is also a gateway to North American cities.

TACA, American Airlines, United Airlines, Continental, Delta Air Lines and Copa Airlines are among others providing services to El Salvador, for details see p300.

BOAT

El Salvador shares the Golfo de Fonseca with Honduras and Nicaragua. Boats occasionally ferry passengers between La Unión (El Salvador), Coyolito, Amapala or San Lorenzo (Honduras), and Potosí (Nicaragua). Going by sea does not save time since there are no scheduled passenger boats and land crossings are relatively close.

BORDER CROSSINGS

Costa Rica & Nicaragua

To/from San Miguel Managua can be reached by a King Quality bus (www.king-qualityca.com; US$27, nine hours) that continues on to San José, Costa Rica (US$47, 19 hours). It stops at San Miguel's Esso gas station (corner Av Roosevelt and Ruta Militar) at about 7:30am and 1:30pm.

From El Amatillo microbuses run from 5:30am to 5pm across the southern tip of Honduras to the Nicaraguan border town of Guasaule (US$5 depending on number of passengers, two hours). Walk 200m for the connections which reach León and Managua. Note that Americans must pay US$7 to enter Nicargaua.

Guatamala

To/from Santa Ana The San Cristóbal–El Progreso border is open 24 hours but you should cross during daylight hours. From Santa Ana, take bus 236 to San Cristóbal (US$0.50, one hour, every 20 minutes 5:30am to 9pm). Buses on the other side of the border go to El Progreso. The last bus back from San Cristóbal is at 6pm.

To/from Metapán Ordinary and *especial* services to Guatemala City via Las Chinamas–Valle Nuevo are offered by **Agencia Puerto Bus** (☎2440-1608; 25a Calle Poniente). Ordinary buses (US$9, four hours) leave hourly 5am to 4pm, except 7am. Especial buses (a well-spent US$11.50, 3½ hours) leave at 7am and 5:30pm. Another option is to catch a 1st-class bus at Las Chinamas.

From Metapán, microbuses run every half-hour to the Anguiatú–Chiquimula border (open 24 hours but more reliably from 6am to 7pm). On the Guatemalan side, buses run frequently to Chiquimula (one hour, last bus at 5:30pm) and onward to Guatemala City (three hours, last bus from Chiquimula at 3:30pm). This is the quickest route to Nuevo Ocotopeque or Copán Ruínas, Honduras. In El Salvador, the last bus from the border to Metapán is at 6:30pm.

To/From Ahuachapán The Las Chinamas–Valle Nuevo border Is open 24 hours but it's best to cross in daylight. Buses leave Ahuachapán from Parque Menéndez every 15 minutes (US$0.50, 5am to 7:30pm) for the Guatemala border. Cross the border 300m to the bus stop for service to Guatemala City via Cuilapa. Tica bus (US$3) passes every half-hour and is safer than 2nd-class service. The last bus from the border to Ahuachapán is at 5:45pm.

To/from Sonsonate The La Hachadura–Ciudad Pedro de Alvarado border is open 24 hours, but it's best to cross in daylight. Bus 259 from Sonsonate drops you right at the border; Salvadoran and Guatemalan immigration posts are at the far side of the complex. In Guatemala, the bus stop is 1km away. Bicycle taxis cost US$0.50. Buses for Guatemala City (US$5, four hours) leave every half-hour via Chiquimulilla and Escuintla. The last bus from La Hachadura to Sonsonate is at 6pm.

Honduras

To/from San Miguel For Tegucigalpa (US$27, five hours), 1st-class King Quality buses stop at San Miguel's Esso gas station (corner Av Roosevelt and Ruta Militar) at around 8am and 3:30pm daily – be early just in case. Buy tickets at the gas station one day in advance.

Otherwise, bus 330 drops you 50m from El Amatillo on the Salvadoran border where a bridge crosses into Honduras. Honduran buses then continue on to Choluteca (US$2.10, 1½ hours) and to Tegucigalpa (US$2, 3½ hours); the last bus for both leaves at 5:30pm. The last bus from El Amatillo to San Miguel goes at 6:30pm.

To/from La Palma The bus from La Palma drops you about 100m from the El Salvador–Honduras border (open 24 hours), where you pay US$3 to enter Honduras. From El Poy, you can take a bus or *colectivo* taxi to Nueva Ocotepeque, Honduras. From there buses leave hourly for San Pedro Sula. For Copán Ruinas, transfer at La Entrada.

The last bus to El Poy from La Palma (bus 119, US$0.50, 30 minutes) leaves at 7pm. The last bus south from El Poy to San Salvador leaves around 4:15pm.

CAR & MOTORCYCLE

If you drive into El Salvador, you must show a driver's license (an international driving permit is accepted) and proof that you own the vehicle you're traveling in. You must also fill out extensive forms. Car insurance is available and advisable but not required. Vehicles may remain in El Salvador for 30 days. If you wish to stay longer, it's best to leave the country and drive back in rather than attempt to deal with the Transport Ministry.

Getting Around

BOAT

You'll need to use a boat to get around the Bahía de Jiquilisco in eastern El Salvador and for any trips in the Golfo de Fonseca, near La Unión. Otherwise, water transportation is rare.

BUS

Hypercolored American school buses run frequently to points throughout the country and are very cheap (US$0.40 to US$5). Some weekend fares increase up to 25%. Routes to some eastern destinations have different categories: *ordinario, especial* and *super especial*. The last two options cost more, but they are faster and more comfortable. Most intercity bus services begin between 4am and 5am and end between 6pm and 7pm.

CAR & MOTORCYCLE

Most roads in El Salvador are paved, but traffic is not easy to negotiate and roads are not particularly well signed. Gas is not cheap either. A gallon of regular unleaded has climbed to about US$4.20.

Police set up checkpoints, especially on roads to border crossings. Carjacking is a problem, as is getting parts stolen off your parked car. Don't drive alone in areas of ill repute and park in safe places. Car insurance is a good idea, but not required.

Rental cars are available in San Salvador and San Miguel and can be delivered elsewhere. The following are in San Salvador:

Alamo Uno Rent a Car (☎2211-2111; Blvd del Hipódromo 426)

Avis (☎2261-1212, airport 2339-9268; www.avis.com.sv; 43a Av Sur 127; per day US$40)

Budget (☎2260-4333; www.budget.com.sv; 1a Calle Poniente 2765; per day US$35)

Quick Rent a Car (☎2229-6959; www.quickrentacar.com.sv) Offers hotel or airport pick-up/drop-off.

HITCHHIKING

Buses or collective pickups go just about anywhere you could want to go, so hitching isn't usually necessary. Both men and women usually hop in the back of pickup trucks, but women might think twice before climbing into a car of only men. Hitching is never entirely safe, and we don't recommend it. Travelers who hitch should understand that they are taking a small but potentially serious risk.

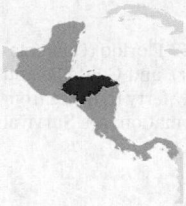

Honduras

☎ 504 / POP 8.45 MILLION

Includes ➡

Tegucigalpa 357
Lago de Yojoa 373
San Pedro Sula..... 374
Copán Ruinas 378
Copán Archaeological Site 384
Gracias 390
La Ceiba.....398
Trujillo.....406
Bay Islands.....408
Roatán 410
Utila 417
La Moskitia.....423
Isla El Tigre.....426

Best Places to Stay

- ➡ D&D Brewery (p373)
- ➡ La Hamaca (p375)
- ➡ Buena Onda (p413)
- ➡ La Casa de Café (p381)
- ➡ Hotel Guancascos (p390)

Best Bars

- ➡ Sol de Copán (p382)
- ➡ Tito Aguacate (p365)
- ➡ Kandil (p391)
- ➡ Babalu (p422)
- ➡ Skid Row (p422)

Why Go?

You've probably heard about the bad boy in the Central American 'hood. Even if you've just glanced at a headline, Honduras and trouble seem inextricably linked. But what's the reality on the ground? Well, despite the country's rep, the vast majority of travelers actually love their time here, for the nation is simply loaded with attractions: the fabled Bay Islands (a dive and party mecca), magical Maya ruins of Copán, seductive beauty of the Lenca highlands, wildlife-rich jungle reserves in La Moskitia. It's also superb value for money: all the adventure sports that have put Costa Rica on the map are available here at backpacking rates. Honduran landscapes are extraordinary, its cultural sights compelling and its people waiting. Sure, take a little extra care, especially in the big cities... but make the move and discover Honduras for yourself.

When to Go

Tegucigalpa

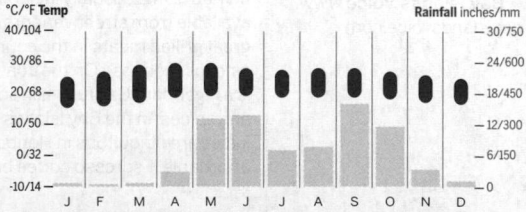

Oct–Feb Rainy season on the north coast and islands but dry in the interior.

Mar–Apr Hot and dry everywhere, with temperatures soaring inland.

Jun–Sep Peak season for viewing whale sharks in Utila.

AT A GLANCE

Currency Lempira (L)

Language Spanish (and some English)

Money ATMs are widespread

Visas Free on arrival for most nationalities

Time GMT minus six hours

Fast Facts

- **Area** 112,090 sq km
- **Capital** Tegucigalpa
- **Emergency** ☎199

Set Your Budget

- **Hostel bed** L95 to L285
- **Evening meal** L57 to L342
- **One-hour local bus trip** L19 to L133

Resources

- **Honduras Tips** www.hondurastips.hn
- **Honduras Weekly** www.hondurasweekly.com
- **Honduras** www.honduras.com
- **Bay Islands Voice** www.bayislandsvoice.com

Connections

Border crossings include Corinto and El Florido (Guatemala), El Amatillo and El Poy (El Salvador), and Guasaule and Las Manos (Nicaragua). There's a weekly ferry to Belize from Puerto Cortés. For more detailed information, see Survival Guide on p436.

FIRST TIME IN HONDURAS

This itinerary should take about two weeks. Entering Honduras at the El Florido border, you'll hit a key attraction immediately: the stunning ruins of **Copán**. Budget at least a couple of days in the area, taking in the temples and surrounding sights before making a short hop west to the atmospheric highland town of **Gracias**, with its hot springs and Lencan villages.

Then it's a long day on the road to the coastal city of **La Ceiba**. Set sail from here for either **Roatán** or **Utila** and indulge in some serious beach and reef time, snorkeling. diving and living the dream.

Back on the mainland, sign up for a rafting trip down the exquisite **Río Cangrejal**, then it's south to **Lago de Yojoa** for an artisan brew or two, hiking and boat trips.

Finish off with a night in either colonial, tranquil **Comayagua** or the bustling capital of **Tegucigalpa**.

Essential Food & Drink

- **Where to Eat** To keep costs down head to *comedores* (simple eateries) where a two- or three-course meal is virtually certain to be under US$3. Buy snacks from *panaderías* (bakeries) and markets. Cafes and restaurants in tourist towns have plenty of international dishes on their menus, including vegetarian choices.
- **What to Eat & Drink** Be sure to try Honduras' national dish, the *baleada* (a wrap-style flatbread stuffed with myriad fillings, usually including refried beans and salad) available from street vendors for US$1 to US$2. You'll find great grilled meats in the country's interior including lots of *pinchos* (kebabs). On the coast, seafood is superb: *tapado* is a legendary Garifuna fish soup prepared with coconut and spices; in the Bay Islands *bando* is a similar dish. Fresh juices are ubiquitous in Honduras and usually excellent and affordable. Espresso coffee bars are found in all main towns.

TEGUCIGALPA

POP 1.13 MILLION / ELEV 975M

Ringed by forested hills in a highland valley, sprawling Tegucigalpa enjoys a relatively fresh, mild climate and a spectacular setting.

Few travelers hang around long enough to savor the capital's delights and sights, but if you're passing through you will find the compact city center boasts some fine colonial architecture and a good museum or two.

Keep your ear to the ground and you'll discover a dynamic young urban scene led by emerging artists and musicians, DJs and designers. There are only a few key venues, so it's relatively easy to connect with this vibrant underground scene in the city's happening cafes and bars.

That's the good news. What's not so great includes the traffic-choked streets and resultant pollution, and, more worryingly, some world-class crime stats. During daylight hours there's little danger, but it certainly pays to keep your wits about you. After dark plan on taking taxis to get around.

The name Tegucigalpa (teh-goos-ee-*gal*-pa) is a bit of a mouthful; Hondurans often call the city Tegus (*teh*-goos) for short. Across the river from Tegucigalpa is Comayagüela, a poorer and dirtier sister city, which has a pretty dodgy reputation. Many buses have terminals here, otherwise there's no reason to visit.

Sights

Downtown Tegus is the neglected heart of the nation, a cluster of once-elegant but now faded streets where *ropa americana* (used clothing) outlets have replaced department stores. For a feel of the city, stroll the (pedestrianized) Calle Peotonal and grab a snack at the market.

★Museo para la Identidad Nacional — MUSEUM

(MIN; Map p364; www.min.hn; Av Miguel Paz Barahona; L60; ⏲9am-5pm Tue-Sat, 10:30am-4pm Sun) If you only hit one sight, head here. The capital's finest museum is housed in an expertly-renovated 19th-century edifice, the former Palace of Ministries. It provides a superb, very comprehensive overview of the history and identity of the nation through a series of modern exhibits. Everything is in Spanish, but audio guides (L50) are available in English and French. The masterstroke here is a 3D film tour of the Copán ruins (L30 extra), shown four times per day.

Plaza Morazán — PLAZA

(Map p364; Av Miguel de Cervantes) At the center of the city is the Plaza Morazán, often called Parque Central. This is Tegucicalpa's hub, with its statue of former president Francisco Morazán on horseback. An elaborate baroque-style cathedral, dating from the 18th century, overlooks the square: step inside and you'll find an intricate altar of gold and silver.

Museo Nacional de Historia y Antropología Villa Roy — MUSEUM

(Map p360; Calle El Telégrafo; L20; ⏲8am-4pm Mon-Sat) Just north of the downtown area, this museum is housed in a grand villa, the opulent former home of ex-president Julio Lozano. The displays chronologically document Honduran history, including early archaeological and pre-Hispanic periods, as well as the rise of the influential fruit companies.

Galería Nacional de Arte — MUSEUM

(Map p364; Calle Bolívar; L30; ⏲9am-4pm Mon-Sat, 9am-1pm Sun) The excellent National Gallery displays the work of Honduras' finest visual artists from the colonial era to the modern, along with some well-preserved religious artifacts. The structure itself (originally a convent) is fascinating, built with adobe walls and dating back to 1654. Just alongside is the 18th-century **Iglesia La Merced**.

Centro de la Cultura Garinagu de Honduras — CULTURAL BUILDING

(Map p364; ☎2222-0511; Plaza Morazán; ⏲8am-5pm Mon-Sat) FREE It's well worth dropping by this cultural centre, situated right on the Parque Morazán, which has handicrafts, a library, CDs and jewelry for sale and information about the Garifuna people. Try to time your visit to coincide with a one-hour dance performance, usually starting at 10am and 4pm Monday to Thursday – some of the most athletic, sensual moves on planet Earth.

Museo del Hombre — MUSEUM

(Map p364; www.museodelhombre.com; Av Miguel de Cervantes; L20; ⏲9am-3pm Mon-Fri) Located in a beautiful colonial-era structure, the Museo del Hombre displays mostly contemporary Honduran art. It's also the location for some cutting-edge fashion shows and gigs.

(Continued on page 362)

Honduras Highlights

1. Immerse yourself in the diver's paradise of **Utila** (p417), with affordable prices and dramatic reefs on its north shore.
2. Marvel at the intricate stone carvings and epic ancient Maya structures of the extraordinary **Copán ruins** (p384).
3. Cruise down the spectacular **Río Cangrejal** (p403) on a raft, then live it up in a jungle lodge.
4. Discover the graceful former capital of Central America, the delightful cobblestoned highland town of **Gracias** (p390).

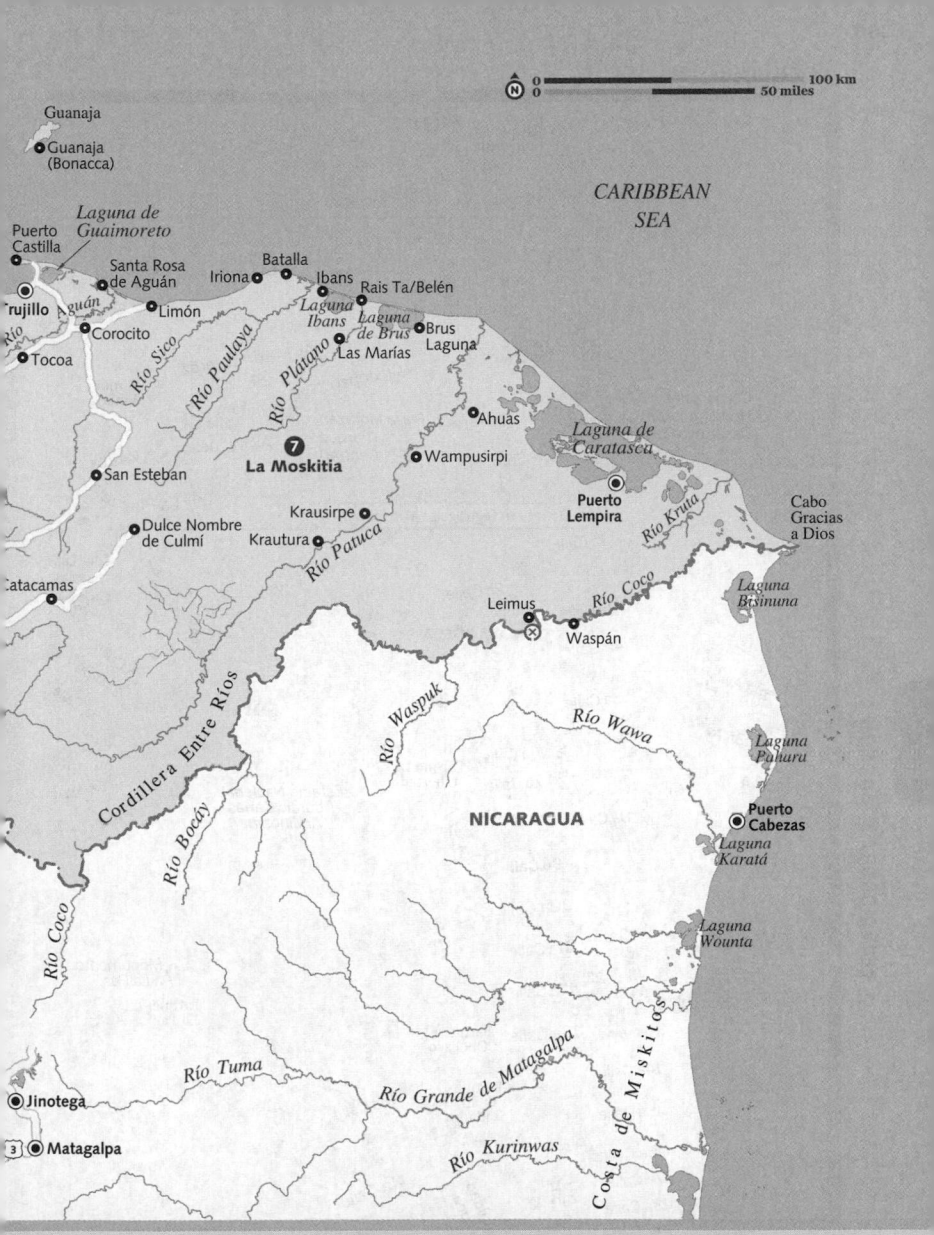

5 Search for a quetzal bird in cloud forests that rise above the cobalt-blue **Lago de Yojoa** (p373), then sample an artisan homebrew.

6 Snorkel wrecks and reefs then explore the far east of the fascinating island of **Roatán** (p410).

7 Go into the wild on an upriver adventure into Central America's last untamed wilderness, **La Moskitia** (p423).

Tegucigalpa

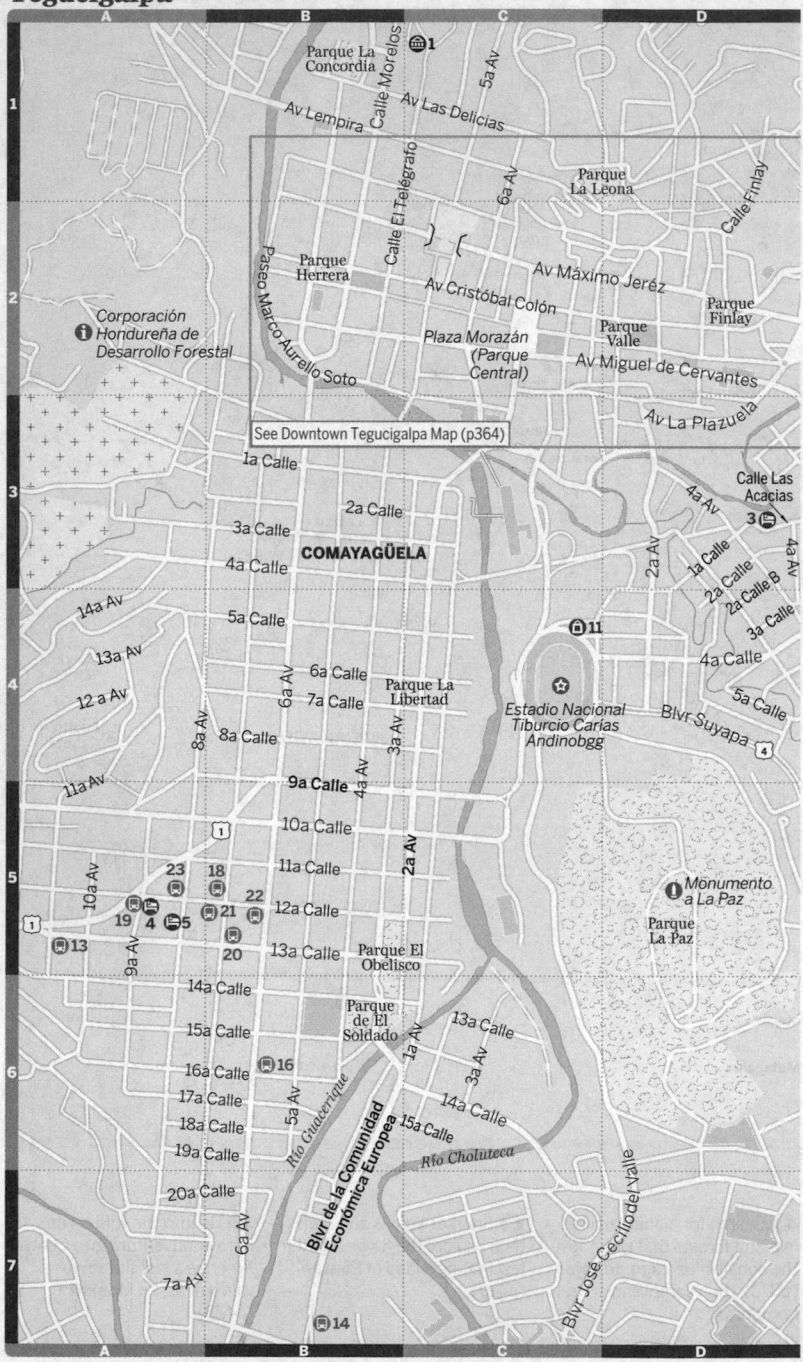

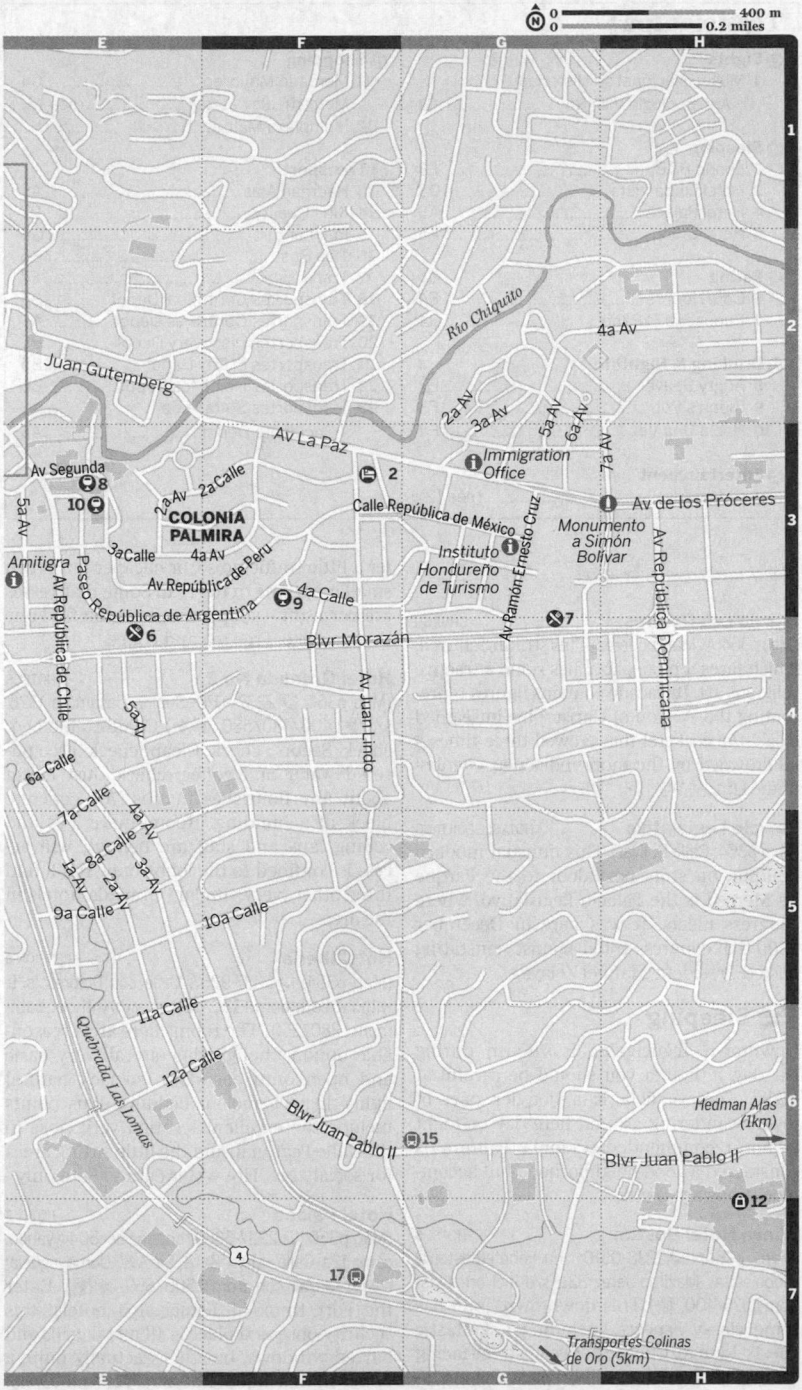
0 400 m
0 0.2 miles
E
F
G
H
1
2
3
4
5
6
7
Río Chiquito
4a Av
Juan Gutemberg
2a Av
3a Av
5a Av
6a Av
7a Av
Av La Paz
Immigration Office
Av Segunda
8
10
2a Av
2a Calle
2
COLONIA PALMIRA
Calle República de México
Av de los Próceres
Monumento a Simón Bolívar
5a Av
3a Calle
4a Av
Instituto Hondureño de Turismo
Av Ramón Ernesto Cruz
Av República Dominicana
Amitigra
Paseo
Av República de Perú
4a Calle
9
Av República de Chile
República de Argentina
6
7
Blvr Morazán
Av Juan Lindo
5a Av
6a Calle
7a Calle
4a Av
8a Calle
1a Av
2a Av
3a Av
9a Calle
10a Calle
11a Calle
Quebrada Las Lomas
12a Calle
Blvr Juan Pablo II
15
Hedman Alas (1km)
Blvr Juan Pablo II
12
4
17
Transportes Colinas de Oro (5km)

Tegucigalpa

Sights
1 Museo Nacional de Historia y Antropología Villa Roy C1

Sleeping
2 Econo B&B F3
3 Hotel Linda Vista D3
4 Hotel Palace A5
5 Hotel Unión A5

Eating
6 Café Honoré E4
7 Pupusería El Patio G4

Drinking & Nightlife
8 Angry Beaver E3
9 Glenn's Pub F3
10 Había Una Vez E3

Entertainment
Cinemark ..... (see 12)

Shopping
11 Mercado Mayoreo C4
Metromedia ..... (see 12)
12 Multiplaza Mall H7

Transport
13 Hedman Alas A5
14 King Quality B7
15 Pullmantur G6
16 Tica Bus B6
17 Trans Nica F7
18 Transportes Contraibal Depot B5
19 Transportes Contreras Depot A5
20 Transportes Discovery Depot B5
21 Transportes El Rey Depot B5
22 Transportes Norteños Depot B5
23 Transportes Sultana de Occidente Depot A5

(Continued from page 357)

Iglesia Los Dolores CHURCH
(Map p364; Av Máximo Jeréz) This striking church, which faces a huge plaza, has some attractive religious art. Its facade contains figures representing the Passion of Christ – his unseamed cloak, the cockerel that crowed three times – all crowned by the more indigenous symbol of the sun.

Palacio Legislativo NOTABLE BUILDING
(Map p364; Calle Bolívar) This unusual modern building on stilts next door to the Parque La Merced is the Palacio Legislativo, where congress meets. It was here in December 2009 that congress voted against reinstating ousted President Manuel Zelaya.

Sleeping

Downtown Tegucigalpa is safe-ish during the day, although you should be careful at night. Comayagüela is a dodgier part of town: wandering around here day or night is not recommended. Colonia Palmira is considered a good neighborhood but accommodations are costly.

Nuevo Hotel Boston HOTEL $
(Map p364; ☎2238-0510; nuevohotelboston@yahoo.es; Av Máximo Jérez 321; s/d incl breakfast from L375/400; @) This downtown hotel has some classy aspects, including a fantastic guests' lounge. Choose between street-facing rooms which are incredibly spacious but suffer a little traffic noise, or cheaper but much smaller options to the rear. Some mattresses are *very* soft – shop around till you find one that you like. Free tea and coffee.

Hotel Granada No 2 HOTEL $
(Map p364; ☎2237-7079; Subida Casamata 1326; s/d/tr L400/480/580; @ ❄) Comfortable bed: check. Secure: check. Clean: check. Free purified water and coffee: check. Just forget about any flourishes in this '70s concrete block of a building. Rooms have TVs and ceiling fans and staff are helpful; wifi access is confined to the lobby only. You'll find three other (very similar) Granada hotels in the area.

Hotel Iberia PENSION $
(Map p364; ☎2237-9267; Calle Los Dolores; s/tr without bathroom L180/360, d with/without bathroom L280/250) The rooms here are a reasonable option, though they are all very basic and open onto corridors (so lack natural light). Expect ancient bedding. Plus points include the excellent location very close to the Calle Peatonal, and the little sitting areas for socializing. Hot water 6am to 8am only.

Hotel Palace HOTEL $
(Map p360; ☎2237-6660; hotelpalace504@yahoo.com; 12a Calle, btwn 8a & 9a Avs, Comayagüela; r with fan/air-con from L500/650; ❄ ❄) Enter the Fort Knox of Tegucigalpa hotels: this security-obsessed place is all metal grills and barred windows, but that's actually quite a bonus in this 'hood. Rooms (over four levels)

are in good shape and have fresh paint and cable TV, but are very plain and functional for the prices charged. Still, staff are friendly and it's a short walk from the bus terminals.

Hotel Unión HOTEL $
(Map p360; ☎2237-4313; 8a Av, btwn 12a & 13a Calles, Comayagüela; s/d/tr L250/350/400;) Just do-able for a night if you're fresh off the bus and funds are tight, this spartan place has small, plain rooms with fans and spring beds. Don't expect much more than a grunt from the receptionist, but at least cleanliness is taken seriously – smell that bleach.

Hotel MacArthur HOTEL $$
(Map p364; ☎2237-9839; www.hotelmacarthur.com; Av Lempira 454; s/d with fan L777/976, with air-con L976/1176;) This hotel has a strong Honduran flavor, with an enjoyably old-fashioned lobby and a large selection of spacious rooms located off long corridors. Decor-wise the accommodation may be a little dated for some tastes, but the dark wood furniture has a certain appeal. There's also an inexpensive cafeteria here serving breakfast and dinner.

Econo B&B B&B $$$
(Map p360; ☎2221-5949; www.econobb.com; Colonia Palmira 555, Colonia Palmira; s/d with breakfast L1200/1400;) Within a few meters of the US embassy, this very welcoming B&B is a real retreat from the Tegus streets. Spacious family-sized rooms, all with kitchens, TV/DVD player and reliable wi-fi are set to one side of a large compound. Breakfast is served in the adjoining home of gracious owner Olympia (who lived in the USA for years). It's a bit tricky to find (especially at night) as the guesthouse lacks a sign: call ahead to gain access.

Hotel Linda Vista GUESTHOUSE $$$
(Map p360; ☎2238-2099; www.lindavistahotel.net; Calle Las Acacias 1438, Colonia Palmira; s/d incl breakfast L1000/1320;) Run by hospitable people, this neat, welcoming hotel has six rooms with mahogany furnishings, big closets and spacious bathrooms. As the name suggests, the city views are outstanding from the rear garden.

Eating

There's a dearth of choice downtown, where fast-food joints rule the streets. For more choice head up to Colonia Palmira where the food is pricier but the eye candy and relative safety come free of charge. There are low-end eateries and street food options strewn about Comayagüela, but it is not a place to wander aimlessly in search of a bite.

Merendero Delia COMEDOR $
(Map p364; Av Cristóbal Colón; meals L50–70; 8am-4pm Mon-Sat) Serves simple, no-nonsense Honduran dishes like *pollo en salsa* (chicken in spicy sauce) and *sopa de frijoles con costilla de res* (black bean soup with beef ribs) for L50 a hit. Expect Fanta-orange walls and plastic fantastic chairs.

Food Stands HONDURAN $
(Map p364; off Av Paulino Valladares; snacks L20–40; 11am-3pm) At the side of Iglesia Los Dolores, these stands offer a variety of tempting cheapie lunchtime street-food dishes including *pupusas* (cornmeal mass stuffed with cheese or refried beans) and *baleadas* (flour tortilla filled with beans and cheese).

★Café Paradiso CAFE $$
(Map p364; Av Miguel Paz Barahona 1351; mains L90-195; 10am-10:30pm Mon-Sat;) An intimate, bohemian hangout *par excellence,* this is a great place to rub shoulders with Tegus's creative types. The decor (including an excess of curios and lots of paintings) and layout (multiple rooms set off a central covered patio) are unusual. Food-wise, you can snack on a croissant for just L25 or feast on a filet mignon for L195. Arthouse movies are shown at 6:30pm Tuesday; poetry readings at 6:30pm Thursday.

Café.Tienda 1331 CAFE $$
(Map p364; Av Miguel de Cervantes; meals L70-L95; 10am-7pm Mon-Fri, 10am-5pm Sat;) This stylish little place (lime-green sculptured concrete walls and monochrome photography) serves excellent salads and sandwiches, or delve into the lunch buffet (noon to 3pm). Popular with artists and Tegus's hip young things.

Restaurante Duncan Maya HONDURAN $$
(Map p364; cnr Av Cristóbal Colón & Calle Salvador Corleto; meals L65-160; 8am-10pm Mon-Sat, to 9:30pm Sun) Enjoyable, atmospheric place that occupies a covered patio with original floor tiles, colossal wooden columns and a full bar, including many imported beers. It's an excellent, economic destination for breakfast (L65) or a set lunch (L67). Dinners (like *carne asada de res* –grilled beef – or *camarones empanadas* – breaded shrimp) are far more costly at around L150.

Downtown Tegucigalpa

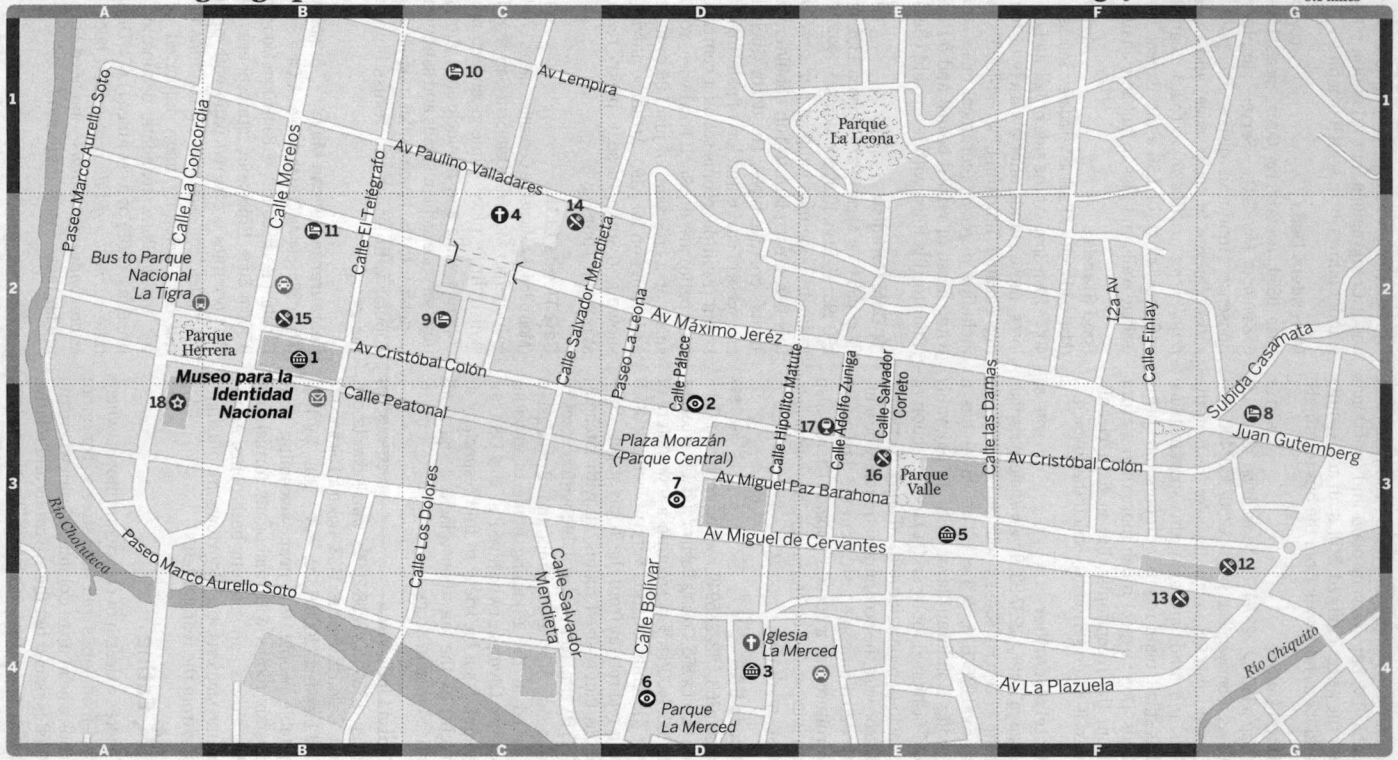

Downtown Tegucigalpa

Top Sights
1 Museo para la Identidad Nacional B2

Sights
2 Centro de la Cultura Garinagu de Honduras D3
3 Galería Nacional de Arte D4
4 Iglesia Los Dolores C2
5 Museo del Hombre E3
6 Palacio Legislativo D4
7 Plaza Morazán D3

Sleeping
8 Hotel Granada No 2 ..... G3
9 Hotel Iberia C2
10 Hotel MacArthur C1
11 Nuevo Hotel Boston B2

Eating
12 Café Paradiso G3
13 Café.Tienda 1331 ..... F4
14 Food Stands C2
15 Merendero Delia B2
16 Restaurante Duncan Maya E3

Drinking & Nightlife
17 Tito Aguacate E3

Entertainment
Café Paradiso ..... (see 12)
18 Teatro Nacional Manuel Bonilla A3

Pupusería El Patio HONDURAN $
(Map p360; Blvr Morazán, Colonia Palmira; pupusas L23-28; ⏲11am-1:30am) On weekends this beer hall of a place can be a riot, with tables overflowing with bottles and families belting out the karaoke. Tacos and typical Honduran dishes are the main items on the menu – groups should go for the *Plato de Variedad* (L188), which introduces all of the Honduran staples and serves three to four people.

Café Honoré INTERNATIONAL, DELI $$$
(Map p360; Paseo República de Argentina 1941, Colonia Palmira; sandwiches/mains from L130/220; ⏲8:30am-9:30pm Mon-Sat, to 6pm Sun; 📶) This is a mecca for the Honduran elite, but if you're yearning for gastro treats this is the place. The deli section has Parma ham and French cheese while the large street terrace, complete with mod-Asian decor, makes a great place to blow the budget on an outrageously pricey gourmet sandwich.

Drinking & Nightlife

Colonia Palmira is your best bet for a night out, with several bars along Blvr Morazán and around Plaza San Martín. You won't be able to party til dawn in this city as there's a 2am curfew.

★Tito Aguacate BAR
(Map p364; Av Cristóbal Colón; ⏲11am-9pm) This legendary downtown dive bar – all peeling yellow paintwork and strip lights – is a scruffy haunt for leftist intellectuals and hard drinkers. The bar has been around since 1945, but women have only recently been admitted. A tapa is served with every drink and you have to try the famous hangover cure *calambre* (made from gin, apple wine, sugar and lime). The sign outside says 'New Bar' but don't pay any attention – everyone calls it Tito's.

Había Una Vez BAR, CLUB
(Map p360; Plaza San Martín 501, Colonia Palmira; ⏲6pm-midnight Tue-Thu, to 2am Fri & Sat) Happening bar perfect for low-key clubbing that draws a hip, sexy, moneyed crowd, with DJs spinning deep house and lounge on weekend nights. During the week it's good for a sociable drink.

Angry Beaver PUB
(Map p360; Plaza Villa Real; ⏲6pm-1am; 📶) An atmospheric new pub run by a Honduran/Canadian couple, with a fine choice of beer (including Newcastle Brown Ale) and welcoming staff. There's a great jukebox and subdued lighting (though an excess of corny posters).

Glenn's Pub PUB
(Map p360; Colonia Palmira; ⏲6pm-2am Mon-Sat; 📶) A long-standing 'secret' among *capitalinos,* this intimate, very sociable bar caters to a mix of free-spirited 20-somethings and hardened local drinkers. The action spills out onto the sidewalk on weekend nights. The owner is a hard-rock fan, so expect a soundtrack of endless guitar solos to accompany your evening here.

Entertainment

Consult www.agendartehonduras.com for a round-up of cultural events in the capital.

Café Paradiso CINEMA
(Map p364; www.paradisoblog.wordpress.com; Av Miguel Paz Barahona 1351; ⏲10am-10:30pm Mon-Sat) Shows arthouse movies every Tuesday

at 6:30pm, and has poetry readings on Thursday at 6:30pm.

Teatro Nacional Manuel Bonilla THEATER, PERFOMING ARTS
(Map p364; ☎2222-4366; Av Miguel Paz Barahona) Hosts a variety of performing arts including theater and concerts.

Cinemark CINEMA
(Map p360; ☎2231-2044; Blvr Juan Pablo II, Multiplaza Mall; tickets from L70) A modern multiscreen cineplex. Mainly shows Hollywood films.

Shopping

Honduran handicrafts are sold at small stores on Av Miguel de Cevantes, east of Plaza Morazán.

Mercado Mayoreo MARKET
(Map p360; ⏲8am-5pm Fri, 6am-3pm Sat) Every Friday and Saturday, this colorful cheap market sets up shop near the Estadio Nacional. There's a dazzling array of produce and stalls, hawking everything from birdcages to vegetables and some great little *pupusa* cafes too.

Multiplaza Mall MALL
(Map p360; Blvr Juan Pablo II; ⏲10am-8pm Mon-Sat, noon-6pm Sun) The most convenient shopping complex for travelers, this mall is southwest of Colonia Palmira, with ATMs, bookstores, internet and a cinema.

Metromedia BOOKS
(Map p360; Blvr Juan Pablo II, Multiplaza Mall) Sells English-language books and magazines, and there's a cafe too.

Information

DANGERS & ANNOYANCES

Like most Central American cities, Tegucigalpa has a very high crime rate. However, with common sense, you should be able to enjoy the city without putting yourself at undue risk. During the day, downtown Tegucigalpa and Colonia Palmira are usually fine to walk around – although beware of pickpockets. Be especially alert and careful in and around the bus terminals of Comayagüela – this area is notorious for crime.

It's best to avoid city buses (which are prone to 'taxing' by gang members). Take taxis at night.

EMERGENCY & MEDICAL SERVICES

Ambulance (☎195; ⏲24hr) Red Cross.

Honduras Medical Center (☎2280-1500; www.hmc.com.hn; Av Juan Lindo; ⏲24hr) One of the best private hospitals in the country.

Police (☎199, 2222-8736; 5a Av; ⏲24hr)

INTERNET ACCESS & TELEPHONE

Multinet (Calle Peatonal; per hr L20; ⏲9am-9pm) Reliable internet cafe and call center.

MONEY

ATMs are dotted about the city: at the airport, on the northeast corner of Parque Central, in the Hedman Alas bus terminal and in the shopping malls.

Banco Atlántida (Parque Central; ⏲9am-4pm Mon-Fri, 9am-2pm Sat) Has a 24-hour ATM.

Citibank (Blvr Morazán, Centro Comercial Plaza Criolla; ⏲8am-4pm Mon-Fri, 9am-1pm Sat) One of several banks here.

HSBC (Blvr Morazán; ⏲8am-5pm Mon-Fri, 9am-1:30pm Sat) With ATM.

POST

Downtown Post Office (cnr Av Miguel Paz Barahona & Calle El Telégrafo; ⏲8am-5pm Mon-Fri, 8am-1pm Sat)

TOURIST INFORMATION

Amitigra (☎2231-3641; www.amitigra.org; 2a Calle Nunciatura Apostolica 210, Colonia Palmira; ⏲8am-5pm Mon-Fri) Manages Parque Nacional La Tigra and can provide information.

Corporación Hondureña de Desarrollo Forestal (Cohdefor; ☎2223-4346; Colonia El Carrizal; ⏲8am-3:30pm Mon-Fri) The national office, located 4km west of the center. You can get information on Honduras' national parks and protected areas here.

Immigration Office (☎2238-5613, 2245-6491; www.migracion.gob.hn; Anillo Periférico, near Universidad Technólogica de Honduras; ⏲8:30am-4:30pm Mon-Fri) Extends visas (US$20 for 30 days) and handles immigration matters.

Instituto Hondureño de Turismo (IHT; ☎2222-2124; www.letsgohonduras.com; cnr Av Ramón Ernesto Cruz & Calle República de México; ⏲9am-5pm Mon-Fri) Helpful tourist office, with good general information and lots of glossy leaflets. But don't expect too much practical information.

TRAVEL AGENCIES

Several reliable travel agencies are clustered around Hotel Honduras Maya. Be aware that some agencies charge just for the *cotización* (pricing an itinerary).

Mundirama Travel (☎2232-3909; www.mundiramatravel.com; Edificio Cicsa, cnr Avs República de Panamá & República de Chile; ⏲8am-5pm Mon-Fri, 8am-noon Sat) Good for flight reservations. Also the local American Express rep.

Getting There & Away

AIR

The airport is 6.5km south of Tegucigalpa.

DESTINATION	COST (L)
La Ceiba	1494
Roatán (via La Ceiba)	1952
Utila (via La Ceiba)	2631

Aerolíneas Sosa (☎2233-5107, airport 2234-0137; www.aerolineasosa.com; Blvr Morazán, Centro Comercial Gallerias Maya; ⏲8am-5pm Mon-Fri, 8am-noon Sat)

American Airlines (☎2216-4800, toll free 800 220-1414; Edif Palmira; ⏲8am-5:30pm Mon-Fri, 9am-noon Sat) Across from Hotel Honduras Maya.

TACA/Isleña (☎2234-2422; www.taca.com; Blvr Morazán; ⏲8am-5pm Mon-Sat, 9am-2pm Sun)

BUS

There's no central station in Tegus. Each bus company has its own depot, and unfortunately most are in Comayagüela. See the bus info table on this page and p367 for departure information. Keep a wary eye on your belongings in this part of town.

International & Long-distance Buses

There are five international bus companies:

Hedman Alas (Map p360; ☎2239-1764; www.hedmanalas.com; Blvr Suyapa, Edif Florencia Plaza) Connects Tegus with San Salvador and Guatemala City. Two departure offices: one in Comayagüela and a far nicer terminal located behind Multiplaza Mall in the southeast of the city.

King Quality (Map p360; ☎2225-5415; www.king-qualityca.com; Blvr de la Comunidad Económica Europea, near 6a Av, Comayagüela) Goes to El Salvador, Guatemala, Nicaragua and Costa Rica.

Pullmantur (Map p360; ☎2232-0216; www.pullmantur.com; Blvr Juan Pablo II, Hotel Marriott) Connects Tegus with San Salvador and Guatemala City.

Tica Bus (Map p360; ☎2220-0579; 16a Calle, btwn 5a & 6a Avs, Comayagüela) Goes to El Salvador, Guatemala and Nicaragua and the Mexican border, and has connections to Costa Rica and Panama.

INTERNATIONAL BUSES FROM TEGUCIGALPA

DESTINATION	COST (L)	DURATION (ONE WAY)	BUS LINE	PHONE	FREQUENCY
Guatemala City (Guatemala)	580-1694	22hr (with overnight in San Salvador)	Tica Bus	2220-0579	1 daily
	–	15hr (with layover in San Salvador)	King Quality	2225-5415	1 daily
	–	14hr	Hedman Alas	2237-7143	2 daily
	1294-1952	11hr	Pullmantur	2232-0216	1 daily
Managua (Nicaragua)	380-724	8hr	Tica Bus	2220-0579	1 daily
	–	7-8hr	King Quality	2225-5415	2 daily
	597	7hr	Trans Nica	2239-7933	1 daily
San José (Costa Rica)	760	2 days (with overnight in Managua)	Tica Bus	2220-0579	1 daily
	996	16hr	Trans Nica	2239-7933	1 daily
San Salvador (El Salvador)	285-952	6½hr	Tica Bus	2220-0579	1 daily
	–	6-7hr	King Quality	2225-5415	2 daily
	796-1095	6½hr	Pullmantur	2232-0216	1 daily
Tapachula (Mexico)	855	40hr (overnight in San Salvador, transfer in Guatamala City)	Tica Bus	2220-0579	1 daily

Trans Nica (Map p360; ☎2239-7933; www.transnica.com; Blvr Suyapa, Hotel Alameda) Heads to Managua and on to San José. Make sure you arrive 45 minutes early before taking any international departures.

Hedman Alas and **Viana** (☎2225-6583; www.vianatransportes.com; Blvr Fuerzas Armadas) offer very comfortable, but also very expensive, buses on domestic routes. If you're heading for San Pedro Sula, Copán Ruinas or the north coast towns of Tela and La Ceiba, there are cheaper alternatives.

Getting Around

TO/FROM THE AIRPORT

Aeropuerto Internacional Toncontín is 6.5 traffic-snarled kilometers south of the center of Tegucigalpa. Local buses marked 'Loarque' (L7) do run from the terminal to Comayagüela, but it's far safer to catch a taxi (see following) due to security concerns on city buses. Another option is to grab a *colectivo* van (L12) which connect the airport with a stop on Calle Morelos, five blocks west of Parque Central.

Cotatyh (☎2238-4985) taxis to/from the airport cost L200.

BUS

City buses are cheap (L3), loud, dirty and can be dangerous. Theft is common and gangs sometimes target buses. Stick to taxis.

CAR & MOTORCYCLE

Before hiring a vehicle be sure to ask about the deductible (the amount you pay before insurance kicks in) – it can be as high as L40,000. Hire rates start at L520 per day.

Econo Rent-a-Car (☎2235-2105, airport 2291-0108; www.econorentacarhn.com; Calle Principle, Col El Trapiche; ⏲7am-7pm Mon-Fri, 7am-5pm Sat & Sun)

National/Alamo (☎2250-1362, airport 2233-4962; Av Segunga, Residencia Modelo; ⏲8am-6pm Mon-Sat)

TAXI

Taxis cruise all over town; a ride costs L60-120 depending on the distance.

There are a couple of useful downtown taxi *colectivo* stops; one on Calle Morelos that is particularly helpful for the airport, and another between Parque Valle and Parque La Mercad that runs to the Mercado Jacaleapa terminal (where buses depart for El Paraíso and Danlí). They charge L12.

LONG-DISTANCE BUSES FROM TEGUCIGALPA

DESTINATION	COST (L)	DURATION	BUS LINE	PHONE	FREQUENCY
Agua Caliente	322	9-10hr	Sultana de Occidente	2237-8101	hourly until 1:30pm
Catacamas	93-137	3½-4hr	Discovery	2222-4256	9 daily
Choluteca	47-60	3hr	Mi Esperanza	2225-2901	hourly 6am-4pm
Comayagua	55	2hr	Contreras Express	2238-8984	12 daily
Copán Ruinas	732-886	7hr	Hedman Alas	2237-7143	2 daily
El Paraíso	66	2hr	Colinas de Oro	9523-1637	hourly 6am-6pm, to 4pm Sun
Juticalpa	86	2½-3½hr	Discovery	2222-4256	9 daily
La Ceiba	830-1365	7½hr	Viana	2225-6583	3 daily
	262	8hr	Cristina	2225-1446	8 daily
La Entrada	226	6hr	Sultana de Occdentei	2237-8101	hourly until 1:30pm
Las Manos*	78	2½hr	Colinas de Oro	9523-1637	3 daily
San Pedro Sula	178	4hr	El Rey Express	2237-8561	10 daily
	545-930	4hr	Viana	2225-6583	5 daily
Santa Rosa de Copán	248	7hr	Sultana de Occidente	2237-8101	hourly 6am-1:30pm
Tela	227	5½hr	Cristina	2225-1446	8 daily
Trujillo	280	10hr	Contraibel	2237-1666	2 daily

*Nicaraguan border; last bus from border to Ocotal (Nicaragua) at 4pm

WORTH A TRIP

PARQUE NACIONAL LA TIGRA

A beautiful national park just a short hop from the capital, **Parque Nacional La Tigra** (L200; ⏲8am-4pm, last entrance 2pm) encompasses a cloud forest and eight hiking trails. There's an abundance of (elusive) wildlife – from pumas to peccaries – and towering trees, lichens and large ferns, bromeliads and orchids. It can be chilly up here – bring adequate clothing.

Amitigra (p366) in Tegus has information and manages overnight visits to the park. La Tigra has two entrances, **Jutiapa** and **El Rosario** – both have good visitor centers with accommodations (L300 per person) and *comedores* (simple eateries). Maps are available; guides are not really needed, as long as you stick to the main trails. For somewhere really special to stay, the two-room **Cabaña Mirador El Rosario** (☎2767-2141; r L650) is perfect, with stunning views and delicious home-cooked food. The German owners Jorge and Monika will pick you up if you call ahead.

The Jutiapa entrance is closest to the capital, 22km northeast. In Tegus, buses (L23, one hour) leave from Parque Herrera (7am, 9am, 2pm, 4pm and 5pm Monday to Friday; 8am, 10am, noon, 1pm and 3pm Saturday and Sunday) for Aldea El Chaparro, a 15-minute walk from the visitor center. Buses return from El Chaparro at 5:30am, 5:45am, 6am, 7am, 9am, 11am, noon and 3pm.

Around Tegucigalpa

The huge gothic **Basílica de Suyapa** (🚌6a Av & 9 Calle in Comayagüela), the most important church in Honduras, dominates the hillsides south of Tegucigalpa. It's famous for its large, brilliant stained-glass windows, and dates back to 1954. La Virgen de Suyapa (patron saint of all Central America) is represented inside by a tiny painted wooden statue, only 6cm tall inside. It's 7km southeast of the city center; buses for Suyapa (L3, 30 minutes) leave from the corner of 6a Av and 7 Calle in Comayagüela.

Perched among pine-covered hills, **Santa Lucía** is a charming old colonial mining town with a spectacular vista over the capital, 14km to the east. There's a striking 18th-century *iglesia* (church) and historic streets to explore. Buses (L9, 45 minutes) depart for Santa Lucía from an Esso station off Av la Paz in Tegucigalpa.

WESTERN HONDURAS

The heartland of Honduras, this mountainous, forested region encompasses a roll call of the nation's outstanding sights. The top attraction has to be the outstanding Maya ruins of Copán, closely followed by the timeless colonial charm of Gracias, gateway to a chain of exquisite traditional communities called the Ruta de Lenca. The historic cities of Comayagua and Santa Rosa de Copán are other key cultural centers.

Hikers will love the spectacular trails inside the Montaña de Celaque cloud forest, while there's dazzling birdlife and scenery around idyllic Lago de Yojoa, which is fast becoming a mecca for travellers.

Big, booming San Pedro Sula is the economic powerhouse of the nation and a travel hub. But as it's a featureless, crime-plagued city, few travellers hang around.

The main routes are all served by speedy, regular bus connections.

Comayagua

POP 80,800

Comayagua, 84km northwest of Tegucigalpa, is the historic first capital of Honduras and was a religious and political center for over three centuries until power shifted to Tegucigalpa in 1880. The town's colonial past is evident in its fine old churches, an impressive cathedral and its colonial plazas. A very Catholic city, it's *the* place in Honduras to witness Easter celebrations.

On the outskirts of the town is a huge air base used by the US military. Known as La Palmerola (or Soto Cano), it formed a base for US forces during the 1980s when the Contra war was raging in Nicaragua. Today about 1000 soldiers are stationed here.

OFF THE BEATEN TRACK

HIGHLAND HIKES

Spanning more than 300 sq km of primary and secondary forest, **Parque Nacional Montaña de Comayagua** (Panacoma; L35) has two main trails leading through the cloud forest, from near the small village of Río Negro, 42km north of Comayagua, to waterfalls (no bathing). The park is managed by Ecosimco (p371).

The first trail is to **Cascada de los Ensueños**, a 75m-high waterfall about an hour's hike through mostly secondary forest. The second trail veers off the first just before reaching Los Ensueños, and leads to another waterfall, **El Gavilán**.

Simple **accommodation** (☎2990-0802; bunks L70-140) is available at the house of Don Velásquez in Río Negro. You can hire a guide (recommended) in Río Negro. Pickup trucks to Río Negro (L35, two hours, four daily) leave from the south side of the Comayagua market.

Sights

Sights are clustered around the beautiful Parque Central.

Cathedral CHURCH
(Parque Central; ⏲7am-8pm) In the heart of town, Comayagua's cathedral is the largest colonial-era place of worship in Honduras. It was built between 1685 and 1715 and is adorned with intricate wooden carvings and gold-plated altars.

The cathedral's most interesting feature is its ancient Moorish **clock**, dating back to around 1100AD, which was originally located in the Alhambra in Granada, Spain. In 1620 it was donated to the town by King Phillip III. Look out for the older Roman-style IIII (rather than IV) on the clock face. Drop by the tourist office and they'll accompany you up the belltower for a closer look: the clock strikes every 15 minutes.

Museo Regional de Arqueología MUSEUM
(6a Calle NO; L80; ⏲8:30am-4pm) This fine museum is housed in a former presidential palace, which adds to its appeal. Inside you'll find some ancient Lenca artifacts, including a stela, polychrome ceramics, jade jewelry and petroglyphs. Descriptions are in Spanish only.

Museo Colonial de Arte Religioso MUSEUM
(Av 2a de Julio, near 3a Calle NE; L25; ⏲8am-noon & 2-4:30pm Tue-Sun) Closed at the time of research for renovation, this museum occupies the site of the first university in Central America, founded in 1632. The museum, which should reopen in 2014, contains an impressive collection of religious art and paraphernalia.

Nuestra Señora de la Caridad CHURCH
(cnr 7a Calle NO & 3a Av NO; ⏲7am-8pm) The much remodeled Nuestra Señora de la Caridad was built at the end of the 16th century and is used as a place of worship for the local indigenous community.

La Merced CHURCH
(1a Av NE) Comayagua's first *iglesia* was La Merced. Building started in 1550 and it was consecrated as a cathedral in 1561. The plaza out the front is very pretty.

Sleeping

Hotel Norimax Colonial HOTEL $
(☎2772-1703; Calle Manuel Bonilla s/n; r with fan/air-con L300/350; ❄) This dusky pink edifice on the southern fringes of the center has clean, inviting rooms with attractive wooden beds, wardrobes and cable TV. There's also a (less attractive) sister hotel, the Norimax, at the western end of Calle Manuel Bonilla.

Hotel America Inc HOTEL $
(☎2772-0530; www.hotelamericainc.com; cnr 1a Av NO & 1a Calle NO; r with fan/air-con from L475/535; ❄📶🏊) A welcoming place in the market area, this place has a fancy (if dated) lobby and a wide selection of rooms. The cheaper options are plain but serviceable; the fancy new ones have refurbished *baños* (bathrooms) and quality furnishings but cost a lot more. The pool is tiny (around 8m).

Eating & Drinking

La Casa de Sandwich CAFE $
(2a Av NE; items L28-60; ⏲9am-9pm Mon-Sat, 11am-6pm Sun; 📶) An excellent Honduran/Puerto Rican-owned cafe where they bake baguette-style bread on the premises. Sit on one of the chunky wooden tables and tuck into a salami or *bistek* (steak) sandwich (around L50) and down a *jugo* (juice; L12). It's a couple of blocks east of the Parque Central.

★Restaurante Plaza Colonial HONDURAN, INTERNATIONAL **$$**
(Parque Central; mains L70-230; ⏲7:30am-9pm) On the east side of the Parque Central, this classy restaurant offers the best view in town from its terrace tables, plus myriad atmospheric dining rooms bursting with curios and character. It's quite classy (and pricey) but the set lunch (L70) is excellent value and you'll find the salads, snacks, seafood and grilled meats well-prepared and fully flavorsome.

La Gota de Limón BAR, CAFE
(5a Calle NO; meals L60–150; ⏲10:30am-7pm Sun-Wed, to 2am Thu-Sat) An upmarket bar-lounge that operates as an (underused) cafe during the day. On weekend nights it morphs into one of the town's best bars, drawing a fashionable crowd with DJs playing a mix of salsa, merengue and Latin hits. There's usually no cover charge.

Orientation

Heading north into town from the main San Pedro Sula to Tegucigalpa highway you pass through the market area after 750m, then hit the Parque Central in another 250m.

Streets are defined according to the compass: NO for *noroeste* (northwest), NE for *noreste* (northeast), SO for *suroeste* (southwest) and SE for *sureste* (southeast).

Information

Banco Atlántida (Parque Central; ⏲8am-5pm Mon-Fri, 9am-1:30pm Sat) Has an ATM machine.

Ecosimco (Ecosistema Montaña de Comayagua; ☎2772-4681; ecosimco@hondutel.hn; Camara de Comercio; ⏲9am-noon & 1-5pm Mon-Fri) Manages the Montaña de Comayagua National Park. It's 500m north of town – look for the big green gates.

L@Red (Parque Central; per hr L25; ⏲9am-7pm)

Police (☎2772-0080)

Post Office (1a Av NE btwn 4a & 5a Calles NO; ⏲8am-4pm Mon-Fri, to noon Sat)

Getting There & Away

Comayagua is connected to Tegucigalpa (L50, two hours, every 20 minutes) by very regular buses including those run by **Transportes Catrachos** (☎2772-0260; cnr 1a Calle SO & 1a Av NO), **Transportes Contreras** (☎2772-4618; Av 3 SO) and **Transportes El Rey**; pick up Transportes El Rey buses on the highway on the south side of town.

Transportes Catrachos and Transportes El Rey also operate buses to San Pedro Sula (L78, three hours, every 30 minutes). Buses to Marcala (L50, 1½ hours) leave just outside the Rivera terminal, departing hourly from 6am until 1pm, and again at 3pm.

La Esperanza

POP 22,000 / ELEV 1770M

Up in the highlands, slow-paced La Esperanza is known for its markets. Indigenous influence is strong here – you will see many women wearing the distinctive, colorful Lenca headdress. For these reasons – and not its muddy streets – it is a more interesting stopover than Marcala. The highest town in Honduras, it can get decidedly chilly here, too.

Two blocks west of the pretty Parque Central, the **Casa de Cultura** (Av Morazán; ⏲noon-4pm Mon-Fri) FREE has a couple of rooms devoted to Lenca culture, including some excellent ceramics and weavings. Continuing up the hill from here you'll soon reach **La Gruta**, a small cave now converted into a chapel.

Sleeping & Eating

Look out for local dishes containing *choros* (wild mushrooms).

TRANSPORT FROM LA ESPERANZA

DESTINATION	COST (L)	DURATION	FREQUENCY
Gracias	70	2½hr	7 daily
San Juan	35	1¼hr	hrly
San Pedro Sula	110	4hr	every 40min
Santa Rosa de Copán	85	3½hr	1 daily
Marcala	40	1½hr	4-5 daily
Tegucigalpa	110	4hr	every 40min

Hotel & Comedor Martiner PENSION, COMEDOR $
(☎2783-0931; martiner10@yahoo.com; Av España; s/d L225/325, meals L35-50) A block and a half east of the *parque*, this welcoming budget hotel has good-value, spacious, clean rooms with cable TV. There's a little *comedor* here too for filling, inexpensive grub, and during the day the roof terrace is a cool hangout-with-a-view.

Hotel Mejía Batres HOTEL $
(☎2783-4189; s without bathroom L170, s/d/tr with bathroom L320/470/550;) Boasts a very convenient central location (one block west of the Parque Central). Its rooms, though a little old-fashioned, are comfortable enough and well presented, though bathrooms are cramped.

El Fogón INTERNATIONAL, HONDURAN $$
(mains L70-160; 9am-9:30pm Sun-Thu, to 12:30am Fri & Sat) The most happening place in town, this atmospheric bar-restaurant a block west of Parque Central is an enjoyable destination for a meal. Dine on succulent grilled meats or Mexican favorites, sip a margartia or slug on a *cerveza*, then dance the night away (weekends only).

Information

The police and post office are on Parque Central. For cash, there's a **Banco Atlántida** (Av Los Proceres) one block north of Parque Central. Check your email at **Explored** (Plaza María; per hr L20; 9am-11pm) opposite the Hotel Mejía Batres.

Getting There & Away

The bus situation in La Esperanza can be confusing. The main 'terminal' for Tegucigalpa, San Pedro Sula and Santa Rosa de Cópan (via Gracias) is 800m east of the center, past the bridge. Other (mainly local) services (including those for Marcala) leave from around *mercado quemado* (burned market), which is a couple of blocks northeast of the Parque Central.

The road between Gracias and La Esperanza is now mostly paved and served by very regular minibuses (you may have to change in San Juan en route).

Marcala

POP 15,300

Marcala is a highland town with a strong indigenous heritage. It lies at the southern end of Honduras' 'Ruta Lenca' – a collection of Lenca villages and stronghold of Lencan culture. The town itself is tranquil but unremarkable, but it sits pretty in prime coffee country – and there are several opportunities to see the world's favorite bean being harvested and prepared. Several hikes in the surrounding area take in picturesque waterfalls and caves.

Activities

The hike to **La Estanzuela** – a pretty waterfall and swimming spot – via the impressive cavern **La Cueva del Gigante**, is a popular excursion. The tourist office has a good leaflet detailing exactly how to get there, as well as other trails.

Cooperativa RAOS GUIDED TOUR
(☎2764-5181; cooperativaraos@yahoo.com; 8am-4pm Mon-Fri, 8am-noon Sat) Cooperativa RAOS, on the road towards La Esperanza, is Honduras' first organic farming cooperative. It now represents over 200 small producers. *Finca* (farm) tours (per person L100 to L300) are a great way to learn about organic coffee cultivation and talk to the farmers.

Sleeping & Eating

Hotel y Cafetería Roxana HOTEL $
(☎2764-5866; s/d from L220/250, mains L45) This unappealing-looking green-and-cream concrete hotel isn't going to win any architectural awards, but its rooms are good value, all with private hot-water bathrooms and cable TV, and some with a balcony. Meals are also offered in the downstairs *comedor*. The

TRANSPORT FROM MARCALA

DESTINATION	COST (L)	DURATION	FREQUENCY
Comayagua	55	2½hr	8 daily
La Esperanza	40	1hr	5 daily
San Pedro Sula	115	5hr	1 daily
Tegucigalpa	78-100	3½hr	hrly

hotel is located opposite the post office, close to the market.

Hotel La Nueva Jerusalén HOTEL $
(☎2764-5909; s/d L220/270;) Motel-style place with two rows of rooms with fans and private hot-water bathrooms, facing a concrete parking lot. It is one block north and two blocks east of the Parque Central.

Casa Gloria HONDURAN $$
(Parque Central; mains L60-150; 8am-9pm;) Attractive colonial-style place that offers buffet dining (*pollo asada* – grilled chicken – *bistek* – steak – and some veggie options) during the day and service with a smile. The premises (reminiscent of Antigua Guatemala) are decorated with some fine Lenca ceramics and art.

Information

For cash head to **Banco Atlántida** (8am-4:30pm Mon-Fri, 8am-noon Sat) at the entrance to town, which has an ATM.

Cooperativa RAOS (☎2764-5181; cooperativaraos@yahoo.com; 8am-4pm Mon-Fri, 8am-noon Sat) and the official **Tourist Office** (☎2764-5858; Parque Central; 9am-6pm, closed Wed) are both excellent for tourist information.

For internet needs, **TIC** (☎2764-4132; per hr L20; 8am-9pm, to 7pm Sun) is two blocks west of and half a block north of the basketball courts.

Getting There & Away

Buses leave from various points, but all pass the Texaco gas station at the east end of the main road in and out of town.

Foreign travelers are not permitted entry to El Salvador at the nearby border-crossing of Sabanetas. Locals are still able to pass through, but save yourself a frustrating journey and use alternative crossings.

Cuevas de Taulabé

On the highway 20km south of Lago de Yojoa, the **Cuevas de Taulabé** (CA-5 Hwy, Km 140; L40; 8am-5pm) are a network of underground caves (over 12km in length) with unusual stalactite and stalagmite formations. The entrance fee includes a guide.

The first section of the caves has lights and a cement pathway; the pathway can be slippery, so wear appropriate shoes.

Lago de Yojoa

Largely undeveloped, and ringed by dense tropical forest, Lago de Yojoa is exceptionally scenic. Thanks to the indefatigable efforts of a local microbrewery owner to promote the region, the lake is now *the* most popular spot to break the journey between the Bay Islands and Nicaragua.

Lago de Yojoa's birdlife is world-class: the latest species count is up to 485 – over half the total in Honduras – including the elusive quetzal. You can also hike to remote waterfalls and to the summit of Santa Bárbara, visit coffee *fincas*, go tubing and zip-lining or row on the lake itself. As the *lago* is very shallow and there are lots of reeds close to shore, swimming is not that great.

The small town of Peña Blanca acts as a transport hub for the lake. There's an ATM here and some cheap hotels, but virtually all travelers stay at the D&D Brewery.

Sleeping & Eating

★D&D Brewery LODGE $
(☎9994-9719; www.ddbrewery.com; Los Naranjos; camping/dm per person L60/120, s/d/cabin L200/300/600;) Rapidly establishing the lake as a backpacking mecca, this excellent place has been transformed by Virginian Bobby Durrette, who first came to Honduras with the Peace Corp. The accommodations are comfortable and good value, but D&D's trump card is its microbrewery, with several superb beers (including a porter and fruit-flavored options) on tap. Food is excellent (try the blueberry pancakes) and the local coffee is fabulously smooth. The lodge does not have lake views, but acts as an excellent base to set up all manner of trips, from hardcore hiking to genteel birdwatching.

El Cortijo del Lago HOTEL $
(☎2608-5527; www.elcortijodellago.com; lakeside; dm/r L150/500, meals from L80;) This place enjoys a lovely setting right on the lake, but the dated accommodations could be in better shape. It's best used as a pit stop for a cold beer with a view, or a bite to eat. Located 2km from the La Guama turnoff.

Pollo Rico's HONDURAN $
(roadside, Pulhapanzak; meals L60; 6am-9pm) Right by the turnoff for the Pulhapanzak waterfall, this open-sided place turns out truly lip-smacking rotisserie chicken. Grab a

WORTH A TRIP

EXPLORING AROUND LAGO DE YOJOA

If you like the great outdoors, the gorgeous region around Lago de Yojoa will keep you busy for days. **D&D Adventures** (☎9994-9719; www.ddadventures.com; Los Naranjos, D&D Brewery; day trips from L460) can get to all the following places.

➡ **Pulhapanzak** (www.letsgopulha.com; L60; ⏲6am-6pm) is a magnificent 43m waterfall on the Río Lindo, just 17km north of the lake (and also an easy day trip from San Pedro Sula). Surrounded by some lush, well-preserved forest it's a well-organized, privately-run beauty spot where guides will lead you along a path directly behind the waterfall. There's good swimming and zip-lining (L500) right across the main body of the falls. Take dry clothes if you do the cave tour. It can get crowded here on weekends and holidays. From San Pedro, take an El Mochito chicken bus (L45, one hour) and get off at San Buenaventura, from where it's a well-marked 15-minute walk. Less frequent but direct Pulhapanzak Express buses also go directly to the entrance. The last bus back passes through San Buenaventura around 4pm.

➡ **Boat trips** on the lake are an essential experience, involving an early start (6am). The less-developed western side of the lake is best for seeing outstanding birdlife (including toucans and fish eagles) as well as large iguanas and monkeys. Expect to pay L250 per person for a two-hour tour in a rowing boat.

➡ **Parque Eco-Arqueológico Los Naranjos** (☎9654-0040; L114; ⏲8am-4pm), northwest of the lake, was first occupied around 1300 BC, and is thought to be the largest Preclassic-era Lenca archaeological site. The park includes trails for viewing semi-excavated ruins and plants and wildlife, particularly birds.

➡ **Parque Nacional Cerro Azul Meambar** (☎9865-9082; www.paghonduras.org/panacamlodge.html; L20) is east of the lake – a well-equipped park with kilometers of trails leading to waterfalls, caves and untouched cloud forest. There is also a **visitors center** (☎2608-5510, in Tegucigalpa 2773-2027), lodge and restaurant here. The entrance is via a turnoff from La Guama on the main CA-5 highway. Frequent pickups head to Santa Elena; from there, walking to the park's PANACAM Lodge takes about one hour.

➡ **Parque Nacional Santa Bárbara** is an isolated national park containing Honduras' second-highest peak, Montaña de Santa Bárbara (2744m), plus extensive cloud forest rich in orchids and epiphytes. It's a tough hike to the summit but you've a very good chance of seeing quetzals on this mountain. A bus leaves Peña Blanca daily at 10:30am for the town of San Luis Planes, where you can hire a guide (essential) in the community association. A bus returns to Peña Blanca daily at 6am.

➡ **Three waterfall hike** runs through the foothills of Parque Nacional Santa Bárbara – a delightful day-hike through coffee country and traditional settlements. The main attraction here is a stunning series of falls locals dub La Escalada de los Gigantes (Giants' Stairs), from where there are sweeping views. D&D Adventures charges L460 for this hike, including transport.

stool, order a cold beer, and chow down with the local *vaqueros* (cowboys).

ℹ Getting There & Away

From San Pedro Sula get a El Mochito-bound chicken bus from the main terminal via Peña Blanca (L50, 1½ hours, every 30 minutes) to the village of Los Naranjos. The bus stops within 300m of the D&D.

From Tegucigalpa, get a San Pedro Sula-bound bus to La Guama (three hours, more than 20 daily). From there, take another bus to Peña Blanca (L10, 15 minutes, every 15 minutes) from where you can either get a bus or *mototaxi* to Los Naranjos, 6km away.

San Pedro Sula

POP 717,000 / TRANSPORT HUB

'Bestowed' the title of the world's most dangerous city in 2012, San Pedro Sula's rep precedes it. Let's be clear – few travelers will want to linger long here: there are no sights, there's little cultural life, and the sultry climate can be oppressive.

The situation on the ground here is that most of the crime is gang-on-gang, so it's very rare for tourists to be targeted. Is San Pedro Sula really more dangerous than places such as Damascus or Mogadishu? Well, some zones within the city obviously are violent, but you probably won't see them: the city remains doable for travelers for a day or two.

San Pedro is the business and industrial capital of Honduras. The nation's engine room, the city generates almost two-thirds of the country's GDP, with thousands of people employed in giant *maquila* (clothes-weaving) factories. Its restaurants and nightlife arguably outstrip those in the capital.

And as San Pedro's international airport is Honduras' main entry point and its bus station a crucial hub for travellers, you're very likely to pass through. See the Safe Travel advice on p435.

Sights

The heart of the city around the Parque Central is rundown but full of life.

Cathedral CHURCH
(Parque Central) San Pedro's cathedral is a mock-colonial structure that actually dates from 1949. It faces the once-majestic (now decrepid) Art Deco Palacio Municipal on the other side of the square.

Museo de Antropología e Historia de San Pedro Sula MUSEUM
(☎2557-1874; cnr 3a Av NO & 4a Calle NO; adult/child L40/20; ⏲9am-4pm Mon & Wed-Sat, 9am-3pm Sun) This fine museum walks visitors through the history of the Valle de Sula from its pre-Columbian days to the modern era.

Sleeping

Aging budget hotels are mostly in the downtown area south of Parque Central, an area which can be dodgy after dark. Hostels and guesthouses tend to be closer to the main bus terminal in the north of the city. Hot water is not that common in many budget places.

★La Hamaca HOSTEL $
(☎9590-5401, 3191-0847; www.lahamacahostel.com; cnr 9a Av & 12a Calle, Colonia Trejo; dm/r L280/640; ❄📶) The number one choice for backpackers, this excellent hostel is a five-minute taxi ride from the bus station. It's run by a dynamic young team of Hondurans, all fluent English speakers, who know exactly what travelers are looking for. Rooms and dorms are spacious, and there's a superb lounge, games room, large kitchen and garden at the rear with a fully-equipped gym (owner Juan Carlos is a personal trainer). Travel advice is second to none and the neighborhood is secure, with a mall a short walk away.

Dos Molinos HOTEL $
(☎2550-5926; www.dosmolinos.hostel.com; cnr 13a Calle & 8a Av, Barrio Paz Barahona; s/d/tr with fan L400/500/720, d with air-con L600; ❄📶) This is an excellently maintained, family-owned place with six very clean rooms (all with a wardrobe, TV and cold-water private bathroom) run by Blanca and Luis, who look after guests very well but speak little English. Transport at any hour to the bus station is included, as is breakfast and drinking water.

Hotel Terraza HOTEL $
(☎2550-3108; 6a Av SO btwn 4a & 5a Calles SO; s/d with fan L300/350, with air-con L400/450 ; ❄📶) Not a bad downtown cheapie, particularly if you like orange tiling, orange paintwork, and, yes, orange curtains. All rooms have hot-water bathroom, cable TV, a rickety old desk and a wobbly chair.

★La Posada B&B $$
(☎2566-3312; www.laposadahn.com; 21 Calle A btwn 9 and 11 Avs, Colonia Universidad casa 172; s/d/tr L800/900/1000; ❄📶🏊) If this is your first night in Honduras you couldn't pick a better start to your trip than booking a room at La Posada. It's not cheap, but given the quality of the elegant house, cleanliness, beautiful rooms and very welcoming and helpful family owners, it represents excellent value. There's a guests' kitchen and garden and it's four blocks from a mall and restaurants in a leafy, wealthy area.

Eating

San Pedro Sula has a wide range of culinary choices. Upmarket places, as well as US fast-food franchises, are mainly located on Circunvalación. There's also a whole bunch of cheap and cheerful *comedores* at Mercado Guimilito.

Plaza Típica HONDURAN $
(3a Av NO; meals L45-80; ⏲6am-4:30pm) Just north of the Parque Central this open-sided

food court is your best bet for an inexpensive daytime meal. There's around 25 stands rustling up delicious *carne asada* (grilled meat), *tapado* (seafood soup with coconut) and amazing tropical fruit juices.

Cafetería Pamplona HONDURAN $
(Parque Central; meals L34-120; ⏲7am-7pm Mon-Sat, 8am-2pm Sun) Enjoyable cafe where you'll find bull-running photos on the walls and groups of earnest intellectuals discussing national politics in the corner. Good for breakfast, a set lunch or club sandwich.

Café Skandia CAFETERIA, INTERNATIONAL $$
(Gran Hotel Sula, Parque Central; snacks/mains from L30/90; ⏲6am-midnight; 📶) An absolute institution in the city center, this classic 1950s-style cafe looks like it's been transplanted from an ocean liner with its marine blue color scheme and vintage chrome-and-white-leather seats.

There's a vast window which overlooks the hotel's palm-fringed pool. All sorts of characters pass through: minor diplomats, sugar daddies with their 'companions' and even air-con-seeking backpackers. Menu-wise there's steaks, burgers, salads and sandwiches, as well as milkshakes and lots of dessert action.

Drinking & Nightlife

The Zona Viva, which hugs the inside of the Circunvalación between 7a Calle SO and 11a Calle SO, is home to the main concentration of bars and clubs.

Doghouse PUB
(Jardines del Valle; ⏲4-11pm Mon-Fri, to 1am Sat; 📶) In the buzzing Jardines del Valle district of San Pedro, this intimate bar looks a lot like a log cabin. It's very popular with visiting gringos, as the beers are cheap (L20 for a SalvaVida) and you can make requests on the YouTube jukebox. Trivia night is Thursdays at 8pm.

Information

The city's malls also have banks with ATMs.

BAC/Bamer (5a Av NO btwn 1a & 2a Calles NO; ⏲9am-5pm Mon-Fri, 9am-noon Sat) With ATM.

Banco Atlántida (Parque Central; ⏲8:30am-5pm Mon-Fri, 9am-1pm Sat) Has an ATM.

Canaturh (☎2521-3814; www.canaturh.org; 12a Av NO btwn 2a & 3a Calle NO; ⏲8am-4pm Mon-Fri) Some tourist information is offered here, but you'll get more up-to-date info from hostels like La Hamaca.

Diosita.net (Parque Central; per hr L25; ⏲7am-5pm) Internet access.

Mesoamérica Travel (☎2557-8447; www.mesoamerica-travel.com; cnr 8a Calle & 32a Avenida NO) Professional agency that does interesting upscale tours, including national park trips.

Post Office (cnr 9a Calle & 3a Av SO; ⏲7:30am-5pm Mon-Fri, 8am-noon Sat)

Tourist Police (☎2550-0001; cnr 12a Av NO & Blvr Morazan; ⏲24hr) No English is spoken!

Information

DANGERS & ANNOYANCES

San Pedro Sula's crime rate is one of the highest in the world. Mostly it involves gangs and narco traffickers, and travelers rarely get caught up in big trouble. However, do be very cautious. Avoid being flashy with your belongings and dress with restraint (save the shorts for the beach). Downtown is dodgy after nightfall. Use taxis to get around – don't risk the local buses.

Getting There & Away

AIR

Aeropuerto Internacional Ramón Villeda Morales (☎6689-3261) San Pedro Sula's modern Aeropuerto Internacional Ramón Villeda Morales is served by daily direct flights to many major cities in Central America and several US cities. Domestically there are connections to Tegucigalpa, La Ceiba, Puerto Lempira and the Bay Islands (usually via La Ceiba). The airport is on SPS-Tela Hwy CA-13, about 12km southeast of the city center.

International Airlines

American Airlines (☎2553-3506, airport 2668-3244; www.aa.com; cnr Av Circunvalación & 5a Calle SO, Edificio Banco Ficohsa) Flies to/from Miami.

Maya Island Air (☎2668-0569; www.mayaislandair.com) Flies to Belize and Guatemala City.

United/Copa (☎2552-9770, airport 2668-3212; www.continental.com; 4a Av NO btwn 1a & 2a Calles NO) Flies to/from Houston and Newark.

TACA (☎2550-8222; www.taca.com; Av Circunvalación, Colonia Trejo, Edif Yude Canahuati) Connects San Pedro with Guatemala City, Miami, New York, San José and San Salvador.

Domestic Airlines

Aerolíneas Sosa (☎2550-6545, airport 2668-3128; www.aerolineasosa.com; 1a Calle SO btwn 7a & 8a Av SO)

CM Airlines (☎2547-2425; www.cmairlines.com)

Isleña (☎2550-8222; www.taca.com; Av Circunvalación, Colonia Trejo, Edif Yude Canahuati)

BUSES FROM SAN PEDRO SULA

International Buses

DESTINATION	COST (L)	DURATION	BUS LINE	PHONE	FREQUENCY
Antigua, Guatemala	1233-1695	9hr	Hedman Alas	2516-2273	1 daily
Guatemala City, Guatemala	560	8hr	Rutas Orientales	2553-1174	1 daily
	670	8hr	Fuente del Norte	9843-0507	1 daily
	1117-1695	8hr	Hedman Alas	2516-2273	2 daily
	1320	8hr	King Quality	2516-2167	1 daily"
Santa Elena (Flores), Guatemala	825	13h	Fuente del Norte	9843-0507	1 daily
Managua, Nicaragua	640	12hr	Tica Bus	2220-0579	1 daily
Panama City, Panama	2260-2540	3 days	Tica Bus	2220-0579	1 daily
San Jose, Costa Rica	1160-1440	2 days	Tica Bus	2220-0579	1 daily
San Salvador, El Salvador	422	7hr	Sultana	2662-0940	1 daily
	800	7hr	King Quality	2553-4547	1 daily

Long-distance Buses

DESTINATION	COST (L)	DURATION	BUS LINE	PHONE	FREQUENCY
Agua Caliente	175-233	5hr	Congolón	2553-1174	every 2hr
Comayagua	74	2½hr	Diaz	2505-9955	8 daily
Copán Ruinas	110	3hr	Casasola	2516-2031	7 daily
	540-760	3hr	Hedman Alas	2516-2273	2 daily
El Mochito	52	2hr	Tima	2659-3161	every 30min
La Ceiba	98-500	3-4hr	7 bus lines incl Hedman Alas, Viana, Diana Express		every 15-30min
Puerto Cortés	48	1hr-1½hr	Impala	2665-0606	every 15min
Pulhapanzak & Lago de Yojoa	46	2hr	Etul	2516-2011	every 20min
	36	2hr	Pulhapanzak Express	No phone	9 daily
Santa Rosa de Copán	89	3hr	Toritos y Copanaecos	2516-2045	every 30min
	121	3hr	Sultana	2237-8101	5 daily
Tegucigalpa	142-545	4hr-4½hr	6 bus lines incl El Rey Express, Hedman Alas, Sultana, Viana		every 15-30min
Tela	78-382	1½hr	7 bus lines incl Hedman Alas, Mirna, Tela Express		every 15-30min
Trujillo	195	7hr	Cotuc	2520-7497	8 daily
	210	6½hr	Contraibal	9908-1509	9 daily

BUS

All buses depart from the modern, well-organised **Terminal Gran Central Metropolitana** (☎2516-1616; Av Circunvalación), 6km south of the Parque Central. Buses use designated bays and there's a large mall and food court here. There's a handy directory at the terminal's entrance; Hedman Alas buses have their own terminal at the rear. The magazine *Honduras Tips* has bus information; the website www.horariodebuses.com is an excellent online resource. Use taxis from the official rank, not freelance drivers.

Getting Around

TO/FROM THE AIRPORT

San Pedro's Aeropuerto Internacional Ramón Villeda Morales is about 14km east of town. **Hedman Alas** (☎2516-2273; www.hedmanalas.com; Terminal Gran Central Metropolitana) provides the only direct bus connections (L120 to L280, four daily) to/from San Pedro Sula's bus terminal. Hedman Alas also has very useful direct buses from the airport to Tela, La Ceiba, Tegucigalpa and Copán Ruinas. If you're really Lempira-light, it's a 2.5km walk from the airport to the main road to catch a local bus into town. Taxis cost L250 to L300.

BUS

It's best not to use local buses as they are subject to frequent robberies and 'taxing' by gangs.

CAR & MOTORCYCLE

Car rental agencies in San Pedro Sula with airport offices:

Econo Rent-A-Car (☎2668-1881; www.econorentacarhn.com)

Thrifty (☎2668-2427; www.thrifty.com)

TAXI

Average fares around town are L50 to L100. From the bus station to the center is around L80; to the airport about L250 to L300. Fares rise substantially after 9pm.

Parque Nacional Cusuco

Parque Nacional Cusuco (L190; ⏲8am-4:30pm), occupying a good chunk of the spectacular Merendón mountain range which fills the horizon west of San Pedro, is an eco-paradise with magnificent biodiversity, untouched cloud forest and unique dwarf forest. Its highest peak is **Cerro Jilinco** (2242m). There's excellent hiking here and the green-world contrast to San Pedro Sula really is quite something.

Huge tree ferns – of up to 20m, the highest in all of Central America – give you the impression of being in a *Jurassic Park* habitat. From March to May one of the typical early morning sounds of Cusuco National Park is the monotonous call of the resplendent quetzal, the sacred bird of the Aztecs and Mayas. Tapir, howler monkeys and the *cusuco* (armadillo) live in the heart of the park, though are very rarely encountered.

The charm of Cusuco does not only come from nature, but also from the quiet and harmonic life in the 38 surrounding coffee settlements. One of these, **Buenos Aires**, a few kilometers short of the park entrance, has a Tourism Commission and visitors center with maps and information about wildlife and plant species. Six marked trails (2km to 5km) lead from here into the forest.

There's no public transport to the park, and as the access road is in such poor condition it's usually only passable in a 4WD vehicle. This is one of those places where a tour makes a lot of sense. **JungleXpedition** (☎9762-6620; www.junglexpedition.org) are the local experts on Cusuco. Owner Juan Carlos is building trails inside the park, has contacts in all the communities and plans to open a travelers' lodge inside Cusuco. Two-day trips start at L800 per person (minimum three people) including 4WD transport and all meals.

Copán Ruinas

POP 8200

The beautiful, tranquil little town of Copán Ruinas, often simply called Copán, is the most traveler-oriented – and pleasant – town in Honduras. It's a stroll from the famous Maya ruins of the same name. Sloping cobblestone streets, white adobe buildings with red-tile roofs and an attractive colonial church give it a highly atmospheric, tranquil air. Most travelers stop here just for the ruins, but that's a mistake: Copán's collection of excellent restaurants and bars, beautiful attractions in the surrounding countryside and friendly population are all reasons to linger.

Sights

The fascinating Copán archaeological site (p384), 1km east of town, is the area's big draw.

Copán Ruinas

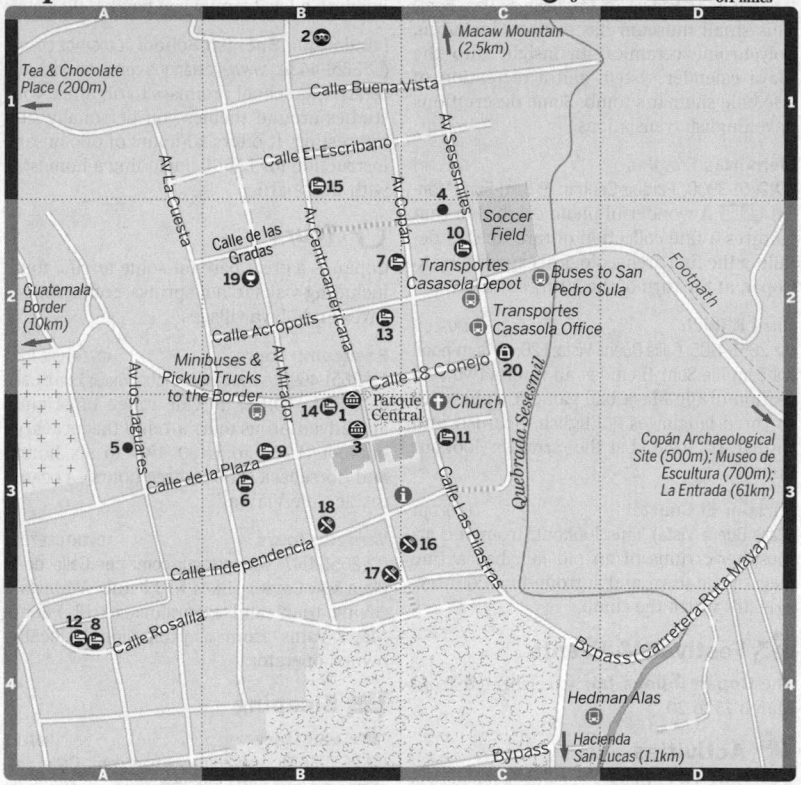

Copán Ruinas

Sights

Casa K'inich ..... (see 2)
1 Memorias Frágiles B3
2 Mirador El Cuartel B1
3 Museo de Arqueología Maya B3

Activities, Courses & Tours

Basecamp Tours ..... (see 6)
4 Guacamaya Spanish Academy C2
5 Ixbalanque Spanish School A3
Yaragua Tours ..... (see 11)

Sleeping

6 Café ViaVia B3
7 Hostal Berekah B2
8 Hostel Iguana Azul A4
9 Hotel Don Moises B3
10 Hotel Mary C2
11 Hotel Yaragua C3
12 La Casa de Café B&B A4
13 La Posada de Belssy B2
14 Lauro's Hotel B3
15 Terramaya B1

Eating

16 Café San Rafael C3
Café ViaVia ..... (see 6)
17 Carnitas Nia Lola B3
Comedor Mary ..... (see 10)
La Casa de Todo ..... (see 20)
18 Twisted Tanya's B3

Drinking & Nightlife

19 Sol de Copán B2

Shopping

20 La Casa de Todo C2

Museo de Arqueología Maya MUSEUM
(☎2651-4437; Parque Central; L285; ⏲9am-5pm) This small museum has exhibits including polychrome ceramics, an insight into the Maya calender system and a recreation of a female shaman's tomb. Some descriptions have English translations.

Memorias Frágiles GALLERY
(☎2651-3900; Parque Central; ⏲8am-5pm Mon-Fri) FREE A wonderful photo exhibition that features a fine collection of rare images detailing the first archaeological expeditions to Copán at the turn of the 20th century.

Casa K'inich MUSEUM
(☎2651-4105; Calle Buena Vista; L20; ⏲8am-noon & 1-5pm Tue-Sun) Includes an interactive recreation of the Maya ball game. Displays are in three languages – English, Spanish and Ch'orti'. It's located at the *mirador* (lookout point).

Mirador El Cuartel LOOKOUT
(Calle Buena Vista) This lookout, from the atmospheric ruins of an old jail, has a fine view of the town and surrounding countryside. It's worth the climb.

Festivals & Events

The **Copán Ruinas fair** is celebrated from March 15 to 20.

Activities

Hacienda San Lucas HORSEBACK RIDING
(☎2651-4495; www.haciendasanlucas.com; 3hr ride L500) Offers excellent, professional horseback riding around the beautiful eastern hills of the Copán Valley. It's essential to book a day ahead.

Finca El Cisne FARM, HORSEBACK RIDING
(☎2651-4695; www.fincaelcisne.com; horseback tour incl accommodations, 3 meals & thermal baths admission from L1900) Highly scenic horseback-riding tours, usually part of a day-long or overnight trip.

Courses

Copán's Spanish schools are both well-regarded and offer one-on-one tuition, after-class activities and guided excursions.

Guacamaya Spanish Academy LANGUAGE COURSE
(☎2651-4360; www.guacamaya.com; Calle de las Gradas, off Av Copán) Offers three study options, with 20 hours of one-on-one tuition costing L2800. Add hostel accommodation and it's L3520; or with full board and lodging with a local family you pay L4500.

Ixbalanque Spanish School LANGUAGE COURSE
(☎2651-4432; www.ixbalanque.com; Av los Jaguares) This school promises to organize your studies around themes you personally find interesting. It offers 20 hours of one-on-one instruction for L5000, including a homestay with full board.

Tours

Copán is a great base for some terrific tours including visits to hot springs, coffee *fincas*, caves and Maya villages.

Basecamp Tours ADVENTURE TOUR
(☎2651-4695; www.basecamphonduras.com; Calle de la Plaza) Offers a wide range of original and adventurous tours around the local area on foot (L200 to L900, two to six hours) and horseback (L300, three hours). Located inside Cafe ViaVia.

Yaragua Tours ADVENTURE TOUR
(☎2651-4147; www.yaragua.com; cnr Calle de la Plaza & Av Copán) Hikes to El Rubi Waterfall, caving tours and excursions to El Puente Maya ruins from a professional, locally-owned operator.

Sleeping

★**Hotel Mary** HOTEL $
(☎2651-4673; www.comedormary.com; Calle Sesesmiles; d/tw L500/900;) One of the best deals in town, this beautifully-presented new place has seven rooms dotted around a pretty garden, all with attractive textile bedcovers, a ceiling fan and hand-carved furniture – the owners even add fresh flowers sometimes, a lovely touch. The (famous) *comedor* next door is under the same management.

Hostel Iguana Azul HOSTEL $
(☎2651-4620; www.iguanaazulcopan.com; Calle Rosalila; dm/s/d L150/270/320;) Keeping standards high, this small, very well set-up place offers real value, with stylishly-presented accommodations that have quality mattresses and fresh linen, high ceilings, bedside tables, screened windows, reliable hot water and lockers. There's lots of good info about transport, tours, sights and restaurants. It's about a seven-minute walk from the *parque*.

Hostal Berekah HOSTEL $
(☎9951-4288; http://hotelberakah.wordpress.com; Av Copán; dm/d L120/300;) Getting good

feedback from readers, this modest hostel has small, though pleasant rooms, a dorm with five beds, a kitchen and clean shared hot-water bathrooms. Best of all, the upper balcony is great for socializing or chilling in a hammock. When we dropped by the receptionist was totally disinterested but, the owner is much more customer-oriented.

La Posada de Belssy HOTEL $
(☎2651-4680; www.laposadadebelssy.com; Calle Acrópolis; s/d with fan L300/350, r with air-con L500-600;) An excellent budget choice, this inviting little pension has smallish, neat rooms all with a fresh feel and TV, and air-con available for a little extra cash. The tiny roof pool is cool-off rather than lap-swimming size. The owners are friendly and offer breakfast (L50) and you'll also find a guests' kitchen.

Café ViaVia HOTEL $
(☎2651-4652; www.viaviacafe.com; Calle de la Plaza; s/d from L240/320;) At the rear of a very popular bar-restaurant, these attractive rooms have private showers and great beds (2m long). If you want to be near the heart of town this is a good option (though on weekends the adjoining nightlife can be loud – pack some ear plugs).

Lauro's Hotel HOTEL $
(☎2651-4068; www.lauroshotel.com; Calle 18 Conejo; s/d with fan L400/500, r with air-con L800;) Half a block from the *parque,* this is a well-managed hotel with a choice of spotless rooms, some with air-con. The owners have gone a bit overboard on the beige color scheme, but hey... rooms on the upper floors are more pricey and have views of the town.

Hotel Yaragua HOTEL $
(☎2651-4147; www.yaragua.com; cnr Av Copán & Calle de la Plaza; s/d L500/600;) The bright-yellow paint job and jungle-style patio area give this place a cheery feel. Rooms are smallish but comfortable and you can't beat the central location.

Hotel Don Moises PENSION $
(☎9867-8593; Calle La Plaza; dm/s/d L120/250/350;) Offering more of a local experience, this family-run guesthouse has a central location and a bustling, welcoming vibe. The dorms and rooms are perhaps a little messy around the edges but the owner is a helpful soul who can arrange shuttle buses and laundry.

★La Casa de Café B&B B&B $$
(☎2651-4620; www.casadecafecopan.com; Calle Rosalila; s/d incl breakfast L895/1150;) An impeccably decorated B&B that has incredibly tasteful rooms adorned with carved wooden doors and Guatemalan masks. The setting is stunning – in the morning mists rise around the Guatemalan mountains to the west. Breakfast is superb, and served in the garden with local coffee and eggs prepared to order.

Terramaya BOUTIQUE HOTEL $$$
(☎2651-4623; www.terramayacopan.com; Av Centroamericana; s/d incl breakfast L1700/1890;) A wonderful place to stay, where the little details (including elegant modernist furniture and chic, Mediterranean-style design) are just perfect. There's a peaceful garden and candlelit terrace with misty-eyed mountain views. Treat yourself: it's actually fine value given the lashings of style, atmosphere and comfort offered.

Hacienda San Lucas HISTORIC HOTEL $$$
(☎2651-4495; www.haciendasanlucas.com; r from L2830;) This is a magical hotel 3km south of town in the countryside. Beautifully restored, utterly unique and with fabulous views of the valley, taking in the town and archaeological site, the place has to be seen to be believed. The recently restored and expanded adobe hacienda is solar-powered, but the rooms are candlelit at night, adding to the serene atmosphere. The food here is highly praised, and many people come just for dinner. Los Sapos archaeological site is on the property. Phone beforehand or drop in to its office in Copán Ruinas town.

Eating

★Café San Rafael CAFE, DELI $$
(Av Centroamericana; meals L100-200; 9am-7:30pm;) This classy cafe has tables set to the side of a garden courtyard. Breakfast choices include *croque madam, omelette du fromage* and great hash browns, while the sandwiches (starting at L99) are pricey but great quality: try a *clásico*. Organic coffee, grown on the owner's *finca* is served, while the deli section features excellent artisan cheeses (manchego, camembert) made on the premises – try a platter for L199. Wine happy hour is 3pm to 6pm.

Comedor Mary COMEDOR $$
(Av Sesesmiles; mains L70-250; 7am–9pm) Now in a new location, this superb *comedor*

WORTH A TRIP

TEA & CHOCOLATE

David Sedat is a US citizen who's lived virtually his whole life in Central America. A prominent archaeologist, he led the team that discovered the tomb of Yax K'uk Mo', the founder of Copán's ruling dynasty, in 1995. His other passion is the environment, a cause he and his family promote via their Copán 2012 Botanical Research Station, dedicated to reforestation and the sustainable cultivation of fruit trees and medicinal plants on the steep slopes above Copán.

Visitors can tour the research station, which was once degraded and eroded farmland but is now a shaded, flourishing habitat. Native plants like agave, yucca, Maya cotton and air potatoes are grown alongside peanuts, yam, ginger, macadamia trees, dragon fruit, lemon grass and other exotica. David's real love is the noni fruit, which is credited with myriad healing and health properties; they grow in prodigious numbers at the station.

You're welcome to drop by his house (between 4pm and 6pm on weekdays), appropriately called **The Tea & Chocolate Place**, and sample some noni tea, juice or creams, all for sale. The family (his daughter Carolina is a fluent English speaker) love talking about Copán and its social and environmental issues.

The Tea & Chocolate Place is about a 10-minute walk northwest of the Parque Central – most motortaxi drivers know it. To set up a visit to the station call first.

offers authentic, flavorsome Honduran cooking including a superb *típico copaneco* (local breakfast, L82), lots of soups and also prime cuts of beef like *entraña*. Service is sharp and friendly and the atmosphere is buzzing in the evenings.

Café ViaVia INTERNATIONAL **$$**
(www.viaviacafe.com/en/copan; Calle de la Plaza; breakfast L60-80, mains L80-140; 7am-10pm;) A great place to hang out, this vast bar/restaurant has all bases covered with an attractive courtyard, sociable bar and a front terrace for people-watching. It specializes in meat-optional, vegetarian-slanted global and local cuisine, including nachos, burgers and filling breakfasts. Movies, concerts and dancing add to the evening vibe.

La Casa de Todo HONDURAN, INTERNATIONAL **$$**
(www.casadetodo.com; Av Sesesmiles; mains L80-150; 7am-8pm;) Colonial-style place that offers Copán specialties including *shepes* (tamales steamed with chicken, beans and herbs) and lots of breakfast choices, salads and *licuados* (fruit drinks: try the mango and strawberry). Tables are set around a patio garden, and you'll also find a bookshop, laundry and souvenir store here.

Carnitas Nia Lola HONDURAN **$$$**
(Av Centroamericana; mains L140-355; 7am-10pm;) This log cabin-like bar/restaurant is something of a Copán institution. The interior is a minimalist's nightmare – plastered with assorted curios including random license plates, vinyl records, an armadillo shell and fake Maya artefacts. The *anafres* (bean-and-cheese appetizers; free with meals) are quite a production here, heated by fiery coals. Renowned for its grilled meats preapared on a *parrilla* before you – try the ribs.

Twisted Tanya's INTERNATIONAL **$$$**
(2651-4182; www.twistedtanyas.com; Calle Independencia; 2-/3-course meals L380/420; 2-10pm Mon-Sat) Run by a larger-than-life British character, this enjoyable restaurant/bar has an ambitious (perhaps slightly over-elaborate) menu including tequila shrimp with linguine and jalapeño filet mignon. There's an extensive cocktail menu. Backpacker specials (L120 to L200) are served from 3pm to 6pm, featuring three courses.

Drinking & Entertainment

★Sol de Copán BAR, BREWERY
(Av Mirador; 1-11pm) Terrific German-owned microbrewery in a large basement northwest of the *parque*. Tomas, the friendly owner, is highly attentive, making sure everyone is regularly topped-up with wheat beer, pilsner or dark ale. Delicious German sausages are served, and there's live music some nights too.

Cafe ViaVia BAR, CINEMA
(www.viaviacafe.com/en/copan; Calle de la Plaza; 7am-10pm) The bar here is the liveliest in town with a highly sociable vibe, drink specials, occasional gigs and DJs playing Latin and western tunes at weekends. Movies are

shown on Sunday, Monday and Tuesday at 7pm on an upstairs terrace.

Shopping

Items to look out for are leatherwear, textiles, cigars and rum. Try **La Casa de Todo** (☎2651-4185; www.casadetodo.com; Av Sesesmiles; ⏲7am-9pm): the 'House of Everything' has just about...well, everything. An incredible selection of books, Lencan ceramics, jewelry and souvenirs.

Orientation

Copán is tiny really, with the Parque Central at its heart. The ruins are 1km east of town, a pleasant 20-minute stroll along a footpath to one side of the highway.

Information

BAC/Bamer (Parque Central; ⏲8am-5pm Mon-Fri, 8:30am-1pm Sat) With an ATM.

Banco Atlántida (cnr Calle Independencia & Av Copán) Changes US dollars and has an ATM.

Police (☎2651-4060; Calle de la Plaza; ⏲24hr) It's 300m west of the *parque*.

Tourist Office (☎2651-3829; www.copanhonduras.org; Calle Independencia; ⏲8am-5pm Mon-Fri, 8am-noon Sat) Has a calendar of activities. When we dropped by no one spoke English here!

La Casa de Todo (Av Sesesmiles; ⏲7am-9pm) Food, internet (per hour L20) and laundry services (wash, dry and fold L20 per lb).

Getting There & Away

Minibuses to/from the Guatemalan border (L20, 20 minutes, every 20 minutes) run between 6am and 5pm from a little terminal on Calle 18 Conejo. On the Guatemala side, buses to Esquipulas and Chiquimula leave the border regularly until about 5pm.

Basecamp Tours (p380) and other operators run shuttle buses between Copán Ruinas and Antigua (L400, six hours, twice daily) via Guatemala City (five hours).

Shuttles also run daily at 4am (and on Mondays, Wednesdays and Fridays at 1pm) to El Salvador stopping at Santa Ana (L560, 4½ hours), San Salvador (L720, five hours) and beaches including El Tunco and El Zonte (both L720, six hours); you can book via Basecamp or other travel agencies.

There are also *busitos* (minibuses) east to La Entrada (L28, 1¼ hours, every 30 minutes) for onward connections in Honduras.

Transportes Casasola (☎2651-4078) has cheap, usually cramped buses that leave from a stop on Calle Acrópolis.

Hedman Alas (☎2651-4037; Km 62 Carretera a San Lucas; ⏲6am-6:30pm) has a modern terminal just south of town where you can make advanced bookings. Arrive at least 40 minutes early for international departures.

Getting Around

Three-wheeled mototaxis whizz around the cobbled streets: expect to pay L20 for a short ride or L60 to L80 for sights outside town like Hacieda San Lucas or the bird park. It costs about L60 to get to the ruins.

Around Copán Ruinas

Macaw Mountain

Macaw Mountain (☎2651-4245; www.macawmountain.com; L200; ⏲9am-5pm) is a beautifully landscaped bird sanctuary and breeding center about 3km northeast of the town center. The setting is lovely, with good trails leading through a thickly forested valley and over a gurgling river. The resident flock of rescued, abandoned and endangered birds here includes five kinds of macaw (including copious numbers of scarlet macaws native

BUSES FROM COPÁN RUINAS

DESTINATION	COST (L)	DURATION	BUS LINE	PHONE	FREQUENCY
Antigua	790–1252	5hr	Hedman Alas	2651-4037	1 daily
Guatemala	674–1252	6hr	Hedman Alas	2651-4037	2 daily
La Ceiba	674–828	7hr	Hedman Alas	2651-4037	2 daily
San Pedro Sula	125	3hr	Transportes Casasola	2651-4078	7 daily
	366-520	3hr	Hedman Alas	2651-4037	2 daily
Santa Rosa de Copán	88	2½hr	Transportes Casasola	2651-4078	1 daily

THE RETURN OF THE MACAW

Sacred to the ancient Maya, **scarlet macaw** imagery and veneration can be witnessed everywhere at Copán's magnificent archaeological site. Giant macaw sculptures adorn the sides of the great ball court, sculptured feathers grace kings' headdresses and the very founder of the ruling dynasty was called Yax K'uk Mo' (First Quetzal Macaw). When you visit the ruins you're certain to be greeted by a dazzling flash of red, blue and yellow and a squawk or two from (semi-domesticated but free-flying) resident scarlet macaws who live by the entrance gate.

Sadly, Honduras' national bird population has been in steep decline for decades. In 2011 teamwork by the Macaw Mountain bird park, World Parrot Trust, local NGO Asociación Copan and the Honduran government resulted in several birds being released from captivity into the Copán Valley. Macaws continue to breed successfully in the bird park and it's hoped that, combined with educational programs and its protected status, numbers will multiply. There are now over 20 free-flying birds in the Copán region, and several macaw pairs are successfully raising chicks.

to Copán), parrots, toucans, grey hawks and great-horned owls.

Some birds are allowed out of their cages at feeding time, squawking and interacting with visitors. The bird enclosures are very well maintained and there's a terrific new permanent exhibition about the relationship between the ancient Maya and the scarlet macaw. There's also a good restaurant and cafe on site. Your entrance ticket is valid for three days. A mototaxi from town costs around L50, or you can walk it in 30 minutes.

Finca El Cisne

Visiting the Finca El Cisne (p380) highlands coffee and cardamom plantation, 24km north of Copán Ruinas, is more a privileged invitation into a hacienda than a tour. Founded in the 1920s the *finca* raises cattle and grows coffee and cardamom, but also produces corn, avocado, breadfruit, plantain, beans, oranges and star fruit.

Day tours include guided horseback riding through the forests and pastures, bathing in hot springs and visits to coffee and cardamom fields and processing facilities. Carlos Castejón, the friendly, English-speaking owner (and US-trained agronomist) leads most tours. Day tours (per person L1500) include transportation to and from Copán Ruinas and a great lunch. You can also stay at the *finca*, with packages from L1900.

Aguas Termales

About 24km north of Copán Ruinas you'll find some hot springs known as **Aguas Termales** (L200; ⏲10am-10pm) – a lovely hour's drive through fertile mountains and coffee plantations. On one side of the river are cheaper, less developed springs, while across the way you'll find the 'spa,' a much more pricey set-up. Tour operators offer trips here, or you can catch a local bus (L21, one hour, every 30 minutes) from Copán Ruinas.

Copán Archaeological Site

One of the most important of all Maya civilizations lived, prospered then mysteriously crumbled around the **Copán archaeological site** (☎2651-4108; general admission L300, museum L140, tunnels L300; ⏲8am-5pm, last entrance 3:30pm), a Unesco World Heritage Site. During the Classic period (AD 250–900), the city at Copán Ruinas culturally dominated the region. The architecture is not as grand as Tikal's but the city produced remarkable sculptures and hieroglyphics.

The ruins are a pleasant 1km stroll outside of Copán. A visitors center, excellent Museum of Sculpture and a cafe/gift shop are close to the main entrance. Guides at the **Asociación Guís Copán** (☎2651-4108; www.asociacionguiascopan.com; 2hr tour for 1-9 people L500) really know their stuff and are a worthwhile investment.

The booklet *History Carved in Stone: A Guide to the Archaeological Park of the Ruins of Copán* by William L Fash and Ricardo Agurcia Fasquelle, is usually available. For further reading see *Scribes, Warriors and Kings* by William Fash (2001), a comprehensible overview of Copán.

History

Pre-Columbian History

From dating pottery discovered in the area, scientists believe people have lived in the Copán valley for more than two millennia – since at least 1200 BC. Craft and trade seemed to thrive early on – excavated artifacts show influences from as far afield as central Mexico.

Around AD 426, one royal family came to rule Copán, led by a mysterious king named K'inich Yax K'uk' Mo' (Great Sun Lord

Copán Archaeological Site

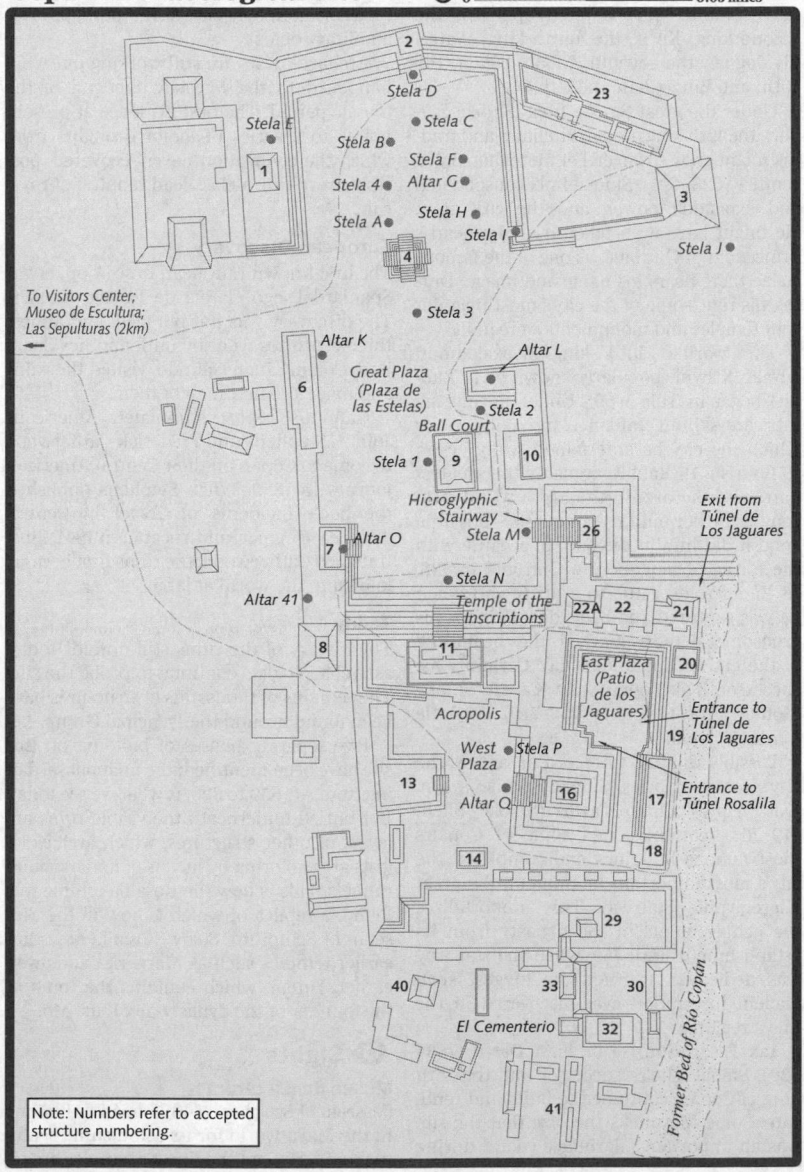

Note: Numbers refer to accepted structure numbering.

Quetzal Macaw). He was associated with the massive urban state in Mexico known today as Teotihuacán. Archaeological evidence indicates that he was a great shaman and warrior; 16 later kings revered him as the semidivine founder of the city. His dynasty ruled throughout Copán's golden age.

The early kings (435–628) mostly remain shrouded in mystery – only a few names have come to light: K'inich Popol Hol, the second king; Ku Ix, the fourth king; Waterlily Jaguar, the seventh; Moon Jaguar, the 10th; and Butz' Chan, the 11th.

Under the great Smoke Imix (Smoke Jaguar), the 12th king, Copán's military and trading might grew stronger. For more than half a century (628–695), Smoke Imix consolidated and expanded power, and the city grew. He might have even taken over the nearby princedom of Quiriguá, as one of the famous stelae there bears his name and image. During his rule, some of the city's most magnificent temples and monuments were built.

The warlike 13th king, Waxaklajuun Ub'aah K'awiil (popularly known as 18 Rabbit), began his rule in 695. Under his rule, the intricate, skillful craftsmen and sculptors for which the city became famed really began to flourish. 18 Rabbit, arguably the greatest patron of the arts in the Maya world, also sought further military conquests – but little good it did him in the end. In a battle with the forces of neighboring Quiriguá in 738, 18 Rabbit's life came to a grisly end when he was captured and beheaded. Perhaps his gruesome demise marked the beginning of the end of Copán's heyday. Certainly his successor, K'ak' Joplaj Chan K'awiil (Smoke Monkey), the 14th king (738–749), left little mark on Copán.

Possibly in a bid to record or restore the city's former glories, Smoke Monkey's son, K'ak' Yipyaj Chan K'awiil (Smoke Shell; 749–763), commissioned some of Copán's most famous buildings and completed the city's most important monument, the great Hieroglyphic Stairway. This immortalizes the achievements of the dynasty from its establishment until 755, when the stairway was dedicated. It bears the longest such ancient inscription ever discovered in the Maya region.

Yax Pasaj (Sunrise or First Dawn; 763–820), Smoke Shell's successor and the 16th king of Copán, continued to build and renovate. Some Mayanists theorize that the site was an important pilgrimage center during Classic Maya times, with chiefs traveling to Copán to acquire kingship insignia for their elite. At the end of the 8th century, the valley of Copán had over a minimum of 20,000 inhabitants.

However, it's clear that by the early 9th century the ruling dynasty's power was declining and its subjects had fallen on hard times. The final ruler, U Cit Tok', had his reign mysteriously cut short – perhaps after a military defeat.

Archaeologists are still working out what happened to the Maya at the end of the Classic period. The best evidence at present points to a series of major droughts from which the civilization never recovered, possibly provoking a class-lead rebuttal of royal rule.

European Discovery

The first known European to see Copán was Spaniard Diego García de Palacio in 1576. The discovery was not pursued, and almost three centuries went by until another Spaniard, Colonel Juan Galindo, visited the ruins and made the first map of them.

Galindo's report stimulated Americans John L Stephens and Frederick Catherwood to come to Copán on their Central American journey in 1839. When Stephens published the book Incidents of Travel in Central America, Chiapas, and Yucatán in 1841, illustrated by Catherwood, the ruins first became known to the world at large.

Today

The history of the ruins still unfolds today, as archaeologists continue to probe the site. The remains of thousands of structures have been found around the Principal Group.

Five separate phases of building on this site have been identified; the final phase, dating from AD 650 to 820, is what we see today. But buried underneath the visible ruins are layers of other structures, which archaeologists are exploring by means of underground tunnels. This is how the Rosalila temple was found, a replica of which is now in the Museum of Sculpture. Below Rosalila are other earlier temples such as Margarita and, even earlier, Hunal, which contains the tomb of the founder of the dynasty, Yax K'uk' Mo'.

Sights

Museo de Escultura MUSEUM

(Museum of Sculpture; L140) Copán is unique in the Maya world for its astonishing sculpture, and some of the finest examples are on display at this impressive museum. Entering the building is an experience in itself: you go through the mouth of a serpent and wind through the entrails of the beast before suddenly emerging into a fantastic world of sculpture and light.

The highlight of the museum is a full-scale replica of the Rosalila temple, which was discovered in near-perfect condition by archaeologists in 1989 by means of a tunnel dug into Structure 16, the central building of the Acropolis. Rosalila, dedicated in AD 571 by Copán's 10th ruler, Moon Jaguar, was apparently so sacred that when Structure 16 was built over it, Rosalila was not destroyed but was left completely intact inside the core of the newer structure.

The Principal Group

The Principal Group is a group of ruins about 400m beyond the visitors center, accessed via a shady avenue of trees. Beautiful (though partly domesticated) macaws greet you as you enter the site.

Stelae of the Great Plaza

ARCHAEOLOGICAL SITE

The huge, intricately carved stone **stelae** portraying the rulers of Copán have come to define this site, and its **Great Plaza** (Plaza de las Estelas). Most of the best stelae date from AD 613 to 738, especially from the reigns of Smoke Imix (628–95) and 18 Rabbit (695–738). All seem to have originally been painted; a few traces of red paint survive on Stela C. Many stelae had vaults beneath or beside them in which sacrifices and offerings could be placed.

Many of the stelae on the Great Plaza portray King 18 Rabbit, including Stelae A, B, C, D, F, H and 4, and are remarkable in the Maya area for being carved in high relief. Some are (amazing) reproductions, the originals can be viewed in the museum.

Doubled-headed **Stela C**, perhaps the most magnificent monument, depicts 18 Rabbit as a young ruler on one side, and as an old man, complete with beard, on the reverse. **Stela A** (731), another stunning work, bears name glyphs of four of the most powerful cities of the Classic Era (Calakmul, Copán, Tikal and Palenque). Nearby are **Stela 4** (731) and **Stela B** (731), depicting 18 Rabbit upon his accession to the throne. **Stela D** (736) also portrays King 18 Rabbit: on its back are two columns of hieroglyphs, while at its base is an altar with fearsome representations of Chac, the rain god.

On the eastern side of the plaza is **Stela F** (721) which has a more lyrical design, with the robes of 18 Rabbit flowing around to the other side of the stone, where there are glyphs. **Stela J**, further off to the east and probably the earliest of 18 Rabbit's stelae, is covered in glyphs forming an intriguing mat design, the symbol for kingship.

Stela E (614), erected on top of Structure 1 on the west side of the Great Plaza, is among the oldest stelae. **Altar G** (800), commissioned by Yax Pasaj and showing twin serpent heads, is among the last monuments carved at Copán.

Ball Court & Hieroglyphic Stairway

ARCHAEOLOGICAL SITE

South of the Great Plaza, across what is known as the Central Plaza, is the **Ball Court** (731), the second-largest in Central America. It's thought competitors kept a hard rubber ball in the air using thighs and hips (but not their hands). The one you see is the third or fourth ball court built in this spot; the other two smaller ones were buried by this construction. Note the macaw heads carved at the top of the sloping walls. The central marker in the court was the work of King 18 Rabbit.

South of the ball court is Copán's most famous monument, the **Hieroglyphic Stairway**, also the work of 18 Rabbit. Today it's protected from the elements by a massive tarp. The flight of 63 steps bears a history – in several thousand glyphs – of the royal house of Copán; the steps are bordered by ramps inscribed with more reliefs and glyphs. The story inscribed on the steps begins by noting the death and burial inside the stairway of the 12th king and goes on to discuss the history of the later dynasty but is still not completely understood, because the stairway was partially ruined and the stones jumbled.

At the base of the Hieroglyphic Stairway is **Stela M** (AD 756), bearing a figure (probably King Smoke Shell) in a feathered cloak; glyphs tell of the solar eclipse in that year. The altar in front shows a plumed serpent with a human head emerging from its jaws.

Acropolis

ARCHAEOLOGICAL SITE

The lofty flight of steps to the south of the Hieroglyphic Stairway is called the **Temple of the Inscriptions**. On top of the stairway, the walls are carved with groups of

WATER WORLD

Some archaeologists, including David Sedat (field director the Early Copán Archaeological Project), believe that the Classic Maya periodically flooded the West Plaza – they've found the entrance channels – to give the sacred space a truly ethereal appearance on key dates in the calendar. An artificial lake would have formed, surrounded by temples, representing a body of primordial water in their cosmovision. Ancient texts found in the Guatemalan highlands record pilgrimages to a 'great city of the east' and it's thought Copán's ancient name could have been Hao' Ha (body of water). Look closely and you'll see conch shells (symbolizing a watery world) on Temple 11's facade. Sedat also believes that the Great Plaza could have been flooded to form a lake on auspicious days in the Maya calendar.

hieroglyphs. South of the stairway are the most secluded areas of the Acropolis, organized into two plazas.

The highly atmospheric **West Plaza** is bordered to the north by Temple 11 and on its east side by Temple 16 (look out for six skulls on its facade), which was constructed by Yax Pasaj. At Temple 16's base rests a replica of Yax Pasaj's famed **Altar Q** (AD 776). Around its sides, carved in superb relief, are the 16 great kings of Copán, ending with the altar's creator, Yax Pasaj. Beneath the altar was a sacrificial vault in which archaeologists discovered the bones of 15 sacrificed jaguars and several macaws. Some Mayanists believe that the West Plaza could have been periodically flooded by the Maya (see boxed text, above).

On the north side of the **East Plaza** (Patio de los Jaguares) sits the throne building of 18 Rabbit, with its serpent-mouth doorway and interior sculpture.

Túnel Rosalila & Túnel de los Jaguares ARCHAEOLOGICAL SITE

(L300) In 1999, archaeologists opened up to the public two tunnels that allow visitors to get a glimpse of pre-existing structures below the visible surface structures. The first tunnel, **Rosalila**, is very short and takes only a few visitors at a time. The famous temple is only barely exposed, and behind thick glass. The other tunnel, **Los Jaguares**, was originally 700m in length, but a large section has been closed, reducing it to about 80m, running along the foundations of Temple 22. While fascinating, it's hard to justify the L300 extra you pay to get in.

Las Sepulturas

Often overlooked by visitors, the excavations at the small site of Las Sepulturas have shed light on the daily life of the Maya of Copán during the city's golden age.

Las Sepulturas was possibly the residential area of rich, powerful nobles and religious leaders. One huge, luxurious compound seems to have housed some 250 people in 40 or 50 buildings arranged around 11 courtyards. The principal structure, called the House of the Bakabs (officials), had outer walls carved with full-size figures of 10 males in fancy feathered headdresses; inside was a massive hieroglyphic bench.

A pleasant 1km-long path connects Las Sepulturas with the ruins of Copán.

Santa Rosa de Copán

POP 47,000

Santa Rosa de Copán is a cool mountain town with cobbled streets and some lovely, restored colonial buildings. It's far less tranquil than Gracias – but there's more going on here, including some great cafes and restaurants. However, it doesn't have any world-class sights like Copán Ruinas and, consequently, not as many tourists, which is part of its charm.

The annual **festival day** is August 30. The town is also renowned for its colorful **Semana Santa** celebrations.

Tours

La Flor de Copán Cigar Factory GUIDED TOUR

(☎2662-0185; tours L40; ⏲tours in English 10am & 2pm Mon-Fri) La Flor de Copán Cigar Factory, 2km out of town, shows visitors the craft behind making hand-rolled cigars. If you just want to smoke some, there's a store on Calle Real Centenario at 3a Av NO; a box of 25 cigars starts at L1280.

Lenca Land Trails GUIDED TOUR

(☎9997-5340; lencatours@gmail.com; Calle Real Centenario, Hotel Elvir, near 3a Av NO; ⏲8am-noon) Run by English speaker Max Elvir, a well-known local guide who offers excellent tours to Lenca villages and Parque Nacional Montaña de Celaque.

Sleeping

Hotel Karolina Boutique HOTEL $
(☎2662-2210; hotelkarolinaboutique@hotmail.com; 2a Calle SO; s/d/tw incl breakfast L400/500/650; ❄📶) Someone has a very keen eye for design at this newly renovated hotel – the lobby is full of mod-Asian influences and lots of scarlet paintwork. The theme continues in the 12 smallish bedrooms, all boasting large LCD TVs and stylish beds, though the plain, cramped bathrooms have not been touched. It's two blocks south of the Parque Central

Hotel Santa Eduviges HOTEL $
(☎2662-0380; 1a Calle NO; r L350-400) This green colonial-style edifice is a tad old-fashioned but kept neat and tidy by the conscientous *señora* owner. Blankets are provided, the mattresses have some spring, and all rooms have cable TV and a private bathroom.

Posada de Carlos y Blanca GUESTHOUSE $$
(☎2662-1028; www.posadacarlosyblanca.com; Calle Real Centenario, near 4a Av SO; s/d incl breakfast L500/700; 📶) There's a warm family setting at this comfy converted home with bright, comfortable accommodations. The English-speaking daughter Astrid helps and hosts in the evenings, and breakfast is wonderful.

Eating

★Ten Napel Café CAFE $
(www.tennapelcafe.com; 1a Calle NO btwn 2a & 3a Avs NO; snacks & meals L18-85; ⏲8am-noon & 2-7pm Mon-Sat; 📶) Owned by a welcoming Honduran/Dutch couple, this beautiful cafe is excellent for a sandwich, croissant or panini (all baked on the premises), cake, crepe, *tartaleta* or just a fully-flavored cup of coffee or glass of wine. Eat inside or in the serene garden at the rear.

Cafe Honor CAFE $
(Parque Central; snacks & meals L40-80; ⏲7:30am-5:30pm) Located in the ornate bandstand in the heart of the central plaza. Cafe Honor offers the best views in town from its upper-floor balcony. Great for a coffee (including organic and single-estate options), or check out one of the fine-value breakfast combos (L40) which include a cappuccino and waffle or sandwich.

Lenca Maya HONDURAN $$
(☎2662-6477; 2a Calle SE; meals L90-200) A five-minute walk southwest of the *parque,* this atmospheric restaurant is a class act, with tables scattered around a colonial-style courtyard. The menu includes *anafre* (beans and cheese cooked in a claypot), seafood, grilled meat, *sopa de gallina* (chicken soup) and a set lunch for L90.

Information

Banet/Unibanc ATM (1a Calle)
Police (☎2662-0214)
Post Office (Parque Central; ⏲8am-4:30pm Mon-Fri, 8am-noon Sat)
Tourist Office (☎2662-2232; www.visitesantarosedecopan.org; Parque Central; ⏲7am-5pm; @) In a kiosk in the central plaza, with helpful (though non-English-speaking) staff. Has a couple of good city maps (L10 to L20) and can advise about the town's cultural significance and historic buildings. Internet access L15 per hour.

Getting There & Away

Most buses use the main terminal on the highway, 1.5km northwest of the center: a *colectivo* into town from here costs L15. **Sultana** (☎2662-0940) buses to Tegucigalpa, San Pedro Sula, Nueva Ocotepeque and Agua Caliente (Guatemala) depart from a separate terminal next door.

BUSES FROM SANTA ROSA DE COPÁN

DESTINATION	COST (L)	DURATION	FREQUENCY
Agua Caliente (Guatemala)	90	2½hr	15 daily
Copán Ruinas	82	3hr	1 daily
Gracias	48	1½hr	every 30min
La Entrada	38	1¼hr	every 30min
Nueva Ocotepeque	70	2hr	15 daily
San Pedro Sula	82-108	3-3½hr	every 30min
Tegucigalpa	198	7hr	5 daily

WORTH A TRIP

BELÉN GUALCHO

Belén Gualcho is a highly picturesque colonial town clinging to the side of a mountain at 1600m above sea level, on the other side of Parque Nacional Montaña de Celaque from Gracias. Access is via a dirt road from Santa Rosa de Copán. Attractions include an interesting *iglesia* and an excellent **Lenca market** on Sunday. There's an entrance to Parque Nacional Celaque here, and a rural trail leading to San Manuel Colohete, but no checkpoint, and no services.

A few buses go between here and Santa Rosa each day. There are a couple of basic places to stay and to eat.

Congolón (☎2662-3834) has a terminal on the highway nearer town and serves San Pedro Sula and Nueva Ocotepeque.

Gracias

POP 12,800

Gracias is a jewel – a small, tranquil cobblestone town 47km southeast of Santa Rosa de Copán that's one of the prettiest and most historic settlements in Honduras. For a brief time in the 16th century, it was the capital of all Spanish-conquered Central America. Traces of its former grandeur remain in its centuries-old buildings, colonial churches and impressive fort. The pace of life here rarely moves much faster than walking.

Founded in 1526 by Spanish Captain Juan de Chávez; its original name was Gracias a Dios (Thanks to God). Eventually the town's importance was eclipsed by Antigua (Guatemala) and Comayagua.

The area around Gracias, including Parque Nacional Montaña de Celaque, is mountainous and beautiful, much of it forested.

Sights & Activities

Gracias has several colonial *iglesias*: **Las Mercedes**, **San Sebastián** and **San Marcos** on the Parque Central. Oddly, the latter's facade does not face the plaza.

Most of the area's other attractions, including some fine hot springs, are a few kilometers out of town.

Castillo San Cristóbal FORT
(⏲7am-5pm) FREE High on a hill west of the center, this pocket-sized fortress affords wonderful views over the town from its whitewashed ramparts. Dating from the 19th century, there's little to see inside the structure today, but you'll find some modern sculpture in the fort's grounds.

Museo Casa Galeano MUSEUM
(☎2625-5407; L30; ⏲9am-6pm) This museum is located in a beautiful restored colonial house with extensive gardens, however its contents (a fossilized turtle, old coins) are pretty mediocre and labeling is only in Spanish.

Tours

Marco Aurelio (☎2656-0627; guiamarcolencas@yahoo.com) the owner of Cafetería Artesenías El Jarrón, can arrange/guide hikes in Celaque (L350 to L1000), trips to La Campa (from L800), horseback-riding trips, bike rental (per hour L30) and tent rental (per night L70 to L80).

Good tours can also be organized at the Hotel Guanacasos.

Sleeping

As a market town, Gracias mainly caters to passing traders. Most budget hotels are very basic and not particularly tourist-oriented.

★Hotel Guancascos HOTEL $
(☎2656-1219; www.guancascos.com; s/d/tr from L520/570/710; @ 📶) A memorable place to stay with immaculately clean and good-value rooms set off shady paths that meander through the hotel's leafy hillside plot, 400m southwest of Parque Central. All plants are labeled, and woodpeckers and hummingbirds are frequently seen. The in-house restaurant is one of the best in town, tourist information is excellent, tours are available and it's all operated on environmentally friendly principals.

Casa Mio HOTEL $
(☎2656-0349; s/d L400/450; ❄ 📶) Just south of the market area and 200m southwest of Parque Central, this new place has very well-presented and spacious modern rooms, all with fresh linen, air-conditioning, attractive furniture and a picture or two gracing the

walls. There's free drinking water and reliable wi-fi.

Hotelito Josue PENSION $
(☎2656 0076; r with/without TV L250/200) Simple place with functional, smallish twins and double rooms off a long slim patio, all with a cold-water bathroom. The family owners are friendly and also run a *lavandería* (laundry) here. It's in the market district, a couple of blocks west of Parque Central.

Hotel Erick PENSION $
(☎2656-1066; r L200-250) For years this place has been a backpackers' base but the owners really could try harder: the rooms lack ventilation and you can expect saggy beds and a rundown feel. There's no sign – ask in the store next door and someone will show you around. It's a couple of blocks northwest of Parque Central.

Eating & Drinking

Cafetería Artesenías El Jarrón HONDURAN $
(Parque Central; mains L50-90; ⏲7am-8pm) Bustling, atmospheric place that does a lot of lunchtime trade: the buffet (L70 to L90) is a great deal, with lots of veggie dishes. You sit on polished logwood tables, and there's a garden patio at the rear. Lencan handicrafts and ceramics are also sold here and tours can be arranged.

Ensaladas Dulces Lorendiana HONDURAN $
(items from L25) An incredible find, this little store has shelves stacked floor-to-ceiling with hundreds (thousands?) of jars filled with pickled vegetables, chutneys and fruit wines, all prepared by the owner. A take-out portion costs L25. It's 250m southwest of the Parque Central.

El Señor de la Sierra CAFE $
(Parque Central; drinks & snacks L15-35; ⏲8am-10pm) Occupying the upper floor of the ornate bandstand in the central plaza, this is the best place in town for an espresso, cappuccino, flavoured coffee or *granita* (iced fruit drink) and a doughnut. Owner Nelson loves to chat about soccer.

Restaurante Guancascos INTERNATIONAL, HONDURAN $$
(Hotel Guancascos; meals L55-130; ⏲7am-9pm; 📶) A wonderful terrace restaurant at the Hotel Guancascos (p390), from where you can gaze over Gracias' terracotta-tiled rooftops and the Lencan highlands. Great for breakfast (L70 to L90), a filling sandwich, veggie plate or pan-fried fish. There's efficient service, excellent fresh juices and wine by the glass.

Rinconcito Graciano HONDURAN $$
(meals L60-120; ⏲7am-9pm) Owner Lizeth Perdomo serves up interesting traditional Lencan dishes (and standard Central American fare) in a bohemian setting. However, as it's rarely busy, it's best to drop by and order ahead. Located 300m southwest of the Parque Central.

★Kandil BAR, CAFE
(⏲11:30am-10pm Tue-Sun; 📶) Flying the flag for contemporary aesthetics in the rustic Lencan hills, Kandil is a beautifully designed place where modish decor juxtaposes with colonial-style tradition. It's famous for its frozen mojitos, and there's good pizza and bruschetta – but the real fun is just lounging with the arty crowd that hangs here. Mainly electronic and indie tunes. You'll find it two blocks north of Parque Central.

Information

Banco de Occidente (Parque Central) With ATM.

Tourist Office (Parque Central kiosk; ⏲8am-noon & 1:30-4:30pm Mon-Fri) Has some useful information binders but keeps irregular hours. You'll need to speak Spanish.

Getting There & Away

Most buses leave from a couple of stops northwest of the market, except those for La Esperanza and San Juan which use a terminal south of the Parque Central. There's no direct service

BUSES FROM GRACIAS

DESTINATION	COST (L)	DURATION	FREQUENCY
La Esperanza	72	2½hr	5 daily
San Juan	36	1hr	8 daily
San Pedro Sula	122	4hr	4 daily
Santa Rosa de Copán	48	1½hr	every 30min

WORTH A TRIP

EXPLORING AROUND GRACIAS

Bathing in the public **Aguas Termales Presidente** (L25; ⏲6am-11:30pm) is a memorable experience. It is a roughshod tourist attraction but the setting, practically within a forest, makes it special – where else can you watch wisps of steam rise from natural springs as lush foliage sways above you? About 6km southeast of town, the hot springs have several pools at various temperatures. There's a restaurant, bar and grubby changing rooms onsite. It's walkable in an hour or so, or L50 in a mototaxi. On weekends and holidays, the springs can get crowded; consider trying the private **Termas del Río** (☎2656-1304; L60; ⏲7:30am-9pm), 7km north of Gracias. These are just as beautiful, better maintained and less crowded. Catch any bus heading to Santa Rosa to reach these pools.

Several small towns near Gracias are also worth a visit. **La Campa**, a lovely little traditional village 16km south of town, has to be one of the most scenic settlements in Honduras, set below towering mountains and bordering a dramatic canyon. There are several great ceramic workshops here and it's possible to hike to the Camapara peak (six hours return; ask at Hostal JB for a guide). **Canopy Extremo** (☎2608-3817; L500) is a truly spectacular new attraction, with six zip lines over the canyon – among the most dramatic zip-line rides in Central America. There are two excellent hotels in La Campa, **Vista Hermosa** (☎2625-4770; r L300–400) and **Hostal JB** (☎9925-6042; hostal_jb@yahoo.com; r L300–450), which also has a great restaurant (meals L75) and garden.

San Manuel Colohete, 16km past La Campa, is another attractive little mountain town with a beautiful (and recently restored) colonial church, famous for its 400-year-old fresco paintings. There is one hotel in town.

Buses head from Gracias to La Campa (L20, five daily), some continuing on to San Manuel Colohete a further hour away.

Consult the website www.colosuca.com for good information about this region.

to Copán Ruinas; catch any bus bound for San Pedro Sula and change at La Entrada.

Parque Nacional Montaña de Celaque

Celaque (which means, oddly, 'box of water' in the local Lenca dialect) is one of Honduras' most impressive national parks. It boasts **El Cerro de las Minas**, the country's highest peak at 2849m, which is covered in lush forest. The park contains the headwaters of several rivers, a majestic waterfall visible from the entire valley, and very steep slopes, including some vertical cliffs.

The park is rich in plant and animal life. Pumas, ocelots and quetzals live here, but they are rarely seen. More common are beautiful butterflies, monkeys, black squirrels and reptiles, but you have to be very quiet and up very early to see much wildlife.

Activities

There are five established **hiking trails** in the Parque Nacional Montaña de Celaque. Two short trails involve a walk of an hour or so; the Mirador de la Cascada is around four hours; while Sendero El Gallo takes five to six hours. The summit itself a hardcore two-day expedition (for which you'll need a guide, tent, warm clothes and hiking boots). Because of clouds and tree cover, you might not see anything from the top, but the cloud forest is magical.

The three longer trails can become unclear in places – look for the colored ribbons. Do not wander off; the forest is so dense it can be hard, or impossible, to find the trail again if you leave it.

You can arrange guides in the village just before the entrance; or in Gracias, Marco Aurelio (p390) is recommended. Guides charge around L300 for half-day hikes and L500 per day for overnight trips.

Information

A **visitors center** (with toilets, information and barbecue areas) marks the entrance to the park. The entrance fee (L50) is payable here; it's an additional L50 per person per night to camp. Information on hiking in the park is available from Hotel Guancascos in Gracias or the tourist office (p391) in Gracias' Parque Central.

Getting There & Away

The main entrance to the park is about 8km uphill from Gracias. A bumpy mototaxi ride will take you there for about L150.

San Juan

This tiny, traditional mountain town is well worth a stop if you've an interest in Lenca life and culture.

Local guides can be arranged through the local tourism cooperative – speak to **Gladys Nolasco** (☎2754-7150), the president, who owns the store Docucentro Israel. Excursions include a trek to **La Cascada de los Duendes**, which goes through cloud forest and a series of waterfalls, ending with a coffee *finca* tour; and **El Cañon Encantado**, a tour of local beauty spots. Horseback riding, visits to traditional artisans, and coffee roasting and tasting tours can also be arranged.

There's very regular transport between San Juan and both Gracias and La Esperanza. Check into the good new **Hotel Junior** (☎9962-2587; r with hot-water bathroom L180-240) if you want to stay.

Nueva Ocotepeque

POP 19,100 / TRANSPORT HUB

Dust-blown Nueva Ocotepeque is a crossroads town, with a lot of traffic to the nearby borders at Agua Caliente (Guatemala) and El Poy (El Salvador). Few travelers stay here but there are adequate hotels, including the good-value **Hotel Turista** (☎2653-3639; Av General Francisco Morazán; d without bathroom L260, s/d L280/380; P). Eateries, hotels and ATMs are on or near Calle Intermedio, which runs through town.

Getting There & Away

Two long-distance bus companies serve Nueva Ocotepeque: **Congolón** (☎2653-3064) is half a block south of the Parque Central, while **Sultana** (☎2653-2405) is two blocks north of the *parque*. Buses to Agua Caliente and El Poy depart the Transportes San José terminal two blocks north of the *parque*. For Tegucigalpa, take a San Pedro Sula bus and transfer. For Santa Rosa de Copán, take any San Pedro Sula bus.

BUSES FROM NUEVA OCOTEPEQUE

DESTINATION	COST (L)	DURATION	FREQUENCY
Agua Caliente	22	30min	every 30min to 6pm
El Poy (Salvadoran border)	15	15min	every 20min to 7pm
San Pedro Sula	160-195	5hr	14 daily
Santa Rosa de Copán	78-92	2hr	14 daily

NORTHERN HONDURAS

The lush, tropical northern region of Honduras has seduced visitors for centuries with its natural wonders and easy Caribbean vibe. Between the beaches are mangrove swamps and jungle reserves – with manatees in Cuero y Salado and howler monkeys in idyllic Parque Nacional Jeannette Kawas – that scream out be explored. Rafting the whitewaters of the Río Cangrejal is *the* big-ticket experience, but there's also fine hiking in Pico Bonito and the unique flavor and rhythms of the coast's Afro-Caribbean Garifuna villages.

However, all this eco-appeal contrasts sharply with the agribusiness which dominates the economy and landscape – banana and African palm plantations fill the narrow coastal plain. Urban decay is all too evident in the region's large towns. Tela will suffice as a base for a day or two, and Trujillo has a welcome slice of historic charm, but that's about it – you won't want to hang around La Ceiba or Puerto Cortés for long.

The coast fills with local tourists during **Semana Santa** (Holy Week before Easter) when prices double. Most places are quiet the rest of the time.

Information

DANGERS & ANNOYANCES

La Ceiba and Tela have sky-high crime rates. During the day there's little danger, but things deteriorate after dark and muggings are common. Travelers have also been accosted and robbed on beaches outside La Ceiba, Tela (especially) and Trujillo. Do not walk along these beaches without company, and never after dark.

DIG THAT BEAT: INSIDE GARIFUNA DANCING

Shaking to live Garifuna music is a highlight of the north coast. Musicians create a throbbing pared-down sound using large drums, a turtle shell, maracas and a big conch shell. Words are chanted, the audience responds and dancers begin to move their hips in physics-defying loops to the *punta*, a traditional Garifuna dance.

During mid-July every year, the **National Garifuna Dance Festival** takes place in the small town of Baja Mar, near Puerto Cortés. All towns and villages have annual fiestas, and cultural events and gatherings of one kind or another happen throughout the year. **Garifuna Day** (Apr 12), a big holiday for all the Garifuna communities, commemorates the day in 1797 when the Garifuna arrived in Honduras.

Near Trujillo, the towns of Santa Fe and Santa Rosa de Aguán have their festivals on July 15 to 30 and August 22 to 29, respectively. The last three days are usually the most frenetic.

Puerto Cortés

POP 116,000 / TRANSPORT HUB

Honduras' main port is a thoroughly depressing and ugly town – if you've just arrived from Guatemala or Belize, things only get better from here. There's nothing of interest to travelers beyond the ferry to Belize. Nearby Omoa is a far more attractive base.

Accommodation options are very limited and poor value: **Hotel El Centro** (2665-1160; 3a Av btwn 2a & 3a Calles E; r with fan/air-con from L359/494; P) is a secure place in the center, while **Prince Wilson Hotel** (2665-6512; s/d with air-con L450/600) is next to the dock for Belize. You'll find ATMs and cheap *comedores* around the Parque Central.

Getting There & Away

BOAT

Two different companies run a weekly ferry to Belize. Bizarrely, they both leave at exactly the same time (11am) on the same day (Monday). Both ferries leave from the same dock next door to Restaurant El Delfin in Barra la Laguna, 3km southeast of the center.

D-Express (9991-0778; www.belizeferry.com) runs to Big Creek and Placencia (both L1200). **Pride of Belize** (8897-4448; www.prideofbelize.com) calls at Dangriga (L1100) and Belize City (L1375). You need to be at the dock by 10am to sign up on the day of travel. To get to the dock take any San Pedro–Puerto Cortés bus, get off at La Laguna and follow the signs to Restaurant El Delfin. You can also change money at the dock.

Note that it may be cheaper and easier for you to get to Belize via the Guatemalan port of Puerto Barrios.

BUS

Buses for San Pedro Sula (L44, 1 hour, every 15 minutes) leave from a terminal on 4a Av between 3a and 4a Calles until 5.30pm. Buses for the Guatemalan border at Corinto leave roughly hourly (L55 to L70, two hours) via Omoa (L16, 30 minutes); the last bus is at 5.20pm.

Omoa

POP 6,200

Snail-paced Omoa, 18km west of Puerto Cortés, is an attracive little resort on a broad curving bay that makes for great sunsets. Due to coastal erosion the brown-sugar beach is slimline, but this is still a relaxed and enjoyable place to spend a day or two. There's an historic fort and a clutch of seafood restaurants along the seafront.

There are no ATMs in Omoa; bring cash.

Sights

Fortaleza de San Fernando de Omoa FORT

(L80; 8am-4pm Mon-Fri, 9am-5pm Sat & Sun) Omoa's claim to historical fame is its colossal Spanish fortress, the Fortaleza de San Fernando de Omoa. Built (of brick and coral) between 1759 and 1777 under orders from King Fernando VII of Spain to protect the coast from rampant piracy, the fortress was captured in 1779 by the British. It's in excellent condition today and the fine new visitors center and museum provide satisfying historical background.

Sleeping & Eating

Roli's Place HOSTEL $

(2658-9082; www.omoa.net/roli.html; campsites/hammock/dm per person L60/60/80, s/d without bathroom L150/180, s/d without air-con L220/250, d/tr with air-con L330/380;) Excellent Swiss-owned hostel that occupies a vast grassy plot – a lovely place to hang out, and just a short walk from the beach.

The well-furnished double rooms, complete with LCD TVs with international channels, are a steal, and you'll also find a decent dorm and shady campground. Freebies include the ocean-going kayaks, bikes and drinking water.

It's worth noting that this isn't a party hostel and there are (numerous) rules, which some find a little excessive, including a 10pm noise curfew.

Hotel Michelle HOTEL $

(2658-9104; www.hotelmichelle.ca; r with fan/air-con L300/450;) Located right on the beach, this Honduran/Canadian-owned place is excellent value with five neat, very well-priced rooms and a small pool. There's also a bar, and meals are available on request.

Burgers & Mariscos HONDURAN, SEAFOOD $$

(Carretera a Guatemala; mains L60-160; 8am-9pm) It's a long haul to get here on foot (about a 15-minute walk from Roli's) but this excellent option on the main highway scores highly for good-value food, including excellent burgers, fresh seafood and tasty *tamarindo* juice.

Getting There & Away

The beach is about 1.5km from the highway. There are hourly connections (L16, 30min) to/from Puerto Cortés; some buses will branch off the highway and drop passengers at the beach.

Roli's Place runs shuttles to La Ceiba or Puerto Barrios in Guatemala on demand.

Tela

POP 37,400

The resort of Tela has a ravishing coastline of pale sandy beaches backed by coconut palms and dotted with fascinating Garifuna villages. So why do few travelers bother to drop by? Well, the stark reality is that Tela's town center is pretty rundown these days and those lovely beaches certainly could be cleaner.

That said, you should consider a night or two here as the two nature reserves – Jeannette Kawas and Punta Izopo – are very special indeed, and within easy striking distance.

Tela is crammed with Honduran vacationers during **Semana Santa** (Holy Week before Easter), but the rest of the year things are pretty *tranquilo*.

Sights & Activities

Tela's main attraction is its **beaches**, which stretch for miles around the bay. Most are littered, but west of town in front of Hotel Villas Telamar there's a pale, powdery stretch which is kept impeccably clean. Beach beds can be rented by nonguests, but only when occupancy is low at the resort. Beaches further afield, while much cleaner, can be risky to visit.

Tours

Garifuna Tours GUIDED TOUR

(2448-2904; www.garifunatours.com; 9a Calle NE at 5a Ave NE; 7:30am-6pm Mon-Sat, to 5pm Sun) A professional, long-established agency that offers tours including boat excursions to Parque Nacional Jeannette Kawas (from L680), kayaking in Punta Izopo (L620) and trips to Cayos Cochinos (L980). All prices are based on a minimum of six people.

Sleeping

Hotel Bertha PENSION $

(2448-1009; 8a Calle NE btwn 8a & 9a Avs NE; r with fan/air-con from L250/350;) A classic old-school *pensión* in a quiet location. What's great about this place is that the friendly family owners aren't doing anything fancy, but provide very decent, clean rooms, all with en-suite bathrooms (cold water) at affordable prices. It's a five-minute walk inland from the beach.

César Mariscos Anexo HOTEL $

(2448-2083; www.hotelcesarmariscos.com; cnr 9a Calle NE & 1a Av NE; s/d L450/550;) A cheaper sister hotel to the (much pricier) beachfront landmark, this place has spacious rooms with exposed-brick walls, good-quality mattresses, cable TV and modern bathrooms. It's a five-minute walk from the shore.

M@ngo Hotel HOTEL $

(2448-0388; www.mangocafe.net; cnr 5a Av & 8a Calle NE; s/d/tr with fan L372/440/555, with air-con L511/627/766;) A lot of backpackers end up here, so it's not a bad place to meet people. However prices have been jacked up recently, and it's not great value – the rooms are pretty ordinary and subject to sonic boom blasts of cheesy merengue and rabid reggaetón from the store opposite.

Maya Vista Hotel y Restaurante HOTEL $$
(☎2448-1497; www.mayavista.com; Barrio Lempira; s/d with fan L570/680, with air-con from L1040/1160; ❄@) Worth considering for a splurge, this lovely place has a fine selection of rooms with tasteful decor, most with sweeping views of the Tela bay. They don't list the cheapest fan-cooled rooms on their website. There is also a very good restaurant on site. It's a 10-minute walk east of the center.

Eating

Seafood is plentiful, delicious and cheap in Tela. Seafood soups are a local delicacy: fish, shrimp, lobster and *caracol* (conch) are found in many restaurants. Another specialty is *pan de coco* (coconut bread). There's a **Despensa Familiar** (Parque Central; ⏲7am-7pm Mon-Sat, to 6pm Sun) on the main square for self-caterers.

Auto Pollo Al Carbón FAST FOOD $
(11a Calle NE at 2a Av NE; half chicken L79; ⏲7am-11pm) Roast chicken served under a corrugated-iron roof in an open-air shack, a wishbone's throw away from the Caribbean. You can grab a quarter of chicken and a salad here for just L47.

Los Manajares HONDURAN $
(4a Av NE; meals L60-100; ⏲11am-5pm) Buffet-style place where there are always four freshly-prepared specials. Take your pick from hearty dishes like *costilla en coco* (ribs in coconut sauce) or *pollo horneado* (roast chicken) and check out the photos of Tela's old railway station while you're here.

Luces del Norte INTERNATIONAL $$
(cnr 11a Calle NE & 5a Av NE; mains L60-250; ⏲7am-10pm; 📶) Boasting pretty wooden Caribbean-style premises, this is a popular restaurant. Renowned for its seafood including paella (L180 for two; order ahead), pasta, omelettes and filling breakfasts (around L100).

Pizzería Bella Italia ITALIAN $$
(☎2448-1055; cnr 4a Av NE & Calle Peatonal; mains from L90; ⏲noon-9pm Tue-Sun; 📶) The pizza here is terrific – from personal to 16-piece *gigantes* (extra large) – but the specialty is the *panzerotti*, a variation of calzone stuffed with salami, ham, mushrooms and more. It's right on the beach.

Information

Banco de Occidente (Parque Central; ⏲8am-5:30pm Mon-Fri, 8:30am-1pm Sat) With ATM.

Fundación Prolansate (☎2448-2042; www.prolansate.org; cnr 7a Av & 8a Calle NE; ⏲8am-5:30pm Mon-Thu, to 4:30pm Fri) Promotes sustainable tourism in Tela and has information on Lancetilla Botanical Gardens and Punta Sal. Can organize educational visits.

Milton.net (cnr 10a Calle & 9a Ave NE; per hr L10; ⏲8am-9pm Mon-Sat; @) Ramshackle little internet cafe and call center.

Post Office (4a Av; ⏲8am-4pm Mon-Fri, 8am-noon Sat)

Tourist Police (☎9713-6731; cnr 11a Calle NE & 4a Av NE; ⏲24hr)

DANGERS & ANNOYANCES

Tela can have an edgy vibe. After about 8pm things get very quiet (unless it's a busy holiday weekend). Avoid walking any dark lanes or along the beach after nightfall. Be warned that the beachside bars north of the market can get rough at night.

Don't take anything of value to the beach. During the day, also avoid walking alone beyond the Hotel Villas Telamar Resort on the western end of the beach and the La Ensenada Beach Resort pier on the eastern end.

Most visitors enjoy their stay in Tela and have no problems.

Getting There & Away

Slow buses leave Tela every 20 minutes for La Ceiba (L52, 2½ hours, 4am to 6pm) from the long-distance terminal at the corner of 9a Calle NE and 9a Av NE. For quicker direct buses, take a taxi to the gas station on the highway, from where buses to La Ceiba and San Pedro Sula pass regularly.

Transportes Tela Express (2a Av NE) operates nine daily (seven on Sunday) direct buses to San Pedro Sula (L76, two hours) from its terminal. **Hedman Alas** (☎2448-3075; Hotel Villa Telemar; ⏲8am-5pm) has a daily connection to San Pedro Sula (L212 to L347, two hours) and also to La Ceiba (L232 to L386, two hours).

Local buses to the Garifuna villages near Tela depart from a dirt lot on the corner of 11a Calle and 8a Av.

Getting Around

Tela has many taxis; a ride in town costs L20. A taxi to Triunfo de la Cruz, La Ensenada or Tornabé is around L120 to L150. Mountain bikes can be rented at the M@ngo Hotel (p395) for L100 per day.

Around Tela

Lancetilla Jardín Botánico

Said to be the second-largest tropical garden in the world, the **Lancetilla Botanical Garden & Research Center** (☎2408-7806; www.esnacifor.hn; L154; ⏲7am-4pm) was founded by the United Fruit Company in 1926 and is still an active center for scientific study today. The gardens are a delight to visit – a tropical wonderland of plant species from all corners of the globe. There are 636 species of Asiatic fruit trees including many varieties of lycee, mango, durian, mangosteen and jackfruit. Trails are well-marked.

Birdlife also thrives at Lancetilla – hundreds of species have been spotted. Each year on December 14 and 15 the Audubon Society conducts a 24-hour bird count; you can participate if you're here at that time. Migratory species are present from November to February.

There's a **visitors center** (☎2408-8806; ⏲7am-4pm) where you can buy an explanatory map (L10) or hire a guide (per hour L100). Bird-watching tours (per hour L100) can be arranged, if you call in advance – expect a very early morning start. Some information is also available from Fundación Prolansate (p396).

Accommodation is available, including **cabins** (L500; ❄) with three individual beds and private bathrooms; book through the visitors center.

Getting There & Away

Lancetilla is 6km southwest of the center of Tela. A good way to get here is by bike, which you can rent in Tela. About 4km from town there's a turnoff from the highway that leads to the main gardens. Taxis charge L100 (one-way).

Parque Nacional Jeannette Kawas

Standing on the beach at Tela, you can look out and see a long arc of land curving to the west to a point almost in front of you. This point, **Punta Sal**, is part of the Parque Nacional Jeannette Kawas.

The park has several white-sand beaches, including the pretty **Playa Cocalito**. Offshore coral reefs make for reasonable **snorkeling**, and howler monkeys, boa constrictors and toucans live in the forest. The park used to be known as Parque Nacional Marino Punta Sal: it was renamed for Jeannette Kawas, an environmental campaigner who was murdered in 1995 following her tireless work to protect the park from developers. There is a L95 fee to enter.

On the park's east side is the **Laguna de los Micos** (Lagoon of the Monkeys) with mangrove forests harboring hundreds of bird species (especially from November to February, when migratory species flock here).

You can arrange day trips, which include hiking, snorkeling and hanging out on Playa Cocalito. Tela's Garifuna Tours (p395) and **Eco di Mare Tours** (☎9932 3552, 2439 0110; www.ecodimaretours.com; cnr 4a Av NE & 10 Calle NE, in front of Bank Atlántida parking lot; ⏲office 7am-5:30pm) run tours here.

Getting There & Away

Aside from day trips with Tela tour companies, you can negotiate a trip with one of the boatmen who tie-up under the main bridge just west of town. You can also make the trip from the village of Miami.

Refugio de Vida Punta Izopo

Standing on the beach at Tela and looking to the east, you can see **Punta Izopo**, part of the Punta Izopo Wildlife Refuge. Rivers entering the wildlife refuge spread out into a network of canals that channel through the tangle of mangrove forest. Monkeys, turtles and even crocodiles live here as well as many species of birds.

Tela tour agencies organise kayak trips to Punta Izopo. Gliding silently through the mangrove canals, you can get close to wildlife. You could also set up a boat or kayak trip yourself in the village of El Triunfo de la Cruz. Entrance fee is L60.

Garifuna Villages

Several Garifuna villages are within easy reach of Tela. Imagine rustic houses right on the beach, fishing canoes resting on the sand and the azure of the Caribbean offshore and you've got the picture. Although you can walk to all these villages by following the shoreline from Tela, it is not always safe due to the occasional assault. A tour or public transport is a safer option.

All villages have places to stay and at least a couple of restaurants beside the beach specializing in seafood and fish cooked in coconut.

GUIFITI: MOONSHINE SECRETS

The local moonshine on the north coast of Honduras is a mysterious concoction known as Guifiti (sometimes spelt Gifiti or Güfiti). Legend has it that it is a natural aphrodisiac, and aficionados claim all sorts of medicinal qualities, from helping diabetes to cleaning arteries. The exact recipe varies from brewer to brewer, although most versions will contain a base of *aguardiente* (a potent local gut-rot), as well as a blend of herbs and spices. In fact, there are rumors that in some versions not all of the ingredients are entirely legal.

Perhaps that is why you cannot pick up a bottle from supermarket shelves. However, make a few discreet enquiries in most north-coast towns and villages, and it won't be long before you track down a dram – even in surprisingly upmarket locations. It's pretty powerful stuff so don't throw too many glasses down your throat too quickly. If you are keen to spread the love and take some home, you can buy bottles in the Mercado Guamilito in San Pedro Sula.

The closest village is attractive little **La Ensenada**, 3km east along the arc of the beach from Tela, just before you reach the point. **Hotel Laguna Mar** (☎9811-5558; d L600; P ❄), just 100m from the beach, has meticulously maintained gardens and neat little rooms. Seafood restaurants in La Ensenada tend to only open on the weekend.

Larger **El Triunfo de la Cruz** can be reached by regular buses that depart from near Tela's market. It's the most developed of the Garifuna villages, lacking the peaceful ambiance of the other settlements. **Cabañas y Restaurante Colón** (☎9989-5622; r L280-480; P ❄) consists of a bunch of rustic *cabañas* a few footsteps away from the sand and a seafood restaurant (mains L70 to L220). Both La Ensenada and Triunfo de la Cruz are accessible via a paved road.

West of Tela it's 8km to **Tornabé**, a large Garifuna settlement where you can set up boat tours. Past Tornabé, the beach road continues for several more kilometers to **Miami**, a beautiful village of *palapa*-roofed huts on a narrow sandbar. Boats can be hired here (L1700 for up to seven people) for trips into Parque Nacional Jeannette Kawas. This area is changing fast as the nearby Los Micos golf resort reaches completion.

Getting There & Away

Although you can walk along the beach from Tela to any of the villages, the walk is not always safe and should not be done alone or at night.

Buses to the Garifuna villages depart from the local bus terminal in Tela. There are two routes: one heading west to Tornabé; another heading east to Triunfo de la Cruz. Buses on both routes depart hourly from around 7am to 5pm Monday to Saturday; the fare ranges from L12 to L17, and journeys take about 30 to 45 minutes to reach the villages.

If you're driving or cycling, you can get to Tornabé by the beach road heading west from Tela. Be careful where you cross the sandbar at the Laguna de los Micos between San Juan and Tornabé – vehicles regularly get stuck in the sand here. You may need a 4WD vehicle to get past Tornabé to Miami. You can also get to Tornabé from the highway: the turnoff, 5km west of Tela, is marked by a sign to 'The Last Resort.' To drive to La Ensenada or Triunfo de la Cruz, take the highway to the turnoff for Triunfo de la Cruz, 5km east of Tela. After 1km the road forks: go left to La Ensenada, or right to Triunfo de la Cruz.

La Ceiba

POP 191,000

La Ceiba is known as Honduras' party town: Tegucigalpa thinks, San Pedro Sula works and La Ceiba has fun, so the saying goes. Certainly this port city's buzzing nightlife makes it a mecca for fiesta-hungry Hondurans. All the action is over the estuary in Barrio La Isla, the city's *zona viva*.

There's very little of interest in Ceiba itself: local beaches are polluted and unsafe and downtown has a crumbling, neglected air. For most travelers Ceiba is nothing more than a jumping-off point for the Bay Islands or the world-class whitewater on the Río Cangrejal.

Expect searing heat and punishing humidity – this is a totally tropical town. Security is a pressing issue: you should be alert and take taxis at night to get around.

Sights

Museum of Butterflies & Other Insects MUSEUM
(Calle Escuela Internacional G-12, Colonia El Sauce; adult/child L80/40; ⏲8am-4pm Mon-Sat) A remarkable collection of over 13,000 butterflies, moths and other insects (most collected in Honduras), all displayed in cases. Highlights include the largest moth in the world, with a 30cm (1ft) wingspan, and a gigantic quarter-pound beetle.

Parque Swinford PLAZA
(Av La República btwn 7a & 8a Calles) Parque Swinford is a lush, tropical botanical oasis in the heart of La Ceiba, complete with a restored train carriage from the area's rail heyday.

Festivals & Events

Carnaval CULTURAL
(⏲late May) The city reaches its good-time peak at Carnaval, when it's rammed with revelers. Saturday is the biggest day, with parades, costumes, music and celebrations in the streets.

Tours

Jungle River Tours ADVENTURE TOUR
(☎2440-1282, 2440-1268; www.jungleriverlodge.com; Av La República) At Banana Republic Guest House, this agency organizes white-water rafting and canopy tours (L872), mountain biking (L436) and other trips.

La Moskitia Ecoaventuras ADVENTURE TOUR
(☎2441-3279; www.lamoskitia.hn; Colonia El Toronjal 2, 504) Jorge Salaverri is the pioneer of tours to La Moskitia (p424). He also offers hiking (L855), sea kayaking (L800) and white-water rafting (L800) from his guesthouse on the Río Cangrejal. Clients snag a free room in his La Ceiba guesthouse near Mall Megaplaza per tour booked.

Tourist Options GUIDED TOUR
(☎9982-7534, 2440-0265; www.hondurastouristoptions.com; Blvr 15 de Septiembre) Trips to Garifuna villages, Pico Bonito, Cuero y Salado and Cayos Cochinos (around L1400 per person). Located in the Viajes Atlántida travel agency.

Sleeping

Accommodations are fairly uninspiring in La Ceiba. Staying in the center is convenient, although it is eerily quiet at night (when you shouldn't walk the streets). There are far better options outside the city amid the tropical jungle by the Río Cangrejal.

★Hotel El Estadio HOSTEL $
(☎3192-2474, 9730-5690; www.hotelelestadio.com; Calle Estadio; dm/s/d L220/360/520; 📶) Owned by Peter, originally from Roatán but who lived in Boston for years, this hostel is well set-up for travelers. The two (four-bed) dorms are small but equipped with quality mattresses, and fresh towels are provided. Private rooms are more spacious, and hammocks (L100) are also available. Tours of the Mosquitia and Cayos Cochinos (L800 in a speed boat) can be organised and transport (including San Pedro Sula airport) arranged. The surrounding area is a little sketchy at night, when you should travel by taxi.

Moskitia Ecoaventuras Hotel HOSTEL $
(☎2441-3279; www.lamoskitia.hn; Colonia El Toronjal 2, 504; dm/d L160/320; ❄📶) Close to Ceiba's biggest mall, this hostel is well set-up for travelers with good travel info and a noticeboard, book exchange, laundry service, free coffee and internet, luggage storage and lockers. It's home base of La Moskitia Ecoaventuras tours which organizes excellent expeditions around northern Honduras.

Hotel Catracho HOTEL $
(☎2440-2312; www.hotelcatracho.com; 12a Calle, Barrio El Iman; s with fan/air-con L350/450, d with fan/air-con L450/600; ❄📶🏊) Once you get past the slightly vacant attitude at reception, this hotel's functional tiled rooms are not a bad deal, with fresh linen provided (though the fan rooms only have cold-water bathrooms). It's in a quiet neighborhood and you'll find a little cafe for cheap meals (from L55). The wi-fi is very weak in the rooms.

Banana Republic Guest House HOSTEL $
(☎2440-1268; www.jungleriverlodge.com; Av La República; dm L160, r with/without bathroom L340/285; @📶) This creaky old wooden house sets itself up as backpacker HQ, but on our last visit it was looking pretty rundown, and the bare rooms could certainly be more easy on the eye. That said, traveler information is good, there's a laundry and a guests' kitchen. The hostel acts as a feeder for Jungle River Tours.

Hotel Iberia HOTEL $$
(☎2443-0401; www.hoteliberia.com; Av San Isidro btwn 5a & 6a Calles; s/d L580/696; ❄📶) A bit of

La Ceiba

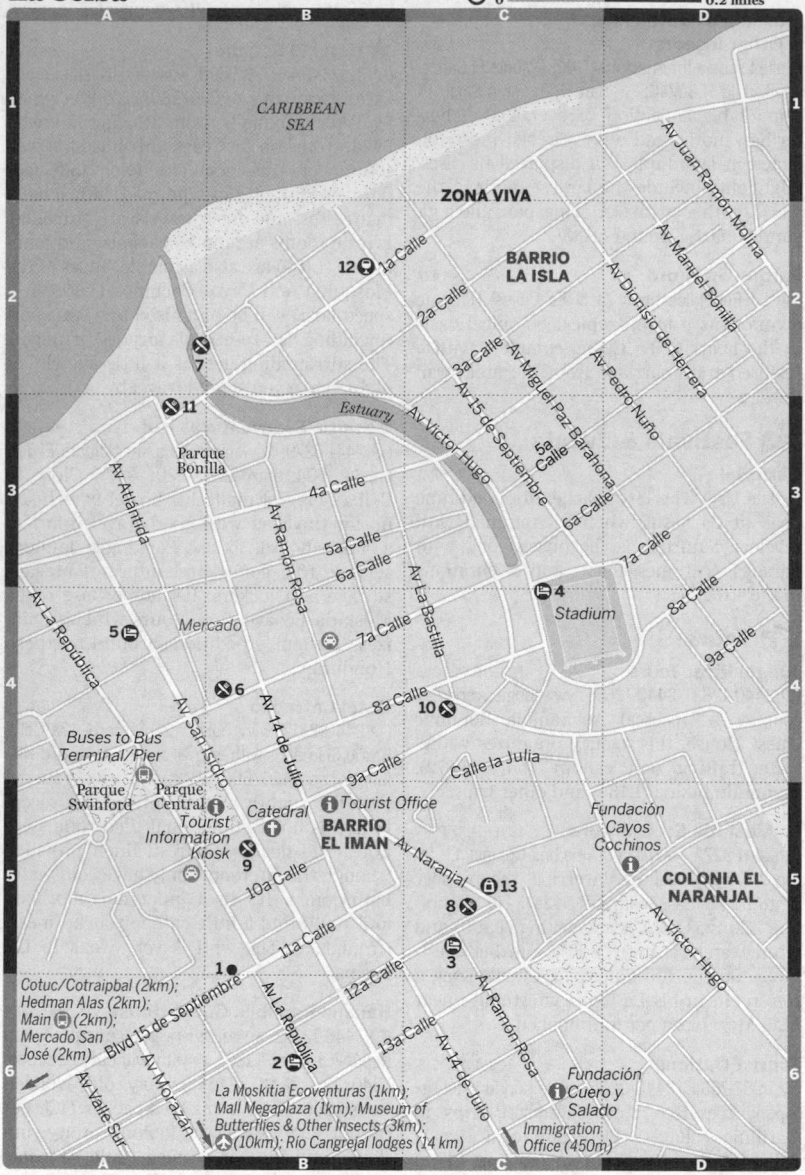

a bizarre set-up, this centrally located hotel has accommodations on the upper floors of a run-down 1960s concrete plaza. Rooms, though in need of a makeover, are very spacious and reasonable value.

Eating

Cafetería Cobel COMEDOR $

(cnr 7a Calle & Av Atlántida; set lunch L60; ⏲6:30am-6pm Mon-Sat) Packed little eatery that serves *plato del días* (set lunch meals). The bustle means it can take a while to

La Ceiba

Activities, Courses & Tours
Jungle River Tours ..... (see 2)
1 Tourist Options B5

Sleeping
2 Banana Republic Guest House B6
3 Hotel Catracho C5
4 Hotel El Estadio C4
5 Hotel Iberia A4

Eating
6 Cafetería Cobel B4
7 Chef Guity A2
8 Expatriates Bar & Grill C5
9 Jugos Chapala B5
10 Ki'boc Café C4
11 Pupusaría Universitaria A3

Drinking & Nightlife
12 La Palapa B2

Shopping
13 Souvenirs El Buen Amigo C5

attract the attention of the pink-uniformed waitresses. There is air-con in the back room.

Pupusaría Universitaria HONDURAN $
(1a Calle, near Av 14 de Julio; pupusas L16, mains L85-90; ⏲10am-11pm) An excellent budget haunt inside a clapboard-and-bamboo building, serving up big flavors at moderate rates: *pupusas*, tacos and succulent *pinchos* (kebabs) are all on offer.

Jugos Chapala JUICE BAR $
(Av San Isidro; drinks L33-55; ⏲7.30am-7pm) Terrific juice bar with a near-encylopedic choice of juices and shakes, which are available with myriad extras (including oats, cornflakes and fibre). Also sells yummy fruit salads. Very clean and just south of the *parque*.

★**Ki'boc Café** HONDURAN, INTERNATIONAL $$
(4a Av btwn Calle 8a & 9a; breakfast/lunch from L60/100; ⏲7am-7pm Mon-Fri, 8am-7pm Sat, 8am-noon Sun; 📶) A civilized, artsy cafe where the staff are very welcoming, coffee is organic, and breakfasts are the best in town (the Occidente-style *chilaquiles* are a real treat). There's a good book exchange, a little terrace and an air-conditioned interior with paintings and mismatched decor.

Expatriates Bar & Grill INTERNATIONAL $$
(12a Calle, Barrio El Imán; mains L120-270; ⏲4pm-midnight Mon-Thu, 4pm-2am Fri, 11am-2am Sat, 11am-11pm Sun; 📶) Classic (some would say clichéd) expat hangout with US sports on the TV and a familiar line-up up of barbecued meats and a few veggie options. There are drinks and food specials virtually every day.

Chef Guity SEAFOOD $$$
(off 1a Calle; mains L110-300; ⏲11am-10pm Tue-Sun) *Zona viva*-located Garifuna-style restaurant famous for its seafood – including conch, fish, lobster and crab – but particuarly *tapado* (a fish stew in coconut sauce).

Drinking & Nightlife

Most of La Ceiba's nightlife centers on and around 1a Calle in Barrio La Isla, known as the *zona viva*.

La Palapa BAR, CLUB
(Av 15 de Septiembre; ⏲11am-11pm Sun-Wed, 11am-2am Thu-Sat) This huge, upmarket, two-story thatched-roof bar/restaurant is just off the beach and draws a rich, hedonistic party crowd. Locals tend to eat seafood then gavitate to the central dancefloor to salsa off the excess.

Shopping

Mall Megaplaza MALL
(Carretera a Muelle Cabotaje; ⏲10am-9pm) Modern mall with a cinema, food court, internet cafes, banks and ATMs.

Souvenirs El Buen Amigo ARTS & CRAFTS
(Av Naranjal s/n, Barrio El Iman; ⏲8am-6:30pm Mon-Sat) Honduran *artesanías* including Lencan pottery, wood carvings and hammocks.

Information

Tour companies are your best bet for booking travel services. All the banks in the Mall Megaplaza have ATMs.

Banco Atlántida (Av San Isidro) With ATM.

Europanet (Parque Central; per hr L20; ⏲8am-6pm Mon-Sat; @) Internet access.

Fundación Cuero y Salado (☎2443-0329; cuero_salado@yahoo.com; cnr Av Ramón Rosa & 15a Calle; ⏲8am-5pm Mon-Fri, 8-11am Sat) Manages the Cuero y Salado Wildlife Reserve.

Hospital Eurohonduras (☎2440-0927; Av Atlántida; ⏲24hr) Between 1a Calle and the beach.

Immigration Office (☎2442-0638; 1a Calle, nr Av 14 de Julio; ⏲7:30am-3:30pm)

Post Office (cnr Av Morazán & 14a Calle; ⏲8am-4pm Mon-Fri, 8am-noon Sat) A bit of a trek from the center.

Tourist Office (☎2440-3044; 9a Calle; ⏲8am-4:30pm Mon-Fri) Offers lots of brochures and a map of the city. There's also a kiosk (☎440-1562; Parque Central; ⏲8am-6pm Mon-Sat) on the Parque Central and a desk at the airport.

Tourist Police (☎2441-0860; Residencial El Toronjal; ⏲24hr) Three blocks south of Carr a Tela.

Getting There & Away

La Ceiba's Aeropuerto Golosón is 10km west of downtown. Flights leave frequently for San Pedro Sula, Tegucigalpa, the Bay Islands and La Moskitia.

AIR

AeroCaribe (☎2442-2569; www.aerocaribehn.com) Flies to Guanaja (twice daily) and several destinations in La Mosquitia including Puerto Lempira, Palacios and Brus Laguna.

Aerolíneas Sosa (☎2443-1399, at airport 2440-0692; www.aerolineasosa.com; Av San Isidro btwn 8a & 9a Calles) Regular connections to Roatán, Utila and Puerto Lempira. There's also a weekly flight (US$176) to Grand Cayman.

Lanhsa (☎2442-1283; www.lanhsa.com) Connects Ceiba with Roatán, Puerto Lempira and Tegucigalpa.

TACA/Isleña (☎2441-3191, airport 2443-2683; www.flyislena.com; 22a Calle at Av Morazán, Mall Megaplaza, 1st fl) To/from Roatán, San Pedro Sula and Tegucigalpa

Flights From La Ceiba

DESTINATION	COST (L)
Guanaja	1100-1450
Puerto Lempira	2200-2670
Roatán	1020-1485
San Pedro Sula	1450-3600
Tegucigalpa	1450-1450
Utila	1110-1320

BOAT

Ferries to the Bay Islands operate from the Muelle de Cabotaje, about 8km east of town.

The modern, comfortable **Galaxy Wave** (☎La Ceiba 2414-5739, Roatán 2445-1795; www.roatanferry.com) sails twice daily to Roatán at 9:30am and 4:30pm (1st/normal class L674/574, 1¾ hours). The beat-up **Utila Princess II** (☎La Ceiba 2408-5163; www.utilaprincess.com; ⏲ticket office 7am-4pm) departs twice daily at 9:30am and 4pm (L472, one hour).

Sea sickness can affect passengers on both services – plan accordingly.

BUS

Most non-luxury buses use the main terminal at Mercado San José, about 1.5km west of the center of La Ceiba – **Diana Express** (☎2441-6460), **Catisa-Tupsa** (☎2441-2539) and **Kamaldy** (☎2441-2028; www.transporteskamaldy.com) all have offices there – but there are some important exceptions. The **Viana** (☎2441-2230; www.vianatransportes.com) bus terminal is another 500m further west along the same road; continue a bit further for **Cotuc** (☎2441-2199) and **Cotraibal** buses for Trujillo. **San Miguel Plus** (☎2441-2280; transportesanmiguel.com) buses also leave from a terminal on this highway. **Hedman Alas** (☎2441-5347; www.hedmanalas.com) has its own terminal on the main highway just east of the center. An additional three companies also head to San Pedro Sula from the main terminal.

Getting Around

TO/FROM THE AIRPORT

La Ceiba's airport is 10km west of the town on the highway to Tela. Any non-express bus heading west from the main bus terminal could drop you there. *Colectivo* taxis from the Parque Central pass the airport (L20); you have to wait for the taxi to fill up. A normal taxi costs around L120.

Coming from the airport, taxis in the official rank charge about L200 for the ride into town; if you go to the main road and flag down a *colectivo* it's L20 per person.

TO/FROM THE BUS TERMINAL

The main bus terminal is at Mercado San José, about 1.5km west of central La Ceiba. Local buses run between this terminal and the central plaza (L6), or you can take a *colectivo* taxi (L20). Buses marked 'Terminal' head to the station from the bus stop at Av La República between 7a Calle and 8a Calle (L6).

TO/FROM THE PIER

Ferries to the Bay Islands operate from the Muelle de Cabotaje, about 8km (20 minutes) east of town. From the bus terminal or from town, taxis charge about L80 to L100. A *colectivo* (L20) goes from the town center at 7a Calle; there's no *colectivo* on the way back.

CAR

There are numerous rental agencies in La Ceiba.

Avis (☎2441-2802; www.avis.com.hn; Entrada Principal a La Ceiba; ⏲7:30am-6pm)

Econo Rent-A-Car (☎2442-8686; www.econorentacarhn.com; Carretera a Tela; ⏲8am-5pm) Located near Megaplaza Mall.

TAXI
Colectivo taxis in La Ceiba charge a standard L20 per person, going up a bit after 8pm.

Around La Ceiba

Río Cangrejal

Surging through the jungle, the turquoise Río Cangrejal is rightly renowned as Central America's premier rafting experience. Even if you've zero intention of dipping an oar in its foaming waters, the region makes a stunning base for all manner of adventure sports, birdwatching or just chilling by the river. The scenery is spectacular, the air is mountain-fresh and there are some excellent places to stay strung out along the riverside.

Activities

Most visitors are here to raft or kayak the Cangrejal, but there's also mountain biking, horseback riding, swimming and great rainforest hiking.

Guaruma Servicios GUIDED TOUR
(☎2442-2673; www.guaruma.org) A worthwhile operation dedicated to boosting opportunities for the local community through sustainable tourism. It's based at the small village of Las Mangas in Río Cangrejal.

White-Water Rafting & Kayaking
The Río Cangrejal offers sublime **white-water rafting**. The scenery is immense, with the river coarsing through rainforest that's part of the Parque Nacional Pico Bonito. There's a good chance of seeing herons, kingfishers and toucans.

There are two main sections of the Cangrejal: the **upper** part is hardcore, offering real Class IV and V thrills, rapids and speed. After very heavy rain it may not be possible to raft here. The **lower** section offers year-

BUSES FROM LA CEIBA

DESTINATION	COST (L)	DURATION	BUS LINE	PHONE	DEPARTURE
Copán Ruinas	674-828	7hr	Hedman Alas	2441-5347	2 daily
El Porvenir	12	45min	Main Terminal	N/A	every 45min Mon-Sat, hourly Sun
La Unión-Cuero y Salado	28	1½hr	Main Terminal	N/A	every 45min Mon-Sat, hourly Sun
Nueva Armenia	28	1½hr	Main Terminal	N/A	6-7 daily
Sambo Creek/ Corazal	17	1hr	Main Terminal	N/A	every 35min
San Pedro Sula	115	3½hr	Diana Express	2449-0388	6 daily
	108	3½hr	Catisa-Tupsa	2441-9539	hourly 5am-6pm
	345-501	3hr	Hedman Alas	2441-5347	4 daily (via San Pedro Sula airport)
	345-556	3hr	Viana	2441-2330	3-4 daily
Tegucigalpa	242	7hr	Kalmaldy	2441-2028	4 daily
	672-1145	6½hr	Viana	2441-2330	3-4 daily
	559-713	6½hr	Hedman Alas	2441-5347	3 daily
	400-600	6½hr	San Miguel Plus	2441-2280	3 daily
Tela	66	2hr	Kamaldy	2441-2028	4 daily
	42	2hr	Main Terminal	N/A	every 25min
	200-300	1½hr	San Miguel Plus	2441-2280	3 daily
Trujillo	110	3hr	Cotuc/ Cotraipbal	2441-2129	hourly
Yaruca/Río Cangrejal	17	30min	Main Terminal	N/A	5 daily, or any Las Mangas bus

round Class III rafting, the river surging around giant boulders.

Whichever section you choose you'll need an experienced, competent guide – accidents have occurred in the upper section of the Cangrejal after heavy rainfall, when conditions can be particularly treacherous. Always check out the situation first with your tour operator. Jungle River Tours (p399; from L700) and La Moskitia Ecoaventuras (p399; from L800) offer budget-friendly prices. **Omega Tours** (☎9631-0295; www.omegatours.info; Omega Lodge, road to Yaruca Km 9) cost more (from L1300), but its trips are better received.

Hiking & Horseback Riding

Just uphill from the Jungle River Lodge, right by the Centro de Visitantes, a rope bridge extends over the Cangrejal to the other side of the river, allowing **hiking** access into the heart of Parque Nacional Pico Bonito. Omega Lodge also has several well-marked trails on its grounds.

Horseback riding is offered at Omega Lodge for L1500 per half-day. All the horses live at the lodge and are very well cared for.

Canopy Tours

Jungle River Tours (p399) operates an eight-cable circuit that lasts two hours and includes a 200m slide across the river (per person L700).

Sleeping & Eating

The following lodges are 14km to 16km from La Ceiba. All except Guaruma offer a free night in a dorm or a discounted room if you book a tour.

★Omega Lodge LODGE $
(☎9631-0295; www.omegatours.info; road to Yaruca Km 9; s/d without bathroom L200/400, cabins L2000; @ 📶 ❄) A beautifully conceived and constructed ecolodge, though it lacks views. The entire (German-owned) complex ticks over efficiently with environmental principals at its core: solar power, a chemical-free pool and ecofriendly waste-management. Food is simply outstanding, with home-cooked healthy eating and lots of vegetarian choices (breakfast L45 to L90; mains L90 to L220). The owners pioneered rafting on the *río,* and offer many excellent trips. However, watch out for additional taxes to your bill when you leave.

Jungle River Lodge LODGE $
(☎2440-1268; www.jungleriverlodge.com; road to Yaruca Km 7; dm/d with bathroom L220/800, meals from L70; 📶) Jungle River Tours' lodge is perched on a ledge with a simply magnificent perspective of the Río Cangrejal valley – the outdoor bar-restaurant here has to have one of Honduras' greatest vistas. Accommodation is far more prosaic, varying from functional dorms to attractive rooms, some with hot-water private bathrooms. There are natural swimming pools below and all kinds of tours can be booked (canopy tours, hiking and white-water rafting). To get a free ride here, rock up to Banana Republic Guest House in La Ceiba.

La Moskitia Adventuras Lodge LODGE $
(☎2441-3279; www.lamoskitia.hn; road to Yaruca Km 9; dm/d L160/320; 📶) This impressive new riverside lodge has a stunning position overlooking the roaring Cangrejal – you'll be mesmerized by the view. Accommodation and restaurant prices are geared to backpacker budgets, and professionally organized rafting, hiking and zip lining trips are offered. Has a sister hostel in La Ceiba, from where transport can be arranged.

Guaruma Community Lodge CABINS $
(☎9917-5325; www.guaruma.org; road to Yaruca Km 12; d/tr/q L350/400/450) In the village of Las Mangas, these well-constructed, clean cabins channel funds back into the community. Good-value meals (L80 to L90), bikes (per day L100) and guides are available. Take a bus heading towards Yaruca.

Parque Nacional Pico Bonito

Looming over La Ceiba, the densely forested mountain of Pico Bonito forms one of Honduras' best-known national parks. It harbours some abundant wildlife, including jaguars, armadillos and monkeys.

There are two entrances. **El Pino** village is about 15km west of La Ceiba on the highway to Tela. Here you'll find rustic cabins at the **Centro Ecoturístico Natural View** (☎2368-8343; r L300). Tours and guides can be arranged here for the moderately difficult three-hour hike to **Cascada Zacate** (per person incl guide, transport & park entrance fee L210) waterfall.

The other entrance is by the **Río Cangrejal**, where a new **visitors center** (road to Yaruca; ⏲7am-4pm) has been built, along with a suspension bridge over the roaring river (L20 to access for photos). Conviently, it's on the same road as the Río Cangrejal river lodges. From the visitors center there's a lovely trail (three hours return) through lush mountainside forest to **El Bejuco waterfall**.

Tour agencies in La Ceiba offer Pico Bonito tours. For additional information about the park, contact the **Fundación Parque Nacional Pico Bonito** (Funapib; ☎2442-3044; www.picobonito.org; Carretera a Tela, Colonia Palmira, La Ceiba; ⏲8am-4pm Mon-Fri)

Entrance to Pico Bonito National Park is L133.

Getting There & Away

Any bus headed toward Tela or San Pedro Sula can drop you at El Pino (L18, 30 minutes).

To get to the Río Cangrejal side, jump on a bus to Yaruca or Las Mangas from the main terminal in La Ceiba.

Cayos Cochinos

The idyllic white sands of the **Cayos Cochinos** (the Hog Islands), just 17km from the mainland, can easily be visited as a day trip from the La Ceiba region. Access is by motorized canoe from Nueva Armenia or Sambo Creek, east of La Ceiba. There's a L200 to entrance fee to enter the Cayos Cochinos.

The two Hog Islands, 13 tiny coral cays and seas around them are a **marine reserve** – it is illegal to anchor on the reef, and commercial fishing is prohibited. Consequently, the reefs are pristine and fish-abundant. Diving and snorkeling are excellent around the islands, with black coral reefs, wall diving, cave diving, seamounts and a plane wreck. The islands are also known for their unique pink boa constrictors and the strength of the local Garifuna culture.

It's possible to go independently to the cays, although you will not save much money, and local boatmen are unlikely to have a radio or life jackets. Day trips cost L700 per person (minimum five people) from Sambo Creek. Lots of La Ceiba tour operators offer tours to the cays: Tourist Options (p399) has a good rep and provides snorkeling gear.

If you want to play Robinson Crusoe for a few days, there are rustic *cabañas* available for L100 to L400 on Chachauate cay, a speck in the Caribbean, or two comfortable cabins with private bathrooms at **Laru Beya** (☎9489-6058; www.cayoscochinoshonduras.webs.com; s/d L250/400) in the east end of the main island.

Contact **Fundación Cayos Cochinos** (☎2442-2670; www.cayoscochinos.org; cnr Av Victor Hugo & 13a Calle 1175, Barrio Colonia El Naranjal, La Ceiba) for more information about the islands or volunteering.

Sambo Creek

Some 21km east of La Ceiba, Sambo Creek is a thriving Garifuna fishing village. It's a slightly scruffy but fascinating place where you'll see women in striking attire and traditional headdresses. A *punta* party (traditional Garifuna dance) is never far away. The beach is a lovely stretch of sand, which most of the year is pretty clean, though trash washes up after storms.

Don't miss the **Sambo Creek Canopy Tour & Spa** (☎3355-6481; canopy tour & spa L855), which whizzes you through the treetops for more than an hour, and finishes in spectacular hillside thermal springs set amid the rainforest. The turnoff is 500m east of Sambo Creek, on the highway to Trujillo.

Overlooking the ocean, **Centro Turístico Sambo Creek** (☎9587-0874; mauriciolvir@yahoo.com; per person L180), owned by Tourist Options in La Ceiba, offers five rather worn, though large rooms. There's a breezy hammock deck and restaurant (open Thursday to Sunday only). Boat trips to Cayo Cochinos leave from here, costing L700 (minimum five people). A short walk east of Sambo Creek there are a couple of midrange guesthouses. **Villa Helen's** (☎2441-2017; www.villahelens.com; r L800-900, cabins from L1000; P ❄ @ ≋) is the best value and has lush gardens and two swimming pools. The rooms at **Paradise Found** (☎9861-1335; www.paradisefoundlaceiba.com; r L1200; P ❄ @) are overpriced, but the cuisine is great (meals from L130). Another good place to eat is **Kay's Place** (meals from L150; ⏲9:30am-10pm), a beachside bar-restaurant in Sambo Creek; there's often live Garifuna music here.

Refugio de Vida Silvestre Cuero y Salado

On the coast about 30km west of La Ceiba, this wetland reseve protects varied and abundant wildlife: manatees are the most famous (and the hardest to see), but there are also howler and white-faced monkeys, sloths, agoutis (rabbit-sized rodents), iguanas, caimans and hundreds of bird species.

The small town of **La Unión** is the gateway to Cuero y Salado. From there you catch a train to a **visitors center** (☎2443-0329) where a L200 entrance fee is collected and tours can be organized. Canoe trips (L130 for two people, plus L210 per guide for a two-hour tour) are by far the best way to explore the reserve.

A well-maintained **dorm** (per person L160) is a short walk away, and simple meals are available at the visitors center cafe.

For further information, contact **Fundación Cuero y Salado** (☎2443-0329; www.cueroysalado.org; cnr 19 Av & Av 14 de Julio, La Ceiba; ⏲8-11:30am & 1-5:30pm Mon-Fri) in La Ceiba.

Getting There & Away

To get to the reserve, take a bus to La Unión from La Ceiba's main terminal (L20, one hour, every 30 minutes). From La Unión, jump on the *trencito* (a railcar) for the 9.5km ride on the old banana railroad to the visitors center (one or two people L250, three or more people L125 each, 45 minutes, hourly 7am to 2pm). The last railcar returns from the visitors center at 2.30pm; the final bus from La Unión to La Ceiba is at 4pm. It's possible to walk to the reserve in 1½ hours along the railway tracks, but it's safest not to as this is a lonely part of the country.

Trujillo

POP 33,000

Sleepy, tropical Trujillo sits above the wide arc of the Bahía de Trujillo, an expanse of water that has seen the sails of Columbus and many a famous buccaneer. It burns a serene crystal blue when the weather cooperates. As it's the end of the road to a certain extent, few travelers end up in Trujillo, but rather come with a purpose. A place to lose yourself for a spell? Perhaps.

For years the town has been talked up as Honduras' next big tourism thing, without ever actually getting there. But with new resort hotels opening around the bay and a cruise ship terminal nearing completion, maybe this time it's for real. Maybe.

History

For a small town, Trujillo has had an important part in the history of Central America. It was near Trujillo, on August 14, 1502, that Columbus first set foot on the American mainland (and here that the first Catholic Mass on the continent was performed).

Founded on May 18, 1525, Trujillo was one of the earliest Spanish settlements in Central America, and a provincial capital until 1537.

The Spanish used the port at Trujillo to ship out gold and silver from the interior of Honduras – and inevitably pirates soon came sniffing around. The Bahía de Trujillo was the scene of several great battles when the town was attacked by pirates, including Henry Morgan.

The Spanish built several fortresses – the ruins of the fort of Santa Bárbara can still be explored today. Despite the fortifications, the buccaneers prevailed, and after a sacking by Dutch pirates in 1643, the town lay in ruins for over a century until it was resettled in 1787. Trujillo was also the stage for American adventurer William Walker's bid to take over Central America. It was doomed to failure – he was captured and executed by firing squad in 1860. His grave is now just outside the town center.

Sights

You can sense the town's tumultuous history during a quick stroll around Trujillo's historical core and cobblestone streets. Many fine Caribbean-style wooden houses remain, and be sure to take in the fort.

Trujillo also has a fine shoreline, though a lot of trash washes up on its beaches.

★Fortaleza Santa Bárbara de Trujillo FORT

(admission L60; ⏲9am-5pm) High above the waves, gazing over the Caribbean towards the European motherland, this 17th-century Spanish fortress could not have a more evocative position. Though its ruined remains are not that impressive visually, it's still an inspirational spot to reflect on the forces and characters that shaped the history of the American continent.

Fifteen cannons face the sea, and a plaque marks the place where North American wanabe conqueror William Walker was executed. The on-site museum has colonial and Garifuna artifacts on display.

Grave of William Walker CEMETERY

FREE Just west of town, where the Río Cristales flows into the sea, lies the town cemetery. Here lies the grave of William Walker, who died in Trujillo following his ill-fated bid to conquer Central America.

Trujillo

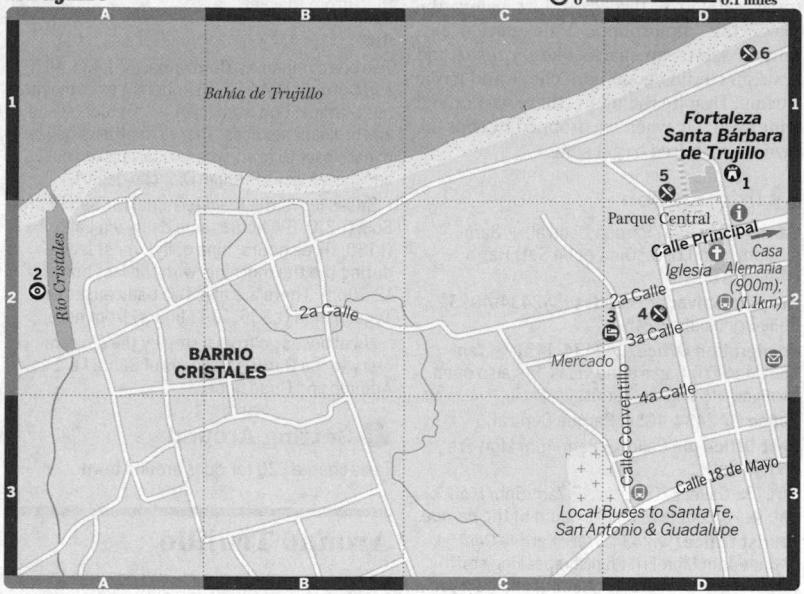

Sleeping

Casa Alemania HOTEL $

(☎2434-4466; d from L350; ❄ 📶 🏊) Jovial German owner Gunter Wassmus' likeable hotel sits beachside just east of central Trujillo. Rooms are modern, well-appointed and fine value, with good quality bedding and mattresses. Expect huge portions in the hotel restaurant (meals from L80). The pool is great for hanging out and there's a small gym too.

Hotel Emperador PENSION $

(☎2434-4446; r with/without air-con L500/250; ❄ 📶) Owned by a (slightly eccentric) local historian, this hotel has 10 functional rooms to the side of a remarkable Caribbean building, which dates back to 1787. Check out the time-warp atmosphere in the adjoining cafe while you're here.

Eating

For cheap eats, stick to the town center; for something more fancy head down to the beach.

Café & Sabores HONDURAN $

(Calle Principal; mains L60-80; ⏲6am-8pm Mon-Sat; ❄) Agreeably old-fashioned diner-like cafe that's good for breakfast (L70) and always has five or six set-lunch choices. Excellent *licuados* are L20 to L30. There's an air-conditioned room at the rear.

Playa Dorada SEAFOOD $$

(mains L60-420; ⏲8am-10pm; 📶) This large beachfront place is often touted as the best seafood restaurant in town, but in truth the menu is a bit hit-and-miss. If you just stick to the outstanding *sopa de mariscos* (seafood soup), which is good value at L160, you can't go wrong.

Trujillo

Top Sights
1 Fortaleza Santa Bárbara de Trujillo D1

Sights
2 Grave of William Walker A2

Sleeping
3 Hotel Emperador D2

Eating
4 Café & Sabores D2
5 Cafe Vino Tinto D1
6 Playa Dorada D1

Cafe Vino Tinto HONDURAN **$$**
(mains L80-150; ⏲11am-9pm) Just below the plaza, this atmospheric little garden restaurant serves up snacks like *pupusas* and mains including good pork chops and garlic shrimp. Despite the name, there was no red wine available when we dropped by (but the owners promised to get some).

Information

Banco Atlántida (Parque Central; ⏲8am-4:30pm Mon-Fri, 8:30am-noon Sat) Has a 24-hour ATM.

Hospital Salvador Paredes (☎2434-4093; Calle Principal; ⏲24hr)

Immigration Office (☎2434-4451; ⏲7am-5pm Mon-Fri) Can extend visas. It's also open some nights and weekends.

Police (☎2434-4054; Parque Central)

Post Office (4a Calle; ⏲8am-4pm Mon-Fri, 8-11am Sat)

SCL (3a Calle; L20 per hr; ⏲7am-5pm Mon-Sat; @) A couple of blocks south of the *parque*.

Tourist Office (☎2434-3140; Parque Central; ⏲8am-4pm Mon-Fri) English-speaking staff (including local character Nelson) can help you here.

Getting There & Away

Note that the highway between Trujillo and La Ceiba passes a notorious drug-smuggling route into La Moskitia. It's lined with many police checkpoints.

BOAT

At the time of research there were no boat connections to Guanaja, one of the Bay Islands, but rumours that a link (might) start again. Similarly, there are no scheduled departures to La Moskitia region, but fishing and cargo boats do sail there from the pier.

BUS

Two bus companies, **Contraibal** (☎2434-4932) and **Cotuc** (☎2444-2181), operate from the main bus terminal 1km from town, with direct (speedy) and ordinary services. There's another small terminal closer to town, where local chicken buses and the services through Olancho depart.

Buses leave the main terminal for San Pedro Sula (L210, 6½ hours, nine daily) via La Ceiba (L130, three hours, nine daily); most leave during the the morning, with the last bus at 12:30pm. There are also two daily buses to Tegucigalpa (L336, 10-11 hours) from here.

Local buses go from a stop by the old cemetery to the Garifuna villages of Santa Fe, San Antonio and Guadalupe.

Getting Around

Taxis charge L20 for rides around town.

WORTH A TRIP

LAGUNA DE GUAIMORETO

Around 5km east of Trujillo, this large lagoon and wildlife refuge has a complex system of canals and mangrove forests that provide shelter to abundant bird, plant and animal life (including the elusive manatee). Thousands of migratory birds refuel here between November and February.

You can hire **rowing boats** or **canoes** (and even someone to paddle for you) by the old bridge between Trujillo and Puerto Castilla. Expect to pay around L250 for a two-hour excursion.

Around Trujillo

Santa Rosa de Aguán

Paul Theroux's novel *The Mosquito Coast,* which was later made into a movie starring Harrison Ford, featured this small tropical town. Just 40km from Trujillo, Santa Rosa de Aguán is a good place to get a taste of La Moskitia if you don't have the time or the money to go all the way out there. The town was severely damaged during Hurricane Mitch in 1988 – 44 people drowned – and it hasn't fully recovered. Still, it has an engaging, frontier-like atmosphere, and you can hire boats to take you up the Río Aguán, where you might catch sight of 3m alligators.

There's an annual **Garifuna festival** here from August 22 to 29. Two very basic hotels charge around L70. Five buses to Santa Rosa de Aguán (L36) leave Trujillo from the gas-station terminal each day at 6:45am, 10am, 1pm, 3pm and 4:45pm. There are four return buses at 5am, 6am, 10am and 3pm.

BAY ISLANDS

Spectacular diving and snorkeling draws visitors from around the world to the three Bay Islands (Islas de la Bahía) – **Roatán**, **Utila** and **Guanaja** – between 25 and 50km off the north coast of Honduras. Their reefs are part of the second-largest barrier reef in

Bay Islands

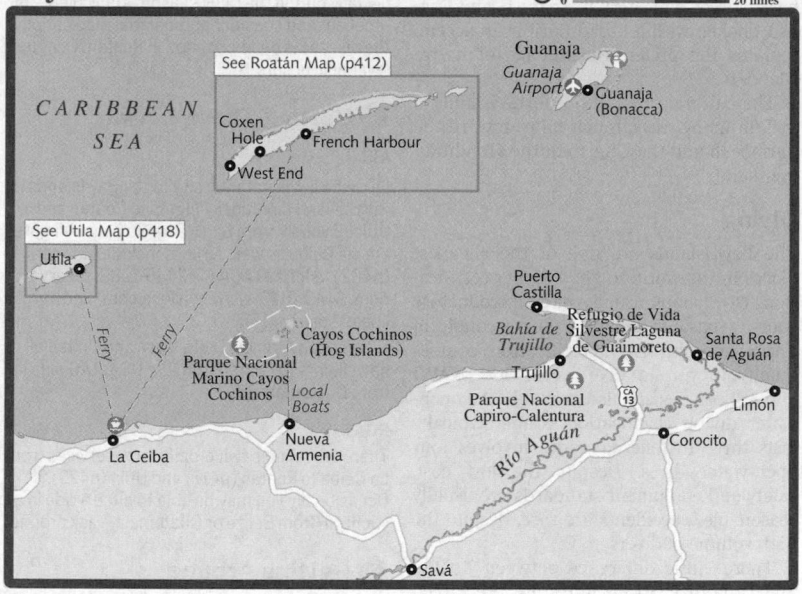

the world, and teem with fish, coral, sponges, rays, sea turtles and even whale sharks.

The islanders have a fascinating heritage that includes African and Carib, European and other ancestry. English is the dominant spoken language, and Spanish is a second language. In Utila, there are still white descendants of early British settlers (with names like Cooper and Thompson); in Roatán there's a Garifuna settlement at Punta Gorda. You'll also find plenty of resident foreigners, working for dive shops and other tourist-oriented businesses.

The islands' economy is based mostly on tourism and fishing, and shrimp and lobster catching. Diving here is very affordable, but lodging and food on the islands are more expensive than on the mainland. Utila is the most affordable island (popular with backpackers), while Roatán has better beaches and a beautiful forested interior. Diving is also good on Guanaja, though the prices here are prohibitive for most travelers. To save costs, look out for free wi-fi (internet costs are sky high in cybercafes) and get a liking for street food (restaurants can be very expensive). And if you're still struggling, rent a snorkel and mask – the reef itself is gratis.

The rainy season here runs roughly from October or November to February. March and August are the hottest months; at other times sea breezes temper the heat.

History

The Bay Islands' history is a compelling tale of conquest and piracy, colonial squabbles between Spain and Britain, and modern migration from the Caribbean and Central American mainland.

Ruins on all three Bay Islands indicate that they were inhabited well before the Europeans arrived, with evidence of Maya, Pech (Paya) and Nahuatl-speaking settlement.

Christopher Columbus landed in Guanaja in 1502, enslaving many islanders. Later, pirates including Henry Morgan used the Bay Islands as a base to raid gold-laden Spanish vessels.

In 1797 thousands of Black Caribs were dumped by the British on Roatán. This group settled at Punta Gorda, survived and mixed with the natives. Migrant groups reached the mainland, setting up villages along the coast. And the Garifuna were born.

Waves of English-speaking settlers, many of them turtle-hunters from the Cayman Islands, migrated to the Bay Islands in the 19th century. The islands remained controlled by the British crown until 1859, when a treaty ceded them to Honduras. However it's only in the last few decades that Tegucigalpa has enforced education in Spanish, and English, spoken with a broad Caribbean accent, remains the preferred language of native islanders.

The cultural orientation of the islands is still, in many ways, much more toward the Caribbean and the USA than the Honduran mainland.

Diving

The Bay Islands are one of the cheapest places in the world to get a diving certification. Dive shops usually offer introductory courses (basic instruction plus a couple of dives) and full PADI-certification courses qualifying you to dive worldwide. NAWI and SSI courses are also available. An open-water diving certification course typically lasts three to four days and involves four open-water dives. Despite the low cost, safety and equipment standards are usually reasonable – accidents are rare, despite the high volume of divers.

There's little difference between Roatán and Utila dive prices. Rates are pre-agreed between dive schools to prevent cut-throat discounting so prices are pretty standardized. However, in Utila many schools offer free dorm beds or throw in a free dive or two – it pays to ask around. Open-water PADI certification costs around L5600 and a 10-dive package around L5000 on both islands.

When choosing a school, speak to the instructors and staff, ask to see their equipment (is it worn and torn or shiny and new?). Some schools specialize in tech dives; all offer deep dives, wreck diving, wall- and cave-diving.

Both islands offer excellent marine life. The shallow coral in Roatán is generally in better condition than Utila's. But Utila has one extraordinary trump card: northeast of the island there's a seamount that's among the best places in the world to view whale sharks.

Information

DANGERS & ANNOYANCES

The islands are generally safer than the mainland, although the crime situation has deteriorated in Roatán in recent years. Remember this is one of the poorest nations in the western hemisphere and a smart phone or laptop represents a huge chunk of money to many locals – be coy with fancy electronics.

Mosquitoes and sand flies are voracious, especially during the rainy season. Apply plenty of repellent and consider antimalarial medication – the disease is quite common in Roatán. Dengue fever also occurs.

Getting There & Away

AIR

La Ceiba is the gateway city to the Bay Islands with several direct daily flights to Roatán and Utila. If you fly from San Pedro Sula most flights are via Ceiba as well. Airlines include Aerocaribe (p402), **Isleña/TACA** (☎2445-1088, reservations 2443-0179; www.flyislena.com) and Aerolineas Sosa (p417).

American Airlines, Delta, Taca and United all have flights to Roatán from the USA; TAG flies in from Guatemala City.

BOAT

There are reliable twice-daily ferry services from La Ceiba to Roatán (p417) and Utila (p423). Occasionally you may be able to hitch a ride in a yacht to/from Belize or Guatemala – ask around.

Getting Around

BOAT

There are currently no ferry services between the Bay Islands – you have to go via La Ceiba. Water taxis are used on Roatán between West End and West Bay and between Utila Town and the Utila cays.

CAR, MOTORCYCLE & BICYCLE

You can rent cars on Roatán (from L900 per day) and motorcycles (L600 per day) on both Roatán and Utila. Bicycles are very popular and cheap in Utila, costing about L100 per day.

TAXI

Taxis ferry people all around Roatán. *Colectivo* fares are reasonable (L30 to L70), but private rates are high (L120 to L200). Most places in Utila are walkable.

Roatán

POP 53,200

Roatán is the largest and most developed of the Bay Islands. Long and thin (50km long but only 2km to 4km wide), the island is a real diving and snorkeling mecca – virtually its entire coastline is fringed by an astonishingly diverse coral reef teeming with tropical fish.

But there's much more to Roatán than its reef. Exquisite white sand beaches like West Bay, a mountainous interior of pine-forested hills and the remote wild east of the island (once a key pirate hangout) beg to be explored.

Unsurprisingly this natural beauty hasn't been ignored by property developers and tour operators, and a slew of fancy resort hotels, a new shopping mall and cruise ship terminal have opened in recent years.

The vast majority of backpackers base themselves in West End.

West End

Curled around two small turquoise bays and laced with coconut palms, West End is an idyllic (if touristy) village close to the western tip of the island. It's the one place in Roatán where independent travelers rather than package tourists predominate, and its quirky 'high street' is lined with sea-facing restaurants, boutiques selling sarongs and jewelry, reggae bars, and (of course) dive schools.

Even though most accommodation and eating options are geared at the midrange market, you'll find some good budget places and there's always a community of backpackers here to socialize with.

Sights

Roatán Marine Park WILDLIFE RESERVE

(☎2445-4206; www.roatanmarinepark.com)

Set up in 2005 with the aim of protecting the reef system around the West End and Sandy Bay, the Roatán Marine Park now covers the whole island. Roatán's reefs are under enormous pressure, both from construction and the sheer amount of visitors, and this nonprofit organization campaigns strongly to conserve the marine environment.

Four boats patrol the shoreline, and people fishing illegally (the use of nets, harpoons or traps is banned) have been jailed. Officers visit local schools to talk about the reef and conservation and children are taken snorkeling.

You can help by:

➡ Making sure you dive with an outfit associated with the marine park. Most dive schools do support it and voluntarily charge all divers a park fee (L100). There's a list of member shops on the marine park's website.

➡ Not eating fish and seafood that's considered at risk. Most pelagic (open-water) fish are fine, but reef fish, conch and small lobster are not. One nasty invader that you *should* definitely try in restaurants is lionfish, an invasive species from Asia (see boxed text, p415).

➡ Never touching coral underwater.

➡ Renting snorkeling gear or buying produce from the Roatán Marine Park HQ in the West End.

Beaches & Snorkeling

Half Moon Bay, which forms the northern part of the West End, is a lovely sheltered sandy bay with shallow water. Snorkeling is good, but it's some distance out to the reef from the shore and there's a lot of boat traffic, so consider heading elsewhere like nearby West Bay.

Snorkeling equipment (L100 per day) can be rented from numerous places in West End: we suggest you go to the Marine Park office as then your money helps protect the reef.

ROATÁN'S BEST DIVE SPOTS

➡ **Green Outhouse** – Great for a first deep dive of the day, with lots of marine life. Two walls: the first from 15ft (4.5m) to 50ft (15m), and then the main wall from 60ft (18m) down.

➡ **West End Wall** – Dramatic vertical wall starting at 20ft (6m) and going straight down. Good marine life: healthy gorgonians with lots of creole wrasse.

➡ **Texas** – Huge barrel sponges and deep water gorgonians, usually lots of current and plenty of barracudas, groupers and marine life.

➡ **Mary's Place** – Lots of deep swim-throughs and an amazing main crack where a peninsula of coral broke away from the wall. Gorgeous coral and schools of Atlantic spadefish in the crack.

➡ **Aguilar Wreck**– Something for everyone: reef, wall, sand bottom, garden eels, lots of blue parrot fish, huge groupers, a resident moray eel and then ending the dive in the shallow reef with lots of marine life.

Roatán

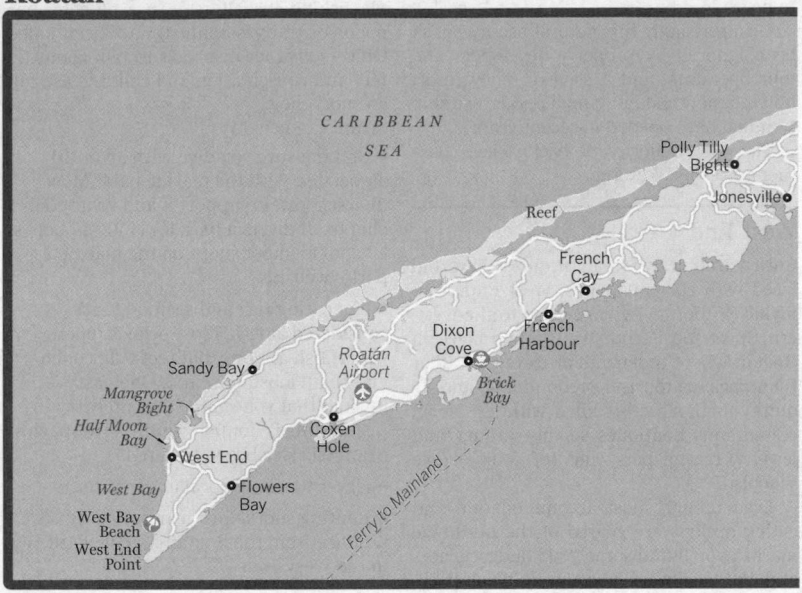

Activities

Diving

The entire coastline of Roatán, especially the western tip, is dotted with dozens of dive sites, many just meters off the shore. With names such as Hole-in-the-Wall and Sponge Emporium, Roatán is truly a diver's paradise, with endless variety and near-perfect diving conditions. Compared with Utila, smaller classes tend to be the norm and Roatán's shallow reef is in slightly better shape. Most sites are nearby, so shops typically offer three or four one-tank dives per day, as opposed to two two-tank dives common on Utila. Prices are pretty standard among the shops.

Training and courses in **freediving** are also now available in West End.

Native Sons DIVING
(☎2445-4003; www.nativesonsroatan.com) Run by Alvin Jackson, a local instructor with three decades of experience. Very popular with backpackers.

InnerSea DIVING
(☎9561-0306; walidapnea@yahoo.fr; Splash Inn, West End) Freediving specialists. One-/three-day courses cost L2000/5000 and involve training using relaxation and breathing techniques.

Ocean Connections DIVING
(☎2327-0935; www.ocean-connections.com) Small classes; also has a dive shop in West Bay.

Roatán Divers DIVING
(☎9803-9389; dive@roatandiver.com) Owned by Reno, an islander who has logged over 5000 dives in Roatán, this small school has new equipment and a welcoming atmosphere.

Reef Gliders DIVING
(☎8413-5099; www.reefgliders.com; next to Purple Turtle) American-owned school that's safety and conservation conscious.

Tyll's Dive DIVING
(☎9698-0416; www.tyllsdive.com) A relaxed, friendly dive shop on the main drag.

West End Divers DIVING
(☎2445-4289; www.westenddivers.com) Always popular, this dive shop caters to a younger crowd.

Deep-sea Submarine

Roatán Institute of Deep Sea Exploration ADVENTURE TOUR
(☎3359-2887; www.stanleysubmarines.com; two-person dives from L17,800) One of Roatán's most

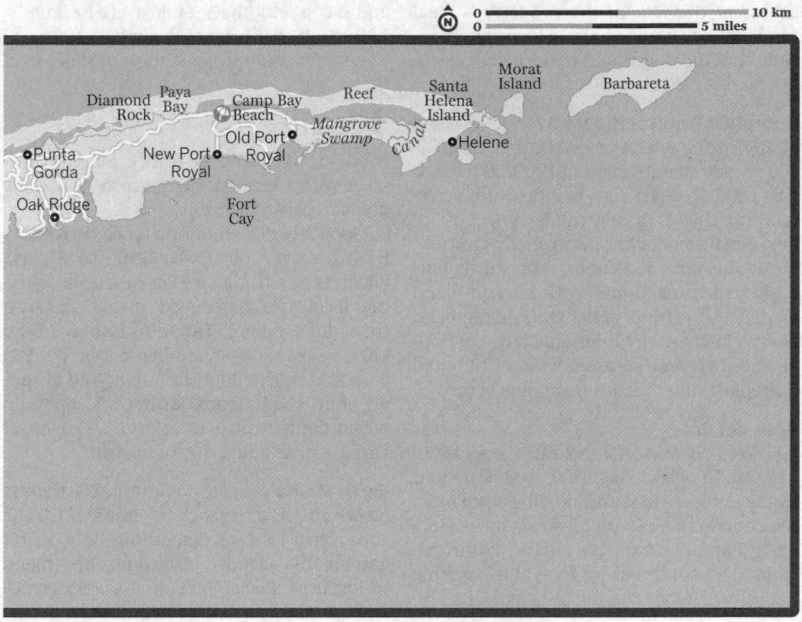

unusual activities is offered by Karl Stanley, the man behind the grandly named Roatán Institute of Deep Sea Exploration. A highly inventive, driven character, Stanley became obsessed with submarines when he was nine years old. Now he has turned his passion into a commercially viable reality, having designed and built his own submersible. He is the subject of the documentary, *A View from Below* (www.aviewfrombelow.com).

Stanley takes passengers in the small yellow submarine to depths of up to 300m, 450m or 600m. Light doesn't penetrate to those depths and those who do dare to take the ride can witness some extraordinary marine life including elusive six-gilled sharks. Stanley freely admits you take the plunge at your own risk (but don't worry, he's piloted over 1400 dives and counting without injury).

Horseback Riding

Roatán's surprisingly lush, undulating interior has some decent horseback-riding country.

El Rancho Barrio Dorcas HORSEBACK RIDING
(☎9687-1067; www.barriodorcasranch.com) Well-organised horseback riding along the beach for L800 per person. Rides on full-moon nights (L1000 per person) are also possible.

Sleeping

Budget choices are limited in West End. Some inexpensive places are linked to dive schools, so if you book a course you get a discounted room.

★Buena Onda HOSTEL $
(☎9770-0158; www.hbuenaonda.com; dm/d L200/300;) Owned and run by a welcoming, worldly Spanish traveler, this excellent new place is perfectly set up with stylish dorms that have lovely bamboo beds, good mattresses, lockers and giant art canvasses. The heart of the operation is a gorgeous open-plan kitchen-lounge with a pool table and sofas – a great place to socialize. There's a barbecue every Saturday, bikes for hire, 24-hour hot water, a sun terrace, activities like yoga and great travel info.

Chillies HOSTEL $
(☎2445-4003; www.nativesonsroatan.com/chillies.htm; Half Moon Bay; dm/d L200/440, cabins with/without bathroom L640/520;) Run by a sweet, welcoming local family (who also own Native Sons diving) this is an ever-popular choice, and for good reason. Budget rooms and dorms in the main building are crammed but kept clean and tidy. If you can shell out a bit more there's a choice of pretty

cabins at the rear of the property – ideal for couples. There are also guests' kitchens. Note that the dorms and budget rooms cannot be reserved ahead.

Georphi's Tropical Hideaway CABINS $
(☎2445-4205; www.roatangeorphis.com; dm L200-300, r with/without bathroom L700/500, cabins from L800; ❄@📶) Just behind Rudy's restaurant, this is a sprawling collection of hexagonal wooden cabins in shady grounds.

All the screened cabins are sturdy-but-basic structures – some with kitchen – and all have a private patio with hammocks. Shared kitchens are miniscule but functional, and there's 24-hour hot water. Unlimited (fairly fast) internet is a huge plus here.

Casa del Sol HOTEL $$
(☎2445-4218; www.casadelsolroatan.com; r L800-1000, studio with kitchen L1300; ❄@📶) Right by the entrance to West End, this place has a selection of rooms with Mexican-style colors and hand-painted porcelain bathroom sinks. The studios sleep four and have big bathtubs. Add air-con for L100 extra.

Posada Arco Iris HOTEL $$
(☎2445-4264; www.roatanposada.com; s/d/tr with fan L840/960/1080, apt from L1320; ❄@📶) A fine choice in a shady setting behind Half Moon Bay, this Argentine-owned place has very well-presented rooms and apartments with kitchens, all brightened up with weavings and tribal art.

For groups it can work out to be reasonably affordable: you'll pay more for air-con and an ocean view. Free kayak use for guests. Prices drop by 20% in low seaon.

Land's End Resort HOTEL $$
(☎9817-8994; www.landsendroatan.com; s/d incl breakfast & air-con L1040/1200, ocean view from L1600; ❄📶🏊) This lovely ocean-facing, upmarket hotel has a few cheaper rooms that lack ocean views but do represent decent value.

Check in and you'll get the run of the saltwater infinity pool, bar-restaurant and easy reef access, and still only be a 10-minute walk from the West End action.

Posada Las Orquideas HOTEL $$
(☎2445-4387; www.posadalasorquideas.com; s/d with fan L840/960, with kitchen L1311/1425; P❄@) Run by the same people who own Posada Arco Iris, with similar amenities, price structure and tasteful decor. This is more secluded and has a jetty that's exclusively for guests, jutting out over pretty Gibson Bay.

It's a five-minute walk north of Half Moon Bay.

Eating

Food in West End is pricey. Staying in a place with a kitchen will cut costs, especially if you're part of a group.

Good street-food options include **Keith's BBQ** (mains L100; ⏲7am-6pm Thu & Sun), which is beachside on Half Moon Bay, serving local-style barbecued meats and fish (including wahoo); **Tacos Al Pastor** (mains L100; ⏲6pm-midnight Mon-Thu, to 3am Fri & Sat) across from the Baptist church; and cheapest of all, the **baleada ladies** who serve up wheat-flour tortillas at L20 to L40 a hit at various spots along the main strip.

Earth Mama's CAFE, INTERNATIONAL $$
(www.earthmamasroatan.com; meals L120-170; ⏲8am-4pm Tue-Sun) Something of a secret garden, this secluded place offers up a menu of inventive dishes including savory crepes with smoked bacon for breakfast and lime shrimp with tomato and cilantro for lunch. There's an incredible smoothie list, too. Prices are steep (watch out for extra food, drink and sales taxes), but the setting is wonderful, with parrots often seen in the high trees overhead) and quality is high.

Creole's Rotisserie Chicken HONDURAN $$
(mains L100-190; ⏲3-10pm) A low-key island institution popular with long-term gringos and locals that offers excellent island-style roast chicken (a quarter is L120) plus shrimp and fish mains. Choose from eight different side dishes (including coconut rice and carrot salad) to accompany your main. Round it off with a slab of rumcake and you're set. Space is limited: you dine on an open-sided deck facing the beach.

Cindy's Place HONDURAN $$
(snacks/meals from L70/100; ⏲8am-5pm) Friendly and cheap, this is a good locally-owned place with a tempting menu and a prime location facing the sea on the main drag. The bacon-and-egg sandwich is a wildly popular grab 'n' go breakfast for divers.

Cannibal Café MEXICAN, INTERNATIONAL $$
(mains L70-230; ⏲10am-10:30pm Mon-Sat; ✎) Seriously large tacos are a specialty at this relaxed Mexican-food eatery. Everything on the menu can be made vegetarian. They also offer wine by the glass or bottle.

Rudy's HONDURAN, INTERNATIONAL **$$**
(www.roatangeorphis.com/restaurant; meals L80-230; ⏲6am-5pm Sun-Fri; 📶) Famous for its breakfasts, with lots of fruit, granola and pancake options on the menu. Also offers fine views of the waves washing in.

Lighthouse Restaurant SEAFOOD, INTERNATIONAL **$$$**
(mains L115-330; ⏲7:30am-10pm) A traditional wooden Caribbean structure that juts out into the bay, this restaurant is the perfect setting for a memorable meal with sea views on three sides. Seafood is the specialty, including grilled fish, shrimp and lobster. There are different, cheaper menus for breakfast and lunch.

Drinking & Entertainment

The West End drag is lined with bars dishing out live music or DJs. Foster's, which juts out into the bay, has by far the best location but its ownership changes all the time.

Blue Marlin BAR
(www.bluemarlinroatan.com; ⏲noon-midnight Mon-Thu, to 2am Fri & Sat, to 10pm Sun) Highly sociable and welcoming bar-restaurant with superb sunset views from the rear deck. Draws a good mix of locals, expats and visitors. There's live music on Fridays and karaoke (oh no!) on Thursdays. Happy hour (4pm to 6pm) features two-for-one cocktails.

Cafe Escondido CAFE, BAR
(⏲7:45am-3pm Thu-Sat & Mon, 7:45am-8pm Sun) Above West End Divers, this fine cafe-bar has a lovely, breezy upper deck with fine harbor views, mags for browsing and sofas for lounging. Sip an espresso during the day or slug on a beer and take it all in. There's live music (funk/reggae/acoustic) on Sunday evenings.

Sundowners BAR
(⏲11am-9:30pm) This open-sided beachfront bar is *the* expat hangout in Roatán, and there's always a crop of grizzly old characters hogging the bar stools from lunchtime onwards. Backpackers also gather here, despite the dated music, and filling bar grub is served.

Information

There are three ATMs in West End. Internet connections in cybercafes are hit-and-miss and prices are painful: try **Barefoot Charlie's** (opposite Foster's Bar; ⏲9am-9pm), which also has a book exchange. Thankfully, free wi-fi is becoming common. For medical attention, Anthony's Key Resort in Sandy Bay operates the best clinic in the area.

West Bay

Imagine a vision of the Caribbean: a paradise beach of white powdery sand fringed with coconut palms, and an azure sea filling the horizon. West Bay is that vision (though pay heed to the cruise ship warning following).

Two decades ago this was still a virgin beach, and backpackers reveled in the sheer unadulterated natural majesty of the scene. Times have changed, and a line of (pretty uninspiring) resort hotels lurk behind the palms and coastal pines. But if you head to the far (southern) end of the kilometer-long beach, close to the volcanic rocks where large

THE NEW PIRATES OF THE CARIBBEAN

Native to the Pacific and Southeast Asia, the voracious **lionfish** is a recent and very unwelcome intruder around the Bay Islands. Characterized by a threatening appearance of protruding venomous spines, these small fish (growing to an average 35cm in length) are originally thought to have escaped from aquariums in Florida and gradually spread south into Honduran waters (and beyond), gobbling up juvenile reef fish on the way. As they have no natural enemies in the western hemisphere, numbers have exploded.

Divers are now licensed to spear lionfish, with regular lionfish derbies held in Utila and Roatán. In 2012, a total of 1211 were killed in just two days. Staff at the Roatán Marine Park are also trying to encourage sharks and barracuda to eat lionfish by presenting them as a fast-food snack on the end of a speargun.

If you do encounter a lionfish while snorkeling or diving, keep your distance. Their poison is extremely painful, and can cause nausea and vomiting (and on very rare occasions, paralysis of the limbs and even death).

Do your bit by ordering lionfish on restaurant menus: it goes down very well as *ceviche*, in a kebab or as a deep-fried fillet.

black iguanas hide out, there are still few better places in Honduras to indulge in some serious beach time.

The exquisite **coral garden** offshore here has suffered in recent years with inexperienced snorkelers stomping over the coral, but there's still some excellent snorkeling.

However, it's essential to time your visit to West Bay carefully: when a **cruise ship** hits the island up to 5000 people can be disgorged on poor old West Bay, and sunbeds that normally go for L100 cost L500.

There are no beachside places that are geared to backpackers' wallets. Bring your own packed lunch, or try the little row of shops directly behind the beach where you'll find **Java Vine** (sandwiches from L110, wine from L105; ⏲7:30am-2pm Mon-Fri, 7:30am-2pm & 5-8pm Sat & Sun) for good sandwiches, cake, coffee and wine.

You can walk to West Bay from West End, but as there have been occasional attacks it's best to take a *colectivo* water taxi (per person each way L50, 10 minutes) which leave regularly all day.

Sandy Bay

About 4km northeast of West End, Sandy Bay is a quiet little community popular with expats. Here the **Carambola Botanical Gardens** (☎2445-3117; www.carambolagardens.com; L200; ⏲8am-5pm) covers a protected hillside, with several nature trails filled with orchids, spice plants, an 'iguana wall' and lots of wandering agoutis (rodent-like animals).

Ocean-facing **Tranquil Seas** (www.tranquilseas.com; Sandy Bay; meals L180-350 ; ⏲7:30am-10pm), owned by a British/Spanish couple, is well worth a look if you're in the area, with authentic Spanish 'tapas and tunes' on Tuesdays and excellent (though pricey) grub the rest of the week.

Coxen Hole

Coxen Hole is the largest town on Roatán, and home to government offices, banks and the post office. The airport is just outside town, but otherwise it's of little interest to travelers.

French Harbour

An important port, French Harbour has a large fishing, shrimp and lobster fleet, but otherwise there's little of interest other than the quirky appeal of **Arch's Iguana Farm** (☎2455-7743; www.archsiguanaandmarinepark.com; admission L160; ⏲9am-4pm) in French Cay, just outside of town. Less a farm than the house of a serious iguanaphile, everywhere you look you see iguanas, some 4000 in all – on the driveway, in the trees, under bushes, everywhere.

Oak Ridge

Oak Ridge is another ramshackle port town on Roatán's eastern side, this one hugging a protected harbor, with wooden houses on stilts all along the shore. Water taxis can take you on a tour through mangrove canals to **Jonesville**, a small town on a nearby bight. A one-hour boat tour costs L500 (for up to eight people).

Far East

East of Oak Ridge a dirt road snakes across a wildly beautiful landscape, with the forested spine of the island rising above some isolated bays, beaches and mangroves. There are turnoffs for the Garifuna settlement of **Punta Gorda** and old pirate stronghold of **Port Royal**, but the main attraction is stunning **Camp Bay Beach** on the north shore – a wonderful, virtually undeveloped strip of pale sand. Here you'll find **La Sirena** (Camp Bay; meals L150-300; ⏲11am-8pm), a lonely shack on stilts that serves up some of the best seafood on the island.

Continue a little further east and you enter the dense pines of the **Port Royal National Park**, where the **Lost Moose** (☎3342-6094; www.lostmooseguesthouse.com; Port Royal; d L1100; 📶), high on a hill overlooking the south coast, provides a superbly remote place to stay. There's wi-fi and excellent home-cooked food here.

Regular buses run as far as Oak Ridge, from where you'll have to make your own way further east.

ℹ Information

DANGERS & ANNOYANCES

Roatán is generally a pretty safe destination. However occasional assaults have occurred on the beachside walk between West End and West Bay. Coxen Hole can get sketchy after nightfall, and you should avoid hitching or waiting for taxis on the main roads outside of the towns after dark – robberies are not uncommon.

Getting There & Away

AIR

Roatán's **Aeropuerto Juan Ramón Galvez** (☎2445-1880) is a short distance east of Coxen Hole.

Isleña/TACA (☎2445-1088; www.flyislena.com), **Aerolineas Sosa** (☎2445-1154; www.aerolineassosa.com) and AeroCaribe (p402) have offices in Roatán's airport; they offer daily flights between Roatán and La Ceiba (L1020 to L1485 each way). **CM Airlines** (☎9522-5304; www.cmairlines.com) flies from Tegucigalpa (L1380 to L2014).

There are several international connections to Roatán: American Airlines flies to Miami; Delta to Atlanta; Taca to Miami; United to Houston and Newark. Seasonally, Sunwing operates charter flights from Montreal and Toronto in Canada. TAG flies from Guatemala City.

BOAT

Galaxy Wave (☎2445-2265; www.roatanferry.com; one-way normal/1st class L574/674; ⏲ticket office 5:30am-3:30pm) is a sleek, comfortable catarmaran that connects Roatán with La Ceiba. It sails from the Dixon Cove terminal at 7am and 2pm, returning from La Ceiba at 9:30am and 4:30pm. There is no direct service from Roatán to Utila.

Getting Around

BICYCLE

Captain Van's (☎2445-4076; www.captainvans.com; West End; ⏲8am-4pm) in West End rents bicycles for L200 per day.

BOAT

In West End, *colectivo* boats to West Bay (per person L50, last one from either end around 5pm) leave from the main strip. You have to wait until they fill up.

BUS

Roatán has two bus routes, both originating in Coxen Hole near the HB Warren supermarket. One route heads west linking Coxen Hole with Sandy Bay (L15, 20 minutes) and West End (L20, 30 minutes). The second route heads east from Coxen Hole past the airport, Dixon Cove, French Harbour and on to Oak Ridge (L40, one hour).

Buses run every 20 to 30 minutes from 6am to 5:30pm.

CAR & MOTORCYCLE

Captain Van's (p417) in West End rents scooters (L780 per day), motorcycles (L1100 to L1200) and cars (from L1100).

TAXI

Taxis operate around the island. As everywhere in Honduras, always clarify the price of the ride before you start. Many taxis are *colectivos* during the day charging very reasonable rates – from West End to the airport or ferry terminal is L45 to L55 per person. It's essential to establish that you want to travel *colectivo* if you are the first passenger.

GETTING TO WEST END

To/From the Airport

Private taxis charge L350 to West End. If you walk to the highway outside the airport, transport is cheaper: *colectivos* charge L35 to Coxen Hole then L20 to West End.

To/From Dixon Cove Pier

There are no direct *colectivos* between Dixon Cove and the West End. From the ferry walk 150m to the main road and catch a *colectivo* to Coxen Hole (L40), then another to West End (L20). Official taxis from the ferry terminal ask for L500 to West End.

Utila

POP 3100

Famous throughout the backpacking globe as *the* place to learn to dive in Latin America, Utila's reputation precedes it. A distinctly quirky little island, Utila has a unique heritage: British and African ancestry and live-and-direct cultural influences from Jamaica and the Central American mainland.

Stroll along the island's main street and you'll hear killer reggae basslines from dancehalls, see elderly English-looking couples enjoying the evening breeze from their rocking chairs, and witness some of the most competitive domino games this side of Kingston.

Utila is small – about 13km long and 5km wide – and flat except for one small hill. Virtually the entire population lives in one settlement, Utila Town, set on a curving bay. There are only two small beaches here, and a cluster of tiny cays off the island's southwest shore.

Today Utila earns its keep from its reef. There are over a dozen dive schools here, and dive sites dotted around the shoreline. Whale sharks are regularly spotted around the island and are a huge draw.

A little rough around the edges, Utila is no manicured Caribbean hideaway. For such a tiny island Utila has an annoying

Utila

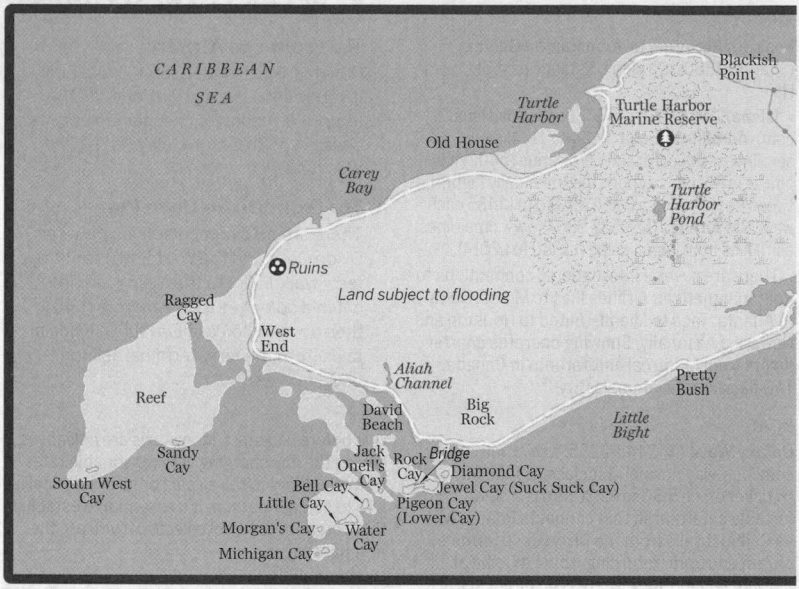

traffic problem: a constant tide of motorcycles, quadbikes, tuk-tuks and pickups curses the island's two streets. Trash is another huge issue.

Sights

Iguana Research & Breeding Station

WILDLIFE CENTER

(www.utila-iguana.de; admission L60; ⏲9:30am-noon & 1:30-5pm Mon-Fri) East of Mamey La, this center studies and protects the highly endangered Utila iguana (swamper) which lives in mangrove forest. Visitors get to see plenty of these fascinating, spiny-tailed critters. There are always volunteer opportunities available, and four tours of the island are offered (to bat caves and beyond – see Nature Tours, p420).

Utila Art Space

ARTS CENTER

(Cola de Mico Rd; ⏲2-6pm Mon-Fri) FREE Locals call this amazing Gaudiesque building (designed by the owner of the Treetanic bar) the 'museum', but it's actually a cultural center providing activities for islanders, particularly children. Visitors and volunteers are very welcome to drop by and help out with the art, sculpture and music workshops and there are occasional events.

Beaches & Cays

Most people come to Utila to dive, but if you're looking for sand, **Chepes Beach** is a pleasant, albeit small, cove, with palm trees, white sand and some beachside bars and snack joints. It's at the far western end of the main street. There's reasonable snorkelling offshore.

Several cays on Utila's southwest shore make good day trips. **Jewel Cay** and **Pigeon Cay**, connected by a small bridge, are home to a charming village and the best fish burgers in Honduras. Kayaks can be rented here. **Water Cay** is a beautiful, uninhabited little island dotted with coconut palms and good snorkeling off the southeastern corner. Utila's annual Sun Jam party is held here in August, when house and techno DJs from across the globe play to a crowd of 1500 in a full-on rave. The rest of the year it's blissfully tranquil.

Trips to the cays cost about L600 (round trip) to Jewel or Pigeon Cay, or around L1000 to Water Cay for up to four people.

Activities

Diving

Utila has some superb **dive sites**. The north side of the island offers spectacular wall diving, with bountiful pelagic life inlcuding

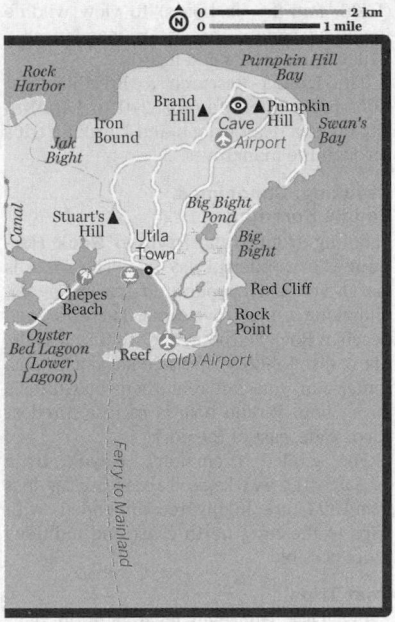

rays and sharks, and usually excellent visibility. It's great for drift and deep diving.

The southern sites are more suited to beginners, with shallower water, though the coral is in a less pristine condition. The seamount Black Hills often offers the most prolific marine life, including schools of horse-eyed jacks, while the wreck *Halliburton 211* is a deep-dive thrill.

Utila is rightly famous for the magnificent **whale sharks** that gather here all year (see boxed text, p420).

Most dive shops start a course every day or two, and many offer instruction in various languages. Prices hardly vary at all, so take a good look around and talk to the instructors before you decide to sign up. Safety and conservation are key concerns – stick with dive shops that are members of UDSEC (Utila Dive Safety & Environment Council). Most schools offer free or discounted accommodation if you take a course.

PADI open-water dive courses take three or four days and range in price from L5360 to L6180, including a L58-per-day reef fee, which goes toward the upkeep of the buoys and coral. A package of 10 fun dives is L5000.

Freediving courses and training are now available in Utila at Gunter's Dive Shop.

Utila Dive Centre DIVING
(UDC; ☎2425-3326; www.utiladivecentre.com) The largest diving operation in Utila, UDC is dead serious about safety and professionalism. Offers five dive boats, lots of tech-diving and rebreather courses and instruction. Students are separated from certified divers and accommodation at the Mango Inn (p421) is excellent.

Underwater Vision DIVING
(☎2425 3103; www.utilascubadiving.com; Main St E) Friendly and sociable dive school that offers professional tuition in English, Spanish, German, French, Swedish and Italian. Discounted accommodation is in great dorms (per person L100) in the classy Trudy's (p421) hotel

Gunter's Dive Shop DIVING
(☎2425-3350; www.ecomarineutila.com) The longest-established dive shop on the island, located a 10-minute walk west of the dock. Low-key and unpretentious, with small classes and solid PADI instruction. Apnea Total freediving courses are also offered (from L3400). The backpacker lodge across the street is free for students.

Alton's Dive Center DIVING
(☎2425-3704; www.diveinutila.com) Friendly and welcoming locally-owned PADI dive school with up-to-date gear and cheap accommodations right on the dock. Attracts a younger backpacker crowd. It's 300m east of the intersection.

Captain Morgan's Dive Centre DIVING
(☎2425-3349; www.divingutila.com) Right opposite the dock, Captain Morgan's trump card is that it offers more trips to the north coast than any other dive center. Accommodation is in a good new hotel, the Pirate's Bay Inn, a short walk away.

Bay Islands College of Diving DIVING
(BICD; ☎2425-3291; www.dive-utila.com) Busy, well-established shop with an onsite pool, free accommodations and gym use and small groups. The on-site recompression chamber is the only one on the island. Located west of the dock.

Cross Creek DIVING
(☎2425-3397; www.crosscreekutila.com; Main St E) Friendly multilingual staff and professional instruction. Rooms at the adjacent hotel are small and clean but get very hot in the sun (cabins are a better option).

Utila Water Sports DIVING
(☎2425-3264; www.utilawatersports.com) Small groups and new gear are key attractions at this professional school, located at the upmarket Palms Hotel. Most courses are SSI not PADI. East of the intersection.

Snorkeling

Utila offers exceptional snorkeling, though you'll have to make a bit of an effort to access a good reef. Many dive shops rent snorkel gear (per day around L150). Most dive schools allow snorkelers to tag along on dive boats for a small fee (around L100). Otherwise there's some snorkeling at **Chepes Beach**, at the western end of Main St, but the water is very shallow close to shore – pick your way carefully across the sandy bottom for access to deeper water.

Nature Tours

Few visitors make it much beyond Utila Town and the reefs offshore, but the swampy interior of the island is fascinating to explore.

Kanahua (☎8737-5334; www.kanahua.com) is an Utilan research and conservation organisation based in Pumpkin Hill. Visitors are welcome to join scientists on study tours (L500, four to six hours) to view wildlife including agouti, the critically-endangered Utilan iguana, bats and lizards.

The Iguana Research & Breeding Station (p418) offers tours (L240 to L400) to bat caves, a dead lagoon and kayaking trips through the mangroves.

Kayaking, Canoeing & Paddle Boarding

Paddling from Utila Town to **Rock Harbour** is a wonderful day trip. The route is via Oyster Bed Lagoon and Lower Lagoon and along a mangrove canal. There's a good beach at Rock Harbour, and it's very private. Many dive schools offer free kayaks for customers, or you can rent them at Gunter's Dive Shop. Paddle boards can be hired at Rico's Cafe, east of the dock.

For guided excursions, **Kayak Utila** (☎3389-4113; www.kayakutila.com; half-day trips from L800) are highly recommended, with trips to the cays, north coast and multiday tours possible.

Boat Trips

Many local fishermen have signs in their windows for boat tours; prices start at

THE BIGGEST FISH

The thrill of the chase is immense. You're in the open ocean, in a dive boat off the north coast of Utila, scanning the horizon. The first sign comes from the sky as seabirds plunge into the sea, picking off small baitfish from huge schools. Next up, 'boils' are created by the frenzied feeding of bonito (black-fin tuna), which also prey on baitfish. And then, with a bit of luck, there's a shout from the captain as a whale shark is spotted, gliding just below the surface, hoovering up great mouthfuls of fish- and plankton-rich seawater.

Whale sharks, the world's biggest fish, are found in Utilan waters year round, but most are seen between March and April and between June and September. They are usually only encountered in the open ocean, not on coral reefs. Currents converge around underwater seamounts, creating an upswell of plankton and baitfish on which the whale sharks feed.

If you're lucky enough to encounter a whale shark, a signal is given by the captain then it's into the big blue with your mask and snorkel. Often the shark surfaces to feed in a vertical position, an astonishing sight, its vast mouth agape sucking in tiny fish and seawater, which it filters through a gill-raker and then expels via five pairs of huge gill slits.

The sharks have a broad, flattened head, and the upperside of their body is covered in white spots and square checkerboard-style markings. By photographing the intricate patterns behind the sharks' gill slits, individuals can be recognized.

Utila's **Whale Shark & Oceanic Research Center** (☎2425-3760; www.wsorc.com; West Main St; ⏲9am-4pm Mon-Sat) FREE compiles a database of sightings, gives presentations and shows videos about this marine giant. Numbers are said to be stable around Utila, though the species is classified as 'vunerable' by the International Union for Conservation of Nature.

Records show whale sharks can reach around 12m (40 feet) in length and 21 tons. And yet speak to an Utilan fisherman over a bottle of rum, and you'll hear whispers about much larger sharks, including one they call Old Tom, said to be 20m or more (depending on who's buying the next bottle, of course).

RENT YOUR OWN ISLAND!

It is not every day you have the chance to step out your front door and let the sands of your own Caribbean island run between your toes. But that's exactly what you can do just off Utila for surprisingly little money. Choose between two different cays – both of which have cabins and facilities – as well as the essential crystal-clear waters lapping at the shore. If you do it in a group, it can work out to be reasonably cheap. **Sandy Cay** is available for L2600 a night (two-night minimum). The two-bedroom cabin there has solar power and a kitchen and can accommodate a maximum of 14 (extra mattresses are available). The slightly more luxurious and larger house on **Little Cay** goes for L2900 a night. It has four bedrooms, a generator and can sleep a maximum of 16. Contact **Barry Jackson** (☎2408-3100; cayosutila@hotmail.com) for bookings and info.

L1000 per boat. They can take you to Water Cay, to Rock Harbour via the mangrove canal, though the lagoon etc.

Sleeping

Expect to be greeted at the pier by a bunch of brochure-carrying touts giving you the hard sell.

Many dive shops, including Underwater Vision, Captain Morgan's Dive Centre and Utila Dive Center, have good, cheap (or free) accommodations if you sign up for a course.

★Rubi's Inn HOTEL $
(☎2425-3240; rubisinn@yahoo.com; Main St E; s/d/tr from L400/500/600; ❄📶) Owned by Tony and Rosa, a charming local couple, this small hotel has 12 spotless, spacious rooms with polished floors and fresh linen (those on the upper deck have sea vistas) in a wooden waterfront building. There's a private dock for swimming and sunbathing, hammocks for horizontal time and a guests' kitchen. Air-con is available but adds (a lot) to the price. Book ahead by phone.

Bayview Hotel GUESTHOUSE $
(☎2425-3114; bayviewinternet@yahoo.com; Main St W; d with fan L500-580, with air-con L900; ❄📶) Owned by a welcoming Utilan family who have relatives in the USA, this traditional guesthouse has an enviable waterfront location (with private dock for chilling) on the road to Chepes Beach. The fine-value rooms are plain but spacious, with firm mattresses – all have bathrooms with hot water; some have a fridge.

Hotel Bird of Paradise GUESTHOUSE $
(☎2425-3387; Cola de Mico; r with fan L300-400; 📶) Just steps from the dock, this good new place has eight tidy, clean rooms with either two or three beds, in an elegant little wooden Utilan house. Bathrooms are shared. You'll find friendly management (though little English was spoken when we dropped by) and a spacious guests' kitchen/living area in the basement. It could not be more centrally located.

Hotel Sea Side Inn HOTEL $
(☎2425-3150; www.hotelseaside.net; Main St W; d with bathroom L400; ❄📶) A 10-minute walk west of the dock, this well-maintained place has a tranquil location close to Chepes Beach. Rooms have two double beds and air-con, there's a guests' kitchen and you'll enjoy the sweeping Caribbean views from the shared balcony.

Tony's Place GUESTHOUSE $
(☎2425-3376; off Cola de Mico; s/d L130/200) Eight basic but clean rooms, stacked on two floors on the same site as the owner's house. Look out for the white-and-green building diagonally opposite the Mango Inn.

Trudy's HOTEL $$
(☎2425 3103; www.utilascubadiving.com; Main St E; dm L160, r/ste with air-con L700/1100; 📶) A delightful base, this locally owned, western-run partnership has an absolutely stunning oceanfront plot to enjoy with a beach volleyball court, docks for swimming and a cafe that makes for a relaxing and sociable stay. Dorms are small but perfectly formed with four beds, polished wooden floors and sea views from the communal balcony. The shared bathrooms have hot water. Book via Underwater Vision (p419); divers get discounted rates.

Mango Inn HOTEL $$
(☎2425-3326; www.mango-inn.com; Cola de Mico; dm L200, d/cabin from L1100/1500; ❄📶🏊) Linked to Utila Dive Center, this excellent place is straight up the hill from the pier.

Well-constructed timber accommodations, mostly midrange, are scattered around a garden shaded by mango trees, and the pool area and cafe are just great. Backpacker dorms (which cannot be booked ahead) are very decent indeed and shared bathrooms are nicer than average.

Eating

Utila Town has a good selection of eating options for such a small settlement. Several places to stay also have kitchens where you can cook. Minimarkets are dotted along Main St.

Bush's Supermarket SUPERMARKET $
(Main St E; 6:30am-6pm Mon-Sat, 6:30-10:30am Sun) Opens early so you can get your day's supplies before you hop on a dive boat. The attached cafeteria run by Carmela is famous for its cinnamon rolls.

Zanzibar HONDURAN, CAFE $
(Main St E; meals L50-110; 7am-4pm) Friendly, inexpensive local place that offers lots of breakfast choices including cornflakes, omelets, pancakes and filling *super baleadas* (L50). Look out for the pale green-and-white wooden building opposite Babalu bar.

Mango Café PIZZA, INTERNATIONAL $$
(Mango Inn, Cola de Mico; pizza L100-300; 6am-2pm & 5-10pm;) Owned by Andrea, an Italian who's lived in Utila since the 1990s, this place specializes in authentic thin-crust pizza from a purpose-built brick oven. There's always a daily special and the cafe also scores for salads, sandwiches, espresso coffee and drinks. If you eat here you're welcome to use the hotel pool and sunbeds.

Munchies INTERNATIONAL $$
(Main St W; mains L70-140; 7:30am-9pm;) Situated in a landmark Utilan building (the wooden structure was built in 1864) this restauant's front porch offers the best perch in town for people-watching. There's friendly service, good vegetarian options, big breakfasts and espresso coffee. At the rear you'll find an iguana garden (though the spiny-tailed ones do play hard to get).

Che Pancho CAFE $$
(Main St E; meals L60-120; 8am-6pm;) In the same premises as Utila's cinema, this small, efficiently-run cafe serves up an excellent selection of salads (try the *de la casa* for L75), Milanese meat dishes, hot dogs, omelettes and fine smoothies and juices.

El Picante MEXICAN $$
(Main St E; mains L125-280; 11am-10pm Sun-Thu, 11am-5pm Fri, 5-10pm Sat;) Now located in a stunning restored Caribbean building on the shorefront, this restaurant has ocean views from its elevated upper deck. Serves up all the Mexican classics you'd expect and want, and if you drop by on Mondays it's two-for-one margaritas.

Drinking & Nightlife

The party scene is strong in Utila, which at times feels like a cool college town revolving around a small diving university. Unfortunately most of the unique (if rough) local dancehalls have closed in recent years, but parties are still occassionally held at the Casino bar on Main St E.

★Babalu BAR
(Main St E; 5-11pm) Terrific waterfront bar that boasts, 'You won't find us in the Lonely Planet'. Er...our sincere apologies. It's owned by Dado, an Italian who's quite possibly the most urbane man on the planet. At the rear there's a hole in the terrace which becomes an 'aquarium' when spotlit at night, attracting myriad reef fish and crabs. The beer is cheap (L28) and music is cool (jazz, funk).

Skid Row BAR
(Main St W; 10am-11pm) Everything a hard-drinking bar should be, with a leaky tin roof, concrete floor, pool table, dart board, an excess of wizened characters and a long-suffering barman. Ladies are cordially invited to take up the 'Giufity Challenge' – downing shots of Garifuna herb-enhanced moonshine. Pub grub including Tex-Mex dishes and burgers also available.

Treetanic BAR
(Cola de Mico; 8pm-midnight, to 1am Wed & Fri) Owned by Neil, an eccentric American artist, this psychedelic mango treetop bar is somewhere you just have to see, even if the Gaudi-like decor is looking faintly ridiculous these days. Always draws a cast of local characters.

La Cueva BAR
(Main St W; 11am-midnight) Dive bar that packs in a curious mix of local characters, hard drinkers and international wandering classes. Try the banana-infused rum.

Tranquila Bar BAR
(Main St W; 4pm-1am Sun-Thu, to 3am Fri & Sat) Jutting out over the bay, this rather uninspiring bar is nevertheless a key evening

hangout – more for its prime location than the appalling music (hard rock, bland Top 40 pap), which everyone moans about.

Entertainment

Reef Video & Cinema CINEMA
(☎2425-3754; Main St E; ⏲9:30am-7pm Mon-Sat) Rents DVDs (L40), and shows different films each night at 7:30pm in a cute little upstairs 60-seater cinema (L50).

Shopping

Gunter's Driftwood Gallery GALLERY
(☎2425-3113; west of Cola de Mico; ⏲hours vary) A quirky workshop a couple of blocks inland, where the eponymous Gunter carves and displays sculptures (lots of sharks) made from driftwood. Turn left just before Mango Inn; you'll see the sign on your right. It is more likely to be open in the afternoon (except Sunday).

Information

The websites www.aboututila.com and www.utilaguide.com both offer good general info and news about Utila. There are two ATMs just up from the main dock: Bush's Supermarket will do a cash advance (around 7% fee) if the ATMs are not functioning. You'll find the post office and immigration right by the public dock. Utila has numerous internet centers, and free (though pedestrian) wi-fi is now common.

Captain Morgan's Dive Centre (☎2425-3349; www.divingutila.com; Main St; ⏲8am-7pm) Across from the pier, Captain Morgan's offers straightforward tourist information and advice, and you can even leave your backpack there while you look for a hotel.

Caye Caulker Cyber Café (Main St E; per hr L40; ⏲8am-8pm) Low-cost connections and cheap international calls.

Morgan's Travel (☎2425-3161; www.utilamorgans travel.com; ⏲8am-noon & 2-5:30pm Mon-Sat) Arranges plane tickets off the island and taxis to and from the airport. Next to the pier.

Police (☎2425-3145)

Utila Community Clinic (☎2425-3137; Main St W; ⏲10am-3:30pm Mon-Fri) Run by Dr John McVay, a well-regarded US doctor. There's also a pharmacy onsite.

Getting There & Away

AIR

With the ferry only taking an hour, few travelers bother with flights these days. Nevertheless two airlines connect Utila and La Ceiba: **Aerolíneas Sosa** (☎2452-3161; www.aerolineassosa.com) flies to Utila from La Ceiba three times weekly; CM Airlines (p417) only flies on Saturdays. Flights cost around L1100 and take about 15 minutes.

BOAT

The **Utila Princess II** (☎2425-3390; ⏲ticket office 8-11am & 2-4:30pm), an ugly converted cargo boat, runs from La Ceiba to Utila at 9:30am and 4pm. Crossings take one hour. The same boat returns from Utila to La Ceiba at 6:20am and 2pm. Tickets are L472 to Utila and L448 to La Ceiba; arrive half an hour in advance.

There are no scheduled boat links between Utila and Roatán.

Getting Around

You can can walk the entirety of Utila's Main St in about 20 minutes.

Bikes are available from many places by the hour/day/week for L25/100/500.

LA MOSKITIA

La Moskitia, that vast part of Honduras you see on maps with very few roads, is one of the region's last frontiers of untamed wilderness. Huge expanses are virtually untouched jungle, and when combined with magnificent wetland and savannah habitats it's no wonder Moskitia is often dubbed Central America's Amazon. In many ways the description is apt, for both are under threat from loggers, cattle ranchers and land-hungry *campesinos* (farmers)

Manatees, tapirs and jaguars all still thrive here – they have learnt to be circumspect around man, and they may not be easy to spot. Crocodiles can be seen in the waters, while the birdlife including macaws and fish eagles is outstanding.

Culturally, La Moskitia is unique. Historically, its people allied themselves with the British against the Spanish, and many people today still claim an English heritage. Tegucigalpa only really started to attempt to control the region from the 1950s. There are five different ethnic groups, with isolated pockets of Pech and Tawahka in the interior, as well as Mískito, Garifuna and ladino populations.

A visit to the region is not for the faint-hearted. Access is tough (unless you fly in) and conditions are rustic at best. Sadly, drug smugglers are here in force and there's a noticeably dodgy vibe in some towns.

Sensibly, many travelers visit La Moskitia as part of a tour. La Moskitia's isolation is such that prices are noticeably higher than elsewhere – expect to up your normal budget considerably if you're traveling independently.

And yet when you're gliding down a pristine jungle-lined river in a dugout canoe, past thatch-and-mud houses with squabbling toucans overhead and crocs in the shallows, there's simply nowhere else like it in Honduras.

Tours

Several travel companies offer excellent tours of La Moskitia, providing an easier (and not necessarily much more expensive) taste of the terrain. Other recommended operators include Basecamp Tours (p380) in Copán Ruinas; **Omega Tours** (☎9631-0295; www.omegatours.info; Omega Jungle Lodge, Calle a Yaruca Km 9) in La Ceiba.

La Moskitia Ecoaventuras ADVENTURE TOUR (☎2441-3279; www.lamoskitia.hn; Colonia El Toronjal, La Ceiba) This company has decades of experience in La Moskitia, and owner Jorge Carranza is a native of the region. They offer a five-day trip to Brus Laguna and Las Marias (US$240 excluding airfares) or a 10-day Río Plátano rafting expedition (US$1467), which is a serious adventure. Prices are based on a minimum of four people.

Laguna de Ibans

The small traditional coastal communities around Laguna de Ibans are likely to be your first overnight stop if you come via the overland route. Pick your base from a cluster of small settlements – **Cocobila**, **Raista** and **Belén** – which all have good budget accommodation and are a short walk apart.

The quiet Mískito village of **Raista** is possibly the nicest of the three, with wooden houses on stilts and the excellent, welcoming **Raista Eco Lodge** (☎8926-5635, 2433-8220; per person L200) which has rustic but comfortable rooms, mosquito nets and good home-cooking (meals around L80). There are beach walks (though trash spoils the scene) and wildlife-spotting hikes can be arranged to look for nesting sea turtles and crocs in the lagoon (no swimming here folks!). If you get the chance, take in **Plaplaya**, a lovely traditional Garifuna village a short boat ride from Raista, where giant leatherback sea turtles nest and are released by volunteers between April and July.

There's an airstrip in Belén, with nine weekly AeroCaribe (p437) flights to/from Trujillo (L2165). *Colectivo* boats to Batalla (L250, two hours), for overland connections to Trujillo, stop in all three villages at ungodly times, betwen 3am and 3:30am. Heading inland, you can arrange transport to Las Marías (round trip L4500, five to six hours). Heading west, an early-morning *colectivo* boat takes passengers to Palacios in time to catch the first speedboat to Iriona.

Reserva de la Biosfera del Río Plátano

The Río Plátano Biosphere Reserve is a magnificent nature reserve, declared a World Heritage Site in 1980. A vast unspoiled, untamed wilderness, it is home to extraordinary animal life, including a number of endangered species. The best time of year to visit is from November to July; the best time for seeing birds is during February and March, when many migratory birds are here.

One of the best places to organize tours is in **Las Marías**, a village in the heart of the reserve with around 100 Mískito and Pech families. There is no running water or electricity here, though there are a few generators. Several basic lodgings will also cook you simple meals: clean, airy **Hospedaje Doña Justa** (☎9966-9234; r without bathroom per person L100, meals L50) is one good option in the center of town.

There are short trails around the village good for birding, but for longer trips it's essential to hire a guide and arrange camping equipment and food. There's a coordinating fee per group of L100, head guides cost L250 to L300 a day, and secondary guides L180. Neither prices nor number of guides per trip are negotiable. Guides are rotated by the coordinating guide, and vary considerably; none speak English. Bookings are difficult to organize in advance and not really necessary. Just turn up and you will be assigned a guide.

Popular short tours include a twilight crocodile-spotting walk (L800 for two people) and a daytrip by boat to see some petroglyphs. Arduous longer trips into primary rainforest include a two-day hike up wildlife-rich **Cerro Baltimore** and a three-day expedition to the summit of **Pico Dama** (840m), both of which require several guides.

The bad news is that there are no scheduled *colectivos* to Las Marías, but if you hang around for a few days you'll probably get lucky, expect to pay L700 per person (one-way). A round-trip *expreso* from Raista costs around L4500 for up to three people (five to six hours); the boatman will wait in Las Marías for two nights for the return leg. It's also possible to set up dug-out canoe trips and hikes (speak to Alberto Tinglas in Cocobila) between the coast and Las Marías.

Palacios

Palacios is a tense, rather lawless place known as a drug-running stronghold. If you miss a boat connection you might get stuck here. If so, head to the vaguely colonial-style **Hotel Moskitia** (☎9996-5648; www.hotelmoskitia.com; r L500) which offers modern rooms with lake-views and balconies.

Colectivo canoes will run you across from Batalla (L60, five minutes).

Brus Laguna

POP 7100

Beside the lagoon of the same name, Brus Laguna is an accessible entry point to La Moskitia, as it has an airport. You can head to Raista or even straight to Las Marías from here. For a bed, check out **Villa Biosfera** (☎9919-9925; s/d without bathroom L180/350), a stilted wooden cabin on the lagoon where the fan-cooled rooms have mosquito nets. There's a couple of internet places here, but no bank. Note that there's now a large US DEA and Honduran military presence in the area due to increased narco activities.

AeroCaribe (p437) connects La Ceiba with Brus Laguna (L2267) nine times a week. From Batalla, direct *colectivos* head to Brus Laguna between 3pm and 5pm (L400, four hours).

Puerto Lempira & Around

POP 8900

Despite being not much more than an overgrown village, **Puerto Lempira** is the largest town in Moskitia. Situated on the inland side of the Laguna de Caratasca, it's not that interesting, though it has good air connections, the only ATM in Moskitia, a hospital and cybercafe. Good sleeping options include the **Backpackers Lodge** (☎9912-7991; hemarmat@yahoo.com; opposite Municipalidad; per person L200) where English-speaking owner Junior is a well-informed host and offers budget-friendly tours and rents bikes. **Hotel Yu Baiwan** (☎2433-6348, 9568-2142; s/d L550/650; ❄) is a more pricey alternative.

Possible daytrips from Puerto Lempira include the serene Mískito village of **Mistruk**, 18km south of town on the banks of the Laguna de Tansing, which can be reached on a bike.

Flights head to/from La Ceiba several times a week (for details see Getting There & Away, below). It's also possible to travel overland (and water) between Brus Laguna and Puerto Lempira but you'll be crossing one of the Americas' principal cocaine smuggling routes. We don't recommend you try.

Foreigners are not permitted to enter Nicaragua at the nearby border post of Leimus.

Information

DANGERS & ANNOYANCES

This is wild country and needs to be treated with respect. Never venture into the rainforest without a guide. Trails are faint and overgrown, and hikers can quickly become hopelessly lost.

Malaria is present: bring insect repellent and consider antimalarial pills. A water purification kit (a filter or iodine tablets) is also a good idea. Most lodging options are equipped with mosquito nets.

Avoid crossing the bigger lagoons late in the day – afternoon winds can create large waves. From November to March, sudden squalls wreak havoc any time of day.

La Moskitia is one of Central America's main drug-running corridors and both the Honduran military and US DEA are here in force. The chances of it affecting you are slim, but ask around to minimize your risk of being caught in the crossfire.

Getting There & Away

AIR

All flights to La Moskitia depart from La Ceiba but schedules changes regularly and can be cancelled at short notice. **AeroCaribe** (p437) hops between La Ceiba and Palacios, Belén, Brus Laguna and Puerto Lempira (L2200) nine times a week. **Aerolineas Sosa** (☎2433-6558; www.aerolineasosa.com; ⏲8:30am-5:30pm Mon-Fri, to noon Sat & Sun) flies to Puerto Lempira (L2600).

OVERLAND

Going overland via the north coast is a rough and complex (but inexpensive) route into La Moskitia. However you should be aware that this remote route is used by drug-smugglers and you'll encounter numerous military road blocks on the way, particularly around Tocoa.

You'll need an early start from La Ceiba to make it to Raista in one day. Take a Trujillo bus (6am, or preferably earlier) to Tocoa (L95, 2½ hours), from where overloaded *pailas* (pickups) leave between 9am and 10am for Batalla (L550, four to six hours), a small Garifuna town. From Batalla *colectivo* boats head to Raista (L200, two hours). Depending on weather and road conditions, this should get you into Belén and Raista before dark. Coming from Trujillo, get a La Ceiba bus and change in Tocoa.

To return, take the 3am to 4am boat from Belén, Raista or Cocobila to Batalla (L250, two hours), for a 5am to 6am truck to Tocoa. Tocoa has bus connections to both La Ceiba and Trujillo (roughly hourly until 4pm).

Getting Around

Different seasons present different challenges in terms of getting around La Moskitia. The rainy reason (November to January) is the most difficult.

AeroCaribe (p437) hops between Palacios, Belén, Brus Laguna and Puerto Lempira nine times a week; flights cost L1000 to L1400 one-way.

Most transportation in Moskitia is by **boat**. A *cayuco* is a motorized boat used for long trips, either as an *expreso* (charter) or a cheaper *colectivo*. Upriver, the most common boat is a *pipantes*, a dug-out canoe.

Irregular **pickups** ply the single dirt road along the Laguna de Ibans passing through Cocobila, Raista and Belén.

SOUTHERN HONDURAS

Honduras touches the Pacific with a 124km coastline on the Golfo de Fonseca. This perpetually (often infernally) hot coastal plain is dominated by agribusinesses: sugarcane, African Palm plantations and shrimp farms.

It's a much traveled region (the Interamericana crosses through Honduras here), though there's little of interest to travelers – except perhaps Isla de Tigre, which has some charm. If you're only in transit, it's less than three hours by bus between the borders of El Salvador and Nicaragua. Heading east to Nicaragua you're sure to pass through the large city and transport hub of **Choluteca**, which has little to detain you, though there are plentiful banks and facilities.

Isla El Tigre

South of the important junction of Jícaro Galán on the Interamericana it's a short hop to the little port of Coyolito, from where boats (L20, every 15 minutes, 15 minutes) head to the inactive volcanic island of Isla El Tigre. Its main town is **Amapala**, a scruffy fishing village with picturesque crumbling clapboard architecture and a **tourist office** (☎2795-8555; ⏲8am-5pm Mon-Fri, 8am-noon Sat) on the dock with a list of accommodations. There are few budget options, but on lovely Playa Grande, 4km south of Amapala, the good-value **Hotel Y Restaurante Dignita** (☎2795-8707; s/d L500/650) has a great seafood restaurant. Black-sand **Playa Negra** in the north of the island is arguably the island's best beach. Minibuses (L10) from Amapala circuit half-way around the island past beaches or you can grab a *mototaxi*.

UNDERSTAND HONDURAS

Honduras Today

The original banana republic, Honduras has been ignored or kicked about for most of its existence. But in 2012 the nation finally became newsworthy and Hondurans joked, using gallows humor, that at last they had won something – the United Nations announced the country had become the murder-rate capital of the world. Not surprisingly, crime levels and the deeply interconnected issues of gang and drug cartel activity have grown to dominate the country's collective consciousness.

Statistics may lie, but Honduras' crime figures ain't great whichever way you spin them. In 2012 there were 91.6 homicides per 100,000 inhabitants (more than four times the level in Mexico and more than 20 times the rate in the USA). Most of the killings are barely investigated, and the impunity rate is 90%.

But it's not only the day-to-day threat of attack or robbery that Hondurans have to consider as they go shopping, drive a car or board a bus. Extortion or 'war taxing' practised by gangs in poor barrios hikes up costs for the whole nation: street vendors have to pay to pitch a stall; transport companies have to pay so their buses can pass through gang-controlled territory. Sky-high crime rates curb inward investment, so prospective employers avoid Honduras because of huge security costs. Armed guards stand in front of just about everything. Tourism suffers,

MEL & PEPE

In many ways, Honduras appears to be perpetually teetering on the brink. But then life has always been a struggle for Hondurans, and crises seem to be part of the nation's DNA. In 2009 President Manuel 'Mel' Zelaya (a cowboy-hat-toting rancher from Olancho) was ousted in a dramatic twilight raid on his home, and forcefully expatriated – an action dubbed a military coup by the international media. However, as Zelaya was attempting to rewrite the constitution (most observers saw this as a thinly-veiled attempt to extend his term of office) and the military were acting on orders issued by the Supreme Court, perhaps it was more an eviction of an unruly tenant than a power-grab by the generals. Democratic elections duly followed, and Nationalist Party candidate Porfirio 'Pepe' Lobo, a center-right conservative with strong backing from the nation's oligarchy, was voted in. Another rancher from Olancho, Pepe left his *sombrero* back on the farm, but the chaos continued.

Lobo's presidency saw the country rack up foreign debts of over US$5 billion while ongoing financial turmoil left state workers, including teachers and the military, unpaid. Doctors protested they had insufficient medicines to do their work. And a new crisis blew up in December 2012 when Congress voted to sack four Supreme Court justices who had repeatedly found new laws to be unconstitutional. Their replacements were more cooperative. Meanwhile, the USA's Drug Enforcement Agency estimated that 25 to 30 tonnes of cocaine blew through Honduras each month as the country became *the* key transit country in the region.

The next elections will be contested in November 2013.

and many hoteliers in the Bay Islands wonder if they'll ever see a high season again. Even the Peace Corps, whose largest mission used to be in Honduras, pulled out in 2012. The country's image has hit rock bottom.

Given the status quo, many have voted with their feet and sought a new life in the USA or elsewhere. An estimated million Hondurans live north of the border; according to *La Prensa* newspaper their remittances for 2012 were some US$3.2 billion, or about 18% of the Honduran economy. There's barely a family in the whole nation which does not have a member in *El Norte*.

And yet somehow the nation soldiers on. Strong exports of coffee, clothing, bananas and sugar helped the economy grow by a respectable 3.3% in 2012. Coffee is a particular success story with production (mainly of high-quality arabica beans) surging ahead; Honduras became the world's fourth biggest exporter by January 2013 according to International Coffee Organization figures. The controversial *maquila* (mainly garment-assembly) sector continued to expand, too: a vast swathe of factories now defines the outskirts of San Pedro Sula and other northern towns, employing 125,000 people. However critics argue that little income flows back into the nation because they operate in special tax-free zones.

Deeply troubled though the nation may be, Honduras is a survivor.

Violence, Gangs & Drugs

Malcolm McLaren, one-time manager of the Sex Pistols, said, 'Any publicity is good publicity'. But he probably never traveled to Honduras – a 'failed state' according to the *Economist* – or dropped by San Pedro Sula, which has the highest murder rate in the world according to the UN's homicide statistics. Imagine working for the Honduras tourist board...

Honduras' problems are huge. It has long been an impoverished country and its neighborhood is a troubled one. As Central America has become the key transit region for cocaine, Honduras' remote regions and long Caribbean coastline have been targeted by drug traffickers. US DEA officials estimate that 79% of all illicit cocaine flights from South America land in Honduras, from where it's a short hop to the US. Go-fast boats laden with coke have transformed the economy of La Moskitia region from lobster-diving to drug-shipping.

An unholy alliance of street gangs and Mexican drug cartels has resulted in spiralling rates of violence in Honduras, with a systemically corrupt police force said to be deeply involved. Honduras' ex-Security

Minister Oscar Alvárez stated publically in 2011 that police were essentially acting as air traffic controlers for drug flights.

From a traveler's perspective, all this violence is actually quite compartmentalized, and you're extremely unlikely to see it. Honduran cities don't appear to be war zones – they look very like any other Central American or Mexican city. You will see a lot of armed guards on the streets, and *barrios seguros* (gated communities) are spreading through the suburbs, but people still walk the downtown districts in the daytime (if less so after dark). The gangs and drug smugglers have no real interest in tourists, but it's essential to minimize your chances of being a victim of crime, just as you would anywhere in the world. Pay particular attention to the Safe Travel advice on p435.

History

Honduras has had a rough deal over the centuries. Things got off to a sparkling start when the Maya civilization emerged in Copán, but then the Spaniards came and trampled all over the territory. Marauding pirates added to the mix in the 17th century.

Independence brought a brief respite, but for virtually the entire 20th century Honduras was dominated by distant, powerful forces as giant US fruit companies and later the US military set up shop in the nation.

Early History

The earliest humans are thought to have arrived in Honduras around 9000BC, though almost nothing is known about their lives other than that they were hunter-gatherers. By around 2000BC there were settlements cropping up across the land.

It was over millennia more before the Maya site of Copán Ruinas began to flourish, as sculptors carved stone stelae unequalled in the Maya world and mathematicians and astronomers calculated uncannily accurate calendars and planetary movements. For hundreds of years, a good slice of the Maya Classic Period (AD 250–900), the city dominated the region culturally, until its decline in the 9th century AD.

Spanish Colonization

Columbus, on his fourth and final voyage, landed near present-day Trujillo in 1502, naming the place Honduras ('depths' in Spanish) for the deep waters off the north coast.

He established a town (Trujillo), Honduras' first capital in 1525, but the gleam of silver from the interior soon caught the conquistadors' eye: in 1537 Comayagua, midway between the Pacific and Caribbean coasts, became their new capital.

Indigenous people put up fierce resistance to the invasion, although this was weakened by their vulnerability to European-introduced diseases. The sternest resistance was from Lempira (chief of the Lenca tribe and considered a national hero), who led a force of 30,000 against the Spanish, before he was assassinated. By 1539 resistance was largely crushed.

British Influence

By the beginning of the 17th century, Spanish colonists were coming under regular attack from rival imperial forces – especially the British. Merchants from Britain, attracted by the mahogany and hardwoods of the Honduran Caribbean coast, established settlements there and on the Bay Islands.

Britain eventually ceded control of the Caribbean coast to the Spanish, but continued to influence the region. In 1797, slaves rebelled on the Caribbean island of St Vincent. The British shipped thousands to the island of Roatán, where they mixed with indigenous people. Eventually these people, the Garifuna, crossed to the mainland and founded settlements along the coast.

Independence

After gaining its independence from Spain in 1821, Honduras was briefly part of independent Mexico and then a member of the Central American Federation. The Honduran liberal hero General Francisco Morazán was elected president in 1830. The union was short-lived, however, and Honduras declared itself a separate independent nation in 1838.

Liberal and conservative factions wrestled and power alternated between civilian governments and military regimes, such that the country's constitution would be rewritten 17 times between 1821 and 1982. Honduras has also experienced literally hundreds of coups, rebellions and power seizures since achieving independence.

The 'Banana Republic'

Around the end of the 19th century, US traders marveled at the rapid growth of bananas on the fertile north coast (just a short sail from southern USA). US entrepreneurs bought land for growing bananas and three companies, including the Standard (later United Fruit) company, bought up huge chunks of land.

Bananas provided 11% of Honduras' exports in 1892, 42% in 1903 and 66% in 1913. The success of the industry made the banana companies extremely powerful within Honduras, with policy and politicians controlled by their interests.

20th-Century Politics

The USA increasingly came to influence Honduran affairs. In 1911 and 1912, US marines were dispatched to the nation to 'protect US investments.'

A two-month strike in 1954 – in which as many as 25,000 banana workers and sympathizers participated – remains a seminal moment in Honduran labor history. Unions were recognized, and workers gained rights that were unheard of in neighboring Central American countries.

From the late 1950s the military steadily began to take a much more important role in the country's governance, via coups and political pressure. Long periods of military rule alternated with civilian presidents throughout the 1960s and 1970s. This cycle was finally ended with the 1981 democratic presidential elections.

The 1980s

During the 1980s Honduras was surrounded by revolutions and conflict. In July 1979 the revolutionary Sandinista movement in Nicaragua overthrew the Somoza dictatorship, and Somoza's national guardsmen fled into Honduras. Civil war broke out in El Salvador in 1980 and internal conflict worsened in Guatemala.

Honduras became the focus of US policy and strategic operations in the region, backed up by General Gustavo Álvarez, who supported an increasing US military presence. Under Ronald Reagan huge sums of money and thousands of US troops were funneled into Honduras and refugee camps of Nicaraguans in Honduras were used as bases for a US-sponsored covert war against the Nicaraguan Sandinista government, known as the Contra War.

Public alarm grew as hundreds of leftists 'disappeared' inside Honduras and the US militarization of Honduras ramped up. By 1984 General Álvarez was exiled by fellow officers, and the Honduran government suspended US training of the Salvadoran military within its borders.

In Washington, the Reagan administration was rocked by revelations it had illegally used money from arms sales to Iran to support anti-Sandinista Contras. Large demonstrations followed in Tegucigalpa, and in

THE FOOTBALL WAR

Legendary football manager Bill Shankly once said, 'Some people believe football is a matter of life and death...it is much more important than that.' Even Mr Shankly might have balked at Honduras' and El Salvador's sporting rivalry, which spilled off the pitch and onto the battlefield in the 1969 Guerra de Fútbol – the notorious Football (Soccer) War.

Tensions did not suddenly break out on the stadium terraces. In the 1950s and 1960s, a flagging economy forced 300,000 Salvadorans to seek better conditions in Honduras. However, the Honduran economy was itself ailing, and Salvadorans began to be targeted as scapegoats. In June 1969, Honduran authorities started throwing Salvadoran immigrants out of the country. A stream of Salvadoran refugees followed, alleging Honduran brutality.

In the same month, the two countries were playing World Cup qualifying matches against each other. At the San Salvador game, Salvadorans attacked Honduran fans, defiling the Honduran flag and mocking the anthem. Across the border, angry Hondurans then turned on Salvadoran immigrants. Tempers frayed further and the El Salvador army invaded Honduran territory on July 14, capturing Nueva Ocotepeque. Honduras retaliated with air strikes. A ceasefire was called after only six days, but around 2000 Hondurans lost their lives, while thousands of Salvadorans fled home.

November 1988 the government refused to sign a new military agreement with the USA. With the election of Violeta Chamorro as president of Nicaragua in 1990, the Contra War ended.

Modern Currents & 'Coups'

Through the presidential administrations of Rafael Leonardo Callejas Romero (1990–94) and Carlos Roberto Reina Idiaquez (1994–98), Honduras struggled economically. Then in 1998 Honduras was dealt a devastating blow as Hurricane Mitch killed thousands and caused widespread devastation (estimated at US$3 billion), setting the economy back years.

In 2001, Ricardo Maduro from the National Party was elected president, largely on the back of his promises to reduce crime. But despite pouring huge resources into the problem, crime levels rose inexorably. In January 2006, a cowboy-hat-wearing rancher from Olancho, José Manuel Zelaya Rosales was elected president. He aligned himself closely with other Latin American left-wing leaders (such as Hugo Chávez) but in 2009 his plan to rewrite the constitution and therefore make himself eligible for a second term, provoked a crisis. The Supreme Court ordered Zelaya be removed from office and despite global indignation (many countries viewed his explusion as a coup) he was dispatched to exile in the Dominican Republic.

Democratic elections in November 2009 saw National Party member Porfirio 'Pepe' Lobo confirmed as president.

The Culture

The National Psyche

Generalizations don't – and shouldn't – come easily for a country with such wide-ranging cultures. The *ladino* (of mixed indigenous and European parentage) businessman will have a different outlook to the Garifuna fisherman, who may not have much in common with a Lencan subsistence farmer. However, Hondurans are less likely to reach a collective flashpoint than their neighbors, at least historically.

It's this easy-going nature which probably defines the national psyche more than anything else. Other Central Americans, particularly those from El Salvador, tend to view it as laziness, which is a tad harsh. For Western visitors this lack of a sense of urgency can be occasionally frustrating, but it is important to remember that attitudes towards service are very different to, say, the USA. For Hondurans, a steady, laid-back demeanour is the way things are done. A sense of reserve is often maintained – few Hondurans are in-your-face loud and assertive.

Lifestyle

Lifestyles in Honduras vary as widely as the country's shockingly unequal social spectrum. The fortunate economic elite often lead an Americanized lifestyle, driving SUVs and shopping in air-conditioned malls. Far more commonly, Hondurans are forced to scratch out a living. Poverty is perhaps at its most shocking in poor urban barrios, where there's a constant threat of violence.

Lack of opportunities have forced many to seek jobs in the USA, where there are an estimated one million Hondurans, over 60% of them undocumented.

Hondurans are hugely family-oriented. They often have a wider family network than many Europeans or North Americans are used to – aunts, uncles, grandparents, cousins and even more distant relatives often play a significant role in family life.

Another attitude in Honduran society is machismo. Women are often still treated as second-class citizens. Women's wages are much lower (women can expect to earn a third of the average male wage, according to a UN Development Program report) and reported levels of domestic abuse are disturbing.

The same macho tendencies mean that gay culture is very much in the closet and the country is one of the most dangerous places in the world to be homosexual. Gay Activist José Pepe Palacios estimates there have been at least 89 LGBT people murdered in Honduras, including many gay rights advocates, since the 2009 coup.

People

Around 90% of Hondurans are *mestizo,* with a mixture of Spanish, indigenous and African heritage.

One of the most ethnically diverse regions of Honduras is La Moskitia, home to Mískito and Pech people as well as tiny numbers of

READING UP

Want more background? Leaf your way through the following books:

➡ *Enrique's Journey* by Sonia Nazario. A runaway from Tegucigalpa searches for his mother in the USA.

➡ *Bananas: How the United Fruit Company Shaped the World* by Peter Chapman. Great insight on the banana giant's impact on Central America.

➡ *The Mosquito Coast* by Paul Theroux. A vivid fictional account of life in the jungle.

➡ *Honduras: A Country Guide* by Tom Barry and Kent Norsworthy. Solid, if dated, historical background.

➡ *The United States, Honduras, and the Crisis in Central America* by Donald E Schulz and Deborah Sundloff Schulz. Discusses the role of the US in Central America during the region's tumultuous civil wars.

* *Prisión Verde* by Ramón Amaya-Amador. Life on a banana plantation by a political writer.

➡ *El Humano y la Diosa* (The Human and the Goddess), *Los Barcos* and *The Big Banana* by Roberto Quesada. One of Honduras' leading novelists.

➡ Juan Ramón Molina (1875–1908) – perhaps the country's best-loved poet.

Tawahka (less than 3000) around the Río Patuca.

Over 50,000 Garinagu (Afro-Carib Garifuna people) live on Honduras' north coast, spread between La Moskitia and the Guatemalan border. Thousands of other people with African ancestry also live on the north coast and Bay Islands.

The indigenous Tolupanes (also called Jicaque or Xicaque) live in small villages dotting the departments of Yoro and Francisco Morazán. Some 38,000 Ch'orti' Maya are found around Copán Ruinas, while the large Lenca group (as many as 300,000) live in southwestern Honduras.

Many of Honduras' elite are of white (Spanish and European) stock, but there are also small numbers in the Bay Islands who trace their (distant) routes back to England.

Honduras also has perhaps 100,000 people of Arab descent, mainly Catholic and Orthodox Christians originally from Palestine and the Levant.

Religion

Honduras has traditionally been an overwhelmingly Roman Catholic country, but this has changed considerably in the last few decades with the rise of the evangelical movement. Exact figures are unreliable but a CID-Gallup poll in 2007 reported that 47% identified themselves as Roman Catholic and 36% as evangelical Protestant.

Unlike neighboring Guatemala, few indigenous customs or beliefs have been integrated into Christian worship. There are also small numbers of Orthodox Christians, Jews and Muslims. Tegucigalpa and San Pedro Sula both have synagogues and mosques.

Arts

Honduras has a small but exciting contemporary arts scene and an intriguing artistic heritage.

Musician/politician Aurelio Martínez (he was a deputy in Honduras' Congress for four years) is the star of the *punta* (traditional Garifuna music and dance) scene, his *Garifuna Soul* and *Laru Beya* albums receiving rave reviews all over the world.

Emerging new artists include bands like Simón (www.bandasimon.com) fusing folk, punk and latin sounds; and Ytterbium (www.ytterbium.bandcamp.com) combining grunge and alt-rock influences. Fernando Rey is a very talented young singer-songwriter. Honduras also contributes significantly to the reggaetón movement, with artists like Raggamofin Killas.

There's a thriving visual arts scene. Julio Visquerra paints in a style that's been called 'magical realist'. José Antonio Velásquez (1906–83) was a renowned primitist painter. Urban Maeztro is a Honduran street artist who makes provocative Banksy-style work.

BIRDS IN HONDURAS

Over 700 bird species have been recorded in Honduras. The Lago de Yojoa (p373) is a mecca, and national parks and reserves provide excellent opportunities for spotting toucans, parrots and raptors. Quetzals are found in cloud forest national parks including Cusuco, Celaque and La Tigra.

Migratory birds flock to wetlands and lagoons along the north coast from November to February. A successful breeding and reintroduction program has resulted in scarlet macaws (Honduras' national bird) recolonizing the Copán valley, where there's also an excellent bird park (see p383).

Lovers of graphic novels should check out Honduran Independent Comics (www.hiccomics.com).

The Garifuna are known for their incredible dances. If you get a chance to see a performance by the Ballet Folklórico Garifuna, don't miss it.

Honduras has some talented filmakers. Independent movies and documentaries are showcased at Cor Fest (www.cor3fest.com), held annually in Roatán.

Landscape & Wildlife

Honduras is a country of breathtaking natural beauty, with a huge range of bird, mammal, reptile and plant species. However, illegal logging, underresourced authorities and construction projects are putting this under threat. While the environment has plenty of defenders, they face a tough struggle against developers, corruption and plain ignorance.

The Land

Countries don't come that big in Central America, but Honduras weighs in as the second-largest (after Nicaragua), with an area of 112,090 sq km. Its coastline includes a 644km Caribbean stretch and 124km on the Pacific side, as well as the Bay Islands and other islets. The fertile north is by far the most developed – its banana plantations have long been a mainstay of the economy.

Much of the Honduran interior is mountainous with peaks reaching 2849m. There are many fertile highland valleys, but no active volcanoes. Extensive wetland areas, swamps and mangrove forests are dotted along the north coast.

Flora & Fauna

There is a dazzling array of flora and fauna in Honduras. Jaguars, tapirs, crocodiles and the mighty Ceiba tree are found in tropical zones; in the cloud forests are rare butterflies among the orchids and magnificent pines; while whale sharks and sea turtles thrive in the country's turquoise Caribbean waters.

It is the sheer variety of habitats here that allows so many different species to thrive. Honduras has mangroves, freshwater lakes, oceans, lagoons, cloud forests, pine forests and tropical rainforests (considerably more than Costa Rica).

Much of the habitat is under threat from deforestation. Endangered species include the scarlet macaw (the national bird), Utilan iguana, manatee, quetzal, jaguar and tapir. Their future depends on just how much protection Honduras' so-called protected areas can really offer.

National Parks & Protected Areas

Approaching one-fifth of Honduran territory is officially protected as a national park or reserve, but all too often the government lacks the resources – or the political will – to stop development and deforestation.

Important protected areas, including marine reserves, include:

➡ **Lancetilla Jardín Botánico** This botanical garden has more than 1200 plant species and hundreds of bird species. Near Tela (p397).

➡ **Parque Nacional Cusuco** A cloud forest with a large population of quetzals. Near San Pedro Sula (p378).

➡ **Parque Nacional Jeanette Kawas** Habitats include mangrove swamps, a small tropical forest, beaches and offshore reefs. Near Tela (p397).

➡ **Parque Nacional Montaña de Celaque** An elevated plateau that includes Honduras' highest peak. Near Gracias (p392).

➡ **Parque Nacional Pico Bonito** High biodiversity, dense forests and many waterfalls. Near La Ceiba (p404).

➡ **Refugio de Vida Punta Izopo** Includes tropical wet forest, mangroves and wetlands. Near Tela (p397).

➡ **Refugio de Vida Silvestre Cuero y Salado** The largest manatee reserve in Central America. Monkeys and birdlife also abound. Near La Ceiba (p405).

➡ **Reserva de la Biosfera del Río Plátano** A World Heritage Site, the Río Plátano covers 5251 sq km of lowland tropical rainforest. In La Moskitia (p424).

➡ **Roatán Marine Park** Protects the entire coastline of Roatán island and includes some outstanding coral formations (p411).

➡ **Tawahka Asangni Biosphere Reserve** Tropical rainforest on the ancestral lands of the Tawahka people. In La Moskitia.

➡ **Turtle Harbor Marine Reserve** Encompasses the north coast of Utila.

Environmental Issues

Deforestation is the most pressing environmental issue facing Honduras today. Though the nation is the most densely forested in Central America, it's disappearing fast – around 2% of Honduras' forests are lost each year. Talks were held in January 2013 between the EU and Honduras to establish a Voluntary Partnership Agreement so that only legally-obtained timber can be exported to Europe. However, illegal timber exports to the USA and Caribbean islands continue.

Activists who oppose loggers, developers or ranchers are reguarly threatened, and even killed. The Punta Sal reserve near Tela is now the Parque Nacional Jeanette Kawas, named after the campaigner who opposed construction plans for years and was murdered in 1995. Two activists in Olancho who opposed loggers were killed (by police officers) in 2006.

There are myriad other environmental concerns. Honduras lost two-thirds of its mangrove forests between 1980 and 2003, mostly for shrimp farms. Mining activity is polluting the Lago de Yojoa (the largest source of freshwater in the country) with heavy metals. Vast plantations of African palms are spreading along the north coast, a monocultural environment that provides little in the way of habitat for wildlife.

SURVIVAL GUIDE

Directory A–Z

ACCOMMODATIONS

Hotels vary wildly in Honduras depending where you are. In most towns you can get a decent, functional clean room with a bathroom and a fan for around L250 to L350. In the big cities it's very important to choose a hotel in a relatively secure neighborhood, and these places tend to cost more (L350 to L500), as do acccommodations in the Bay Islands.

You'll find hostels with dorm beds where travelers gather, including Copán Ruinas, Utila, Roatán, La Ceiba and San Pedro Sula. Costs vary considerably for dorms, from L150 to L300 a bed.

Note that, as elsewhere in Central America, a *sencilla* (single) usually indicates that the room has one double bed, while a *doble* has two beds – save money and sleep next to a friend.

In resort areas like the Bay Islands, prices peak around Christmas and New Year and during Semana Santa (Easter week).

Air-conditioning is an expensive luxury, particularly in the Bay Islands. Free wi-fi is becoming quite common in many accommodations.

There are no organized campsites in Honduras, so leave the tent at home.

ACTIVITIES

If you're up for outdoor stuff, you've come to the right place, with hiking, zip lining, riding, birdwatching and outstanding white-water rafting and kayaking available. Head to the Bay Islands for some of the best snorkeling and diving in the western hemisphere.

CLIMATE

Confusingly, there are two rainy seasons in Honduras. On the north coast it rains year-round, but the wettest months are from September to February. During this time floods can occur, impeding travel and occasionally causing severe damage. The south and west of the country has a different, distinct rainy season between May and October.

SLEEPING PRICE RANGES

The following price ranges refer to a double room with bathroom. Unless otherwise stated tax is included in the price.

$	Less than L600
$$	L600–1200
$$$	More than L1200

The mountainous interior is much cooler than the humid coastal lowlands. Altitude affects temperatures greatly: in places like Tegucigalpa (975m) and Gracias (803m) the heat rarely gets too oppressive.

Hurricane season is June to November.

EMBASSIES & CONSULATES

Most embassies are in Tegucigalpa.

Belizean Embassy (☎2238-4614; consuladobelice@yahoo.com; Av República de Chile, Centro Comercial Hotel Honduras Maya)

Canadian Embassy (☎2232-4551; www.canadainternational.gc.ca/costa_rica; Blvr San Juan Bosco, Centro Financiero Banexpo, Local 3)

Dutch Consulate (☎2239-8090; info@cgholanda.hn; 3a Av 2315, Colonia Florencia Norte)

El Salvadoran Embassy (☎2239-7017; www.embajadahonduras.rree.gob.sv; Diagonal Aguán 2952)

German Embassy (☎2232-3161; www.tegucigalpa.diplo.de; Av República Dominicana 925)

Guatemalan Embassy (☎2232-5018; embhonduras@minex.gob; Calle Alfonso XIII 3716, Colonia Lomas del Guijaro)

Nicaraguan Embassy (☎2239-5225; embanic@amnettgu.com; Avenida Choluteca, Bloque M-1, No 1130, Colonia Lomas de Tepeyac)

UK Honorary Consulate (☎2237-6577; www.ukimmigration.org.uk/uk_embassies/honduras.php; Calle Principal 2402, Colonia La Reforma)

US Embassy (☎2236-9320; http://honduras.usembassy.gov; Av La Paz)

FESTIVALS & EVENTS

Just about every city, town and village in Honduras has a patron saint and celebrates an annual festival around their saint's day.

April 12, the anniversary of the arrival of the Garifuna people in Honduras in 1797, is a joyful occasion celebrated in all Garifuna communities. Utila's **Sun Jam** (www.sunjam.com), held annually in early August, is a DJ-driven beach party on a desert island. Other major festivals include:

Feria de Suyapa The patron saint of Honduras is celebrated in Suyapa, near Tegucigalpa, from around February 2 to 11. February 3 is the saint's day.

Carnaval at La Ceiba Celebrated during the third week in May. The third Saturday is the biggest day, with parades, costumes, music and celebrations in the streets.

EATING PRICE RANGES

The following price ranges refer to the typical cost of a meal excluding drinks and taxes.

$	less than L75
$$	L75–150
$$$	more than L150

FOOD & DRINK

Honduran cuisine may be not be globally-renowned, but there are many distinctive dishes: see p356 for some of these and what kind of restaurants you'll find. While you're on the North coast, two Garifuna specialties are *pan de coco* (coconut bread) and *casabe* (a crispy flat bread).

Most basic restaurants' prices include **tax**, but anywhere midrange and above tends to exclude it. **Tipping** is not common in cheap places, but appreciated; upmarket restaurants automatically add 10% to your bill.

Honduras has several **beers** on offer – SalvaVida and Port Royal are favorites among travelers, followed by the blander Imperial. They are all produced by the same brewery, Cerveceria Hondureña. All are cheap – from L20 in bars. For excellent, home-brewed beer, visit D&D Brewery (p373) in Lago de Yojoa or Sol de Copán (p382) in Copán Ruinas.

Flor de Caña **rum** is widely available and excellent.

GAY & LESBIAN TRAVELERS

The legal age of consent is 15. However, Honduras is very much 'in the closet' when it comes to homosexuality and open displays of affection between gay or lesbian couples can be targeted with abuse. Anti-gay attacks (including murders) have recently increased. Organizations serving the gay, lesbian and transsexual/transgender communities include **Asociación LGTB Arcoiris de Honduras** (☎2206-2408; arcoirisghn@yahoo.com) and **Colectiva Violeta** (☎2237-4905; colectivo_violeta@yahoo.com).

INTERNET ACCESS

Every city and most towns and villages usually have at least one **internet cafe**. Connections tend to be slow, and cost L15 to L20 per hour – much more in the Bay Islands (around L100 per hour).

Many accommodations, cafes and restaurants have free **wi-fi**, though expect connection drop-offs and pedestrian speeds.

LANGUAGE COURSES

Copán Ruinas is a delightful place to study Spanish and has two good language schools (see p380).

LEGAL MATTERS

Police officers in Honduras aren't immune to corruption. If you plan to rent a car, for example, be aware that police are not above looking for infractions to get a little money for gas.

There are tourist police in towns including San Pedro Sula and Tela, but as very few officers speak English, don't expect too much help.

MONEY

The unit of currency in Honduras is the lempira (L), which is divided into 100 *centavos*. Over the last decade the lempira has been steadily sliding against the US dollar; for exchange rate information see p731.

ATMs

There are cash machines in cities and towns throughout the country. Foreign cards are accepted (with four-digit PINs).

Cash

Banks will exchange US dollars and occasionally euros. Bring your passport and go in the morning. Your hotel may let you pay in US dollars (worth doing to avoid the bank queues), or exchange them for you, as may some places in the more touristy areas.

Credit Cards

Visa and MasterCard are accepted at most midrange hotels and major supermarkets, but don't expect to use plastic as freely as you would in North America or Europe. Expect a 5% to 10% credit card surcharge at some hotels and restaurants.

Cash advances on cards are available at most banks in case of emergency.

Traveler's Checks

Traveler's checks are extremely difficult to cash or use anywhere in Honduras. Most banks, hotels and other retailers want nothing to do with them.

OPENING HOURS

Businesses are generally open during the following hours.

- **Banks** 8:30am to 4:30pm Monday to Friday and 8:30am to noon Saturday.
- **Restaurants** 7am or 8am until 9pm daily.
- **Shops** 9am to 6pm daily.

PUBLIC HOLIDAYS

New Year's Day January 1
Day of the Americas April 14
Semana Santa (Holy Week) Thursday, Friday and Saturday before Easter Sunday.
Labor Day May 1
Independence Day September 15
Francisco Morazán Day October 3
Día de la Raza (Columbus Day) October 12
Army Day October 21
Christmas Day December 25

SAFE TRAVEL

Most travelers enjoy their time in Honduras and their trips pass without unpleasant incidents. That said, Honduras does have a very serious crime problem.

The country's ingrained gun culture may unsettle visitors, but the chances of a firearms assault are slim – petty theft is a far more likely risk. You should be cautious – but not paranoid – in the cities, especially San Pedro Sula and Tegucigalpa, which both have gang problems (again, travelers are rarely targeted). Walking in the center in the daytime is usually fine, although don't flash your belongings about. Take cabs at night.

In general, small towns are much safer than the big cities. Watch yourself on the north coast, especially on the beach. It's best not to walk alone on city beaches in Tela or La Ceiba day or night as thefts, muggings and even rapes have occurred.

Avoid travel (especially driving) at night, when banditos and drug runners do their dirty work.

Malaria and dengue fever are present in Honduras. The humid north coast, Bay Islands and Moskitia are high-risk zones. Biting sand flies can be a real annoyance too.

Beware of poisonous snakes, especially the fer-de-lance (known locally as *barba amarilla*); the coral snake is also present. Crocodiles and caimans live in the waterways of La Moskitia. Honduras also has scorpions (not lethal), black widow spiders, wasps and other stinging insects. You probably will never see a dangerous animal, but be aware that they exist.

TELEPHONE

The country code for Honduras is ☎504. There are no area codes.

If you haven't got a cell phone, internet cafes are your best best for inexpensive calls, using Skype or their in-house system. The call centers of the state phone company **Hondutel** (www.hondutel.hn) are notoriously inefficient and expensive and should be seen as a last resort.

Cell Phones

Honduras has widespread cellular coverage. Claro and Tigo are the two main providers.

Most North American phones function well in Honduras, but phones bought in Europe, Australia, New Zealand and many Asian countries often won't work at all.

If you need to buy a local phone they are available from L350. SIM cards cost around L100 but have to be registered first in a branch, which can be a hassle.

Phone credit *(saldo)* can be topped up in many places, including small stores. Certain days are *doble* or even *quadruple*, so you get two or four-times the credit. Calling the USA is quite cheap, especially when you top up on a *quadruple* day (around L2 per minute), but Europe and elsewhere are much more costly.

TOURIST INFORMATION

There are very few tourist information offices in Honduras, and those that exist offer limited practical advice. The national office is the Instituto Hondureño de Turismo (p366) in Tegucigalpa.

TRAVELERS WITH DISABILITIES

Honduras lacks facilities for disabled travelers, other than in upmarket hotels and resorts. Wheelchair-bound visitors will find it difficult to negotiate towns because of poor-quality sidewalks and cobblestones. Public transport is not geared to less-able travelers, though the ferries to Roatán do offer wheelchair access.

VISAS & DOCUMENTS

Citizens of most western European countries, Australia, Canada, Japan, New Zealand and the United States normally receive free 90-day tourist cards when entering the country. This also applies to the countries signed up to the CA-4 border agreement – Guatemala, Nicaragua, Honduras and El Salvador. Other nationalities, including most Asian and African countries, have to apply for a visa in advance from a Honduran embassy, and pay a fee of US$30.

Once inside Honduras you can apply for a one-time 30-day extension (L400) at the main immigration office in Tegucigalpa (travelers have reported problems gaining extensions in other offices). Or, just take a trip outside the CA-4 (Belize and Costa Rica are nearest) for at least three days, then get a new 180-day visa on re-entering Honduras.

VOLUNTEERING

A number of organizations offer volunteer opportunities in Honduras, on projects ranging from building homes to teaching English.

The website www.travel-to-honduras.com has a long list of groups that run volunteer programs here, from large operations like Casa Alianza to the tiny Utila Iguana Conservation Project.

WOMEN TRAVELERS

Honduras is still a male-dominated society. Personal safety is the biggest concern for female travelers. Most women do not feel threatened while traveling alone in Honduras, but it certainly pays to adopt an assertive demeanor.

As elsewhere, you'll probably attract less attention if you dress modestly. On the Bay Islands, where lots of foreign tourists congregate, things are more relaxed, though topless bathing is most definitely out. It's best to only head to clubs and bars with male company, or in a group.

DEPARTURE TAX

If you fly out of Honduras, you must pay L760 (US$38) departure tax at the airport. The domestic departure tax is L40 (US$2).

Getting There & Away

Flights, tours and rail tickets can be booked online at www.lonelyplanet.com/bookings.

AIR

Frequent direct flights connect Honduras with other Central American capitals and destinations in the USA. There are no direct flights to Europe.

The busiest and largest airport is in San Pedro Sula, followed by Tegucigalpa. There are also a few direct flights between Atlanta, Houston and Miami in the US and Roatán.

BOAT

The only scheduled international passenger boat services to/from Honduras are the two small boats that run (on the same day at the same time!) weekly from Puerto Cortés to Belize.

If you arrive or depart from Honduras by sea, be sure to clear your paperwork (entry and exit stamps, if necessary) immediately with the immigration office in Puerto Cortés.

LAND

Bus

There are five main luxury-class international bus companies serving Honduras: King Quality, Pullmantur, Tica Bus, Hedman Alas and Trans Nica. Three other companies (Rutas Orientales, Fuente del Norte and Sultana) offer less pricey alternatives.

The two hubs for international departures are San Pedro Sula and Tegucigalpa. From these two cities you can get to San Salvador (El Salvador); Guatemala City, Antigua, Santa Elena/Flores (Guatemala); Managua (Nicaragua); San José (Costa Rica); and Panama City.

It's also possible to take local buses, crossing the border on foot and picking up another bus on the other side.

BORDER CROSSINGS

Guatemala

To Guatemala, the main crossings are at El Florido, Agua Caliente and Corinto. There's no official fee to leave Honduras or enter Guatemala but immigration officials often ask for a dollar or two.

The 24-hour border at **Agua Caliente** is a half-hour bus ride from Nueva Ocotepeque (L22, 30 minutes, every 30 minutes to 6pm). Buses (Q10) connect the Honduran and Guatemalan immigration posts, which are 2km apart. From the Guatemalan side buses go to **Esquipulas**, where you can connect to **Guatemala City** or **Flores**.

The 24-hour border at **El Florido** is 9km west of Copán Ruinas and connected by very regular minibus services (L20, 20 minutes, every 20 minutes). If you're on a trans-border bus or shuttle bus you'll have to get off and clear customs and immigration on both sides of the frontier. Moneychangers will approach you, usually offering decent rates. There's also a bank on the Guatemalan side.

The Guatemalan border at **Corinto** (open 6am to 9pm) is a 51km bus ride southwest of Omoa (L40, 1½ hours, every hour). Buses to the border leave from the main highway and will drop you at a set of *comedores*. From there, walk through immigration procedures. Microbuses waiting on the Guatemalan side connect to **Puerto Barrios**.

El Salvador

To El Salvador, the main crossings are El Poy and El Amatillo; the crossing at Sabanetas near Marcala is *not* open for foreigners.

The El Salvador border at **El Poy** (24-hour) is a short bus ride from Nueva Ocotepeque (L15, 15 minutes, every 20 minutes to 7pm). On both sides, the bus drops you about 100m from the border, from where you walk across and catch a bus onward. On the Salvadoran side, buses leave frequently for **San Salvador** and **La Palma**.

There are buses from Choluteca in Honduas' south to the Salvadoran border at **El Amatillo** (L52, two hours, every 20 minutes until 6:30pm).

Nicaragua

Crossings to Nicaragua are at Guasaule, El Espino and Las Manos.

In southern Honduras, buses run from Choluteca to the Nicaraguan border at **Guasaule** (L28, 45 minutes, every 20 minutes 6am to 6pm).

For the border at **El Espino** border you'll have to travel via San Marcos de Colón, from where there's very regular transport (L15, 15 minutes).

For **Las Manos**, buses run from Tegucigalpa (L78, 2½ hours, three daily).

Getting Around

AIR

Domestic air travel in Honduras is relatively inexpensive, and the safety record is generally good. There are connections from La Ceiba, Tegucigalpa and San Pedro Sula to Utila and Roatán, and also between the three major cities.

Air routes also open up La Moskitia, though these routes are quite pricey.

AeroCaribe (☎2442-1085; www.aerocaribehn.com)

Aerolíneas Sosa (☎La Ceiba 2443-1894, Roatán 2445-1658, San Pedro Sula 2550-6545, Tegucigalpa 2233-5107; www.aerolineasosa.com)

TACA/Isleña (☎La Ceiba 2441-3191, Roatán 2445-1088, San Pedro Sula 2516-1061, Tegucigalpa 2236-8222; www.taca.com)

BOAT

Two passenger ferries, the luxury catamaran *Galaxy Wave* and the beat-up *Utila Princess II*, operate between La Ceiba and the Bay Islands. There is no ferry service between the two islands.

In La Moskitia, almost all transportation is via the waterways. There are also water taxis on Roatán from West End to West Bay, and from Coyolito on the Golfo de Fonseca over to the Isla del Tigre.

BUS

Buses are a cheap and easy way to get around Honduras, and there are some very fancy (and costly) services. The first buses of the day often start very early in the morning; the last bus usually departs in the late afternoon. Buses on major highways run later.

On major bus routes, you'll often have a choice between taking a *directo* (direct) or a *parando* (ordinary bus which makes many stops). Microbuses or *rapiditos* are minivan-like buses.

City buses are not recommended due to safety issues – gangs 'tax' transport companies and occassionally assault drivers.

CAR & MOTORCYCLE

Driving on the highway in Honduras is like playing in the advanced level of a video game. Many locals drive at insane speeds (to avoid the perceived threat of carjacking).

The main highways are paved, mostly in reasonable condition. Away from the highways, roads tend to be dirt: conditions can vary wildly according to rainfall and the time of year, ranging from acceptable to impassable.

Rental cars are available in Tegucigalpa, San Pedro Sula, La Ceiba and on Roatán. Prices start at L550 a day for an economy car with a hefty deductable.

TAXI

Taxis are everywhere in Honduran towns. It's very common to share a ride in many places, so each passenger pays around L20. If you want a private ride, rates start at about L60. Fares increase at night.

In the major cities, *colectivos* (shared taxis) ply a number of prescribed routes, costing around L15 to L25 per passenger.

Three-wheeled *mototaxis* (tuk-tuks) are very common in small towns and villages, but they're not allowed to operate in big city centers. Expect to pay about half what you would in a taxi.

Nicaragua

☎505 / POP 5,869,859

Includes ➡

Managua.....442
Granada.....456
Masaya 467
Isla de Ometepe & Around 470
San Juan del Sur 476
León.....481
Estelí.....491
Matagalpa.....498
Caribbean Coast 500
Bluefields.....501
Pearl Lagoon 503
Corn Islands 504
San Carlos & Around 508

Best Places to Eat

- ➡ Tercer Ojo (p463)
- ➡ Cevicheria El Chino (p502)
- ➡ Café-Arte Tipiscayán (p494)

Best Places to Stay

- ➡ Surfing Turtle Lodge (p489)
- ➡ Playa Hermosa Beach Hotel (p481)
- ➡ Hotel Los Arcos (p493)

Why Go?

There are few places that are everything for everyone. But Nicaragua has just about all you could ask for in a tropical paradise.

Want 90-octane waves and beach-blanket-bohemia days on lost beaches? Nicaragua's got you covered with two long coastlines of peaced-out surf camps, hippie enclaves and remote fishing villages that are only now entering the tourist game.

Or are you thinking about diving into history, tromping through colonial villages and exploring the region's unique cultural patrimony? Well, Nicaragua's got that, too. Colonial cities like León and Granada offer crimson-hued snapshots of the past, while remote Caribbean fishing villages provide glimpses into present-day life in this diverse, proud and optimistic nation.

Beyond that there are volcanoes to be climbed (and surfed down), lagoons to be explored, islands to be Robinson Crusoed, and spirited locals to take you there and beyond.

When to Go

Managua

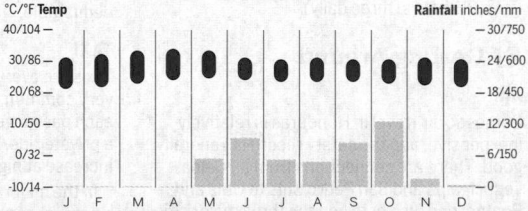

Nov–May High season means dry weather, sunny days, but slightly bigger crowds.

Mar–Nov It's rainy, but green, and you get the biggest, brawniest waves for Pacific Coast surf safaris.

Sep–Nov Hotels are cheaper, but the tail end of hurricane season can screw up your plans.

Connections

Nicaragua's border with Honduras can be crossed at Las Manos, El Espino or El Guasaule. From Costa Rica, you can enter by road at Peñas Blancas or by boat via Los Chiles. From Potosí, you can hop on a small boat to El Salvador. For more detailed information, see the Survival Guide on p525.

FIRST TIME IN NICARAGUA

If you've got limited time in Nicaragua, a trip through the southwest is big on awesome and small on hours in the bus. Kick off your trip in charismatic **Granada**. Spend three nights taking in the wonderful streetscapes and visiting the museums and churches. From here, you can head out for day trips or overnighters to the lush crater at **Laguna de Apoyo**, the characterful artisan-villages known as **Pueblos Blancos**, or to the **Mombacho** and **Masaya** volcanoes and protected wild preserves.

Next head down the highway to San Jorge, from where you'll take the ferry across to the out-of-this world **Isla de Ometepe** with its twin volcanoes and endless outdoor activities. From there, it's across the isthmus to the **Southern Pacific Beaches**. Most people begin and end their beach time in the funked-out international beach village of **San Juan del Sur**, but definitely plan on spending a night or two on the surf beaches north and south of here. If you are headed north, you won't want to miss a stop off in **León**.

Essential Food & Drink

➡ **Where to eat** Budget eateries – generally *comedores* or *cafetínes*, *fritangas* and market stalls – serve a limited range of filling dishes and set meals from US$2 to US$5.

➡ **What to eat** *Gallo pinto* (mixed rice and beans) is a staple. On the coasts, you can sample wonderful seafood, while the interior has some of the best grass-fed beef in Central America. Be sure to keep an eye out for local specialties, including *nacatamles* (banana-leaf packed with cornmeal and other goodness), *baho* (steamed beef, plantains and yucca), *rondón* (coconut seafood stew served in the Caribbean) and *quesillo* (mozzarella and onions wrapped in a tortilla and topped with sour cream).

➡ **What to drink** Flor de Caña is the national rum; local beers include Toña and Victoria, both light pilsners.

AT A GLANCE

Nicaragua is considered one of the safest countries in Latin America. Spanish is spoken throughout much of the country. On the Caribbean Coast you'll find English is more common. You can get by on US$20 to US$30 per day. Visas are pretty straightforward here for most nationalities for up to three months. Nicaragua is on GMT minus six hours (no daylight savings).

Fast Facts

➡ **Area** 129,494 sq km (approximately the size of Greece or New York State)

➡ **Capital** Managua

➡ **Emergency** ☎115 (fire), ☎118 (police), from cell phones ☎911

Set Your Budget

➡ **Hostel Bed** US$8-20

➡ **Evening Meal** US$2-5

➡ **Bus Ticket** US$1-3

Resources

➡ **Vianica.com** (www.vianica.com/traveling)

➡ **Intur** (www.visitanicaragua.com/ingles)

➡ **Latin American Network Information Center** (www.lanic.utexas.edu/la/ca/nicaragua)

Nicaragua Highlights

1. Scramble to the summits for views to everywhere and beyond on lush and lovely **Isla de Ometepe** (p471).
2. Swim through crystal-clear Caribbean waters in the far-out **Corn Islands** (p504).
3. Savor the colonial delights, spirited streetways and mystical churches in **Granada** (p456).
4. Find out exactly why the revolution wasn't televised in the irreverent, off-beat and turbo-charged bars of colonial **León** (p482).
5. Charge the big waves in the chiller-than-thou surf towns along the **Southern Pacific Coast** (p476).
6. Laze out for several days of zen in the tranquil corners of **Reserva Natural Laguna de Apoyo** (p466).
7. Board a riverboat to explore the picturesque **Río San Juan** (p510), home to abundant birdlife and an unexpected fortress.
8. Discover the heart of the hard-working highlands in the earthy town of **Matagalpa** (p498).
9. Bargain with local fishermen to take you boating in the intriguing Mískito area of **Pearl Lagoon** (p503).

85°W
84°W
Cabo Gracias a Dios
Laguna Bismuna
Río Coco (Segovia)
Leimus
Waspám
Bismuna Tara
La Troquera
Río Patuca
Cordillera Entre Ríos
San Andres
Río Waspuk
Río Wawa
Luciana
Dákura
Sisin
Atlántico Norte
Reserva de Biosfera Bosawás
Laguna Pahara
BILWI (PUERTO CABEZAS)
Yulú
Kukalaya
Lamlaya
14°N
Laguna Karatá
Río Bocay
Rosita
Costa de Miskitos
Jinotega
Siuna
El Ocote
El Empalme
Laguna Wounta
Wiwili
El Cuá
Isabelia
Valle Kuikuinita
Río Prinzapolka
Cordillera
Yaoska
Kangrina
Río Tuma
Matagalpa
Río Grande de Matagalpa
13°N
San José
Barrera
Karawala
Barra de Río Grande
San Ramón
Matiguás
Chamarro
Río Kurinwas
Tortuguero
Tasbapauni
Atlántico Sur
Orinoco
Boaco
BOACO
El Ayote
Laguna de Perlas
Pearl Keys
Camoapa
Río Rama
9 Pearl Lagoon
Chontales
El Alto
San Lorenzo
Río Escondido
El Rama
Corn Islands 2
JUIGALPA
Isla El Muerto
BLUEFIELDS
12°N
Río Ojecuapa
7
Río Rama
San Ubaldo
Bahía de Bluefields
CARIBBEAN SEA
Isla Zapatera
Lago de Nicaragua
Morrito
Río Tepenaguasapa
Altagracia
Volcán Concepción (1610m) 1
Monkey Point
Río Punta Gorda
San Jorge
San Miguelito
Punta Gorda
La Virgen
Isla de Ometepe
Río San Juan
Sapoá
Archipiélago de Solentiname
Río Maíz
Bahía Punta Gorda
Peñas Blancas
SAN CARLOS
Boca de Sábalos
El Ostional
La Cruz
1
Los Chiles
El Castillo
11°N
San Juan del Norte (Greytown)
Río Frío
Río San Juan 7
COSTA RICA
Barra del Colorado
85°W
84°W

MANAGUA

POP 1,028,800

Managua is a shambles. It is chaotic and broken, poetic and mesmerizing all at the same time.

And while most travelers are now skipping the city altogether – and arranging quick airport transfers from nearby Granada – stay a day or two and you will see that big, bad Managua ain't so bad after all, and that this truly is the heartstring that holds the nation's culture, commerce and consciousness together.

Aside from diving into the whir of a magnificent beehive of honking horns, sprawling markets, garbage and rancor, this low-rise city with its improbable trees, remarkable street art and spirited monuments also gives you easy access to nearby lagoons, nature reserves at Montebelli and Chocoyero-El Brujo, a smattering of fun beaches like Pochomil, and the hot springs at El Trapiche.

History

At the time of the Spanish conquest, Managua was an indigenous lakeshore settlement whose inhabitants practiced agriculture, hunting and fishing. These early Managuans put up a vigorous resistance to the Spanish, who responded by destroying their city. Managua subsequently remained a village until the mid-19th century.

The city rose out of obscurity in 1852 after conflicts between liberal León and conservative Granada repeatedly erupted into civil war. Lying midway between the two, Managua was chosen as a compromise capital.

Since then, a series of natural disasters has thrashed the capital. The gracious old city center was destroyed by earthquake and the ensuing fire in March 1931, and burned again five years later. It was completely rebuilt into one of the most developed cities in the region, only to be razed by an even more devastating earthquake in 1972.

When geologists found the downtown area riddled with faults, the decision was made to leave the site behind. President Somoza and his partners saw great potential for profit in the disaster and bought up large tracts of land on the outskirts of the city on which to build new housing developments, leading to the sprawl that characterizes Managua today.

Sights & Activities

Plaza de la Revolución & Malecón

This quiet collection of pre-earthquake and post-revolutionary monuments, parks, museums and government offices was once the pulsing heart of Managua; the *malecón* (pier) now has a handful of run-down restaurants. Then came the 1972 earthquake, and two decades of war and privation, and the center was all but abandoned. Some work is ongoing to repair this area.

★Plaza de la Revolución PARK
(Map p448) Inaugurated in 1899 by national hero and original anti-American General José Santos Zelaya, this open plaza has been the scene of countless protests, parades, romances and more. On the northeast of the plaza rests the **tomb** (Map p448) of Sandinista commander Carlos Fonseca. Head toward the lake to the **Monumento a Rubén Darío** (Map p448), Nicaragua's most famous poet.

Antigua Catedral CATHEDRAL
(Map p448) Built in 1929, shattered by the 1972 earthquake, and, despite promises, never restored.

Palacio de la Cultura y Biblioteca Nacional MUSEUM
(Map p448; admission US$2; ⏲8am-5pm Mon-Fri, 9am-4pm Sat & Sun) Adjacent to the Antigua Catedral, the 1935 palace houses the **Museo Nacional** (Map p448; admission US$2; ⏲8am-5pm). The timeline starts only 500 million years ago, as Nicaragua is one of the newest places on earth. Other exhibits whiz through the Spanish-colonial period before landing in the Sandino, then the Sandinista, eras.

Centro Cultural Managua CULTURAL BUILDING
(Map p448; Plaza de la Revolución, 1c S) Located in the remnants of the Gran Hotel, this cultural center hosts changing art exhibits, concerts and dances, plus handicrafts fairs on the first Saturday of the month.

Concha Acústica MONUMENT
(Map p448) The trippy Acoustic Shell overlooks **Plaza de la Fé Juan Pablo II**. Other monuments in this area include the statue of Latin American liberation superhero **Simón Bolívar**, the slightly overgrown **Plaza de la Cultura de Guatemala**, and the unabashedly political, disturbingly disproportionate **Estatua al Soldado** (Nameless Guerrilla

Soldier) on the western side of Av Bolívar, on the corner diagonally opposite the Centro Cultural Managua. A block away, the **Monumento al Trabajador Nicaragüense** celebrates the Nicaraguan worker.

★Parque de la Paz PARK
(Map p448) It was here that the weapons from the 1980s conflict were gathered to be destroyed and buried, and it is still possible to glimpse twisted gun barrels sticking out of the concrete that encircles a burned-out tank. Ironically, the peace park is notorious for muggings, so make a beeline to the security office, from where the guards will gladly escort you around for a small tip.

Puerto Salvador Allende BOAT TOUR
(Map p448; ☎2222-2745; www.epn.com.ni) This relatively modern port offers 45-minute boat tours Tuesday to Sunday to Isla del Amor at 11am, 1pm, 3pm and 5pm (US$3 to US$5). You can also head out at 10am and 1pm Friday to Sunday for a two-hour tour to the small village of San Francisco Libre (US$8).

Barrio Martha Quezada & Around

★Parque Historico Nacional Loma de Tiscapa PARK
(Map p448; ⏲8am-8pm Tue-Sun) Home to what's easily Managua's most recognizable landmark, Sandino's somber silhouette, this national historic park was once the site of the Casa Presidencial, where Sandino and his men were executed in 1934. Begin your ascent at the Hotel Crowne Plaza. You'll pass **Monumento Roosevelt**, constructed in 1939, with lovely lake views.

The top of the hill is actually the lip of Volcán Tiscapa's beautiful little crater lake, with incredible views of the city, both cathedrals and Volcán Momotombo, plus Canopy Tiscapa, a small but fun 1.2km, three-platform, 25-minute tour. Keep in mind that, despite a vigorous clean-up campaign, the lake is polluted with untreated sewage.

Arboretum Nacional GARDENS
(National Arboretum; Map p448; admission US$0.30; ⏲8am-5pm Mon-Fri) These modest gardens feature more than 200 species of plants divided into Nicaragua's five major life zones.

Other Neighborhoods

★Huellas de Acahualinca ARCHAEOLOGICAL SITE
(Map p444; ☎2266-5774; admission US$4, photography fee US$1; ⏲9am-4pm) These ancient footprints are Managua's most fascinating attraction, and highly recommended for the glimpse of a long-vanished human past that it affords. Buried 4m deep under compacted volcanic material, the tracks were discovered by quarrying workmen in 1874.

There are 10 sets of human footprints (men, women and children) that have been dated to some 6000 years ago; they pace in one direction, toward the lake. There are also tracks of deer and *mapache* (a type of raccoon) present. An additional area excavated in 1978 shows the prints continuing nearby, and it is thought there could be many more in the surrounding area. The entry fee includes an optional guided tour in Spanish.

The neighborhood around here is a little sketchy, and you are well advised to take a taxi to the door.

Nueva Catedral CATHEDRAL
(Map p448; ☎2278-4232) South of Tiscapa along the road to the Rotonda Rubén Darío, this Managua landmark was inaugurated in 1993. It's a curious building studded with dozens of domes that help provide structural support during earthquakes and represent the 63 churches in the Managua diocese.

Courses

Viva Spanish School LANGUAGE COURSE
(Map p448; ☎2270-2339; www.vivaspanishschool.com; Edificio FNI, 2c S) This school offers intensive Spanish courses for US$175 a week (US$225 for a couple) and can arrange flexible homestays. It's just east of Metrocentro mall.

Alianza Francesa COURSE
(Map p448; ☎2267-2811; www.alianzafrancesa.org.ni; Planes de Altamira, de la Embajada de México ½c N) Offers classes in painting, drawing, French, German and Portuguese, along with occasional art exhibits and poetry readings.

Festivals & Events

Managua celebrates all the major national festivals, and has a few of its own.

Managua

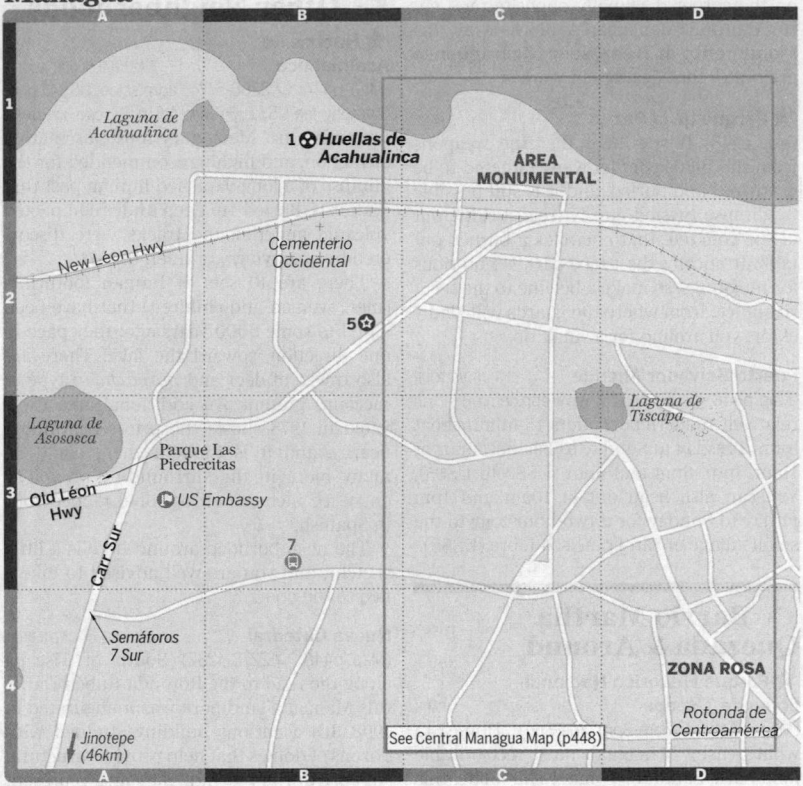

Annual Taxi Grand Prix EVENT
(Last week in March) Drivers modify a licensed taxi's exhaust system, then head to the pit at the Antigua Catedral.

Day of the Revolution NATIONAL HOLIDAY
(July 19) You'll finally understand why people still love Daniel Ortega when you see the master work a crowd of 100,000 red-and-black-flag-waving faithful.

Festival of Santo Domingo de Guzman RELIGIOUS
(August 1 to August 10) Managua's *fiestas patronales* (patron saint parties) last for more than a week and feature a carnival, sporting events, *hípicos* (horse parades) and a procession of *diablitos,* which takes Santo Domingo to his country shrine at the Sierritas de Managua, followed by music and fireworks.

Sleeping

Barrio Martha Quezada, better known to *taxistas* as 'Tica Bus,' is a compact residential district west of Hotel Crowne Plaza with many cheap guesthouses and places to eat. Crime is on the rise here at night. The Carretera a Masaya has just one budget lodging option nearby, but is the best nightlife spot in town. Also worth checking out is Rotonda Bello Horizonte, another nightlife district with a decent guesthouse.

Managua Backpackers Inn HOSTEL $
(Map p448; 2267-0006; www.managuahostel.com; El Muelle, 75m S, Carretera a Masaya; dm with fan/air-con US$10/14, s/d without bathroom $23/29, d with air-con $34;) This is the best hostel in Managua. It's minutes away from Metrocentro mall and endless nightlife and restaurant options. Rooms are basic but breezy, open and comfortable. And all the hostel amenities are here – DVD

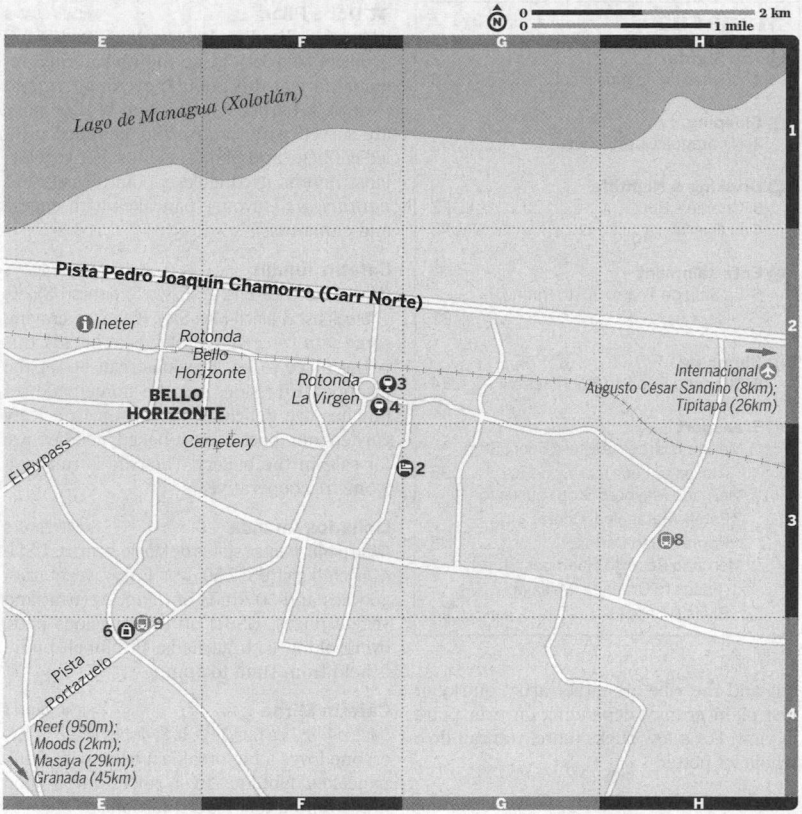

room, good-sized pool, well-stocked kitchen and heaps of tourist info.

Hotel Los Felipe HOTEL $
(Map p448; ☎2222-6501; www.hotellosfelipe.net.ni; Tica Bus, 1½c O; s/d with fan US$15/20, with air-con US$25/30; P ❄ 📶 ≋) If you're planning on doing anything more than crashing the night and moving on, this is where you want to be. Rooms are a decent size, spotless and dotted around a lush garden with a (relatively) huge pool. Small discounts apply for more than three days, bigger ones for a month.

Casa Vanegas HOTEL $
(Map p448; ☎2222-4043; casavanegas1@hotmail.com; Tica Bus, 1c O; s/d US$12/20, s without bathroom $12; 📶) Clean and secure, this friendly family-run spot offers decent-sized, unexciting rooms around a small patio. Hammocks, a spacious lounge area, cable TV and a shared kitchen make it a good option.

Hostal Dulce Sueño HOTEL $
(Map p448; ☎2228-4195; www.hostaldulcesueno.com; Tica Bus, 70m E; s/d US$10/16; 📶) This simple guesthouse has spotless, no-frills rooms, and a central patio with a TV and a shared kitchen. It's a few steps from the Tica Bus terminal, but this block is reputedly quite dangerous at night.

Jardín de Italia HOTEL $
(Map p448; ☎2222-7967; www.jardindeitalia.com; Tica Bus, 1c E, ½c N; r per person US$10; @ 📶) Rooms are styled with cutesy, homey decorations, and run alongside a pretty garden. The rooms are passable, but the service is just a bit odd.

Casa de Huéspedes Santos HOTEL $
(Map p448; ☎2222-3713; www.casadehuespedessantos.com.ni; Tica Bus, 1c N, 1½ O; r per person US$7; P 📶) This rambling classic has a variety of rooms arranged around a couple of covered courtyards. The murals, the lay-

Managua

Top Sights
1 Huellas de Acahualinca B1

Sleeping
2 Nicaragua Guest House G3

Drinking & Nightlife
3 Charlie's Bar F2
4 El Puerto F2

Entertainment
5 La Sala de Teatro Justo Rufino Garay B2

Shopping
6 Mercado Roberto Huembes E4

Transport
7 Mercado Israel Lewites (Bóer) Stop (buses to León) B3
8 Mercado Mayoreo Stop (buses to Estelí, Matagalpa, Ocotal, Rama & San Carlos H3
9 Mercado Roberto Huembes Stop (buses to Granada, Masaya, Rivas & Sapoá) E4

out and the vibe are either artsy, quirky or just plain grungy, depending on your point of view. For a few bucks more, you can do a whole lot better.

Hotel y Apartamento Los Cisneros HOTEL $$
(Map p448; ☎2222-3235; www.hotelloscisneros.com; Tica Bus, 1c N, 1½ O; s/d with fan US$30/40, with air-con US$46/56, apt from US$40; P ❄ @ 📶) A great deal on quirky, colorful, relative luxury, it's got hot water, phones, art, and potted plants everywhere.

Nicaragua Guest House GUESTHOUSE $$
(Map p444; ☎2249-8963; www.3dp.ch/nicaragua; Rotonda de La Virgen, 2c S, 2½c O; s/d with fan US$15/20, with air-con $28/35; ❄ 📶) Basic but comfortable rooms a short ride from all the action in the Bello Horizonte neighborhood. The only catch? The 11pm curfew.

Eating

With an abundance of cheap eateries catering to office workers, Barrio Martha Quezada is a great place to get a taste for Nicaraguan cuisine. Most of Managua's popular restaurants are located around Carretera a Masaya to the south of the Metrocentro mall.

★Doña Pilar NICARAGUAN $
(Map p448; Tica Bus, 1c O, ½c N; dishes US$2-4; ⏲6-9pm Mon-Sat) Get mouthwatering regional fare at this popular evening *fritanga* (sidewalk barbecue). Chicken, beef or pork are served with *gallo pinto,* chopped pickled cabbage and plantain chips. For vegetarians there is fried cheese, potato cakes and *manuelitas* (savoury pancakes with cheese and cinnamon).

Cafetín Tonalli NICARAGUAN $
(Map p448; Tica Bus, 2c E, ½c S; dishes US$2-6; ⏲breakfast & lunch Mon-Sat) If you're craving some *pan integral* (wholewheat bread), this is the place to be. Breakfast can be on the disappointing side, but the homemade set lunches are delicious, served up in a leafy garden out back. Fresh-baked goodies are for sale in the bakery. The cafe is run by a women's cooperative.

Licuados Ananda VEGETERIAN $
(Map p448; frente Estatua de Montoya; mains US$1-4, lunch buffet US$2.50; ✎) Enjoy vegetarian goodies and 50 kinds of *licuados* (fruit and veggie juices; US$1) on this spacious patio overlooking lush gardens; the lunch buffet is held from 11am to 3pm.

Cafetín Mirna NICARAGUAN $
(Map p448; Tica Bus, 1c O, 1c S; dishes US$2-5) Everyone loves a big breakfast here, with fluffy pancakes, fabulous fresh juices and a good lunch buffet, too. It's a tradition.

Tercer Ojo FUSION $$
(Map p448; Seminole Plaza, 3½c S; mains US$5-14; 📶) Managua's best fusion restaurant doesn't even really bother fusing – it just goes straight out for delicious Asian flavors that you can't get anywhere else in the country (apart from its sister restaurant in Granada). A wide balcony for street-side people-watching adds to the appeal.

La Casa del Café CAFE $$
(Map p448; www.casadelcafe.com.ni; Lacmiel, 1c E, ½c S; sandwiches US$6; ⏲8am-7pm) With a breezy upstairs balcony, wi-fi access and all your favorite caffeinated beverages, this upmarket cafe is the perfect place to escape the chaos of the city. The food is overpriced, but no one will hurry you along if you sip frozen mochaccinos all day.

Cocina Doña Haydee NICARAGUAN $$
(Map p448; lacocina.com.ni; Pharaoh's Casino, 1c O; mains US$3-8; ⏲breakfast, lunch & dinner) This spot does rustic right, all the way down to

the traditional costumes and classic menu, from *gallo pinto* to *guiso de chilote* (cheese soup with baby corn) to steak with all the trimmings.

La Hora del Taco MEXICAN $$
(Map p448; Monte de los Olivos, 1c N; mains US$4.50-7.50; ⏲lunch & dinner) This sprawling Mexican bar and restaurant has a well-considered menu that includes standards like nachos and fajitas plus a few southern Mexican favorites such as *cochinita pibil* (suckling pig).

Drinking & Nightlife

There are bars all over town, but the best ones can be found in Barrio Martha Quezada, around Metrocentro mall and at the Rotonda Bello Horizonte. Take a cab home!

Shannon Bar IRISH PUB
(Map p448; Tica Bus, 1c E, ½c S) The classic bar in this area, this Irish pub is an expat gathering spot and one of the only places in town where you can get a cold Guinness tallboy.

Caramanchel BAR
(Map p448; Hotel Crowne Plaza, 1c S, ½c E) For the extremely down-to-earth, bohemian side of Bolonia, hit the dance floor at this mostly outdoor neighborhood bar. Dress is extremely casual (jeans and flip-flops OK), and the DJ spins laidback dance tunes into the early morning.

El Grillito BAR
(Map p448; Intur, ½c N) There are a few little outdoor bars like this in the area, but this one consistently gets a good crowd. A range of snacks and more substantial meals are on the menu and the music volume is conversation-friendly.

Zona Hippo's BAR
(Map p448; Seminole Plaza, 1c S; ⏲noon-2am) Wanna go where everybody knows your name? Globalization has arrived and it's called Hippo's Grill & Tavern, with nine different burgers, next door to affiliated Woody's Sports Bar, with 15 types of hot wings. Both have Caesar salads, plenty of 'flair,' nonthreatening rock music and very full bars.

El Puerto BAR
(Map p444; Rotonda Bello Horizonte, 80m E) Ignore the lame disco out back (there are much better ones in the area); this is the place to grab a beer on the front deck and do a bit of people-watching, before slipping inside for a couple of games of pool on surprisingly good tables.

Reef LOUNGE
(Galeria Santo Domingo) The most popular spot in the emerging *zona viva* (nightlife zone) out back of the Santo Domingo mall, this is a favorite pre-dance spot for scenesters.

Moods DANCE
(www.moodsclubmanagua.com; Galeria Santo Domingo; cover US$3-10) Pretty much *the* club in town, with a dress code, Euro styling, imported DJs, dry ice, polished chrome, laser lighting...you get the picture. It's south of the city.

WORTH A TRIP

EASY DAY TRIPS FROM MANAGUA

➡ **Lagunas De Xiloá & Apoyeque** Half a dozen crater lakes lie near Managua. The best for swimming is Laguna de Xiloá, on the Península de Chiltepe, about 20km northwest of Managua off the road to León. It's a steep 30-minute hike from Laguna de Xiloá to less accessible but more picturesque Laguna de Apoyeque, deep within a steep crater. Take bus 110 from UCA to Ciudad Sandino, where you can catch an onward bus to the lagoons.

➡ **Mateare** Back out on the main highway, take a right to get to this lazy little fishing village sloping down to the banks of Lago de Managua. From here, you can hire a boat for around US$80 (up to seven people) to take you to Isla Momotombo. Look out for snakes. Buses leave Mateare's Parque Central every two hours between 6am and 6pm for the 40-minute ride to Managua's Mercado Israel Lewites; the fare is US$0.35.

➡ **El Trapiche** Located 22km from Managua in the town of Tipitapa, the **Centro Turístico El Trapiche** (admission US$0.25; ⏲7am-6pm) has therapeutic waters surrounded by gardens and restaurants. Buses to Tipitapa depart from Mercado Roberto Huembes.

Central Managua

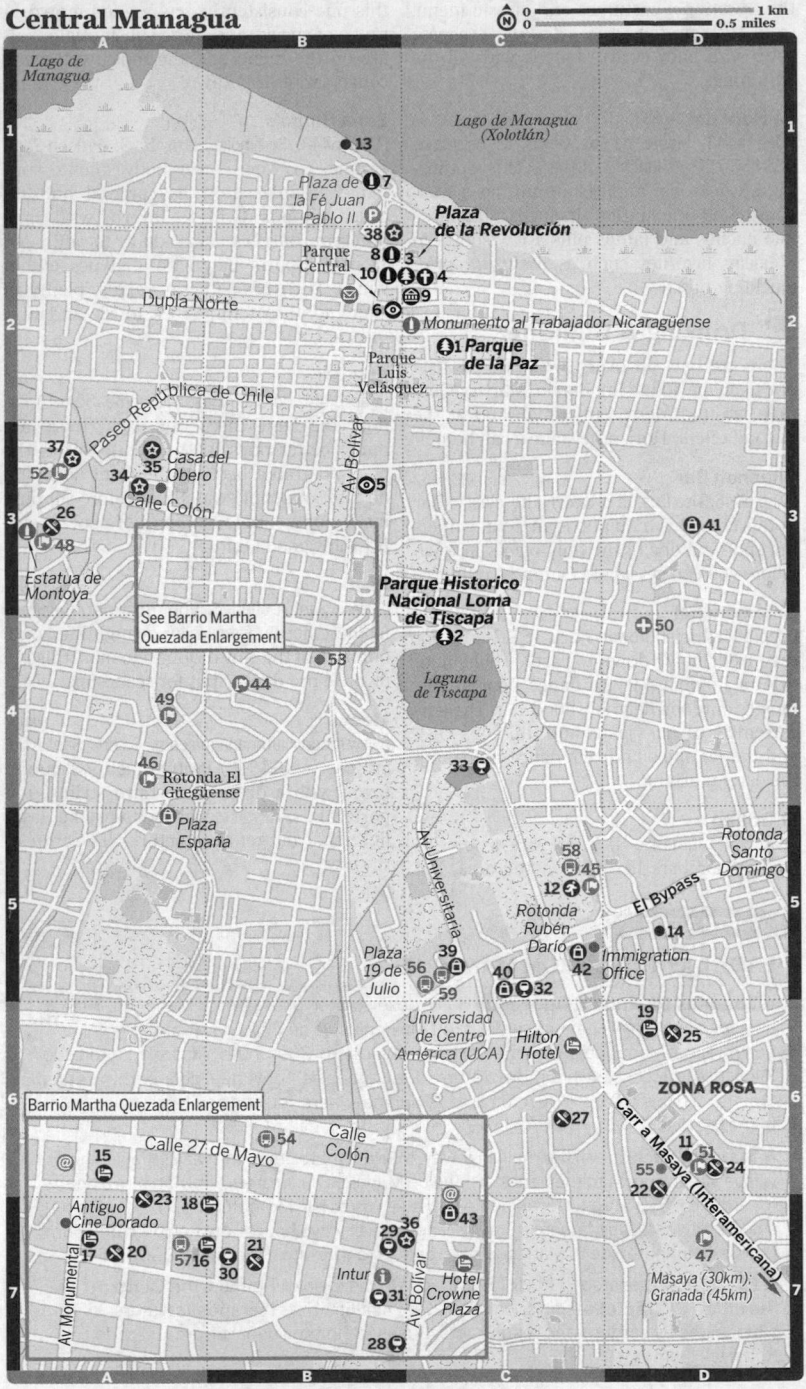

Central Managua

Top Sights
1 Parque de la Paz C2
2 Parque Historico Nacional Loma de Tiscapa C4
3 Plaza de la Revolución C2

Sights
4 Antigua Catedral C2
5 Arboretum Nacional B3
6 Centro Cultural Managua B2
7 Concha Acústica B1
8 Monumento a Rubén Darío B2
Museo Nacional ..... (see 9)
9 Palacio de la Cultura y Biblioteca Nacional C2
10 Tomb of Carlos Fonseca B2

Activities, Courses & Tours
11 Alianza Francesa D6
12 Nueva Catedral C5
13 Puerto Salvador Allende B1
14 Viva Spanish School D5

Sleeping
15 Casa de Huéspedes Santos A6
16 Casa Vanegas B7
Hostal Dulce Sueño ..... (see 16)
17 Hotel Los Felipe A7
Hotel y Apartamento Los Cisneros ..... (see 15)
18 Jardín de Italia B7
19 Managua Backpackers Inn D6

Eating
20 Cafetín Mirna A7
21 Cafetín Tonalli B7
22 Cocina Doña Haydee D6
23 Doña Pilar A7
24 La Casa del Café D6
25 La Hora del Taco D6
26 Licuados Ananda A3
27 Tercer Ojo C6

Drinking & Nightlife
28 Caramanchel B7
29 El Grillito B7
30 Shannon Bar B7
31 Tabú B7
32 Zona Hippo's C5
33 Zona Latino C4

Entertainment
Bar La Cavanga ..... (see 6)
34 Estadio Cranshaw A3
35 Estadio Denis Martínez A3
36 La Casa de los Mejía Godoy C7
37 Ruta Maya A3
38 Teatro Nacional Rubén Darío B2

Shopping
39 El Parnaso C5
40 Librería Hispamer C5
41 Mercado Oriental D3
42 Metrocentro C5
43 Plaza Inter C7

Information
44 Canadian Embassy B4
45 Costa Rican Consulate C5
46 Danish Embassy A4
47 Dutch Embassy D7
48 French Embassy A3
49 German Embassy A4
50 Hospital Bautista D4
51 Mexican Embassy D6
52 Panamanian Embassy A3

Transport
53 Alamo B4
54 Central Line B6
55 Easy Rent-a-car D6
King Quality ..... (see 36)
56 Microbuses to Masaya, Granada & León (UCA) C5
57 Tica Bus A7
58 Transnica C5
59 UCA Minivans C5

Zona Latino DANCE
(Map p448; Rotonda Rubén Darío, 600m N) This is the place to be for Latin grooves: salsa, merengue and *cumbia* (Colombian dance tunes) are in heavy rotation at this sprawling club in an oddly removed location.

Charlie's Bar DANCE
(Map p444; Rotonda Bello Horizonte, 60m E; cover US$1) The original and still one of the best, Charlie keeps the dance floor packed with a good selection of new hits and classics, all in the Caribbean vein.

Tabú GAY
(Map p448; Intur, 100m S) One of the few gay bars with any longevity in town. Tabu's dance floor gets going on weekends.

☆ Entertainment

Live Music

Bar La Cavanga LIVE MUSIC
(Map p448; Centro Cultural Managua; cover US$4; ⏲Thu-Sat) Take a taxi out to this 1950s-era gem, which stages live folk and jazz shows in the sketchy neighborhood near the Antigua Catedral.

La Casa de los Mejía Godoy LIVE MUSIC
(Map p448; ☎2222-6110; www.losmejiagodoy.com; frente Hotel Crowne Plaza; cover US$8-15; ⏲opening hours vary) Living legends Carlos and Luis Enrique Mejía Godoy, whose folk-music explorations into the heart of Nicaraguan culture have become church hymns and revolutionary standards since they first started laying down riffs in the 1960s, have moved from their original intimate venue to a larger premises with a restaurant. Make reservations if you're planning on seeing the brothers play.

Bar Art Café LIVE MUSIC
(Estatua de Montoya, 3c O, 50m N; ⏲Wed-Sat) Always worth a look, this bohemian little space in front of Parque Las Palmas hosts poetry and open-mic nights on Wednesday, electronica DJs on Thursday and other underground-type events the rest of the week.

Ruta Maya LIVE MUSIC
(Map p448; ☎2268-0698; www.rutamaya.com.ni; Estatua de Montoya, 150m E; cover US$1-5) Look around for flyers (or check the website) for happenings at this thatch-roofed venue.

Theater & Cinema
Every mall has a cinema inside screening international blockbusters.

Teatro Nacional Rubén Darío THEATER
(Map p448; ☎2266-3630; www.tnrubendario.gob.ni; Área Monumental) This impressive theater hosts high-quality plays, concerts, and exhibitions by national and visiting artists.

La Sala de Teatro Justo Rufino Garay THEATER
(Map p444; ☎2266-3714; www.rufinos.org; Estatua de Montoya, 3c O, 20m N; tickets US$2) Artsy movies at 7pm Wednesday.

INCH PERFORMING ARTS
(Instituto Nicaragüense de Cultura Hispanica; ☎2276-0733; nichispanica@gmail.com; Av del Campo 40-42, Las Colinas; ⏲9am-3pm Mon-Fri) Located in the very ritzy hill suburb of Las Colinas to the south of Managua, this center hosts some of the city's best cultural events.

Sport
Managua's Bóer baseball team faces its rivals in the professional league and national championship (October to January) at the **Estadio Denis Martínez** (Map p448), just northwest of Barrio Martha Quezada. Check www.lnbp.com.ni for schedules. Reflecting football's secondary status in Nicaragua, **Estadio Cranshaw** (Map p448) is a more humble affair that squats in the shadows of its big brother, just to the south.

Shopping

Mercado Oriental MARKET
(Map p448) Stash your cash in a couple of places (sock, bra) and try to find a local guide for Central America's largest market and scariest shopping experience.

Mercado Roberto Huembes HANDICRAFTS
(Map p444) This is more than just the southbound bus terminal; it has the best selection of souvenirs in Managua, from all over the country.

Librería Hispamer BOOKS
(Map p448; www.hispamer.com.ni; UCA, 1c E, 1c N) This bookstore has the country's best selection of Nicaraguan and Latin American literature, history and poetry, plus local news and arts periodicals.

El Parnaso BOOKS
(Map p448; Rotonda Rubén Darío, 300m O) Across from the UCA, this lefty bookstore has a great selection of magazines.

Metrocentro MALL
(Map p448) Upscale mall with restaurants, movie theaters and more.

Galeria Santo Domingo MALL
(Carretera a Masaya, Km 8) See and be seen at the discos, eateries and shops of Managua's most upscale mall.

Plaza Inter MALL
(Map p448) Adjacent to Barrio Martha Quezada, it's convenient, with a movie theater (with subtitled movies), lots of discount shops, a couple of department stores and a solid food court.

Orientation

Managua's spread-out collection of barrios (neighborhoods) sits on the southern shore of Lago de Managua (Xolotlán). The former center on the lakeshore is now largely derelict, having been left vacant after the 1972 quake, but has several visitor attractions. South of here, Volcán Tiscapa and its crater lake is the city's main landmark. To its west is the pyramidal Hotel Crowne Plaza and the Barrio Martha Quezada, home of many of the city's budget accommodations, while to the south is a thriving commercial zone running along the city's main thoroughfare, Carretera a Masaya.

WHERE THE STREETS HAVE NO NAME – NAVIGATING MANAGUA

Like other Nicaraguan cities and towns, Managua has few street signs and only the major roads are named. Large buildings, *rotondas* (traffic circles) and traffic lights serve as de facto points of reference, and locations are described in terms of their direction and distance, usually in *cuadras* (blocks), from these points. Just to complicate matters, many of these references no longer exist, so you may get addresses that begin with something like '*de donde fue Sandy's*' (from where Sandy's used to be...).

In addition, in Managua a special system is used for the cardinal points, whereby *al lago* (to the lake) means 'north' while *arriba* (up) is 'east' and *abajo* (down) is 'west,' the latter expressions deriving from the sun's movement. South is just plain old *sur*. Thus you might hear: '*del antiguo Cine Dorado, una cuadra al lago, dos cuadras arriba,*' meaning from the old Dorado Cinema, one block north, two blocks to the east.

Confused? You get used to it. Places in Managua give the address in Spanish – but we use the cardinal points N (norte; north), S (sur; south), E (este; east) and O (oeste; west) – so you can ask locals or just let the cab driver figure it out. *Cuadra* is abbreviated to 'c' in addresses for listings.

Managua's central market, Mercado Roberto Huembes, lies 2km southeast of Metrocentro; other major markets (and adjacent bus terminals) are at the western (Bóer), northern (Oriental, confusingly) and eastern (Mayoreo) ends of town.

Information

DANGERS & ANNOYANCES

Managua is nowhere near as dangerous as it seems, and a vast majority of visits to the capital are incident free. That said, crime has risen here in recent years, and like in any large city in the region, it pays to take some basic precautions. Keep your camera and iPod hidden, look at your map before you set out and only carry as much money as you realistically are going to need during the day. Except in the upmarket areas, always take a taxi after dark, and take one in the Área Monumental even during daylight hours. Barrio Martha Quezada has its share of incidents, mostly on its northern edge and between it and Plaza Inter; take a taxi through here, even if it's just a couple of blocks. For information on taxi safety, see the boxed text p525.

EMERGENCY

Ambulance (☎128; Red Cross)

Fire (☎115)

Police (☎118)

IMMIGRATION

Immigration Office (www.migracion.gob.ni; Metrocentro; ⏲10am-6pm Mon-Fri, 10am-1pm Sat & Sun) The main office is located near the Ciudad Jardín area but this is a more convenient office, in the Metrocentro mall.

INTERNET ACCESS

All the large shopping malls have free wi-fi access. There are numerous internet cafes throughout Managua. Convenient ones:

Kafe Internet (Av Monumental; per hr US$0.70)

Plaza Inter (per hr US$2) Inside the food court.

MEDICAL SERVICES

Pharmacies, found all over Managua, are usually open until 10pm.

Hospital Alemán-Nicaragüense (☎2249-3368; Carretera Norte, Km 6) Has some German-speaking staff and modern equipment.

Hospital Bautista (Map p448; ☎2264-9020; www.hospitalbautistanicaragua.com; Casa Ricardo Morales Aviles, 2c S, 1½c E, Barrio Largaespada) Professional and reasonably priced emergency and outpatient services. Some staff speak English.

Hospital Metropolitano Vivian Pellas (☎2255-6900; www.metropolitano.com.ni; Carretera a Masaya, Km 9.75) State-of-the-art facility.

MONEY

Managua has scores of banks and ATMs, most on the Visa/Plus system. BAC, with machines at Metrocentro, the international airport and Plaza España, accepts MasterCard/Cirrus debit cards and gives US dollars and córdobas. Any bank can change US dollars.

POST & TELEPHONE

Most people are now calling internationally using VOIP.

Palacio de Correos (Plaza de la Revolución, 2c O) The main post office (inside the former

Enitel building) has poste restante services (mail is held for up to 45 days).

TOURIST INFORMATION

Ben Linder House (☎2266-4363; www.casabenlinder.org; de donde fue el Banco Popular, 2c N, 2c E, Monseñor Lezcano) This cultural center primarily serves the English-speaking volunteer community.

Intur (Nicaraguan Institute of Tourism; ☎2222-3333; www.visitanicaragua.com; Hotel Crowne Plaza, 1c S, 1c O) Has helpful maps and can recommend hotels and attractions in Managua and beyond. There is another office in the airport.

Marena Central (Ministry of the Environment & Natural Resources; ☎2263-2830; www.marena.gob.ni; Carretera Norte, Km 12.5) Bring ID to the inconveniently located headquarters (out past the airport, a US$8 taxi ride) to gain access to maps, flyers and management plans for most of Nicaragua's 82 protected areas.

Getting There & Away

AIR

Managua International Airport (MGA; www.eaai.com.ni; Carretera Norte, Km 13) is a small, manageable airport located about 30 to 45 minutes from most hotels. **Intur** (⏲8am-10pm) has an office inside the international terminal, next to the luggage belt in the arrivals area, where English-speaking staff can recommend hotels, confirm flights and share flyers.

The smaller, more chaotic domestic terminal is adjacent to the main building.

The internal carrier **La Costeña** (☎2263-2142; www.lacostena.com.ni; Managua International Airport) has regular service to Bluefields, the Corn Islands, Las Minas, Puerto Cabezas and Waspán.

BUS

Managua is the main transportation hub for the country, with four major national bus and van terminals, plus a handful of international bus lines, most grouped in Barrio Martha Quezada.

International Bus

Tica Bus (Map p448; www.ticabus.com) is in a newly remodeled terminal at the heart of Barrio Martha Quezada. **King Quality** (Map p448; ☎2222-2075; www.king-qualityca.com; Calle 27 de Mayo, frente Plaza Inter) has in-flight...er, in-ride meal service and less intense air-conditioning. **Transnica** (Map p448; www.

NATIONAL BUS SERVICES FROM MANAGUA

DESTINATION	COST (US$)	DURATION	FREQUENCY	LEAVES FROM
Boaco	2	3 hr	every 15 min	Mayoreo
Carazo (serving Diriamba & Jinotepe)	1	1 hr	every 20 min	Bóer
Chinandega/El Viejo	2.50	2½ hr	every 30 min	Bóer
Chinandega minibus	3	2 hr	when full	Bóer
El Rama *expreso*	7.50	5 hr	3 daily	Mayoreo
El Rama *ordinario*	7.50	5 hr	5 daily	Mayoreo
El Sauce	3	3 hr	3 daily	Bóer
Esquipulas	3	4 hr	6 daily	Mayoreo
Estelí	3	2 hr	hourly	Mayoreo
Granada	0.75	1 hr	every 15 min	Huembes
Granada minibus	1.25	1 hr	when full	UCA
Jinotega	3.50	4 hr	hourly	Mayoreo
Jinotepe minibus	1.15	1 hr	when full	UCA
Juigalpa	2	4 hr	every 20 min	Mayoreo
La Paz Centro	0.90	1½ hr	every 30 min	Bóer
León *expreso* (via New Hwy & La Paz Centro)	1.85	1½ hr	every 2 hr	Bóer
León *ordinario* (via Old Hwy)	1.50	2 hr	every 20 min	Bóer

transnica.com) is the odd one out, with offices over the other side of the laguna.

As well as the services listed below, other alternatives include **Del Sol Bus** (www.busesdelsol.com) and **Central Line** (Map p448; ☎2254-5431; www.transportescentralline.com; Calle 27 de Mayo, 4½c O, Esso). Del Sol Bus has one bus leaving for San Salvador (US$45) and continuing to Guatemala City (US$70) at 4am daily, and Central Line offers services to San José, Costa Rica (US$23, eight hours, 10am), with stops in Masaya and Liberia.

Buses departing from Tica Bus:

Costa Rica (US$29 to US$40, 10 hours, six daily) For Liberia and San José.

Guatemala (US$55, 30 hours, twice daily) There is a continuing service to Tapachula, Mexico (US$69, 48 hours).

Honduras (US$23, seven hours, 5am) There is a continuing service from Tegucigalpa to San Pedro Sula (US$31, 11 hours).

Panama City (US$92, 34 hours) Via San Jose.

San Salvador (US$34 to US$49, 11 hours, twice daily)

Buses departing from King Quality:

Costa Rica (US$44, eight hours, 1:30pm)

Guatemala (US$75, 32 hours, 3am) For Guatemala City.

El Salvador (US$53, 10 hours, 3am) For San Salvador.

Honduras (US$44, 10 hours, 3am) For Tegucigalpa.

Buses departing from Transnica:

Costa Rica (US$23, nine hours, three daily) There's a luxury bus (US$35) at noon; for San José.

Honduras (US$29, 10 hours, 5am) For Tegucigalpa.

National Buses & Minivans

Buses leave from three main places: **Mercado Roberto Huembes** (Map p444) for Granada, Masaya and southwest Nicaragua; **Mercado Israel Lewites** (Map p444), commonly known as Bóer, for León and the northern Pacific; and **Mercado Mayoreo** (Map p444) for the Caribbean coast and the northern highlands. Some also leave from the Mercado Oriental, mainly to rural destinations not covered here. It's faster, more comfortable and a bit more expensive to take minivans from **UCA** (Map p448) (pronounced 'ooka') or *expreso* (express) rather than *ordinario* (regular) service.

DESTINATION	COST (US$)	DURATION	FREQUENCY	LEAVES FROM
León minibus	2.75	1½ hr	when full	Bóer
León minibus	2.75	1½ hr	when full	UCA
Masatepe minibus	1.10	1 hr	every 20 min	Huembes
Masaya	0.50	1 hr	every 30 min	Huembes
Masaya minibus	0.75	½ hr	when full	UCA
Matagalpa	2.10	2¾ hr	hourly	Mayoreo
Mateare	0.30	40 min	every 2 hr	Bóer
Nagarote	0.70	1 hr	every 30 min	Bóer
Naindame	1	1½ hr	every 20 min	Huembes
Ocotal	4.25	3½ hr	hourly	Mayoreo
Peñas Blancas	3.50	3 hr	2 daily	Huembes
Pochomil/Masachapa	1.10	2 hr	every 20 min	Bóer
Río Blanco	5	4 hr	hourly	Mayoreo
Rivas *expreso*	3.25	1½ hr	every 30 min	Huembes
Rivas *ordinario*	2	2 hr	every 30 min	Huembes
San Carlos	7.50	9 hr	6 daily	Mayoreo
San Juan del Sur	3.25	2½ hr	2 daily	Huembes
San Marcos minibus	1	1 hr	when full	Huembes
Siuna	9	10-12 hr	3 daily	Mayoreo
Somoto	4	4 hr	8 daily	Mayoreo
Ticuantepe minibus	0.35	40 min	when full	Huembes

Shuttle Buses

With frequent, inexpensive public minibuses running to León, Granada and other popular destinations, Managua's shuttle-bus scene is not huge. The biggest draws here are safety and the direct airport departure, meaning you don't have to catch a cab into town to connect with an onward bus.

Managua Backpackers offers shuttles to San Juan del Sur (US$70), León (US$50) and Granada (US$35) for one to four people. **Paxeos** (☎2552-8291; www.paxeos.com) serves Granada (US$40) and León ($70) for up to three people, and **Adelante Express** (☎8850-6070; www.adelanteexpress.com) serves San Juan del Sur (US$45 per person, three hours, leaving Managua's airport at 1pm daily).

Getting Around

TO/FROM THE AIRPORT

The airport is 11km from town and has its special, more expensive taxis (US$15 to US$20 to most Managua destinations), which don't stop to pick up other passengers. At night this is worth it, but during the day you can just run across the very busy Carretera Norte to the bus stop, where *colectivo* taxis cost US$5 to go into town. Even cheaper (and only advisable during broad daylight) are regular buses, charging US$0.20 for the ride all the way to Mercado Roberto Huembes. Look for buses with 'Huembes' above the windshield.

BUS

Local buses are frequent and crowded. They're also known for their professional pickpockets, but stay alert and you'll be fine. Routes run every 10 minutes from 4:45am to 6pm, then every 15 minutes until 10pm. Buses do not generally stop en route – look for the nearest bus shelter. The fare is US$0.15. Useful routes:

No 101 Linda Vista to Mercado Mayoreo, via Rotonda Bello Horizonte.

No 109 Plaza de la República to Mercado Roberto Huembes, stopping en route at Plaza Inter.

No 110 Mercado Israel Lewites (Bóer) to Mercado Mayoreo, via UCA, Metrocentro, Rotonda de Centroamérica, Mercado Roberto Huembes and Mercado Iván Montenegro.

No 116 Estatua de Montoya, Plaza Inter, Mercado Oriental and Rotonda Bello Horizonte.

No 118 From Parque Las Piedrecitas, heads down Carretera Sur, then east, passing by Mercado Israel Lewites (Bóer), Rotonda El Güegüense (Plaza España), Plaza Inter and Mercado Oriental on its way to Mercado Mayoreo.

No 119 From Linda Vista to Mercado Roberto Huembes, with stops at Rotonda El Güegüense and UCA.

CAR

Driving in Managua is crazy, man! But once you get out of town, with some Spanish under your belt, you should be OK. The airport has major international rental chains (and some locals).

Alamo (Map p448; ☎2277-1117; www.alamonicaragua.com; Hospital Militar, 100m E)

Easy Rent-a-car (Map p448; ☎2270-0654; www.easyrentacar.com.ni; Carretera a Masaya, Km 7.5)

TAXI

Most taxis in Managua are *colectivos*, which pick up passengers as they go. There are also more expensive private taxis based at the airport, shopping malls, Mercado Roberto Huembes and other places. These are safer, but regular taxis also always congregate close by. Licensed taxis have red plates and the driver's ID above the dash; if yours doesn't, you're in a pirate taxi. This is probably OK, but don't go to the ATM, and beware of scams no matter what kind of taxi you're in. At night, take only licensed taxis – there has been an increase in reports of taxi drivers robbing passengers after dark. For more information, see the boxed text on p525.

Fares are US$1 to US$4 per person within the city. From Barrio Martha Quezada, taxis go to the airport (US$6/8/12 for one/two/three people), Mercado Roberto Huembes (US$2/3 for one/two people), Mercado Israel Lewites (US$1.50/2), Mercado Mayoreo (US$4/5), Zona Rosa (US$2/3) and Huellas de Acahualinca (US$2/3). Prices rise at night.

Around Managua

Masachapa & Pochomil

The twin Pacific beach towns of Masachapa and Pochomil are so close together that they might as well be one. You arrive in Masachapa, a small fishing village with a handful of bars, hotels and restaurants on the beach.

Buses and pedicabs ply the 2km between Masachapa and the government-operated **Centro Turistico Pochomil** (car/pedestrian US$1/free) tourist center. This run-down tourist ghetto has about 30 businesses, mostly waterfront restaurants and bars, almost all with palapa (thatched) roofs, fronting a truly spectacular beach.

There is no ATM in either town, so bring plenty of cash.

Activities

There's great surfing – a left point break just north of Montelimar, and a hollow right reef

Around Managua

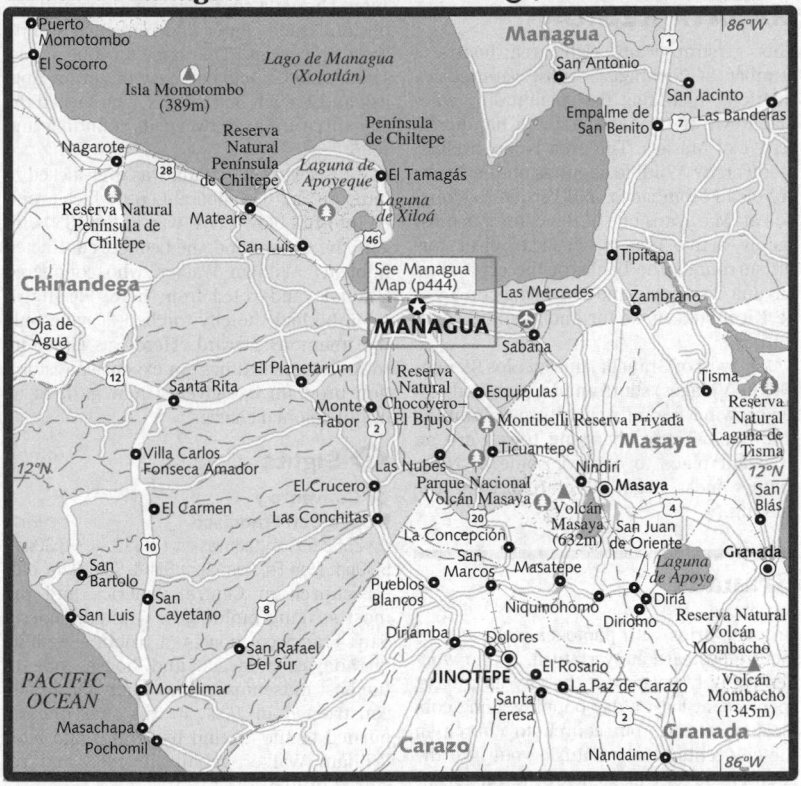

break to the south; Quizala, a beach break, is closer to Masachapa. South towards Pochomil there are scores of smallish, predictable peaks that would be perfect to learn on.

There's a suprisingly clean river between Masachapa and Pochomil that makes for a fun dip.

Masachapa Surf and Sportfishing SURFING

(☎8984-2464; www.sanjuandelsursurf.com; 200m E of beach on Main Rd, Masachapa) This small place rents surf boards (US$20 per day), runs sunset cruises (US$25 per person) and can charter surf/fish safaris (half/full day US$285/420). To learn to surf, take a US$40 day-long lesson (including board rental).

Sleeping

Hotel Alta Mar HOTEL $

(☎2269-9204; Centro Turístico Pochomil; r without bathroom US$10, r with air-con US$40; P ❄) By far the best deal in Pochomil, and the only hotel within the central tourist area really worth considering, this place has a decent restaurant with good ocean views and small, spotless rooms.

Hospedaje Flipper HOTEL $

(☎2269-6509; Masachapa; r US$17) Right at the entrance to Masachapa, this is the cheapest option in town, with OK cement rooms and cleanish private bathrooms; it caters to couples on a beach break.

Getting There & Away

Buses arrive first at Masachapa – if you're planning on staying here, get off at the *empalme* (T-intersection).

Buses run from Pochomil and Masachapa through to Managua's Mercado Israel Lewites (US$1.10, two hours) every 20 minutes from 8am to 6pm.

GRANADA & THE MASAYA REGION

This geographically rich area boasts a number of Nicaragua's most vaunted attractions, including the spellbinding colonial town of Granada and the handicraft center of Masaya. The area is also rich in biodiversity. Wildlife abounds on the flanks of Volcán Mombacho, and Parque Nacional Volcán Masaya is one of the country's most visibly active craters. Lush tropical forest surrounds the banks of the crystalline Laguna de Apoyo, and Las Isletas on Lago de Nicaragua make for another fine swim setting.

Just west of Granada, the Pueblos Blancos (White Villages) stand amid a highland coffee-growing region rich in pre-Columbian traditions. These charming towns are an excellent place to observe some of Nicaragua's most beautiful craftwork in the making.

Granada

POP 123,000

Granada drips with photogenic elegance, a picture postcard at every turn. It's no wonder many travelers use the city as a base, spending at least a day bopping along cobblestone roads from church to church in the city center, then venturing out into the countryside for trips to nearby attractions.

Just out of town half-day adventures take you to an evocative archipelago waterworld at Las Isletas and fun beaches at the Peninsula de Asese. Volcán Mombacho has walking trails, a canopy tour and a butterfly sanctuary, not to mention a few hot springs dotted around its foothills.

Culturally curious travelers may consider a trip to community tourism operations in nearby villages like Nicaragua Libre, or out to Parque Nacional Archipiélago Zapatera, home to one of the most impressive collections of petroglyphs and statues in the country.

History

Nicknamed 'the Great Sultan' in reference to its Moorish namesake across the Atlantic, Granada is Nicaragua's oldest colonial city. Founded in 1524 by Francisco Hernández de Córdoba, it stands at the foot of Volcán Mombacho on the northwestern shore of Lago de Nicaragua. With access to the Caribbean Sea via the lake and the Río San Juan, Granada soon became a rich and important trade center and remained so into the 19th century. This same Caribbean passage made Granada an easy target for English and French buccaneers, who sacked the city three times between its founding and 1685.

Conservative Granada was ever-locked in bitter rivalry with liberal León, which erupted into full-blown civil war in the 1850s. To gain the upper hand, the Leonese contracted filibuster William Walker, who conquered Granada and ruled from here. Fleeing in 1856, he had the city torched, leaving only the infamous placard, 'Here was Granada.' In more recent times, an expensive restoration program has given a new glow to its bright colonial charms.

Sights

★Convento y Museo San Francisco CHURCH

(☎2552-5535; admission US$2; ⏲8:30am-5:30pm Mon-Fri, 9am-4pm Sat & Sun) The oldest church in Central America and the most striking building in Granada, Iglesia San Francisco boasts a robin's-egg-blue birthday-cake facade and houses one of the best museums in the region. Originally constructed in 1585, it was subsequently burned to the ground by pirates and later William Walker, rebuilt in 1868 and restored in 1989.

The museum is through the small door on the left, where guides (some of whom speak English) are available for tours; tips are appreciated. Museum highlights include top-notch primitivist art, a scale model of the city, and a group of papier-mâché indigenous people cooking, relaxing in hammocks and swinging on comelazatoaztegams, a sort of a 360-degree see-saw.

★Iglesia de La Merced CHURCH

(Calle Real Xalteva; bell tower admission US$1) Arguably the most beautiful church in the city, this landmark is fronted by a plaza popular with young lovers. The caretaker usually takes people up to the **bell tower** at 11am, but you can ask any time.

Originally completed in 1539, it was razed by pirates in 1655 and rebuilt with its current baroque facade between 1781 and 1783. Damaged by Walker's forces in 1854, it was restored with the current elaborate interior in 1862.

WORTH A TRIP

BOAT TOUR OF LAS ISLETAS

An easy morning or afternoon trip from Granada takes you by boat to this miniature archipelago of 365 (OK, maybe fewer) tiny tropical islands. Keep your eye out for ospreys, king fishers, caimans and howler monkeys (along the mainland).

There's even a Spanish fortress. **Castillo San Pablo** was built in 1784 and has great views of Granada and Volcán Mombacho, plus a fine swimming hole nearby.

Most tours also pass **Isla de los Monos** (Monkey Island), where the spider and Capuchin monkey residents brought here by a veterinarian living on a nearby island are friendly but may run off with your picnic lunch.

Most tour companies run trips to Las Isletas, or you can do it yourself with **Inuit Kayaks** (☎2552-6695; marielo_q75@hotmail.com; Centro Turístico, 1.5km S), about 1km from the Centro Turístico entrance, which runs several guided kayak tours (from US$10 per hour). Touts will offer to hook you up with a boat tour from pretty much the moment you enter the Centro Turístico. If you're on your own or in a small group, wait around until a larger group forms (unless you want to pay for the whole boat yourself – around US$20 for a one-hour tour) and the boatmen start offering discount seats just to fill up their boat. For the best bird-watching, you'll want to arrange your trip the day before to get out at dawn. Sunset is also quite nice, though the tour is quicker, with less exploration of further afield corners of the island group. You may be able to arrange a short sunset cruise to Castillo San Pedro for around US$5 per boat.

Taking a turnoff to the right just after Inuit Kayaks (look for the sign saying 'Marina Cocibolca') takes you out onto the other side of the Peninsula de Asese to **Puerto Asese**, where you can also hire boats to tour the *isletas* over this side. It's a fun bike ride out here, but travel in groups, as some robberies have been reported.

There are numerous restaurants in the island chain. Ask your boatman to include a stop at one, where a large meal of locally caught fish will run around US$7.50.

Casa de los Leones & Fundación Casa de los Tres Mundos

CULTURAL BUILDING

(Parque Central, 50m N; child/adult US$0.25/0.40; ⏲8am-7pm Mon-Fri, 8am-6pm Sat & Sun) Founded in 1986 by Ernesto Cardenal, the Fundación Casa de los Tres Mundos moved to elegant 1720 Casa de los Leones in 1992. At the entrance, a board lists special events: poetry readings, classical ballet, folkloric dance and free movies. During regular business hours, your entrance fee buys you a look at a beautiful mansion and a few art displays.

Nicaragua Butterfly Reserve

PARK

(☎8895-3012; www.backyardnature.net/nbr; admission US$7; ⏲8am-4pm Mon-Sat) About 4km from Granada on the dirt road that leads from the cemetery to Laguna de Apoyo, this *mariposario* (butterfly farm) offers interesting tours. It's about a 45-minute walk – take Calle de las Comedias where it branches off to the right of the cemetery at the western edge of town.

Mi Museo

MUSEUM

(☎2552-7614; Calle Atravesada, Cine Karawala, ½c N; ⏲8am-5pm) **FREE** This museum displays an incredible private collection of ceramics dating from at least 2000 BC to the present. Hundreds of beautifully crafted pieces were chosen with as much an eye for their artistic merit as their archaeological significance. They are displayed in the grand old adobe with the same aesthetic awareness. Guided tours are worth it.

Fortaleza La Polvora

FORT

(donations appreciated; ⏲8am-5pm) Originally called the Fortaleza de Armas when it was constructed in 1748, this lavishly turreted Spanish fortress still has the best view in town, over ancient, water-stained church domes all the way to Lago de Nicaragua. You can also check out a roomful of paintings and a couple of artifacts. It was undergoing renovations at press time.

Antigüa Estación del Ferrocarril

LANDMARK

(Old train station) Nine long blocks north of the town center along Calle Atravesada you'll find the old train station, next to Parque Sandino, where a few well-preserved railroad cars are on display. Out front of the station is the Parque de los Poetas, dedicated to Nicaragua's literary giants.

Granada

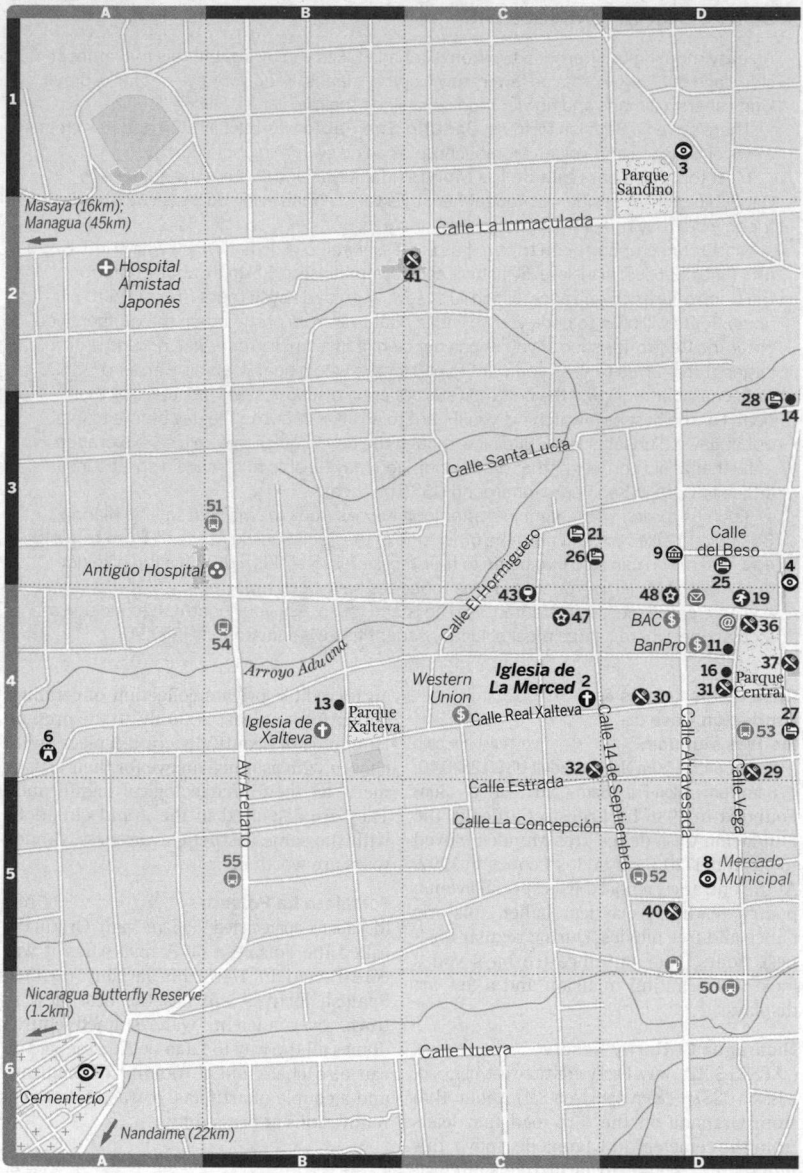

Granada Cementario CEMETERY
(Nandaime s/n) Used between 1876 and 1922, this cemetery has lots of picturesque mausoleums and tombs, including those of six Nicaraguan presidents. Most people come to see the 1880 neoclassical stone **Capilla de Animas** (Chapel of Spirits), a scale model of the French chapel of the same name.

Mercado Municipal MARKET
(Calle Atravesada) Head to the overflowing and fun (if not particularly good for souvenir

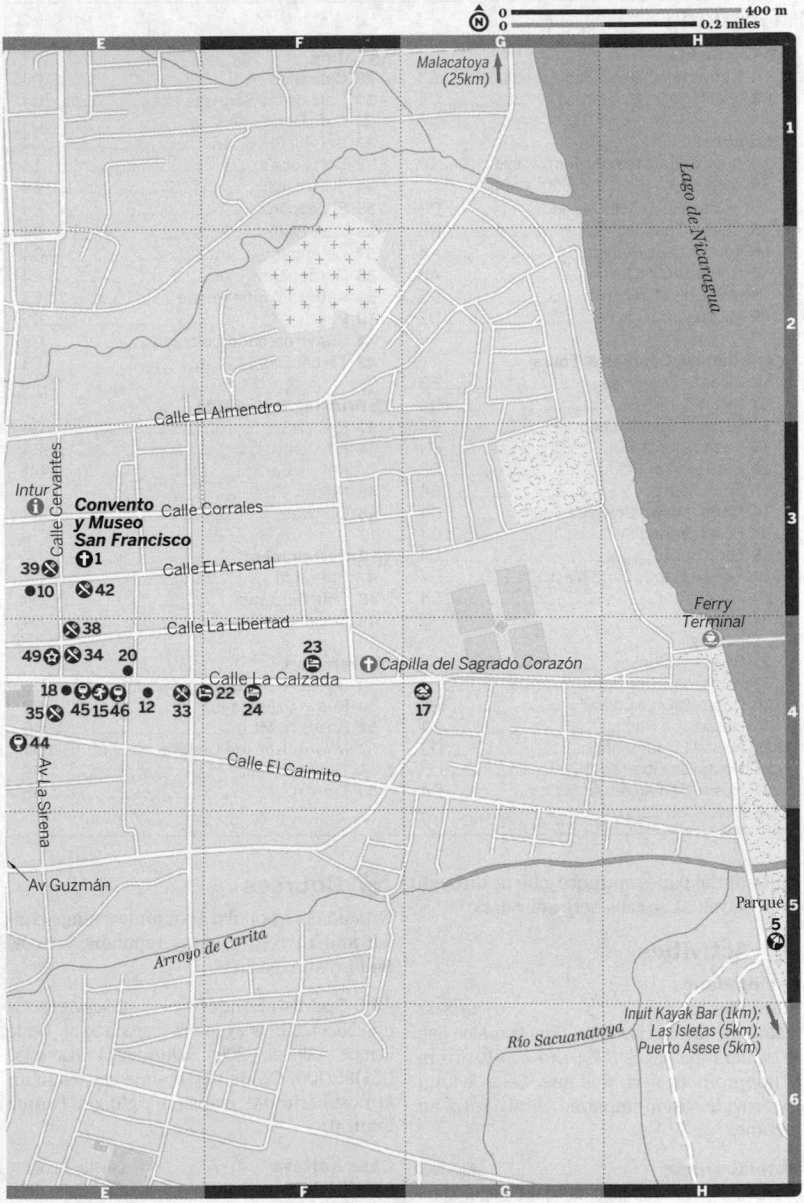

shopping) Mercado Municipal, located in a neoclassical building constructed in 1892. The building may be beautiful, but there's really no way of knowing until somebody gets up there and scrubs the facade.

Centro Turístico BEACH

FREE This tourist center has restaurants, discos, sandy beaches, kids' play areas and picnic spots, and is the place to go to hire a launch or kayak for a Las Isletas excursion (hire boats at Cabinas Amarillas – 3km

Granada

Top Sights
1 Convento y Museo San Francisco E3
2 Iglesia de La Merced C4

Sights
3 Antigüa Estación del Ferrocarril D1
4 Casa de los Leones & Fundación Casa de los Tres Mundos D3
5 Centro Turístico H5
6 Fortaleza La Polvora A4
7 Granada Cementario A6
8 Mercado Municipal D5
9 Mi Museo D3

Activities, Courses & Tours
10 Alliance Française E3
11 APC Spanish School D4
12 Calzada Spanish School E4
13 Casa Xalteva B4
14 Corazón Tours D3
15 Erick Tours E4
16 Horse-Drawn Carriage Tour D4
17 Hotel Granada G4
18 Leo Tours E4
19 Seeing Hands Blind Massage D4
20 Tierra Tour E4

Sleeping
21 Bearded Monkey C3
22 Hospedaje Cocibolca F4
23 Hospedaje La Calzada F4
24 Hospedaje Ruiz F4
25 Hostal El Momento D3
26 Hostal La Libertad C3
27 Hostal San Angel D4
28 Hotel Con Corazón D3

Eating
29 Café Blue D4
30 Café de las Sonrisas D4
31 Café Don Simon D4
32 Cafetín El Volcán C4
33 Don Luca's E4
34 El Pizzaiol E4
35 El Zaguán E4
36 Euro Café D4
37 Fritangas D4
38 Garden Café E4
39 Kathy's Waffle House E3
40 Palí D5
41 Supermercado Colonia C2
42 Tercer Ojo E3

Drinking & Nightlife
43 El Club C4
44 Encuentros E4
Kelly's Bar ..... (see 44)
45 Nectar E4
46 O'Sheas E4

Entertainment
47 Café Nuit C4
48 Cine Karawala D4
49 Imagine E4

Transport
50 Buses to Destinations South D6
51 Buses to Managua B3
52 Buses to Masaya D5
53 Microbuses to Managua D4
54 Tica Bus B4
55 Transnica B5

south of the park's entrance gate or through Inuit Kayak). Use cabs here after dark.

Activities

Seeing Hands Blind Massage MASSAGE

(Euro Café, Calle La Libertad; ⏲9am-6pm Mon-Sat; 👪) Offers massages (US$3 to US$10) from a nonprofit project that has been set up to provide vision-impaired locals with an income.

Hotel Granada SWIMMING

(☎2552-2974; www.hotelgranadanicaragua.com; Calle La Calzada, frente Iglesia de Guadalupe; pool admission US$7) While the hotel ain't worth the expense, it does offer day passes for its big, beautiful pool to tempt travelers on hot days.

Courses

Granada is a popular spot for learning Spanish and there are many reputable schools and private teachers.

APC Spanish School LANGUAGE COURSE

(☎2552-4203; www.spanishgranada.com; frente Parque Central; 20hr with/without homestay US$185/100) Offers one-on-one classes in an atmospheric old mansion right on Parque Central.

Casa Xalteva LANGUAGE COURSE

(☎2552-2436; www.casaxalteva.com; Calle Real Xalteva, Iglesia Xalteva, 25m N; 20hr without homestay US$135) Nonprofit Spanish school.

Alliance Française LANGUAGE COURSE

(www.alianzafrancesa.org.ni; Calle El Arsenal s/n) French and Spanish courses, plus franco-fantastic cultural events.

Calzada Spanish School LANGUAGE COURSE
(☎8402-7820; www.spanishonlinenicaragua.com; Galería Calzada, Calle La Calzada) Online or one-on-one tutoring for US$5.50 to US$7 per hour.

Tours

The classic Granada tour takes a **horse-drawn carriage** (up to 5 people US$15) from Parque Central for an hour-long whirl past churches, the cemetery, the *malecón* and more with your Spanish-speaking guide. They'll also wait while you take the other classic Granada trip, a boat ride through Las Isletas.

You can arrange trips all over the country from Granada, with recommended splurges including the Granada city tour (per person US$20 to US$25), Reserva Natural Volcán Mombacho (with/without canopy tour US$70/35), Masaya's Mercado Artesanías (US$30) and Volcán Masaya (US$25 to US$40, including Catarina).

Most operators also rent out bikes (US$1 per hour) and kayaks (US$9 per hour), and can arrange Las Isletas tours.

Prices are lower for larger groups, so solo travelers should shop around to see who is already going or hook up with groups at your hostel.

Corazón Tours TOUR
(www.hotelconcorazon.com; Calle Cervantes, Parque Central 3c N) Located inside the Hotel Con Corazón, this nonprofit tour operator offers well-done trips.

Leo Tours TOUR
(☎8422-7905; www.leotourscomunitarios.com; Parque Central, 1½c E) Enthusiastic locally owned business that offers all the usual options as well as some interesting visits to local communities.

Tierra Tour TOUR
(☎2552-8723; www.tierratour.com; Calle La Calzada, Catedral, 2c E) Slightly upscale (read: more expensive) tour operator.

Festivals & Events

International Poetry Festival CULTURAL
(www.festivalpoesianicaragua.com; ⏲February) Local and international poets take over the town for this event that also includes concerts by some of Nicaragua's best musicians.

Fiestas de Agosto RELIGIOUS
(⏲3rd week of August) Granada celebrates the Assumption of Mary, with fireworks, concerts, rodeos and horse parades by the lakefront.

Inmaculada Concepción RELIGIOUS
(Purísimas; ⏲November 28 to December 7) Neighborhoods bear elaborate floats through the streets in honor of Granada's patron saint, the Virgen Concepción de María.

Sleeping

These prices are for high season (December to May); at pricier hotels rates may drop around 15% outside of the peak season. Make reservations and expect to pay more around Christmas, Semana Santa, the mid-August *fiestas* and Independence Day (September 15).

Bearded Monkey HOSTEL $
(☎2552-4028; bearded@yahoomail.com; Calle 14 de Septiembre, Parque Central, 2c O, ½c N; dm/d/tr without bathroom US$5/15/18; @📶) A backpackers' favorite and Granada institution, the Monkey is a rambling colonial monster, partially renovated in the grunge-chic style that backpackers will be familiar with. The bar is always hopping at this party-forward hostel. The dorms have decent mattresses and are a little bigger than neighboring hostels, and of course you get hammocks, shared kitchen, book exchange and more.

Hostal El Momento HOSTEL $
(☎2552-7811; www.hostelgranadanicaragua.com; Calle del Beso; dm/s/d/tr/q US$8/14/18/34/40; @📶) Catering to the mature backpacker set, this hip new offering has cool chill areas throughout, iPads in the lobby, a book exchange and shared kitchen. The dorm room sleeps 11 and has great, firm mattresses and lockers. Bring your earplugs. Private rooms are a good bet, some maintaining the historic character of the building.

Hostal La Libertad HOSTEL $
(www.hostallalibertad.com.ni; Calle 14 de Septiembre; s/d US$15/20, dm/s/d without bathroom US$5/10/12; @📶) This hostel caters to a younger party set, with massive 16-bed dorms, a shared kitchen and a brightly painted courtyard framed by hammocks. The rooms are clean, but the mattresses can be a bit shoddy. There's a girls-only dorm.

Hospedaje Ruiz HOTEL $
(☎2552-2346; hospedajeycaferuiz@gmail.com; Calle La Calzada s/n; s/d US$18/22, d with air-con US$35;) Walk through the friendly family's restaurant and kitchen area to find this excellent little budget choice. The freshly painted rooms are simple and spacious, with good, firm beds. Bathrooms are on the small side but spotless and recently renovated.

Hostal San Angel HOTEL $
(☎2552-6373; mariacampos118@hotmail.com; Av Guzmán s/n; s/d US$12/22;) Half a block from Parque Central, this super-friendly colonial-style hotel is a good budget buy. The rooms are slightly cramped with hard beds and cold-water showers, but you get a shared kitchen, easy access to everything in town and a warm family atmosphere.

Hospedaje La Calzada GUESTHOUSE $
(☎961-7128; Calle La Calzada, Parque Central, 3½c E; s/d US$11/17, without bathroom US$7/13) A back-to-basics budget hotel – rooms are smallish and the beds have a definite sag to them – but the price is right (for some) and the location's a killer.

Hospedaje Cocibolca GUESTHOUSE $
(☎2552-7223; hospedaje_@hotmail.com; Calle La Calzada, Parque Central, 3c E; s/d with fan US$16/19, with air-con US$35/40;) For the price you can probably do better, but this decent and centrally located budget spot does have some sweet 1980s headboards with inlaid mirrors. The common areas are dominated by giant water tanks, hardly an aesthete's dream.

★Hotel Con Corazón HOTEL $$$
(☎2552-8852; www.hotelconcorazon.com; Calle Cervantes, Parque Central, 3c N; s/d/tr/q US$62/73/94/121;) An elegant nonprofit hotel that directs earnings to the development of local educational programs. The rooms are simple and pleasing, spacious enough without being luxurious.

It has salsa classes on Monday nights that are open to the public.

Eating

The classic Granada dining experience is relaxing over a light meal in a shady corner of the Parque Central. Four cute **kiosks** anchoring the plaza at each corner serve *vigorón* (mashed yucca topped with coleslaw and pork rinds), best washed down with *chicha* (fruit juice mixed with sugar and water or milk).

There are two grocery stores: **Supermercado Colonia** (Calle La Inmaculada, Parque Sandino, 4c O) and **Palí** (Calle Atravesada, frente Mercado Municipal).

Granada has excellent street food, with bags of fruit salad (with fork US$0.30) and other goodies on sale between the Parque Central and the Mercado Municipal (p458) in the morning. Just before sunset, **fritangas** (sidewalk barbecues; snacks US$1-3) set up in the Parque Central and Calle La Calzada, dishing up barbecue, *gallo pinto* and all things fried onto washed banana leaves for you to enjoy.

Garden Café SANDWICHES $
(Calle La Libertad, Parque Central, 1c E; sandwiches US$4-5; 7am-9pm;) Offering the best salads and sandwiches in town, this tranquil little spot also does excellent coffee and a range of breakfasts.

Don Luca's PIZZERIA $
(Calle La Calzada s/n; pizza US$2.50-4, mains US$5-10) While the pizza is on the bland side of scrumpdiddiliumptious, this friendly outdoor eatery offers a great vantage point for people-watching and a wide selection of Italian faves.

Café de las Sonrisas NICARAGUAN $
(www.tioantonio.org; Calle Real Xalteva; dishes US$2.50-4; 7am-5pm Mon-Fri, 7am-2pm Sat & Sun) Practice your international communication at this nonprofit cafe run by hearing-impaired staff. There's a picture-gram menu, sign charts and basic Nicaraguan fare that's hearty and wholesome. It also sells hammocks made by blind people.

Euro Café CAFE $
(Calle La Libertad, Parque Central, 10m O; dishes US$3-4) One of the better cafes in town serves up a huge range of hot and iced coffees, juices, sandwiches, bagels, wraps and more in a plant-filled courtyard.

Café Don Simon SANDWICHES $
(Parque Central, costado O; breakfast & sandwiches US$2.50-5) A surprisingly moderately priced cafe, considering its five-star location, with tables overlooking the plaza. There's a wide range of breakfasts (including bagels) and a good selection of hot and cold drinks.

Kathy's Waffle House BREAKFAST $
(Calle El Arsenal, frente Convento San Francisco; dishes US$3-5; 7am-2pm) Anybody doubting the rejuvenating qualities of *gallo pinto* and bacon and eggs should drop into this cute

little cafe with a steaming hangover. Zing! Problem solved. There are all sorts of waffles, snacks and pancakes on offer, along with bottomless coffee and great views of the convent from the front balcony.

Cafetín El Volcán NICARAGUAN $
(Calle 14 de Septiembre, Iglesia de La Merced, 1c S; quesillos US$0.50-2) You could come for the good-value set lunches (US$3), but pretty much everyone in town agrees that the real draw here are the *quesillos*, some of the tastiest around. Also a good range of traditional drinks including *tiste* (a toasted corn beverage; US$0.50), *grama* (wheatgrass) and carrot juice.

Café Blue SNACKS $
(Calle Vega, Parque Central, 1c S; dishes US$2-4; P) A refreshingly simple little cafe serving up good American and Nica breakfasts, some spicy huevos rancheros, pancakes and a range of sandwiches under a cane ceiling.

★Tercer Ojo FUSION $$
(☎2552 6451; Calle El Arsenal, frente Convento San Francisco; meals US$5-14; ⏲11am-11pm; 📶) Specializing in Asian cuisine (but taking you across at least three-quarters of the world with its expansive menu and wine list), the Third Eye is your go-to for tofu, Indian, sushi and Thai food.

El Pizzaiol ITALIAN $$
(Calle La Libertad s/n; mains US$7-12.50; ⏲noon-10pm) You'll love the ambiance in this Italian trattoria. The food is pretty authentic – with a few regional variations, and the dessert list is to die for. The thin-crust pizza tops the menu, though you will do equally well with the savory pasta and meat dishes.

El Zaguán STEAKHOUSE $$
(☎2552-2522; Av La Sirena s/n; meals US$7-13; ⏲noon-11pm; 👪) Scoring consistent props for the best steak in town, this large yet somehow cozy restaurant just behind the cathedral specializes in melt-in-your-mouth locally grown steaks, flame grilled right before your very eyes. Some solid chicken and fish dishes and a good wine list round out the menu. Make reservations in the high season.

Drinking & Nightlife

A popular way to start the night is at one of the bars along Calle La Calzada. By the lake, there are some *discotecas,* packed with young locals at weekends, and a couple of dancing spots, frequented by an older crowd. They are fun but volatile, and you should definitely get a cab down here at night.

O'Sheas IRISH PUB
(Calle La Calzada s/n) One of the most popular pubs along the Calzada pedestrian strip, with friendly service and good pub grub.

Encuentros LOUNGE
(Calle El Caimito s/n; meals US$7-12; ⏲5pm-2am) This studied lounge and restaurant has be-bop-tastic atmosphere, made even groovier by the fedora-sporting waiters, acid jazz and modern menu that features contemporary cuisine like chicken in plum sauce and an assortment of tapas.

Nectar LOUNGE
(Calle La Calzada, Parque Central, 1½c E; dishes US$4-6) A seductive little lounge-bar with a good list of cocktails and some cozy sitting areas. In high season it often gets visiting DJs and live bands to liven up the place. Some delicious light meals and snacks make up the small, creative menu.

El Club LOUNGE
(☎2552 4245; www.elclub-nicaragua.com; Calle La Libertad, Parque Central, 3c O; cover US$2-5; ⏲Thu-Sat) A stylish and sophisticated venue hosting visiting DJs on a regular basis. This seems to be the preferred venue for the visiting A-list crowd from Managua – dress to impress. It has a US$8 open bar some nights.

Kelly's Bar IRISH PUB
(cnr Av La Serena & Calle El Caimito) Belfast meets Granada in this friendly pub that features an excellent patio out back, sports on the TV and good times.

☆ Entertainment

Everyone's favorite hostel, the Bearded Monkey (p461), screens indie and foreign films at 6pm and 8pm nightly.

Café Nuit LIVE MUSIC
(Calle La Libertad, Parque Central, 2½c O; cover Sat & Sun US$0.50; ⏲Tue-Sat) One of the most consistent and atmospheric live-music venues in town, set in a leafy courtyard. There's a small dance floor in front of the stage that gets packed when the band starts cooking.

Imagine LIVE MUSIC
(Calle La Libertad s/n) Just like John Lennon would have liked it (before Yoko got into

the picture), this chilled-out bar and well-overpriced restaurant features live music most days (based of course on an eight-day week).

Cine Karawala CINEMA
(Calle Atravesada; tickets US$1.50) Shows semi-recent films on weekends.

Information

DANGERS & ANNOYANCES

There have been some reports of robberies on the road leading down to the lake and south into the Centro Turístico – take a cab after dark. Assaults have been reported on the bike trip to the Peninsula de Asese (take a tour to avoid problems).

INTERNET ACCESS

There are internet places all over town. Most charge US$0.70 to US$1 per minute.

Alhambra Internet C@fe (Calle La Libertad, frente Hotel Colonial; per hr US$0.80) Very air-conditioned, with some of the fastest machines in town.

LAUNDRY

Fernanda's Laundry Service (Galeria La Calzada, Calle La Calzada; per 2-4 pounds US$3.75) Fast and friendly.

Laundry (Calle Consulado, Parque Central, 1½c O; per 450g US$0.75) Convenient for those staying out west.

MEDICAL SERVICES

Hospital Amistad Japonés (☎2552-2719; Calle La Inmaculada, Esso station, 2km O) On the road to Managua.

MONEY

BAC (Calle La Libertad, Parque Central, 1c O)

BanPro (Calle Consulado, Parque Central, 1c O)

Western Union (Calle Real Xalteva) International money transfers.

POST

Post Office (Calle Atravesada, BanCentro, ½c S) Opposite Cine Karawala.

TOURIST INFORMATION

Intur (☎2552-6858; www.visitanicaragua.com/ingles; Calle Corrales) Up-to-date transport information, a passable city map and heaps of flyers.

UCA (Union of Agricultural Cooperatives; www.ucatierrayagua.org) Organizes community-based tours to rural villages.

Getting There & Away

BOAT

Ferries leave the **ferry terminal** (☎2552-2966; Calle La Calzada, final; ⏲8am-1:30pm) at 2pm Monday and Thursday, stopping at Altagracia (Isla de Ometepe; lower/upper deck US$2/5, three hours), San Miguelito (lower/upper deck US$3/7.50, nine hours) and San Carlos (lower/upper deck US$4/9, 14 hours). First-class seats, on the upper deck, have padded chairs and access to the TV, which will be on all night. Stake out a sleeping spot early and don't forget your seasickness medication. If you're thinking about doing the Granada–Altagracia run one-way only, it's best to leave from Granada – you travel in the day, get some views and arrive late afternoon. Leaving Altagracia for Granada, you travel at night and arrive in the early hours of the morning.

Puerto Asese (☎2552-2269), about 2km southeast of town, has boats for Las Isletas and Parque Nacional Archipiélago Zapatera.

BUS

Transnica (☎2522-6619; www.transnica.com; Calle El Tamarindo, Iglesia Xalteva, 1c O, 1½c S) has buses to Costa Rica (US$29, eight hours) at 6am, 8am (express to San José) and 11am. **Tica Bus** (☎2552-8535; www.ticabus.com; Av Arellano, Antigüo Hospital, ½c S) leaves for San José (US$29 to US$40, eight hours) at 7am and 1pm. For other international services, you'll need to go to Rivas or Managua.

Granada doesn't have one central bus terminal. **Buses to Managua** (US$.075, one hour, 4am to 7pm, every 20 minutes), arriving at that city's Mercado Roberto Huembes, depart from the lot just north of the old hospital on the western edge of town. **Microbuses to Managua** (US$1, one hour, 5am to 7.30pm, every 15 minutes), arriving at UCA in that city, leave from the convenient lot just south of the Parque Central on Calle Vega. **Buses to Masaya** (US$0.50, 30 minutes, 5am to 6pm, every 20 minutes) leave from two blocks west of the market, around the corner from Palí.

Buses to destinations south of Granada leave from a block south of the market, across from the Shell station.

Carazo (US$0.70, 50 minutes, every 20 minutes) For San Marcos, Diriamba (with connections to the Carazo beaches) and Jinotepe.

Catarina & San Juan de Oriente (US$0.50, 30 minutes, every 20 minutes) Also serves Niquinohomo.

Nandaime (Reserva Natural Volcán Mombacho; US$0.45, 20 minutes, half-hourly)

Pueblos Blancos/Carazo (US$0.40 to US$0.70, four daily) For Diriomo, Diría, Catarina, Niquinohomo, Masatepe, San Marcos and Jinotepe.

WORTH A TRIP

DAY TRIPS FROM GRANADA

There are several great day trips from Granada. Here are some off-the-beaten-track options.

Nicaragua Libre, La Granadilla and La Nanda Rural tourism at its best. UCA (p464) can tell you more.

Aguas Termales La Calera (☎2552-6330; osorio@invernic.com) FREE Hot springs a short trip away.

Reserva Silvestre Privada Domitila (☎8881-1786; www.domitila.org; r per person incl 3 meals US$90) It's expensive getting to this wildlife reserve. Go with a tour operator from Granada for around US$30.

Parque Nacional Archipiélago Zapatera (lodge dm incl 3 meals US$15, tour per person US$60-80) Isla Zapatera, a dormant volcano rising to 629m from the shallow waters of Lago de Nicaragua, is an ancient ceremonial island of the Chorotega and male counterpart to more buxom Isla de Ometepe, whose smoking cone can be seen after you take the three-hour hike to the top. The 45-sq-km island and surrounding archipelago of 13 islands are part of Parque Nacional Archipiélago Zapatera, designated to protect not only the remaining swaths of virgin tropical dry and wet forest but also the unparalleled collection of petroglyphs and statues left here between 500 and 1500 years ago. You can camp here for US$3 per person. Community boats (one way US$5) leave Puerto Asese on Tuesday, Friday and Sunday, or you can hire a private boat from there for US$38/75 one way/return. Contact UCA in Granada for more information.

Rivas (US$1.25, 1½ hours, nearly hourly) Catch the 1:30pm bus to make the last boat to Isla de Ometepe.

Shuttle Bus

Considering that Managua is a one-hour, one-dollar hop in a minibus (and that León buses leave from the spot where you arrive) and that other destinations are nearly equally accessible, shuttle service is not so popular in Granada.

Erick Tours (☎8974-5575; ericktour@hotmail.com; Calle La Calzada s/n) has airport transfers for US$35 for two people.

Bearded Monkey Has shuttles at 10:30am Monday, Wednesday and Friday to Laguna de Apoyo (US$4/10 guests/nonguests at the Monkey Hut).

Casa San Francisco Shuttles leave Tuesday to Sunday at 8am to Laguna de Apoyo (US$10 return).

TAXI

Taxis are plentiful. Always agree on a fare before getting into the taxi, which should be US$0.50 per person during the day and US$0.70 at night in the city. Always take a taxi between the beach bars and downtown.

It's inexpensive and convenient to take taxis to other destinations, including Masaya (US$12/17 market/volcano), Laguna de Apoyo (US$12), Rivas (US$24), San Juan del Sur (US$30) and Managua (US$24), keeping in mind that fares vary according to gas prices and your bargaining skills.

Around Granada

Reserva Natural Volcán Mombacho

It's been a few decades since this 1345m **volcano** (☎2552-5858; www.mombacho.org; park entrance US$15, mariposario adult US$1; ⏲8am-5pm Thu-Sun), the defining feature of the Granada skyline, has acted up but it is still most certainly active and sends up the periodic puff of smoke, just to keep locals on their toes. It's easy to get to the crown of cloud forest, steamed up with fumaroles and other volcanic bubblings beneath the misty vines and orchids.

Get here early to take the short trail through the **organic coffee farm**, or check out the **mariposario** (butterfly garden) and **orchid garden** (free with entrance) close to the parking lot.

Once you get to the top, where three species of monkeys, 168 species of birds and over 100 types of orchids are just part of the jungle canopy this park is intent on preserving, you have a choice of three trails.

You can also make reservations to sleep dorm-style in the ten-bed **biological station**, with latrines outside, for US$30 per person.

Several operators in Granada arrange tours to Mombacho. There are two canopy tours on-site, that take you across more than 1.5km of platforms and cables, each for US$28.75 per person.

Reserva Natural Laguna de Apoyo

Set in a picturesque valley brimming with wildlife, the lovely Apoyo crater lake is another one of Nicaragua's many natural wonders. Dry tropical rainforest along the surrounding slopes contains much biodiversity, including howler monkeys and many species of bats. But the real attraction is the pristine water of the lagoon, a massive, mineral-infused pool that is without doubt the best swim in the country.

Activities

There's a free **beach** at the bottom of the road; look for the trail just to the right of the T-intersection. Otherwise, pay a few dollars to any of the hotels for day-use privileges at their docks.

Apoyo Dive Center DIVING
(☎8631-1890; Triangulo, 500m N; one tank US$40) Located in the Hotel Selva Sur, this PADI operation also has certification courses.

Estación Biológica DIVING
(☎8882-3992; www.gaianicaragua.org; Triangulo 1km N; one tank US$60) This ecological research station hosts scientists studying the region's endemic fish population and offers dives for PADI-certified divers.

Courses

Spanish School Laguna de Apoyo LANGUAGE COURSE
(☎8882-3992; www.gaianicaragua.org; Triangulo, 1km N) Located at the Estación Biológica, this school offers 20 hours of language instruction plus room and board for US$240.

Sleeping & Eating

There's a basic store 50m north of the T-intersection. Otherwise, most hotels also have restaurants.

Monkey Hut HOSTEL $
(☎8887-3546; www.themonkeyhut.net; Triangulo, 450m N; dm/d/cabin US$14/34/56; P) Operated by Granada's popular Bearded Monkey hostel, this waterfront property has a beautiful dock.

Paradiso Hotel HOSTEL $
(www.paradisolaguna.com; Triangulo, 550m N; dm US$10, r with/without bathroom US$40/25; P) The large 12-bed dorm has lake views, making it a good bet for budgeteers.

Pucha's Inn INN $
(☎2522 5505; Triangulo, 1.5km N; r US$20) Simple budget rooms a bit up the hill from the water's edge. If you're coming, call ahead as the place is often left unattended.

★San Simian BUNGALOW $$$
(☎8850-8101; www.sansimian.com; Triangulo, 3km S; cabins incl breakfast US$55; P) These beautiful little cabins blend into the jungly hillside. Most have stone-walled, al fresco bathrooms, and all have big-screened windows, mosquito nets over the beds, and plenty of air and light.

Getting There & Away

You can walk here from Granada: ask for directions at your hostel.

The main entrance is from a road off the Carretera a Masaya at Km 37.5. Buses run every half-hour between the crater rim and Masaya (US$0.30, 6am to 6pm). Only three buses, which read 'El Valle de la Laguna,' descend all the way to the waterfront (US$0.70). The half-hour, 2km descent isn't a bad walk, but going uphill is hard work.

Hitchhiking is common on this stretch, but taxis are not (except on Sunday). Taxis from Granada (US$10) and Masaya (US$6) may charge less to drop you off at the top. The Bearded Monkey (p461) hostel runs shuttles here from Granada.

Pueblos Blancos

This charming mountainous region a short distance from both Masaya and Granada has a refreshing climate and is dotted with pretty villages famed for their skilled craftspeople and colorful traditions. Named after the pale white stucco homes that once dominated the area, the Pueblos Blancos (White Towns) are extremely compact, with villages practically growing into one another, which makes them easy to visit on a stress-free day trip.

The gorgeous village of **Catarina** is known for its **mirador** (lookout point; admission US$1), which offers sweeping views of Laguna de Apoyo, Lago de Nicaragua and the city of Granada. You can rent a horse (US$5 per hour) for the steep decent to the *laguna*, at least a two-hour round trip.

Nearby, sleepy **San Juan de Oriente** may be home to fewer than 3000 people, but it is the most important centre of artisanal pottery in Nicaragua. You can go to workshops all over town and watch the artists at work, or stop by the Centro de Artesania Nabotiva, a cooperative market.

Rarely visited by tourists, the friendly village of **Diria** is the gateway to the Mirador el Boquete, an alternate lookout over Laguna de Apoyo.

Buses to these villages (US$1 to US1.20, 30 minutes, every 20 minutes until 5pm) leave regularly from one block south of the market in Granada.

Carazo Towns

Southwest of the Pueblos Blancos, in Carazo department, **San Marcos** and the 'twin cities' of **Jinotepe** and **Diriamba** are set in a citrus- and coffee-cultivation area. The three towns celebrate a distinctive religious and folklore ritual known as 'Toro Guaco,' in which the Nicarao town of Jinotepe and Diriamba, its Chorotega rival before the European conquest, commemorate their relationship. Jinotepe's patron is Santiago (St James), whose day is July 25; Diriamba's is San Sebastián (January 20). These two towns, along with San Marcos, carry out ceremonial visits to each other, livened up with striking costumes and masks displayed in dances, mock battles and plays satirizing their Spanish invaders. The pantomime figure of 'El Güegüense' is a symbol of Nicaraguan identity.

Buses to Diriamba, Jinotepe and San Marcos depart from one block south of the market in Granada (US$0.75, 45 minutes, hourly until 6pm). There are extremely frequent departures from Masaya and Managua as well.

Masaya

POP 166,500

Coming from Granada, Masaya may seem a little down at heel. This is a very workaday little town, unexceptional but for two things – a wonderful, crumbling *malecón* (waterfront walkway) and the famous artisan market, Mercado Artesanías, where you can stock up for every birthday, Christmas and anniversary for the rest of your life without buying two of the same thing. Nicaraguan tourists, by the way, always make sure their visit coincides with one of Masaya's many spectacular festivals, and there are cultural exhibitions and dances every Thursday evening.

Masaya is 29km southeast of Managua and 16km northwest of Granada. The city sits at the edge of Laguna de Masaya, beyond which rises Volcán Masaya, which can be visited on day trips from here or Granada.

Sights & Activities

One of the best ways to see the town is in a **horse-drawn carriage**, about US$2.50 per person for the grand tour. If you're here between Thursday and Sunday, consider taking the cute little **tourist train** (US$2) from Hotel Madera's Inn on a 40-minute guided tour of Masaya.

★ Mercado Artesanías — MARKET

The most concentrated area of *artesanías* is in the original market, the fabulous Mercado Artesanías, restored to its former glory after destruction in the revolution. Thursday nights feature live music.

★ Museo del Folklore — MUSEUM

(Mercado Artesanías; admission US$2; ⏲ 8am-5pm Fri-Wed, 8am-7pm Thu) This new museum inside the Mercado Artesanías walls focuses on dance, local myths and the cultural traditions of Masaya.

Malecón & Laguna de Masaya — WATERFRONT

Seven blocks west of the Parque Central is one of the most inspiring views in a region famed for them.

Fortaleza De Coyotepe — FORT

(admission US$0.70; ⏲ 8am-6pm) Built in 1893 atop Cerro de los Coyotes, this eerie fortress witnessed the last stand of Benjamín Zeledón, the 1912 hero of resistance to US intervention. You can walk 2km north on the Interamericana (Pan-American Hwy), but it's worth getting a Managua-bound bus (US$0.30) or taxi (US$1) to avoid the scary traffic.

Churches

There are 12 major barrios in Masaya, all of which were once separate communities with their own churches, plazas and identities: Monimbó, San Jerónimo, Santa Teresa, Villa Bosco Monge, Aserrio, Santa Susana, Las Malvinas, El Palomar, La Ceibita, Cerro Fortaleza de Coyotepe, Sylvio Renazco and Cerro la Barranca.

At the center of it all is the 1750 **Parroquia de la Asunción**, an attractive but

Masaya

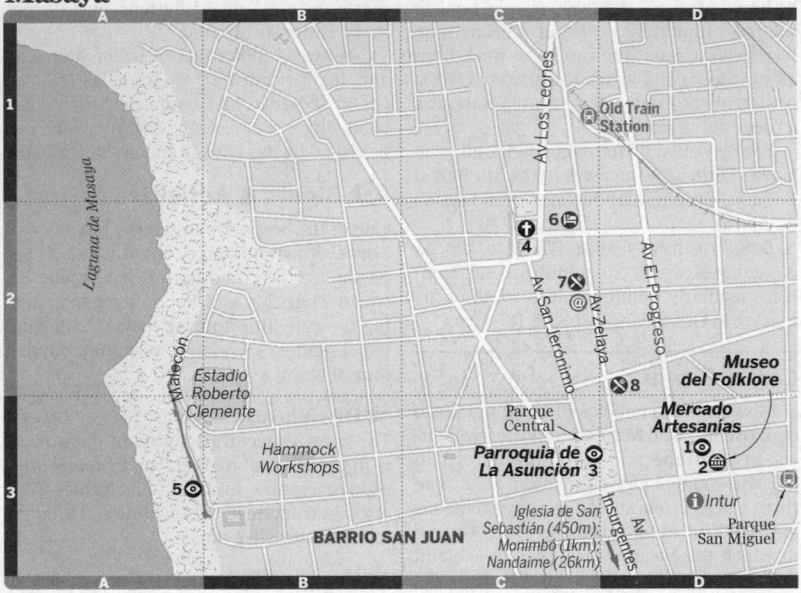

scarred late-baroque beauty that the Spanish government has offered to help repair. It watches over the Parque Central, formally known as **Parque 17 de Octubre**.

Monimbó is Masaya's most famous neighborhood, its ancient center now marked by the 1935 **Iglesia San Sebastián** (cnr Av Real de Monimbó & Calle Las Cuatro Esquinas). Perhaps more important, **Iglesia María Magdalena** (Av Magdalena), sort of the female counterpart to San Sebastián, is where many of Monimbó's most important festivals begin or end.

Among the major buildings worst hit by the earthquake, which also destroyed about 80 homes, was 1928 **Iglesia de San Jerónimo** (cnr Av San Jerónimo & Calle Palo Blanco), the spiritual heart of Masaya and one of the most recognizable silhouettes on the skyline.

Tours

Masaya Tours TOUR

(☎8666-7754; in front of Museo del Folklore) This home-grown operation offers trips to the nearby pueblos (villages; US$25 per person), Volcán Masaya (US$35) and other tourist spots.

Festivals & Events

Masaya is party central. Check in at the Museo del Folklore (p467) to see if a festival is on.

San Lázaro RELIGIOUS

(⏲week before Palm Sunday) Includes a procession of costumed dogs.

San Jerónimo RELIGIOUS

(⏲September 30) Officially it's eight days of festivities, but folks have stretched out Nicaragua's most famous festival to three months. Fireworks, marimbas, parades, drag queens and more make this a fiesta to remember.

Noche de Agüizotes CULTURAL

(last Friday in October) Not to be confused with Halloween or Day of the Dead, this spooky festival features legends come to life and ghosts of the dead.

Sleeping

Hostal Mi Casa HOSTEL $

(☎2522-2500; mantonabermudez@hotmail.com; Av Zelaya; dm/r US$7/20, r with air-con $25; P ❄ 📶) Mi Casa has a nice garden area dominated by chattering birds. The three-bed dorm rooms have private bathrooms, making this a step up for the shared-room set.

Hotel Madera's Inn HOTEL $

(☎2522-5825; www.hotelmaderasinn.com; Av Zelaya, Iglesia San Jerónimo, 1c E, ½c N; dm/d US$5/15, tr with air-con $45; ❄ 📶) Although it

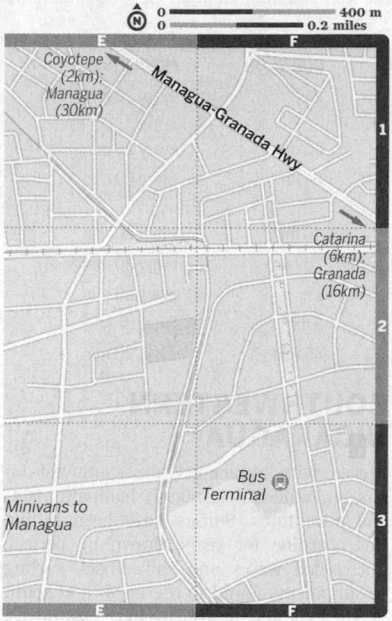

Masaya

Top Sights
1 Mercado Artesanías D3
2 Museo del Folklore D3
3 Parroquia de La Asunción C3

Sights
4 Iglesia de San Jerónimo C2
5 Malecón & Laguna de Masaya A3

Activities, Courses & Tours
Masaya Tours ..... (see 1)
Tourist Train ..... (see 6)

Sleeping
Hostal Mi Casa ..... (see 7)
6 Hotel Madera's Inn C2

Eating
7 Fruti Fruti C2
8 Taquería La Jarochita D2

smells a bit smoky, this simple hotel is one of your best bets in Masaya. There are nice firm mattresses and friendly service – ask for a room upstairs. There's an annex across the street with dorm rooms sleeping four that can get a bit cramped with just a fan to keep you cool.

Eating

Inexpensive *comedores* (basic eateries) cling to the outside of the Mercado Municipal Ernesto Fernández, just outside the bus terminal. Plastic baggies of *vigorón*, fruit salad and *gallo pinto* can be had for less than US$1. There's also snack stalls on the Parque 17 de Octubre and in the Mercado Artesanías.

Fruti Fruti SANDWICHES $
(Av Zelaya, Parque Central, 3c N; snacks US$2-6; ⏲7am-10pm) Right among the budget accommodations is this refreshing option that serves rather excellent smoothies to beat the heat.

Taquería La Jarochita MEXICAN $$
(Av Zelaya, Parque Central, 1c N; dishes US$7-12; ⏲11:30am-late) A block north of Parque Central, La Jarochita prepares good Mexican fare such as tacos and enchiladas. It's a colorful, characterful place; grab yourself a table on the small terrace if you can.

Drinking & Nightlife

Discos are clustered around the entrance to the *malecón* – go for a walk and see which thumping beat suits you best.

Information

Intur (☎2522-7615; www.visitanicaragua.com/ingles; Av El Progreso, Mercado Artesanías, ½c S) Sells a city map and staff can point you to local crafts workshops.

Kablenet Café (Av Zelaya, Iglesia San Jerónimo, 1c E, 1c S; per hr US$0.70) Reliable internet access.

Getting There & Away

Taxis and horse-drawn carriages both charge around US$0.75 for a ride across town.

Minivans to Managua's Universidad Centro America (US$0.80, 30 minutes) leave the park in front of Iglesia de San Miguel when full. Other buses and minivans arrive and depart from the **bus terminal** at the eastern side of the Mercado Municipal (see table, p470).

Parque Nacional Volcán Masaya

Volcán Masaya (☎2528-1444; admission US$4, guide per 3hr US$15; ⏲9am-4:45pm) is the most heavily venting volcano in Nicaragua, and in a more litigious nation there is no way you would ever be allowed to drive up to the lip of a volcanic cone as volatile as the Santiago crater.

BUS SERVICES FROM MASAYA

DESTINATION	COST (US$)	DURATION	FREQUENCY
Carazo (San Marcos, Diriamba and Jinotepe)	0.30-0.50	1¼ hr	every 20 min
Catarina, Diriomo and Diriá	0.30-0.50	40 min	every 20 min
Catarina, San Juan de Oriente, Niquinohomo, Masatepe and San Marcos	0.50	1¼ hr	every 20 min
Granada	0.50	40 min	every 20 min
Laguna de Apoyo entrance	0.35	20 min	every 20 min
Managua	0.50	1 hr	every 20 min
Matagalpa	3	3 hr	twice daily
Ticuantepe	0.50	45 min	every 20 min

There's always lava bubbling at the bottom (you probably won't see it, though), and a column of sulfurous gases rising above.

Try to arrive in the afternoon, when the crater's thousands of *chocoyos* (parakeets) return to their nests in the crater walls, apparently unharmed by the billowing toxic gases.

There are more than 20km of hiking trails. The shorter, most accessible treks require **guides** (per group US$0.70 to US$2), which you pay for with your admission. If you speak Spanish, ask your guide to show you around the attractive **museum** (admission free) at the visitor center, with impressive natural-history displays and beautiful murals, and the **butterfly garden**.

The park entrance is 7km north of Masaya. It's 5km of paved road to the crater and **Plaza de Oviedo**, which honors the intrepid priest who went down into the volcano with a sample dish, to find out whether or not the lava was (as he suspected) pure gold. Park officials limit your time here to just five minutes. From here, community-run **horseback tours** (US$4) can take you toward the summit.

There's a night tour (US$10 per person, 5pm to 7pm) where you can witness millions of bats leaving a nearby cave...spooky.

Getting There & Away

Any Managua-bound bus from Masaya or Granada can drop you at the entrance, but it's a steep, hot climb to the crater; hitching is possible. Consider a round-trip taxi from Masaya (US$8) or Granada (US$15), including an hour's wait at the top. Most tour outfits in Granada come here as part of a Masaya day trip, including the markets and Catarina overlook, for around US$15 per person.

SOUTHWESTERN NICARAGUA

Packed with attractions, the southwest offers up some of Nicaragua's hallmark vistas and adventures. Surfers have been hitting this coastline for years, drawn by perfect, uncrowded waves and chilled-back surfing encampments found to the north and south of San Juan del Sur. No trip to the southwest would be complete without a few days on Isla de Ometepe.

Isla de Ometepe & Around

To get to Isla de Ometepe from this side of the mainland, you'll need to pass first through rough-and-tumble Rivas, then get a boat from San Jorge.

Rivas

POP 50,600

Rivas has its fans – people say it's authentic and lively with some wonderful buildings downtown. Maybe. But with the beaches, lake and Ometepe beckoning, few travelers pause here long enough to find out.

Sights

Iglesia Parroquial de San Pedro CHURCH
(Parque Central) This 1863 church on the eastern side of Parque Central is worth a look for its attractive classical facade.

Museo de Antropología MUSEUM
(Mercado, 1c S, 1c E; admission US$1; ⏲8:30am-noon & 2-5pm) This anthropology museum is set in a fabulous historic mansion.

Sleeping & Eating

Rivas has plenty of cheap eats, with the very cheapest clinging to the outside of the chaotic market. The biggest grocery store is **Palí** (Parque Central, 1½c O).

Hospedaje Lidia GUESTHOUSE $
(☎2563-3477; Uno, ½c O; s/d US$15/22, without bathroom US$10/18;) Opposite Intur, this amiable, family-run operation offers the nicest budget lodging in town, with well-scrubbed rooms and a good attitude.

Rosti-Pizza PARRILLA $$
(Parque Central, costado S; dishes US$5-10) This is one of the better restaurants in town, with good ambiance. Grab a table out front and chow down on good steaks and decent burgers and watch as what seems like the entire town crosses the Parque Central at least once.

Information

BAC (frente Hotel Cacique Nicarao) Has an all-card ATM.

Intur (☎2563-4914; rivas@intur.gob.ni; Texaco station, ½c O; ⏲Mon-Fri)

Getting There & Around

Rivas is the regional transport hub. Both **Transnica** (☎2563-5397; www.transnica.com; Uno, ½c N) and **Tica Bus** (☎8877-1407; www.ticabus.com; Uno, 1½c N) have offices in town and daily buses to San José, Costa Rica (US$29 to US$40). For services north, you'll need to go through Managua.

The **bus terminal** (☎8669-0330) is adjacent to the market, about 10 blocks west of the Interamericana. You can catch more luxurious long-distance buses (most headed to Managua, not Granada) at the bus stop just north of the exit to San Jorge. Bus services include the following:

Granada (US$1.25, 1½ hours, hourly) Alternatively, take any Managua-bound bus and change at Nandaime.

Managua (US$2, 2½ hours, every 25 minutes)

Refugio de Vida Silvestre La Flor & El Ostional (US$1.80, two to three hours, three daily)

Salinas & Tola beaches (US$1.70, two hours, 5:30am, 6am and 8:30am) Returns at noon and 2pm.

San Jorge (US$0.30, 20 minutes, half-hourly)

San Juan del Sur (US$0.75, 45 minutes, half-hourly) With continuing service to La Flor and El Ostional at 11:30am, 3pm and possibly 4pm.

Sapoá/Peñas Blancas, Costa Rica (US$0.75, 45 minutes, half-hourly)

Southern beaches (US$2.50, two to three hours, three daily) Service to San Juan del Sur, Playa el Coco, La Flor and El Ostional.

San Jorge

This relaxed spot, 6km east of Rivas, is where most travelers head to cross over to Isla de Ometepe. The center of town is 1km from the ferry dock.

Isla de Ometepe

POP 29,800

Ometepe never fails to impress. The island's twin volcanic peaks, fertile soil, clean waters, wide beaches, wildlife population, archaeological sites and dramatic profile are quickly propelling it up traveler tick lists.

More than 1700 petroglyphs have been found on Ometepe, making this a traveler's adventure fantasy island.

The island's two major settlements, Altagracia and Moyogalpa, both offer accommodations and restaurants, but to experience the true charms of Ometepe, travel further out: Charco Verde, Playa Santo Domingo, Balgüe and Mérida all offer lovely settings amid the island's rich biodiversity.

Moyogalpa and Altagracia have unreliable ATMs (bring enough cash for your trip).

Activities

Ometepe is great for hiking, exploring and swimming. However, the terrain is rough, signage minimal and trails hard to follow. Since a number of tourists got lost and died while climbing the volcanoes, authorities have made local guides mandatory for these trips. Guides can be hired at tour operators in Moyogalpa and Altagracia or through hotels.

Both of the volcanoes are challenging. **Volcán Maderas** is the more accessible of the two, a tough, muddy scramble through cloud

A FIERY PAST

According to legend, pre-Hispanic inhabitants of the Volcán Masaya area would throw young women into the boiling lava at the bottom of the crater to appease Chaciutique, the goddess of fire.

The cross overlooking Cráter Santiago is a replica of the one placed there in the 16th century by the Spanish, who hoped to exorcise the demons who dwelled within.

Isla de Ometepe

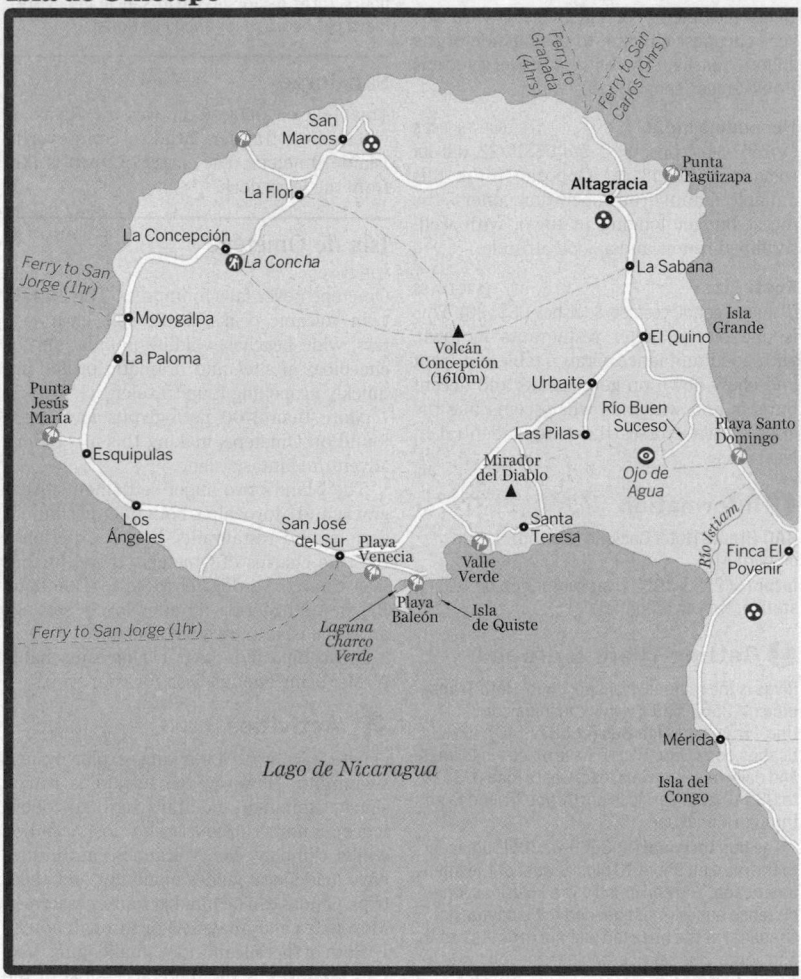

forest to the crater, where there's a greenish lake below. It's about eight hours there and back. There are several routes to the top; the trails leaving from Finca Magdalena, Mérida and El Porvenir are the most used.

Volcán Concepción is a pretty serious 10- to 12-hour hike, the last bit up steep and slippery volcanic scree. Be prepared for intense heat (sun, not lava), and also for chills at the summit. The two main trails leave from points near Altagracia and Moyogalpa.

On the Maderas side, there are also several trails to see petroglyphs. The **petroglyphs** near the hotel of El Porvenir are a 45-minute horseback ride from Santo Domingo; ask hotel staffers for directions. Others are found at El Socorro, Finca Magdalena and El Corozal. On the south side of Maderas, an impressive 35m-high **waterfall** is located a couple of hours' hike above San Ramón.

There are great beaches and **swimming** spots all around the island; check out Punta Jesús María, Playa Venecia and the Isla de Quiste, a beautiful islet not far from Charco Verde. The most popular beach, Playa Santo Domingo, is on the isthmus connecting the two volcanoes, and has plenty of places to stay and eat.

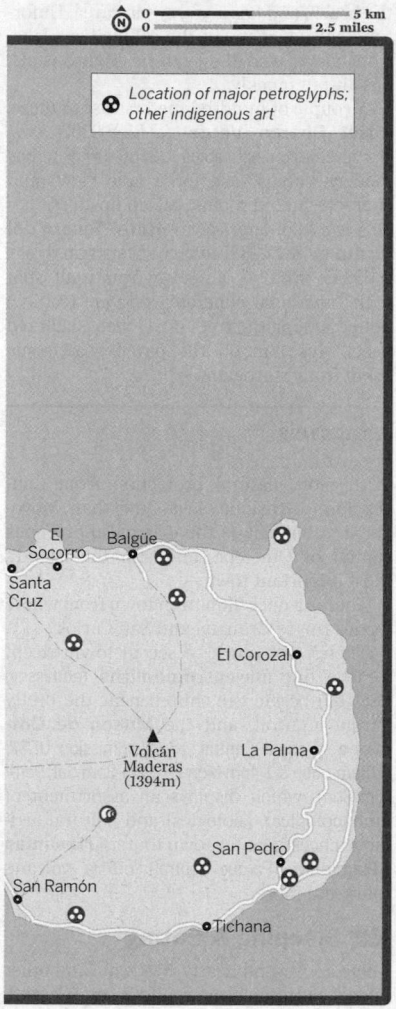

Many of the sleeping options have horses, bikes or kayaks to hire at reasonable rates. A growing number of farms on the island are signing up to the **Fincas Verdes agrotourism program** (www.fincasverdes.com), offering farmstays. Check out **Fundación Entre Volcánes** (☎2569-4118; www.fundacionentrevolcanes.org; frente Enitel) for volunteer ops.

Tours

Inexpensive local guides are highly recommended during hikes, for safety, to increase your chances of spotting wildlife and for enhanced insight into the island's culture. Guides basically live off your tips, so be generous. Any hotel can arrange a guide.

Moyogalpa

POP 10,000

Not just the ferry terminal for hourly boats from the mainland, Moyogalpa is the nerve center for Ometepe's nascent tourist industry, with several hotels and restaurants and most of the island's tour companies. It's also base camp for the climb up Volcán Concepción. It's a bit of a tourist ghetto, and those looking for chillaxed island days should hightail it outta here.

The **Sala Arqueológica Ometepe** (☎2569-4225; Muelle, 4½c E; admission US$1; ⏲8am-9pm) is worth a look. The small museum displays a decent little collection of pre-Columbian pieces. On the same block, Banco Pro Credit has a Visa/Plus ATM.

Around 5km south of Moyogalpa, and easily reached by bicycle, is the remarkable **Punta Jesús María**, a narrow sandbar that juts out into the lake, forming a natural pier perfect for swimming and picnics.

Sleeping

Hotel Escuela Teosintal HOTEL $

(☎2569-4105; Muelle, 2c E, 1½c S; s/d US$12/18;) Run by an agricultural coop, these are by far the sweetest rooms for the price. They're spacious and spotless, with cable TV, modern bathrooms and a lush little garden out back.

Hospedaje Central HOTEL $

(El Indio Viejo; ☎2569-4262; www.hostelometepe.com; Muelle, 3c E, 1c S; dm US$5.50-7.50, r US$10.50, d with air-con US$25;) About as hippy-trippy as things get in town, the Central is all murals and hammocks. Rooms are definitely basic, but OK for the price.

Hotelito Aly HOTEL $

(☎2569-4196; www.hotelitoaly.com; Muelle, 2½c E; r per person US$10, without bathroom US$7;) While the downstairs restaurant is cheery enough, the rooms surrounding it may be a bit grim for some. Upstairs, the situation improves, with spacious, airy rooms and good beds.

Eating & Drinking

Pizzeria Buon Appetito PIZZERIA $$

(Muelle, 100m E; mains US$6-12;) Grab a table out front to watch the action on the main drag at the island's best pizza-pie place.

Café Bistro Cocibolca NICARAGUAN $
(Muelle, 3c E, 1c S; dishes US$2-4) Serves up a great range of international foods and some really yummy sandwiches. The music is chilled most of the week, and the place converts into the town's biggest disco on weekends.

Yogi's Bar BURGERS $
(Hospedaje Central, ½c S; burgers US$4) Yogi's offers US-style burgers and sandwiches, yummy homemade brownies, big breakfasts and movies on the big screen nightly.

Timbo al Tambo BAR
(Muelle, 2½c E; ⏲3pm-late Tue-Sat) Your best bet for action on any given night, this cozy bar has a big screen showing sporting events and a sweaty disco area upstairs where young locals gather to grind to reggaetón hits.

Moyogalpa to Altagracia

A kilometer or so down the road from the turnoff to Punta Jesús María, Esquipulas is home to the **Galería de Arte Carlos Vargas** (⏲9am-6pm Mon-Sat, 9am-noon Sun), Ometepe's most prolific artist-photographer. A little further out of town, past the cemetery, is the turnoff to **Finca Samaria** (☎8695-5215; http://samariahotelrestaurante.wordpress.com; r per person US$7, breakfast US$2), a beautiful little farmstay option a 500m walk down a dirt road – take a left just before you hit the water.

About halfway between Esquipulas and San José del Sur, look for the turnoff to the **Museos el Ceibo** (☎8874-8706; www.elceibomuseos.com; admission per museum US$3; ⏲8am-5pm), 2km down a shady lane off the main road, the best museums on the island with archaeological and coin museums.

Around 10km from Moyogalpa on the Altagracia road, you'll find the **Reserva Charco Verde** (www.fincasverdes.com; admission US$0.75). There is a hiking trail through the woods, and you'll likely see monkeys and plenty of birds. The lovely Playa Bancón looks across at the swimmable **Isla de Quiste**, a prime camping spot. Ask one of the hotels if you want to organize a boat service across.

There are three places to stay here, run by members of the same family. Bookings are often necessary. **Hotel Finca Playa Venecia** (☎8887-0191; www.fincavenecia.com; cabins with fan/air-con US$30/45; P ❄ 📶) is a decent bet on this side of the island. The grouping of 20 cabins and four basic rooms sits near the beach, and has a grassy play area. Unfortunately, not many of the cabins have lakefront views, and they can be slightly stale, but air out quickly.

A couple of hundred meters east of these, **Hotel Charco Verde** (☎8887-9302; www.charcoverde.com.ni; cabins US$60; ❄ 📶) has modern cabins (ask for a lake view) and characterful old rooms – sleep upstairs.

A few kilometers away, **Hotel Tesoro del Pirata** (☎8927-2831; tesorodelpirata@gmail.com; d US$35; ❄ 🏊) is an away-from-it-all spot with functional concrete *cabañas* (cabins) dotted among the trees on a lovely sheltered beach. It's 1km off the paved road some 14km from Moyogalpa.

Altagracia

POP 7000

With more natural protection from Concepción's occasional lava flow than Moyogalpa, Altagracia is the original indigenous capital of Ometepe, and still the island's most important town.

There's a dock 2km from town from where ferries run to Granada and San Carlos.

There's not much to see in town except for the fine ancient **monoliths** (admission US$0.50) beside the church near the pretty Parque Central, and the **Museo de Ometepe** (Parque Central, 1c O; admission US$2; ⏲8am-noon & 1-4pm Mon-Fri, 9am-3pm Sat, 9am-1pm Sun), which displays an assortment of archaeological, geological and cultural artifacts; check here for town tours. **Artesanías Altagracia** (Parque Central) offers volcano tours and more.

Sleeping & Eating

There are several hearty *fritangas* and other budget eating options around Parque Central.

Hotel Central HOTEL $
(☎2569-4420; www.hotelcentraldeometepe.com; Iglesia, 2c S; r per person US$9.30, cabin per person US$12, cabin with air-con US$45; ❄ 📶) The best-looking rooms in town are a simple affair but a good deal. Rooms out front are arranged around a pretty garden, and have bathrooms with river-pebbled accents.

Hotel Castillo HOTEL $
(☎2569-4403; www.hotelcastillo-ometepe.blogspot.com; Iglesia, 1c S, ½c O; dm/s US$6/10, r with air-con US$20; ❄ @ 📶) Nothing fancy going on here, but it's fairly clean and brightly painted, with a couple of good hangout areas.

Hospedaje Kencho HOTEL $
(☎8944-4087; www.hotelkencho.com; Iglesia, ½c S; r per person without bathroom US$3, s/d with fan US$5/7, r with air-con US$30; ❄) This is a bargain basement option with slightly rundown rooms. Everything is clean, however, and the owners are friendly.

Playa Santo Domingo

Windswept (sometimes a little too windswept) beaches and the island's finest accommodations lie southeast of Altagracia, on the long and lovely lava isthmus that cradles Playa Santo Domingo.

There's plenty to do here. Follow a well-signed trail to the **Presa Ojo de Agua** (admission US$2; ⏲comedor daylight hours), a shady swimming hole about 1.5km north of Playa Santo Domingo, head out by kayak on the **Río Istiam**, on foot from the north of town to the **Sendero Peña Inculta** (admission US$2.50), or launch into the air at the **Canopy Sendero Los Monos**, a 500m zipline located opposite the Hotel Finca Santo Domingo.

Sleeping & Eating

Hospedaje Buena Vista HOTEL $
(☎2569-4864; s/d US$15/20; 📶) The best (well, only) budget spot along this stretch, with a tidy garden, good hangout areas and plenty of waterfront hammock action. Room 1 is best.

Hotel Finca Santo Domingo RESORT $$
(☎2569-4862; www.hotelfincasantodomingo.org; s/d US$25/30, cabin US$45-55; P❄📶) More like a resort than anywhere else on the island, this class act sprawls out along the beachfront. Rooms upstairs have a pleasant nautical feel to them but unfortunate slumping beds. Rooms 3 and 4 have the best views.

Natural Restaurant Vegetariano VEGETARIAN $
(juices US$2, dishes US$3-4; ✎) Right at the northern entrance to Santo Domingo, this little beachside beauty serves up some tasty vegetarian meals.

Santo Domingo to Balgüe

Beyond Santo Domingo, the road divides at Santa Cruz, with the left fork heading to Balgüe and the right to Mérida.

Sleeping & Eating

Most hotels also serve food.

Casa Istiam HOTEL $
(☎2569-4879; r with fan/air-con US$15/30) About halfway between Playa Santo Domingo and Santa Cruz, rooms are basic but cute, with fresh, bright paint jobs and cool stone floors.

Hostal Espirales HOSTEL $
(☎8573-4998; www.hostalespirales.com; dm/s/d US$7/15/20, r with air-con US$25) Across the road from the beach on your way to Balgüe, this farm-hotel has simple rooms and a basic dormitory.

El Zopilote Finca Ecológica HOSTEL $
(☎8961-8742; www.ometepezopilote.com; 200m up trail from road; hammocks US$3, tents per person US$3, dm US$6, cabins US$14-18; 📶) By far the most laidback hippy option on the island, this organic farm offers a range of accommodations scattered around a lush hillside on a sizeable working farm.

Finca Magdalena HOSTEL $
(☎8498-1683; www.fincamagdalena.com; hammocks or campsites per person US$3, dm/tr/q US$3.50/15/24, cabins US$40; @) This Ometepe original setup on the slopes of Volcán Maderas is a classic backpacking spot. Rooms and dorms on this working coffee *finca* are set in a rickety old wooden farmhouse.

Hospedaje Así es Mi Tierra GUESTHOUSE $
(☎8493-0506; www.mitierraometepe.com; r US$18, without bathroom US$12) At the southern end of Balgüe is a sweet little family-run affair offering basic but functional rooms. The best part is the 50m jungle trail that leads down to a pebble beach.

Café Campestre HOSTEL $
(☎8571-5930; fincacampestre@gmail.com; dm US$10; 📶) This good-vibes hostel has basic dorm rooms with mosquito-net-covered beds.

Café Isabel NICARAGUAN $
(dishes US$3-4.50) Balgüe has a cluster of cafes just to the north of town, including this place which features a huge fixed plate with your choice of meat and freshly made *nacatamales* (banana-leaf-wrapped bundles of cornmeal, meat, vegetables and herbs; US$1.50).

Mérida & San Ramón

On the other side of Maderas lies the beautiful, windswept shoreline of Mérida, a spread-out town with a couple of thousand inhabitants. Further south, San Ramón is a simple agricultural village, typical of the Maderas side of the island. Beyond here, the road degenerates even further but passes through some friendly and fascinatingly isolated plantain-farming communities before emerging at Balgüe.

Don't miss the hike from the Estación Biológica de Ometepe to the 40m-high **Cascada San Ramón** (admission US$3) waterfall.

Sleeping & Eating

★Hacienda Mérida HOTEL $
(☎8868-8973; www.hmerida.com; campsites or hammock per person US$3, dm US$7, r downstairs/upstairs US$23/32; P @) On the north side of Mérida, this is by far the lushest budget option around (with some very nice midrange rooms thrown in), offering every activity you could possibly want.

Albergue Ecológico El Porvenir LODGE $
(☎2569-4420; www.hotelkabanas.com/bienvenidosporvenir.html; r per person US$8; P) A kilometer past where the road splits is the entrance to this sunny hilltop lodge and restaurant that has it all – great volcano views and petroglyphs amid attractive gardens, a restaurant serving good-value meals, plus excellent, spacious rooms. Check here for nearby trails.

Caballito's Mar HOSTEL $
(☎8842-6120; www.caballitosmar.com; dm US$5) About 1km before Mérida, look for a sign to a simple little Spanish-Nica-run place right on the beach, with great lake views from the waterfront bar-restaurant. This is the best place to start **kayak tours** of the Río Istiam (US$15 per person) or your own trips to nearby Isla del Congo.

Getting There & Away

The most convenient way to get to Isla de Ometepe is the one-hour, 17km boat ride from San Jorge to Moyogalpa or San José del Sur. The **Hacienda Mérida** (☎8868-8973; www.hmerida.com) does sailboat tours and transfers. You'll need a minimum of four (and a maximum of six) people for the following prices: San Jorge (US$25 per person, one hour), San Carlos (US$80 per person, nine to 11 hours) and Granada (US$60 per person, eight to nine hours).

Ferries cross the lake between Granada and San Carlos twice weekly, stopping in Altagracia (unless the weather is really bad) en route. One-way fares from San Jorge to Moyogalpa are US$3, and you'll need to pay a US$0.40 dock fee. Schedules change frequently:

Moyogalpa to San Jorge 6am, 7:45am, 11am, 12:30pm, 4pm, 5:30pm

San Jorge to Moyogalpa 7am, 7:45am, 10:30am, noon, 2:30pm, 4pm, 5:30pm

Altagracia to Granada (US$4.25, four hours, 3pm Tuesday)

Altagracia to San Carlos (US$6, nine hours, 6pm Monday and Thursday) Also serves San Miguelito.

Granada to Altagracia (US$4.25, four hours, 2:30pm Monday, 2pm Thursday)

San Carlos to Altagracia (US$6, nine hours, 2pm Tuesday and Friday)

Getting Around

The lack of traffic makes hitching a problem (although any passing pickup will almost certainly give you a ride). Bicycling (rental US$5 per day) and motorcycling (rental US$25 per day) is a breeze.

Bus service is solid, but the southern island's terrible roads take their toll on buses and schedules change frequently. Fewer buses run on Sunday. Between Moyogalpa and Altagracia there are hourly buses. All buses from Moyogalpa to the Maderas side of the island stop in Altagracia about one hour later, then head down the isthmus past Playa Santo Domingo.

At Santa Cruz, buses go right (south) to Mérida and San Ramón, and left (east) to Balgüe, perhaps continuing to La Palma. Buses do not serve the southeastern portion of the island, between San Ramón and La Palma, at all.

Buses from Moyagalpa:

Altagracia (US$0.75, one hour, hourly)

Balgüe (US$1.10, two hours, 2:40pm)

Mérida (US$1.25, 2½ hours, three daily)

San Ramón (US$1.10, three hours, twice daily)

SOUTHERN PACIFIC COAST

To get to the Tola beaches – El Astillero down to Playa Gigante – you'll need to pass through Rivas and Tola, then head toward the beach. San Juan del Sur seves as the access point for the beaches between Playa Marsella in the north downward to El Ostional.

San Juan del Sur

POP 15,500

This is the hub for exploration of Nicaragua's toned-and-tanned Southern Pacific beaches. And while the once-sleepy fishing village doesn't have an amazing beach – you need to head either 30 minutes north or south for that – it does have the best restaurants and nightlife around.

The town itself, with its clapboard Victorian houses and steady influx of young and beautiful international travelers and scenesters, is quite fun. The half-moon brown-sugar beach provides splendid sunset views. Top it all off with a towering statue of Christ on a neighboring hillside and you have all the workings to kick off an amazing adventure in paradise.

Activities

The best surfing is generally April to December, but waves are less crowded in the low season. There's a **beach break** on bigger swells at the northern end of the beach, but most surfers hire boats or stay at the beaches north and south of town. Casa Oro Hostel runs a daily shuttle out to Playa Maderas. Watch for boat traffic if you swim here.

There are a few fun hikes just outside of town. **Hospedaje Elizabeth** (☎458-2270) rents out mountain bikes (US$6 per day).

Arena Caliente SURFING
(☎8815-3247; www.arenacaliente.com; Mercado, ½c N) A one-stop shop for all your surfing needs.

Good Times Surf Shop SURFING
(☎8980-2951; Gato Negro, 100m S) Laidback surf center specializing in trips to less crowded beaches.

Neptune Watersports DIVING
(www.neptunewsn.com; Mercado 1c O, 10m N; 2-tank dive US$85) Check here for dives and boat excursions.

Courses

Casa de Cultura COURSE
(Av del Mar s/n) This arts center offers classes, arts exhibits and more.

Escuela Español San Juan del Sur LANGUAGE
(☎8639-7377; int Casa de Cultura; 20hr with/without homestay US$165/100) Activities, which cost an extra US$30 per week, include beach trips and tours to Ometepe, Granada and Rivas. There are also free activities like city tours, and dance and cooking classes.

Tours

In addition to surfing and fishing tours, there are lots of other ways to see San Juan del Sur.

Casa Oro Hostel TOUR
(☎2568-2415; www.casaeloro.com; Av del Cine, Parque Central, 1c O, 50m N) Offers budget excursions, including sailing tours and fishing trips, turtle tours and more.

Da Flying Frog CANOPY TOUR
(☎8613-4460; daflyingfrog@hotmail.com; per person US$30; ⏲8am-4pm Mon-Sat) This canopy tour is made up of 17 platforms and 2.5km of zipline that passes through some forested hills on the outskirts of town. Ask your hotel to call for a pick-up.

Rana Tours BOAT TOUR
(☎2568-2066; ranatours@gmail.com; Av del Mar s/n) Offers water-taxi services out to Playas Majagual, Maderas, Marcella and Hermosa (US$15 to US$20 per person).

WORTH A TRIP

TOLA BEACHES

The Pacific beaches accessed from Tola retain some of that lost-beach paradise feel, with top-notch surf and good vibes.

➡ **Playa Gigante** This surf town on a white crescent has expensive surf camps and a few budget options near the beach. The best spot is the Hostel Camino del Gigante.

➡ **Playa Popoyo** Big waves and a peaced-out surf scene with good budget hotels that include Sunset Villas Hostel, Hotel Magnific Rock and Casa Maur.

➡ **Getting there** There are no banks or real grocery stores, and internet and cell-phone coverage is patchy at best. Do what you need to do before you hit the trail. Bus access is reliable but inconvenient, though it is improving along with the atrocious roads. The road is paved to Tola, and they are currently paving the road from Tola to Playa Gigante. Buses leave Rivas for Las Salinas at 5:30am, 6am and 8:30am, and return at noon and 2pm. Note that Playa Gigante is a 7km walk from the bus stop. You can also get here by taxi from Rivas (see p471).

San Juan del Sur

Sleeping

San Juan del Sur is one of the few places in Nicaragua with marked seasonal rates. At Easter and other Nicaraguan holiday times, prices can double.

Casa Oro Hostel HOSTEL $

(☎2568-2415; www.casaeloro.com; Av del Cine, Parque Central, 1c O, 50m N; dm US$8-9, d with fan/air-con US$28/35, all incl breakfast; ❄ @) This backpacker standby has all the amenities – great info center, discount internet, kitchen, and lounge areas. Rooftop bar (party ends at 11pm), and good vibes 24-7.

Hostel Esperanza HOSTEL $

(☎8754-6816; www.hostelesperanza.com; Av del Mar s/n; dm US$8-9, d US$25, without bathroom US$18;) This up-and-coming hostel has a great location right across the street from the beach. It also has clean, simple rooms, a fun central garden area and a shared kitchen. The dorms are pretty big (14 and nine beds each), so bring your earplugs.

Posada Puesto del Sol GUESTHOUSE $

(☎2568-2532; lalacard98@yahoo.com; Calle Iglesia, Iglesia, 1½c O; r per person US$10;) Smallish but lovingly decorated rooms in a family home. Some share a bathroom with one other – ask to look around if this is a problem. It can get hot here.

Hotel Estrella HOTEL $

(☎2568-2210; infosanjuan10@gmail.com; Av del Mar, Mercado, 2c O; r per person without bathroom US$8-10) This high-ceilinged century-old landmark is a basic, atavistic beauty with run-down rooms and wonderful balconies with some of the best views in town. Bathrooms are downstairs in the backyard.

El Coco Azul HOTEL $$

(☎2568-2697; www.elcocoazul.com; Calle Iglesia s/n; d US$58, without bathroom US$46;) This

San Juan del Sur

Activities, Courses & Tours

1 Arena Caliente....C2
2 Casa de Cultura....B4
Casa Oro Hostel....(see 7)
Escuela Español San Juan del Sur....(see 2)
3 Good Times Surf Shop....B2
4 Hospedaje Elizabeth....C2
5 Neptune Watersports....C2
6 Rana Tours....B3

Sleeping

7 Casa Oro Hostel....C3
8 El Coco Azul....B3
9 Hostel Esperanza....B3
10 Hotel Estrella....B3
11 Posada Puesto del Sol....C3

Eating

12 Big Wave Dave's....B2
13 El Colibrí....D3
14 El Gato Negro....B2
15 Mercado....C2
16 Mesón Español....B1
17 Pan de Vida....C2
18 Super Frutto....B3

Drinking & Nightlife

19 Traditional Irish Bar....C2

young, affordable boutique hotel has detail-oriented service, colorful common areas, and clean and airy rooms in a contemporary-style setting just 30m from the beach.

Eating

The cheapest meals in town are served in the tidy **mercado** (dishes US$2-4).

★ Super Frutto ICE CREAM $
(Calle Central s/n; ice cream US$2-3) The best gelato in all of Nicaragua is served up at this after-dinner favorite. Note: in the heat, you are better off avoiding cones.

El Gato Negro SANDWICHES $
(Texaco station, 2c O; sandwiches & light meals US$4-6) The coolest cafe around has a great selection of espresso-based drinks, yummy cakes, comfy lounges, and a large selection of new and used books for sale.

Pan de Vida BAKERY $
(Entrance Rd; baked items US$1-3; ⏲8am-6pm) This bakery does the best breads in town.

El Colibrí INTERNATIONAL $$
(Texaco station, 5c S; dishes US$7-10; ⏲dinner Tue-Sun; ✎) One of the best menus in town can be found at this relaxed indoor-outdoor Mediterranean restaurant. The regular dishes are good and the specials board is always full of winners.

Mesón Español SPANISH $$
(Av del Mar s/n; mains US$6-13; ⏲11am-10:30pm) One of the more upscale beachfront eateries, this tapas joint also has a good selection of beef and seafood on offer.

Big Wave Dave's BURGERS $$
(Texaco station, 2½c O; dishes US$5-8; ⏲Tue-Sun) A looong-time expat favorite, Dave serves up all sorts of comfort food including excellent burgers and big breakfasts. Beer it here.

Drinking & Nightlife

Most of the beachfront restaurants double as bars and lounges.

Crazy Crab Disco DANCE
(final, Av del Mar; ⏲Fri-Sun) The original SJDS disco. The mirrored balls and colored lights start spinning at 9pm, but the in-crowd doesn't show up until at least 11pm, primed for an all-night party. This area's a bit desolate – it's best to get a cab home.

Traditional Irish Bar IRISH PUB
(Av del Mercado s/n) Don't think you'd find this one in Dublin, but it does its best.

Information

Most hostels have wi-fi and computers. **Cyber Leo's** (Av del Cine, Gato Negro, ½c S; per hr US$1) is a cheap internet cafe.

BAC (Av del Mar, Hotel Casa Blanca)

Intur (☎2568-3022; Calle Iglesia, frente Parque Central) Well stocked with brochures and staff willing (if not always able) to answer questions about the town and surrounds.

Santini Lavandería (Calle Iglesia s/n) Laundry priced by the eye.

Police (☎8453-3732, 2453-3732; final, Av del Mar)

Post Office

San Juan del Sur Info (www.sanjuandelsur.org.ni) English-language, traveler-savvy site.

DANGERS & ANNOYANCES

Don't walk alone on the beach at night. And when you head home from the bar, walk in a large group or ask for a cab.

Getting There & Around

Getting to the beaches north and south of town can be expensive, so ask at the surf shops if they have a boat going with extra space for you. Casa

Oro Hostel's regular beach shuttle to Playa Maderas (US$5 return) leaves at 8:15am, 10:45am, 1pm and 5pm.

Big Wave Dave's offers shuttles to Managua, Granada and Masaya (US$25) leaving at 7am. Casa Oro Hostel has shuttles to Granada (US$15), Rivas (US$5), Managua (US$30) and San Jorge (US$7). Book well in advance for either of these options.

Work is underway to open an international border to Costa Rica on the road south of El Ostional – keep your ears open.

BUS

Tica Bus (☎2568-2427; www.ticabus.com; Calle Central s/n) has an office here to buy tickets from Rivas to Costa Rica.

Bus service to the beaches depends very much on road conditions – if you're here in the wet season, you may find it drastically reduced (or even cancelled). There is regular **bus service** from the bus stop in front of the market to destinations including the following:

Managua (*expreso* US$3.30, three hours, 4:30am, 5am, 5:30am, 6am and 7am; *ordinario* US$2.50, four hours, at least hourly)

Northern beaches (US$1, two hours, twice daily) Service to Toro Mixcal, Nacascolo, Marsella, Playa Maderas (Los Playones), Majagual, Ocotal and Rivas.

Rivas (US$1, 40 minutes, every 25 minutes)

Southern beaches (US$1, two hours, 1:10pm, 3pm and 4:30pm) Service to Empalme de Remanso, Playa El Coco, Refugio de Vida Silvestre La Flor and El Ostional; returning buses leave El Ostional at 5am, 6am and 4pm.

TAXI

The Taxi Cooperative of San Juan del Sur charges US$0.70 to anywhere in town, US$1.50 for *colectivo* taxis to Rivas. Each driver has a list of set rates for other destinations, including Morgan's Rock (US$20), Playa El Coco or Reserva La Flor (US$40), El Ostional (US$50), the Costa Rican border (US$25), Masaya or Granada (US$50), and Managua (US$80). Taxis congregate close to the market.

Beaches North of San Juan del Sur

If you're taking the bus out to these beaches, bear in mind that there'll be at least a 2km walk from the bus stop to the water. Hitching is common (but traffic isn't), though you can always put a bike on top of the bus and do it that way. **Playa Marsella** is 9km north of SJDS. It's a good swimming beach with expensive hotels.

Playa Maderas

A good-time-vibes backbacker and surfer hangout, this stunning beach, with rocky expanses that offer excellent tide pooling and wide, wonderful sandy stretches for sunbathing, is famed for having one of the best beach breaks in the country.

Sometimes called Los Playones, it's a slow wave in fairly deep (2m) water, good for beginners, with two right and two left breaks that get hollow on a rising tide.

There's a faster, intermediate-level reef break between Madera and Majagual called Panga Drops, accessible by boat only. Many surf shops and hostels in San Juan del Sur offer shuttles here.

North of here, the beaches at Bahía Majahual (stay at **Matilda's** (☎8456-3461; permatents per person US$6-7, s/d US$15/25)) and Playa Ocotal (stay at **Morgan's Rock** (☎2254-7989; www.morgansrock.com; s/d from US$224/360) 🍃) are worth a look.

Sleeping

Casa Maderas Ecolodge LODGE $

(☎8786-4897; www.casamaderas.com; dm/d/tr/q/ste US$13.50/39/49/60/69; 📶 🏊) 🍃 Set on 3 hectares of lush jungle and terraced permaculture, it does rustic-modern to perfection. Six-bed dorms are spacious, with double beds, mosquito nets and stylish bathrooms.

There's also a shared kitchen, yoga classes and free beach shuttle.

Hotel 3 Hermanos HOSTEL $

(☎8879-5272; los3hermanosarena@hotmail.com; beachfront; dm US$10) Shoestringing surfers love this rasta-bar restaurant and hostel, just steps away from one of the country's best breaks.

Café Revolución CAMPGROUND $

(100m inland from beach; campsites per person US$2; 📶) This catch-all restaurant offers wi-fi (US$2), yoga (US$10), pizza (US$6 to US$10), and cheap camping spots that include use of the restaurant's bathrooms.

Beaches South of San Juan del Sur

The first beach to the south is **Playa Remanso**, which has a smallish beach break ideal for beginners, and has caves and tidal pools to explore. The next beach south, **Playa Tamarindo**, is a half-hour walk from

Playa Remanso. Surfers come with the rising tide to try for a long wave with right and left breaks. From there, you hit the cooled-out beach towns of Playa Hermosa, Playa El Coco and El Ostional.

Playa Hermosa

This beach (admission US$3) with its own surf camp has some dope-ass surfing (with five breaks on the beach alone), a cool lost-beach-in-paradise vibe and plenty of toned surfers running around.

The **Playa Hermosa Beach Hotel** (☎8671-3327; www.playahermosabeachhotel.com; dm/d incl breakfast US$21/52) is the best beach hostel on the southern Pacific coast of Nicaragua. The open-air six-bed dorm rooms in this rustic paradise catch the breeze to stay cool at night. Private rooms upstairs have giant mosquito nets (ask for the oceanfront room). There's a great vibe and surf scene here, with a chilled-out open-air restaurant.

Transfers to and from San Juan del Sur are included in the price. It also offers surf rentals (US$10) and horseback riding trips (US$12).

Playa El Coco

This is a world-class beach, a spectacular stretch of sparkling sand punctuated by cliffs so pretty that they grace about half of the country's tourist literature.

Your best accommodation option in town is **Lug's Place,** (☎8381-6976; www.lugsplace.com; r without bathroom US$25, with air-con US$75; 📶) located on the southern section of the beach. The rooms are really simple – a brick room with a ceiling fan and clean sheets – with two new upper-scale options on the way. The bar and lounge are a good bet, with cheap(ish) international fare (US$6 to US$18). Check here for private house rentals and camping.

Refugio de Vida Silvestre La Flor

One of the principal laying grounds for endangered olive ridley and leatherback turtles, this **wildlife refuge** (☎8419-1014; admission US$8, campsites per tent US$20) is 20km south of San Juan del Sur. It's easy to visit on a guided tour from San Juan del Sur, or you can stay in the attractive campground. Park guards sell water and soft drinks, but there's no food or insect repellent, so come prepared.

Turtles lay their eggs here, usually between 9pm and 2am, between July and January, peaking in September and October. Leatherbacks usually arrive solo, but olive ridleys generally come in *arribadas* (flotillas), when more than 3000 of them pack the beaches at a time. Some people time these arrivals by moon cycles, but no one really knows for sure until the ladies arrive; call the ranger station if you want to be sure.

When there aren't any turtles around, the park still has an attractive, undeveloped beach, a couple of monkeys on-site and a few short trails; there's a decent beach break (right and left) at the northern end. It's off-limits during turtle season.

El Ostional

This fishing village, practically a stone's throw from the Costa Rican border, has an attractive brown-sugar beach with a well-known point break called 'Los Senos' (The Breasts). You can arrange accommodations and tours here with **Coopertur** (☎8353-7091; communitytours@yahoo.es; north end of beach; homestay per person per night US$10).

The rooms at **Manta Raya** (☎8353-7091; north end of beach; s/d/tr US$15/25/35) are quite basic (a bed, fan and lamp), but some come with ocean views (and a slight breeze).

Three buses leave daily from the Parque Central to San Juan del Sur (US$1.50, one hour).

LEÓN & NORTHWESTERN NICARAGUA

This is Nicaragua at its fieriest and most passionate. The regional capital of León is – and will always be – a hotbed of intellectualism and independence. Just out of León, more than a dozen volcanic peaks wait to be climbed (or surfed). This region has some of the best beach accommodation – and gnarliest surfing – in the country. And the virgin wetlands of the Reserva Natural Isla Juan Venado are not to be missed. Further afield, you'll find the biggest mangrove forest in Central America, awe-inspiring beauty at Reserva Natural Volcán Cosigüina and unique windows into everyday Nicaraguan life in the little towns along the way.

León

POP 201,100

Intensely political, buzzing with energy and, at times, drop-dead gorgeous (in a crumbling, colonial kind of way), León is what Managua should be – a city of awe-inspiring churches, fabulous art collections, stunning streetscapes, cosmopolitan eateries, fiery intellectualism, and all-week, walk-everywhere, happening nightlife. Many people fall in love with Granada, but most of them leave their heart in León.

History

León was originally founded in 1524 by Francisco Hernández de Córdoba near the foot of Volcán Momotombo. After a series of natural disasters, the Spanish abandoned the site in 1610 to rebuild the city near the important indigenous settlement of Subtiava, where it remains.

León served as the nation's capital for most of the colonial period and also served as the ecclesiastical center for the entire region, resulting in an impressive legacy of many fine churches and colonial buildings. The Universidad Autónoma de Nicaragua (UNAN), Nicaragua's first university, was founded here in 1912.

Traditionally León has been the most politically progressive of Nicaraguan cities. During the revolution, virtually the entire town fought against Somoza. Dramatic murals around town serve as reminders of that period and the city remains a strong Sandinista heartland.

Sights

Other colonial churches worth visiting include **Iglesia de San Francisco**, **Nuestra Señora de Guadalupe**, **Capilla San Juan de Dios** (1a Calle SO), **Iglesia de La Merced** and **Iglesia San Juan** (3a Av SE).

★Museo de Arte Fundación Ortiz-Guardián — MUSEUM

(3a Av SO, Iglesia San Francisco, ½c S; admission US$0.80; ⏲10am-6pm Tue-Sat, 8am-4pm Sun) Probably the finest contemporary-art museum in all of Central America, the Ortiz-Guardián Collection is packed with artwork.

Begin surrounded by the luxurious realism of the Renaissance and spare beauty of the colonial period, then wander through romanticism, modernism, postmodernism and actually modern pieces by Cuban, Peruvian and other Latin American schools. Rubens, Picasso, Chagall and other big names make an appearance, but it's the work by Latin American masters – Diego Rivera, Rufino Tamayo, Fernando Botero, Roberto Matta and more – that define the collection. A Spanish-speaking guide costs an extra US$1.25 and is well worth it.

★Catedral — CATHEDRAL

(Roof tour admission US$1; ⏲roof tour 8am-noon & 2-4pm Mon-Sat) Officially known as the Basílica de la Asunción, León's cathedral is the largest in Central America, its expansive design famously, and perhaps apocryphally, approved for construction in much more important Lima, Peru.

Leónese leaders originally submitted a more modest but bogus set of plans, and then architect Diego José de Porres Esquivel, the Capitan General of Guatemala (also responsible for San Juan Bautista de Subtiava, La Recolección and La Merced churches, among others), pulled the switcheroo and built this beauty right here.

This is the cathedral's fourth incarnation. The 1610 original was replaced in 1624 with a wood-and-adobe structure that pirate William Dampier burned to the ground in 1685. Another adobe was used until work began on this enormous 'Antigüeño,' Central American baroque-style masterpiece in 1747. Construction, done primarily by indigenous laborers from Subtiava and Posoltega, went on for more than 100 years.

The cathedral is a sort of pantheon of Nicaraguan culture. The tomb of Rubén Darío, León's favorite son, is on one side of the altar. Nearby rest the tombs of lesser-known Leónese poets Alfonso Cortés and Salomón de la Selva, as well as Miguel Larreynaga.

Among the magnificent works of art within are the Stations of the Cross by Antonio Sarria, considered masterpieces, and *El Cristo Negro de Pedrarias,* possibly the oldest Catholic image in the Americas.

If it's a clear day, take the roof tour, with a spectacular view of the city and smoking volcanoes beyond. The cathedral was having a face-lift at press time but should be completed by the time you read this. Regardless it will still be open to the public.

Museo de Leyendas y Tradiciones — MUSEUM

(4a Calle SO, frente Ruinas San Sebastián; admission US$2; ⏲8am-noon & 1-5pm) León's most entertaining and eclectic museum, the Museum of Myths & Traditions is now housed in La

XXI (the 21st Garrison). What makes it unmissable is the striking contrast of its main subjects: a quirky collection of life-sized papier-mâché figures from Leónese history and legend, handmade by founder Señora Toruña, and murals graphically depicting methods the Guardia Nacional used to torture prisoners.

Museo-Archivo Rubén Darío MUSEUM
(cnr Calles Central Rubén Darío & 4a Av SO; admission US$1; ⏲8am-noon & 2-5pm Tue-Sat, 8am-noon Sun) Exhibits are displayed throughout the house where Nicaragua's most famous poet lived until he was a teenager, ranging from everyday items – more a window into well-to-do Nicaragua in the late 1800s – to handwritten manuscripts of Darío's famous works.

★Iglesia de la Recolección CHURCH
(1a Av NE) Three blocks north of the cathedral, the 18th-century Iglesia de La Recolección has a magnificent yellow baroque facade, with carved vines wound around stone pillars, and symbols in bas-relief medallions that portray the life of Christ.

Iglesia Dulce Nombre de Jesús el Calvario CHURCH
(Calle Central Rubén Darío) The 18th-century El Calvario is a hodgepodge of neoclassical and baroque styles. The interior is nice, with predictably gory, full-sized statues of Jesus and the thieves being crucified, but you're here for the vividly painted facade between the red-brick bell towers.

El Fortín de Acososco FORT
For great views over the city, climb the hill to the former Guardia Nacional stronghold of El Fortín de Acososco on the southern outskirts of town. The building is located in a somewhat sketchy area next to the municipal garbage dump, so leave your valuables in the hotel and travel in a group.

★Galería de Héroes y Mártires MUSEUM
(1a Calle NO, Iglesia de la Merced, ½c O; donation US$1; ⏲10am-5pm) An homage to León's more recent history is found at the Galería de Héroes y Mártires run by mothers of Frente Sandinista de Liberación Nacional (Sandinista National Liberation Front; FSLN) member veterans and fallen heroes.

Museo Entomológico MUSEUM
(☎2311-6586; www.bio-nica.info; cnr 3a Av NE & 2a Calle NE; admission US$0.50; ⏲9am-noon & 2-4pm) For a truly comprehensive collection of creepy crawlies, butterflies, scorpions and other critters.

Cimac GARDENS
(☎2311-0752; Puente Martín, ½c E, 1c N; admission US$1; ⏲8am-noon & 2-5pm) These excellent botanic gardens occupy 9 sq km on the edge of downtown.

Barrio Subtiava

This western neighborhood is rich in tradition and well worth an afternoon. Highlights include the **Museo de Arte Sacre** (☎2311-8288; frente Iglesia Parroquial de San Juan Bautista de Subtiava; admission US$0.70; ⏲8am-noon & 2-5pm Mon-Fri, 8am-noon Sat), **Museo Adiáct** (Iglesia Parroquial de San Juan Bautista de Subtiava, 2c N, Calle Central Rubén Darío; admission US$0.70; ⏲8am-noon & 2-5pm Mon-Fri, 8am-noon Sat), **Museo Insurreccional Luís Manuel Toruño** (Casa El Buzón; Iglesia Parroquial de San Juan Bautista de Subtiava, 2c E, 1½c S; ⏲Sat) and **El Tamarindón** (Iglesia Parroquial de San Juan Bautista de Subtiava, 3c S, 2c O), a tree where Adiáct, the chief of the Subtiava tribe, was hanged during the conquest.

It's a solid 20-minute walk or US$0.70 taxi ride to Subtiava from the León cathedral, or you can take one of the covered trucks (US$0.18) plying the streets.

Iglesia Parroquial de San Juan Bautista de Subtiava CHURCH
(13 Av SO) In the neighborhood of Subtiava lies the recently restored Iglesia Parroquial de San Juan Bautista de Subtiava, the oldest intact church in the city. Built in the first decade of the 18th century, it features a typical arched timber roof upon which is affixed an extraordinary sun icon, said to have been a device to attract the indigenous community to worship.

Courses

UNAN COURSE
(Universidad Nacional Autónoma de Nicaragua León; www.unanleon.edu.ni/centrodeidiomas; continguo Iglesia de la Merced) Nicaragua's first and most important university was founded in 1812. Wander around or drop in for some guerrilla learning. It also offers top-notch language learning programs and homestays.

La Casa de Cultura COURSE
(☎2311-2116; Parque La Merced, 2c O) Decorated with elaborate murals, this relaxed cultural center offers cheap art, dance and music.

León

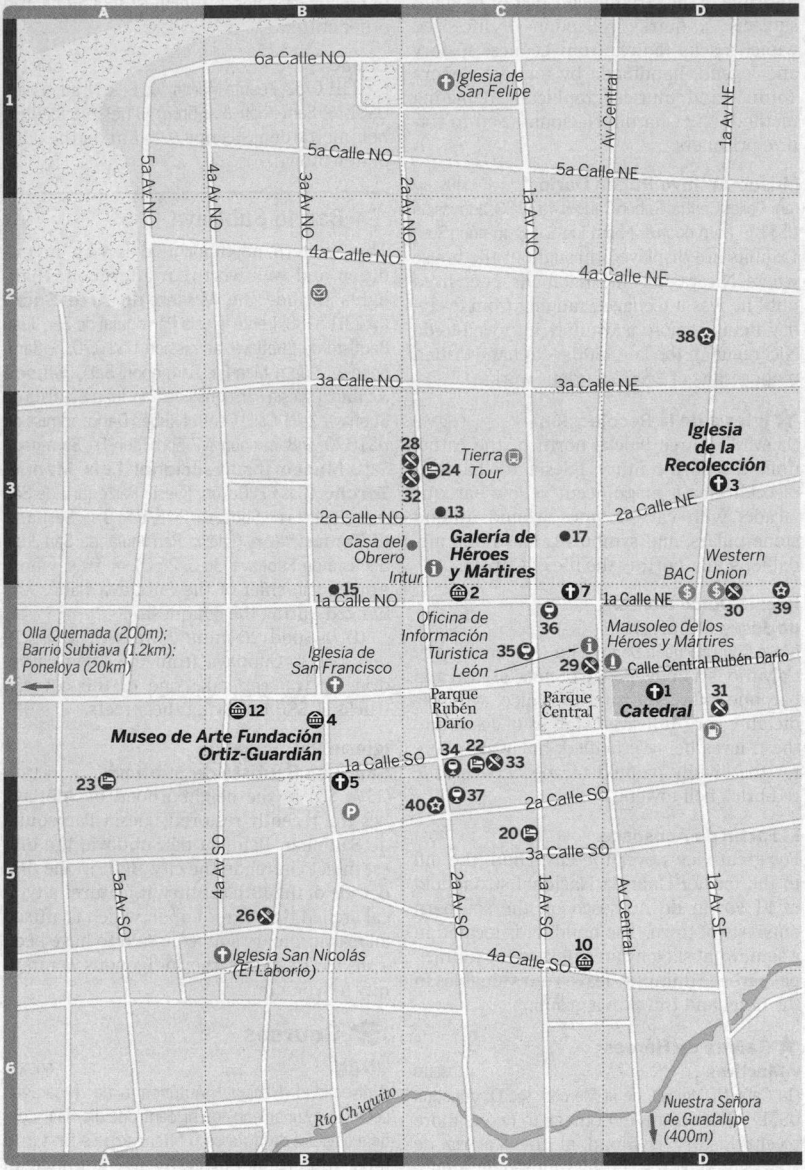

Escuela de Español León COURSE
(☎2315-5540; www.leonspanishschool.org; int La Casa de Cultura; 20hr with/without homestay US$224/140) Based in La Casa de Cultura, this is a professional operation with plenty of cultural activities and out-of-town excursions.

Tours

Volcano surfing, just so you know, involves hauling yourself to the top of somewhere like steaming Cerro Negro, then riding a 'sandboard' (something like a modified snowboard) or toboggan down its black-

gravel 45-degree slopes. The standard tour offerings available from most agencies in León include Cerro Negro (US$28), Laguna Verde (US$65), León Viejo (US$45) and Consigüina (US$90, two days).

León

Top Sights

1 Catedral D4
2 Galería de Héroes y Mártires C4
3 Iglesia de la Recolección D3
4 Museo de Arte Fundación Ortiz-Guardián B4

Sights

5 Capilla San Juan de Dios B5
6 Cimac F5
7 Iglesia de La Merced C4
8 Iglesia Dulce Nombre de Jesús el Calvario F4
9 Iglesia San Juan E2
10 Museo de Leyendas y Tradiciones C5
11 Museo Entomológico E3
12 Museo-Archivo Rubén Darío B4

Activities, Courses & Tours

13 Eco-Camp Expeditions C3
Escuela de Español León ..... (see 15)
14 Green Pathways E3
15 La Casa de Cultura B4
16 Quetzaltrekkers E3
17 UNAN C3

Sleeping

18 Bigfoot Hostel E3
19 Casona Colonial E2
20 Hostel La Clínica C5
21 Hotel Real E3
22 La Siesta Perdida C4
23 La Tortuga Booluda A5
24 Lazybones Hostel C3
25 Vía Vía E3

Eating

26 CocinArte B5
27 Comedor Lucia E3
28 El Mediterraneo C3
29 El Sesteo C4
30 La Unión Supermercado D4
31 Mercado Central D4
32 Mesón Real C3
33 Taquezal C4

Drinking & Nightlife

34 Bar Baro C4
35 Disco Bohemios C4
36 Don Señor C4
Oxygene ..... (see 34)
37 Solero C5

Entertainment

38 Alianza Francesa D2
39 Plaza Siglo Nuevo D4
40 Teatro Municipal José de la Cruz Mena C5

Quetzaltrekkers ADVENTURE TOUR
(☎2311-6695; www.quetzaltrekkers.com; 2a Calle NE, Iglesia de La Recolección, 1½c E) Profits from this outstanding operator go to a charity. Volunteers are very welcome.

Green Pathways ADVENTURE TOUR
(☎2315-0964; www.greenpathways.com; opposite Bigfoot Hostel) Socially conscientious operator with a focus on rural tourism.

Eco-Camp Expeditions ADVENTURE TOUR
(☎2311-1828; www.ecocampexpeditions.com; Parque Rubén Darío 2c N, 10m E) A solid operation for camping and other adventure activities outside León.

Festivals & Events

Every Saturday, from early afternoon till midnight, the Parque Central comes alive for the Tertulia Leónesa, inviting everyone outside to eat, drink and dance.

La Gritería Chiquita HISTORIC
(August 14) Dates back to 1947 when an erupting Cerro Negro threatened to bury the city in ash only to stop suddenly when a local priest vowed to initiate a preliminary *gritería* (shouting), similar to December's Día de la Purísima but changing the response to ¡La asunción de María! ('The ascension of Mary!').

Día de la Virgen de Merced RELIGIOUS
(September 24) León's saint's day, solemnly observed with religious processions through the streets of the city. The preceding day is more festive: revelers don a bull-shaped armature lined with fireworks, called the *toro encohetado,* then charge at panic-stricken onlookers as the rockets fly.

Día de la Purísima Concepción RELIGIOUS
(December 7) A warm-up for the Día de la Concepción de María (December 8), celebrated throughout Nicaragua.

Sleeping

★La Tortuga Booluda HOSTEL $
(☎2311-4653; www.tortugabooluda.com; Catedral, 4½c O; dm US$6, s/d from US$17/24; @) Quiet yet sociable and boasting value-adding extras such as a free pancake breakfast, a top-notch kitchen, organic coffee and the best book exchange in town, the 'Lazy Turtle' immediately feels like a home away from home. Rooms are simple but stylish, the dorms are spacious and there is a chilled lounge area.

Lazybones Hostel HOSTEL $
(☎2311-3472; www.lazyboneshostelnicaragua.com; 2a Av NO, Parque Rubén Darío, 2½c N; dm US$8, r US$30, without bathroom US$20; P @) Part of the new wave of hostels, this quiet, less party-oriented spot has trim grounds, excellent rooms and dorms, and a very laidback atmosphere.

Bigfoot Hostel HOSTEL $
(☎8505-1284; www.bigfootnicaragua.com; 2 Av NE; dm US$6, r without bathroom US$18, q US$33;) With kitchen access, a miniature swimming pool and handmade mojitos on offer, it wouldn't really matter what the rooms were like, but they're a good deal. There's a good travelers' vibe at this party hostel – it swears the party shuts down at 10pm.

Vía Vía HOSTEL $
(☎2311-6142; www.viaviacafe.com; 2a Av NE, Iglesia de La Recolección, 1c E, ½c S; dm/s/d US$7/19/29;) The Vía Vía chain of hostels, which stretches from Kathmandu to Buenos Aires, consistently comes up with the goods. This is no exception, offering beautiful, colonial-style rooms with great bathrooms, and spacious six-bed dorms with their own bathroom!

Hostel La Clínica HOSTEL $
(☎2311-2031; 1a Av SO, Parque Central, 1½c S; dm US$5, r US$12, without bathroom US$8;) A good location and friendly owners make up (kind of) for small rooms, Sponge-Bob beds and rough bathrooms that sit around a cramped and unkempt courtyard.

La Siesta Perdida HOSTEL $
(☎2311-2289; www.siestaperdida.com; Parque Central, 50m O; dm/d US$5/12;) You are likely to lose sleep here, as the bar out front is one of the most popular in town. But it's a fun place all in all, with a large book exchange, shared kitchen and rougher edge than other hostels in town.

Casona Colonial HISTORIC HOTEL $$
(☎2311-3178; www.casonacolonialguest.com; 4a Calle NE, Parque San Juan, ½c O; s/d with fan US$17/22, r with air-con US$42;) With more character than many in this price range, the medium-sized rooms are long on colonial atmosphere without all the costly little extras.

Hotel Real HOTEL $$
(☎2311-2606; www.hotelrealdeleon.net; 2a Calle NE, Iglesia de La Recolección, 1½c E; s/d incl breakfast US$38/48;) The 'Royal Hotel' has a

quaint front sitting area, and old-style *casona* (historic mansion) feel but with relatively modern rooms bedecked with flatscreens and Flintstone-firm beds.

Eating

The best place to eat on the cheap or buy fresh veggies is the beautiful, clean **Mercado Central** (⏲6am-5pm), with several inexpensive eateries serving *comidas corrientes* (set meals). After hours, two of the best *fritangas* in town set up right outside, on the street behind the cathedral, where you can enjoy a huge meal for around US$2. **La Unión Supermercado** (1a Calle NE) is your best super-sized market option.

Many hotels and hostels also have decent restaurants/bars/cafes.

Comedor Lucia NICARAGUAN $
(2a Av NE, Bigfoot Hostel, 10m N; mains US$2-4; ⏲Mon-Sat) In 'backpacker alley'; gets a predictable mix of locals and travelers.

El Mediterraneo MEDITERRANEAN $$
(☎8895-9392; 2a Av NO, Parque Rubén Darío, 2½c N; dishes US$6-10; ⏲dinner) Date night? Check out the most frequently recommended fine-dining option in town.

CocinArte VEGETARIAN $$
(4a Calle SO, frente El Laborío; mains US$4-7; ✎) This cute little restaurant offers vegetarian versions of dishes from around the world in relaxed and arty surrounds.

Taquezal NICARAGUAN $$
(1a Calle SO, Parque Central, ½c O; dishes US$4-7; ⏲4pm-late) With a grand, high-ceilinged dining room kept cool by a battalion of ceiling fans, this is one of León's most atmospheric eating spots.

El Sesteo NICARAGUAN $$
(Calle Central Rubén Darío, frente Parque Central; dishes US$5-13; ⏲11am-10pm) You can't beat the location (although you can beat the prices) of this pleasant plaza-side cafe.

★Mesón Real CONTEMPORARY $$$
(www.elmesonreal.com; Parque Rubén Dario, 220m N; mains US$6-15; ⏲dinner Mon-Sat, lunch Fri-Sat) Travel your way through a tapas menu that includes an eyeball popping crab bisque, and bull's balls and clams in garlic sauce, or check out the grilled grouper or other well-conceived dishes.

Drinking

Most nights start along 1a Calle, west of the park or at the Bigfoot, La Siesta Perdida and Vía Vía hostels. There are some snooty discos just out of town on the bypass road.

Bar Baro BAR
(cnr 1 Calle SO & 2 Av SO) The corner bar offers a wide selection of international dishes and is a popular drink spot.

Olla Quemada BAR
(Calle Central Rubén Darío, Iglesia de San Francisco, 3c O) Latin dance nights, and a good mix of locals and travelers all week.

Solero BAR
(2a Av SO, frente Teatro; ⏲7pm-late) Attracting a slightly older crowd.

Oxygene DANCE
(1a Calle SE, Parque Central, ½c O; ⏲8pm-late Wed-Sat) The hottest dance club in the city center with plenty of sleek, modern styling, bright young things, a pool table and occasional live bands.

Don Señor DANCE
(1a Calle NO, frente Iglesia de La Merced; cover US$1-3) There is a disco upstairs, a relaxed bar (with dance floor) downstairs, and the restaurant-pub El Alamo around the corner.

Disco Bohemios DANCE
(1a Av NO, Parque Central, ½c N; ⏲8pm-late Fri & Sat) In the unsigned orange building in front of the basketball court, this is your classic Latin disco.

Entertainment

La Casa de Cultura often has folk music and other events, while **Plaza Siglo Nuevo** (1a Calle NE, La Unión, 20m E; tickets US$3), León's cinema, shows mostly big-budget American films. The **Alianza Francesa** (☎2311-0126; 1a Av NE, Iglesia de la Recolección, 1½c N; ⏲8am-noon & 2-5pm Mon-Fri) hosts a range of cultural events – drop in for this month's program.

Teatro Municipal José de la Cruz Mena PERFORMING ARTS
(2a Av SO, Parque Central, 1c O, 1c S) Check the board in front of this attractive 1885 theater to see what's on during your visit. It's been impressively restored, and for less than US$2 you may be able to catch anything from Salvadorian rock groups to art films.

Information

Most budget spots have wi-fi and do laundry.

BAC (1a Calle NE, La Unión, 10m E)

BanPro (Bigfoot Hostel, 20m N)

Clean Express Lavandería (cnr Av Central & 4a Calle NE; ⏲7am-7pm)

Intur (☎2311-3382; www.intur.gob.ni; 2a Av NO, Parque Rubén Darío, 1½c N) Busy staff can arrange hookups with local guides but are not really traveler focused.

León Online (www.leononline.net) Useful Spanish-language portal.

Ministry of the Environment & Natural Resources (Marena; ☎2311-3776; mareleon@ibw.com) Located across from the Shell station at the southern entrance to the León bypass road, this office administers the volcanic national reserves of Telica-Rota, Pilas-El Hoyo and Momotombo, and nonvolcanic Isla Juan Venado (your best bet is going to the Isla Juan Venado ranger station in Las Peñitas or with a private tour).

Oficina de Información Turistica León (☎2311-3528; Av Central, Parque Central, 25m N; ⏲8:30am-noon & 2-6pm Mon-Fri, 9am-5pm Sat & Sun) This place closes down a lot, but when it's open, it's a good source for local info.

Post Office (3 Av NO)

Western Union (1 Calle NE)

Getting There & Around

Take **taxis** (per person day/night US$0.70/1) at night. You can rent bikes for around US$5 per day from Bigfoot Hostel, Lazybones Hostel and La Tortuga Booluda.

BUS

Buses headed south stop first in Managua, with an often lengthy wait between connections – it's better to make your own way there.

Check with your hostel about shuttle services, which you will need to book early, and find out when a group is leaving (most shuttles don't leave without at least four passengers).

Tierra Tour (☎2315-4278; www.tierratour.com; 1a Av NO, Iglesia de La Merced, 1½c N) has departures for Granada and Managua. Bigfoot Hostel has departures for Antigua, Guatemala (US$75), Managua (US$10), Granada (US$15),

NATIONAL BUS SERVICES FROM LEÓN

Most buses leave from León's chaotic **main bus terminal** (☎2311-3909; 6a Calle NE, Palí, 1½km E), which has a fun market area nearby. Watch your wallet.

For trips to Rota (Cerro Negro) note that Rota is 5km from the base of the volcano. The San Isidro bus has connections to frequent Matagalpa and Estelí buses.

DESTINATION	COST (US$)	DURATION	FREQUENCY
Chinandega bus	1	1½ hr	every 20 min
Chinandega microbus	1.25	50 min	depart when full
El Corinto	1.25	1½ hr	half-hourly
El Sauce	2.50	2½ hr	hourly
Estelí	2.50	2½ hr	4 daily
Granada microbus	3	2-3 hr	hourly
Hervideros de San Jacinto	0.75	40 min	half-hourly
La Paz Centro	0.75	40 min	every 45 min
Managua microbus	2	1¼ hr	depart when full
Managua (Carr Nueva, via La Paz Centro) *expreso*	1.70	1¼ hr	almost hourly
Managua (Carr Vieja, via Puerto Sandino) *ordinario*	1.50	1¾ hr	every 20 min
Masaya	2.75	2½ hr	hourly
Matagalpa	3	2½ hr	3 daily
Nagarote	1	1 hr	every 45 min
Rota (Cerro Negro)	0.75	2¼ hr	3 daily
Salinas Grandes	0.80	2 hr	4 daily
San Isidro	2.25	2½ hr	half-hourly

San Juan del Sur (US$25), and Poneloya (US$2), leaving most days.

Tica Bus (☎2311-6153; www.ticabus.com; 6a Calle NE, Palí, 1c O) Has departures for Guatemala City, Guatemala (US$70); San Salvador, El Salvador (US$50); Tegucigalpa, Honduras (US$23); and Tapachula, Mexico (US$92).

Beni Tours (☎2315-2349; 3a Av NE, Iglesia de San Juan, 25m N) You can buy your tickets for Transnica buses to San José, Costa Rica (US$35) and Tegucigalpa, Honduras (US$35) here. It also offers school-bus service to San Salvador, El Salvador (US$30), and Guatemala City, Guatemala (US$40), leaving at 10am daily.

Poneloya & Las Peñitas Beaches

The most accessible beaches from León are Poneloya and Las Peñitas, both an easy 20-minute bus ride from Mercadito Subtiava in León. The road splits at the sea: go right for Poneloya proper, left for more developed La Peñitas and Reserva Natural Isla Juan Venado.

Reserva Natural Isla Juan Venado is is an 18km-long, sandy barrier island (in some places only 300m wide), with swimming holes and lots of wildlife including nesting turtles and mosquitoes galore.

Several wilder beaches further south are a bit more difficult to reach, including Salinas Grandes, with regular bus service from León and its own access to Reserva Natural Isla Juan Venado.

From La Bocanita in Poneloya you can hire a private *panga* (small motorboat) seating four (US$70 to US$100) up to El Corinto, over to the Surfing Turtle Lodge on neighboring Isla Brasiles (US$0.75), or just out and back to explore the coastline.

Check at Hotelito Oasis for Isla Juan Venado tours (US$15), surf lessons (US$15) and board rentals (US$5/9, half-/full day).

Sleeping

Olazul HOSTEL $

(☎8435-7936; www.hotelolazul.com; empalme, 1km S; dm US$10, r with fan/air-con US$45/50; P ❄ ≈) Set on a wide stretch of open beach, these are the best digs in town. The restaurant overlooks the waves, and out back are five cute little cabins. There's a six-bed dorm and a dirty pool here, too.

Hotelito Oasis HOSTEL $

(☎8839-5344; www.oasislaspenitas.com; empalme, 3km S; dm/s/d US$7/18/20;) A long-time surfer favorite, the Oasis definitely has that lazy backpacker vibe, helped along by its absolute beachfront location. Rooms are big and plain. The four-bed dorm is a bit dark and cramped.

★Surfing Turtle Lodge LODGE $$

(☎8640-0644; www.surfingturtlelodge.com; Isla los Brasiles, across estuary from La Bocanita; tent US$5, dm US$10-12, r without bathroom US$32, cabin with bathroom US$40-60;) Getting to this utopian beach paradise is half the fun. From La Bocanita in Poneloya, you catch a small launch (US$0.75 each way), then take a 15-minute walk (or US$0.50 horse-carriage ride) to this beachfront lodge and hippie hideout on the 7km-long Isla los Brasiles. There's good surf right out front (mostly lefts), bonfires at night and a good chance you'll stay here...like forever.

The second-story dorm is one of the coolest spots in all of Central America with a giant view to the ocean. Electricity starts here at 6pm, and there's an on-site restaurant and turtle protection program. Day visitors are welcome as are long-term volunteers.

Playa Roca HOTEL $$

(☎8428-8903; www.playaroca.com; empalme, 2km S; r US$35, without bathroom US$25;) Looking out onto a rocky outcrop with a sweet patch of sand either side, this is the most scenic setting on the beach. Rooms are OK – big and bare, with cool tiled floors.

Getting There & Away

Buses leave for León (US$0.75, every 50 minutes) from the clutch of restaurant-bars just north of Barco de Oro. You can also arrange private boats seating at least four to Salinas Grandes (US$60, three hours), including a tour of the reserve.

Cosigüina Peninsula Beaches

The Cosigüina Peninsula is well on its way to becoming an island, worn away on two sides by brilliant estuaries and fringed with sandy beaches, ranging from the pearl grays of Jiquilillo to coal black at Playa Carbón.

Playa Aserradores

Worth the bumpy ride from the well-signed exit off the Chinandega–Potosí Hwy, this long, smooth stretch of sand has excellent surfing. Chancletas offers fishing tours

OFF THE BEATEN TRACK

VOLCANOES & BEACHES IN THE NORTHWEST

There are plenty of exploration opportunities in northwestern Nicaragua.

- **San Jacinto** is base camp for assaults on three volcanoes: Telica, Rota and Santa Clara. There are hot springs and boiling mud pools in town.
- **Volcán Momotombo** is 35km south of León. It is a hot, arduous full-day hike to the summit. It is far more convenient to go with a tour from León.
- **León Viejo** lies at the foot of Volcán Momotombo. Founded in 1524, Old León was abandoned less than a century later after being hit by a series of earthquakes. The settlement was subsequently completely buried under layers of ash from Momotombo. You can take a tour here from León, but it's easy to visit by yourself. Regular buses run from León to La Paz Centro (US$0.80, 45 minutes) meeting buses to Puerto Momotombo (US$0.50), less than 1km from the site.
- **Reserva Natural Pilas-El Hoyo** is home to the Cerro Negro volcano, where most people end up volcano surfing.
- **Puerto Sandino** is a workaday port town with Hawaii-sized waves.
- **El Transito** is pretty far south on the Pacific Coast, and features easy beginner-style waves.
- **Volcán Cosigüina** has spectacular views over the Golfo de Fonseca to Honduras and El Salvador.

(US$120, four hours), kayak tours (US$30, six hours), surfboard rentals (US$15 per day), and horses (US$20) and bikes (US$6).

Perched up on a grassy hillside overlooking the famed Boom-wavos break, **Hotel Chancletas** (☎8868-5036; www.hotelchancletas.com; Asseradores; r without bathroom with fan US$35, r with bathroom and air-con US$80; P ❄ 📶) is a surfer's spot with shared rooms that may have some mysterious animal droppings on the sheets, and nice upscale rooms.

Buses here from Chinandega depart at 2:30pm and 4pm, and leave for Chinandega at 5am and 7:45am (US$1, 1½ hours).

Playa Jiquilillo

This picture-perfect fishing village fronts a dramatic rocky point. There's excellent surf here, and the **Reserva Natural Estero Padre Ramos** protects the largest remaining mangrove forest in Central America. There is a **visitors center** (Los Zorros, 500m E of Y-Junction) in the community of Los Zorros, next to Finca Ecológica Trinchera, with some basic info. Finca Ecológica Trinchera and Jiquilillo hostels offer boat tours (US$35 to US$40), two-hour birding tours (US$10) and an interesting nighttime shrimping tour (US$10 to US$20) where locals show you both the commercial and ecological sides of the reserve.

Buses to Chinandega (US$1, 1½ hours) leave at 6am, 7:30am, 9:30am, 1:15pm and 3:30pm, returning from the Chinandega Mercadito at 6:30am, 10am, 11:30am, 3pm and 4:30pm.

Sleeping

★Rancho Tranquilo HOSTEL $

(☎8968-2290; www.rancho-tranquilo-nicaragua.com; dm US$7, cabins without bathroom US$20; P) The best budget spot in town, this collection of bungalows and a small dorm on a private stretch of beach is great. There's a cool bar and common area, and vegetarian dinners (US$3 to US$5) are served family style.

Hospedaje Rancho Esperanza GUESTHOUSE $

(☎8879-1795; www.rancho-esperanza.com; dm US$6, cabañas s/d US$10/16) Let staff know you're on your way to this quiet collection of simple bamboo huts scattered across a grassy field a bit back from the beach.

Finca Ecológica Trinchera FARM $

(☎8382-8560; www.fincatrinchera.com; Los Zorros, 500m E of Y-Junction; dm US$8, r per person without bathroom US$12) Don't want to be on the beach? Check out this inland option on a 2-hectare fruit farm.

Monty's Surf Camp LODGE $$
(☎8949-1952; www.nicaraguasurfbeach.com; dm US$20, s/d US$65/70, without bathroom US$35/40; @) The most upscale option here is this hotel–surf camp set right on the waterfront. The lounge and common areas are sweet with a wasting-away-in-paradise feel par excellence.

NORTHERN NICARAGUA

You've officially escaped Central America's backpacker superhighway and arrived in a place where colorful quetzals nest in misty cloud forests, and Nicaragua's best coffee and tobacco are cultivated with both capitalist zeal and collective spirit. With a little time and commitment you'll duck into ancient, crumbling cathedrals, get pounded by countless waterfalls, explore recently discovered canyons, and pay tribute to the pirates, colonists, revolutionaries, artists and poets who were inspired by these fertile mountains and mingled with the humble, open-hearted people who've lived here for generations.

Estelí

POP 122,900

A Sandinista stronghold, a university town, a market center for the thousands of farmers that populate its surrounding hills, Estelí has a multifaceted soul. On weekdays you can wake up with sunrise yoga before Spanish class, and on Saturday you can mingle with farmers at the massive produce market, then see them again at midnight, dancing like mad in a *ranchero* bar. And we haven't even mentioned the world-class cigars or the zeal with which a city with socialist roots has taken to slot machines. Yes, you don't have to be a Che Guevara devotee to dig this town.

Set on the Pan-American Hwy close to the Honduran border, Estelí was a strategic stronghold that saw heavy fighting and helped turn the revolution and, later, the Contra War. Makes sense, then, that it has remained one of the Sandinistas' strongest support bases. You'll see the murals and probably take in a political rally or three, and you won't want to miss the nearby collective farms in the cloud forests.

Sights

Although Estelí's most impressive attractions are in the surrounding mountains, the 1823 **Catedral** has a wonderful facade, and is worth a wander. Keep an eye out for the interesting **murals** that crop up about town, many of which were painted by participants in the **Funarte** (www.funarte.org.ni) children's mural workshop.

★Galería de Héroes y Mártires MUSEUM
(☎2714-0942, 8419-3519; galleryofheroesandmartyrs.blogspot.com; Av 1a NE, Calle Transversal, ½c N; donations appreciated; ⏲9:30am-4pm Tue-Fri) Be sure to stop by this moving gallery devoted to fallen revolutionaries, with displays of faded photos, clothes and weaponry.

Museo de Historia y Arqueología MUSEUM
(☎2713-3753; Catedral, 2c E, 3c N; ⏲8am-noon & 2pm-5pm Mon-Fri) In a large concrete faux indigenous pyramid on the north side of town, Estelí's museum has a small but interesting collection of pottery and petroglyphs from local pre-Hispanic cultures.

Casa de Cultura Leonel Rugama CULTURAL BUILDING
(☎2713-3021; esq Av 1a NE & Calle Transversal; ⏲8am-8pm) In the bullet-hole-marked former home of a high-ranking Somoza official, the Casa de Cultura offers a range of art, dance and music classes.

Courses

Escuela de Héroes y Mártires LANGUAGE COURSE
(☎8419-3519; inside Galería de Héroes y Mártires; per week with/without homestay US$180/100) Spanish classes right in the middle of town.

CENAC Spanish School LANGUAGE COURSE
(☎2713-5437; www.spanishschoolcenac.com; Panamericana, btwn Calles 5a SE & 6a SE; per week with/without homestay US$180/110) Professionally run Spanish school with classes for all levels.

Tours

★Tree Huggers GUIDED TOUR
(☎8496-7449; treehuggersnicaragua.wordpress.com; Av 2a NE & Calle 3a NE; ⏲8am-8pm) This friendly and vibrant tour operator is the specialist in trips to Miraflor but also offers other interesting community tourism trips around town and a great value cigar tour.

Estelí

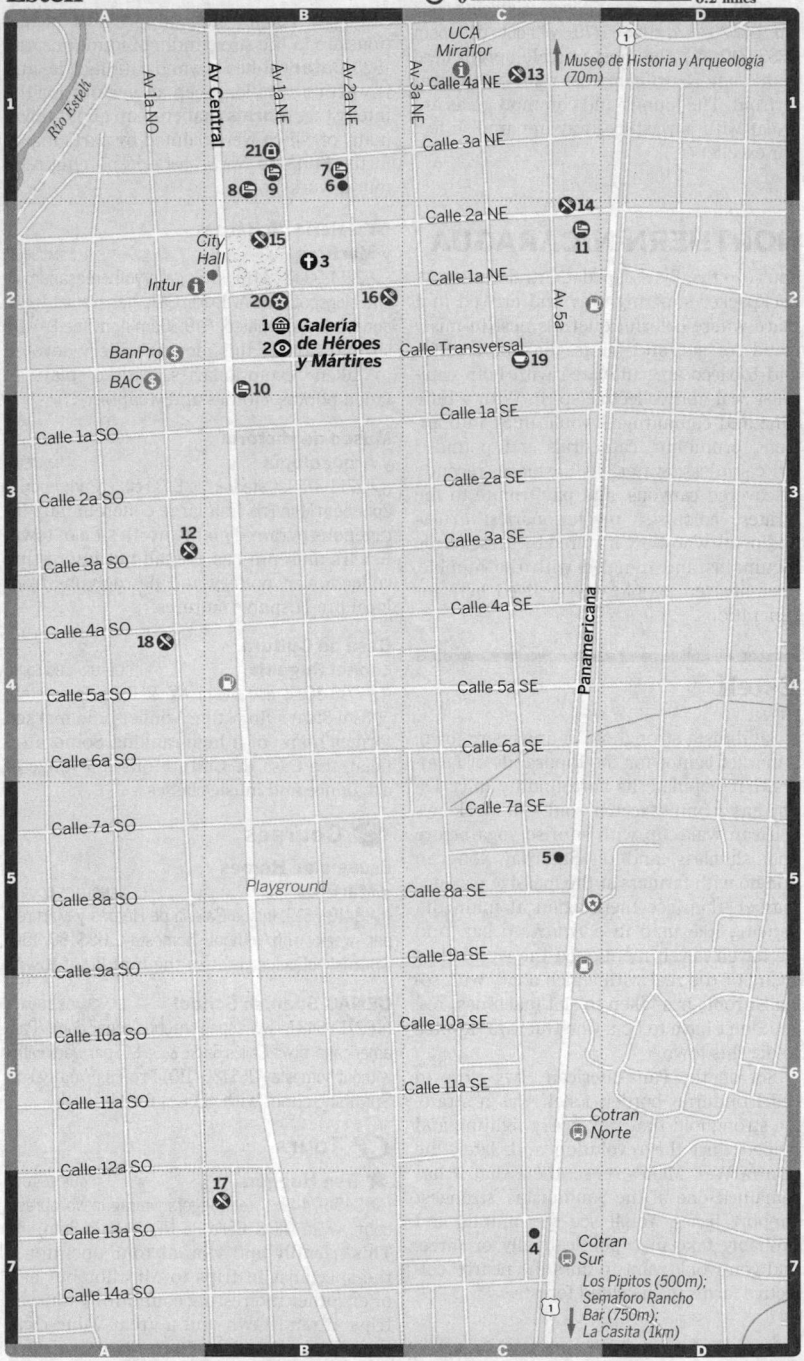
0 400 m
0 0.2 miles
A B C D
1 2 3 4 5 6 7
Río Estelí
Av 1a NO
Av Central
Av 1a NE
Av 2a NE
Av 3a NE
Av 5a
UCA Miraflor
Museo de Historia y Arqueología (70m)
Calle 4a NE
Calle 3a NE
Calle 2a NE
Calle 1a NE
Calle Transversal
Calle 1a SE
Calle 2a SE
Calle 3a SE
Calle 4a SE
Calle 5a SE
Calle 6a SE
Calle 7a SE
Calle 8a SE
Calle 9a SE
Calle 10a SE
Calle 11a SE
Calle 1a SO
Calle 2a SO
Calle 3a SO
Calle 4a SO
Calle 5a SO
Calle 6a SO
Calle 7a SO
Calle 8a SO
Calle 9a SO
Calle 10a SO
Calle 11a SO
Calle 12a SO
Calle 13a SO
Calle 14a SO
City Hall
Intur
BanPro
BAC
Galería de Héroes y Mártires
Playground
Panamericana
Cotran Norte
Cotran Sur
Los Pipitos (500m); Semaforo Rancho Bar (750m); La Casita (1km)
1
2
3
4
5
6
7
8
9
10
11
12
13
14
15
16
17
18
19
20
21

Estelí

Top Sights
1 Galería de Héroes y Mártires B2

Sights
2 Casa de Cultura Leonel Rugama B2
3 Catedral B2

Activities, Courses & Tours
4 CENAC Spanish School C7
Escuela de Héroes y Mártires ..... (see 1)
5 Tabacalera Cubanica C5
6 Tree Huggers B1

Sleeping
7 Hospedaje Luna B1
8 Hostal Miraflor B1
9 Hotel Los Arcos B1
10 Hotel Nicarao B2
11 Sonati C2

Eating
12 Buffet Castillo A3
13 Café-Arte Tipiscayán C1
14 El Quesito C2
15 Farmers' Market B2
16 Koma Rico B2
17 Mercado B7
18 Supermercado Las Segovias A4

Drinking & Nightlife
19 Mocha Nana Café C2

Entertainment
20 Cinema Estelí B2

Shopping
21 Artesanías La Esquina B1

Tabacalera Cubanica CIGAR TOUR
(☎ 2713-2383; Panamericana & Calle 7a SE) This pioneering factory produces Padrón cigars, Nicaraguás most prestigious (and costly) brand.

Drew Estate CIGAR TOUR
(www.cigarsafari.com; Barrio Oscar Gamez 2) Estelí's most innovative cigar company.

Plasencia Cigars CIGAR TOUR
(☎ 2713-4074; Escuela Normal, 200m N) Large company that produces more than 30 brands of *puros* including a selection of organic cigars.

Sleeping

Hotel Nicarao GUESTHOUSE $
(☎ 2713-2490; hotelnicarao79@yahoo.es; Av Central, Calle Transversal, ½c S; r per person US$19, without bathroom US$12;) This charming garden gem looks grubby from the street, but inside you'll find pleasant rooms at exceptional value set around a spacious courtyard with sofas and rocking chairs.

Hostal Miraflor GUESTHOUSE $
(☎ 2713-2003; Av Central, Calle 2a NE, ½c N; s/d/tr US$12/17/25;) Friendly family-run place offering basic rooms with new tiled bathrooms and hot water. Sure, the beds sag and there are stains on the walls, but the price is comfy. Cheap meals are available.

★ Hotel Los Arcos HOTEL $$
(☎ 2713-3830; hotelosarcos@hotmail.com; esq Av 1a NE & Calle 3a NE; s/d with fan US$45/50, with aircon US$55/60, all incl breakfast; P) Run by a nonprofit organization, Los Arcos remains the best hotel in town, with a dream location one block north of the cathedral, a roof deck with kick-ass mountain and city views, and spotless rooms with soft sheets, Spanish tiles and high ceilings.

Hospedaje Luna HOSTEL $$
(☎ 8441-8466; www.cafeluzyluna.com; esq Av 2a NE & Calle 3a NE; dm/s/d/tr US$7/15/25/30;) With a central location, clean rooms, courtyard common area and a wealth of information on Estelí and the surrounding area, this nonprofit hostel is the budget traveler's favorite.

Sonati HOSTEL $$
(☎ 2713-6043; sonati.esteli@gmail.com; Catedral, 3½c E; dm US$6-7, s/d/tr US$15/25/40;) This chilled hostel feels a lot like a houseshare with plenty of communal space, a spacious shared kitchen and a pleasant rear garden.

Eating

Self-caterers can visit **Supermercado Las Segovias** (cnr Calle 4a SO & Av 1a NO), a solid supermarket with great deals on gourmet coffee. Estelí's municipal **market** (cnr Calle 12a SO & Av 1a SO) is always stocked with amazingly fresh produce. There's a **farmers' market** (Parque Central; ⏲ 7am-noon) every Friday morning on the Parque Central.

Buffet Castillo NICARAGUAN $
(☎ 2713-0337; Parque Central, 4c S, ½c O; meals US$2-3.50; ⏲ 7am-3pm Mon-Sat) Often packed at lunchtime, this neat diner offers restaurant-quality meals, including ribs, fried fish and jalapeño chicken, at a budget price.

El Quesito NICARAGUAN $
(cnr Calle 2a NE & Av 4a NE, Del Asoganor, 1c N; items US$1-2, meals US$3-4; ⏲ 6:30am-8pm)

Pull up a handmade wooden chair at this rustic corner diner and enjoy homemade yogurt flavored with local fruits, *quesillos* and *leche agria* (sour milk) – yes, what most of us pour down the sink is a delicacy in Nicaragua! It also prepares excellent, nongreasy Nica breakfasts and set meals.

La Casita CAFE $
(Panamericana; snacks US$1-2; ⏲9am-7pm Tue-Sun) Hidden about 1km south of town (US$1 in a cab), La Casita is surrounded by gardens shading a trickling stream. Sip coffee or chai, munch muesli with homemade yogurt, or snack on rustic loaves of brown bread served with spreads or chunks of cheese.

Koma Rico NICARAGUAN $
(Cinema Estelí, 2c E; dishes US$2-3; ⏲6-10pm, closed Fri) Stack your plate high at this popular *fritanga* that's based upon the tried-and-tested marriage of tasty barbecued meats and ice-cold beer.

★**Café-Arte Tipiscayán** NICARAGUAN $$
(☎2713-7303; Calle 4a NE, Av 4a NE, 10m E; snacks US$2-4, mains US$6-8; ⏲noon-10pm Thu-Tue) The family of San Juan de Limay soapstone sculptor Freddy Moreno serves ultra-traditional fare such as *güirílas* (corn pancakes) and cheese curd, *montucas* (Nicaraguan *tamales*) and grilled meats, as well as excellent coffee.

Drinking & Nightlife

Most nightlife is out on the Panamericana.

★**Semaforo's Ranchon Bar** BAR, RESTAURANT
(Panamericana, Hospital 300m S; ⏲8pm-5am Thu-Sun) This indoor-outdoor club with the *palapa* roof and bandstand brings terrific live music to a crowd that is here to dance in their boots and cowboy hats.

Cigarszone CLUB
(Panamericana) Expansive club big on bling and high-tech lights.

Mocha Nana Café CAFE
(☎2713-3164; Calle Transversal, Av 4a SE, ½c E; drinks US$1.50; ⏲11am-9pm) Where Estelí intellectuals gather to sip caffeine, debate politics and culture, and munch tasty waffles. On Friday evenings there is usually live music by local bands (cover US$1.50).

Entertainment

Cinema Estelí CINEMA
(Calle 1a NE; tickets around US$2.25) Old-time movie theater.

Shopping

For custom-made cowboy boots (around US$80) and other leather goods check out the workshops to the south of Supermercado Las Segovias on Av 1a SO.

Artesanías La Esquina HANDICRAFTS
(☎2713-3239; cnr Av 1a NE & Calle 3a NE; ⏲8am-noon & 2-6pm) Look for the wonderful local pottery.

Information

BAC (cnr Calle Transversal & Av 1a NO) MasterCard/Cirrus/Visa/Plus ATM.

BanPro (cnr Calle Transversal & Av 1a NO) Reliable ATM.

Lavanderia Express (☎2714-1297; Av 3a SE, Calle 1a SE, 30m S, Migracion, ½c N; per pound US$1 ; ⏲9am-5pm) Economical wash and dry service.

Intur (☎2713-6799; Plaza Plator, Parque Central, ½c O; ⏲8am-1pm) Official tourist office with an abundance of regional brochures, but not a lot of expertise.

Police (☎118; Panamericana)

UCA Miraflor (Unión de Cooperativas Agropecuarias de Miraflor; ☎2713-2971; www.ucamiraflor.com; cnr Av 4a NE & Calle 4a NE; ⏲8am-noon & 12:30-5:30pm Mon-Sat) Information and booking for Reserva Natural Miraflor.

Getting There & Away

Estelí has two bus terminals, blue collar **Cotran Norte** (☎2713-2529), with plenty of slot machines and a soft-rock soundtrack, and the more refined **Cotran Sur** (☎2713-6162). Both are located at the southern end of the city on the Panamericana.

Buses departing from Cotran Norte:

Jalapa (US$3.50, 2¾ hours, twice daily)

Jinotega (via Concordia, San Rafael) (US$1.80, 2½ hours, six daily)

León (US$2.80, 2½ hours, 3:10pm; microbus US$3, two hours, depart when full) Alternatively, take the Matagalpa bus and change at San Isidro.

Managua (*expreso* US$3, 2½ hours, four daily) First three buses don't run on Sunday.

Masaya (US$3, three hours, twice daily)

Ocotal (US$1.25, 1½ hours, hourly) Buses run from 6am to 11am.

San Juan de Limay (US$1.80, two hours, seven daily)

Somoto (US$1.15, 1½ hours, hourly)

Buses departing from Cotran Sur:

León (US$2.80, 2½ hours, 5am, 5:45am, 6:45am) First two buses don't run on Sunday.

Managua (*expreso* US$3, 2½ hours, hourly; *ordinario* US$2.25, 3½ hours, half-hourly) First two express buses don't run on Sunday.

Matagalpa (*ordinario* US$1.25, 1¾ hours, half-hourly)

Área Protegida Miraflor

Enticing Miraflor, located some 30km northeast of Estelí, is a vast expanse of private land that is managed by the community and has been declared a nature reserve. It's predominantly farmland, covering three climatic zones from dry to wet, stretching from 800m to 1450m.

Miraflor is a great place to get away from it all, immerse yourself in the lifestyle of traditional coffee-growing communities, and do some low-key walking, bird-watching or horseback riding. There are also several volunteer projects that you can get involved with. There is no central town; *fincas* (farms) are scattered widely across the area, and around several small community hubs.

UCA Miraflor (p494) in Estelí manages the reserve and can help you plan a visit, hook you up with an English-speaking guide and book family homestays. Alternatively, Tree Huggers (p491) provides detailed, impartial advice on planning a trip and also makes reservations.

Sights & Activities

Local **guides** (per day US$15, horses per person US$10) usually meet incoming buses and are both inexpensive and a great resource. They know all the best hikes and climbs and can share insights into Miraflor's unique history and local daily life.

Specialty coffee (with/without tasting session US$70/30, up to 10 participants), orchid (US$30, up to 10 participants) and bird (US$60, up to six participants) tours are held seasonally and should be arranged via UCA Miraflor in advance.

Some landowners charge admission to visit sights or pass through their property; bring plenty of change.

Most people come here to visit within the local communitiies. **Coyolito** has a cool lookout and waterfalls. **Cebollal** caters to tourists and offers easy access to **Los Volcancitos**, a stand of virgin cloud forest. **Sontule** is a great spot to learn about coffee. **La Perla** has a nearby lagoon. **La Pita** has a cool swimming hole nearby.

Sleeping & Eating

There are several choices of accommodations within the reserve, all of which should be booked through UCA Miraflor or Tree Huggers in Estelí.

Farmhouse rooms (per person with/without meals US$19/8) allow the most interaction with local families; **cabañas** (per person with/without meals US$24/10) have more privacy. Both options are rustic and some accommodations have pit latrines.

If creature comforts are important, **Finca Neblina del Bosque** (☎8701-1460; www.visitamiraflor.com; Cebollal; dm with/without meals US$7/19, cabañas per person incl meals US$25-38), owned by a Nica-German couple, is the most comfortable option in Miraflor but it has decidedly less rural farming flavor.

Note that the entire reserve is a dry zone and no alcoholic beverages are sold.

Getting There & Away

There are bus services from Estelí's Cotran Norte to various parts of the reserve (around US$0.70 for all destinations). Buses to El Coyolito (one hour), in the lower southwestern zone, and La Pita leave from the Pulperia Miraflor in the northern outskirts of Estelí. Swing by the UCA Miraflor office in Estelí to find out the best bus for your destination.

Área Protegida Cerro Tisey-Estanzuela

This small park just 10km south of Estelí is smaller, drier and less populated but every bit as gorgeous as Área Protegida Miraflor. It's possible to visit Tisey on a day trip from Estelí; however, the park's attractions are spread out all over its 9344 hectares and public transportation is limited so you'll see more if you spend the night.

The main entrance is accessed from the dirt road beside Hospital San Juan de Dios in Estelí. In the park's lower elevations, just 5km from Estelí, is the inspiring **Salto Estanzuela** (admission US$1), a gushing 36m waterfall that careens over a bromeliad-studded cliff. There have been reports of robberies recently on the path to the falls from the main Tisey road – travel in a group and don't take any valuables.

After the falls, the road begins to climb high into the mountains before arriving at the Eco-Posada, where you'll find a handful of Spanish-speaking guides (US$20 to US$25 per day). The nearby, 2km **Mirador de Tisey**

Trail is absolutely spectacular. A short walk further along the road is the entrance to Alberto Gutiérrez's singular **Galería del Arte el Jalacate** (admission by donation).

About 3km beyond the *galería* is the cute hamlet of **La Garnacha**, known for a chapel that housed huddled refugees of a Contra invasion during the war, and a **dairy co-operative** (☎8658-1054; garnachaturistica@yahoo.es; Comunidad La Garnacha) that produces artisanal Italian-style goat cheese. The progressive cooperative organizes several interesting activities. You'll also find the best beds in Tisey in this little town.

Sleeping & Eating

The *comedor* in La Garnacha prepares excellent meals (US$3 to US$5) using local organic produce.

Cabañas La Garnacha LODGE $

(☎8658-1054; garnchaturistica@yahoo.es; La Garnacha; r US$15, cabañas US$20-40) Overlooking a small lake, these community-run cabins have hot water and can sleep two to 10 guests. Basic rooms (US$3) in local homes can also be organized from here.

Eco-Posada LODGE $

(☎8386-1427, 2713-6213; r per person US$6, cabañas US$14) Offers comfortable cabins with flush toilets, and front porches slung with hammocks overlooking a small creek.

Getting There & Away

Tisey is served by two buses a day (US$1, 1½ hours), which are marked 'La Tejera' and leave from Estelí Cotran Sur at 6:30am and 1:30pm. The buses pass Salto Estanzuela and Eco-Posada before arriving at the La Garnacha turnoff, a 1.5km walk from the community. Buses return to Estelí from the La Garnacha turnoff at 8:30am and 3:30pm. On Wednesday there is no service.

In the dry season, you can also charter a taxi from Estelí (about US$40 to US$50 for five to six hours), which is a good idea for day-trippers.

Salto Estanzuela is about a 90-minute walk or 40-minute bicycle ride from the hospital in Estelí. Expect to pay around US$8 to US$10 in a taxi.

Somoto

POP 37,000

Diminutive Somoto has not always been a shoe-in on the itineraries of visitors to northern Nicaragua. In fact, until 2003 this was just another sleepy colonial town in the Honduran shadow famed for its donkeys and *rosquillas* (baked corn snacks). Then two Czech scientists stumbled onto a rift in the rugged, overgrown clay earth outside town and, just 75 million years after these charcoal granite cliffs pierced the earth's surface, Europeans 'discovered' Cañon de Somoto (Somoto Canyon), where the Río Coco is born.

Of course, the locals living nearby have known about it all along and formerly referred to the site as 'La Estrechura,' while it is said that the area's original inhabitants, the Chorotegas, referred to the region as Tepezonate (Mountain of Water).

Sights

Monumento Nacional Cañon de Somoto PARK

(admission US$2) This is an unmissable experience. There are three routes to explore the canyon. The full six-hour, 12km circuit will take you to two bat caves well above the rim before you hike down to the river, boulder hop, swim through (small) rapids and leap off 8m rocks into deep swimming holes.

The most popular option is the four-hour, 6km classic loop that will get you straight into the canyon, where you'll swim, hike and leap beneath slate-rock faces and jagged peaks.

For those that are averse to exercise, there is also a three-hour 'lite' tour where you are paddled up the gorge in a small boat and float back down in an inflatable tube.

Guides (half-/full day up to five people US$15 to US$20) are not technically mandatory if you just want to hang around the lower reaches, but are absolutely essential if you want to venture into the canyon. Guides from the local community of Sonis at the entrance to the reserve have formed a **co-operative** (☎8676-5883; Carretera Somoto–El Espino, Km 229.5) and work on a rotation basis. They offer a fantastic package including taxi transportation from Somoto, life vest and water shoes, a dry bag, entrance fee, guide, lunch and a boat trip for US$25 per visitor. They also offer horseback-riding tours to the surrounding mountains to get a bird's-eye view of the area and organize homestays in the community so you are able to spend more time exploring. Another option is to visit the site with one of the professional guides from **Cosermuturma** (☎2722-2340, 8630-0704; reymen2008@hotmail.com; Enitel, 7½c S) in Somoto.

If you are just in Somoto to see the canyon, consider staying with one of the local families as part of their community-based tourism project in the village of **Sonis**, right at the canyon entrance (US$5-7 a night). Contact **Henry Soriano** (☎8610-7642; Carretera Somoto–El Espino, Km 229.5) to reserve a room.

To visit the canyon take any El Espino–bound bus (US$0.40, 30 minutes) from the bus terminal to the trail head at Km 231 near the community of Sonis. A taxi will cost around US$5. From here it's a 3km hike to the canyon including a river crossing that may be over 1m deep. The last bus back to Somoto passes at around 5:30pm.

The canyon often closes in October, when the water is too high. Call the guides to check on conditions.

Jinotega

POP 46,000 / ELEV 995M

Hidden in a cat's eye of a valley, the City of Mists is enclosed on all sides by mountains dappled in cloud forests, crowned with granite ridges and pocked with deep gorges.

While coffee tourism percolates in Matagalpa, Jinotega, which brims with adventure and promise, still sees far more foreign-aid workers than tourists. So walk these cobbled streets, visit nearby Lago de Apanás, and hike into the misty mountains, where you can harvest coffee with locals and stroll through primary forest. Just make sure to get to Cerro La Cruz on a clear day to glimpse the cat's eye in all her jade glory.

That City of Mists moniker is no joke. The average temperature is just 20°C (68°F) and the town can get 2600mm of rain annually. Bring rain gear and a fleece for the cool evenings.

Sights & Activities

The beauty of Jinotega's **Catedral San Juan** (c 1805) is in the sanctuary, where you'll marvel at the chestnut and gold-leaf altar, pristine white arches and rows of heavenly saints. Opposite the cathedral is a terrific, split-level **Parque Central** shaded by palms and towering laurel trees.

★Cerro La Cruz RELIGIOUS

A steep yet worthwhile hour's hike from the cemetery and embedded in a boulder-crusted ridge is the town's cross, originally placed here in 1703 by Franciscan Fray Margíl de Jesús.

La Biosfera FARM

(☎8698-1439, 8427-8414; www.hijuela.com/labiosferaretreat; Carretera vieja Matagalpa) This American-run permaculture farm just 3km outside town has fantastic views and 7 hectares of forest to explore. It offers subsidized accommodation for those that want to volunteer on the farm.

Tours

Cuculmeca CULTURAL TOUR

(☎2782-3579; www.cuculmeca.org; Barrio Daniel Teller, Salida al Guayacán; ⏲9am-5pm Mon-Fri) This dynamic NGO arranges accommodation and guides for visits to farms and sustainable tourism projects in the Reserva Natural Cerro Datanlí–El Diablo and around San Rafael del Norte.

Sleeping

Hotel Primavera GUESTHOUSE $

(☎2782-2400; Parque Central, 5c N, 1c E; s/d US$8.50/12.50, without bathroom US$5/10) The sunniest and cleanest cheapie has new tile and decent mattresses in the rooms, and is owned by a lovely family who hang out in the lobby. The door shuts at 10pm sharp, so make arrangements if you intend to stay out late.

Hotel Bosawás HOTEL $

(☎2782-6689; Parque Central, 4c N; s/d US$10.50/14.50, without bathroom US$6.50/8.50;) Pass through the bright lobby to get to the basic but excellent-value rooms at this budget classic. Those at the front with shared bathrooms and windows onto the street are actually nicer than the more expensive ones with private bathrooms at the rear.

Hotel Central HOTEL $$

(☎2782-2063; Parque Central, 1c E, ½c N; s/d/tr US$10.50/19/25.20; P) The friendly staff rents comfy rooms with hot water and cable TV, although the walls are somewhat thin. The rooms on the north side are brighter as they have outside-facing windows.

Eating & Drinking

There are a few street-food stalls around the park, and *fritangas* fire up around town in the evenings.

★La Casa de Don Colocho BAKERY $

(☎2782-2584; Parque Central, 3c E, 3c S; pastries US$0.60-1.10; ⏲7am-8pm;) A bakery every town would love. The cinnamon rolls are dense and sugary; the pineapple triangles are addictive.

Soda El Tico NICARAGUAN $
(☎2782-2059; Parque Central, 1c E, ½c S; buffet meals US$4, mains US$6; ⏲7:30am-10pm) By far the most appetizing restaurant in town, Soda El Tico is a classic steam-table buffet.

Asados Gloria BARBECUE $
(Hospital, ½c O; meals US$2-2.50; ⏲noon-9pm) At last a cheap *fritanga* with inviting ambience and real salad.

La Terraza CAFE $$
(contiguo Banco Procredit; mains US$6-7; ⏲noon-10pm) This flash new cafe-restaurant above Soda El Tico feels just a tad too stylish for hard-working Jinotega with elegant wrought-iron tables.

Café Flor de Jinotega CAFE
(☎2782-2617; www.soppexcca.org; Cotran Norte, 1½c N; espresso drinks US$0.50-0.75; ⏲8am-6pm) Quite simply the best cup of coffee in town, and possibly on all of the Ruta de Café.

Bar Jinocuba BAR
(Alcaldía, 5c N; ⏲noon-midnight, closed Tue) Groovy alternative rock bar.

La Taverna BAR
(Parque Central, 2c O; ⏲noon-midnight) The coolest dive in the northern highlands.

Getting There & Away

There are two bus terminals. **Cotran Norte** is on the highway east of town, while **Cotran Sur** sits near the town's southern entrance.

Buses departing from Cotran Norte:

Estelí (US$2, 1¾ hours, six daily)

Pantasma (San Gabriel) (US$1.80, 1½ hours, hourly)

Pantasma (Asturias) (US$2, 1½ hours, hourly)

San Rafael del Norte (*ordinario* US$0.80, 40 minutes; *expreso* US$1, 30 minutes; half-hourly)

Yalí (US$2, two hours, five daily)

Buses departing from Cotran Sur:

Managua (US$3.40, 3½ hours, 4am to 4pm, 10 daily) Via new road; does not enter Matagalpa.

Matagalpa (US$1, 1¼ hours, half-hourly)

Matagalpa

POP 89,100 / ELEV 902M

If you love coffee, mountains and urbanity, then have your cake and eat it in Matagalpa, a town where for decades an ever-increasing number of Liberal coffee patriarchs and subsistence Sandinista farmers have rubbed shoulders during city festivals and at market.

And when you've sipped your last cup of city, head for the hills, where you can hike through primary forest to gushing waterfalls, pick coffee, explore mineshafts and listen to *ranchero* troubadours jam under a harvest moon.

Sights

★Casa Museo Comandante Carlos Fonseca MUSEUM

(Parque Rubén Darío, 1c E; donations appreciated; ⏲9am-5pm) Commander Carlos Fonseca, the Sandinista equivalent of Malcolm X, grew up desperately poor in this humble adobe

OFF THE BEATEN TRACK

BOSAWÁS

If you are the kind of traveler that relishes dropping off the radar, the **Reserva de Biosfera Bosawás** is the place for you. The largest rainforest in the Americas after the Amazon, it's a magical place of spectacular forested peaks and fast-flowing rivers that rush past tiny indigenous villages. With no roads, no hotels and no electricity, it's a tough place to visit, but the potential for adventure is enormous.

The easiest way into the reserve is via the town of **Wiwili** on the Río Coco in northern Jinotega department. There is no public transportation on the river, but if you're not in a hurry, it's possible to travel all the way to the Caribbean using the boats of local traders and organizations.

Another option is to travel from Jinotega to the village of **Ayapal**, from where boats leave irregularly for the trip down the narrow Río Bocay, past the mysterious caves of Tunawalan, to the Mískito village of San Andrés on the Río Coco.

Once you get into the reserve proper, the only places to stay are in indigenous Mayanga and Mískito villages, where you can often arrange some sort of accommodation. It can get cold at night, so bring warm clothes as well as plenty of food, water purification tablets and a flashlight.

WORTH A TRIP

CAFFEINATED ADVENTURES

For a glimpse into the life of Nicaragua's hard-working *campesinos* (farmers) in the northern highlands, head to the small town of **San Ramón**, 12km east of Matagalpa, where local agricultural cooperative **UCA San Ramon** (☎2772-5247; www.agroecoturismorural.com; guides per day US$15) has developed a tempting menu of fantastic activities in four nearby rural villages: La Pita, La Reina, La Corona and El Roblar. Tours include sustainable agriculture, Nicaraguan rural culture and cooking, and coffee-harvesting (in season), as well as activities such as horse-riding and wildlife-spotting. Buses to San Ramón (US$0.45) leave half-hourly from Cotran Norte in Matagalpa, but it is much faster to take a shared taxi (US$1.20). From San Ramón you can hike to the communities or hire a bicycle (US$10 per day).

with his single mother and four siblings. Now it's a tiny but enthralling museum that follows his evolution as a leader from childhood until his death.

Iglesia Catedral San Pedro CHURCH
(Parque Morazán) Built in 1874, Matagalpa's glorious whitewashed neoclassical cathedral is flooded with light.

Museo de Café MUSEUM
(Av José Beníto Escobar, Parque Morazán, 1c S; ⏲8am-12:30pm & 2-5pm Mon-Fri) FREE Recently overhauled, this absorbing museum features large, glossy printed displays in Spanish and English on the roots of regional cafes and modern coffee production.

Iglesia San José CHURCH
Originally constructed in 1751 and used as a jail for indigenous rebels in the late 1800s, this church was rebuilt in 1917.

Activities

Reserva Natural Cerro Apante PARK
(admission US$1.50) Matagalpa's most popular hiking trail leads from Finca San Luis, a 20-minute walk (or US$1 taxi ride) south of Parque Dario, into this reserve. It's a two-hour round-trip hike to the *mirador*.

Café Girasol HIKING
(☎2772-6030; www.familiasespeciales.org; ⏲6:30am-10pm) A charitable setup that accepts volunteers, Café Girasol sells detailed leaflets (US$1) for a number of self-guided walks in the Matagalpa area that vary in length from four to eight hours.

Tours

★**Matagalpa Tours** ADVENTURE TOUR
(☎2772-0108, 8647-4680; www.matagalpatours.com; ⏲8am-12:30pm & 2-6pm Mon-Fri, 8am-4pm Sat) A well-run, English-speaking setup that offers a wide range of excursions in Matagalpa and the surrounding hills.

Courses

Escuela de Español Matagalpa LANGUAGE COURSE
(☎2772-0108; www.matagalpa.info) Run from the same office as Matagalpa Tours.

Sleeping

Hotel El Castillo HOTEL $
(☎2772-0034; hotelelcastillomt@gmail.com; Parque Morazán, 3c E; s/d/tr US$15/17/24; 📶) This excellent-value new hotel set on a hillside has great views and is only three blocks from the park.

Hotel Central HOTEL $
(☎2712-3140; Av José Beníto Escobar, Parque Rubén Darío, 2½c N; s/d/tr US$11.50/15.50/21; 📶) Vacillates between dumpy and bright depending upon the rooms, which all come with cable TV, plump pillows and new spring mattresses.

Hospedaje Vic Pal GUESTHOUSE $
(☎2772-6735; Parque Morazán, 3½c N; r US$8, s/d without bathroom US$3/6) Really cheap and basic, it's also clean, quiet and friendly.

Luna International Hostel HOSTEL $
(☎8496-3408; www.cafeluzyluna.com; Gasolinera Uno, 3½c E; dm/r US$7/20) This new branch of the popular Estelí hostel was just finding its feet when we passed through, but has clean and spacious rooms, a large kitchen and plenty of information for travelers.

La Buena Onda HOSTEL $$
(☎2772-2135; www.hostelmatagalpa.com; cancha Brigadista, 2½c E; dm/s/d US$8/25/30; 📶) Clean, centrally located and with a chilled vibe, this fine hostel ticks all the boxes. It's located in a cozy converted house with well-

furnished rooms, spacious dorms with private bathrooms and big lockers.

Eating

Look to the smoky booths that set up at sunset just north of Palí supermarket and the cathedral for the regional specialty, *güirílas*. Made with a fresh corn *masa*, they are sweeter and thicker than your average tortilla.

Repostería Gutiérrez CAFE $
(☎2772-2502; Parque Morazán, ½c S; pastries US$0.50-1.50; ⏲7am-8pm) Serves tasty fresh pastries and excellent local coffee to a dedicated clientele.

El Mexicano MEXICAN $
(Parque Morazon, 1c N, 2½c E; mains US$3; ⏲noon-10pm; ✎) It looks posh from the outside, but go in to enjoy cheap authentic Mexican food prepared by the owner/chef from Guadalajara and served in a casual dining area.

Maná de Cielo NICARAGUAN $
(Av Martínez, Parque Morazán, 3c S; meals US$3-5; ⏲7am-9pm) The best-loved steam table in Matagalpa.

★La Vita é Bella ITALIAN $$
(☎2772-5476; Parque Morazán, 2½c E, 1½c N; pastas US$3-4, mains US$5-8; ⏲noon-10pm; ✎) This local institution serves up flavorful authentic Italian dishes at low prices in a relaxed bistro atmosphere. The thin-crust pizza is some of the best in Nicaragua.

Drinking

Artesanos BAR
(☎2772-2444; www.artesanoscafebar.blogspot.com; Parque Morazán, 1c S, ½c E; ⏲9am-midnight) Hands down the grooviest bar-cafe in town.

Entertainment

Centro Cultural Guanuca CULTURAL CENTER
(☎2772-3562; Guadalupe, 1½c S; ⏲10am-10pm) Run by a nonprofit women's organization, this great venue shows art-house movies and hosts concerts.

Orientation

Bordered on its western edge by the river, Matagalpa's central zone is concentrated around two one-way streets that link the city's principal plazas, Parque Morazán on the north side and Parque Rubén Darío to the south. The municipal cathedral faces Morazán; budget accommodations are concentrated around Rubén Darío.

Information

BAC (Parque Morazán, ½c S)
Correos de Nicaragua (Parque Morazán, 1c S; ⏲8am-1pm)
Intur (☎2772-7060; Av Martínez, Parque Morazán, 3c S; ⏲8am-2pm) Useful for flyers but not much else.

Getting There & Away

There are two main bus terminals in Matagalpa. Clean, well-organized **Cotran Sur** (☎2772-4659), about 800m west of Parque Rubén Darío, generally serves Managua and points south.

Buses departing from Cotran Sur:
Chinandega (US$3.40, 3½ hours, twice daily)
Ciudad Darío (US$0.85, one hour, six daily)
Estelí (US$1.20, 2¼ hours, half-hourly)
Jinotega (US$1, 1½ hours, half-hourly)
León (US$3, 2½ hours, four daily)
Managua (*ordinario* US$2.10, 2¾ hours, half-hourly; *expreso* US$3, 2¼ hours, hourly)
Masaya (US$3, three hours, twice daily)

Chaotic and disorienting by comparison, **Cotran Norte** (Cotramusun) goes to the following destinations:
El Cuá (US$3.20, four hours, six daily)
Esquipulas (US$1.75, 1½ hours, nine daily)
San Ramón (US$0.45, 30min, half-hourly)

CARIBBEAN COAST

A ramble along Nicaragua's Caribbean coast would be the perfect terrain for an epic novel. Your settings would include wide, muddy rivers surrounded by thick jungle, a fascinating tropical port town and an expanse of mangrove-shrouded black water that is home to more than a dozen ethnic fishing enclaves. And we haven't even got to the pristine offshore islands ringed by white sand with a turquoise trim.

Your cast will feature tough and insightful characters from English-speaking Creole towns and indigenous Mískito, Mayangna, Rama and Garifuna communities. And there will be plenty of action too, with scuba diving, epic treks through dense rainforest, beach combing, and fishing in the mangroves.

The coast is divided into two autonomos regions: to the north is the Región Autónoma del Atlántico Norte (RAAN), and south is the Región Autónoma del Atlántico Sur (RAAS).

Bluefields

POP 54,800

With brick streets etched into a series of jade peninsulas, Bluefields (the city) stretches into Bluefields (the bay) like so many fingers. In between is a series of docks, floating restaurants, shipwrecks, and fish and produce markets. The city was once full of old wood Victorian charm before Category IV Hurricane Juana wiped it off the map in 1988.

Today's Bluefields is rather thick with new concrete boxes, especially in the loud knot of streets downtown that eventually gives way to poor tin-roof neighborhoods that ramble over nearby hillsides and inland along brackish creeks.

The capital of the RAAS is the the beating heart of Creole culture, famed for its its distinctive music, colorful dances and delicious cuisine. Still, you probably won't linger too long. After all, you are just a boat ride away from the intriguing Pearl Lagoon basin, the spectacular Pearl Keys and those luscious Corn Islands.

Sights & Activities

Moravian Church CHURCH

The town's most striking building is the Moravian church, a lovely building with characteristic stained glass. Although it dated from 1849, what you see now is a concrete replica of the wooden original, flattened by Hurricane Juana (Joan).

Parque Reyes PARK

Parque Reyes is a popular meeting point with impressive 25m trees and a monument to the six ethnic groups of the region.

El Bluff PORT, BEACH

Across the bay, the port El Bluff has a long beach that while not particularly attractive is the only real place to swim around here. Boats to El Bluff (US$1.40) leave regularly from the dock by the market.

Rama Cay ISLAND

(☎tel, info 628-1112; castrofrancis@hotmail.com)

Around 15km south of town in the southern reaches of Bahía de Bluefields lies the tiny island of Rama Cay, unofficial capital of the Rama nation. Home to more than half of the remaining Rama people, it is a crowded place with groups of wooden houses jostling for space under the fruit trees.

The real reason to come to the island is Hotel Surpise Dream, a hotel and ecotourism project run by the Rama Nation in conjunction with BICU. There's currently no regular boat service to Rama Cay, so independent travelers can choose a pricey private *panga* or try to hitch a ride with a Rama fisher, who may or may not speak Spanish.

GETTING THERE & STAYING SAFE

You can travel overland from Managua to the Caribbean coast, but most visitors take the frequent, inexpensive La Costeña (p503) flights. There are active commercial airstrips in Bilwi, Waspám, Bluefields, Great Corn Island and two of the three Las Minas towns. Still, if you have more time than cash and enjoy the (really) slow lane, there are two overland routes into the region.

There are irregular passenger-boat services between Bluefields and Bilwi via Great Corn Island, but don't count on it if your schedule is tight.

➡ **Las Minas–Bilwi overland** We won't sugar coat this. You're in for a grueling ride on a beat-up old school bus packed to the gills. It begins with a 10- to 12-hour bus ride from Managua to Siuna in Las Minas, where you can access the Reserva de Biosfera Bosawás (Bosawás Biosphere Reserve). From Siuna it's another 10 to 12 hours on a horrendous road to Bilwi. Waspám and the Río Coco are a smoothish six hours north from there.

➡ **Boaco–Juigalpa–El Rama–Bluefields overland** The (much!) preferred trip to the crystalline Caribbean Sea unfurls on the smooth, paved road to El Rama, with rejuvenating side trips to the mountain towns of Boaco and Juigalpa. From El Rama, you can hop on a testing five-hour bus along the rutted dirt road to Pearl Lagoon or take a convenient two-hour fast boat ride down the Río Escondido to Bluefields, from where there are twice-weekly boat services to the Corn Islands and daily speedboats to Pearl Lagoon.

➡ **Staying safe** This region sits along the cocaine drug smuggling route from South America to the US. Use big-city smarts to stay safe and avoid the white stuff.

AROUND THE MAYPOLE

Never afraid to kick up its heels on Friday night, Bluefields really pushes the boat out for its annual May fiesta, **Palo de Mayo** (Maypole Festival; May). Deriving in part from traditional British maypole celebrations, it's a riotous party that celebrates fertility (and, in many cases, puts it to the test).

Throughout the month, Bluefields' main barrios stage block parties with concerts, traditional games and plenty of dancing. But things really heat up at the end of the month when the carnival winds its way through the city's streets.

Reserva Silvestre Greenfields NATURE RESERVE
(2779-0589; www.greenfields.com.ni; r incl 2 meals US$100, day admission 1-2 visitors US$30; by appointment) This privately managed, 284-hectare wildlife reserve near Kukra Hill has tracts of both mangroves and jungle.

Sleeping

Avoid the cheap lodgings around the market and the dock which mainly cater to prostitutes and their clients.

Hostal Doña Vero GUESTHOUSE $
(2572-2166; Galileo, ½c N; r US$14, without bathroom US$11.50;) A great centrally located budget option with clean, comfortable rooms with private bathroom, unlimited coffee and filtered water.

Guesthouse Campbell GUESTHOUSE $
(8827-2221; Galileo, 2½c S; r with/without aircon US$11/20) A bit out of the way but great value, this family-run guesthouse has clean, comfortable rooms with private bathroom and cable TV.

Los Pipitos GUESTHOUSE $
(2572-1590; Mercado, 1½c S; r with/without aircon US$20/15) Walk through the diner to reach these simple, quiet rooms set around a small courtyard. Party animals will be given a key to the side gate so you won't have to rouse anyone in the early hours.

Hotel Caribbean Dream HOTEL $$
(2572-0107; Mercado, 1c O, ½c S; r US$27-32;) A sweet downtown hotel that strikes a good balance between price and amenities.

Eating

Bluefields' favorite snack is the *paty*, a savory spiced meat pastry sold for US$0.25 by roaming vendors all over town.

★Cevicheria El Chino SEAFOOD $
(frente Colegio Bautista; ceviche US$1.80; 7am-9pm) Don't leave Bluefields without trying El Chinós' marvelous ceviche, prepared fresh daily and served in small polystyrene cups at this unremarkable grocery shop.

Maranatha Vineyard Bakery BAKERY $
(items US$0.25-1; 8am-7pm) Traditional Creole bakery of local preacher and career politician Rayfield Hodgson.

Comedor de Las Platas NICARAGUAN $
(contiguo Galileo; meals US$2.50; noon-8pm) A quiet *comedor* serving budget lunches during the day, this local institution transforms into the best *fritanga* in town in the evenings.

Pesca Frito NICARAGUAN $$
(Mercado, 1c O; mains US$4-7.50; 11am-10pm) If you don't mind (really) loud reggae and domino slamming, this lively bar serves great-value seafood.

Drinking & Nightlife

★Four Brothers CLUB
(Parque Reyes, 6c S; 8pm-4am Thu-Sun) Dance up a storm to dancehall, country and reggae. Go in a group, it sometimes gets a little rough later on.

Midnight Dream (LaLa's) BAR
(Iglesia, 2c N; 11am-midnight) There is an open-air deck that feels like it is floating on the bay and ridiculously loud reggae numbers.

Cima Club CLUB
(2572-1410; Mercado, 2c O, 1c N; 8pm-late) A popular, massive late-night venue.

Orientation

Most of Bluefields' commerce, *hospedajes* (guesthouses) and restaurants are found in the blocks between Parque Reyes and the bay. Internet spots are all over the town center and most offer cheap international calls. The airport is about 3km south of town.

Information

BanPro (frente Iglesia) Reliable Visa/MasterCard ATM.

Correos de Nicaragua (Post Office; Moravian College, 1c O; 8am-2pm Mon-Sat)

Intur (☎2572-0221; Iglesia, 2c S; ⏲8am-2pm Mon-Fri) A block west of the Moravian church.

Police (☎2572-2448; Barrio Punta Fria)

Getting There & Away

Take a taxi (US$0.50) to the Bluefields Airport, where **La Costeña** (☎2572-2500, 2572-2750; Aeropuerto; ⏲6am-5pm) has daily flights to Managua and Great Corn Island, and flies to Bilwi three days a week:

Bilwi (one way/return US$96/148, 50 minutes, 10:10am Monday, Wednesday and Friday)

Corn Island (one way/return US$64/99, 20 minutes, 7:25am and 3:10pm)

Managua (one way/return US$82/127, 70 minutes, 8:35am, 10:10am and 4:20pm)

There are several scheduled boat services to Corn Island. The government-run *Rio Escondido* (US$10, five hours) has the most reliable schedule, departing from the Muelle Municipal (Municipal Dock) at 9am on Wednesday. Larger and more comfortable but slightly slower, the **Captain D** (☎8850-2767; seat/bunk US$10/12) leaves an hour later, and occasionally has continuing service to Bilwi. The **Island Express** (☎8847-5137; per seat US$10) leaves from El Bluff between 3am and 5am on Friday. You'll need to take the *panga* from Bluefields the night before. There are also a number of cargo boats making the trip on irregular schedules.

Transporte Vargas (☎2572-0724, 2572-1510; Muelle Municipal; ⏲5am-4pm) has collective *pangas* to El Rama (US$10, 1¾ hours, 5:30am, 1pm and 3pm) and Pearl Lagoon (US$7, one hour, 7am, 11am and 3pm). Service to El Bluff (US$1.60, 30 minutes) departs continually when full. **Transporte Jipe** (☎2572-1871; contiguo Mercado; ⏲5am-4pm) next to the market also runs *pangas* to El Rama (US$10, 1¾ hours, 6am and 3pm).

Pearl Lagoon

At last, you've arrived in the real Caribbean. Here are dirt roads and palm trees, reggae music, and an English-speaking Creole community that fishes the local waters for shrimp, fish and lobster, and still refers to Spanish-speaking Nicaraguans as 'the Spaniards.' There are no banks in Pearl Lagoon, so come with ample cash and plan on staying longer than anticipated. You can receive emergency cash transfers at **Western Union** (frente Muelle; ⏲9am-5pm Mon-Fri). You can get online at **Taylor's Cyber** (contiguo Muelle; per hr US$0.80; ⏲8am-8pm).

Sights & Activities

If you are here on the weekend, make sure to catch a baseball game at the impressive **stadium**. A 30-minute walk through the wetlands behind the town is **Awas**, a Mískito village that has the best swimming beach in the area.

A short boat ride across the lagoon from Awas lies the laidback village of **Kakabila**, one of the most traditional Mískito communities in the area. It's a US$200 to US$300 boat ride to the amazing nearby **Pearl Keys**. Group up to save money.

Heading north from here, **Orinoco** is the heart of the Garifuna community in Nicaragua. While similar in appearance to the other dark-skinned residents of the coast, the Garifuna have a very different history and culture. Descendants of escaped slaves and indigenous Carib who trace their origins back to the Caribbean islands of Dominica and San Vincent, the Garifuna have maintained many of their indigenous traditions as well as their unique music and dance.

Tours

★Captain Sodlan McCoy BOAT TOUR

Anyone can take you to the Pearl Keys, but few know the area even half as well as Captain Sodlan McCoy. Ask for him at Fry Fish.

Queen Lobster Tours BOAT TOUR

(☎8662-3393, 8499-4403; www.queenlobster.com; Muelle, 200m N) Offers trips to the Pearl Keys and a number of other inventive activities around town including traditional cooking classes. Rents bikes for US$1 per hour.

Sleeping

Comfort Zone GUESTHOUSE $

(Muelle, 2c S, ½c E; r US$12.50-14.50) Next to the family store, these brand-new tiled rooms with flatscreen TV, small desks, fans and private bathroom are the best value in town.

Green Lodge HOTEL $

(☎2572-0507; Front Rd, Muelle 75m S; s/d with air-con US$30/35, r without bathroom US$10-14) Half a block from the dock, this long-running hotel is a fine choice. The cheaper rooms upstairs in the family home are a little cramped, but those in the new wing are clean, spacious and comfortable.

Slilma Guesthouse GUESTHOUSE $

(☎2572-0523; slilma_gh1@yahoo.com; Enitel, 1c S, 1c E; r with/without air-con US$30/20, r without bathroom US$10) Take the first left after the cell tower to find this budget guesthouse offering small but very clean rooms.

Casa Blanca HOTEL **$$**
(☎2572-0508; Enitel, 250m O; s/d with air-con US$35/40, s/d/tr without bathroom US$20/25/35) This lovely white house has wooden floors and furnishings made in the attached workshop.

Eating & Drinking

Coconut Delight BAKERY **$**
(Miss Betty's; Muelle, 30m S; ⏲7am-8:30pm) Follow the sweet smells to this pink wooden hut to discover Caribbean baking at its finest.

★Casa Ulrich INTERNATIONAL **$$**
(Up Point, Muelle 350m N; mains US$5.50-12.50; ⏲7am-10pm) Everything on the menu is top-notch, but make sure to try the tender fillet steaks that arrive at your table on a sizzling platter or the delicate shrimp pasta.

Queen Lobster SEAFOOD **$$**
(☎8662-3393; www.queenlobster.com; Front Rd, Muelle, 200m N; mains US$3.50-8.50; ⏲noon-midnight) Some of the best seafood in town is served in this utterly picturesque thatched dining room jutting over the lagoon.

Fry Fish BAR
(Point View; ☎8410-5197; Up Point; ⏲11am-9pm) Follow the road from the dock all the way north to find this breezy thatched neighborhood bar with cold beers and great reggae.

Getting There & Away

Boats run to Bluefields (US$7) at 6:30am and 1pm. Sign up the day before for the early boat.

Every Monday, Wednesday, Thursday and Saturday a *panga* makes the run to Orinoco from Bluefields via Pearl Lagoon (US$12, two hours, 9am); it returns to Pearl Lagoon and Bluefields the following day. There are *pangas* from Bluefields to Tasbapauni (US$12, 2½ hours, 11am) that pass Pearl Lagoon daily except Sunday. Times are liable to shift depending upon the season, so you'll need to ask about departure times at the dock.

One bus (US$6.30, five hours) daily leaves Pearl Lagoon at 5am for El Rama.

Corn Islands

The Caribbean coast's biggest tourist draw is actually 70km offshore on a pair of enchanting islands with horseshoe bays, crystalline coves and underwater caves. Great Corn is larger and peopled by a Creole population that lives in colorful wooden houses, many of which are sprinkled along the main road that encircles the island. And though tourism is the second-largest industry, behind lobster fishing, you won't see mega-developments here. Little Corn, a tiny, jungled, car-less jewel, actually attracts more tourists, with most visitors heading for funky, creative beachside *cabañas* that are the perfect setting for Robinson Crusoe 2.0. The dive sites are more diverse on Little Corn, the jungle is thick and the food is outrageously good, which explains why so many ignore the larger island and indulge in car-free tranquility. But there is a catch. During high season there can be more foreigners than locals.

Dangers & Annoyances

Bare-bones law enforcement and a growing tourist industry has seen theft becoming a problem on the Corn Islands, especially from hotel rooms. While muggings are uncommon, tourists on Great Corn are discouraged from walking around Bluff Point without a local chaperone.

Great Corn Island

POP 7100

Great Corn is on the shortlist for most authentic Caribbean island. Here are barefoot bars, commercial fishing wharfs, pick-up baseball games on the beach, smiling young lobster divers catch-in-hand, an ever-present armada of elders sitting in rocking chairs on creaky front porches and elegant virgin beaches backed by picturesque headlands. It's a place where reggae and country music can coexist without irony. Where fresh lobster is a staple ingredient rather than a luxury. And the longer you stay, the less you want to leave.

Sights & Activities

Long Bay is where you'll find the island's best stretch of golden sand. **Southwest Bay** beckons with another outstanding wide beach.

Walk up the dirt trail behind the Sunrise Hotel in South End past the banana groves and you will be rewarded with panoramic views from **Mt Pleasant** as the sun plunges beneath the Caribbean Sea. Or make your way to **Quinn Hill**.

Next to the stadium is the non-quite-worth-your-time **Culture House** (☎8702-8519; Mt Pleasant, contiguo Alcaldía; ⏲8am-8pm Mon-Fri) museum.

The **tourist office** (☎2575-5091; shereleeivel@gmail.com; contiguo Estadio; ⏲8am-4pm Mon-Fri) is able to organize guides (US$20 to US$50) for hikes all over the island, including to the wild **Bluff Point**.

There's terrific snorkeling along the reef off the **Sally Peachie** coast. Mr Dorsey at Yellow Tail (p505) offers highly recommended guided snorkeling tours. **El Paraiso** (☎2575-5111; www.paraisoclub.com; Waula Point) rents out snorkel gear (US$10 per half-day), as well as arranging chartered snorkeling tours (US$30 per person) and fishing trips (US$40 per person).

Nautilus Dive Center DIVING
(☎2575-5077; www.nautilus-dive-nicaragua.com; Brig Bay, Muelle, 150m N; ⏲8am-6pm) Great Corn's only diving outfitter.

Sleeping

Mayflower GUESTHOUSE $
(Brig Bay, Pasenic, 600m S; r/tw US$15/25) Walking distance from town, but on a nice, quiet stretch of beach, this relaxed guesthouse offers a handful of neatly painted, clean rooms a stone's throw from the water.

Casa Blanca GUESTHOUSE $
(☎8629-4529; Brig Bay, Pasenic, 250m S; r US$10) Cheap and basic, this family-run *hospedaje* on Brig Bay beach is a budget travelers' favourite with six small rooms in a wooden house.

Hotel Morgan HOTEL $
(☎2575-5502; North End; r with/without air-con US$25/15, cabañas US$40; ❄) Efficient hotel offering a range of accommodations, the best of which are found in split-level duplexes.

Yellowtail GUESTHOUSE $$
(☎8659-3634; r US$25) Just east of Seva's restaurant, this relaxed place has just two cabins with fridge, cooker and private bathroom in a lovely part of the island.

Lodge at Long Bay GUESTHOUSE $$
(☎8660-6785, 8339-7745; lodgeatlongbay@gmail.com; Long Bay; r US$45-50) You won't find better value than these two small, comfortably furnished apartments alongside the best beach on the island.

Eating

South End Pulpería BAKERY $
(South End; items US$0.50-1; ⏲8am-9pm) It sells fresh-baked coconut loaves and soda cakes.

Doña Lola SEAFOOD $$
(☎8519-4332; btwn South End & Sally Peachie; mains US$6-12.50; ⏲noon-10pm) Perched on an isolated point on the east side of the island, this colorful and airy restaurant serves up delicious local cuisine. Try the *mofongo* (garlic-infused mashed plantains topped with seafood).

Comederia Mari SEAFOOD $$
(☎8650-6811; Sally Peachie; mains US$7.50-10.50; ⏲noon-9pm) Eat at your Corn Island mom's house. You will sit right outside the mother chef's home, under the palms with a cricket serenade, and taste kingfish braised in tomato sauce, shrimp sautéed in garlic and lobster *al gusto* (to your liking).

Fisher's Cave SEAFOOD $$
(☎2575-1191; contiguo Muelle, Brig Bay; mains US$5-16; ⏲7am-11pm) It's no wonder that this is the locals' preferred fish house.

Seva's SEAFOOD $$
(Sally Peachie; dishes US$6.50-10.50; ⏲7am-10pm) Lobster, shrimp and fish come grilled, garlic sautéed, fried and smothered in tomato sauce. The food is just OK, but the ambience makes up for it.

Drinking & Nightlife

★**Nico's** BAR
(South End; ⏲noon-2am Thu-Sun) Part lobster cooperative, part rocking bar, Nico's is a truly authentic island experience.

Bambule CLUB
(South End; ⏲9pm-3am Thu-Sun) Corn Island's hottest disco is an indoor/outdoor affair right by the water. It's down a dark, bumpy road in South End – take a taxi.

Island Style BAR
(Long Bay; ⏲10am-10pm) The only bar and restaurant on Long Bay is the barefoot, palm-thatched variety.

Getting There & Away

Great Corn's small airport is served by La Costeña, which runs flights to Bluefields (one way/return US$64/99, 20 minutes), with continuing service to Managua (one way/return US$107/164, 70 minutes), at 8am and 4:10pm.

Several regular boats make the five- to six-hour trip to Bluefields via El Bluff. The government-run *Rio Escondido* (US$10) leaves at Thursday at 9am. More comfortable is the *Captain D* (seat/bunk US$10/12), a large cargo ship that leaves at 11pm on Saturday. It also runs once a month from Corn Island to Bilwi (US$22, 10 hours), usually leaving Thursday evening.

Little Corn Island

POP 500

This jade *islita* is a dreamy escape with imaginative bungalow properties encamped on otherwise virgin beaches. Locals live, drink, dine, shoot pool and dance in the Village, which is set on a serene harbor sheltered from the north winds.

Sights & Activities

The island's best and most picturesque beaches are on opposite ends of the island. From Casa Iguana you can stroll south along the windward shore, scramble over the rocks and arrive on **Big Fowl House Beach**, then **Jimmy Lever Beach**. Or walk 20 minutes north from the Village through the jungle to **Otto Beach**. Then navigate the rugged northern shore until you find the spectacular **Goat Beach**, framed by two headlands.

On the way back, don't forget to climb the **lighthouse**, a steel tower jutting 6m above the mango trees.

There is great snorkeling on the east and north sides of the island. Many hotels in these areas rent snorkeling gear, as do the dive shops. If you want a guide, ask in the village for **Alfonso** (☎8434-2520; School, 300m N), who runs tours in his boat (US$20 per person) and also organizes fishing trips (US$40 per person).

OFF THE BEATEN TRACK

CARIBBEAN WATER ADVENTURES

➡ **Mískito Keys** Convince a local fisherman to take you to this biological reserve of fabulous islets, coral reefs and stilt houses 50km from Bilwi (Puerto Cabezas).

➡ **Río Coco** The heart of Mískito country runs beside the Honduran border along this river. Waspám, the main settlement, is reachable by plane from Managua or bus from Bilwi.

➡ **Monkey Point** Located 60km south of Bluefields, this little Creole community lies near some kick-butt swimming spots.

Dolphin Dive DIVING
(☎8917-9717; www.dolphindivelittlecorn.com; 1/10 dives US$35/280; ⏲8am-6pm) Professional yet laidback, this locally owned dive shop has good equipment and experienced instructors.

Dive Little Corn DIVING
(☎8856-5888; www.divelittlecorn.net; Village; 1/10 dives US$35/280; ⏲8am-6pm) Little Corn's original dive shop is owned and managed by Casa Iguana.

Kite Little Corn KITESURFING
(www.kitelittlecorn.com; inside Dolphin Dive; ⏲8am-6pm) Soar over the turquoise waters of Little Corn Island with this new kitesurfing school run by Nacho. It offers two-day intensive courses (US$270) and group tuition (US$30 per hour).

Sleeping

You can stay either in the Village, which is convenient and offers the most restaurant and nightlife options, or in one of the more secluded slices of paradise. Most businesses have signs in the Village telling you which path to take.

Three Brothers GUESTHOUSE $
(☎8658-8736; Escuela, 50m S; s/d/tr US$12/15/25, r without bathroom US$10) A favorite among budget travelers, this guesthouse in the middle of the Village is run by the extremely laidback Randy and has a communal, hostel-like vibe.

Lobster Inn HOTEL $
(☎8847-1736; r with/without TV US$20/15) Sit back in the rocking chairs and admire the sea views from the balcony of this sweet hotel safe in the knowledge that you've snagged one of the best-value rooms on the island.

Hotel Los Delfines HOTEL $$
(☎8892-0186; s/d/tr US$40/50/60; ❄) These tiled bungalows scattered among the citrus trees could do with an overhaul, but if you desire air-con, hot water and cable TV, you'll find it here.

Ensueños BUNGALOW $$
(www.ensuenos-littlecornisland.com; cabañas without bathroom US$25, casas US$45-70) Surrounded by forest and fruit orchards, and perched on a golden crescent of sand and a sheltered turquoise cove, are three rustic candlelit *cabañas* made from rocks and driftwood and three delightful wind- and solar-powered *casas* with small kitchens.

Elsa's Place BEACH HUT $$
(☎2575-5014, 8437-5210; r US$25-40, r without bathroom US$12-20) Miss Elsa sticks to a winning formula: cheap, comfortable rooms right by the water.

Cool Spot BEACH HUT $$
(Grace's Place; ☎8617-4491; r US$25, without bathroom US$10) This rocking backpacker haunt was destroyed by fire just after we passed through, but at press time rebuilding work was already underway.

Sunrise Paradise BEACH HUT $$
(Carlito's Place; ☎2570-0432, 8461-7395; www.carlitosplacelittlecorn.com; huts US$30-40, apt US$60-80) A little quieter than its neighbors, Carlito's features spartan cabins right on the beach with firm beds and little porches that are kept cool by ocean-facing windows.

Eating & Drinking

Sweet Oasis NICARAGUAN $$
(Snacks US$1.80-4.20, meals US$6-8.50; ⏲7am-10pm; 📶) Sit in small kiosks or at the bar and tuck into tasty, if a little greasy, lobster, fish, shrimp or chicken dishes at this popular pathside diner.

Comedor Bridget NICARAGUAN $$
(☎8437-7295; meals US$7-8.50; ⏲7am-10pm) Order the superb salt-dusted, lightly fried fish at this local joint behind the Dive Little Corn shop.

Rose's NICARAGUAN, VEGETARIAN $$
(Meals US$4-8.50; ⏲6:30am-9:30pm) This humble *comedor* on the trail to town has vegetarian pastas and coconut curries.

★Habana Libre CUBAN $$$
(☎2572-9086; mains US$10-14; ⏲noon-10pm) Long considered the Corn Islands' best restaurant, this Cuban-run kitchen serves up outstanding plates of fish, shrimp, roast pork and *ropa vieja* (a Cuban shredded-beef delicacy) in a swank dining patio. But the absolute star of the show is the lobster in jalapeño sauce.

Aguila's BAR
(⏲11am-1am) Little Corn's most popular after-hours hangout.

Tranquilo Cafe CAFE
(⏲8am-late; 📶) Feeling homesick? Head to this hip open-air cafe for great burgers, buffalo wings and bruschetta with an indie-rock soundtrack.

Getting There & Around

Little Corn is only about 1.5 sq km. You can walk end to end in an hour.

Collective *pangas* to Little Corn (US$6, 40 minutes) leave from the dock on Great Corn at 10am and 4:30pm; if you're staying on the northern end of Little Corn, you should take the morning boat. Boats leave Little Corn at 7am and 1:30pm from the main pier. If you're taking the morning flight to Managua, you need to travel the day before. It can get very rough and you may get soaked. Bring garbage bags to cover your luggage. For a smoother ride, it's possible to ride on the large cargo ships (US$2 to US$3, 1¼ hours) that supply the *islita*, but there are only a handful of departures each week.

Bilwi (Puerto Cabezas)

POP 48,500

This impoverished Caribbean port town and ethnic melting pot sprawls along the coast and back into the scrubby pines on wide brick streets and red-earth roads, full of people and music, smiles and sideways glances. Sure, this city has systemic problems (poverty, decay, crime), and it's never good when international aid is a town's biggest source of income. But with tasty seafood, great-value historic lodging options, and seaside indigenous communities a boat ride away, it can also be as alluring as a sweet, yet slightly sketchy, new friend.

Sights

Beaches around Bilwi are nobody's idea of the Caribbean dream. **La Bocana**, an old pirate hangout at the river mouth north of town, has a stretch of decent beach, but crooks still dig it here. Come with a local.

Check at **Intur** (☎2792-1564; puertocabezas@intur.gob.ni; Parque Central, 2c N; ⏲8am-2pm) for info on nearby attractions.

★Casa Museo Judith Kain MUSEUM
(☎2792-2225; Parque Central, 4c N, 1c O; ⏲8am-3pm Mon-Fri) FREE Set in the former home of a prolific local painter, this museum provides a window into what it was like to live in Bilwi in the good old days.

Muelle Viejo PORT
Take a stroll along the wooden boards of the historic Muelle Viejo (Old Pier), where both Sandino and the Contras received arms smuggled in from abroad.

Mercado Municipal MARKET
(⏲7am-3pm) This ramshackle collection of stalls selling ripe produce, traditional fried-fish breakfasts and sweet, savory *rondón* (gumbo) is a popular place to pass the morning.

Tours

Amica CULTURAL TOUR
(Association of Indigenous Women on the Atlantic Coast; ☎2792-2219; asociacionamica@yahoo; Parque Central, 3c S; ⏲8am-noon Mon & 2-5:30pm Mon-Fri, 8am-noon Sat) Your ticket into the area's natural reserves and indigenous communities is through Amica.

Sleeping

Casa Museo Judith Kain HOTEL $
(☎2792-2225; casamuseojudithkain@hotmail.com; Parque Central, 4c N, 1c O; s/d/tr with fan US$12/15/20, with air-con US$23/27/30; P ❄ 📶) In a town with an abundance of great-value lodging, this may be the best of the bunch. Rooms set in two superb old craftsman gems are super-clean and charming.

Hospedaje Rivera GUESTHOUSE $
(☎2792-2471; Parque Central, 1½c S; r US$11) The clean rooms on the 2nd story of this fine, centrally located family home are a terrific budget choice.

Hotel Liwa Mairin HOTEL $
(☎2792-2315; Parque Central, 2c E, 1c S; s/d US$15/20, with air-con US$25/30; ❄) This centrally located hotel right by the Caribbean Sea offers large air-con rooms with firm mattresses and high ceilings.

El Cortijo II GUESTHOUSE $$
(☎2792-2340; cortijoarguello@yahoo.com; Parque Central, 3c N, 1c E; s/d/tr US$22/26.50/29) This 60-year-old craftsman gem is your Caribbean grandma's house. Rooms are spotless with worn wooden floors and high ceilings.

Eating & Drinking

Comedor Alka NICARAGUAN $
(frente Parque Central; meals US$2.75-3; ⏲11am-9pm) Stop here for savory and cheap eats where barbecued beef and chicken are served with a bit of attitude.

Restaurante Faramhi SEAFOOD $$
(☎2792-1611; frente Aeropuerto; mains US$7.50; ⏲11am-10pm) Close to the airport, this popular restaurant serves some of the best seafood in town.

Kabu Payaska SEAFOOD $$
(Parque Central, 1.5km N; seafood dishes US$7.50-8.50; ⏲noon-10pm) Bilwi's best-loved seafood house is set on one large concrete patio overlooking the swirling Caribbean.

Bar Titi BAR
(⏲noon-late) Sounds like a strip club but it's actually one of Bilwi's most chilled bars.

Kabu Yula BAR
(Parque Central, 5c S; ⏲2pm-2am) A two-story *palapa* with unbroken sea views.

Karibbean Sol CLUB
(⏲8pm-3am) Sooner or later anyone out on a big night ends up at this rustic dancehall half a block from Parque Central. It's a little sketchy but has plenty of atmosphere.

Getting There & Away

La Costeña (☎2792-2282; Aeropuerto; ⏲8am-noon & 3-6pm) offers regular flights to Managua and Bluefields. Book tickets in advance. Departure tax is US$2. Flights include the following:

Bluefields (one way/return US$96/148, 50 minutes, 11:20am Monday, Wednesday and Friday)

Managua (one way/return US$97/149, 1½ hours, 7:40am, noon and 3:40pm Monday to Saturday, 7:40am and noon Sunday)

Buses depart from the bus terminal, 2km west of town, to the following destinations:

Managua (US$25.20, 20 to 24 hours, twice daily)

Rosita (US$7.50, six to to 10 hours, twice daily)

Siuna (US$10, eight to 12 hours, 7am)

Waspám (US$6, six hours, twice daily)

The only regular boat service to/from Bilwi is the **Captain D** (☎8850-2767), which runs between Corn Island and Bilwi (US$22, 10 to 12 hours) about once a month depending on demand. Call to check the schedule.

San Carlos & Around

The steamy riverside town of San Carlos is a key hub for river transport, and launchpad for a number of highly appealing attractions including the Archipiélago de Solentiname, several wildlife reserves and the fabulously unlikely Spanish castle at El Castillo.

San Carlos

POP 12,100

The capital of the isolated Río San Juan department is the gateway to some of Nicaragua's most compelling countryside but is itself a curious place with a bit of an identity crisis. During the day it's a busy international port filled with herds of travelers in transit, which explains the bustling and festive *malecón* (waterfront) lined with restaurants. But when night falls, and the magnificent views disappear with the setting sun, it reverts to a rather lackluster small town where gossiping is the main form of entertainment.

Centro Cultural Jose Coronel Urtecho is set within the crumbling walls of **Fortaleza de San Carlos** (admission free; ⏲9am-5pm). It's no El Castillo, but it was built in 1724 and has amazing lake and Río San Juan views. There's another old **Spanish observation post**, with cannon, at Restaurant Mirador.

Check at **Intur** (☎2583-0301; riosanjuan@intur.gob.ni; contiguo a Migración; ⏲8am-1pm) for nearby tours.

Sleeping & Eating

The cheapest eats in town are at the cluster of bus-station *comedores*, the best of which is **Comedor Alondra** (meals US$2.50).

Hospedaje Peña GUESTHOUSE $

(☎2583-0298; Parque Central, 1c S; r per person without bathroom US$3) Don't expect many frills (or toilet seats) in this original San Carlos flophouse but it's cheap and just a block from the *malecón*.

Gran Lago Hotel HOTEL $$

(☎2583-0075; Parque Central, 1c O, 1c S; s/d incl breakfast US$35/40; ❄📶) The four air-con rooms here are clean and comfortable but don't take advantage of the great lakeside location.

Hotel Carelhys HOTEL $$

(☎2583-0389; Parque Central, ½c S; r with/without air-con US$30/15) This budget favorite half a block from Parque Central has a selection of slightly shabby rooms with cable TV and private bathroom.

Soda La Fortaleza CAFE $

(Malecón; meals US$2-6; ⏲6am-10pm) This lively spot on the lakefront serves up filling breakfasts and cheap, tasty Nica dishes.

Restaurante Kaoma NICARAGUAN $$

(☎2583-0293; Parque Central, 1½c S; mains US$7-11; ⏲8am-midnight) A beautiful terrace restaurant with old wooden floors, beamed ceilings and massive lake views.

Getting There & Away

The San Carlos airport is a 3km, US$1 cab ride from downtown San Carlos. The compact, 12-seat planes leave for Managua (one way/return US$76/116, 45 minutes) at 2pm.

Buses leave from the bus terminal in San Carlos for the following destinations:

El Rama (US$6.50, seven hours, 9am)

Juigalpa (US$4, four hours, four daily)

Managua (US$6.50, six hours, eight daily)

San Miguelito (US$2, two to four hours) Direct buses leave at 12:20pm and 1pm, but you can hop on any Managua- or Juigalpa-bound bus and get off at the San Miguelito turnoff.

WORTH A TRIP

WETLAND WANDERINGS

A great spot to visit near San Carlos is the **Refugio de Vida Silvestre los Guatuzos**, a fabulous wetland zone that abuts the Costa Rican border and was once a minefield (it's safe now!).

There are two excellent nature-focused accommodations on the Río Papaturro. **Cabañas Caiman** (☎506-8704-3880, 8676-2958; aillenm@hotmail.com; r per person incl breakfast US$14) and the **Centro Ecológico los Guatuzos** (☎2270-3561, 8877-5096; www.losguatuzos.com; r per person with/without bathroom US$13/11), a professionally run research station that welcomes tourists. It offers guided hikes and a moonlight alligator tour (US$45 per person). Kayaks are also available to rent.

There are slow collective boats from San Carlos to Papaturro (US$4, four hours) at 9am Tuesday, Wednesday and Friday, returning to San Carlos from Río Papaturro at 8am Monday, Tuesday and Thursday. It costs around US$130/240 one way/round-trip from San Carlos in a private *panga*. It's cheaper to rent a boat (round-trip boat/*panga* US$70/100) in Solentiname.

Nestled on the Río Frio, **Reserva Esperanza Verde** (☎2583-0459; r per person incl 3 meals US$50) is a 5000-hectare, humid tropical forest reserve. You can do it in a day trip from San Carlos (US$30 per person, two-person minimum).

Collective riverboat services to Boca de Sábalos (US$3.10, 2¼ hours) and El Castillo (US$3.40, 3½ hours) leave from the **Muelle Municipal** (Municipal Dock), half a block west of the market, at 8am, noon, 2:30pm and 3:30pm Monday through Saturday; 8am and 1:30pm on Sunday. Express boats to Sábalos (US$4.75, one hour) and El Castillo (US$5.70, 1½ hours) leave at 6:30am and 10am.

The government-run ferry leaves the dock at 2pm Tuesday and Friday for San Miguelito (US$3, two to three hours), Altagracia (Isla de Ometepe; US$6.50, nine hours) and Granada (US$9.50, 12 to 14 hours). Stake out a sleeping spot early, bring extra layers, and don't forget your hammock or you may be sleeping on the cold, hard deck.

The ferry returns from Granada at 2pm Monday and Thursday, stopping at the same ports and arriving in San Carlos at sunrise.

Islas Solentiname

The isolated Archipiélago de Solentiname (Solentiname Archipelago), in the southern part of Lago de Nicaragua, is a traditional haven for artists and a fascinating place to visit. Ernesto Cardenal, the versatile artist-poet-monk who was minister of culture during the Sandinista years, set up a communal society here for craftspeople, poets and painters, inspired by the principles of liberation theology. A distinctive school of colorful primitivist painting arose out of these revolutionary-era workshops and has become world famous.

Solentiname comprises 36 islands; the largest are Mancarrón, San Fernando (also called Isla Elvis Chavarría) and Venada (Isla Donald Guevara). The first two have the principal facilities for travelers. **Mancarrón** also has the islands' most famous sight, the simple yet beautiful adobe **church** that was the spiritual and communal center of Cardenal's community. Near here is an interesting archaeological exhibition, while a short walk away is **El Refugio**, the main community on the island, where you can wander among the local homes watching artisans create brightly painted balsa carvings. **San Fernando** has an excellent museum, with informative displays on the pre-Columbian residents of the archipelago, as well as a gallery that showcases the work of some of the islands' best artists. There are many **petroglyphs** scattered around the islands, which make appealing destinations for hikes – there are also caves to explore on **Isla Venada**. Fishing is good around here, and **Isla Zapote** has fantastic bird-watching possibilities. Otherwise, the islands are just great for taking it easy.

Sleeping & Eating

Hostal Buen Amigo GUESTHOUSE $
(☎8869-6619; hostalbuenamigo@gmail.com; El Refugio; r per person with/without bathroom US$10/6) On Mancarrón, this is an appealing budget spot, with comfy and colorful rooms and local artists whittling away outside.

★Hotel La Comunidad GUESTHOUSE $$
(☎8966-7056, 2277-3495; contiguo Muelle; r per person with/without meals US$35/15) Your best lodging bet on Mancarrón. Located next to the dock, it has two solar-powered wooden houses overlooking the bay.

Hospedaje Mire Estrellas GUESTHOUSE $$
(☎8561-4943; r per person with/without bathroom US$12/10) On Isla San Fernando, Hospedaje Mire Estrellas offers small wooden rooms right on the water by the dock. If you are planning on staying here, bring supplies from San Carlos or arrange meals in one of the bigger hotels on the island.

Getting There & Around

Transol (☎8828-3243, 8555-4739; www.transol.com.ni; ⏲24hr) runs a fast boat service (US$10, 90 minutes) between San Carlos and the islands, leaving San Carlos at 3pm and returning at 9am.

If the service is discontinued (which it might be), you'll need either time or money to visit the archipelago. Slow and inexpensive public boats (US$4, two to three hours) run twice a week, leaving San Carlos at 1pm Tuesday and Friday (US$4), with stops at San Fernando and Mancarrón. They leave Mancarrón, stopping about 30 minutes later at San Fernando, at 4:30am Tuesday and Friday (US$4). If that doesn't work with your schedule, you can hire a private boat (seating at least six) for US$120 to US$150 between San Carlos and the islands.

Most visitors hire private *pangas* between the islands; it's at least US$20 round-trip between San Fernando and Mancarrón. A cheaper and more adventurous way to explore the archipelago is to paddle. Kayaks and canoes are available for rent on both Mancarrón and San Fernando.

Río San Juan

The river that makes Nicaraguan hearts stir with pride flows 199km from Lago de Nicaragua to the Caribbean Sea. For much of its length, the river forms the border between Nicaragua and its neighbor Costa Rica, and

OFF THE BEATEN TRACK

EXPLORING THE INDIO-MAÍZ

For nature lovers it doesn't get much better than this. One of Central America's most impressive rainforests, the **Reserva Biológica Río Indio-Maíz** begins a few kilometers downstream from El Castillo and continues all the way to the Caribbean Sea. You can book trips to the reserve from El Castillo for US$120 per group (maximum four people) including transportation and a guide. For a splurge, check out the **Refugio Bartola** (☎8376-6979, 8885-7386; www.refugiobartola.com; r per person incl meals US$50, day-use fee US$5, guides per day US$20), a wonderfully rustic lodge and private reserve set on the confulence of the Ríos San Juan and Bartola.

Continuing east, the reserve forms an impenetrable wall of forest along the Nicaraguan side of the Río San Juan (unfortunately the Costa Rican side is heavily deforested) until you reach the isolated community of **San Juan del Norte**. Surrounded by magical hidden lagoons, dense rainforest and Caribbean beaches, this rarely visited town has plenty to offer. From here you can organize multiday boat trips to indigenous communities in the heart of the reserve via the spectacular Río Indio or explore the ruins of Greytown, the once-thriving British outpost across the bay that has been completely swallowed by the jungle. There are a couple of decent places to stay in town, including **Hostal Familiar** (☎8446-2096; Muelle, 300m S; r with/without river view US$20/14).

Slow boats leave from San Carlos for San Juan del Norte (US$14, nine to 12 hours, 6am Tuesday, Thursday and Friday) stopping in Boca de Sábalos at 9:15am and El Castillo at 10am. Fast boats leave San Carlos for San Juan del Norte (US$25, six hours) at 6am Tuesday and Friday and 10am Wednesday and Sunday, stopping in Boca de Sábalos and El Castillo one hour/90 minutes later respectively.

Slow boats return from San Juan del Norte at 5am Thursday, Saturday and Sunday. Fast boats return at 5:30am Thursday and Sunday and at 8:30am Monday and Friday.

has been a frequent source of tension between the two nations.

A trip on the San Juan is a fabulous experience – it's a bird-watching paradise, and you may well spot caimans sunning themselves on logs. These creatures will likely face eviction should Nicaragua's grand plans of a transisthmian canal ever come to fruition.

BOCA DE SÁBALOS

It feels like that thick jungle looming on its edges is about to reclaim this muddy, dusty town set at the confluence of the Río San Juan and Río Sábalos (Tarpon River).

Río Sábalos effectively splits the town in half, with the inexpensive *hospedajes* and main road on one side, and a smaller community, threaded by a slender footpath past rustic homes and gardens, on the other. It's two córdobas (US$0.10) to cross the canal in a dugout canoe.

The 90-hectare **Reserva Privada El Quebracho** (☎2583-0035; www.fundaciondelrio.org; admission US$5) borders the Reserva Biológica Indio-Maíz. Take a taxi to Buena Vista, and walk the last hour to the reserve.

The **Asociación de Guías Jacamar** (☎8970-0007, 8441-5958; asociacionguiasjacamar@yahoo.com; frente Muelle; ⏲8am-5pm) and its young nature guides are your one-stop ticket to adventure.

Sleeping

Hospedaje y Comedor Clarissa GUESTHOUSE $

(☎8364-3588; Muelle, ½c N; s/d without bathroom US$4/8, r US$10; ❄) Rooms in this nice wooden home are basic but clean.

★Sábalos Lodge LODGE $$

(☎2583-0046; www.sabaloslodge.com; Muelle, 1km E; d US$35-60) This collection of stilted, thatched bungalows set in one meandering riverside row achieves the *Robinson Crusoe* ideal.

Getting There & Away

Boat services from Boca de Sábalos:

El Castillo (US$0.55, one hour, 10am, 2pm, 4:30pm and 5:30pm Monday to Saturday, 10am and 2:30pm Sunday; express US$1, 30 minutes, 7:30am and 11am)

San Carlos (US$3.50, 2½ hours, 6am, 7am, 8am and 3pm Monday to Saturday, 6am and 3pm Sunday; express US$4.75, one hour, 6am and noon)

EL CASTILLO

POP 1000

El Castillo is a fortress built by the Spanish in 1675 at a strategic bend in the river to try to halt the passage of pirates heading for the fabled gold of Granada. It's an utterly memorable spot, with the unlikely castle looking over the lively rapids below.

Bitter battles were fought at El Castillo against flotillas of assailants. In 1762 the British and their Mískito allies attacked the fort, but Spanish forces, led by the daughter of their fallen commander, managed to hold off the invaders. The **fort** (admission US$2, camera fee US$1; ⏲8am-noon & 1-4:30pm) offers top views and has decent Spanish-language displays on its turbulent history. Admission includes a well-informed guided tour.

Right opposite the dock, a **tourist office** (⏲8am-noon & 2-5pm) offers a well-organized system of guided excursions in the area, including horseback riding, night caiman tours and visits to the Reserva Biológica Río Indio-Maíz. You can also organize similar tours through private operators including the recommended **Nena Tour** (☎8821-2135; www.nenalodge.com), downstream on the main drag.

Sleeping & Eating

Many basic lodging options are found on the waterfront close to the dock. Be sure to try *camarones* (river shrimp) while in town.

★Hotel Tropical HOTEL **$$**

(☎8447-8213, 8699-8886; Muelle 130m E; r with/without air-con incl breakfast US$30/25; ❄) Lie back and listen to the rushing water of El Castillo outside your window at this fantastic small hotel above Restaurant Vanessa.

Casa de Huesped Chinandegano GUESTHOUSE **$$**

(☎2583-3011; Muelle, 240m E; r per person US$9, without bathroom US$7; 📶) This creaky wooden house done up with potted tropical plants and a shabby-chic dining area is the best cheapie in town.

★Borders Coffee CAFE **$$**

(☎8408-7688; detras Base Militar; meals US$3.50-13; ⏲7am-10pm; ✎) By the time you read this, this fun cafe should be settled into its expansive new open-air locale behind the military base. There you'll find a full menu of burgers, pasta, river shrimp and several vegetarian options.

Getting There & Around

From El Castillo, collective boats leave for San Carlos (US$3.50, three hours) via Boca de Sábalos (US$0.50, 30 minutes) at 5am, 6am, 7am and 2pm. On Sunday there are only services at 5am and 2pm.

Fast *pangas* to San Carlos (US$5.70, 1½ hours) via Boca de Sábalos (US$1, 15 minutes) leave at 6am and 10am.

UNDERSTAND NICARAGUA

Nicaragua Today

Like him or loathe him, President Daniel Ortega's re-election in 2011 has delivered something that Nicaragua has lacked for a long time: a sense of stability. Gone are the transport strikes, debilitating power rationing and unpredictable rallies. And, after being devastated by the civil war, the country's economy and infrastructure are slowly being reconstructed.

But all is not rosy; Nicaragua remains one of the poorest nations on the American continent and questions continue to be raised at home and abroad over perceived erosion of democracy that has marked the Sandinista National Liberation Front's (FSLN in Spanish) return to power.

While the hunger-eradication programs, new houses and other initiatives have been well received by FSLN supporters, the lack of transparency of their funding has caused controversy.

Many analysts suggest the Nicaraguan economy is overly dependent on Venezuelan handouts and the 2013 death of Venezuelan President Hugo Chávez could signal rough roads ahead for Nicaragua and other members of the Bolivarian Alliance.

Simmering tensions over Nicaragua and Costa Rica's favorite patriotic flash point, the Río San Juan, once again boiled over in late 2010 over Managua's dredging operations in the river's delta. The dispute is ongoing, with the International Court of Justice getting involved.

History

Early History

Fascinatingly, the earliest traces of human habitation in Nicaragua are some 6000-year-old footprints found near the banks of Lago de Managua, within the area occupied by the present-day capital.

Nicaragua was home to several indigenous groups, including the ancestors of today's Rama who live on the Caribbean coast, and the Chorotegas and Nicaraos, on the Pacific side. The latter spoke a form of Nahuatl, the language of the Aztecs. Many Nicaraguan places retain their Nahuatl names.

European Arrival

The indigenous inhabitants' first contact with Europeans was in 1502, when Columbus sailed down Nicaragua's Caribbean coast.

The next exploratory mission, led by Gil González de Ávila, came north from the Spanish settlement at Panama, arriving in 1522. It found a chieftain, Cacique Nicarao, governing the southern shores of Lago de Nicaragua and the tribe of the same name. The Spaniards thus named the region Nicaragua.

Two years later the Spanish were back to colonize, led this time by Francisco Hernández de Córdoba, who founded the cities of Granada and León in 1524. Both were established near indigenous settlements whose inhabitants were subjugated and put to work. Attempts at founding a similar city near Managua were resisted; the indigenous settlement was destroyed as punishment.

Colonial Settlement

The gold that had initially attracted the Spaniards soon gave out, but Granada and León remained. Granada, with a direct connection to the Caribbean and Europe via Lago de Nicaragua, became a comparatively rich colonial trading center. With its wealthy business class, the city was the natural center for the Conservative Party, which favored traditional values of monarchy and ecclesiastical authority.

Originally founded on Lago de Managua, León became the center for radical clerics and intellectuals, who formed the Liberal Party and supported the unification of Central America and reforms based on those of the French and American revolutions.

The difference in wealth between the two cities, and the political supremacy of León, led to conflicts that raged until the 1850s, at times erupting into outright civil war. The continual fighting between them stopped only when the capital was moved to the neutral location of Managua.

While the Spanish were settling the Pacific lowlands, the English were the dominant influence on the Caribbean side of Nicaragua. English, French and Dutch pirates plying the Caribbean established settlements and attacked the east coast in the 17th century, at times even penetrating to Granada via the Río San Juan.

Early Independence

Along with the rest of Central America, Nicaragua gained independence from Spain in 1821, was briefly part of Mexico, was then incorporated into the new Central American Federation and finally achieved complete independence in 1838. The cities of León and Granada continued to feud.

After independence, the Liberals and Conservatives weren't the only groups vying for power. With the Spanish out of the picture, Britain and the USA both became interested in Nicaragua and its strategically important passage from Lago de Nicaragua to the Caribbean. Both countries wanted to build an interoceanic canal through Central America, and Nicaragua looked the likeliest spot.

The Late 19th Century

In 1857 the Liberals, disgraced after inviting William Walker into the country, lost power to the Conservatives and were unable to regain it for the next 36 years. The new government set up shop in Managua, then little more than a village, which had been nominated as capital in 1852 in an attempt to quell the rivalry between Granada and León.

In 1860 the British signed a treaty ceding the Caribbean region to the now-independent governments of Honduras and Nicaragua. The Nicaraguan section remained an autonomous region until the 1890s.

Zelaya's Coup & US Intervention

In 1893 a Liberal general named José Santos Zelaya deposed the Conservative president and became president himself. Zelaya soon antagonized the US by seeking a canal deal with Germany and Japan. Encouraged by Washington, which sought to monopolize a transisthmian canal in Panama, the Conservatives rebelled in 1909. After Zelaya ordered the execution of two US mercenaries accused of aiding the Conservatives, the American government forced his resignation. In 1912 the US responded to another rebellion, this time against the corrupt Conservative administration, by sending 2500 marines to Nicaragua.

For most of the next two decades the US dominated politics in Nicaragua, installing presidents it favored and ousting those it didn't, using its marines as persuasion. In 1914 the Bryan-Chamorro Treaty was signed, granting the US exclusive canal rights in Nicaragua; America actually had no intention of building such a canal, but wanted to ensure that no one else did.

Sandino & the Somoza Era

The Conservative regime was opposed by a group of Liberal rebels including Augusto C Sandino, who eventually became leader of a long-term guerrilla campaign resisting US involvement. The marines headed home in 1933 after handing over military power to the US-trained Guardia Nacional, led by Anastasio Somoza García.

In February 1934 Somoza engineered the assassination of Sandino, who was abducted and gunned down after being summoned to dinner at the presidental palace to discuss disarmament. Somoza, with his main enemy out of the way, then set his sights on supreme power. Overthrowing Liberal president Sacasa a couple of years later, he established himself as president in 1937, founding a family dynasty that was to rule for four decades.

After creating a new constitution to grant himself more power, Somoza García ruled Nicaragua as an internationally notorious dictator for the next 20 years, sometimes as president, at other times behind a puppet president. He amassed huge personal wealth by corrupt means (the Somoza landholdings attained were the size of El Salvador). Of course, the majority of Nicaraguans remained entrenched in poverty.

Somoza supported the USA (the CIA used Nicaragua as a launchpad for both the 1954 overthrow of Guatemalan leader Colon Jacobo Arbenz Guzmán and the 1961 invasion of Cuba) and was in turn supported by the US government.

After his assassination in León in 1956, Somoza was succeeded by his elder son, Luis Somoza Debayle.

Rising Opposition

In 1961 Carlos Fonseca Amador, a prominent figure in the student movement that had opposed the Somoza regime in the 1950s, joined forces with Colonel Santos López (an

DOING THINGS THE WILLIAM WALKER WAY

Latin America's turbulent history is littered with colorful characters, but there were few messiah complexes bigger than that of William Walker, an American adventurer who directed and starred in *Conquistador 2,* more than three centuries after Cortéz took the New World by storm with the original hit. He started his one-man mission in 1853, leading a small party to attack Mexico, where he declared himself president of 'independent' Sonora before being ignominiously driven out.

In 1855 the Liberals of León asked Walker to help them seize power from Granada's Conservatives. Walker entered Nicaragua with 56 followers, attacked Granada and prevailed. Instead of ceding it to his employers, he soon had himself elected president of Nicaragua (in 'free and fair elections', no doubt), and the US recognized his government. He then reinstituted slavery, declared English the country's official language, mortgaged the entire nation to fund personal borrowing and invaded Costa Rica, announcing his intention to control the whole of Central America. This was a step too far, and those nations united to drive him out. Walker fled Granada, leaving the city alight, and was forced to return to the USA.

Not easily put off, he landed with a small army at Greytown six months later, only to be arrested and deported by the US Navy. He tried again in 1860; this time the British Navy captured him and turned him over to the Hondurans, who ended his adventures with a volley of rifle fire in 1860. His grave is in Trujillo's old cemetery.

old fighting partner of Sandino's) and other activists to form the Frente Sandinista de Liberación Nacional (Sandinista National Liberation Front), or FSLN.

On December 23, 1972, at around midnight, an earthquake devastated Managua, leveling more than 250 city blocks, killing more than 6000 people and leaving 300,000 homeless. As international aid poured in, the money was diverted to Anastasio Somoza and his associates, while the people who needed it suffered and died. This obvious abuse dramatically increased opposition to Somoza among all classes of society. Wealthy businesspeople also turned against Somoza as they saw their own ventures being eclipsed by the Somoza family's corrupt empire.

By 1974 opposition was widespread. Two groups were widely recognized – the FSLN (Sandinistas), led by Carlos Fonseca, and the Unión Democrática de Liberación, led by Pedro Joaquín Chamorro, popular owner and editor of the Managua newspaper *La Prensa,* which had long printed articles critical of the Somoza regime.

In December 1974 the FSLN kidnapped several leading members of the Somoza regime, gaining ransoms and the freeing of political prisoners in exchange for the release of the hostages. The Somoza government responded with a campaign of systematic killings over the following 2½ years. Fonseca was killed in a skirmish in 1976.

Revolution & the FSLN

The last straw for the Nicaraguan public was the assassination in January 1978 of Chamorro. Violence erupted and a general strike was declared. Business interests united with moderate factions in the Frente Amplio Opositor (Broad Opposition Front; FAO) and unsuccessfully attempted to negotiate an end to the Somoza dictatorship.

In August 1978 the FSLN occupied the Palacio Nacional and took more than 2000 hostages, demanding freedom for 60 imprisoned Sandinistas. The government acceded, and the hostages were released. Nevertheless, the revolt spread, with spontaneous uprisings in many major towns. The Guardia Nacional responded swiftly and ruthlessly, shelling those cities and killing thousands.

The FAO, having exhausted its negotiating efforts, threw in its lot with the Sandinistas, which they now perceived as the only viable way to oust the dictatorship. This broad alliance formed a revolutionary government provisionally based in San José, Costa Rica, which gained recognition from some Latin American and European governments and military support in the form of arms shipments. Thus the FSLN was well prepared to launch its final offensive in June 1979. The revolutionary forces took city after city, with the support of thousands of civilians. On July 17, as the Sandinistas were preparing to enter Managua, Somoza resigned the presidency and fled the country. (He was assassinated by Sandinista agents a year later in Asunción, Paraguay.) The Sandinistas marched victorious into Managua on July 19, 1979.

They inherited a shambles. Poverty, homelessness, illiteracy and staggeringly inadequate health care were just a few of the widespread problems. An estimated 50,000 people had been killed in the revolutionary struggle, and perhaps 150,000 more left homeless.

The FSLN and prominent anti-Somoza moderates (including Violeta Barrios de Chamorro, widow of the martyred Pedro Joaquín Chamorro) set up a five-member junta to administer the country. The constitution was suspended, the national congress dissolved and the Guardia Nacional replaced by the Sandinista People's Army.

However, the alliance between moderates and the FSLN didn't last long. In April 1980 Chamorro and the one other moderate resigned from the ruling junta when it became clear that the FSLN intended to dominate the council of state, which was being set up to serve as the nation's interim legislature. The junta thus was reduced from five members to three, with revolutionary commander Daniel Ortega Saavedra appointed coordinator.

Trying to salvage what it could of its influence over the country, the US (under President Jimmy Carter) authorized US$75 million in emergency aid to the Sandinista-led government. However, by late 1980 it was becoming concerned about the increasing numbers of Soviet and Cuban advisors in Nicaragua and allegations that the Sandinistas were beginning to provide arms to leftist rebels in El Salvador.

The Contra War

After Ronald Reagan became US president in January 1981, relations between Nicaragua and the US took a turn for the worse. Reagan suspended all aid to Nicaragua and began funding the counterrevolutionary military groups known as Contras, which operated out of Honduras and eventually Costa Rica as well. Most of the original Contras were ex-soldiers of Somoza's Guardia Nacional, but as time passed, their ranks filled with disaffected local people.

The Contra war escalated throughout the 1980s. As US money flowed to the Contras, their numbers grew to more than 15,000 fighters. Honduras was heavily militarized, with large-scale US–Honduran maneuvers threatening an invasion of Nicaragua. The Sandinistas responded by instituting conscription and building an army that eventually numbered 95,000. Soviet and Cuban military and economic aid poured in, reaching US$700 million in 1987. A CIA scheme to mine Nicaragua's harbors was revealed in 1984 and resulted in a judgment against the US by the International Court of Justice.

Elections in November 1984 were boycotted by leading non-Sandinistas, who complained of sweeping FSLN control of the nation's media. Daniel Ortega was elected president with 63% of the vote, and the FSLN won 61 of the 96 seats in the new national assembly.

In May 1985 the USA initiated a trade embargo of Nicaragua and pressured other countries to do the same. The embargo lasted for the next five years and helped to strangle Nicaragua's economy.

After the US Congress rejected further military aid for the Contras in 1985, the Reagan administration secretly continued funding them through a scheme in which the CIA illegally sold weapons to Iran and diverted the proceeds to the Contras. When the details leaked out, the infamous 'Iran-Contra Affair' blew up.

After many failed peace initiatives, the Costa Rican president, Oscar Arias Sánchez, finally came up with an accord that was signed in August 1987 by the leaders of Costa Rica, El Salvador, Nicaragua, Guatemala and Honduras. Though a great stride forward (Arias won the Nobel Peace Prize), it proved difficult to implement, as participating nations failed to follow through on their commitments, while the US took measures that seemed intentionally aimed at undermining the peace process.

The 1990 Election

By the late 1980s the Nicaraguan economy was again desperate. Civil war, the US trade embargo and the inefficiencies of a Soviet-style centralized economy had produced hyperinflation, falling production and rising unemployment. As it became clear that the US Congress was preparing to grant the Contras further aid, Daniel Ortega called elections that he expected would give the Sandinistas a popular mandate to govern.

The FSLN, however, underestimated the disillusionment and fatigue of the Nicaraguan people. Economic problems and the daily grind had eclipsed the dramatic accomplishments of the Sandinistas' early years: redistributing Somoza lands to small farming cooperatives, reducing illiteracy from 50% to 13%, eliminating polio through a massive immunization program and reducing the rate of infant mortality by a third.

The Unión Nacional Opositora (UNO), a broad coalition of 14 political parties opposing the Sandinista government, was formed in 1989. UNO presidential candidate Violeta Barrios de Chamorro had the backing and financing of the US, which had promised to lift the embargo and give hundreds of millions of dollars in economic aid to Nicaragua if UNO won. With such bribes in place, the UNO handily took the elections of February 25, 1990, gaining 55% of the presidential votes and 51 of the 110 seats in the national assembly, compared with the FSLN's 39. Ortega had plenty of grounds for complaint, but, to his credit, in the end he went quietly, perhaps avoiding further conflict.

Politics in the 1990s

Chamorro took office in April 1990. The Contras stopped fighting at the end of June with a symbolic and heavily publicized turning-in of their weapons. The US trade embargo was lifted, and US and other foreign aid began to pour in.

Chamorro faced a tricky balancing act in trying to reunify the country and satisfy all interests. The promised economic recovery was slow in coming; growth was sluggish, and unemployment remained stubbornly high. Nevertheless, in 1996, when Nicaragua went to the polls again, the people rejected the FSLN's Ortega and opted for former Managua mayor Arnoldo Alemán of the PLC, a center-right liberal alliance.

Alemán's achievements included investing heavily in infrastructure and reducing the size of the army by a factor of 10, but his administration was plagued by scandal, as corruption soared and Alemán amassed a personal fortune from the state's coffers. Meanwhile, however, the Sandinistas had their own image problems, as the ever-present Ortega was accused by his step-daughter of sexual abuse. In a gesture of mutual self-preservation, Ortega and Alemán struck a deal, popularly known as *el pacto* (the pact), aimed at nullifying the threat of the opposition, pulling the teeth of anticorruption watchdogs and guaranteeing Alemán immunity from further investigation.

Currents in the New Millennium

After losing three successive elections, FSLN leader Ortega finally returned to power in the November 2006 elections, capitalizing on disillusionment with neoliberal policies that had failed to jump-start the country's economy and *el pacto*–sponsored law that lowered the threshold for a first-round victory to 35% of the votes (Ortega received 38%).

Taking office in January 2007, Ortega proclaimed a new era of leftist Latin American unity, leaving the USA and some international investors a little jumpy. The early days of Ortega's presidency were a flurry of activity, with Nicaragua's energy crisis seemingly solved via a deal with Venezuela's Hugo Chávez, and Ortega pledging to maintain good relations with the USA while at the same time courting closer ties with US arch-rival Iran.

But as the Ortega government found its feet, there was no sign of radical land reforms or wave of nationalizations that the business sector had dreaded and some die-hard FSLN supporters had hoped for. Ortega for the most part followed the economic course set by the previous government and continued to honor Nicaragua's international financial obligations.

The first test for Nicaraguan democracy under the new Ortega government surfaced in 2008, with countrywide municipal elections. The FSLN claimed victory in more than 70% of municipalities. Opposition forces claimed widespread voter fraud and *La Prensa* labeled the election 'the most fraudulent elections in Nicaraguan history.'

Nevertheless Ortega weathered the storm and by the end of his return term was able to point to solid economic growth alongside the reintroduction of free health care and education among the achievements of his government.

The Culture

The National Psyche

Nicaragua has a fierce cultural streak and prides itself on homegrown literature, dance, art, music and cuisine. This spiritual independence is a holdover from the revolution and Contra War, but also goes back all the way to Spanish colonization, when indigenous nations won limited autonomy at enormous personal cost.

Nicaragua also still suffers from a bit of post-traumatic stress disorder. Spanish speakers will hear plenty of stories involving tanks, explosions and aerial bombings. Former Sandinistas and Contras work, play and take communion together, however, and any tensions you might expect seem to have been addressed and worked through.

Of course, attitudes differ from place to place. Residents of the English- and Mískito-speaking Atlantic coast rarely consider themselves part of Nicaragua proper, and many would prefer to be returned to the British Empire than suffer further oppression by the 'Spaniards' on the other side of the country. The cattle ranchers of the central highlands resist interference from the federal government, while coffee pickers in

FEVER PITCH

When you hear someone talk about 'El Presidente,' they may not be referring to the country's leader, but to former Montreal Expos pitcher Denis Martínez, a Nicaraguan legend in the national sport *beisbol* (baseball), which pushes soccer into a distant second place. The sport was first played competitively in Bluefields in the late 19th century, but it didn't really take off until the arrival of US marines in the country a couple of decades later. Since then Nicaraguans have been fanatical about it, with games played everywhere from dusty city lots to cattle fields. There is a professional league too; in Managua crowds of 20,000 or more gather to see its Bóer club play against the three other major league teams: Granada, León and Chinandega (teams vary depending on who can raise the annual registration fee). Check www.lnpb.com.ni for fixtures.

Matagalpa or students in León are willing to walk to Managua to complain to the government if they perceive that an injustice has been done.

Lifestyle

Nicaragua is a country in motion. One in five Nicas live outside the country. Most people moving within Nicaragua are young women, and most go to Managua; men tend to follow the harvest into rural areas and the surrounding countries. Regular jobs are difficult to find, and more than half of employed Nicaraguans are in the 'informal sector' – street vendors, maids, artisans – without benefits or job security.

Despite the country's Catholic background, couples often live together and have children without being married, especially in larger cities. Nicaraguans are generally fairly accepting of the LGBT community, although the community is still fighting for full legal recognition.

Wealth is distributed unequally, with the moneyed elite living much as they would in Miami or elsewhere. For the vast majority of Nicaraguans, however, just putting food on the table is a daily struggle, with 46% living below the poverty line and perhaps a third of the country subsisting on two meals or fewer per day.

People

With 6.1 million people spread across 130,000 sq km, Nicaragua is the second-least densely populated country in Central America after Belize. The CIA World Factbook estimates that 69% of the population is *mestizo* (mixed indigenous and white), 17% white, 9% black and 5% indigenous. The most recent census reports that just over 440,000 people describe themselves as indigenous: the Mískito (121,000), Mayangna/Sumo (9800) and Garifuna (3300), all with some African heritage, occupy the Caribbean coast alongside the Rama (4200). In the central and northern highlands, the Cacaoperas and Matagalpas (15,200) may be Maya in origin, while the Chorotegas (46,000), the Subtiavas (20,000) and the Nahoas (11,100) have similarities to the Aztecs.

European heritage is just as diverse. The Spanish settled the Pacific coast, while a wave of German immigrants in the 1800s has left the northern highlands surprisingly *chele* (white, from *leche,* or milk). And many of those blue eyes you see on the Atlantic coast can be traced back to British, French and Dutch pirates.

The original African immigrants were shipwrecked, escaped or freed slaves who began arriving soon after the Spanish. Another wave of Creoles and West Indians arrived in the late 1800s to work on banana and cacao plantations in the east.

Religion

Although Nicaragua's majority religion is Catholic – about 59% of the population identifies as such – Nicaraguan Catholicism retains many indigenous elements. Liberation theology also made its mark on Nicaraguan Catholicism. On the Atlantic coast, Moravian missionaries from Germany began arriving in the early 1800s, and today their red-and-white wooden churches are the centerpieces of many Creole and Mískito towns. More recently, over 100 Protestant sects, most US-based and collectively referred to as *evangelistas,* have converted at least 21% of the population. Perhaps most interesting, nearly 16% of Nicaraguans say they are atheist or agnostic, unusual in Latin America and a huge relief if you're one too.

Arts

Nicaragua is a bright star in the firmament of Latin American literature, and poetry is the country's most important and beloved art. Rubén Darío (1867–1916), a poet who lived in León, is one of the most renowned authors in the Spanish language, and his writings have inspired literary movements and trends throughout the Latin world.

Three outstanding writers emerged soon after Darío, and their works are still popular: Azarías Pallais (1884–1954), Salomón de la Selva (1893–1959) and Alfonso Cortés (1893–1969). In the 1930s the experimental 'Vanguardia' movement came on the scene, led by José Coronel Urtecho, Pablo Antonio Cuadra, Joaquín Cuadra Pasos and Manolo Cuadra. A number of leading personalities in the Sandinista leadership, including Sergio Ramírez, Rosario Murillo and Ernesto Cardenal, made literary contributions as well as political ones.

Cardenal, in fact, was responsible for a whole new style of Nicaraguan art when he harnessed the talents of the local population of the Solentiname archipelago. The result, a distinctive, colorful, primitivist style of painting, is famous worldwide.

The Caribbean coast, with its distinct culture, has its own art forms, too. In Bluefields, the calypso-influenced *palo de mayo* (maypole) is a widely popular musical genre.

Landscape & Wildlife

The Land

Nicaragua, comprising 129,494 sq km, is the largest country in Central America. It is bordered on the north by Honduras, the south by Costa Rica, the east by the Caribbean Sea and the west by the Pacific Ocean.

The country has three distinct geographical regions.

PACIFIC LOWLANDS

The western coastal region is a broad, hot, fertile lowland plain broken by 11 major volcanoes. Some of the tallest are San Cristóbal (1745m), northeast of Chinandega; Concepción (1610m), on Isla de Ometepe in Lago de Nicaragua; and Mombacho (1345m), near Granada.

The fertile volcanic soil and the hot climate, with its distinct rainy and dry seasons, make this the most productive agricultural area in the country. It holds the country's major population centers.

Also in the area are Lago de Nicaragua (also known by its indigenous name, Cocibolca), the largest lake in Central America, studded with more than 400 islands, and the smaller Lago de Managua (Xolotlán).

NORTH-CENTRAL MOUNTAINS

The north-central region, with its high mountains and valleys, is cooler than the Pacific lowlands and also very fertile. About 25% of the country's agriculture is concentrated here, including most coffee production. The highest point in the country, Pico Mogotón (2438m), is near the Honduran border, in the region around Ocotal.

CARIBBEAN COAST

The Caribbean ('Atlantic') region occupies about half of Nicaragua's area. The 541km coastline is broken by many large lagoons and deltas. Twenty-three rivers flow from the central mountains into the Caribbean, including the Río Coco (685km), Nicaragua's longest river, and the Río San Juan (199km), which flows from Lago de Nicaragua. These define much of the borders with Honduras and Costa Rica respectively. The Caribbean region gets an immense amount of rainfall. It is sparsely populated and covered by tropical rainforest. The largest towns are Bluefields and Bilwi (Puerto Cabezas), both coastal ports. Several small islands, including the much-visited Corn Islands (Islas del Maíz), lie off the Caribbean coast, surrounded by coral reefs.

Wildlife

Boasting some of the largest forest reserves in the region and one of the lowest population densities, Nicaragua's incredible biodiversity is appreciated by scientists and tourists alike.

ANIMALS

Three species of sea turtle make their annual nesting grounds along the extensive undeveloped beaches of Nicaragua's Pacific coast and on islands off the Caribbean coast. Other reptiles and amphibians found in Nicaragua include green iguanas, black iguanas, and numerous species of lizard and caiman.

The country has a wealth of birdlife, from tropical species that are resident in a variety of forest environments to waterbirds on the lakes and rivers, and migrants passing between North and South America. Urracas (white-throated magpie jays) are found throughout the country, but scissor-tailed flycatchers, scarlet macaws and the colorful national bird, the *guardabarranco* (blue-crowned motmot), may be more difficult to spot.

Mantled howler monkeys are perhaps the easiest primates to find, as their mighty roar gives their location away, but Nicaragua also hosts Geoffroy's spider monkeys and white-faced capuchin monkeys, both of which are also common.

Among the more curious aquatic species are the sharks of Lago de Nicaragua. A member of the bull shark family, *Carcharhinus leucas* is the world's only known shark species that can pass between saltwater and freshwater. These were once in great abundance in the lake; today, owing to massive overfishing, they are rarely seen.

PLANTS

Nicaragua's plant life is at least as diverse as its animal life. The various ecosystems, ranging from dry tropical forest to cloud forest to rainforest, provide fertile territory for botanical exploration. Tree varieties include tamarind, kapok, frangipani and *palo de sal,* which adapts to its high-salinity coastal environment by excreting salt crystals. Orchids, including the nocturnally blooming *huele de noche,* flourish in the cloud forests of Mombacho and Miraflor.

National Parks & Protected Areas

About 18.2% of Nicaragua's land is federally protected as part of 76 wildlife areas.

Nicaragua's national parks and reserves are unlike those in many other countries in that the majority have next to no facilities for visitors.

Accommodations within park boundaries are rare, dedicated zones to pitch a tent even more so.

There are very few marked trails, which makes hiring local guides even more important, and reliable maps of the reserves are also hard to come by.

Marena administers most wildlife areas, often through other public and private organizations.

Environmental Issues

With a developing economy, poor infrastructure and limited resources, Nicaragua faces a tough task in protecting the environment at the same time as lifting its citizens out of poverty.

Like its neighbors on the Central American isthmus, Nicaragua is beset by grave environmental problems. High on the list is the rapid loss of its forests, degradation of soil quality and disappearance of species. Pesticides from the ranches invade the water table and ultimately the food chain. Nicaragua's two major lakes are also both polluted, with Lago de Managua being particularly toxic.

It's not all doom and gloom, though. Environmental consciousness is growing within Nicaragua. The government has declared the environment a national priority and has made a measurable commitment to fighting deforestation and other pressing environmental issues. And each municipality now has a department devoted to natural resources.

SURVIVAL GUIDE

Directory A–Z

ACCOMMODATIONS

Budget hotels, sometimes called *hospedajes,* are inexpensive compared to the rest of Central America. You can almost always get your own clean wooden room, with a window and a shared bathroom, for under US$6 per person per night. Double that and you get a bigger room and a private bathroom; prices are higher

NATURE'S PLAYGROUNDS IN NICARAGUA

MAJOR PARK OR NATURAL AREA	FEATURES	ACTIVITIES
Parque Nacional Volcán Masaya	Most heavily venting volcano in Central America, possible gateway to hell; lava tunnels; parakeets	Driving to the edge of an active crater, bird-watching, hiking
Reserva Natural Volcán Concepción & Parque Nacional Volcán Maderas	1 island, 2 volcanoes: gently smoking Concepción & dormant Maderas, crowned in cloud forest	Hiking, petroglyph hunting, swimming, kayaking
Reserva Biológica Indio-Maíz	Epic riverboat rides, macaws, walking trees, frogs	Canoeing, kayaking, hiking
Monumento Nacional Cañon de Somoto	The Río Coco is born – in the 'Grand Canyon' of Nicaragua	Hiking, rock scrambles, freezing-cold water
Refugio de Vida Silvestre La Flor	Leatherback & olive ridley turtles, primary dry tropical forest, beaches	Surfing, camping, sea-turtle ogling
Reserva Natural Volcán Mombacho	Volcanic views of Granada & Cocibolca, dwarf cloud forest, 100 species of orchid, fumeroles, butterfly garden	Hiking, camping, riding in military transport

SLEEPING PRICE RANGES

Price indicators for sleeping options in this chapter denote the cost of a standard double room with private bathroom.

$	Less than US$20
$$	US$20–50
$$$	More than US$50

in A-list destinations, where there are always cheap dorm beds (US$8 to US$10) if you're on a shoestring. In less-developed regions, you may be using bucket-flush toilets and bucket showers in this price range. Budget travelers should always bring candles and a flashlight (torch), just in case. If there's no mosquito net, just ask.

ACTIVITIES

Nicaragua has almost unlimited opportunities for outdoor activities but few places to rent or buy equipment, so come prepared. Well-established sports include canoeing and kayaking, diving and snorkeling, hiking, fishing and surfing. Sports with particular promise for development (once there's money invested) include windsurfing, parasailing and kitesurfing.

Diving & Snorkeling

Reefs full of marine life near Little and Big Corn Islands offer outstanding opportunities for snorkelers and divers (with equipment rental and guided dives available on both islands). There's also diving at Laguna de Apoyo and San Juan del Sur.

Hiking

There are some great hikes around Volcán Mombacho, the Cañon de Somoto and the highlands around Matagalpa. Fit walkers will want to hike the country's many volcanoes: one of the two on Isla de Ometepe, for example, or one of several in the northwest of the country.

Surfing

Surfing is huge here right now, with prime spots along the Pacific coast, many only reachable by boat. San Juan del Sur is the jumping-off point for several decent beaches. Surf camps are springing up left, right and center: keep your ear to the ground. Even remote spots are becoming more crowded – be considerate to locals anywhere you go.

EMBASSIES & CONSULATES

Most embassies are in Managua. Check www.cancilleria.gob.ni/acreditados for additional information.

The following offices are located in Managua.

Canadian Embassy (Map p448; ☎2268-0433; Los Pipitos, 2c abajo, Bolonia)

Costa Rican Consulate (Map p448; ☎2251-0429; consuladocrmanagua@yahoo.com; Rotonda Rubén Darío, 2c E, 500m N; ⏲8am-3pm)

Danish Embassy (Map p448; ☎2276-8630; Plaza España, 2c N, 1½c O)

Dutch Embassy (Map p448; ☎2276-8643; Colegio Teresiano, 1c S, 1c O)

French Embassy (Map p448; ☎2228-1056; www.ambafrance-ni.org; Iglesia El Carmen, 1½c O)

German Embassy (Map p448; ☎2266-7500; Rotonda El Güegüense, 1½c N)

Guatemalan Embassy (☎2279-9606; Carretera a Masaya, Km 11.5)

Honduran Embassy (☎2276-2406; Av del Campo 298, Las Colinas; ⏲9am-5pm Mon-Fri)

Mexican Embassy (Map p448; ☎2278-1859; http://embamex.sre.gob.mx/nicaragua; Altamira d'Este, frente Claro)

Panamanian Embassy (Map p448; ☎2266-8633; Cuartel General de Bomberos, 1c E)

Salvadoran Embassy (☎2276-2132; Av del Campo 142, Las Colinas)

US Embassy (☎2266-6010; Carretera Sur, Km 5.5)

FOOD & DRINK

Food

A variety of restaurants serving international and vegetarian cuisine can be found in Managua, León, Granada and San Juan del Sur, but the most typical (and inexpensive) fare can usually be found in street stands, market stalls and *comedores* (basic eateries). Local favorites include: *gallo pinto* (a blend of rice and beans often served with eggs for breakfast); *nacatamales* (banana-leaf-wrapped bundles of cornmeal, pork, vegetables and herbs, traditionally served on weekends); *quesillos* (soft cheese and onions folded in a tortilla); and *vigorón* (yucca steamed and topped with *chicharrón* – fried pork rind – and cabbage salad). In the evenings, *fritangas* open up on street corners, at door fronts and around the central plazas offering an artery-hardening double act of grilled meats and fried sides.

Drinks

Many restaurants serve fresh *jugos* (juices) and *refrescos naturales*, made from local fruits, herbs and seeds blended with water and sugar and poured over crushed ice. These can be a delightful treat or a sugary mess depending on how they are prepared. Look out for unusual flavors including *pithaya*, a purple cactus fruit; *tamarindo*, from the tamarind tree; and *chía*, a mucilaginous seed usually blended with lemon. *Tiste* is a traditional drink made from cocoa beans and corn.

EATING PRICE RANGES

Price indicators for eating options in this book denote the cost of a typical main course.

$	Less than US$5
$$	US$5–10
$$$	More than US$10

In spite of the importance of coffee farming, instant is what is most commonly served outside the tourist areas. There are two major national beers. Most Nicaraguans prefer the refreshing but rather bland Toña, while many visitors opt for the slightly more flavorful Victoria.

GAY & LESBIAN TRAVELERS

While consensual gay sex was recently decriminalized in Nicaragua, attitudes may take a bit longer to change. As in most of Latin America, gay and lesbian travelers will run into fewer problems if they avoid public displays of affection, and ask for two beds and then push them together. That said, lots of Nicaraguan gays and lesbians flaunt their sexuality, so you probably won't have much difficulty figuring out the scene.

Get started on the web at www.gaynicaragua.org, which has some listings. There are a small selection of gay and lesbian bars and clubs in Managua and a vaguely tolerant scene in Granada, but apart from that, it's a pretty straight (acting) country.

INTERNET ACCESS

Internet access on the Pacific coast is fast, cheap (US$0.70 to US$1 per hour) and widely available even in small towns. The Caribbean coast has slightly slower, slightly more expensive internet, which is not widely available. Many hotels and restaurants now have wi-fi networks.

LANGUAGE COURSES

Most population centers have a Casa de Cultura (House of Culture) where you can enrol in all sorts of classes – painting, folkloric dance, makeup and hair care – dirt cheap, often for less than US$1 per class, or US$6 per month.

Nicaragua is also a good place to learn Spanish, although it's a bit more expensive than Guatemala, which is a favorite among budget-minded backpacking students. Classes cost US$100 to US$120 for 20 hours of instruction at a respected school, and usually include study materials and field trips; homestays, with three meals daily, are arranged for US$80 per week.

LEGAL MATTERS

Nicaragua's police force is professional and visible, and very approachable by Central American standards. Some people advocate slipping traffic cops a 100-córdoba (US$4) bill with your ID to smooth out minor traffic violations, but that could always backfire, and if you get caught with drugs or committing a more serious crime, it won't be that easy to get away from the law.

MAPS

Detailed maps are hard to find inside Nicaragua so consider purchasing before you arrive if you plan to get off the beaten track.

Intur (www.intur.gob.ni) Offices have tourist-oriented regional and city map.

Ineter (Nicaragua Institute for Territorial Studies; www.ineter.gob.ni; frente Dirección de Migración y Extranjeria, Managua) Has the best selection of detailed maps in the country. Many are out of print, but bring a flash drive and they'll upload the files.

International Travel Maps & Books (www.itmb.ca) Publishes a detailed road map (US$12.95), but don't trust it completely for secondary roads.

Mapas Naturismo (www.mapas-naturismo.com) Has the most current road map on the market (US$9).

MONEY

Nicaragua's currency is the córdoba (C$), sometimes called a 'peso' or 'real' by locals. Córdobas come in coins of C$0.25, C$0.50, C$1, C$5 and C$10, and bills of C$10, C$20, C$50, C$100, C$200 and C$500. The plastic bills are flimsy and tear easily. Bills of C$100 and larger can be difficult to change; try the gas station.

US dollars are accepted almost everywhere, but they will be rejected if they are even slightly marked, ripped or damaged. Córdobas are usually easier to use, particularly at smaller businesses and anywhere off the beaten track –

FAVORITE LOCAL SAYINGS

Latin American Spanish vocabulary is rich in regional variations. Impress the locals with your mastery of local slang:

bacanal – party

Chele – white person

chunche – thing, small object

Nicas – Nicaraguan guys and gals

palmado – broke, penniless

tuani – cool

tuanis – right on

NICARAGUA'S TOP SURF SPOTS

Here are some favorite waves, which we've listed northeast to southwest. All of these beaches are on the Pacific coast. For a comprehensive list of the best breaks pick up a map (US$8) from **Surf Maps** (www.surfmaps.com).

Playa Aserradores Just northeast of Chinandega, this beach is also called Boom-wavos for the powerful, hollow beach break making all that noise. There's another left five minutes offshore and plenty more waves around.

El Corinto One of the best waves in the country goes almost unsurfed out there beyond Playa Paso Caballos, but it's boat access only; just north is a rivermouth break with left-breaking peaks.

Poneloya and Las Peñitas Only decent surfing, but the easiest access on Nicaragua's north Pacific, just 20km from León.

Puerto Sandino The stretch from Puerto Sandino to El Velero has half a dozen reef and rocky-bottomed beach breaks, including one spectacular left.

Playa Huehuete Now is that golden time between when the road is paved and when the gated communities go up: check out the point, beach and rivermouth break at this sweet spot just south of Casares!

Popoyo This collection of sandy-floored surf lodges may be Nicaragua's next bona fide surf town, with at least four named waves: Popoyo, a right and left point break; aggressive Bus Stop; fast and rocky-floored Cobra; and the best wave in the region, Emergencias, with a left for the long boards and hollow right for short boards. Best accessed from Tola.

Playa Gigante Accessing another handful of named waves, most of them a boat ride away, it's no wonder that surf lodges are springing up all over this beautiful beach, reached via Tola.

Playa Maderas Sometimes called Los Playones, this excellent surf spot with easy access from San Juan del Sur has a slow wave with two rights and two lefts that's perfect for beginners.

always keep at least 200 córdoba on you, preferably in smaller bills.

The córdoba is devalued according to a fixed plan against the US dollar. All prices in this guide are given in US dollars (US$), as costs in córdoba are more likely to fluctuate with the exchange rate.

ATMs & Credit Cards

ATMs *(cajeros automaticos)* are the easiest way to access cash in Nicaragua. They are available in most major towns and tourist regions. Most ATMs charge around US$2.50 per transaction on top of whatever your bank charges. It's also possible to organize cash advances over the counter in many banks. Travelers checks are inconvenient and may be changed at only some banks for a steep fee but it may be worth bringing a small amount for an emergency stash.

Branches of the following banks have reliable ATMs:

BAC Visa/Plus and MasterCard/Cirrus.
Bancentro Visa/Plus.
BanPro Visa/Plus and MasterCard/Cirrus.
Banco ProCredit Visa/Plus.

Black Market

Street moneychangers *(coyotes)* change money at around the same rate as banks, minus the long queues. They're generally honest, but you should know the exchange rate and do the math before completing the transaction.

OPENING HOURS

General office hours are from 9am to 5pm Monday to Friday and 9am to noon on weekends. Many offices, most museums and some shops take a lunch break from noon to 2pm.

POST

Considering that there are no real addresses in Nicaragua, the mail service is surprisingly effective. It costs about US$0.80 to send a standard letter or postcard to the US, about US$1 to Europe. You can receive mail at any post office by having it addressed as follows: *(your name)*, Lista de Correo, Correo Central, *(town name)*, Nicaragua.

Make sure you bring your passport when you go to check your mail, and don't leave mail sitting there for more than two weeks.

ADDRESSES

As few streets have names and fewer houses are numbered, Nicaraguans use a unique system for addresses. They take a landmark, then give the distance from it in blocks, using cardinal points for directions; eg *catedral, 2c N* (two blocks north of the cathedral).

Abbreviations for addresses:

c	*cuadra*	block
E	*Este*	east
N	*Norte*	north
O	*Oeste*	west
S	*Sur*	south

Other landmark-based addresses, such as *frente catedral* (in front of the cathedral), are given in Spanish in the text, so that locals can point you in the right direction.

SAFE TRAVEL

Despite the fact that Nicaragua has one of the lowest crime rates in Central America, as a 'wealthy' foreigner you will at least be considered a potential target by scam artists and thieves. Make sure you stay alert and take precautions against theft and mugging. Several areas are considered dangerous enough to merit their own warnings, including Managua, with big-city problems; San Juan del Sur, with bohemian tourist-industry problems; and most of the Caribbean coast, with narco-inspired security problems.

Always play it extra safe in the rural Caribbean coast, undeveloped nature reserves and anywhere that infrastructure is limited and communications are weak.

Back-country hikers should be aware that while Nicaragua has been officially declared free of land mines, there still may be other kinds of unexploded ordinance in remote areas, particularly along the Honduran border in the northern highlands and RAAN (Región Autónoma del Atlántico Norte). If in doubt, take a local guide.

TELEPHONE

Nicaragua's calling code is ☎505. There are no area codes within Nicaragua. Many homes and businesses 'rent' their phone for a fee (usually around US$0.25 per minute) for national calls to landlines and cell phones.

Direct calls abroad using the phone network or cell phones are expensive – any internet cafe will offer much cheaper rates.

Many travelers simply buy a phone upon arrival – prices start around US$15, and there are phone shops at the airport. You can also buy a SIM card (around US$3.50) and insert it into any unlocked North American phone. The two phone companies are Claro, which has better coverage, and Movistar. Electronic top-ups are available at *pulperías* (corner stores) and gas stations all over the country.

TOURIST INFORMATION

The tourist board **Intur** (www.intur.gob.ni) has an office in nearly every major town, and usually has plenty of flyers and, if you're lucky, a map. Some are excellent with detailed information on hotels, transport and guides; however most are staffed by bureaucrats with little real interest in local attractions.

Backpacker hostels, many of which have information centers, are a better bet for practical information.

The environmental ministry **Marena** (www.marena.gob.ni) also has offices everywhere that can provide information on national parks and can sometimes organize guides.

In small towns, the local *alcaldía* (mayor's office) is often a great source of information on nearby sights.

TRAVELERS WITH DISABILITIES

While Nicaraguans are generally accommodating toward people with mobility issues, and will gladly give you a hand getting around, the combination of cobbled streets, cracked sidewalks and steps in pretty much every building can make life tough.

There are few regular services for disabled travelers and because of difficulties in finding suitable transport, it's easiest to go through a tour company. **Kool Tour** (cmejia@kool-tour.com; Ciudad Jardin q-12, Managua) is a specialist that arranges tours for travelers with disabilities.

There are very few wheelchair-accessible toilets and bathrooms in Nicaragua, so bringing toilet-seat extensions and wall-mountable mobility aids is highly recommended. For general mobility-impaired advice, go to www.able-travel.com.

VISAS

Visitors from most countries can stay in Nicaragua for up to 90 days without a visa, as long as they have a passport valid for the next six months, proof of sufficient funds (US$200 or a credit card) and an onward ticket (rarely checked).

Citizens of some parts of Eastern Europe and Latin America and many African and Asian nations need visas to enter Nicaragua. Check the Nicaraguan Foreign Ministry website, www.cancilleria.gob.ni/servicios/visas.shtml, for the full lists.

Nicaragua is part of the CA-4, a regional agreement covering Nicaragua, Honduras, El Salvador and Guatemala. Officially, you can only stay for 90 days maximum in the *entire* CA-4, at which point you can get one extension of 90 days from the **immigration office** (Dirección de Migración y Extranjeria; ☎2244-3989; www.migracion.gob.ni; ⏲8-11:30am & 1:30-3pm Mon-Fri) in Managua for around US$10 per month. After those 90 days, you must leave the region (this means going to Costa Rica, basically) for 72 hours, which automatically renews your visa.

Don't bet on it, but flying between CA-4 countries tends to get you another 90 days on landing. Land border officials are stricter in adhering to the regulations.

VOLUNTEERING

Nicaragua has a very developed volunteer culture traceable to the influx of 'Sandalistas' (young foreign volunteers) during the revolution. Many hostels and Spanish schools maintain lists of organizations or check out **Volunteer South America** (www.volunteersouthamerica.net) and **Go Abroad** (www.goabroad.com).

Following are some organizations that accept foreign volunteers:

Building New Hope (www.buildingnewhope.org) Many Granada opportunities. Intermediate Spanish essential.

Quetzaltrekkers (☎2311-6695; www.quetzaltrekkers.com; 2a Calle NE, Iglesia de La Recolección, 1½c E, León) Guide hikes and help street kids.

WOMEN TRAVELERS

There are no special dangers for women traveling in Nicaragua, but the same advice applies as for the rest of Central America about dress, catcalls and so on. In fact, with the normal precautions, many women find Nicaragua to be a surprisingly pleasant country in which to travel. The Caribbean coast, however, is definitely a place to be more careful if traveling solo.

Getting There & Away

Nicaragua is accessible by air via the international airport in Managua, by road using five major border crossings with Honduras and Costa Rica, and by boat between El Salvador and Potosí.

AIR

Nicaragua's main international hub is **Managua International Airport** (MGA; www.eaai.com.ni; Carretera Norte, Km 13). It has connecting flights to Miami, Fort Lauderdale, Atlanta and Houston in the US, and several major cities within Central America. It's worth checking fares to neighboring Costa Rica, which may be significantly cheaper.

BORDER CROSSINGS
Costa Rica

If you've booked an international bus from Rivas or Managua, the border crossing between Sapoá, Nicaragua, and Peñas Blancas, Costa Rica, will be a snap, as they do everything but hold your hand. Make reservations in advance during the high season. It's often cheaper and more convenient, however, to take local buses and cross on your own.

The 1km-long, enclosed border is fairly simple, although the sudden (and strategic) crush of 'helpers' can be intimidating. Pedicabs (US$1) not only roll you through, they also protect you from the masses.

On the Nicaraguan side, get your passport stamped at a window in the large, poorly marked cement building just east of the main road. It costs US$5 to enter Nicaragua, US$2 to exit, payable in córdobas. The Municipality of Sapoá charges US$1 extra to enter or exit the border zone.

Leaving or entering Costa Rica is free. Everyone entering Costa Rica technically needs a ticket leaving the country, which is rarely asked for. If it's your unlucky day, Dendu Transport and Transnica, both located right outside, sell US$10 tickets from San José to Managua.

Buses from Sapoá run at least hourly to Rivas (US$10, one hour) between 6am and 5:30pm, where you can make connections throughout Nicaragua. *Taxistas* (taxi drivers) may tell you Nicaraguan buses aren't running, or are unsafe, but that isn't correct.

Transnica runs buses from Peñas Blancas to San José (US$10, five hours) at 5:15am, 7:30am, 9am (direct), 10:45am, noon, 1:30pm, 3:30pm and 6pm. Pulmitan de Liberia goes to Liberia

TAXI SAFETY

Express kidnappings – where a taxi driver holds the passenger hostage by knifepoint and then takes them to ATMs around town until their bank account is depleted – are on the rise in Managua, and have also been reported in Granada, Masaya, San Juan del Sur and San Jorge. Take radio taxis with a bubble on top. The ones with the bubble on the roof and/or red plates are considered safer. There should be a nametag with the driver's information on the dashboard. Ask your hotel to call you a cab. But don't trust just anybody. There are reports of people being kidnapped after a friendly stranger on the street helped them hail a cab.

ENTRY FEES & DEPARTURE TAX

Upon entering the country, visitors are required to purchase a tourist card for US$10 and a US$2 processing fee. Anyone flying out of the country must pay US$32 international departure tax, usually included in your ticket price. Domestic departure tax is US$2.

(US$2, two hours) at 6:30am, 8:30am, 9:30am, 12:30pm, 2:30pm and 5:30pm.

It's always faster and easier to take a taxi, which may be prohibitively expensive on the Costa Rican side (US$50 to Liberia), but much more reasonable from Sapoá to Rivas (US$12), San Jorge (US$15), San Juan del Sur (US$20) and Granada (US$50).

Note: there are plans to pave the Pacific Coast road from El Ostional south to Costa Rica, opening a new international border crossing here, but it's still several years away.

It's also possible to cross to Costa Rica by boat. From San Carlos, you can take a small boat up the jungle-clad Río Frio to the Costa Rican border station at Los Chiles (US$10, one hour). Boats depart from the San Carlos immigration office a block west of the dock at 10:30am, 1:30pm and 4pm Monday to Saturday, and noon and 4pm Sunday. Come half an hour before the departure time to get your exit stamp (US$2).

El Salvador

There are plans to open a ferry port in Potosí (some say as early as 2015) for transfers to La Unión in El Salvador and perhaps to Honduras. For now, you can do it by hiring a boat (1½ hours) with **Ecodetur** (☎ 8320-3481; www.ecodetour.com; entrance to Potosí) for US$35 per person, with a six-person minimum. There's a passport checkpoint in both Potosí and La Unión (open daily 8am to 5:30pm).

Honduras

The most popular land route into Honduras passes through northern Nicaragua in the town of Ocotal. The bus terminal is on the Panamericana, 1km south of the Central Plaza. Buses (US$0.40, one hour) leave hourly for the border crossing at Las Manos, from where it's 132km (2½ hours by bus) to Tegucigalpa. Las Manos is a major crossing, open 24 hours, although there's only bus service from 5am to 4:30pm. Other routes:

Somoto to Choluteca, Honduras A high-altitude crossing that comes with an amazing granite canyon. Buses for El Espino (US$0.40, 30 minutes) leave the Somoto bus terminal hourly from 4:15am to 5:15pm. The border is open from 8am to about 5pm daily.

El Guasaule to Choluteca, Honduras The fastest route from Nicaragua, an easy cruise north from lovely León. The El Guasaule crossing is hot, hectic and disorganized.

Bus

International buses have reclining seats, air-conditioning, TVs, bathrooms and sometimes even food service, and are definitely safer for travelers with luggage. Crossing borders on international buses is generally hassle-free. At many borders the helper will take your passport, collect your border fees, get your stamp and return your passport to you as you get back on the bus. At the Costa Rican border post at Peñas Blancas you must complete the formalities in person.

There are direct bus services (without changing buses) to Costa Rica, Honduras, El Salvador and Guatemala, and connecting services to Panama and Mexico.

Car & Motorcycle

You can drive over any of Nicaragua's land borders but you will need registration papers in your name, insurance, your passport and a driver's license. You will get a 30-day permit and a special stamp in your passport. If you leave without the vehicle, you will be charged a (hefty) import duty. Your home driver's license is valid for 90 days after entering the country, after which you technically need to apply for a Nicaraguan license. In reality, this is rarely an issue.

Getting Around

AIR

There is one domestic carrier, **La Costeña** ☎ 2263-2142; www.lacostena.com.ni; Managua International Airport), which offers regular services from Managua to Bluefields, the Corn Islands, Las Minas, San Carlos, San Juan del Norte (Greytown), Bilwi and Waspám. Many domestic flights use tiny single-prop planes where weight is important and bags necessarily get left behind, so keep all necessities in your carry-on luggage.

Note La Costeña is one of the few airlines that actually charges more to book online – a US$15 surcharge.

BOAT

Many destinations are accessible only, or most easily, by boat. Public *pangas* (small motorboats) with outboard motors are much more expensive than road transport – in general it costs around US$6 to US$8 per hour of travel. In places without regular service, you will need to hire your own private *panga*. Prices vary widely, but you'll spend about US$50 to US$100 per hour for four to six people; tour operators can usually find a better deal.

Following are the major departure points with regular boat service:

Bluefields To Pearl Lagoon, El Rama and Corn Island. Regular boats run between Great Corn and Little Corn Islands.

El Rama To Bluefields.

Granada To Isla de Ometepe and San Carlos.

San Carlos To Granada, the Islas Solentiname, the Río San Juan, the scenic border crossing to Costa Rica and several natural reserves.

Waspám The gateway to the Río Coco.

BUS

Bus service in Nicaragua is excellent if basic. Public transport is usually on old Bluebird school buses, which means no luggage compartments. Try to avoid putting your pack on top of the bus, and instead sit toward the back and put it with the sacks of rice and beans.

Pay your fare after the bus starts moving. You may be issued a paper 'ticket' on distance buses – don't lose it, or you may be charged again. Some bus terminals allow you to purchase tickets ahead of time, which should in theory guarantee you a seat. While buses generally cruise around town before getting underway, you're more likely to get a seat by boarding the bus at the station or terminal.

Bus terminals, often huge, chaotic lots next to markets, may seem difficult to navigate, particularly if you don't speak much Spanish. Fear not! If you can pronounce your destination, the guys yelling will help you find your bus – just make sure they put you on an *expreso* and not an *ordinario* or you'll be spending more time on the road than you planned.

CAR & MOTORCYCLE

The roads in western Nicaragua are generally good between major towns, but it's ideal if you speak at least some Spanish, because signage sucks. Get off the beaten track a little and the quality deteriorates sharply. There are no particularly unusual traffic regulations, and Managua driving is the only experience likely to get your pulse racing.

Renting a car is an excellent way to see more remote parts of the country and is neither complicated nor overly expensive. There are several car-rental agencies in Managua.

HITCHHIKING

Hitchhiking is very common in Nicaragua, even by solo women – just stick out your thumb. Foreign women, particularly those carrying all their bags, should think twice before hitchhiking solo. Never hitchhike into or out of Managua.

In rural areas where bus service is rare, anyone driving a pickup truck will almost certainly stop for you. Climb onto the back tray (unless specifically invited up front) and when you want to get off, tap on the cabin roof a couple of times.

You should always offer to pay the driver, which will almost always be refused.

LOCAL TRANSPORTATION

In smaller towns there are fewer taxis and more *tuk tuks* (motorized three wheelers) and *triciclos* (bicycle rickshaws). They're inexpensive – around US$0.50 per person to go anywhere in town – and kinda fun (although the *triciclo* driver pedaling around Rivas wearing the 'I love my job' T-shirt was probably overstating the case slightly).

TAXI

Almost all taxis in Nicaragua are *colectivos*, which stop and pick up other clients en route to your destination.

Managua taxis are unmetered and notorious for ripping off tourists. Taxis at major border crossings may also overcharge, given the chance. Most other city taxis have set in-town fares, usually around US$0.50 to US$0.70, rising slightly at night. Ask a local how much a fare should cost before getting into the cab.

Hiring taxis between cities is a comfortable and reasonable option for midrange travelers. Prices vary widely, but expect to pay US$10 for every 20km.

Costa Rica

506 / POP 4.7 MILLION

Includes ➡

San José 529
Monteverde & Santa Elena 571
La Fortuna & Volcán Arenal 580
Liberia 586
Península de Nicoya 591
Montezuma 601
Mal País & Santa Teresa 604
Manuel Antonio 610
Southern Costa Rica & Península de Osa 613

Best Places to Eat

- ➡ Bread & Chocolate (p570)
- ➡ Café Caburé (p578)
- ➡ Restaurant Mary (p604)
- ➡ Taco Bar (p606)
- ➡ Café Milagro (p609)

Best Places to Stay

- ➡ Hotel Pura Vida (p568)
- ➡ Arenal Hostel Resort (p582)
- ➡ Chilamate Rainforest Eco Retreat (p584)
- ➡ Luna Llena (p601)
- ➡ Casa Mariposa (p615)

Why Go?

The bellowing of howler monkeys echoes across the treetops. Magnificent frigate birds circle high overhead, while less-than-sonorous squawking uncovers a pair of scarlet macaws. Morning breaks in the coastal rainforest.

Similar scenes unfold across Costa Rica, from the dry tropical forest along the Pacific coast to the misty cloud forest at higher altitudes. One-third of this country's area is protected, making it a wildlife wonderland.

The flora and fauna are only part of the appeal. Annually Costa Rica attracts more than one million visitors eager to catch a wave, climb a volcano or otherwise partake of paradise.

It's never easy to maintain the delicate balance between preserving natural resources and cashing in on economic opportunity, but Ticos are tireless in their efforts. These peace-loving people are eager to share the staggering scenery, bountiful biodiversity and complete contentment of *pura vida*, the 'pure life' of Costa Rica.

When to Go

San José

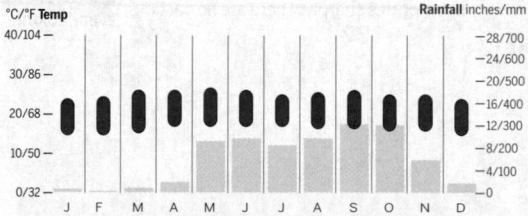

Jan–Apr The 'dry' season sees consistently hot temperatures and sunny skies.

May–Jul Crowds thin out and prices drop at the beginning of the 'green' rainy season.

Dec The holidays are festive, though accommodation prices skyrocket.

Connections

You can enter overland from Nicaragua (at Peñas Blancas or Los Chiles) and from Panama (at Sixaola, Paso Canoas or Río Sereno). For more detailed information, see Survival Guide on p634.

FIRST TIME IN COSTA RICA

One Week

From San José, beeline north to **La Fortuna** to hike on the flanks of **Volcán Arenal** and soak in the area's hot springs. Then catch a boat across Laguna de Arenal, and a bus to **Monteverde**, where you might just encounter the elusive quetzal on a stroll through the **Reserva Biológica Bosque Nuboso Monteverde**. Head south to Quepos and finish your week exploring the rainforest and soaking up the sun at **Parque Nacional Manuel Antonio**.

Two Weeks

Continue south to discover the under-explored southern sector. Scale the country's highest peak (3820m) at **Parque Nacional Chirripó** or blaze a trail through the pristine rainforest of **Parque Nacional Corcovado**. End your trip on the culturally distinct Caribbean coast, where you can paddle a maze of canals around **Tortuguero** or indulge in surf, sun and fun in **Puerto Viejo de Talamanca**.

Essential Food & Drink

- The Tico diet consists largely of rice and beans and – when it's time to change things up – beans and rice.
- Breakfast for Ticos is usually *gallo pinto* (literally 'spotted rooster'), a stir-fry of rice and beans, usually served with eggs, cheese or *natilla* (sour cream).
- Most restaurants offer a set meal at lunch and dinner called a *casado*, or a 'married man's' lunch, featuring meat, beans, rice and salad. An extremely popular *casado* is the ubiquitous *arroz con pollo*, or chicken and rice.
- Seafood is plentiful, fresh and delicious. While it's not traditional Tico fare, you'll find *ceviche* on most menus (raw fish or shrimp, marinated in lime juice and served chilled).
- On the Caribbean coast, the cuisine shows off its Caribbean roots. Don't miss a chance to sample *rondón*, a spicy seafood gumbo.

AT A GLANCE

Currency Costa Rican colón; US dollars (US$) also accepted

Language Spanish & English

Money ATMs are ubiquitous; credit and debit cards widely accepted

Visas Generally not required for stays less than 90 days

Time GMT minus six hours; no daylight saving time

Fast Facts

- **Area** 51,100 sq km
- **Capital** San José
- **Emergency** 911

Set Your Budget

- **Dorm bed** US$12 to US$16
- **Casado** US$3 to US$6
- **Bus fare** US$3 to US$10
- **National park admission** US$10
- **Zip-line canopy tour** US$40 to US$60

Resources

- **Tico Times** (www.ticotimes.net)
- **Costa Rica Tourism Board** (www.visitcostarica.com)
- **Lonely Planet** (www.lonelyplanet.com)

Costa Rica Highlights

1. Glide through the waterways of **Parque Nacional Tortuguero** (p557), spying on howlers, sloths, crocs and manatees
2. Groove to a reggae beat and slurp up spicy *rondón* in **Puerto Viejo de Talamanca** (p566)
3. Soak in the volcano-heated springs around **La Fortuna** (p580)
4. Get your head into the clouds in the misty, mystical setting of the nature preserves around **Monteverde and Santa Elena** (p572)
5. Catch the waves and the rays on the windswept beaches of **Mal País** (p604)
6. Explore alternative music, art and lifestyles at the **Envision Festival** (p611) in Dominical
7. Scale Costa Rica's highest peak (3820m) at **Parque Nacional Chirripó** (p616), where the panorama yawns from the Atlantic to the Pacific
8. Hike across **Parque Nacional Corcovado** (p620) to commune with monkeys, macaws and other rainforest residents

84°W
83°W
NICARAGUA
0 50 km
0 25 miles
11°N
Río San Juan
CARIBBEAN SEA
Río Colorado
Barra del Colorado
Trinidad
Río San Carlos
Boca Tapada
Río Chirripó
Puerto Lindo
Río Toro
Río Sarapiquí
Tortuguero
Parque Nacional Tortuguero
Pital
Puerto Viejo de Sarapiquí
Aguas Zarcas
La Virgen
Cariari
Ciudad Quesada (San Carlos)
San Miguel
Parque Nacional Braulio Carrillo
Cordillera Central
Guápiles
Guácimo
Río Reventazón
Zarcero
Volcán Poás (2704m)
Volcán Barva (2906m)
Siquirres
San Ramón
Matina
ALAJUELA
HEREDIA
Volcán Irazu
Monumento Nacional Archaeológico Guayabo
Moín
PUERTO LIMÓN
10°N
Río Tárcoles
Ciudad Colón
SAN JOSÉ
CARTAGO
Turrialba
Santiago de Puriscal
Paraíso
Moravia
Puerto Viejo de Talamanca
San Ignacio de Acosta
San Marcos de Tarrazú
Tapantí
Pandora
Cahuita
Punta Uva
Cerro de la Muerte (3491m)
Bribrí
Manzanillo
Santa Maria de Dota
Parque Nacional Chirripó
Río Teliré
Parrita
San Gerardo de Dota
Shiroles
Amubri
Sixaola
Guabito
Reserva Indígena Cocles/Kékölöldi
Isla Damas
Herradura
Quepos
San Gerardo de Rivas
Cordillera de Talamanca
Manuel Antonio
San Isidro de El General
Parque Nacional Manuel Antonio
Dominical
Río General
Ujarrás
Uvita
Buenas Aires
Playa Bahía
Isla Ballena
Tortuga Abajo
Ciudad Cortés
Paso Real
Potrero Grande
9°N
Palmar Norte
Santa Elena
Bahía de Coronado
Palmar Sur
Las Mellizas
Sierpe
San Vito
Sabalito
Río Sereno
Chacarita
Bahía Drake
Agua Buena
Rincón
Río Claro
Isla del Caño
Golfito
Neily
Parque Nacional Corcovado
Golfo Dulce
Coto 47
PANAMA
Paso Canoas
Península de Osa
Puerto Jiménez
Zancudo
David (Panama)
Carate
Pavones
84°W
83°W

SAN JOSÉ

POP 1,188,000

San José is not a pretty city, what with the unremarkable concrete structures, clogged pedestrian arcades and fast-food monstrosities dominating its cityscape. And how delightful can a city really be when you're constantly dodging homicidal drivers, evading pickpockets and trying to tune out the cacophony of honking horns and ear-splitting reggaetón?

But once you get the hang of it, Chepe – as San José is affectionately known – quickly reveals its charms. Take your time poking around the more historic neighborhoods, where colonial mansions have been converted into contemporary art galleries, refined international restaurants and boutique hotels. Colorfully arresting murals and hipster buskers pop up on the most unexpected corners. And in its museums of gold and jade and national history lie all the layers of indigenous heritage, colonial past and great minds that made Costa Rica the environmental champion and military-free country we love today.

Sights

★Plaza de la Cultura PLAZA

(Avs Central & 2 btwn Calles 3 & 5) For many Ticos, Costa Rica begins here. This architecturally unremarkable concrete plaza in the heart of downtown is usually packed with locals slurping ice-cream cones and admiring the wide gamut of San José street life: juggling clowns, itinerant vendors and cruising teenagers. It is perhaps one of the safest spots in the city since there's a police tower stationed at one corner.

Museo de Oro Precolombino y Numismática MUSEUM

(☎2243-4202; www.museosdelbancocentral.org; Plaza de la Cultura, Avs Central & 2 btwn Calles 3 & 5; adult/student/child US$11/8/free; ⏲9:15am-5pm) This three-in-one museum houses a glittering collection of pre-Columbian gold artifacts, a small exhibit detailing the history of Costa Rican currency and a temporary display space for local art. Security is tight – all visitors must leave bags at the door.

Teatro Nacional NOTABLE BUILDING

(☎2221-5341; www.teatronacional.go.cr; Av 2 btwn Calles 3 & 5; admission US$7; ⏲9am-4pm Tue-Sun) The 1897 national theater is the city's most impressive public building, featuring a columned neoclassical facade. It is flanked by statues of Beethoven and Calderón de la Barca, a 17th-century Spanish dramatist. Paintings depicting 19th-century life line the lavish lobby and auditorium. The most famous is *Alegoría al café y el banano,* portraying idyllic coffee and banana harvests, painted by an Italian with no apparent experience in the matter (observe how the laborers hold the banana bunches).

Parque Nacional PARK

(Avs 1 & 3 btwn Calles 15 & 19) One of the nicest of San José's green spaces is the Parque Nacional, a shady spot where retirees read newspapers and young couples smooch coyly on concrete benches. At its center is the Monumento Nacional, a dramatic statue (erected in 1953) that depicts the Central American nations driving out American filibuster William Walker.

Museo Nacional de Costa Rica MUSEUM

(☎2257-1433; www.museocostarica.go.cr; Calle 17 btwn Avs Central & 2; adult/child US$8/4; ⏲8:30am-4:30pm Tue-Sat, 9am-4:30pm Sun) Located inside the Bellavista Fortress, the Museo Nacional offers a quick survey of Costa Rican history. You'll find a wide range of pre-Columbian artifacts as well as numerous colonial objects and religious art. The natural-history wing has flora and fauna specimens, minerals and fossils.

Parque España PARK

(Avs 3 & 7 btwn Calles 9 & 11) Wedged between MADC and the Museo de Jade, Parque España may be small, but it becomes a riot of birdsong every day at sunset when the local avian population comes in to roost. In addition to being a good spot for a shady break, the park is home to an ornate statue of Christopher Columbus that was given to the people of Costa Rica in 2002 by his descendants, commemorating the quincentennial of the explorer's landing in Puerto Limón.

Museo de Arte y Diseño Contemporáneo MUSEUM

(☎2257-7202; www.madc.cr; Av 3 btwn Calles 13 & 15; admission US$3, Mon free; ⏲9:30am-5pm Mon-Sat) Commonly referred to as MADC, the Contemporary Art & Design Museum is housed in the historic National Liquor Factory building, which dates from 1856. The largest and most important contemporary art museum in the region, MADC is focused on showing the works of contemporary Costa Rican, Central American and South American artists and occasionally features temporary exhibits devoted to interior design, fashion and graphic art.

★Museo de Jade MUSEUM
(☎2287-6034; www.ins-cr.com; 1st fl, Edificio INS, Av 7 btwn Calles 9 & 11; adult/child US$9/free; ⏲8:30am-3:30pm Mon-Fri, 10am-2pm Sat) San José's most famous museum is located in the Instituto Nacional de Seguros (National Insurance Institute). It houses the world's largest collection of American jade (pronounced *ha*-day). Archaeological exhibits of ceramics and stonework offer insight into Costa Rica's pre-Columbian cultures.

Parque La Sabana PARK
Parque La Sabana, at the west end of Paseo Colón, is the most popular retreat from the grit and the grime. La Sabana is home to two museums, a lagoon, a fountain and a variety of sports facilities including the Estadio Nacional, where international and division-one soccer matches are played. During the daytime, it's a great place for a stroll, picnic or a relaxed jog. During the nighttime, it's a great place for getting mugged.

Museo de Arte Costarricense MUSEUM
(☎2256-1281; www.musarco.go.cr; east entrance of Parque La Sabana; ⏲9am-4pm Tue-Sun; 👪) FREE
At the eastern entrance to the Parque La Sabana is the Museo de Arte Costarricense, housed in a Spanish-style structure that served as San José's main airport terminal until 1955. The newly remodeled museum features regional art and other exhibits. The on-site sculpture garden and free admission make it a great option for families.

Catedral Metropolitana CHURCH
(Avs 2 & 4 btwn Calles Central & 1) To the east of the Parque Central is the 1871 Renaissance-style Catedral Metropolitana, a pilgrimage site for devout Ticos. The interiors, in keeping with the period, are graceful neoclassical, with colorful Spanish tile floors, stained-glass windows, and a Christ figure that was produced by a Guatemalan workshop in the late 17th century.

Courses

The San José area has fine Spanish-language schools, many of which offer homestays for students. Most also organize volunteer placements, a great way to learn Spanish while giving back to those who need it most.

Amerispan Study Abroad LANGUAGE COURSE
(☎in USA & Canada 800-879-6640, worldwide 215-531-7917; www.amerispan.com) Located 300m south of Radio Columbia in Zapote, this place offers a variety of educational programs, as well as volunteer placements and medical Spanish.

Costa Rican Language Academy LANGUAGE COURSE
(☎2280-1685, in USA 866-230-6361; www.learnspanish.com; Calle Ronda, Barrio Dent) In addition to Spanish, this place – 175m west of San Pedro Mall – offers cooking and dance classes.

Institute for Central American Development Studies LANGUAGE COURSE
(ICADS; ☎2225-0508; www.icads.org; Montes de Oca, San Pedro) Month-long programs, with and without homestays, are combined with lectures and activities focused on environmental and political issues. ICADS is located in San Pedro, about 3km east of downtown San José.

Personalized Spanish LANGUAGE COURSE
(☎2278-3254; www.personalizedspanish.com; Tres Ríos) Like the name implies, private classes that cater to your needs, including special programs for health-care workers, children, business and law. Located about 15km east of San José in the suburb of Tres Ríos.

Tours

The city is small and easily navigable, but if you're looking for a walking tour that will guide you to key sites, here are some recommendations:

Barrio Bird Walking Tours WALKING TOUR
(☎8926-9867; www.toursanjosecostarica.com; tours US$18-30) The knowledgeable and engaging Stacey Corrales shows visitors San José's famous and not-so-famous sights, providing history and insights on the city's architecture, murals and urban art. Specialized tours also cater to gourmands, photographers and bar-crawlers.

Costa Rica Art Tour TOUR
(☎8359-5571, 2288-0896; www.costaricaarttour.com; per person US$95) A small outfit, run by Molly Keeler, organizes a recommended day tour that visits five different artists' studios, where you can view (and buy) the work of local painters, sculptors, printmakers, ceramicists and jewelers. Lunch and hotel pick-up

San José

A
B
C
D
1
2
3
4
5
6
7
BARRIO MÉXICO
Interamericana (2km); Internacional Juan Santamaria (17km); Alajuela (18km)
Iglesia Barrio Mexico
Plaza
Av 13
Calle 10
Gran Terminal del Caribe
Av 11
Transportes Blanco
Transportes Deldú
Calle 8
Calle 18
Calle 16
Av 9
Calle 12
Terminal San Carlos
Av 7
Av 13
Av 11
Av 9
Av 5
Calle 14
Empresas Alfaro
Av 7
Buses to Heredia
16
Av 5
Transportes Bocatoreños
Panaline
King Quality
Av 5
Av 3
Calle 18
Calle 16
Av 3
Calle 6
Calle 4
Calle 2
Calle Central
Calle 1
Calle 3
Av 3
Terminal Coca-Cola
Machu Picchu (750m); Kabata Hostel (900m)
Av 1
Av 1
34
Paseo Colón
Av Central
Club Vertigo (1km); Museo de Arte Costarricense (1.2km); La Sabana (1.2km)
Buses to Alajuela, Volcán Poás & Airport (Tuasa)
Plaza de la Cultura
2
30
Av 2
Parque La Merced
Hospital San Juan de Dios
Parque Central
3
Av 4
Buses to Volcán Irazú
Av 6
Av 8
Calle 16
Calle 14
Calle 12
Calle 10
Calle 8
Calle 6
Calle 4
Calle 2
Calle Central
Calle 1
29
Calle 3
Calle 5
Av 10
Av 12
Empresarios Unidos
Av 12
Av 14
27
Av 16
Calle 16
Terminal Tracopa (300m); Green House Hostel (350m); Transportes Musoc (600m)

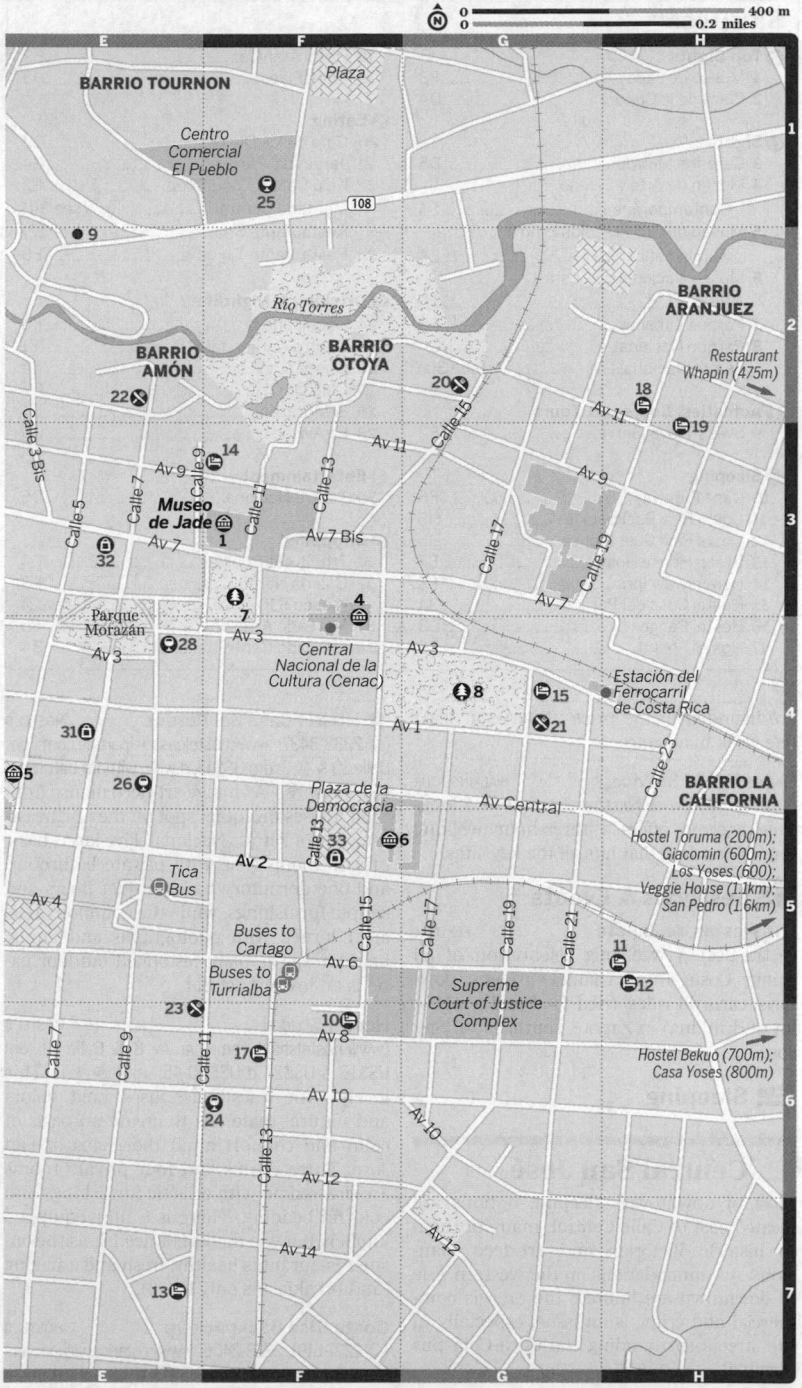
0 400 m
0 0.2 miles
E
F
G
H
1
2
3
4
5
6
7
BARRIO TOURNON
Plaza
Centro Comercial El Pueblo
25
108
9
Río Torres
BARRIO ARANJUEZ
BARRIO AMÓN
BARRIO OTOYA
Restaurant Whapin (475m)
22
20
18
19
14
Av 11
Calle 15
Av 9
Calle 3 Bis
Calle 5
Calle 7
Calle 9
Calle 11
Calle 13
Calle 17
Calle 19
Museo de Jade
1
32
Av 7
Av 7 Bis
4
7
Parque Morazán
28
Av 3
Central Nacional de la Cultura (Cenac)
8
15
21
Estación del Ferrocarril de Costa Rica
Av 1
31
5
26
Calle 23
BARRIO LA CALIFORNIA
Plaza de la Democracia
Av Central
33
6
Hostel Toruma (200m); Giacomin (600m); Los Yoses (600); Veggie House (1.1km); San Pedro (1.6km)
Av 2
Tica Bus
Av 4
Calle 21
Buses to Cartago
Av 6
11
12
Buses to Turrialba
Supreme Court of Justice Complex
23
10
Av 8
17
Hostel Bekuo (700m); Casa Yoses (800m)
Av 10
24
Av 12
Av 14
13

San José

Top Sights
1 Museo de Jade F3
2 Plaza de la Cultura D4

Sights
3 Catedral Metropolitana D5
4 Museo de Arte y Diseño Contemporáneo F4
5 Museo de Oro Precolombino y Numismática E4
6 Museo Nacional de Costa Rica F5
7 Parque España F3
8 Parque Nacional G4
Teatro Nacional ..... (see 30)

Activities, Courses & Tours
9 Swiss Travel Service E2

Sleeping
10 Casa Ridgway F6
11 Costa Rica Backpackers H5
12 Costa Rica Guesthouse H5
13 Green House Hostel E7
14 Hemingway Inn F3
15 Hostel Casa del Parque G4
16 Hostel Pangea D3
17 Hostel Shakti F6
18 Hotel Aranjuez H2
19 Kaps Place H3

Eating
20 Café de los Deseos G2
21 Jardín del Parque G4
22 Kalú Café & Food Shop E2
Mercado Central ..... (see 34)
Restaurante Shakti ..... (see 17)
23 Restaurante Tin-Jo E6

Drinking & Nightlife
24 Bochinche F6
25 Centro Comercial El Pueblo F1
26 Chelle's E4
27 Club Oh! C7
28 El Morazán E4
29 La Avispa D6

Entertainment
30 Teatro Nacional D5

Shopping
31 7th Street Books E4
32 Galería Namu E3
Kiosco SJO ..... (see 22)
33 Mercado Artesanal F5
34 Mercado Central B4

are included in the price. Reserve at least one week in advance.

Swiss Travel Service WALKING TOUR
(☎2282-4898; www.swisstravelcr.com) A long-time agency; offers a three-hour walking tour of San José that hits all the key sites.

Festivals & Events

Las Fiestas de Zapote FESTIVAL
(late Dec) A weeklong celebration of all things Costa Rican (namely rodeos, cowboys, carnival rides, fried food and a whole lot of drinking) in Zapote, southeast of San José.

Sleeping

Central San José

Most of downtown's sleeping options are located east of Calle Central, many of them in historic Victorian and art-deco mansions. Accommodations on the western side of downtown are limited: the area is commercial and crime is an issue, especially in the streets surrounding the Coca-Cola bus terminal.

★Hostel Casa del Parque HOSTEL $
(☎2233-3437; www.hostelcasadelparque.com; cnr Calle 19 & Av 3; dm US$13, d with/without bathroom US$44/34;) A vintage art-deco manse from 1936 houses this quiet spot on the northeastern edge of Parque Nacional. Five large, basic private rooms (one with private bathroom) and one dormitory have parquet floors and simple furnishings, while the common areas are adorned with photographs and family heirlooms. The plant-festooned outdoor patio is an inviting retreat.

Hostel Shakti HOSTEL $
(www.hostelshakti.com; cnr Av 8 & Calle 13; dm US$16, s US$27, d US$40-45;) This lovely little guesthouse uses bold colors and natural materials to create an oasis of calm and comfort amid the chaos of San Jose. Three dorms and four private rooms are dressed up with eclectic furnishings and colorful bedding. There is a fully equipped kitchen, but you might not need it, as the on-site restaurant is healthy, fresh and amazing (and breakfast is only US$3).

Costa Rica Backpackers HOSTEL $
(☎2221-6191, 2223-2406; www.costaricabackpackers.com; Av 6 nr Calle 21; dm US$13, d without bathroom

US$32; P @) East of the downtown area, this extremely popular hostel has 15 dormitories and 13 private double rooms spread out over several structures that surround a nice garden with hammocks and a free-form pool. Rooms and shared bathrooms are basic, but clean, and decorated with tropical-themed murals.

Hostel Pangea HOSTEL $
(2221-1992; www.hostelpangea.com; Av 7 btwn Calles 3 & 3bis, Barrio Amón; dm US$14, d with/without bathroom US$45/34, ste US$60-70; P @) This industrial-strength, Tico-owned hostel – 25 dorms and 25 private rooms – has been a popular 20-something backpacker hangout in San José for years. It's not difficult to see why: it's smack in the middle of the city and comes stocked with a pool, a rooftop restaurant-lounge with stellar views and a combination bar/movie theater furnished with bean bags and a stripper pole. Needless to say, this is a party spot.

Casa Ridgway GUESTHOUSE $
(2222-1400, 2233-2693; www.casaridgwayhostel.com; cnr Calle 15 & Av 6bis; dm US$15, s/d US$25/38, without bathroom US$22/34; P) This small, welcoming guesthouse, located on a quiet side street near the Supreme Court complex, is run by the adjacent Friends' Peace Center, a Quaker organization that promotes social justice and human rights. The rooms are sparse but immaculate, as are the shared showers and communal kitchen – and the atmosphere is, well, peaceful.

Green House Hostel HOSTEL
(2258-0102; www.greenhousehostel.altervista.org; btwn Avs 14 & 18; dm with bathroom US$15, s/d/tr US$27/37/42; P) An electric-green block on the outside, this hostel is attractive on the inside, adorned with hanging plants, historic photographs and antiques. The rooms themselves are austere, though the perk here is that they all have private bathrooms (even the dorms).

Costa Rica Guesthouse GUESTHOUSE $
(2223-7034; www.costa-rica-guesthouse.com; Av 6 nr Calle 21; dm US$16, d with/without bathroom from US$39/32, all incl breakfast; P @) This guesthouse, dating from 1904, has simple, graceful rooms with spacious bathrooms and hallways lined with Spanish tiles. Furnishings are basic (creaky beds), but it's a tranquil, couples-friendly spot. It has a small internet lounge and an outdoor patio adorned with epiphytes.

★Hotel Aranjuez HOTEL $$
(2256-1825; www.hotelaranjuez.com; Calle 19 btwn Avs 11 & 13; s/d from US$32/49, without bathroom US$25/30, all incl breakfast; P @) This rambling hotel in Barrio Aranjuez consists of several nicely maintained vintage homes that have been strung together with connecting gardens. The 35 spotless rooms come in an infinite variety of configurations and the private ones are equipped with lockboxes and cable TV. The hotel's best attribute, however, is the lush garden patio, where a legendary breakfast buffet is served every morning.

Kaps Place GUESTHOUSE $$
(2221-1169, 8647-7190; www.kapsplace.com; Calle 19 btwn Avs 11 & 13; s US$25-50, d US$45-60, tr US$55-70, apt US$85-125; P @) A colorful little guesthouse on a residential street in Barrio Aranjuez, Kaps has 24 small, homey rooms of various configurations spread over two buildings. Run by Karla Arias, this is most decidedly a family place: expect to see kids playing in the yucca-plant-filled courtyard or hopping on the trampoline. The kitchen is immaculate, the patios are strung with hammocks and the communal areas are wonderfully decorated in bright mosaics.

Hemingway Inn HOTEL $$
(2221-1804, 2257-8630; www.hemingwayinn.com; cnr Calle 9 & Av 9; s US$35-60, d US$60-75, all incl breakfast;) This funky little spot in

GETTING TO YOUR HOTEL

It's a good idea to make advance arrangements for transportation to your hotel from the airport or bus station. (Most hotels and hostels offer this service for a fee.) If not, play it safe by following these simple dos and don'ts:

- Do try to take an official taxi.
- Don't believe your driver if he tells you the hotel is closed, full or otherwise unavailable.
- Do have a telephone on hand so you can call your hotel or hostel for directions and/or confirmation.
- Don't let your taxi driver call on your behalf.
- Do ask to see a room before paying if you have any concerns about the hotel.

Barrio Amón has 17 rooms in a rambling *cafetalero* house dating to the 1920s. With a garden, shared kitchen and murals adorning the walls, the inn has a relaxed and friendly ambience. All of the rooms come with safes (US$3 per day) and each is simple, comfortable and unique.

La Sabana & Surrounds

About 4km west of Plaza de la Cultura, the ciy's congested center gives way to private homes, shopping areas and the sprawling Parque Metropolitano La Sabana. The quiet neighborhoods around the park are home to a few excellent hostels.

Mi Casa Hostel HOSTEL $

(☎2231-4700; www.micasahostel.com; Sabana Norte; dm US$13, r with/without bathroom from US$32/25, all incl breakfast; P @) A converted modernist home in La Sabana, it has polished wood floors, vintage furnishings and half a dozen eclectic guest rooms to choose from (two of which are dormitories). It has a pleasant garden, where a tiny bar stocks cold beer for guests, as well as a pool table, free internet and a laundry service. Find it on the north side of the park, 50m west and 150m north of the ICE building.

Galileo Hostel HOSTEL $

(☎2248-2094; www.hostelgalileo.com; cnr Calle 40 & Av 2; dm US$9-11, r without bathroom US$24-30; @) In an old house east of Parque La Sabana, this snug little hostel has several dormitories and a handful of private rooms with shared bathroom. The freshly painted dorms are tight (bunk to bunk), but the owner and staff are friendly and the prices are the cheapest in town.

Gaudy's HOSTEL $

(☎2248-0086; www.backpacker.co.cr; Casa 3636, Av 5 btwn Calles 36 & 38; dm US$12, d with/without bathroom US$36/22; P @) You'll find this homey hostel inside a sprawling modernist house in a residential area east of Parque La Sabana. Popular among shoestring travelers for years, it has 13 private rooms and two dormitories. The design scheme is basic and the vibe is mellow. But the place has plenty of fun features, including a TV lounge, a pool table, a foosball table and a courtyard strung with hammocks.

Kabata Hostel HOSTEL $

(☎2283-2000, 2255-0355; www.kabatahostel.com; Calle 36 btwn Avs 1 & 3; dm US$13, d without bathroom US$40-46;) Run by a Tico family, this modern, no-frills hostel has a new location a few blocks east of Parque La Sabana. Rooms are basic but clean. The place prides itself on personalized service and hospitality, which includes plenty of expert insights on traveling around the country.

Los Yoses & San Pedro

These suburbs provide an enticing (and convenient) alternative to staying in central San Jose. The neighborhoods are safe and vibrant, with easy access to good restaurants and great nightlife. It's a long walk (20 minutes) or a short bus ride (five minutes) to get into the center.

★Hostel Bekuo HOSTEL $

(☎2234-1091; www.hostelbekuo.com; Av 8 btwn Calles 39 & 41, Los Yoses; dm US$13, d with/without bathroom US$38/32, d with bathroom & TV US$45, all incl breakfast; P @ ; San Pedro, taxi) This restful spot feels more like a home than a hostel. The airy modernist structure has nine rooms (four of which are dormitories, one of which is reserved especially for women), as well as large tile bathrooms, an expansive TV lounge dotted with bean bags, and an interior courtyard with a pre-Columbian granite sphere right in the center. It's in Los Yoses in the heart of the university district.

Stolas Hostel HOSTEL $

(☎2225-5185; www.hostelstolas.com; Calle 35, Los Yoses; dm/s/d incl breakfast US$12/20/30; P @ ; Zapote-Corte) The newest addition to the scene in Los Yoses is this fun, funky hostel, where your hosts are committed to making you feel at home. The rooms are clean and comfortable enough, but the idea here is to relax and hang out in the common areas, which are equipped with plush chairs, a big TV, movies, Wii and – most importantly – good company.

Hostel Toruma HOSTEL $

(☎2234-8186; www.hosteltoruma.com; Av Central btwn Calles 29 & 33, Los Yoses; dm US$13, r without bathroom US$38, s/d/tr with bathroom US$38/52/64; P @) A former presidential mansion, this graceful neoclassical home how houses a 'luxury budget' accommodation option. A recent makeover preserved the Spanish-tile floors and decorative friezes, converting the living space into four dormitories and 17 spacious private rooms. All have access to an internet lounge dotted with bean bags and a small poolside restaurant and bar.

Casa Yoses HOSTEL $
(☎2234-5486; www.casayoses.com; Av 8, Los Yoses; dm US$11-14, r per person with/without bathroom US$20/17, all incl breakfast; P @ ; San Pedro) Another mellow spot, this nine-room Spanish Revival–style house is perched on a hill that offers lovely views of the valley from the front garden.

It's a family-friendly place that offers dorms (including an all-female option), as well as cramped singles and more spacious doubles and quads. They vary in decor and style, but all have wood floors and tiled hallways. TV, pool table and foosball are at your disposal.

Hotel Milvia GUESTHOUSE $$
(☎2225-4543; www.hotelmilvia.com; San Pedro; s/d/tr incl breakfast US$69/80/87) This lovely Caribbean-style plantation building once served as the home of Ricardo Fernández Peralta, an artillery colonel who fought in Costa Rica's 1948 civil war. Now owned by a Brit expat and his Tica wife, it serves as a hotel and art gallery. Nine eclectic rooms – some carpeted, others with shining wood floors, all dotted with bright pieces of art – surround a pleasant courtyard with a trickling fountain. An upstairs terrace provides incredible views of the mountains in the distance. It's two blocks northeast of Av Central in San Pedro.

Eating

Central San José

Mercado Central MARKET $
(Avs Central & 1 btwn Calles 6 & 8; 6:30am-6pm Mon-Sat) One of the cheapest places for a good lunch is at the market, where you'll find a variety of restaurants and *sodas* (cheap lunch counters) serving *casados*, tamales, seafood and everything in between.

Café de los Deseos CAFE $
(☎2222-0496; www.cafedelosdeseos.com; Calle 15 btwn Avs 9 & 11, Barrio Otoya; mains US$4-10; 2-10pm Tue-Sat) Full of young artsy types, this colorful cafe offers up delicious visions for the eye as well as tasty *bocas* (appetizers) that include salads and individual pizzas. Smoothies, desserts, cocktails and other temptations round out the menu. The setting is cozy and colorful, its walls hung with the work of local artists and rooms adorned with beaded curtains, branches entwined with fairy lights and hand-painted tables.

Restaurante Shakti VEGETARIAN $
(☎2222-4475; cnr Av 8 & Calle 13; mains US$5-9; 7:30am-7pm Mon-Fri, 8am-6pm Sat;) Attached to the hostel of the same name, this informal neighborhood health food outpost serves up simple, organic-focused cooking as well as freshly baked goods. Favorites here include veggie burgers, along with various fish dishes, but most people arrive for the *casado* of the day – which is always vegetarian.

★ Jardín del Parque VEGETARIAN $$
(☎2248-4979; Calle 19 btwn Avs 1 & 3; meals US$7-12; 8am-5pm Mon-Fri;) Focusing on organic, local ingredients, this vegetarian oasis offers hearty breakfasts, crispy pizzas and delicious sandwiches served on homemade bread. Take your pick from three different veggie burgers or, for something different, sample the daily special. All of this delicious healthiness is served on a delightful shady terrace overlooking the Parque Nacional.

Restaurante Tin-Jo ASIAN $$
(☎2221-7605; www.tinjo.com; Calle 11 btwn Avs 6 & 8; mains US$10-18; 11:30am-3pm & 5:30-10pm Mon-Thu, 11:30am-3pm & 5:30-11pm Fri & Sat, 11:30am-10pm Sun;) The interiors of this popular Asian standard-bearer are a riot of pan-Asian everything, just like the menu. Expect a wide range of fare from various regions – from *kung pao* shrimp to spicy tuna *maki* to *pad thai* – as well as an extensive vegetarian menu. Credit cards accepted.

Kalú Café & Food Shop CAFE $$
(☎2221-2081; www.kalu.co.cr; cnr Calle 7 & Av 11, Barrio Amón; mains US$11-18; noon-6pm Mon, noon-9:30pm Tue-Sat;) Sharing a sleek space with the Kiosco SJO (p542) design store, this style-conscious cafe is run by noted chef Camille Ratton. The menu is a modern global fusion of salads, sandwiches, pastas and tapas. Whatever you do, save room for a mind-melting dessert.

La Sabana & Surrounds

Soda Tapia FAST FOOD $

(☎2222-6734; www.sodatapia.com; cnr Av 2 & Calle 42; mains US$5-7, desserts US$3-4; ⏲6am-2am Mon-Thu, 24hr Fri & Sat, 6am-midnight Sun; P) An unpretentious '50s-style diner, it's perpetually filled with couples and families noshing on grilled sandwiches and generous *casados*. The place is a little pricey for soda fare, but the food is filling and the atmosphere is fun.

Machu Picchu PERUVIAN $$

(☎2222-7384, 2255-1717; www.restaurantemachupicchu.com; Calle 32 btwn Avs 1 & 3; mains US$8-22, children's menu US$6-9; ⏲10am-10pm Mon-Sat, 11am-6pm Sun; P) This locally renowned Peruvian restaurant will do you right if you have a hankering for all things Andean. A popular spot for a leisurely Sunday lunch, it has an encyclopedic menu that features tasty Peruvian classics such as *pulpo al olivo* (octopus in olive sauce), *ají de gallina* (a nutty chicken stew) and *causa* (chilled potato terrines stuffed with shrimp and avocado).

Los Yoses & San Pedro

Veggie House VEGETARIAN $$

(☎2280-9949; www.restaurantveggiehouse.com; Blvd Los Yoses; mains US$6-10; ⏲7:30am-7:30pm Mon-Fri, 8am-5pm Sat;) With a name like Veggie House, you know this place takes care of the herbivores. But the food here, west of Mall San Pedro, is so scrumptious and satisfying that even non-veggies will enjoy it – from salads and smoothies to more substantial fare like burgers, lasagna and more. Fancy coffee drinks and decadent desserts provide a fine finish.

Giacomin BAKERY $

(☎2224-3463; www.pasteleriagiacomin.com; Av Central, Los Yoses; pastries from US$1.30; ⏲8am-noon & 2-7pm Mon-Sat) *Josefinos* swear that this small pastry shop, east of Calle 37, is the best in town. Your sweet tooth will be sated by chocolates, cakes and cookies, but the place is also known for tasty pizzas, savory pastries and quiche. Look carefully: the bakery is obscured by a parking lot to the east of the Automercado.

Comida Para Sentir VEGETARIAN $

(☎2224-1163; Calle Central, San Pedro; casados US$3-7; ⏲10am-6pm Mon-Fri;) This informal, bustling student spot serves an international menu of veggie everything including curried rice with cashews, vegetable *casado* and whole-grain sandwiches. Don't miss the *tardes de maíz* (afternoons of corn), from 3pm to 6pm, featuring delicious corn-based treats like tamales and *pupusas* (cornmeal mass stuffed with cheese or beans). It's 100m north of Parque de San Pedro.

★**Restaurant Whapin** CARIBBEAN $$

(☎2283-1480; www.whapincr.com; cnr Calle 35 & Av 13, Barrio Escalante; mains US$13-21; ⏲8am-11pm Mon-Fri, 11:30am-11pm Sat) If you don't make it to the Caribbean, then make sure you eat here: an intimate corner spot painted Rasta red, yellow and green, and serving up spectacularly delicious meals. Enjoy a steamy bowl of *rondón* (seafood gumbo cooked in coconut milk), a plate of rice and red beans, or fish simmered in spicy coconut sauce.

Drinking & Nightlife

Whether you prefer Imperial beer, a shot of *guaro* or a smooth *batido* with a shot of rum, you'll find a suitable drinking establishment in San Jose. The price of a beer will vary depending on the venue, but count on spending US$2.50 and up. Take your ID; some places card everyone upon entering.

Calle La Amargura STREET

(Calle 3, San Pedro, north of Av Central) North of Av Central in San Pedro, Calle 3 is known as the Calle La Amargura (Street of Sorrow). However, it should be called Calle de la Cruda (Street of Hangovers) because it has the city's highest concentrations of bars, many of which are packed with customers (mainly university students) even during daylight hours. Places come and go, but **Terra U** (☎2283-7728; www.terrau.com; Calle La Amargura, San Pedro; ⏲10am-2:30am Mon-Sat, 3pm-2:30am Sun), 50m north of Calle Central, and **Caccio's** (www.caccios.com; Calle de la Amargura, San Pedro), 150m north of Av Central, are longtime party spots. The area gets rowdy in the wee hours: watch out for drunks and pickpockets.

Centro Comercial El Pueblo BAR

(☎2221-9434; www.centrocomercialelpueblo.com; Barrio Tournon; ⏲hours vary) This Spanish Medi-

GAY & LESBIAN SAN JOSÉ

The city is home to a thriving gay and lesbian scene – at least by Central American standards. Cover prices at these venues vary depending on the night and location (usually from US$4 to US$10). Smaller places come and go, but there are a few long-standing mainstays. Take a taxi to the clubs listed below, which are on the sketchy south side of town.

La Avispa (☎2223-5343; www.laavispa.co.cr; Calle 1 btwn Avs 8 & 10; ⏲8pm-1am Fri & Sat, 5-9pm Sun) This is a long-standing gay establishment that hosts a stylish crowd for drinking and dancing. Twice monthly ladies nights are for women only. Otherwise, the place is usually packed with well-dressed, good-looking men shooting pool and getting their groove on.

Bochinche (☎2221-0500; Calle 11 btwn Avs 10 & 12; ⏲8pm-5am Wed-Sat) A club that features everything from classic disco to electronica, as well as special themed nights.

Club Oh! (☎2221-9341; Calle 2 btwn Avs 14 & 16; ⏲from 9pm Fri & Sat) A massive dance club with an attached lounge attracts a mixed crowd of gay men, lesbians and their allies. There's drinking, dancing and midnight drag shows every Friday.

terranean outdoor mall is a warren of bars, clubs and music venues. The proximity of one place to the next makes it ideal for a pub crawl and there is stringent security, which keeps the atmosphere generally safe (though it can get unruly as the night wears on). Things usually get going at about 9pm and shut down by 3am.

El Morazán BAR
(☎2256-5110; cnr Calle 9 & Av 3; cocktails US$5-7; ⏲noon-midnight) On the east side of Parque Morazán, this exposed-brick, Spanish tile–clad space dates back to 1904. Throughout its long life it has hosted all manner of historical figures (including Che Guevara, according to one account). With beer, cocktails and live music, it is a popular hangout among Chepe's boho set.

Chelle's BAR
(☎2221-1369; cnr Av Central & Calle 9; ⏲24hr) If you're boozing the night away with Ticos, you might find yourself here at 4am, clutching a cold one and telling people you just met that you love them. If you feel at home at a good old-fashioned dive bar, Chelle's is for you.

Club Vertigo CLUB
(☎2257-8424; www.vertigocr.com; Paseo Colón btwn Calles 38 & 40; cover US$6-10; ⏲10pm-dawn) The city's premier club is located on the ground floor of a nondescript office tower, but Club Vertigo packs in Chepe's beautiful people with a mix of house, trance and electronica. Downstairs is an 850-person-capacity sweatbox of a dance floor, while upstairs you'll find a chill-out lounge lined with red sofas. Dress to the nines and note that cover charges can skyrocket on guest-DJ nights.

☆ Entertainment

Pick up *La Nación* on Thursday for a complete listing (in Spanish) of the coming week's nightlife and cultural events. The *Tico Times* 'Weekend' section (in English) has a calendar of events. Available at the tourist office, *Guía de Ciudad,* published by *El Financiero,* features local happenings. Visit www.entretenimiento.co.cr for more up-to-date movie, bar and club listings across the San José area.

Teatro Nacional THEATRE
(☎2221-5341; www.teatronacional.go.cr; Calles 3 & 5 btwn Avs Central & 2) Costa Rica's most important theater stages plays, dance, opera, symphony, Latin American music and other major events. The main season runs from March to November, but there are performances throughout the year.

Jazz Café LIVE MUSIC
(☎2253-8933; www.jazzcafecostarica.com; Av Central, San Pedro; cover US$6-10; ⏲6pm-2am) Jazz Café is *the* destination in San José for live music, with bands ranging from traditional salsa to jazz fusion. Countless performers have taken to the stage here, including legendary Cuban bandleader Chucho Valdés and Colombian pop star Juanes. It's 50m east of Antiguo Banco Popular in San Pedro.

Shopping

★Galería Namu HANDICRAFTS
(☎2256 3412; www.galerianamu.com; Av 7 btwn Calles 5 & 7; ⏲9am-6:30pm Mon-Sat, 1-5pm Sun Jan-Apr) For a quick education about local indigenous cultures, Galería Namu does a wonderful job of bringing together artwork and crafts from a diverse population of regional ethnicities. It can also help arrange visits to remote indigenous territories in different parts of Costa Rica.

Mercado Central MARKET
(Avs Central & 1 btwn Calles 6 & 8; ⏲6am-6pm Mon-Sat) Assuming you dress down and stick a wad of cash in your sock, the gritty Mercado Central is the best place for hammocks *hecho en* (made in) Nicaragua and '*Pura Vida*' tees *hecho en* China. Get some export-quality coffee beans here for a fraction of the boutique price.

Mercado Artesanal MARKET
(Crafts Market; Plaza de la Democracia, Avs Central & 2 btwn Calles 13 & 15; ⏲midmorning-sunset) One of the city's best shopping experiences, the Mercado Artesanal has 100 open-air stalls hawking handcrafted jewelry, elaborate woodwork, Guatemalan sarongs and Cuban cigars.

Kiosco SJO ARTS & CRAFTS
(☎2258-1829; www.kioscosjo.com; cnr Av 11 & Calle 7, Barrio Amón; ⏲11am-6pm Mon, 11am-10pm Tue-Sat) With a focus on sustainable design by Latin American artisans, this sleek shop stocks handmade jewelry, hand-tooled leather boots and bags, original photography, artisanal chocolates, fashion and contemporary home decor by established regional designers. It's pricey, but the quality is exceptional.

7th Street Books BOOKS
(☎2256-8251; Calle 7 btwn Avs Central & 1; ⏲9am-6pm Mon-Sat, 10am-5pm Sun) The headquarters of all things English-language. Stock includes fiction, guidebooks and children's books, but the specialty is the flora, fauna and natural history of Costa Rica. There is also a selection of maps.

Orientation

San José's center is arranged in a grid with avenidas running east to west and calles running north to south. Av Central, the nucleus of the city, becomes a pedestrian mall between Calles 6 and 9. It turns into Paseo Colón west of Calle 14.

The center has several loosely defined *barrios* (districts). The downtown is a commercial area with bus stops and cultural sights. Perhaps the most interesting district to visitors is Barrio Amón, north of Av 5 and east of Calle 1, with its concentration of landmark mansions, largely converted into hotels and fine-dining establishments. Just west of downtown is La Sabana, named after the park.

About 2km east of central San José, the barrios known as Los Yoses and San Pedro are home to a number of embassies as well as the most prestigious university in the country, La Universidad de Costa Rica (UCR). The area serves as the nightlife hub of under-30 *josefinos*, with trendy bars, restaurants and nightclubs. Much like a Latin love affair, hot spots sizzle and fizzle quickly.

While we have indicated streets and avenues, most locals instead use landmarks to guide themselves.

Information

DANGERS & ANNOYANCES

Though Costa Rica has the lowest crime rate of any Central American country, crime in urban centers such as San José is a problem. Not surprisingly, in a city where one in five people live below the poverty line, the most common offense is theft. Readers have reported pickpockets and snatch-and-grab theft, as well as muggings.

You'll see the tourism police (*policía turística*) in the major tourist gathering spots in San José, wearing white polo shirts. These officers can be helpful in the event of an emergency and most of them speak some English.

Neighborhoods reviewed here are generally safe during the day, though you should be especially careful around the Coca-Cola bus terminal and the red-light district south of Parque Central, particularly at night. It is wise to take an official taxi when traveling any significant distance after dark.

EMERGENCY

Organismo de Investigacíon Judicial
(☎2222-1365, 2221-5337; Calle 17 btwn Avs 6 & 8; ⏲9am-5pm Mon-Fri) If you find yourself the victim of a crime, you'll have to file a report in person in the Supreme Court of Justice building.

Red Cross (Cruz Roja Costariccense; ☎128, in San José 2542-5000; www.cruzroja.or.cr; Av 8 btwn Calles 14 & 16)

Traffic Police (Policía de Tránsito; ☎2222-9330, 2222-9245; www.transito.go.cr)

INTERNET ACCESS

Checking email is easy in San José, where cybercafes are more plentiful than fruit peddlers.

Rates are generally less than US$1 per hour, though these days most hotels (even budget hostels) provide free internet access, mostly via wi-fi.

MEDICAL SERVICES

Clínica Bíblica (☎2522-1000, emergency 2522-1030; www.clinicabiblica.com; Av 14 btwn Calles Central & 1) The top private clinic in the downtown area. Doctors speak English, French and German, and an emergency room is open 24 hours.

Hospital La Católica (☎2246-3000; www.hospitallacatolica.com; Guadalupe) A pricey private clinic located northeast of downtown. In 2009, the hospital debuted an adjacent 34-room hotel – geared at patients who arrive for treatments from abroad.

Hospital San Juan de Dios (☎2257-6282; cnr Paseo Colón & Calle 14) The free public hospital is, incidentally, Costa Rica's oldest (founded 1845). It offers a wide variety of medical services and there is a children's wing. Expect long waits.

MONEY

Any bank will change foreign currency into colones, but US dollars are by far the most accepted currency for exchange. ATMs are widespread in the city.

POST

Correo Central (Central Post Office; ☎2223-9766; www.correos.go.cr; Calle 2 btwn Avs 1 & 3; ⏲7:30am-5:30pm Mon-Fri, 7:30am-noon Sat) The most efficient place in Costa Rica to send and receive mail.

TELEPHONE

Local and international calls can be made from most public phones, which are widespread. Chip and Colibrí phone cards are sold at souvenir shops, newsstands and Más X Menos supermarkets. Hotels usually have lobby phones.

TOURIST INFORMATION

Instituto Costarricense de Turismo (ICT, Costa Rica Tourism Board; ☎2299-5800, in USA & Canada 866-267-8274; www.visitcostarica.com; Plaza de la Cultura, Calle 5 btwn Avs Central & 2; ⏲9am-5pm with flexible lunch Mon-Fri) The government tourism office is good for a copy of the master bus schedule and handy free maps of San José and Costa Rica.

Getting There & Away

AIR

Aeropuerto Internacional Juan Santamaría (SJO) handles international air traffic at its main terminal. Immediately to the north of the main terminal, a diminutive blue building houses the operations of **Sansa** (☎2290-4100; www.flysansa.com), one of the country's two domestic airlines.

Aeropuerto Tobías Bolaños (SYQ), which lies in the San José suburb of Pavas, services domestic flights on **NatureAir** (☎2299-6000; www.natureair.com), the country's other domestic airline.

BUS

Bus transportation in San José can be bewildering. There is no public bus system and no central terminal. Instead, dozens of private companies operate out of stops scattered throughout the city. Many bus companies have no more than a

INTERNATIONAL BUSES FROM SAN JOSÉ

DESTINATION	COMPANY	COST (US$)	DURATION (HR)	DEPARTURES (DAILY)
Bocas del Toro, Panama	Transportes Bocatoreños	10	6	9am or 10am
David, Panama	Tracopa	25	9	2
Managua, Nicaragua	King Quality	44	9	3am
	Tica Bus	27-40	9	4
	TransNica	27-38	9	4
Panama City, Panama	Panaline	25	15	1pm
	Tica Bus	42-58	15	2
San Salvador, El Salvador	King Quality	62	19	3am
Tegucigalpa, Honduras	King Quality	65	17	3am
	TransNica	50	18½	4am

stop (in this case pay the driver directly); some have a tiny office with a window on the street, while some operate from a terminal. Companies include the following:

Pulmitan (☎2666-0458; Calle 24 btwn Avs 5 & 7)

Transportes Deldú (☎2256-9072; www.transportesdeldu.com; Av 9 btwn Calles 10 & 12)

Empresas Alfaro (☎2222-2666; Av 5 btwn Calles 14 & 16)

Tralapa (Calle 20 btwn Avs 3 & 5)

Transportes Jacó (☎2290-2922; Terminal Coca-Cola, Av 1 btwn Calles 16 & 18)

Empresarios Unidos (☎2222-8231; cnr Av 12 & Calle 16)

Transportes Blanco (☎2257-4121; Calle 12 btwn Avs 9 & 11)

Transportes Musoc (Calle Central btwn Avs 22 & 24)

The bigger stations service entire regions.

Gran Terminal del Caribe (Calle Central, north of Av 13) Serves the Caribbean coast.

Terminal Coca-Cola (Av 1 btwn Calles 16 & 18) A well-known, labyrinthine landmark. Scores of buses leave from here to points all over Costa Rica, including the Central Valley and the Pacific Coast. Thefts are common around here, so stay alert.

Terminal San Carlos (Terminal del Atlántico Norte; cnr Av 9 & Calle 12)Serves northern destinations such as Monteverde, La Fortuna and Sarapiquí, as well as a few destinations on the Península de Nicoya.

Tracopa (☎2221-4214; www.tracopacr.com; Calle 5 btwn Avs 18 & 20) Serves San Isidro de El General and points south.

Buses are crowded on Friday evening and Saturday morning, even more so during Christmas and Easter. Bus schedules change regularly and prices change with fluctuating fuel costs. Get a master bus schedule at the ICT office or online at www.visitcostarica.com.

International Buses

International buses get booked up fast. Buy your tickets in advance – and take your passport. The following companies run services from San José:

Transportes Bocatoreños (☎2227-5923; cnr Av 5 & Calle 16)

Tracopa (see above)

King Quality (☎2258-8834; www.king-qualityca.com; Calle 12 btwn Avs 3 & 5)

Tica Bus (☎2221-0006; www.ticabus.com; cnr Calle 9 & Av 4)

TransNica (☎2223-4123; www.transnica.com; Calle 22 btwn Avs 3 & 5)

Panaline (☎2256-8721; cnr Av 5 & Calle 16)

Shuttle Bus

Several companies shuttle passengers in air-con minivans from San José to the most popular destinations around Costa Rica. They are more expensive than the standard bus service, but they offer door-to-door service and can get you there faster. Plus you can book online.

Grayline's Fantasy Bus (☎2220-2126; www.graylinecostarica.com; US$33-89) Routes extend from the Nicoya to the Caribbean, with a few destinations in the far north and far south. Also offers weekly passes that allow unlimited travel on the scheduled routes.

Interbus (☎2283-5573; www.interbusonline.com; US$37-57) Also offers convenient airport transfers (US$15) and a useful three-time flexipass.

ℹ Getting Around

TO/FROM THE AIRPORT

You can reserve a pick-up with **Taxi Aeropuerto** (☎2221-6865), which charges a flat rate of between US$21 and US$30 to/from most parts of San José. (These taxis are a bright orange color.) You can also take a street taxi, but the rates may vary wildly. Make sure the driver starts his meter.

Interbus (p544) runs an airport shuttle service that will pick you up at your hotel and take you to either airport (US$15 per person); good value if you're traveling alone.

The cheapest option is the regular bus service:

➡ To Aeropuerto Internacional Juan Santamaría, take the red bus bound for Alajuela operated by **Tuasa** (Av 2 btwn Calles 12 & 14; ☎2442-6900), which departs every 10 minutes from Av 2 between Calle 12 and Calle 14. Be sure to tell the driver that you are getting off at the airport.

➡ Buses to Tobías Bolaños depart every 30 minutes from Av 1, 250m west of the Terminal Coca-Cola.

TO/FROM THE BUS STATIONS

If traveling by bus, you'll arrive at one of several international bus terminals sprinkled around the western and southern parts of downtown. Much of this area is walkable provided you aren't hauling a lot of luggage and are staying nearby. But, if you're arriving at night, take a taxi, since most terminals are in dodgy areas.

Note that many taxi drivers in San José are commissioned by hotels to bring them customers, and the hotel scene is so competitive that drivers will say just about anything to steer you to the places they represent. See the box on p537 to ensure you make it to the hotel of your choosing.

BUS

Local buses are useful to get you into the suburbs and surrounding villages, or to the airport.

DOMESTIC BUSES FROM SAN JOSÉ

DESTINATION	POINT OF DEPARTURE	COST (US$)	DURATION (HR)	FREQUENCY (DAILY)
To Central Valley				
Alajuela	Av 2 btwn Calles 12 & 14	1.50	35 min	every 10 min 4am-10pm
Turrialba	Calle 13 btwn Avs 6 & 8	2.50	2	hrly 5am-9pm
To Northwestern Costa Rica				
La Fortuna	Terminal San Carlos	6	4	3
Liberia	Pulmitan	5	4½	hrly 6am-8pm
Monteverde/Sana Elena	Terminal San Carlos	5	5	2
Peñas Blancas, Nicaragua border crossing	Transportes Deldú	9	6	21 (direct bus 4:30am & 7am)
To Península de Nicoya				
Montezuma & Mal País	Terminal San Carlos	14	6	2
Playa del Coco	Pulmitan	7	5	3
Sámara	Empresas Alfaro	8	5	noon
Tamarindo	Empresas Alfaro	9	5½	2
Tamarindo	Tralapa	9	5½	2
To the Central Pacific Coast				
Dominical & Uvita	Tracopa	5	7	2
Jacó	Transportes Jacó	4	2½	8
Puntarenas	Empresarios Unidos	3.50	2½	hrly 6am-7pm
Quepos/Manuel Antonio	Tracopa	8	4	12
To Southern Costa Rica & Península de Osa				
Golfito	Tracopa	10	8	2
Paso Canoas, Panama border crossing	Tracopa	10	6	7
Puerto Jiménez	Transportes Blanco	12	8	2
San Isidro de El General	Tracopa	5	3	hrly 5am-6:30pm
San Isidro de El General	Transportes Musoc	5	3	hrly 5:30am-5:30pm
To the Caribbean Coast				
Cariari, for transfer to Tortuguero	Gran Terminal del Caribe	3.25	2¼	9
Puerto Limón	Gran Terminal del Caribe	5	3	every 30 min 5am-7pm
Puerto Viejo de Talamanca	Gran Terminal del Caribe	9	4½	4
Sixaola, Panama border crossing	Gran Terminal del Caribe	11	6	4
To the Northern Lowlands				
Los Chiles, Nicaraguan border	Terminal San Carlos	4.50	5	2
Puerto Viejo de Sarapiquí	Gran Terminal del Caribe	3.20	2	10

Most buses run between 5am and 10pm and cost in the vicinity of US$0.50 to US$1.

➡ Buses from Parque La Sabana head into town on Paseo Colón, then go over to Av 2 at the San Juan de Dios hospital. They then go various ways through town before heading back to La Sabana. Buses are marked Sabana–Estadio, Sabana–Cementerio or Cementerio–Estadio. These buses are a good bet for a cheap city tour.

➡ Buses going east to Los Yoses and San Pedro go back and forth along Av 2 and then switch over to Av Central at Calle 29. (These are easily identifiable by the big sign that says 'Mall San Pedro' on the front window.) The route starts at the corner of Av 2 and Calle 7, near Restaurante El Pollo Campesino.

TAXI

Red taxis can be hailed on the street day or night, or you can have your hotel call one for you.

Marías (meters) are generally used, though a few drivers will tell you they're broken and try to charge you more – especially if you don't speak Spanish. (Not using a meter is illegal.) Make sure the *maría* is operating when you get in, or negotiate the fare up front. Short rides downtown cost US$2 to US$4. There's a 20% surcharge after 10pm that may not appear on the *maría*.

CENTRAL VALLEY & HIGHLANDS

It is on the coffee-cultivated hillsides of the Central Valley that you'll find Costa Rica's heart and soul. This is not only the geographical center of the country, but also its cultural and spiritual core. It is here that the Spanish first settled, here that coffee built a prosperous nation, here that picturesque highland villages still host centuries-old fiestas. It is also here that you'll get to fully appreciate Costa Rica's country cooking: artisanal cheeses, steamy corn cakes and freshly caught river trout.

Curvy mountain roads and cattle traffic force travelers to slow their roll. Quaint (and some quirky) agricultural towns invite leisurely detours to farmers markets and church processions, a refreshing break from the tourist-industrial complex on the coasts. But it's not all cows and coffee – world-class rapids, resplendent quetzals and close encounters with active volcanoes all show off the rich landscape in which Costa Rica's character is rooted.

Alajuela

POP 47,900

Alajuela is by no means a tourist 'destination.' Much of the architecture is unremarkable, the streets are often jammed and there isn't a lot to see. But it's warm and welcoming, with an an upbeat vibe that is virtually absent in the capital. Its best features seem undeniably provincial: the mango-lined plaza, old-fashioned shops and a soaring alabaster cathedral.

The proximity to Aeropuerto Internacional Juan Santamaría, just 3km outside the city, makes Alajuela a highly convenient transit point if you are entering or leaving the country. It's also a pleasant base when visiting Volcán Poás to the north.

Sights

Museo Juan Santamaría MUSEUM

(☎2441-4775; Av 1 btwn Calles Central & 2; ⏲10am-5:30pm Tue-Sun) FREE Costa Rica's second city is also home to one of the country's most famous figures: Juan Santamaría, the humble drummer boy who died putting an end to William Walker's campaign to turn Central America into slaving territory in the Battle of Rivas in 1856. Learn all about it at this small museum, northwest of the parque central. Once the town jail, it now houses maps, paintings and historic artifacts.

Festivals & Events

Día de Juan Santamaría FESTIVAL

(Alajuela; ⏲April 11) Commemorating Costa Rica's national hero, this week-long celebration includes parades, concerts, dances.

Sleeping

Hotel Cortéz Azul HOSTEL $

(☎2443-6145; www.hotelcortezazul.com; Av 5 btwn Calles 2 & 4; dm US$12, d with/without bathroom US$35/30; P) The owner, Eduardo Rodríguez, is a local artist who has painted murals and hung other unique pieces throughout the property. The hotel has 10 homey, clean rooms with polished wood floors, a plant-strewn courtyard and an open-air kitchen. Rave reviews for friendly, helpful staff.

Hotel Trotamundos HOSTEL $

(☎2430-5832; www.hoteltrotamundos.com; Av 5 btwn Calles 2 & 4; dm US$12, d with/without bathroom US$35/30, all incl breakfast; @) This spot is as basic as it gets, but the rooms are clean and the service is super-friendly. Three dorms and seven private units are nestled into a two-story house that surrounds a tiny interior courtyard. Extra points for the satisfying Tico-style breakfast.

Hostel Maleku HOSTEL $
(☎2430-4304; www.malekuhostel.com; dm US$15, s/d without bathroom incl breakfast US$25/38; @) A sweet little backpackers' abode located on the south edge of town, 50m west of the San Rafael Hospital, Maleku has tight spic-and-span rooms tucked in a vintage home on a quiet street. It's a wonderful, serene spot and the staff is very helpful.

Vida Tropical B&B B&B $$
(☎2443-9576; www.vidatropical.com; Calle 3 north of Av 11; s/d without bathroom incl breakfast US$45/60; P @) In a quiet residential neighborhood, this Colombian-American–run house has five snug, simple guest rooms awash in bright murals (all but one share a bathroom). The well-tended backyard is perfect for catching some sun in a hammock, and laundry service is available. Rates include a free pick-up or drop-off at the airport.

Hotel Los Volcanes GUESTHOUSE $$
(☎2441-0525; www.hotellosvolcanes.com; Av 3 btwn Calles Central & 2; d with/without bathroom incl breakfast from US$60/46; P @) This refurbished 1920s home has 15 rooms – from vintage units with wood floors, period-style furniture and clean, shared bathrooms, to contemporary rooms with flat-screen TV and safe. There's also an enjoyable courtyard in the back, complete with gurgling fountain. For an easy day-trip to Volcán Poás, take advantage of the hotel's round-trip shuttle for US$30.

Villa Pacandé GUESTHOUSE $$
(☎6077-7565; www.villapacande.com; Rd to Volcán Poás; d/tr/q incl breakfast from US$40/50/60; P @) Located 3km north of Alajuela center, this Spanish-style home is set on gorgeous grounds, festooned with blooms and buzzing with hummingbirds. The nine rooms are simple and comfortable, some offering a lovely view of the garden. This is a perfect choice for your first or last night if you're not interested in exploring the charms of Alajuela.

Alajuela Backpackers Boutique Hostel HOTEL $$
(☎2441-7149; www.alajuelabackpackers.com; cnr Av 4 & Calle 4; dm/r/ste US$17/55/70; @) Facing Parque de los Niños, this four-story inn is more hotel than hostel, with private rooms and dorms surrounding a plant-draped atrium. Watch movies on the flat-screen TV in the beanbag lounge, or sip beers on the 4th-floor bar terrace and watch planes take off in the distance. The dorms house only four people per room, and each has its own bathroom. Big bonus: free airport transfers (book one day ahead).

Eating

Mercado Central MARKET
(Calles 4 & 6 btwn Avs 1 & Central; 7am-6pm Mon-Sat) For the cheapest meals, head to the enclosed Mercado Central for produce stands, inexpensive lunch counters and much, much more.

Jalepeños Central MEXICAN $
(☎2430-4027; Calle 1 btwn Avs 3 & 5; mains US$3-8; 11:30am-9pm Mon-Sat) Run by an animated Colombian-American from New York City, this popular Tex-Mex spot will introduce some much-needed spice into your diet. Good food, good service, good times.

Coffee Dreams Café CAFE $
(☎2430-3970; cnr Calle 1 & Av 3; mains US$2-9; 8am-8pm Mon-Sat;) For a variety of traditional dishes and rich desserts, this cute cafe is a reliably good place for food or coffee. Window seats are an inviting place to sip your java, eat a sweet and watch the street scene.

La Mansarda COSTA RICAN $$
(☎2441-4390; 2nd fl, Calle Central btwn Avs Central & 2; mains US$5-16; 11am-11pm) Grilled fish and chicken dishes are the specialty at this casual balcony restaurant overlooking the street. Save room for the *flan de coco* (coconut flan) or, better yet, a belt of Flor de Caña rum.

Shopping

Goodlight Books BOOKS
(☎2430-4083; www.goodlightbooks.com; Av 3 btwn Calles 1 & 3; 9am-6pm) One of the country's best English-language bookstores, well stocked with new and used books and a decent selection on Costa Rica and the region.

Central Valley & Highlands

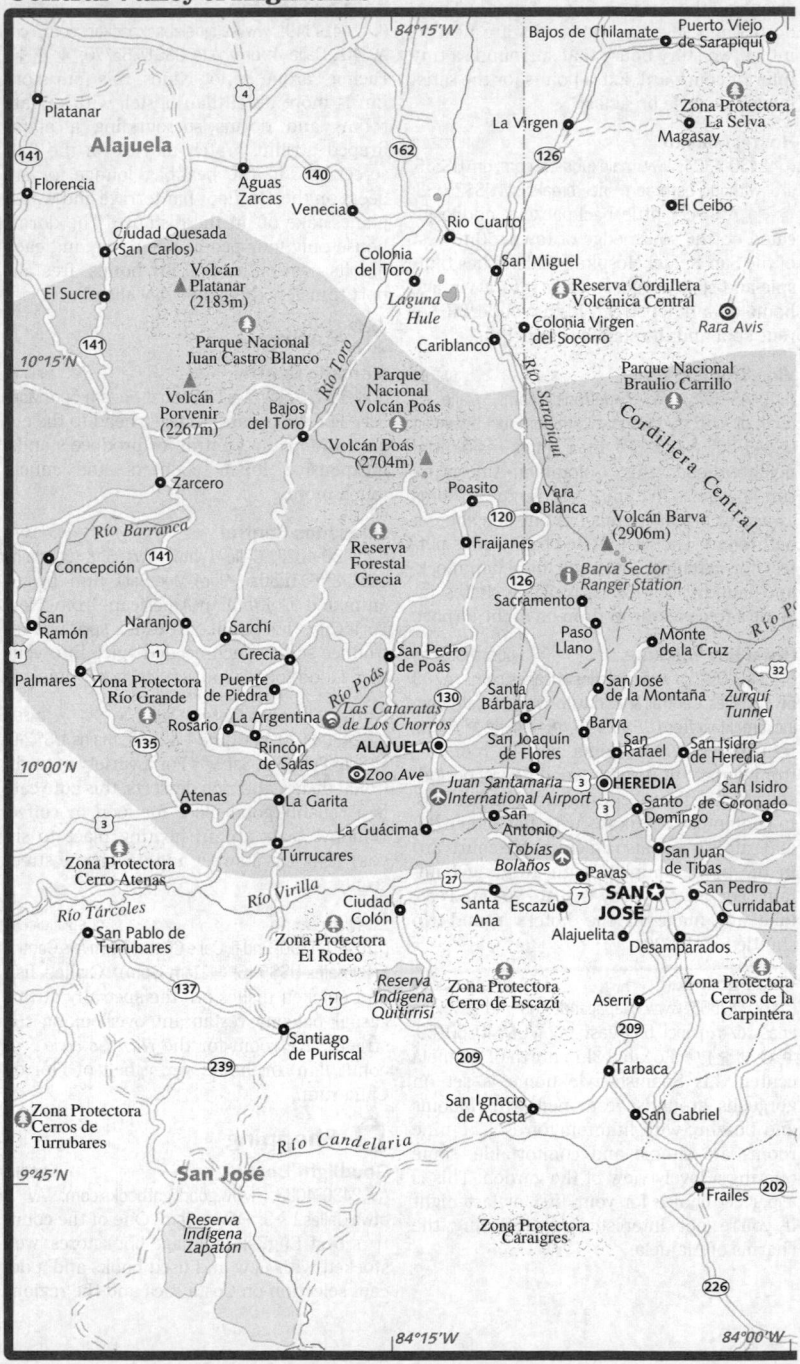

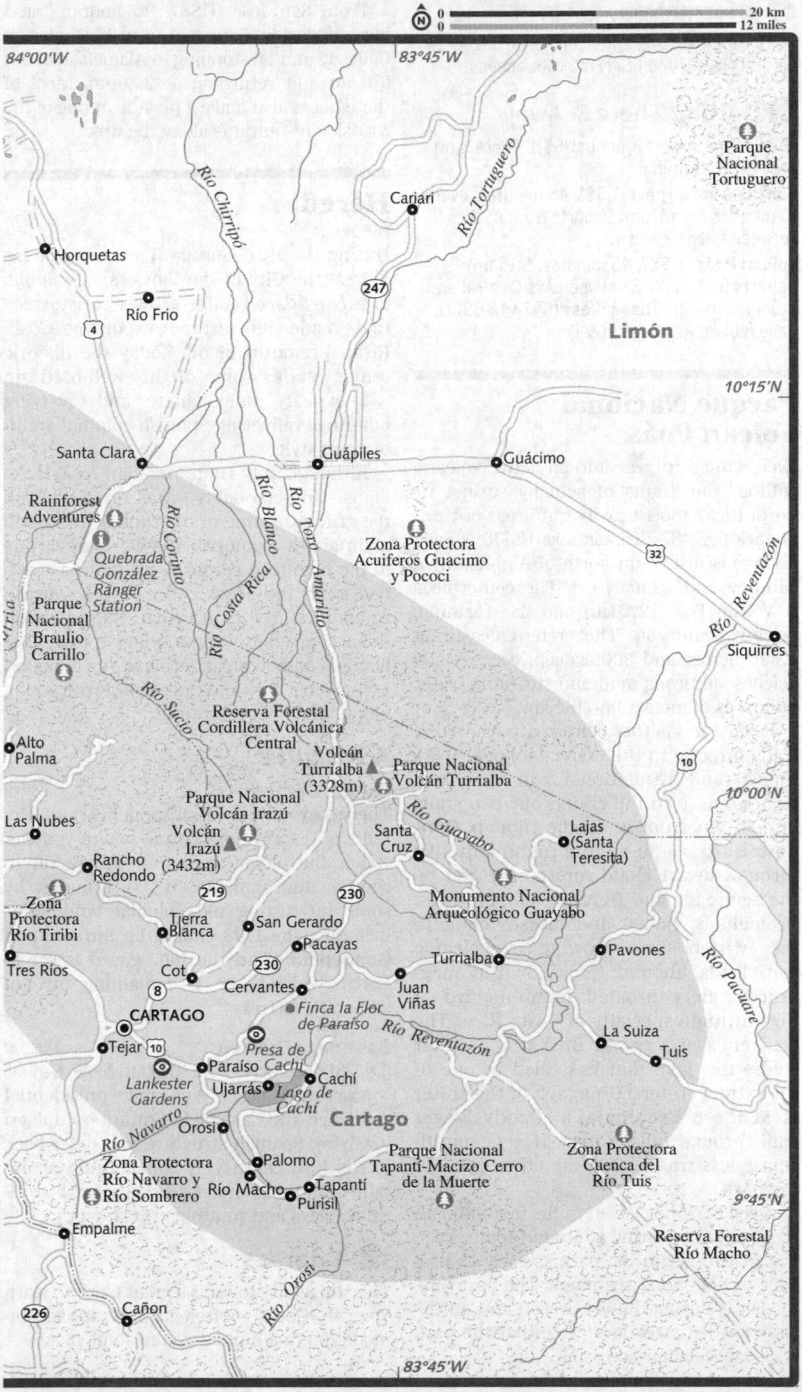
0 20 km
0 12 miles
84°00'W
83°45'W
Parque Nacional Tortuguero
Río Tortuguero
Cariari
Río Chirripó
Horquetas
Río Frio
247
4
Limón
10°15'N
Santa Clara
Guápiles
Guácimo
Rainforest Adventures
Quebrada González Ranger Station
Río Corinto
Río Blanco
Río Toro Amarillo
Zona Protectora Acuíferos Guacimo y Pococi
32
Río Reventazón
Parque Nacional Braulio Carrillo
Río Costa Rica
Siquirres
Río Sucio
Reserva Forestal Cordillera Volcánica Central
Alto Palma
Volcán Turrialba (3328m)
Parque Nacional Volcán Turrialba
10
10°00'N
Parque Nacional Volcán Irazú
Las Nubes
Volcán Irazú (3432m)
Río Guayabo
Santa Cruz
Lajas (Santa Teresita)
Rancho Redondo
219
230
Monumento Nacional Arqueológico Guayabo
Zona Protectora Río Tiribi
Tierra Blanca
San Gerardo
Pacayas
Turrialba
Pavones
Río Pacuare
Tres Ríos
Cot
230
8
Cervantes
Juan Viñas
CARTAGO
Finca la Flor de Paraíso
Río Reventazón
La Suiza
Tejar
10
Presa de Cachí
Tuis
Paraíso
Cachí
Lankester Gardens
Ujarrás
Lago de Cachí
Cartago
Río Navarro
Orosi
Zona Protectora Río Navarro y Río Sombrero
Palomo
Parque Nacional Tapantí-Macizo Cerro de la Muerte
Zona Protectora Cuenca del Río Tuis
Río Macho
Tapantí
Purisil
9°45'N
Empalme
Reserva Forestal Río Macho
Río Orosi
226
Cañon
83°45'W

Information

BYTE (2441-1142; 2nd fl, cnr Calle 3 & Av 1; per hr US$1; Mon-Sat) Internet access.

Getting There & Away

A taxi to the airport is about US$8. There is no central bus terminal.

San José via airport (US$1, 45 minutes, every 10 minutes 5am-11pm) Departs from Av 4 between Calles 2 and 4.

Volcán Poás (US$7, 45 minutes, 9:15am) Departs from Calle 8 between Avs Central and 1. Service run by **Tuasa West** (2442-6900; Calle 8 btwn Avs Central & 1).

Parque Nacional Volcán Poás

Ever wanted to peer into an active volcano without the drama of actually scaling it? Costa Rica's most heavily trafficked **national park** (2482-2165; admission US$10; 8am-3:30pm) is just 37km north of Alajuela by a winding and scenic road. The centerpiece is Volcán Poás (2704m) and its steaming, belching cauldron. The crater, measuring 1.3km across and 300m deep, occasionally belches sulfurous mud and steaming water hundreds of meters into the air.

From the visitors center, a paved road leads directly to the crater lookout. Toxic fumes (and regulations) will keep you from going into the crater, but two trails branch out from it. To the right is **Sendero Botos**, a 30-minute round-trip hike through dwarf cloud forest nurtured by the acidic air and freezing temperatures. Bromeliads, lichen and mosses cling to the twisted trees growing in volcanic soil. Birds abound; look for the magnificent fiery-throated hummingbird, a high-altitude specialty of Costa Rica. The trail ends at **Laguna Botos**, a peculiar cold-water lake that has filled in one of the extinct craters. Going left of the crater is **Sendero Escalonia**, a slightly longer trail through taller forest. It gets significantly less traffic than the other parts of the park.

A veil of clouds envelops the mountain almost daily, appearing at around 10am. Even if it's clear, get to the park as early as possible or you won't see much. The best time to visit is during the dry season and on the less-crowded weekdays. Note that the park is also wheelchair-accessible.

From San José (US$7, 1½ hours), Tuasa buses depart 8:30am daily from Av 2 between Calles 12 and 14, stopping in Alajuela at about 9:15am and returning at 2:30pm. Most of these buses also make a pit stop at one of the roadside restaurants along the way.

Heredia

POP 21,500

During the 19th century, La Ciudad de las Flores (the City of the Flowers) was home to a *cafetalero* (coffee grower) aristocracy that made its fortune exporting Costa Rica's premium blend. Today the historic center retains some of this well-bred air, with a leafy main square, and low-lying buildings reflecting Spanish-colonial architectural style.

Although only 11km from San José, Heredia is – in personality – well removed from the grit and grime of the capital. Yet it still maintains a cosmopolitan vibe – largely due to the high-tech corporations that have settled amid the area's coffee *fincas* (farms). In addition, the Universidad Nacional (National University) keeps things a touch bohemian, and on any afternoon, you're bound to find local bars and cafes abuzz with young folk idling away their time.

Sights

Parque Central PARK

The geographic and cultural heart of Heredia is the Parque Central, where you can watch the older generation square off in checker tournaments. It's surrounded by some interesting old colonial landmarks, including the 1798 church **La Inmaculada Concepción** and the 1867 guard tower **El Fortín**, which is the last remaining turret of a Spanish fortress.

Casa de la Cultura MUSEUM

(2261-4485; cnr Calle Central & Av Central; hours vary) FREE A former presidential residence, the Casa de la Cultura occupies a low-lying Spanish structure that dates back to the 18th century. It is beautifully maintained and now houses permanent historical displays and rotating art exhibits.

Courses

This university town is a great place to learn Spanish. Courses often incorporate accommodation in a homestay and some meals.

Centro Panamericano de Idiomas LANGUAGE COURSE
(☎2265 6306; www.cpi-edu.com; 5-day course with/without homestay US$525/375) Based in San Joaquín de la Flores, just outside Heredia. Price includes two meals per day.

Intercultura LANGUAGE COURSE
(☎2260-8480, in USA & Canada 866-978-6668; www.interculturacostarica.com; cnr Calle 10 & Av 4; 5-day course with/without homestay US$483/315) This Heredia school also arranges volunteer opportunities and offers cooking and dance classes. Language course prices include two meals per day.

Sleeping & Eating

Hotel Las Flores HOTEL $
(☎2261 8147; www.hotel-lasflores.com; Av 12 btwn Calles 12 & 14; s/d/tr US$16/30/42; P) At the southern end of town – and a bit of a walk from the action – this spotless family-run place has 29 rooms painted in citrus colors. The furnishings are basic, but the mattresses are thick, and all rooms have private bathrooms with hot water and TV sets.

Hotel América HOTEL $$
(☎2260-9292; www.hotelamericacr.com; Calle Central btwn Avs 2 & 4; s/d/tr incl breakfast US$60/70/80; @) Of the four hotels in this local chain, this is the best deal. It is centrally located just south of the church, and though unspectacular in design, it's clean and comfortable. Tile-floor rooms come equipped with cable TV, safe and fan.

Espigas COSTA RICAN $
(☎2237-3275; cnr Av 2 & Calle 2; breakfast US$7, mains US$4-8; ⏲7am-9pm) Espigas is the go-to cafe for delicious set breakfasts and filling lunches. Order sit-down meals at the counter, stop by the front window to pick up fresh *batidos* (fruit shakes) or pop in for a look at the tantalizing pastry case.

Vishnu Mango Verde VEGETARIAN $
(☎2237-2526; Calle 7 btwn Avs Central & 1; dishes US$3-7; ⏲8am-7pm Mon-Sat;) This branch of the San José chain is the top spot in town for vegetarian fare, including a wide array of colorful salads and cheap, gut-filling *casados*.

Cowboy Steakhouse STEAKHOUSE $$
(☎2237-8719; Calle 9 btwn Avs 3 & 5; dishes US$5-15; ⏲5-11pm Mon-Sat) This yellow-and-red joint has two bars, patio seating and the best cuts of beef in town.

Getting There & Away

There is no central bus terminal, and buses leave from bus stops scattered around the southern part of town.

Alajuela (US$1, 20 minutes, every 15 minutes, 6am to 10pm) Departs from the corner of Av Central and Calle 9.

San José (US$0.90, 20 minutes, every 20-30 minutes, 4:40am to 11pm) Departs from Av 8 between Calles Central and 1.

Parque Nacional Braulio Carrillo

Thick virgin forest, gushing waterfalls, swift rivers and deep canyons – it's hard to believe that you are only 30 minutes north of San José while walking around this under-explored national park. Braulio Carrillo's extraordinary biodiversity is attributed to its range in altitude, from Volcán Barva's misty cloud forest to the lush, humid lowlands reaching toward the Caribbean.

Founded in 1978, the park protects primary forest threatened when the highway between San José and Puerto Limón was built. Driving through it will give you an idea of what Costa Rica looked like prior to the 1950s – rushing rivers and rolling hills steeped in mountain rainforest.

Several rivers traverse the park: the Río Sucio (Dirty River), whose yellow waters carry volcanic minerals, and the crystal-clear Río Hondura. They intersect next to the main highway, and it's fascinating to see the contrast of colors. Volcán Barva is located at the southwestern corner of the park.

There have been reports of thefts from cars parked at entrances to the trails, as well as an armed robbery inside the park. Don't leave your car parked anywhere along the main highway. And as a general rule, you should always register at a ranger station before setting out on a hike.

Quebrada González Sector

The most popular hiking area is accessed at the northern end of the park at the **Quebrada González ranger station** (☎2261-2619; admission US$10; ⏲7am-4pm), 22km past the Zurquí tunnel to the east of the San José–Limón highway. From the ranger station, you can follow the 2.8km **Sendero La Botella** (about 90 minutes) past a series of waterfalls into Patria Canyon. The ranger station has a guarded parking lot, toilets and well-marked trails.

From San José, the bus to Guápiles (US$2, 50 minutes, departs hourly) departs from the Gran Terminal del Caribe. It can drop you off at the park entrance, but it's a 2km walk back along the highway to reach the restaurant where returning buses stop. Take precautions, as muggings have been reported along this stretch.

Barva Sector

Climbing Volcán Barva is a strenuous five-hour round trip along a well-maintained trail. Begin on the western side of the park at the **Barva Sector ranger station** (☎2266-1883; admission US$8; ⏲7am-4pm) near the village of Sacramento, north of Heredia. From the ranger station a signed track climbs to two lagoons at the volcano's summit, and several spur trails lead to waterfalls and other scenic spots along the way. Trails are often muddy, and you should be prepared for rain any time of the year.

Camping is allowed at basic **campsites** (per person US$3) near the ranger station; bring your own drinking water.

From Heredia (Calle 1, between Avs 4 and 6), take a bus to Paso Llano (US$1, two hours, three daily). From there, it's a 5km walk to Sacramento and then another 3km to the park entrance.

Rainforest Adventures

Sharing a border with the national park, this 1200-acre **private reserve** (☎2257-5961; www.rainforestadventure.com; Hwy 32, btwn San José & Guápiles) also shares much of the same ecology and the easy access from the capital. The park offers a variety of adventure tours that allow visitors to explore the rainforest, including the Rainforest Aerial Tram (adult/child US$60/30) that carries visitors to the heights of the forest canopy in a gondola. The 2.6km ride takes 40 minutes each way, affording unusual plant-spotting and bird-watching opportunities. Other activities include guided birding and hiking (US$128 to US$132), a zip-line canopy tour (adult/child US$50/35) and a butterfly and frog garden (US$10).

Hourly buses between San José and Guápiles can drop you at the refuge entrance. Alternatively, a Rainforest Adventures shuttle bus will pick you up at your hotel for US$30.

Cartago

POP 24,900

Peace rules Cartago, where the quiet of the central plaza is only broken by rogue pigeons and the shouts of the lottery lady. Once the colonial capital, Cartago's grandeur has been somewhat diminished by Mother Nature's rumblings. Still, it retains great religious significance and a certain conservative charm. For most visitors, Cartago is the spot to catch your breath, a peaceful modern city with attractions nearby.

Sights

Basílica de Nuestra Señora de Los Ángeles CHURCH

(cnr Av 2 & Calle 16) The most venerated religious site in the country, this basilica exudes airy Byzantine grace, with fine stained-glass windows, hand-painted interiors and ornate side chapels. Though the structure has changed many times since 1635, the relic that it protects – the revered La Negrita – remains unharmed inside.

Las Ruinas de la Parroquia RUIN

(Iglesia del Convento; cnr Av 2 & Calle 2) Las Ruinas de la Parroquia was built in 1575 as a shrine to St James the Apostle. After being destroyed by successive earthquakes in the 19th and 20th centuries, the shrine's shell has been left

DON'T MISS

LA NEGRITA

La Negrita (The Black Virgin) is a statuette of an indigenous Virgin Mary found on the spot where the Basílica de Nuestra Señora de Los Ángeles now stands by a native woman on August 2, 1635. As the story goes, when she tried to take the statuette with her, it miraculously reappeared back where she'd found it. Twice. So the townspeople built a shrine around her. In 1824, she was declared Costa Rica's patron Virgin. She now resides on a gold, jewel-studded platform at the main altar. Each August 2, on the anniversary of the statuette's miraculous discovery, pilgrims from every corner of the country (and beyond) walk the 22km from San José to the basilica in Cartago, many of them arriving on their knees.

as an evocative historical landmark. Nowadays, the walls contain a blooming garden.

Lankester Gardens BOTANICAL GARDEN
(☎2552-3247; www.jbl.ucr.ac.cr; adult/student US$7.50/5; ⏲8:30am-4:30pm) The University of Costa Rica runs the exceptional Lankester Gardens, started by a British orchid enthusiast. Orchids are the big drawcard, with 800 varieties at their showiest from February to April. A trail through the winding gardens passes through tropical forest filled with bromeliads, palms and heliconias. The gardens are 6km east of Cartago: take the bus bound for Paraíso and ask the driver to drop you off at the turnoff – from there, walk 750m to the entrance.

Festivals & Events

Costa Rican Independence Day HOLIDAY
With events all over the country, Costa Rica's Independance Day is a fun party. The center of the action is the relay race that passes a 'Freedom Torch' from Guatamala to Costa Rica. The torch arrives at Cartago in the evening of the 14th, when the nation breaks into the national anthem.

Sleeping & Eating

Los Ángeles Lodge B&B $$
(☎2591-4169, 2551-0957; Av 4 btwn Calles 14 & 16; s/d incl breakfast US$35/50; P ❄ 📶) With its balconies overlooking the Plaza de la Basílica, this decent B&B stands out with spacious and comfortable rooms, hot showers and breakfast made to order by the cheerful owners.

La Puerta del Sol COSTA RICAN $$
(☎2551-0615; Av 4 btwn Calles 14 & 16; mains US$6-10; ⏲8am-10pm Sun-Thu, 8am-midnight Fri & Sat) Located downstairs from Los Ángeles Lodge, this pleasant restaurant has been around since 1957 and serves myriad Tico specialties as well as burgers and sandwiches. Don't miss the vintage photos of Cartago displayed on the walls.

Getting There & Around

Most buses arrive along Av 2 and reach La Basílica de Nuestra Señora de los Ángeles before returning to the main terminal on Av 4.

Orosi (US$0.80, 40 minutes, hourly 5:30am to 10pm Mon-Sat) Departs corner Calle 4 and Av 1.

Paraíso and Lankester Gardens (US$0.50, 40 minutes, hourly 7am to 10pm) Corner Calle 4 and Av 1.

San José (US$1, 45 minutes, every 5 minutes) Corner Calle 2 and Av 6, north of Parque Central.

Turrialba (US$1.40, 1½ hours, every 45 minutes weekdays, five daily Sat & Sun) Av 3 between Calles 8 and 1, in front of Tribunales de Justicia.

Río Orosi Valley

Resplendent mountain vistas, crumbling churches and lazy hot springs define the appeal of this valley of coffee plantations southeast of Cartago.

Beyond Paraíso, head south 8km to the pleasant village of **Orosi**, named after a 16th-century Huetar chief. From Orosi, a loop road heads north and parallels the Río Orosi before swinging around the artificial **Lago de Cachí**. After the village of Ujarrás, the road continues for a few more kilometers before looping back to **Paraíso**.

Public transportation is scarce in the valley, but there are infrequent minibuses connecting the villages for a couple of hundred colones per ride.

Sights & Activities

Iglesia de San José Orosi CHURCH
Orosi is one of the few colonial-era towns to survive Costa Rica's frequent earthquakes, which have thankfully spared the photogenic village church. Built in 1743, it is the oldest religious site still in use in Costa Rica.

Parque Nacional Tapantí-Macizo Cerro de la Muerte PARK
(admission US$10; ⏲8am-4pm) This 580-sq-km national park has a rainy claim to fame: it is the wettest park in the country, getting almost 8000mm of precipitation a year. Dense woods, waterfalls and over 200 bird species flourish in this lush, rugged terrain. The entrance to Tapantí is about 3km south of Purisil.

Hot Springs SWIMMING
Being in a volcanic region also means Orosi has the perks of thermal springs. Though not on the scale of the steaming-hot waters found near Fortuna, Orosi does offer a couple of nice modest pools with warm water. **Los Balnearios** (☎2533-2156; admission US$3.60; ⏲7:30am-4pm Wed-Mon), 25m from Orosi Lodge, has several pools, right in town. **Los Patios** (☎2533-3009; admission US$4; ⏲8am-4pm Tue-Sun) is a larger complex with a few more pools, 1.5km south of Orosi.

Aventuras Orosi RAFTING
(☎2533-4000; www.aventurasorosicr.com; Motel Río; tours US$75; ⏲9am-4pm) Operated by the charming Luis, this small outfit on the north side of the hanging bridge offers local rafting expeditions and waterfall-drenched canopy tours. Prices include transportation from San Jose.

Sleeping & Eating

Montaña Linda HOSTEL $
(☎2533-3640; www.montanalinda.com; dm US$8.50, d US$30, s/d/tr without bathroom US$15/22/30, guesthouse s/d with bathroom US$30/35; P@) Southwest of the bus stop is this great, chilled-out hostel, with tidy dorms and brightly accented private rooms surrounding a homey terrace. This place also operates one of the most affordable Spanish-language schools in the country.

★Orosi Lodge INN $$
(☎2533-3578; www.orosilodge.com; d/tr US$66/77, d chalet US$107; P) Wake up and smell the coffee! This quiet haven, run by a friendly German couple, has eight bright rooms with wood-beam ceilings and tile floors (each equipped with coffeemaker and free organic coffee). Delicious, wholesome breakfasts and homemade pastries are worth a stop even if you are not staying here. It's located south of the park, near the entrance to Los Balnearios.

Parque Nacional Volcán Irazú

Named Thunderpoint *(ara-tzu)* by indigenous people, the large and looming Irazú is Costa Rica's tallest (3432m) active volcano. One of the most memorable eruptions was on March 19, 1963, welcoming the visiting US President John F Kennedy by throwing a blanket of hot volcanic ash over most of the Central Valley. In recent years, activity has dissipated to a few hissing fumaroles and tremors.

You'll find a small **visitors center** (☎2551-9398, 2200-5025; park admission US$10; ⏲8am-3:30pm) and a basic cafe, but no accommodations or camping facilities. A paved road reaches the summit. From the parking lot, a 1km-long trail leads to a lookout over the bare landscape of craters and ash. When the clouds clear there are amazing views of the Pacific and Caribbean, but most days you have to use your imagination.

The park is 19km north of Cartago. Most visitors arrive with an organized tour or private transportation. The only public transportation to Irazú departs from San José (US$6) from Av 2 (between Calles 1 and 3) at 8am, stops in Cartago to pick up passengers at about 8:30am and arrives at the summit around 10am. The return bus departs from Irazú at 12:30pm.

Turrialba

POP 31,100

In the vicinity of Turrialba, at an elevation of 650m above sea level, the Río Reventazón gouges a mountain pass through the Cordillera Central. In the 1880s this geological quirk allowed the 'Jungle Train' to roll through, and the mountain village of Turrialba grew prosperous from the coffee trade. Things changed at the end of the next century, when the straight, smooth Hwy 32 was built to bypass the town, and an earthquake shut down the railway for good. Suddenly, Turrialba found itself off the beaten path.

Nowadays, that's what makes this mellow town so appealing. The area is renowned for its mountain air, strong coffee and Central America's best white-water rafting.

Sights

Catie GARDENS
(Centro Agronómico Tropical de Investigación; Center for Tropical Agronomy Research & Education; ☎2556-2700; www.catie.ac.cr/jardinbotanico; admission US$10, guided tours US$25-50; ⏲7am-4pm Mon-Fri, 8am-4pm Sat & Sun) Catie, 3km east of Turrialba, consists of 1000 hectares dedicated to tropical agricultural research and education. Agronomists from all over the world recognize this as one of the most important centers in the tropics. You need to make reservations for one of several guided tours through laboratories, greenhouses, a seed bank, experimental plots and one of the most extensive libraries of tropical agriculture literature in the world. Alternatively, pick up a map and take a self-guided walk.

Activities

Rafting is the main draw, but the area is also prime for birding, mountain biking, kayaking and canyoning. Expect to pay anywhere from US$80 to US$120 for a daytrip. These companies also offer tours to the local volcanoes, coffee plantations and pre-Columbian ruins.

Explornatura RAFTING
(☎2556-2070, in USA & Canada 866-571-2443; www.explornatura.com; Av 4 btwn Calles 2 & 4)

Río Locos RAFTING
(☎2556-6035; www.whiteh2o.com)

Tico's River Adventures RAFTING
(☎2556-1231; www.ticoriver.com)

Sleeping

★Casa de Lis Hostel HOSTEL $
(☎2556-4933; www.hostelcasadelis.com; Av Central near Calle 2; dm US$10, d/tr/q US$40/45/50, without bathroom US$25/35/40; 📶) Just what Turrialba needed – a bright hostel right in the center of town. This sweet four-room place is spotless, with a fully equipped kitchen, a small garden and a roof terrace for enjoying volcano views. Inexpensive breakfasts (topping out at US$4) and laundry service are available.

Hotel Interamericano HOTEL $
(☎2556-0142; www.hotelinteramericano.com; Av 1 near Calle 1; s/d/tr US$25/35/45, without bathroom US$15/20/30; P 📶) On the south side of the old train tracks is this simple 22-room hotel, regarded as *the* meeting place in Turrialba by rafters. The showers are immaculate (and hot!), the tiled rooms are bright and the 2nd-story lounge is an ideal spot to sip beer and share adventure stories. The staff here is a great source of local information.

WHITE-WATER RAFTING IN THE TURRIALBA AREA

There are two major rivers in the Turrialba area that are popular for rafting – the Río Reventazón and the Río Pacuare. The following is a quick guide to the ins and outs (and ups and downs) of each.

Río Reventazón

This storied rock-lined river has its beginnings at the Lago de Cachí, an artificial lake created by a dam of the same name. From there, 1000m above sea level, it splashes down the eastern slopes of the cordilleras to the Caribbean lowlands. It is one of the most difficult, adrenaline-pumping runs in the country – and with more than 65km of rapids, you can get as hard core as you like.

Tour operators divide the river into four sections between the dam and the take-out point in Siquirres. **Las Máquinas** (Power House) is a Class II-III float that's perfect for families, while **Florida**, the final and most popular segment, is a scenic Class III with a little more white water to keep things interesting. The **Pascua** section has 15 Class IV rapids – featuring names like 'The Abyss' – and is considered to be the classic run. The Class V **Peralta** segment is the most challenging; tours do not always run it due to safety concerns.

Water levels stay fairly constant year-round because of releases from the dam. There are no releases on Sunday, however, and although the river is runnable, it's generally considered the worst day.

Río Pacuare

The Río Pacuare is the next major river valley east of the Reventazón, and has arguably the most scenic rafting in Costa Rica, if not Central America. The river plunges down the Caribbean slope through a series of spectacular canyons clothed in virgin rainforest, through runs named for their fury and separated by calm stretches that enable you to stare at near-vertical green walls towering hundreds of meters above.

The Class III-IV **Lower Pacuare** is the more accessible run: 28km through rocky gorges and isolated canyons, past an indigenous village, untamed jungle and lots of wildlife curious as to what the screaming is all about. The **Upper Pacuare** is also classified as Class III-IV, but there are a few sections that can go to Class V depending on conditions. It's about a two-hour drive to the put-in, though it's worth it – you'll have the prettiest jungle cruise on earth all to yourself.

The Pacuare can be run year-round, though June to October are considered the best months. The highest water is from October to December, when the river runs fast with huge waves. March and April is when the river is at its lowest, though it is still challenging.

Turrialba B&B B&B $$
(☎386-246-2184; www.turrialbabedandbreakfast.com; Calle 1 north of Av 6; s/d/tr US$40/60/80; ❄📶) This charming and tranquil spot has clean, bright, well-appointed rooms, a cozy living-room and a lovely garden patio hung with hammocks. The on-site library is chock full of travel guides. Breakfast (not included) is highly recommended.

Eating

Panadería La Castellana BAKERY $
(☎2556-9090; www.lacastellanacr.com; cnr Calle 2 & Av 4; breakfast US$2.50-5, pizza US$8-13; ⏲24hr) Whether it's pizza by the slice, *gallo pinto* (a common meal of blended rice and beans) and eggs, or coffee and a pastry, La Castellana does it well and at all hours. It even offers half-orders for smaller appetites. Dine in, or pick up some whole-wheat bread or desserts for eats on the road.

Restaurant Betico Mata BARBECUE $
(☎2556-8640; Hwy 10; gallos US$2; ⏲ 11am-midnight, to later Sat & Sun) This carnivore's paradise at the south end of town specializes in *gallos* (open-faced tacos on corn tortillas) piled with succulent, fresh-grilled meats, including beef, chicken, sausage or pork, all soaked in the special house marinade. Recommended accompaniment: ice-cold beer.

La Feria COSTA RICAN
(☎2556-5550; Calle 6 north of Av 4; casados US$5, mains US$4-11; ⏲11am-10pm Wed-Mon, 11am-2pm Tue; ✎) This unremarkable-looking spot has friendly service and excellent, inexpensive home cooking.

Information

There's no official tourist office, but most hotels and rafting outfits can organize tours, accommodations and transportation throughout the region.

Banco de Costa Rica (cnr Av Central & Calle 3; ⏲9am-4pm Mon-Fri) Has a 24-hour ATM.

Cafe Internet (☎2556-4575; cnr Av 2 & Calle 4; per hr US$0.80; ⏲8am-8pm)

Getting There & Away

Buses depart from the modern terminal at the western edge of town off Hwy 10.

Monumento Nacional Arqueológico Guayabo (US$1; 1hr; 4 Mon-Sat, 2 Sun)

San José (US$2.75, 2 hour, every 30 to 60 minutes 5am-6:30pm) Via Paraíso and Cartago.

Siquirres (US$2.25, 1¾ hour, six daily) For transfer to Puerto Limón.

CARIBBEAN COAST

The Caribbean coast's rain-drenched, malarial wildness thwarted the first 16th-century Spaniards who settled here, and subsequently isolated this region for centuries. Thus, the Caribbean culture – influenced by indigenous peoples and West Indian immigrants – is distinct from the rest of Costa Rica. You'll taste the difference in the *rondón*

WORTH A TRIP

MONUMENTO NACIONAL ARQUEOLÓGICO GUAYABO

Guayabo is the largest and most important **archaeological site** (☎2559-1220; admission US$6; ⏲8am-3:30pm) in Costa Rica. Only 19km north of Turrialba, this area was occupied as early as 1000 BC, its peak population reaching around 10,000. It featured paved streets, an aqueduct and decorative gold. Archaeologists are unsure of the site's exact significance: it is thought to be an ancient ceremonial center. The site was abandoned around AD 1400, though the exact reason is unknown.

Although Guayabo is not nearly as impressive as Mayan and Aztec archaeological sites in northern Central America, excavations have unearthed sophisticated infrastructure and mysterious petroglyphs. The still-functioning **aqueduct** is considered the most impressive find (especially considering some of the plumbing in modern-day coastal towns). There's an information and **exhibit center**, but many of the best pieces are displayed at the Museo Nacional in San José.

Aside from the historical significance, Guayabo is also an excellent spot for **birding**, thanks to the open areas. Camping (per person US$5) is permitted, and services include latrines and running water.

Buses (US$1, one hour) from Turrialba depart three times a day. Unless you are spending the night, the only practical option is at 11:15am Monday through Saturday or 9am on Sunday. The return is at 12:30pm or 4pm.

(spicy seafood gumbo), hear it in the lilt of patois and see it on the uncrowded stretches of black-sand beaches.

Tortuguero

Located within the confines of Parque Nacional Tortuguero, accessible only by air or water, this bustling little village with strong Afro-Caribbean roots is best known for attracting hordes of sea turtles (the name Tortuguero means 'turtle place') – and the hordes of tourists who want to see them. While the peak turtle season is in July and August, the park and village attract travelers year-round, thanks to the lush canals that are swarming with birds, monkeys, manatees, sloths and crocs.

Sights & Activities

Parque Nacional Tortuguero PARK

This misty, green coastal park sits on a broad flood plain parted by a jigsaw of canals. Referred to as the 'mini-Amazon', Parque Nacional Tortuguero's intense biodiversity includes over 400 bird species, 60 species of frogs, 30 species of freshwater fish and three species of monkey, as well as the threatened West Indian manatee. Caimans and crocodiles can be seen lounging on river banks, while freshwater turtles bask on logs.

Over 50,000 visitors a year come to boat the canals and see the wildlife, particularly to watch turtles lay eggs. This is the most important Caribbean breeding site of the green sea turtle, 40,000 of which arrive every season to nest. Leatherback, loggerhead and hawksbill turtles also nest here. Various volunteer organizations address the problem of poaching with vigilant turtle patrols.

Park headquarters is at **Cuatro Esquinas** (☎2709-8086; park admission US$10; ⏲5:30am-6pm with breaks for breakfast & lunch), just north of Tortuguero village.

Sharks and strong currents make the beaches unsuitable for swimming.

Boating & Canoeing

The best way to see the park (and its inhabitants) is to take a boat tour (p558) of the canals.

Four aquatic trails wind their way through the Parque Nacional Tortuguero. The **Río Tortuguero** acts as the entrance way to the network of trails. This wide, still river is often covered with water lilies and frequented by aquatic birds such as herons and kingfishers, as well as peacocks.

> **SSSHHH!**
>
> For optimum wildlife-spotting around Tortuguero, forego the noisy motors. Opt for a guided tour of the canals by canoe or in Daryl Loth's super-silent electric motorboat (p558).

The **Caño Chiquero** is a waterway thick with vegetation, especially artichoke trees and red guacimo trees. Black turtles and green iguanas hang out here. Caño Chiquero leads to the narrow **Caño Mora** and **Caño Harold**, popular with Jesus Christ lizards and caimans.

Hiking

Behind Cuatro Esquinas station, **El Gavilan Land Trail** is the park's only public trail. The muddy, 2km-long loop traverses tropical humid forest and follows a stretch of beach. Green parrots and several species of monkeys are commonly sighted here. It is well-marked and does not require a guide.

Turtle-Watching

Visitors are allowed to check out the green-turtle rookeries at night from March to October (late July through August is prime time) and observe eggs being laid or hatching. Obviously, turtle sightings are not guaranteed. But if you're lucky, it is truly amazing and awe-inspiring to see a 180kg turtle haul itself up onto the beach, dig a nest, lay 120 eggs the size of table-tennis balls and scoot back to sea, exhausted.

A guide must accompany all visitors. Camera flashes and flashlights are prohibited by law, as they disturb the egg-laying process.

If you're unable to visit during the peak green turtle breeding season, the next best time is between February and July, when leatherback turtles nest in small numbers (especially from mid-April to mid-May). Hawksbill turtles nest sporadically from March to October, and loggerhead turtles are also sometimes seen. Tours cost US$20 (a flat rate established by the village), which includes the purchase of a US$4 sticker that pays for the patrols that help protect the nesting sites from scavengers and looters.

Tours

Signs all over town advertise guide services for canal tours and turtle walks. Going rates are about US$20 per person for a two or three-hour tour.

Castor Hunter Thomas BOAT TOUR
(☎8870-8634; castorhunter.blogspot.com; Soda Doña María) A local who has worked as a guide for more than 20 years leads turtle tours (in season), guided hikes and wonderful canoe tours.

Daryl Loth BOAT TOUR
(☎8833-0827, 2709-8011; safari@racsa.co.cr) A personable Canadian-born naturalist (formerly of Coterc) offers excellent boat trips in a super-silent electric motorboat, as well as turtle tours (in season) and guided hikes.

Tinamon Tours BOAT TOUR
(☎2709-8004, 8842-6561; www.tinamontours.de) Barbara Hartung offers hiking, canoe and turtle tours in German, English, French or Spanish. Also offers a unique tour about Tortuguero history, culture and medicinal plants.

Sleeping

El Icaco HOTEL $
(☎2709-8044; www.hotelelicaco.com; s/d/tr/q incl breakfast US$25/35/50/60;) This simple oceanfront lodging offers clean, brightly painted rooms and friendly service. The beachfront location is ideal, and there are plenty of hammocks from which to enjoy it. Reserve your room in advance and somebody will meet you upon arrival at the boat dock.

Cabinas Balcon del Mar CABINA $
(☎2709-8124, 2767-7412; per person US$8-12) This beachfront option is super quiet, thanks to its prime location on the edge of town and next to the national park. Perks include comfortable beds, hot-water showers, clean communal kitchen and lots of hammocks.

La Casona CABINA $
(☎2709-8047, 2709-8092; s/d US$18/25, d with kitchenette US$35;) Ten painted cement rooms with rustic touches surround a garden at this family-run spot on the north side of the soccer field. Three units have kitchenettes with hot plates. In addition, Jenny and her sons offer canoe rental, as well as canoe tours to a local farm on Caño Harold.

Cabinas Tortuguero CABINA $
(☎2709-8114, 8622-8137; cabinas_tortuguero@yahoo.com; s/d without bathroom US$10/16, s/d/tr US$20/25/30) Across from the food shop Tienda Bambú, you'll find 11 brightly painted bungalows surrounding a tidy garden at this popular budget spot. Rooms are clean and there are hammocks for lounging.

Cabinas Miss Miriam II CABINA $
(☎2709-8107, 8873-2671; s/d US$20/30;) This beach-side branch of Miss Miriam's budget *cabinas* has clean tiled rooms, firm mattresses and hot water. Rooms surround a small garden courtyard, and there's an on-site *soda* and free wi-fi. It's south of the soccer field, 25m east of the Adventist church.

★Casa Marbella B&B $$
(☎8833-0827, 2709-8011; casamarbella.tripod.com; s US$35-60, d US$40-65, extra person US$10, all incl breakfast;) This charming B&B opposite the Catholic church manages to be wonderfully serene while also being in the middle of it all. Ten simple whitewashed rooms have good lighting and ceiling fans, as well as super-clean bathrooms with electric showers. Hearty breakfasts (think fresh pancakes with tropical fruit) are served on an outdoor deck with views of the canal.

Hotel Miss Junie CABINA $$
(☎2709-8102; www.iguanaverdetours.com; s/d standard US$45/50, superior US$55/60, all incl breakfast) Miss Junie's place is set on wide grounds, shaded by palm trees and strewn with hammocks and wooden armchairs. Spotless, wood-paneled rooms in a nicely kept tropical plantation–style building are tastefully (if minimally) decorated with wood accents and bright bedspreads. Upstairs rooms share a breezy balcony overlooking the canal. Credit cards accepted. It's at the northern end of the main road.

La Baula Lodge LODGE $$
(☎2709-8041, 8951-8951; www.labaulalodge.com; s/d/tr US$40/70/75, all incl breakfast;) This laid-back, long-running lodge has rustic *cabinas*, painted in bright Caribbean colors. Wood-panelled rooms have hot water, ceiling fans and garden views. There's an on-site restaurant, which often hosts live music. It's north of the village (accessible by boat), so be sure to ask the boat driver to drop you there.

Eating

Budda Cafe EUROPEAN $
(pizzas US$7-9, dishes US$7-18; ⏲11am-9pm; ✉) This riverside spot keeps a hipster vibe with ambient club music on the sound system and Buddhist 'om' symbols stenciled onto just about everything. It's a lovely place, with excellent pizzas, rich coffee and scumptious crepes (both savory and sweet).

Soda Doña María COSTA RICAN $
(☎8870-8634; dishes US$3-6; ⏲7am-8pm) Recover from a hike in the park at this riverside *soda*, serving fresh *jugos* (juices), burgers and tasty fish *casados*. It's about 200m north of the park entrance.

La Casona ITALIAN $
(casados US$6, mains US$6-12; ⏲7:30-11am & 1:30-8:30pm; ✉) La Casona offers a variety of Italian specialties, including a well-rendered lasagna made with hearts of palm. On the northern edge of the soccer field.

Miss Miriam's CARIBBEAN $$
(mains US$4-16; ⏲8am-8pm) This little place dishes out huge plates of flavorful local food, like its well-spiced Caribbean chicken. The extensive menu is displayed above the kitchen (ask for prices). It's on the northern side of the soccer field.

Wild Ginger FUSION $$
(mains US$10-30; ⏲noon-9pm) This beachfront standout is a fantastic addition to village

GETTING TO TORTUGUERO INDEPENDENTLY

If you want to get to Tortuguero independently, it can be done. Here is what to do:

From San José to Cariari

Take a morning bus from San José's Gran Terminal del Caribe to Cariari (US$3.25, two hours, 6:30am, 9am or 10:30am). In Cariari, you will arrive at a bus station at the south end of town (known as the *estación nueva*). From here, you can walk or take a taxi 500m north to the *estación vieja* (old station), otherwise referred to as the Terminal Caribeño.

Public Transportation from Cariari

The cheapest option is by public transportation on **Clic Clic** (☎2709-8155, 8844-0463) or **Coopetraca** (☎2767-7590), both of which charge US$5 per person for the bus-boat service from the *estación vieja* all the way to Tortuguero. For these two options, the bus service will be the same, but the boat service will be different. Buses depart Cariari at 6am, 11:30am and 3pm.

If you choose Clic Clic, buy only the bus ticket to La Pavona (US$2); if you choose Coopetraca, you'll buy the combined bus-boat ticket (US$5) up front. After a ride through banana plantations, you will arrive at the Río Suerte, where a number of boat companies will be waiting at the dock. (Get ready to be solicited.) If you're riding with Clic Clic, you will pay the remainder of your fare (US$3) to the boatman. Boats depart daily at 7:30am, 1pm and 4:30pm. These companies will take you to the public boat dock in Tortuguero.

Private Transportation from Cariari

For less complicated, more expensive private service, there is Viajes Bananero, which has an office inside the San José bus terminal in Cariari. Buy your boat ticket here (US$10 per person). From this same point, you will then take a bus (US$1.20 per person) to its proprietary boat dock. Bus departure times are at 11:30am and 2pm. Pay the driver directly; take small change. The trip ends at the company's private dock on the southern edge of Tortuguero.

Private Transportation from Moín

Theoretically, the Asociasión de Boteros de los Canales de Tortuguero (p561) operates a regular service from Moín (near Puerto Limón) to Tortuguero, every day at 10am. This is primarily a tourist route, however, so the service is not super reliable, especially in the low season. **Tropical Wind** (☎2798-6059, 8327-0317, 8313-7164; per person 1-way US$30) and **Viajes Bananero** (☎2709-8005; per person 1-way US$35) are two Tortuguero-based agencies that make the run regularly.

dining options. Well-balanced fusion cuisine utilizes fresh ingredients and includes such specialties as filet mignon with tamarind sauce, crispy golden shrimp and a highly recommended Wild Ginger burger. Leave room for dessert. It's 150m north of the elementary school.

Information

There are no banks or ATMs in town and only a few businesses accept credit cards, so bring all the cash you'll need. Internet connections can be iffy.

Beyetty Internet (Cabinas Beyetty; per hr US$4; 8:30am-9pm) Two vintage machines and a friendly proprietor.

Tortuguero Info Center (2709-8055; tortuguero_info@racsa.co.cr; internet per hr US$4; 8am-7pm) Independent information center that sells Sansa airline tickets and provides internet access; may be closed in slower seasons. It's across from the Catholic church.

Tortuguero Village (www.tortuguerovillage.com) A solid source of information, listing local businesses and providing comprehensive directions on how to get to Tortuguero.

Getting There & Away

It's not hard to get here on your own (see box, p559). However, if you don't care to go it alone, these package tours can take care of everything from the moment your plane lands in San José. Costs vary widely depending on accommodations and transportation.

Exploradores Outdoors (2222-6262; www.exploradoresoutdoors.com)

Jungle Tom Safaris (2221-7878; www.jungletomsafaris.com) Offers recommended one-day (US$92), overnight (from US$120) and two-night packages (from US$152) or just round-trip transportation (US$45) – useful for independent travelers who want to be free upon arrival.

Riverboat Francesca Nature Tours (2226-0986; www.tortuguerocanals.com)

Puerto Limón

POP 58,500

The biggest city on Costa Rica's Caribbean coast, the birthplace of United Fruit and the capital of Limón Province, this ragged city sits removed from the rest of the country. Around here, business is measured by truckloads of fruit, not busloads of tourists.

Limón has not aged gracefully. It is a grid of dilapidated buildings, overgrown parks and sidewalks choked with street vendors. Crime is a problem (though tourists are not usually targeted). Most travelers zip through on their way to points north or south, but Limón can be a compelling destination for adventurous urban explorers.

Sights & Activities

Parque Vargas PARK

The city's main attraction is the waterfront Parque Vargas, an incongruous expanse of bench-lined sidewalks beneath a lost little jungle of tall palms and tropical flowers, centered on a crumbling bandstand. From here, you can head inland along Av 2, the **pedestrian mall** that caters to the cruise-ship traffic.

From the park, it's also a pleasant walk north along the **sea wall**, where views of the rocky headland are set to steady crashing of waves against the concrete jetty. After dark this is a popular mugging and make-out spot.

Playa Bonita BEACH

Limón itself has no beach, but Playa Bonita, 4km northwest of town, is a pleasant, sandy beach that's good for swimming. Surfers head there for its point/reef break, which makes for a powerful (and sometimes dangerous) left. Any Limón–Moín bus will drop you there.

Sleeping

Budget hotels in Limón are pretty gloomy: ask to see a room and check security before committing.

Hotel Miami HOTEL $

(2758-0490; hmiamilimon@yahoo.com; Av 2 btwn Calles 4 & 5; s/d US$26/35, with air-con US$35/48; P ❄ @) For its location on the main drag, this clean, mint-green place feels surprisingly serene, especially in the rooms in back. All 34 tidy rooms are equipped with cable TV and fan. Rooms with air-conditioning have hot water. Welcoming staff, common balconies overlooking the street and secure setup add up to the best value in town.

Oasys del Caribe BUNGALOW $

(2795-0024; oasysdelcaribe@ice.co.cr; s/d/f US$35/40/60, without air-con US$30/35/50; P ❄) If you're not excited about staying in Limón, head about 3km north on the way to Playa Bonita and Moín (convenient if you're departing to Tortuguero). These cozy pink bungalows surround a small pool, which is a perk, as there is no beach access. There are a few pricer options on the ocean.

Hotel Palace HOTEL $
(☎2758-1068; 2nd fl, Calle 2 btwn Avs 2 & 3; d US$20) For seasoned budget travelers, this woman-owned place is a reasonably safe though dilapidated choice. The six rooms surround an interior courtyard and have built-in cold-water bathrooms in a cubicle in the corner.

Park Hotel HOTEL $$
(☎2798-0555; www.parkhotellimon.com; Av 3 btwn Calles 1 & 2; s/d standard US$52/72, superior US$58/82, deluxe US$70/98; P ❄ ❄ @) Downtown Limón's most attractive hotel has 32 rooms in a peach-colored building that faces the ocean. Tiled rooms are tidy and sport clean bathrooms with hot water. There's also a semi-swanky restaurant on site. Credit cards accepted.

Eating

★Caribbean Kalisi Coffee Shop CARIBBEAN $
(☎2758-3249; Calle 6 btwn Avs 3 & 4; mains from US$5; ⏲7:30am-7:30pm Mon-Fri, 8am-7:30pm Sat, 8am-5pm Sun) Belly up to the cafeteria-style counter at this friendly family spot and cobble together a plate of coconut rice, red beans and whatever's cooking that day – typically a wide variety of fabulous Caribbean meat and veggie dishes.

Fruit & Veggie Land VEGETARIAN $
(☎2758-4142; Calle 7 btwn Avs 2 & 3; smoothies from US$2; ⏲8am-8pm; ✎) This great breakfast or lunch spot squeezes fresh fruit and blends it into smoothies of every color and flavor.

Taquería y Antojería Yenori MEXICAN $
(☎2758-8294; Calle 7 btwn Avs 3 & 4; mains US$4-10; ⏲9am-9pm) This cute little Mexican spot serves tacos (US$1.20) and *casados* (US$4). You have to ring the bell to get buzzed in, where you'll find clean tables, chilled soda and a blaring air-con unit.

Central Market MARKET
(Av 2 btwn Calles 3 & 4; ⏲6am-8pm Mon-Sat) For the cheapest budget eats, hit the central market, which has several *sodas* and plenty of groceries.

Information

If traveling onward to Tortuguero, Limón will be your last opportunity to get cash.

Banco de Costa Rica (☎2758-3166; cnr Av 2 & Calle 1)

Hospital Tony Facio (☎2758-2222) On the coast at the northern end of town; serves the entire province.

Scotiabank (cnr Av 3 & Calle 2; ⏲9am-5pm Mon-Fri, 9am-1pm Sat)

DANGERS & ANNOYANCES

Theft is a problem: take precautions against pickpockets during the day, particularly in the market and along the sea wall. In addition, people do get mugged here, so stick to well-lit main streets at night.

Getting There & Away

BOAT

Boats to Tortuguero depart from the main transportation dock, which is 7km north of town in Moín. If you're feeling lucky, you can just show up in Moín in the morning and try to get on one of the outgoing tour boats. But you are better off reserving in advance, particularly during slower seasons when boats don't travel the route on a daily basis. Fares to Tortuguero generally cost US$35 to US$40 one way.

Asociación de Boteros de los Canales de Tortuguero (Abacat; ☎8360-7325) Regular service to Tortuguero, normally departing Moín at 10am.

Tortuguero Wildlife Tours & Transportation (William Guerrero, TUCA; ☎2798-7027, 8371-2323; www.tortuguero-wildlife.com) This operation is run by master sloth-spotter William Guerrero and his wife; ideal for leisurely rides to Tortuguero.

Tropical Wind (☎8327-0317, 8313-7164, 2798-6059) Almost-daily shuttles in high season.

Viajes Bananero (☎8833-1066, in San José 2222-8973) Regular (though not daily) trips to Tortuguero.

BUS

Buses to and from San José, Guápiles and Moín arrive at **Terminal Caribeño** (Av 2 btwn Calles 7 & 8) on the west side of the baseball stadium. Buses to points south all depart from **Autotransportes Mepe Terminal** (☎2758-1572; Calle 6 btwn Avs 1 & 2), on the east side of the stadium.

Guápiles (US$4, 2 hour; hourly 5am to 6pm) For transfer to Turrialba.

Moín (US$0.60, 20 minutes, hourly 5:30am to 6:30pm) For boats to Tortuguero.

Puerto Viejo de Talamanca (US$3.20; 1½hr; hrly 5am-7pm) Via Cahuita.

San José (US$5.50, 3 hour, hourly 5am to 7pm)

Cahuita

POP 600

Even as tourism has mushroomed on Costa Rica's southern coast, Cahuita has managed to hold onto its laid-back Caribbean vibe. The roads are made of dirt, many of the older houses rest on stilts and chatty neighbors still converse in Mekatelyu. A graceful black-sand beach and a chilled-out demeanor hint at a not-so-distant past, when the area was little more than just a string of cocoa farms.

Cahuita proudly claims the area's first permanent Afro-Caribbean settler – a turtle fisherman named William Smith, who moved his family to Punta Cahuita in 1828. Now his descendants, along with the descendants of so many other West Indian immigrants, run the tasty backyard eateries and brightly painted bungalows that hug this idyllic stretch of coast.

Sights & Activities

★Parque Nacional Cahuita PARK

Among the country's most visited parks, Parque Nacional Cahuita is small but beautiful. Humidity nurtures a dense tropical foliage of coconut palms, mango trees and sea grapes. The forest skirts white sandy beaches on a tranquil bay. Easy to access, it attracts scads of visitors who loll in the mild surf, scan the trails for sloths and monkeys and snorkel the coral reef. (Note that snorkeling is permitted only with a licensed guide.)

At the east end of Cahuita, **Kelly Creek Ranger Station** (☎2755-0461; admission by donation; ⏲6am-5pm) sits next to Playa Blanca stretching 2km east. Signs for the first 500m warn not to swim, but beyond this point the waves are gentle. After the rocky Punta Cahuita you'll find Vargas Beach and **Puerto Vargas Ranger Station** (☎2755-0302; admission US$10; ⏲8am-4pm Mon-Fri, 7am-5pm Sat & Sun). An easily navigable 7km-long coastal trail leads through the jungle from Kelly Creek to Puerto Vargas. Beware, Río Perezoso, near the end of the first beach, can be thigh-deep at high tide or dangerous to cross in rainy season.

Camping is permitted at Playa Vargas, less than 1km from the Puerto Vargas ranger station. The facilities include cold outdoor showers, drinking water and pit latrines. Don't leave anything unattended and be especially careful about storing food, as monkeys will scarf it up if they can.

Tree of Life GARDENS

(☎8610-0490, 2755-0014; www.treeoflifecostarica.com; adult/child US$12/6, guided tour US$15; ⏲9am-3pm Tue-Sun Nov–mid-Apr, daily tour 11am Jul-Aug, closed mid-Apr–Jun & Sep-Oct) This wildlife center and botanical garden is 2km northwest of town on the Playa Negra road. The beautiful place rescues and rehabilitates animals, while also promoting conservation through education. Among the animals in residence, there's a kinkajou, a pair of peccaries, sloths and monkeys.

Mariposario de Cahuita GARDENS

(☎2755-0361; admission US$10; ⏲8:30am-3:30pm Mon-Fri, to noon Sat; 👪) On the highway, at the entrance to town, you'll find this wonderful garden aflutter with lovely butterflies (great for kids). Stroll around the fountain-filled grounds and admire the local residents, including many friendly caterpillars. Descriptions are posted in several languages; guided tours are available.

★Playa Negra BEACH

At the northwest end of Cahuita, Playa Negra is a long, black-sand beach flying the *bandera azul ecológica*, a flag that indicates the beach is kept to the highest ecological standards. This is undoubtedly Cahuita's top spot for swimming. Most importantly, it is generally never crowded. When the swells are big, this spot also has an excellent beach break. It is not one of the regular stops on the Costa Rica surfer circuit, which means more waves for you.

Tours

Snorkeling, horseback riding, chocolate tours and visits to nearby indigenous territories are standard offerings.

Cahuita Tours TOUR

(☎2755-0101, 2755-0000; www.cahuitatours.com) One of the most established agencies in town, especially for snorkeling (US$50) and tours of nearby parks and reserves.

Centro Turístico Brigitte HORSE RIDING

(☎2755-0053; www.brigittecahuita.com; Playa Negra) Brigitte specializes in horseback-riding tours along the beach or to jungle waterfalls (one/three/five hours per person US$35/60/85).

Roberto's Tours FISHING

(☎2755-0117, 8396-9864) Specializes in sportfishing tours and has a restaurant for cooking up your catch.

Willie's Tours TOUR
(☎2755-1024, 8917-6982; www.willies-costarica-tours.com; ⏲8am-noon & 3-7pm Mon-Sat) A full-service tour agency that can also arrange further-flung tours and transport.

Sleeping

There are two possible areas for lodgings in Cahuita: the town center (which can be a little noisy if you're anywhere near Coco's Bar), or north of town along Playa Negra.

Center

Secret Garden CABINA $
(☎2755-0581, 8772-1846; koosiecostarica@live.nl; dm US$9, s/d US$15/25; ❄@📶) Managed by a friendly and forthright Dutch owner named Willeke, this small spot has a lush and tranquil garden, surrounded by five spacious tiled units with fans, mosquito nets and hot-water showers. One dormitory has five beds. The rooms are spotless; unfortunately the communal kitchen is not.

Spencer Seaside Lodging CABINA $
(☎2755-0027; s/d downstairs US$16/26, upstairs US$20/30; P) The only place that's in town and on the beach. Rooms are basic, but big. Upstairs units have sea views and sea breezes, as well as a shared terrace strung with hammocks.

Villa Delmar CABINA $
(☎2755-0375, 2755-0392; www.villadelmarcr.com; d US$19-25; P) In an out-of-the-way spot close to the national park, the Villa Delmar is a good deal for the price. The 10 ramshackle *cabinas* vary widely, but they all have access to a shared kitchen and laundry service.

Cabinas Smith 1 CABINA $
(☎2755-0068; older s/d/tr US$12/16/21, newer s/d/tr/q US$25/31/36/46; P❄📶) A total of 11 rooms of various configurations are set on two properties (Cabinas Smith 1 and **Cabinas Smith 2**) that lie around the corner from each other in a quiet part of town. Newer rooms have ceramic tiled floors, cable TV, minifridges and bright mirror mosaics, while the cheaper units are far more basic.

★Bungalows Aché BUNGALOW $$
(☎2755-0119; www.bungalowsache.com; bungalows US$50-55; P📶) In Nigeria, *Aché* means 'Amen,' and you'll likely say the same thing when you see these spotless octagonal bungalows on a peaceful property bordering the national park. The three charming, polished wood cabins have bright red-and-white linens and come stocked with a lockbox, minifridge, kettle and private decks with hammocks.

Alby Lodge BUNGALOW $$
(☎2755-0031; www.albylodge.com; d/tr/q US$50/55/60; P📶) This fine German-run lodge on the edge of the park has spacious landscaped grounds that attract howler monkeys and birds. Four raised bungalows are spread out, allowing for plenty of privacy. High ceilings, mosquito nets and driftwood details make for pleasant jungle decor. A common *rancho* (thatched gazebo) has excellent communal kitchen facilities.

Playa Negra

About 1.5km northwest of town, Playa Negra is quieter and pleasant, with a limited choice of restaurants and services. If you want to bar-hop, stay in town as walking back at night is not recommended.

Cabinas Tito BUNGALOW $
(☎2755-0286, 8880-1904; www.cahuita-cabinas-tito.com; d with/without hot water US$30/25, additional person US$10; P) Surrounded by extensive tropical gardens and banana plants, this charming spot offers seven clean, brightly painted cabins. Rooms are furnished in wicker, with mosquito nets and jungle accents.

Cabinas Algebra BUNGALOW $
(☎2755-0057; www.cabinasalgebra.com; bungalows US$20-35; P📶) Cabinas Algebra has four cabins that channel a rustic *Swiss Family Robinson* vibe. Each of the cozy units is crafted from wood and strung with hammocks. The onsite restaurant is a bonus, since it's a 2km trek into town.

Centro Turístico Brigitte CABINA $
(☎2755-0053; www.brigittecahuita.com; s/d/tr US$35/40/50, s without bathroom US$15; P@📶) The brightly painted wood *cabinas* each have a private terrace overlooking the garden (with hammock, of course). You can also camp (US$3 per person) provided you have your own gear. Amazing banana pancakes are served for breakfast (US$5). Extra points for proximity the beach.

La Piscina Natural CABINA $$
(☎2755-0146; piscinanatural@cahuita.cr; d/tr US$40/50; P🏊) This gem – run by inimitable Cahuita natives Walter and Patty – is

Cahuita

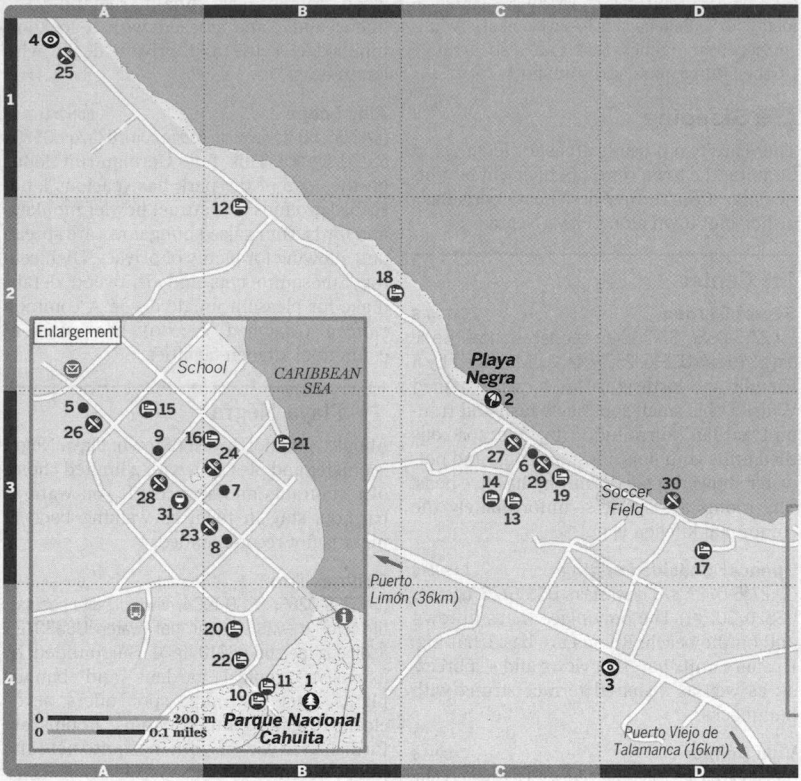

about 1km northwest of the soccer field. What makes this little place so special are the lush grounds and the natural pool (great for a dip) amid the rocks. There is a huge shared kitchen, an outdoor lounge studded with intriguing driftwood sculptures and plenty of chilled beer on hand for guests.

Cabinas Nirvana CABINA **$$**

(☎2755-0110; d US$35-60, additional person US$10; ❄ 📶 🏊) Seven attractive *cabinas* surround a swimming pool at this lush garden spot. Monkeys, toucans and even sloths are frequent visitors to the jungly grounds. A fresh fruit-filled breakfast is available for an extra fee. The amiable owner Alex goes above and beyond to satisfy his guests, offering free pick-up at the bus station and other perks.

Cabinas Iguana CABINA **$$**

(☎2755-0005; www.cabinas-iguana.com; d bungalow US$45-55, d without bathroom US$25; P 📶 🏊) Set back from the beach road, several bungalows are nestled into the lushly forested grounds. Simple cabins of various sizes (one of which sleeps six) have lots of wood accents, tile floors and beds with mosquito nets. Bicycles are available to rent.

Playa Negra Guesthouse BUNGALOW **$$**

(☎2755-0127; www.playanegra.cr; s/d US$60/75, cottage US$95-140; P 📶 🏊) This beautiful Caribbean-style plantation house, with several freestanding storybook cottages (equipped with full kitchens), is meticulously decorated and maintained. Guest rooms are painted sherbety colors and feature charming tropical accents – such as colorful mosaics in the bathrooms and cozy wicker lounge chairs on the private decks.

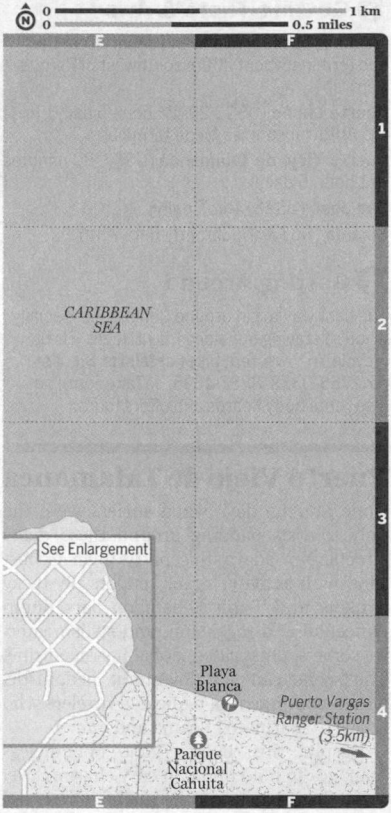

Cahuita

Top Sights
1 Parque Nacional Cahuita B4
2 Playa Negra C3

Sights
3 Mariposario de Cahuita D4
4 Tree of Life A1

Activities, Courses & Tours
5 Cahuita Tours A3
6 Centro Turístico Brigitte C3
7 Mister Big J's B3
8 Roberto's Tours B3
9 Willie's Tours A3

Sleeping
10 Alby Lodge B4
11 Bungalows Aché B4
12 Cabinas Algebra B2
13 Cabinas Iguana C3
14 Cabinas Nirvana C3
15 Cabinas Smith 1 ..... A3
16 Cabinas Smith 2 ..... B3
17 Cabinas Tito D3
Centro Turístico Brigitte ..... (see 6)
18 La Piscina Natural B2
19 Playa Negra Guesthouse C3
20 Secret Garden B4
21 Spencer Seaside Lodging B3
22 Villa Delmar B4

Eating
23 Cafe Chocolatte 100% Natural B3
24 Café del Parquecito B3
25 Caribbean Coconut A1
26 Cha Cha Cha A3
27 Chao's Paradise C3
28 Cocoricó A3
29 Reggae Restaurant C3
30 Sobre Las Olas D3

Drinking & Nightlife
31 Coco's Bar A3

Eating

Center

Cafe Chocolatte 100% Natural INTERNATIONAL $
(dishes US$3-11; ⏲ 6:30am-2pm Mon-Fri) There's no better place in Cahuita to greet the morning with a cup o' joe or unwind in the afternoon with a refreshing *jugo*. Hearty sandwiches on homemade whole-grain bread are perfect for beach picnics at the national park.

Cocoricó PIZZA $
(pizzas US$4-13; ⏲ 4-10pm Mon-Thu, noon-10pm Sat & Sun) Sweet spot for pizza and a movie (nightly).

Café del Parquecito COSTA RICAN $
(breakfast US$4-6; ⏲ 6am-3pm & 6pm-close) Five words: crepes stuffed with tropical fruit.

★ **Cha Cha Cha** INTERNATIONAL $$
(☎ 8394-4153; mains US$9-20; ⏲ noon-10pm Tue-Sun; ✎) In a corner veranda of an old house, this attractive expat favorite is adorned with the chef's artwork and offers sophisticated world cuisine. Exquisite sauces star in dishes from filet mignon with wild mushrooms and truffle oil to mussels in Dijon sauce. Kick it off with an evocatively named cocktail, like the Dulce Amor (Sweet Love), made with starfruit and *guaro*.

Playa Negra

Reggae Restaurant CARIBBEAN $
(mains US$4-10; ⏲7-11am & noon-9pm) With a friendly, laid-back vibe, this *soda* serves Caribbean-style standards.

Caribbean Coconut ITALIAN $$
(☎2755-0483; www.caribbeancoconut.net; Playa Grande; mains US$7-20; ✎) Even if you are staying in town, it's worth the 3km trek north to Playa Grande to indulge in an Italian feast. The chef's special lobster penne tops the charts, but there is a great selection of seafood, steaks, pizza and pasta. Enjoy it with a glass of Italian red with a view of the Caribbean blue. Credit cards are accepted.

Sobre Las Olas SEAFOOD $$
(☎2755-0109; pastas US$12-15, mains US$12-25; ⏲noon-10pm Wed-Mon; ✎) Dine on the beach at this atmospheric spot 'over the waves.' It is owned by a lively Tico-Italian couple who serve a variety of Mediterranean-influenced specialties.

Chao's Paradise CARIBBEAN $$
(☎2755-0480; seafood mains US$8-15; ⏲11am-11pm) Follow the wafting smell of garlic and simmering sauces to this highly recommended Playa Negra outpost. It serves fresh catches cooked up in spicy 'Chao' sauce.

Drinking & Nightlife

Coco's Bar BAR
(⏲noon-last man standing) This low-key town is home to one crazy loud drinking hole: Coco's Bar. You can't miss it at the main intersection, painted in Rasta red, yellow and green, and cranking the reggaetón to 11. On some nights (usually on weekends) there is live music. If you're not looking to burst your eardrums, try one of the mellower drinking establishments situated right across the street.

Information

Banco de Costa Rica (⏲9am-4pm Mon-Fri) Located at the bus terminal.

Cahuita.cr (www.cahuita.cr) Website with ample information about the town's restaurant and lodging options.

Centro Turístico Brigitte (☎2755-0053; www.brigittecahuita.com; per hr US$2; ⏲7am-6pm) Internet access. Also offers tours.

Internet Palmer (per hr US$2; ⏲9am-8pm)

Getting There & Away

All public buses arrive at and depart from the bus terminal about 200m southwest of Parque Central.

Puerto Limón (US$3.20, 1½ hour, 5 daily) To the Autotransportes Mepe terminal.

Puerto Viejo de Talamanca (US$2, 30 minutes to 1 hour, 5 daily)

San José (US$8, 4hr; 5 daily)

Sixaola (US$3.50; 2hr; hrly 6am-7pm)

Getting Around

The best way to get around Cahuita – especially if you're staying out along Playa Negra – is by bicycle. In town, rent bikes at **Mister Big J's** (☎2755-0353, 8887-4695; ⏲7am-6pm); he also rents body boards and offers tours.

Puerto Viejo de Talamanca

Gone are the days when surfers were the only tourists padding around these dusty streets. Nowadays, this party town is bustling with activity: street vendors ply tacky trinkets and T-shirts, bamboo bars pump dancehall and reggaetón, and stylish eateries serve sophisticated global fusion cuisine. The scene can get downright hedonistic, with a contingent of dedicated revelers who arrive to marinate in ganja and *guaro*.

Despite this, Puerto Viejo nonetheless manages to hold on to an easy charm. Stray a couple of blocks off the main commercial strip and you might find yourself on a sleepy dirt road, savoring a spicy Caribbean stew in the company of local families. Nearby, you'll find rainforest fruit farms set to a soundtrack of cackling birds and croaking frogs, and wide-open beaches where the daily itinerary revolves around surfing and snoozing.

So, chill a little. Party a little. Eat a little. You've come to the right place.

Sights & Activities

Jaguar Centro de Rescate WILDLIFE REFUGE
(☎2750-0710; www.jaguarrescue.com; admission US$15; ⏲tours 9:30am & 11:30am Mon-Sat) Named in honor of its original resident, this wildlife rescue center in Playa Chiquita now focuses mostly on sloths and monkeys. Founded by Spanish zoologist Encar and her partner Sandro, an Italian herpetologist, the center rehabilitates orphaned, injured and rescued animals for reintroduction into the wild whenever possible. It's located near Playa Chiquita, just east of Puerto Viejo.

Finca La Isla GARDENS
(☎2750-0046, 8829-4929; www.costaricacaribbean.com; self-guided/guided tour US$5/10; ⏲10am-4pm Fri-Mon) West of town, Finca La Isla is a working tropical farm and botanical garden ideal for bird-watching and wildlife observation (look for sloths and poison dart frogs).

Surfing

Breaking on the reef that hugs the village is the famed **Salsa Brava**, a shallow break that is also one of the country's most infamous waves. Novices will prefer the beach break at **Playa Cocles** – where the waves are almost as impressive and the landing far less damaging. Cocles is about 2km east of town. Conditions are usually best early in the day, before the wind picks up.

Waves in the area generally peak from November to March, and there is a surfing miniseason from June to July. From late March to May, and in September and October, the sea is at its calmest.

Several surf schools around town charge about US$50 for two hours of lessons. Stands around town rent boards from about US$20 per day. Try **Totem Surf School** (☎2750-0758; totemsurfschool.blogspot.com; Playa Cocles) or ATEC (p568).

Cycling

The forested road to **Manzanillo** (13km) offers a scenic ride. Take your swimsuit and watch for howler monkeys and butterflies on the way.

Diving & Snorkeling

Costa Rica's only two living reef systems form a naturally protected sanctuary from Cahuita to Manzanillo. They are home to 35 species of coral and over 400 species of fish, not to mention dolphins, sharks and, occasionally, whales. Underwater visibility is best when the sea is calm. If the surfing is bad, snorkeling is good.

Snorkel just south of **Punta Uva** (in front of the Arrecife restaurant), where you will find stunning examples of reindeer coral, sheet coral and lettuce coral. The reef at Manzanillo is also easily accessible. You can rent equipment at Aquamor Talamanca Adventures (p571) in Manzanillo. Tour companies offer guided trips for about US$45 per person.

Dive outfitters include **Reef Runner Divers** (☎2750-0480; www.reefrunnerdivers.net; 1-/2-tank dive US$65/90; ⏲8am-6pm) and Aquamor Talamanca Adventures, in Manzanillo.

Swimming

Just northwest of town, **Playa Negra** offers the area's safest swimming, as well as excellent body boarding. Southeast of town at **Playa Cocles**, the jungle meets the sea and the waves are perfect for swimming and body surfing.

Riptides and undertows can be dangerous. Inquire at your hotel or with local tour operators about current conditions.

SURFING SALSA BRAVA

One of the biggest breaks in Costa Rica, the **Salsa Brava** is named for the heaping helping of 'spicy sauce' it serves up on the sharp, shallow reef, continually collecting its debt of fun in broken skin, boards and bones. The wave makes its regular, dramatic appearance when the swells pull in from the east, pushing a wall of water against the reef, in the process, generating a thick and powerful curl. There's no gradual build up here: the water is transformed from swell to wave in a matter of seconds. Ride it out and you're golden. Wipeout and you'll rocket head-first into the reef. In his memoir, *In Search of Captain Zero,* surfer and screenwriter Allen Weisbecker describes it as 'vicious.' Some mordant locals have baptized it 'the cheese-grater.'

Interestingly, this storied wave helped turn Puerto Viejo into a destination. Thirty years ago, the town was barely accessible. But that did not dissuade dogged surfers from the bumpy bus rides and rickety canoes that hauled them and their boards on the weeklong trip from San José. They camped on the beach and shacked up with locals, carbo-loading at cheap *sodas*. Other intrepid explorers – biologists, Peace Corps volunteers, disaffected American veterans looking to escape the fallout of the Vietnam War – also materialized during this time, helping spread the word about the area's luminous sunsets, lush rainforests and monster curls. Today, Puerto Viejo has a fine paved road, global eateries and wi-fi. The fierceness of the Salsa Brava, however, remains unchanged.

Puerto Viejo de Talamanca

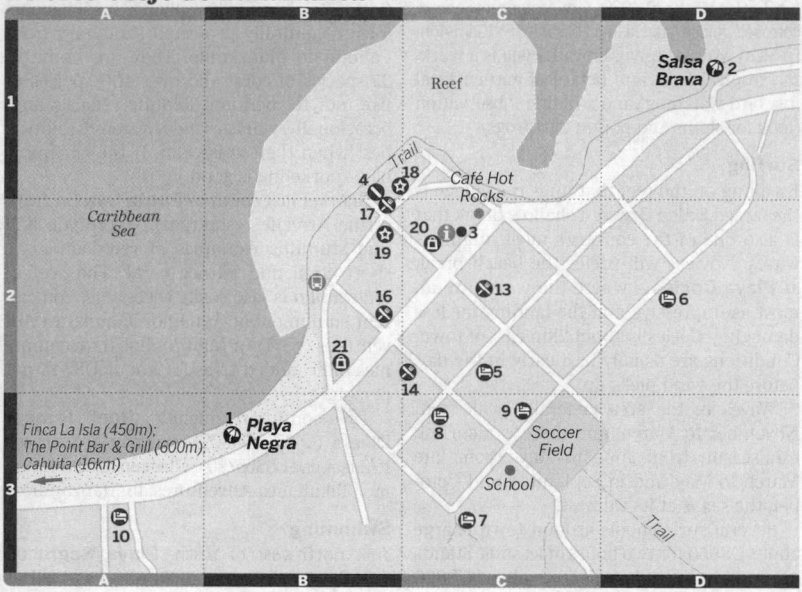

Tours

ATEC HIKING

(Asociación Talamanqueña de Ecoturismo y Conservación; ☎2750-0191, 2750-0398; www.ateccr.org; ⏲8am-9pm) This highly reputable not-for-profit organization promotes environmentally sensitive tourism by working with local guides and supporting local communities. Hiking, horseback riding and canoe trips involve bird-watching and visiting indigenous territories and local farms. Depending on the activity, half-day excursions start at about US$25 and go up to US$80 for overnight trips.

Sleeping

★Hotel Pura Vida HOTEL $

(☎2750-0002; www.hotel-puravida.com; s/d/tr US$34/38/48, s/d/tr without bathroom US$28/32/42; P) Although this place offers budget prices, the atmosphere and amenities are solidly midrange. Ten breezy, immaculate guest rooms, clad in polished wood, bright linens and ceramic-tile floors, make up this homey inn on a quiet street.

Alongside a lovingly tended garden, you'll find a serene lounge with easy chairs and hammocks.

Hostel Pagalú HOSTEL $

(☎2750-1930; www.pagalu.com; dm US$12, d with/without bathroom US$32/26; P) A brand new hostel on a quiet street, this place offers a break from Puerto Viejo's party scene. Superclean, airy dormitories and half a dozen private doubles are painted white and come with polished-wood accents. Niceties include large lockers, charging stations for MP3 players and reading lamps installed above each bunk.

Rocking J's HOSTEL $

(☎2750-0657; www.rockingjs.com; camping per person US$6-8, hammock US$7, dm US$11, d US$26, 3-4-person ste US$60-70; P) Puerto Viejo's grooviest hostel and 'hammock hotel' is owned by the charismatic, mischievous 'J,' who organizes full-moon toga parties and round-the-table drinking games. Good times, good vibes and new friends await here. The accommodations are basic. Tight rows of tents, hammocks, snug dorms and private doubles share rickety showers in a concrete structure that is brightened by a veritable explosion of psychedelic mosaics.

Monte Sol CABINA $

(☎2750-0098; www.montesol.net; d with/without bathroom US$33/27, d/q bungalows with kitchen US$47/67; P @) Clean, basic *cabinas* in

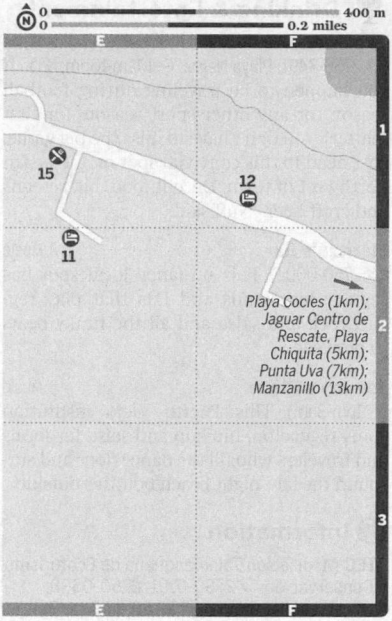

Puerto Viejo de Talamanca

Top Sights
1 Playa Negra B3
2 Salsa Brava D1

Activities, Courses & Tours
3 ATEC C2
4 Reef Runner Divers B1

Sleeping
5 Cabinas Guaraná C2
6 Cabinas Tropical D2
7 Coco Loco Lodge C3
8 Hostel Pagalú C3
9 Hotel Pura Vida C3
10 Kaya's Place A3
11 Monte Sol E2
12 Rocking J's F1

Eating
13 Bread & Chocolate C2
14 Sel & Sucre C2
Soda Mirna ..... (see 3)
15 Stashu's con Fusion E1
16 Veronica's Place B2
17 Zion Cafe B2

Entertainment
18 Johnny's Place B1
19 Maritza's Bar B2

Shopping
20 Organic Market C2
21 Super el Buen Precio B2

a quiet locale east of town have tile floors, mosquito nets and hammocks. Guests have access to a welcoming, woody lounge area, shaded by an almond tree.

Kaya's Place INN $
(☎2750-0690; www.kayasplace.com; s/d without bathroom US$20/30, d with/without ocean views US$45/35; P) This super-friendly inn just west of town has 17 snug, basic rooms and apartments (some of which share cool-water showers). The cheapest rooms are dim but the 2nd-floor lounge is filled with hammocks and offers prime views over Playa Negra.

★ Cabinas Guaraná CABINA $$
(☎2750-0244; www.hotelguarana.com; s/d/tr/q US$35/43/53/60; P @) Amid a riotous tropical garden, 10 brightly painted concrete *cabinas* are decorated with wooden furniture and colorful folk tapestries, and each one comes with a small private terrace with hammock. There is a spacious shared kitchen and a vertigo-inducing tree house that offers spectacular sea views. This place is excellent value; credit cards are accepted.

Cabinas Tropical CABINA $$
(☎2750-0283; www.cabinastropical.com; s/d US$38/42, d with air-con US$48; P) Ten spacious rooms – decorated with varnished wood and shiny tiles – surround a primly landscaped garden on the eastern end of town. The comfortable quarters are just part of the appeal: biologist owner Rolfe Blancke leads excellent bird-watching hikes at dawn (per person US$60, minimum three people, breakfast provided).

Coco Loco Lodge BUNGALOW $$
(☎2750-0281; www.cocolocolodge.com; d US$57, d bungalow US$63-75; P @) You'll find various accommodations at this quiet Austrian-run hotel. The most charming are the palm-thatched bungalows, equipped with shining wood floors, minifridge and coffeemakers. All of these have private terraces with hammocks, offering views of the expansive garden. Discount for cash payment.

Eating

Get groceries at **Super El Buen Precio** (6:30am-8:30pm) or at the weekly **Organic Market** (6am-6pm Sat), which offers produce and typical regional snacks.

★Bread & Chocolate BREAKFAST $
(2750-0723; meals US$4-10; 6:30am-6:30pm Tue-Sat, to 2:30pm Sun;) Ever had a completely homemade PB&J (ie bread, peanut butter *and* jelly all made from scratch)? That and more can be yours at this dream of a cafe in the center of town. Coffees are served in individual French presses; mochas come unconstructed so you have the pleasure of mixing your own homemade chocolate, steamed milk and coffee; and everything else – from the gazpacho to the granola – is lovingly and skilfully made in-house.

Veronica's Place VEGETARIAN $
(2750-0263; www.veronicasplacepv.com; dishes US$4-7; 10am-8pm Sun-Thu, to 4pm Fri;) A delightful vegetarian cafe, this place offers fresh, healthy interpretations of Caribbean food, using fresh fruits and vegetables, as well as soy products.

Sel & Sucre FRENCH $
(2750-0636; meals US$4-10;) Dark coffee and fresh-fruit smoothies offer a nice complement to the menu of crêpes, both savory and sweet. These delights are all prepared by one talented French man, so service can be slow but it's worth the wait.

Zion Cafe VEGETARIAN $
(2750-2083; breakfast US$4-6, lunch US$6-8;) This cool, contemporary cafe is the perfect place to de-tox. Grab a seat at a sidewalk table or on the rooftop terrace, cool down with the Caribbean breeze and feast on healthy salads, wraps and delicious veggie fare.

Soda Mirna CARIBBEAN $
(mains US$5-8; noon-10pm) This humble little *soda* on the main drag offers excellent people-watching and highly tasty (and inexpensive) Caribbean-style dishes.

★Stashu's con Fusion FUSION $$
(2750-0530; meals US$7-18; 5-10pm Thu-Tue;) Stroll 250m out of town toward Playa Cocles to this romantic candlelit patio cafe serving up creative cuisine that combines elements of Caribbean, Indian, Mexican and Thai. Owner and chef Stash Golas is an artist inside the kitchen and out.

Drinking & Entertainment

The Point Bar & Grill SPORTS BAR
(2756-8491; Playa Negra; 10am-10pm;) If you happen to be traveling during football season (or any other sport season, for that matter), you don't have to miss the big game. Just head to this convivial spot on the beach northwest of town. Decent food, big screens and craft beer. 'Nuff said.

Maritza's Bar LIVE MUSIC
(2750-0003) This un-fancy local spot has regular live bands and DJs that play reggae, rock and salsa and all the funky beats in between.

Johnny's Place MUSIC
(1pm-3am) This Puerto Viejo institution spins reggaetón, hip-hop and salsa for locals and travelers who fill the dance floor and surround the late-night beach bonfires outside.

Information

ATEC (Asociación Talamanqueña de Ecoturismo y Conservación; 2750-0191, 2750-0398; www.ateccr.org; per hr US$2.50; 8am-9pm) Internet access; also a reliable source of information on tours and activities in the area.

Banco de Costa Rica (9am-4pm Mon-Fri) The ATM here works on the Plus and Visa systems. It sometimes runs out of cash on weekends.

Green Coast (www.greencoast.com) A network of hotels and tour operators that is dedicated to promoting sustainable tourism along the southern Caribbean coast.

Jungle Internet (2750-2003, 2750-2086; www.junglec.com; per hr US$3; 8am-11pm) Decent laptops and wireless access.

Puerto Viejo Satellite (www.puertoviejosatellite.com) All the ins and outs of Puerto Viejo.

DANGERS & ANNOYANCES

A cottage industry of drug dealers has become a permanent part of the landscape in Puerto Viejo and it can get quite aggressive. Be firm and be aware that the use of marijuana is illegal, even though it is common in Puerto Viejo.

Getting There & Away

BUS

All public buses arrive at and depart from the bus terminal half a block southwest of Maritza's Bar.

Bribrí/Sixaola (US$3, 30/90 minutes; hourly 6:30am to 7:30pm)

Cahuita/Puerto Limón (US$3.50, 30/90 minutes, hourly 5:30am to 7:30pm)

Manzanillo (US$1, 30 minutes, 5 daily)

San José (US$9.50, 5 hours, 4 daily)

SHUTTLE BUS

In addition to the regular shuttle bus companies that service major Costa Rican destinations, **Gandoca Tours** (☎8762-8848, 6075-1720; www.gandocawildlifetours.com) operates a daily shuttle to Bocas del Toro in Panama (US$25), which departs at 8:30am.

Getting Around

Bicycle is a fine way to get around town, and pedaling out to other beaches east of Puerto Viejo is one of the highlights of this corner of Costa Rica. You'll find rental outlets all over town (in addition to many hotels).

Manzanillo

The 13km route to Manzanillo slips past sandy beaches and dense canopy, passing beach villages and the Reserva Indígena Cocles/Kekoldi, and ending in Refugio Nacional de Vida Silvestre Gandoca-Manzanillo. Take a cruiser; the road is paved, but don't get too distracted spotting wildlife as the potholes are doozies. The town itself is part of **Refugio Nacional de Vida Silvestre Gandoca-Manzanillo**, a pristine remnant of wild Caribbean coastline stretching to Panama.

Gandoca-Manzanillo's stunning coastal trail leads 5.5km through the rainforest and desolate beaches to Punta Mona. Wildlife includes the rare harpy eagle, monkeys and toucans. The coral reef 200m offshore is 10 times the size of the Cahuita reef, with the clearest waters and best diversity of sea life in Costa Rica. The best resource on the area is the long-term resident Larkin family at **Aquamor Talamanca Adventures** (☎8835-6041, 2759-9012; www.greencoast.com/aquamor.htm), 100m west of Maxi's Cabinas. It runs a PADI dive school, rents snorkeling gear (US$4 per hour) and kayaks, and offers dolphin-observation trips with excellent naturalist guides.

Sleeping & Eating

Cabinas Manzanillo CABINA $

(☎8839-8386, 2759-9033; r US$35; P) Run by the ever-helpful Sandra Castillo and Pablo Bustamante, these eight *cabinas* on the western end of town are so clean, you could eat off the tile floors. Cheery rooms have big beds, industrial-strength ceiling fans and spacious bathrooms. There's also a shared kitchen.

Getting There & Away

Buses depart to Puerto Limón (US$3.20, 2½ hours) five times a day, passing through Puerto Viejo and Cahuita along the way.

Sixaola

This is the end of the road – literally. A bumpy tarmac leads to an old railroad bridge over the Río Sixaola that serves as the border crossing into Panama. Like most border towns, Sixaola is hardly scenic: it's an extravaganza of dingy bars and roadside stalls selling rubber boots.

There's no good reason to stay in Sixaola, but if you get stuck, head for safe, clean **Cabinas Sanchez** (☎2754-2105; r US$15). It's about 200m from the border along the lower road.

The bus station is one block north of the border crossing, on the east side of the main drag. Buses to either San José (US$11.60, six hours, four daily) or Puerto Limón (US$3.30, three hours, departs hourly from 5am to 6pm) all stop at Bribrí and Cahuita.

See p634 for information on getting to Guabito and Bocas del Toro, Panama.

WORTH A TRIP

PUNTA MONA

Five kilometers south of Manzanillo, **Punta Mona** (☎8321-8788; www.puntamona.org; campsites per person US$35, r per person US$65, all incl 3 organic meals; @) is an organic farm and retreat center that offers yoga training, permaculture design and other educational opportunities. To arrange a stay and transportation, email ahead or visit the farm's office in Puerto Viejo, which is located behind ATEC.

NORTH CENTRAL COSTA RICA

The spark of adventure lures travelers to this sector – to careen through the canopy of the cloud forest at Monteverde, and to soak in volcano-heated springs at Volcán Arenal. The most popular circuit makes the connection between Santa Elena and La Fortuna with a jeep-boat-jeep shortcut across the Laguna de Arenal. Travelers with time to get off the beaten track can go further and discover where the volcanic mountains give way to flat, tropical lowlands, extending all the way to the Nicaraguan border.

Monteverde & Santa Elena

Snug in the misty greenbelt of two cloud-forest reserves, this slim corridor of human habitation consists of the Tico village of Santa Elena and the Quaker settlement of Monteverde. The area was first settled by loggers and farmers in the 1930s. The Quakers arrived in 1951, emigrating from the US to avoid being drafted to fight in the Korean War. In order to protect the vital watershed, the Quaker community established the private reserve that is now Reserva Biológica Bosque Nuboso Monteverde.

A 1983 *National Geographic* feature described this unique landscape, and subsequently billed the area as *the* place to view one of Central America's most famous birds – the resplendent quetzal. Suddenly, hordes of tourists armed with tripods and telephoto lenses started braving Monteverde's notoriously awful access roads, and tourism has not waned since.

The cloud forests near Monteverde and Santa Elena are one of Costa Rica's premier destinations for everyone from budget backpackers to well-heeled retirees. Sometimes it feels like they are all here at once. Take heart in the fact that the local community continues to fight to maintain the fragile balance of nature and commerce.

Sights

Donning rubbery rain gear and mud boots is a rite of passage for those visiting in search of resplendent quetzals, hummingbirds, howler monkeys, sloths, snakes and more. Just remember that wildlife absconds in the mist, so hold back wild expectations.

★Reserva Biológica Bosque Nuboso Monteverde WILDLIFE RESERVE

(Monteverde Cloud Forest Wildlife Biological Reserve; ☎2645 5122; www.cct.or.cr; adult/concession US$17/8.50; ⏲7am-4pm) When Quaker settlers first arrived, they agreed to preserve about a third of their property in order to protect the watershed above Monteverde. Fighting off squatters with the help of the Nature Conservancy and the World Wildlife Fund, they began what is now known as one of the country's most eminent reserves.

Trails in the reserve are clearly marked. The **Sendero Bosque Nuboso** is a pretty 2km walk through the cloud forest to the continental divide. From there you can return via the wide **Sendero El Camino**, which branches off to a 25m-high suspension bridge. The circuit takes two to three hours. Recommended half-day tours (US$17 plus admission) in English leave at 7:30am; call ahead to reserve a space or to arrange a night walk or bird-watching tour. Near the entrance, there is a visitors center with a gift shop and a restaurant.

Visitors should note that some of the walking trails are very muddy, and even during the dry season the cloud forest is wet. Because of the fragile environment, the reserve allows a maximum of 160 people at any given time. Arrive early (or come off season) so as not to miss out.

The reserve is 6km south of Santa Elena village. Public buses (US$1.20, 30 minutes) depart from the Banco Nacional three times a day.

★Bosque Eterno de los Niños WILDLIFE RESERVE

(Children's Eternal Forest; ☎2645-5003; www.acmcr.org; adult/student US$12/8; ⏲7:30am-5:30pm) Founded by school children fed up with the childish squandering of our natural resources, Bosque Eterno de los Niños is an enormous 220-sq-km reserve providing a home for local wildlife among the primary and secondary forest (and to allow former agricultural land to be slowly reclaimed by the jungle). The reserve is largely inaccessible, except for the **Bajo del Tigre** sector, where 4km of trails wind through a unique premontane landscape. Daily bird walks (US$28, 5:30am) and night walks (US$20, 5:30pm) are recommended and should be reserved in advance.

El Jardín de las Mariposas ZOO

(Butterfly Garden; ☎2645-5512; www.monteverdebutterflygarden.com; adult/student/children 12yr & under US$9/7/3; ⏲9:30am-4pm) Everything you ever wanted to know about butterflies, with four gardens representing different habitats, home to more than 50 species. Up-close observation cases allow visitors to witness the butterflies as they emerge from the chrysalis. Other exhibits feature the industrious leafcutter ant. Explore on your own or take advantage of the knowledgeable naturalist guides.

Ranario ZOO

(Frog Pond; ☎2645-6320; ranariomv@racsa.co.cr; adult/student & child US$13/10; ⏲9am-8:30pm) About 25 species of frogs and toads reside in the transparent enclosures lining the winding jungle paths. Sharp-eyed guides lead informative tours in English or Spanish, pointing out frogs, eggs and tadpoles with flashlights. Many resident amphibians are more active by night, so come back in the evening for another look (included).

Bat Jungle ZOO
(☎2645-7701; www.batjungle.com; adult/child US$11/9; ⏲9:30am-7:30pm) Learn about echolocation, bat-wing aerodynamics and other amazing flying-mammal facts. The so-called Bat Jungle is small but informative, with good bilingual educational displays and a free-flying bat habitat housing almost 100 bats.

Serpentario ZOO
(Serpentarium; ☎2645-6002; per person US$9; ⏲9am-8pm) The serpentarium houses about 40 species of snakes, lizards, turtles and other cold-blooded creatures. It's pricey, but interesting – if you're into slithering slimy things.

Jardín de Orquídeas GARDENS
(Orchid Garden; ☎2645-5308; www.monteverdeorchidgarden.com; adult/child under 12yr US$10/free; ⏲8am-5pm) This sweet-smelling garden has shady trails winding past more than 400 types of orchid organized into taxonomic groups.

Activities

Canopy Tours

All of the canopy tour companies offer transportation from your hotel in Santa Elena or Monteverde (free unless otherwise indicated). In addition to the zip-lines, most of these facilities also have hanging bridges, which allow you to see the canopy at a slower pace.

Aventura CANOPY TOUR
(☎2645-6388; www.monteverdeadventure.com; adult/child US$45/35; ⏲7am-4pm) Aventura has 19 platforms that are spiced up with a Tarzan swing, a 15m rappel and a Superman zip line that makes you feel as if you really are flying.

Extremo Canopy CANOPY TOUR
(☎2645-6058; www.monteverdeextremo.com; canopy US$40, super cable US$30, bungee US$60, tarzan swing $35; ⏲8am-4pm) When they say 'extremo,' they mean it. In addition to the regular canopy tour, there's a 1km-long 'Super Cable'; the highest and most adrenaline-addled Tarzan swing in the area; and a bungee jump. One way or another, you will scream.

Original Canopy Tour CANOPY TOUR
(☎2645-5243; www.canopytour.com; adult/student/child US$45/35/25; ⏲7:30am-4pm) On the grounds of Cloud Forest Lodge, this has the fabled zip lines that started the

WORTH A TRIP

RESERVA SANTA ELENA

Though Monteverde gets all the attention, the misty **Reserva Santa Elena** (☎2645-7107, 2645-5390; www.reservasantaelena.org; adult/student US$14/7; ⏲7am-4pm) has plenty to recommend it.

While Monteverde Crowd...er...Cloud Forest entertains almost 200,000 visitors annually, Santa Elena sees fewer than 20,000 tourists each year, which means its dewy trails through mysteriously veiled forest are usually far quieter. Here, you can practically hear the canopy, draped with epiphytes, breathing with humid exhalations as water drops on to the leaf litter and mud underfoot. The odd call of the three-wattled bellbird or low crescendo of a howler monkey punctuates the higher-pitched bird chatter.

This is slightly higher in elevation than Monteverde, and as some of the forest is secondary growth, there are sunnier places for spotting birds and other animals throughout. There's a stable population of monkey and sloth. Unless you're a trained ecologist, the old-growth forest in Santa Elena will seem fairly similar in appearance to Monteverde, though the lack of cement blocks on the trails means that you'll have a much more authentic (note: muddy) trekking experience.

At 310 hectares, it's much smaller than the other forest. More than 12km of trails are open for hiking, including four circular trails of varying difficulty and length. Guided hikes (US$15 plus entrance fee) depart from the visitors center at 7:30am and 11:30am daily.

The reserve is about 6km northeast of the village of Santa Elena. Catch the bus (US$2, 30 minutes, four daily) from the Banco Nacional in town.

Monteverde & Santa Elena

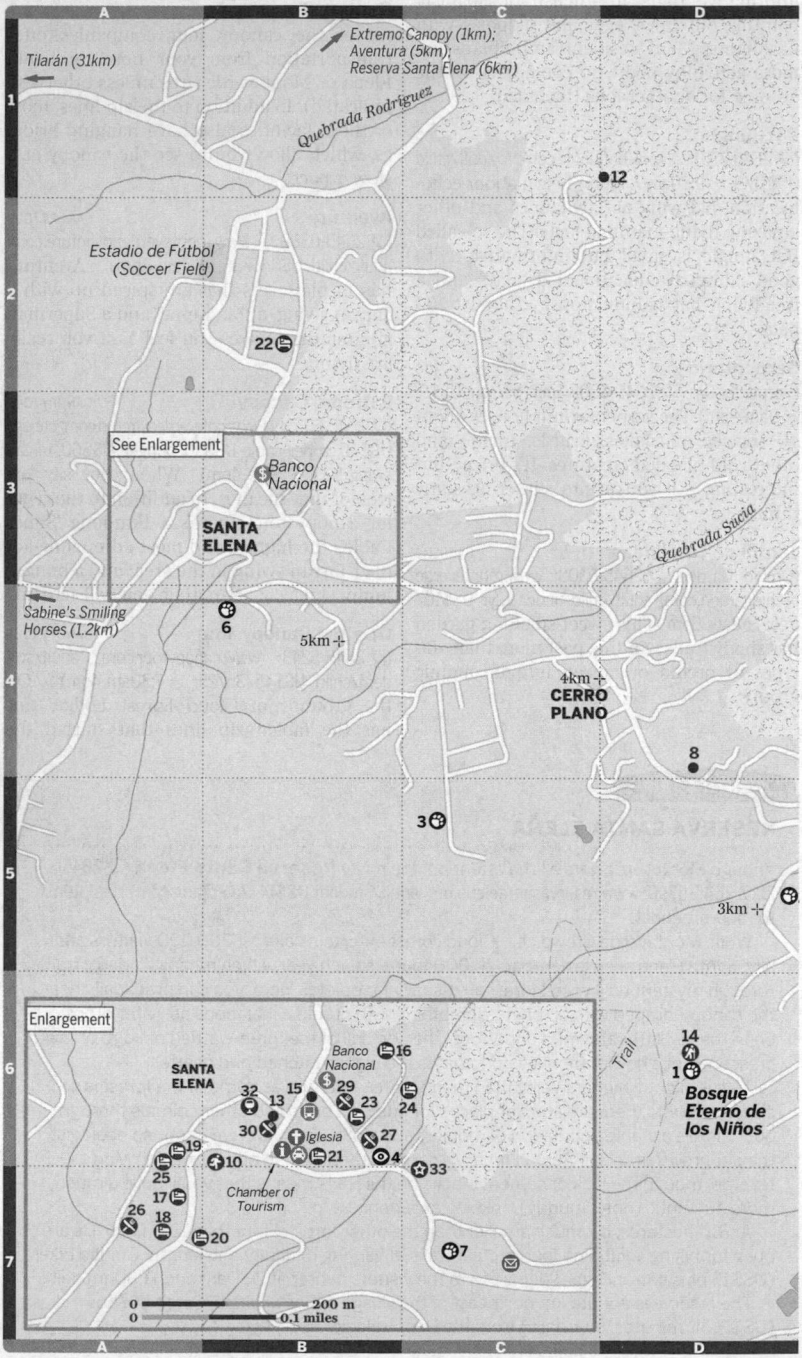

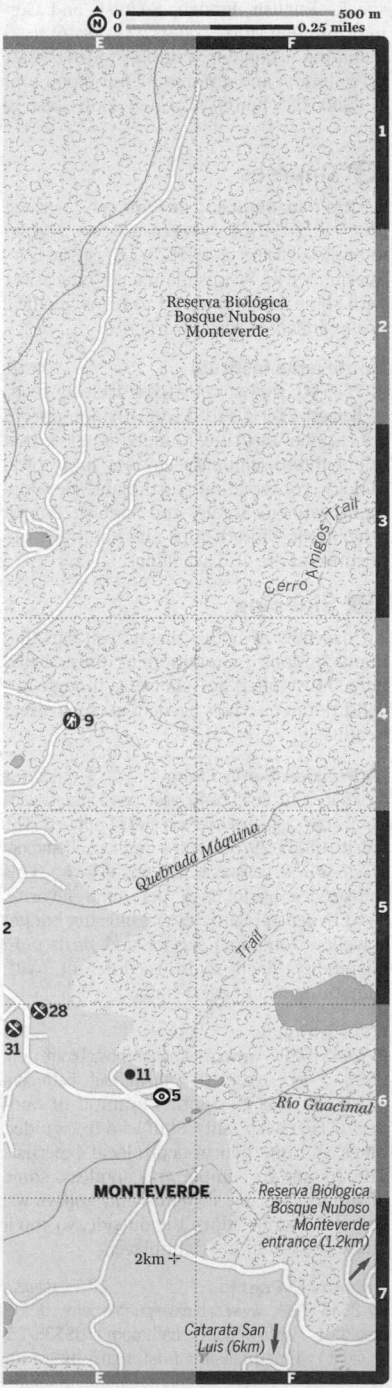

Monteverde & Santa Elena

Top Sights

1 Bosque Eterno de los Niños D6

Sights

2 Bat Jungle D5
3 El Jardín de las Mariposas C5
4 Jardín de Orquídeas B6
5 Monteverde Cheese Factory E6
6 Ranario B4
7 Serpentario C7

Activities, Courses & Tours

8 Centro Panamericano de Idiomas D4
9 Cerro Amigos E4
10 Desafío Adventure Company B6
11 Monteverde Institute E6
12 Original Canopy Tour D1
13 Selvatura B6
14 Sendero Bajo del Tigre (Jaguar Canyon Trail) D6
15 SkyTrek B6

Sleeping

16 Arco Iris Ecolodge B6
17 Cabinas & Hotel Vista al Golfo A7
18 Cabinas Eddy A7
19 Cabinas El Pueblo A6
20 Casa Tranquilo A7
21 Hotel El Sueño B6
22 Mar Inn B&B B2
23 Pensión Santa Elena B6
24 Quetzal Inn C6
25 Sloth Backpackers A6

Eating

Café Caburé ..... (see 2)
26 La Carambola Art Cafe A7
27 Morpho's Restaurant B6
28 Stella's Bakery E6
29 Taco Taco B6
30 Tree House Restaurant & Café B6
31 Whole Foods Market E6

Drinking & Nightlife

32 Bar Amigos B6

Entertainment

33 Green Park C7

Shopping

Casem ..... (see 31)

adventure tourism. These lines aren't as elaborate as the others, but it's a piece of history, complete with 14 platforms, a rappel through the center of an old fig tree and 5km of private trails that are worth a wander.

Selvatura CANOPY TOUR
(☎2645-5929; www.selvatura.com; canopy US$45, walkways US$30, each exhibit US$15; ⏲7:30am-4pm) One of the bigger games in town, Selvatura has 3km of cables, 18 platforms and one Tarzan swing through primary forest. For the less adventurous, there's a series of treetop walkways and a slew of nature museums, including a huge insect exhibit.

SkyTrek CANOPY TOUR
(☎2645-5238; www.skyadventures.travel; adult/student/child US$83/63/53, transportation US$3-5; ⏲7:30am-5pm) This seriously fast canopy tour consists of 11 platforms attached to steel towers. We're talking serious speeds of up to 64km/h. The price includes admission to the SkyTram gondola and SkyWalk hanging bridges; cheaper packages are also available.

Hiking

Take a free hike up 1842m **Cerro Amigos** on a clear day for great views of Volcán Arenal, 20km away to the northeast. The trail leaves Monteverde from behind Hotel Belmar (the road behind the gas station), ascending roughly 300m in 3km. From the hotel, take the dirt road going downhill, then the next left.

The strenuous hike to the **Catarata San Luis** (San Luis Waterfall), about 7km south of Monteverde, rewards you with views of a gorgeous stream cascading from the cloud forests into a series of swimming holes just begging for a picnic. It's only a few kilometers, but it's steep and the rocky, mud-filled terrain can get very slick. A taxi from town costs about U$12.

Horseback Riding

Almost all of the outfitters offer guided horse rides between Monteverde and La Fortuna. See p579 for details.

Desafío Adventure Company HORSE RIDING
(☎2645-5874; www.monteverdetours.com) Day trips to Cataratas San Luis (US$80, six hours) and Monteverde Reserve (US$50, four hours), as well as several multiday rides.

Sabine's Smiling Horses HORSE RIDING
(☎2645-6894, 8385-2424; www.horseback-ridingtour.com; ⏲depart 8am) Run by Sabine, who speaks English, French, Spanish and German, Smiling Horses offers a variety of treks including a popular waterfall tour (US$50, three hours) and a romantic full-moon tour (US$50, 2½ hours). Located 2km west of town.

Courses

Centro Panamericano de Idiomas LANGUAGE
(CPI; ☎2265-6306; www.cpi-edu.com; classes with/without homestay US$525/375; ⏲8am-5pm) Specializes in Spanish-language education, with some courses geared to teens, medical professionals or social workers.

Monteverde Institute COURSES
(☎2645-5053; www.monteverde-institute.org; courses/homestay per week US$320/140) A nonprofit educational institute, founded in 1986, that offers interdisciplinary courses in tropical biology, conservation, sustainable development, women's studies and Spanish, among other topics. Internships and volunteer opportunities are also available.

Sleeping

An overflow of hotels means you can find many options in addition to those listed here. Most offer hot showers, though air-conditioning is not needed at such great heights.

★Pensión Santa Elena HOSTEL $
(☎2645-5051, 2645-6240; www.pensionsantaelena.com; camping per person US$7, dm US$12, s/d/tr US$19/29/36, s/d/tr without bathroom US$16/24/36, cabinas US$47-65; P@📶) This full-service hostel is a perennial favorite, right in central Santa Elena, offering budget travellers top-notch service and *pura vida* hospitality. Each room is different, with something to suit every budget.

Casa Tranquilo B&B $
(☎2645-6782; www.casatranquilohostel.com; dm US$7, d incl breakfast with/without bathroom US$25/20; P@📶) Another example of wonderful Tico hospitality. Staff lead free guided hikes, sharing their in-depth local expertise. The rooms are simple and spotless, some of them featuring skylights and golf views. Colorful murals adorn the outside, so you'll know you are in the right place.

Cabinas El Pueblo CABINAS $
(☎2645-6192; www.cabinaselpueblo.com; d incl breakfast with/without bathroom US$35/25; P@📶) This pleasant hostel run by an at-

tentive Tico couple is one of the best value deals in town. Marlenny and Freddy are eager to please, fetching guests at the bus station, booking tours and serving up big, filling breakfasts. The cute place also has a fully equipped kitchen, balcony, garden and hammocks.

Cabinas Eddy CABINAS $
(☎2645-6635; www.cabinas-eddy.com; d US$35-50, without bathroom US$30; P @) This reader-recommended budget spot continues to get raves for its delightful staff and the marimba-playing owner and manager. The rooms vary but service is consistently congenial.

Sloth Backpackers HOSTEL $
(☎2645-5793; www.monteverdeslothbackpackers.com; d/tr US$20/30) A colorful, corrugated tin and cinder block hostel that is well priced and comes with friendly management and a peaceful, back-roads location. Guests share communal bathrooms.

Cabinas & Hotel Vista al Golfo CABINAS $
(☎2645-6321; www.cabinasvistaalgolfo.com; dm US$7, s/d/tr US$20/25/36, without bathroom US$15/20/30; P) This is a very comfortable locale run by a congenial Costa Rican family. Rooms are well kept, the showers are hot and the owners will make you feel right at home. The upstairs balcony rooms (US$5 extra) have great views of the rainforest and, on a clear day, the Golfo de Nicoya. The hostel is in a separate location on the main drag, offering four-person dorms and a great common area.

Arco Iris Ecolodge LODGE $$
(☎2645-5067; www.arcoirislodge.com; s economy/standard US$30/65, d economy/standard/superior US$40/85/110; P @) This clutch of pretty cabins is on a little hill overlooking Santa Elena and the surrounding forests, and has the privacy and intimacy of a mountain retreat. The lodge features a system of private trails that wind throughout the property, including one that leads to a lookout point where you can see the Pacific on a clear day. There are a variety of different room sizes and styles to choose from, so you can either go rustic or live it up.

Mar Inn B&B B&B $$
(☎2645-5279; www.monteverdemarinn.com; s/d/tr incl breakfast US$45/62/68; P @) On a hill about 50m north of the high school, this family-run B&B is a great option, as the managers are welcoming and the breakfasts filling. Wood-paneled rooms are rustic and airy, and the quiet location means a restful night's sleep. It has a communal kitchen and a shared balcony where rocking chairs are oriented toward those lovely sunset views.

Quetzal Inn LODGE $$
(☎2645-6076; www.quetzalinn.com; d with/without balcony US$50/40; P @) On a quiet lane, this place has all the advantages of a central location, but still attracts birds, monkeys and wildlife. With wood-plank walls, high-sloped ceilings and green surroundings, this family-run lodge has a perfect combination of thoughtfully designed accommodations and a personable, hospitable ambience.

Finca Terra Viva LODGE $$
(☎2645-5454; www.terravivacr.com; d/q incl breakfast US$50/80, extra person US$10; P @) This 135-hectare *finca*, 3.5km or so out on the road toward Reserva Santa Elena, is being gradually returned to the forest; about 60% is already there. In the meantime, cattle, pigs, goats, horses and chickens offer guests a typical Costa Rica *finca* experience. There are six rustic, wooden rooms, as well as a few free-standing *casitas* (huts) with kitchenettes.

Hotel El Sueño HOTEL $$
(☎2645-5021; www.hotelelsuenocr.com; d incl US$40-60; P) This friendly, Tico-run hotel has spacious wooden rooms and a good

WORTH A TRIP

MONTEVERDE CHEESE FACTORY

Until the upswing in ecotourism, Monteverde's number-one employer was this **cheese factory** (La Lechería; ☎2645-7090; www.monteverdecheesefactory.com; adult/child US$12/10; ⏲tours 9am & 2pm Mon-Sat, store 7:30am-5pm Mon-Sat, 7:30am-4pm Sun). Started in 1953 by Monteverde's original Quaker settlers, the factory produces everything from a creamy Gouda to a very nice sharp, white cheddar, as well as other dairy products – most importantly, ice cream. Reservations are required for the two-hour tour of the factory, but you can pop in at any time to sample the creamy goodness.

BUSES FROM MONTEVERDE & SANTA ELENA

DESTINATION	POINT OF DEPARTURE	COST (US$)	DURATION (HR)	FREQUENCY (DAILY)
Puntarenas	Banco Nacional	3	3	3
Reserva Biológica Bosque Nuboso Monteverde	Banco Nacional	1.20	30 min	3
Reserva Santa Elena	Banco Nacional	2	30 min	4
San José	bus terminal	5	5	2
Tilarán, with connection to La Fortuna	bus terminal	3	7	6am

on-site restaurant. It's right in the center of town, so it can get noisy unless you request a room toward the back. Enjoy sweeping views from the balcony.

Eating

In addition to the big supermarkets in town, the tiny **Whole Foods Market** (7:30am-5:30pm) – no relation to the global behemoth – in Cerro Plano does has a smallish selection for self-caterers. Profits are reinvested in the community (it's part of the Casem cooperative).

La Carambola Art Cafe CAFE $

(2645-5465; lacarambolacafe@gmail.com; mains US$6-12; 11am-9pm;) A cute, bohemian cafe serving something different from standard fare. Here you'll find 100% fruit smoothies, freshly made hummus and pita sandwiches packed with Indian or Thai spiced chicken, and ample vegetarian choices too. It also serves beer and wine – cheers!

Taco Taco MEXICAN $

(mains US$5-8; noon-8pm;) This fast and friendly *taquería* (taco stall) offers tasty Tex-Mex tacos, burritos and quesadillas filled with shredded chicken, slow-roasted short rib, pork *al pastor* (cooked on a spit), roasted veggies and battered mahi mahi.

Stella's Bakery BAKERY $

(2645-5560; mains US$4-8; 6am-10pm) Order your choice of sandwich on delicious homemade breads with a convenient order form (one side is in English), and don't skimp on the veggies, many of which are locally grown (and organic). Bird nerds: an emerald toucanet is a regular visitor to the feeder out back.

★Café Caburé CAFE $$

(2645-5020; www.cabure.net; mains US$10-12; 9am-8pm Mon-Sat;) The Argentinean cafe above the Bat Jungle specializes in creative and delicious everything, from sandwiches on homemade bread and fresh salads, to more elaborate fare like tortillas stuffed with chicken mole, chipotle-rubbed steak, curried potatoes, or lemon shrimp. Save room for dessert because the chocolate treats are high art.

Morpho's Restaurant INTERNATIONAL $$

(2645-5607; mains US$7-20; 11am-9pm;) Dine among gushing waterfalls and pretty butterflies at this romantic downtown restaurant. The sophisticated menu combines local ingredients with gourmet flair – the results are sure to please any palate.

Tree House Restaurant & Café CAFE $$

(2645-5751; mains US$7-18; 11am-10pm;) Built around a half-century-old *higuerón* (fig) tree, this hip cafe serves up decent (if overpriced) food in a unique setting. It's a lively space to have a bite, linger over wine or (occasionally) catch live music.

Drinking & Entertainment

★Bar Amigos BAR

(2645-5071; www.baramigos.com; noon-3am) This is the one consistent place in the area at which to let loose. There are DJs, karaoke, all the sports from the US, and a billiard room downstairs. Things get going around 11pm.

Green Park LIVE MUSIC

(La Taberna; 2645-5883; 8pm-1am) Known by many names in recent years, this drinking establishment will always be remembered as La Taberna. No matter what you call it, you'll find a friendly outdoor bar, drink specials, pub fare and live music.

Shopping

Casem HANDICRAFTS
(Cooperativa de Artesanía Santa Elena Monteverde; ☎2645-5190; www.casemcoop.org; ⏲8am-5pm Mon-Sat, plus 10am-4pm Sun Dec-Apr) Casem, a women's arts and crafts cooperative, sells crafts and souvenirs with profits benefiting the community.

Orientation

In the cloud forest at 1200m to 1600m, the community of Monteverde is scattered along the road that leads to the reserve. Most budget hotels and restaurants are in the village of Santa Elena, while the more expensive lodges are found along the road. The Monteverde reserve is 6km southeast of Santa Elena, and the Santa Elena reserve is 5km northeast of Santa Elena village.

Information

Chamber of Tourism (☎2645-6565; www.monteverdecr.com; ⏲8am-8pm) Operated by the local Chamber of Commerce.

Libreria Chunches (☎2645-5147) Travel and natural history books, US newspapers, laundry service and snacks.

Pensión Santa Elena (www.pensionsantaelena.com) A more objective source of information than the Chamber of Tourism.

Red Cross (☎2645-6128; ⏲24hr) A hospital located just north of Santa Elena.

Getting There & Away

BUS

All arriving buses stop at the **bus terminal** (☎2645-5159; ⏲5:45-11am & 1:30-5pm Mon-Fri, closes 3pm Sat & Sun) in downtown Santa Elena. Keep a close eye on your luggage on the bus.

Note that the journey to La Fortuna takes longer than you'd think, because you have to hang around for two hours in Tilarán. If you have a few extra dollars, the jeep-boat-jeep option to La Fortuna is much faster.

JEEP-BOAT-JEEP

The fastest route between Monteverde–Santa Elena and La Fortuna is a jeep-boat-jeep combo (around US$25 to US$30, three hours), which can be arranged through almost any hotel or tour operator in either town. A 4WD minivan takes you to Río Chiquito, meeting a boat that crosses Laguna de Arenal, where a taxi on the other side continues to La Fortuna. This is increasingly becoming the primary transportation between La Fortuna and Monteverde, as it's incredibly scenic, reasonably priced and saves half a day of rough travel. Even if you may be confused as to why there are absolutely no jeeps involved in the process whatsoever.

HORSEBACK

There are a number of outfitters that offer transportation on horseback (per person US$65 to US$185, five to six hours) to La Fortuna, usually in combination with jeep rides. There are three main trails used: the Lake Trail (safe year-round), the Chiquito Trail (safe most of the year) and the gorgeous but infamous Castillo Trail (passable only in dry season by experienced riders). According to sources, the best among the horseback outfitters is Desafio Adventure Company (p576).

Tilarán

POP 8100

On the slopes of the Cordillera de Tilarán at the western end of Laguna de Arenal, this ranching boomtown makes a pleasant rest stop for travelers. Friendly and western, Tilarán showcases its first love – bulls – the last weekend in April with a rodeo, and on June 13 with a bullfight (note that the bull isn't killed in the Costa Rican version of the event) dedicated to San Antonio. At other times, it's a quiet town with some middle-class charm.

You can check email while waiting for your bus at **Cybercafé Tilarán** (☎2695-9010; per hr US$1.20; ⏲9am-10pm Mon-Sat), which has speedy connections.

BUSES FROM TILARÁN

DESTINATION	PRICE (US$)	DURATION (HR)	FREQUENCY(DAILY)
Cañas	1	30 min	7
La Fortuna	5	3	3
Puntarenas	4	2	2
San José	7	4	5
Santa Elena/Monteverde	3	2½	departs 12:30pm

Sleeping & Eating

Hotel Guadalupe HOTEL $
(☎2695-5943; www.hotelguadalupe.co.cr; r from US$30; P ❄ 📶) This modern hotel attracts traveling business types, who make themselves at home in simple rooms, dressed up with jewel tones and tile floors. Service is friendly and efficient, and there is a decent restaurant on site.

Hotel Tilarán HOTEL $
(☎2695-5043; r with/without bathroom US$11/7; P) On the west side of Parque Central, this is a solid budget choice. The rooms are tiny but mostly clean (and quiet if you can get one facing the rear).

Hotel Cielo Azul HOTEL $$
(☎2695-4000; www.cieloazulresort.com; s/d/tr US$40/60/75; P ❄ 📶 🏊) About 500m outside town, this hillside property has nine spiffy rooms overlooking a parking lot, a lovely pool and the Tilarán hills. With a catalog of tours, it's not a bad base to explore the surrounding area.

Getting There & Away

Buses depart from the terminal just west of Parque Central. The route between Tilarán and San José goes via the Interamericana, not La Fortuna.

La Fortuna & Volcán Arenal

POP 10,000

Prior to 1968, La Fortuna was a sleepy agricultural town, 6km from the base of Cerro Arenal. However, on the morning of July 29, 1968, Arenal erupted violently after nearly 400 years of dormancy, and buried some nearby villages. Suddenly, tourists from around the world started descending on La Fortuna in search of fiery night skies and the inevitable blurry photo of creeping lava.

Since then, La Fortuna has served as the principal gateway for visiting Volcán Arenal, and it's still one of the top destinations for travelers in Costa Rica. However, be aware that the great mountain has stopped spewing its molten discharge, and there are no longer lava photo ops. But the mountain is still glorious, offering a playground of cascading waterfalls, steep trails and luxurious hot springs.

As rapid development has taken its toll, you might find yourself batting off tour-hawkers the minute you step off the bus. Relax, once you get settled in, these hawkers disperse and you can enjoy nature's many distractions – probably a good thing since it takes time for Volcán Arenal to peek out from the cloud cover.

Sights & Activities

Parque Nacional Volcán Arenal PARK
(☎2461-8499; admission US$10) After the initial excitement in 1968, Volcán Arenal continued to produce ash columns, explosions and red streamers of molten rock almost daily. It all ended quite abruptly in 2010, leaving the alarmed tourist industry to gasp and spew in its place. While the molten night views are gone for now, the mighty mountain is still worthy of your time, as its slopes are home to great hiking trails and fantastic wildlife.

The park entrance is about 15km west of La Fortuna. Independent travelers can take an 8am bus toward Tilarán (ask to get off at the park). From the 'Parque Nacional' sign off the main road, a 2km dirt road leads to the park. From the ranger station grab a trail map to choose from trails through old lava flows, tropical rainforest or to the lake. The bus returns to La Fortuna at 2pm.

La Catarata de la Fortuna WATERFALL
(admission US$10; ⏲8am-5pm) A ribbon of cold, clear water called La Catarata de la Fortuna pours through a sheer canyon thick with bromeliads and ferns. Though it's dangerous to dive beneath the thundering 70m falls, you can take a dip in its perfect swimming holes (though keep an eye on your backpack). Rent a bike or walk. It's 7km from La Fortuna – all uphill – through pastureland and papaya trees. This is also the trailhead for the strenuous five-hour climb up to the lake-filled volcanic crater at Cerro Chato.

Arenal 1968 HIKING
(☎2462-1212; www.arenal1968.com; per person US$10; ⏲7am-10pm) Near the highway turnoff to the park, this is a private network of trails and lookouts along the original 1968 lava flow. The entrance is located 1.2km from the turnoff, just before the ranger station.

Hot Springs

What's the consolation prize if you can't actually see the volcano spewing hot rocks and lava? Why, hot springs, of course. There are several free, public hot springs in the area that any local can direct you to. If you're after a more comfortable experience, consider one of the area's resorts. They are all located along the road between La Fortuna and the turn-off to the park.

Eco-Termales HOT SPRING
(☎2479-8484; www.anywherecostarica.com; adult/child US$34/24, with dinner US$51/38; ⏲10am, 1pm & 5pm; 👪) Understated yet luxurious. Entry is restricted to just 100 visitors per time slot, so reservations are required.

Springs Resort & Spa HOT SPRING
(☎2401-3313, in USA 954-727-8333; www.thespringscostarica.com; 2-day admission US$50; P 👪) Eighteen free-form pools with various temperatures, volcano views, landscaped gardens, waterfalls, water slides and swim-up bars. It's pricey, but you can come back the next day for free.

Baldi Hot Springs HOT SPRING
(☎2479-9917; www.baldihotsprings.cr; with/without buffet US$51/31; ⏲10am-10pm; P 👪) A club on water, with three swim-up bars, blaring music and boozy drinks.

Tabacón Hot Springs HOT SPRING
(☎2519-1900; www.tabacon.com; day pass incl lunch or dinner adult/child US$85/30, day pass without meals US$60/10, evening pass without meals US$45; ⏲10am-10pm; P) Broad-leaf palms, rare orchids and other florid tropical blooms part to reveal a 40°C (104°F) waterfall pouring over a (fake) cliff, with hordes of overheated tourists lounging on the rocks.

Tours

Canoa Aventura CANOEING
(☎2479-8200; www.canoa-aventura.com; full-day trip to Caño Negro incl breakfast & lunch US$131; ⏲6:30am-9:30pm) About 1.5km west of town, Canoa Aventura specializes in canoe and float trips led by bilingual naturalist guides. Popular paddles include the full-day trip to Caño Negro.

Aventuras Arenal TOUR
(☎2479-9133; www.arenaladventures.com; Av Central; ⏲7am-8pm) Has been around for over 15 years, organizing a variety of local day tours via bike, boat and horseback.

Desafío Adventure Company TOURS
(☎2479-0020; www.desafiocostarica.com; Calle 2; horsetourbtwnMonteverde&ArenalUS$65; ⏲6:30am-9pm) This highly recommended company offers a variety of tours including rafting, horseback riding, mountain biking, canyoneering and more.

OFF THE BEATEN TRACK

VIENTO FRESCO WATERFALLS

If you're passing through Tilarán with your own wheels, consider a detour to **Viento Fresco Waterfalls** (☎2695-3434; www.vientofresco.net; adult/student/child US$15/12/10; ⏲7:30am-5pm; 👪). This series of five cascades includes the amazing Arco Iris (Rainbow Falls), which drops 75m into a refreshing shallow pool. There are plenty of opportunities for swimming and 'showering' under the falls. It's located 11km south of Tilarán on the road to Santa Elena/Monteverde.

Eagle Tours TOURS
(☎2479-9091; www.eagletours.net; ⏲6:30am-9pm) Budget travelers rave about this professionally run tour agency, with an office about 150m west of the church.

Jacamar Tours HIKING
(☎2479-9767; www.arenaltours.com; Av Central; ⏲7am-9pm) Recommended for its incredible variety of naturalist hikes.

Sunset Tours TOUR
(☎2479-9800; www.sunsettourcr.com; Calle 2; ⏲6:30am-9pm) This is La Fortuna's most established tour company, recommended for high-quality tours with bilingual guides.

Canopy Tours

Ecoglide CANOPY TOUR
(☎2479-7120; www.arenalecoglide.com; adult/student & child US$55/45; ⏲7am-4pm; 👪) Opened in 2008, Ecoglide is the biggest canopy game in town, with 13 cables, 15 platforms and a 'Tarzan' swing. It's 3.5km west of La Fortuna.

Arenal Paraíso Canopy Tours CANOPY TOUR
(☎2479-1100; www.arenalparaiso.com; US$45; ⏲8am-5pm) About 5km west of La Fortuna, this resort's 12 zip lines offer views of the Arenal river canyon and waterfalls.

Canopy Los Cañones CANOPY TOUR
(☎2479-1000; www.canopyloscanones.com; US$45) Located at the Hotel Los Lagos, Canopy Los Cañones has 15 cables, from 50m to 500m long, over the rainforest. Recover from your adventure by soaking in the hotel's thermal pools for no additional cost.

Sleeping

★Arenal Hostel Resort HOSTEL $
(☎2479-9222; www.arenalhostelresort.com; Av Central; dm/s/d/tr/q US$16/48/58/75/88; P ❄ ⊛ ≋) Offering the best of hostel and resort, this welcoming place is arranged around a landscaped garden, complete with hammocks, pool and volcano view. All rooms are clean, spacious and air-conditioned, and service is top-notch. It's right in the middle of town.

Sleeping Indian Hostel HOSTEL $
(☎8843-7101, 2479-8431; Av Fort; s/d US$25/30; ⊛) Ethnic insensitivities aside, this is a bright, cheery 2nd-story hostel, just north of the church. Its six fan-cooled, tiled rooms are furnished with wooden beds. It's run by a mellow, sophisticated local who offers plenty of communal space accented by drums, handicrafts and inviting hammocks.

La Fortuna Backpackers HOSTEL $
(☎2479-9700; www.fortunabackpackers.com; cnr Calle 5 & Ave Fort; dm/d US$10/25; P @ ⊛) Two blocks east of Parque Central, this humble peach-tinted *casa* (house) contains a surprisingly excellent hostel, with spotless rooms and an updated kitchen. Service is friendly, breakfast is delicious and prices are among the cheapest in town.

La Choza Inn INN $
(☎2479-9361; www.lachozainnhostel.com; Av Fort btwn Calles 2 & 4; dm US$10, s/d US$30/45, all incl breakfast; P @ ⊛) This popular budget inn 100m west of Parque Central has dark, palmwood dorm rooms to nicer doubles. There's a well-stocked communal kitchen, a reliable tour agency and personable staff.

Arenal Backpackers Resort HOSTEL $
(☎2479-7000; www.arenalbackpackersresort.com; Av Central; dm US$15-16, tents s/d US$25/35, d with/without bathroom US$56/45; P ❄ @ ⊛ ≋) Located two blocks west of the church, this is a self-proclaimed 'five-star hostel' with volcano views. Dorm rooms have private hot-water bathrooms and thick, orthopedic mattresses, while furnished tents offer another comfortable budget option. The real draw is the landscaped pool with swim-up bar.

Hotel Cerro Azul BUNGALOWS $$
(☎2479-7360; www.ranchocerroazul.com; d/tr/q US$64/76/90; P ❄ ⊛) Nothing fancy here, just four cute, shingled cabins with decks overlooking the trees, the river and the volcano beyond. Think: simple, natural, beautiful, comfortable. It's south of La Fortuna on the road to the waterfall.

Hotel Las Colinas HOTEL $$
(☎2479-9305; www.lascolinasarenal.com; Calle 1 btwn Avs Central & Arenal; s/d/tr incl breakfast from US$68/75/96; P ❄ @ ⊛) Modern, airy rooms have amenities like cable TV and solar-powered hot water, while the 2nd-story terrace has great views of the volcano.

Eating & Drinking

Rainforest Café CAFE $
(☎2479-7239; Calle 1 btwn Avs Central & Arenal; pastries US$1-5; ⏲7am-8:30pm; ⊛) Superb coffee and free wi-fi with a dash of industrial chic. There's an urban coffeehouse atmosphere with burlap coffee bags on the floor and coffee beans under the glass tabletops. Pastries and sandwiches will complement your joe.

Flying Tomato Cafe VEGETARIAN $
(☎2479-9913; www.lostresgatos.com; cnr Calle 5 & Av Volcan; mains US$5-10; ⏲8am-9pm; ✎) An exclusively veggie kitchen, serving pasta, veggie burgers, stir-frys and soups. It might be the only place in Fortuna to offer soy milk for espresso drinks and *batidos* (fruit shakes).

Soda Viquez SODA $
(☎2479-7133; cnr Calle 1 & Av Arenal; mains US$6-10; ⏲7am-10pm) Insanely popular among travelers, this friendly spot takes *tipica* and adds something to it. Prices are reasonable, portions ample.

Soda la Hormiga SODA $
(Av Arenal; mains US$3-5; ⏲6am-8pm) Locally beloved and set conveniently next door to the bus station, this open-air lunch counter is one of the quaintest, cheapest *sodas* in town. It does all the *casados*, as well as big breakfasts and burgers too.

La Cascada RESTAURANT $$
(☎2479-9145; cnr Av Fort & Calle 1; mains US$6-26; ⏲11am-late) This thatched-roof landmark has been around so long the *palapa* roof is almost as big an institution as the volcano it mimics. It has a small bar and acquires a drinking crowd at night but tourists go for lunch and dinner too. It has all the roast and grilled meat dishes, as well as veggie options.

Rockoco BAR
(Av Central; ⏲5pm-3am) You can't miss this place, west of town, due to its magic bus facade. Inside, it's all surfboard decor and graphed up Marilyn, Mona and Frida por-

traits on the back wall. The arced bamboo bar is wide and welcoming with cocktails, burgers and beers.

Information

Arenal Rocks Internet (☎8854-2898; Av Central; per hr US$1.20; ⏲8am-11pm) Located under the Hotel Arenal Carmella.

Expediciones (☎2479-9101; cnr Av Central & Calle 1; per 30/60min US$0.80/1.20; ⏲7am-9pm Mon-Sat) Most tour operators in town also provide internet access, but if you're not interested in hearing a sales pitch, there are no hassles here.

Getting There & Away

BUS

All domestic buses stop at the **Centro Comercial Adifort** (Av Arenal) bus terminal.

Ciudad Quesada for transfer to San José (US$1.60, 1 hour, 15 daily 5am to 7pm)

San José direct (US$4.25, 4½ hours, 12:45pm & 2:45pm)

Tilarán for transfer to Monteverde (US$3.60, 6 hours to 8 hours, 8am)

The Tica Bus to Nicaragua (US$27) passes by El Tanque between 6:30am and 7am daily; to catch the bus you'll have to take an early taxi to El Tanque (15 minutes, US$12).

JEEP-BOAT-JEEP

The fastest route between La Fortuna and Monteverde–Santa Elena is a jeep-boat-jeep combo (around US$25 to US$30, three hours), which can be booked through any tour agency.

HORSEBACK

Several tour companies offer horseback-riding trips between La Fortuna and Monteverde. The trip (a combination of horse, taxi or boat) takes five to seven hours and costs about US$85, including separate transport of your luggage. One recommended company is Desafío Adventure Company (p581).

Los Chiles

Sweltering and sleepy, Los Chiles sits three rutted kilometers south of Nicaragua. Originally settled by merchants and fishermen, it later served as an important supply route for Nicaraguan Contras, with a strong US military presence throughout the 1980s. Today gringo-traffic refers to travelers exploring the scenic water route to Caño Negro or the river route to Nicaragua, a one- to two-hour boat ride. Travelers crossing here must stop in Los Chiles for the necessary paperwork.

The Banco Nacional in town has an ATM and changes cash.

Sleeping & Eating

Hotel y Cabinas Carolina CABINAS $

(☎2471-1151; r from US$30; ❄📶) Not your typical border-town accommodations. This friendly, family-run option gets rave reviews for attentive English-speaking staff, spotless rooms and excellent local food. It's further from the boat dock than the other options, but it's worth the walk.

Hotel Wilson Tulipán HOTEL $

(☎2471-1414; www.hoteleswilson.com; cnr Ave 0 & Calle 4; s/d/tr incl breakfast US$30/48/60; P🏊❄@📶) Brand new rooms are set in a strange, ghost-town motel that is right down the road from the boat dock. There are older but still comfortable rooms in the main building too, but those get plenty of night noise from the lively bar and restaurant (mains US$5 to US$8), which flaunts tasty seafood *tipica* and bad behavior.

Getting There & Away

Regular boat transportation is limited to quick shuttles across the Nicaraguan border to San Carlos (US$12), departing daily at 12:30pm and 3:30pm. Get here early as space is limited and immigration lines are long. See p634 for details.

All buses arrive and leave from the terminal behind Soda Pamela, near the intersection of Hwy 35. Timetables are flexible, so play it safe and inquire locally.

Ciudad Quesada (US$2.25, 2 hours, every 45 minutes 4:30am to 6pm) For transfer to La Fortuna.

San José (US$6, 5 hours, 5am to 3pm)

Upala (US$4, 2½ hours, 3 daily) Via Caño Negro.

La Virgen

Steeped in the tangled shores of the wild and scenic Río Sarapiquí, La Virgen prospered in the heyday of the banana trade. Today it's a little-known destination for world-class kayaking and rafting, which is best in December. All the buses between San José and Puerto Viejo de Sarapiquí make stops in La Virgen.

Activities

Sarapiquí Outdoor Center RAFTING

(☎8322-5597, 2761-1123; www.costaricaraft.com; 2-/4-hr rafting trip US$65/110, guided kayak trips US$120-150) Here is your local paddling authority. In addition to offering its own rafting excursions, it offers kayak rental (per day US$45) and instruction, as well as info about local conditions.

Hacienda Pozo Azul Adventures ADVENTURE SPORTS
(☎2761-1360, in USA & Canada 877-810-6903; www.pozoazul.com; tours US$38-55;) Specializes in adventure activities, including horseback-riding tours, a canopy tour over the lush jungle and river, rappelling, and assorted river trips.

Sleeping & Eating

Rancho Leona LODGE $
(☎2761-1019, 2761-0048; www.rancholeona.com; r without bathroom per person US$12;) Kayakers congregate at this shady, riverside spot to swap tales of white-water adventure. The simple, spotless rooms in the wood-plank lodge share hot-water bathrooms. In addition to arranging river trips, the super-friendly staff sometimes prepare family-style dinners.

Tirimbina Lodge LODGE $$
(☎2761-1579; www.tirimbina.org; Tirimbina Rainforest Center; s/d/tr from US$45/56/68) Set on a 345-hectare private reserve, this rustic lodge offers an immersive rainforest experience at affordable prices. The accommodation is not fancy, but excellent guided tours and 9km of trails provide up-close wildlife-watching opportunities. This non-profit center reinvests its profits into environmental research and education.

Puerto Viejo de Sarapiquí

POP 7100

At the scenic confluence of two rivers, Puerto Viejo de Sarapiquí was once the most important port in Costa Rica, sending off boats laden with fruit, coffee and other commercial exports. Today, it is simply a gritty palm-shaded market town, but it offers excellent opportunities for bird-watching, rafting, kayaking and hiking.

Taking the launch from Puerto Viejo to Trinidad, at the confluence of the Ríos Sarapiquí and San Juan, provides a rich opportunity to see crocodiles, sloths, birds, monkeys and iguanas sunning themselves on the muddy riverbanks. The river system is still off the beaten tourist track, revealing rainforest and ranches, wildlife and old war zones, pasture land and protected forest.

If you don't care to go all the way to Trinidad, you can still take a shorter river cruise (90 minutes) on the Ruta Los Heroes with the **Associacion de Turismo Rural** (☎2766-5858; tour per person US$20; ⏲8am-3pm).

Sleeping & Eating

Cabinas Laura CABINA $
(☎2766-6316; s/d US$20/24;) A sparkling, quiet choice on the road to the pier. Rooms are simple with new tile, wood furnishings and cable TV.

★Chilamate Rainforest Eco Retreat LODGE $$
(☎2766-6949; www.chilamaterainforest.com; dm US$30, s/d incl breakfast US$76/96) Built on

WORTH A TRIP

CAÑO NEGRO

The remote 102-sq-km **Refugio Nacional de Vida Silvestre Caño Negro** (☎2471-1309; ⏲8am-4pm) has long lured anglers seeking that elusive 18kg snook, and birders hoping to glimpse rare waterfowl. During the dry season water levels drop, concentrating the birds and fish in close quarters. From January to March, when migratory birds land in large numbers, avian density is world class.

The Río Frío defines the landscape – south of the main Caño Negro dock it's a table-flat, swampy expanse of marsh and lagoon. North of town, it's a slender river that carves looming forest.

Tour operators offer wildlife-watching trips to Caño Negro from La Fortuna and San José. Los Chiles is a more convenient base, allowing you to get on the river earlier. Inquire at the dock to book a half-day trip for US$45 per person, or make your way to Caño Negro village where you can book a tour through the local tour-guide cooperative, known as **Real Tour** (☎2471-1621; real.tour@hotmail.com; 1hr tour US$40, 2-3hr tour US$60, 4hr tour US$70; ⏲8am-4pm).

Buses to Caño Negro depart from Los Chiles three times a day.

MISTAKEN IDENTITY

Don't confuse Puerto Viejo de Sarapiquí with the *other* Puerto Viejo (de Talamanca) on the Caribbean coast.

20 hectares of secondary forest, the five large solar-powered cabins are basic but full of character, with comfy hand-crafted furniture. Out back, the bunkhouse has 12 dorm beds with shared bathroom and kitchen. Behind the lodge, 6km of paths wind through the jungle, where you might spot sloths, monkeys, toucans, frogs, snakes and more. The resort is 6km west of town on the road to La Virgen.

Posada Andrea Cristina B&B CABINA **$$**
(☎2766-6265; www.andreacristina.com; s/d incl breakfast US$32/52; P) About 1km west of the center, this recommended B&B has eight quaint cabins in its garden, each with a colorful paint job, stone tile, high beamed ceilings, hot water and outdoor table and chairs. It's situated on the edge of the forest, so there are plenty of opportunities for birdwatching on the grounds.

Getting There & Away

The small port has a regular service to the small ranching outpost of Trinidad, which is just across the Río San Juan from Nicaragua. Boats to Trinidad depart at 2pm and return the following morning at 5am and cost US$10 per person.

Right across from the park, the **bus terminal** (☎2233-4242; 5am-7pm) sells tickets to the following destinations:

Guápiles (US$2, 1 hour, 10 daily) Empresarios Guapileños buses.

La Virgen (US$1, 30 minutes, hourly 6am to 8pm)

San José (US$2.50, 2 hours, 9 daily) Autotransportes Sarapiquí and Empresarios Guapileños buses.

GUANACASTE

Like the prized, gnarled shade tree the region is named after, there is something singular and stubborn about Guanacaste. Call it the backwater blessing – a slow, colonial pace means that locals are laidback and cordial, and roads still lead to nowhere.

Volcanoes, hot springs and horse packing trips take travelers high above the cowboy plains. Rare, dry tropical forests lead into remote Pacific beaches, turtle havens with riotously sweet surf breaks. And with a shiny new airport terminal, it's never been easier to explore the great northwest.

Cañas

POP 25,500

Sabanero (cowboy) culture is evident on the sweltering streets of Cañas, where custom pickup trucks share the road with swaggering cowboys on horseback. It's typical rural Latin America, where the gait is slow and businesses lock up for lunch. Don't miss the striking **Catholic Church**, covered with mosaics by the famed local artist Otto Apuy.

At the crossroads of the Interamericana and the eastern road to Monteverde, Cañas provides visitors with a base for organizing rafting trips on the nearby Río Corobicí. Book with **Safaris Corobicí** (☎2669-6091; www.safaricorobici.com; Interamericana Km 193; 2hr tour US$52, 3hr bird-watching tour US$60; departures 7am-3pm;), whose office is on the Interamericana, 4km north of Cañas.

Sleeping & Eating

Hotel Cañas HOTEL **$**
(☎2669-5118; www.hotelcanascr.com; cnr Calle 2 & Av 3; s/d US$24/32; P) This professionally run hotel is quiet and super clean, but those potted (silk!) plants offer merely the illusion of nature.

Caña Brava Inn HOTEL **$$**
(☎2669-1294; www.canabravainn.com; cnr Interamericana & Av 5; s/d US$45/60; P) This newish, upscale hotel has all the modern amenities including well-insulated rooms with flat-screen TV, huge comfy bedding and contemporary, dark wood furnishings.

Rincón Corobicí COSTA RICAN **$$**
(☎2669-1234; www.rinconcorobici.com; mains US$6-12; 8am-6pm) This attractive Swiss-run restaurant is 4km north of Cañas on the banks of the Río Corobicí. A terrace provides river and garden views, and a short trail follows the riverbank where you can take a cool dip. You can also book rafting trips here.

Getting There & Away

Terminal Cañas sits at the north end of town.

Liberia (US$3, 1½ hours, 10 daily 4:30am to 5:30pm)

Puntarenas (US$3, 2 hours, 7 daily 6am to 4:30pm)

San José (US$5, 3½ hours, 9 daily 4am to 5:30pm)

Tilarán (US$1, 45 minutes, 8 daily 6am to 5:45pm)

Parque Nacional Palo Verde

The 184-sq-km **Parque Nacional Palo Verde** (☎2524-0628; www.ots.ac.cr; adult/child US$10/1; ⏲8am-4pm) is a wetland sanctuary in Costa Rica's driest province. Palo Verde has the greatest concentrations of waterfowl and shorebirds in Central America, with over 300 recorded bird species. Visitors can spot large flocks of herons (including rare black-crowned night herons), storks, spoonbills and scarlet macaws. When the dry season begins in December, birds congregate in lakes and marshes, trees lose their leaves and the flocks become easier to see.

Find good accommodations and information at the **Hacienda Palo Verde Research Station** (☎2524-0607; www.ots.ac.cr; r incl breakfast per person US$72; P), run by the Organization of Tropical Studies (OTS). It also offers naturalist-guided **hiking tours** (per person US$24) and **bird-watching tours** (per person US$36) Tours depart from OTS headquarters at 8am and 3pm.

Palo Verde is 30km west of Cañas: look for the turnoff in Bagaces. Buses running between Cañas and Liberia can drop you at the ACT office in Bagaces. If you call the office in advance, rangers may be able to drive you the remaining 22km into the park.

Liberia

POP 63,000 / TRANSPORT HUB

The sunny, rural capital of Guanacaste has long served as a transportation hub connecting Costa Rica with Nicaragua, as well as being the standard-bearer of Costa Rica's *sabanero* culture. Nowadays, tourism is fast becoming a significant contributor to the economy. With an expanding international airport, Liberia is a safe and surprisingly chilled-out gateway to the rest of Costa Rica. It's an especially good launching pad

Liberia

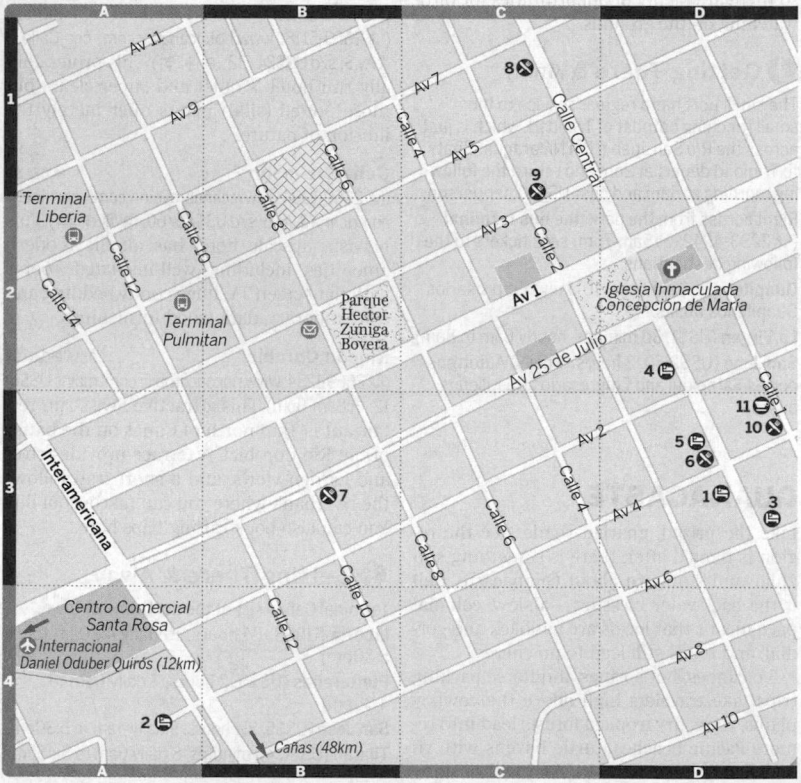

for exploring Rincon de la Valle National Park and the beaches of the Península de Nicoya.

Sleeping

La Posada del Tope GUESTHOUSE $
(☎2666-3876; hotelposadadeltope@gmail.com; Calle Real btwn Avs 2 & 4; r with/without bathroom US$30/20; P) Set around an awesome garden and furnished with an eclectic collection of art and antiques, this place has a lot of personality for a budget hotel. Rooms are decidedly basic but the price is right. The bilingual Tico owner, Denís, is a wealth of information.

Hotel Liberia HOTEL $
(☎2666-0161; www.hotelliberiacr.com; Calle Real btwn Avs Central & 2; dm US$10, s/d from US$20/32; P) Rooms in this rambling, century-old building surround an outdoor lounge complete with TV, hammocks and jet-lagged backpackers. The atmosphere is vibrant, but the rooms are ragged.

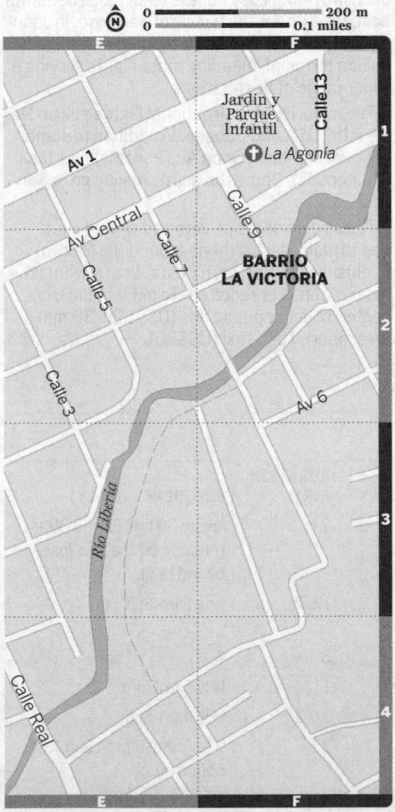

Hotel La Casona HOTEL $
(☎2666-2971; casona@racsa.co.cr; cnr Calle Real & Av 6; d US$36; P) This pink, wooden house has adequate rooms and friendly management. Prices are often negotiable.

★Casa del Papel B&B $$
(Posada de la Calle Real; ☎2666-0626; posadadelacallereal@gmail.com; cnr Calle Real & Av 4; s US$20-55, d US$30-75, all incl breakfast; P) This historic house has been artfully converted into an exquisite guesthouse, easily recognizable by its newsprint facade. The rooms are simply and tastefully decorated, most with shared bathrooms. The common lounge is hung with original art and vintage furnishings, while gorgeous gardens, swimming pool with jacuzzi and hammocks are at your disposal.

El Punto Hotel HOTEL $$$
(☎2665-2986; www.elpuntohotel.com; cnr Interamericana & Av 4; r from US$100; P) This converted elementary school is now a chic contemporary hotel. Saturated in tropical colors, the loft apartments are equipped with hammocks, kitchenettes and bold modern art. The young bilingual owner, Mariana, is charm personified.

Eating & Drinking

Los Comales COSTA RICAN $
(☎2666-0105; Calle Central btwn Avs 7 & 5; dishes US$3-8; 6:30-9pm) This convivial, popular local spot is run by a women's collective, and serves native Guanacaste dishes as well as typical cuisine. The specialty is

Liberia

Sleeping
1 Casa del Papel D3
2 El Punto Hotel A4
3 Hotel La Casona D3
4 Hotel Liberia D2
5 La Posada del Tope D3

Eating
6 Café Liberia D3
7 Jauja B3
8 Los Comales C1
9 Pan y Miel C1
10 Pizza Pronto D3

Drinking & Nightlife
11 Mariajuana D3

chicken and salsa, but the *casados* are just as tasty.

Pan y Miel BAKERY $
(☎2666-0718; Calle 2 btwn Avs 3 & 5; mains US$2-6; ⏲6am-6pm) If you're looking for breakfast, this local bakery serves its excellent bread as sandwiches and French toast. There's also a buffet line with filling *casado* fixings, pastries and fresh fruit.

Mariajuana CAFE
(Calle 1 btwn Avs 2 & 4; mains US$2-6; ⏲11:30am-10pm Mon-Sat; 📶 👪) This funky, colorful, al fresco bar is a welcoming place for burritos, grills and fresh-fruit *batidos*.

★Café Liberia ORGANIC $$
(☎2665-1660; Calle Real btwn Avs 2 & 4; mains US$8-12; ⏲7am-10pm Mon-Sat; ❄ 📶 ✎) This beautifully restored colonial building has heavy wood furniture and a frescoed ceiling, creating a romantic ambiance for rich coffee and gourmet fare. It's an atmospheric setting for occasional live music and other perfomances.

Jauja RESTAURANT $$
(☎2665-2061; cnr Av 25 de Julio & Calle 10; mains US$8-18; ⏲11am-1am; P 📶) This stylish indoor-outdoor bar serves wood-fired pizza, tender grass-fed steaks and burgers on home-baked buns. A solid new venture from a young, born-and-raised Liberia chef.

Pizza Pronto ITALIAN $$
(☎2666-2098; cnr Av 4 & Calle 1; mains US$8-17; ⏲11am-11pm) This very cute, old-world pizzeria, where the wood is stacked next to the smoking courtyard oven, keeps it romantic and simple – just pizza, pasta and salads. Choose from a long list of toppings for your wood-fired pizza, including fresh seafood or local pineapple.

Information

Cyberm@nia (☎2666-7240; Av 1 btwn Calles 2 & Central; per hr US$1.20; ⏲8am-10pm) With the friendliest staff ever, this spot is also good for cheap long-distance calls.

Hospital Dr Enrique Baltodano Briceño (☎2666-0011, emergencies 2666-0318) The hospital is behind the stadium, on the northeastern outskirts of town.

Planet Internet (☎2665-3737; Calle Real btwn Avs Central & 2; per hr US$1; ⏲9am-9pm) Has speedy machines set up for internet calling.

Getting There & Away

AIR

Since 1993, Aeropuerto Internacional Daniel Oduber Quirós (p634), 12km west of Liberia, has served as the country's second international airport, providing easy access to all those beautiful beaches without the hassle of San José. In January 2012, it unveiled its sleek, mod new US$35 million terminal, meaning more flights serving a wider range of destinations.

The majority of international flights still arrive from the USA and Canada, in addition to some regional flights on Copa Air (Panama) and Taca (Guatemala). Domestic flights mainly go to San José.

The airport offers private and shared shuttles to many destinations around the Nicoya Peninsula and Northern Costa Rica. Advanced reservations are required. To get into Liberia's center, take the public bus (US$1.20, 30 minutes, hourly) or a taxi (US$20).

BUSES FROM LIBERIA

DESTINATION	POINT OF DEPARTURE	PRICE (US$)	DURATION (HR)	FREQUENCY (DAILY)
Cañas	Terminal Liberia	2	2	every 30 min 5am-9:30pm (or jump off the San José-bound bus)
La Cruz/Peñas Blancas	Terminal Liberia	2.50	1½-2	hrly 5am-6:30pm
Managua, Nicaragua	Liberia Cruce	30	5	4
Playa del Coco	Terminal Pulmitan	1.20	1	hrly 5am-7pm
Playa Tamarindo	Terminal Liberia	2.75	1½-2	hrly 4am-6pm
Puntarenas	Terminal Liberia	3	3	9 (or jump off the San José–bound bus)
San José	Terminal Pulmitan	6	4½	11

BUS

Buses depart from **Terminal Liberia** (Av 7 btwn Calles 12 & 14) and **Terminal Pulmitan** (Av 5 btwn Calles 10 & 12). The TransNica bus to Managua pulls over at the Liberia Cruce, the traffic light on the Interamericana.

Shuttle Bus

If you're trying to reach the Península de Nicoya, there are numerous shuttle services, including **Tropical Tour Shuttles** (☎2640-1900; www.tropicaltourshuttles.com).

Parque Nacional Rincón de la Vieja

Active Volcán Rincón de la Vieja (1895m) is the steamy star of this park, which bubbles with fumaroles, tepid springs, and steaming, flatulent mud pits, as well as a young and feisty *volcancito* (small volcano). Much of the park is accessible on sometimes steep, well-maintained trails. The crater itself is off-limits, since a series of eruptions in early 2012 has made it unsafe.

The park is home to 300 bird species as well as morpho butterflies, tapirs, monkeys and pumas. The park i s also home to the country's highest density of Costa Rica's national flower, the increasingly rare purple orchid (*Cattleya skinneri*), locally known as *guaria morada*. Take precautions against ticks, especially in grassy areas – wear closed shoes and trousers.

Most visitors enter through the **Las Pailas sector** (☎2661-8139; www.acguanacaste.ac.cr; adult/child US$10/1; ⏲7am-3pm, closed Mon) on its western flank. Going east from the ranger station, a circular trail (about 3km) takes you past boiling mud pools known as **Las Pailas**, or 'the caldrons', as well as sulfurous fumaroles and a miniature volcano. West of the ranger station, the Sendero Cangreja leads 5km to **Catarata La Cangreja**, a waterfall plunging from a high cliff into a blue lagoon ideal for swimming.

From the **Santa María ranger station** (☎2661-8139; www.acguanacaste.ac.cr; adult/child US$10/1; ⏲8am-5pm) you can follow a 2.8km trail to the sulfurous **hot springs**. There's also a 1.1km trail to the Catarata Bosque Encantado, Santa Maria's best waterfall.

Sleeping

Camping is permitted only at the Santa Maria ranger station (US$2 per person). The campground has water, pit toilets, showers, tables and grills, but you'll have to be self-sufficient. Dry-season camping in December, March and April is recommended, but be prepared for cold and foggy weather year-round.

Rinconcito Lodge LODGE $

(☎2200-0074; www.rinconcitolodge.com; standard s/d US$25/39, superior s/d incl breakfast US$36/63/81/93; P) Just 3km from the Santa María sector of the park, this recommended budget option has attractive, rustic cabins that are surrounded by some of the prettiest pastoral scenery imaginable. Cheaper rooms are just as clean and fresh as the larger variety, but they're tiny. Inexpensive tours and transportation are also available.

El Sol Verde CAMPGROUND $$

(☎2665-5357; www.elsolverde.com; campsites US$7, tent houses US$25, d/q US$48/69; P) A lovely Dutch couple in Curubandé village offers three sweet Spanish-tiled, wood-walled rooms. Alternatively, bed down in the camping area where there's a few furnished tent houses, a shared outdoor kitchen and plenty of space to pitch your own tent. Transportation to the park is available, and you'll find hiking, swimming and wildlife in the immediate vicinity.

Getting There & Away

The Las Pailas sector is accessible via a 20km gravel road beginning at a signed turnoff from the Interamericana 5km north of Liberia. To reach the park, you must use a private road (US$1.50 per person). Drivers must have a 4WD in the rainy season. There's no public transportation, but hotels and lodges can arrange transportation from Liberia for around US$30 each way.

The Santa María ranger station is accessible via a rougher road beginning at Barrio La Victoria in Liberia. There is no public bus service. Taxis cost around US$45 each way.

Santa Rosa

Part of the Area de Conservacion Guanacaste, the **Santa Rosa Sector** (2666-5051; admission US$10) was established mainly for historical and patriotic reasons, but Santa Rosa also has botanical and biological interest. The rare tropical dry forest is populated by primordial acacia thorn trees and tall *jaragua* grass, as well as cacti and bromeliads. Playa Nancite is famous for its *arribadas* (mass nesting) of olive ridley sea turtles that can number up to 8000 at a time. However, the majority of travelers are here for one reason – the chance to surf at Playa Naranjo and Ollie's Point.

Make reservations in advance to stay in the basic dorm at the park's **research station** (☎2666-5051; www.acguanacaste.ac.cr; dm US$15, meals US$6-7), where there is also a cheap cafeteria. Otherwise, there's a shady developed **campground** (per person US$2) close to the park headquarters, with picnic benches, grills, flushing toilets and cold-water showers. Playa Naranjo is also popular for camping, though there's no potable water.

Sights & Activities

La Casona HISTORIC BUILDING
(☎2666-5051; www.acguanacaste.ac.cr; ⏲8-11:30am & 1-4pm) This reconstructed building is on the grounds of the old Hacienda Santa Rosa, which is where the battle of 1856 was fought. It now contains a good museum, with exhibits on the military action, as well as the region's natural history. The museum was closed for renovation at the time of research, but will likely reopen before you arrive. Two hiking trails leave from behind the museum, one of which leads to the **Monumento a Los Héroes**.

Playa Naranjo BEACH
The surfing at Playa Naranjo is truly world-class, especially near **Witch's Rock**, a beach break famous for its fast, hollow 3m rights (although there are also fun lefts when it isn't pumping). Although this is a beach break, there are rocks near the river mouth. Be especially careful near the estuary, as it's a rich feeding ground for crocodiles during the tide changes. The surfing is equally legendary off Playa Portero Grande at **Ollie's Point**, which boasts the best right-hander in Costa Rica (though this remote beach is only accessible by boat from Playa del Coco or Tamarindo).

Playa Nancite BEACH
The best turtle beach is Playa Nancite in the south, and during September and October as many as 8000 olive ridley turtles show up on the beach at once. Nancite is a restricted area, but permission can be obtained from the park service to see this spectacle. Flashlights and flash photography are prohibited, as is fishing and hunting.

Getting There & Away

The park entrance is on the west side of the Interamericana, 35km north of Liberia. Take any bus headed to the Nicaragua border at Peñas Blancas and ask the driver to let you off at the park entrance. You can also arrange private transportation from Liberia for about US$20 per person round trip.

From the highway, it is another 7km to the ranger station, where you'll find the information center, campground, museum, research station and nature trail. A 12km trail leads down to the coast and Playa Naranjo. To drive, you need a high-clearance 4WD vehicle for river crossings; inquire with rangers for road conditions.

La Cruz

POP 4800

La Cruz is the closest town to the Peñas Blancas border crossing with Nicaragua, and it's the principal gateway to **Bahía Salinas**, Costa Rica's premier kitesurfing destination. La Cruz itself is a gritty and fairly sleepy provincial town set on a mountain plateau, with magical views of the wind-swept Bahía Salinas from nearly every corner.

Sleeping & Eating

Hotel La Mirada HOTEL $
(☎2679-9702; www.hotellamirada.com; s/d US$27/40; P ❄ 📶) Despite the name, there are no views to speak of, but this place is family-owned and lovingly maintained. Rooms are a bit oddly laid out but super clean with beamed ceilings, cable TV and loft sleeping spaces for the kids.

Amalia's Inn INN $
(☎2679-9618; s/d US$20/30; P ❄ 🏊) The shared terracotta terraces at Amalia's have stupendous bay views. The white stucco house on a cliff isn't a bad place to spend the night, either. Walls in the meandering house are hung with modernist paintings by Amalia's late husband.

Hotel Bella Vista HOTEL $
(☎2679-8050; r with/without bathroom US$16/12; P ❄ 🏊) With a lovely mosaic-bottomed pool and breezy restaurant at the top of the hill, this Dutch-run hotel has stuffy but reasonably clean rooms. Those on the second level get more light and have outstanding views.

Getting There & Away

Most buses depart from the bus station, which is three blocks west of the Interamericana, across from the city administration building.

Transportes Deldú (www.transportesdeldu.com; 7:30am-12:30pm & 1:30-6pm), based at the bus station, sells tickets and stores bags. To catch a TransNica bus to Peñas Blancas, you'll need to flag a bus down on the Interamericana.

Liberia (US$2.50, 1½ hours, 8 daily)

Peñas Blancas (US$1.50, 45 minutes, 10 daily)

San José (US$7, 5 hours, hourly 5:30am to 5:30pm) Via Liberia.

PENÍNSULA DE NICOYA

The allure of the Península de Nicoya needs no explanation. Maybe you're here to sample sapphire waters that peel left and right, and curl into perfect barrels up and down the coast. Or you want to dive, snorkel, fish or paddle in the life-affirming Pacific. Burn days and nights on the beach, spot nesting leatherbacks, or bound across rugged roads, fording rivers and navigating ridges with massive coastal views.

In any case, there's no shortage of groovy boutique nests, yoga studios and tasteful kitchens to nourish and shelter you between adventures. Whether you've set aside days or weeks, it's time to get busy.

Playa del Coco

Easily the most accessible of the peninsula's beaches is Playa del Coco, 37km west of Liberia. Its name is derived from the cocoa-colored sand that lies between its two rocky headlands. Sportfishing is the engine that built this place, and you'll mingle with the American anglers at happy hour (it starts rather early here).

Sights & Activities

The northern peninsula is one of the best and most easily accessible dive destinations in the country. Dives are made off the coast at **Isla Santa Catalina** (about 20km southwest) or **Isla Murciélago** (40km northwest). Plenty of turtles and pelagics meander through, including mantas, sharks and whales, and you'll be lost in huge schools of smaller tropical fish.

The preferred beach for snorkeling and swimming is **Playa Ocotal**, 4km south of town. Playa del Coco is also a jumping-off point for surfing at Witch's Rock and Ollie's Point in Santa Rosa. The surf shops in town can set you up.

Rich Coast Diving DIVING
(2670-0176, in USA & Canada 800-434-8464; www.richcoastdiving.com; 2 tanks per person US$100, Open Water Course US$450) On the main street, this Dutch-owned dive shop is the area's largest.

Summer Salt DIVING
(2670-0308; www.summer-salt.com; 2 tanks per person US$100-120) This friendly Swiss-run dive shop has professional, bilingual staff. On the main street, 100m south of the park.

Festivals & Events

Fiesta de La Virgen del Mar FESTIVAL
(Festival of the Virgin of the Sea; mid-Jul) Held in Puntarenas and Playa del Coco, it involves colorful regattas and boat parades.

Sleeping

Budget lodgings – mostly with cold water only – primarily cater to Tico weekenders. Some of the best options are along La Chorrera, the road that runs parallel to the beach, heading northeast from the main drag.

Pure Vibes Backpackers Resort HOSTEL $
(2670-0273; www.purevibesesorts.com; La Chorrera; dm US$12-19, d US$60-70;) Everything you ever wanted in a hostel: clean rooms of varying sizes (including all-female dorms), en suite bathrooms, a huge pool and plenty of hammocks, friendly management and loads of on-site fun. Super bonus: the hostel pays your taxi fare from the bus stop.

Cabinas Coco Azul CABINA $
(2670-0431; cabinascocoazul_cr@yahoo.com; d from US$25;) This white brick building is the best of several budget *cabinas* located in a quiet, gated complex behind the church. Rooms are sparkling clean and comfy.

Hotel Mar & Mar HOTEL $$
(2670-1212; s/d US$20/40;) A romantic beachfront hacienda whose fan-cooled rooms have ceramic-tiled floors. Singles are clean but cramped; double rooms are worth the extra cash.

Laura's House B&B B&B $$
(2670-0157; www.laurashousecr.com; La Chorrera; s/d/tr/q incl breakfast US$50/62/74/85;) Laura's homey B&B has a prime

Península de Nicoya

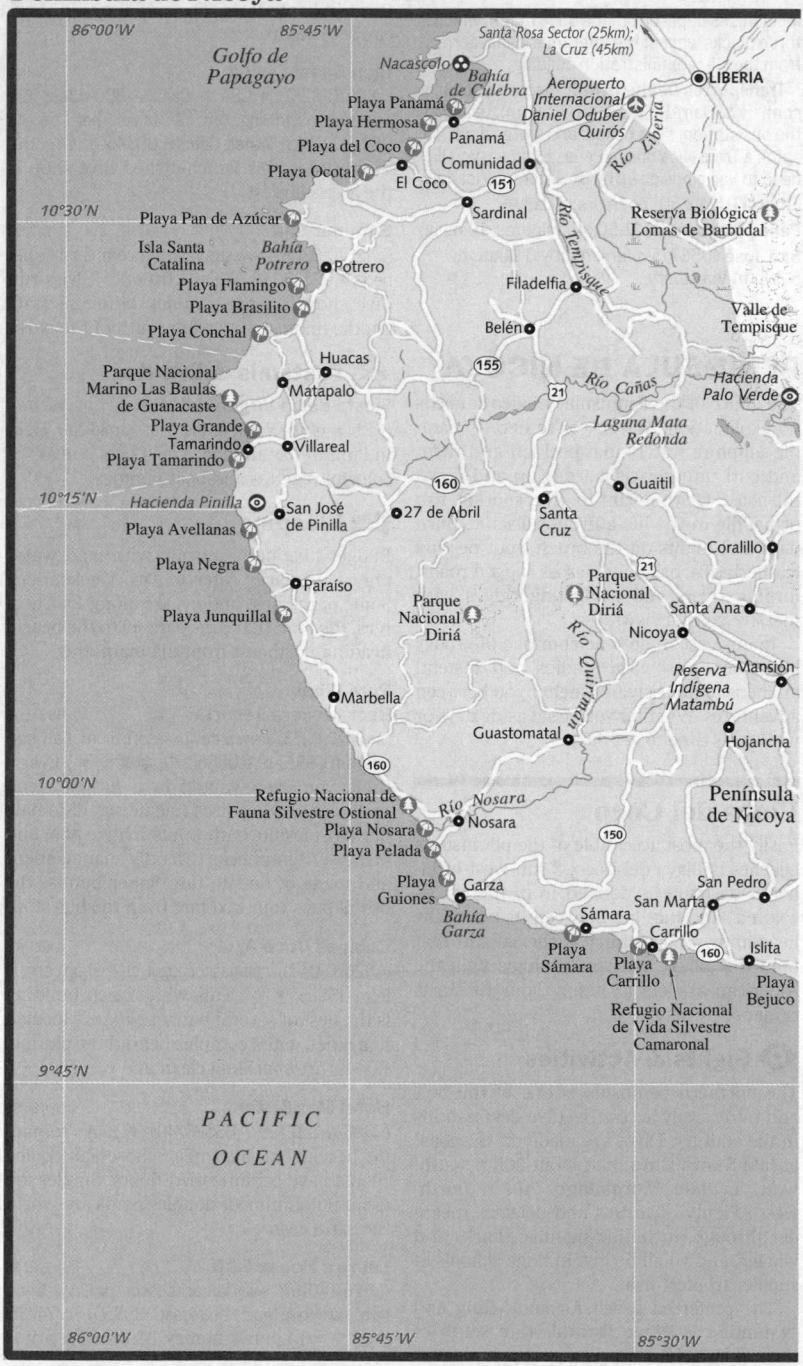

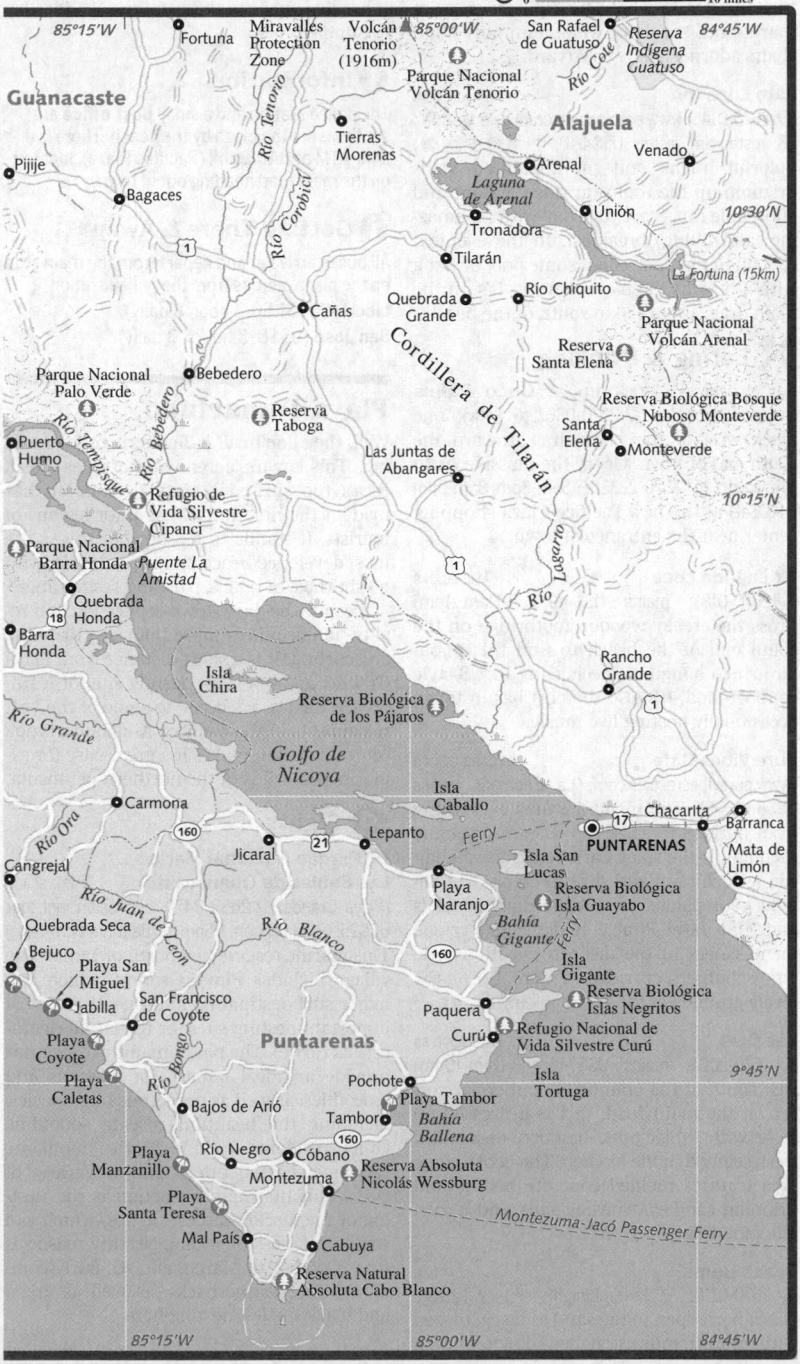
0 20 km
0 10 miles
85°15'W
Fortuna
Miravallés Protection Zone
Volcán Tenorio (1916m)
85°00'W
San Rafael de Guatuso
Reserva Indígena Guatuso
84°45'W
Parque Nacional Volcán Tenorio
Río Coto
Guanacaste
Río Tenorio
Alajuela
Tierras Morenas
Venado
Pijije
Arenal
Bagaces
Laguna de Arenal
Unión
Río Corobicí
Tronadora
10°30'N
1
Tilarán
La Fortuna (15km)
Río Chiquito
Quebrada Grande
Cañas
Parque Nacional Volcán Arenal
Reserva Santa Elena
Cordillera de Tilarán
Parque Nacional Palo Verde
Bebedero
Río Bebedero
Reserva Taboga
Reserva Biológica Bosque Nuboso Monteverde
Santa Elena
Puerto Humo
Río Tempisque
Monteverde
Las Juntas de Abangares
Refugio de Vida Silvestre Cipanci
10°15'N
Parque Nacional Barra Honda
Puente La Amistad
Río Lagarto
Quebrada Honda
18
Barra Honda
Rancho Grande
Isla Chira
Reserva Biológica de los Pájaros
Río Grande
Golfo de Nicoya
Isla Caballo
Carmona
Chacarita
Barranca
Río Ora
160
21
Lepanto
Ferry
17
PUNTARENAS
Mata de Limón
Jicaral
Isla San Lucas
Cangrejal
Playa Naranjo
Reserva Biológica Isla Guayabo
Río Juan de León
Río Blanco
Bahía Gigante
Ferry
Quebrada Seca
Bejuco
Isla Gigante
Playa San Miguel
Reserva Biológica Islas Negritos
Jabilla
San Francisco de Coyote
Paquera
Curú
Refugio Nacional de Vida Silvestre Curú
Playa Coyote
Puntarenas
Río Bongo
Isla Tortuga
9°45'N
Playa Caletas
Pochote
Playa Tambor
Bajos de Arió
Tambor
Bahía Ballena
Río Negro
Cóbano
Playa Manzanillo
Reserva Absoluta Nicolás Wessburg
Montezuma
Playa Santa Teresa
Montezuma-Jacó Passenger Ferry
Mal País
Cabuya
Reserva Natural Absoluta Cabo Blanco
85°15'W
85°00'W
84°45'W

location one block from the beach and a friendly, family vibe. The eight rooms are spartan but spacious, while hammocks and chairs adorn a shady courtyard.

Pato Loco Inn GUESTHOUSE **$$**
(☎2670-0145; www.patolocoinn.com; d/tr US$58/68, restaurant dishes US$4-10; P ❄ @ 📶 🏊 🐾) Colorful linens and mural-painted walls brighten up the rooms at this pleasant and affordable inn. Start your day with an amazing (and filling) breakfast. In the evening, cool off in the pool, shoot some pool or hang with a beer at the bar out front. It's on the main drag, about 1.5km south of the beach.

Eating & Drinking

For groceries, stock up at **Coco Palms Supermercado** (☎2670-0367; ⏲24hr), one block west of the main drag, toward the south end of town. Or try the massive **Auto Mercado** (☎2670-2232; ⏲8am-8pm, 8am-9pm Fri & Sat) at the new Pacifico Plaza shopping center near the entrance of town.

★La Vida Loca AMERICAN **$**
(☎2670-0181; mains US$4-9; ⏲11am-11pm) Cross the creaky wooden footbridge on the south end of the beach to find this popular gringo hangout, specializing in US-style comfort food. It's also the best bar in town, occasionally hosting live music.

Pure Vibes Cafe CARIBBEAN **$**
(www.purevibesresorts.com; La Chorrera; mains US$8-10; ✎) The menu features everything from burgers to salads to *casados*, but the highlight is the spicy Caribbean fare. Jamaican jerk chicken and shrimp creole will delight your palate, as will the daily specials and 'One Love Punch'. A dedicated veggie menu caters to the meat-free, with veggie wraps, burgers, curries and more. Set on the lovely grounds of the backpackers' resort.

Las Olas SEAFOOD **$$**
(☎2670-2003; mains US$7-16; ⏲11am-10pm) Just south of the cramped commercial vortex on the main road, this is a dressed-up *soda* with tablecloths, bamboo decor and fresh seafood in the kitchen. The cool lounge area features molded concrete booths and dripping candles, whirling fans and a gurgling fountain.

Beach Bums BAR
(☎2670-0110; ⏲11am-midnight; 📶) A huge beach barn open to the sand and sea, blazed with graffiti murals, nailed down with a surfboard bar, icing the coldest beer in town. It has live music in the evenings, Wednesday to Sunday.

Information

The police station and a small **post office** are southeast of the plaza by the beach. There is a 24hr ATM at **BAC Bank** (Pacífico Plaza), located on the main road heading out of town.

Getting There & Away

All buses arrive at and depart from the main stop on the plaza, across from the police station.
Liberia (US$1.50, 1 hour, 8 daily)
San José (US$8, 5 hours, 3 daily)

Playa Tamarindo

Well, they don't call it Tamagringo for nothing. This town's perennial status as Costa Rica's top surf and party destination has made it the first and last stop for legions of tourists. It stands to reason that this is the most developed beach on the peninsula, with no shortage of hotels, bars and restaurants.

Despite the party-town reputation and reality, Tamarindo is more than just drinking and surfing. It is a short distance from Playa Grande, an important nesting site for leatherback turtles. It's home to some of the best restaurants in the country. And Tamarindo's central location makes it a great base for exploring the wilds of the northern peninsula.

Sights

★Parque Nacional Marino Las Baulas de Guanacaste PARK, BEACH
(Playa Grande; ☎2653 0470; admission incl tour US$25; ⏲8am-noon, 1-5pm, turtle tours 6pm-2am) This marine reserve just north of Tamarindo village includes **Playa Grande**, which is a major surf destination and one of the most important nesting sites for the *baula* (leatherback turtle). The park's mangrove swamps provide an ideal habitat for caimans and crocodiles, as well as numerous bird species, including the beautiful roseate spoonbill. Other residents include howler monkeys, raccoons, coatis, otters and a variety of crabs. But the main attraction is the nesting of the world's largest turtles, which can weigh in excess of 400kg. Nesting season is from October to March, and it's fairly common to see leatherbacks, as well as green and black turtles, nesting here.

During the day, the beach is free and open to all, which is a good thing as the breaks off Playa Grande are fast, steep and consistent. You can get here by boat (US$2, from 7am to 4pm) from the north end of Tamarindo village, near the park office (☎2653-1687). At night, it is only possible to visit the beach on a guided tour, which should be booked in advance (also at the park office or through your hotel). Tours with transportation run for about US$45.

Activities

Surfing

The most popular wave around Tamarindo is a medium-sized right-hander that breaks directly in front of the Diriá Hotel. The waters here are full of beginner surfers learning the ropes. There is also a good left that's fed by the river mouth, a spot also popular with crocodiles during the rising tide (coincidentally, the best time to surf). Locals know a few other spots in the area, but we're certainly not going to ruin their fun – ask around.

Surf lessons hover at around US$40 for 1½ to two hours; most operators will let you keep the board for a few hours beyond that.

Kelly's Surf Shop SURFING
(☎2653-1355; www.kellysurfshop.com; board rental per day/week US$20/120; ⏲9am-6pm) One of the very best surf shops in the area, it has a terrific selection of newish boards that it rents by the day or week.

Matos Surf Shop SURFING
(☎2653-0845, 2653-0734; www.matossurfshop.com; Sunrise Commercial Center; ⏲8am-8pm, lessons 9-11am & 2-4pm) The granddaddy of local surf shops is owned by a Uruguayan DJ–photo-entrepreneur. It offers lessons and rents boards at the cheapest rates in town.

Witch's Rock Surf Camp SURFING
(☎2653 0239; www.witchsrocksurfcamp.com; ⏲8am-8pm) Board rentals, surf camps, lessons and regular excursions to Witch's Rock and Ollie's Point. There are beachside accommodations for surfers who sign up for multiday packages.

Other Activities

Agua Rica Diving Center DIVING
(☎2653-0094, 2653-2023; www.aguarica.net; 2 tanks US$80-105) Italian-owned Agua Rica Diving Center, the area's scuba-diving expert, offers snorkeling and an assortment of dives in the Catalina Islands, including diving certification classes and trips to the Cocos Islands.

Blue Trailz CYCLING, SURFING
(☎2653-1705; www.bluetrailz.com; bike rental per day US$25, bike tours US$55-75, dm/r US$14/US$59; ⏲7am-7pm Mon-Sat) Surf boards and mountain bikes. Sweet. Besides renting the equipment, it also organizes mountain-biking tours in the vicinity.

Papagayo Excursions BOAT TOUR
(☎2653-0254; tamarindobeach.net/papagayo) The longest-running outfitter in town organizes a wide variety of tours, including to hard-to-reach national parks and nearby turtle-nesting sites.

Courses

There are several language schools in Tamarindo, all of which charge about US$420 to US$440 for a week-long intensive course (beginner to advanced), including 'homestay' accommodations with a Tico family. Check out the 'Spanish & Surf' packages that also include surf classes and board rentals.

Coastal Spanish Institute LANGUAGE COURSE
(☎2653-2673; www.coastalspanish.com)

Wayra LANGUAGE COURSE
(☎2653-0359; www.spanish-wayra.co.cr)

Sleeping

★La Oveja Negra HOSTEL $
(☎2653-0005; www.laovejanegrahostel.com; dm/d US$15/35; P @) The hippest hostel in town attracts an international crowd. You'll like the sufficiently clean, tiled rooms (with shared bathrooms); the funky art on the walls; and the groovy furniture and open kitchen in the common areas. It also offers board rentals and surf lessons (group/private US$30/45).

Blue Trailz Hostel HOSTEL $
(☎2653-1705; dm US$14, r US$59; ❄ @) Across the street from the beach, this immaculate and intimate hostel is popular among the surfer set and other party people. Super-attentive staff go out of their way to make sure everyone is having a good time. Two dorm rooms have air-con, new tile floors and kitchenette, while identical private rooms sleep up to six. Guests get reduced rates on boards, bikes, lesson and tours. Sweet!

Playa Tamarindo

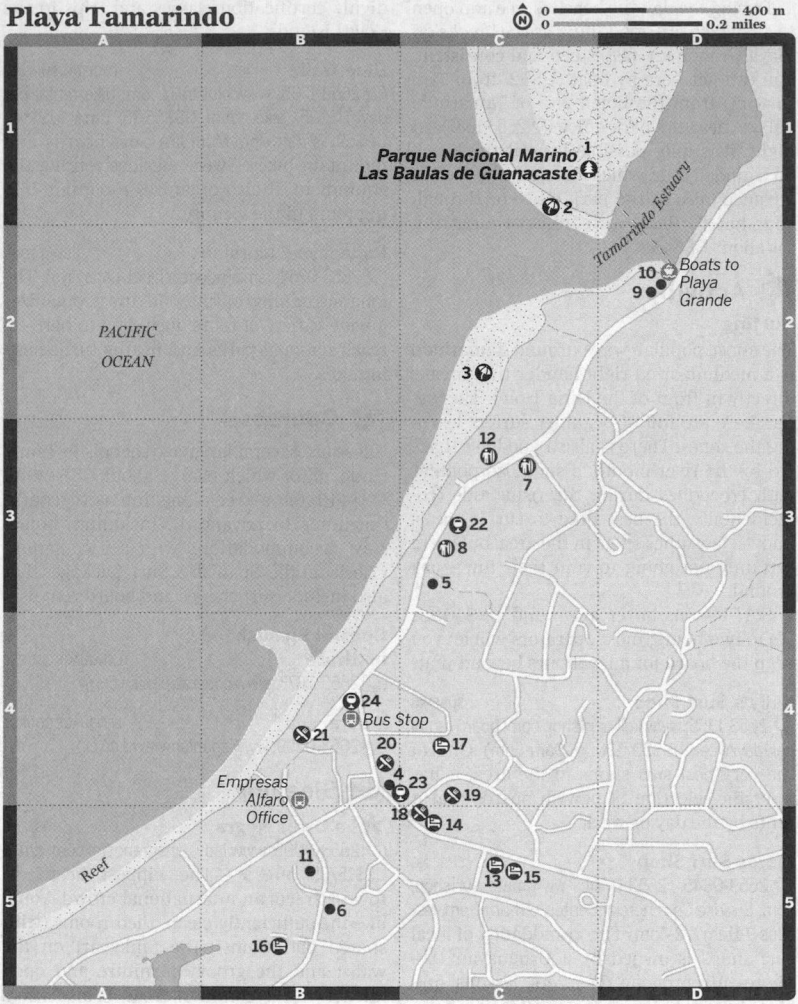

Tamarindo Backpackers HOSTEL $
(☎2653-4545; www.tamarindobackpackers.com; dm US$16, d from US$40; P ❄ @ 📶 🏊) This intimate, all-star backpacker spot is in a gorgeous yellow hacienda down a quiet cul-de-sac that's a bit of a hike from the beach. The doubles with private bathrooms are almost luxurious with Spanish-tiled floors, beamed ceilings and fat flat-screens. The dorms are quite clean but otherwise unspectacular. Outside you'll find lovely tropical gardens, a small pool and hammocks, all surrounded by woods inhabited by howler monkeys.

Pura Vida Hostel HOSTEL $
(☎8747-8780; www.puravidahostel.com; dm US$12-15, s/d US$35/45; 🏊 ❄ @ 📶) Inside this leafy compound are dorms and private rooms accented by hand-painted flourishes and mirrored mosaics. It's not much of a party place, but the vibe is friendly and super chill, especially in the common *rancho*, furnished with hammocks and rocking chairs.

La Botella de Leche HOSTEL $
(☎2653-0189; www.labotelladeleche.com; dm US$13-16, s/d US$30/38; P ❄ @ 📶 🏊) With a relaxed vibe and over-the-top cow theme,

Playa Tamarindo

Top Sights
1 Parque Nacional Marino Las Baulas de Guanacaste C1

Sights
2 Playa Grande C1
3 Playa Tamarindo C2

Activities, Courses & Tours
4 Agua Rica Diving Center B4
5 Blue Trailz C3
6 Coastal Spanish Institute B5
7 Kelly's Surf Shop C3
8 Matos Surf Shop C3
9 Papagayo Excursions D2
10 Parque Nacional Marina Las Baulas De Guanacaste office D2
11 Wayra B5
12 Witch's Rock Surf Camp C3

Sleeping
Blue Trailz Hostel ..... (see 5)
13 La Botella de Leche C5
14 La Oveja Negra C5
15 Pura Vida Hostel C5
16 Tamarindo Backpackers B5
17 Villas Macondo C4

Eating
18 Falafel Bar C5
19 La Baula C4
20 Longboards B4
21 Nogui's B4

Drinking & Nightlife
22 Aqua Disco C3
23 Bar 1 ..... C4
Eat@Joe's ..... (see 12)
24 Le Beach Club B4

this spot is highly recommended for its attentive management, air-conditioned rooms and dormitories with en suite bathrooms, and quiet location at the eastern edge of town. It is not recommended for its grim shared kitchen. Other nice perks include surfboard racks, hammocks and TV lounge.

Villas Macondo HOTEL **$$**
(☎2653-0812; www.villasmacondo.com; s/d/tr US$40/50/60, with air-con US$65/65/85, apt US$110-150; P ❄ @ 📶 🏊) Although it's only 200m from the beach, this establishment is an oasis of serenity in an otherwise frenzied town – it's also one of the best deals around. Beautiful modern villas with private hot showers and hammock-strung patios surround a solar-heated pool and tropical gardens.

Eating

Longboards AMERICAN **$**
(☎2653-0027; mains US$4-11 ; ⏲11am-10pm Thu-Tue) An American-style barbecue joint and expat favorite, with excellent pulled pork, ribs and beef brisket. Belly up to the surfboard-shaped tables and grind some proper barbecue.

Falafel Bar MEDITERRANEAN **$**
(☎2653-1268; mains US$5-8 ; ⏲9am-11pm) This Mediterranean cafe serves all the faves: shwarma, falafel, tabbouleh, hummus and kebabs. And like any good shwarma joint it routinely (if not regularly) stays open into the wee smalls.

Nogui's SEAFOOD **$$**
(☎2653-0029; mains US$8-22; ⏲11am-11pm) A fish shack with Mediterranean charm, this romantic gem on the beach flaunts local seafood. Make a dinner reservation, or get sloshed at the bar with the occasionally rowdy (but not too rowdy) regulars.

La Baula PIZZERIA **$$**
(☎2653-1450; mains US$9-13; ⏲5:30-11pm; 👪) This casual open-air restaurant has real wood-fired pizzas, pastas and other Italian fare. It's also one of the most family-friendly restaurants in town, with a playground to keep the kids entertained.

Drinking & Nightlife

On weekends, all you really have to do is follow the scene wherever it happens to go. Cruising the main drag has the festive feel of spring break, and nearly every bar hosts a ladies' night.

Bar 1 SUSHI BAR
(☎2653-2586; ⏲6:30pm-2am Thu-Tue) The classy Bar 1 is an open-air people-watching jewel on the 3rd floor at Plaza Tamarindo. If you're hungry, the sushi is recommended, but there's also fresh-fruit cocktails, pool tables and a DJ working the wax.

Eat@Joe's AMERICAN
(☎2653-1262; ⏲7am-10pm) The best happy hour in town is at this bar at Witch's Rock Surf Camp, where you can order the famous 'Nachos as Big as Your Ass' and watch the

sunset while sucking down cold ones on the beach. Can't beat it.

Aqua Disco CLUB
(☎2653-2782; www.aquadiscoteque.com) Aqua Disco is the only real nightclub in Tamarindo. The best nights are Monday (ladies' night) and Saturday, when for a US$4 cover charge it has an open bar for two hours.

Le Beach Club CLUB
(☎2653-0178; ⏲11am-close) This place has beds and hammocks on the sand and live DJs on Saturday. It also gets an excellent sundowner crowd who feel the throbbing bass as the orb melts into the sea.

Information

Coastal Emergency Medical Service
(☎2653-0611, 2653-1974; ⏲24hr) It does house calls! Can you say that about your hometown doc?

Internet Bakanos (per hr US$2.50; ⏲8am-10pm) On the 2nd floor above an Italian deli; offers high-speed internet connections and international phone calls.

Tamarindo News (www.tamarindonews.com) Keep up with the local happenings by picking up a copy of the English-language newspaper.

DANGERS & ANNOYANCES

Tamarindo has a growing drug and prostitution trade, with vendors openly plying their wares on the main road by the rotunda. Theft is also a problem. Don't leave valuables on the beach or in your car; use a safe or locker at your hotel.

It's always important to keep your wits about you. If you're alone, tell somebody where you're going. Don't get so wasted that you become vulnerable to crime or accident. Take common-sense precautions.

Getting There & Away

Buses to San José depart from the **Empresas Alfaro** office, behind Babylon bar. Other buses depart from the bus stop across the street from Zullymar Hostel.

Liberia (US$3, 2½ hours, hourly 4:30am to 6:30pm)

San José (US$11, 6 hours, 2 daily) Alternatively, take a bus to Liberia and change for frequent buses to the capital.

Playas Avellanas & Negra

About 15km south of Tamarindo, these popular surfing beaches have some of the best, most consistent waves in the area, made famous in *Endless Summer II*. Avellanas is a long stretch of white sand backed by mangroves, and Negra, a few kilometers further south, is a darker, caramel-color beach broken up by rocky outcrops.

At Avellanas, **Little Hawaii** is a powerful and open-faced right at medium tide, while **Beach Break** barrels at low tide (though the surfing is good any time of day). Negra has a world-class right that barrels, especially with a moderate offshore wind. In between is the community of **Playa Lagartillo**, with a few *cabinas* and *sodas* scattered along the road.

The recommended **Avellanas Surf School** (☎2653-4484; avellanas-surf-school.com; ⏲8am-5pm) offers surf lessons (US$50) and board rentals. **Café Playa Negra** (☎2652-9351; www.playanegracafe.com; ⏲7am-9pm) has a laundry service and internet access. There's no ATM and many places do not accept credit cards, so bring the cash you will need.

Sleeping & Eating

Playa Avellanas

Casa Surf GUESTHOUSE $
(☎2652-9075; www.casa-surf.com; per person US$10, room, board & board per person US$30; P) Look for the 'Casa Surf' across from Cabinas Las Olas, and pull over for a clean, quiet place to stay. This place has five simple rooms with shared bathroom and a full kitchen. It also offers an excellent-value room, board and board option, which includes two meals and surf-board rental.

Lola's on the Beach CAFE $$
(☎2652-9097; meals US$8-13; ⏲10am-5pm Tue-Sun) If the water is looking glassy, Lola's is the place to hang. Stylish slanted wood chairs are planted in the sand beneath thatched umbrellas, and the tree stump bar overlooks a gorgeous open kitchen. Beachy cuisine includes an epic tuna poke, an overstuffed spicy grilled chicken pita, papaya salad and classic Dutch-style fries. The smoothies are likewise terrific.

Playa Negra

Kontiki HOSTEL $
(☎2652-9117; www.kontikiplayanegra.com; r with/without bathroom per person US$25/15; P📶) Along the road from Avellanas, this low-key place has a rambling collection of treehouses on stilts that are frequented by both surfers and howler monkeys. In the middle

of it all is a pavilion where guests swing in hammocks and feast on pizza.

Hotel Rocky Point CABINAS $
(Cabinas Playa Negra; ☎2652-9270; www.cabinasplayanegra.com; s/d/tr/q US$35/40/50/60, s/d without bathroom US$20/30, all incl breakfast; ❄📶🏊) The quaint *cabinas* at Rocky Point are set around a gorgeous tropical garden, teeming with hummingbirds, butterflies and parakeets. The simple rooms have wood-stained walls and artistic details, and the on-site Jalapeño Taco Grill is fresh, fast and delicious.

Café Playa Negra HOTEL $$
(☎2653-4360, 8818-9092; www.cafeplayanegra.com; s/d/tr/q US$35/55/70/80, air-con extra US$10; P❄@📶🏊) These stylish, minimalist digs – upstairs from a charming cafe – have polished concrete floors and elevated beds dressed with colorful bedspreads. There's a groovy shared deck with plush lounges. The downstairs cafe (7am to 9pm, Wednesday to Monday) serves tasty Peruvian-fusion fare, in addition to international standards.

Getting There & Away

There is no public transportation to/from Playa Tamarindo, though surf camps often organize trips. The only bus connections are heading inland, via Santa Cruz (US$1.50, 1½ hours, two daily).

Playa Sámara

Is Sámara the black hole of happiness? That's what more than one expat has said after stopping here on vacation and never leaving. On the surface it's just an easy-to-navigate beach town with barefoot, three-star appeal, and a crescent-shaped strip of pale-gray sand spanning two rocky headlands. Not spectacular, just safe, mellow, reasonably developed, easily navigable on foot and accessible by public transportation. But be careful, the longer you stay the less likely you are to leave.

Activities

Experienced surfers will probably be bored with Sámara's inconsistent waves, though beginners can have a blast here.

C&C Surf School SURFING
(☎2656-0590; cncsurfsamara.webs.com; board rentals per day US$16, lessons semi-private/private US$30/40; ⏲8am-8pm) A great choice, offering private and semi-private lessons; the fee includes another hour of board rental afterwards. It also rents kayaks and surfboards and arranges a variety of tours and trips throughout Costa Rica.

Wing Nuts CANOPY TOUR
(☎2656-0153; www.wingnutscanopy.com; adult/child US$60/40; ⏲tours 7am, 10:30am & 2pm) One entrepreneurial family found a way to preserve their beautiful, wild patch of dry tropical forest: by setting up a small-scale canopy tour. Family-owned but professionally run, this 10-platform operation is unique for its personal approach, as groups max out at 10 people. The price includes transportation from your hotel in Sámara.

Courses

Centro de Idiomas Intercultura LANGUAGE COURSE
(☎2260-8480, 2656-0127; www.samaralanguageschool.com; courses per week with/without homestay US$483/315) Centro de Idiomas Intercultura claims to be the only Spanish school directly on the beach, which makes for a pleasant – if not always productive – place to study.

Sleeping

Hotel Matilori HOSTEL $
(☎2656-0291; posadamatilori@racsa.co.cr; dm/r US$$15/45; P❄📶) Offering terrific value, this colorful hostel has spotless four-person dorm rooms as well as private rooms with shared bathrooms. The communal kitchen is clean and fully stocked. And the endearing owners go above and beyond to ensure their guests' comfort. Best of all, it's steps from the beach.

Hostel Mariposas HOSTEL $
(☎8703-3625; www.hostelmariposas.com; campsite US$8, dm US$16, d without bathroom US$36; 📶) This fun and funky hostel is down the dirt road by the language school, just 60m from the sand. It's got a super-chill atmosphere, swaying hammocks, a big communal kitchen and two resident dogs. On the downside, it has a shortage of bathrooms, lacks security, is noisy and has two resident dogs.

Entre Dos Aguas GUESTHOUSE $$
(☎2656-0998; www.hoteldosaguas.com; d US$45-50, tr/q US$59/66, ste US$85-98; P@🏊) This fantastic little inn offers the charming personality and artistic atmosphere of a

boutique hotel, at the price of a roadside motel. Seven brightly colored rooms have private stone showers with hot water, vibrant woven linens and many homey little touches – all with access to an inviting common courtyard and lush garden. It's just north of the main intersection on the road to Nicoya.

Sámara Palm Lodge GUESTHOUSE **$$**
(☎22656-1169; www.samarapalmlodge.com; d US$60; P ❄ 📶 🏊) An inviting little lodge on the western edge of town (250m from the main intersection). Eight spotless rooms feature tropical decor, with natural wood furniture, tile floors and bold colorful artwork. They face a lush garden and enticing swimming pool. Your hosts, Brigitte and Lothar, are delightful.

Eating & Drinking

Lo Que Hay MEXICAN **$**
(☎2656-0811; tacos US$2, meals from US$6; ⏲7am-late) This rocking beachside *taquería* offers four delectable taco fillings (fish, chicken, beef or pork), and mains like blackened fish, slow-roasted pork and beef fajitas. The grilled avocados stuffed with *pico de gallo* are delish. Tacos or no, the bar crowd sips into the wee smalls.

★Ahora Si VEGETARIAN **$$**
(☎2656-0741; mains US$5-11; P 📶 ✎) A Venetian-owned, vegetarian restaurant and all-natural cocktail bar. It does smoothies with coconut milk; gnocchi with nutmeg, sage and smoked cheese; soy burgers and yucca fries; wok stir-fries; and thin-crust pizzas too. All served on a lovingly decorated tiled patio.

Casa Esmeralda SODA **$$**
(☎2656-0489; mains US$6-17; ⏲noon-9:30pm Mon-Sat) A favorite with locals, the place is dressed up with tablecloths and faux-adobe walls. The menu features tasty salads, pastas, meat, chicken and fish dishes. The fish in avocado sauce comes highly recommended.

Al Manglar ITALIAN **$$**
(☎2656-0096; mains US$8-18; ⏲5-10pm; P ✎) This thatch-roofed, open-air restaurant serves gnocchi and ravioli, as well as pizza-perfect pies.

La Vela Latina BAR
(☎2656-2286; ⏲noon-1:30am; 📶) Settle into a comfy chair on the sand and order a bucket of icy beers or a perfectly blended cocktail. There's also a menu of sophisticated *bocas* and sushi to nosh on.

Bar Olas BAR
(⏲noon-late) This archetypal seafront dive on the north end of the beach makes almost no effort, but it's open early and serves late, and drinks are cheap.

Information

Internet Sámara (☎2656-1102; per hr US$2; ⏲9am-1pm & 3-9pm) On the main road next to Bar Arriba.

Sámara Beach (www.samarabeach.com) Get the skinny on Sámara, with links to hotels, restaurants, activities and more.

Sky Net Tours (Sámara Adventure Company; ☎2656-0920; www.samara-tours.com; per hr US$2; ⏲9am-9pm) Formerly the Samara Travel Center, this extremely helpful place has an internet cafe, and can book flights and Interbus tickets and arrange tours.

Getting There & Away

There are two daily buses to San José (US$8; five hours) that depart from the main intersection just south of Entre Dos Aguas. Buy your bus tickets at the nearby Alfaro office.

To reach Liberia, head first to Nicoya (US$2.50, two hours, hourly) on a bus departing from the *pulpería* by the soccer field.

Playa Naranjo

This small port on the eastern side of the peninsula (not to be confused with the peninsula's west-coast beach of the same name) has neither a beach nor oranges. It serves only as the terminal for the Puntarenas car ferry. There isn't any reason to hang around, and you probably won't have to, as the ferries tend to run reasonably on time.

All transportation is geared to the arrival and departure of the Puntarenas ferry. The **Coonatramar ferry** (☎2661-1069; www.coonatramar.com; adult/child/bicycle/motorcycle/car US$2/1/4/6/18) to Puntarenas departs daily at 8am, 12:30pm, 5:30pm and 9pm and takes 1½ hours. You must have your ticket before boarding. Buses meet the ferry and take passengers on to Nicoya (US$3, three hours) for transfer to Playa Sámara.

Paquera

The tiny village of Paquera is about 25km by road from Playa Naranjo and 4km from the ferry terminal. Paquera is more of a population center than Playa Naranjo, though there's little reason to stay here longer than you have to.

All transportation is geared to the arrival and departure of the Puntarenas ferry. If either is running late, the other will wait. **Ferry Naviera Tambor** (☎2661-2084; www.naviera tambor.com; adult/child/bicycle/motorcycle/car US$1.65/1/4.50/7/23) departs daily (one hour) at 6am, 9am, 11am, 2pm, 5pm and 8pm.

Buses meet arriving passengers at the ferry terminal to take them to Montezuma (US$3, two hours). Alternatively, get off in Cóbano for transfer to Mal País (US$2, 45 minutes). The bus can be crowded, so get off the ferry quickly to get a seat.

Many taxi drivers will tell you the bus won't come, but this isn't true. With that said, getting several travelers together to share a taxi is a good option since the ride will take half as long as the bus.

Montezuma

Montezuma is an endearing beach town that demands you abandon the car and instead stroll, swim and surf. The warm and wild ocean, and that remnant, ever-audible jungle, has helped this rocky nook cultivate an inviting, boho vibe. Typical tourist offerings do a brisk trade here, but you'll also bump up against Montezuma's internationally inflected, artsy-rootsy beach culture in yoga classes, volunteer corps, festivals, veggie-friendly dining rooms, and neo-Rastas hawking uplifting herbs. No wonder locals lovingly call this town 'Montefuma.'

Sights & Activities

★Montezuma Waterfalls WATERFALL

A 20-minute (500m) river hike leads to a waterfall with a delicious swimming hole. Further along the trail, a second set of falls offers an exhilarating 10m leap from the top into deep water below. (Reach the 'diving platform' from the trail: do not try to scale the slippery rocks!) Countless travelers enjoy these thrills but a few of them have died; so do it at your own risk.

Swimming & Snorkeling

Picture-perfect white-sand beaches are strung out along the coast, separated by small rocky headlands and offering great beachcombing and tide-pool studying. The beaches in front of the town are nice enough, but the further northeast you walk, the more isolated and pristine they become. During low tide, the best snorkeling is in the tide pools, and at **Playa Las Manchas**, 1km south of downtown.

Surfing

There's great surf if you're willing to walk the 7km up the coastline to **Playa Grande**, or if you head south about 3km to **Playa Cedros**.

Montezuma Surf School with Chris Johnson SURFING

(☎2642-1256; www.montezumasurf.com; lesson US$40, surf safari US$60) Dedicated to getting you hooked on surfing in two hours or less. Also organizes 'surf safaris' to the best waves all around the peninsula.

Young Vision Surf School SURFING

(☎8669-6835; youngvisionsurf@gmail.com; lessons from US$40) Manny and Alvaro get rave reviews for their knowledge, enthusiasm and patience with new surfers of all ages. Daily lessons include two hours of instruction, the use of the surf board, rash guard and fresh fruits.

Tours

Montezuma Bike Tours CYCLING

(☎8871-1540; www.montezumabiketours.com; per person US$38-60, rental half/full day US$18/25) Rides range in terrain and difficulty and last up to four hours, taking in hidden beaches, waterfalls and rugged mountains. The business has no storefront; it brings the bikes to you or meets you at a designated starting point.

Sun Trails CANOPY TOUR

(☎2642-0808; www.montezumatraveladventures.com; tour US$40; ⏲9am-3pm) After you've flown down nine zip lines, this 2.5-hour canopy tour winds up with a hike down to the waterfalls; bring your swimsuit.

Zuma Tours TOURS

(☎2642-0024; www.zumatours.net) Snorkeling trips to Isla Tortuga, horseback riding in Cabo Blanco and more. This office also has the only public internet access in town.

Sleeping

Take precautions as theft from hotel rooms is common in Montezuma.

★Luna Llena HOSTEL $

(☎2642-0390; www.lunallenahotel.com; dm US$10, s US$25, d US$35-50; P📶) On the northern edge of town on a hilltop overlooking the

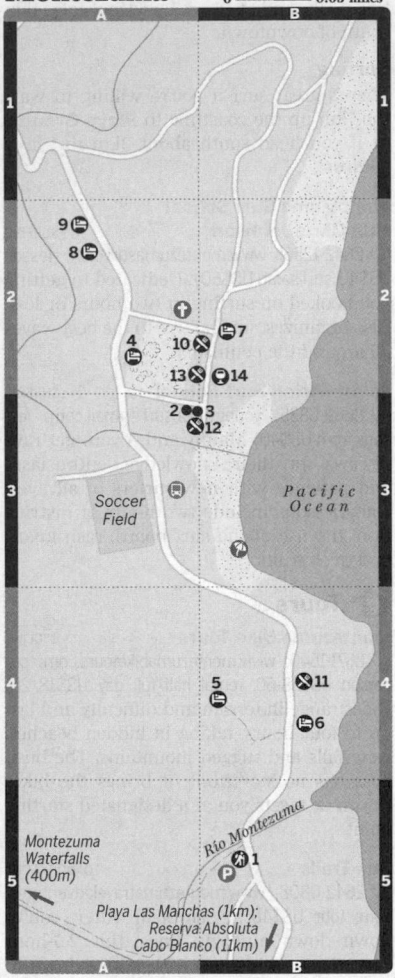

Montezuma

Activities, Courses & Tours

1 Montezuma Waterfalls Trailhead B5
2 Sun Trails A3
3 Zuma Tours A3

Sleeping

4 Hotel La Aurora A2
5 Hotel Los Mangos B4
6 Hotel Lucy B4
7 Hotel Pargo Feliz B2
8 Luna Llena A2
9 Luz en el Cielo A2

Eating

10 Orgánico B2
11 Playa de los Artistas B4
12 Soda Monte Sol A3
13 Vaca Loca A2

Drinking & Nightlife

14 Chico's Bar B2

bay is this delightful budget option with 12 varied rooms, all of them spotless, most with balconies and shared bathroom facilities. Wildlife abounds in the vicinity (keep your food in the communal kitchen).

Luz en el Cielo HOSTEL, B&B $

(☎2642-0030, 8811-3700; www.luzenelcielo.com; dm US$15-27, s/d/tr/q US$54/78/98/112, all incl breakfast; P) In the jungle but two only minutes from town, this homey hostel and B&B is an inviting retreat. Crowded dorm rooms are super clean with sturdy wood furniture and lockers, while the new 'luxury' dorms are more spacious, with TVs, private balconies and en suite bathrooms. The treetop *cabinas* are also wonderful. Amazing breakfast, enticing hammocks and super-friendly staff.

Hotel Pargo Feliz CABINA $

(☎2642-0064; d US$30-45;) You can't beat the location of these beachfront *cabinas* in the heart of Montezuma. Rooms are simple, clean and fan-cooled. The communal balcony and garden terrace have relaxing hammocks with sea views, and at night the surf will lull you to sleep.

Hotel Lucy GUESTHOUSE $

(☎2642-0273; dm/d US$15/35; P) This beachside *pensión* is popular with budget travelers, thanks to the hammocks on shared terraces overlooking a rocky beach. Rooms are drab and service is lackluster but the views from the upstairs veranda are terrific.

Hotel La Aurora HOTEL $$

(☎2642-0051; www.hotelaurora-montezuma.com; r from US$40, air-con extra US$10; P) Reader-recommended Hotel La Aurora is housed in a pretty, vine-covered yellow building overlooking the park. The 15 rooms are plain but comfortable, with perks like hot-water showers, orthopedic beds and private balconies. Communal space includes a kitchen and plenty of hammocks for chilling out. It's not the most charming or interesting place you'll ever stay, but it's decent value for the money.

Hotel Los Mangos HOTEL $$
(☎2642-0076; www.hotellosmangos.com; d with/without bathroom US$65/35, tr bungalows US$95; P ❄ 📶 🏊) Scattered across mango-dotted gardens, this whimsical hotel has simple, bright, jewel-toned rooms in the main building, and attractive (though dark) octagonal bungalows that offer more privacy. Monkeys populate the mango trees, and yoga classes are held in the gorgeous, ocean-view yoga pavilion.

Eating & Drinking

Soda Monte Sol COSTA RICAN $
(☎8849-4962; mains US$5-14; ⏲7am-9pm) This colorful, mural-painted hole-in-the-wall does authentic, tasty and affordable *casados*, pasta, burgers and a variety of juices and smoothies. All is served in a humble dining room touched with grace. Great people-watching spot.

Vaca Loca CAFE $
(mains US$6-9; ⏲7am-6pm Mon-Fri, 7am-10pm Sat, 8am-6pm Sun) A cute cafe with one long, built-in, wrap-around booth and a crazy-cow theme. The menu is wide-ranging, including excellent breakfasts, unique sandwiches and delectable fish tacos.

★**Orgánico** ORGANIC $$
(www.montezumabeach.com/cafe-organico; mains US$7-11; ⏲8am-9pm; ✎) When they say 'pure food made with love,' they mean it – this healthy cafe turns out nine vegetarian dishes including spicy Thai burgers, a *sopa azteca* with tofu, burritos, falafel, smoothies and other meat-free treats. But it does meat dishes, like spaghetti Bolognese, too. Whaddaya want? They're Italian. They have live music almost nightly, including an open mic on Monday nights.

Playa de los Artistas INTERNATIONAL $$
(☎2642-0920; www.playamontezuma.net/playadelosartistas; mains US$9-13; ⏲noon-9pm Mon-Sat) This artfully decorated beachside spot is the most romantic restaurant in town. The Mediterranean menu changes daily depending on locally available ingredients, though you can always count on fresh seafood roasted in the wood oven and presented impeccably.

Chico's Bar BAR
(⏲11am-2am) A sprawling complex of bars, tables, beach chairs and a wide dance floor. It can get loud, especially on Thursday, which is reggae night. If you can score a table outside, it can be sort of romantic.

Information

The only ATM in town is located across from Chico's Bar, but it's regularly empty of cash on busy weekends. You can go online at Zuma Tours (p601).

El Parque (☎2642-0164; laundry per kg US$2, bikes/scooters/ATVs per day US$10/40/75; ⏲7am-8pm) Laundry, bikes and scooters.

Librería Topsy (☎2642-0576; ⏲8am-4pm Mon-Fri, 8am-noon Sat) Has American newspapers and magazines, and a large lending library with books in several languages. It also serves as the unofficial post service.

Getting There & Away

BOAT

Zuma Tours (p601) runs a water taxi from Montezuma to Jacó (US$40, one hour, departs daily at 9:30am). The price includes van transfer from the beach to Jacó bus terminal. Dress appropriately; you will get wet.

Tour operators can also book a boat-van service to San José, Manuel Antonio and Dominical.

BUS

Buses depart Montezuma from a sandy lot on the beach, across from the soccer field. Buy tickets directly from the bus driver. To get to Mal País and Santa Teresa, go to Cóbano and change buses.

Cabo Blanco (US$1, 45 minutes, 2 daily)

Cóbano (US$1, 30 minutes, every 2 hours 8am to 8pm)

Paquera (US$3, 2 hours, 6 daily)

San José (US$14, 6 hours, 2 daily)

SHUTTLE BUS

Montezuma Expeditions (www.montezumaexpeditions.com) Operates private shuttles to San José (US$45), La Fortuna (US$50), Tamarindo (US$45) and Sámara (US$45). Picks up from lodgings.

Reserva Natural Absoluta Cabo Blanco

On the southwestern tip of Península de Nicoya, this is Costa Rica's oldest protected wilderness area, established by pioneering conservationists. Encompassing evergreen forests, pristine white-sand beaches and offshore islands, the reserve is 11km south of Montezuma by dirt road.

Prior to the late 1980s, visitors were not permitted to Cabo Blanco, which is why it is called an 'absolute' nature reserve. Now, a limited number of trails are open to visitors, though the reserve remains closed on Monday and Tuesday to minimize environmental impact.

From the **ranger station** (☎2642-0093; adult/child under 12yr US$10/1; ⏲8am-4pm Wed-Sun), the **Sendero Sueco** (Swedish Trail) leads 4.5km down to a wilderness beach at the tip of the peninsula, while the **Sendero Danes** (Danish trail) is a spur that branches from Sendero Sueco and reconnects a kilometer later. Be advised that the trail can get very muddy (especially in the rainy season), and fairly steep in certain parts – plan for about two hours in each direction for the longer trail. The wide, sandy pebble beach at the end of the trail is magnificent.

Buses (US$1.50, 45 minutes) depart from the park entrance for Montezuma at 9am and 4pm. A taxi from Montezuma to the park costs about US$16.

Mal País & Santa Teresa

Get ready for tasty waves, creative kitchens and babes in board shorts and bikinis. This duo has collectively become one of Costa Rica's most life-affirming destinations. Here, the sea is almost perfect when it comes to shape, color and temperature. The hills are dotted with stylish boutique sleeps and surprisingly diverse eats. The entire area unfurls along one coastal road that rambles from Santa Teresa in the north through Playa El Carmen, terminating in the authentic Tico fishing hamlet of Mal País.

Surfing is the be all and end all for most visitors to Mal País, and the entire area is saturated with surf shops and surf schools that can give you the skinny on where to catch what waves. When you care to take a break from your board, many accommodations can arrange horseback-riding tours and fishing trips.

Sleeping & Eating

Malpaís Surf Camp & Resort LODGE $
(☎2640-0357; www.malpaissurfcamp.com; Mal País; camp US$11, dm US$17, d with/without bathroom US$73/40; P ❄ @ 📶 🏊) There are comfortable, private *cabanas* and more luxurious digs, but the best deal at this surfers' lodge is the open-air *rancho*, with a tin roof and pebble floors, which you can share with three other surfers. Wander the landscaped tropical grounds, swim in the luscious pool, grab a cold beer in the open-air lounge and soak up the good vibes.

Casa Zen GUESTHOUSE $
(☎2640-0523; www.zencostarica.com; Santa Teresa; dm US$15, d/tr/q US$34/42/40 all incl breakfast; P @ 📶) This recommended Asian-inspired guesthouse is decked out in celestial murals and happy Buddha sculptures. All bathroom facilities are shared, as are an impressive kitchen and a beautiful tiled *rancho*. Twice-daily yoga classes are held in the open-air studio. *Namaste*.

Cuesta Arriba HOSTEL $
(☎2640-0607; www.cuestaarribahostel.com; Santa Teresa; dm/d incl breakfast US$15/50; P ❄ 📶 🏊) This is a thinking person's hostel attracting an older, more polished crowd. Colorful, loft-style dorms have six beds, en suite bathrooms and creative mosaic tile embellishments.

The private rooms are also lovely. Communal areas include a big, well-stocked kitchen area, a breezy terrace upstairs and a garden hung with hammocks. Located near the end of the bus line in Santa Teresa.

★**Restaurant Mary** INTERNATIONAL, ORGANIC $$
(☎2640-0153; Mal País; mains US$7-17; ⏲5:30-10pm Thu-Tue) Hidden in plain sight in Mal País village, this charming restaurant has a concrete floor and a chalkboard menu. Delicious pizzas, tasty menu staples and sensational specials are all made from local, organic ingredients.

Getting There & Away

All buses begin and end at Ginger Café, 100m south of Cuesta Arriba hostel; you can flag the bus down anywhere along the road up to Frank's Place, at which point buses turn left and head inland toward Cóbano.

A direct bus to San José via the Paquera ferry departs at 6am and 2pm (US$13, six hours). To get to Montezuma, take a local buses to Cóbano (US$2, 45 minutes, two daily) and transfer.

Montezuma Expeditions (see p603) runs private shuttles to San José (US$50), La Fortuna, Liberia, and Monteverde (US$55). It also services various other destinations on the Península de Nicoya (US$50) and the central Pacific coast.

CENTRAL PACIFIC COAST

Stretching from the rough-and-ready port of Puntarenas to the tiny town of Uvita, the central Pacific coast is home to both wet and dry tropical rainforests, sun-drenched sandy beaches and a healthy dose of wildlife. On shore, national parks protect endangered squirrel monkeys and scarlet macaws, while offshore waters are home to migrating whales and pods of dolphins. With so much biodiversity packed into a small geographic area, it's no wonder the coastal area is often thought of as Costa Rica in miniature.

Puntarenas

POP 70,600

The 'Pearl of the Pacific' is a battered port city at the tip of a sandy peninsula (8km long but only 100m to 600m wide). Lively and hot, this provincial capital served as a major coffee port during the 19th century. During the dry season, Tico vacationers pack the beaches. Otherwise, it's the home of rowdy dockworkers and sailors alongside elderly ladies who scrub their sidewalks and keep the bougainvilleas blooming.

Most travelers come here just to catch the ferry to the Nicoya peninsula. If you're stuck for the night, **Hotel Cabezas** (☎2661-1045; Av 1 btwn Calles 2 & 4; s/d from US$25/30; P) and **Cabinas Joyce** (☎2661-4290, 8706-9101; cnr Calle 4 & Av 2; s US$20, d US$40-60; ❄ ❄ 📶) are good options.

Getting There & Away

BOAT

Car and passenger ferries bound for Paquera and Playa Naranjo depart from the **northwestern dock** (Av 3 btwn Calles 31 & 33). Purchase tickets before boarding.

To Playa Naranjo (for transfer to Nicoya and points west) **Coonatramar** (☎2661-1069; www.coonatramar.com; adult US$1.75, bike/car US$4/18) ferries depart at 6:30am, 10am, 2:30pm and 7.30pm for the two-hour trip. See p600 for more information.

To Paquera (for transfer to Montezuma and Mal País) **Naviera Tambor** (☎2661-2084; www.navieratambor.com; adult/child US$1.60/US$1) has six daily departures between 5am and 8:30pm for the 1½-hour trip. See p600.

BUS

Buses for San José depart from the large navy-blue building on the north corner of Calle 2 and Paseo de los Turistas. Buses for other destinations leave from across the street, on the beach side of the Paseo.

Jacó (US$2, 1½ hours, 7 daily 4:30am to 5:30pm)
Santa Elena (US$3, 3 hours, 3 daily 7:50am to 2:15pm)
Quepos (US$4, 3 hours, 8 daily 5am to 5:30pm)
San José (US$3, 2½ hours, hourly 4am to 7pm)

Parque Nacional Carara

Situated at the mouth of the Río Tárcoles, this 52-sq-km park is a green haven during the dry season and an important oasis for wildlife. As the northernmost tropical wet forest on the Pacific coast, its diverse wildlife includes the increasingly rare scarlet macaw, sloths, squirrels and crocodiles. The dry season (December to April) is the best time to go. Visitors can walk the **Sendero Laguna Meándrica**, which penetrates deep into the reserve. From the Río Tárcoles bridge, it is 3km south to the **Carara ranger station** (admission US$10; ⏲7am-4pm) where you can get info. Don't travel alone or carry valuables as occasional muggings are reported.

Parque Nacional Carara is 50km southeast of Puntarenas. Take any bus bound for Jacó or Quepos (often packed on weekends, which can be problematic for the return).

Jacó

POP 9500

Few places in Costa Rica generate such divergent opinions and paradoxical realities as Jacó. Partying surfers, North American retirees and international developers laud Jacó for its devil-may-care atmosphere, bustling streets and booming real-estate opportunities. Observant ecotourists, marginalized

DON'T MISS

CROCODILE BRIDGE

If you're driving between Puntarenas and Jacó, make a quick stop next to the Río Tárcoles bridge, also known as Crocodile Bridge. Here, you'll have an excellent chance of spotting enormous crocodiles basking on the sandbanks below the bridge – sometimes as many as 30 at a time. Although they're visible year-round, the best time for viewing is low tide during the dry season (December to April). Binoculars help.

Ticos and loyalists of the 'old Costa Rica' absolutely despise the place for the exact same reasons. While Jacó's ramshackle charm is not for everyone, the surfing is excellent, the restaurants and bars are cosmopolitan and the nightlife is an adventure.

Activities

Surfing

Although the rainy season is considered best for Pacific coast surfing, Jacó is blessed with consistent year-round breaks. More advanced surfers head south to **Playa Hermosa**, but the waves at Jacó are also strong and steady. Rent a board or sign up for a lesson at **Carton Surf Shop** (☎2643-3762; www.cartonsurfboards.com; Calle Madrigal), at the southern end of the main drag.

Hiking

The hiking trail up **Mt Miros** winds through primary and secondary rainforest, offering spectacular views of Jacó and Playa Hermosa. The trailhead is located near the entrance to the canopy tour, but it's unmarked, so ask a local to point it out.

Tours

Virtually every shop, hotel and restaurant in town books tours, as Jacó operates on a lucrative commission-based system. Note that the canopy tours in this area are more expensive than in other parts of the country.

Discovery Horseback Tours HORSE RIDING

(☎8838-7550; www.horseridecostarica.com; rides from US$75) This recommended outfit offers an extremely high level of service and professionalism on its beach and rainforest rides.

Kayak Jacó Costa Rica Outriggers KAYAKING

(☎8869-7074, 2643-1233; www.kayakjaco.com; tours from US$70) This reliable company facilitates kayaking and sea-canoeing trips that include snorkeling excursions to tropical islands.

Sleeping

Beds on Bohio HOSTEL $

(☎2643-5251; www.bedsonbohio.com; Calle Bohio; dm with/without air-con US$14/12, r from US$40;) An excellent addition to the surf scene in Jacó, this hostel is steps from the beach and is totally chill. Perks include a courtyard strung with hammocks, cheap surfboard rental and a great restaurant on site. Calle Bohio is one block southeast of the bridge.

Hotel de Haan HOSTEL $

(☎2643-1795; www.hoteldehaan.com; Calle Bohío; dm US$10, d with/without air-con US$36/30;) This outpost is one of the top budget bets in town, and is perennially popular with backpackers from around the world. Freshly tiled rooms with steamy hot-water showers are clean and secure. The upstairs balcony is a draw for congregating with fellow backpackers and swapping travel stories until the wee hours of the morning. One block southeast of the bridge.

Las Camas Hostel HOTEL $

(☎8533-7619, 8639-4241; www.lascamashostel.com; Dorado Sol; dm with/without air-con US$13/11, r US$30-45;) Offering the most basic facilities and the minimum level of cleanliness, this laidback hostel is full of personality (and personalities). The Hungarian transplant owners pride themselves on a no-rules policy, which means that 'you can jump off the waterfalls into the pool at 4am if that's what you'd like.' It's a fun party place, but there are also quieter, private rooms in the annex across the street. Look for the Rasta-painted gate near the KFC at the western end of town.

Camping El Hicaco CAMPGROUND $

(☎2643-3004; Calle Hicaco; campsites per person US$5;) The only proper campground in town (at the eastern end). There are picnic tables, bathrooms and a lockup for gear, though its proximity to the bars and clubs means you might not get much shut-eye. Don't leave valuables in your tent, as theft is a big problem here.

★Buddha House GUESTHOUSE $$

(☎2643-1111; www.hostelbuddhahouse.com; Av Pastor Diaz; d with/without bathroom US$65/35;) An oasis of calm in the midst of hustling Jacó. Bold colours and modern art create an artistic atmosphere at this 'boutique hostel'. Communal areas include a breezy patio and a spotless kitchen. Surfboard rental and spa treatments are available on site. It's located on the main drag, just east of the river.

Eating

★Taco Bar MEXICAN $

(Calle Pops; meals US$6-12, breakfast US$3; ⏲8am-6pm;) A one-stop shop for Mexican, seafood, salads and smoothies, as well as filling, cheap brekkies. Most importantly, it promises 'Killer Fish Tacos' and it delivers.

Wok CHINESE $
(☎2643-6168; Av Pastor Díaz; mains US$4-8; ⏲11:30am-10pm Mon-Sat; ✎) The Wok's pan-Asian menu is reliably good – especially the stir-fries and the ribs (only available on Wednesdays). The tables facing Jacó's main street also provide primo people-watching.

Tsunami Sushi JAPANESE $$
(☎2643-3678; Av Pastor Díaz; meals US$7-15; ⏲5-10pm Sun-Thu, to 1am Fri) Don't miss this modern, lively place north of Calle Pops. It serves up an exquisite assortment of sushi, sashimi and rolls. Pacific sportfish – dolphinfish, tuna and wahoo – are the freshest.

Drinking & Entertainment

There are numerous raging bars and dance clubs that cater to good-times-seeking expats and travelers, but be advised that a good portion of the nightlife in Jacó revolves around prostitution.

Surf Dogs BAR
(☎2643-3342; www.surfdogsbar.com; Av Pastor Diaz; ⏲10am-late Tue-Sun) Chill out with pub fare, icy beers and decadent daiquiris served at tables crafted from surfboards. It's definitely a surfer bar (think foosball and dartboards). But it's also a daiquiri bar, with at least eight different kinds on the menu. The food is a pleasant surprise.

Le Loft DJ
(Av Pastor Díaz) Jacó's sleekest nightlife offering. Live DJs spin essential mixes while glam-aspiring customers do their best to look beautiful and act fabulous. The party starts late and ends early.

Information

DANGERS & ANNOYANCES

Aside from petty crime such as pickpocketing and car break-ins, Jacó is not a dangerous place. That said, the city's high concentration of wealthy foreigners has resulted in thriving sex and drugs trades. Travelers should take the normal precautions, namely, secure valuables and avoid walking home late at night.

Getting There & Away

BOAT

To reach the Peninsula de Nicoya, Zuma Tours (p601) runs one daily taxi boat from Jacó to Montezuma (US$40, one hour, departs 11am). The jet-boat departs from Playa Herradura, which is 2km north of town. Reservations can be made at most tour operators in town. It's a beach landing, so wear the right shoes.

BUS

Buses for San José stop at the Plaza Jacó mall, north of the center. The bus stop for other destinations is opposite the Más X Menos supermarket. (Stand in front of the supermarket if you're headed north; stand across the street if you're headed south.) All buses originate in Puntarenas or Quepos.

Puntarenas (US$1.75, 1½ hours, 8 daily)
Quepos (US$1.75, 1½ hours, 6 daily)
San José (US$4, 3 hours, 7 daily)

Quepos

POP 12,900

Located just 7km from the entrance to Parque Nacional Manuel Antonio, the tiny town of Quepos serves as the gateway to the park, as well as a convenient port of call for travelers in need of goods and services. Although the Manuel Antonio area was rapidly and irreversibly transformed following the ecotourism boom, Quepos has largely remained an authentic Tico town. Exuding a traditional Latin American charm, Quepos is a low-key alternative to the tourist-packed trail not far beyond.

Activities

The beaches in town are polluted and are not recommended for swimming. The following agencies are located on the main street in Quepos, near the soccer field.

H2O Adventures ADVENTURE TOUR
(Rios Tropicales; ☎2777-4092; www.h2ocr.com) White-water rafting trips on the Río Naranjo (Class III-IV). This company, which sometimes goes by the other name of Rios Tropicales, also runs a kayaking trip to Isla Damas and tubing on the Río Savegre.

Iguana Tours ADVENTURE TOUR
(☎2777-2052; www.iguanatours.com) With tours that leave for destinations all over the central Pacific coast, this adventure-travel shop offers reputable river rafting, sea kayaking, horseback riding, mangrove tours and dolphin-watching excursions.

Oceans Unlimited DIVING, SNORKELING
(☎2777-3171; www.scubadivingcostarica.com) Offers local dives as well as longer trips south

Manuel Antonio Area

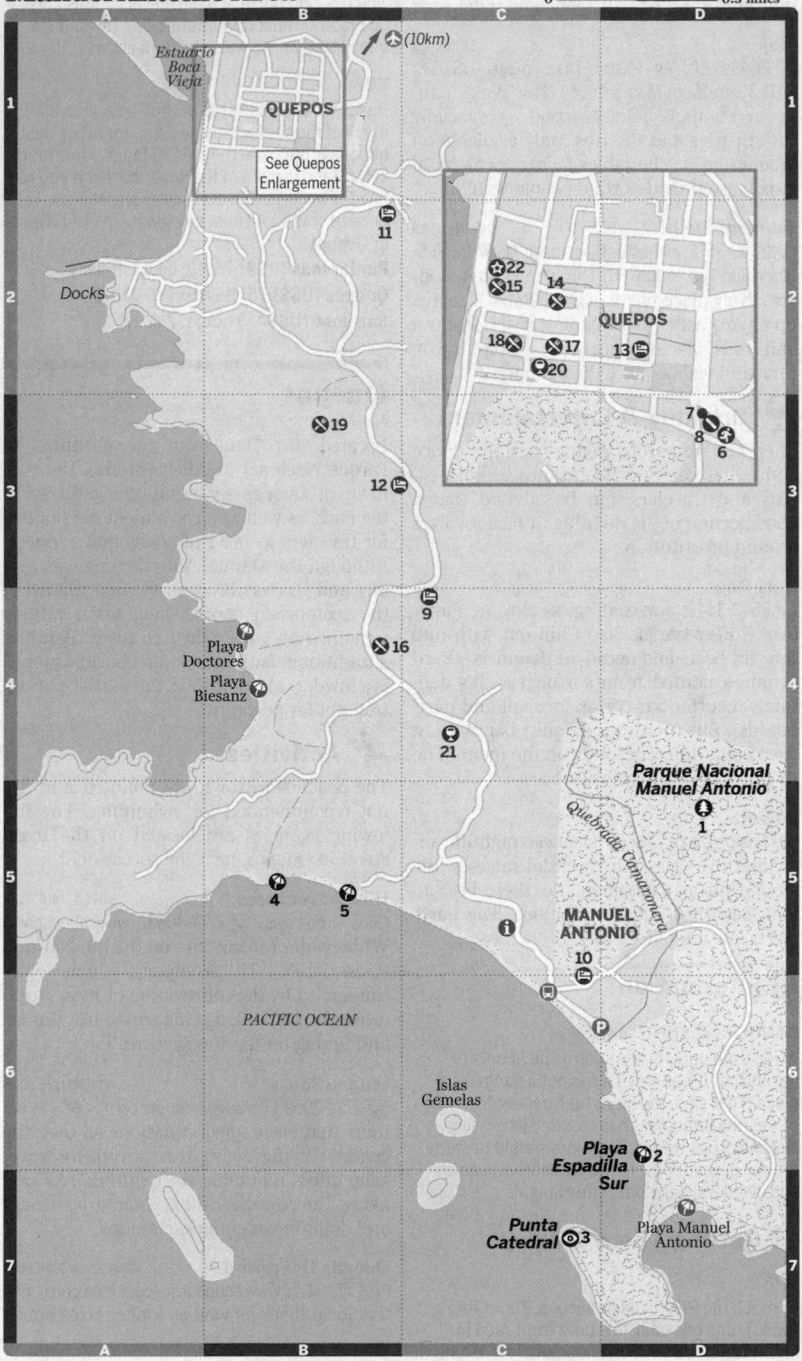

Manuel Antonio Area

Top Sights
1 Parque Nacional Manuel Antonio D5
2 Playa Espadilla Sur D6
3 Punta Catedral C7

Sights
4 La Playita B5
5 Playa Espadilla B5

Activities, Courses & Tours
6 H2O Adventures D3
7 Iguana Tours D3
8 Oceans Unlimited D3

Sleeping
9 Backpackers Manuel Antonio C4
10 Backpackers Paradise Costa Linda C6
11 Pura Vida Hostel B2
12 Vista Serena Hostel B3
13 Wide Mouth Frog Backpackers D2

Eating
14 Bohemia Café C2
15 Café Milagro C2
16 El Patio de Café Milagro B4
17 Mercado Central C2
18 Monchados C2
19 Ronny's Place B3

Drinking & Nightlife
20 Dos Locos C2
21 El Avión C4

Entertainment
22 Republik Club C2

to Bahía Drake (which requires a two-hour bus trip).

Sleeping

Wide Mouth Frog Backpackers HOSTEL $
(☎2777-2798; www.widemouthfrog.org; dm US$12, r with/without bathroom US$50/35, all incl breakfast;) Tiled rooms are spread around an inviting pool with plenty of lounge chairs, where backpackers can catch some rays and swap stories. All the essentials are here, including a communal kitchen, a TV lounge with a DVD library and a couple of lazy dogs padding around the place. Good vibes radiate throughout the premises, which are northwest of the soccer field.

Pura Vida Hostel HOSTEL $
(☎2777-2321; www.puravidahostelmanuelantonio.com; dm US$10-15, r per person US$15-20, all incl breakfast; 7am-10pm;) From the rainbow hued facade to the interior murals, this place is nothing if not colorful. The rooms have tropical-colored walls, bright linens, tile floors and lockers. Big, shared balconies overlook the jungle-covered hills, where you're likely to spot squirrel monkeys passing through. It's on the southern edge of town on the road to Manuel Antonio.

Eating

★**Café Milagro** CAFE $
(www.cafemilagro.com; meals US$5-8; 6am-10pm;) This quaint cafe is famous for its coffee drinks, brewed from the finest Costa Rican beans (which you can buy in the store next door). But the food is also excellent, especially its decadent breakfasts. Free w-ifi and English-language newspapers encourage dallying.

Bohemia Café CAFE $
(☎2774-0109; meals US$5-10; 9am-9pm Mon-Sat;) Wild with colors and animal print, this eclectic cafe draws a pleasant mix of travelers clacking away on keyboards, wolfing down excellent burritos and sipping fresh-fruit smoothies. For upscale fare it does creative international dishes with tropical flair.

Monchados CARIBBEAN $$
(dishes US$8-15; 5pm-midnight) Something of a Quepos institution, this long-standing Mex-Carib spot is always bustling with dinner-goers who line up to try traditional Limónese dishes and Mexican standards.

Mercado Central MARKET
(Central Market; hours vary) If you want to go local, you can't go wrong with the mercado central, a vast complex in the center of town that hosts plenty of budget-friendly *sodas* and cafes in addition to fruit-and-vegetable vendors.

Drinking & Entertainment

Dos Locos BAR
(☎2777-1526; 7am-11pm Mon-Sat, 11am-10pm Sun) This popular Mexican restaurant also serves as a regular drinking spot for the local expat community, and as a venue for the occasional live band.

Republik Club CLUB
(cover charge for men US$3; ⏲6:30pm-2:30am) Republik hosts the most reliable party in central Quepos. As the night wears on, the volume gets louder, the drinks get pricier and things tend to careen out of control.

Getting There & Away

All buses arrive and depart from the main terminal in the center of town. Buy tickets for San José well in advance at the **Transportes Morales ticket office** (☎2777-0263; ⏲7-11am & 1-5pm Mon-Sat, 7am-1pm Sun) at the bus terminal.

Jacó (US$1.50, 1½ hours, 4 daily)
Puntarenas (US$4.25, 3½ hours, 7 daily)
San Isidro de El General (US$4, 3 hours, 3 daily) Via Dominical.
San José (US$8, 4 hours, 5 daily)

Manuel Antonio

From the port of Quepos, the road swings inland for 7km before reaching the beaches of Manuel Antonio Village and the entrance to the national park. This serpentine route passes over a number of hills awash with picturesque views of forested slopes leading down to the palm-fringed coastline. Note that this stretch is hopelessly expensive, though there are a handful of hostels and eateries offering good value.

Sights & Activities

★Parque Nacional Manuel Antonio PARK
(☎2777-0644; park entrance US$10, parking US$3; ⏲7am-4pm Tue-Sun) Replete with swaying palms and playful monkeys, sparkling blue water and riotous tropical birds, Costa Rica's smallest national park (16 sq km) embodies the country's postcard-perfect appeal. Unfortunately, huge volumes of visitors descend on this small space. Avoid the crowds by going early in the morning, midweek and/or off-season.

To reach the park entrance, wade through the narrow estuary or ferry across for about US$1. At the entrance, you can hire naturalist guides (US$25 per person), who are licensed by the official agency Aguila.

Once inside, clearly marked trails wind through rainforest-backed tropical beaches and rocky headlands. Hikers are bound to spot resident populations of iguanas, howlers, capuchins, coatis, sloths and possibly the elusive squirrel monkeys. (Visitors report that hiring a guide virtually guarantees wildlife sightings.)

From the park entrance, it's a 30-minute walk to the park's idyllic beaches, **Playa Espadilla Sur** and **Playa Manuel Antonio**. The two beaches are separated by a rocky peninsula with a thick forest center. A trail leads around the peninsula to **Punta Catedral**, with great views of the Pacific and rocky islets inhabited by brown boobies and pelicans. A nearby visitors center has drinking water, toilets and beach showers.

Beyond Playa Manuel Antonio, the trail divides. The steep lower trail descends to the quiet **Playa Puerto Escondido**. The upper trail climbs to a stunning lookout. Rangers limit the number of hikers on this trail.

Buses leave from near the national park entrance and will stop along the road to Quepos if you flag them down.

Playa Espadilla BEACH
Be wary of rip currents at this attractive beach near the park entrance. This is the only beach in the area that is patrolled by lifeguards.

La Playita BEACH
At the far western end of Playa Espadilla, beyond a rocky headland, this gay beach is frequented primarily by young men. This used to be the place for nude sunbathing but local authorities have been cracking down on this. Make sure you bring your passport to minimize unwanted hassle.

Sleeping

★Vista Serena Hostel HOSTEL $
(☎2777-5162; www.vistaserena.com; dm US$10-16, bungalows without bathroom US$45-60, all incl breakfast; P @) Perched scenically on a quiet hillside, this memorable spot offers spectacular ocean sunsets from a hammock-filled terrace. A short trail hike through local farmland leads to a remote wilderness beach. The white-tiled rooms are spic-and-span, though there seems to be a shortage of bathrooms.

Backpackers Manuel Antonio HOSTEL $
(☎2777-2507; www.backpackersmanuelantonio.com; dm/d incl breakfast US$12/35; P @) Located in front of the football field (about 2.5km from the park), this locally owned hostel has decent facilities and a fun, sociable vibe. The place has white-washed rooms with wooden bunkbeds and lockers, tiled bathrooms and a communal kitchen and TV lounge. A breezy

balcony overlooks the jungle-covered hillside leading down to the pool.

Backpackers Paradise Costa Linda HOSTEL $
(☎2777-0304; www.costalinda-backpackers.com; r per person from US$10; P ❄ @ 📶) It's not in the same class as competing hostels due to shoddy rooms, but this shoestringers' crash pad is a decent option considering the rock-bottom price tag and beachside location. All bathrooms are shared. Excellent meals are served at the on-site garden cafe.

Eating & Drinking

El Patio de Café Milagro FUSION $$
(☎2777-2272; www.cafemilagro.com) The cafe is an obligatory stop for excellent coffee, aka 'black gold.' The patio is even better for decadent breakfasts (banana pancakes with macadamia nuts), amazing sandwiches (mango mahi mahi wrap) and sophisticated interpretations of Tico fare (Creole pork tenderloin). It's a lovely setting, surrounded by tropical gardens, but you can also order your sandwich packed for a picnic in the park.

Ronny's Place BURGERS, SEAFOOD $$
(☎2777-5120; www.ronnysplace.com; mains US$6-14; ⏲noon-10pm; P) Head 800m west from the main drag, on a well-signed dirt road, for an incredible panorama featuring two pristine bays and 360 degrees of primitive jungle. It's a glorious setting to chow down on big burgers and fresh seafood, washed down with sweet, refreshing sangria.

El Avión BAR
(☎2777-3378; mains US$6-14; 📶 👪) This unforgettable airplane bar-restaurant was constructed from the body of a 1954 Fairchild C-123. It was originally purchased in the 1980s for the Nicaraguan Contras, but it never made it out of its hangar as the Iran-Contra scandal unfolded. It's a fun, atmospheric spot for a beer, guacamole and a Pacific sunset. There's often live music during the dry season. You can't miss the airplane on the main road, about 2km north of the park entrance.

Information

La Buena Nota (☎2777-1002; buennota@racsa.co.cr), at the northern end of Manuel Antonio Village, serves as an informal information center. It sells maps, guidebooks, books in various languages, English-language newspapers, beach supplies and souvenirs.

Getting There & Away

Inter-city buses to San José and other destinations depart from the bus station in Quepos.

Local buses between Quepos and Manuel Antonio (US$0.35) depart roughly every 30 minutes between 6am and 7:30pm, and less frequently after 7:30pm. The last bus departs Manuel Antonio at 10:25pm.

Colectivo taxis between Quepos and Manuel Antonio will usually pick up extra passengers for a few hundred colones, the equivalent of about US$0.50. A private taxi to the park will cost around US$15.

Dominical

Dominical hits a real sweet spot with the travelers who wander up and down its rough dirt road with a surfboard under their arm, balancing the day's activities between the intense adrenaline rush of riding perfect waves and the lazy swing of a hammock. Dominical recalls the mythical 'old Costa Rica' when the coast was dotted with lazy little towns that drew a motley crew of surfers, backpackers and affable do-nothings. Dominical has no significant cultural sights, no paved roads and no chain restaurants. If you're not here to surf or swing in a hammock, it might not be the place for you.

Activities

Dominical owes its fame to its seriously sick point and beach breaks, though surf conditions here are variable. If you're just getting started, stay in the white water or head to the nearby beach of **Dominicalito**, which is tamer. Incidentally, the quality of surf instruction here is among the best and most affordable in the country.

Costa Rica Surf Camp SURFING
(☎8812-3625, 2787-0393; www.crsurfschool.com; Hotel Diu Wak; individual lessons from US$40, all inclusive packages per week from US$1050)

Sunset Surf SURFING
(☎8917-3143; www.sunsetsurfdominical.com) Inland 50m from Dominical beach at Domilocos.

Festivals & Events

Envision Festival FESTIVAL
(www.envisionfestival.com) Held in Dominical during the first week of March, this is a festival with a New Age bent, bringing together fire dancers, yoga and jam bands.

Sleeping

Most of the recommended sleeping options are located at the southern end of town.

Piramys Beachfront Hostel HOSTEL $
(☎8353-6428, 8353-6538; www.hosteldominical.com; dm US$8-14, d US$28; @) The operative word is 'beachfront'. Taking full advantage of ocean views, the Piramys has an open-air dormitory, with single and double beds draped in mosquito nets. There is a huge lounge with hammocks and TV, a kitchen and a fully-equipped gym. For more privacy, you can upgrade to an artistic mural-painted private room, but you won't have access to the other communal facilities. Great burger joint on site. This place is 100m past El Coco restaurant.

Montañas de Agua HOTEL $
(☎2787-0200; www.montanasdeagua.com; d with/without air-con US$50/30, apt US$75; P) This excellent option is hidden amongst the lush foliage on a small side street east of the main drag. Even the cheapest rooms have tile floors, wide-plank ceilings, hot-water showers and small porches strung with hammocks. The grounds are beautiful and it's steps from the beach.

Antorchas Camping CAMPGROUND $
(☎2787-0307; campsites per person US$5, dm US$10; P) Just a few meters from the beach, this campground is one of the most secure in town, though you should still be diligent about locking up your valuables in the provided lockers. Campers can take advantage of basic amenities, including cold showers and a shared kitchen, while more finicky shoestringers can bed down in spartan dorms for a few extra dollars a night.

Domilocos HOTEL $$
(☎2787-0244; www.domilocos.com; r US$75; P @) This Italian-owned property is a solid if overpriced midrange option, with Mediterranean-inspired grounds lined with potted plants and one of the town's best restaurants. Fairly ordinary rooms with squeaky beds and bamboo furniture are nothing to write home about, but they're a step up from most of the budget options in town.

Eating & Drinking

Chapy's Healthy Subs & Wraps DELI $
(☎2787-0283; meals US$5-10; ⏲9am-3pm Mon-Sat;) With crunchy wraps and thick, grilled veg sandwiches stacked high on homemade focaccia, Chapy's is a vegetarian's dream come true. As healthy as they are delicious, the sandwiches can be dressed in spicy hummus and homemade sauces. If you need a lunch to grab and go, this place has the best stuff in town.

San Clemente Bar & Grill BREAKFAST $
(meals US$5-12; ⏲9am-midnight) A classic Dominical watering hole – complete with broken surfboards on the walls – serving up big breakfasts and Tex-Mex dishes.

Maracutú VEGETARIAN, ORGANIC $$
(☎2787-0091; http://maracatucostarica.com; meals US$6-12; ⏲11am-1am;) Advertising a 'natural restaurant and world music,' this funky joint serves up eclectic culinary offerings highlighted by fresh seafood and delicious vegetarian and vegan fare. At night, the place transforms into a hip club scene with dance parties, live music and a young, cool crowd.

Tortilla Flats BAR
Right on the beachfront, Tortilla Flats has become the de facto place for surfers to enjoy session beers and tacos after a morning in the water. Its open-air atmosphere is pleasant, the surf videos on the televisions are on a continuous loop and the staff is friendly. There are also a few *cabinas* if you want to crash here.

Information

There are no banking facilities in town – the only ATM is up on the highway – but San Clemente Bar & Grill will exchange traveler's checks. There's a postal service upstairs in the same small shopping center.

Dominical Internet (per hr US$2; ⏲9:30am-7pm Mon-Sat) Above the San Clemente Bar & Grill.

DANGERS & ANNOYANCES

Waves, currents and riptides in Dominical are very strong, and there have been drownings in the past. Watch for red flags (which mark riptides), follow the instructions of posted signs and swim at beaches that are patrolled by lifeguards.

Getting There & Away

Buses pick-up and drop-off along the main road in Dominical. There are six daily buses to Quepos (US$6, three hours) and four daily buses to Uvita (US$1.20, one hour). Buses to San San Isidro de El General and San José originate in Uvita and reach Dominical about one hour later.

Uvita

A loose straggle of farms with back roads swallowed in tall grass, this hamlet 17km south of Dominical shows what coastal Costa Rica was like before the tourist boom. While nightlife may be limited to stargazing, Uvita boasts fantastic stretches of flat sand that comprise **Parque Nacional Marino Ballena**.

This stunner of a marine park (☎2743-8236; admission US$7) protects the coral and rock reefs surrounding **Isla Ballena**. It's a small area with huge importance, protecting colonies of sea birds, pods of dolphins, nesting sea turtles (May to November) and – most famously – **migrating humpback whales** (August to October and December to April). The beaches are a stunning combination of golden sand and polished rock. All of them are virtually deserted and perfect for peaceful swimming and sunbathing. From the ranger station you can walk out onto **Punta Uvita** and snorkel (best at low tide). Or hire a boat (per person US$45) from Playa Bahía Uvita to Isla Ballena for a two-hour **snorkeling** trip.

Sleeping & Eating

Flutterby House HOSTEL $

(☎8341-2730; www.flutterbyhouse.com; campsites US$5, dm US$12-15, d US$30-60; P @ ❄ 🐾) This ramshackle collection of colorful tree houses and dorms is friendly, fun and within walking-distance of the beach. The list of perks is long: boards and bikes for rent; beer for a pittance; a tidy, open-air communal kitchen; and a delectable nightly dinner featuring local fare. Located near the south entrance to the park.

Tucan Hotel HOSTEL, CAMPGROUND $

(☎2743-8140; www.tucanhotel.com; campsites, hammocks & dm US$6, d from US$25; P ❄ @ ❄) About 150m east of the highway, this self-proclaimed 'traveler's refuge' is a fun and funky place that will make you feel at home, whether you need a hammock to swing in or a private room to call your own. The kitchen has only the basics, but the on-site restaurant is excellent. Super bonus: free shuttle to the beach.

Cascada Verde HOSTEL $

(☎2743-8191; www.cascadaverde.org; shared loft per person US$12, dm/d US$12/45; P) About 2km inland from Uvita, this organic permaculture farm and holistic retreat attracts legions of dedicated alternative lifestylers determined to calm down and connect with nature. Accommodations are basic and somewhat exposed to the elements, though there is ample outdoor communal space for yoga and quiet meditation. The on-site restaurant serves vegetarian and raw-food specialties.

Getting There & Away

Most buses depart from the two sheltered bus stops on the Costanera in the main village.

San Isidro de El General (US$1.25, 2 hours, 4 daily)

San José (US$5, 7 hours, 2 daily)

SOUTHERN COSTA RICA & PENÍNSULA DE OSA

Wild, vast and largely unexplored, southern Costa Rica is cut through the middle by the jagged range of the Cordillera de Talamanca and finished off at the bottom by the 'biologically intense' Osa peninsula. The mist-shrouded mountain range is marked with clear, turbulent rivers plunging to the lowlands, while the Osa's pristine beaches are lapped by rainforest.

For thrill-seekers, southern Costa Rica packs a punch with the country's highest peak and its richest wildlife. From the slopes of the Talamanca to the beaches of the Osa, this region beckons travelers with youthful hearts, intrepid spirits and a yearning for something truly wild.

San Isidro de El General

POP 62,500

'El General' is the region's largest population center and major transportation hub. If you're traveling to the southern Pacific beaches or Chirripó, a brief stop is inevitable, though there's little reason to linger.

Sleeping & Eating

Hotel Chirripó HOTEL $

(☎2771-0529; www.hotelchirripo.com; Av 2 btwn Calles Central & 1; s/d from US$16/24; P ❄) Overlooking the Parque Central, this is a popular spot for budget travelers passing through town. You'll find whitewashed rooms that are utterly barren but surprisingly dirt- and grime-free. A few flowering plants and a festive mural in the lobby brighten otherwise stark surroundings.

Península de Osa & Golfo Dulce

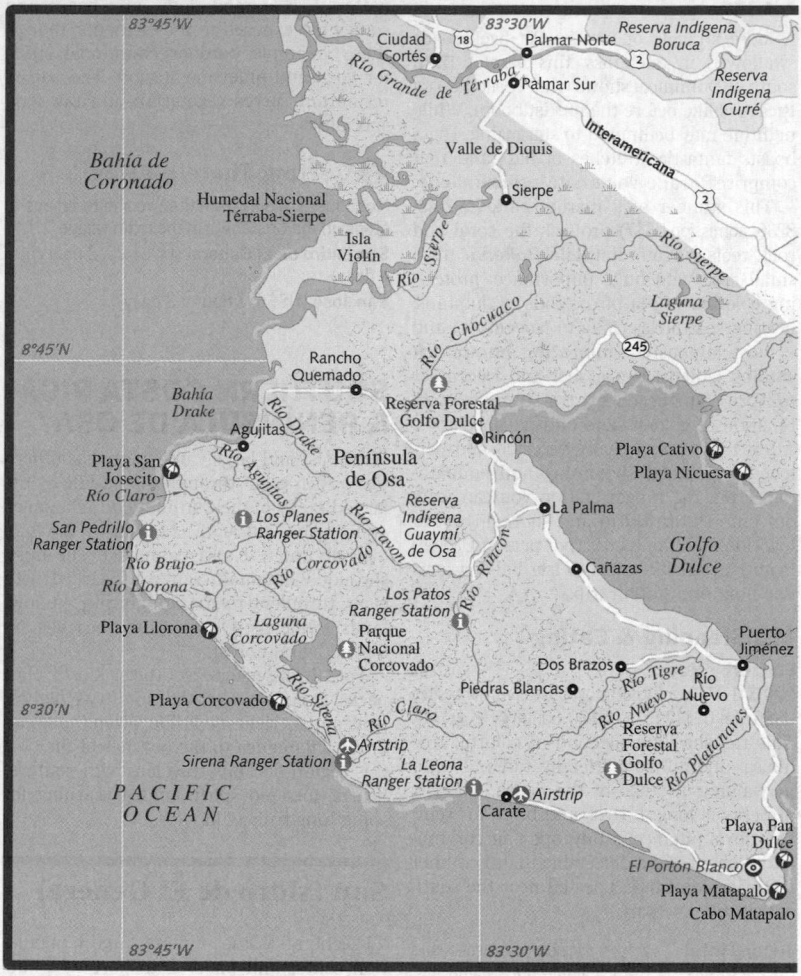

Hotel Los Crestones HOTEL $$

(☎2770-1200, 2770-1500; www.hotelloscrestones.com; cnr Calle Central & Av 14; s/d from US$40/50; P ❄ 📶) South of the soccer field, this sharp motor court is decked with blooming flowerboxes and climbing vines outside – a welcome sight to the road-weary traveler. Inside, functional rooms feature modern furnishings and fixtures, while attentive staff keep this place running efficiently.

Kafe de la Casa CAFE $

(☎2770-4816; Av 3 btwn Calles 2 & 4; meals US$6-13; ⏲7am-8pm) Set in an old Tico house one block west of the Interamericana, this bohemian cafe features eclectic artwork, an open kitchen and breezy garden seating. The menu has excellent breakfasts, light lunches, gourmet dinners and plenty of coffee drinks.

ℹ Information

Minae Park Service Office (Sinac; ☎2771-5116, 2742-5083; aclap@sinac.go.cr; Calle 2 btwn Avs 2 & 4; ⏲8am-noon & 1-4pm Mon-Fri) If you're hiking Chirripó, you can try to make reservations for the mountaintop hostel here. Please note a deposit is required to hold your reservation.

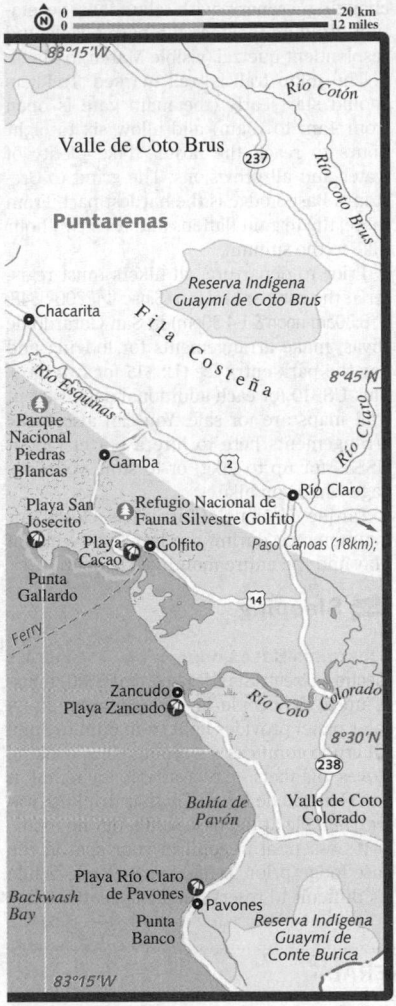

Getting There & Away

BUS

Long-distance buses leave from various points along the Interamericana. Buy your tickets early.

Buses to San José and to Southern Costa Rica depart from the **Terminal Tracopa** (☎2771-0468) on the Interamericana, just south of Av Central. On the side street south of the Tracopa terminal you'll find **Terminal Quepos** (☎2771-2550), also called Transportes Blanco, which services the Pacific coast. See table, p616, for departure information.

San Gerardo de Rivas

If you have plans to climb to the summit of Chirripó, then you're in the right place – the tiny but tranquil town of San Gerardo de Rivas marks the entrance to the national park. Here, you can make arrangements for accommodations within the park, pick up a few last-minute supplies and – perhaps most important of all – get a good night's rest before embarking on the trek. Note that there is no ATM in the village.

Do not fret if you have to hang around for a day or two. You can hike to the waterfalls in the mystical, magical **Cloudbridge Nature Reserve** (☎in USA 212-362-9391; www.cloudbridge.org; admission by donation; ⏲sunrise-sunset) or soak in the hot springs at **Aguas Termales Gevi** (☎2742-5210; Herradura; admission US$6; ⏲7am-5pm) in nearby Herradura.

Sleeping & Eating

★Casa Mariposa HOSTEL $
(☎2742-5037; www.hotelcasamariposa.net; dm US$14, d US$36-56; P@) This warm and welcoming backpacker hostel offers an excellent communal atmosphere that is conducive to picking up a few travel companions for the Chirripó trek. Carved out the side of the mountain near the trailhead, the close but cozy quarters have shared bathrooms, rustic stone walls and playful adornments. Bird-filled garden, communal kitchen and strategically hung hammocks complete the pretty picture.

Cabinas Roca Dura CABINAS $
(☎2262-7218; campsites US$5, r US$15-35; P) Located in the center of town just opposite the soccer field, this hip hostelry is built right into the side of a giant boulder, lending a Flintstones ambience to the quarters. Wall murals brighten the smallest stone rooms, while pricier rooms have tree-trunk furniture and fixtures and views of forested hillsides. The wooden bar is a friendly place for a drink (or a meal).

El Urán Hotel y Restaurante HOSTEL $
(☎2742-5003; www.hoteluran.com; dm/d/tr US$13/40/60; P) Just 50m below the trailhead, this no-nonsense youth hotel is something of an institution for hikers heading to/from Chirripó. Budget-friendly rooms of varying shapes and sizes are perfect for a restful snooze, while the onsite restaurant,

grocery store and laundry facilities all cater to the shoestring set.

Hotel de Montaña El Pelícano HOTEL $$
(☎8382-3000; www.hotelpelicano.net; r with/without bathrooms US$66/30, cabins from US$72; P @) About 300m below the ranger station, this simple but functional lodge has a collection of comfortable rooms overlooking the river valley. The highlight of the property is the gallery of the owner, a late-blooming artist who sculpts whimsical wood pieces.

Information

The Chirripó ranger station is about 1km below the soccer field on the road from San Isidro. Stop by early to check for availability at Crestones Base Lodge (p616), and to confirm and pay fees before setting out. The Base Lodge holds 10 first-come-first-served beds, which can only be reserved the day prior to arrival.

Getting There & Away

Buses to San Isidro depart from the soccer field at 5:15am, 11:30am and 4pm (US$1.60, 1½ to two hours).

Parque Nacional Chirripó

At 3820m, Cerro Chirripó is Costa Rica's highest peak and the centerpiece of a gorgeous national park set in the rugged Cordillera de Talamanca. The landscape is defined by lush cloud forest, high alpine lakes and bare *paramó* (a highland shrub and tussock grass habitat typical of the southern zone). The steep ascent traverses constantly changing scenery with abundant vegetation. Wildlife includes the harpy eagle and resplendent quetzal (visible March to May).

The 16km trail is well marked. Trekkers should start early (the main gate is open from 4am to 10am) and allow six to eight hours to reach the hostel. Take plenty of water and all provisions. The grind to Crestones Base Lodge is the hardest part. From there, the terrain flattens and it's a two-hour hike to the summit.

Prior to departure, all hikers must register at the **ranger station** (Sinac; ☎2200-5348; ⏲6:30am-noon & 1-4:30pm) in San Gerardo de Rivas, make arrangements for lodging and pay the park entry fee (US$15 for two days, plus US$10 for each additional day). Decent trail maps are for sale. You can also make arrangements here to hire a porter (about US$35 for up to 15kg) or to store your luggage while you hike.

Parque Nacional Chirripó is closed for maintenance during the last two weeks of May and the entire month of October.

Sleeping

Crestones Base Lodge LODGE $
(Centro Ambientalista el Parámo; dm US$10) houses up to 60 people in dorm-style bunks. A solar panel provides light from 6pm to 8pm. All crude comforts – sleeping bags, cooking stoves, blankets – are available for rental in San Gerardo de Rivas. There is drinking water available at the base camp, but no food.

It's essential to confirm your spot at the base lodge prior to making the trek. While it's difficult to reserve in advance, the lodge

BUSES FROM SAN ISIDRO DE EL GENERAL

DESTINATION	POINT OF DEPARTURE	PRICE (US$)	DURATION (HR)	FREQUENCY (DAILY)
Dominical	Terminal Quepos	3.80	2	3 daily
Neily	Terminal Tracopa	7	6	4 daily
Palmar Norte	Terminal Tracopa	4	2½	10 daily
Paso Canoas	Terminal Tracopa	6	5	6 daily
Puerto Jiménez via Palmar Norte	Terminal Quepos	6	5	2 daily
Quepos	Terminal Quepos	4	3	3 daily
San Gerardo de Rivas (for Parque Nacional Chirripó)	Local Terminal	1.60	1½	3 daily
San José	Terminal Tracopa	4.25	3	hrly 5am-8:30pm
Uvita	Terminal Quepos	1.60	1½	2 daily

sets aside 10 spaces per night for travelers who show up in San Gerardo and are ready to hike on the following day.

Getting There & Away

From San Gerardo de Rivas there is free transportation to the trailhead at 5am from opposite the ranger station. Several hotels also offer early-morning trailhead transportation for their guests.

Palmar

POP 4900

This hot and dusty banana-belt town is split into two by the Río Grande de Térraba. For travelers it is the northern gateway to the Osa peninsula. Palmar Sur has a local airstrip, while facilities such as banks, buses and hotels are in Palmar Norte. Note that if you are heading to Bahía Drake, this is your last chance to get cash. It also offers a rare opportunity to check out the **granite spheres** left by pre-Columbian cultures, some exceeding 2m in diameter.

Otherwise, there is little reason to spend any more time here than it takes to change buses. If you need to spend the night, get a room at the modest, family-run **Hotel Vista al Cerro** (☎2786-6663; www.vistaalcerro.com; d from US$30, apt negotiable; P ❄ @), on the western edge of town, or a sun-filled bungalow at **Brunka Lodge** (☎2786-7489; r from US$60; ❄ @ 📶 🏊), which is on the Interamericana just east of the intersection with 34.

Getting There & Away

The bus ticket office is inside the Panadería Palenquito.

Neily (US$1.60, 1½ hours, 8 daily) Departs from Supermercado Térraba.

San Isidro de El General (US$4, 3 hours, 4 daily) Departs Interamericana, east side.

San José (US$5.75, 6 hours, 7 daily) Departs Interamericana, east side.

Sierpe (US$1.40, 40 minutes, 7 daily) Departs Panadería Palenquito.

Sierpe

This sleepy village on the Río Sierpe is the gateway to Bahía Drake. If you've made a reservation with any of the jungle lodges further down the coast, you will be picked up here by boat. Beyond its function as a transit point, there is little reason to spend any time here.

The **Centro Turístico Las Vegas** (⏲6am-10pm), next to the boat dock, is a catch-all place for tourist information, distributing a wide selection of maps and brochures. It also offers internet access and serves a broad range of food to waiting passengers.

Your lodge will make arrangements for the boat transfer. If for some reason things go awry, there is no shortage of water taxis milling about. Buses to Palmar Norte (US$1.40, 40 minutes) depart from in front of the Pulpería Fenix from 5:30am to 6pm.

Bahía Drake

This area feels like an appendage of the Parque Nacional Corcovado (p620), as macaws, monkeys and other wildlife frolic in the treetops, and pods of dolphins flit through the waters offshore. Bahía Drake is a remote and expensive destination, but shoestringers can take advantage of a few budget options in the scenic village of Agujitas, which sits between the great green tangle of the national park and the shimmering blue of the bay. There are no banking facilities in Bahía Drake, so bring your cash with you.

Activities

Hiking

A public trail follows the coastline for the entire spectacular stretch from Agujitas to Corcovado, which takes four to six hours to hike in its entirety. It's excellent for spotting wonderful wildlife. Look (and listen) for squawking scarlet macaws and hooting chestnut-mandible toucans, as well as white-faced capuchin and howler monkeys, kinkajous and sloths. Scenic little inlets punctuate this entire route, each with a wild, windswept beach.

All of the lodges offer tours to Parque Nacional Corcovado, usually a full-day trip to San Pedrillo ranger station (from US$75 to US$150 per person), including boat transportation, lunch and guided hikes. These tours can be disappointing, as the trails around the ranger station get crowded and most tours start well after sunrise, when activity in the rainforest has already quieted down.

Swimming & Snorkeling

Lodges run snorkeling trips to **Isla del Caño,** which is about 20km west of Agujitas. There are other opportunities for snorkeling on the coast between Agujitas and Corcovado. **Playa San Josecito** attracts scores of colorful species, which hide out among the coral reef and rocks. Another recommended spot is **Playa Cocalito**, a small, pretty beach that is near Agujitas and is pleasant for swimming and sunbathing.

Kayaking & Canoeing

The idyllic **Río Agujitas** conveniently empties out into the bay, which is surrounded by hidden coves and sandy beaches ideal for exploring in a sea kayak. Paddling at high tide is recommended because it allows you to explore more territory. Most accommodations options in the area have kayaks and canoes for rent for a small fee.

Tours

Nighttime Walking Tour TOUR

(☎8701-7356; www.thenighttour.com; admission US$35; ⏲7:30-10pm) Tracie the 'Bug Lady' has created quite a name for herself with a fascinating nighttime walking tour in the jungle. Tracie is a walking encyclopedia on bug facts, and not just the boring scientific detail – one of her fields of research is the military use of insects!

Corcovado Expeditions TOUR

(☎8846-4734; www.corcovadoexpeditions.net) Offers competitively priced tours to Corcovado and Isla del Caño, as well as a wide variety of specialty hikes including unique excursions to look for rare tropical birds and poison-dart frogs. The office is located between the clinic and the school.

Original Canopy Tour CANOPY TOUR

(☎8371-1598; jinetesdeosa.com/canopy_tour.htm; admission US$35; ⏲8am-4pm) At Hotel Jinetes de Osa, the Original Canopy Tour has nine platforms, six cables and one 20m observation deck from where you can get a new perspective on the rainforest. Tours take two to three hours.

Sleeping & Eating

Pura Vida Drake Bay CABINA $

(☎8720-0801; www.puravidadrakebay.com; s/d from US$20/30; 📶) This economical option in the middle of town is a great bet for shoestringers. The owner, Martina, offers a few simple fan-cooled rooms, a communal kitchen and a wealth of information about Corcovado. The on-site *soda* is one of the best eating options in town.

★Finca Maresia BUNGALOW $$

(☎2775-0279, 8888-1625; www.fincamaresia.com; Camino a Los Planes; budget s/d US$30/40, standard s/d US$50/60, superior s/d US$75/90, all incl breakfast) Stretching across a series of hills, Finca Maresia entices travelers with low prices, high value and delightful design sense. Overlooking lush environs, the eight rooms' decor has been inspired by the owners' extensive travels, exhibiting eclectic features from modernist glass walls to Japanese-style sliding rice-paper doors. The finca is 2km from Agujitas on the road to Los Planes.

Casita Corcovado B&B $$

(☎2775-0627; www.casitacorcovado.com; s/d incl breakfast US$45/80; 🏊❄📶) At the end of the road in Agujitas, Jamie and Craig's lovely little oceanfront home has three rooms, each carefully furnished with tile floors and wood furniture, and all sharing a bathroom. Guests have access to two breezy patios and plenty of inviting hammocks, with the amenities of the village at the doorstep. Delicious, home-cooked meals are also available.

Cabinas Murillo CABINA $$

(☎2256-2748, 8892-7702; www.drakecorcovadocabins.com; r s/d US$30/40, cabin s/d US$40/50; P📶) This family-run place has simple, tidy rooms that are right in the middle of Agujitas. The cabins up on the hillside are even better: for only a few dollars more, enjoy a balcony overlooking the entire bay, perfect for whale-watching.

Cabinas El Mirador Lodge CABINA $$

(☎8836-9415; www.miradordrakebay.com; per person incl meals from US$50; P📶) High on a hill at the northern end of Agujitas, El Mirador (Lookout Point) lives up to its name, offering spectacular views of the bay from its eight cozy cabins. The hospitable Vargas family ensures all guests receive a warm welcome, as well as three square meals a day of hearty, home-cooked Costa Rican fare. Discount for email booking and cash payment.

Getting There & Away

All of the hotels offer boat transfers between Sierpe and Bahía Drake with prior arrangements. If you have not made advanced arrangements with your lodge for a pick-up, you can always grab a private water taxi in Sierpe for a negotiable price.

From Agujitas, it's a 16km, four- to six-hour hike along the beachside trail to San Pedrillo ranger station at the north end of Corcovado. If you are heading into the park, make sure you have reservations to camp at the ranger stations.

Puerto Jiménez

POP 3000

Once a gold-mining center, Port Jim (as the gringos call it) retains the air of a flat-out frontier post. While walking through the dusty streets, it's not unusual to spot scarlet macaws roosting on the soccer field, or white-faced capuchins swinging in the treetops adjacent to the main street. It's not hard to understand why Puerto Jiménez is brimming with wildlife, given that the town lies on the edge of Parque Nacional Corcovado. As the preferred jumping-off point for travelers heading to the Sirena ranger station (famed for wildlife-watching opportunities), the town is a great place to organize an expedition, stock up on supplies, eat a hot meal and get a good night's rest before hitting the trails.

About 5km east of town, the secluded – and often deserted – **Playa Platanares** is excellent for swimming, sunning and recovering from too much adventure. The nearby mangroves of **Río Platanares** are a paradise for kayaking and bird-watching.

Tours

Osa Wild ECOTOUR

(www.osawildtravel.com; Rte 245, downtown Puerto Jimenez; day ecotours from US$17) This innovative outfit is a great resource for travelers to connect with community-oriented initiatives, including homestays, farm tours and sustainable local cultural exchanges.

Aventuras Tropicales ADVENTURE TOUR

(☎2735-5195; www.aventurastropicales.com) An operation that offers all sorts of tropical adventures, including snorkeling, kayaking and fishing.

Sleeping

Cabinas Back Packers HOTEL $

(☎2735-5181; d with/without air-con US$32/20; ❄) Puerto Jiménez has loads of budget digs, but this is among the best of the bunch – it's squeaky clean, relatively quiet and situated directly next to the *colectivo* (collective car/truck) station leading to the park. The rooms vary but they're all simple and spotless, as is the well-stocked kitchen.

Cabinas the Corner HOSTEL $

(☎2735-5328; www.jimenezhotels.com/cabinasthecorner; dm/d US$10/12; P📶) While this ultra-budget crash pad provides little more than a bed in a fan-cooled room for the night, the Corner is kept admirably clean and secure, and resultantly has a growing legion of devoted fans. This is as good a place as any to link up with other potential trekkers, form an expedition party and stock up on invaluable local advice. It's half a block from Restaurant Carolina.

Cacao Monkeys CABINA $$

(☎2735-5248; www.cacaomonkeys.com; s/d incl breakfast from US$40/60; P📶) On the southwestern fringes of town, this cocoa plantation has five brightly painted wooden *cabinas,* each of a unique design, all with shiny hardwood floors and porches. On 3.5 hectares of secondary forest, there are also walking trails and an excellent riverside café (meals US$8). Wildlife abounds.

Cabinas Tropicales CABINAS $$

(☎2735-5298, 8997-1445; www.cabinas-tropicales.com; s/d from US$35/40; P❄@) The tidy accommodations at Cabinas Tropicales range from simple standards to roomy lofts and a deluxe suite. Each is unique, but they all have sturdy furniture, air-con and access to the gorgeous gardens and well-stocked open-air kitchen. Your host, Mark, is both personable and knowledgeable, making this one of the best-value options in town. Located near the airstrip.

Cabinas Jiménez CABINA $$

(☎2735-5090; www.cabinasjimenez.com; d from US$50; P❄@📶🏊) This long-standing clutch of cabins has a prime location on the northern edge of town, overlooking the gulf. Rooms feature underwater murals in the bathrooms, carved wooden furniture and woven textiles. Pricier rooms have fantastic views of the lagoon.

Cabinas Marcelina HOTEL $$

(☎2755-5286; www.jimenezhotels.com/cabinasmarcelina; d with/without air-con US$50/45; P❄) Marcelina's place is a long-standing favorite among cost-conscious travelers. Near the Catholic church, the salmon-pink concrete building is surrounded by blooming trees, lending it a homey atmosphere that invites good dreams. Modern furniture, fluffy towels and tile bathrooms are a welcome sight.

Eating & Drinking

Restaurant Carolina COSTA RICAN $
(dishes US$3-8) This is *the* hub in Puerto Jiménez. Expats, nature guides, tourists and locals all gather here for food, drinks and plenty of carousing. The cell-like rooms are also a cool option (as in, air-conditioned) if you're stuck for somewhere to stay. It's on the main drag, one block south of the soccer field.

Pizzamail.it PIZZERIA $$
(pizzas US$9-18; ⏲4-10:30pm; 📶) It does not instill much confidence when a restaurant is named after a website. Still, all doubts will be cast aside when a server at Pizzamail.it brings out the pie: a thin-crust, wood-fired piece of Italy in the middle of the jungle. Opposite the soccer field.

Juanita's BAR
(www.juanitasmexican.com; ⏲5pm-2am) You can get halfway decent food at Juanita's, but it's more popular for the margaritas. One block south of the soccer field, just east of Rte 245.

Information

Banco Nacional de Costa Rica (⏲8:30am-3:45pm Mon-Fri) Due to completely inscrutable bureaucracy, money orders for the park must be purchased at this, the Banco Nacional de Costa Rica, opposite the church.

Cafenet El Sol (☎2735-5719; www.soldeosa.com; per hr US$1; ⏲7am-10pm)

Oficina de Área de Conservación Osa (Osa Conservation Area Headquarters; ☎2735-5580; ⏲8am-noon & 1-4pm Mon-Fri) Make reservations here to camp in Corcovado. It's east of downtown, opposite the airstrip.

Getting There & Away

BOAT

Two passenger ferries travel to Golfito (US$6, 1½ hours), departing two or three times daily. You can also hire a private water taxi to shuttle you across the bay.

BUS

Most buses arrive at the terminal on the west side of town. All of these pass La Palma (23km away) for the eastern entry into Corcovado. Buy tickets to San José in advance.

Neily (US$5, 3 hours, 2 daily)

San Isidro de El General (US$7, 5 hours, 3 daily)

San José (US$12, 8 hours, 2 daily)

TAXI

Colectivo Transportation (☎8832-8680, 8837-3120; Soda Deya) runs a jeep-taxi service to Carate (three hours, US$10) on the southern tip of the national park. Departures are from the Soda Deya at 6am and 1:30pm, returning at 8:30am and 4pm.

Otherwise, you can call and hire a 4WD taxi from **Taxi 348** (☎8849-5228; taxicorcovado@racsa.co.cr) or from the **Central Taxi Center** (☎2735-5481). Taxis usually charge up to US$80 for the ride to Carate and more than US$100 for the overland trek to Drake.

Parque Nacional Corcovado

Famously labeled by *National Geographic* as 'the most biologically intense place on earth,' this **national park** is the last great original tract of tropical rainforest in Pacific Central America. The bastion of biological diversity is home to Costa Rica's largest population of scarlet macaws, as well as countless other endangered species, including Baird's tapir, the giant anteater and the world's largest bird of prey, the harpy eagle. Corcovado's amazing biodiversity has long attracted a devoted stream of visitors who descend from Bahía Drake and Puerto Jiménez to explore the remote location and spy on a wide array of wildlife.

The best wildlife-watching is at Sirena station, but the coastal trails are also excellent for birds and monkeys. The Los Patos trail is famous for its agressive peccaries. (Climb a tree to avoid being bitten or trampled.)

Activities

Hiking

Paths are primitive and the hiking is hot, humid and insect-ridden, but the challenge of the trek and the interaction with wildlife at Corcovado are thrilling. The main routes across Parque Nacional Corcovado are well marked, making this journey easy enough to complete independently, but hiring a guide will increase your chances of seeing wildlife and eliminate any possibility of losing the trail. Remember:

- Hike in the dry season (December to April).
- Carry plenty of food, water, sun block and insect repellent.

➡ Always verify your route with the rangers before setting out.

La Leona to Sirena to Los Patos

The most popular route traverses the park from La Leona to Sirena, then exits the park at Los Patos (or vice versa). Both of these end points are easily accessible from Puerto Jiménez, which serves as a convenient jumping-off point. From the park entrance at Carate, it's a one-hour, 3.5km hike to La Leona ranger station, where you can camp (or not). From there it takes six to seven hours to complete the 16km hike to Sirena. The trail follows the shoreline through coastal forest and deserted beaches, including one major river crossing.

From Sirena, hike inland 18km through the heart of Corcovado to Los Patos ranger station. The six-hour slog involves two river crossings, and the last 6km requires some steep uphill climbs (which may be a reason to do this hike in the opposite direction). Camp at Los Patos or continue another 14km to La Palma, which takes about four hours. From there buses travel to Puerto Jiménez.

Sirena to San Pedrillo & Los Planes

The trek between Sirena and San Pedrillo (or the new station at Los Planes) is difficult, both physically and logistically. This beach trail is closed from April to November when the estuaries flood. At the time of writing, it was closed year-round for reasons of safety, and it may be closed permanently.

When it's open, the hike requires three river crossings, which are impossible at high tide, so it's important to time your hike accordingly. The 23km hike to San Pedrillo takes 10 to 12 hours. It involves stunning beach scenery, which also means loose sand and little shade. Experienced guides recommend that the first part of this hike should be completed at night to avoid the hot sun.

Camp at San Pedrillo ranger station, then continue 15km to Drake, which takes another five to seven hours. Alternatively, it's usually possible to get a lift back to Drake from one of the tour operators leading a day hike.

Sleeping & Eating

There is camping at the ranger stations (per person US$4); facilities include potable water and latrines. Camping is not permitted in areas other than the ranger stations.

Simple dormitory lodging (per person US$12) and excellent meals (breakfast US$20, dinner US$25) are available at Sirena station only. You must make advance reservations for lodging and meals through the Oficina de Área de Conservación Osa (p620) in Puerto Jiménez.

Otherwise, campers must bring all their own food. Note that ranger stations face a challenge with trash disposal, so all visitors are required to pack out all of their trash.

Information & Orientation

Corcovado Guide (www.corcovadoguide.com) is an excellent source of information.

If you intend to camp in the park or use any of the facilities at Sirena station, be sure to make reservations a few days in advance at the Oficina de Área de Conservación Osa (p620) in Puerto Jiménez.

Park headquarters are at Sirena ranger station on the coast in the middle of the park. Other ranger stations are located on the park boundaries: San Pedrillo ranger station in the northwest corner on the coast; the new Los Planes ranger station on the northern boundary (near the village of the same name); La Leona ranger station in the southeast corner on the coast (near the village of Carate); and Los Patos ranger station in the northeast corner (near the village of La Palma).

Getting There & Away

FROM BAHÍA DRAKE

Walk the 16km coastal trail that leads to San Pedrillo station (about four hours from Agujitas), or any lodge can drop you here as a part of its regular tours to Corcovado. Alternatively, you can consider heading inland to the Los Planes station, though this is a longer, more heavily forested route.

You can also charter a boat to San Pedrillo (US$80 to US$125) or Sirena (US$125 to US$165).

FROM LA PALMA

From the north, the closest point of access is the town of La Palma. All buses heading to/from Puerto Jímenez pass through La Palma.

You might be able to find a taxi to take you partway to Los Patos; however, the road is only passable to 4WD vehicles (and not always), so be prepared to hike the 14km to the ranger station.

FROM CARATE

In the southeast, the closest point of access is Carate, from where La Leona station is a one-hour, 3.5km hike west along the beach.

Carate is accessible from Puerto Jiménez via a poorly maintained, adventure-filled 45km dirt road. A 4WD *colectivo* jeep taxi travels this route (US$10, 1½ hours), departing Carate *pulpería* at 8:30am and 3:30pm daily.

Golfito

POP 7600

A rough-and-ready little city with a long and sordid history, Golfito is a ramshackle port that stretches out along the Golfo Dulce. Ticos enthusiastically shop duty-free here, but for backpackers it's merely a springboard to Puerto Jiménez or Pavones. If you get stuck, **Cabinas Princesa de Golfito** (☎2775-0442; s/d US$15/25; P ❄ 📶) is a safe, welcoming option, just north of the bus depot.

Two passenger ferries (US$6, 1½ hours) travel to Puerto Jiménez from the Muellecito (Small Dock), departing two or three times a day. You can also hire a private water taxi at the smaller dock, north of the Muelle Bananero.

Most buses stop at the depot in front of the Muellecito.

Neily (US$1.30, 1½ hours, hourly 6am to 7pm)

Pavones (US$5, 3 hours, 2 daily) Service may be affected by road and weather conditions, especially in rainy season.

San José, (US$11, 8 hours, 2 daily) Via San Isidro de El General. Departs from the terminal near Muelle Bananero.

Pavones

POP 2700

Home to what is reportedly the longest left-hand surf break on the planet, Pavones is a legendary destination for surfers the world over. This is Costa Rica's southernmost point, and you'll work hard to get down here. That's one reason why the palm-lined streets are still not paved, the pace of life is slow and the overall atmosphere remains tranquil.

Buses arrive first at Pavones, then head further south to Punta Banco where the road ends and jungle stretches to Panama. Transportation between the two areas is scant, but it is a pleasant long walk. Pavones has no bank or gas station, so make sure you have plenty of money and gas.

Sleeping

Rancho Burica LODGE $

(☎2776-2223; www.ranchoburica.com; r per person US$15-35; P) This friendly Dutch-run outpost is the end of the road in Punta Banco (literally). All rooms have bathrooms and fans, while the pricier ones have mosquito-netted beds and attractive wood furniture. Excellent, filling set-menu meals (US$7 to US$10) provide sustenance for surfers. Hammocks interspersed around the property offer ample opportunity for chilling out. And of course, the waves are at your doorstep.

Cabinas Mira Olas CABINA $

(☎2776-2006; www.miraolas.com; d/tr from US$35/45; P 📶) This 4.5-hectare farm is full of wildlife and fruit trees. Clean, comfortable cabins all have cool fans, hot showers and wide hammock-strung porches overlooking the orchard. To find Mira Olas, follow the signs up the steep hill: it's worth the climb!

★Yoga Farm LODGE $$$

(www.yogafarmcostarica.org; dm/s/d incl meals & yoga US$43/50/90) It's an invigorating 15-minute uphill walk from Rancho Burica. But once you arrive, it's an inspirational lesson in intentional, sustainable, healthy living. Accommodations are in simple, clean rooms with wood bunk beds. Bathrooms have composting toilets. Vegetarian meals are prepared with ingredients from the organic garden. Daily yoga classes take place in an open-air studio overlooking the ocean. Namaste.

Drinking & Nightlife

Esquina del Mar Cantina BAR

A Pavones institution that has great views of the left break; this is where you should grab a drink after your last ride.

Getting There & Away

Two daily buses go to Golfito (US$3, three hours), departing at 5am from the end of the road at Rancho Burica (though you can pick it up in town) and at 12:30pm from the Esquina del Mar Cantina.

Neily

POP 11,100 / TRANSPORT HUB

Although it is southern Costa Rica's second-largest 'city,' Neily has retained the friendly atmosphere of a rural town, much like neighboring Palmar. At just 50m above sea level, steamy Neily also serves as a regional transportation hub and agricultural center, though it is decidedly lacking in tourist appeal. A **Banco Coopealianza** (⏲8am-3pm Mon-Fri), just southwest of the *mercado*

BUSES FROM NEILY

DESTINATION	PRICE (US$)	DURATION (HR)	FREQUENCY (DAILY)
Dominical	4	3	3
Golfito	1.65	1½	hrly 6am-7:30pm
Palmar	1.65	1½	7
Paso Canoas	0.75	30 min	at least hrly 6am-6pm
Puerto Jiménez	4	3	2
San Isido de El General	7	6	4
San José	11	8	5

(market), has a 24-hour ATM on the Cirrus network.

Few people have a good reason to stick around town, though you can always grab a clean room and a hot meal at **Hotel Andrea** (☎2783-3784, 2783-3715; www.hotelandreacr.com; d without/with AC $37/46; P ❄ @), across from central market. Clean, secure and decent value, the place also has one of Neily's best restaurants on-site.

Buses leave from the main terminal on the east side of town.

Paso Canoas

The main port of entry between Costa Rica and Panama is like most border outposts the world over: hectic, slightly seedy and devoid of charm. As you might imagine, most travelers leave Paso Canoas with little more than a passing glance at their passport stamp.

Báncredito (⏲8am-4:30pm), near the **Costa Rican Migración and Customs** (⏲6am-11pm), changes traveler's checks and there is an ATM near the border. Colones are accepted at the border, but are difficult to get rid of further into Panama.

Tracopa buses leave for San José (US$12, six hours, four daily) from the **Tracopa bus terminal** (☎2732-2201), which is just north of the border post on the east side of the main road. Sunday-afternoon buses are full of weekend shoppers, so buy tickets as early as possible. Buses for Neily (US$0.75, 30 minutes) leave from in front of the post office at least once an hour from 6am to 6pm.

See p634 for information about getting to David, Panama.

UNDERSTAND COSTA RICA

Costa Rica Today

Despite the economic tumult that has rocked the world in recent years, Costa Rica's economy has remained relatively stable, thanks to consistently growing returns on tourism.

Tourism now outweighs both agriculture and industry as the biggest slice of the economy. The success of the 'green revolution' has created a new concern, namely the need for *sustainable* tourism. The increasing number of visitors to Costa Rica has led to more hotels, more transportation and more infrastructure upgrades. This tourist-driven encroachment inevitably places stress on the fragile ecosystem that people are flocking to see.

Poverty levels are largely kept in check by strong welfare programs. That said, the proportion of Ticos living below the poverty line has increased to 21%. Nicaraguans continue to cross the border in record numbers, with as many as half a million living in Costa Rica. Rightly or wrongly, immigrants are often blamed for increases in crime, fueling ongoing animosity between Nicas and Ticos.

Another problem that has seeped over the borders from neighboring states is the violent drug trade. Once merely a bridge for the flow of drugs between South and North America, Costa Rica is rapidly becoming a storage and trading center for drug cartels. Between 2009 and 2012 authorities seized over 90 tons of cocaine. After years on the sideline Costa Rica has finally entered the drug war.

History

Lost Civilization

About 500 years ago, on the eve of European discovery, as many as 400,000 people lived in today's Costa Rica. The Central Valley hosted roughly 20 small tribes, organized into chiefdoms, with a *cacique* (chief) leading a hierarchical society that included shaman, warriors, workers and slaves. To the east, the fierce Caribs dominated the Atlantic coastal lowlands. Adept at seafaring, they provided a conduit of trade with the South American mainland.

Concentrated tribes of indigenous people in the northwest tended cornfields and were connected to the great Meso-American cultures. Aztec religious practices and Maya jade and craftsmanship are in evidence on the Península de Nicoya, while Costa Rican quetzal feathers and golden trinkets have turned up in Mexico. The three chiefdoms found in the southwest showed the influence of native Andean cultures, including coca leaves, yucca and sweet potatoes.

Heirs of Columbus

On his fourth and final voyage to the New World in 1502, Christopher Columbus was forced to drop anchor near today's Puerto Limón after a hurricane damaged his ship. Waiting for repairs, Columbus ventured into the verdant terrain and exchanged gifts with welcoming natives. He returned from this encounter claiming to have seen 'more gold in two days than in four years in Spain.' Anxious to claim its bounty, Columbus petitioned the Spanish Crown to have himself appointed governor. However, by the time he returned to Seville, his royal patron Queen Isabella was on her deathbed, and King Ferdinand awarded the prize to a rival. Columbus never returned to the New World, and worn down by ill health and court politics, he died in 1506.

To the disappointment of his conquistador heirs, the region did not abound with gold and the locals were not so affable. The pestilent swamps, volcano-topped mountains and oppressive jungles made Columbus' paradise seem more like hell for new colonies.

Balboa's crossing of Panama in 1513 found a western beachhead from which to assault Costa Rica, so the Spanish targeted the indigenous groups living near the Golfo de Nicoya. Intercontinental germ exchange caused outbreaks of feverish death on both sides. Scarce in mineral wealth and indigenous laborers, the Spanish eventually came to regard the region as the poorest and most miserable in all the Americas.

It was not until the 1560s that a Spanish colony was established at Cartago. This small community in the interior settled to cultivate the rich volcanic soil of the Central Valley.

Central Valley Sunday

Central America formed a loosely administered colony. Its political-military headquarters was in Guatemala and the closest bishop was in Nicaragua. Lacking strategic significance or exploitable riches, Costa Rica was a minor provincial outpost.

Costa Rica's colonial path diverged from the typical Spanish pattern in that a powerful landholding elite and slave-based economy never gained prominence. Instead of large estates, mining operations and coastal cities, modest-sized villages of small-holders developed in the interior Central Valley. Workers toiled six days a week, while Central Valley Sundays were just for prayer and rest. There were several well-connected families whose lineage went back to the founding of the colony, but anyone could acquire wealth by agricultural processing or trade. In national lore, this relative egalitarianism is touted as 'rural democracy.'

Colonial life centered on agriculture. Costa Ricans grew corn, beans and plantains for subsistence, and produced sugar, cacao and tobacco for sale. However, indigenous raids and pirate attacks kept villagers on nervous guard. When Cartago was leveled in 1723 by Volcán Irazú, new settlements sprouted in Heredia, San José and Alajuela. As the 18th century closed, the population topped 50,000.

As Spanish settlement expanded, the indigenous population plummeted. From 400,000 at the time Columbus first sailed, the number was reduced to 20,000 a century later, and to 8000 a century after that. While disease was the main source of death, the Spanish exploited native labor relentlessly. Outside the valley, several tribes managed to prolong their survival under forest cover, staging occasional raids, but eventually they were defeated by military campaigns.

A Sovereign Struggle

In 1821 the Americas wriggled free of Spain's imperial grip. The newly liberated colonies pondered their fate: stay together in a United States of Central America or go their separate national ways. The first solution, the Central American Federation (CAF), suffered from an imbalance of power and no ability to raise taxes or have defense. Costa Rica formally withdrew in 1938.

An independent Costa Rica took shape under Juan Mora Fernandez, first head of state (1824–33). In 1824 the Nicoya-Guanacaste province seceded from Nicaragua and joined its more easygoing southern neighbor, defining the territorial borders. In 1852 Costa Rica received its first diplomatic emissaries from the USA and Great Britain.

As one empire receded, another rose. In the 19th century, the USA was in an expansive mood and Spanish America looked vulnerable. In 1856 the soldier of fortune William Walker landed in Nicaragua intending to conquer Central America, establish slavery and construct an interoceanic canal. When Walker marched on Costa Rica, he faced a hastily mobilized volunteer army of 9000 civilians. They stopped the Yankee mercenaries at Santa Rosa, chasing them back into Nicaragua. During the fight, a daring drummer boy from Alajuela, Juan Santamaría, was killed while setting fire to Walker's defenses. The battle became a national legend and Santamaría a national hero (and inspiration for an airport).

Coffee Rica

In the 19th century, the introduction of the caffeinated red bean transformed the impoverished nation into the wealthiest in the region.

When an export market emerged, the government promoted coffee to farmers by providing free saplings. By the 1840s, local merchants scoped out their own overseas markets, persuading the captain of the HMS *Monarch* to transport several hundred sacks of Costa Rican coffee to London, percolating the beginning of a beautiful friendship.

In the 1940s, children learned to read with a text that stated, 'Coffee is good for me. I drink coffee every morning.' Coffee's quick fix made it popular among working-class consumers in the industrializing north. Enterprising German immigrants improved the technical and financial aspects of the business. By century's end, more than one-third of the Central Valley was dedicated to coffee cultivation, and coffee accounted for more than 90% of all exports.

An elite group of coffee barons monopolized the processing, marketing and financing of the coffee economy, but they lacked the land and labor to monopolize the crop. As such, the coffee economy in Costa Rica created a wide network of high-end traders and small-scale growers (unlike in the rest of Central America, where a narrow elite controlled large estates, worked by tenant laborers). However, with three-quarters of the coffee barons descended from just two colonial families, the coffee elite's economic interests became a priority in national politics. Today Costa Rica has an estimated 130,000 coffee farms.

The Banana Boom

The coffee trade unintentionally gave rise to Costa Rica's next export boom – bananas. Getting coffee out to world markets necessitated a rail link from the central highlands to the coast and Limón's deep harbor made an ideal port. But inland was dense jungle and infested swamps. In 1871 the government contracted the building of the railroad to Minor Keith, nephew of an American railroad tycoon.

The project was a disaster. Malaria and accidents forced a constant replenishing of workers. Tico recruits gave way to US convicts and Chinese indentured servants, who were replaced by freed Jamaican slaves. Keith's two brothers died during the arduous first decade that laid 100km of track. The government defaulted on funding and construction costs soared over budget. To entice Keith to continue, the government turned over 3240 sq km of land along the route and a 99-year lease to run the railroad. In 1890 the line was finally completed, and running at a loss.

Bananas were first grown along the railroad tracks as a cheap food source for workers. Desperate to recoup his investment, Keith shipped some to New Orleans. Consumers went, well, bananas. *Fincas* (plantations) replaced lowland forests and bananas surpassed coffee as Costa Rica's most lucrative export by the early 20th century. Although Costa Rica became the world's leading banana exporter, the profits shipped out along with the bananas.

Joining with another American importer, Keith founded the infamous United Fruit Company, soon the largest employer in Central America. Known as *el pulpo* (the octopus) to locals, United Fruit owned huge swathes of lush lowlands, much of the transportation and communication infrastructure, and bunches of bureaucrats. A wave of migrant laborers arrived from Jamaica, changing the country's ethnic complexion and provoking racial tensions.

In 1913, a banana blight known as 'Panama disease' shut down many Caribbean plantations and the industry relocated to the Pacific. Eventually United Fruit lost its banana monopoly.

Unarmed Democracy

Early Costa Rican politics followed the Central American pattern of violence and dictatorship. In the 19th century, a few favored aristocrats competed to control patronage in the new state. The military, the Church and especially the coffee barons were the main sources of influence. Presidents were more often removed at gunpoint than by the ballot box.

But by the early 20th century, Costa Rica began to implement more equitable policies. The eligible electorate had expanded from 2% to 10% of the adult population. Higher taxes on the coffee barons were financing social reform, and the country enjoyed free public education, a guaranteed minimum wage and child protection laws. Disenfranchised groups resorted to protest politics, forcing the resignation of at least one president.

In the 1940s, tension mounted, as activists continued to champion the rights of the working class and the poor. Civil war broke out after disputed elections in 1948. Led by coffee grower and utopian democrat José Figueres Ferrer, armed workers battled military forces, and Nicaraguan and US forces joined in the fray. Peace was restored in under two months at the cost of 2000 deaths.

Figueres became head of a temporary junta government. His 1949 constitution granted full citizenship and voting rights to women, blacks, indigenous groups and Chinese minorities. His copious decrees taxed the wealthy, nationalized banks and built a modern welfare state. Most extraordinarily, Figueres abolished the military, calling it a threat to democracy. These actions became the foundation for Costa Rica's unique and unarmed democracy.

The Contra Conflict

The sovereignty of the small nations of Central America was limited by their northern neighbor, as the USA was hostile toward leftist politics. During the 1970s, radical socialists forced the military regimes of Guatemala, El Salvador and Nicaragua onto the defensive. When they toppled the American-backed Somoza dictatorship in Nicaragua in 1979, President Ronald Reagan decided to intervene. The Cold War arrived in the hot tropics.

Under intense US pressure, politically moderate Costa Rica was reluctantly dragged in. The Contras set up camp in Costa Rica, from where they staged guerrilla raids and built a secret jungle airstrip to fly in weapons and supplies. Costa Rican authorities were bribed to keep quiet. Diplomatic relations between Costa Rica and Nicaragua grew nastier and border clashes became bloodier.

The war polarized Costa Rica. Conservatives pushed to re-establish the military and join the anticommunist crusade. On the opposing side, in May 1984, over 20,000 demonstrators marched through San José to give peace a chance. The debate peaked with the 1986 presidential election. The victor was 44-year-old Oscar Arias Sánchez, an intellectual reformer in the mold of Figueres.

Once in office, Arias affirmed his commitment to a negotiated resolution and reasserted Costa Rican national independence. He vowed to uphold neutrality and kick out the Contras. Soon, the US ambassador quit his post and a public ceremony had Costa Rican schoolchildren planting trees on the secret CIA airfield. Most notably, Arias became the driving force in uniting Central America around a peace plan, which ended the Nicaraguan war. In 1987, he was awarded the Nobel Peace Prize.

Paradise Found

The same dense rainforest that conquistadors had cursed 500 years earlier revealed a hidden wealth: ecotourism.

An oversupply of coffee caused a crash in prices in the 1970s. The new market unpredictability brought together an unusual alliance of big business and environmentalists. If wealth could not be sustained through the country's exports, then what about imports – of tourists? Costa Rica embarked on a green revolution. By 1995, there were more than 125 government-protected sites. Almost one-third of the entire country is under some form of environmental protection.

Success encouraged private landholders to build reserves as well. It started slowly: Monteverde reserve recorded only 500 tourists in 1975; 20 years later the number surpassed 50,000. Tourism contributed more than US$750 million in 1995, passing coffee and bananas as the main source of foreign currency earnings.

Modern Currents

In the 2010 presidential elections, the victor was the former Vice President Laura Chinchilla. Chinchilla campaigned on similar economic platforms as her political mentor, Oscar Arias Sánchez, namely the promotion of free trade and further access to US markets. Unlike Arias, President Chinchilla is a social conservative who is opposed to legalized abortion, same-sex marriage and emergency contraception.

Chinchilla has spent much of her time in office dealing with tensions on the Nicaraguan border and struggling with a budget deficit. As a result, her approval ratings have been low, as constituents claim she should be focusing on reducing crime. She has made efforts to draw international attention to Costa Rica's battles against drug running, including receiving US President Obama in 2013 to emphasize the two countries' cooperation.

The Culture

People

Most Costa Ricans are *mestizo*, having a mix of Spanish and indigenous and/or African roots (though the majority of Ticos consider themselves to be white). Indigenous groups comprise only 1% of the population. These groups include the Bribrí and Cabécar, the Brunka, the Guaymí and the Maleku.

Less than 3% of the population is black, concentrated on the Caribbean coast. Tracing its ancestry to Jamaican immigrants who were brought to build railroads in the 19th century, this population speaks Mecatelyu: a creole of English, Spanish and Jamaican English.

Chinese (1% of the population) also first arrived to work on the railroads and since then have had regular waves of immigration. Taiwanese immigration has been particularly strong.

Lifestyle

With the lack of war, long life expectancy and a relatively sturdy economy, Costa Rica enjoys the highest standard of living in Central America. Indeed, Costa Rica often tops lists of the 'happiest' places in the world.

Significantly, life expectancy in Costa Rica is almost the same as in the USA, thanks to a comprehensive socialized health-care system and proper sanitation systems.

Still, the divide between rich and poor is broad. The middle and upper classes largely reside in San José and other major cities. For the vast majority of *campesinos*

PURA VIDA

'Pura vida' – pure life – is more than just a slogan that rolls off the tongues of Ticos and emblazons souvenirs; this phrase is a bona fide mantra for the Costa Rican way of life. Perhaps the essence of the pure life is something better lived than explained, but hearing *'pura vida'* again and again while traveling across this beautiful country – as a greeting, a stand-in for goodbye and an acknowledgement of thanks – makes it evident that the concept is deep within the DNA of this country.

The living seems particularly pure when Costa Rica is compared with its Central American neighbors: there's little poverty, illiteracy or political tumult; the country is crowded with ecological jewels and has high standards of living. What's more, Costa Rica has flourished without an army for the past 60 years.

The sum of the parts makes for a country that's an oasis of calm in a corner of the world that has been continuously degraded by warfare. And although the Costa Rican people are justifiably proud, a compliment to the country is likely to be met simply with a warm smile and an enigmatic two-word reply: *pura vida*.

(farmers) and *indígenas* (people of indigenous origin), life is harder, poverty levels are higher and standards of living are lower. This is especially true along the Caribbean coast, where the descendants of Jamaican immigrants have long suffered from a lack of attention by the federal government.

As in the rest of the world, globalization is having a dramatic effect on Costa Ricans, who are increasingly mobile, international and intertwined in the global economy – for better or for worse.

Landscape & Wildlife

Landscape

Despite its diminutive size – at 51,000 sq km it is slightly smaller than the USA's West Virginia – Costa Rica's land is an explosion of technicolor, topographical contrasts. On one coast are the breezy skies and big waves of the Pacific. Only 119km away lie the muggy and languid shores of the Caribbean. In between there are active volcanoes, alpine peaks and crisp high-elevation forest. Few places on earth can compare with this little country's spectacular interaction of natural, geological and climatic forces.

The national-park system protects 35 national parks, covering 11% of the country. Scores of other protected zones include wetlands and mangroves, in addition to a slew of privately owned and operated reserves. Authorities claim that one-third of the country is under conservation. Unfortunately, some of this land is still at risk – partly because the government lacks the funds and infrastructure to enforce its protection policies.

ENDANGERED SPECIES

The number-one threat to most of Costa Rica's endangered species is habitat destruction, followed by hunting and trapping.

➡ The legendary resplendent quetzal – topping every naturalist's must-see list – approaches extinction as its home forests are felled.

➡ A booming pet trade has extirpated the population of large, squawky scarlet macaws.

➡ Sea turtles have suffered from the destruction of beaches, which directly affect their ability to reproduce, as well as from hunting and the harvesting of eggs.

Wildlife

ANIMALS

Poison arrow frogs, giant tarantulas and spider monkeys inhabit our imagination of the tropics. In reality, few places live up to our wild expectations – but Costa Rica does. Considered the world nucleus of wildlife diversity, it has over 615 species per 10,000 sq km. (Compare that to the USA's 104 species.)

Birders have recorded over 850 avian species in Costa Rica. Some 200-plus species of migrating birds come from as far away as Alaska and Australia, so it's not unusual to see your backyard birds feeding alongside trogons and toucans. Because many birds in Costa Rica have restricted ranges, you are guaranteed to find different species everywhere you travel.

Visitors will almost certainly see one of Costa Rica's four types of monkey or two types of sloth, but there are an additional 230 types of mammals awaiting the patient observer. More exotic sightings might include the amazing four-eyed opossum or the silky anteater, the elusive tapir or the sly jaguarundi.

PLANTS

Costa Rica's floral biodiversity is staggering: close to 12,000 species of vascular plants have been described in Costa Rica, and the list gets longer each year. Orchids alone account for about 1400 species.

The diversity of habitats that created this many species is a wonder – one day you're canoeing in a muggy mangrove swamp, and the next day squinting through bone-chilling fog to see orchids in a montane cloud forest. While the country's beaches are beautiful, travelers would be remiss to visit Costa Rica without seeing some of its distinctive plant communities, including rainforests, mangrove swamps, cloud forests and dry forests.

SURVIVAL GUIDE

Directory A–Z

ACCOMMODATIONS

Accommodations come at every price and comfort level, and there is usually at least one excellent option for budget travelers. The variety and number of rooms on offer means that advance booking is not usually mandatory (unless you have your heart set on a particular place).

In tourist towns, you'll find plenty of *cabinas*, a loose term for cheap to midrange lodging. In general, dorm rooms cost between US$12 and US$15, and a budget double costs up to US$40. Cheaper places generally have shared bathrooms, but it's still possible to get a double with a private bathroom for US$25 in some towns.

High-season (December to April) prices are quoted in this book. Many lodges lower their prices during the 'green' season (May to November). Expect to pay a premium during Christmas, New Year and Easter week (Semana Santa). Prices are inclusive of tax and given in US dollars, which is the preferred currency for listing rates in Costa Rica.

Most destinations have at least one campground, which usually includes toilets and cold showers. Campsites are available at many national parks as well; take insect repellent, food and supplies. Camping prices are generally per person, per night.

If you're traveling in from another part of Central America, you'll notice that prices in Costa Rica are much higher than in the rest of the region.

CHILDREN

Mischievious monkeys and steaming volcanoes, mysterious rainforests and palm-lined beaches – Costa Rica is a safe, exhilarating tropical playland that makes a huge impression on younger travelers. Adventure comes in a spectrum of age-appropriate intensity levels, and the family-friendly culture is always welcoming to little ones. From a practical (parental) point of view, Costa Rica is certainly the best destination for family travel in Central America, thanks to its decent transportation infrastructure, low crime rate and world-class health-care system. For an exhaustive number of travel suggestions for families, check out Lonely Planet's *Travel with Children*.

Practicalities

- Baby food, formula and disposable diapers are readily available in most towns, but stock up before going to remote areas.
- Tap water is safe to drink throughout the country.
- Most restaurants do not have children's menus, but Costa Rican food is simple and hearty and suitable for finicky young eaters.
- High chairs and booster chairs are not common in restaurants. Special facilities for changing diapers are also rare.
- Most lodges and hotels offer accommodation options that are suitable for families, but you'll probably need to bring your own travel crib. Rates are often reduced for children under 12.
- Children pay reduced rates on ferries, tourist bus services and domestic airline flights.
- Car-rental agencies may offer car seats for infants and toddlers but they are often in poor condition, so you are probably better off bringing your own.
- While childcare 'agencies' are nonexistent, the owner or manager of your hotel will probably be able to help you find somebody to look after your kids.
- Look for surf lessons, language courses, horseback riding tours and other activities that are specially designed for kids.

CUSTOMS

All travelers over the age of 18 are allowed to enter the country with 5L of wine or spirits and 500g of processed tobacco (400 cigarettes or 50 cigars). Camera gear and binoculars, and camping, snorkeling and other sporting equipment, are readily allowed into the country.

EMBASSIES & CONSULATES

Australia and New Zealand do not have consular representation in Costa Rica; the closest embassies are in Mexico City. All embassies and consulates listed here are located in San José.

Canadian Embassy (☎2242-4400; www.costarica.gc.ca; Oficentro Ejecutivo La Sabana, 3rd fl, Edificio 3, Sabana Sur) Located behind the government office building known as La Contraloria.

French Embassy (☎2234-4167; www.ambafrance-cr.org; Curridabat) On the road to Curridabat, 200m south and 50m west of the Mitsubishi dealer.

German Embassy (☎2290-9091; www.san-jose.diplo.de; 8th fl, Torre La Sabana, Sabana

SLEEPING PRICE RANGES

The following price ranges refer to the price for a double room with private bathroom in the high season (December to April). All prices include taxes.

$	Less than US$40
$$	US$40–US$80
$$$	More than US$80

Norte) On the 8th floor of Torre La Sabana, on Sabana Norte, 300m west of the ICE building.

Guatemalan Embassy (☎2291-6172, 2220-1297; www.minex.gob.gt; Sabana Sur) About 100m south and 50m west of Gimnasio Fitsimons.

Honduran Embassy (☎2231-1642; Blvd Rohrmoser) Off Calle Humboldt, about 50m south and 75m east of Parque la Amistad.

Mexican Embassy (☎2257-0633; embamex.sre.gob.mx/costarica; Av 7 btwn Calles 13 & 15) About 250m south of the Subaru dealership.

Netherlands Embassy (☎2296-1490; www.costarica.nlambassade.org; Calle del Golf, Oficentro Ejecutivo La Sabana, 3rd fl, Edificio 3, Sabana Sur) Behind La Contraloría.

Nicaraguan Embassy (☎2221-2284; Av Central 2540 btwn Calles 25 & 27, Barrio La California)

Panamanian Embassy (☎2281-2442; San Pedro) Head 200m south and 25m east from the *antiguo higuerón* (old fig tree).

Salvadoran Embassy (☎2257-7855; cnr Calle 38 & Av 9)

Spanish Embassy (☎2222-1933; Calle 32 btwn Paseo Colón & Av 2)

UK Embassy (☎2258-2025; www.ukincostarica.fco.uk.gov; 11th fl, Edificio Centro Colón, Paseo Colón btwn Calles 38 & 40)

US Embassy (☎2519-2000; http://costarica.usembassy.gov; Carretera a Pavas) Opposite Centro Commercial del Oeste.

FOOD & DRINK

The most popular eating establishment in Costa Rica is the *soda*, which is a small, informal lunch counter. Other popular cheapies include the omnipresent fried- and rotisserie-chicken stands. A regular *restaurante* is usually higher on the price scale and has slightly more atmosphere.

For something smaller, *pastelerías* and *panaderías* are shops that sell pastries and bread, while many bars serve snacks called *bocas*, which are snack-sized portions of main meals.

Lunch is usually the day's main meal and is typically served around noon. Dinner tends to be a lighter version of lunch and is eaten around 7pm.

EATING PRICE RANGES

The following price ranges refer to a standard meal. Unless otherwise stated tax is included in the price.

$ Less than US$9

$$ US$9–US$15

$$$ More than US$15

GAY & LESBIAN TRAVELERS

Homosexual acts between two consenting adults (aged 18 and over) are legal in Costa Rica. Acceptance is much greater here than in other Central American countries, but that tolerance exists mostly at a 'don't ask, don't tell' level. Same-sex couples are unlikely to be the subject of harassment, though public displays of affection might attract unwanted attention.

The Pacific resort town of Manuel Antonio is a popular gay vacation center, and San José also has some decent nightclubs and bars.

CIPAC (Center of Investigation & Promotion of Human Rights in Central America; ☎2280-7821; www.cipacdh.org) The leading gay activist organization in Costa Rica.

Gente 10 (www.gente10.net) This gay magazine is distributed at bars and clubs in San José.

International Gay & Lesbian Travel Association (IGLTA; ☎954-630-1637; www.iglta.org) Maintains a list of hundreds of travel agents and tour operators all over the world.

Travel Costa Rica Now (www.travelcostaricanow.com) Longtime residents Michael Alan and D'Angelo provide custom-designed vacations and loads of straight-up information about gay travel in Costa Rica, including listings of LBGT-friendly lodging.

INTERNET ACCESS

- Costa Rica has plenty of internet cafes, and many businesses have wi-fi.
- Expect to pay US$1 to US$2 per hour in San José and tourist towns.
- Wi-fi is common in all midrange and top-end hotels.

LEGAL MATTERS

- If you are arrested, your embassy can offer limited assistance. Embassy officials will not bail you out and you are subject to Costa Rican laws, not the laws of your own country.
- Drivers should carry their passport and driver's license at all times. In case of an accident, leave the vehicles in place and call the police immediately to make a report.
- Prostitution is legal in Costa Rica, but child prostitution (under 18 years) is strictly prohibited and severely prosecuted.
- Marijuana and recreational drugs of any sort are illegal.
- Keep in mind that travelers may be subject to the laws of their own country in regard to sexual relations.

MAPS

Detailed maps are unfortunately hard to come by in Costa Rica. An excellent option is the 1:330,000 Costa Rica sheet produced by International Travel Map, which is waterproof and includes a San José inset.

➡ The **Fundación Neotrópica** (www.neotropica.org) publishes a 1:500,000 map showing national parks and other protected areas. These are available in some local bookstores.

➡ The Instituto Costarricense de Turismo (ICT) publishes a 1:700,000 Costa Rica map with a 1:12,500 Central San José map on the reverse. These are free at ICT offices in San José.

➡ Online, **Maptak** (www.maptak.com) has maps of Costa Rica's seven provinces and their capitals.

➡ Few national park offices or ranger stations have maps for hikers. Topographical maps are available for purchase from the **Instituto Geográfico Nacional** (IGN; ☎2257-7798; Calle 9 btwn Avs 20 & 22; ⏲7:30am-noon & 1-3pm Mon-Fri) in San José.

MONEY

ATMs

➡ ATMs, or *cajeros automáticos*, are ubiquitous in all but Costa Rica's smallest towns.

➡ Most ATMs dispense both US dollars and Costa Rican colones.

Cash

➡ The Costa Rican currency is the colón (plural colones), named after Cristóbal Colón (Christopher Columbus).

➡ Bills come in 500, 1000, 5000, 10,000, 20,000 and 50,000 notes, while coins come in denominations of 5, 10, 20, 25, 50 and 100.

➡ Paying for things in US dollars is common, and at times is encouraged, especially for hotels and tours. Meals, local and intercity bus fares, taxis and small-ticket purchase items should be paid for in colones.

➡ Newer US dollars (ie big heads) are preferred throughout Costa Rica.

Credit Cards

➡ Cards are widely accepted at midrange and top-end hotels, as well as top-end restaurants and some travel agencies.

➡ All car-rental agencies require drivers to have a credit card.

➡ Expect a transaction fee on all international credit-card purchases.

➡ Holders of credit and debit cards can buy colones in some banks, though you can expect to pay a high transaction fee.

Moneychangers

Hotels and travel agencies are willing to change money for travelers but be aware that many charge hefty commissions. Changing money on the streets is not recommended, except possibly at land borders.

Tipping

Bellhop/porter	US$1-5 per service
Housekeeper	US$1-2 per day
Restaurant server	0-10% (may be included in bill)
Taxi driver	NA
Tour guide	US$5-15
Tour driver	US$2-6

Traveler's Checks

With the popularity of ATMs and credit cards, traveler's checks are increasingly uncommon in Costa Rica. They can be exchanged at banks, typically only for US dollars or Costa Rican colones.

OPENING HOURS

Restaurants Usually open from 7am and serve dinner until 9pm, though upscale places may open only for dinner. In remote areas, even the small *sodas* (inexpensive eateries) might open only at specific meal times.

Government offices Typically open between 8am and 5pm Monday to Friday, but often close between 11:30am and 1:30pm.

Banks Hours are variable, but most are open at least from 9am to 3pm Monday to Friday.

Shops Most are open from 8am to 6pm Monday to Saturday.

Unless otherwise stated, count on sights, activities and restaurants to be open daily.

WHAT'S THAT ADDRESS?

Though some larger cities have streets that have been dutifully named, signage is rare, and finding a Tico who knows what street they are standing on is even rarer. Everybody uses landmarks when providing directions: an address may be given as 200m south and 150m east of a church. (A city block is *cien metros* – literally 100m – so '250 *metros al sur*' means 2½ blocks south, regardless of the distance.)

Churches, parks, office buildings, fast-food joints and car dealerships are the most common landmarks used – but these are often meaningless to the foreign traveler who will have no idea where the Subaru dealership is to begin with. Better yet, Ticos frequently refer to landmarks that no longer exist. In San Pedro, outside of San José, locals still use the sight of an old fig tree *(el antiguo higuerón)* to provide directions.

Confused? Get used to it...

PUBLIC HOLIDAYS

Días feriados (national holidays) are taken seriously in Costa Rica. Banks, public offices and many stores close, and public transportation may be reduced.

New Year's Day (January 1)

Semana Santa (Holy Week; March or April) The Thursday and Friday before Easter Sunday is the official holiday, though most businesses shut down for the whole week.

Día de Juan Santamaría (April 11)

Labor Day (May 1)

Día de la Madre (Mother's Day; August 15) Coincides with the annual Catholic Feast of the Assumption.

Independence Day (September 15)

Día de la Raza (Columbus' Day; October 12)

Christmas Day (December 25) Christmas Eve is also an unofficial holiday.

Last week in December Many business close during the week between Christmas and New Year, though tourist attractions are open.

SAFE TRAVEL

Hiking Hazards

Hikers setting out into the wilderness should be adequately prepared for their trips.

- Know your limits and don't set out to do a hike you can't reasonably complete.
- Carry plenty of water, even on very short trips. Carry maps, extra food and a compass.
- Let someone know where you are going, so they can narrow the search area in the event of an emergency. Stick to the trail.
- Be aware that Costa Rica's wildlife can pose a threat to hikers, particularly in Corcovado National Park (p620).

Ocean Hazards

Approximately 200 drownings a year occur in Costa Rican waters, 90% of which are caused by riptides, which are strong currents that pull the swimmer out to sea. If you are caught in a riptide, do not struggle. Simply float and let the tide carry you out beyond the breakers, after which the riptide will dissipate; then swim parallel to the beach and allow the surf to carry you back in.

Theft & Muggings

The biggest danger that most travelers face is theft. There is a lot of petty crime in Costa Rica, especially on buses, on the beach and in hotels. Keep your wits about you and take precautions.

TELEPHONE

- Cellular service now covers nearly all of the country that is accessible to tourists.
- Public phones are found all over Costa Rica and Chip or Colibrí phone cards are available in 1000, 2000 and 3000 colón denominations.
- Chip cards are inserted into the phone and scanned. Colibrí cards (more common) require you to dial a toll-free number (199) and enter an access code. Instructions are provided in English or Spanish.
- The cheapest international calls from Costa Rica are direct-dialed using a phone card. To make international calls, dial the international access code (00) followed by the country code and number.
- Skype and other voice-over IP services are also widely available at internet cafes and accommodations.
- Pay phones cannot receive international calls.
- To call Costa Rica from abroad, use the country code (506) before the eight-digit number.

TIME

Costa Rica is six hours behind GMT, so Costa Rican time is equivalent to Central Time in North America. That means it is one hour behind Panama and the same time as Nicaragua. There is no daylight-saving time.

DISCOUNT CARDS

Note that discount cards are not universally accepted at museums and parks.

CARD	DISCOUNTS	REQUIREMENTS	COST	APPLY
Costa Rica Card	Hotel & restaurant discounts through affiliated network	Must be picked up in-country & used with photo ID	individual/ couple/family US$30/40/60	www.costaricacard.org
Student Identity Card (ISIC)	Museum & tour discounts	Any full-time student	US$20-30 depending on country of origin	www.isic.org
International Student Exchange (ISE)	Museum & tour discounts	Full-time student btwn 12 & 26yr	US$25	www.isecard.com

TOILETS

➡ Public restrooms are rare, but most restaurants and cafes will let you use their facilities, sometimes for a small charge – never more than 500 colones.

➡ Bus terminals and other major public buildings usually have toilets, also at a charge.

* Don't flush your toilet paper. Costa Rican plumbing is often poor and often has very low pressure.

➡ Dispose of toilet paper in the rubbish bin inside the bathroom.

TOURIST INFORMATION

The government-run tourism board, the Instituto Costarricense de Turismo (ICT), has an information office in the capital at the Plaza de la Cultura (p543). It can provide you with free maps, a master bus schedule and information on road conditions in the hinterlands. English is spoken.

TRAVELERS WITH DISABILITIES

Independent travel in Costa Rica is difficult for anyone with mobility constraints. Although Costa Rica has an equal-opportunity law, the law applies only to new or newly remodeled businesses and is loosely enforced. Therefore, very few hotels and restaurants have features specifically suited to wheelchair use. Many don't have ramps, and room or bathroom doors are rarely wide enough to accommodate a wheelchair.

Outside the buildings, streets and sidewalks are potholed and poorly paved, making wheelchair use frustrating at best. Public buses don't have provisions to carry wheelchairs and most national parks and outdoor tourist attractions don't have trails suited to wheelchair use. Notable exceptions include Volcán Poás (p550), and the **Rainforest Aerial Tram** (☎ 2257-5961; www.rainforestrams.com; adult/student & child US$55/28, full-day tour with lunch & guided hike US$99/56; ♿).

VISAS

Passport-carrying nationals of the following countries are allowed 90 days' stay with no visa: Argentina, Canada, Israel, Japan, Panama, the USA, and most western European countries.

Citizens of Australia, Iceland, Ireland, Mexico, New Zealand, Russia, South Africa and Venezuela are allowed to stay for 30 days with no visa. Others require a visa from a Costa Rican embassy or consulate. Note that visas cannot be obtained at the border. For the latest info on visas, check with the ICT.

Extensions

➡ Extending your stay beyond the authorized 30 or 90 days is time-consuming, making it easier to leave the country for 72 hours and then re-enter.

➡ Extensions can be handled by the office of **Migración** (Immigration; ☎ 2220-0355; ⏲ 8am-4pm) in San José, opposite Channel 6, about 4km north of Parque La Sabana.

➡ Requirements for extensions change, so allow several working days.

VOLUNTEERING

While there are many opportunities to volunteer in Costa Rica, most of them are self-funded, meaning that volunteers are responsible for covering their own travel and living costs. Often, the host organization can help place volunteers in homestays or other affordable accommodations. Almost all placements require a commitment of two weeks or more.

Community Service

Fundación Corcovado (www.corcovadofoundation.org) Wide-ranging volunteer opportunities include environmental education, protection of sea turtles and information services at the national park.

Monteverde Institute (www.monteverde-institute.org) A nonprofit educational institute offering training in tropical biology, conservation and sustainable development.

Sustainable Horizon (www.sustainablehorizon.com) Organizes 10-day trips that include five days of work on a service project.

Forestry Management

At Bosque Eterno de los Niños (p572), volunteers are needed to help manage the extensive rainforest preserve, with work assignments ranging from reception to ranger stations.

Cloudbridge Nature Reserve (www.cloudbridge.org) Trail building, tree planting and construction are all part of the job description.

Tropical Science Center (www.cct.or.cr) This longstanding NGO offers volunteer placement at Monteverde Cloud Forest Reserve for trail maintenance and conservation work.

Organic Farming

Finca La Flor de Paraíso (www.la-flor.org) Offers programs in a variety of disciplines from animal husbandry to medicinal-herb cultivation.

Punta Mona (www.puntamona.org) An organic farm and retreat center that is based on organic permaculture and sustainable living.

Rancho Margot (www.ranchomargot.org) This self-proclaimed life-skills university offers a natural education emphasizing organic farming and animal husbandry.

Reserva Biológica Dúrika (www.durika.org) A sustainable community that is centered upon a 75-sq-km biological reserve.

WWOOF Costa Rica (www.wwoofcostarica.org) This loose network of farms is part of the large international network of Willing Workers on Organic Farms (WWOOF).

Wildlife Conservation

Canadian Organization for Tropical Education & Rainforest Conservation (Coterc; ☎2709-8052, in Canada 905-831-8809; www.coterc.org; per week US$200) A reputable Canadian not-for-profit outfit that has various volunteer opportunities at its research station in Tortuguero.

CCC (www.cccturtle.org) Assist scientists with turtle tagging and research on green and leatherback turtles.

Earthwatch (www.earthwatch.org) Teams of volunteers join expeditions to study the link between climate change and caterpillars, work with community coffee growers or protect dolphins and sea turtles.

Profelis (www.grafischer.com/profelis) A feline conservation program that takes care of confiscated wild cats, both big and small.

Sea Turtle Conservancy (www.conserveturtles.org) From March to October, this Puerto Límon organization hosts 'eco-volunteer adventures' working with sea turtles and birds. Other opportunities at the Tortuguero research station.

WORKING

It's difficult for foreigners to find work in Costa Rica, as labor laws favor Costa Ricans.The only foreigners legally employed in Costa Rica work for their own businesses, possess skills not found in the country, or work for companies that have special agreements with the government.

Getting a bona fide job necessitates obtaining a work permit – a time-consuming and difficult process. The most likely source of paid employment is as an English teacher at one of the language institutes, or working in the hospitality industry in a hotel or resort. Naturalists or river guides may be able to find work with private lodges or adventure-travel operators, though you shouldn't expect to make more than survival wages from these jobs.

ℹ Getting There & Away

AIR

Airports & Airlines

Costa Rica is well connected by air to other Central and South American countries, as well to the USA. The US Federal Aviation Administration has assessed Costa Rica's aviation authorities to be in compliance with international safety standards.

Aeropuerto Internacional Juan Santamaría (☎2437-2400; www.sanjose-costaricaairport.com) Most international flights arrive at this airport, which is located 17km northwest of San José, in the town of Alajuela.

Aeropuerto Internacional Daniel Oduber Quirós (LIR; www.liberiacostaricaairport.net) This smaller airport in Liberia also receives flights from USA and Canada, as well as some charter flights. International flights are expected to increase with the opening of a new terminal in 2012.

> **DEPARTURE TAX**
>
> There is a US$26 departure tax on all international outbound flights. The tax is payable in cash or credit card, and Banco de Costa Rica has an ATM next to the departure-tax station.

BORDER CROSSINGS

Costa Rica shares land borders with Nicaragua and Panama. Many travelers enter the country by bus since an extensive bus system links the Central American capitals and it's vastly cheaper than flying. Note that international buses may cost slightly more than taking a series of local buses, but they're worth it. These better-quality buses travel faster and can help you cross borders efficiently.

Nicaragua

From Peñas Blancas Costa Rica's northern terminus of the Interamericana is a busy border crossing, open 6am to 8pm daily. You won't be charged to exit or enter Costa Rica, but entering and leaving Nicaragua costs US$10. You'll also be charged US$1 to enter the state of Rivas. Banks on either side will change local colones and córdobas for dollars but, inconveniently, not for each other. Independent money changers will happily make the exchange for you – at whatever rates they feel like setting.

The border posts are about 1km apart. Hordes of touts will offer to 'guide' you through the simple crossing – let them carry your luggage if you like, but agree on a fee beforehand.

From Sapoá on the Nicaraguan side, it's a 37km bus ride to Rivas (US$1, 45 minutes, every 30 minutes). You can also take a taxi for about US$30 but you'll have to bargain hard.

From Los Chiles There's a 14km dirt road between Los Chiles in Costa Rica and San Carlos, Nicaragua, but this crossing requires special permission that is generally reserved for federal employees. Most regular folk go across by boat on the Río Frío, which is easily arranged in Los Chiles.

You must first get an exit stamp in your passport at **Migración** (Immigration; Calle 4 & Av 0; ⏲8am-noon & 1:30-4pm), about 100m east of the dock (directly across the street from Hotel Tulipán). If you are coming from Nicaragua, you must make *migración* your first stop.

Regular boats (US$10 to US$12, 90 minutes) leave Los Chiles at 12:30pm and 3:30pm daily, with extra boats if demand is high. Boats leave

San Carlos for Los Chiles at 10:30am and 4pm. Of course, the Nicaragua–Costa Rica border is not known for its reliability, so confirm these times before setting out.

Nicaragua charges a US$7 entry fee and US$2 exit fee. Los Chiles municipality charges a US$1.10 exit and entry fee; after getting your passport stamped at *migración*, walk down to the docks and pay the exit fee at the yellow Recaudador Municipal office. Reverse this procedure if you are arriving here from Nicaragua.

Your boat will make a stop at the actual border post about halfway through the trip; note the psychedelic 'camouflage' paint job on the building where your friendly, gun-wielding Nicaraguan border personnel are based.

Panama

From Paso Canoas At the southern end of the Costa Rican leg of the Interamericana, this border crossing is open from 6am to 11pm and is the place to cross for David, Panama. It is crowded and confusing, especially during vacation periods when hordes of shoppers pass through.

The Costa Rican *migración* (6am to 11pm) is on the eastern side of the highway, north of the Tracopa bus terminal. There is no exit or entrance fee at this border crossing.

About 400m east, all incoming travelers must stop at the Panamanian immigration post to purchase a tourist card (US$5) to enter Panama. You might be asked to show an onward ticket and evidence of financial solvency (a credit card should suffice).

From the Panama side of the border, minivans depart constantly to David (US$2, 1½ hours).

From Sixaola An old railroad bridge spanning the waters of the Río Sixaola connects Sixaola in Costa Rica to Guabito in Panama. From here, most travelers make for Bocas del Toro, a picturesque archipelago of Panamanian jungle islands.

The border is open 7am to 5pm (8am to 6pm in Guabito, which is an hour ahead of Costa Rica), though one or both sides may close for lunch at around 1pm. Be sure to stop at both immigration offices, which are at either end of the bridge. To enter Panama, you need to purchase a tourist card for US$5. If you aren't carrying proof of onward travel out of Panama, you may be 'required' to purchase a bus ticket, conveniently sold on the road below.

Guabito has no hotels or banks, but in a pinch you can exchange colones at the market across the street.

- From the border, buses (US$1, one hour, every half-hour) run to Terminal Piquera in Changuinola, where you can transfer to one of the frequent buses to Almirante (US$1.50, 45 minutes) for the water taxi.

> **ONWARD TICKETS**
>
> Officially, travelers are required to have a ticket out of Costa Rica before they are allowed to enter. This is rarely and erratically enforced. To be safe, those arriving on land with no onward ticket can purchase one from international bus companies in Managua, Nicaragua or Panama City.

- Alternatively, from Guabito you can take a collective taxi (per person US$10, one hour) straight to Almirante.
- From Almirante, water taxis (US$5, 25 minutes) make the trip to Bocas del Toro every hour from 6:30am to 7pm.

Getting Around

AIR

- Costa Rica's domestic airlines are **Nature Air** (☎2220-3054; www.natureair.com) and **Sansa** (☎2290-4100; www.flysansa.com). Sansa is linked with Grupo TACA.
- Both airlines fly small passenger planes, and you're allocated a baggage allowance of no more than 12kg.
- Space is limited and demand is high in the dry season, so advance reservations are recommended.
- All domestic flights originate and terminate at San José. Destinations include Golfito, Liberia, Neily, Palmar Sur, Playa Sámara, Playa Tamarindo, Puerto Jiménez, Quepos and Tortuguero.

BICYCLE

With an improving network of paved secondary roads, Costa Rica is emerging as one of Central America's most comfortable cycle-touring destinations. Mountain bikes and beach cruisers can be rented in towns with a significant tourist presence, for US$10 to US$15 per day. A few companies organize bike tours around Costa Rica.

BOAT

Caribbean Coast & Northern Lowlands

- On the Caribbean coast, several bus-boat services link Cariari and Tortuguero.
- Boats also ply the canals that run along the coast from Moín to Tortuguero, although no regular service exists.
- A daily water taxi connects Puerto Viejo de Sarapiquí with Trinidad on the Río San Juan. The San Juan is Nicaraguan territory, so take your passport.

Península de Nicoya

Ferries cross the Golfo de Nicoya, connecting the central Pacific coast with the southern tip of Península de Nicoya.

- The Coonatramar Ferry (p600) links the port of Puntarenas with Playa Naranjo four times daily.
- Naviera Tambor (p605) travels between Puntarenas and Paquera six times a day, for a bus connection to Montezuma.
- Zuma Tours (p601) runs a daily water taxi between Montezuma and Jacó.

Península de Osa

- Crossing the Golfo Dulce, two ferries link Golfito with Puerto Jiménez, making the crossing two or three times daily (though the schedule is not reliable).
- On the other side of the Península de Osa, water taxis connect Bahía Drake with Sierpe.

BUS

Local Bus

- Local buses are a cheap and reliable way of getting around Costa Rica. The longest domestic journey out of San José costs less than US$20.
- San José is the transportation center for the country, though there is no central terminal.
- Buses can be very crowded, but don't usually pass up passengers on account of being too full. Note that there are no buses from Thursday to Saturday before Easter Sunday.
- There are two types of bus: *directo* and *colectivo*. The *directo* buses should go from one destination to the next with few stops; the *colectivos* make more stops and are very slow going.
- Trips longer than four hours usually include a rest stop as buses do not have toilets.
- Theft from overhead racks is rampant.
- Bus schedules fluctuate, so always confirm the time when you buy your ticket and arrive early for your departure.
- The master bus schedule is available from the Instituto Costarricense de Turismo (p543).

Shuttle Bus

The tourist-van shuttle services (aka gringo buses) are an alternative to the standard intercity buses. These buses have online reservations and they offer door-to-door service. The buses are smaller, cooler, more comfortable and significantly more expensive than local buses. The following companies service a wide variety of destinations:

Grayline's Fantasy Bus (☎2220-2126; www.graylinecostarica.com)

Interbus (www.interbusonline.com)

Montezuma Expeditions (☎2642-0919; www.montezumaexpeditions.com; Centro Comercial Playa El Carmen)

Tropical Tours (☎2640-1900, 8849-8569; www.tropicaltourshuttles.com)

CAR & MOTORCYCLE

- Drivers in Costa Rica are required to have a valid driving license from their home country or an International Driving Permit (IDP).
- Gasoline (petrol) and diesel are widely available. In remote areas, fuel might be sold at the neighborhood *pulpería* (corner store).
- The quality of roads varies from the quite smoothly paved (though winding) Interamericana to the barely passable rural back roads. It's always recommended (and sometimes required) to invest in a 4WD vehicle.
- Roads often suffer from landslides, sudden flooding and fog. Always inquire about road conditions before setting out.
- There are speed limits of 100km/h or less on all primary roads and 60km/h or less on secondary roads. Seatbelts are required.
- Rental cars are widely available. Car rental requires a valid driver's license, a major credit card and a passport. Costa Rican insurance is mandatory, even if you have insurance at home.
- Thieves can easily recognize rental cars and break-ins are common. Never leave anything in sight in a parked car and park in a guarded lot whenever possible.

HITCHHIKING

Hitchhiking is never entirely safe in any country and Lonely Planet doesn't recommend it. People who hitchhike will be safer if they travel in pairs and let someone know where they are planning to go.

Hitchhiking in Costa Rica is unusual on main roads (due to frequent buses), but it's more common on minor rural roads. Hitchhikers should offer to pay upon arrival: *¿Cuanto le debo?* (How much do I owe you?) Many will wave the offer aside, but it is polite to offer, nonetheless.

TAXI

Taxis are considered a form of public transportation in remote areas that lack good public-transportation networks. They can be hired by the hour, the half-day or full day, or you can arrange a flat fee for a trip. Meters are not used on long trips, so arrange the fare ahead of time. Fares can fluctuate due to worse-than-expected road conditions and bad weather in tough-to-reach places.

Panama

507 / POP 3.4 MILLION

Includes ➡

Panama City 639
Panama Canal 657
Santa Catalina 666
David 668
Boquete 672
Parque Nacional Volcán Barú 677
Bocas del Toro Province 679
Colón 693
Comarca de Kuna Yala 698
Darién Province 702

Best Places to Eat

- ➡ Anachoreo (p668)
- ➡ Cuatro (p670)
- ➡ Mercado de Mariscos (p650)
- ➡ La Rosa Mexicano (p651)
- ➡ Raw (p687)

Best Places to Stay

- ➡ Eco Venao (p665)
- ➡ Magnolia Inn (p648)
- ➡ Hibiscus Garden (p666)
- ➡ Lost & Found Lodge (p680)
- ➡ Al Natural Resort (p691)

Why Go?

Consider Panama a place of discovery: explore the ruins of Spanish forts on the Caribbean coast or boat deep into indigenous territories in a dugout canoe. There are plenty of beaches to choose from, from deserted islands to chill Caribbean hang-outs to Pacific surf. Panama City – culturally diverse, driven, rough-edged yet sophisticated – is to be among Latin America's most vibrant and outward-looking capitals, where English is widely spoken. In the last century, Panama was defined by the canal; what lies just beyond may define it for the next. The canal expansion spells growth and even more glitz, but for now you can still pick an empty islet and play *Survivor* for a day.

When to Go

Panama City

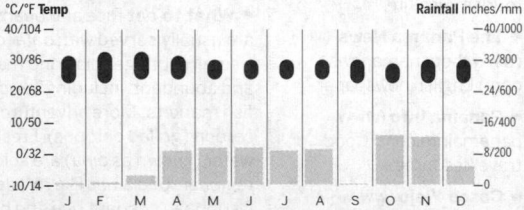

Dec–Apr High season on the Pacific coast is also the dry season. Best time to hike or dive.

May–Nov Rainy season means low-season travel rates.

Aug–Oct Migrating humpback whales in the Pacific; shoulder season in Bocas.

AT A GLANCE

Currency US dollar ($)

Language Spanish

Money ATMs widely available. Credit cards accepted in some areas.

Visas Generally not required for stays of 90 days or less.

Time GMT minus five hours

Fast Facts

- **Area** 78,200 sq km
- **Capital** Panama City
- **Police** 104

Set Your Budget

From US$35 per day:

- Air-conditioned dorm bed: US$13
- Dinner at a food cart or self-catering: US$5; at a midrange restaurant: US$18
- Four-hour bus ride: US$9

Resources

- **ATP/Visit Panama** (www.atp.gob.pa; www.visitpanama.com) Official tourism website.
- **The Panama News** (www.thepanamanews.com) English newspaper.
- **Panama Info** (www.panamainfo.com) Good travel resource.
- **Casco Viejo** (www.cascoviejo.org) Panama City info.

Connections

The principal crossing to Costa Rica is on the Interamericana at Paso Canoas. Guabito on the Caribbean side and Río Sereno in the highlands are less chaotic border posts. For more detailed information, see Survival Guide on p723.

FIRST TIME IN PANAMA

Charge the capital, seek out a rainforest adventure and end with a Caribbean getaway on this one-week itinerary.

Start by imbibing the rush of **Panama City**. Visit **Panamá Viejo**, destroyed in a massive pirate raid, and explore **Casco Viejo**, a cobblestone neighborhood with plaza cafes and rooftop bars.

Take a day trip to nearby **Miraflores Locks** to witness mammoth ships squeezing through the canal. At nearby **Parque Nacional Soberanía** climb a canopy tower to search for toucans and sloths, or kayak down **Lago Gatún** alongside howler monkeys and sunbathing crocodiles.

Next, head to **Bocas del Toro** for four days of chill Caribbean vibes. Snorkel in the aquamarine waters with tropical fish and coral reefs, and explore Isla Colón by cruiser bike. Alternatively, escape to **Isla Bastimentos**, with its thatched resorts and jungle lodges. For a dose of culture, take a chocolate tour on the mainland or visit indigenous groups on other islands with a community tourism initiative.

Got a second week? Head over the divide to highland **Boquete** to explore coffee farms and cloud forests before hitting the great beaches of the **Pacific coast** and circling back to the capital.

Essential Food & Drink

- **Where to eat** Budget eateries like *cafeterías* (simple eateries), *panaderías* (bakeries), stands and market stalls sell a range of filling dishes and set meals from US$3 to US$6.
- **What to eat** Rice and beans are a staple in Panama and are usually served with *patacones* (fried green plantains), a small cabbage salad and meat. Seafood is inexpensive and abundant, including *ceviche* (marinated raw fish) at fish markets. More adventurous palates should try *pulpo al carbon* (grilled octopus). Fresh tropical juices and coconut water (known as *pipa*) are sold on the street. Don't miss regional specialties like *tortilla de maíz* (fried cornmeal cake), Caribbean coconut rice and bottled D'Elida's hot pepper sauce.

PANAMA CITY

POP 699,500

The most cosmopolitan capital in Central America, Panama City is both vibrant metropolis and gateway to tropical escapes. Always a work in progress, construction is underway to add a subway, complete the massive canal expansion and open the biodiversity museum. But it's the particulars – homespun galleries, a graffiti-clad underground bar and the titillating tropical cuisine – that make it unique. Pedal the coastal green space, explore the historic Casco or attend an avant-garde performance and you will realize this capital isn't just about salsa. That's just the backbeat.

History

Panama City was founded in 1519 by the Spanish governor Pedro Arias de Ávila (Pedrarias) not long after Balboa first saw the Pacific. The Spanish settlement quickly became an important center of government and church authorities. In 1671 the city was ransacked and destroyed by Welsh pirate Henry Morgan, leaving only the stone ruins of Panamá Viejo.

Three years later, the city was re-established in the peninsular area of Casco Viejo. After the destruction of the Caribbean port at Portobelo in 1746, the Spanish overland trade route declined. Panama City subsequently faded in importance, though it returned to prominence in the 1850s when gold seekers on the way to California flooded across the isthmus by the Panama Railroad.

After Panama declared its independence from Colombia on November 3, 1903, Panama City was firmly established as the capital. Completed in 1914, the Panama Canal spurred the city on to become a hub of international business and trade.

The canal is the main reason why Panama City is by far the wealthiest city in Central America today. While foreign investment waned with the 2009 world economic crisis, the expansion of the Panama Canal, set to be completed by 2015, signals possible future prosperity.

Sights

★Museo de Arte Contemporáneo MUSEUM

(Map p646; ☎262-3380; www.macpanama.org; Av de los Mártires, Ancón; admission US$3; ⏲9am-4pm Mon-Fri, to noon Sat, to 3pm Sun) This wonderful, privately owned museum features the best collection of Panamanian art anywhere, an excellent collection of works on paper by Latin American artists, and the occasional temporary exhibition by a foreign or national artist.

Museo Afro-Antilleano MUSEUM

(Map p646; ☎262-5348; cnr Av Justo Arosemena & Calle 24 Este; admission US$1; ⏲8:30am-4:30pm Tue-Sat) The small Afro-Antillean museum has exhibits on the history of Panama's West Indian community, particularly their work building the railroad and later the canal.

Museo de Ciencias Naturales MUSEUM

(Map p646; ☎info 225 0645; Av Cuba btwn Calles 29 Este & 30 Este; admission US$1; ⏲9am-3:45pm Tue-Sat) Features works on the natural sciences, flora, fauna, geology and paleontology of Panama.

Baha'i House of Worship TEMPLE

(☎231-1137; ⏲10am-6pm) On the outskirts of Panama City, the white-domed Baha'i House of Worship is the mother temple for all of Latin America. It looms like a giant egg atop the crest of a hill, with a beautiful, breezy interior.

Readings from the Baha'i writings (in English and Spanish) are held Sunday mornings at 10am. Any bus to Colón can let you off on the highway, but it's a long walk up the hill. The temple is 11km northeast of the city center on the Vía Transístmica.

Casco Viejo

Following the destruction of the old city by Henry Morgan in 1671, the Spanish moved their city 8km southwest to a rocky peninsula on the foot of Cerro Ancón. The new location was easier to defend as the reefs prevented ships from approaching the city except at high tide. The new city was also easy to defend as it was surrounded by a massive wall, which is how Casco Viejo (Old Compound) got its name.

In 1904, at the time construction began on the Panama Canal, all of Panama City existed where Casco Viejo stands today. As population growth and urban expansion pushed the boundaries further east, the city's elite left and the neighborhood rapidly deteriorated into an urban slum.

Today, Casco Viejo is half crumbling, half high-end. The newly restored architecture gives a sense of how magnificent the area must have looked in past years.

Panama Highlights

1 While the days away sipping coconuts and snorkeling at laid-back resorts in the **Archipiélago de Bocas del Toro** (p679)

2 Fuel up for highland adventures with local mountain-grown coffee in **Boquete**, the town of eternal spring (p672)

3 In **Panama City**, spend the day admiring the faded glory of the old city (p639) then revel till sunrise on Calle Uruguay (p651)

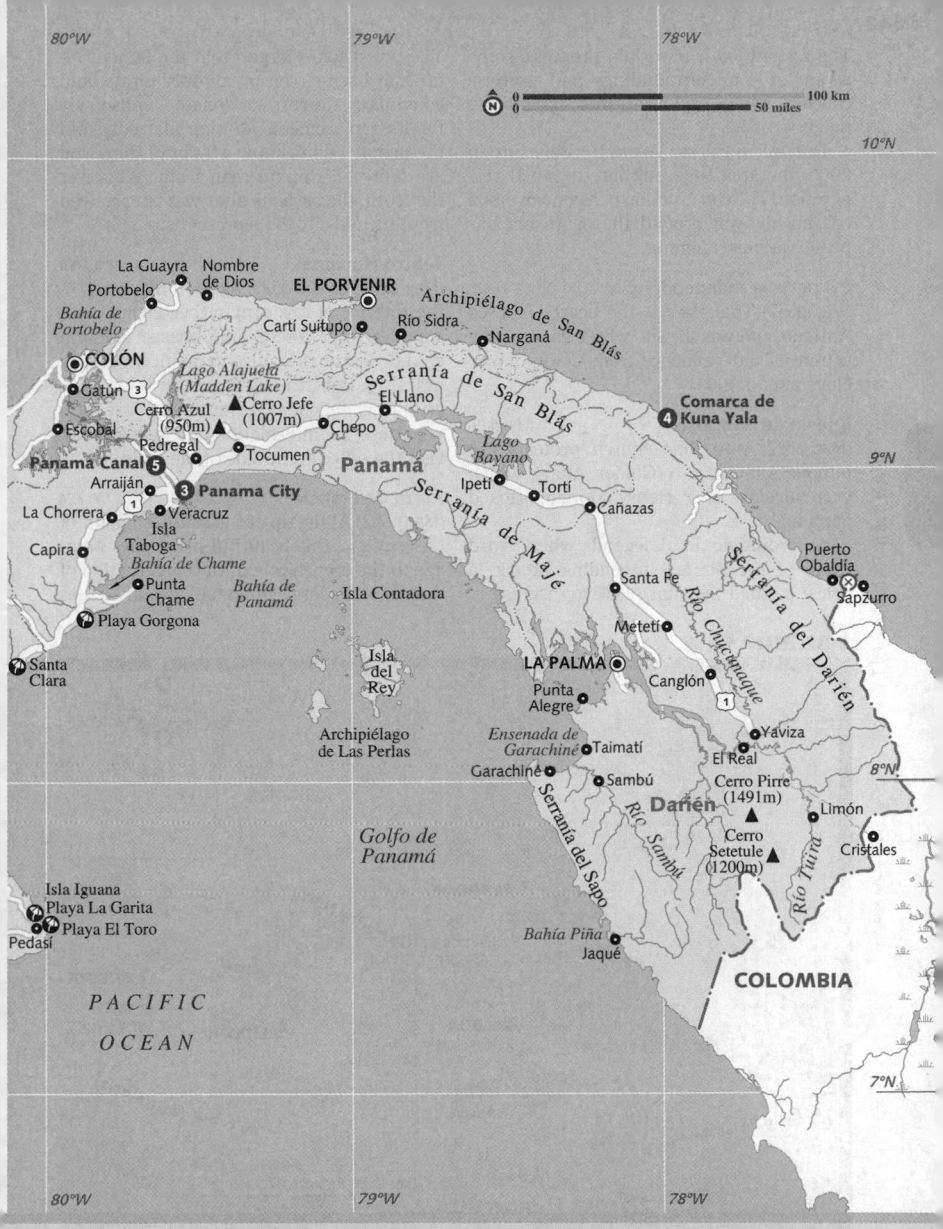

4 Cruise white-sand cays, swim in clear waters and soak up sunrise on a sailboat in the **Comarca de Kuna Yala** (p698)

5 Lay eyes on the awe-inspiring **Panama Canal** (p657), an engineering marvel in the midst of an expansion

The restoration is a work in progress, so be aware of your surroundings and exercise caution while exploring this fascinating neighborhood.

Declared a Unesco World Heritage Site in 2003, the area is getting international recognition. The construction of a controversial coastal highway around the peninsula has preservationists fuming.

Plaza de la Independencia PLAZA
(Map p652) This plaza is the heart of Casco Antiguo, and was the site where Panama declared its independence from Colombia on November 3, 1903.

Iglesia de San José CHURCH
(Map p652; Av A) This church protects the famous Altar de Oro (Golden Altar), which was salvaged after Henry Morgan sacked Panamá Viejo.

According to local legend, when word came of the pirate's impending attack, a priest painted the altar black to disguise it. The priest told Morgan that the famous altar had been stolen by another pirate, and convinced Morgan to donate handsomely for its replacement. Morgan allegedly told the priest, 'I don't know why, but I think you are more of a pirate than I am.' Whatever the truth, the baroque altar was later moved from the old city to its present site.

Teatro Nacional THEATER
(Map p652; ☎262-3525; Av B) Built in 1907, the interior of this ornate theater has been completely restored, and boasts red and gold decorations, a once-magnificent ceiling mural by Roberto Lewis and an impressive crystal chandelier. Performances are still held here; for information or a look around, visit the office at the side of the building.

Plaza de Francia PLAZA
(Map p652) At the tip of the southern point of Casco Viejo, this beautiful plaza pays homage to the French role in the construction of the canal. Its large stone tablets and statues

Panama City

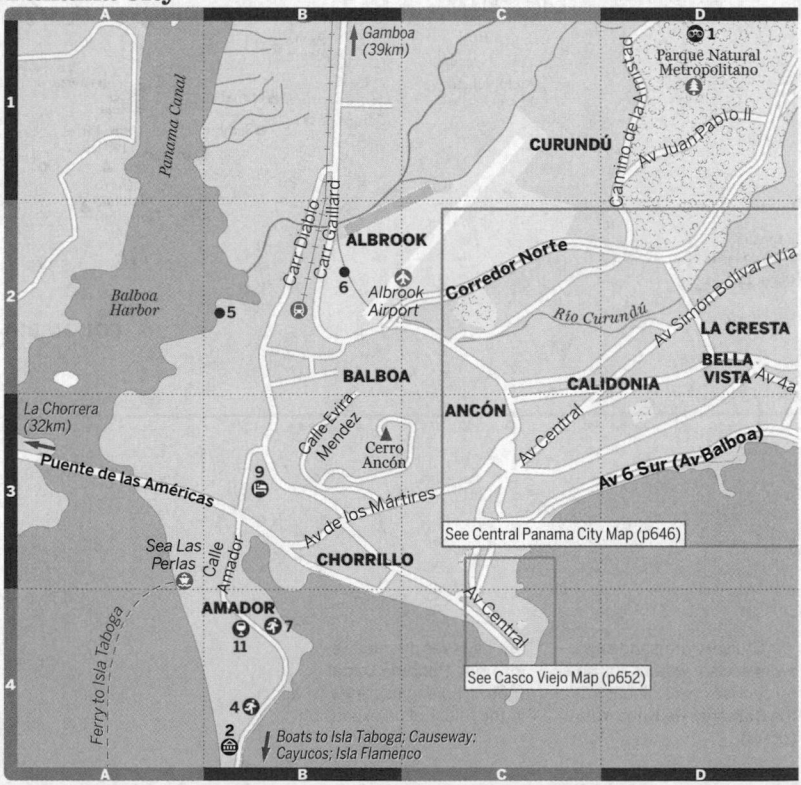

are dedicated to the memory of the 22,000 workers who died trying to build the canal.

Paseo las Bóvedas LANDMARK
(Map p652) This esplanade runs along the top of the sea wall built by the Spanish to protect the city. From here, you can see the Puente de las Américas (Bridge of the Americas) arching over the waterway and the ships lining up to enter the canal.

Palacio de las Garzas HISTORIC BUILDING
(Presidential Palace; Map p652; Av Alfaro) The presidential palace is named after the great white herons that reside here. The president of Panama lives on the upper floor.

Museo de Arte Religioso Colonial MUSEUM
(Museum of Colonial Religious Art; Map p652; ☎228-2897; cnr Av A & Calle 3a Este; admission US$1; ⏲8am-4pm Tue-Sat) Housed beside the ruins of the Iglesia y Convento de Santo Domingo, this art museum has a collection of colonial-era religious artifacts, some dating from the 16th century.

Just inside the doorway of the ruins is the Arco Chato, a long arch that has stood here, unsupported, for centuries. It reportedly played a part in the selection of Panama over Nicaragua as the site for the canal: its survival was taken as proof that the area was not subject to earthquakes. The arch suddenly collapsed in 2003.

Museo del Canal Interoceánico MUSEUM
(Panama Canal Museum; Map p652; ☎211-1649; www.museodelcanal.com; Calle 6a Oeste; admission US$5; ⏲9am-5pm Tue-Sun) This impressive museum is housed in the former headquarters for the original French canal company. The museum presents excellent exhibits on the famous waterway, framed in its historical and political context. Signs are in Spanish, but English-speaking guides and audio tours are available.

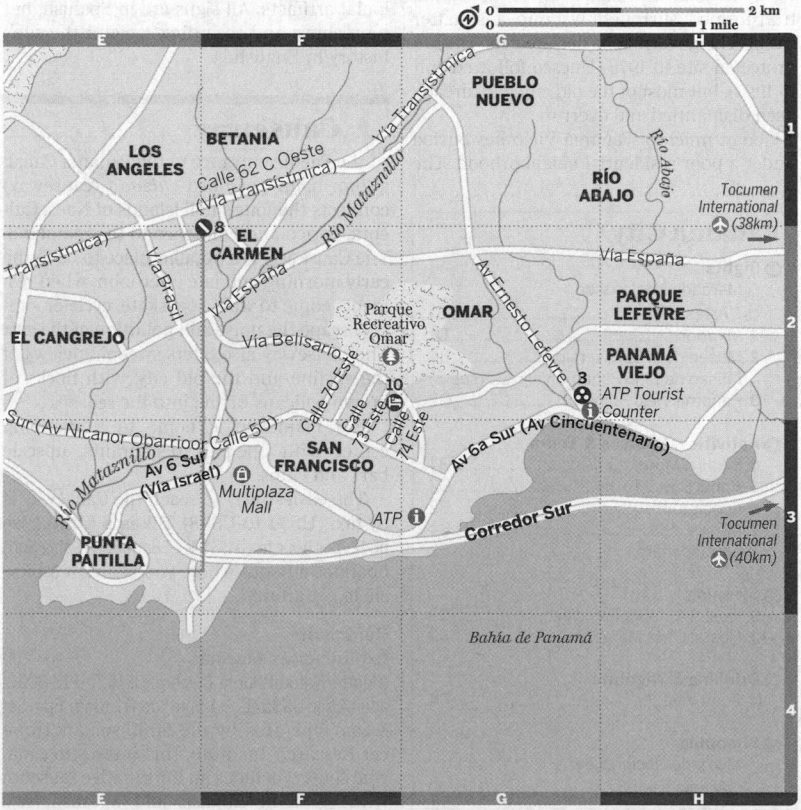

Museo de Historia de Panamá MUSEUM
(Map p652; ☎501-4128; Calle 6a Oeste, Palacio Municipal; ⏲8am-4pm Mon-Fri) FREE This modest museum has a small selection of exhibits covering Panamanian history from the colonial period to the modern era.

Panamá Viejo

For over 150 years, the city of Panamá, founded in 1519, was the metropolis of the Pacific, its riches the envy of pirates the world over. In addition to being a gateway to the riches of Peru, it was also a major trading post for Oriental silks and spices.

When Panamá fell to Henry Morgan in 1671, the city contained a magnificent cathedral, several beautiful churches, thousands of colonial homes and hundreds of warehouses stocked with foreign goods. Plundering reduced Panamá Viejo to mere beams and stone blocks.

Although the ruins were left intact as recently as 1950, the expansion of the capital transformed surroundings into a squatter camp. The government declared the ruins a protected site in 1976 (Unesco followed suit in 1997), but most of the old city had already been dismantled and overrun.

Today, much of Panamá Viejo lies buried under a poor residential neighborhood. The ruins are definitely worth visiting, however, even if only to stand on the hallowed grounds of one of North America's important colonial cities.

Panamá Viejo Ruins RUINS
(Map p642) The ruins of Panamá Viejo cover a large area. You can still see the cathedral with its stone tower, the plaza beside it, the convent of Santo Domingo, the Iglesia de San José, the hospital of San Juan de Dios and the city hall.

Mercado Nacional de Artesanías MARKET
(National Artisans Market; Map p642; Av 6 Sur; ⏲9am-4pm Mon-Sat, to 1pm Sun) Panamá Viejo buses will drop you off at this artisans market, behind the first remnant of ruins as you approach from Panama City.

Museo de Sitio Panamá Viejo MUSEUM
(Map p642; ☎226-8915; www.panamaviejo.org; Av 6 Sur; admission US$3; ⏲9am-5pm Tue-Sun) Features a cool scale model of Panamá Viejo prior to 1671, as well as a few surviving colonial artifacts. All signs are in Spanish, but a brochure and recording recount the site's history in English.

Panama City

Sights
- Mercado Nacional de Artesanías ..... (see 3)
- 1 Mirador D1
- 2 Museo de la Biodiversidad B4
- Museo de Sitio Panamá Viejo ..... (see 3)
- 3 Panamá Viejo Ruins G2

Activities, Courses & Tours
- 4 Bikes n More B4
- 5 Canal Bay & Tours B2
- 6 Ecocircuitos B2
- 7 Moses B4
- 8 Scubapanama F2

Sleeping
- 9 Hostal Amador Familiar B3
- 10 Hostal Casa Margarita F2

Drinking & Nightlife
- 11 Zona Viva B4

Shopping
- Mercado Nacional de Artesanías ..... (see 3)

Causeway

At the Pacific entrance to the Panama Canal, a 2km palm-tree-lined *calzada* (causeway) connects the four small islands of Naos, Culebra, Perico and Flamenco to the mainland. The Causeway is a popular place to be in the early morning and late afternoon, when residents come to walk, jog, skate, cycle or simply escape the noise and pollution of the city. The Causeway also offers sweeping views of the skyline and the old city, with flocks of brown pelicans diving into the sea.

Isla Flamenco is home to a shopping center with open-air restaurants, upscale bars and clubs.

The easiest way to reach the Causeway is by taxi (US$4 to US$8). **Bikes n More** (Map p642; per hour from US$4; ⏲8am-6pm Sat & Sun) operates a booth where you can rent a bicycle to get around.

Centro de Exhibiciones Marinas MUSEUM
(Centro Natural Punta Culebra, CEM; ☎212-8000; adult/child US$5/1; ⏲1-5pm Tue-Fri, 10am-6pm Sat & Sun) Operated by the Smithsonian Tropical Research Institute, this interesting marine center includes an informative museum with signs in English and Spanish, two

THE JAZZ SOLUTION IN CASCO VIEJO

This once down-and-out section of the city is writing a new chapter. Making a strong push towards revitalization, Casco Viejo is home to dozens of new restaurants, cafes, shops and renovated historic buildings. In the midst of this architectural revival, another less tangible one struggles to take place: that of the Panamanian community.

Jazz great and native Panamanian Danilo Perez returned here to establish **Fundación Danilo Perez** (Map p652; ☎211-0272; www.fundaciondaniloperez.com; Av A 1069), a musical foundation that has generated over a million dollars in scholarships, many to underprivileged youth. According to Perez, 'Through the discipline of music we can create relevant leaders and good citizens. We can solve many of society's problems.'

The foundation also sponsors the Panama Jazz Festival (p646), a wildly popular citywide event featuring artists from all over the world. The weeklong festival, held every January, culminates in a free Saturday concert at the Casco's Plaza de la Independencia. The foundation in Casco Viejo also houses a library and musical museum, and is open to the public.

small aquariums and a nature trail through a patch of dry forest containing sloths and iguanas.

Museo de la Biodiversidad MUSEUM
(Museum of Biodiversity; Map p642; www.biomuseopanama.org) Panama's new landmark museum, with extensive botanical gardens, was designed by world-renowned architect Frank Gehry, and has a controversial look of crumpled multicolor forms. Located near the tip of the Causeway, it is slated to open in 2013.

Parque Natural Metropolitano

Up on a hill, north of downtown, this 2.65-sq-km national park protects a wild area of tropical forest within the city limits. Main walks, the **Nature Trail** and the **Tití Monkey Trail**, join to form one long loop. The 150m-high **mirador** (Lookout; Map p642) offers views of Panama City, the bay and the canal, all the way to the Miraflores Locks.

Mammals include *tití* monkeys, anteaters, sloths, white-tailed deer, iguanas, turtles and tortoises. More than 250 bird species have been spotted here.

The park was the site of an important battle during the US invasion to oust Noriega. Concrete structures just past the park entrance were used during WWII as a testing and assembly plant for aircraft engines.

It's bordered on the west and north by Camino de la Amistad; Av Juan Pablo II runs right through the park.

For a self-guided tour, get a pamphlet in Spanish and English at the **visitors center** (☎232-5516; www.parquemetropolitano.org; admission US$1; ⏲8am-5pm Mon-Fri, to 1pm Sat), about 40m north of the park entrance.

Courses

Casco Antiguo Spanish School LANGUAGE COURSE
(Map p652; ☎228-3258; www.cascospanish.com; Calle 4a Oeste, Casco Viejo; 20hr intensive per week from US$195) This new Spanish school sits in the heart of the Casco. In addition to private and group lessons, they also offer accommodations and activities.

Institute for Spanish Language Studies LANGUAGE COURSE
(ILERI; ☎260-4424; www.isls.com/panama; Camino de la Amistad, El Dorado) Located in the suburban El Dorado neighborhood, this language school offers four hours of one-on-one instruction per day, five days a week. Costs start at US$275 for the first week, with optional extra homestays (US$175 per week).

Tours

Barefoot Panama TOUR
(☎6780-3010; www.barefootpanama.com; city tour per person US$79) Prompt and professional, this tiny US-run agency does a great city tour of Panama that takes in everything from the history to the flora and fauna. There's also day trips to San Lorenzo and Gamboa, with visits to a Wounaan indigenous village.

City Sightseeing Panama BUS TOUR
(Map p646; ☎392-6000; www.citysightseeingpty.com; Av Justo Arosemena & Calle 29 Este; 24hr ticket adult/child US$29/24) These red double-deckers loop the city and are a good way to get your bearings. Stops include Multicentro

Central Panama City

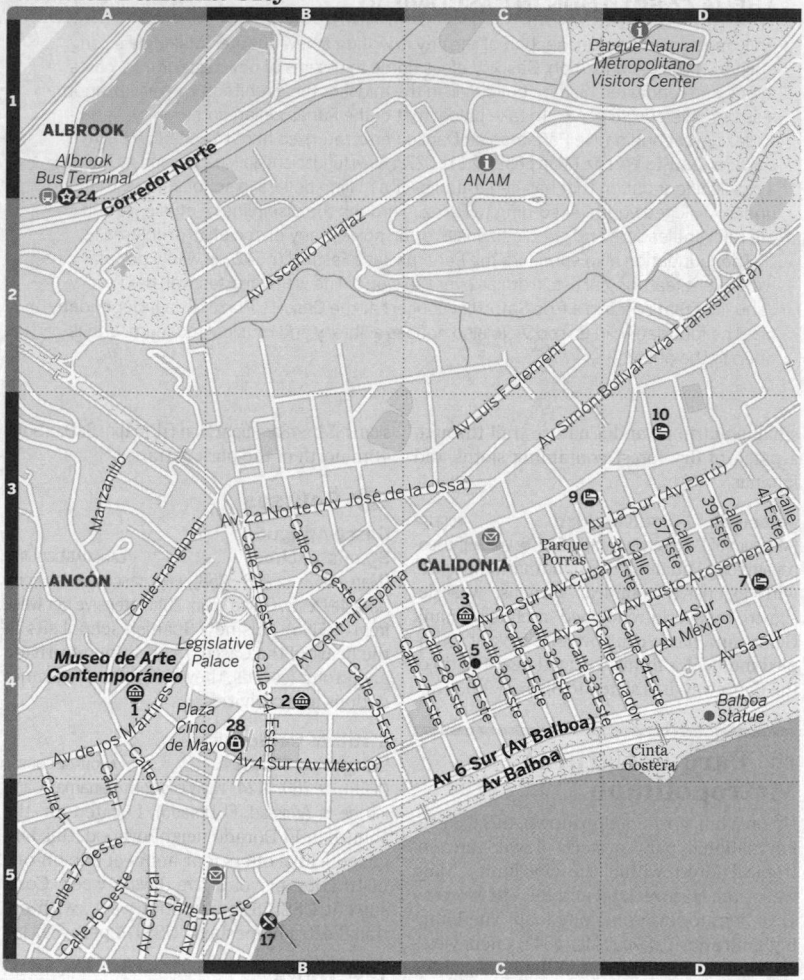

Mall, Calle Uruguay, Casco Viejo and the Amador Causeway. Service is hop-on, hop-off, so you can explore the sights all you want with hourly pickups. Departures run between 9am to 4pm, except for the night tour. Tickets are good for 24 or 48 hours. They also offer a tour of the canal zone.

Festivals & Events

Local events are listed in the arts section in the Sunday edition of *La Prensa,* as well as the back pages of *The Panama News*.

Carnaval FESTIVAL

Carnaval is celebrated in Panama City with merriment and wild abandon in the days preceding Ash Wednesday. From Saturday until the following Tuesday, work is put away, and masks, costumes and confetti come out. For 96 hours almost anything goes.

Panama Jazz Festival FESTIVAL

(www.panamajazzfestival.com) A blast, the Panama Jazz Festival is gaining momentum as one of the biggest musical events in Panama, drawing hundreds of thousands of spectators for a weeklong festival. Open-air events

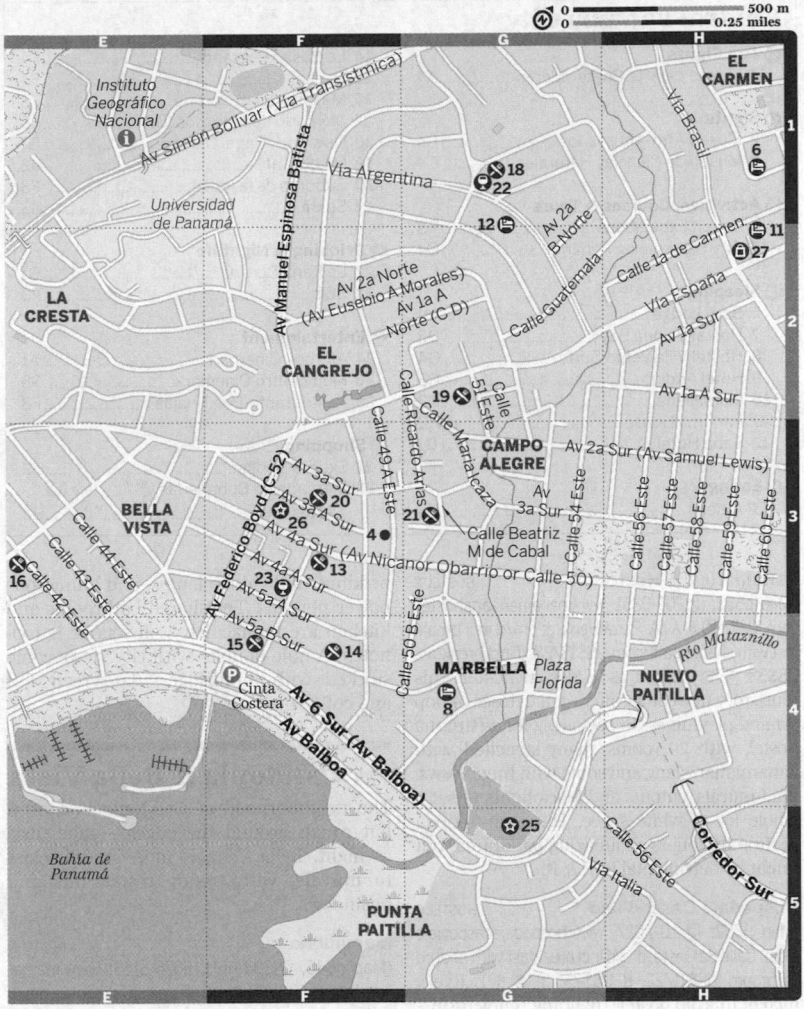

are usually free, while big-draw theater spectacles require tickets. It's held all over the city.

Sleeping

Casco Viejo

As Casco Viejo sees extensive renovation, this old-world charmer is becoming an excellent option for lodging. Advantages include the great number of restaurants and cafes, and its walkability.

★ Luna's Castle HOSTEL $

(Map p652; ☎262-1540; www.lunascastlehostel.com; Calle 9a Este; dm/d/tr incl breakfast US$13/30/39; @) Housed in a creaky mansion, Luna's masterfully blends Spanish colonial architecture with funky, laid-back backpacker vibes and great service. A bit looney and very friendly, it's the kind of hostel people keep talking about long after their trip. Its latest feature is a helpful activities concierge whose expertise ranges from planning a sailboat trip to finding the best mojito.

Central Panama City

Top Sights
1 Museo de Arte Contemporáneo A4

Sights
2 Museo Afro-Antilleano B4
3 Museo de Ciencias Naturales C4

Activities, Courses & Tours
4 Ancon Expeditions F3
5 City Sightseeing Panama C4

Sleeping
6 Baru Lodge H1
7 Hostal Balboa Bay D3
8 Hostel Villa Vento Surf G4
9 Hotel Andino C3
10 Mamallena D3
11 Panama House H2
12 Saba Hotel G1

Eating
13 Athens F3
14 La Rosa Mexicano F4
15 Market F4
16 Masala Indian Cuisine E3
17 Mercado de Mariscos B5
18 New York Bagel Café G1
19 Niko's Café G2
20 Sabores de la India F3
21 Sukhi G3

Drinking & Nightlife
22 La Rana Dorada G1
23 S6is F3

Entertainment
24 Albrook Cinemark A1
25 Multicentro Cinemark G5
26 Restaurante-Bar Tinajas F3

Shopping
27 Exedra Books H2
28 Mercado de Buhonerías y Artesanías B4

Panamericana Hostel HOSTEL $

(Map p652; ☎ 202-0851; www.panamericanahostel.com; Calle 10 & Av A, Plaza Herrera; dm/d incl breakfast with shared bathroom US$13/28, d incl breakfast US$38; @) Billed as a 'design hostel,' this four-story newcomer offers equal doses of pop art and playfulness. It seems big for a Panama hostel, with 29 rooms, many stenciled with Panamanian slang and some with huge views. Wall murals, cutouts and black lights offset a whole lot of white space. The soon-to-open rooftop bar offers an amazing panorama, but might be detrimental to R & R.

Hospedaje Casco Viejo HOSTEL $

(Map p652; ☎ 211-2027; www.hospedajecascoviejo.com; Calle 8a Oeste; dm/d incl breakfast with shared bathroom US$11/22, d US$25; P @) Every inch of this old hostel – pending renovation – has seen heavy use, but it's hard to get picky at these prices. The best room is the dormitory, with well-spaced single beds. Perks include a communal kitchen and an open-air courtyard. It's on a quiet side street near the Iglesia de San José.

★ Magnolia Inn INN $$

(Map p652; ☎ 6551-9217, 202-0827; www.magnoliapanama.com; Calle Boquete at Calle 8a Este; dm US$15, r US$80-135;) Every little detail speaks to the thoughtfulness of this cool inn, a restored three-story colonial run by US expats. Air-conditioned dorms are grown-up friendly, with orthopedic mattresses, quality bedding, individual lamps and numerous power plug-ins. The shared bathrooms and kitchen are immaculate and service is top-notch. Ample doubles with city views come stocked with minifridges, flat-screen TVs and coffee makers.

Calidonia & Bella Vista

The neighborhood of Calidonia is central but rough around the edges – take taxis at night. Bella Vista is more middle-class to upscale, with trendy restaurants and businesses.

Mamallena HOSTEL $

(Map p646; ☎ 393-6611, 6676-6163; www.mamallena.com; Calle Primera Perejil, Calidonia; dm/d incl breakfast US$13/33; @) This small, homey hostel nails the mark on service. Amenities include 24-hour desk service, pancake breakfasts and DVD library. High-ceiling dorms have air-con at night and the cute motel-style doubles offer considerable privacy. The onsite travel agency arranges sailing to San Blás and popular day trips. Renovations with more doubles and a swimming pool are coming.

Hostal Balboa Bay GUESTHOUSE $

(Map p646; ☎ 227-6182; Calle 39 Este No 21, Bella Vista; dm incl breakfast US$13, s/d US$35/50; @) Though quiet and clean, rooms are of widely varying quality and service can be spotty as well. It's currently undergoing renovations – check for changes in rates. Though central, it gets less traffic than the competition. The neighborhood becomes deserted at night, so take taxis.

Saba Hotel HOTEL $$
(Map p646; ☎ 201-6100; www.thesabahotel.com; Vía Argentina s/n, Bella Vista; d US$120; ❄ @ 📶) Modern and cheerful, the Saba is a great-value addition to Bella Vista. With lots of glass and bamboo, there's a sustainable theme that's probably more stylish than substantive. Still, you can practice yoga, get a carrot juice at the detox bar or order room service while watching your flat-screen TV. Service is great and there's a restaurant on site.

Hotel Andino HOTEL $$
(Map p646; ☎ 225-1162; www.hotelandino.net; Calle 35 Este, Calidonia; s/d US$49/55; P ❄ 📶) Rooms at the Andino come up short on charm, but they're big, clean and equipped like start-up apartments. Request a king-sized room and you can also get a two-burner stove for some self-catering adventures. If you don't feel like leaving the hotel, there's a bar and restaurant onsite, making it a convenient choice to crash overnight between bus departures.

El Cangrejo & San Francisco

The modern banking district of El Cangrejo is central but also one of the noisier spots in town. San Francisco is a higher-end neighborhood but it's largely residential, without many options for nightlife.

Panama House B&B $
(Map p646; ☎ 263-4366; www.panamahousebb.com; Calle 1a de Carmen 32, El Carmen; dm/s/d with shared bathroom incl breakfast US$15/35/45, s/d incl breakfast US$55/65; P ❄ @ 📶) In a cozy colonial near Vía Brasil, this congenial home sports fresh rooms with high ceilings. Guests of all ages congregate in the communal kitchen, lounge area or on the lush hammock patio. The owners offer a wealth of knowledge of the city and countryside. Be sure to book ahead.

Hostel Villa Vento Surf HOSTEL $
(Map p646; ☎ 397-6001, 6101-4841; hostelvillaventosurf.com; Calle 47 No 7, Marbella; dm/s/d/tr incl breakfast US$15/35/40/45; ❄ @ 📶 🏊) This relaxed newcomer sits in a suburban-style home around the corner from nightlife hotspot Calle Uruguay. Young internationals come for the swimming pool or the easy-access partying, though it's a relatively calm spot (all laptops engaged) and the staff is nice. It's a bit disheveled. Bunks crowd larger dorms, but air-con keeps them cool. Breakfast is pancakes and coffee.

Baru Lodge B&B $$
(Map p646; ☎ 393-2340; www.barulodge.com; Calle 2nda Norte H-7, El Carmen; s/d incl breakfast US$60/70; ❄ @ 📶) Tasteful and cordial, this subdued inn sits on a residential street central to the action. Rooms are sleek and modern with soft lighting. The English-speaking owner makes guests feel right at home. Cable TV, fast wi-fi and air purifiers are among the perks. The garden patio, where continental breakfasts are served, has wicker seating.

Hostal Casa Margarita B&B $$
(Map p642; ☎ 394-5557; www.hostalcasamargarita.com; Casa 97, Calle Los Claveles; s/d/tr incl breakfast US$75/88/115; P ❄ @) Irresistibly cozy and chic, this stucco house features seven smart and impeccable rooms with colorful touches, flat-screen TVs and minifridges. A huge garden and breakfast patio allows ample space to lounge or dally over a complete breakfast with fresh fruit. Guests also have kitchen use, but the real treasures here are the warm hosts.

Canal Zone

For quiet digs, this is your best bet. The neighborhood of Balboa sits right before the Causeway, while Clayton is further out, adjacent to Miraflores Locks. You're a taxi ride away from downtown, but also from the noise and congestion of Panama City.

Hostal de Clayton HOSTEL $
(☎ 317-1634; www.hostaldeclayton.com; Edificio 605B, Calle Guanabana, Clayton; dm US$15, d with/without bathroom US$45/38; P ❄ @ 📶) Reminiscent of an army barracks, this friendly hostel is located on the site of the former US army base of Clayton, a well-heeled residential area. The rooms and amenities are perfectly suited to the budget traveler, but for those without a rental car or the budget for taxis, the location leaves you adrift in suburbia.

Hostal Amador Familiar INN $
(Map p642; ☎314-1251; www.hostalamador-familiar.com; Casa 1519, Calle Akee, Balboa; dm incl breakfast US$15, d with fan/air-con US$30/35; P ❄ @ 📶) Hostal Amador Familiar is a big, yellow canal house with high-ceiling bedrooms and a private garden with open-air kitchen. Breakfast includes cereal or eggs, toast and coffee. Tiled rooms with rod-iron beds and sashed windows sport the quirks and creaks of old buildings, but the dorm is cramped and unpopular. The location is just off the Causeway. It costs US$3 to downtown by taxi.

★Dos Palmitos B&B $$
(☎391-0994; www.dospalmitos.com; Guayacan Terrace 0532B, Ancon Hill; s/d incl breakfast US$75/88; ❄ @ 📶) If your attraction to Panama is more about wildlife than wild life, check out this tucked-away canal house B&B. There's just four rooms decorated with *molas* (hand-stitched textiles made by Kuna indigenous people) and vintage news clips and featuring immaculate wooden floors, king beds and wicker furniture. The backyard terrace offers bird-watching and abundant breakfasts featuring homemade bread and fresh juice. Host Angeline also offers transportation and tours.

Eating

Casco Viejo

★Mercado de Mariscos MARKET $
(Map p646; Av Balboa; mains US$2.50-14; ⏲lunch Mon-Sat) Above a bristling fish market, an unassuming restaurant is *the* place to get your seafood fix. Lunchtime gets packed, so come early for whole fried fish and cavernous bowls of 'Get Up Lazarus' soup (a sure hangover cure). Outside, stands ladle out delicious US$2.50 plastic cups of *ceviche* – varieties include Mediterranean-style (with olives) and curry.

La Petite Bretagne CREPERIE $
(Map p652; Av Central; mains US$8; ⏲10am-5pm Tue-Fri, to 10pm Sat, to 3pm Sun) Authentic buckwheat crêpes from Brittany, fresh salads and tarts – like savory caramelized onion – that are melt-in-your-mouth good. It's also good for espresso and dessert, namely an endorphin-enducing velvety chocolate fondant.

Café Per Due ITALIAN $
(Map p652; ☎6512-9311; Av A; pizza US$5-12; ⏲9am-10pm Tue-Sun; ✎) Our pick for a quick bite, this casual Italian-run eatery serves scrumptious thin-crust pizzas. Check out the bacon and blue cheese or the fresh tomato, basil and garlic. Mozzarella is not skimped on. For privacy, try the tiny brick courtyard with a couple of tables.

Granclement ICE CREAM $
(Map p652; Av Central; gelato US$2.80-4.20; ⏲1-3pm & 4-7pm) Pure pleasure defines these tropical fruit gelatos and intense, creamy flavors like basil, orange-chocolate and ginger. A few scoops of these fussy French creations sweeten any stroll through the Casco.

Café Coca Cola PANAMANIAN $
(Map p652; Av Central; plates US$3-6; ⏲7:30am-11pm; ❄) A neighborhood institution, this old-school diner serves hearty platefuls of rice, beans and the featured meat of the day, all with air-conditioning.

Super Gourmet DELI $
(Map p652; Av A; mains US$5-9; ⏲7am-7pm Mon-Sat, 10am-3pm Sun) Stocking gourmet goods from wine to wasabi peas, this is the perfect pre-picnic stop. You can also grab soup or a baguette deli sandwich; the half-portion is probably enough. For breakfast, eggs on English muffins or *arepas* (savory corn cakes) hit the spot.

Diablo Rosso CAFE $
(Map p652; ☎262-1957; www.diablorosso.com; cnr Calle 6a Oste & Av A; mains US$4-10; ⏲11am-7pm Tue-Sat; 📶) This art cafe with biting social commentary and quirky folk art would be perfectly at home in Buenos Aires' Palermo. You can also enjoy a frothy cup of cappuccino, cheesy *arepas* piled high with eggs, hearty vegetarian soup or spinach *quesadillas*. Check for art openings or Tuesday night art cinema.

Manolo Caracol PANAMANIAN $$$
(Map p652; ☎228-4640; www.manolocaracol.net; Av Central; tasting menu US$36; ⏲noon-3pm & 7-10:30pm Mon-Fri, 7-11pm Sat) Manolo immerses you in tropical tastes. Tiny courses pair opposite flavors and textures, such as beef tongue sprinkled in sea salt, fire-roasted lobster drizzled in olive oil, and tart mango salad with crunchy greens. Not every dish sings, but the fun is adventuring through them in a lovely colonial atmosphere. Drinks are extra.

El Cangrejo & Bella Vista

New York Bagel Café CAFE $

(Map p646; Plaza Cabeza de Einstein near Vía Argentina, El Cangrejo; mains US$3-9; 7am-8pm Mon-Fri, 8am-8pm Sat, 8am-3pm Sun;) More San Francisco than Brooklyn, this fully US creation nonetheless packs in expats, with freshly baked bagels, lox and oversized breakfasts. They also serve handsome burgers. The setting offers jazz, soft sofas and your assortment of laptop geeks.

Sabores de la India INDIAN $

(Map p646; Calle 51, Bella Vista; mains US$3-10;) With Bollywood on the telly and cooks from the continent, this unassuming spot is a fast track to your spicy food fix. Vegetarian options (with tofu) are plenty, there's also a succulent chicken tikka, garlic naan and spicy daal. Big appetites should score the US$10 lunch buffet.

Niko's Café CAFETERIA $

(Map p646; Calle 51 Este, El Cangrejo; mains US$3-8; 24hr) A Greek immigrant who once sold food from a cart, Niko now has a successful Panama City chain. These sprawling 24-hour cafeterias serve hearty portions of inexpensive food including made-to-order breakfasts, Panamanian dishes and desserts. Near Vía España.

Athens GREEK $

(Map p646; Calle 50, Bella Vista; mains US$5; 11am-11:30pm Thu-Tue) Fresh and casual, this Greek eatery serves warm pitas with hummus, satisfying Greek salads, gyros and pizzas. It's ideal for families and large groups, with long hours and plenty of indoor and outdoor seating.

★El Caribe JAMAICAN $$

(214-6207; Vía Argentina, El Cangrejo; mains US$7-12; 11:30am-9:30pm Mon-Thu, to 10:30pm Fri-Sun) You can't get more authentic than this Jamaican via NYC restaurant serving set lunches (US$8.50). Seafood garlic dishes with coconut rice and jerk chicken (spicy upon request) are fresh and very flavorful. Jazz plays the last Saturday of the month.

Sukhi THAI $$

(Map p646; 395-6081; Calle Beatriz M de Cabal, Bella Vista; mains US$8-13; 11:30am-10pm Mon-Sat) In a cheerful cafe, this casual newcomer offers lovely, though not the most authentic, southeast Asian food. Start with fried calamari with ginger-and-cilantro dipping sauce. Flavors pop in the green-bean green curry, while Ladna comes in fragrant beef broth with broccoli rabe. Service is good and the price is right.

Masala Indian Cuisine INDIAN $$

(Map p646; 225-0105; Av Justo Arosemena, Bella Vista; mains US$8-18; noon-11pm) A fiery plate of Indian curry and an ice-cold Kingfisher lager are a perfect match for the tropical climate. Cozied up with floor pillows and colorful textiles, Masala offers a full complement of traditional dishes, ranging from tikka masala to lamb vindaloo, with a good selection for vegetarians.

★La Rosa Mexicano MEXICAN $$$

(Map p646; 301-0488; Av 5a B Sur, Bella Vista; mains US$10-28) No soggy burritos here. This chic eatery offers modern Mexican in a Cirque du Soleil setting. Start with guacamole handmade at your table. The watermelon margarita – topped with a sprig of rosemary – is a stunner. Picks include red snapper, salad with jicama and roast pumpkin seeds and, for dessert, a dizzy-good *cajeta* (caramel) with sea salt. Service is sterling. Near Calle Aquilino de la Guardia.

Market INTERNATIONAL $$$

(Map p646; www.marketpanama.com; cnr Calles Uruguay & 47, Bella Vista; mains US$9-28) With blackboard specials, brick and bustle, this bistro is more Manhattan than Calle Uruguay. Salads come in oversized bowls and you can top off your order of Angus beef with interesting sides such as creamed spinach or green beans with bacon. Weekend brunch is wildly popular.

Drinking & Nightlife

Bars and clubs open and close with alarming frequency in Panama City, where the nightlife is stylish, sophisticated and fairly pricey. The well-to-do denizens love a good scene, so it's worth scrubbing up, donning nice threads and parting with a bit of dough. You might regret blowing your budget in the morning, but that's the price you pay to party with the beautiful people.

Big areas for nightlife include Casco Viejo, Bella Vista and the Causeway. Vía Argentina is an up-and-coming spot – look for new bars and clubs on this fashionable avenue. The district of Bella Vista is home to Calle Uruguay, a strip of trendy bars and

Casco Viejo

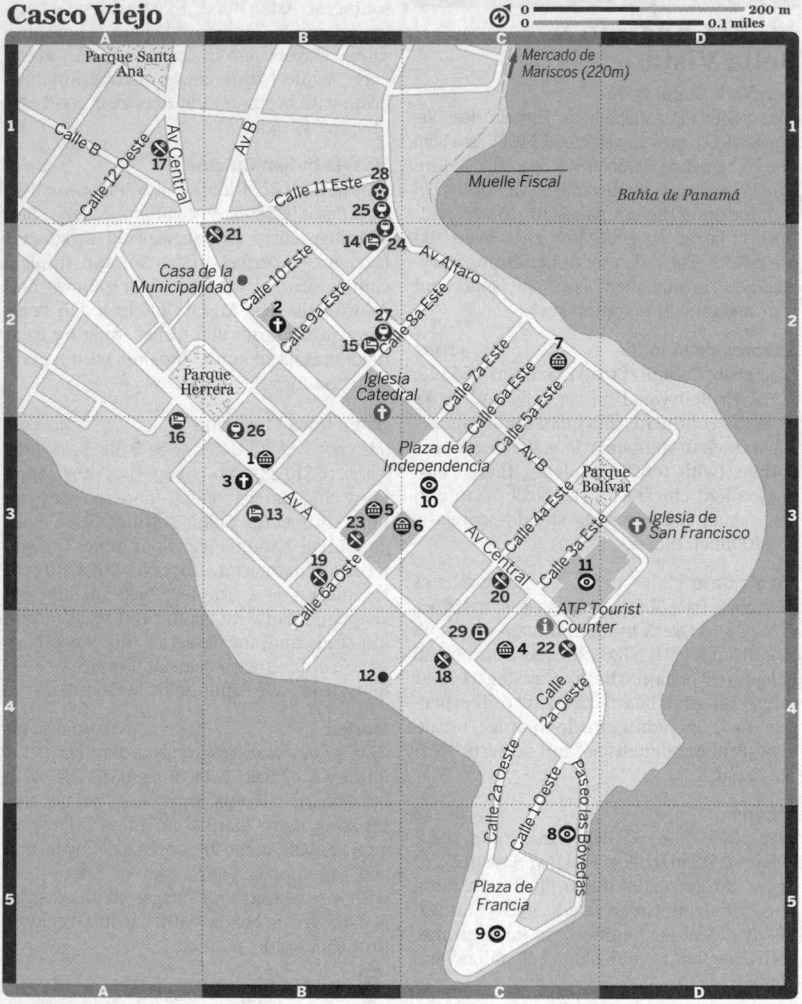

clubs reminiscent of Miami's South Beach. The scene is young and you can expect to pay to play here. Moreover, clubs change hands quickly in this neighborhood, so it's best to ask locals about the latest and greatest additions.

For what's happening in the city, be sure to pick up a copy of **La Prensa** (www.prensa.com). Weekend listings are available in the Thursday and Friday editions or on its website; look for the 'De Noche' section. Generally, the best gay scene in Panama City is actually found at the city's hippest bars and clubs, not at gay-specific establishments.

Although half the fun of partying it up in Panama City is finding a hidden gem, here's a few of our favorite spots to get you started.

Bar Relic BAR

(Map p652; www.relicbar.com; Calle 9a Este, Casco Viejo; ⏲9pm-2am Tue-Sat) At this cavernous hostel bar service is friendly and patrons (both travelers and Panamanian hipsters) easily mingle in the ample courtyard. Hungry? Try the pulled-pork sandwich. Not only are you partying outside (a rarity in Panama City) but you're next to the historical wall of the city.

Casco Viejo

Sights
1 Fundación Danilo Perez B3
2 Iglesia de La Merced B2
3 Iglesia de San José B3
4 Museo de Arte Religioso Colonial C4
5 Museo de Historia de Panamá B3
6 Museo del Canal Interoceánico C3
7 Palacio de las Garzas C2
8 Paseo las Bóvedas C5
9 Plaza de Francia C5
10 Plaza de la Independencia C3
11 Teatro Nacional C3

Activities, Courses & Tours
12 Casco Antiguo Spanish School B4

Sleeping
13 Hospedaje Casco Viejo B3
14 Luna's Castle B2
15 Magnolia Inn B2
16 Panamericana Hostel A3

Eating
17 Café Coca Cola A1
18 Café Per Due C4
19 Diablo Rosso B3
20 Granclement C3
21 La Petite Bretagne B2
22 Manolo Caracol C4
23 Super Gourmet B3

Drinking & Nightlife
24 Bar Relic B2
25 La Rana Dorada B1
26 Mojito sin Mojito B3
27 Tántalo Bar B2

Entertainment
28 Havana Panamá B1
Teatro Nacional ..... (see 11)

Shopping
29 Karavan C4

Mojito sin Mojito BAR
(Map p652; cnr Av A & Calle 9a Este, Casco Viejo) With a stripped down, warehouse atmosphere, this very local bar welcomes both flip-flops and stilettos. It's best for beer on tap and a burger (either veggie or regular). If you're feeling smart, chat up the trivia-giving bartender.

Tántalo Bar COCKTAIL BAR
(Map p652; cnr Calle 8a Este & Av B, Casco Viejo; cover US$5-10; ⏲rooftop deck 5pm-2am) Though it serves reasonably priced lunches, this ultra-hip cafe-bar is best known for sunset happy hours on its rooftop deck. Pair your cocktail with some delectable tapas. Cover is charged after 10pm, but to get a spot on the tiny roof deck you need to show up around 7pm.

Cayucos CAFE
Located on the Causeway, this open-air resto-bar sits on the water with excellent views of the city. While more restaurant than bar, it's perfect for the first cold beer of the evening.

S6is CLUB
(Map p646; Calle Uruguay, Bella Vista; ⏲from 9pm Tue & Thu-Sat) Pronounced 'seis' (as in the number 'six'), this club caters to *miembros del club,* aka, the beautiful people. There's a fine selection of electronic music worthy of the megaclub scene, but a more intimate and loungy vibe.

La Rana Dorada BREWERY
(Map p652; Av Alfaro, Casco Viejo) Panama City's first brewpub of small craft beers gets packed during the after-work happy hour. Along with a draft, pizzas are popular. A second location is on **Vía Argentina** (Map p646).

Zona Viva CLUB
(Map p642; Causeway) Located on the Causeway, Zona Viva is not unlike a mall – a closed compound hosting a number of nightlife spots, ranging from packed dance clubs to more low-key watering holes.

☆ Entertainment

If you're not looking to get blotto, there are numerous ways to spend a moonlit (or rainy) evening in the city. A good place to start is the arts section in the Sunday edition of *La Prensa,* or the back pages of the *Panama News.*

★ Havana Panamá LIVE MUSIC
(Map p652; Av Alfaro, Casco Viejo; cover US$10; ⏲Thu-Sat) Old school rules this vintage salsa bar replete with bandstand and leather booths. You'll have to don your finest threads (there's a dress code) and enter behind a swooshy velvet curtain. A salsa band rocks the house.

Restaurante-Bar Tinajas TRADITIONAL DANCE
(Map p646; ☎263-7890; www.tinajaspanama.com; Av 3a A Sur, Bella Vista; entry US$5; ⏲Mon-Sat) A good place to see traditional Panamanian folk dancing, this Panamanian dinner show

is a classic. Sure, it's touristy, but nicely done just the same. Shows are Wednesday to Saturday nights at 9pm, with a US$12 minimum per person for drinks and food. Reservations recommended. Near Av Frederico Boyd.

Teatro Nacional THEATER
(Map p652; ☎262-3525; Av B, Casco Viejo) For a little culture, the Teatro Nacional offers dance, music and live performances, though just sitting in this historic theater is enjoyable enough.

Multicentro Cinemark CINEMA
(Map p646; Multicentro Mall) Mainstream cinema, with some dubbed titles and some with subtitles. Near Punta Paitilla.

Albrook Cinemark CINEMA
(Map p646; Albrook Mall) Next to the Albrook bus terminal. There's also one in the Multiplaza Mall.

Shopping

★Karavan ART
(Map p652; ☎228-7177; www.karavan-gallery.com; Calle 3a Oeste, Casco Viejo; ⏲9:30am-5pm Mon-Fri, 10am-5pm Sat, noon-5pm Sun) An excellent place to find original Kuna embroidery with modern designs, and Congo art from Portobelo, with artisans working onsite. Karavan commissions local artists and works to develop new talent.

Mercado de Buhonerías y Artesanías MARKET
(Map p646; Av Central España; ⏲9am-5pm Mon-Sat) A bustling outdoor market where authentic handicrafts can be found.

Mercado Nacional de Artesanías MARKET
(National Artisans Market; Map p642; Panamá Viejo; ⏲9am-4pm Mon-Sat, to 1pm Sun) This crafts market near the Panamá Viejo ruins is a good choice for memorable souvenirs.

Exedra Books BOOKS
(Map p646; ☎264-4252; cnr Vías España & Brasil; ⏲9:30am-9:30pm Mon-Sat, 11am-8:30pm Sun) Among Central America's best bookstores.

Orientation

Panama City stretches about 20km along the Pacific coast, from the Panama Canal at its western end to the ruins of Panamá Viejo at the east. City streets can go by several names; for taxis it's best to use landmarks to orient drivers.

Near the canal are Albrook airport, the Fuerte Amador Causeway and the wealthy Balboa and Ancón suburbs, which were first built for the US canal and military workers. The Puente de las Américas (Bridge of the Americas) arches gracefully over the canal.

The colonial peninsula of Casco Viejo (also called Casco Antiguo), juts into the sea on the southwestern side of town. From here, two major roads head east through the city.

The main drag is Av Central, which runs past the cathedral in Casco Viejo. At a fork further east, the avenue becomes Av Central España; the section that traverses the El Cangrejo business and financial district is called Vía España. The other part of the fork becomes Av 1 Norte (José D Espinar), Av Simón Bolívar and finally Vía Transístmica as it heads out of town and across the isthmus toward Colón.

Along Av Balboa, the Cinta Costera is a waterfront green space with walking and biking paths that extends from downtown to Casco Viejo.

Generally, *avenidas* (avenues) run east–west, while *calles* (streets) run north–south. Av Central and Vía España form the boundary – *avenidas* south of Vía España are labeled *sur* (south) while *calles* east of Vía España are labeled *este*.

MAPS

Just off Av Simón Bolívar opposite the Universidad de Panamá, **Instituto Geográfico Nacional** (Tommy Guardia; ☎236-2444; Transistmica, near Av Arturo del Valle; ⏲8am-4pm Mon-Fri) has an excellent map collection for sale.

Information

DANGERS & ANNOYANCES

Casco Viejo is the focus of an ambitious urban renewal program, though it's still a work in progress. The tip of the peninsula southeast of the Iglesia de la Merced is safe for tourists and heavily patrolled by police officers.

Moving to the base of the peninsula, there are high-density slums where many tourists have been the target of criminals. Other high-crime areas include Curundú, El Chorrillo, Santa Ana, San Miguelito and Río Abajo.

Calle Uruguay, the clubbing hub of the city, also attracts opportunists. Don't take your full wallet out at night. We have heard reports of women embracing male travelers to take their wallets.

When walking the city streets, be aware that drivers do not yield to pedestrians. Also, be on the lookout for missing storm and sewer covers, downed wires and high curbs.

EMERGENCY

Police (☎104)

INTERNET ACCESS

Most lodgings have wi-fi, and internet cafes are plentiful, especially in the El Cangrejo banking district.

MEDICAL SERVICES

Centro Médico Paitilla (☎265-8800, 265-8883; cnr Calle 53 & Av Balboa) Has well-trained physicians who speak both Spanish and English.

Centro Metropolitano de Salud (☎512-6600; Corosel Los Ríos; ⏲7:30am-noon & 1-3pm Mon-Fri) Offers yellow-fever vaccinations with international certificate (required for travel to Colombia if returning to Panama) for a minimal charge.

MONEY

There are plenty of 24-hour ATMs throughout the city.

HSBC (Vía España) Changes Amex traveler's checks with no fee; US$5 transaction for other types.

Panacambios (☎223-1800; Vía España, Ground fl, Plaza Regency Bldg; ⏲8am-5pm Mon-Fri) Buys and sells international currencies.

POST

Many hotels sell stamps and some will mail guests' letters.

Main Post Office (Av Balboa btwn Calles 30 & 31; ⏲7am-5:45pm Mon-Fri, to 4:45pm Sat) Holds poste-restante items for 30 days.

Post Office (Plaza las Americas; ⏲7am-5:45pm Mon-Fri, to 4:45pm Sat) Only post office for mailing packages.

TELEPHONE

Tarjetas (phone cards) in denominations of US$3, US$5 and US$10 can be purchased at pharmacies for local and regional calls, which can be made from any card phone.

TOURIST INFORMATION

ATP (Autoridad de Turismo Panama; ☎226-7000; www.atp.gob.pa; Vía Israel, San Francisco; ⏲8:30am-4:30pm Mon-Fri) Panama's tourism bureau is headquartered at the Centro Atlapain in the San Francisco neighborhood. ATP offices give out free maps but few employees speak English. Enter at the rear of the large building. There are also information counters in Panamá Viejo and Casco Viejo.

ANAM (Autoridad Nacional del Ambiente; ☎315-0855, 500-0855; www.anam.gob.pa; Bldg 804, Albrook; ⏲8am-4pm) ANAM can occasionally provide maps and information on national parks, but they are not organized to provide much assistance to tourists.

Getting There & Away

AIR

International flights arrive at **Tocumen International Airport** (☎238-4322, 238-4160; www.tocumenpanama.aero), 35km northeast of the city center.

For domestic flights, the only carrier currently serving the country is **Air Panama** (☎316-9000; www.flyairpanama.com). Domestic flights depart from **Albrook airport** (Aeropuerto Marcos A Gelabert; ☎315-0403), near the bus terminal.

All flights within Panama last under one hour and prices vary according to season and availability. Sample one-way fares are Bocas del Toro (US$116), David (US$117), Achutupu in San Blás (US$80), Isla Contadora (US$70) and Sambú in the Darién (US$48).

BOAT

Barcos Calypso (☎314-1730; round-trip US$12) Ferry departures from Panama City to Isla Taboga at 8:30am and 3pm Monday and Friday, 8:30am on Tuesday, Wednesday and Thursday, and 8am, 10:30am and 4pm on weekends.

National Tours (☎6617-0450, 6615-1392; round-trip US$14) This fast ferry to Isla Taboga (under 30 minutes) is a small boat. There are daily departures from Panama City's Balboa Yacht Club at 8:30am and 3pm. There is no indoor seating, so it;s not ideal for bad weather. Phone service is poor, so buy tickets onsite.

Sea Las Perlas (☎391-1424; www.sealasperlas.com; adult/child one-way US$45/35) Catamaran ferry service (one hour 40 minutes) leaves from Balboa Yacht Club for Contadora Island daily at 8am, returning at 3pm. Sunday also has an 11am departure.

BUS

Albrook bus terminal is a convenient and modern one-stop location for most buses leaving Panama City. The terminal includes a food court, banks, shops, a sports bar, storage room, bathrooms and showers. There's a mall next door, complete with a supermarket and cinema.

Both **Panaline** (☎227-8648; www.viajeros.com/panaline) and **Tica Bus** (☎262-2084; www.ticabus.com) serve San José and Costa Rica; see their websites for hours.

Canal Zone buses depart from Albrook to Balboa and Clayton, Miraflores Locks and Gamboa, leaving every 45 minutes. In transition, these buses will soon be run by Metrobus with the same card system.

Albrook Bus Terminal (☎303-3030; www.grantnt.com) The city's main bus terminal. Passengers must buy a multiuse card or *tarjeta* to pay the US$0.10 terminal tax before entering the bus area by turnstile (also swiped for bus station bathrooms). You can avoid this inconvenience by offering another person in line cash to swipe their card for you. An information booth offers assistance.

Metrobus (www.tarjetametrobus.com; fare US$0.25-1.25) All local buses are on the new Metrobus system with designated bus stops and clean, new buses. Cash is not accepted. Buy rechargable orange cards or *tarjetas* at a special kiosk in the Albrook bus terminal or at designated stops or kiosks listed on the website. If you don't have one, try offering another passenger reimbursement for swiping their card.

CAR & MOTORCYCLE

Daily rates start from US$35 per day for the most economical cars, including insurance and unlimited kilometers. The following car rental agencies have locations at Albrook and Tocumen airports.

Avis (☎238-4056; www.avis.com.pa)

Budget (☎Tocumen 238-4069; www.budget-panama.com)

Hertz (☎238-3751; www.hertz.com.pa)

National (☎238-4144; www.nationalpanama.com)

TRAIN

Note that the Panama City terminus is actually located in the town of Corazal, a 15-minute cab ride from the capital.

Panama Railway Company (PCRC; ☎317-6070; www.panarail.com; Carretera Gaillard; one-way adult/child US$25/$15) This glass-domed luxury passenger train takes a lovely ride from Panama City to Colón daily, leaving at 7:15am and returning at 5:15pm. The train follows the canal, at times surrounded by nothing but thick vine-strewn jungle. If you want to relive the heyday of luxury train travel for an hour or two, this is definitely the way to do it.

ℹ Getting Around

BICYCLE

The only spot to rent bicycles in Panama City is at the start of the Causeway. Both **Moses** (Map p642; ☎221-3671; ⏲9am-7pm Sat & Sun) and Bikes n More (p644) operate booths with rentals starting at US$4 per hour for mountain bikes. You can also rent tandems and rickshaw bikes.

BUS

Panama City is almost done phasing out its *diablos rojos* or 'red devils' for modern, safe, air-conditioned buses by Metrobus (p656). Rides cost US$0.25 to $1.25, with the higher cost for corredor routes.

Buses run along the three major west-to-east routes: Av Central–Vía España, Av Balboa–Vía Israel, and Av Simón Bolívar–Vía Transístmica. The Av Central–Vía España streets are one-way going west for much of the route; eastbound buses use Av Perú and Av 4 Sur – these buses will take you into the banking district of El Cangrejo. Buses also run along Av Ricardo J Alfaro (known as Tumba Muerto).

Metrobuses stop at official bus stops and the Albrook bus terminal near the Albrook airport.

TAXI

Taxis are plentiful but problematic. Some drivers do not travel (or even know) the whole city, so

BUSES FROM PANAMA CITY

DESTINATION	COST (US$)	DURATION (HR)	FREQUENCY
Changuinola	28	10	daily
Chitré	9	4	hourly
Colón	3.50	2	every 20min
David	15-19	7-8	15 daily
El Valle	4.25	2½	hourly
Las Tablas	10	4½	hourly
Penonomé	5.25	2½	48 daily
Pesé	9.65	4½	6 daily
San José, Costa Rica	40	16	2 daily
Santiago	9	4	20 daily
Soná (for Santa Catalina)	10	6	6 daily
Villa de Los Santos	9	4	18 daily
Yaviza	14	6-8	8 daily

GETTING INTO TOWN

From the Airport

Tocumen International Airport is 35km northeast of the city center. The cheapest way to get into the city is to exit the terminal, cross the street (to the bus shelter) and catch a city-bound bus. Much faster and costlier, taxis (from US$27) can be hired at the Transportes Turísticos desk at the airport exit, next to posted prices.

From the Albrook terminal, airport buses (US$1.25, one to 1½ hours) marked 'Tocumen Corredor' depart every 15 minutes. You can also take a taxi.

The Albrook airport north of Cerro Ancón handles domestic flights. The easiest way to get to/from the airport is by taxi; the ride should cost between US$3 and US$5.

From the Bus Terminal

All long-distance buses arrive at the Albrook bus terminal; from here there are connections throughout the city. Routes (such as Vía España, Panamá Viejo) are displayed in the front window and cost US$0.25. If you arrive after dark, it is recommended that you take a taxi (US$3 to US$5) to your destination.

don't be surprised if they leave you standing on the sidewalk upon hearing your destination.

Taxis are not metered, but there is a list of standard fares that drivers are supposed to charge, measured by zones. One zone runs a minimum of US$2; Canal Zone destinations run up to US$6. An average ride, crossing a couple of zones, would cost US$3 to US$4, more for additional passengers or if it's late. Always agree on a fare before you get into the cab or, better, ask your hotel to estimate the fare to your destination and then simply hand the driver the money upon arriving. Taxis can also be rented by the hour.

Watch out for unmarked large-model US cars serving hotels as cabs. Their prices are up to four times that of regular street taxis. Reputable companies include **America** (☎223-7694), **America Libre** (☎223-7342) and **Latino** (☎224-0677).

AROUND PANAMA CITY

No visit to Panama City would be complete without taking a day trip to its famous waterway – just remember that the Canal Zone is much, much more than just the canal. The rainforest surrounding the canal is easily accessed and one of the best places to view a variety of Central American wildlife.

Panama Canal

The canal is truly one of the world's greatest engineering marvels. Stretching for 80km from Panama City on the Pacific side to Colón on the Atlantic side, the canal cuts right through the continental divide. Around 13,000 vessels pass through the canal each year and ships worldwide are built with the dimensions of the Panama Canal's locks (305m long and 33.5m wide) in mind. In 2010, the canal brought in US$2 billion in revenue.

Ships pay according to their weight, with the average fee around US$30,000. The highest amount paid was around US$376,000, paid in 2010 by the cruise ship *Norwegian Pearl;* the lowest amount was US$0.36, paid in 1928 by Richard Halliburton, who swam through.

The pre-expansion canal has three sets of double locks: Miraflores and Pedro Miguel Locks on the Pacific side and Gatún Locks on the Atlantic side. Between the locks, ships pass through a huge artificial lake, Lago Gatún, created by the Gatún Dam across the Río Chagres (when created they were the largest dam and largest artificial lake on Earth), and the Gaillard Cut, a 14km cut through the rock and shale of the isthmian mountains. With the passage of each ship, a staggering 52 million gallons of fresh water is released into the ocean.

Panamanians voted to expand the canal in 2006. The US$5.25 billion plan will widen and deepen existing navigation channels as well as enable the construction of two new locks. Originally planned for inauguration at the canal's 100-year anniversary, it now looks like the expansion will not open until 2015.

Sights

The easiest and best way to visit the canal is to go to the Miraflores Visitors Center,

Panama Canal

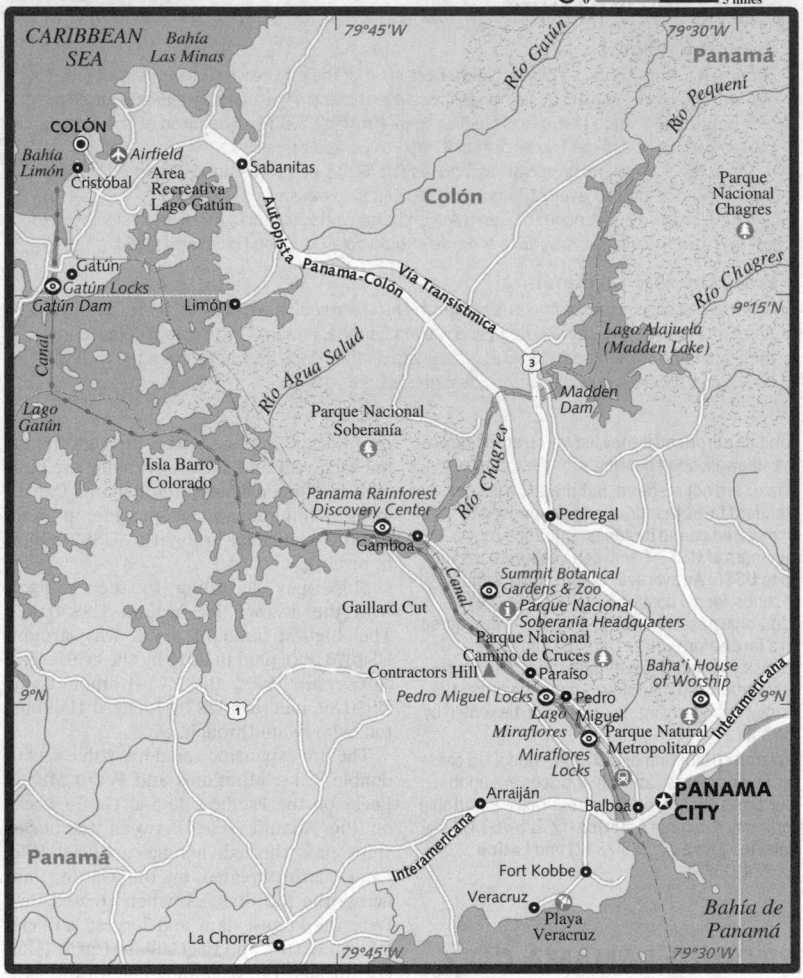

located just outside Panama City. You can visit the new Canal Expansion Observation Center (p695) and Gatún Locks as a trip from Colón.

Miraflores Locks CANAL

(☎ 276-8325; www.pancanal.com; viewing deck/full access US$5/8; ⏲ 9am-5pm) Here there are shaded viewing platforms, a visitors center with a four-story museum, and an excellent restaurant overlooking the locks. The best times to view big liners passing through are from 9am to 11am and 3pm to 5pm. Take any Paraíso or Gamboa bus (US$0.35) and walk 15 minutes from the sign. A taxi costs around US$20 round-trip.

Pedro Miguel Locks CANAL

FREE North of the Miraflores Locks are the Pedro Miguel Locks. You will pass them if you're taking the highway to Gamboa. The only facilities here are a parking lot, from where you can see the locks.

Activities

Canal Bay & Tours BOAT TOUR

(Map p642; ☎ 314-1339; www.canalandbaytours.com; partial transit US$115) Offers partial canal transits every Saturday morning. Boats depart from Muelle (Pier) 19 in Balboa, a western suburb of Panama City, travel through the Miraflores Locks to Lago Miraflores and back. Make reservations in advance. One Saturday every month, the company also offers full transits.

★Yala Tours ADVENTURE TOURS
(☎232-0215, 6641-6676; www.yalatourspanama.com) This small Swiss-run operation provides specialized trips throughout Panama, and also day trips to Gamboa and the Canal area. A highlight is kayaking in Río Chagres and Lago Gatún while watching canal ships mow through. There's also a canal boat tour in Lago Gatún, wildlife-watching and hiking in Parque Nacional Soberanía, and cultural visits to an Emberá village.

Panama Canal Fishing FISHING
(☎315-1905, 6678-2653; www.panamacanalfishing.com; day trips for 2 anglers all inclusive from US$445) If you're looking to reel in a big one, get in touch with Panama Canal Fishing. Its signature tour is fishing for peacock bass on Lago Gatún and the Río Chagres. Introduced by an American looking to boost his pastime, peacock bass are now considered a plague; fishing them does the lake a great favor.

Around the Canal

Although no trip to Panama would be complete without visiting the world-famous canal itself, the surrounding area is also home to impressive attractions, especially wildlife-watching and bird-watching. On a day trip from Panama City, you could first visit the Miraflores Locks, then Parque Nacional Soberanía and the Panamá Rainforest Discovery Center. The last two stops are only 25km from the center of Panama City, but they seem like a different world.

These attractions are located along the highway that runs from Panama City to Gamboa, the small town where the Río Chagres enters Lago Gatún. They can be reached by taking the Gamboa bus from Albrook bus terminal (p655).

Parque Nacional Soberanía

A few kilometers past Summit, across the border into Colón Province, the 221-sq-km **Parque Nacional Soberanía** (admission US$5) is one of the most accessible tropical rainforest areas in Panama. It extends much of the way across the isthmus, from Limón on Lago Gatún to just north of Paraíso, and boasts hiking trails that brim with wildlife.

You can pay the entrance fee at the **park headquarters** (Autoridad Nacional del Ambiente; ☎276-6370) at the turnoff to Summit. Maps, information about the park and camping permits are available here, including a brochure for self-guided walks along the nature trail. If you plan on hiking, note that the trailheads are quite a distance from the park headquarters. If arriving by taxi, have the driver wait for you to pay the fee and then take you to the trailhead.

Hiking trails in the park include a section of the old **Sendero Las Cruces** (Las Cruces Trail), used by the Spanish to transport gold by mule train between Panama City and Nombre de Dios, and the 17km **Camino del Oleoducto** (Pipeline Rd), providing access to Río Agua Salud, where you can walk upriver for a swim under a waterfall. A shorter, very easy trail is the **Sendero El Charco** (the Puddle Trail), signposted from the highway, 3km past the Summit Botanical Gardens & Zoo.

Pipeline Rd is considered to be one of the world's premier **bird-watching sites** – not surprisingly, it's intensely popular with bird-watchers, especially in the early morning hours. Over 500 different species of birds have been spotted on the trail, and it's fairly likely you will see everything from toucans to trogons.

The Río Chagres, which flows through the park and supplies most of the water for the Panama Canal, is home to several **Emberá communities**. Although the Darién is the ancestral home of the Emberá, a wave of migration to the shores of the Río Chagres commenced in the 1950s. The Emberá community of **Ella Puru** (☎6537-7223) and community of **San Antonio** (☎6637-9503) regularly receive visitors. With prior notice you can arrange a pickup from the docks in Gamboa. There is no shortage of possible excursions, ranging from taking guided rainforest walks to watching traditional dances.

Panama Rainforest Discovery Center

Geared toward ecotourism and environmental education, this **center** (☎6588-0697; www.pipelineroad.org; adult/child US$20/4; ⏲6am-4pm) is an excellent facility for bird-watchers and nature lovers. If you roll out of bed early, you will be rewarded for the effort. Those arriving after 10am pay US$5 less in admission – a sure sign that coming later is of lesser value. During premium hours, only 25 visitors are admitted to minimize impact on wildlife. A 32m-high observation tower is great for spotting blue cotinga and toucans. The sustainably built visitors center provides information and has 13 species of hummingbirds feeding nearby.

You can also contact the center to participate in bird migration counts. These are run by the non-profit **Fundación Avifauna Eugene Eisenmann** (☎264-6266; www.avifauna.org.pa) with the mission to protect Panama's bird fauna and rainforest habitat.

No buses access the park. It is best to negotiate with a taxi, rent a car or go with an organized tour. The center is 1.6km from the entrance to Pipeline Rd. You must pass the town of Gamboa, at the end of Gaillard Rd, and follow the signs.

Monumento Nacional Isla Barro Colorado

This lush island in the middle of Lago Gatún is the most intensively studied area in the Neotropics. Isla Barro Colorado (BCI) was formed by the damming of the Río Chagres and the creation of the lake and in 1923 it became one of the first biological reserves in the New World. Home to 1316 recorded plant species, 381 bird species and 120 mammal species, the island also contains a 59km network of marked and protected trails. It is managed by the Smithsonian Tropical Research Institute (STRI), which administers a world-renowned research facility here.

Although the 15-sq-km island was once restricted to scientists, visitors can now enter as part of a guided tour. The trip includes an STRI boat ride down an attractive part of the canal, from Gamboa across the lake to the island. Tour reservations are essential – book as far in advance as possible. Reserve through the Panama City visitor services office of **STRI** (☎212-8000; www.stri.org; Av Roosevelt, Tupper Bldg, Ancón; adult US$70; ⏲8:30am-4:30pm Mon-Fri).

A 45-minute boat ride leaves Gamboa pier at 7:15am on weekdays and at 8am on weekends. Hikes are demanding and last two to three hours. The entire trip lasts four to six hours, depending on the size of the group and the weather. A buffet lunch (with vegetarian options) is included. For more information, you can download the free pdf on the STRI website.

Isla Taboga

A tropical island with only one road and no traffic, Isla Taboga is a pleasant place to escape the hustle and bustle of Panama City, just 20km offshore.

History

Taboga is part of a chain of islands once inhabited by indigenous peoples who resided in thatched huts and lived off the bounty of the sea. In 1515, Spanish soldiers announced their arrival by killing or enslaving the islanders and establishing a small colony. A number of pirates, including Henry Morgan and Francis Drake, frequented the island and used it as a base from which to attack Spanish ships and towns. Aside from a few live rounds fired by the US Navy during a WWII session of target practice, recent years have been peaceful.

Sights & Activities

Fine **beaches** lie in either direction from the ferry dock. Many visitors head right, to the island's most popular beach, arcing between Taboga and tiny Isla El Morro.

On weekends, fishermen at the pier take visitors around the island to good **snorkeling** spots and caves on the western side rumored to hold pirate treasure. During the week you can snorkel around Isla El Morro, which doesn't have coral, but attracts some large fish.

Walk left from the pier to the village. After a fork, a high road leads to a modest **church** with a simple square. Founded in 1550, it's the second-oldest church in the Western Hemisphere; inside is a handsome altar and lovely artwork. Further down the road, a beautiful public **garden** bears a statue of the island's patroness, Nuestra Señora del Carmen.

Refugio de Vida Silvestre Isla Taboga y Urabá is home to one of the largest breeding colonies of brown pelicans in the world. May is the height of nesting season, but pelicans can be seen from January to June.

Occasionally during August, September and October, migrating humpback and sei whales can be seen in spectacular displays. Keep an eye out when on the ferry.

Festivals & Events

Nuestra Señora del Carmen FESTIVAL
Island patroness Nuestra Señora del Carmen is honored with a seafaring procession every July 16. Seemingly everyone partakes in games, fire-breathing or dancing.

Fiesta del Mar FESTIVAL
(www.fiestadelmarpanama.com) Launched in 2012, this festival highlights local culture with live Panamanian Calypso music, dancing, a pageant and food events. Held at the end of January, it draws 4000 guests to this tiny island.

Sleeping & Eating

Most people choose to visit Isla Taboga as a day trip from Panama City, though there are a few affordable places to stay.

Zoraida's Cool GUESTHOUSE $
(☎6471-1123, 6566-9250; s/d/tr US$35/45/50) Overlooking the bay, this turquoise house is run by Rafael, the widower of Zoraida. Small rooms with plastic-wrapped mattresses are the cheapest around. The hammock deck serves for a snooze with Pacific views. Turn left as you exit the dock and walk for a few minutes until you see a sign leading you up the hill.

Cerrito Tropical B&B $$
(☎390-8999; www.cerritotropicalpanama.com; d incl breakfast US$88, 2-person apt US$110-220; ❄📶) This smart Canadian-owned B&B occupies a quiet nook at the end of a steep road. Rooms are stylish, some small, with access to a large shady deck. Extras range from Spanish lessons to barbecues and picnic lunches. To arrive, go right uphill at the end of Calle Francisco Pizarro.

Vereda Tropical Hotel HOTEL $$
(☎250-2154; www.hotelveredatropical.com; d with fan/air-con incl breakfast US$72/83; ❄📶) Atop a hill with commanding views (it's about 100m up a winding path), this boutique hotel charms with tropical tones, mosaic tiles and rod-iron railings. The dining patio has gaping views and Julio Iglesias serenading from the speakers. Unfortunately, service is slack.

Donde Pope Si Hay PANAMANIAN $
(mains US$4-7; ⏲8am-8pm) A simple cement eatery serving fresh fish, green coconut water and *patacones* (fried plantains).

Information

For more information on the island, check the excellent English-language site, www.taboga.panamanow.com.

Getting There & Away

From Panama City's Causeway, **Barcos Calypso** (☎314-1730; round-trip US$12) and National Tours (p655) have ferry departures twice daily, with an extra departure on weekends.

PACIFIC COAST & HIGHLANDS

Between Chiriquí and Panama City, the regions of Veraguas, Península de Azuero and Coclé have long been overshadowed by the flash of the capital, the coolness of the highlands and the lure of the Caribbean. But for Panama's heart and soul, this may be the best place to look.

Dominated by agriculture, these are friendly provinces of laid-back colonial towns, farms and hillside villages. Founded by the Spanish four centuries ago, traditions live on in original colonial architecture, dazzling festivals and exquisite handicrafts.

Highlights include Santa Catalina, one of the best surf destinations in Central America, as well as the scenic mountain towns of Santa Fé and El Valle. The Pedasí coast

WORTH A TRIP

ARCHIPIÉLAGO DE LAS PERLAS

With hundreds of islands, white-sand beaches and turquoise waters, the Pearl Islands are everybody's idea of paradise. Though *Survivor* was filmed here, you can stay without a majority vote. There is plenty of snorkeling, diving and sunning, but prices for lodging and food tend to be steep. Our pick is **Perla Real** (☎250-4095, 6513-9064; www.perlareal.com; d/ste/villa incl breakfast US$95/125/185; ❄📶) a comfortable inn that's a 10-minute walk from the beaches of Isla Contadora. Snorkeling and diving trips can be arranged at **Coral Dreams** (☎6536-1776; www.coral-dreams.com). There are daily flights and a ferry from Panama City.

is an up-and-coming destination for off-the-beaten-track beaches and surf.

El Valle

POP 5700

Picturesque El Valle de Antón is nestled in the crater of a giant extinct volcano that blew its top three million years ago. It's a popular weekend getaway for urbanites seeking a little fresh air and scenery.

Sights & Activities

The hills around El Valle are excellent for walking and horseback riding; **Residencial El Valle** hires out both bikes and horses. The trails are well defined since they're frequently used by locals. **Piedra El Sapo** (Toad Stone), west of town near **La India Dormida** (a mountain ridge that resembles a sleeping indigenous girl), is said to have some of the most beautiful trails. Nearby, in the neighborhood of La Pintada, are some unusual ancient **petroglyphs** depicting humans, animals and other shapes.

El Valle Amphibian Conservation Center WILDLIFE RESERVE
(EVACC; www.fightforthefrogs.com/valle.html) The excellent El Valle Amphibian Conservation Center works to save amphibians from the deadly kitrid virus threatening amphibians around the world. You can see native Panamanian species including the golden frog. It's on the grounds of El Níspero zoo, 1km north of Av Central.

Square-Trunked Trees OUTDOORS
(Calle Club Campestre; suggested donation US$2) El Valle's famous *arboles cuadrados* (square trees), an unusual native species, are located in a thicket along a hiking trail behind the Hotel Campestre, east and north of the town center.

Pozos Termales HOT SPRINGS
(Thermal Baths; Calle los Pozos; admission US$2.25; ⏲8am-5pm) On the west side of town (follow the signs), Pozos Termales is the perfect place to soak the afternoon away. In a remote, forested area, the recently renovated complex features a series of pools with varying temperatures and supposed curative properties.

Chorro El Macho WATERFALL
(Manly Falls; admission US$3.60; ⏲dawn-dusk) The most famous waterfall in the El Valle area is the 85m-high Chorro El Macho, accessed via a short hike. The waterfall is 2km northwest of town, reachable by the bus to La Mesa (US$0.35). There's a lovely rainforest swimming hole just below the falls – bring your swimsuit.

Sleeping & Eating

La Casa de Juan GUESTHOUSE $
(☎6453-9775, 6807-1651; www.lacasadejuanpanama.blogspot.com; Calle Cocorron No 4; campsite per tent US$10, dm/s/d US$10/15/20; 📶) This bare-bones Sanford and Son setup brims with the clutter of ATV vehicles, outdoor weight-lifting equipment and wagon wheels. Though decrepit, the house is clean and Señor Juan is a social host who also offers guided walks.

Santa Librada GUESTHOUSE $
(☎6591-9135; Av Central; d US$20-35) Behind the popular restaurant, a passageway leads to three basic but clean doubles, adding another much-needed value option ideal for couples.

Residencial El Valle HOTEL $$
(☎983-6536; www.hotelresidencialelvalle.com; Av Central; d/tr/q US$55/66/83; P 📶) Visitors become loyalists, given the high level of service offered at this motel-style lodging. This long-standing hotel offers clean no-fuss rooms, a nice roof deck and bike rentals. Attached is a popular restaurant.

Buon Appetito PIZZERIA $
(☎6401-6301; mains US$6-9; ⏲6-9pm Thu, noon-9pm Fri & Sat, to 8pm Sun) Run by a couple from Milan, locals say this is the real deal, serving pastas, lasagna, focaccia and pizza, Italian-style. Watch for the daily special with dessert. The pizzeria is run out of the family home. There's no real street address; it's on the 'calle de la Panadería Cano.'

Restaurante Santa Librada PANAMANIAN $
(Av Central; mains US$3-5) Cheap and cheerful, the Santa serves hearty portions of Panamanian staples such as *bistec picado* (spicy shredded beef), as well as sandwiches and breakfast.

Shopping

Mercado de Artesanía MARKET
(Av Central; ⏲8am-6pm) A main attraction is the Sunday handicrafts market where Ngöbe-Buglé, Kuna, Emberá and Wounaan peoples sell quality baskets, woodwork, ceramics, soapstone carvings, flowers and plants (including orchids), and a variety of

fresh produce. A smaller version is open daily.

Getting There & Away

Buses leave Panama City hourly for El Valle (US$4.25, 2½ hours).

The center of town is small, but many of El Valle's attractions are a distance away. Taxis within town cost US$2 to US$3. Buses to La Mesa (US$0.50) pass by Chorro El Macho, and run along El Valle's main street.

Chitré

POP 41,600

The mellow, cowboy-esque capital of Herrera Province links visitors to the lovely Península de Azuero.

Sleeping & Eating

Hotel Santa Rita HOTEL $

(☎996-4610; cnr Calle Manuel Maria Correa & Av Herrera; d with/without air-con US$29/23; P ❄ 📶) One of the city's first hotels, Santa Rita has slid in status to simply economical. High-ceiling rooms feel musty around the edges and bathrooms smell scoured with bleach. Perks include some private balconies, very friendly attention and cable TV.

Hotel Rex HOTEL $$

(☎996-4310; Calle Melitón Martín s/n; d/tr US$55/72; P ❄ 📶) With a prime location on Parque Union and good dining downstairs, Rex is a solid midrange choice. Clean tiled rooms have brick walls, fresh towels and water thermoses. There's TV in the rooms, two terminals with internet and wi-fi available throughout.

Restaurante El Meson PANAMANIAN $$

(☎996-4310; Calle Melitón Martín s/n; mains US$4-12; ⏲7:15am-10pm; 📶) This place has a long list of offerings, from sandwiches to steak and seafood. The chicken tacos will satisfy small appetites. Full breakfasts include fried yucca or *tortillas de maíz* with eggs and coffee. The decor includes glass tables and tall wooden chairs.

Getting There & Away

Chitré is a regional bus transportation center. Buses arrive and depart from the **Terminal de Transportes de Herrera** (☎996-6426), 1km south of downtown. Buses go to Las Tablas (US$1.50, 40 minutes, every 20 minutes) and on to Pedasí (US$3.25, one hour, hourly) and other places on the peninsula. To get there, **Radio Taxi** (☎996-4442) charges US$1 to US$2. The 'Terminal' bus (US$0.35) leaves from the intersection of Calle Aminta Burgos de Amado and Av Herrera.

To get to David or Panama City from Chitré, take a bus to Divisa and then catch a *directo* (direct bus) to either city (US$8, four hours). Buses leave every half hour from the Delta station at the intersection of the Interamericana and the Carretera Nacional.

Pedasí

POP 1700

For years, this sleepy retreat bloomed only at festival times. But outsiders are discovering the big appeal of small-town life and wilderness beaches. Almost without warning, Pedasí has become the focus of an intensive push to develop the southwestern coastline, with lofty comparisons to Tuscany and California.

DON'T MISS

LOS FIESTAS DE AZUERO

Famous throughout Panama, the traditional festivals in Azuero were started by Spanish settlers. Few foreigners see this wild side of Panama. While you may sacrifice a day or two to a thumping head, these are parties you'll never forget. Some of the best:

Carnaval The four days before Ash Wednesday (February/March) in Chitré, Parita, Las Tablas and Villa de Los Santos.

Semana Santa March/April in Pesé and Villa de Los Santos.

Feria de Azuero Late April/early May in Villa de los Santos.

Fiesta de Corpus Christi Forty days after Easter in Villa de Los Santos.

Patronales de San Pablo & San Pedro June 29 in Pedasí and La Arena.

Feria de la Mejorana, Festival de la Virgen de las Mercedes September 23 to 27 in Guararé.

Sights & Activities

Pedasí serves as the gateway to the Azuero coastline; the closest beaches are **Playa El Toro** and **La Garita**, both reached by a 2km road (walk or take a taxi for US$6 to US$8).

Isla de Cañas WILDLIFE RESERVE
(admission US$10) Every year, thousands of olive ridley sea turtles nest at Isla de Cañas. There is no public transportation to the island but trips can be arranged through the ATP office.

Refugio de Vida Silvestre Isla Iguana PARK
(admission US$10) A 0.5-sq-km island wildlife refuge off the peninsula. Though ravaged by El Niño, the surviving coral is pretty spectacular and the water is shallow enough to snorkel in. Humpback whales also inhabit the surrounding waters from June to November. ATP has boat listings (around US$60 per group).

Pedasí Sports Club DIVING
(☎995-2894; www.pedasisportsclub.biz; Calle Central s/n) The PADI-certified Pedasí Sports Club offers two-tank dives (US$95 and up) to Isla Frailes and Isla Iguana. Snorkelers (US$65) can join dive trips to Iguana. Also on offer are a river kayak tour (US$65), sportfishing (US$180), turtle-watching (US$65) and horseback riding (US$65). Staff speak English.

Sleeping

Peak Hostel HOSTEL $
(☎6258-1875, 995-2776; peakhostel@gmail.com; dm/s/d/tr US$10/45/55/65; ❄) Pedasí's first hostel has a prime location on the plaza with a nice backyard garden. The attractive concrete slab rooms with murals could use some fixing (look for leaks), though some are fine. Showers have hot water. On the other hand, dorms are musty and overstocked with bunks.

Dim's Hostal GUESTHOUSE $
(☎995-2303; mirely@iname.com; Av Central s/n; s/d incl breakfast US$33/49; P ❄ @ 📶) Dim's Hostal has a family atmosphere and a coveted backyard patio, complete with breakfast tables, hammocks and a mango tree. Rooms vary in quality (some beds sag) but the owners are delightful and service-oriented. A highlight is the huge breakfast spread, where your friendly host cooks up eggs and *tortillas de maíz* made to order.

Hostal Doña María HOTEL $$
(☎995-2916; www.hostaldonamaria.com; Av Central s/n; s/d/tr incl breakfast US$40/55/70; P ❄ @) With double beds and a quiet atmosphere, this caring, family-run lodging is ideal for couples and has good tiled rooms with firm beds in plush quilted covers. The upstairs patio has soft sofas that peer out onto the street and a stack of magazines to peruse. Showers have hot water and there's an open-air kitchen for guest use. An upgrade to a room with cable TV or a queen-sized bed costs US$5.

Eating

★Fonda Mama Fefa PANAMANIAN $
(Calle Los Estudiantes s/n; set meal US$2.25; ⏲5am-2pm Mon-Sat) Matriarch of creole cooking, Mama Fefa usually runs out of lunch food by noon (though you can linger longer). Cheap and cheerful, these huge *platos típicos* include meat or fish, rice, salad and a drink. Devotees share the space at a few outdoor tables.

Bakery CAFE $
(☎995-2878; www.thebakerypedasi.com; Av Central s/n; mains US$4-7; ⏲7am-10pm) Known for exquisite breakfasts with homemade wheat or sourdough breads and organic coffee, this Israeli-run bakery does a brisk business. There's also bread-bowl soup and sandwiches with vegetarian options. The shady porch overlooks the main street.

Maudy's Café CAFE $
(Av Central s/n; mains US$3-6; ⏲8am-5pm Mon-Sat ; 📶) Pineapple mint or banana beet with carrot and OJ are refreshing zingers at this serious juice bar. You can also get fruit salad, baguette sandwiches or fruit sorbet at open-air tables flanked by resident parrots. It's closed September through October.

Pasta e Vino ITALIAN $
(☎6695-2689; mains US$5; ⏲6:30-10pm Tue-Sun) The essence of simplicity, this Italian-run restaurant has three chalkboard offerings nightly: pastas, a wine list and salad. Food is simple but authentic, like the pesto with black olives and fresh cheese. It's all about service (you are actually in Danilo and Elena's living room). The yellow house is three blocks past the plaza, on the road to Playa El Toro.

Information

ANAM (⏲8am-4pm Mon-Fri) The ANAM office in the south of town has extremely poor service (and no phone), but in theory it provides information about Isla Iguana and Isla de Cañas.

ATP (☎995-2339; ⏲9:30am-5:30pm) Helpful but slow, the ATP office lies one block past the main road in the north of town. They have a list of boat contacts for Isla de Cañas.

Banco Nacional de Panama (Av Central s/n) Has an ATM (one of two in town on Av Central) near the entrance to town.

Getting There & Away

Buses to Las Tablas leave every 45 minutes between 6am and 4pm (US$3, one hour) from next to the Centro Comercial. Buses to Playa Venado (US$2, 30 minutes) leave at 7am, noon and 2pm. Buses to Cañas (US$2, 45 minutes) leave at 7am.

The coastline is easily accessed by private vehicle or **taxi** (☎995-2275); the taxi stand sits on Av Central. Standard one-way fares include Playa El Toro US$3.50, Playa La Garita US$5 and Playa Venado US$24.

Playa Venao

Past Pedasí, the long, protected beach of Playa Venao is transforming from a wild beach to an outright destination. Surfers lay the first claim to its waters – waves are consistent and break in both directions.

A short skip to the waves, **La Choza** (www.playavenaohostel.com; campsite per person US$7, dm US$15, d with/without air-con US$55/40; ❄📶) is perfect for shoestringers. Somewhat cramped dorms have polished cement floors, fans, comfortable beds and hot showers. Some private rooms feature bunks and all rooms have shared bathrooms. There's a kitchen for guest use, a mini-market a short distance away and a swank open-air restaurant nearby on the beach.

On the jungle side of the main access road, **Eco Venao** (☎832-0530; www.venao.com; campsite per person US$5.50, dm/d with shared bathroom US$11/28, 2-person cabin US$44, 6-person house US$275; P❄📶🏊) offers a cool mountain ambience and good prices. The eight-person dorm (no reservations accepted) is rustic but comfy, with mosquito nets, kitchen and shady porch ringed with hammocks.

The modern and colonial-style guesthouses are simply lovely. You can also rent horses (US$10), surfboards (US$15 per day), kayaks (US$25 per day) and do beachfront yoga. 'Eco' means that trash separation and recycling are practiced, and there's minimal infrastructure, with small footpaths that lead to the beach.

There's a decent onsite restaurant with backpacker specials. Post-surfing you can hike 15 minutes to a waterfall.

The Playa Venao turnoff is 33km by road southwest of Pedasí. The Cañas–Las Tablas bus (US$2) passes between 8am and 9am and makes the return journey in the evening. Confirm exact times with your hotel. You can also take a taxi from Pedasí (US$30).

OFF THE BEATEN TRACK

WESTERN AZUERO

Most visitors access the Azuero via Chitre, but a few hours south of Santiago, the west coast of the peninsula is an amazing off-the-beaten-path attraction.

Between December and February, three species of turtles hatch on the beaches of Malena. To join community volunteers working toward their preservation, contact **Malena Beach Conservation Association** (Asociación Conservacionista de Playa Malena; www.playamalena.org; tours per person from US$10, lodging per person incl breakfast US$10). Basic Spanish is necessary. The organization also offers horseback riding, boat tours and nature walks.

In nearby Palmilla, **Hotel Heliconia** (Tanager Tourism; ☎6676-0220; http://hotelheliconia-panama.com; tented rancho s/d US$18/30, s/d incl breakfast US$50/75; ❄) provides luxury camping mid-December through mid-May, meals and smart rooms. The excellent retreat was thoughtfully crafted by Dutch biologists who also offer recommended area tours. They also work with the local community on sustainable tourism projects. From Santiago, coaster buses leave hourly to Mariato, which then go on to Palmilla (US$4, 1½ hours)..

Santa Catalina

The secret about one of Central America's top surf spots is out. The right and left beach breaks of Santa Catalina are comparable to Oahu's Sunset Beach on a good day. The fishing village has a laid-back feel, with a handful of thatched restaurants and little else for nightlife.

Since the recent paving of the access road, foreign investment has been shoring up. Though cell-phone service was recently added, there are still no banks and very few places take credit cards. Make sure you arrive with cash. For general information and surf forecasts, check out www.santacatalinabeach.com.

Activities

The best waves are generally from December to April, though there's surf here year-round. Unlike the Caribbean, the Pacific offers fairly consistent sets, though a good swell will really give a boost to the surfing here. Be advised that many of the breaks in the area are over rocks, and can easily snap your board if you don't know what you're doing. Most of the accommodations in town rent boards and offer surfing lessons.

★Panama Dive Center DIVING
(☎6665-7879; www.panamadivecenter.com; ⏲7am-7pm) A friendly and professional operation, this PADI-certified dive center offers snorkeling (US$60), all-day two-tank dive trips (US$130) and courses. It's on the main road toward the beach.

Santa Catalina Surf Shop SURFING
(☎6963-0831; www.santacatalinasurfshop.com; ⏲8am-3pm) Run by a friendly Southern California couple, this surf shop specializes in getting good gear to those loathe to travel with extra baggage. Rents, buys and sells quality boards and accessories. Located on the main road. Also open by appointment.

Surf & Shake SURFING
(www.surfandshake.com; ⏲9am-6pm) On the road to the beach, just 150m in from the main street, Surf & Shake rents boards and sells leashes, boards and surf wear. Run by a duo of German surfers, it's also a good spot for surf info in English and German. If it's after hours you can try knocking.

Sleeping

If you want to be on the beach, follow the road out of town – a number of signed turnoffs advertise accommodations. Most are a 1km walk to the center on mostly flat but unshaded terrain.

Cabañas Rolo CABIN $
(☎6494-3916; www.rolocabins.net; dm US$11, d with/without bathroom US$55/20, tr with/without bathroom $65/30; P) These rustic cabins are a favorite of baby-faced surfers from around the world. Each has one to three good beds, a fan, and a shared cold-water bathroom that sees much traffic. Truckstop-quality coffee is free in the morning and guests have use of an open-air kitchen. The owner Rolo Ortega speaks Spanish and English, offers surf lessons and can arrange surf trips to Isla Cébaco (per group US$200).

Blue Zone HOSTEL $
(☎6458-5305; www.bluezonepanama.com; campsite per tent US$5, dm/s/d US$10/18/20; P @) This attractive adobe hostel has a cluster of dark cement rooms arranged around circular spaces. There's also a campsite and long-term rates. There's hot showers, free coffee and homemade goodies too.

Surfer's Paradise HOSTEL $
(☎6709-1037; surfcatalina@hotmail.com; campsite per person US$8, dm US$13, s/d/tr US$36/48/55; P ❄) You could watch the tubes roll in all day at this hilltop campground with a box seat to the waves. While the location is prime, the rooms are just long, adequate cement boxes with fans and single beds. There is also a thatched restaurant with views. Guests can take surf classes and rent boards. Air-con is extra.

★Hibiscus Garden LODGE $
(☎6615-6097; www.hibiscusgarden.com; Playa La Gartero; dm US$10, s with/without bathroom US$25/18, d with/without bathroom US$40/30; P ❄ @ 📶) On Playa La Gartero (10km before Santa Catalina), these relaxed German-run lodgings fuse modern and rustic, with stylish installations and minimal fuss. There's playful mosaics throughout. Rooms have recycled driftwood beds and private hammock terraces. An open-air dorm catches the breeze and views. Unlike the beaches of Santa Catalina, this gulf beach is calm, secluded and very swimmable.

For some, the distance from town is a drawback, though a town shuttle (round-trip US$5) is offered. You won't get bored: horseback riding (three-hour trip US$20), wakeboarding, surf lessons and fishing trips are offered. Children under 14 years stay free. The restaurant (mains US$6.50 to US$15) serves wonderful salads, sandwiches on homemade German bread and a daily special, or you can use the community kitchen.

La Buena Vida CABIN $$
(☎6572-0664; www.labuenavida.biz; cabins from US$66; P ❄ 📶) Three bright cabins feature sea-themed mosaics and colorful tiles, original designs crafted by the American couple that has welded, tiled and painted the place into eclectic perfection. The owners have ironed out every little detail here, from local tips and recommendations to quality lunchboxes for tours. La Buena Vida composts and recycles, and offers yoga. Located on the main street.

Oasis Surf Camp CABIN $$
(☎6588-7077; www.oasissurfcamp.com; campsite per person US$10, d with fan/air-con US$40/50, ste US$150; P ❄ 📶) This Italian-run surf camp has long been a local staple and its beachfront setting is one of the best. Cabins overlooking the black-sand beach have simple but adequate facilities including cold-water showers and ample hammocks. Meals are served at the open-air restaurant. The camp also rents a variety of surf boards. It's 2km from Santa Catalina's main road, on Playa Estero near the mouth of the river.

Eating

La Panaderia BAKERY $
(The Bakery; ☎6549-7464; ⏲6:30am-4pm) On the main street, this tiny bakery run by a French and Spanish couple is a local institution. Come before 9:30am, as bread sells out, and breakfasts (think omelets and pancakes) are slow to get served. There's also great coffee, lunchboxes to go, cakes and delectable muffins.

Pizzeria Jamming PIZZERIA $
(pizzas US$5-8; ⏲from 6:30pm) A much-loved local institution on the road to the beach-facing hotels. Delicious thin-crust pizzas are made from fresh ingredients, and the open-air *rancho* (small house) is Santa Catalina's liveliest gathering spot.

La Buena Vida AMERICAN $
(www.labuenavida.biz; mains from US$5; ⏲6am-2pm) Great bets are the breakfast burritos or the Greek scrambles with feta, olives, tomatoes and eggs in this funky tiled cafe perched above the main street. There are also fresh fruit drinks and a lunchtime selection of salads, tacos and sandwiches on homemade bread.

Los Pibes ARGENTINE $
(mains US$5-12; ⏲6:30-10pm Thu-Tue) This good-vibe Argentine eatery is an original – from its menus of nachos, steak and small Argentine-style empanadas to its margs and mojitos drenched in crushed ice. Surfers can gorge on mammoth burgers topped with bacon or eggs. It's 1km from town.

Getting There & Away

To reach Santa Catalina from Panama City, first take a bus to Santiago (see p656), then another to Soná where buses leave for Santa Catalina (US$4.65, 1½ hours) at 5am, 11am, 2pm and 4:30pm. Taxis also go from Soná to Santa Catalina (from US$60). Direct Panama City–Soná buses run every two hours.

From Santa Catalina, three buses serve Soná daily, leaving at 7am, 8:20am and 1:15pm. In Santa Catalina, the bus stops at the beach road intersection. If you're staying outside of the center, most lodgings are a 1km walk on mostly

WORTH A TRIP

ISLA DE COIBA

With the exception of the Galápagos and Isla de Coco, few Latin destinations are as exotic (and difficult to access) as this island. It's part of the marine park Parque Nacional Coiba, just 20km offshore from the Golfo de Chiriquí.

Coiba is a veritable lost world of pristine ecosystems and unique fauna. Left alone for the past century while it hosted a notorious penal colony on its shores, Coiba offers intrepid travelers the chance to paddle the Pacific, hike through primary rainforest, snorkel and dive in a marine park and come face to face with increasingly rare wildlife.

With virtually no tourist infrastructure in place, a tour is key. For tours that include hiking and snorkeling, contact recommended local guide **Javier Elizondo** (☎6544-1806; www.birdcoiba.com; full day per person US$110-250). Prices decrease with the number of participants, so it's worth getting a group together.

flat terrain. Note that there are only taxis in town when someone is arriving from Soná.

To get to the ocean-side surf hotels from the bus terminal, take the dirt road on the left side of the road into Santa Catalina just before the road ends. Each hotel has its own sign marking the turnoff.

Santa Fé

In the shadow of the continental divide, this tiny mountain town is a perfect destination for independent-minded hikers and bird-watchers looking to escape the crowds.

A number of lovely waterfalls, empty mountain streams and accessible swimming spots are all within walking distance from town. The swimming hole at **Río Bulava** is a 20-minute walk. Head along the right branch of the fork at the southern edge of town, take the second right, and you'll soon reach several spots that make for a nice dip. The refreshing **Cascada de Bermejo** is an excellent half-day hike – you can get directions at your lodgings.

To see an organic family farm up close, visit **Chong & María** (☎6525-4832; half-day tour per person US$5), hospitable *campesino* hosts happy to show you around their very small-scale operation. Make sure you book ahead. For horseback rides and waterfall hikes, **Aventuras Cesamo** (☎6972-0571, 954-0807; www.aventurascesamo.blogspot.com) offers outings with a reputable local guide.

A sweet base camp, **Hostal La Qhia** (☎954-0903, 6592-5589; www.panamamountainhouse.com; dm US$11, d & tr with/without bathroom US$39/33; P) offers an oasis of lovely gardens and comfortable beds. It's also an excellent source of information, offering maps and detailed instructions for area hikes and river trips. Another good option is **Hotel Anachoreo** (☎6053-4310; www.anachoreo.com; s/d/tr/q incl breakfast US$33/44/56/68), a guesthouse with panoramic views. With just a few tables, the onsite restaurant **Anachoreo** (☎6911-4848; mains US$7-10; ⏲5-9pm Wed-Sun) serves gorgeous steamed fish wrapped in banana leaves, heaped salads from the organic backyard garden and delicacies from the chef's native Cambodia.

Argentine-run **La Matera** (☎6053-4310; Calle Principal; pizza US$9; ⏲5-8:30pm Thu & Fri, 11am-8:30pm Sat & Sun; 📶) cooks up thin-crust pizzas in a very mod cafe with table games and wine. For simple fare, **Restaurante de la Terminal** (Bus Terminal; mains US$3; ⏲11am-7:30pm) does good *comida típica* (regional specialties) at the bus terminal.

Buses from Santiago to Santa Fé (US$2.90, 1½ hours) depart every 30 minutes from 5am to 6pm. From Santiago you can catch frequent buses to David (US$9, three hours) and Panama City (US$9.50, four hours).

CHIRIQUÍ PROVINCE

Chiricanos claim to have it all and there's more than an element of truth to it: they have Panama's tallest mountains, longest rivers and most fertile valleys. There are spectacular highland rainforests as well as the country's most productive agricultural and cattle-ranching regions. Not surprisingly, many *chiricanos* often dream about creating an independent República de Chiriquí.

Bordering Costa Rica to the west, Chiriquí is often the first province in Panama encountered by overland travelers. It also serves as a suitable introduction to the beauty of Panama. Although the mist-covered mountains near Boquete are slowly being colonized by waves of North American and European retirees, the town serves as a good base for exploring the flanks of towering Volcán Barú, Panama's only volcano and its highest point (3475m). The region is also home to the Parque Internacional La Amistad, a bi-national park shared by Costa Rica and Panama, with lush rainforests unfettered by tourist crowds.

David

POP 104,500

Panama's second-largest city is the capital of Chiriquí Province and a major agricultural center. Though David has a large-town feel, it's rapidly growing in terms of wealth and importance as foreign capital arrives via international retirees moving in. But the trend has somewhat stabilized.

For most travelers, David serves as an important transportation hub for those heading to or from Costa Rica, the Chiriquí highlands, Golfo de Chiriquí, Panama City and Bocas del Toro. Although the city has few attractions in its own right, David is a pleasant enough place to stay, and there's no shortage of interesting things to see and do in the surrounding area. From here, it is possible to do day trips that involve white-water rafting on the Río Chiriquí or the Río Chiriquí Viejo;

David

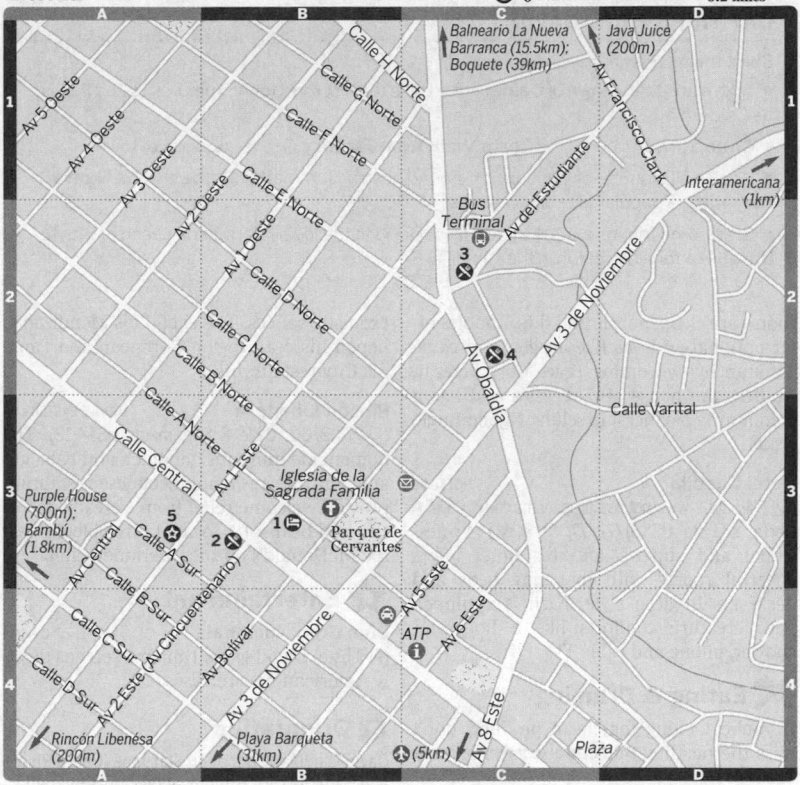

the tours originate in Boquete but will pick up passengers in David (see p673).

Festivals & Events

Feria de San José de David FESTIVAL

This big international fair is held for 10 days each March; contact the ATP tourist office for exact dates, as they vary from year to year.

Sleeping

Bambú HOSTEL $

(☎730-2961; www.bambuhostel.com; Calle de la Virgencita, San Mateo Abajo; dm US$10-12, d with/without bathroom US$30/25; P ❄ 📶 🏊) This chill little house is run by a friendly Cantonese-speaking NYC musician. There's a regular dorm and Darién-style dorm (a thatched hut on stilts) with mosquito nets out back. Includes electric hot-water showers in so-so bathrooms. There's cable TV and air-con in the double rooms. The star features are the sprawling garden with swimming pool, bar (open until 11pm) and the requisite hammocks.

David

Sleeping
1 Hotel Castilla B3

Eating
2 Casa Vegetariana B3
3 Cuatro C2
4 Mercado C2

Entertainment
5 Cine Gran Nacional A3

Purple House HOSTEL $

(☎774-4059; www.purplehousehostel.com; cnr Calle C Sur & Av 6 Oeste; dm US$8, d with/without bathroom US$27/25; P ❄ @ 📶) Guests have use of a communal kitchen, cable TV, DVD rentals and a splash patio for cooling off. Tiled bunk

WORTH A TRIP

DAY TRIPS FROM DAVID

Spice things up with these excursions:

- Take a bus to the town of **Caldera**, and hike the dirt road for 45 minutes to Los Pozos de Caldera.
- Go on a private tour of the **Carta Vieja Rum Factory** on the outskirts of town.
- Hop on a Boquete- or Concepción-bound bus and jump off at **Balneario La Nueva Barranca**, a popular local swimming spot.
- Grab some friends and take a taxi from David to the lovely dark-sand beach of **Playa Barqueta** for a day of fun in the sun.

rooms are clean, purple and tidy. Doubles offer optional add-ons like air-con and cable TV. Run by welcoming Peace Corp veteran Andrea, the house also recycles and has a community partnership selling Ngöbe-Buglé crafts.

Hotel Castilla HOTEL **$$**
(☎774-5260; www.hotelcastillapanama.com; Calle A Norte; s/d/ste US$61/72/77; P ❄ @) Professional and super-clean, this hotel offers cheerful rooms with matching beds and desk sets in deco style. Each is equipped with creature comforts like a hot-water shower, phone and cable TV.

Eating & Drinking

If you're looking for cheap produce, don't miss the bustling **mercado** (cnr Avs Bolívar & Obaldía).

Casa Vegetariana CAFETERIA **$**
(Av 2 Este; meals US$2; ⏲7am-4pm; ✎) This cheerful Chinese-style mini-cafeteria packs in the crowds for inexpensive plates of sautéed greens, eggplant, fried rice and beans served on no-nonsense metal plates.

Java Juice CAFE **$**
(Interamericana; mains US$2.50-6; ✎) Iced coffee, fresh fruit smoothies, healthy salads and grilled burgers are the fare at this charming outdoor cafe northeast of the bus terminal.

★Cuatro PANAMANIAN **$$**
(☎730-5638; cnr Avs Obaldía & del Estudiante; mains US$12-16; ⏲noon-3pm & 6:30-10:30pm Mon-Sat) Only one spot does great local food in David, with sophistication and even happy surprises. Classic Panamanian basics – like cassava, tamales and new corn – get gourmet treatment. Start with hot corn blinis with red onion marmalade. Honey-glazed pork ribs are tender and fish come in exquisite sauces. The chef, Luis Mendizábal, honed his craft in top European and Panama City restaurants.

Rincón Libenésa MIDDLE EASTERN **$$**
(☎774-2700; Calle F Sur; mains US$4-12) The homemade hummus, tabouleh and baba ghanooj at this authentic Lebanese restaurant provide welcome relief from a steady diet of rice and beans. It's located three blocks past the McDonald's off the Interamericana.

Entertainment

Cine Gran Nacional CINEMA
(Av 1 Este) David's small cinema screens mostly American new releases.

Orientation

David is halfway between San José (Costa Rica) and Panama City – about seven hours by road from either place. The Interamericana does not enter the town, but skirts around its northern and western sides. The city's heart is its fine central plaza, the Parque de Cervantes, about 1.5km southwest of the highway.

Information

ANAM (☎775-7840; fax 774-6671; ⏲8am-4pm Mon-Fri) Provides tourist information and gives permits to camp in the national parks. It's near the airport.

ATP (☎775-2839; Calle Central; ⏲8:30am-4:30pm Mon-Fri) Provides information on Chiriquí Province.

Chiriquí Hospital (☎777-8814; cnr Calle Central & Av 3 Oeste) One of the best hospitals in the country.

HSBC (Av Central) With branches on Calle C Norte near the park and on Av Obaldía north of the bus station.

Post Office (Calle C Norte; ⏲7am-6pm Mon-Fri, to 4:30pm Sat)

Getting There & Away

AIR

David's airport, the **Aeropuerto Enrique Malek** (☎721-1072), is about 5km from town. There are no buses to the airport; take a taxi (US$5) or a shared taxi (US$2).

Air Panama (☎721-0841; www.flyairpanama.com) Has multiple flights daily from Panama City (US$117, 45 minutes).

BUS

The David **bus station** (Av del Estudiante) is about 600m northeast of the central plaza. Most buses begin service by 7am. See table below for departure information.

For Guadalupe, passengers can get on a Cerro Punta bus, which continues on; passengers for Volcán also take the Cerro Punta bus, but will need to get off earlier. For Las Lajas, continue to the beach via taxi (US$6).

Tracopa (☎775-0585; www.tracopacr.com) Direct buses between David and San José, Costa Rica (US$21, eight hours), daily at 8:30am and 12pm from the David bus station.

Golfo de Chiriquí

The undisputed gem of the Chiriquí lowlands is **Parque Nacional Marino Golfo de Chiriquí**, a national marine park with an area of 147 sq km protecting 25 islands, 19 coral reefs and abundant wildlife. The marine park also includes the 30-sq-km **Isla Boca Brava** (accessed via mainland Boca Chica), a lovely little island crisscrossed with hiking trails and home to monkeys, nesting sea turtles and 280 recorded bird species. Whether you want to lie on the beach, snorkel clear waters or go wildlife-watching under the rainforest canopy, there's something for everyone at this off-the-beaten-path destination.

Ideal for mingling with other travelers, **Hotel Boca Brava** (☎851-0017; www.hotelbocabrava.com; Isla Boca Brava; hammock/dm US$8/11, d with/without bathroom US$50/39, ste US$94; ❄) offers rooms from rustic to deluxe. Budget travelers might pick the hammock room over the too-warm dorm. Doubles are snug; the best deal is the 'hostel' option with shared bathroom. The hotel can arrange excursions like snorkeling, whale-watching or just lounging on an uninhabited island. Only some rooms have air-con. The attached **Restaurante Bar Boca Brava** (meals from US$7) occupies a cool space on an overhanging deck with expansive water views. It's the perfect setting for a sunset cocktail like a Brava Colada. Reasonably priced meals range from fresh fish to burgers.

To reach Boca Chica, first take a David bus (US$2) to the Horconcitos turnoff, located 39km east. You can also take any passing bus heading from David to Panama City and ask the driver to stop at the Horconcitos turnoff.

From the turnoff, take a bus (US$3, 50 minutes) that leaves four times daily for Boca Chica, or a taxi (US$20). For transportation hours, call **Jimi** (☎6857-2094). At the Boca Chica dock, hire a water taxi (per person US$3) to take you 200m to the Boca Brava island dock at Restaurante Boca Brava.

BUSES FROM DAVID

DESTINATION	COST (US$)	DURATION	FREQUENCY (DAILY)
Boquete	1.75	1hr	every 20min until 9:30pm
Caldera	2.40	45min	hourly until 7:30pm
Cerro Punta	3.50	2¼hr	every 20min until 8pm
Changuinola	9.70	4½hr	hourly until 6:30pm
Guadalupe	3.50	2½hr	every 20min until 8pm
Horconcitos	2	45min	11am & 5pm
Las Lajas	5	1½hr	four daily
Panama City	15-18	7-8hr	every 45min, 6:45am-8pm
Paso Canoas	2.10	1½hr	every 10min until 9:30pm
Puerto Armuelles	3	2½hr	every 15min until 9pm
Río Sereno	5.10	2½hr	every 30min until 5pm
Santiago	9	3hr	hourly until 9pm
Volcán	3	1½hr	every 20min until 8pm

Punta Burica

This lush peninsula jutting into the Pacific is a lovely spot for absorbing the beauty of both the rainforest and the coastline.

A very remote and rustic getaway, **Mono Feliz** (☎6595-0388; monofeliz@gmail.com; campsite/cabin per person US$8/25; 3 meals US$25; P) offers cabins with mosquito nets, a freshwater pool frequented by monkeys and an outdoor kitchen for guest use. With your own gear you can camp on the beach and have access to the pool and bathrooms. Activities include nature walks (an excursion to Isla Burica at low tide is a highlight), fishing, surfing, bird-watching and horseback riding. English is spoken.

To arrive, start with an early bus from David to Puerto Armuelles (US$3, 2½ hours). From the Puerto Armuelles *mercado municipal* take a truck to Bella Vista. From here, it's a one-hour downhill walk. Or get off at El Medio, the last coastal stop, from where it's an hour's walk along the beach. Mono Feliz is directly in front of Isla Burica. For private transportation from Puerto Armuelles, contact Spanish-speaking **Tonio** (☎6595-0388; per person one way US$10) or **Eric** (☎6652-9930; US$35), who runs boat shuttles from the marina, weather permitting. With a 4WD, there is dry season (mid-December to mid-April) access.

From Puerto Armuelles keep heading south along the coast toward Costa Rica. Go through the Petroterminal and then veer directly onto the beach (attempt only at low tide). Continue up to a dirt road marked with a 'Mono Feliz' sign, about 30 minutes on.

Playa Las Lajas

With one of the longest beaches of Central America, the 20km palm-fringed Playa Las Lajas seems to stretch forever. Lodgings are popping up, improving options for travelers and making the beach an overnight destination for more visitors. Crowds gather on the weekends, but during the week you can have serious stretches of sand all to yourself.

Run by a young Italian couple, **Casa Laguna B&B** (☎6896-0882; www.casalagunapanama.com; d with/without bathroom incl breakfast US$100/70;) is a popular option for couples. Rooms are ample and cool. There's also open-air ranchos around the property for relaxing and it's a three-minute walk to the beach. Immense breakfasts include yogurt, fruit and pancakes, and other meals are available upon request. The pool is small and above ground.

With open-air *ranchos* and attractive earthy constructions, the Italian-run **La Spiaza** (☎6620-6431; www.laspiazapanama.com; dm US$8, d US$20-30;) is the best bargain lodging/pizzeria at the beach. It sits across the road from the beach in a shadeless compound.

To reach Las Lajas, take any bus from David (US$2.70, 1½ hours) that passes the Las Lajas turnoff on the Interamericana. At the turnoff, take a taxi (US$6) to where the road reaches the sea.

Boquete

POP 6000

The mountain town of Boquete, the Napa Valley of coffee, is known throughout Panama for its cool, fresh climate and pristine natural setting. Flowers, coffee, vegetables and citrus fruits flourish in Boquete's rich soil, and the friendliness of the locals seems to rub off on everyone who passes through.

Boquete was very much intent on remaining a small town, but was faced with a change beyond anyone's control – baby boomers started getting old. When the American Association for Retired Persons's *Modern Maturity* magazine named Boquete one of the four top places in the world to retire, foreign retirees started snatching up mountain plots. Today, gated communities dot the hillsides and the face of Boquete is slowly being transformed.

For travelers, Boquete is one of the country's top destinations. Outdoor lovers can hike, climb, raft or go on a canopy tour. You can also visit coffee farms, soak in hot springs and study Spanish here. And there's nothing quite like starting your day with a glass of freshly squeezed OJ, or perking up with a cup of locally grown coffee.

Sights

Mi Jardín es Su Jardín GARDENS

(dawn-dusk) FREE A magnificent garden surrounding a luxurious private estate. The residence is off-limits to the public, but you are free to stroll around.

El Explorador GARDENS

(☎775-2643; Calle Jaramillo Alto; adult/child US$5/2; 10am-6pm daily mid-Dec–mid-Apr, Sat & Sun mid-Apr–mid-Dec) A private garden in a hilly area 45 minutes' walk from the town center. It's like something out of *Alice in Wonderland,* with no shortage of quirky eye-catching displays.

Activities

Hiking

With its breathtaking vistas of mist-covered hills and nearby forests, Boquete is one of the most idyllic regions for hiking and walking. Several good paved roads lead out of town into the surrounding hills, passing coffee plantations, fields and farms, gardens and virgin forest.

Although some will be content with picturesque strolls along the river, the more ambitious can climb **Volcán Barú**, Panama's highest point and only volcano. There are several entrances to the park, but the trail with easiest access to the summit starts near Boquete.

You can also access the Sendero Los Quetzales (p677) from Boquete; the trail is uphill from here though – you'll have an easier time if you start hiking from Cerro Punta.

A pleasant day hike is along the **Sendero El Pianista** (Pianist Trail), which winds through dairy land and into humid cloud forest. To access the trailhead, take the first right fork out of Boquete (going north) and cross over two bridges. Immediately before the third bridge, about 4km out of town, a track leads off to the left between a couple of buildings. You need to wade across a small river after 200m, but then it's a steady, leisurely incline for 2km before you start to climb a steeper, narrow path. The path winds deep into the forest, and you can turn back at any time.

White-Water Rafting

Excellent white-water rafting is within a two-hour drive of Boquete. Ríos Chiriquí and Chiriquí Viejo both flow from the fertile hills of Volcán Barú. At some places, waterfalls can be seen, and both pass through narrow canyons with awesome, sheer rock walls.

The Chiriquí is most often run from May to December, while the Chiriquí Viejo is run the rest of the year; the rides tend to last four and five hours, respectively. Depending on the skill level of your party, you can tackle thrilling Class III and Class IV rapids or some seriously scary Class V ones.

Boquete Outdoor Adventures ADVENTURE SPORTS
(☎720-2284; www.boqueteoutdooradventures.com; Av Central, Plaza Los Establos) This reliable outfitter offers quality rafting trips (US$90) and tailored vacations ideal for families. Its sportfishing adventures on the Golfo de Chiriquí are value-priced (US$600 to US$800 for four passengers). Guides are bilingual and the company uses local service providers.

Hot Springs

Los Pozos de Caldera HOT SPRINGS
(admission US$1; ⏲dawn-dusk) An undeveloped hot spring rumored to have health-giving properties. Arrange a tour (US$25) which includes a petroglyph site or take a taxi (US$40 round-trip) with the caveat that you will have to walk the last part of a very rough dirt road for one hour one-way. A Boquete bus goes to Caldera (US$1.50) every two hours.

Tours

Cafe de la Luna TOUR
(☎6677-7748; per person US$15-30) If you are looking to learn about small-scale organic coffee production, check out this extended tour that includes roasting and tasting. The tour takes 1½ to 2½ hours and cost depends on the number of participants.

Café Ruíz TOUR
(☎720-1392; www.caferuiz.com; 3-hour tour US$30; ⏲9am Mon-Sat) Panama's most famous coffee-grower makes the award-winning Gesha coffee. Tours start at 9am daily except Sundays and holidays; advance reservations are required. Located on the main road about 600m north of the town center.

Kotowa Coffee Estate TOUR
(☎720-3852) A gourmet grower offering the most comprehensive coffee-estate tour in the area. The estate requests 24 hours' notice prior to your visit. You can also have a cup at an outlet in the ATP information center.

Boquete Tree Trek ADVENTURE TOUR
(☎720-1635, 6450-2599; www.aventurist.com; Av Central, Plaza Los Establos; canopy tour US$65; ⏲7:30am-1pm & 2-4:30pm) Travelers love the three-hour canopy tour with 12 zip lines, a rappel and a Tarzan swing in secondary forest. The lines pick up some serious speed, so you might want to consider going a little heavy on the handbrake. The company sells other tours and also offers lovely

Boquete

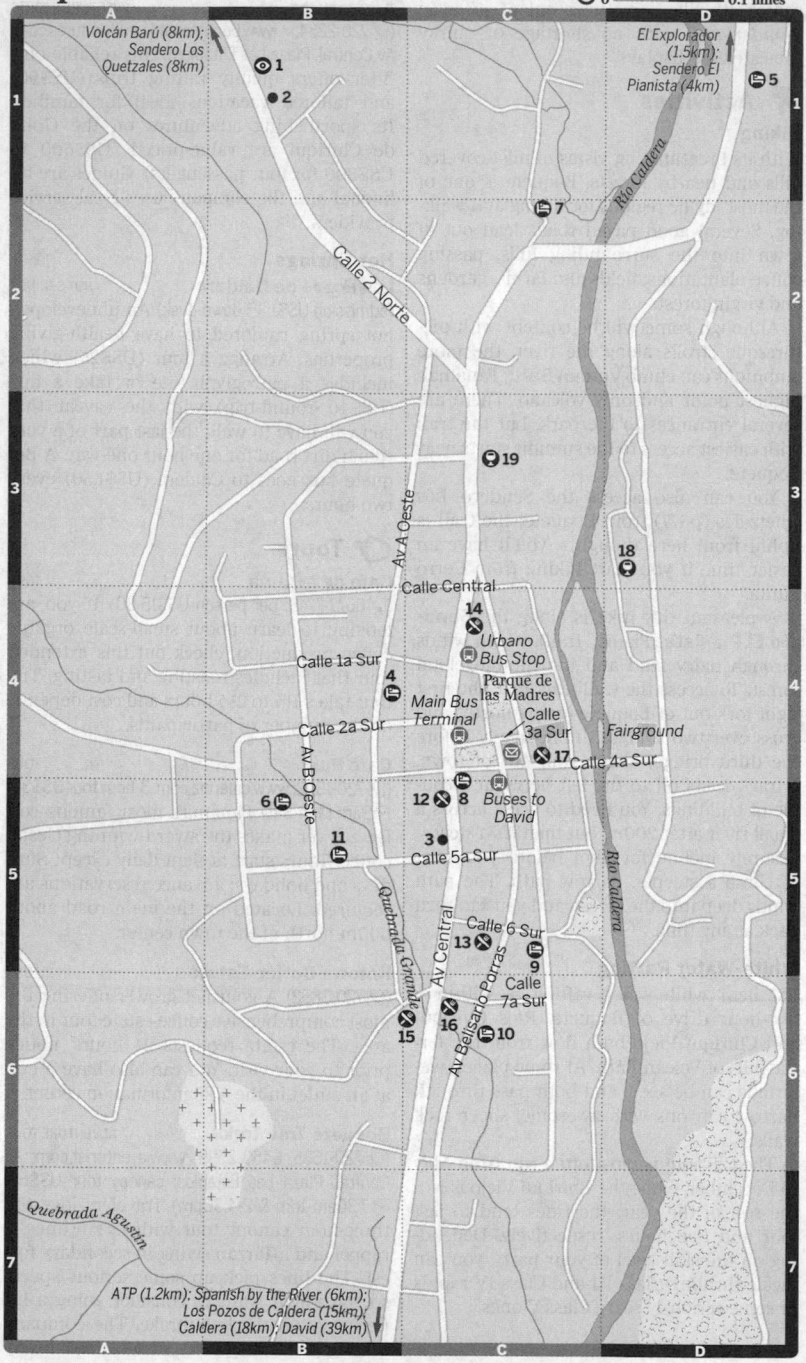
0 200 m
0 0.1 miles
A
B
C
D
1
2
3
4
5
6
7
Volcán Barú (8km); Sendero Los Quetzales (8km)
El Explorador (1.5km); Sendero El Pianista (4km)
Río Caldera
Calle 2 Norte
Av A Oeste
Calle Central
Calle 1a Sur
Calle 2a Sur
Av B Oeste
Urbano Bus Stop
Parque de las Madres
Main Bus Terminal
Calle 3a Sur
Fairground
Calle 4a Sur
Buses to David
Calle 5a Sur
Quebrada Grande
Av Central
Calle 6 Sur
Av Belisario Porras
Calle 7a Sur
Quebrada Agustín
ATP (1.2km); Spanish by the River (6km); Los Pozos de Caldera (15km); Caldera (18km); David (39km)

Boquete

Sights
1 Mi Jardín es Su Jardín B1

Activities, Courses & Tours
Boquete Outdoor Adventures ..... (see 3)
Boquete Tree Trek ..... (see 3)
2 Café Ruíz B1
3 Habla Ya Language Center C5

Sleeping
4 Hostal Nomba B4
5 Hotel Ladera D1
6 Isla Verde B5
7 La Casa de La Abuela C2
8 Mamallena C5
9 Pensión Marilós C5
10 Pensión Topas C6
11 Refugio del Río B5

Eating
12 Big Daddy's Grill C5
13 Café de Encuentro C5
14 El Sabrosón C4
15 Mike's Global Grill C6
16 Sugar & Spice C6
17 Supermercado Romero C4

Drinking & Nightlife
18 La Cabaña D3
19 Zanzibar C3

accommodations in rural cabins, with transportation from the center.

Courses

Both of the following language schools can arrange tours and hook up travelers with homestays and volunteer opportunities in the area.

Habla Ya Language Center LANGUAGE COURSE
(☎720-1294; www.hablayapanama.com; Av Central, Plaza Los Establos; ⏲8am-6pm Mon-Fri, 9am-noon Sat) Habla Ya Language Center offers both group and private lessons. A week of group lessons starts at US$175.

Spanish by the River LANGUAGE COURSE
(☎720-3456; www.spanishatlocations.com) The sister school to the popular Spanish school in Bocas del Toro is located 5km south of Boquete near the turnoff to Palmira. Standard/intensive lessons are US$185/275 for a one-week course. Discounts come with longer stays.

Festivals & Events

Feria de las Flores y del Café EVENT
(Flower & Coffee Fair) The town's annual fair, the Feria is held for 10 days each January. While there's coffee in the name, it's strangely missing from exhibits, though you will find plenty of rum and children's carnival rides.

Feria de Las Orquídeas EVENT
(Orchid Fair) Showing over 150 varieties, the orchid fair is held every April in Boquete. It's not all flowers – sundown brings rock concerts and dancing. Contact ATP for exact dates.

Sleeping

Because of the cool climate, all the places to stay in Boquete have hot showers.

Refugio del Río HOSTEL $
(☎720-2088; www.refugiodelrio.com; Av B Oeste; dm US$11, d with/without bathroom US$33/28, cabin US$35; P @) With the comfy feel of a large, well-kept home, this budget stop features a huge guest kitchen and good location. Sprawling rooms are pleasant and well furnished, though could be tidier. The dormitory features a row of single beds with snug covers but saggy mattresses. Reserve ahead for the cool tree house cabin overlooking the babbling river out back.

Mamallena HOSTEL $
(☎730-8342; www.mamallenaboquete.com; Av Central; dm US$11, d with/without bathroom US$28/25, tr with/without bathroom US$37/33, q US$47; P) On the plaza, this ex-boarding house is backpacker central, complete with kitchen, coin-op laundry and free pancake breakfasts. For its huge capacity it seems rather cozy. Four-bed dorms boast orthopedic mattresses. Smokers retreat to the sheltered patio area. Service-oriented, the hostel runs tours and shuttles (to Bocas and Volcán) through an onsite agency, and offers local information.

Pensión Topas GUESTHOUSE $
(☎720-1005; www.coffeeadventures.net/topas.html; Av Belisario Porras; s/d US$25/35; P) Built around a small organic garden and pool, this German-run lodging features Tintin murals and tidy rooms. A shady outdoor patio provides ample shared space and perks include a slackline, foosball and volleyball. Hosts can

get unexpectedly boisterous, leading guests to give it mixed reviews.

Hostal Nomba HOSTEL $
(☎720-2864, 6497-5672; www.nombapanama.com; Av A Oeste; dm/d without bathroom US$10/24; P) This pared-down chill-out hostel is fairly sterile but good for tight budgets (there's a slight discount for smaller rooms). An onsite bar, darts and foosball keeps it lively. The in-house outfitter offers regular excursions and bike rentals.

Pensión Marilós GUESTHOUSE $
(☎720-1380; marilos66@hotmail.com; cnr Av A Este & Calle 6 Sur; s with/without bathroom US$15/10, d with/without bathroom US$20/14; P) With the feel of a well-worn family home, Marilós offers a bit of peace and quiet at bargain rates. Rooms with assorted knick-knacks and doo-dads are reminiscent of the guest bedroom at grandma's house. There's even a mild-mannered dog to pet and the owner Frank can help you make the most of your time in Boquete.

La Casa de La Abuela HOTEL $$
(☎730-9484; www.lacasadeabuela.com; Av Central s/n; s/d incl breakfast US$80/112;) This new brick hotel is a smart addition to Boquete. Eighteen earthtone rooms, some with balconies, have tiled floors, flat-screen TVs, hot showers and modern installations. There is nice outdoor patio seating, though the roadside location can be noisy at times.

★Isla Verde CABIN $$
(☎720-2533; islaverde@cwpanama.net; Av B Oeste; d apt US$150, cabins from US$90; P @) Set riverside in a beautiful, lush garden with Buddha statues, these delicious two-story alpine cabins feature luxurious mattresses, vaulted ceilings, complete kitchens and roomy bathrooms. It's probably the best in-town retreat, with prompt service and even professional massages available. Cabins cost US$20 extra for each additional person (US$10 for kids). Look for the highly anticipated restaurant opening onsite.

Hotel Ladera HOTEL $$$
(☎730-9000; www.hotel-ladera.com; Camino a Palo Alto; s/d incl breakfast US$98/119; P) This good value, upscale roadside hotel features an appealing ultra-modern style and attentive staff at the front desk. Rooms feature an outdoor terrace or balcony and two queen-sized beds with wicker headboards. There's onsite dining as well as room service. The hotel often hosts events and art shows.

Eating & Drinking

★Big Daddy's Grill SEAFOOD $
(☎6683-3354; Av Central; mains US$5-10; noon-9pm Tue-Sat, to 8pm Sun) The next best thing to dining in Baja, this friendly eatery serves the most enormous and satisfying fish tacos. Floridians Larry (the big daddy) and Elizabeth use fresh fish they catch off the Chiriquí coastline. There's also lovely salads, margaritas rimmed with chili salt and (if you must) corn dogs. The backyard patio offers privacy and better ambience.

Sugar & Spice BAKERY, DELI $
(Av Central & Calle 7a Sur; sandwiches US$4; 8am-6pm Thu-Sat & Mon-Tue, to 4pm Sun) An artisan bakery with a couple of patio tables for American-style sandwiches, organic salads and oh-so-good brownies. You can also take away fresh breads, including wholegrain and ciabatta.

Café de Encuentro CAFE $
(Calle 6 Sur; mains US$3-7; 7am-noon) In a converted carport and garden, this family-run eatery is a find. All guests are *mi amor* to the affectionate Olga, who cooks breakfast like nobody's business. The menu ranges from Panamanian fare to pancakes and bacon. Expect to wait.

El Sabrosón CAFETERIA $
(Av Central; mains US$2-5; 7am-12am daily) This much-loved local institution cooks up cheap and filling Panamanian cuisine served cafeteria style.

Supermercado Romero SUPERMARKET $
(Av A Este; h24hr) One block east of the plaza, this has the best selection of groceries.

★Il Pianista ITALIAN $$
(Palo Alto; mains US$5-15) Husband cooks and wife serves at this creekside Sicilian restaurant with riverstone walls and just a few tables. A bottle of wine and pizza or calzones make the perfect leisurely lunch but don't come in a rush. Service is as slow as magma. Local buses in the hillsides loop by here.

Mike's Global Grill INTERNATIONAL $$
(☎730-9360; Av Central Oeste; mains US$6-12; 11am-10pm Wed-Mon) This restaurant is the lovechild of a couple who met at the South Pole. To further the wanderlust theme, dishes range from Asian fusion to Ameri-

can chili, falafel and brick-oven pizzas. The ambience is friendly and chill, and there's a long bar, sofas and stacks of magazines. At night it's a popular watering hole for expats, with occasional live music.

La Cabaña CLUB
(Calle de la Feria; cover US$2; ⏲7pm-2am Fri & Sat) Boquete's only disco is riverside, with DJs, reggaetón, a young crowd and a steady current of rum and colas to keep it flowing.

Zanzibar BAR
(Av Central; ⏲6-11:30pm Mon-Sat) This low-key jazz bar is the place to mingle with travelers and locals. Your best chance of hearing live music is on weekends. Happy hour runs from 5pm to 7pm.

Information

ATP (☎720-4060; ⏲8am-5:30pm) About 1.5km south of Boquete, this office sits atop a bluff overlooking town. Here you can grab a Kotowa coffee, pick up maps and obtain information on area attractions. A 2nd-floor exhibit details the history of the region (Spanish only).

Banco Nacional de Panama (Av Central) Has a 24-hour ATM.

Centro Medico San Juan Bautista (☎720-1881; Calle 2 Norte) For medical care.

Global Bank (Av Central) Bank with ATM.

Post Office (Av Belisario Porras s/n; ⏲7am-6pm Mon-Fri, to 5pm Sat)

Getting There & Around

Buses to Boquete depart from David's main bus terminal regularly (US$1.75, one hour, every 30 minutes) from 6am to 9:30pm. Buses to David depart from the south side of Boquete's plaza every 30 minutes from 5am to 6:30pm.

Boquete's small size lends itself to easy exploration. The *urbano* (local) buses winding through the hills cost US$0.50. They depart on the main road one block north of the plaza. Taxis charge US$2 to US$3 for most places around town.

For scooter or bike rentals (about US$3 per hour), check out local hostels.

Parque Nacional Volcán Barú

This 143-sq-km **national park** (admission US$5) is home to Volcán Barú, which is Panama's only volcano as well as the dominant geographical feature of Chiriquí. Volcán Barú is no longer active (there is in fact no record of its most recent eruption), and it has not one but seven craters. Its summit, which tops out at 3475m, is the highest point in Panama; on a clear day it affords views of both the Pacific and Caribbean coasts.

The national park also contains the Sendero Los Quetzales, one of the most scenic treks in the country. It is home to its namesake bird, plus over 250 other bird species, pumas, tapirs and the *conejo pintado* (a spotted raccoon-like animal).

Landslides can shut down the trail but the recent addition of a bridge should help transit. Inquire with rangers before setting out.

Activities

Hiking Volcán Barú

With summit views of both oceans, climbing the volcano is a goal of many visitors. But it might not be worth it in poor weather, as the going is strenuous and rough. In addition, there is little to see in cloud cover. You can enter the park on the eastern and western sides of the volcano. The eastern access, known as 'El Salto,' includes a drive through beautiful forest.

From Boquete, the eastern summit access is the easiest, but it involves a strenuous uphill hike along a 14km road that goes from the park entrance – about 8km northwest of the center of Boquete – to the summit. The road is paved to the ranger station and 2km beyond. If you drive or taxi as far up as possible and then walk the rest of the way, it takes about five or six hours to reach the summit from the park gate; walking from town would take another two or three hours each way.

On this route, it's best to camp on the mountain at least one night; and you should be prepared for the cold. Camping will also allow you to be at the top during the morning, when the views are best.

The other park entrance is just outside the town of Volcán, on the road to Cerro Punta. This rugged road into the park (requiring a 4WD) goes only a short way off the main road to the foot of the volcano. The view of the summit and the nearby peaks from this entrance is impressive, and there's a lovely loop trail that winds through secondary and virgin forest. Access from this side is steep and technical.

Hiking Sendero Los Quetzales

The park's most accessible trail is the scenic **Sendero Los Quetzales** (Quetzals Trail) near Cerro Punta. One of the most beautiful in Panama, this trail runs for 8km between Cerro Punta and Boquete, crossing back and forth over the Río Caldera. The trail can be done in either direction, but is easiest from west to east: the town of Cerro Punta is almost 1000m higher than Boquete, so hiking east is more downhill.

Note that a recent landslide has made sections of this trail very difficult to follow. It is under repair, but progress will surely be slow. Always check on the state of the trail before starting your hike as a guide may be required.

In good conditions, the trail itself takes about four to five hours walking west to east, though getting to and from the trailhead will take another couple of hours of walking on either side. A 4WD taxi can take you to the start of the trail on the Cerro Punta side for about US$12; taxi drivers know the area as Respingo. The trail is 5km uphill from the main road and 2km from the last paved road. When you exit the trail, it's another 8km along the road to Boquete, though you may be able to catch a taxi along the way.

In total, the hike is about 23km, so plan accordingly if you intend to walk the entire length.

After arriving in Boquete, you can stay overnight or take a bus to David and then Cerro Punta; note that the last Cerro Punta bus leaves David at 6pm. You can also leave your luggage at one of the hotels in David and save yourself the hassle of backtracking. Take only the bare essentials with you on the walk (and a little cash for a good meal and/or lodging in Boquete).

Sleeping

Parque Nacional Volcán Barú Camping CAMPGROUND $

(campsite US$5) Camping is available in the park and on the trail to the summit from the Boquete side, along the Sendero Los Quetzales or at the ranger station at the entrance to the Sendero Los Quetzales on the Cerro Punta side.

Information

Admission to the park (US$5) is paid at either of the trailheads leading to the summit or at the ranger station on the Cerro Punto side of the Sendero Los Quetzales.

The best time to visit is during the dry season, especially early in the morning when wildlife is most active.

Overnight temperatures can drop below freezing, and it may be windy and cold during the day, particularly in the morning – dress accordingly.

Getting There & Away

The trailhead leading to the summit of Volcán Barú is best accessed from the town of Boquete, while the Sendero Los Quetzales is best approached from Cerro Punta.

Cerro Punta

At an altitude of 1800m, this small town is surrounded by beautiful, rich agricultural lands, and offers spectacular views across a fertile valley to the peaks of Parque Internacional La Amistad. Although the scenery is inspiring enough, the main reason travelers pass through here is to access the Sendero Los Quetzales or the Parque Internacional La Amistad.

The modest **Hotel Cerro Punta** (☎771-2020; http://hotelcerropunta.zxq.net; s/d/tr US$24/30/36; P) offers a row of mint-green concrete rooms that are a bit tired and beat up. If you're on your way to either national park, enjoy the private hot-water bathroom – it's the last one you'll see for a while.

Buses run from David to Cerro Punta (US$3.50, 2¼ hours, every 20 minutes). If you're coming from Costa Rica, you can catch this bus at the turnoff from the Interamericana at Concepción.

Parque Internacional La Amistad

This 4070-sq-km **national park** (admission US$5, campsite US$5; ⏲8am-4pm) was established jointly by Panama and Costa Rica – hence its name, La Amistad (Friendship). In Panama, the park covers portions of Chiriquí and Bocas del Toro Provinces, and is home to members of three indigenous groups: the Teribe, the Bribrí and the Ngöbe-Buglé.

The bi-national park also contains large swaths of virgin rainforest that are home to a recorded 90 mammal species (including jaguars and pumas) and more than 300 bird species (including resplendent quetzals and harpy eagles). Although most of the park's area is high up in the Talamanca mountains and remains inaccessible, there is no shortage of hiking and camping opportunities available for intrepid travelers.

Admission to the park is paid at either of the two Panamanian entrances: one at Las Nubes, near Cerro Punta on the Chiriquí side, and one at Wekso, near Changuinola on the Bocas del Toro side. Permits to camp in the park are available at the ranger station.

Las Nubes

Three main trails originate at the Las Nubes ranger station. The **Sendero La Cascada** (Waterfall Trail) is a 3.4km round-trip hike that takes in three *miradors* (lookout points) as well as a 45m-high waterfall with a lovely bathing pool. The **Sendero El Retoño** (Rebirth Trail) loops 2.1km through secondary forest, crosses a number of a rustic bridges and winds through bamboo groves. The **Vereda La Montaña** (Mountain Lane) is a more strenuous 8km round-trip hike that ascends Cerro Picacho.

The ranger station at Las Nubes has a **dorm** (dm US$12) with bunk beds. Due to its popularity, guests need to reserve ahead via ANAM (p670) in David. Guests have kitchen access; stock up on provisions in Cerro Punta. Bring your own bedding and warm clothes as this side of the park, at 2280m above sea level, has a cool climate. Temperatures are usually around 24°C (75°F) in the daytime and drop to about 3°C (38°F) at night.

The Las Nubes entrance is about 7km from Cerro Punta; a sign on the main road in Cerro Punta marks the turnoff. The road starts out paved, but by the time you reach the park, it's a rutted track suitable only for 4WDs. A taxi (US$6 for two people) will bring you here from Cerro Punta.

Wekso

Wekso is accessed by a jungle river blanketed with rainforest and intermittent waterfalls; the backdrop is the glorious Talamanca range. After about 45 minutes on the river, you'll see a sign on the right bank that announces your arrival at Wekso, which is actually a protected area but still some way from the park. There's a 3.5km loop trail at Wekso that cuts through secondary and virgin rainforest, with excellent bird-watching. You can also take a dip in the river (the water is too swift for crocodiles), but be careful not to wade out very far or the current will carry you downstream.

A Naso-run **Guest Lodge** (☎6574-9874; http://odesen.bocas.com; lodging per person US$20, 3 meals US$14), which benefits the tribe, is staffed by members of the local community. Rooms are basic but there is a secure water supply, flush toilets and an outdoor shower. Workers can also prepare meals for you, lead you on guided tours through the jungle and answer all your questions about Naso culture and history. It's a five-hour hike from Wekso to the Parque Internacional La Amistad.

Wekso is administered by **Odesen** (Organization for the Sustainable Development of Naso Ecotourism; ☎6569-3869; http://odesen.bocas.com), a community-based development organization that promotes ecotourism in the park as well as the cultural preservation of the Naso. Their direct contact is Raul Quintero.

To reach Wekso, you first have to catch a bus from Changuinola to the hamlet of El Silencio (US$0.80, 40 minutes), and then take a 45-minute boat ride up the Río Teribe. In El Silencio, you can hire a five-person boat for around US$60 to US$75. If you contact the ANAM office in Changuinola about visiting Wekso, they can radio ahead and make sure there is someone at the river's edge.

BOCAS DEL TORO PROVINCE

Where primary rainforest meets banana plantation and Caribbean islands dot a shock of blue waters, Bocas del Toro Province promises all that is tropical. Located 32km from the Costa Rican border, the Archipiélago de Bocas del Toro consists of six densely forested islands, scores of uninhabited islets and Panama's oldest marine park, Parque Nacional Marino Isla Bastimentos. Naturally beautiful and half-tame, Bocas is Panama's principal tourist draw, the place for a hefty dose of sun and surf. Isla Colón, home to the regional capital town of Bocas del Toro, is the main destination for travelers. Other islands host resort-style accommodations and indigenous communities.

In addition to being the longtime roost of Chiquita Banana, the mainland is home to the Panamanian half of the bi-national Parque Internacional La Amistad, home of megafauna such as the elusive jaguar, as well as Ngöbe-Buglé settlements. Deep in the forest live the last remaining Naso, one of the only tribes in the Americas to retain their traditional monarchs.

Few visitors are disappointed with the perfect Bocas cocktail of water, fun and

WORTH A TRIP

LOST & FOUND LODGE

On the way to Bocas del Toro province in the Talamanca mountain range, this original cloud forest lodge offers a utopian take on jungle living. Only accessible on foot, **Lost & Found Lodge** (☎6432-8182; www.lostandfoundlodge.com; dm/d/tr without bathroom US$14/33/48) is a backpacker community perched on a steep hill facing a gaping mountain panorama.

The Canadian owners have plotted every detail, from foosball tournaments to a tricked-out treasure hunt that takes visitors mucking through rivers and labyrinths, competing for a coveted bottle of cheap wine. Bunks are stacked high, but you can also choose a private room that's basic but clean. Shared bathrooms are stall-style and well maintained.

The open-air kitchen is stocked with basic provisions (pasta, eggs, sauces and vegetables) for sale, though you can also order meals. There's also a minipub set up far from sleepers.

Activities are varied and well priced. A highlight is the Lost World Tour, which takes hikers to an impressive waterfall and an indigenous community. You can also visit a local coffee producer or hike the trails.

While Rocky the resident kinkajou is here because he cannot be released into the wild, other animals come for the buffet of bananas occasionally left out for them – not the best wildlife practice, but one you might see throughout the country and should discourage.

Given the isolation, it's necessary to call or email reservations 24 hours in advance. From David, the lodge provides a shuttle (US$30), or you can take the bus (US$3.50). After one hour, the bus reaches a sign for the lodge near Km 42. From here, hike 15 minutes. You can also take a bus from the Bocas side, starting in Changuinola or Almirante (around US$8).

Discounts are given for longer stays. The lodge also provides good shuttle tours between Bocas and Boquete, making active stops at places of interest.

thatched luxury. Unfortunately, the secret has leaked, and there's no sign that development will slow down. The real-estate boom has brought bulldozers and bullying interests, making locals debate the merits of increased tourism when there may not be the infrastructure to support it.

Isla Colón

Relaxed as it is, Isla Colón has ridden a major development boom. Since the mid-1990s, foreign investors have been buying up land like crazy, with new hotels, restaurants and condos constantly springing up. Fortunately, there's still a heavy dose of local flavor, and the lack of beachside Pizza Huts is testament to the fact that development is still years behind similar destinations in nearby Costa Rica.

Activities

Diving & Snorkeling

With nearly 40 rivers unloading silt into the seas around Bocas del Toro, the archipelago's waters are notorious for poor visibility. If it has rained a lot in recent days, visibility may be limited to only 3m; at best visibility is about 15m. Although experienced divers accustomed to crystal-clear Caribbean diving may be disappointed with Bocas, the islands still have much to offer.

The emerald-green waters of the archipelago are home to barracuda, stingrays, dolphins and nurse sharks. Better sites nearby include **Dark Wood Reef** (Map p682), northwest of Bastimentos; **Hospital Point**, a 50ft wall off Cayo Nancy; and the base of the **Punta Juan buoy** (Map p682) north of Isla San Cristóbal.

Boat Tours

The most popular tours in the area are all-day snorkeling trips, which are perfect for nondivers who want a taste of the area's rich marine life. A typical tour costs US$20 per person, and goes to Dolphin Bay, Cayo Crawl, Red Frog Beach ($2 entry) and Hospital Point. A trip to the distant Cayos Zapatillas costs US$25 (plus an additional US$10 for admission to the marine park), and includes lunch, a laze on the beach and a jungle walkabout on Cayo Zapatilla Sur.

Many 'tours' are really little more than boat transportation to a pretty spot. If you have your own snorkel gear (or if you rent it), you can also get the local boatmen to take you around the area in their small, motorized canoes. Agree on a price before you go.

Surfing

Still emerging as an international surf destination, Bocas offers an excellent mix of beginner beach breaks, ripping reefs breaks and some seriously suicidal breaks.

Beginner surfers looking for a bit of reef experience should check out **Playa Punch**, which offers a good mix of lefts and rights. Although it can get heavy when big, Punch generally offers some of the kindest waves around.

Just past Punch on route to Playa Bluff is a popular reef break known as **Dumps**. This left break can get up to 3m, and should only be ridden by experienced surfers as wiping out on the reef here is a dangerous affair. There is also an inner break known as **Inner Dumps**, which also breaks left, but is more forgiving than its outer brother.

Be careful walking out on the reefs as they are sharp and full of urchins – wear booties. If you get cut up, be sure to properly disinfect your wounds.

Playa Bluff, the island's most notorious surf spot, throws out powerful barreling waves that break in shallow water along the beach, with a reputation for snapping boards. Though waves close quickly, the tubes here are truly awesome, especially when the swells are strong.

Kayaking

Although you will need to be wary of boat traffic and the occasional swell, a great way to travel between islands is by sea kayak. Dive shops rent kayaks for US$5 per hour.

Cycling

Whether you're heading to Boca del Drago on the paved road or pedaling to Playa Bluff, a bike can seriously increase your mobility. Note that the ride to Boca del Drago is taxing, especially when the sun is beaming. It's an easier (though shadeless) ride to Punta Bluff; be aware that the road can flood after heavy rains. Bikes are available from some hostels and from **Ixa's Bike World** (Map p684; Av H; ⏲ 8am-6pm) in Bocas town.

Hiking

If you're looking to get well off the beaten path, there is a network of undeveloped hiking trails that fan out across the island. One of the more popular hikes starts at the end of the coastal road in Mimbi Timbi and carries on along the coast to Boca del Drago. You will need about six hours of daylight to complete the hike and you must carry in all your fresh water. The trail winds past caves, caverns and plenty of vine-entangled jungle. A bike will help speed things up a bit, though you will be carrying it part of the way, especially if it's recently rained.

Fishing

The best budget option for aspiring anglers is to go surf casting with the local water taxi drivers. The hand lines are a bit tricky at first, though you'll get the hang of it. It's best to go early in the morning when the fish are biting. Prices are negotiable.

Bocas del Toro

As the archipelago's largest and most developed island, Isla Colón is home to the provincial capital of Bocas del Toro – a colorful town of wooden houses built by the United Fruit Company in the early 20th century. Today, Bocas is a slow-paced community of West Indians, Latinos and resident gringos. It serves as a convenient base for exploring the marine national park; *taxis marinos* (water taxis) can whisk you away to remote beaches and snorkeling sites.

It rains a lot in Bocas – even in the dry season, there can be long periods of constant showers.

Sights

Boca del Drago BEACH

This beach, on the west side of Isla Colón, is among the best on the island, with good swimming and snorkeling, especially when the sea is calm. The lack of surge here means that this is the safest spot in the archipelago for nonsurfers. There is a regular bus and water taxi to the beach from Bocas town.

Playa Bluff BEACH

This secluded wilderness beach is pounded by intense waves. Although you wouldn't want to get into the water here without a board, the soft, yellow sand and palm-fringed shores are pristine. It serves as a nesting area for sea turtles from May to September. The

Archipiélago de Bocas del Toro

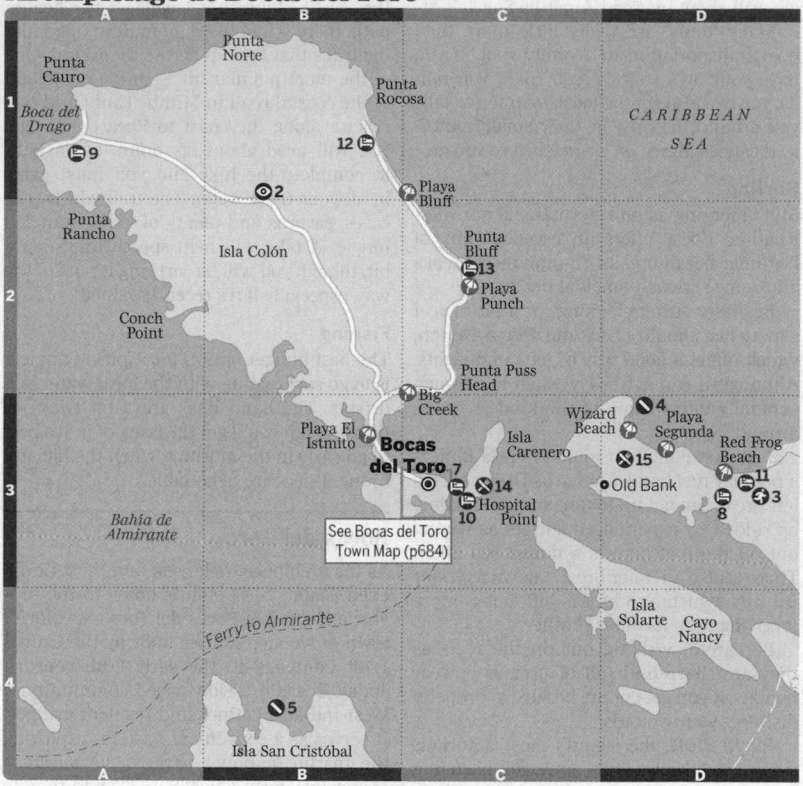

beach is 8km from Bocas town, next to the road after you round Punta Bluff.

La Gruta CAVE

(The Cavern; Map p682; admission US$1; ⏲dawn-dusk) Adventurers will love this bat cave in the indigenous Communidad Bahía Honda. It's reached by wading through waist-high water with thousands of sleeping bats overhead. The entrance is marked by a Virgin Mary statue, 8km from Bocas town on the road to Boca del Drago. There is also a small community restaurant.

Bocas Butterfly Farm GARDENS

(Map p684; ☎757-9008; adult/child US$5/2; ⏲9am- 3pm Mon-Sat, to noon Sun) A great morning trip from Bocas town is the adorable Bocas Butterfly Farm, which houses species from every corner of Panama. There is no road access; hire a water taxi for US$1 one way.

Playa El Istmito BEACH

This beach, also called Playa La Cabaña, is the closest to town, though it's on Sand Fly Bay and the *chitras* (sand flies) that live here have an itchy bite. This is not the most attractive beach and, unless you're walking, it's worth heading further north.

Playa Punch BEACH

Further up the coast is Playa Punch, which is dangerous for swimming but good for surfing.

Activities

★Anaboca TOUR

(La Asociación Natural Bocas Carey; ☎6843-7244, 6529-7153; www.anaboca.org; per person hiking/turtle tours US$10/15) This nonprofit run by the local community addresses marine turtle conservation. In season, certified guides offer nighttime tours to view turtle hatching on Playa Bluff. There's also community stays

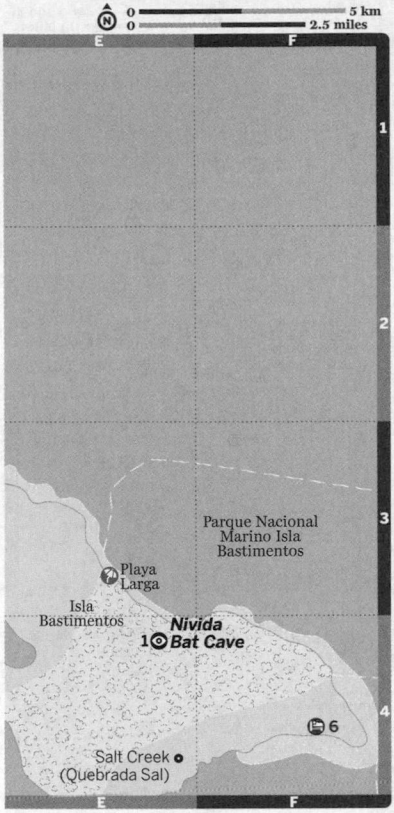

Archipiélago de Bocas del Toro

Top Sights
1 Nivida Bat Cave E4

Sights
2 La Gruta B1

Activities, Courses & Tours
3 Bastimentos Sky D3
4 Dark Wood Reef D3
5 Punta Juan Buov B4

Sleeping
6 Al Natural Resort F4
7 Aqua Lounge C3
8 Bocas Bound Hostel D3
9 Cabañas Estefany A1
10 Casa Acuario C3
Gran Kahuna Hostel ..... (see 10)
11 Palmar Tent Lodge D3
12 Playa Bluff Lodge B1
13 Tesoro Escondido C2

Eating
14 Pickled Parrot C3
15 Up In the Hill D3

(food and lodging US$45), which is a good idea if you're there to watch hatching in the wee hours.

Starfleet Eco Adventures DIVING
(Map p684; ☎757-9630; www.starfleetscuba.com; Calle 1) PADI open-water and advanced-diver courses are available. Starfleet offers instruction in English and enjoys a strong reputation among locals and travelers.

La Buga DIVING
(Map p684; ☎757-9534; www.labugapanama.com; Calle 3; ⏲8am-8pm) A well-regarded dive shop. Highlights include night dives and visiting the caves off Bastimentos (US$70). It also offers surf rentals and lessons, stand-up paddles (US$20 per day) and kayak rentals.

Bocas Water Sports DIVING
(Map p684; ☎757-9541; www.bocaswatersports.com; Calle 3) A longtime PADI dive center operating in Bocas.

Transparente Tours TOUR
(Map p684; ☎6583-0351, 757-9915; transparentetours@hotmail.com; Calle 3; ⏲9:30am-5:30pm) This recommended tour operator provides guides, gear, drinks and radios on excursions.

Tropix Surf SURFING
(Map p684; ☎757-9727; Calle 3; ⏲9am-7pm) You can rent surfboards from Tropix Surf. If heading out to Isla Bastimentos, arrange your board in advance.

Catamaran Sailing Adventures SAILING
(Map p684; ☎757-7048; www.bocassailing.com; Av Sur; snorkel tour US$45; ⏲8:30-11am & 4-8pm) With affordable overnight adventures and options for snorkeling, fishing and dolphin-watching, Catamaran Sailing Adventures has popular kid-friendly tours on a 42-foot catamaran.

Courses

Habla Ya LANGUAGE COURSE
(Map p684; ☎757-7352, 730-8344; www.hablayapanama.com; Av G & Calle 9 Sur; ⏲8am-5:30pm) With a great reputation, this Spanish school offers intensive courses on Spanish for travelers. There's air-conditioned classrooms and

Bocas del Toro Town

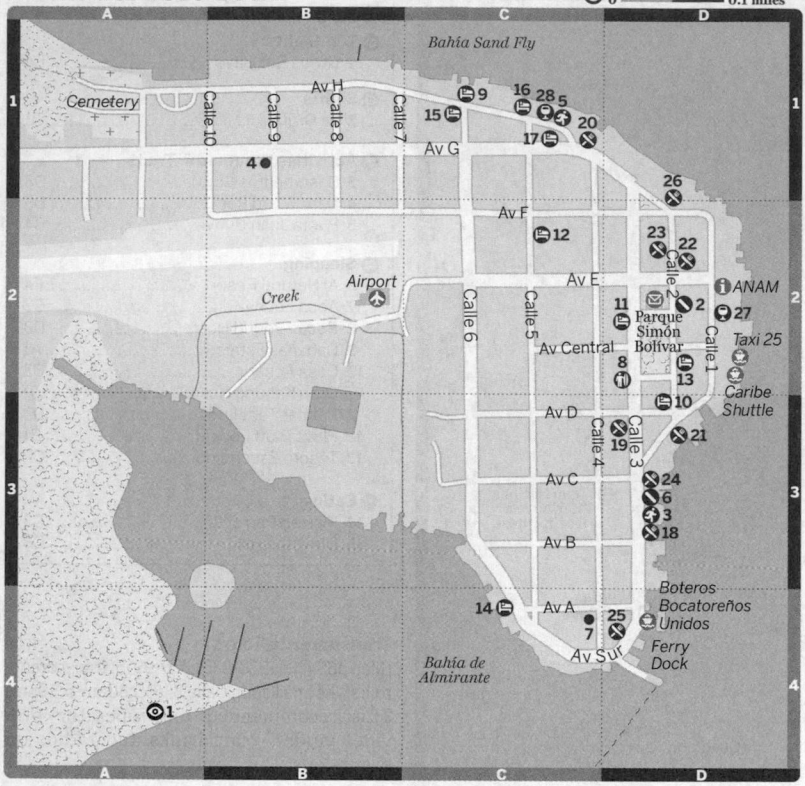

Bocas del Toro Town

Sights
1 Bocas Butterfly Farm A4

Activities, Courses & Tours
2 Bocas Water Sports D2
3 Catamaran Sailing Adventures D3
4 Habla Ya B1
5 Ixa's Bike World C1
6 La Buga D3
7 Spanish by the Sea C4
Starfleet Eco Adventures ..... (see 6)
Transparente Tours ..... (see 3)
8 Tropix Surf D2

Sleeping
9 Cocomo C1
10 Hostal Hansi D3
11 Hostel Heike D2
12 Hotel Cala Luna C2
13 Hotel del Parque D2
14 Hotel Dos Palmas C4
15 Lula's C1
16 Lula's Hostel C1
17 Mondo Taitú C1

Eating
Alberto's Pizzeria ..... (see 12)
18 Buena Vista Bar & Grill D3
19 El Chitré D3
20 La Casbah C1
21 Lilli's Cafe D3
22 Om Café D2
23 Panadería & Dulceria Alemana D2
24 Raw D3
25 Super Gourmet D4
26 Tom's D1

Drinking & Nightlife
27 Barco Hundido D2
Mondo Taitú Bar ..... (see 17)
28 Riptide C1

special rates on tours and lodging in the school's own dorms and private rooms.

Spanish by the Sea LANGUAGE COURSE
(Map p684; ☎757-9518; www.spanishbythesea.com; Calle 4) Group lessons in a relaxed setting are US$185 per week for 20 hours at this language school. Homestays can be arranged (US$18 per night), or you can bunk down in clean and comfy dorms (US$10) or private rooms (US$25).

Festivals & Events

Bocas celebrates all of Panama's holidays, with a few enjoyable local ones besides.

May Day EVENT
A Maypole dance performed by local girls. Celebrated May 1.

Día de la Virgen del Carmen FESTIVAL
Bocatoreños make a pilgrimage to La Gruta cave for a mass in honor of the Virgen del Carmen on the third Sunday in July.

Feria del Mar FESTIVAL
Held on Playa El Istmito, a few kilometers north of Bocas, from September 28 to October 2.

Fundación de la Provincia de Bocas del Toro EVENT
A big affair celebrating the foundation of the province in 1904, with parades and other events. Held November 16.

Día de Bastimentos EVENT
Bastimentos Day is celebrated on November 23 with a huge parade and drumming exhibitions.

Sleeping

Reservations are a good idea between December and April and during national holidays and local festivals.

BOCAS TOWN

★Hostel Heike HOSTEL $
(Map p684; ☎757-9708; www.hostelheike.com; Calle 3; dm with/without air-con US$12/10, r per person US$11; ❄@📶) Awash with colorful murals and natural woods, Heike is the perfect spot for chilling, Caribbean-style. Expertly managed by a friendly Panamanian, there are free basic Spanish classes daily at 2pm, purified water and hot drinks. A sprawling roof deck with hammocks is the perfect spot for a cold beer and a good book. Private rooms feature bunks, not double beds.

Hostal Hansi GUESTHOUSE $
(Map p684; ☎757-9085; http://hostalhansi.bocas.com; cnr Av D & Calle 2; s without bathroom US$13, s/d/tr US$15/25/30; @📶) The idea here is family-friendly and the German-owned guesthouse prides itself on having a quiet interior and hot showers. Rooms have fans and are generally spotless and comfortable. Doubles sport their own balcony. Guests can cook in an ample kitchen, where fridge space precisely organized by room number – surely a UN-worthy model of hosteling.

Mondo Taitú HOSTEL $
(Map p684; ☎757-9425; www.mondotaitu.com; Av G; dm with/without air-con US$12/10, d without bathroom US$24; ❄@📶) Though it looks like a strong wind could collapse it, this is Bocas' backpacker hub. Built on good vibes, this hostel has a chill social atmosphere, freebies and nightlife. There's a communal kitchen, lounge area, laundry facilities, and free bikes and surfboards.

Hotel Dos Palmas HOTEL $
(Map p684; ☎757-9906; residencialdospalmas@yahoo.com; Av Sur; d/tr US$28/35; ❄) Proudly '100% Bocatoreño,' Dos Palmas offers basic wooden rooms with old-fashioned furnishings. Run by a friendly matriarch, it's not some cookie-cutter lodging. Some might find it a little musty. It sits above the water and boasts exceptional views of the bay.

Lula's Hostel HOSTEL $$
(Map p684; ☎757-9057; www.lulabb.com/hostel-lulas; Av H; dm/d without bathroom US$20/60; ❄📶) It's not every day that your hostel has it's own swim-off dock. This super cute

LOCAL KNOWLEDGE

SUSTAINABLE TOURISM ON BOCAS

Mass tourism has been hard on Bocas, so when you go, think sustainable. Avoid using small plastic water bottles. Support sustainable tourism with a visit to the Ngöbe-run restaurant in Comunidad Bahía Honda. Make sure your boat in Dolphin Bay keeps a respectable distance from dolphins, and use the co-op of local boaters who show more consciousness in their boating practices.

Daniel Suman, environmental law professor

DON'T MISS

OREBA CHOCOLATE TOUR

Lauded by travelers, this guided **tour** (☎6649-1457; quintero2380@gmail.com; per person US$25) takes you to an organic chocolate farm run by the indigenous Ngöbe community. Swiss experts have classified the chocolate as some of the highest grade cacao in the world. Tour the farm, see tree sloths, sample chocolate and enjoy a traditional lunch. The trip (four-person minimum) is guided in Spanish and English.

Though it's on the mainland near Almirante, most visitors book the tour through their Bocas hostel or Super Gourmet (p687). The cost does not include the boat trip from Bocas (US$7 round-trip).

mint-green cottage features big solid bunks and recent renovations. With no onsite host, guests are on their own after leaving a deposit for keys. The owners rent kayaks for US$10 per half day.

Lula's B&B $$
(Map p684; ☎757-9057; www.lulabb.com; Av Norte; d/tr/q incl breakfast US$55/77/88; ❄@📶) A place of rockers and porches, this B&B is lovely. Rooms are immaculate, with hot showers and a snug design. The US hosts provide first-rate service, in addition to big southern breakfasts.

Cocomo B&B $$
(Map p684; ☎757-9259; www.cocomoonthesea.com; cnr Av Norte & Calle 6A; s/d/tr incl breakfast US$60/80/90; ❄📶) A sweet clapboard house with a tropical garden and waterfront hammock deck, Cocomo wants for nothing. If the weather's bad, this is a snug spot to hole up. Rooms have hot water. All-you-can-eat breakfast includes pastries, fruit, yogurt and omelets. There's kayak rentals (US$10) and you can swim right off the dock.

Hotel del Parque HOTEL $$
(Map p684; ☎757-9008; www.hdelparque.webs.com; Calle 2; s/d/tr US$37/45/50; ❄📶) A classic Caribbean house fronting the plaza, this tranquil place has B&B style within budget reach. Ample rooms have big windows, cool cement floors and firm beds with crisp linens. The terraces provide views of the action on the plaza and hammocks for cat naps.

Hotel Cala Luna HOTEL $$
(Map p684; ☎757-9066; www.calalunabocas.com; Calle 5; s/d/tr US$55/65/80; ❄@) Atop Alberto's Pizza, the Italian-owned Cala Luna features cathedral windows, tasteful wood details and crisp, functional rooms. As an added bonus, guests can watch planes coming in for a landing 30m above their heads from a pair of lookouts on the roof.

AROUND THE ISLAND

Cabañas Estefany CABIN $
(Map p682; ☎6956-4525; gilbertosanchez-25@hotmail.com; dm US$12, d with kitchen US$35, 6-person cabin US$75; @) Located at Boca del Drago, these wooden *cabañas* are bare bones – some without fans and all with cold showers. Secure a room with a fan as it can get quite buggy. Cabins are often booked up with scientific researchers, so it's recommended that you call ahead.

★**Tesoro Escondido** CABIN $$
(Map p682; ☎6782-0512; www.tesoroescondido.info; d/tr from US$35/50, 2-/3-/4-person cabins US$65/80/95) Exuding a very homespun charm, this seafront lodge with thatched cottages works its magic. It's not for everyone – the overgrown rainforest means there might be visitors. Mosaic tables and recycled bottle construction lend a bohemian air, but the most remarkable feature is the Swiss cooking. Can you say, 'best chocolate ever tasted'? Guests dine on fixed menus (US$10 to US$14) with fab desserts.

Snorkeling gear is free to borrow. It's on the right, just before Playa Bluff.

Playa Bluff Lodge LODGE $$
(Map p682; ☎6798-8507; www.playablufflodge.com; d incl breakfast US$110; 🏊) This highly recommended lodge is run by a welcoming Dutch family. Modern and attractive rooms are nestled into a rainforest location, with lily ponds and huge trees that host the occasional sloth. A boon for families, its casual onsite bar-restaurant (open to the public) features a billiards table and kids area. There's also a pool, exotic frog diorama and jungle treks (US$45).

The location is literally the end of the road, 8km from Bocas, across from the beach. Transfers are included with a three-night stay.

Eating

Food carts sell roast chicken and fresh smoothies and juices, but ask for bottled water in your *batido* (fruit shakes made with milkor water).

★Raw SUSHI $
(Map p684; ☎6938-8473; Calle 2; mains US$8-10) Just a little plank restaurant on the water, but the offerings are spot on. Carafes of sake accompany fresh tofu spring rolls and amazing tacos with tuna tartar and pickled onions. The salads are wonderful and service is attentive. At night candles are lit and the full bar specializing in original martinis starts humming.

Tom's PANAMANIAN $
(Map p684; ☎6776-9280; Av H; mains US$6-10; ⏲10am-5pm Mon-Sat) Locals of every stripe agree that Tom's is the spot for a tasty lunch that doesn't break the bank. Head upstairs in a concrete market building; it's on a shaded 2nd-floor terrace overlooking the water. Seafood or chicken is usually paired with rice or fries. They also deliver.

Lilli's Cafe CAFE $
(Map p684; Calle 1; plates US$5-8) Whether you feast on eggs Benedict with crab or an oversized burger, be sure to try the homemade 'Killin' Me Man' pepper sauce. After all, nothing says the Caribbean like an ocean view and fire on the palate.

Panadería & Dulceria Alemana BAKERY $
(Map p684; Calle 2; snacks US$1-5; ⏲7am-8pm Mon-Sat, 8am-4pm Sun) The best real coffee on the island, whole-grain bread and moist slabs of carrot cake are the order of the day at this German bakery.

El Chitré PANAMANIAN $
(Map p684; Calle 3; plates US$2-4; ⏲8am-10pm Mon-Sat) Patronized by locals and travelers alike, this no-frills cafeteria is the best spot in town for cheap but tasty grub.

Super Gourmet SUPERMARKET $
(Map p684; Calle 3; ⏲9am-7pm Mon-Sat) Stocks specialty items such as local organic chocolate, Mexican food, wine and frozen bagels.

Alberto's Pizzeria PIZZERIA $
(Map p684; Calle 5; pizzas US$10; ⏲noon-10pm Mon-Sat) Sardinian-run Alberto's is a favorite local haunt where you can play ping-pong while anticipating your dinner. Fresh pizzas with toppings such as artichokes, kalamata olives and gorgonzola satisfy big appetites.

La Casbah MEDITERRANEAN $$
(Map p684; ☎6477-4227; Av H; mains US$8-15; ⏲6-10pm Tue-Sat) Popular with locals and travelers alike, this Mediterranean restaurant serves up gazpacho, goat's cheese salad and well-prepared meat and seafood. The fish of the day comes in cucumber and coconut sauce and there's a nice baked veggie plate for non-meat-eaters. Reserve ahead.

Om Café INDIAN $$
(Map p684; cnr Av E & Calle 2; mains US$6.50-15; ⏲8am-noon & 6-10pm Fri-Tue) Guaranteed to make your brow sweat, this welcoming Indian cafe cooks up classic curries and vindaloo with crisp, hot naan. Service may be slow, so order up a cocktail to keep you company (try the Tipsy Turban – a dizzy mix of passion fruit, rum and sugar).

Buena Vista Bar & Grill AMERICAN $$
(Map p684; Calle 1; mains US$7-13; ⏲8am-10pm Wed-Mon) This waterfront restaurant serves nachos, bacon cheeseburgers and brownie sundaes to hungry expats. Dinner ups the ante with seafood and fish dishes.

Drinking & Nightlife

Mondo Taitú Bar BAR
(Map p684; Av G; ⏲7pm-late) It's a guaranteed good time here. On Tuesday and Friday, the party-loving owners entertain with themed events, though the creative cocktail list and hookahs make Mondo a good choice any night. If you're feeling brave, order a tequila suicide – a snort of salt, a squeeze of lime in the eye and a shot of bad tequila (at least it's free!)

Barco Hundido BAR
(Map p684; Calle 1; ⏲8pm-midnight) Most nights in Bocas end at this open-air bar, affectionately known as the 'Wreck Deck' – the name comes from the sunken banana boat that rests in the clear Caribbean waters in the front. A short boardwalk extends from the bar to an island seating area perfect for stargazing.

Riptide BAR
(Map p684; Av H; ⏲9am-midnight) If you haven't the budget to booze it up with your buddies on a private yacht, this weathered boat-bar may be the next best thing. A gringo magnet, it's a good spot to gather around a horseshoe-shaped bar and shoot the breeze.

There are daily food specials – some swear by the fried chicken, but general reviews are very mixed.

Orientation

Bocas del Toro town is laid out in a grid pattern with most of the hotels and restaurants on Calle 3. The airport is on Av E, four blocks from Calle 3.

Note that the town, the archipelago and the province all share the name Bocas del Toro. Isla Colón and Bocas del Toro town are also referred to as Bocas Isla.

Information

For more information on the islands, see the useful English website www.bocas.com, check out the **National Geographic** (www.gobluecentralamerica.org) page on Bocas or check out the island's monthly bilingual publication, **The Bocas Breeze** (www.thebocasbreeze.com).

ANAM (Autoridad Nacional de Ambiente; ☎757-9442; Calle 1) Not really set up as a tourist information office, though they can answer questions about the national park or other protected areas. If you want to camp out in any of the protected areas, you must first get a permit from an ANAM office.

ATP (Autoridad de Turismo Panama; ☎757-9642; ⏲8:30am-3:30pm Mon-Fri) In Centro de Facilidades Turísticas e Interpretación (Cefati) on the eastern waterfront. A color map in English and Spanish is available.

Banco Nacional de Panamá (cnr Calle 4 & Av E; ⏲8am-2pm Mon-Fri, to noon Sat) Exchanges traveler's checks and has a 24-hour ATM.

Bocas Sustainable Tourism Alliance (☎6956-9520; www.discoverbocasdeltoro.com) English-speaking staff with good reference information for travelers. There's no office but you can get help with sustainable tours online or by phone. Arranges visits to a Ngöbe crafts workshop on Isla San Cristóbal.

Cable & Wireless (Calle 1) International calls can be made here.

Hospital (☎757-9201; Av G; ⏲24hr) The island's only hospital has a 24-hour emergency room.

Post Office (Calle 3, Governmental Bldg)

DANGERS & ANNOYANCES

The surf can be quite dangerous on some beaches, with frequently strong riptides – use caution when going out into the waves. If you get caught in a rip, swim parallel to the shore and don't panic.

Tap water is not safe to drink in Bocas del Toro. Bocas Sustainable Tourism Alliance refills water bottles.

Bocas del Toro is a conservative place and local law prevents both men and women from walking down the streets topless. Even if you are on your way to the beach, wear a shirt or you will be sent back to your hotel if spotted by the police.

DON'T MISS

GEMS OF THE ARCHIPELAGO

Skip the crowds by hiring a boat and checking out:

Cayo Crawl Get lost in these mangrove-dotted channels near Isla Bastimentos.

Cayos Zapatillas Set out for these pristine white-sand beaches and virgin forests.

Dolphin Bay Spot dolphins frolicking at this densely populated breeding ground.

Swan Cay Spot red-billed tropic birds and white-crowned pigeons in this cay near Isla de Los Pájaros.

Getting There & Away

AIR

Air Panama (☎757-9841; www.flyairpanama.com) Flies to Panama City (US$116, one hour, once or twice daily). Office at the airport.

Nature Air (☎in USA 800-235-9272; www.natureair.com) Flies from San José, Costa Rica (US$135, 1½ hours) in the early morning several times per week.

BOAT

If you don't fly into Bocas you'll have to take a water taxi (US$4) from Almirante on the mainland. On the waterfront, **Taxi 25** makes the half-hour trip every half hour from 6am to 6:30pm.

Caribe Shuttle (☎757-7048; www.caribeshuttle.com) To reach Puerto Viejo, Costa Rica, this combination boat-bus trip (US$32) runs twice daily. There's also an option to go on to Cahuita (US$38) or San Jose (US$70). They provide a hotel pick-up but you must reserve one day in advance.

Getting Around

A cross-island bus goes to Bocas del Drago from Bocas plaza (US$2.40, one hour, six daily between 5:30am and 8:30pm). The latest schedule is in the *Bocas Breeze*.

To reach nearby islands, you can hire boaters operating motorized boats and canoes along the waterfront. As a general rule, you should always sort out the rate beforehand, and clarify if it is for one way or a round-trip. Always pay on the return leg – this guarantees a pickup – though most boaters will want some money upfront to buy petrol. Although rates vary, you will get a better deal if you speak Spanish, are with a group and arrange for a pickup.

Locals claim **Boteros Bocatoreños Unidos** (☎6022-9554; Calle 3; ⏲6:30am-6:30pm) consistently offers fair prices; the staff is also trained in safe boating and sustainable tourism practices.

Isla Carenero

A few hundred meters from Isla Colón, the oft-forgotten Isla Carenero takes its name from 'careening' – nautical talk for leaning a ship on one side for maintenance. In October 1502, Columbus docked his fleet here for careening while he recovered from a bellyache.

Today, the wave of development that transformed Isla Colón is also making headway on Isla Carenero, though staying on the latter is a quieter alternative.

Activities

Those serious about surfing can tackle Silverbacks, an enormous barreling right that breaks over a reef, with heights of over 5m. This world-class break wouldn't look out of place on Hawaii's North Shore. Take a water taxi to reach it.

Escuela de Mar SURFING
(☎6785-7984, 757-9137; www.bocasbuccaneer-resort.com/surfing-school; ⏲8am-6pm) For quality surf classes (US$45 per three hours) or rentals of kayaks ($10 per three hours), stand-up paddles (US$30 per day) and boards (US$15 per day), check out this surf school run by Argentine Luis. It's located on the water at the Buccaneer Resort. Call ahead if you can.

Sleeping & Eating

Although not as popular as Isla Colón or Isla Bastimentos, Isla Carenero is a good option for travelers who want a different view of the islands.

★Gran Kahuna Hostel HOSTEL $
(Map p682; ☎757-9551; www.grankahunabocas.com; dm/d US$12/45; ❄@📶) Wildly popular in its new waterfront location, this surfer inn is adorable, with yellow cement cabins, bright rooms and even a picket fence. Plus there's a huge flat-screen TV and house guitars. The cleanliness is impressive; not so the service when we visited. There's also a kitchen and onsite bar.

Aqua Lounge HOSTEL $
(Map p682; ☎757-9042; www.bocasaqualounge.info; dm/d/tr incl breakfast US$11/25/36; 📶🏊) This backpacker palace is a rustic matchstick construction on the dock facing Bocas. Guests love it or leave it, but it says Spring Break in so many ways. The onsite bar is hugely popular. Then there's the aquatic trampoline…

Casa Acuario INN $$
(Map p682; ☎757-9565; www.casaacuario.com; d US$88-102; ❄📶) Visually dreamy, this tropical inn sits above crystal-blue waters teeming with tropical fish. Rooms are impeccably outfitted with smart fixtures and rustic, crafty touches. The big draws are the private decks and open-air dining.

Pickled Parrot INTERNATIONAL $
(Map p682; ☎757-9093; mains US$5.50-10; ⏲11am-9pm) Locals claim the best food on the island is served at this seaside deck. Burgers with blue cheese, stuffed chilies, firecracker shrimp and *ceviche* are lovingly prepared by a cantankerous chef. And there's drinks too.

Orientation

Water taxis dock at the small marina on the tip of the island. From here, a path leads to the fledgling town and continues across the island.

Getting There & Away

Isla Carenero is a quick and easy US$1 boat ride from Bocas del Toro town.

Isla Bastimentos

Although it's a mere 10-minute boat ride from the town of Bocas del Toro, Isla Bastimentos is a different world. The northern coast is home to palm-fringed wilderness beaches that serve as nesting grounds for sea turtles, while most of the southern coast consists of mangrove islands and coral reefs within the boundaries of the Parque Nacional Marino Isla Bastimentos. The main settlement is the historic West Indian town of Old Bank, which has its origins in the banana industry. The island is also home to the Ngöbe-Buglé village of Salt Creek (Quebrada Sal), separated from Old Bank by a huge swath of jungle.

Long the stronghold of Afro-Caribbean culture in Bocas, Bastimentos is changing in nature, not in small part due to the development of Red Frog Beach.

Sights

Bastimentos has some amazing beaches, though be careful swimming as the surf can really pick up on the north coast.

The most beautiful beach on the island is **Wizard Beach** (also known as Playa Primera), which is awash in powdery yellow sand and backed by thick, vine-strewn jungle. Although Wizard Beach is connected to Old Bank via a wilderness path, the mere 30-minute walk can turn into an all-day trek through the muck if it's been raining heavily.

Assuming the weather is cooperating, you can continue walking along the coast to **Playa Segunda** (Second Beach) and **Red Frog Beach**. You can access Red Frog Beach by water taxi via a small marina on the south side of the island; entrance to the beach is US$3. While you are on Red Frog Beach, keep an eye out for the *rana rojo* (strawberry poison-dart frog) as they might not be on the island for too much longer.

The path continues past Red Frog Beach to **Playa Larga** (Long Beach), where sea turtles nest from April to August. Playa Larga and much of the eastern side of the island fall under the protection of Parque Nacional Marino Isla Bastimentos.

Old Bank NEIGHBORHOOD

Although very poor and somewhat depressed, Old Bank has a much more pronounced Caribbean vibe than Bocas town, and it's a relaxing place to stroll around and soak up the atmosphere. You may hear Guari-Guari, the Spanish-English Creole language.

Parque Nacional Marino Isla Bastimentos PARK

(admission US$10) Established in 1988, Panama's first marine park protects parts of the Archipiélago de Bocas del Toro, including parts of Isla Bastimentos and the Cayos Zapatillas. It's also an important nature reserve for countless species of Caribbean wildlife. Campers must first obtain a permit from ANAM in Bocas del Toro (see p688).

★Nivida Bat Cave CAVE

(Bahía Honda; Map p682) A massive cavern complete with swarms of nectar bats and a subterranean lake suitable for swimming. Half the fun of the place is getting there via motorboat through a channel of lush vegetation. Go only with a reliable guide (around US$25 per person).

Salt Creek VILLAGE

(Quebrada Sal) On the southeastern edge of Bastimentos, at the end of a long canal cut through the mangrove forest, is the Ngöbe-Buglé village also known as Quebrada Sal.

OFF THE BEATEN TRACK

ISLA SAN CRISTÓBAL

One-and-a-half-hours away from Bocas town is another world – the Ngöbe community on Isla San Cristóbal. These subsistence farmers and fishers have a strong sense of Ngöbe identity, though they live mostly in difficult circumstances.

On a day trip, you can see how the Ngöbe prepare and dye fibers to make chacara bags, tour medicinal gardens and enjoy a traditional meal cooked over a wood fire. Visitor fees (day tours including lunch US$20 per person) benefit the local community.

The Peace Corps has helped develop **Isla San Cristóbal Hostel** (☎6832-9118; www.keteka.com/destinations/latin-america/panama/isla-san-cristobal; tours, meals and 2-night lodging US$75), a community-run ecolodge with basic mosquito-net draped beds, rainwater catchment showers and composting toilets. Boat taxis (US$60 per round-trip) charge by boat, not per person. For arrangements, you can also contact Bocas Sustainable Tourism Alliance (p688).

Also on the island, **Dolphin Bay Hideaway** (☎6417-7351, 6772-9917; www.dolphinbayhideaway.com; d incl 2 meals US$120-160; 📶) is a charming and highly recommended inn run by Transylvanian Erika and her husband, who is from the island. On the mangrove, the lovely two-story home features a big wooden deck, docks with hammocks and a lily pond. Rooms are romantic and well appointed, with canopy beds and pitchers of water, and you are entitled to 'all the coconuts you can drink.' The owners also offer tours around the area.

The community consists of 60-odd thatch and bamboo houses, an elementary school, handicrafts store, general store and soccer field. Visitors pay a US$1 entry fee and sign the visitors' log. Access is by water taxi.

Laguna de Bastimentos LAKE
Getting to this jungle lake surrounded by dense vegetation is a challenging hike. This swath of rainforest is the terra firma section of the Parque Nacional Marino Isla Bastimentos. Go only with a reliable guide.

Activities

If you're looking for a solid beach break, both Wizard Beach and Red Frog Beach offer fairly constant sets of lefts and rights that are perfect for beginner and intermediate surfers. When the swells are in, Wizard occasionally throws out some huge barrels, though they tend to close up pretty quickly.

Bastimentos Sky ZIP LINE
(Map p682; ☎757-8001, 6507-4646; www.redfrogbeach.com/bocas-del-toro-zipline.html; per person US$55) Seven zip lines, a swinging bridge and vertical rappel are a few of the highlights of this new attraction, brought to you by the Red Frog Beach development and a well-known Costa Rican zip-line designer. The tour lasts two hours and reaches heights of 45m.

Uwe SNORKELING
(☎6741-1535; 3-hour tour US$15) A standout guide for snorkeling tours (there must be a reason he's called the 'fish whisperer'), Uwe speaks several languages and takes groups to lesser-known destinations, like wonderful mangrove areas covered in sponges. Four-person group minimum.

Señora Kony Gonzales TOUR
(☎6092-7259; Salt Creek) English-speaking guide to Salt Creek. Leads community tours (US$2), and visits to a bat cave (US$12) and Playa Larga (US$12). Monkeys and sloths might be viewed as well.

Sleeping

Hostel Bastimentos HOSTEL $
(☎757-9053; Old Bank; dm US$6, d US$12-18, d with air-con US$30; @📶) On a hill off the main path, this sprawling yellow clapboard has a bright selection of 28 rooms and hammock decks. Spaces are creaky but serviceable and the host, Dixon, couldn't be nicer. Backpacker-ready, it has two kitchens and a common room with a bar, TV and dartboard.

Pension Tío Tom GUESTHOUSE $
(☎757-9831; tiotomscabin@gmail.com; Old Bank; d US$22-27, 2-person bungalow US$34; 📶) This plank-and-thatch building has been offering cheap, clean and unfussy rooms for years. All rooms now come with private bathrooms and a waterfront deck is strewn with hammocks. German-run, they can also provide hearty meals (dinner US$7), organize tours and rent kayaks.

Bocas Bound Hostel HOSTEL $
(Map p682; ☎757-8012; www.bocasbound.com; dm US$13, d with/without bathroom US$50/30; ❄📶) From the public dock it's a five-minute walk to this popular new cement hostel, part of the original plans for a high-end resort. Large concrete structures have long dorms in narrow rooms and an open-air kitchen, all tidy and clean. There's a separate restaurant (mains US$6 to US$17) and general store. While short on charm, it's functional.

It's 15 minutes further on foot to Red Frog Beach.

Palmar Tent Lodge GLAMPING $$
(Map p682; ☎6880-8640; www.palmartentlodge.com; dm tent US$15, d/tr tent from US$50/60) On the edge of the jungle and famous Red Frog Beach, Palmar introduces glamping to Bocas, with accommodations in solar-powered circular tents, some with private outdoor showers. The thatched lounge offers open-air meals and socializing. A laid-back attitude is required as there's no locked area for your stuff and scorpions do live here. Most guests love it anyway.

Transfers from Isla Colón are US$10 round-trip, plus the $3 beach entry fee.

★Al Natural Resort RESORT $$$
(Map p682; ☎757-9004; www.alnaturalresort.com; d incl 3 meals from US$260) This desert-island hideaway lends a bohemian twist to all-inclusive. Based on traditional Ngöbe-Buglé architecture, the round wood-and-palm bungalows have an open design that delivers sea views. Being exposed to the elements is not everyone's cup of organic, young-leaf tea, especially if the rain and wind pick up. Still, the hosts are gracious and the meals (wine included) are well prepared.

It's ideal for surfers and divers. The resort also loans kayaks to paddle out to snorkel spots. Rates dip by US$80 after the first night.

OFF THE BEATEN TRACK

ADVENTURE IN NASO COUNTRY

On the border of Parque Internacional La Amistad and the proposed Naso reservation, this unique jungle lodging and sustainable tour operator is a recommended step off the gringo trail. At **Soposo Rainforest Adventures** (☎6631-2222; www.soposo.com; per person day tour US$90, 2-day package with tours, lodging & meals US$140), guests stay in stilted thatched huts, eat traditional foods and immerse themselves in Naso culture.

The project, spearheaded by an ex-Peace Corps volunteer and her Naso husband, has been lauded by travelers. It was created to offer the Naso people an alternative income, bolster cultural self-esteem and protect natural resources in the face of a massive hydroelectric project that is changing the nature of the area. A highlight is a three-day trip up the Teribe river to the village of the Naso monarch. They also offer trips to San-San Pond Sak to see the manatees and search for hatching turtles.

From Changuinola, it's a 30-minute taxi ride to the village of El Silencio, from where there's river access to the lodging.

Eating & Drinking

★Up In the Hill CAFE $

(Map p682; www.upinthehill.com; chocolate from US$2) Organic chocolate and gourmet coffee are reason enough to hike to this charming outpost on Bastimentos. To get there, head right from the Old Banks docks onto the main road and follow the signs. It's a 15-minute walk.

Roots CARIBBEAN $

(Old Bank; mains US$4-15; ⏲11:30am-9pm Wed-Mon) A deck bar with boat docking, this Bocas institution is famous for local meat and seafood, perfectly accented with fresh coconut milk. Co-owner Oscar Powell has also done much for the community of Isla Bastimentos and he's a personable fellow with a sharp sense of humor.

Orientation

The small village of Old Bank has no roads, just a wide, concrete footpath lined on both sides with colorfully painted wooden houses. From the town, there is a path leading across the island to Wizard Beach and Red Frog Beach, though the route can turn into a virtual swamp following the rains.

On the southeastern side of the island is the remote Ngöbe-Buglé village of Salt Creek. Tropical forest covers the interior of the island; you can explore it, but go only with a guide as it's very easy to get lost.

Information

Readers have reported daytime muggings on the trail between Old Town and Red Frog Beach (an alternate trail). Never go on any trail after dark and always travel with a friend. Don't take valuables, including a camera, to the beach.

Getting There & Away

To get to Isla Bastimentos from Bocas del Toro town, just walk down to the waterfront and ask a boatman to take you over. The ride will cost about US$4 to Old Bank or the public dock for Red Frog Beach (the beach lies 20 minutes further on by footpath).

Almirante

A clutch of stilted homes on the water, this unkempt village has seen better days. From Almirante, you can reach Bocas del Toro by water taxi, or a water shuttle run by Taxi 25 (US$4, 30 minutes). Seeing disoriented travelers arrive, local taxis will try to charge US$5 for the trip between the bus station and the dock, but the walk only takes five minutes.

An air-conditioned bus to Changuinola (US$1.50) leaves every 15 minutes between 6am and 8pm. Taxis to Changuinola (US$20) can be bargained, particularly if you start your walk from the dock to the bus station.

Changuinola

POP 32,600

Headquarters of the Chiriquí Land Company, the very same people that bring you Chiquita bananas, Changuinola is a hot and rather dusty town surrounded by a sea of banana plantations. Although there is little reason to linger, overland travelers en route from Costa Rica to Isla Colón stop here.

Changuinola also serves as the access point for the Wekso entrance to the Parque Internacional La Amistad. The **ANAM** (☎758-6603, 767-9485; ⏲8am-4pm Mon-Fri) office near the center of town has information on the park.

Sleeping & Eating

Hotel Hawaii HOTEL $
(☎758-6025; Av 17 de Abril; s/d/tr US$24/26/33; ❄@📶) These ample, plain rooms have clean bathrooms with spigot showers and beds clad in white sheets. There's an internet cafe in the lobby.

Resto Cotty's PANAMANIAN $
(Av 17 de Abril; meals US$2.50; ⏲24hr) On the main road, this clean cafeteria-style restaurant serves Panamanian fare. A plate of curried chicken and rice is gratifying and quick.

Getting There & Away

Buses depart near the city center, close to a number of restaurants, bars, markets and hotels. Buses for Costa Rica depart next to the Shell gas station. Other buses depart from **Terminal Urrica** (☎758-8115) with departures between 6am and 7pm.

COLÓN PROVINCE

With an edgy reputation more true crime than travel, Colón rarely makes travel wish lists. But there is more to this Caribbean province than its downtrodden capital. Extending for over 200km along the Caribbean coast from Veraguas Province in the west to the Comarca de Kuna Yala in the east, Colón Province is mostly undeveloped and virtually inaccessible. However, the province is also home to the Spanish colonial city of Portobelo, once the most prominent port on the Caribbean, as well as the famed tropical getaway of Isla Grande.

Although the city of Colón can be rough, the province boasts treasures from pristine beaches and lowland rainforests to colonial splendors and modern engineering marvels. Portobelo, with its growing music and art scene, shows the best of vibrant Congo culture. The luxury train between Panama City and Colón remains one of the greatest rail journeys in the Americas.

Colón

POP 134,000

With its colonial grandeur crumbling and its neighborhoods marginalized, historical Colón is sadly the city that Panama forgot, in spite of vigorous renovations meant to court Caribbean cruise ships. Prior to 1869, the railroad connecting Panama City and Colón was the only rapid transit across the continental Western Hemisphere. However, the establishment of the US transcontinental railroad put Colón out of business almost overnight. The last whiff of prosperity was seen during the construction of the Panama Canal.

In an attempt to revive the city, the Zona Libre (Free Zone) was created on the city's edge in 1948. Today, it's the largest free-trade zone in the Americas. Unfortunately, little of the US$10 billion in annual commerce seems to benefit locals.

Recent improvements in city safety are attributed to tighter gang control and an arms-for-food program that got many guns off the streets.

BUSES FROM CHANGUINOLA

DESTINATION	COST (US$)	DURATION	FREQUENCY
Almirante (with boat connections to Isla Colón)	1.50	45min	every 30min
David	10	4¾hr	every 45min
El Silencio (Parque Internacional La Amistad)	0.80	30min	every 20min
Guabito–Sixaola	1	30min	every 30min
Las Tablas (Las Delicias)	2	1¾hr	hourly
Panama City	29	12hr	daily 7am
San José (Costa Rica)	12	6hr	daily 10am

History

Colón was founded in 1850 as the Caribbean terminus of the Panama Railroad, though it faded into obscurity less than 20 years later. At the peak of its economic depression in 1881, the French arrived in Colón to start construction of an interoceanic canal. Four years later, a Colombian hoping to spark a revolution burned the city to the ground. In the years to follow, Colón entered a second golden age, rebuilt in French Colonial architectural style. Rivaling Panama City in beauty and wealth, life in the top of the Canal Zone was pleasurable and highly profitable. Following its economic ruin in 1914, the city spiraled into the depths of depravity. Today, most of the colonial city is still intact, though the buildings are on the verge of collapse.

Sights

Zona Libre SHOPPING CENTER

(Free Zone) Second only to Hong Kong's in terms of business volume, Colón's duty-free zone is a huge fortress of big-box stores selling duty-free items in bulk merchandise. It's not set up to sell to individual items to tourists. Individual purchases go to Tocumen International Airport in Panama City, where they may be retrieved upon a visitor's departure. To enter, present your passport at the security office.

Colón 2000 NEIGHBORHOOD

Only a decade old, this sterile shopping and entertainment sector, with shops and a casino geared toward cruise-ship travelers, sits on the east side of Colón.

Sleeping & Eating

There's no shortage of hotels in Colón, though most are in seedy areas and have serious security issues.

Meryland Hotel HOTEL $$

(441-7055; www.hotelmeryland.com; cnr Calle 7 & Av Santa Isabel; s/d US$44/55; P) A massive stone building, this business hotel fronts an attractive city park. Small, tiled rooms with gold tones and rod-iron furniture have air-con, cable TV and hot-water bathrooms, though you're paying for the 24-hour security, not luxury. The onsite restaurant saves you the trouble of having to leave the hotel at night.

Radisson HOTEL $$

(446-2000; www.radisson.com; Colón 2000; d/ste US$119/169; P) Really, you could be anywhere, but this luxury chain hotel has the friendliest staff and the best digs in Colón. Rooms are comfortable and sufficiently stylish, with minibar and flat-screen TVs. Get big off-season discounts with web specials. There is 24-hour security.

Arrecifes SEAFOOD $$

(info 441 9308; cnr Calle 3 & Paseo Gorgas; mains US$10-12; noon-8pm Mon-Sat) Local business owners lunch at this nondescript building cooking up great Caribbean seafood in the gated port area. Expect no frills and no water views, just generous portions of *criollo*-style (Creole-style) seafood, stewed in onions, peppers and tomatoes, and whole fried snappers.

Orientation

The city is reached via two major roads on the southern side of town. The roads become Av Amador Guerrero and Av Bolivar at the entrance to the town, and run straight up the grid-patterned city, ending near Colon's northern waterfront.

Perpendicular to these avenues are numbered streets. Calle 16 is the first of these you'll cross as you enter the town while Calle 1 is at the northern end of town. The Zona Libre occupies the southeastern corner of the city; just north of this is the city's cruise-ship port, Colón 2000.

Information

Apart from the cruise port on the eastern side of the city and the bustling Zona Libre, Colón has a dangerous reputation. Violent crime rates have lowered, but visitors should exercise caution when walking around, even during the day. Paseo de Washington, the renovated waterfront area, and Av Bolívar are safe to peruse by day. Always travel by taxi at night.

Given Colón's high rate of crime, the safest place to withdraw money is the Banco Nacional de Panama ATM at the Colón 2000 cruise port.

Getting There & Away

Plans are in the works to add an overnight ferry to Cartagena, which would be Panama's only direct boat service to Colombia outside the Darién.

BUS

From Panama City, a regular bus service to Colón (US$3.50, one to 1½hrs, every 30 minutes) departs from the Albrook bus terminal.

Colón's *terminal de buses* (bus terminal) is at the intersection of Calle Terminal and Av Bolívar. Hourly departures include La Guayra (US$3, two hours; from here you can catch the boat to Isla Grande), Nombre de Dios (US$3.80, 2½ hours) and Portobelo (US$1.60, 1½ hours).

If you are headed east of Colón from Panama City, these buses can be boarded at Sabanitas, the turnoff for Portobelo, thus avoiding a trip into Colón. Be aware that buses may be standing room only, particularly on weekends.

TRAIN

If you are arriving via train from Panama City (p656), the bus terminal is within walking distance.

Getting Around

While in Colón, it's a good idea to not wander around on foot. Fortunately, taxis congregate at the bus station, train station and the Zona Libre, and fares across the city are usually under US$2.

Around Colón

Sights

Canal Expansion Observation Center LOOKOUT

(Centro de Observación de la Ampliación del Canal; ☎276-8325; www.micanaldepanama.com; adult/child US$15/10; ⏲8:30am-3:30pm) Still a work in progress, this new and pricey observation center offers an exclusive view of the Panama Canal expansion, slated to be completed in 2015. Visits take slightly over an hour. Covered decks look out onto Lago Gatún and the locks. There is also a theater with videos in English, exhibits, a cafe and gift shop. A short rainforest trail has sloths and monkeys.

The turnoff for the new observation center is just past the railroad tracks, to the left; for the locks, continue straight at the turnoff. The center is accessible for travellers with disabilities.

Gatún Locks CANAL

(adult/child US$5/free; ⏲8am-4pm) The Gatún Locks raise southbound ships 29.5m from Caribbean waters to the level of Lago Gatún. From there, the ships travel 37km to the Pedro Miguel Locks, which lower southbound ships 9.3m to Lago Miraflores, a small body of water that separates the two sets of Pacific locks. The ships are then lowered to sea level at the Miraflores Locks.

Not only are the Gatún Locks the largest of the three current sets, but their size is simply mind boggling. Workers poured a record-setting 1,820,000 cu meters of concrete to construct the locks, a process which took four years.

A viewing stand opposite the control tower offers a prime view of the locks in action. A brochure in English clearly describes the two-hour process.

It's 10km south of Colón. Buses to the Gatún Locks leave the Colón bus terminal hourly (US$1.25, 20 minutes). A taxi ride from Colón to the locks and dam and back should cost US$60 per party, but agree on a price before leaving.

Parque Nacional San Lorenzo PARK

(www.sanlorenzo.org.pa) Centered on the ruins of the crumbling Spanish colonial fortress of Fuerte San Lorenzo, the 97-sq-km park is perched at the mouth of the Río Chagres. This river floated Welsh pirate Henry Morgan to the interior in 1671, enabling him to sack the original Panama City.

The Spanish fortress is built of blocks of cut coral with rows of old cannons jutting out. Among the many Spanish cannons, you might spot a British one – evidence of the time when British pirates overcame the fort. Much of the fort is well preserved, including the moat, the cannons and the arched rooms.

There is no public transportation to Fuerte San Lorenzo from Colón. Tours from Panama City are well priced, considering that a round-trip taxi ride from Colón costs around US$60.

Portobelo

POP 4100

This Caribbean fishing village is so laid-back and languorous, it's incredible to ponder that it was once the greatest Spanish port in Central America. Mules once carried Peruvian gold and Oriental treasures to Panama City via the fortresses at Portobelo. Though English privateers destroyed them several times throughout their history, many of these atmospheric colonial fortresses still stand. Throughout the village, homes are situated among these atmospheric ruins.

Portobelo is experiencing something of a cultural rival, with recent interest surging in

PORTOBELO'S TOP ESCAPES

- Take a water taxi to Puerto Francés for private swims and jungle hikes.
- Snorkel around Spanish cannons encrusted in the coral landscape.
- Kayak up the tranquil Río Claro.
- Watch a sunset from El Fuerte de San Fernando.
- Join a Congo dance workshop and sweat to cool African rhythms.

Congo art and dancing. Visitors can explore the extensive ruins, take a boat to remote beaches and dive at interesting underwater attractions.

History

Portobelo, the 'beautiful port,' was named by Columbus in 1502, when he stopped here on his fourth New World voyage. For the next 200 years, Portobelo served as the principal Spanish Caribbean port in Central America.

Aiming to disrupt the Spanish treasure route, British admiral Edward Vernon destroyed Portobelo in 1739. Discouraged, the Spanish abandoned the overland Panama route, and instead started sailing the long way around Cape Horn to and from the western coast of South America.

Though rebuilt in 1751, Portobelo never attained its former prominence, and in time became a virtual ruin. The outermost fortress was dismantled to build the Panama Canal, with larger stones used in the construction of the Gatún Locks. Yet there are still considerable parts of the town intact, protected as a national park and historic site.

Sights

The remnants of **Fuerte Santiago**, 500m west of Portobelo's center, include officers' quarters, an artillery shed, a sentry box, a barracks and batteries. If short on time, San Jerónimo is more complete and makes for a better visit than Santiago. The ruins of **Fuerte San Fernando** occupy a grassy flat across the bay.

Fuerte San Jerónimo FORT
Fuerte San Jerónimo, closer to Portobelo center, was the largest fortress ever built to protect the bay. Eighteen cannon embrasures face the mouth of the bay, some exactly where the Spanish troops left them in 1821, the year Panama declared independence. Beyond the impressive gateway of San Jerónimo are the remains of the officers' quarters, barracks and a guard room.

Real Aduana de Portobelo HISTORIC BUILDING
(admission US$1; ⏲8am-4pm) Also known as the *contaduría*, this restored colonial customs house has interesting exhibits of Portobelo's history as well as a three-dimensional model of the area.

Iglesia de San Félipe ARCHITECTURE
This large colonial church, built in 1776, contains a life-size statue of the Black Christ, which is believed to have miraculous powers.

Activities

Although the clarity of the water here is not spectacular, Portobelo enjoys a good diving reputation due to two unique sites off the coast, namely a 33m cargo ship and a C-45 twin-engine plane.

Water taxis leave from Fuerte Santiago. Co-op Santiago de La Gloria charges a two-person minimum to Playa La Huerta (US$30), Playa Blanca (US$45) and the beach at Puerto Francés (US$35); all fees are round-trip.

Scubaportobelo DIVING
(☎261-3841; www.scubapanama.com) Outfitter Scubaportobelo offers all-inclusive scuba packages with waterfront lodgings. It's located on the road into town, on the left.

Festivals & Events

Festival de Cristo Negro FESTIVAL
(Black Christ Festival) Every October 21, pilgrims from all over Panama partake in this festival honoring a miracle-giving statue of the Black Christ housed in the Iglesia de San Félipe. After the sun sets, the statue is paraded down the streets, while pilgrims bedecked in purple robes and thorned crowns dance and drink until the wee hours.

Festival de Diablos y Congos FESTIVAL
The most intriguing local tradition is Festival de Diablos y Congos, a festival of rebellion and ridicule that mocks the colonial Spaniards. During the festivity, blacks assume the role of escaped slaves and take 'captives.' It is held two weeks after Carnaval, sometimes coinciding with Portobelo's patron saint day on March 20.

Sleeping & Eating

Captain Jack's HOSTEL $
(☎448-2009; www.captainjackvoyages.com; dm US$13; @) Run by a sailboat captain from New Jersey, this bare-bones hostel (think plastic-covered mattresses and funky showers) is nonetheless a hub of merrymaking. Perhaps its best feature is the upper deck restaurant-bar serving great grub (US$7 to US$26) from 11am to 10pm. Unfortunately, we are not sure if the Vietnamese cook (responsible for the pho and spring rolls) is staying on.

★Casa de la Bruja GUESTHOUSE $$
(☎226-2035, 6764-0725; sandraeleta@gmail.com; d US$50, 4-person loft US$80, 2-bedroom house US$175; P) Quite out of the ordinary, this chill photographer's home is adapted for guests. There are two ample, lovely houses side by side, with a grassy seafront perfect for lounging. The bright, open interiors showcase photography and local Congo art. It is fine to cook here or you can pay extra for prepared meals. Guests can organize excursions to snorkel and sightsee or take a Caribbean cooking workshop (US$15 per person) from Doña Cecelia.

Casa Rayo Verde GUESTHOUSE $$
(☎202-0111; info.rayoverde@gmail.com; d US$60;) A recent addition, this attractive four-room home is recommended by guests. The property faces the water, and quaint rooms have minifridges and private bathrooms. Guests can enjoy the shared terrace. The guesthouse helps fund art, music and carpentry initiatives in the local community.

Coco Plum Eco Lodge HOTEL $$
(☎448-2102; www.cocoplum-panama.com; s/d/tr US$45/55/65; P) An attractive, motel-style lodging, the friendly Coco Plum has been around for years. At the time of writing, the scuba shop was undergoing transition to new management. On the waterfront, the feel of the place is ocean kitsch, replete with nets, shells and pastels, but the effect is cozy. A salon has games and TV. The attached bar-restaurant (mains US$6 to US$15) is popular with travelers – try the octopus in coconut milk or the seafood stew.

Orientation

Located 43km from Colón, Portobelo consists of about 15 blocks of homes and businesses that line a paved, two-lane road. This road intersects with the Panama City–Colón road at the town of Sabanitas, 33km to the west.

East of Portobelo, the road forks after 9km. The left branch extends 11km to the village of La Guayra, where you can hire boats to Isla Grande.

Information

ATP (☎448-2200, 6485-7028; ⏲9:30am-5:30pm Tue-Fri & Sun) Just off the main road. Ask Mireya Jimenez for information about Congo dance workshops or volunteering with the school. Spanish-only spoken.

Getting There & Away

Buses to Portobelo (US$1.60, 1½ hours, every 30 minutes) depart from Colón's bus terminal from 6:30am to 6pm.

From Panama City, take the Colón bus and get off at El Rey supermarket in Sabanitas, 10km before Colón. Next, catch the bus coming from Colón to Portobelo when it passes through Sabanitas (US$1.25, 1¼ hours). Since it's often full, take as little luggage as possible.

Isla Grande

Palm trees and white-sand beaches form the backdrop to this lovely island 15km northeast of Portobelo. A popular getaway for Panama City folk, Isla Grande is an ideal setting for snorkeling, scuba diving or simply soaking up the island's relaxed vibe. About 300 people of African descent live on the island, most of whom eke out a living from fishing and coconuts – you'll get a taste of both when you sample the fine island cuisine.

Activities

Some lovely **beaches** on the northern side of the island can be reached by boat (hire a water taxi at the dock in front of Cabañas Super Jackson) or on foot (there's a water's-edge trail that loops around the 5km long, 1.5km wide island, as well a slippery cross-island trail).

If you're looking for a good **surf** break, take a water taxi out to La Guayra where you can find a good reef break that peaks right and left.

For around US$50, one of the boatmen in front of Cabañas Super Jackson will take you on a half-day adventure – the possibilities are quite appealing. The mangroves east of Isla Grande are fun to explore, or you could go snorkeling off the coast of the nearby islets.

Festivals & Events

The **Festival of San Juan Bautista** is celebrated on June 24, with swimming and canoe races. The **Virgen del Carmen** is honored on July 16, with a land and sea procession, baptisms and masses.

Carnaval is also celebrated here in rare form. Along with the dancing, there are also satirical songs about current events and a lot of joking in the Caribbean calypso tradition.

Sleeping & Eating

Cabañas Super Jackson CABIN $

(☎448-2311; d/tr/q US$30/40/50; ❄) Close to the main pier, this Isla Grande landmark offers a handful of cheap and cheerful rooms with private bathrooms. There are definitely more comfortable spots on the island, but it's hard to beat the price, the convenience factor and the humorous name.

Sister Moon Eco Lodge LODGE $$

(☎6948-1990; www.hotelsistermoon.com; dm US$25, s/d/tr/q US$40/69/89/109; ≋) The best bang for your buck, this lovely clutch of hillside cabins is surrounded by swaying palms and crashing waves. The fabulous views are best appreciated from a porch hammock. 'Ecolodge' here means no hot water or air-conditioning. The hotel bar-restaurant is built right over the water and features the island's famous coconut-infused seafood. Day passes are US$20.

Bananas Village Resort RESORT $$$

(☎263-9510; www.bananasresort.com; d incl breakfast from US$153, oceanfront ste from US$203; P ❄ @ ≋) Located on the northern side of the island and only accessible by boat or trail, Grande's most upscale accommodation consists of two-story A-frame jungle cottages fronted by the sea. Guests can kayak, play volleyball and use snorkeling gear without extra charges. Weekend prices climb steeply. Day-trippers pay US$35 for use of the facilities, a welcome cocktail and lunch. Some fine snorkeling and dive sites are within a 10-minute boat ride of the island.

Getting There & Away

Buses from Colón go to La Guayra (US$3, 1½ hours, hourly). A 10-minute boat ride from there to Isla Grande costs US$3 to US$5 per person. Parking costs US$3.50 per day.

COMARCA DE KUNA YALA

Imagine a turquoise archipelago that has one island for every day of the year. With white sand and waving palms, these Caribbean islands cheat no one's version of paradise. The Comarca is home to the Kuna, the first group in Latin America to gain indigenous autonomy. Though they have had contact with Europeans since Columbus sailed these waters in 1502, clan identity is paramount, and many make tenacious efforts to preserve a traditional way of life.

In 2009 the road to Cartí was completed, making the region far more accessible than it has ever been. Still off the beaten track, this narrow, 226km-long strip on the Caribbean coast stretches from the Golfo de San Blás to the Colombian border.

Community islands are acre-sized cays packed with bamboo huts, livestock and people. Visitors often prefer the more remote outer islands with few inhabitants. Most areas require landing fees.

History

The Kuna have lived in Eastern Panama for at least two centuries, though scholars fiercely debate their origins. Language similarities with people who once lived several hundred kilometers to the west would indicate that the Kuna migrated eastward. However, oral tradition has it that the Kuna migrated to San Blás from Colombia after the 16th century, following a series of devastating encounters with other tribes armed with poison-dart blowguns.

Scholars agree that life on the islands is relatively new for the Kuna. Historians at the end of the 18th century wrote that the only people who used the San Blás islands at the time were pirates, Spaniards and the odd explorer.

Today, there are an estimated 70,000 Kuna; 32,000 live on the district's islands, 8000 live on tribal land along the coast and 30,000 live outside the district. So communal are the island Kuna that they inhabit only 40 of the 400 cays – the rest are coconut farms with sea turtles and iguanas. The inhabited islands are packed with traditional bamboo-sided, thatched-roof houses in sometimes unsanitary conditions.

Historically, the Kuna subsisted on freshly caught seafood, including fish, lobster, shrimp, Caribbean king crab and octopus. This was accompanied by food crops, including rice, yams, yucca, bananas and pineapples grown on the nearby mainland. Today, this traditional diet is supplemented by food products obtained by bartering coconuts with passing Colombian ships.

Activities

Most lodgings offer complete packages, where a fixed price gets you a room, three meals a day and boat rides to neighboring islands for swimming, snorkeling and lounging on the beach. If you seek community life, you can also arrange visits to more populated islands. Before swimming off the shores of a heavily populated island, however, take a look at the number of outhouses built over the ocean – they may change your mind.

Snorkeling is good in places, but many of the coral reefs in the region are badly damaged. You can often rent snorkeling equipment from lodgings, but serious snorkelers should bring their own gear. Jaunts to mainland jungles are arranged with a guide. Activities aside, most travelers to Kuna Yala are content with simply soaking up the Caribbean sun and perfecting their hammock-swaying.

Sleeping & Eating

In a protectionist move to preserve local culture, the Kuna Congress passed a law several years ago that prohibits outsiders from owning property in the Comarca. Hotels in the Comarca are 100% owned by local families.

Since there are no restaurants, each hotel provides meals for guests. Seafood features widely; quality varies as stocks have been depleted through overfishing. There is always a healthy stock of fresh coconuts on hand. It's a good idea to bring nonperishable snacks with you.

Cabañas Tigre CABIN $

(☎6099-2738; r per person US$10, child US$5; meals from US$4) On a quiet tip of a lovely community island, these bamboo-and-thatch *cabañas* have cement floors and shared facilities. Guests have an ample space with hammocks and a good beach but also get to see a fair amount of typical village life. Three new bamboo-and-thatch cabins under construction will raise rates since they feature private bathrooms. Fly into Corazón de Jesus.

RESPONSIBLE TRAVEL IN KUNA YALA

When visiting the Comarca de Kuna Yala, consider how your visit may affect the community. Tourism revenue can play a vital role in the development of the region, particularly for Kuna artisans or guides. However, indigenous tourism can be an exploitative force. Western interests have already caused an irreversible amount of damage to the region. Be aware of your surroundings and be sensitive to your impact.

One look at the paradisiacal setting, the rainbow flag and the distinctive Kuna dress and you might feel transported into the pages of *National Geographic*. Don't snap that shutter just yet. If the Kuna appear unfriendly, consider their predicament. When cruise ships visit, the number of people on an already congested island can triple. Then nearly two-thirds of the populace (the tourists) turns paparazzi on the other third (the Kuna). It's an unsavory scene that is repeated again and again.

Trash is a problem on the islands, and there is no effective plan for its removal. You may see litter and burning piles of plastics. For the Kunas, the removal of rubbish to the mainland is too costly and there is no designated site or 'culture' of waste management, since all refuse was relatively innocuous until outside influence prevailed. With no current solution to the issue, do what you can to pack out your own garbage and try to consume fresh products with minimal packaging (for example, choose coconut water over bottled drinks).

The way you dress (or fail to) is another issue. Kuna men never go shirtless and Kuna women dress conservatively, with their cleavage, bellies and most of their legs covered. Arriving in Kuna villages in bikinis or shirtless is a sign of disrespect. In general, it is not worth the risk of offending local sensibilities.

To rein in the situation, the Kuna charge fees for photographs taken of them as well as visitation fees for each island. Forget the way things work back home. Remember this is their territory and their rules apply. If you can't afford the photo fee, strike up a conversation instead.

KUNA LIVING 101

Lodging considerations in the Comarca are vastly different from those on the mainland. Here, a spot in a thatched hut with sand floor can cost anywhere between US$30 and US$130 per night. What's the difference?

Often it has more to do with access, ambience and organization than anything. Densely populated community islands are more likely to have budget options, but they will not live up to your image of a remote tropical paradise. Resort islands generally have a higher price tag, but may not offer many opportunities to interact with locals. When planning, consider why you're going and the following:

Space Does the island have shade? Privacy? Are there pleasant areas to swim or do you have to take a boat to swim and snorkel sites?

Access Is the island too remote, requiring expensive transfers to do anything?

Hospitality Ask other travelers about their experience.

Water Is it potable? Consider bringing a filter.

Bathrooms Are there modern installations or does the toilet sit at the end of a dock?

Safety Do excursion boats have life vests and good motors?

Lodgings generally include three meals (but not drinks), one outing per day (eg snorkeling, a community visit) and usually transportation to or from the airport or Cartí, but confirm ahead. Fees for visiting Kuna islands and provision of drinking water may be separate. It is always wise to bring snacks, insect repellent, a first-aid kit and a flashlight. Rates are generally lower from April to November.

When booking, remember that internet is not prevalent and any cell phone number is only good until that phone accidentally falls into the ocean. But approach your hosts with good humor and patience and they will probably reciprocate in spades.

Cabañas Franklin CABIN $

(Tuba Senika; ☎6902-2863; dm US$26, cabin per person US$30) Franklin is a bit of a personality among Kunas: a blue-eyed older gent conversant in English, whose thatched office bears signs in Hebrew. His lodging is consistently popular, with cabins scattered under palms, cement and tiled stall bathrooms, and sand that is regularly raked.

Guests play volleyball in the water and can take snorkeling excursions (US$6). Transfers are extra (US$20 round-trip).

Robinson's Cabins CABIN $

(☎6721-9885; r per person incl 3 meals & tours US$30) For shoestringers who want nothing more than some thatch over their head and sand beneath their toes, this is it. The charismatic Robinson is good for wacky conversation – he studied in the US and has plenty to say. There is little to do here, but dining outdoors around the picnic table provides the perfect opportunity to mix with fellow travelers.

In low season, rates are discounted but transfers to Cartí (US$15) are charged separately. If Robinson is full, his cousin Ina's place next door offers identical rates and lodgings.

Cartí Homestay HOSTEL $

(☎6734-3454, 6517-9850; www.cartihomestay-kunayala.blogspot.com; r per person incl 3 meals & tour US$35; @) Catering to backpackers, this is the best place around to meet young Kunas and strike up a conversation, though the inflatable Jägermeister bottle in the corner is a good indicator of the kind of cultural interactions you might expect. Internet via stick modem is US$1 per hour. The hosts can also coordinate speedboats to Puerto Obaldía for Colombia-bound travelers.

★Cabañas Kuanidup CABIN $$

(☎6635-6737, 6742-7656; www.kuanidup.com; r per person incl 3 meals & tours US$90) A clutch of solar-powered bamboo-and-thatch cabins with sandy floors and private bathrooms. Outings include a waterfall hike, and a visit to the prized Cayos Holandeses or a nearby nudist island. The clincher is the stunning beach. There's billiards and volleyball, but most guests pass the time by simply swinging in the hammocks and meditating to the sounds of lapping waves.

Some huts have tarps under the thatch, which kills a bit of the ambience. But the place is well managed, with secure boats, a septic system, purified drinking water and regional transportation included.

Hotel Corbiski HOTEL **$$**
(☎6708-5254; www.corbiski.com; r without bathroom per person incl 3 meals & tour US$65) A bamboo-walled lodging with laminated floors and neat and spacious rooms on a busy community island. Clean, shared bathrooms occupy cement stalls. Lodgings include purified water and transportation to and from Cartí or Porvenir. The owner, Elias Pérez, speaks English and can arrange local excursions or facilitate volunteering at the school.

Yandup Lodge CABIN **$$$**
(☎261-7229; www.yandupisland.com; s/d cabin incl 3 meals & tours US$160/230) Just five minutes by boat from Playón Chico, tiny islet Yandup is run by an attentive Spaniard-Kuna family. The octagonal thatched-roof cabins have private bathrooms, solar-generated light and clean water. Guests can request vegetarian meals and get tailored excursions, which include cultural visits as well as the usual snorkeling and hiking. The island's grassy grounds and powder-fine beach might be reason enough to just stay put.

Shopping

Molas are the most famous of Panamanian traditional handicrafts. Made of brightly colored squares of cotton fabric sewn together, the finished product reveals landscape scenes, birds, sea turtles or fish – often surrounded by a mazelike pattern. Craftsmanship varies considerably between *molas,* and prices start at US$10 and go into the hundreds. You can find *molas* on the islands (or rather, the *mola* sellers will find you).

Orientation

Formerly inaccessible by road, there is now paved access to Cartí from Panama City. From here, boat transportation can be arranged to islands with basic hotels. If you're planning on staying at any of the far-flung islands, you can also fly into Río Sidra or Playón Chico.

Information

Although a trip to the Archipiélago de San Blás may not fit in the budget, these culturally rich Caribbean islands are a good place for a splurge if you can swing it. Prices vary, but if you stick to the cheaper hotels, you can survive on about US$45 per day; this includes meals, lodging and daily boating excursions. Reserve lodgings ahead.

There's no ATM, so hit one before you touch down on the islands.

The Kuna are very particular about what foreigners do on their islands. As a result, they require that tourists register and pay a visitation fee (between US$3 and US$12) on the main islands. On smaller, privately owned islands, visitors must seek out the owner, receive permission and pay a fee (around US$5).

If you want to take someone's photo, ask their permission first and be prepared to pay (US$1 per photo or subject). You may not be expected to pay for a photo taken of an artisan from whom you buy crafts from, but it depends on the subject. Some islands may charge you US$50 just for possessing a video camera.

Getting There & Away

AIR

Book as far in advance as possible as demand far exceeds supply. Note that planes may stop at other islands in the archipelago, loading and unloading passengers or cargo before continuing on.

Flights depart from Albrook airport in Panama City and arrive at their destinations in about 30 minutes to an hour. A one-way ticket to each destination is around US$40 to US$80; prices vary according to season and availability.

Air Panama (☎316-9000; www.airpanama.com) Daily flights to Achutupu, Cartí, Corazón de Jesús, Playón Chico and Río Sidra.

BOAT

Sailboats travel to Colombia via the archipelago, but most board in Colón Province. Lodgings in Panama City have more information about these privately run trips.

San Blas Adventures (The Darién Gapster; www.sanblasadventures.com; per person all-inclusive US$350) More of a tour than just transport, this popular new four-day service takes backpackers between Cartí and La Miel (the Colombian border), visiting Kuna communities, camping on beaches and snorkeling along the way. Fiberglass boats have outboard engines. A good alternative to the sailboat crossing (avoiding cramped overnight quarters) and rough seas. The website has useful planning details.

CAR & MOTORCYCLE

The El Llano–Cartí road is the only road that leads into the district. It connects the town of El Llano, on the Interamericana 70km east of Panama City, to the San Blás coastal hamlet of Cartí. The road begins near El Llano at the turnoff for Nusagandi.

It's best to take a shared 4WD with a powerful engine, a winch and good tires. Ask your Panama City hostel to arrange transportation. Both **Kuna Yala Expeditions** (☎6708-5254) and driver **Germain Perez** (☎6734-3454; www.cartihome-

OFF THE BEATEN TRACK

SAILING THE KUNA YALA TO COLOMBIA

If you're a backpacker, or don't mind living like one in the name of adventure, consider this: small sailboats can take passengers to Colombia via the scenic Archipiélago de San Blás for the same price as a flight. But the trip may not be for everyone.

Potential guests should know that these boats are not official charters. Passengers help out in exchange for cheap passage and usually few days of sun and sand in the San Blás, often with a snorkeling trip or two. The rough open-sea passage to Cartagena accounts for half the duration of the trip. Before you book, find out the following:

- Are accommodations a cabin or floor space?
- What is the size of boat and the number of passengers?
- Is the boat equipped with adequate life boats and life vests for all passengers?
- Does the boat have an adequate safety equipment and a functioning radio?
- Does the captain have a charter license?
- What are the meals like? (Some boats serve beans and rice three times a day.)

We have heard happy reports, but travelers have also complained about boats skimping on meals, overcrowding or traveling despite bad weather in order to process more trips. Bring snacks and ask ahead about whether the boat needs fresh groceries (hard to stock when boats spend extended periods in the islands). Don't skimp on research – check a boat or captain's existing references with hostels and other travelers before committing. If you are only traveling for the novelty of sailing, consider a trip that sticks to the Kuna Yala.

The best place to inquire about scheduled departures is at any of the youth hostels in Panama City. A typical five-day sailing trip including food and activities (but not island fees) costs around US$500. Another alternative is the motorboat trip offered by San Blas Adventures (p702) that stops to camp on beaches.

staykunayala.blogspot.com; per person US$25) offer transfers for US$50 round-trip per person.

DARIÉN PROVINCE

One of world's richest biomes is the 5760-sq-km Parque Nacional Darién, where the primeval meets the present with scenery nearly unaltered from a million years ago. Even today in the Darién, the Emberá and Wounaan people maintain many of their traditional practices and retain generations-old knowledge of the rainforest. In a stroke of irony, the Darién has remained so pristine because of its volatile reputation.

But while the southern Darién is home to Panama's most spectacular rainforests, the north is home to scenes of habitat destruction. Safety is a real concern here, yet regional issues are complex and require careful consideration. It is not for everyone, but with careful planning and the right destinations, the Darién offers spectacular opportunities for intrepid travelers yearning for something truly wild.

If traveling beyond Yaviza, you are required to receive advance permission from the Servicio Nacional de Fronteras (SENAFRONT) in Panama City.

History

Indigenous groups living within the boundaries of the Darién emigrated from the Chocó region of Colombia thousands of years ago. Anthropologists place the Chocóes in two linguistic groups – the Emberá and the Wounaan. With the exception of language, their cultural features are virtually identical, but they prefer to be distinguished as two separate peoples.

Before the introduction of the gun, the Emberá and Wounaan were expert users of the *boroquera* (blowgun) and they envenomed their darts with lethal toxins from poisonous frogs and bullet ants. Many scholars believe that they forced the Kuna out of the Darién and into the Caribbean coastal area.

During the US occupation, the US Air Force turned to the Emberá and Wounaan for jungle survival. Since both groups thrive in the tropical wilderness, many were added to the corps of instructors that trained US astronauts and air force pilots at Fort Sherman, near Colón.

Today, the majority of the 8000 Emberá and Wounaan in Panama live deep in the rainforests of the Darién, particularly along the Sambú, Jaqué, Chico, Tuquesa, Membrillo, Tuira, Yape and Tucutí rivers. Along with engaging in subsistence agriculture, hunting, fishing and poultry raising, they also work on nearby commercial rice and maize plantations.

Orientation

The Interamericana terminates in the frontier town of Yaviza, beyond which lies the vast wilderness region of the Darién. The highway starts again 150km further on in Colombia. This break between Central and South America is known as the Darién Gap – literally the end of the road.

Information

Printed information on the Darién becomes rapidly outdated. Always seek up-to-date information, usually best from a guide who leads frequent trips to the area.

Local ANAM offices in towns such as Yaviza or La Palma can provide information on the park and help you find guides (usually rangers with days off). Travelers must also check in with the police in these towns before heading out into the jungle.

Panama City's Instituto Geográfico Nacional (p654) usually sells topographical maps for some regions of the Darién.

DANGERS & ANNOYANCES

The greatest hazard in the Darién is the difficult environment. Trails, when they exist at all, are often poorly defined and never marked. Many large rivers that form the backbone of the Darién transportation network create their own hazards. Any help at all, much less medical help, is very far away.

Consult your doctor before you go about necessary medication and cover up as much as possible, especially at dawn and dusk. Dengue and malaria are serious risks. Areas of the Parque Nacional Darién are prime territory for the deadly fer-de-lance snake. The odds of getting a snake bite are remote, but be careful and always wear boots on treks. Although they don't carry Lyme disease, ticks are widespread. Bring tweezers and a few books of matches to remove them.

The US State Department warns travelers against visiting remote areas of the Darién off the Interamericana. This blanket advisory includes the entirety of Parque Nacional Darién, although certain destinations may be OK to visit.

Although the no-go zones in the Darién are well removed from the traditional tourist destinations, their dangers cannot be underestimated. Narco-traffickers who utilize these jungle routes don't appreciate encountering travelers trekking through the woods. Parts of the Darién Gap are areas of activity for former Colombian guerrillas or runaways. Missionaries and travelers alike have been kidnapped and killed in the southern area of the Darién.

Despite these warnings, parts of the Darién can be visited safely. To minimize these risks, it's recommended that you explore the Darién either as part of an organized tour or with the help of a qualified guide.

Tours

The Darién is the only major part of Panama where a guide is necessary. If you speak Spanish, you can hire guides locally for about US$15 to US$30 per day. But transportation costs can be very expensive. If you go with a tour operator, they will take care of all arrangements without a language barrier, teach you about the incredible local ecology, cook for you and humor you when you have blisters.

★ Jungle Treks ADVENTURE TOUR
(☎6438-3130; www.jungletreks.com) Run by a veteran naturalist guide, this recommended outfitter specializes in expedition-style travel for groups of six or more. Destinations include Río Sambú and the Pacific coast. Custom trips are possible, with a three-day minimum. English-speaking.

Ancon Expeditions TOURS
(☎269-9415; www.anconexpeditions.com) The sole operator in the Darién for many years, Ancon has the most experienced guides. Trips run from four days to two weeks. Destinations include a private lodge in Punta Patiño on the Pacific coast and visits to remote indigenous communities. Special programs for birdwatchers and hikers are recommended.

Panama Exotic Adventures TOUR
(☎in Panama City 223-9283; www.panamaexoticadventures.com) With an ecolodge in Metetí, this French-run outfit offers three- to eight-day trips with hands-on visits to indigenous communities, kayaking and other outings.

Getting There & Away

The Interamericana journeys 266km from Panama City to Yaviza. Serving these towns, there are eight buses daily from Panama City to Yaviza between 3:30am and 7am (US$16, 4½ hours).

Darién Province

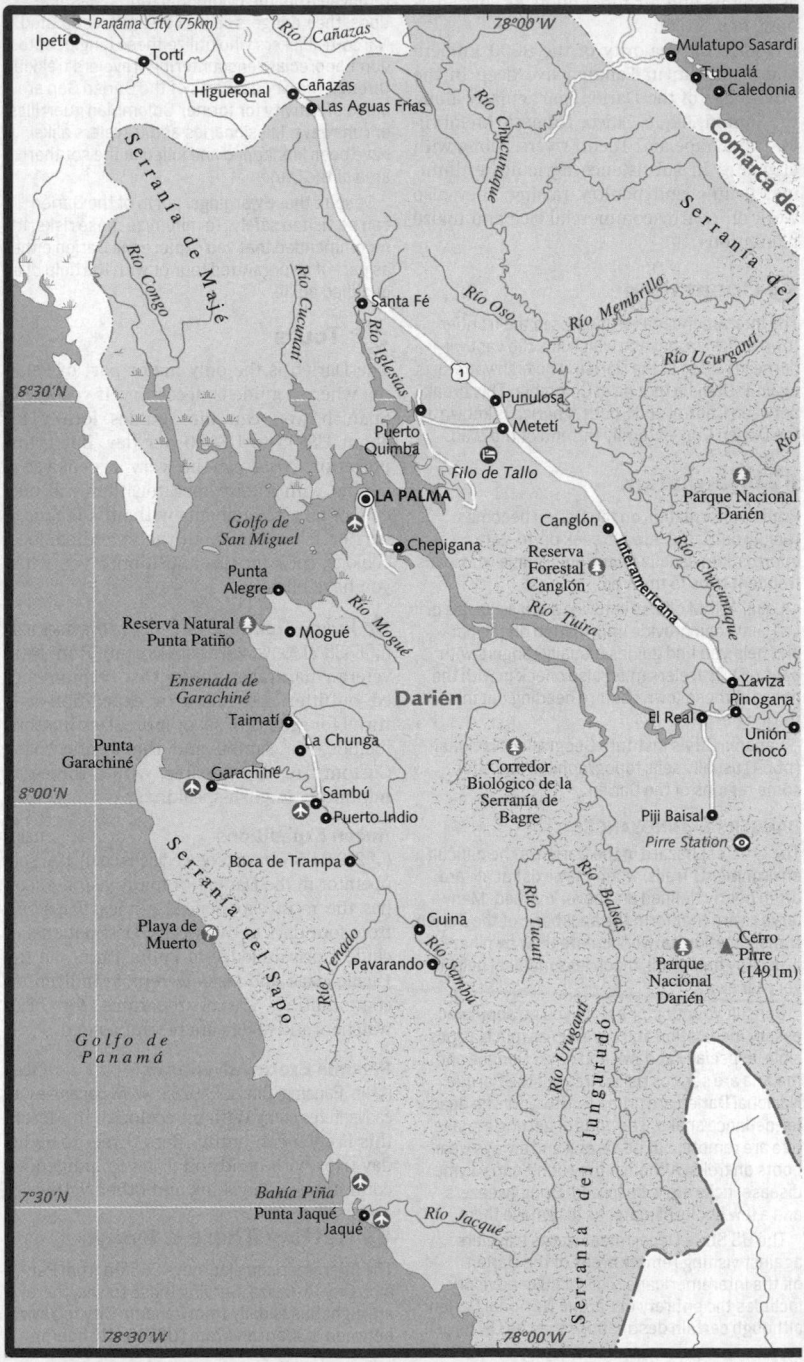

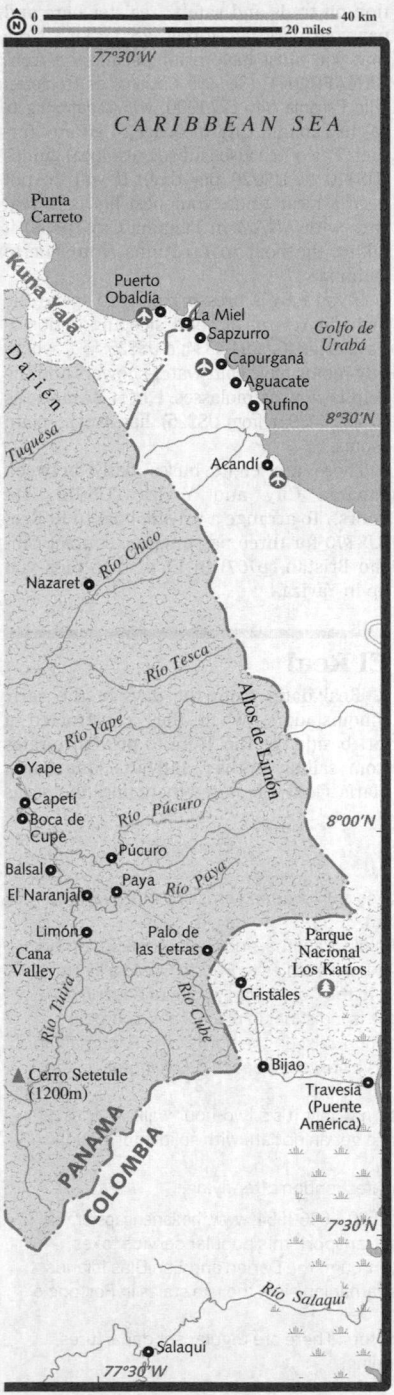

Police checkpoints are frequent on this road, so have your passport ready and be prepared to discuss your travel plans. Occasionally, a soldier will lecture you about the dangers near the border – that's because it's their job to go there if something happens.

With irregular frequency, **Air Panama** (☎ 316-9000; www.flyairpanama.com) has flights to Jaqué, El Real Sambú and Puerto Obaldia. There is also a ferry from Panama City to La Palma.

Getting Around

In the vast jungles of the Darién Province, rivers are often the only means of getting from one point to another, with *piraguas* (dugout canoes) providing the transport. In La Palma you can hire a motorized boat for US$175 to US$200 per day, which can take you to the Río Mogué or the Río Sambú. From either of these rivers you'll have to negotiate with indigenous villagers (in Mogué or La Chunga) to take you further upriver in *piraguas*. Hiring boats in Río Jaqué is possible but strongly ill-advised owing to the dangers of guerrilla activity. A shorter (and cheaper) boat trip goes from Puerto Quimba to La Palma.

Metetí

On the road to Yaviza, Metetí buzzes with passing traffic. It's also a key stepping stone to La Palma via a scenic boat ride. Lodging options here are preferable to those in Yaviza. For last-minute purchases there is a good-sized grocery store.

The bleach-scented **Hotel Felicidad** (☎ 299-6544; d US$23; ❄) is one of the decent hotels, with clean cement rooms. The nearby **Restaurante Johana** (mains US$3.50) serves meat dishes with rice and plantains, and fresh juice (but no beer).

Run by Panama Exotic Adventures, ecolodge **Filo de Tallo** (☎ 6673-5381, in Panama 223-9283; www.panamadarien.com; 4-day package per person from US$1050) is an elegant take on jungle living, with three well-spaced thatched huts containing beds draped with mosquito netting and attached bathrooms set with pastel river stones. Activities include crabbing in the mangroves, kayaking and visiting a Wounaan village. Although it's on a deforested sector just entering the Darién, it's one of the best lodgings in the region. It is also certified as carbon neutral by Forest Finance. Packages include all meals and activities and transportation to and from Panama City.

Traveling to La Palma by boat from Puerto Quimba is an excellent alternative to flying straight in from Panama City. The scenery along this 30-minute river trip is virgin jungle and dense mangrove forests – and you're bound to meet interesting characters onboard.

For the boat to La Palma, take the 20km road for Puerto Quimba, a port on the Río Iglesias. A passenger pickup shuttles between Metetí and Puerto Quimba every 30 minutes from 6am until 9pm (US$3), or take a taxi (US$10).

From Puerto Quimba, unscheduled boats to La Palma leave several times a day between 7:30am and 6:30pm (US$5); they depart from La Palma roughly between 5:30am and 5pm. A one-way charter (US$40) may also be an option.

Yaviza

POP 3300

Part bazaar and part bizarre, this concrete village is the end of the road. Here the Interamericana grinds to a halt and beyond lies the famous Darién Gap. Rough-edged and misshapen, it's hardly a holiday destination. For travelers, it is an essential stop to check in for entry to Parque Nacional Darién.

The **ANAM** (☎299-4495) office of Parque Nacional Darién can offer updated information on trails and safety; register here and pay your park fee (foreigners US$15). Note that you must have prior permission from **SENAFRONT** (Servicio Nacional de Fronteras; ☎in Panama City 527-1000; www.senafront.gob.pa) in Panama City in order to go any further. The office also can suggest local guides (US$10 to US$20 per day). If you do not need a local guide, your best bet is to register with ANAM in Panama City (p655) if taking the boat to La Palma from Puerto Quimba.

If you have a pressing need to spend the night in Yaviza, the best sleeping option is **Ya Darien** (☎294-4334; d US$25; ❄), where tidy rooms have cold-water showers and the help is slow as molasses. **Hotel 3Americas** (☎299-4439; r from US$25) has worn, plain rooms.

There are eight buses daily between Panama City and Yaviza (US$16, 4½ hours). To arrange a private boat to El Real (US$70 for three passengers), contact Chicho Bristan (p707) in El Real to pick you up in Yaviza.

El Real

El Real dates from the days of the early conquistadors, when they constructed a fort beside the Río Tuira to prevent pirates from sailing upriver and attacking Santa María. Gold was stored there until there was

GETTING TO COLOMBIA

Since the Interamericana stops at Yaviza, it leaves only overland crossings through the Darién Gap on foot, which are not recommended.

The Caribbean crossing between Puerto Obaldía, Panama, and Capurganá, Colombia, has become a better option than in the past. Air Panama flies to Puerto Obaldía. From here, there are no buses. You must boat or walk to the Colombian village of Sapzurro. On foot, this takes about 2½ hours, but the track is indistinct in places, and sporadic regional insecurity makes boating the better option. Just on the border, the Panamanian village of La Miel is building a hostel and features a gorgeous beach (20 minutes on foot to Sapzurro).

From Sapzurro, ferries go to Capurganá; alternatively, it's a two-hour walk. As the security situation constantly changes, it's best to get an update with solid information about the route beforehand.

Sailing or boating to Colombia is by far the safest option after flying.

San Blas Adventure (Darien Gapster; ☎6731-2530, 6696-1554; www.thedariengapster.com; 4-day trip US$350) More of a tour than just transport, this popular service takes backpackers between Colombia and Panama, through the Darién and San Blás Islands, camping and snorkeling on the way. On the Panamanian side, the trip starts in Portobelo or Cartí and ends in Sapzurro, Colombia.

Travel is on a covered boat with outboard motors. There are regular set departures and the website features useful details for planning.

a quantity sufficient to warrant assembling an armada and moving the bullion to Panama City. Today, El Real is one of the largest towns in the Darién, though it's still very much a backwater settlement.

El Real is the last sizable settlement before the national park. Those heading up to Rancho Frío must either hire a local guide or be part of a tour – ANAM will not let you proceed unescorted. Before your arrival, you must register at SENAFRONT in Panama City and ANAM in Yaviza or Panama City, where you can pay the entry fee (foreigners US$15).

Options are slim here and it is really best to make food purchases prior to the hike. If you arrive in town too late to start the trek to Rancho Frío, you can spend the night at a rustic *pensión* (guesthouse). At **Fonda Doña Lola** (meals US$3) you can have a heaping plate of rice and chicken.

Currently, El Real is only accessed by boat or air charter. Veteran boatman **Chicho Bristan** (☎299-6566, 6539-2007) offers charter boat trips from Yaviza. Though the park cannot be accessed by vehicle, Chicho can arrange a 4WD (US$30) to take you partway, leaving you in Pirre 1, a 1½-hour hike to Rancho Frío.

Rancho Frío

Thirteen kilometers south of El Real, as the lemon-spectacled tanager flies, is the Rancho Frío sector of Parque Nacional Darién. It's home to **Pirre Station**, the most accessible section of the national park, with two good hiking trails. A two-day hike to Mount Pirre ridge requires a tent and complete self-sufficiency. A second trail winds through jungle to a series of cascades about an hour's hike away. Neither should be attempted without a ranger or local guide as they are not well marked and if you get lost out here, you're finished.

Pirre Station has **barracks** (per person US$15) with fold-out cots, a rustic dining area and kitchen, cold stall showers and an outhouse. There is also a shady **campsite** (per person US$6) where you can either pitch a tent or string up a hammock. Electricity is run off batteries and use must be kept minimal.

Visitors must bring their own food and purified water. Cooking fuel is scarce, so let the rangers do the cooking (US$10 a day is most appreciated).

Pirre Station can only be reached by hiking or a combination of hiking and boating or 4WD transportation. The four-hour hiking route takes the 'road' connecting El Real and Rancho Frío, yet this barely discernible path is pretty much impossible without a guide (you can contract one in Pirre 1).

La Palma

POP 1400

The provincial capital of Darién Province, La Palma is a one-street town located where the wide Río Tuira meets the Golfo de San Miguel. Pastel stilt houses lord over the muddy waterfront, a scene abuzz with commerce, bars and evangelist messages.

Most travelers pass through La Palma to take transport to somewhere else. The two most popular boating destinations are Reserva Natural Punta Patiño and the Emberá villages that line the banks of the Río Sambú.

Every facility of possible interest to the traveler is located on the main street. La Palma is home to the only bank in the Darién Province, the Banco Nacional de Panamá.

Hotel Biaquira Bagara (☎299-6224; d with/without bathroom US$25/17; ❄) is simple and sweet, with hardwood decks, wicker furniture and firm beds. Below, there is a basic market; if you're boating upriver, stock up on groceries here.

There's no shortage of cheap and somewhat cheerful eateries in town. **La Unción** (☎299-6372; mains US$2-5) offers decent *comida criollo* (typical food) served along with fiery sermons on the satellite TV.

At the time of writing, there were no regular flights from Panama City. To hire a boat and a guide, look in the vicinity of the dock for a responsible captain with a seaworthy motorboat (US$120 to US$300 per day, gas included).

Reserva Natural Punta Patiño

Twenty-five kilometers south of La Palma, Punta Patiño is a private **wildlife reserve** owned by the government conservation group Ancon. The 263-sq-km preserve contains species-rich primary and secondary forest, and is one of the best places in Panama to spot harpy eagles. It is also a great place to rack up the bird count, and

SURVIVING THE DARIÉN

Parque Nacional Darién is the most ecologically diverse land-based national park in all of Central America, but it is also one of the least-visited. Chalk it up to reputation – with its high stakes and poisonous snakes, the Darién isn't for everyone. Yet as a destination it is fascinating and fulfilling – provided you take the necessary precautions and go prepared.

Security

When planning your trip, first consider your destination. Established routes are recommended both for your safety and for legal reasons. The police have been known to detain those on unauthorized routes and suspect their activity – even if they are with a guide.

Safety

Even if you have crossed Central America by bus alone, solo travel here is not recommended. Trails are unmarked and it is terribly easy to get lost, and no one is likely to come to your aid. Poisonous snakes and scorpions could end your trip (or your life) unexpectedly.

Preparations

Though remote, the Darién is not cheap, especially considering fuel costs. Travelers should make a careful trip budget. Those who contract a local guide should speak Spanish themselves, so solutions can be discussed when problems arise.

Engines break and flights can get canceled – travel delays are about as common as raindrops in the Darién. Go with extra food and cash, a flashlight, matches, good personal equipment and flexibility in your schedule.

Guides

Paying more usually means getting more. A naturalist guide will have a different skill set than a *guía local* (local guide). Consider your needs and criteria when making a selection. The following are essential:

- Experience in the area.
- Extensive local contacts and problem-solving skills.
- A planned itinerary with realistic travel times and contracted transportation.
- Good equipment (tents, etc) if you do not have your own.
- Any necessary permits.

The following are desired:

- Skill at spotting animals.
- Knowledge of local history, animals and plants.
- Knowledge of English (or another language).
- First-aid kit and skills.
- Handheld radio and/or cell phone for areas with coverage.

Fellow travelers can be excellent guide references but it is important to meet your guide, particularly if you will be traveling solo. If contracting your guide in the Darién, converse with locals, find someone you trust and ask them for references.

Find out ahead of time if gas, transportation, food and fees are included. Perhaps the most important factor for a local guide is that they have extensive contacts in the region who can help arrange logistics, and know the actual terrain. Don't assume that a local guide is experienced – some have never set foot in the national park. ANAM is a good point of reference.

there's a good chance of seeing everything from three-toed sloths and howler monkeys to crocodiles. The only way to reach the preserve is by boat or plane.

Ancon Expeditions (p703) offers a package tour that includes the round-trip airfare between Panama City and Punta Patiño, lodging, food and activities. You can book lodgings at the reserve without a guided tour, but you must provide notification in advance of your arrival.

Sambú

Riverside Sambú is an interesting stop, populated by Emberá people and *cimarrones* (whose ancestors escaped the slave trade by living in the jungle). Urban by Darién standards, it has an airstrip, hospital and pay phone. Given the ease of flying in here, it makes a good launch point to visit riverside Emberá and Wounaan communities and absorb the slow jungle pace.

From Sambú, visitors can plan trips to **Puerto Indio** (with permission from the Emberá and Wounaan) and visit petroglyphs or mangrove forests. **Bocaca Verano** is a lagoon with crocodiles and prolific birdlife. Local guide Lupicinio, who can be found in front of Sambú House, guides hiking excursions ($15 per person) to see harpy eagles and takes tours to Bocaca Verano in dry season. For boat tours, Juan Murillo takes visitors **fishing** (four passengers US$120) in the Golfo de San Miguel in his 75-horsepower boat. Ask around for either guide.

Sambú House (☎268-6905, 6687-4177; www.sambuhausedarienpanama.com; s/d incl meals US$75/125) is the only jungle B&B around. It's an attractive yellow clapboard run by friendly Mabel. Cozy but simple, this might be the only place to get pancake breakfasts in the Darién. You can also arrange cultural tours here. Near the airstrip, **Mi Lindo Sueño** has plain concrete rooms. You can get cheap and tasty meals at **Comidas Benedicta** (meals US$2.50), where Anthony Bourdain dined when in Sambú.

Air Panama (☎316-9000; www.flyairpanama.com) flies twice weekly from Panama City (US$150 round-trip, one hour). Always confirm your return ticket in advance. If the airline cannot fill a flight, it may be delayed indefinitely. This also goes for flights out of Sambú.

The *panga* (small motorboat) to Puerto Quimba (US$20) goes three times a week, with one stop in La Palma. Trips are not scheduled far in advance; ask around and try to confirm a date for a return trip.

UNDERSTAND PANAMA

Panama Today

The fastest growing economy in Latin America in recent years, Panama owes much of its prosperity to the Panama Canal. It already hauls in US$2 billion yearly, but the current US$5 billion expansion will certainly up the stakes. Among the world's largest transportation projects, the expansion will triple canal traffic by digging deeper to accommodate bigger vessels and by adding a third lane. The canal is also expected to shift trade patterns, upsetting the prosperity of North American west coast ports.

Yet prosperity may only be skin deep. While poverty declined 10% in the last decade, Panama still has the second-worst income distribution in Latin America. The lack of opportunity in the provinces has created an exodus to the capital. City dwellers blame the most recent influx for increasing traffic, pollution and crime.

The 2009 world economic crisis somewhat calmed Panama's huge growth spurt of mega-developments and real-estate speculation. Today, whispers of opportunity have investors trickling back. Government investment in a new subway system and other infrastructure costing US$20 billion has residents nervous about later repaying the bill.

There is hope that these investments will pay off. But even the middle class is weary of increasing political cronyism. More and more, disgruntled citizens are protesting the privatization of public resources and taking it to the streets. For Panama, it's time to get back to the essentials.

History

The crossroads of the Americas, the narrow isthmus of Panama has always played a central and even strategic role in the history of the Western Hemisphere, from hosting the biological exchange of species to periodic encounters – and clashes – between many cultures. Once an overland trade route that linked the great civilizations of ancient Peru and Mexico, in the post-Columbian conquest it became the overland route for the siphoning off of Inca treasures. With two oceans so near, transit is a longtime theme. The Panama Railroad once brought prospectors to the California gold rush: today the Panama Canal has become the roaring engine of global commerce.

Lost Panama

The coastlines and rainforests of Panama have been inhabited by humans for at least 11,000 years. Indigenous groups, including the Kuna, the Ngöbe-Buglé, the Emberá, the Wounaan, the Bribrí and the Naso, were living on the isthmus prior to the Spanish arrival. However, the tragedy of Panama is that despite its rich cultural history, there are virtually no physical remains of these great civilizations.

What is known about pre-Columbian Panama is that early inhabitants were part of an extensive trading zone that extended as far south as Peru and as far north as Mexico. Archaeologists have uncovered exquisite gold ornaments and unusual life-size stone statues of human figures, as well as distinctive types of pottery and *metates* (stone platforms that were used for grinding corn).

Panama's first peoples lived beside both oceans, and fished in mangrove swamps, estuaries and coral reefs. It seems only fitting that the country's name is derived from an indigenous word meaning 'abundance of fish.'

New World Order

In 1501 the discovery of Panama by Spanish explorer Rodrigo de Bastidas marked the beginning of the age of conquest and colonization in the isthmus. However, it was his first mate, Vasco Núñez de Balboa, who earned lasting fame following his discovery of the Pacific Ocean 12 years later.

On his fourth and final voyage to the New World in 1502, Christopher Columbus saw 'more gold in two days than in four years in Spain' in present-day Costa Rica. Although his attempts to establish a colony at the mouth of the Río Belén failed due to fierce local resistance, Columbus petitioned the Spanish Crown to have himself appointed as governor of Veraguas, the stretch of shoreline from Honduras to Panama.

Following Columbus' death, King Ferdinand appointed Diego de Nicuesa to settle the newly claimed land. These various attempts would fail miserably. Much to the disappointment of conquistadors, Panama was not rich in gold. Add tropical diseases, inhospitable terrain and less than welcoming natives, and it's easy to see why early Spanish colonies struggled and often failed.

In 1513, Balboa heard rumors about a large sea and a wealthy, gold-producing civilization across the mountains – likely the Inca Empire of Peru. Driven by ambition, Balboa scaled the continental divide and on September 26, 1513, became the first European to set eyes on the Pacific Ocean. He claimed the ocean and all the lands it touched for the king of Spain.

The Empire Expands

In 1519 a cruel and very vindictive Spaniard named Pedro Arias de Ávila (called Pedrarias by contemporaries) founded the city of Panamá on the Pacific, near present-day Panama City. The governor ordered the beheading of Balboa in 1517 on a trumped-up charge of treason. He is also remembered for murderous attacks against the indigenous population, whom he roasted alive or fed to dogs.

Pedrarias nonetheless established Panamá as an important Spanish settlement, a commercial center and a base for further explorations, including the conquest of Peru. From Panamá, vast riches of Peruvian gold and Oriental spices were transported across the isthmus by foot. This famous trade route, known as the Sendero Las Cruces (Las Cruces Trail), can still be walked.

As the Spaniards grew plump on the wealth of plundered civilizations, the world began to notice the prospering colony, especially English privateers lurking in coastal waters. In 1573 Sir Francis Drake destroyed the Nombre de Dios settlement and set sail for England with a galleon laden with Spanish gold.

The Spanish responded by building large stone fortresses at San Lorenzo and Portobelo. Still, Welsh buccaneer Sir Henry Morgan overpowered Fuerte San Lorenzo and sailed up the Río Chagres in 1671. After crossing the isthmus, Morgan destroyed the city of Panamá, burning it to the ground and returning to the Caribbean coast with 200 mules loaded with Spanish loot.

The Spanish rebuilt the city a few years later on a cape several kilometers west of its original site. The ruins of the old settlement, now known as Panamá Viejo, and the colonial city of Casco Viejo are within the city limits of the present-day metropolis.

British privateering continued. After Admiral Edward Vernon destroyed the fortress of Portobelo in 1739, the Spanish abandoned the Panamanian crossing in favor of sailing the long way around Cape Horn to the west coast of South America.

The Empire Ends

On October 27, 1807, Spain and France signed the Treaty of Fontainebleau. It defined the occupation of Portugal. In an act of treachery and military genius, Napoleon moved tens of thousands of troops into Spain, under the guise of reinforcing the Franco-Spanish army occupying Portugal. He then ordered his troops to seize key Spanish fortifications.

The resulting Peninsular War crippled both countries. The conflict, along with the subsequent power vacuum and decades of internal turmoil, caused Spain to lose nearly all of its colonial possessions in the first third of the century.

Panama gained independence from Spanish rule in 1821 and immediately joined Gran Colombia, a confederation of present-day Colombia, Bolivia, Ecuador, Peru and Venezuela – a united Latin American nation that had long been the dream of Simón Bolívar. Internal disputes lead to the abolishment of Gran Colombia in 1831, but fledgling Panama remained a province of Colombia.

Birth of a Nation

Panama's future changed forever when world powers caught on that the isthmus was the narrowest point between the Atlantic and Pacific Oceans. In 1846 Colombia signed a treaty permitting the USA to construct a railway across the isthmus, granting free transit and the right to protect the railway with military force. At the height of the California gold rush in 1849, tens of thousands traveled from the USA's east coast to the west coast via Panama in order to avoid hostile tribes in the central states. Colombia and Panama grew wealthy from the railway, and the first talks of a canal across Central America began to surface.

The idea of a canal across the isthmus was first raised in 1524 when King Charles V of Spain ordered a survey to determine the feasibility of a waterway. Later, Emperor Napoleon III of France also considered the idea. Finally, in 1878, French builder Ferdinand de Lesseps, basking in the glory of the recently constructed Suez canal, was contracted by Colombia to build the canal, bringing his crew to Panama in 1881. Much like Napoleon, Lesseps severely underestimated the task, and over 22,000 workers died from yellow fever and malaria in less than a decade. In 1889 insurmountable construction problems and financial mismanagement drove the company bankrupt.

The USA saw the French failure as a business opportunity. In 1903 Philippe Bunau-Varilla, one of Lesseps' chief engineers, agreed to sell concessions to the USA, though the Colombian government refused. Bunau-Varilla approached the US government to back Panama if it declared independence from Colombia.

On November 3, 1903, a revolutionary junta declared Panama independent, and the US government immediately recognized its sovereignty – the first of a series of American interventions. Although Colombia sent troops by sea to try to regain control, US battleships prevented them from reaching land. Colombia only recognized Panama as a legitimately separate nation in 1921, when the USA compensated Colombia with US$25 million.

The US & the Canal

Following independence, Bunau-Varilla was appointed Panamanian ambassador to the USA, with his first act of office paving the way for future American interventions. Hoping to profit from the sale of canal concessions to the USA, Bunau-Varilla arrived in Washington, DC, before Panama could assemble a delegation. On November 18, 1903, Bunau-Varilla and US Secretary of State John Hay signed the Hay-Bunau-Varilla Treaty, which gave the USA far more than had been offered in the original treaty. In addition to owning concessions to the canal, the USA was also granted 'sovereign rights in perpetuity over the Canal Zone,' an area extending 8km on either side of the canal, and a broad right of intervention in Panamanian affairs.

Despite opposition from the tardy Panamanian delegation as well as lingering questions about its legality, the treaty was ratified, ushering in an era of friction between the USA and Panama. Construction began again on the canal in 1904 and despite disease, landslides and harsh weather, the world's greatest engineering marvel was completed within a decade. The first ship sailed through the canal on August 15, 1914.

In the following years, the US military repeatedly intervened in political affairs. In response to growing Panamanian disenchantment, the Hay-Bunau-Varilla Treaty was replaced in 1936 by the Hull-Alfaro Treaty. The USA relinquished its rights to use its troops outside the Canal Zone and to seize land for canal purposes, and the annual sum paid to Panama for use of the Canal Zone was raised. However, a wave of Panamanian opposition to US occupation grew. Tensions reached a boiling point in 1964 during a student protest that left 27 Panamanians dead and 500 injured. Today, the event is commemorated as Día de Los Mártires (National Martyrs Day).

As US influence waned, the Panamanian army grew more powerful. In 1968 the Guardia Nacional deposed the elected president and took control of the government. Soon after, the constitution was suspended, the national assembly was dissolved, the press censored and the Guardia's General Omar Torrijos Herrera emerged as the new leader. Though he plunged Panama into debt with a massive public works program, Torrijos did convince US president Jimmy Carter to cede control of the canal. The resulting Torrijos-Carter Treaty guaranteed full Panamanian control of the canal as of December 31, 1999, as well as a complete withdrawal of US military forces.

Rise & Fall of Noriega

In 1981, with Panama still basking in the glory of the most recent treaty, a plane crash killed Torrijos. Rumors of foul play swept the country. In 1983 Colonel Manuel Antonio Noriega seized the Guardia Nacional, promoted himself to general and made himself the de facto ruler of Panama. Noriega, a former head of Panama's secret police, a former CIA operative and a graduate of the School of the Americas, quickly began to consolidate his power. He enlarged the Guardia Nacional, significantly expanded its authority and renamed it the Panama Defense Forces. He also created a paramilitary 'Dignity Battalion' in every city, town and village, its members armed and ready to inform on any of their neighbors showing less than complete loyalty to the Noriega regime.

Things went from bad to worse in early 1987 when Noriega was publicly accused of involvement in drug trafficking with Colombian drug cartels, murdering his opponents and rigging elections. Many Panamanians demanded Noriega's dismissal, with general strikes and street demonstrations that resulted in violent clashes with the Panama Defense Forces. In February 1988, Panamanian President Eric Arturo Delvalle attempted to dismiss Noriega, but was forced to flee Panama. Noriega subsequently appointed a president more sympathetic to his cause.

Noriega's regime became an international embarrassment. In March 1988, the USA imposed economic sanctions against Panama, ending a preferential trade agreement, freezing Panamanian assets in US banks and refusing to pay canal fees. A few days after the sanctions were imposed, an unsuccessful military coup prompted Noriega to step up violent repression of his critics. After Noriega's candidate lost the presidential election in May 1989, the general declared the election null and void. Guillermo Endara, the winning candidate, and his two vice-presidential running mates, were badly beaten by Noriega's thugs, with the entire bloody scene captured by a TV crew and broadcasted internationally. A second failed coup in October 1989 was followed by even more repressive measures.

On December 15, 1989, Noriega's legislature declared him president, and his first official act of office was to declare war on the USA. The following day an unarmed US marine dressed in civilian clothes was killed by Panamanian soldiers while leaving a restaurant in Panama City.

The US reaction was swift and unrelenting. In the first hour of December 20, 1989, Panama City was attacked by aircraft, tanks and 26,000 US troops. The invasion, intended to bring Noriega to justice and create a democracy better suited to US interests, left more than 2000 civilians dead, tens of thousands homeless and destroyed entire tracts of Panama City.

On Christmas Day, Noriega claimed asylum in the Vatican embassy. US forces surrounded the embassy and pressured the Vatican to release him. They bombarded the embassy with blaring rock music. Mobs of angry Panamanians surrounded the embassy, calling for Noriega to be ousted.

After 10 days of psychological warfare, the Vatican embassy persuaded Noriega to give himself up by threatening to cancel his asylum. Noriega surrendered to US forces on January 3, and was flown to Miami where he was convicted of conspiracy to manufacture and distribute cocaine.

After his US prison sentence ended in 2007 he was extradited to Paris in April, 2010. A re-trial found Noriega guilty and sentenced him to seven years in prison, but he was conditionally released in order to serve 20 years in Panama, starting in December, 2011, where he is incarcerated today.

Modern Struggles

After Noriega's forced removal, Guillermo Endara, the legitimate winner of the 1989 election, was sworn in as president, and Panama attempted to put itself back together. The country's image and economy were in shambles, and its capital had suffered damage from both the invasion and the widespread looting that followed. Unfortunately, Endara proved to be an ineffective leader whose policies cut jobs and cost his administration its early popularity. He was voted out of office in 1994 with single-digit approval ratings.

Ernesto Pérez Balladares took office next. Under his direction, the Panamanian government implemented a program of privatization that focused on infrastructure improvements, health care and education. Although Pérez Balladares allocated unprecedented levels of funding for Panama's development, he would later be investigated for corruption in 2010.

In 1999 Mireya Moscoso, the widow of popular former president Arnulfo Arias, and Panama's first female leader and head of the conservative Arnulfista Party (PA), took office. Moscoso's ambitious plans never materialized. As Panama celebrated its centenary in 2003, unemployment hit 18% and parts of the country went hungry – yet Moscoso paid US$10 million to bring the Miss Universe pageant to Panama. She was also accused of looking the other way during Colombian military incursions into the Darién.

Martín Torrijos, a member of the Revolutionary Democratic Party (PRD) and the son of former leader Omar Torrijos, took over in 2004. Although there is still debate regarding the success of his administration, he did implement much-needed fiscal reforms, including an overhaul of the nation's social security system. Furthermore, his proposal to expand the Panama Canal was overwhelmingly approved by national referendum.

Current Climate

On May 3, 2009, Panama bucked the Latin American leftist trend by electing conservative supermarket magnate Ricardo Martinelli president. Part of the conservative party Democratic Change (CD), Martinelli was a pro-business choice who has proved even more ambitious in political and development plans than the public had first expected. In 2012, residents united in massive protests when the government planned to sell the Colón free trade zone to private interests.

After the world economic crisis, high inflation kept international investors at bay. But signs of returning prosperity may herald a comeback of the gold-rush aplomb that gave Panama the highest growth rate in the Americas before the election of Martinelli. As his government winds down and Panama looks toward 2014 elections, the future is anyone's guess.

Culture

National Psyche

The narrow isthmus of Panama bridges not only two continents but two vastly different paradigms of Panamanian culture and society. While one sphere of Panama embraces tradition, the other looks to the modernizing influences of a growing economy.

In some ways, these opposing forces are only natural given the many years that Panama has been the object of meddling for other countries. From the US-backed independence of 1903 to the strong-armed removal of Noriega in 1989, with half-a-dozen other interventions in between, the USA left a strong legacy in the country. Nearly every Panamanian has a relative or acquaintance living in the USA. Parts of the country seem swept up in mall fervor, with consumer inspiration straight out of North America.

Others, however, are not so ready to embrace gringo culture. Indigenous groups such as the Emberá and Kuna are struggling to keep their traditions alive, as more and more of their youth are lured into the Westernized lifestyle of the city.

Given the clash between old and new, it's surprising the country isn't suffering from a serious case of cognitive dissonance. Somehow, the exceptionally tolerant Panamanian character weathers many contradictions – the old and the new, the grave disparity between rich and poor, and the gorgeous natural environment and its rapid destruction.

Lifestyle

In spite of the skyscrapers and gleaming restaurants lining the wealthier districts of Panama City, nearly a third of the country's population lives in poverty. Furthermore, almost a quarter of a million Panamanians struggle just to satisfy their basic dietary needs. The poorest tend to live in the least populated provinces: Darién, Bocas del Toro, Veraguas, Los Santos and Colón. There is also substantial poverty in the slums of Panama City, where an estimated 20% of the urban population lives. Countrywide, 9% of the population lives in *barriados* (squatter) settlements.

For *campesinos*, life is hard. A subsistence farmer in the interior might earn as little as US$8 per day, far below the national average of US$12,770 per capita. In the Emberá and Wounaan villages of Darién, traditional living patterns persist as they have for hundreds of years. Thatched hut communities survive on subsistence agriculture, hunting, fishing and pastoralism. The life expectancy in these frontier villages is about 10 years below the national average. The majority of the Emberá and Wounaan communities lack access to clean water and basic sanitation.

The middle and upper class largely reside in and around Panama City, with a level of comfort similar to their counterparts in Europe and the USA. They live in large homes or apartments, have a maid, a car or two, and, for the lucky, few a second home on the beach or in the mountains. Cell phones are de rigueur. Vacations are often enjoyed in Europe or the USA. Most middle-class adults can speak some English and their children usually attend English-speaking schools.

People

The majority of Panamanians (70%) are *mestizo*, which is generally a mix of indigenous and Spanish descent. In truth, many non-black immigrants are also thrown into this category, including a sizable Chinese population – some people estimate that as much as 10% of the population is of Chinese ancestry. There are also a number of other large groups: about 14% of Panamanians are of African descent, 10% of Spanish descent, 5% of mixed African and Spanish descent, and 6% are indigenous. Generally, black Panamanians are mostly descendants of English-speaking West Indians, such as Jamaicans and Trinidadians, who were originally brought to Panama as laborers.

Of the several dozen native tribes that inhabited Panama when the Spanish arrived, few remain. The Kuna live on islands along the Caribbean coast in the autonomous region of the Comarca de Kuna Yala. Considered the most politically organized, they regularly send representatives to the national legislature. The Emberá and Wounaan inhabit the eastern Panamá province and the Darién; Panama's largest tribe, the Ngöbe-Buglé live in Chiriquí, Veraguas and Bocas del Toro. The Teribe inhabit Bocas del Toro Province, while the Bribrí are found along the Talamanca Reserve. Despite modernizing influences, each of Panama's indigenous groups maintains its own language and culture.

Religion

Panama City is home to scores of Catholic churches, Anglican churches filled with West Indians, synagogues, mosques, a shiny Greek Orthodox church, an impressive Hindu temple and a surreal Baha'i house of worship (the headquarters for Latin America).

Freedom of religion is constitutionally guaranteed in Panama, although the preeminence of Roman Catholicism is also officially recognized, with 85% of the country filling its ranks. School children study theology, though it is not compulsory. Protestant denominations account for 12%, Muslims 4.4% and Baha'i 1.2%. Additionally, the country has approximately 3000 Jews (many of them recent immigrants from Israel), 24,000 Buddhists and 9000 Hindus.

In addition to the mainstream world religions, the various indigenous tribes of Panama have their own belief systems, although Christian missionary influence is eradicating traditional beliefs. As in other parts of Latin America, the evangelical movement is prominent.

Catholics represent the majority but only about 20% attend church regularly. The religious orders aren't particularly strong in Panama either – only about 25% of Catholic clergy are Panamanian while the rest are foreign missionaries.

Arts

Panama's all-embracing music scene includes salsa, Latin and American jazz, traditional music from the central provinces, reggae, reggaetón and Latin, British and American rock 'n' roll. Their biggest export is world-renowned salsa singer Rubén Blades, who even ran for president in 1994, finishing third. The jazz composer and pianist Danilo Pérez is widely acclaimed by critics, while Los Rabanes produces classic Panamanian rock. Heavy on the accordion, Panamanian folk music (called *típico*), is well represented by Victorio Vergara and Samy and Sandra Sandoval. These days reggaetón (also known as *punta*) permeates all social levels in Panama, and its stars include Flex and the now-deceased Danger Man.

Several of Panama's best novels were written in the mid-20th century. *El ahogado* (The Drowned Man), a 1937 novel by Tristán Solarte, blends elements of the detective, gothic and psychological genres with a famous local myth. *El desván* (In the Garret), a 1954 novel by Ramón H Jurado, explores the emotional limits of the human condition. *Gamboa Road Gang,* by Joaquín Beleño, is about the political and social events surrounding the Panama Canal. Today's notable authors include poet and novelist Giovanna Benedetti, historical novelist Gloria Guardia and folk novelist Rosa María Britton.

The first prominent figure on Panama's art scene, French-trained Roberto Lewis (1874–1949) painted allegorical images in public buildings; look for those in the Palacio de las Garzas in Panama City. In 1913 Lewis became the director of Panama's first art academy, where he and his successor, Humberto Ivaldi (1909–47), educated a generation of artists. Among the school's students were Juan Manuel Cedeño and Isaac Benítez, and mid-20th-century painters Alfredo Sinclair, Guillermo Trujillo and Eudoro Silvera. Newer artists include Olga Sinclair and Brooke Alfaro.

Sports

Owing to a strong US legacy, baseball is the national pastime. Although Panama has no professional teams, amateur leagues play in stadiums throughout the country. In the US major leagues, Mariano Rivera, the record-setting pitcher for the New York Yankees, is a national hero. The batting champ Rod Carew, another Panamanian star, was inducted into the Hall of Fame in 1991. Former NY Yankee Roberto Kelly is also fondly remembered.

Boxing is another popular spectator sport, and a source of local pride since Panama City native Roberto Durán won the world championship lightweight title in 1972. A legend, he went on to become the world champion in each of the welterweight (1980), light middleweight (1983) and super middleweight (1989) categories. Currently, Panama also has three reigning world boxing champions.

Panama's first Olympic gold came in 2008 when Irving Saladino won the long jump in Beijing.

Landscape & Wildlife

Land

Panama is both the narrowest and the southernmost country in Central America. The long S-shaped isthmus borders Costa Rica in the west and Colombia in the east. Its northern Caribbean coastline measures 1160km, compared to a 1690km Pacific coastline in the south, and its total land area is 78,056km. By comparison, Panama is slightly bigger than Ireland or Austria.

The Panama Canal effectively divides the country into eastern and western regions. Two mountain ranges run along Panama's spine in both the east and the west. The highest point in the country, Chiriquí's Volcán Barú, is also the country's only volcano.

Like all Central American countries, Panama has large, flat coastal lowlands, with huge banana plantations. There are about 480 rivers in Panama and 1518 islands near its shores. The two main island groups are the San Blás and Bocas del Toro Archipelagos on the Caribbean side, but most of the islands are on the Pacific side.

Wildlife

Panama's position as a narrow land bridge between two huge continents has given it a remarkable variety of plant and animal life. Species migrating between the continents have gathered in Panama, which means that it's possible to see South American armadillos, anteaters and sloths alongside North American tapirs, jaguars and deer. With its wide variety of native and migratory species, Panama is one of the world's best places for bird-watchers.

Panama has more than 940 recorded bird species and more than 10,000 plant species, in addition to 125 animal species found only here. The country's 105 rare and endangered species include scarlet macaws, harpy eagles (the national bird of Panama), golden frogs, jaguars and five species of sea turtle. Panama is one of the best places to see a quetzal, and among the primates there are capuchins, tamarins and squirrel, spider and howler monkeys.

Tropical rainforest is the dominant vegetation in the canal area, along the Caribbean coast and in most of the eastern half of the country. The Parque Nacional Darién protects much of Panama's largest tropical rainforest region. Other vegetation zones include Pacific coast grasslands, highland mountain forest, cloud forest on the highest peaks and mangrove forest on both coasts.

National Parks & Reserves

Panama has 12 national parks and more than two dozen officially protected areas. About one-quarter of Panama is set aside for conservation, while about 40% of land remains covered by forest. Panama also has more land set aside for habitat protection than any other Central American country, and its forests contain the greatest number of species of all New World countries north of Colombia. Yet these statistics do not reflect the fact that protected lands are often poorly protected.

In many of the national parks and protected areas, *mestizo* and indigenous villages are scattered about. In some scenarios, these communities help protect and maintain parks and wildlife. National environmental authority ANAM (see p655) manages the national-park system. The admission fee of US$5 (US$20 for marine parks) is paid at either the ANAM headquarters in Panama City, a regional ANAM office or a park ranger station. Permits to camp or stay at an ANAM ranger station (US$5 to US$10) are obtained at the same places.

A few highlights include the following:

Parque Internacional La Amistad Home to several indigenous groups, this park comprises pristine rainforest and abundant wildlife (p678).

Parque Nacional Darién Unesco World Heritage Site with 576,000 hectares of world-class wildlife-rich rainforest (p702).

Parque Nacional Isla de Coiba Includes the 493-sq-km Isla de Coiba, regarded by scientists as a biodiversity hot spot (p667).

Parque Nacional Marino Golfo de Chriquí Protects 25 islands and numerous coral reefs.

Parque Nacional Marino Isla Bastimentos An important nature reserve for many species of Caribbean wildlife, including sea turtles (p689).

Parque Nacional Soberanía A bird-watcher's paradise in lush rainforest (p659).

Parque Nacional Volcán Barú Surrounds Panama's only volcano and highest peak, 3475m Volcán Barú (p677).

Parque Natural Metropolitano Tropical semideciduous forest within the city limits (p645).

Environmental Issues

Unfortunately, deforestation is one of the country's gravest environmental problems. And with Panama's national parks grossly understaffed, illegal hunting, settling and logging take place even inside parks.

Another major concern is mining. Roughly 26% of Panama is mined or under mining concessions, raising concerns about contaminated water sources, and causing the destruction of forest and human habitats. In spite of objections by prominent environmental groups, the government has approved and expedited large-scale mining projects, most notably a US$6.2 billion project – an investment greater than the present expansion of the Panama Canal – to extract gold and copper.

A major victory was the 2012 passing of law 415, which prohibits extraction in indigenous territories and requires their approval for hydro-electric projects. The change came after a shut down of Ngöbe-Bugle community protests earlier in February 2012 left two protesters dead.

SURVIVAL GUIDE

Directory A–Z

ACCOMMODATIONS

Prices cited are high-season rates including Panama's 10% tax on hotel rooms. High season is from mid-December to mid-April. Rates may spike up to 50% higher for Easter week and between Christmas and New Year. Low-season rates are generally about 15% lower.

There is usually no shortage of places to stay in Panama, except during holidays or special events outside Panama City, when advance reservations may be necessary.

ACTIVITIES

Bird-Watching

With more than 900 species of birds in Panama, all you need to do to spot feathered friends is get a good pair of binoculars and hit the trails. Two popular spots include **Pipeline Rd** (Camino del Oleoducto) in Parque Nacional Soberanía and **Parque Nacional Volcán Barú**, home of the resplendent quetzal, the Maya bird of paradise.

Panama's avian species are at their best in the legendary Cana Valley, which is regarded as one of the top bird-watching destinations in the world. This phenomenal wildlife preserve can only be accessed via organized tour with Ancon Expeditions (p703).

Panama Audubon Society (☎232-5977; www.audubonpanama.org), located in Panama City, organizes the annual Christmas bird count on Pipeline Rd, and runs bird-watching expeditions throughout the country.

Diving & Snorkeling

Panama has numerous islands with good snorkeling and diving sights. On the Caribbean coast, **Bocas del Toro** and the **Archipiélago de San Blás** are prime spots. Dive shops on Bocas del Toro rent snorkeling and diving gear, and offer PADI-certified classes, while snorkeling in San Blás is more of the do-it-yourself variety. There is also good diving and snorkeling around **Portobelo**, and there are a couple of reputable dive shops in town.

On the Pacific coast, there is good snorkeling on the **Golfo de Chiriquí** and in the **Archipiélago de las Perlas**. Although coral reefs in the Pacific are not as vibrant as their Caribbean counterparts, you're bound to see some big fish here, as well as the occasional pelagic creature.

You can rent equipment at most destinations, but avid snorkelers should bring their own. Scubapanama (p722), based in Panama City, offers diving trips throughout the country.

Fishing

With 1518 islands, 2988km of coast and 480 rivers, there's no problem finding a fishing spot in Panama. Possibilities include deep-sea fishing, fishing for bass in **Lago Gatún** on the Panama Canal, trout fishing in the rivers running down **Volcán Barú**, and surf casting on any of Panama's Pacific and Caribbean beaches.

Hiking

Hiking opportunities abound in Panama. In the Chiriquí highlands, the **Sendero Los Quetzales** winds through Parque Nacional Volcán Barú, and is regarded as the country's top hike – check conditions before going. **Parque Internacional La Amistad** also has some fine, short trails, starting near its Cerro Punta entrance.

From Boquete, you can summit **Volcán Barú**, Panama's highest point and only volcano. **El Valle**, nestled in a picturesque valley, is a fine place for casual walkers.

Near Panama City on the shores of the canal, **Parque Nacional Soberanía** contains a section of the old Sendero Las Cruces, used by the Spanish to cross between the coasts. **Parque Natural Metropolitano**, on the outskirts of Panama City, also has some good walks leading to a panorama of the city.

You can also trek through lush rainforests in the **Parque Nacional Darién**, though this is best arranged through a reputable guide owing to dangers in the region.

Surfing

The country's top surfing destination is the Caribbean archipelago of **Bocas del Toro**, which attracts strong winter swells and surfers from around the world. Although it remains an off-the-beaten-path destination, **Santa Catalina** on the Pacific coast has some of the most challenging breaks in Central America. There is also uncrowded surfing on the laid-back Caribbean island of **Isla Grande** and at **Playa Venao** on the Península de Azuero.

White-Water Rafting & Kayaking

Whether you take to the water by raft or kayak, Panama boasts some excellent opportunities for river running. The country's most famous white-

SLEEPING PRICE RANGES

The following price ranges refer to a double room with bathroom in high season. Unless otherwise stated, tax is included in the price.

$	Less than US$48
$$	US$48–$120
$$$	More than US$120

TRANSPANAMA TRAIL

Linking all of Panama by trail, this **cross-country circuit** (www.transpanama.org) has spectacular landscapes spanning from coastline to rainforest and mountains. The trail is a work in progress and is currently 60% finished, running from the border of Costa Rica toward Panama City. The Camino Real – the historic land crossing made redundant by the Panama Canal – is part of it.

The trail can be done in short three- to four-day segments, accessed by public transportation. Highlights include the segments between Boquete and Costa Rica, Parque Nacional Campana and El Valle (three to four days), and the Cocle–Veraguas crossing from Huacas el Quise to Laguna de La Yeguada. More information is available on the website, where you can also download GPS tracks for free.

water runs are the Ríos Chiriquí and Chiriquí Viejo, though there are also opportunities for sea kayaking in both Bocas del Toro and Chiriquí Provinces.

The unofficial river-running capital of Panama is the highland town of Boquete, located near the Ríos Chiriquí and Chiriquí Viejo. River kayak trips are also run during the rainy season (April to November).

CLIMATE

Panama's tourist season is the dry season (from mid-December to mid-April). This is true for the Pacific slope, but the Caribbean side can get rain throughout the year. The weather can be hot and steamy in the lowlands during the rainy season, when the humidity makes the heat oppressive. But it won't rain nonstop; rain in Panama, as elsewhere in the tropics, tends to come in sudden short downpours that freshen the air, and is followed by sunshine. It's more comfortable to do long, strenuous hiking in the dry season.

CUSTOMS REGULATIONS

You may bring up to 10 cartons of cigarettes and five bottles of liquor into Panama tax-free. If you try to leave Panama with products made from endangered species – such as jaguar teeth, ocelot skins and turtle shell – you'll face a steep fine and jail time.

ELECTRICITY

Electrical current is 120 volts in Panama City and 110 volts, 60Hz elsewhere. Plugs are two-pronged, as in the US and Canada.

EMBASSIES & CONSULATES

More than 50 countries have embassies or consulates in Panama City. Their contact details can be found in the Panama white pages, listed under 'Embajada de' followed by the country name in Spanish. Many embassies appear in the yellow pages under 'Embajadas' or 'Consulados.' With the exception of the USA and France, most embassies are located in the Marbella district of Panama City.

Ireland, Australia and New Zealand have no consulates or embassies in Panama.

Canadian Embassy (☎294-2500; www.canada-international.gc.ca/panama; Piso 11, Tower A, Torre de las Americas, Punta Pacifica)

Colombian Embassy (☎264-9266; Calle 53 Este, World Trade Center, Marbella)

Costa Rica David (☎264-2980; www.embajadacostaricaenpanama.com; Av Samuel Lewis, Edificio Omega, 3rd fl, Obarrio; ⏲9am-1pm Mon-Fri); Panama City (☎264-2980; fax 264-4057; Av Samuel Lewis)

French Embassy (☎211-6200; www.ambafrance-pa.org; Plaza de Francia, Las Bóvedas, Casco Viejo)

German Embassy (☎263-7733; www.panama.diplo.de; Calle 53 Este, Piso PH, World Trade Center, Marbella)

Netherlands Consulate (☎264-7257; http://dutch-embassy.com/panama.html; Calle 50, Marbella)

UK Embassy (☎297-6550; www.ukinpanama.fco.gov.uk/en; Calle 53 Este, MMG Tower, 4th fl, Marbella)

US Embassy (☎207-7000; www.panama.usembassy.gov; Av Demetrio Basillo Lakas 783, Clayton)

FOOD & DRINK

Food

Panama's national dish is *sancocho* (meat and vegetable stew). *Ropa vieja* (literally 'old clothes'), a spicy shredded beef combination served over rice, is also common. Rice is the staple of Panama.

Breakfast staples and snacks are *tortillas de maíz* (thick, fried cornmeal cakes) and *hojaldras* (deep-fried mass of dough served hot and covered with sugar). For lunch, simple *comida corriente* is an inexpensive set meal of beef, chicken or fish served with rice, black beans, fried plantain, chopped cabbage and maybe an egg or an avocado.

Specialties include *carimañola,* a yucca roll filled with chopped meat and baked egg. The most common snack is the *empanada* (turnover filled with ground meat and cheese). Tamales (cornmeal with a few spices and chicken or pork, wrapped in banana leaves and boiled) are another favorite. Seafood is abundant and includes shrimp, Caribbean king crab, octopus, lobster and *corvina* (sea bass). Along the Caribbean coast you'll also find a West Indian influence to the dishes, such as coconut rice and coconut bread, or seafood mixed with coconut milk.

In Panama City you'll often see vendors pushing carts and selling *raspados* – cones filled with shaved ice topped with fruit syrup and sweetened condensed milk.

Drinks

Fresh fruit drinks, sweetened with sugar and mixed with water or milk, are called *chichas*, and are extremely popular. *Chicheme* is a concoction of milk, sweet corn, cinnamon and vanilla.

Coffee is traditionally served very strong and offered with cream or condensed milk. Milk is pasteurized and safe to drink. Espresso drinks are available only in major cities and tourist destinations.

The national alcoholic drink is made of *seco*, milk and ice. *Seco*, like rum, is distilled from sugarcane, but it doesn't taste anything like the rum you know. This is the drink of *campesinos* (farmers). Popular in the central provinces, *vino de palma* is fermented sap extracted from the trunk of a palm tree called *palma de corozo*. By far the most popular alcoholic beverage in Panama is *cerveza* (beer).

GAY & LESBIAN TRAVELERS

Panamanians are more out than in recent years, though the trend is much more prevalent in the capital than anywhere else. More than in other parts of Central America, you will probably meet openly gay locals, though the culture generally follows an unspoken 'don't ask, don't tell' policy.

Panama City has a few gay and lesbian clubs advertised only online. Outside the capital, gay bars are hard to come by and discrimination is more prevalent. In most instances, gays and lesbians just blend in with the straight crowd at the hipper places and avoid beer halls and other conventional lairs of homophobia.

Panamanian website www.farraurbana.com lists upcoming gay and lesbian events and parties, new club openings and political issues in Panama City. You'll need at least a little Spanish to maneuver through the site.

HEALTH

There are no required vaccines for Panama, but among those recommended are yellow fever, typhoid, rabies and hepatitis A and B. See your doctor well ahead, since most vaccines don't produce immunity until at least two weeks after being given. Request an International Certificate of Vaccination (aka the yellow booklet); it's mandatory for countries that require proof of yellow-fever vaccination.

Tap water is generally drinkable in Panama, except for in Bocas del Toro and Comarca de Kuna Yala. Visitors who have recently arrived may want to start with bottled water and minimum amounts of tap water.

A superb book called *International Travel and Health*, revised annually and available online at no cost, is published by the **World Health Organization** (www.who.int/ith). Another website of general interest is **MD Travel Health** (www.mdtravelhealth.com), with complete travel-health recommendations for every country, updated daily, also at no cost.

Good medical care is widely available in Panama City and also David, and even sought after with a brisk business of medical tourism, though it's limited elsewhere. Most doctors and hospitals expect cash payment, regardless of whether you have travel health insurance.

INSURANCE

Prior to your trip, signing up for a travel insurance policy to cover theft, loss and medical problems is a good idea. Be advised, however, that some policies specifically exclude dangerous activities, which can include scuba diving, motorcycling, and even trekking.

You may prefer a policy that pays doctors or hospitals directly, rather than you having to pay on the spot and claim later. If you have to claim later, ensure you keep all documentation.

Check that the policy covers ambulances or an emergency flight home.

INTERNET ACCESS

Most cities and towns in Panama have inexpensive internet cafes. Public wi-fi access is increasingly common in bus stations, plazas, libraries and restaurants. Hotels and hostels in more tourist-oriented areas are likely to have both internet and wi-fi. The Kuna Yala and Darién regions are exceptions to this.

LEGAL MATTERS

Individuals are legally required to carry identification at all times, preferably a passport. Although this may seem like an inconvenience, there have been cases of travelers spending the night in prison for failure to produce proper ID.

It is illegal for men and women to go topless, even if heading to the beach. This rule is strictly enforced in Bocas del Toro, and you can expect the police to strike up an uncomfortable chat if you're baring all.

EATING PRICE RANGES

The following price ranges refer to a main dish.

$	Less than US$10
$$	US$10–$16
$$$	More than US$16

The legal drinking age in Panama is 18.

Penalties for possession of even small amounts of illegal drugs are much stricter than in the USA, Europe, Australia and almost everywhere else. For example, you can expect to go to jail if the car you are in is stopped and found to contain illegal drugs, even if they aren't yours. Most lawyers won't even accept drug cases because conviction is a near certainty. Defendants often spend years in prison before they are brought to trial and, if convicted (as is usually the case), can expect sentences.

If accused of a serious crime in Panama, you will be taken to jail, where you will likely spend several months before your case goes before a judge.

If you are jailed, your embassy will offer only limited assistance. This may include a visit to make sure that your human rights have not been violated, contacting your family and putting you in contact with a lawyer (whom you must pay yourself). Embassy officials will not bail you out.

MAPS

The Instituto Geográfico Nacional (p654) in Panama City sells topographical maps of selected cities and regions. Various free tourist publications distributed in Panama also have maps.

MONEY

Panama uses the US dollar as its currency. The official name for it here is the balboa, but it's exactly the same bill, and in practice people use the terms '*dólar*' and 'balboa' interchangeably. Panamanian coins are of the same value, size and metal as US coins; both are used. Coins include one, five, 10, 25 and 50 *centavos* (or *centésimos*); 100 *centavos* equal one balboa. Be aware that most businesses won't break US$50 and US$100 bills and those that do may require you to present your passport.

ATMs

Throughout Panama, ATMs are readily available except in the most isolated places. Look for the red '*sistema clave*' signs to find an ATM. They accept cards on most networks (Plus, Cirrus, MasterCard, Visa and Amex).

The following places have no banks, and it's a long way to the nearest ATM: Santa Catalina, Santa Fé, Boca Brava, Isla Contadora, Isla Grande, Portobelo, Isla de Coiba and the Darién.

SPEAK PANAMEÑO

You can express your appreciation with *chévere* (cool) and *buena leche* (good luck). *Una pinta* means 'a beer' while *vaina* just means 'thing'.

Credit Cards

Although accepted at travel agencies, upscale hotels and many restaurants, credit cards can be problematic almost everywhere else. In short, carry enough cash to get you to the next bank or ATM.

Taxes

A tax of 10% is added to the price of hotel rooms – always ask whether the quoted price includes the tax. A 5% sales tax is levied on nonfood products.

Tipping

The standard tipping rate in Panama is around 10% of the bill; in small cafes and more casual places, tipping is not necessary. Taxi drivers do not expect tips.

Traveler's Checks

Although they can be cashed at a few banks, traveler's checks are rarely accepted by businesses, and traveler's checks in currencies other than US dollars are not accepted anywhere in Panama. Some banks will only accept American Express traveler's checks. The banks that do accept traveler's checks typically charge an exchange fee equal to 1% of the amount of the check.

OPENING HOURS

- **Banks** 8:30am to 1pm or 3pm weekdays; some have Saturday hours as well.
- **Bars** From around noon to 10pm; later on Friday and Saturday nights (typically 2am).
- **Government offices** 8am to 4pm weekdays; they don't close for lunch.
- **Supermarkets** 8am to around 8pm or 9pm; the El Rey chain stays open 24 hours.
- **Nightclubs** From around 10pm or 11pm to 3am or 4am in Panama City.
- **Post offices** 7am to 6pm weekdays; to 4:30pm Saturday.
- **Restaurants** Breakfast from 7am to 10pm, lunch from noon to 3pm and dinner from 6pm to 10pm. On Sunday, many restaurants close. In Panama City and David, restaurants open to about 11pm or midnight on Friday and Saturday nights.
- **Shops & pharmacies** Around 9am or 10am to 6pm or 7pm, Monday to Saturday.
- **Travel agencies & tour operators** 8am to noon and 1:30pm to 5pm weekdays, and from 8am to noon Saturday.

POST

Correos de Panama handles mail. In Panama City, packages can only be mailed from the Plaza de las Americas Post Office. Bring all packing materials yourself.

PUBLIC HOLIDAYS

New Year's Day January 1
Martyrs' Day January 9
Carnaval February to March
Semana Santa (Holy Week) March to April
Labor Day May 1
Founding of Old Panama August 15
All Souls' Day November 2
Independence from Colombia November 3
First Call for Independence November 10
Independence from Spain November 28
Mothers' Day December 8
Christmas Day December 25

SAFE TRAVEL

Crime is a problem in certain parts of Panama City. The city's better districts are safer than in many other capitals: witness the all-night restaurants and activity on the streets at night. On the other hand, it is not safe to walk around at night on the outskirts of Casco Viejo – be careful in the side streets of this district even in the daytime. In general, stay where it's well lit and there are plenty of people around.

Colón is widely known for street crime. Consult staff at your hotel on areas to avoid.

Certain areas in the Darién Province bordering Colombia are extremely dangerous. Few travelers have reason to be in these areas. In the past, it has been used as a staging ground by criminals, human traffickers, the Colombian paramilitary and guerrillas. The area that is particularly treacherous goes beyond Boca de Cupe to Colombia, the traditional path through the Darién Gap.

Numerous Colombian boats travel the Caribbean through the Archipiélago de San Blás between the Zona Libre in Colón and Cartagena, Colombia. There have been cases of boats trafficking drugs on northbound voyages. Take this possibility into account if you plan on taking one of these slow cargo boats. On the Pacific there have been incidents as well.

Hiking

Though tropical, Panama runs the gamut from hot to cold and hiking is not easy here. You should go adequately prepared. Always ask about the conditions of the trail before heading out – either with local outfitters or rangers. Carry plenty of water, even on short journeys, and always bring food, matches and adequate clothing – jungles get quite a bit colder at night, particularly at higher elevations.

Hikers have been known to get lost in rainforests, even seemingly user-friendly ones such as Parque Nacional Volcán Barú and the Sendero Los Quetzales. Landslides, storms and vegetation growth can make trails difficult to follow. In some cases, even access roads can deteriorate enough for transport to leave you a few miles before your intended drop-off point. This is just the reality of the jungle. Many hikers have gotten lost and there is no official rescue organization to help. If you are heading out without a guide, tell your hotel about your plans and the number of days you will be gone.

Never walk in unmarked rainforest. Always plan your transportation in advance – know where and when the last bus will pass your terminus, or arrange for a taxi pickup with a responsible, recommended transporter.

Police

Police corruption is not as big a problem in Panama as it is in some other Latin American countries. But it's not unheard of for a Panamanian police officer to stop a motorist for no obvious reason, accuse him or her of violating a law, and levy a fine to be paid on the spot. If there are people around, making a big scene will sometimes fluster the officer into letting you go. Most of the time, however, you become an unwilling participant in a waiting game.

Your best option, unless you want to try to wait out the officer, is to negotiate the fine down. Failure to pay anything can result in your being led to jail with the officer insisting you really did break some law.

Some cities in Panama have tourist police – a division created to deal specifically with travelers. Identifiable by armbands on their uniform, officers in this division may be more helpful.

Swimming

In recent years there have been fatalities – about 80% are caused by rip currents. A rip current is a strong current that pulls the swimmer out to sea. It occurs when two currents that move parallel to the shore meet, causing the opposing waters to choose the path of least resistance, which is a path out to sea. It is most important to remember that rip currents will pull you *out* but not *under*.

If you find yourself caught in a rip current, stay calm and swim parallel to the shore to get out of it – rip currents dissipate quickly. When the current dissipates, swim back in at a 45° angle to the shore to avoid being caught by the current again. Do not try to swim directly back in, as you would be swimming against the rip current and would only exhaust yourself.

If you feel a rip current while you are wading, try to come back in sideways, thus offering less body surface to the current. If you cannot make headway, walk parallel to the beach so that you can get out of the rip current.

TELEPHONE

Panama's country code is ☎507. To call Panama from abroad, use the country code before the seven-digit Panamanian telephone number.

There are no local area codes in Panama. Mobile numbers are eight digits and start with ☎6.

Pay phones can make national calls with change or phone cards (purchased at pharmacies), though they are increasingly rare. Many internet cafes have headphones to make internet phone calls.

If traveling for an extended period, consider getting a Panamanian SIM card if you have an unlocked cell phone. Otherwise, mall kiosks sell pay-per-use phones for as cheap as US$20; many come with minutes loaded. Having a phone can be invaluable for last-minute reservations or directions.

TOURIST INFORMATION

Autoridad de Turismo Panamá (ATP, Panama Tourism Authority; ☎226-7000; www.atp.gob.pa; Vía Israel, Centro Atlapa, San Francisco; ⏲8:30am-4:30pm Mon-Fri) is the national tourism agency. In addition to this head office in Panama City, ATP runs offices in Bocas del Toro, Boquete, Colón, David, Paso Canoas, Penonomé, Portobelo, Santiago, Villa de Los Santos, Las Tablas, El Valle and Pedasí. There are smaller information counters at the ruins of Panamá Viejo, in Casco Viejo, and in both the Tocumen International Airport and the Albrook domestic airport.

ATP has a few useful maps and brochures, not always in stock. Most staff speak only Spanish, and the helpfulness of any particular office depends on the person at the counter.

TOURS

Though increasingly navigable for the independent traveler, Panama does have special conditions (complex logistics, limited public access and big wilderness) which make contracting a tour operator a good option. The Darién is relatively inaccessible without a guide. Some recommended operators:

Ancon Expeditions (Map p646; ☎269-9415; www.anconexpeditions.com; Calle 49 A Este, El Dorado Bldg, Panama City) Operating all over Panama, Ancon employs the country's best nature guides. The company is also the exclusive operator for the world-famous Cana field station popular with bird-watchers, and the Punta Patiño lodge, both in the Darién.

Ecocircuitos (Map p642; ☎314-0068; www.ecocircuitos.com; Albrook Plaza, 2nd fl, No 31, Ancón, Panama City) With a focus on sustainable tourism, Ecocircuitos offers a range of tours throughout the country, including wildlife-watching, kayaking in the Comarca de Kuna Yala and volunteer vacations in the Darién.

Jungle Treks (☎6438-3130; www.jungletreks.com) A new company started by a bilingual naturalist guide, Jungle Treks runs a number of unique, recommended expeditions. Destinations include the Darién, the Chiriquí Highlands, Veraguas and the Canal watershed. Trips can be custom-made but require six participants and a three-day minimum.

Scubapanama (Map p642; ☎261-3841; www.scubapanama.com) Located in the El Carmen area of Panama City, Scubapanama is the country's oldest dive operator, and offers a variety of dive trips.

Sendero Panama (☎393-0747; www.senderopanama.com) A reputable outfitter offering a variety of private tours around Panama, as well as day trips from Panama City. Options include walking, birding, family options and multisport activities. English-speaking and also a member of **APTSO** (Asociación Panameña de Turismo Sostenible, Panamanian SUstainable Tourism Association).

TRAVELERS WITH DISABILITIES

The government-created **Instituto Panameño de Habilitación Especial** (IPHE, Panamanian Institute for Special Rehabilitation; ☎261-0500; www.iphe.gob.pa; Camino Real, Betania, Panama City; ⏲7am-4pm) assists all disabled people in Panama, including foreign tourists. But the law does not require – and Panamanian businesses do not provide – discounts for foreign tourists with disabilities.

Panama is not wheelchair-friendly; with the exception of wheelchair ramps outside a few upscale hotels, parking spaces for the disabled and perhaps a few dozen oversized bathroom stalls, accommodation for people with physical disabilities rarely exists in Panama, even at top hotels. The international **Travelin' Talk Network** (TTN; ☎in USA 303-232-2979; www.travelintalk.net; membership US$20) is a member-based organization offering those with various disabilities a network about travel.

VISAS

Every visitor needs a valid passport and an onward ticket to enter Panama, but further requirements vary by nationality and change occasionally. Note that US citizens can no longer enter Panama with just a driver's license and a birth certificate.

Anyone planning a trip to Panama would be advised to check online to obtain the latest information on entry requirements. Ticketing agents of airlines that fly to Panama and tour operators that send groups there can often provide this information.

You will generally be given a 90-day stamp in your passport when you enter Panama. This means you are allowed to remain in Panama for 90 days without having to obtain further permission from the authorities. After 90 days, visas and tourist cards can be extended at *migración* (immigration) offices.

Tourist cards are included in the price of your air ticket.

At the time of research, people holding passports from the following countries needed to show only their passports to enter Panama: Argentina, Austria, Belgium, Chile, Colombia, Costa Rica, Czech Republic, Denmark, England, El Salvador, Finland, France, Germany, Greece, Guatemala, Holland, Honduras, Hungary, Ireland, Israel, Italy, Luxembourg, Paraguay, Poland, Portugal, Singapore, South Korea, Spain, Sweden, Switzerland, the UK and Uruguay.

People from the following countries need a passport and a tourist card: Antigua, Australia, Bahamas, Barbados, Belize, Canada, Dominican Republic, Granada, Guyana, Jamaica, Japan, New Zealand, Taiwan, Thailand, Tobago, Trinidad, the USA and Venezuela.

Citizens from countries not on the above list will need to obtain a visa, available at Panamanian embassies or consulates. Contact the one nearest you or call Migración y Naturalización in Panama City.

Travelers entering Panama overland will probably be asked to show an onward ticket and proof of sufficient funds (US$500) or a credit card.

If you lose your passport while in Panama, you'll need proof of when you entered the country to be able to leave. Go to your airline's main office in Panama City and request a certification of your entry date *(certificación de vuelo)*. There's no charge, but you'll likely be asked to return the next day to pick it up. Upon leaving the country, present your *certificación de vuelo* to an immigration agent, along with your new passport (obtained from your embassy in Panama City).

WOMEN TRAVELERS

While there is no doubt Panama is a Latin culture, female travelers usually find it safe. A minority of Panamanian men may make flirtatious comments, hiss, honk their horn or stare, even if you're accompanied. Don't take it as a challenge. A kind of hormonal babble, this behavior is as much about male bonding as the female passerby. The best response is to follow the lead of Panamanian women: give these men a broad berth, ignore their comments and look away.

While locals might get away with skimpy, stretchy clothing, travelers will naturally attract less attention with a more conservative approach. Wearing shorts outside of a beach setting marks you as a tourist. In the interior, dress is more formal, with skirts and nice sandals the norm. Even in beach towns, women should save their bathing suit for the beach.

Women traveling solo will get more attention than those traveling in pairs or groups. Although assault and rape of foreign travelers is rare, avoid placing yourself in risky scenarios. In general, don't walk alone in isolated places, don't hitchhike and always pay particular attention to your surroundings.

If you are taking a long-distance bus, sit down next to a woman or a family if you are nervous about come-ons. Be picky about your taxis: though shared taxis may be the norm (between unknown parties), avoid those with more than one man in them. If the driver tries to pick up another fare, you can offer to pay more to travel alone.

WORK

It's difficult for foreigners to find work in Panama. The government doesn't like anyone taking jobs away from Panamanians, and the labor laws reflect this sentiment. The only foreigners legally employed in Panama work for their own businesses, possess skills not found in Panama, or work for companies that have special agreements with the Panamanian government.

Getting There & Away

Passengers entering Panama by air are less scrutinized than those crossing by land. Upon arrival, travelers may have to fill out a tourist card depending on their nationality; the fee is incorporated into the price of the ticket.

The most popular overland crossing is from Costa Rica at Paso Canoas. You may be asked to show an onward ticket – a return bus ticket to Costa Rica will suffice – and a credit card or US$500. It is not recommended to cross overland to Colombia; travelers need permits from SENAFRONT just to enter this region, though many travelers have made successful crossings by boat. See p706 for more information.

AIR

Panama has two International airports. Panama City's **Tocumen International Airport**, 35km from downtown, receives most international flights. In David, **Aeropuerto Enrique Malek** is 75km southeast of the Costa Rican border, and frequently handles flights to and from San José, Costa Rica.

Panama's national airline, **COPA** (☎200-2100; www.copaair.com) is compliant with international aviation standards. Flights go to and from the USA, numerous Latin and South American countries, and the Caribbean.

Panama City is a common destination for travelers flying to/from the region on an open-jaw ticket.

BORDER CROSSINGS

At all three border crossings with Costa Rica you can approach the border via local buses on either side, cross over, board another local bus and continue on your way. Be aware that the last buses leave the border crossings at Guabito and Río Sereno at 7pm; the last bus leaves Paso Canoas for Panama City at 9:30pm. Note that

DEPARTURE TAX

Panama levies a US$40 departure tax for outbound passengers on international flights, included in the cost of the ticket.

Costa Rica is one hour behind Panama – opening and closing times here are given in Panamanian time.

Panaline (☎227-8648; www.viajeros.com/panaline) and **Tica Bus** (☎262-2084; www.ticabus.com) have daily direct departures between San José in Costa Rica, and Panama City, departing from the Albrook bus terminal. Reserve a few days in advance.

Costa Rica

The most heavily trafficked Panama–Costa Rica border crossing is at **Paso Canoas** (⏲24hr), 53km west of David on the Interamericana. Allow at least one to two hours to get through the formalities on both sides. Buses from David depart for the border (US$2.75, 1½ hours) from 4:30am to 9:30pm, every half-hour. On the Costa Rican side of the border, you can catch regular buses to San José or other parts of the country. From David, there are also taxis to Paso Canoas (US$40 to US$50).

The least trafficked crossing into Costa Rica is the border post at **Río Sereno** (9am-5pm Mon-Sat, to 3pm Sun), located 47km west of Volcán. Buses to the border depart half-hourly from David and travel via La Concepción, Volcán and Santa Clara (US$6.50, three hours). On the Costa Rican side of the border you can take a 15-minute bus or taxi ride to San Vito, from where you can catch buses to other destinations. From David, taxis to Río Sereno cost US$70.

The border post at **Guabito–Sixaola** (8am-5pm), north of Changuinola, is a straightforward, less-traveled post, and most travelers find it hassle-free. Buses from Changuinola depart for the border (US$1.80, 30 minutes) from 6am to 7pm, every half-hour. On the Costa Rican side of the border, you can catch regular buses on to Puerto Limón and San José, as well as regional destinations. You can take a taxi from Changuinola to the Costa Rican border at Guabito (US$3 per person, 15 minutes).

Colombia

It's possible to cross to Colombia by sea, though it can be a rough crossing. Multiday motorboat and sailboat trips depart from Colón Province or Comarca de Kuna Yala.

CAR & MOTORCYCLE

You can drive your own car from North America to Panama, but the costs of insurance, fuel, border permits, food and accommodations will be much higher than the cost of an airline ticket. As a result, most people opt to fly down and rent cars when they arrive in Panama City.

If you decide to drive to Panama, get insurance, have your papers in order and never leave your car unattended. US license plates are attractive to some thieves, so you should display these from inside the car.

If you are bringing a car into Panama, you must show a passport, valid driver's license, proof of ownership and insurance papers. Complete information is available at the government website: www.ana.gob.pa/portal/index.php/regimenes-aduaneros/120 -vehiculos-de-turistas.html.

ℹ Getting Around

AIR

Panama currently only has one domestic carrier: **Air Panama** (www.flyairpanama.com). Domestic flights depart Panama City from Albrook airport and arrive in destinations throughout the country. For most flights it's wise to book as far in advance as possible.

Even if you're on a tight budget, one-way domestic flights are never more than US$80, and you can sometimes turn a one- or two-day bus/boat journey into a 45-minute flight.

BICYCLE

You can cycle through Panama easily enough, but cycling within larger Panamanian cities – particularly Panama City – is not wise. Roads are narrow, there are no bike lanes, motorists drive aggressively and frequent rains reduce motorists' visibility.

Outside the cities, roads tend to be in fine shape, although parts of the Interamericana are narrow, leaving little room to move aside should a car pass by. Lodging is rarely more than a day's bike ride away.

BOAT

Boats are the chief means of transportation in several areas of Panama, particularly in Darién Province, the Archipiélago de Las Perlas, and the San Blás and Bocas del Toro island chains. While at least one eccentric soul has swum the entire length of the Panama Canal, a boat simplifies the transit enormously.

The backpacker mecca of Bocas del Toro on Isla Colón is accessible from Almirante by speedy and inexpensive water taxis.

Colombian and Kuna merchant boats carry cargo and passengers along the San Blás coast between Colón and Puerto Obaldía, stopping at up to 48 islands to load and unload passengers and cargo. But these boats are occasionally used to traffic narcotics, and they're often dangerously overloaded. Hiring a local boatman is a wiser option and usually included in lodging.

Since there aren't many roads in eastern Darién Province, boat travel is often the most feasible way to get from one town to another, especially during the rainy season. The boat of choice here is a *piragua* (long canoe), carved from the trunks of giant ceiba trees. Their shallow hulls allow them to ride the many rivers of eastern Panama. Many are motorized.

BUS

You can take a bus to just about any community in Panama that is reachable by road. Some are huge, new Mercedes Benzes equipped with air-con, movie screens and reclining seats. These top-of-the-line buses generally cruise long stretches of highway.

The more frequently used Toyota Coaster buses seat 28 people. Affectionately called *chivas,* these provide inexpensive transit to the interior and along the Interamericana.

Panama City is phasing out its converted school buses known as *diablos rojos* (red devils). Replacing them is the Metrobus system. Riders can obtain swipe cards at the Albrook terminal or main bus stops. Official bus stops are used and the buses are air-conditioned.

CAR & MOTORCYCLE

Due to the low cost and ready availability of buses and taxis, it isn't necessary to rent a vehicle in Panama unless you intend to go to places far off the beaten track. There are car-rental agencies in Panama City, David and Chitré. Several agencies also have offices at Tocumen International Airport in the capital.

To rent a vehicle in Panama, you must be 25 years of age or older and present a passport and driver's license, though some places will rent vehicles to 21-year-olds if you ask politely, pay higher insurance costs, and supply them with a major credit card.

Prices for rentals in Panama run from US$35 per day for economy models to US$115 per day for a 4WD (*cuatro por cuatro).* When you rent, carefully inspect the car for minor dents and scratches, missing radio antennae, hubcaps and the spare tire. Any damages *must* be noted on your rental agreement, otherwise you may be charged for them when you return the car.

There have been many reports of theft from rental cars, so don't leave valuables or luggage unattended. Many hotels provide parking areas for cars.

HITCHHIKING

Hitchhiking is never entirely safe in any country. The practice is not as widespread in Panama as elsewhere in Central America, but is fairly common in remote areas. Most Panamanians travel by bus and travelers would do best to follow suit. The exception is holiday weekends, when buses are overflowing and hitchhiking may be the only way out of a place. If you get a ride, offer payment upon arrival – *'¿Cuánto le debo?'* ('How much do I owe you?') is the standard courtesy.

SUBWAY

Panama City is building a new subway system known as Metro. With its first phase expected to be finished in 2014, the line will link Albrook with Vía Transitsmica, Vía España and Calidonia. The plan is to extend it to Tocumen Airport. The terminal, under construction at the time of writing, is across from the Albrook bus terminal. Fares will be paid with the same cards used for the Metro bus system.

TAXI

Panamanian taxis don't have meters, but there are some set fares. Taxis are cheap, and generally plentiful. But they can be difficult to hail late at night and just before and during holidays. During these times, it's best to call for a radio taxi. Listings for reliable radio taxis can be found in the Yellow Pages of phone directories throughout Panama, under the heading 'Taxis'.

More expensive 'sedan' taxis operate from upscale hotels and malls. These drivers charge at least twice what you'd pay for a hailed cab.

TRAIN

The train trip between Panama City and Colón is scenic.

Survival Guide

DIRECTORY A-Z 728

Accommodations..... 728
Activities 729
Climate..... 730
Customs Regulations..... 730
Discount Cards..... 730
Electricity 731
Embassies & Consulates 731
Exchange Rates 731
Gay & Lesbian Travelers 732
Health.....732
Insurance.....732
Internet Access.....732
Language Courses.....732
Maps.....733
Money.....733
Opening Hours 733
Photography & Video ... 734
Post..... 734
Safe Travel..... 734
Telephone 735
Toilets.....735
Tourist Information 735
Travelers with Disabilities.....735
Visas & Documents..... 736
Volunteering 736
Women Travelers 737
Work.....737

TRANSPORTATION...738

GETTING THERE & AWAY..... 738
Entering Central America 738
Air 738
Land 739
Sea 740
GETTING AROUND..... 740
Air 740
Bicycle 741
Boat 741
Bus 741
Car & Motorcycle.....742
Train 742

LANGUAGE 743

Glossary.....748
Food & Drink Glossary... 750

Directory A-Z

Accommodations

We will list accommodation in order of preference. For those nights when you need a break from shared showers and thin mattresses, we've also included a few midrange options as well as a few splurges.

Accommodation costs vary from country to country. Generally Nicaragua, Honduras and Guatemala are the cheapest countries; Mexico and Belize (and many beach destinations), the most expensive. Features like a private bathroom, hot water and air-con drive up prices.

Reservations are necessary in tourist areas during peak season, particularly during Semana Santa (Easter Week) and the week between Christmas and New Year, when locals are also traveling around the region.

Prices do change; use any prices listed here as a gauge only.

Camping

If you plan on camping, it's best to bring your own gear. Organized campgrounds aren't common. Facilities at campgrounds can vary; only some have fire pits, latrines and water. Another option is *refugios* (huts), usually found in national parks.

Some hostels set aside areas for campers. Some national parks and reserves (particularly in Costa Rica) have basic facilities, but they can be hit-and-miss – sometimes packed and noisy. Prices start at US$7 per person per night. In some places it's feasible to ask to camp on private land.

Hostels

Hostels are found throughout Central America and mostly serve all ages. They generally charge around US$7 to US$15 for a bunk. Except for in Mexico and Costa Rica, Hostelling International (HI) membership isn't particularly useful as many hostels are independently run.

Guesthouses & Hotels

Guesthouses are generally small, family-run lodgings. Most rooms have a fan and shared bathroom. Many do not provide a towel or soap. Options range from nice rooms with shared bath to a dumpy bed with smeared mosquito remains on the walls and a smelly, leaky-faucet shower down the hall.

In hotels, rooms with air-con and TV start at double the price of a room with fan. Generally breakfast is not included in the overnight rate.

'Hot water' can be lukewarm and working only at certain hours of the day. Be sure to ask if water is cold, as it may just be a matter of turning on the hot water heater. Beware of the electric shower: a cold-water showerhead juiced by an electric heating element. Don't touch it, or anything metal, while in the shower or you may get a shock.

Used toilet paper should be placed in the receptacle provided.

We've done our best to avoid including places used by the 'hourly' crowd or prostitutes. If you stumble on some we've included, please let us know.

Hammocks & Cabins

Sleeping in a hammock can make for a breezier night than sleeping in a stuffy room. Many beach towns have hammock rooms or areas for the same price as a dorm. *Cabañas* (or *cabinas*) provide memorable stays on the beach or in the jungle. Amenities vary – many are simple thatched-roof huts with a dirt or sand floor.

BOOK YOUR STAY ONLINE

For more accommodations reviews by Lonely Planet authors, check out www.lonelyplanet.com/central-america/hotels. You'll find independent reviews, as well as recommendations on the best places to stay. Best of all, you can book online.

Homestays

Spanish-language schools arrange homestays in towns where the language-school scene is strong, such as Antigua or Quetzaltenango in Guatemala, Granada in Nicaragua, Copán, Honduras or Bocas del Toro, Panama. A similar option is *turismo rural*; community tourism initiatives with rural homestays.

Activities

Coastal fun is Central America's most popular draw: surfers hit the Pacific while divers generally go to the calmer Caribbean. Mountains, tropical rainforest and volcanoes run through most of the region, offering many compelling (and often tough) hiking and cycling options.

Canopy Tours

Zip-line trips through the treetops have become popular throughout Central America, from the highlands to beaches and rainforests. Do your homework on the safety history of the outfitter you choose. Costs run from US$25 to US$45 per trip.

Cycling

Many shops rent out bicycles for local exploration. Some offer guided cycling trips – such as to Maya villages from San Cristóbal de Las Casas, Mexico (p73) and coffee plantations or ridge rides from Antigua, Guatemala. Cycling is also a fine way to tour countries, though it is best to bring your own bike for these trips (along with proof that you own the bike).

Diving & Snorkeling

Some of Latin America's (and the world's) finest diving and snorkeling spots are found along the barrier reefs off Central America's Caribbean shores. Sites up and down the coast – from Mexico to Panama – offer rich marine life, sunken ships and deep holes. Some of the most famous dive spots can be found at Bay Islands, Honduras; Cozumel, Mexico; the reefs off Belize's northern cays; and the more low-key Corn Islands in Nicaragua.

Honduras' Bay Islands are famous for good-value dives and scuba courses; taking the four-day Professional Association of Diving Instructors (PADI) open-water diving certification course here costs about US$275. Free diving is also taking off, with day courses starting at US$50 in Honduras. Another good-value location for diving is Panama.

Region-wide, snorkeling day trips out to a couple of reef spots can be taken for US$5 to US$45. Dives start at around US$36 in Honduras or US$80 in Mexico. Most dive shops will rent diving equipment – always check it carefully before going under. Be sure to bring evidence of your certification if you plan to dive.

It's possible to dive in the Pacific too, though conditions may be murkier. The best time for diving in the Pacific is October to February. In Nicaragua, San Juan del Sur has a dive shop (p477) and the crater lakes in Laguna de Apoyo (p466) are another good option.

Mexico offers otherworldly dives in cenotes (freshwater limestone sinkholes). There are some options reachable from **Tulum** (☎871-2953; www.xibalbadivecenter.com; Andromeda 7; 1-/2-tank cenote dive M$940/1500, snorkeling M$390-585).

Also check out Lonely Planet's *Cozumel: Diving & Snorkeling* guide.

SAFETY GUIDELINES FOR DIVING

Before scuba diving or free diving, carefully consider the following points to ensure a safe and enjoyable experience.

- You need a current diving certification card from a recognized scuba-diving instructional agency (if scuba diving).
- Be sure you are healthy and feel comfortable diving.
- Obtain reliable information about physical and environmental conditions at the dive site (eg from a reputable local dive operator).
- Be aware of local laws, regulations and etiquette relating to marine life and the environment.
- Dive only at sites within your realm of experience; engage the services of a competent, professionally trained dive instructor or dive master.
- Be aware that underwater conditions vary significantly depending on region, season, and even from one site to another.

Hiking

Central America's stunning natural environment, volcanoes and abundant wildlife make for great hiking. The terrain ranges from cloud forests and rainforests to lowland jungles, river trails and palm-lined beaches.

Jungle trekking can be strenuous, and hikers should be prepared. If you want to camp, bring your own gear as its availability is limited here.

Popular hikes in the region range from volcanoes around Antigua in Guatemala (p113) or the tropical mountain forests of Parque Nacional El Imposible in El Salvador, to prehistoric petroglyphs on Nicaragua's Isla de Ometepe (p471), Honduras' Lago de Yojoa (p373), or coffee-scented hills around Panama's only volcano, Volcán Barú, in the Chiriquí highlands (p677).

The ultimate would be the 60km hike to Guatemala's El Mirador (p209), a sprawling, largely unexcavated Maya city reached by an intense hike into the El Petén jungle, a couple of days each way. Less demanding, but no shorter, is the hike through modern Maya villages from Nebaj (p143) to Todos Santos Cuchumatán, also in Guatemala.

Surfing

Surfing's popularity is on the rise in Central America, with many places renting boards to tackle 'perfect' breaks. Costa Rica has the most developed scene, but low-key spots in El Salvador and Nicaragua are, to some, the best places. If you've never surfed, you can find cheap surf lessons and board rentals starting at US$10. Hot spots include El Salvador's Balsam Coast, San Juan del Sur in Nicaragua, and Costa Rica's increasingly popular Mal País on the Península de Nicoya.

White-Water Rafting

Some of the best white-water rafting in the tropics can be found in Central America and rafting is fast becoming popular all over Latin America. Guatemala, Honduras and Panama are developing a rafting industry and have a number of rivers offering anything from frothing Class IV white water to easy Class II floats. Costa Rica leads the pack in river adventure sports (see p555).

Wildlife-Watching

The unexpected appearance of a toucan, howler monkey, sloth, crocodile, iguana, dolphin or puma makes for the greatest rush on your trip, and the wildlife-viewing and bird-watching opportunities in every part of Central America are world-class. A system of national parks, wildlife refuges, biosphere reserves and other protected areas throughout the region facilitates independent bird- and wildlife-viewing. Even private areas such as gardens around hotels in the countryside can yield a sample of birds, insects, reptiles and even monkeys.

Early morning and late afternoon are the best times to watch for wildlife activity anywhere.

Costa Rica boasts high wildlife density and a developed tour infrastructure, with remarkable places such as the pristine Parque Nacional Corcovado (p620) and many others. Panama also offers incredible wildlife-watching opportunities.

The elusive quetzal – and hordes of other implausibly colorful birds – can be seen in Honduras' Lago de Yojoa and Panama's Volcán Barú in the Chiriquí highlands. Belize's Crooked Tree Wildlife Sanctuary (p246) is another hot spot for bird-watchers. Morning bird-watching tours at Tikal (p205) in Guatemala add to the experience of seeing the ruins.

Howler monkeys (named for their frightening tiger-like roar) can be seen in treetops around the region, such as on an unforgettable walk through the Yaxchilán Maya ruins (p84), throughout Panama and on the Mexico–Guatemala border. The black howler monkey lives only in Belize and can be seen at the Bermudian Landing Community Baboon Sanctuary.

The best places to see sea turtles are Parque Nacional Tortuguero in Costa Rica (p557), Isla de Cañas in Panama (p664) and Refugio de Vida Silvestre La Flor in Nicaragua (p481). Coral reefs are an excellent place to see sea turtles, stingrays, sharks and tons of smaller, more colorful creatures.

TOP SURFING SPOTS

Costa Rica Experts-only Salsa Brava, at Puerto Viejo de Talamanca, or Pavones' three-minute left.

El Salvador Punta Roca, at La Libertad.

Guatemala Sipacate.

Nicaragua Las Salinas (west of Rivas).

Panama Waves at Santa Catalina and the Archipiélago de Bocas del Toro.

Climate

For information on climate around the region, see p18 and each individual country chapter.

Customs Regulations

All visitors leaving and entering a Central American country go through customs. Be prepared for quick bag checks at airports and land borders too. Most are just a quick gaze-and-poke, more of a formality than a search – but not always. Be polite with officials at all times.

Discount Cards

A Hostelling International (HI) membership card isn't terribly useful in Central America, except in Mexico and Costa Rica where some hostels offer minimal discounts to cardholders. Those going on to South America, however, may want to invest in the membership as the card is more commonly accepted there (see www.iyhf.org for information).

Carriers of the International Student Identity Card (ISIC) can get very good discounts on travel insurance, as well as discounted air tickets. Check www.isic.org for details.

Electricity

Most countries in Central America use plug type A or B – which are also used in the United States – with the exception of Belize, which may use type G plugs. Voltage varies between 110v and 220v.

For more information see www.electricaloutlet.org.

Embassies & Consulates

For embassy phone numbers and addresses, see the Survival Guide section of individual country chapters.

As a visitor in a Central American country, it's important to realize what your own country's embassy can and can't do for you. Generally speaking, it won't be much help in emergencies when you're even remotely at fault. Remember that you are bound by the laws of the country you are in. Your embassy will not be sympathetic if you end up in jail after committing a crime locally, even if such actions are legal in your own country.

In genuine emergencies you may get some assistance, but only if other channels have been exhausted. For example, if you have all your money and documents stolen, the embassy might assist in getting a new passport, but a loan for onward travel is out of the question.

Exchange Rates

Belize

Australia	A$1	BZ$1.91
Canada	C$1	BZ$1.98
Euro zone	€1	BZ$2.69
Guatemala	Q1	BZ$0.26
Japan	¥100	BZ$2.10
Mexico	1peso	BZ$0.16
New Zealand	NZ$1	BZ$1.60
UK	UK£1	BZ$3.16
USA	US$1	BZ$2.02

Costa Rica, El Salvador, Nicaragua & Panama

US dollars are widely accepted in both Costa Rica and Nicaragua.

Because many lodgings and activities in these countries list their prices in dollars rather than local currency, we have followed suit here for consistency.

Australia	A$1	US$0.95
Canada	C$1	US$0.98
Euro zone	€1	US$1.33
Japan	¥100	US$1.04
New Zealand	NZ$1	US$0.79
UK	£1	US$1.56

Guatemala

Australia	A$1	Q7.41
Canada	C$1	Q7.68
Euro zone	€1	Q10.42
Japan	¥100	Q8.12
New Zealand	NZ$1	Q6.18
UK	UK£1	Q12.24
USA	US$1	Q7.82

Honduras

Australia	A$1	L19.17
Canada	C$1	L19.87
Euro zone	€1	L26.97
Japan	¥100	L21.01
New Zealand	NZ$1	L15.67
UK	UK£1	L31.69
USA	US$1	L20.26

Mexico

Australia	A$1	M$12.16
Canada	C$1	M$12.60
Euro zone	€1	M$17.09
Japan	¥100	M$13.32
New Zealand	NZ1	M$10.15
UK	UK£1	M$20.09
USA	US$1	M$12.84

For current exchange rates see www.xe.com.

Gay & Lesbian Travelers

On the whole, Central America can be an unwelcoming place for gay men and lesbians. The silver lining is in Mexico, where same-sex marriage was made legal in 2009. Advocacy groups in other Central American countries are eager to follow suit.

Consensual gay sex has been decriminalized in Nicaragua. However, official harassment is possible anywhere in Central America. In Honduras, violence against gays (and even murder) is all too common.

In general, public displays of affection will not be tolerated and gay men (and possibly women) could find themselves the target of verbal or physical abuse.

Discretion is definitely the rule, especially in the countryside of Central America. Lesbians are generally less maligned than gay men and women traveling together should encounter few, if any, problems.

For more information, a useful website is www.gaymexico.com.mx.

Venues

There is usually at least one gay bar in big cities, which makes meeting people easier. Some of the more public gay and lesbian scenes:

Costa Rica San José's thriving scene; beach hangout Manuel Antonio.

El Salvador San Salvador's Blvd de los Héroes; mountain town San Vicente.

Guatemala Bars in Guatemala City.

Mexico Cancún's bars; Playa del Carmen's clubs.

Panama Gay float at Panama City's **Carnaval**.

Health

There are no required vaccinations for Central America, though if you are coming from a yellow fever–infected country in Africa or South America, you must have a yellow fever vaccine. Among others recommended are typhoid, rabies and Hepatitis A and B. Visit your doctor well ahead of your trip, since most vaccines don't produce immunity until at least two weeks after they're given. Ask your doctor for an international certificate of vaccination (the yellow booklet), which will list all the vaccinations you've received. This is mandatory for countries that require proof of yellow-fever vaccination.

It's usually a good idea to consult your government's travel health website before departure, if one is available. The **World Health Organization** (www.who.int/ith) publishes a superb book called *International Travel and Health,* revised annually and available on its website at no cost. The website lists updated risks and worldwide vaccination-certificate requirements. Another useful website, **MD Travel Health** (www.mdtravelhealth.com), provides complete travel health recommendations for every country, updated daily, also at no cost.

If your health insurance does not cover you for medical expenses abroad, consider supplemental insurance.

Insurance

A travel insurance policy covering theft, loss, accidents and illness is highly recommended. Some policies compensate travelers for misrouted or lost luggage. Also check that the coverage includes worst-case scenarios: ambulances, evacuations or an emergency flight home. Some policies specifically exclude 'dangerous activities', which can include scuba diving, motorcycling or even trekking. Read the small print.

There is a wide variety of policies available and your travel agent can make good recommendations. Policies handled by student-travel organizations usually offer good value. If a policy offers lower and higher medical-expense options, the low-expenses policy should be OK for Central America – medical costs are not nearly as high here as elsewhere.

If you have baggage insurance and need to make a claim, the insurance company may demand a receipt as proof that you bought the stuff in the first place. You must usually inform the insurance company by airmail and report the loss or theft to local police within 24 hours. Make a list of stolen items and their value. At the police station, you need to complete a *denuncia* (statement), a copy of which is given to you for your claim.

Worldwide travel insurance is available at www.lonelyplanet.com/travel_services.

Internet Access

Internet access is widely available. Many hostels have guest computers and wi-fi is increasingly common, including at higher-end cafes and restaurants. Internet cafes are less prevalent than before; rates range from US$0.50 in cities and touristy destinations to US$6 in remote areas. Either Alt + 64 or Alt-G + 2 is the command to get the @ symbol on Spanish-language keyboards.

Language Courses

Spanish-language courses are available in many Central American cities. Antigua or Quetzaltenango in Guatemala and Estelí in Nicaragua are three of Central America's best-value destinations.

Maps

The best map of the region is the fold-up color 1:1,100,000 *Central America Travel Reference Map* (US$13), produced by International Travel Maps & Books (www.itmb.com) in Canada. ITMB also publishes separate maps covering each of the Central American countries and various regions of Mexico, as well as several maps of South America.

Money

Prices are given mostly in local currencies. US dollars, which is the official currency in El Salvador and Panama, and widely accepted in Costa Rica and Nicaragua, is used in these country chapters.

ATMs

Bring an ATM (or debit) card. ATMs are available in most cities and large towns and are almost always the most convenient, reliable, secure and economical way of getting cash. The exchange rate from ATMs is usually as good as (if not better than) at any bank or legal money changer. Many ATMs are connected to the MasterCard/Cirrus or Visa/Plus networks. Notify your bank of your travel plans so foreign-made transactions are not barred.

Bargaining

The art of bargaining can be acquired through practice and you'll get some in Central America's markets, particularly when shopping for souvenirs and craft goods. Most accommodations prices are fixed, but for long-term stays (or during low season) it's worth asking for a discount. Indoor shops (such as groceries) generally have fixed prices. You may need to negotiate a price with a taxi driver. If you always approach bargaining with patience and humor, you'll often end up with a price agreeable to both you and the seller.

Black Market

The black market *(mercado negro)* – also known as *mercado paralelo* (parallel market) – is generally limited to money changers at borders, who may or may not be legal. They are known to slip in torn bills or shortchange on occasion, though they accept local currencies that banks elsewhere sometimes don't take. Such unofficial exchange rates for the US dollar can be lower than official bank rates.

Cash

It's a good idea to always have a small amount of US dollars handy – enough to get a room, a meal and a taxi, at least – because they can be exchanged practically anywhere. It's particularly useful when crossing the border or when an ATM isn't available. Central American currencies don't always fly in the next country but generally it's possible to use US dollars. Plan ahead before you head to remote areas; take more than enough cash.

Getting change for bigger notes in local currency is a daily concern. Notes worth even US$20 can sometimes be difficult to change.

Credit Cards

American Express, Visa and MasterCard are the most widely accepted credit cards in Central America. Some card companies also charge a fee (from 2% to 10%) for international transactions. Some banks issue cash advances on major credit cards.

Exchanging Money

➡ Change traveler's checks or foreign cash at a bank or a *casa de cambio* (currency exchange office).

➡ Rates are usually similar, but in general *casas de cambio* are quicker, less bureaucratic and open longer or on weekends. Street money changers, who may or may not be legal, will only handle cash.

➡ Sometimes you can change money unofficially at hotels or in shops that sell imported goods (electronics dealers are an obvious choice).

➡ Compare exchange rates and commission fees first. Big cities tend to offer better exchange rates.

➡ Don't accept torn notes, as most locals won't when you try to use them.

Tipping

Though more basic cafes and bars usually do not expect tips, diners should tip about 10% at more formal restaurants. Some include a service charge of 10% to 20% on the bill. To be sure, ask *¿La cuenta incluye el servicio?* (Does the bill include service charge?)

A small tip for taxi drivers or hotel cleaning staff isn't necessary but appreciated.

Traveler's Checks

Traveler's checks are not nearly as convenient as ATM cards and you may have difficulty cashing them – even at banks. If you must, use only widely accepted brands, such as American Express, Visa, Thomas Cook and Citibank. To facilitate replacement, keep a record of check numbers and the original bill of sale in a safe place.

In some countries traveler's checks are nearly impossible to cash, like Honduras, and banks and *casas de cambio* charge high commissions. Check if there's a fixed transaction fee (regardless of the value of the checks) or a percentage fee (from 3% up to 10%).

Opening Hours

Standard opening hours for each country are given in the chapter directories.

Photography & Video

Always ask before photographing individuals, particularly indigenous people. Paying people for a portrait is a personal decision; in most cases subjects will tell you straight off the going rate for a photo. Some tourist sites charge an additional fee for video cameras or cameras. Don't photograph military installations or personnel; it may be illegal in some areas. In churches photography or the use of flashes is often prohibited.

Post

International postal rates can be quite expensive. Generally, important mail and parcels should be sent by registered or certified service; otherwise they may go missing. Sending parcels can be awkward, as often a customs officer must inspect the contents before a postal clerk can accept them, so don't seal them until the packages have been inspected. The place for posting parcels overseas is sometimes different to the main post office.

UPS, FedEx, DHL and other shipping and private courier services are available in some countries, providing an efficient but expensive alternative.

Safe Travel

Parts of Central America are known for high crime rates and gang activity. While much of it doesn't involve foreign visitors, there have been occasions of grab-and-run theft, assault, rape, carjacking and murder. Capital cities tend to have the highest rates of crime. Many sexual assaults occur on isolated beaches.

Avoid night buses (with the possible exception of Mexico and Panama), as highway robberies often happen at night. Parts of Nicaragua's sparse north still have unexploded land mines from the 1980s conflict. Areas in Panama's Darién Province, which borders Colombia, have restricted access.

Despite the ongoing drug conflicts in Mexico, the Yucatán region is considered very safe for travelers.

It's wise to seek updates from other travelers, tourist offices, police, guesthouse owners and Lonely Planet's **Thorn Tree** (www.lonelyplanet.com/thorntree).

Drugs

Marijuana and cocaine are available in many places but are illegal everywhere in the region and penalties are severe. Avoid any conversation with someone who offers you drugs. If you are in an area where drug trafficking is prevalent, ignore it and do not show any interest whatsoever, since drugs are sometimes used to set up travelers for blackmail and bribery. A relatively new law in Mexico allows drugs for personal use. Roll-your-own cigarettes or cigarette papers may arouse suspicion.

Natural Hazards

Central America is prone to a wide variety of natural disasters, including earthquakes, hurricanes, floods and volcanic eruptions. General information about natural-disaster preparedness is available from the **US Federal Emergency Management Agency** (www.fema.gov).

Police & Military

Corruption is a very serious problem among Latin American police, who are generally poorly paid and poorly supervised. In many countries, they are not reluctant to plant drugs on unsuspecting travelers or enforce minor regulations to the letter in the hope of extracting *coimas* (bribes).

If you are stopped by someone claiming to be a plainclothes policemen, never get into a vehicle with them. Don't give them any documents or show them any money and don't take them to your hotel. If the police appear to be the real thing, insist on going to a police station on foot.

Military checkpoints are frequent in places such as Chiapas, Panama's Darién Province and El Salvador. Most involve routine passport checks.

In police stations, English-speaking interpreters are a rarity. Some cities have a tourist police service that may be more helpful.

Robbery & Theft

Thefts take place, particularly in larger cities and transit points such as bus stations. Most is of the pickpocket or grab-and-run variety. Be wary of food, drinks, sweets or cigarettes from strangers on buses or trains or in bars, as they could be laced with sedatives.

To protect yourself:

- Don't use an iPhone or laptop in public places: thieves will be aroused!
- Wear a money belt to keep a bigger stash of money or passport out of sight. Have small amounts of cash in your pockets; use zip pockets.

TRAVEL ADVICE

The following government websites offer travel advisories and information on current hot spots.

- **UK Foreign & Commonwealth Office** (www.fco.gov.uk/travel)
- **US Department of State** (www.travel.state.gov)

➡ Purses or bags can be slashed or grabbed. Use a cheap, nondescript bag for walking around cities.

➡ Be wary of anyone pointing out a spilled substance (mustard, dog feces) on your clothes. It's a classic pickpocketing ploy: one thief helps to clean the victim, the other robs them.

➡ Avoid night buses.

➡ It's worth splurging on taxis after dark, particularly in cities. Don't wander alone down empty city streets or in isolated areas.

➡ When possible, keep valuables sealed in a signed envelope in a hotel safe.

➡ Make sure your room lock and window locks work and use them.

➡ Don't camp overnight on beaches or in the countryside unless you can be sure it's safe.

➡ Get local safety news from guesthouse owners, tourist offices and other travelers.

➡ Don't resist a robbery. Many thieves are armed. Go to the police after a robbery to report the theft and to get a police statement to present to your insurance company. Say '*Quiero poner una acta de un robo*' (I want to report a robbery). You may have to write up the report yourself, then present it for an official stamp and signature.

Photocopies or photos of original passports, visas and air tickets and careful records of credit-card numbers prove invaluable during replacement procedures. Replacement passport applications are usually referred to the home country, so it helps to have someone back home with a copy of passport details.

Swimming Safety

Hundreds of people drown each year at Central America's beaches. Of the drownings 80% are caused by riptides – strong currents that pull the swimmer out to sea. They can occur even in waist-deep water. The best advice: ask about conditions before entering the water. If it's dangerous, don't tempt the ocean.

Telephone

Internet cafes with net-to-phone service provide the cheapest way to make international calls, with rates varying between US$0.10 and US$0.50 per minute to the USA and Europe.

From traditional landlines, the most economical way of calling abroad is by phone cards purchased at kiosks or corner stores. You can also try direct-dial lines, accessed via special numbers and billed to an account at home. It is sometimes cheaper to make a collect or credit-card call to Europe or North America than to pay for the call where you are.

Many towns and cities have a telephone office with phone booths for local and international calls. Rates can be high. Avoid credit-card phones in Mexico and the black 'press button' phones in Guatemala, which charge extortionate rates.

Cell Phones

Cell (mobile) phones are widely used around Central America's bigger towns and cities. Calling a cell phone is always more expensive than calling a land line.

If you plan to carry your own cell phone, a GSM tri- or quad-band phone is your best bet. Another option is purchasing a prepaid SIM card in-country. You will need a compatible GSM phone that's SIM-unlocked. Or purchase a cheap cell, available in kiosks from around US$20.

Toilets

The toilets of Central America are fine; it's just the plumbing that has issues. Nowhere in the region should you deposit toilet paper or anything else in the toilet unless a sign specifies that it's OK to do so. Wastebaskets are generally provided for that purpose.

Some public toilets have attendants who charge a small fee (US$0.10 or so) and provide paper. It's a good idea to keep a spare roll of toilet paper handy.

Tourist Information

Travelers will find a tourist office in the capital city of each country; some countries have them in outlying towns as well. If you're a student, look for student travel agencies in the capital cities of Costa Rica and Panama and in Cancún, Mexico.

Check www.visitcentroamerica.com (in Spanish only), which has standard tourist-board coverage of all countries.

Travelers with Disabilities

Latin America generally isn't well equipped for disabled travelers, and services (such as phones, toilets, or anything in braille) are rare to the point of nonexistence. Expensive international hotels are more likely to cater to guests with disabilities than cheap hotels; prearranged transportation or air travel will be more feasible than most local buses; off-the-beaten-track destinations will be less accessible than well-developed ones. Careful planning and communication is a must, though information isn't always easy to come by.

If you have a disability and want to communicate with a person with disabilities who might have been to Central America recently, consider becoming a member of **Travelin' Talk Network** (TTN; ☎in USA 303-232-2979; www.travelintalk.net; member-

VIVA EL CA-4!

Guatemala, Honduras, El Salvador and Nicaragua's 'CA-4 Border Control' agreement allows free travel for up to 90 days within this subregion for citizens of the four countries and many foreign nationals (including residents of the USA, Canada, the UK and Australia). On paper, at least, you should only have to pay a tourist fee once to enter these four countries. Yet border patrols may charge a few dollars (for 'paperwork') to which you don't have much alternative.

ship US$20). This organization offers a worldwide directory of members with various disabilities who communicate among themselves about travel.

Other organizations:

Access-Able Travel Source (☎in USA 303-232-2979; www.access-able.com; PO Box 1796, Wheat Ridge, CO 80034, USA) An excellent website with many links.

Visas & Documents

Visas

Presently citizens of the USA, EU, Canada, Australia, New Zealand and many other nations can arrive in all Central American countries (including Mexico) without arranging a visa beforehand. Check ahead from your country before planning your trip, as this may change.

Many countries charge an entry or tourist fee upon arrival – from US$5 to US$20.

Note that if you need a visa for a certain country and arrive at a land border without one, you will probably have to return to the nearest town that has a consulate and obtain a visa. Airlines will not normally let you board a plane to a country for which you don't have the necessary visa. Also, a visa in itself may not guarantee entry: in rare cases, you may still be turned back at the border if you don't have 'sufficient funds' or an onward or return ticket.

Sufficient Funds & Onward Tickets

Checking passports is a routine procedure upon arriving in a country, but some officials may ask about your financial resources either verbally or on the application form. If you lack 'sufficient funds' for your proposed visit, officials may limit the length of your stay. (US$500 per month for your planned stay is generally considered sufficient; traveler's checks, and sometimes a credit card, should qualify toward the total amount.)

Several Central American countries require you to have a ticket out of the country.

Visa Extensions

Once you are inside a country, you can always apply for an extension at the country's immigration office *(migración)*. Usually there is a limit to how many extensions you can receive; if you leave the country and re-enter, your time starts over again.

Volunteering

Considering that well over half the population of countries such as Nicaragua and Guatemala live in poverty, volunteering can both make a trip more meaningful and help out the region you visit. On offer are programs to teach those who can't afford classes, help build homes, work to preserve the environment, or help out at hill-town medical clinics. Many who volunteer end up staying longer than expected and find it to be the best part of a bigger trip. Volunteers – sometimes working alone, seven days a week – usually work hard. Note that studying Spanish at schools that pool profits to help communities is another way of contributing.

You can find volunteering organizations once in Central America (which is cheaper), or arrange programs with international organizations before your trip. Be aware that some volunteering organizations seek a minimum-period commitment and may prefer that you organize your visit before turning up at the doorstep.

For more information on volunteering, get a copy of Lonely Planet's *Volunteer: A Traveller's Guide to Making a Difference Around the World*.

International Organizations

Many international organizations will help you peg a program to match job/school requirements, and get college credit for it. Nearly all programs cost money – usually a bit more than you'd pay on a trip. Some volunteers find sponsors – at school or privately – to fund a program. Spanish is not mandatory for all. Often programs begin with a few weeks of Spanish classes, as part of the on-location transition. Costa Rica has the most opportunities (such as in Monteverde), and Guatemala and Mexico have many too.

Travel agencies such as **STA Travel** (www.statravel.com) can arrange volunteering projects. A few other organizations that offer a variety of programs for Latin America include the following. (Prices don't include transportation to the region unless otherwise noted.)

AmeriSpan (☎215-751-1100, in UK 020-8123 6086, in USA 800-879-6640; www.amerispan.com) Sends volunteers to Costa Rica, Guatemala and the Yucatán on varied programs such as building homes, teaching children and working with animals.

Amigos de las Américas (www.amigoslink.org) Youth-oriented summer programs (including flight to/from USA) range from national-park work to community development in Honduras, Costa Rica and Mexico.

Habitat for Humanity (www.habitat.org) Generally is more about funding than on-field programs, though it listed several options in Costa Rica at research time.

i-to-i (www.i-to-i.com) Has UK, US and Ireland offices; four- to 24-week volunteer and study programs in Guatemala, Honduras, Costa Rica and Mexico, with no language requirement.

Idealist.org (www.idealist.org) Hundreds of links for volunteering opportunities around the world.

International Volunteer Programs Association (www.volunteerinternational.org) Lists many programs in Latin America.

ResponsibleTravel (www.responsibletravel.com) UK-based ecofriendly tour operator with many volunteer trips.

Transitions Abroad (www.transitionsabroad.com) Heaps of volunteer links; look under Central America.

Women Travelers

Women traveling solo through Central America typically find that popular perceptions overestimate the dangers faced. Take all the normal precautions you would in any new territory or big city. The biggest adjustment is getting used to a very vocal male population who hoot, hiss and whistle. Ignore this behavior and most of the time you will be simply left alone. That said, some bars or *cantinas* are simply the haunt of men – if you don't see many females, it's probably best to seek nightlife in restaurant-bars.

Dress according to local norms to avoid unwanted attention (often this means avoiding shorts). Talk to locals to find out which areas to avoid. Certain bars and soccer games tend to be testosterone territory and your incursion will draw attention.

Locals, particularly families, will often go out of their way to help a single female traveler. Keep in mind, though, that it's more typical for Latin American women to socialize with other women. Women in Central America's more conservative societies rarely have male friends. Befriending someone's husband can attract resentment and befriending guys in general is a little unusual – it's probable that they will think you want more than their friendship.

In rape cases, it's best to contact your embassy and see a doctor.

Work

According to law you must have a permit to work in Central America. In practice people may get paid under the table or through some bureaucratic loophole, if they can find suitable work. Many travelers work short-term jobs – through the aforementioned loophole – in restaurants, hostels or bars geared to international travelers, for survival wages. Before taking such a job, consider volunteering instead, as many of these jobs could just as well be performed by locals.

Teaching English is another option, though wages do not match international standards. Big cities offer the best possibilities for schools or private tutoring. Many schools will require Teaching English as a Foreign Language (TEFL) teaching certificates.

Some international organizations help place individuals in various jobs.

Online magazine **Transitions Abroad** (www.transitionsabroad.com) has many useful links to work- and study-abroad options.

Transportation

GETTING THERE & AWAY

Most visitors reach Central America by air or overland from Mexico. Flights, tours and rail tickets can be booked online at www.lonelyplanet.com/bookings.

Entering Central America

Make sure your passport is valid for at least six months beyond the projected end of your trip and has plenty of blank pages for stamp-happy officials. Always keep it with you while traveling between destinations.

Air

All Central American countries have international airports. The major ones are Cancún, Mexico (airport code CUN); Guatemala City, Guatemala (GUA); Belize City, Belize (BZE); San Salvador, El Salvador (SAL); San Pedro Sula (SAP) and Tegucigalpa (TGU), Honduras; Managua, Nicaragua (MGA); San José, Costa Rica (SJO); and Panama City, Panama (PAC). A limited number of international flights also reach Flores, Guatemala (FRS); Roatán, Honduras (RTB); and David, Panama (DAV). Other than South American flights, nearly all go via US gateways (particularly Houston, Miami or New York's JFK) or Mexico City.

Tickets

Central America's slender isthmus shape makes 'open-jaw' tickets – flying into one place (say Cancún or Guatemala City) and out from another (eg Panama City) – an attractive option, and the good news is that it's often not much more expensive than a round-trip ticket. If you're flexible on where you start and end, shop around – discount fares come and go.

You might think going to a hub city – such as San Salvador on TACA – would save money, but sometimes it's *more* expensive; we found some tickets through San Salvador to Belize City from Los Angeles, for example, to be cheaper than return tickets to San Salvador. The reason – in the confusing world of airline ticket pricing – is airlines trying to compete with more direct options. Again, shop around.

Typically, Panama City is more expensive to reach from the US gateways than Guatemala City, but otherwise no Central American city is consistently cheaper than another.

High-season rates (generally July and August, Christmas to New Year, and around Semana Santa) can be considerably more expensive.

Student travel agencies such as **STA Travel** (www.statravel.com) offer student discounts for those under 26.

If you're flying from Europe or Australia, chances are you can get a free stopover in a US gateway city such as Los Angeles or Miami.

RTW TICKETS

Round-the-world (RTW) tickets are an option if coming from the US or Europe, but lack of flight connections between Australasia and Central America have all but put Latin America off RTW ticket options from that part of the world.

From South America

TACA and COPA airlines connect Central American cities to and from Venezuela, Colombia, Ecuador, Peru, Chile and Argentina. LAN, with bases in Chile, Peru and Argentina, does as well. Some USA airlines, such as American Airlines, have a few connections too.

DEPARTURE TAXES

Air taxes in Central American countries vary. These taxes are generally included in fares quoted by travel agents (but not when booking online), both abroad and in Central America.

ONWARD-TICKET REQUIREMENTS

If you're planning on flying into one country and back from another, note that immigration officials may require proof of onward or continuing travel. The restriction mainly ensures nonresidents don't stay long-term without permission.

Showing 'continuing travel' from another country (say, a flight home) and explaining how you'll get there is almost always enough. Most travelers are never asked. It's still a good idea to ask the airlines, as they can be fined for bringing in a passenger without proper documentation. Also, it may be worth showing a print-out of a 'bus reservation' leaving the country.

This requirement also may pop up at land borders. Crossing into Costa Rica, for instance, it's sometimes necessary to purchase a bus ticket at the border leaving Costa Rica – even if you don't plan to use it. For private cars entering no onward ticket is required but proper documentation for the car is needed.

If you're continuing on to South America, check for similar restrictions in those countries.

If you're planning to visit both Central America and South America on a trip, note that TACA (and other airlines) often allows a free stopover (in San José for TACA), meaning you can visit Central America for no extra charge. Panama City is generally the cheapest link to and from South America, with Colombia, Ecuador and Venezuela, unsurprisingly given their proximity to Panama, offering the least expensive deals.

Note that many South American countries require onward air tickets upon arrival.

Land

Border Crossings

There are ample border crossings in Central America, so you generally never have to travel too far out of your way to reach your next destination. Most crossings are by road (or bridge), but there are a few that involve boat travel.

With an influx of foreigners in the region, border police are used to backpackers turning up. That said, the crossing is always easier if you appear somewhat put together (vs disheveled), treat the guards with respect and make an attempt at Spanish.

Before heading to a border crossing, be sure to get the latest information on visas – whether or not you need one – with a little on-the-ground research.

From Mexico

BUS

It's possible to bus from the USA or Canada into Mexico and directly into Central America. The three most convenient land borders between Mexico and Central America are at the Chetumal–Corozal (Belize) border in Quintana Roo (Yucatán Peninsula); as well as Ciudad Cuauhtémoc–La Mesilla (Guatemala) and Ciudad Hidalgo–Ciudad Tecún Umán (Guatemala) in Chiapas state (about 38km to the south of Tapachula).

Another popular border crossing is by boat across the Río Usumacinta at the Frontera Corozal–Bethel (Guatemala) border, south of Palenque.

CAR & MOTORCYCLE

Most people driving to Central America do so from the USA (or Canada). Buying a car in the region (including Mexico) is very complicated. If you drive, you will *not* save money, but it can make for a great trip. But there are a lot of fees, paperwork, red tape, tolls and parking worries involved. You'll need to be prepared to stop for passport checks at military checkpoints. Also, highway robberies aren't unknown. Avoid driving at night.

Note that you'll need liability insurance that covers Mexico and Central America – your policy back home isn't recognized here. It's available at many border towns. Texas-based **Sanborn's Insurance** (☎800-222-0158; www.sanbornsinsurance.com) sells separate coverage (only) for Mexico and Central America. Policies are daily or semi-annual; in Central America, sadly, coverage doesn't include Belize or Nicaragua. It's possible to get a policy by phone or online – so you can get Mexico coverage on the road in Central America for your return through Mexico.

A few other things to consider pretrip:

- You need a valid driver's license from your home country.
- Unleaded gas/petrol is now available throughout Central America.
- Make sure that the shock absorbers and suspension are in good shape for the bumpy roads.
- A spare fuel filter, and other spare parts, could be invaluable.
- Check with a national tourist board or consulate for any changes to the rules on bringing a car into Mexico,

HINTS FOR BORDER CROSSINGS

Going from one of Central America's seven countries (or Mexico) into another can be a frenetic, confusing experience. But with a little planning it's usually a breeze (make that a *slo-o-ow* breeze). Some considerations:

➡ Before you leave one country for another, read up on that country's entry requirements.

➡ Don't leave a country without getting your passport stamped at that country's immigration office. Occasionally, agents are not vigilant so be on the lookout.

➡ Crossings often require changing buses at the border, walking a few hundred meters across, or catching a *colectivo* (shared taxi or minibus taxi) to the nearest bus station. Not all of the borders are open 24 hours, but bus schedules tend to match opening hours.

➡ Many travel agents offer organized trips across the border; many travelers prefer the ease of having someone there (a driver, for example) to help if things get sticky.

➡ Money changers linger around nearly all borders; rates can be fair but some changers do try to shortchange; count carefully. If you're carrying only local currency, try to change at least some before moving on, as it's possible no one will accept it once you're across the border.

➡ Note that, technically, there's a border agreement between Guatemala, Honduras, El Salvador and Nicaragua allowing travel up to 90 days in the four-country region – and you shouldn't have to pay to cross into another country.

or Central America, before showing up in your vehicle.

From South America

There are no road connections between South America and Central America (via Panama), and instability in the border region with Colombia, plus the difficulty of travel, have essentially made the trip over the Darién Gap on foot an impossibility. Visitors to the Darién must register with the police, who currently do not permit crossing on foot.

Sea

Unless you're a yachtie or on a cruise ship, options for boat travel heading to/from the region are very limited and very expensive. The most plausible way is going on a chartered sailboat from the Archipiélago de San Blas, Panama, to Cartagena in Colombia (per person US$500) or La Miel (by motorboat US$350). The five-day trip usually includes a few days on the islands and two days' transit to/from Colombia.

In Cartagena, check with the hostel **Casa Viena** (☎05-664-6242; www.casaviena.com) for schedule information. Note that cargo boats are a risky business; smuggling is common on the Colón–Cartagena cargo route.

GETTING AROUND

Like buses? They are the cheapest and most accessible way to get around Central America, particularly along the Pan-American Hwy (also called the Panamericana or Interamericana – we've alternated usage based on local parlance), which runs through all of the countries except Belize.

In Honduras, most long-distance buses have their own private terminals.

Because of the region's skinny stature, a flight can save several hours of backtracking. Islands and some borders are served by various types of boat.

Air

Many flights connect the region by international carriers as well as the national airlines. Some smaller domestic airlines provide services too. Occasionally it will be necessary to change planes in the carrier's hub city (eg a Managua–Panama City flight may change planes up north in San Salvador).

Prices are an obstacle. Despite relatively short distances, individual one-way and round-trip tickets within Central America (either bought abroad or in the region) can be very expensive. Note that if you fly to Central America on TACA, the airline sometimes sells regional flights – generally to or from San José – at a discount. Not infrequently, one-way tickets run just a few dollars less than a round-trip ticket.

➡ Flights can sometimes be overbooked; reconfirm your ticket before arriving at the airport.

➡ Airfares can vary wildly – depending on the length of stay, time of year and special promotions – so treat high-season fares as a rough gauge only in identifying potential routes.

➡ Note that San Salvador and San José are the most popular hubs. Occasionally a promotional return flight may be even cheaper than a one-way fare.

➡ Worthwhile domestic flights include Managua to Corn Islands (about US$99 return), which saves a two-day bus/boat trip each way. Flights within Panama can also be cheap.

Bicycle

Long-distance cycling in the region can be dangerous, as few drivers are accustomed to sharing narrow streets in cities or (often) shoulderless two-lane highways with bikes. That said, cycling is on an upswing – with mountain rides and coffee-plantation tours (including guide and bike) available all over Central America.

You can rent bicycles in several cities and traveler hangouts, such as San Cristóbal de Las Casas (Mexico), Flores (Guatemala), Granada (Nicaragua) and Panama City. There are many mountain-bike tours available (notably in cooler locales such as Guatemala's highlands and San Cristóbal de Las Casas). Consider the seasons if you're planning to cycle a lot. The dry season (roughly December to April) should spare you from any major soakings.

If you're planning to bike across borders, keep a document of your ownership of the bicycle handy for immigration officials.

Check out www.downtheroad.org, which documents the ongoing worldwide cycling odyssey of Tim and Cyndie Travis; entries are detailed and include Central America. Though dated, the staple guide to cycling the region is *Latin America by Bike: A Complete Touring Guide* (1993), by Walter Sienko. Ian Benford and Peter Hodkinson's *Cycle Central America* covers southern Mexico, Belize, Guatemala and Honduras.

Boat

A few water journeys connect Central American countries. Travelers between Palenque, Mexico, and Flores, Guatemala, cross the Río Usumacinta near Frontera Corozal, Mexico, and Bethel, Guatemala. Another interesting crossing is between Punta Gorda, Belize, and Puerto Barrios (and sometimes Livingston), Guatemala. There's a rather off-track river border crossing between San Carlos, Nicaragua, and Los Chiles, Costa Rica.

Key domestic water journeys include the ride down the Río Escondidas to Bluefields, Nicaragua, and then out to the Corn Islands in the Caribbean. Guatemala's Río Dulce is another famous ride. Other Caribbean islands reached by boat include Honduras' Bay Islands, Belize's Caye Caulker and Mexico's Cozumel and Isla Mujeres.

The Panama Canal is one of the world's most important waterways, connecting the Caribbean and the Pacific.

Bus

Many memories of your trip will be of how you got around by bus. Bus service is well developed throughout the region, though not always comfortable. While some buses are air-conditioned with reserved seats that may recline, you're sure to bounce a time or 20 in one of the famed 'chicken buses'. These are often colorfully repainted former US school buses with a liberal policy toward lugging merchandise (ie chickens).

Avoid night buses throughout the region (with the possible exception of Mexico and Panama), as these have been popular targets for highway robbers.

First-class and some 2nd-class buses depart at scheduled times from a *terminal de autobuses* (long-distance bus station); others leave from parking-lot bus terminals once they are full (these stop to collect more passengers all along the way – thus, you're likely to get a lift from the highway if need be). Be aware that many cities have

CLIMATE CHANGE & TRAVEL

Every form of transport that relies on carbon-based fuel generates CO_2, the main cause of human-induced climate change. Modern travel is dependent on airplanes, which might use less fuel per kilometer per person than most cars but travel much greater distances. The altitude at which aircraft emit gases (including CO_2) and particles also contributes to their climate change impact. Many websites offer 'carbon calculators' that allow people to estimate the carbon emissions generated by their journey and, for those who wish to do so, to offset the impact of the greenhouse gases emitted with contributions to portfolios of climate-friendly initiatives throughout the world. Lonely Planet offsets the carbon footprint of all staff and author travel.

SAMPLE BUS DURATIONS

Remember that bus connections and border-crossing formalities can add extra time to the trip.

ORIGIN	DESTINATION	DURATION (HR)
Cancún, Mexico	Belize City	9-10
Flores, Guatemala	Guatemala City	8-10
Guatemala City	Copán Ruinas, Honduras	5
Managua, Nicaragua	San José	9
San Cristóbal de Las Casas, Mexico	Antigua, Guatemala	11
San José, Costa Rica	Panama City	14
San Salvador, El Salvador	Tegucigalpa	8
Tegucigalpa, Honduras	Managua	8

more than one bus station. Bus companies can have their own terminals as well. Frequency varies.

Luggage may be stored in a lower compartment or piled on the roof of the bus. Keep an eye on your luggage on bus trips if you can, particularly on the easily accessible racks in a packed bus. Always keep your valuables tucked away on your person. Watch out for pickpockets on crowded buses and in bus stations.

In some places, travel agents run shuttle services (mostly vans with air-con) to popular destinations. They're more comfortable and more expensive.

Colectivos & Minibuses

Connecting hub towns with smaller ones on short-haul trips, there's an array of minibuses (called *rapidito* in Honduras, *chiva* in Panama, and *colectivo* in Costa Rica and Mexico). When available, these are cheaper than 1st-class buses and frequent. The catch: they make frequent stops and the driver knows no word for 'full'.

Car & Motorcycle

Driver's License

Potential drivers should check before traveling if their country's driver's license is honored in the destination countries. You may need an International Driving Permit (IDP), issued by automobile associations worldwide.

Be prepared for police checkpoints – always stop and have your papers handy.

Hire & Insurance

Central America is relatively easy to explore by private vehicle and would be more popular if it weren't for the cost (rental and gas) and hassle. Rentals range from about US$15 per day in Nicaragua to US$80 per day in Belize. Still, renting can make for a memorable splurge and get you into areas you might otherwise miss (such as isolated beaches south of Tulum in Mexico and around Costa Rica's Península de Nicoya).

Rentals are usually not allowed to leave the country – though Budget, for example, allows travel from Nicaragua or Guatemala only.

In many cases it's cheaper to arrange (even same-day) rentals with major car-rental agencies on their websites; during research in Tulum we saved 50% on the quoted local fare by going to an internet cafe next door and booking a car online!

4WD vehicles are more expensive (generally US$80 to US$100 per day), and gas is about US$1.25 to US$2.50 per liter.

Insurance is required – and your coverage back home isn't recognized here. Make sure you have at least collision-damage insurance coverage.

To rent a car, you'll need a passport and a driver's license. Some agencies rent to those 21 and over, while others to only those 25 and over. All of Central America drives on the right-hand side of the road.

Scooters and bigger motorcycles are available in some places, the latter usually costing about the same price as a compact car.

Hitchhiking

Hitchhiking (*tomando un jalón* – literally 'taking a hitch') is never entirely safe in any country in the world, and Lonely Planet does not recommend it. Travelers who hitchhike should understand that they are taking a small but potentially serious risk. However, it is common in parts of Central America. If you hitch, try to do it in groups. If you get a ride, offer to pay gas money, even if the driver may turn it down.

Train

The only train trip in the region is a very scenic, glass-domed luxury ride from Panama City to Colón, Panama, alongside the Panama Canal.

Language

Latin American Spanish is the language of choice for travelers in all of Central America except for Belize (where English is the official language, but both Spanish and a local Creole are also widely spoken). Maya and Náhuatl are the most common of a number of indigenous languages spoken throughout the region.

Latin American Spanish pronunciation is easy, as most sounds are also found in English. Note that kh is a throaty sound (like the 'ch' in the Scottish *loch*), v and b are similar to the English 'b' but softer (between a 'v' and a 'b'), and r is strongly rolled. There are some variations in spoken Spanish across Central America, the most notable being the pronunciation of the letters *ll* and *y*. In our pronunciation guides they are represented with y because they are pronounced as the 'y' in 'yes' in most of Central America. In some parts of the region, though, you may hear them pronounced like the 'lli' in 'million'. If you read our colored pronunciation guides as if they were English, you'll be understood. The stressed syllables are indicated with italics in our pronunciation guides.

Where both polite and informal options are given in this section, they are indicated by the abbreviations 'pol' and 'inf'. The masculine and feminine forms are indicated with 'm' and 'f' respectively.

WANT MORE?

For in-depth language information and handy phrases, check out Lonely Planet's *Latin American Spanish Phrasebook*, *Mexican Spanish Phrasebook* and *Costa Rican Spanish Phrasebook*. You'll find them at **shop.lonelyplanet.com**, or you can buy Lonely Planet's iPhone phrasebooks at the Apple App Store.

BASICS

Hello.	*Hola.*	o·la
Goodbye.	*Adiós.*	a·*dyos*
How are you?	*¿Qué tal?*	ke tal
Fine, thanks.	*Bien, gracias.*	byen *gra*·syas
Excuse me.	*Perdón.*	per·*don*
Sorry.	*Lo siento.*	lo *syen*·to
Please.	*Por favor.*	por fa·*vor*
Thank you.	*Gracias.*	*gra*·syas
You are welcome.	*De nada.*	de *na*·da
Yes.	*Sí.*	see
No.	*No.*	no

My name is ...
Me llamo ... me *ya*·mo ...

What's your name?
¿Cómo se llama Usted? *ko*·mo se *ya*·ma oo·*ste* (pol)
¿Cómo te llamas? *ko*·mo te *ya*·mas (inf)

Do you speak English?
¿Habla inglés? *a*·bla een·*gles* (pol)
¿Hablas inglés? *a*·blas een·*gles* (inf)

I don't understand.
Yo no entiendo. yo no en·*tyen*·do

ACCOMMODATIONS

I'd like a single/double room.
Quisiera una habitación individual/doble. kee·*sye*·ra *oo*·na a·bee·ta·*syon* een·dee·vee·*dwal/do*·ble

How much is it per night/person?
¿Cuánto cuesta por noche/persona? *kwan*·to *kwes*·ta por *no*·che/per·*so*·na

Does it include breakfast?
¿Incluye el desayuno? een·*kloo*·ye el de·sa·*yoo*·no

air-con	*aire acondicionado*	*ai*·re a·kon·dee·syo·*na*·do
bathroom	*baño*	*ba*·nyo
bed	*cama*	*ka*·ma
campsite	*terreno de cámping*	te·*re*·no de *kam*·peeng
guesthouse	*pensión*	pen·*syon*
hotel	*hotel*	o·*tel*
youth hostel	*albergue juvenil*	al·*ber*·ge khoo·ve·*neel*
window	*ventana*	ven·*ta*·na

DIRECTIONS

Where is ...?
¿Dónde está ...? — *don*·de es·*ta* ...

What's the address?
¿Cuál es la dirección? — kwal es la dee·rek·*syon*

Could you please write it down?
¿Puede escribirlo, por favor? — *pwe*·de es·kree·*beer*·lo por fa·*vor*

Can you show me (on the map)?
¿Me lo puede indicar (en el mapa)? — me lo *pwe*·de een·dee·*kar* (en el *ma*·pa)

at the corner	*en la esquina*	en la es·*kee*·na
at the traffic lights	*en el semáforo*	en el se·*ma*·fo·ro
behind ...	*detrás de ...*	de·*tras* de ...
in front of ...	*enfrente de ...*	en·*fren*·te de ...
left	*izquierda*	ees·*kyer*·da
next to ...	*al lado de ...*	al *la*·do de ...
opposite ...	*frente a ...*	*fren*·te a ...
right	*derecha*	de·*re*·cha
straight ahead	*todo recto*	*to*·do *rek*·to

EATING & DRINKING

Can I see the menu, please?
¿Puedo ver el menú, por favor? — *pwe*·do ver el me·*noo* por fa·*vor*

What would you recommend?
¿Qué recomienda? — ke re·ko·*myen*·da

Do you have vegetarian food?
¿Tienen comida vegetariana? — *tye*·nen ko·*mee*·da ve·khe·ta·*rya*·na

I don't eat (red meat).
No como (carne roja). — no *ko*·mo (*kar*·ne *ro*·kha)

That was delicious!
¡Estaba buenísimo! — es·*ta*·ba bwe·*nee*·see·mo

Cheers!
¡Salud! — sa·*loo*

The bill, please.
La cuenta, por favor. — la *kwen*·ta por fa·*vor*

KEY PATTERNS

To get by in Spanish, mix and match these simple patterns with words of your choice:

When's (the next flight)?
¿Cuándo sale (el próximo vuelo)? — *kwan*·do *sa*·le (el *prok*·see·mo *vwe*·lo)

Where's (the station)?
¿Dónde está (la estación)? — *don*·de es·*ta* (la es·ta·*syon*)

Where can I (buy a ticket)?
¿Dónde puedo (comprar un billete)? — *don*·de *pwe*·do (kom·*prar* oon bee·*ye*·te)

Do you have (a map)?
¿Tiene (un mapa)? — *tye*·ne (oon *ma*·pa)

Is there (a toilet)?
¿Hay (servicios)? — ai (ser·*vee*·syos)

I'd like (a coffee).
Quisiera (un café). — kee·*sye*·ra (oon ka·*fe*)

I'd like (to hire a car).
Quisiera (alquilar un coche). — kee·*sye*·ra (al·kee·*lar* oon *ko*·che)

Can I (enter)?
¿Se puede (entrar)? — se *pwe*·de (en·*trar*)

Could you please (help me)?
¿Puede (ayudarme), por favor? — *pwe*·de (a·yoo·*dar*·me) por fa·*vor*

Do I have to (get a visa)?
¿Necesito (obtener un visado)? — ne·se·*see*·to (ob·te·*ner* oon vee·*sa*·do)

I'd like a table for ...	*Quisiera una mesa para ...*	kee·*sye*·ra *oo*·na *me*·sa *pa*·ra ...
(eight) o'clock	*las (ocho)*	las (*o*·cho)
(two) people	*(dos) personas*	(dos) per·*so*·nas

Key Words

appetisers	*aperitivos*	a·pe·ree·*tee*·vos
bottle	*botella*	bo·*te*·ya
bowl	*bol*	bol
breakfast	*desayuno*	de·sa·*yoo*·no
children's menu	*menú infantil*	me·*noo* een·fan·*teel*
(too) cold	*(muy) frío*	(mooy) *free*·o
dinner	*cena*	se·na
food	*comida*	ko·*mee*·da

fork	*tenedor*	te·ne·*dor*
glass	*vaso*	*va*·so
hot (warm)	*caliente*	kal·*yen*·te
knife	*cuchillo*	koo·*chee*·yo
lunch	*comida*	ko·*mee*·da
main course	*segundo plato*	se·*goon*·do *pla*·to
plate	*plato*	*pla*·to
restaurant	*restaurante*	res·tow·*ran*·te
spoon	*cuchara*	koo·*cha*·ra
with	*con*	kon
without	*sin*	seen

Meat & Fish

beef	*carne de vaca*	*kar*·ne de *va*·ka
chicken	*pollo*	*po*·yo
duck	*pato*	*pa*·to
lamb	*cordero*	kor·*de*·ro
lobster	*langosta*	lan·*gos*·ta
pork	*cerdo*	*ser*·do
shrimps	*camarones*	ka·ma·*ro*·nes
tuna	*atún*	a·*toon*
turkey	*pavo*	*pa*·vo
veal	*ternera*	ter·*ne*·ra

Fruit & Vegetables

apple	*manzana*	man·*sa*·na
apricot	*albaricoque*	al·ba·ree·*ko*·ke
artichoke	*alcachofa*	al·ka·*cho*·fa
asparagus	*espárragos*	es·*pa*·ra·gos
banana	*plátano*	*pla*·ta·no
beans	*judías*	khoo·*dee*·as
beetroot	*remolacha*	re·mo·*la*·cha
cabbage	*col*	kol
carrot	*zanahoria*	sa·na·*o*·rya
celery	*apio*	*a*·pyo
cherry	*cereza*	se·*re*·sa
corn	*maíz*	ma·*ees*
cucumber	*pepino*	pe·*pee*·no
grape	*uvas*	*oo*·vas
lemon	*limón*	lee·*mon*
lentils	*lentejas*	len·*te*·khas
lettuce	*lechuga*	le·*choo*·ga
mushroom	*champiñón*	cham·pee·*nyon*
nuts	*nueces*	*nwe*·ses
onion	*cebolla*	se·*bo*·ya
orange	*naranja*	na·*ran*·kha
peach	*melocotón*	me·lo·ko·*ton*
peas	*guisantes*	gee·*san*·tes
pepper (bell)	*pimiento*	pee·*myen*·to
pineapple	*piña*	*pee*·nya
plum	*ciruela*	seer·*we*·la
potato	*patata*	pa·*ta*·ta
pumpkin	*calabaza*	ka·la·*ba*·sa
spinach	*espinacas*	es·pee·*na*·kas
strawberry	*fresa*	*fre*·sa
tomato	*tomate*	to·*ma*·te
watermelon	*sandía*	san·*dee*·a

Other

bread	*pan*	pan
butter	*mantequilla*	man·te·*kee*·ya
cheese	*queso*	*ke*·so
egg	*huevo*	*we*·vo
honey	*miel*	myel
jam	*mermelada*	mer·me·*la*·da
oil	*aceite*	a·*sey*·te
pasta	*pasta*	*pas*·ta
pepper	*pimienta*	pee·*myen*·ta
rice	*arroz*	a·*ros*
salt	*sal*	sal
sugar	*azúcar*	a·*soo*·kar
vinegar	*vinagre*	vee·*na*·gre

Drinks

beer	*cerveza*	ser·*ve*·sa
coffee	*café*	ka·*fe*
(orange) juice	*zumo (de naranja)*	*soo*·mo (de na·*ran*·kha)
milk	*leche*	*le*·che
red wine	*vino tinto*	*vee*·no *teen*·to
tea	*té*	te
(mineral) water	*agua (mineral)*	*a*·gwa (mee·ne·*ral*)
white wine	*vino blanco*	*vee*·no *blan*·ko

Signs

Abierto	Open
Cerrado	Closed
Entrada	Entrance
Hombres/Varones	Men
Mujeres/Damas	Women
Prohibido	Prohibited
Salida	Exit
Servicios/Baños	Toilets

EMERGENCIES

Help!	*¡Socorro!*	so·ko·ro
Go away!	*¡Vete!*	ve·te
Call ...!	*¡Llame a ...!*	ya·me a ...
a doctor	*un médico*	oon me·dee·ko
the police	*la policía*	la po·lee·see·a

I'm lost.
Estoy perdido/a. es·toy per·dee·do/a (m/f)

Where are the toilets?
¿Dónde están los baños? don·de es·tan los ba·nyos

I'm ill.
Estoy enfermo/a. es·toy en·fer·mo/a (m/f)

I'm allergic to (antibiotics).
Soy alérgico/a a (los antibióticos). soy a·ler·khee·ko/a a (los an·tee·byo·tee·kos) (m/f)

SHOPPING & SERVICES

What time does it open/close?
¿A qué hora abre/cierra? a ke o·ra ab·re/sye·ra

I'd like to buy ...
Quisiera comprar ... kee·sye·ra kom·prar ...

I'm just looking.
Sólo estoy mirando. so·lo es·toy mee·ran·do

Can I look at it?
¿Puedo verlo? pwe·do ver·lo

I don't like it.
No me gusta. no me goos·ta

How much is it?
¿Cuánto cuesta? kwan·to kwes·ta

That's too expensive.
Es muy caro. es mooy ka·ro

Can you lower the price?
¿Podría bajar un poco el precio? po·dree·a ba·khar oon po·ko el pre·syo

There's a mistake in the bill.
Hay un error en la cuenta. ai oon e·ror en la kwen·ta

Question Words

How?	*¿Cómo?*	ko·mo
What?	*¿Qué?*	ke
When?	*¿Cuándo?*	kwan·do
Where?	*¿Dónde?*	don·de
Which?	*¿Cuál?* (sg) *¿Cuáles?* (pl)	kwal kwa·les
Who?	*¿Quién?*	kyen
Why?	*¿Por qué?*	por ke

ATM	*cajero automático*	ka·khe·ro ow·to·ma·tee·ko
market	*mercado*	mer·ka·do
post office	*correos*	ko·re·os
tourist office	*oficina de turismo*	o·fee·see·na de too·rees·mo

TIME & DATES

What time is it?
¿Qué hora es? ke o·ra es

It's (10) o'clock.
Son (las diez). son (las dyes)

It's half past (one).
Es (la una) y media. es (la oo·na) ee me·dya

morning	*mañana*	ma·nya·na
afternoon	*tarde*	tar·de
evening	*noche*	no·che
yesterday	*ayer*	a·yer
today	*hoy*	oy
tomorrow	*mañana*	ma·nya·na
Monday	*lunes*	loo·nes
Tuesday	*martes*	mar·tes
Wednesday	*miércoles*	myer·ko·les
Thursday	*jueves*	khwe·ves
Friday	*viernes*	vyer·nes
Saturday	*sábado*	sa·ba·do
Sunday	*domingo*	do·meen·go
January	*enero*	e·ne·ro
February	*febrero*	fe·bre·ro
March	*marzo*	mar·so
April	*abril*	a·breel
May	*mayo*	ma·yo
June	*junio*	khoon·yo
July	*julio*	khool·yo
August	*agosto*	a·gos·to
September	*septiembre*	sep·tyem·bre
October	*octubre*	ok·too·bre
November	*noviembre*	no·vyem·bre
December	*diciembre*	dee·syem·bre

TRANSPORTATION

Public Transportation

boat	*barco*	bar·ko
bus	*autobús*	ow·to·boos
plane	*avión*	a·vyon
train	*tren*	tren

Numbers

1	*uno*	oo·no
2	*dos*	dos
3	*tres*	tres
4	*cuatro*	kwa·tro
5	*cinco*	seen·ko
6	*seis*	seys
7	*siete*	sye·te
8	*ocho*	o·cho
9	*nueve*	nwe·ve
10	*diez*	dyes
20	*veinte*	veyn·te
30	*treinta*	treyn·ta
40	*cuarenta*	kwa·ren·ta
50	*cincuenta*	seen·kwen·ta
60	*sesenta*	se·sen·ta
70	*setenta*	se·ten·ta
80	*ochenta*	o·chen·ta
90	*noventa*	no·ven·ta
100	*cien*	syen
1000	*mil*	meel

first	*primero*	pree·me·ro
last	*último*	ool·tee·mo
next	*próximo*	prok·see·mo

airport	*aeropuerto*	a·e·ro·pwer·to
aisle seat	*asiento de pasillo*	a·syen·to de pa·see·yo
bus stop	*parada de autobuses*	pa·ra·da de ow·to·boo·ses
cancelled	*cancelado*	kan·se·la·do
delayed	*retrasado*	re·tra·sa·do
ticket office	*taquilla*	ta·kee·ya
timetable	*horario*	o·ra·ryo
train station	*estación de trenes*	es·ta·syon de tre·nes
window seat	*asiento junto a la ventana*	a·syen·to khoon·to a la ven·ta·na

A ... ticket, please.	*Un billete de ..., por favor.*	oon bee·ye·te de ... por fa·vor
1st-class	*primera clase*	pree·me·ra kla·se
2nd-class	*segunda clase*	se·goon·da kla·se
one-way	*ida*	ee·da
return	*ida y vuelta*	ee·da ee vwel·ta

What time does it arrive/leave?
¿A qué hora llega/sale? a ke o·ra ye·ga/sa·le

Does it stop at ...?
¿Para en ...? pa·ra en ...

Which stop is this?
¿Cuál es esta parada? kwal es es·ta pa·ra·da

Could you tell me when we get to ...?
¿Puede avisarme cuando lleguemos a ...? pwe·de a·vee·sar·me kwan·do ye·ge·mos a ...

I want to get off here.
Quiero bajarme aquí. kye·ro ba·khar·me a·kee

How much is it (to the airport)?
¿Cuánto cuesta ir (al aeropuerto)? kwan·to kwes·ta eer (al a·e·ro·pwer·to)

Please take me to (this address).
Por favor, lléveme a (esta dirección). por fa·vor ye·ve·me a (es·ta dee·rek·syon)

Driving & Cycling

I'd like to hire a ...	*Quisiera alquilar ...*	kee·sye·ra al·kee·lar ...
4WD	*un todo-terreno*	oon to·do·te·re·no
bicycle	*una bicicleta*	oo·na bee·see·kle·ta
car	*un coche*	oon ko·che
motorcycle	*una moto*	oo·na mo·to

child seat	*asiento de seguridad para niños*	a·syen·to de se·goo·ree·da pa·ra nee·nyos
diesel	*petróleo*	pet·ro·le·o
helmet	*casco*	kas·ko
mechanic	*mecánico*	me·ka·nee·ko
petrol/gas	*gasolina*	ga·so·lee·na
service station	*gasolinera*	ga·so·lee·ne·ra
truck	*camion*	ka·myon

Is this the road to ...?
¿Se va a ... por esta carretera? se va a ... por es·ta ka·re·te·ra

Can I park here?
¿Puedo aparcar aquí? pwe·do a·par·kar a·kee

The car has broken down.
El coche se ha averiado. el ko·che se a a·ve·rya·do

I had an accident.
He tenido un accidente. e te·nee·do oon ak·see·den·te

I've run out of petrol/gas.
Me he quedado sin gasolina. me e ke·da·do seen ga·so·lee·na

I have a flat tyre.
Se me pinchó una rueda. se me peen·cho oo·na rwe·da

GLOSSARY

alcaldía – mayor's office
apartado – post-office box
artesanía – handicraft
Av – abbreviation for avenida (avenue)
ayuntamiento – municipal government

bahía – bay
bajareque – traditional wall construction, where a core of stones is held in place by poles of bamboo or other wood then covered with stucco or mud
balneario – public beach or swimming area
barrio – district; neighborhood
Black Caribs – see *Garífuna*

caballeros – literally 'horsemen,' but corresponds to the English 'gentlemen'; look for the term on bathroom doors
cabaña – cabin or bungalow
cabina – see *cabaña;* also a loose term for cheap lodging in Costa Rica (in some cases it refers to cabins or bungalows, in others it refers merely to an economical hotel room)
cajero automático – automated teller machine (ATM)
calle – street
callejón – alley; small, narrow or very short street
calzada – causeway
camión – truck; bus
camioneta – pickup truck
campesino – farmer
Carretera Interamericana – Interamerican Hwy, or Interamericana (also referred to as the Pan-American Hwy, or Panamericana); the nearly continuous highway running from Alaska to Chile (it breaks at the Darién Gap in Panama)
casa de cambio – currency exchange office
casa de huéspedes – guesthouse
cascada – waterfall
catedral – cathedral
cay – small island of sand or coral fragments; also caye, cayo
cayuco – dugout canoe
cenote – large, natural limestone cave used for water storage or ceremonial purposes
cerro – hill
cerveza – beer
Chac – Maya rain god; his likeness appears on many ruins
chac-mool – Maya sacrificial stone sculpture
chamarra – thick, heavy woolen blanket (Guatemala)
chapín – citizen of Guatemala; Guatemalan
chicken bus – former US school bus used for public transportation
cine – movie theater
ciudad – city
cofradía – Maya religious brotherhood, particularly in highland Guatemala
colectivo – shared taxi or minibus that picks up and drops off passengers along its route
colón – national currency of Costa Rica
comedor – basic and cheap eatery, usually with a limited menu
conquistador – any of the Spanish explorer-conquerors of Latin America
Contras – counterrevolutionary military groups fighting against the Sandinista government in Nicaragua throughout the 1980s
cordillera – mountain range
córdoba – national currency of Nicaragua
corte – piece of material 7m to 10m long that is used as a wraparound skirt
costa – coast
criollo – Creole; born in Latin America of Spanish parentage; on the Caribbean coast it refers to someone of mixed African and European descent; see also *mestizo* and *ladino*
cuadra – city block
cueva – cave

damas – ladies; the usual sign on bathroom doors
edificio – building
entrada – entrance
expreso – express bus

faja – waist sash that binds garments and holds what would otherwise be put in pockets
finca – farm; plantation; ranch
fritanga – sidewalk barbecue, widely seen in Nicaragua
fuerte – fort

Garífuna – descendants of West African slaves and Carib Indians, brought to the Caribbean coast of Central America in the late 18th century from the island of St Vincent; also referred to as *Black Caribs*
Garinagu – see *Garífuna*
gibnut – small, brown-spotted rodent similar to a guinea pig; also called *paca*
golfo – gulf
gringo/a – mildly pejorative term used in Latin America to describe male/female foreigners, particularly those from North America; often applied to any visitor of European heritage
gruta – cave

hacienda – agricultural estate or plantation; treasury, as in Departamento de Hacienda (Treasury Department)
hospedaje – guesthouse
huipil – long, woven, white sleeveless tunic with intricate, colorful embroidery (Maya regions)

iglesia – church
indígena – indigenous
Interamericana – see *Carretera Interamericana*
invierno – winter; Central America's wet season, which extends roughly from April through mid-December
isla – island
IVA – *impuesto al valor agregado;* value-added tax
ladino – person of mixed indigenous and European parentage, often used to describe a *mestizo*

who speaks Spanish; see also *mestizo* and *criollo*

lago – lake

laguna – lagoon; lake

lancha – small motorboat

lempira – national currency of Honduras

malecón – waterfront promenade

mar – sea

marimba – xylophonelike instrument

mercado – market

Mesoamerica – a geographical region extending from central Mexico to northwestern Costa Rica

mestizo – person of mixed ancestry, usually Spanish and indigenous; see also *criollo* and *ladino*

metate – flat stone on which corn/maize is ground

migración – immigration; immigration office

milpa – cornfield

mirador – lookout

mola – colorful hand-stitched appliqué textile made by Kuna women

muelle – pier

municipalidad – town hall

museo – museum

Navidad – Christmas

oficina de correos – post office

ordinario – slow bus

paca – see *gibnut*

PADI – Professional Association of Diving Instructors

palacio de gobierno – building housing the executive offices of a state or regional government

palacio municipal – city hall; seat of the corporation or municipal government

palapa – thatched, palm-leaf-roofed shelter with open sides

Panamericana – see *Carretera Interamericana*

panga – small motorboat

parada – bus stop

parque – park; sometimes also used to describe a plaza

parque nacional – national park

peña – folkloric club; evening of music, song and dance

pensión – guesthouse

petén – island

playa – beach

pozo – spring

propina – tip; gratuity

pueblo – small town or village

puente – bridge

puerta – gate; door

puerto – port; harbor

pulpería – corner store; minimart

punta – point; traditional Garífuna dance involving much hip movement

quebrada – ravine; brook

quetzal – national currency of Guatemala, named after the tropical bird

rancho – thatched-roof restaurant

río – river

Ruta Maya – Maya Route, describing travels to the Maya sites of Mexico, Guatemala and Belize (chiefly), but also El Salvador and Honduras

sacbé (pl **sacbeob**) – ceremonial limestone avenue or path between Maya cities

salida – exit

santo – saint

Semana Santa – Holy Week, the week preceding Easter

sendero – path or trail

sierra – mountain range; saw

stela, stelae – standing stone monument of the ancient Maya, usually carved

supermercado – supermarket; anything from a corner store to a large, Western-style supermarket

templo – temple; church

terminal de autobus – bus terminal

Tico/a – male/female inhabitant of Costa Rica

tienda – small shop

típica – see *típico*

típico – typical or characteristic of a region, particularly used to describe food; also a form of Panamanian folkloric music

traje – traditional handmade clothing

turicentro – literally 'tourist center'; outdoor recreation center with swimming facilities, restaurants and camping (El Salvador)

venado – deer; venison

verano – summer; Central America's dry season, roughly from mid-December to April

volcán – volcano

Zapatistas – members of the left-wing group Ejército Zapatista de Liberación Nacional (EZLN), fighting for indigenous rights in Chiapas, Mexico

FOOD & DRINK GLOSSARY

aguardiente – clear, potent liquor made from sugarcane; also referred to as *caña*

aguas de frutas – fruit-flavored water drink

batido – milkshake made with fresh fruit and milk or water

bocas – savory side dishes or appetizers

bolitas de carne – snack of mildly spicy meatballs

cafetería – informal restaurant with waiter service

cafetín – small *cafetería*

caña – see *aguardiente*

carne ahumada – smoked, dried (jerked) meat

ceviche – raw seafood marinated in lemon or lime juice, garlic and seasonings

chicha – heavily sweetened, fresh fruit drinks

chicharrón – pork crackling

cocina – literally 'kitchen'; small, basic restaurant, or cookshop, usually found in or near municipal markets

comedor – cheap, basic eatery, usually with a limited menu

comida a la vista – meal served buffet- or cafeteria-style

comida corriente or corrida; casado – set meal of rice, beans, plantains and a piece of meat or fish

comida típica – typical local-style meal or food

empanada – turnover stuffed with meat or cheese, baked or fried, sometimes with fruit filling as a dessert.

fritanga – sidewalk barbecue, widely seen in Nicaragua

gallo pinto – common meal of mixed rice and beans

garnaches – fried corn tortillas, served open faced or wrapped, with chicken, fish or beef, shredded cabbage and sometimes cheese

gaseosa – soft drink

guacamole – a dip of mashed or chopped avocados

guaro – local firewater made with sugarcane (Costa Rica)

horchata – sweet rice milk drink with cinnamon

huevos fritos/revueltos – fried/scrambled eggs

licuado – fresh fruit drink, blended with milk or water

menú del día – fixed-price meal of several courses

mondongo – tripe soup

pan de coco – coconut bread

panadería – bakery

patacones – fried green plantains cut in thin pieces, salted, pressed and then fried

plato del día – plate (or meal) of the day

pico de gallo – fresh salsa

pipa – coconut water, served straight from the husk

plátano maduro – ripe plantains baked or broiled with butter, brown sugar and cinnamon; served hot

plato típico – meal typical or characteristic of a place or region

pupusa – cornmeal pocket filled with cheese or refried beans, or a mixture of both (El Salvador)

raspados – shaved ice flavored with fruit juice

refresco – soda, or soft drink; in Costa Rica a drink made with local fruits

rellenitos – refried black beans in mashed plantain dumplings

ropa vieja – literally 'old clothes'; spicy shredded beef

rotisería – restaurant selling roast meats

salbutes – see *garnaches*

sancocho – a spicy stew usually made with chicken

seco – alcoholic drink made from sugarcane

soda – place that serves a counter lunch; soda or soft drink (Panama)

tamales – spiced ground corn with chicken or pork, boiled in banana leaves

tapado – rich Garífuna stew made from fish, shrimp, shellfish, coconut milk and plantain, spiced with coriander

tortilla de maíz – a fried cornmeal cake in Panama

vegetariano/a – male/female vegetarian

MEAL TIMES

desayuno	breakfast
almuerzo	lunch; set lunch
cena	dinner

FRUITS & VEGETABLES

aguacate	avocado
ensalada	salad
fresa	strawberry
guanábana	soursop
manzana	apple
maracuya	passion fruit
naranja	orange
piña	pineapple
zanahoria	carrot

SEAFOOD

camarón	shrimp
langosta	lobster
langostino	jumbo shrimp
pescado	fish
pulpo	octopus

MEATS

bistec	steak
carne	beef
chuleta	pork chop
hamburguesa	hamburger
salchicha	sausage

DRINKS

agua	water
bebida	drink
cafe	coffee
cerveza	beer
leche	milk
ron	rum
vino	wine

Behind the Scenes

SEND US YOUR FEEDBACK

We love to hear from travelers – your comments keep us on our toes and help make our books better. Our well-traveled team reads every word on what you loved or loathed about this book. Although we cannot reply individually to postal submissions, we always guarantee that your feedback goes straight to the appropriate authors, in time for the next edition. Each person who sends us information is thanked in the next edition – the most useful submissions are rewarded with a selection of digital PDF chapters.

Visit **lonelyplanet.com/contact** to submit your updates and suggestions or to ask for help. Our award-winning website also features inspirational travel stories, news and discussions.

Note: We may edit, reproduce and incorporate your comments in Lonely Planet products such as guidebooks, websites and digital products, so let us know if you don't want your comments reproduced or your name acknowledged. For a copy of our privacy policy visit lonelyplanet.com/privacy.

OUR READERS

Many thanks to the travelers who used the last edition and wrote to us with helpful hints, useful advice and interesting anecdotes:

A Amir Sagiv, Andrew Stiffman, Andreas Stephan, Andrew Robarts, Anna Kronborg Haar, Ask Gudmundsen **B** Brenda Dragonne, Brodie Kurczynski **C** Carolein Kuijpers, Caroline Cotton, Celine Vincent, Chelsey Anglin, Craig Murphy **D** Darren Francis, David Taylor **F** Farsan Ghassim, Frans Smit **G** Gabriel Trainer, Gijs de Reeper, Guy Raven **H** Haley White, Harald Wilmersdorf, Helen Bonser **I** Inge Yarzagaray, Isabel von Au **J** Jackie Deverall, Jacqueline Ramos, Jane Wilks, Jason White, Johan Lahti, Johanna Norin, John Munday, Juliette Giannesini **L** Laura Hughes, Liam Hanlon **M** Marek Tretera, Marleen Kaag, Mary O'Sullivan, Meagan Simpson **N** Nadya Waziri, Navin Kaicker, Nolan Shulak **O** Olga Gomez **P** Paolo Votino, Paul Griffin, Paulo Martins **R** Ricky Feigin **S** Sam Hathaway, Sara Koch, Sarah Bolt, Sarah Hundt, Simon Sagewka, Steve Bogaerts, Steve Genner, Susan Cherry **T** Teck Ree Law, Tom De bock, Troels Kolln **W** Wolfgang Seel **Z** Zsofia Ujpal

AUTHOR THANKS

Carolyn McCarthy

I am indebted to the many locals, experts and travelers who shared their version of this paradise. Ignacio and Judit were Caribbean dream captains. Kind thanks to Ruth Metzel, Rainald, Carla Rankin, Jim Omer, Andrew, Andrea, Obedin and Koby, Alexandra Dennis, Daniel Smetana, Bobby and Katrina, Cherie and Reggie, taxi Karloz, KC, Douglas and Igua. Annie, Jennie, Iker, David and Rachel offered respite and support. Thanks guys. *Hasta la proxima!*

Greg Benchwick

Thanks to Cat and the crew at Lonely Planet, to my coordinating author, to Pipo in Managua, and my fearless and peerless travel companion Violeta Benchwick.

Joshua Samuel Brown

At the tail end of the fourth month of my fourth journey through Belize, I'd like to thank first and foremost the entire nation and everyone who calls it home, from the northern edge of Corozal to the remotest jungles of the furthest ruins of Toledo. As for individuals who have made this trip particularly worthwhile, in no particular order: my mad henchman of month one Dave Narby; Christopher and Celini in Toledo; Demian and Nicole in Belize City; David and Nikki in Dangriga; Jacki, Nick, John and

Pam in Placencia; Matthew; Yosiah and Linda in Cayo and Gwyn in Corozal.

Special thanks to Misty for the last one and Bill K and Aimee for being a small part of yet another long, strange trip.

John Hecht

Many thanks to all the good folks in the Yucatán who helped make this wonderful journey possible. Special gratitude goes to commissioning editor Cat Craddock-Carrillo, coordinating author Carolyn McCarthy, Mexico coauthor Sandra Bao, the book's current and previous writers, Raul LiCausi, Pepe Treviño and my loyal buddy, *el campeon*. Last but not least, all my love to my wife, Laura, and a big hug for Carlos, the bravest person I've ever known.

Tom Spurling

Thanks to Cat Craddock-Carrillo for getting me to go around again. High fives to Luis and Jorge for hanging out like true professionals. To Rene, thanks for your kind advice, friendly company and that beach house. To Muzza and Matpat, great effort to get on board. Finally to Lucy, Oliver and Poppy, for supporting my absenteeism over the past 10 books, I love you all like *loco*.

Iain Stewart

I had incredible help in Honduras. In San Pedro, Juan Carlos and Tesla were outstanding company, and the book would be so much the poorer with out the efforts and friendship of Bobby by the lake; Julián in La Moskitia; David Sedat and Howard in Copán; Maria, Sandy Pereira and pals in Tegus; Adi in Roatán; UDC in Utila and the Instituto Hondureño de Turismo.

Lucas Vidgen

Thanks firstly to the Guatemalans, for making my adopted country such an amazing place to live, work and travel. To all the travelers and tourism people along the way, especially Brenda Orantes in Guate, Thomas Ansems in Lanquín and Geert Van Vaeck in Copán. In LP land, thanks to Jonathan Ricketson for whatever patience he has left with me and to all the greasemonkeys in the author pool – it's been quite a ride and the support was much appreciated.

Mara Vorhees

Muchas gracias to the many charming Ticos who lent a hand along the way, especially Jose and the extended Caldo family at Natural Paradise in Turrialba, and the Wierniks at Villa Yerbabuena in Monteverde. The hardest part about travel writing is balancing work life with family life. As such, my most heartfelt thanks go to my own family, for tolerating, encouraging and even participating in this adventure.

ACKNOWLEDGMENTS

Climate map data adapted from Peel MC, Finlayson BL & McMahon TA (2007) 'Updated World Map of the Köppen-Geiger Climate Classification', *Hydrology and Earth System Sciences*, 11, 163344.

Illustrations p52-3, p202-3 by Michael Weldon.

Cover photographs: Costa Rica Waterfall near San Miguel, Giovanni Simeone/4Corners; Keel-billed toucan, Belize, Frans Lanting/Corbis; Granada, Nicaragua, Regula Heeb-Zweifel/Corbis; two Emberá girls, Panama, Bruno Morandi/Corbis.

THIS BOOK

This 8th edition of Lonely Planet's Central America on a Shoestring guidebook was coordinated by Carolyn McCarthy (who also wrote the Panama chapter and the front and back sections of the book), Greg Benchwick (Nicaragua), Joshua Samuel Brown (Belize), John Hecht (Mexico's Yucatán & Chiapas), Tom Spurling (El Salvador), Iain Stewart (Honduras), Lucas Vidgen (Guatemala) and Mara Vorhees (Costa Rica). Alex Egerton's work on the 3rd edition of Nicaragua contributed to this book's Nicaragua chapter, Daniel C Schechter's work on the 5th edition of Guatemala contributed to the Guatemala chapter, Mara Vorhees's work on the 5th edition of Belize contributed to the Belize chapter and Sandra Bao's work on the 6th edition of Cancún, Cozumel & the Yucatán contributed to the Mexico's Yucatán & Chiapas chapter. The previous edition was researched and written by Carolyn McCarthy (coordinating author), Greg Benchwick, Joshua Samuel Brown, Alex Egerton, Matthew D Firestone, Kevin Raub, Tom Spurling and Lucas Vidgen. This guidebook was commissioned in Lonely Planet's Oakland office, and produced by the following:

Commissioning Editor Catherine Craddock-Carrillo

Coordinating Editor Lorna Parkes

Senior Cartographers Mark Griffiths, Alison Lyall

Coordinating Layout Designer Wendy Wright

Managing Editors Sasha Baskett, Bruce Evans

Managing Layout Designer Jane Hart

Assisting Editors Laura Gibbs, Carly Hall, Paul Harding, Lauren Hunt, Gabrielle Innes, Kate James, Bella Li, Rosie Nicholson, Kristin Odijk, Charles Rawlings-Way, Fionnuala Twomey, Simon Williamson

Assisting Cartographers Jeff Cameron, Corey Hutchison, Valentina Kremenchutskaya

Assisting Layout Designer Carol Jackson

Cover Research Brendan Dempsey

Language Content Branislava Vladisavljevic

Thanks to Anita Banh, David Carroll, Ryan Evans, Larissa Frost, Chris Girdler, Genesys India, Jouve India, Trent Paton, Kerrianne Southway, Gerard Walker

Index

ABBREVIATIONS

Bel	Belize
Cos	Costa Rica
El S	El Salvador
Gua	Guatemala
Hon	Honduras
Mex	Mexico
Nic	Nicaragua
Pan	Panama

A

accommodations 728-9, *see also individual locations*
activities 729-30, *see also individual locations & activities*
Actun Tunichil Muknal (Bel) 258
Ahuachapán (El S) 314-16
air travel 738-9, 740-1, *see also individual locations*
Ak'Txumbal (Gua) 144
Alajuela (Cos) 546-50
Aldea Loma Linda (Gua) 163
Alegría (El S) 324-5
Almirante (Pan) 692
Altagracia (Nic) 474-5
Altun Ha (Bel) 17, 245-6, **17**
Amapala (Hon) 426
Ambergris Caye (Bel) 240-5
animals, *see* wildlife-watching, turtles
anthropology museums
  Gulisi Garifuna Museum (Bel) 263
  Museo de la Medicina Maya (Mex) 73
  Museo Nacional de Antropología David J Guzmán (El S) 288
  Museo Popol Vuh (Gua) 96
  Museo Regional de Antropología (Mex) 55
Antigua (Gua) 108-21, **110-11**, **2**
  accommodations 115-16
  activities 113
  attractions 109-13
  courses 113
  drinking & entertainment 118-19
  food 116-18
  safe travel 119
  shopping 119
  tours 114-15
  travel to/from & within 120-1
Apaneca (El S) 318-19
Arcatao (El S) 340
archaeological museums
  Gran Museo del Mundo Maya (Mex) 55
  Mi Museo (Nic) 457
  Museo Cultura Cotzumalguapa (Gua) 166
  Museo de Escultura (Hon) 386
  Museo de Oro Precolombino y Numismática (Cos) 532
  Museo El Baúl (Gua) 165
  Museo Lítico (Gua) 205
  Museo Maya de Cancún (Mex) 43-90
  Museo Regional de Arqueología (Gua) 167
  Museo Regional de Arqueología (Hon) 370
  Museo Regional del Sureste de Petén (Gua) 194
  Museo Tikal (Gua) 205
archaeological sites 24
  Altun Ha (Bel) 17, 245-6, **17**
  Bilbao Stones (Gua) 166
  Bonampak (Mex) 84
  Cahal Pech (Bel) 254
  Calakmul (Mex) 69
  Caracol (Bel) 258
  Ceibal (Gua) 191
  Cerros (Bel) 248
  Chenes (Mex) 69
  Chichén Itzá (Mex) 15, 51-4, **15**, **52-3**
  Chinkultic ruins (Mex) 72
  Cihuatán (El S) 302
  Cobá (Mex) 67-8
  Copán Archaeological Site (Hon) 16, 384-8, **385**, **16**
  Dzibilchaltún (Mex) 55
  Edzná (Mex) 69
  Ek' Balam (Mex) 66
  El Baúl (Gua) 165
  El Cedral (Mex) 63
  El Mirador (Gua) 209
  El Perú (Gua) 208
  El Pilar (Bel) 254, 256
  El Zotz (Gua) 208
  Huellas de Acahualinca (Nic) 443
  Isla de Ometepe petroglyphs 472
  Ixcún (Gua) 194
  Ixímché (Gua) 131
  K'umarcaaj (Gua) 142
  Lamanai (Bel) 246
  Lubaantun (Bel) 273
  Mixco Viejo (Gua) 170
  Monte Alto (Gua) 167
  Monumento Nacional Arqueológico Guayabo (Cos) 556
  Nim Li Punit (Bel) 274
  Pacbitun (Bel) 259
  Palenque Ruins (Mex) 13, 80-1, **81**, **13**
  Palmar (Cos) 617
  Panamá Viejo Ruins (Pan) 644
  Parque Arqueológico Takalik Abaj (Gua) 164
  Parque Eco-Arqueológico Los Naranjos (Hon) 374
  Ruinas de Quelepa (El S) 328-54
  Ruinas de San Andrés (El S) 303
  Ruinas de Tazumal (El S) 314
  Ruta Puuc (Mex) 55
  San Gervasio (Mex) 63
  San Miguelito (Mex) 43
  Tikal (Gua) 10, 82, 200-7, **11**, **202-3**
  Toniná (Mex) 72
  Tulum Ruins (Mex) 65
  Uaxactún (Gua) 207-9
  Uxmal (Mex) 55
  Xunantunich (Bel) 260
  Yamil Lu'um (Mex) 43
  Yaxchilán (Mex) 84
  Yaxhá (Gua) 208
  Zaculeu (Gua) 158
  Zona Arqueológica El Rey (Mex) 43-90
Archipiélago de Bocas del Toro (Pan) 10, 680-92, **682-3**, **10**
Archipiélago de Las Perlas (Pan) 661
Archipiélago de San Blás (Pan), *see* Comarca de Kuna Yala
area codes
  El Salvador 351
  Guatemala 222
  Honduras 435
  Mexico 88
  Nicaragua 524
  Panama 721
Área Protegida Cerro Tisey-Estanzuela (Nic) 495-6
Área Protegida Miraflor (Nic) 495
Argueta, Manlio 345
Arrué, Salvador Efraín Salazar 345
art galleries, *see* galleries
Asturias, Miguel Ángel 214
Ataco (El S) 319-20
ATMs 733
  Belize 278
  Costa Rica 631

Map Pages **000**
Photo Pages **000**

El Salvador 351
Guatemala 220
Honduras 435
Mexico 87
Nicaragua 523
Panama 720
Ávila, Pedro Arias de 710
Awas (Nic) 503
Ayapal (Nic) 498

B

Bahía de Jiquilisco (El S) 326-7
Bahía Drake (Cos) 617-19
Balgüe (Nic) 475
banana republics 429, 625
Barra de Santiago (El S) 16, 320
Barranco (Bel) 273
bathrooms 735
Bay Islands (Hon) 12, 408-23, **409**, **12**
beaches 24
Boca del Drago (Pan) 681
Camp Bay Beach (Hon) 416
Chepes Beach (Hon) 418
El Bluff (Nic) 501
Great Corn Island (Nic) 504-6
Isla Grande (Pan) 697
Isla Taboga (Pan) 660
La Garita (Pan) 664
La Playita (Cos) 610
Las Peñitas (Nic) 489
Little Corn Island (Nic) 506, **7**
Montezuma (Cos) 601
Parque Nacional Cahuita (Cos) 562
Playa Aserradores (Nic) 489-90
Playa Barqueta (Pan) 670
Playa Blanca (Gua) 187
Playa Bluff (Pan) 681
Playa Bonita (Cos) 560
Playa Cocalito (Cos) 618
Playa Cocalito (Hon) 397
Playa Cocles (Cos) 567
Playa del Coco (Cos) 591-4
Playa El Coco (Nic) 481
Playa El Cuco (El S) 332
Playa El Espino (El S) 325
Playa El Istmito (Pan) 682
Playa El Sunzal (El S) 307
Playa El Toro (Pan) 664
Playa El Tunco (El S) 16, 305, **16**
Playa El Zonte (El S) 307
Playa Espadilla (Cos) 610
Playa Espadilla Sur (Cos) 610
Playa Esteron (El S) 332
Playa Gigante (Nic) 477
Playa Hermosa (Cos) 606
Playa Hermosa (Nic) 481
Playa Jaguey (El S) 332
Playa Jiquilillo (Nic) 490
Playa Las Lajas (Pan) 672
Playa Las Tunas (El S) 332
Playa Maderas (Nic) 480
Playa Majahual (El S) 333
Playa Manuel Antonio (Cos) 610
Playa Marsella (Nic) 480
Playa Nancite (Cos) 590
Playa Naranjo (Cos) 590
Playa Negra (Cahuita, Cos) 562
Playa Negra (Puerto Viejo de Talamanca, Cos) 567
Playa Negra (Tamarindo, Cos) 598-9
Playa Negra (Hon) 426
Playa Ocotal (Cos) 591
Playa Palancar (Mex) 63
Playa Platanares (Cos) 619
Playa Popoyo (Nic) 477
Playa Punch (Pan) 682
Playa Quehueche (Gua) 187
Playa Remanso (Nic) 480
Playa Sámara (Cos) 599-600
Playa San Josecito (Cos) 618
Playa Tamarindo (Cos) 594-8, **596**
Playa Tamarindo (Nic) 480
Playa Venao (Pan) 665
Poneloya (Nic) 489
Red Frog Beach (Pan) 690
Reserva Natural Absoluta Cabo Blanco (Cos) 603-4
Tulate (Gua) 166
Uvita (Cos) 613
Wizard Beach (Pan) 690
Belén (Hon) 424
Belén Gualcho (Hon) 390
Belize 227-82, **230-1**
accommodations 277
arts 275-6
climate 227, 277
culture 275
disabilities, travelers with 280
embassies & consulates 277
food & drink 228
gay & lesbian travelers 277
highlights 230-1
history 274-5
landscape & wildlife 276
money 278
planning 37
safe travel 279
travel to/from 228, 280-1
travel within 281-2
women travelers 280
Belize City 229-36, **232**, **234**
accommodations 229
attractions 229
drinking & entertainment 233
food 232-3
shopping 233
travel to/from 235-6
travel within 236
Belmopan (Bel) 251-4
Bermudian Landing (Bel) 245
bicycle travel, *see* cycling
Bilwi (Nic) 507-8
Biotopo del Quetzal (Gua) 170-1
Biotopo Mario Dary Rivera, *see* Biotopo del Quetzal
bird-watching, *see also* wildlife-watching
Biotopo Monterrico-Hawaii (Gua) 168
Bosque Eterno de los Niños (Cos) 572
Celestún (Mex) 55
Cerro Alux (Gua) 121
Finca La Isla (Cos) 567
Honduras 432
Isla Barro Colorado (Pan) 660
Lago de Yojoa (Hon) 373
Lancetilla Jardín Botánico (Hon) 397
Macaw Mountain (Hon) 383-4
Monumento Nacional Arqueológico Guayabo (Cos) 556
Panama 717
Panama Rainforest Discovery Center 659-60
Parque Nacional Chirripó (Cos) 616
Parque Nacional Isla Contoy (Mex) 48
Parque Nacional Laguna del Tigre (Gua) 208
Parque Nacional Palo Verde (Cos) 586
Parque Nacional Rincón de la Vieja (Cos) 589
Parque Nacional Soberanía (Pan) 659
Parque Nacional Tortuguero (Cos) 557, **31**
Parque Natural Metropolitano (Pan) 645
Perquín (El S) 335
Playa Jiquilillo (Nic) 490
Puerto Viejo de Sarapiquí (Cos) 584-5
Refugio de Vida Silvestre Isla Taboga y Urabá (Pan) 660
Reserva Biológica Bosque Nuboso Monteverde (Cos) 14, 572, **14**
Reserva Natural Punta Patiño (Pan) 707
Río Platanares (Cos) 619
Sarteneja (Bel) 251
Tikal (Gua) 205
Blue Creek (Bel) 273
Blue Hole National Park (Bel) 240, 261, **23**
Bluefields (Nic) 501-3
boat travel 740, 741, *see also individual locations*
Boca de Sábalos (Nic) 511
Bocas del Toro Province (Pan) 679-93, *see also* Archipiélago de Bocas del Toro
Bocas del Toro Town (Pan) 681-9, **684**
Bolas de Fuego (El S) 27
Bonampak (Mex) 84
Boquete (Pan) 672-7, **674**, **32**
border crossings 739, 740
Belize–Guatemala 281-2
Belize–Honduras 281-2

border crossings *continued*
Belize–Mexico 281-2
CA-4 agreement 736
Costa Rica–Nicaragua 634
Costa Rica–Panama 635
El Salvador–Costa Rica 352
El Salvador–Guatemala 353
El Salvador–Honduras 353
El Salvador–Nicaragua 352
Guatemala–Belize 225
Guatemala–El Salvador 224
Guatemala–Honduras 224
Guatemala–Mexico 225
Honduras–El Salvador 437
Honduras–Guatemala 436-7
Honduras–Nicaragua 437
Mexico–Guatemala 82
Nicaragua–Costa Rica 525
Nicaragua–El Salvador 526
Nicaragua–Honduras 526
Panama–Colombia 724
Panama–Costa Rica 724
budget 19
bus travel, *see also individual locations*
fares 742
to/from Central America 739
within Central America 741
business hours 733, *see also individual locations*

C

Cacaopera (El S) 333-4
Cahuita (Cos) 562-6, **564-5**
Caldera (Pan) 670
Campeche (Mex) 68-72, **70-1**
Cañas (Cos) 585
Cancún (Mex) 43-8, **46**
accommodations 43-5
attractions 43
drinking & nightlife 47
food 45-7
shopping 47
travel to/from 48
travel within 48
Caño Negro (Cos) 35, 584
canoeing & kayaking
Bahía Drake (Cos) 618
Isla Colón (Pan) 681
Jacó (Cos) 606
La Fortuna (Cos) 581
Lago de Atitlán (Gua) 123
Panama 717
Parque Nacional Tortuguero (Cos) 557
Playa Santo Domingo (Nic) 475
Puerto Viejo de Sarapiquí (Cos) 584
Río Cangrejal (Hon) 403
Río Sarapiquí (Cos) 583
San Ignacio (Bel) 256
Turrialba (Cos) 554
Utila (Hon) 420
canyoning 554
Caracol (Bel) 258
Carazo Towns (Nic) 467
Carnaval (Mex) 25
car travel 739-40, 742, *see also individual locations*
Cartago (Cos) 552-3
Casco Viejo (Pan) 639-44
Catarina (Nic) 466
caves
Actun Tunichil Muknal (Bel) 258
Barton Creek Cave (Bel) 259
Centro Turístico Cueva de las Minas (Gua) 179
Che Chem Ha (Bel) 256
Cuevas de Ak'tun Kan (Gua) 194
Cuevas de Taulabé (Hon) 373
Gibnut Cave (Bel) 273
Grutas de Lanquín (Gua) 175
La Cueva del Gigante (Hon) 372
Loltún (Mex) 55
Nivida Bat Cave (Pan) 690
Río Frio Cave (Bel) 259
St Herman's Cave (Bel) 261
Tiger Cave (Bel) 272
Caye Caulker (Bel) 14, 236-40, **238**, **14**
Cayos Cochinos (Hon) 405
Celestún (Mex) 55
cell phones 735
cenotes
Blue Hole National Park (Bel) 261, **23**
Cenote Azul (Mex) 64, 65
Cenote Dzitnup (Mex) 51
Cenote Samulá (Mex) 51
Cenote Zací (Mex) 51
Cristalino Cenote (Mex) 64
Cuzamá (Mex) 55
El Jardín del Edén (Mex) 64
Gran Cenote (Mex) 67
Central America
basics 18-19
itineraries 28-35
travel to/from 19, 738-40
travel within 740-2
Central Valley & Highlands (Cos) 546-71, **548-9**
Cerro Chirripó (Cos) 616
Cerro El Pital (El S) 341
Cerro Punta (Pan) 678
Chalatenango (El S) 339-40
Chalchuapa (El S) 314
Champerico (Gua) 164
Changuinola (Pan) 692
Chapín Abajo (Gua) 34, 182
Chiapas (Mex) 72-85, **74-5**, *see also* Mexico's Yucatán & Chiapas
Chichén Itzá (Mex) 15, 51-4, **15**, **52-3**
Chichicastenango (Gua) 138-42, **29**
children, travel with 629
Chinchilla, Laura 627
Chiquimula (Gua) 177-8
Chiquistepeque (Gua) 166
Chitré (Pan) 663
Choluteca (Hon) 426
Cihuatán (El S) 302
Cinquera (El S) 338
civil wars
Costa Rica 626
El Salvador 334, 336, 343
Guatemala 131, 138, 209, 211
Nicaragua 512, 516
climate 18, *see also individual countries*
Cobá (Mex) 67-8
Cobán (Gua) 171-5, **172-3**
Cocobila (Hon) 424
Cocop (Gua) 144
coffee
Boquete 673
Chicoj Cooperative (Gua) 173
Cooperativa RAOS (Hon) 372
Costa Rica 625
Finca El Cisne (Hon) 384
Finca Santa Leticia (El S) 318
Finca Santa Margarita (Gua) 173
Matagalpa (Nic) 498
Reserva Natural Volcán Mombacho (Nic) 465
San Ramón (Nic) 499
Cojutepeque (El S) 323
Colón (Pan) 693-5
colonial cities 23-4
Comarca de Kuna Yala (Pan) 698-702
Comayagua (Hon) 369-71
Concepción Quezaltepeque (El S) 340
Conchagua (El S) 330
consulates 731, *see also individual countries*
Contra War 515-16
Copán Archaeological Site (Hon) 16, 384-8, **385**, **16**
Copán Ruinas (Hon) 378-83, **379**
Corn Islands, *see* Great Corn Island, Little Corn Island
Corozal (Bel) 248-50, **249**
Corral de Mulas (El S) 326-30
Cosigüina Peninsula (Nic) 489-91
Costa del Sol (El S) 291
Costa Rica 528-636, **530-1**
accommodations 629
children, travel with 629
climate 528
disabilities, travelers with 633
embassies & consulates 629
food & drink 529, 630
gay & lesbian travelers 541, 630
highlights 530
history 624-7
itineraries 529
landscape & wildlife 628
money 631
planning 38
safe travel 632
travel to/from 529, 634-5
travel within 635-6
Costa Rican Independence Day 27, 553
Cotzal (Gua) 144

Coxen Hole (Hon) 416
Crooked Tree (Bel) 246
Cubulco (Gua) 170
customs regulations 730, *see also individual countries*
cycling 729, 741
Antigua (Gua) 113
Isla Colón (Pan) 681
Lago de Atitlán (Gua) 123
Montezuma (Cos) 601
Puerto Viejo de Talamanca (Cos) 567
Quetzaltenango (Gua) 147
San Cristóbal de las Casa (Mex) 73
Tours Ciclista de Montaña (El S) 335

D

Dalton, Roque 345
dangers, *see* safety
Dangriga (Bel) 261-4, **262**
Darién Province (Pan) 702-9, **704**
David 668-71, **669**
Desfile de Bufos (Gua) 25
Día de Juan Santamaria (Cos) 26, 546
Día de los Muertos (Mex) 27
Día de Todos los Santos (Gua) 27, 162
Diria (Nic) 467
Diriamba (Nic) 467
disabilities, travelers with 735-6
Belize 280
Costa Rica 633
El Salvador 351
Guatemala 223
Honduras 436
Nicaragua 524
Panama 722
diving 22, 729, *see also* snorkeling
Archipiélago de Las Perlas (Pan) 661
Bay Islands (Hon) 12, 410, **12**
Blue Hole (Bel) 240
Caye Caulker (Bel) 236
Cayos Cochinos (Hon) 405
Great Corn Island (Nic) 505
Isla Colón (Pan) 680
Isla Cozumel (Mex) 63
Isla Grande (Pan) 697
Isla Mujeres (Mex) 49
Little Corn Island (Nic) 506
Los Cóbanos (El S) 320
Museo Subacuático de Arte (Mex) 43
Panama 717
Placencia (Bel) 266
Playa del Carmen (Mex) 59
Playa del Coco (Cos) 591
Puerto Viejo de Talamanca (Cos) 567
Refugio Nacional de Vida Silvestre Gandoca-Manzanillo (Cos) 571
Roatán (Hon) 411
San Juan del Sur (Nic) 477
San Salvador (El S) 290
Santa Catalina (Pan) 666-9
Santa Cruz La Laguna (Gua) 137
Tulum (Mex) 65
Utila (Hon) 12, 418
Dominical (Cos) 611-12
driving, *see* car travel

E

El Boquerón (El S) 303
El Castillo (Nic) 512
El Estor (Gua) 185
El Manzano (El S) 340
El Mirador (Gua) 209
El Mozote (El S) 336
El Ostional (Nic) 481
El Petén (Gua) 191-209, **192-3**
El Pino (Hon) 404
El Real (Pan) 706-7
El Remate (Gua) 199-200
El Rosario (Hon) 369
El Salvador 283-354, **286-7**
accommodations 348
activities 348
arts 345-6
climate 283
culture 345
dangers & annoyances 349
disabilities, travelers with 351
embassies & consulates 349
food & drink 284
gay & lesbian travelers 350
highlights 286-7
history 342-5
itineraries 284
landscapes & wildlife 346-8
money 350
planning 37
religion 345
travel to/from 284, 352-3
travel within 353-4
visas & documents 352
women travelers 352
El Transito (Nic) 490
El Trapiche (Nic) 447-8
El Triunfo de la Cruz (Hon) 398
El Valle (Pan) 662-3
electricity 731
embassies & consulates 731, *see also individual countries*
Escuintla (Gua) 167-8
Esquipulas (Gua) 178-80
Estanzuela (Gua) 177
Estelí (Nic) 491-5, **492**
etiquette 21
events, *see* festivals & events
exchange rates 731

F

Far East (Hon) 416
Fería de Cultura de las Flores y las Palmas (Cos) 26, 303
Fernandez, Juan Mora 625
Ferrer, José Figueres 626
Festival de Diablos y Congos (Pan) 25, 696
Festival de Invierno (El S) 27
festivals & events
Annual Taxi Grand Prix (Nic) 444-5
Apparition of the Archangel Michael (Gua) 157
Bolas de Fuego (El S) 27
Carnaval (El S) 329
Carnaval (Hon) 399
Carnaval (Mex) 25
Carnaval (Pan) 698
Copán Ruinas fair (Hon) 380
Costa Rican Independence Day 27, 553
Day of the Revolution (Nic) 444-5
Desfile de Bufos (Gua) 25
Día de Bastimentos (Pan) 685
Día de Juan Santamaria (Cos) 26, 546
Día de la Purísima Concepción (Nic) 486
Día de la Virgen de Merced (Nic) 486
Día de la Virgen del Carmen (Pan) 685
Día de los Muertos (Mex) 27
Día de Todos los Santos (Gua) 27, 162
Envision Festival (Cos) 611
Feast of Santo Tomás (Gua) 140
Feast of the Immaculate Conception (Gua) 140
Fería de Cultura de las Flores y las Palmas (Cos) 26, 303
Feria de San José de David (Pan) 669
Feria del Mar (Pan) 685
Feria Titular de San Miguel Arcángel (Gua) 157
Festival de Cristo Negro (Pan) 696
Festival de Diablos y Congos (Pan) 25, 696
Festival de Invierno (El S) 27
Festival de Montaña (El S) 335
Festival of San Juan Bautista (Pan) 698
Festival of Santo Domingo de Guzman (Nic) 444-5
Festival Tradicional de Danza (Gua) 157
Fiesta de La Virgen del Mar (Cos) 591
Fiesta de San Francisco de Asís (Gua) 155
Fiesta del Mar (Pan) 661
Fiestas de Agosto (Nic) 461
Fiestas Elenas (Gua) 142
Fiestas Patronales (El S) 329
Fundación de la Provincia de Bocas del Toro (Pan) 685
Garifuna National Day (Gua) 188
Garifuna Settlement Day (Bel) 27, 261
Inmaculada Concepción (Nic) 461

festivals & events *continued*
International Poetry Festival (Nic) 461
La Feria de San Isidro (Hon) 26
La Gritería Chiquita (Nic) 486
Las Fiestas de Zapote (Cos) 27, 536
Lobsterfest (Bel) 26, 266
Los Fiestas de Azuero (Pan) 663
May Day (Pan) 685
Mistletoe Ball (Bel) 266
Nicaraguan Baseball Championship 25
Noche de Agüizotes (Nic) 27, 468
Nogapope (Pan) 27
Nuestra Señora del Carmen (Pan) 661
Palo de Mayo (Nic) 26, 502
Panama Jazz Festival 25
Placencia Arts Festival (Bel) 266
Quema del Diablo (Gua) 140
Rabin Ajau (Gua) 27
San Jerónimo (Nic) 468
San Lázaro (Nic) 468
Semana Santa (El S) 320
Semana Santa (Gua) 26, 115, 188
Succotz festival (Bel) 260
Sun Jam (Hon) 27
Toledo Cacao Festival (Bel) 26
Wajshakib Batz' (Gua) 157
Finca El Paraíso (Gua) 184
Finca Ixobel (Gua) 193
Flores & Santa Elena (Gua) 194-9, **195**
FMLN 338, 340, 342-4
Fray Bartolomé de Las Casas (Gua) 177
freediving
Roatán (Hon) 412
Utila (Hon) 419
French Harbour (Hon) 416
FSLN 515-17
Fuentes Georginas (Gua) 155
Funes, Mauricio 342

Map Pages **000**
Photo Pages **000**

G

galleries
El Arbol de Dios (El S) 288
Galería La Pinacoteca (El S) 288
Galería Nacional de Arte (Hon) 357
Memorias Frágiles (Hon) 380
Museo de Arte Contemporáneo (Pan) 639
Museo de Arte de El Salvador (El S) 288
Museo de Arte Fundación Ortiz-Guardián (Nic) 482
Museo de Arte y Diseño Contemporáneo (Cos) 532
Museo Nacional de Arte Moderno (Gua) 97
Garifuna
communities 187-91, 273, 397-8, 405, 424, 503
culture 263, 265, 357, 432
festivals 188, 261, 394, 408
music 189, 394
Garifuna Settlement Day (Bel) 27, 261
gay & lesbian travelers 732
Belize 277
Costa Rica 541, 630
El Salvador 350
Guatemala 218
Honduras 434
Nicaragua 522
Panama 719
Golfito (Cos) 622
Golfo de Chiriquí (Pan) 671
Golfo De Fonseca Islands (El S) 332-3
Gonzáles, Gaspar Pedro 214
Gracias (Hon) 390-2
Gran Cenote (Mex) 67
Granada (Nic) 12, 456-65, **458-9**, **12**
Great Corn Island (Nic) 504-6
Guanacaste (Cos) 585-91
Guatajiagua (El S) 334
Guatemala 91-226, **94-5**
accommodations 216
arts 214
budget 92
children, travel with 217
climate 91
culture 212-13
disabilities, travelers with 223
embassies & consulates 217
food & drink 92, 217-18
gay & lesbian travelers 218
highlights 94
history 210-12
itineraries 92
landscapes & wildlife 214-16
planning 36
religion 213-14
resources 92
safe travel 221
travel to/from 92, 224-5
travel within 225
visas & documents 223
women travelers 224
Guatemala City 93-108, **98**, **100-1**
accommodations 97-9
drinking & entertainment 102-3
food 99-102
safety 104
shopping 103
travel to/from 104-6
travel within 106-8
Guayabo (Cos), *see* Monumento Nacional Arqueológico Guayabo
Guerra de Fútbol 429

H

health 732
Heredia (Cos) 550-1
Herradura (Cos) 615
Highlands (Gua) 121-62
travel to/from & within 121
hiking 22, 729
Bahía Drake (Cos) 617-36
Boquete (Pan) 673, **32**
Chalatenango (El S) 339
El Mirador (Gua) 209
Great Corn Island (Nic) 504
Isla Colón (Pan) 681
Isla de Ometepe (Nic) 471
Jacó (Cos) 606
La Palma (El S) 340
Lago de Atitlán (Gua) 123
Lago de Yojoa (Hon) 373, 374
Marcala (Hon) 372
Monteverde (Cos) 576
Monumento Nacional Cañon de Somoto (Nic) 496-7
Nebaj (Gua) 143
Panama 717
Parque Internacional La Amistad (Pan) 679
Parque Nacional Braulio Carrillo (Cos) 551
Parque Nacional Chirripó (Cos) 616
Parque Nacional Corcovado (Cos) 620-1
Parque Nacional Cusuco (Hon) 378
Parque Nacional El Imposible (El S) 316, 321-3
Parque Nacional Manuel Antonio (Cos) 610
Parque Nacional Montaña de Celaque (Hon) 392
Parque Nacional Montaña de Comayagua (Hon) 370
Parque Nacional Rincón de la Vieja (Cos) 589
Parque Nacional Soberanía (Pan) 659
Parque Nacional Tortuguero (Cos) 557
Parque Nacional Volcán Arenal (Cos) 580
Parque Nacional Volcán Barú (Pan) 677
Parque Nacional Volcán Poás (Cos) 550
Perquín (El S) 335
Puerto Viejo de Sarapiquí (Cos) 584
Quetzaltenango (Gua) 147
Reserva de la Biosfera del Río Plátano (Hon) 424
Reserva Natural Absoluta Cabo Blanco (Cos) 604
Río Cangrejal (Hon) 404
San Ignacio (El S) 341
San Juan del Sur (Nic) 477
San Miguel (El S) 328-54
San Pedro La Laguna (Gua) 133
San Vicente (El S) 323
Santa Elena (Cos) 576
Santa Fé (Pan) 668
Santiago Atitlán (Gua) 132
Suchitoto (El S) 336
Tikal (Gua) 205
Todos Santos Cuchumatán (Gua) 162
volcanoes 113, 133, 147, 155

history, *see individual locations*
history museums
Casa de Montejo (Mex) 54
Casa MIMA (Gua) 93
Casa Museo Comandante Carlos Fonseca (Nic) 498
Casa Museo Judith Kain (Nic) 507
El Campamento Guerrillero Simulado (El S) 334
Galería de Héroes y Mártires (Nic) 483, 491
Museo de la Revolución Salvadoreña (El S) 334
Museo del Canal Interoceánico (Pan) 643
Museo para la Identidad Nacional (Hon) 357
hitchhiking 742
Belize 282
Costa Rica 636
Nicaragua 527
Honduras 355-437, **358-9**
accommodations 433
arts 431-2
climate 355, 433
culture 430-1
disabilities, travelers with 436
embassies & consulates 434
food & drink 356, 434
gay & lesbian travelers 434
highlights 358-9
history 428-30
itineraries 356
landscape & wildlife 432-3
money 435
planning 37
religion 431
safe travel 435
travel to/from 356, 436-7
travel within 437
women travelers 436
Hopkins (Bel) 264-6
horseback riding
Antigua (Gua) 113
Copán Ruinas (Hon) 380
El Castillo (Nic) 512
Gracias (Hon) 390
Jacó (Cos) 606
Mal País (Cos) 604
Monteverde (Cos) 576
Montezuma (Cos) 601
Monumento Nacional Cañon de Somoto (Nic) 496
Pueblo Viejo (Bel) 273
Río Cangrejal (Hon) 404
Roatán (Hon) 413
San Juan (Hon) 393
Santa Elena (Cos) 576
Santa Fé (Pan) 668
Suchitoto (El S) 337
hot springs
Aguas Termales (Hon) 384
Aguas Termales La Calera (Nic) 465
Aguas Termales Presidente (Hon) 392
Canton El Progreso (El S) 334
Fuentes Georginas (Gua) 155
Herradura (Cos) 615
La Fortuna (Cos) 580-1
Los Pozos de Caldera (Pan) 673
Orosi (Cos) 553
Parque Nacional Rincón de la Vieja (Cos) 589
Pozos Termales (Pan) 662
San Lorenzo El Tejar (Gua) 121
Termas del Río (Hon) 392
Huehuetenango (Gua) 158

I

Ilobasco (El S) 323
indigenous peoples
Bribrí (Pan) 678
Emberá (Pan) 659, 703
Honduras 430-1
Kakawira (El S) 334
Kuna (Pan) 698
Lenca (Hon) 371, 372, 388
Nahual (El S) 322
Ngöbe (Pan) 678, 690
Panama 714
Pipil (El S) 343
Teribe (Pan) 678
Wounaan (Pan) 645, 659, 703
insurance 732, 739, 742
internet access 732
Isla Barro Colorado (Pan) 660
Isla Bastimentos (Pan) 10, 689-92
Isla Boca Brava (Pan) 671
Isla Carenero (Pan) 689
Isla Colón (Pan) 680-9
Isla Conchagüita (El S) 333
Isla Cozumel (Mex) 61-4, **62**
Isla de Cañas (Pan) 664
Isla de Coiba (Pan) 667
Isla de Ometepe (Nic) 17, 471-3, **472-3**, **17**
Isla El Tigre (Hon) 426
Isla Grande (Pan) 697-8
Isla Holbox (Mex) 48
Isla Martín Pérez (El S) 332
Isla Meanguera (El S) 34, 333
Isla Méndez (El S) 326-7
Isla Montecristo (El S) 325
Isla Mujeres (Mex) 49-50
Isla Murciélago (Cos) 591
Isla San Cristóbal (Pan) 690
Isla San Sebastian (El S) 326-7
Isla Santa Catalina (Cos) 591
Isla Taboga (Pan) 660-1
Isla Zacatillo (El S) 332
Islas Solentiname (Nic) 510
itineraries 28-35, *see also individual locations*
Izalco (El S) 320, 322
Izamal (Mex) 66

J

Jacó (Cos) 605-7
Jaibalito (Gua) 136
Jinotega (Nic) 497-8
Jinotepe (Nic) 467
Joya de Cerén (El S) 303
Juayúa (El S) 317-18, **16**
Jutiapa (Hon) 369

K

Kakabila (Nic) 503
kayaking, *see* canoeing & kayaking
Keith, Minor 625
kitesurfing
Ambergris Caye (Bel) 240
Bahía Salinas (Cos) 590
Caye Caulker (Bel) 236
Little Corn Island (Nic) 506
Mexico 65
K'umarcaaj (Gua) 142

L

La Campa (Hon) 34, 392
La Ceiba (Hon) 398-403, **400**
La Costa del Bálsamo (El S) 305-8
La Cruz (Cos) 590-1
La Democracia (Gua) 167
La Ensenada (Hon) 398
La Esperanza (Hon) 371-2
La Feria de San Isidro (Hon) 26
La Fortuna (Cos) 580-3
La Garnacha (Nic) 496
La Libertad (El S) 303-5
La Moskitia (Hon) 423-6
La Negrita 552
La Palma (El S) 340-2
La Palma (Pan) 707
La Unión (El S) 330-2, **331**
La Virgen (Cos) 583-4
Lago de Atitlán (Gua) 15, 121-38, **122**, **15**
Lago de Coatepeque (El S) 308-9
Lago de Izabal (Gua) 181-5
Lago de Nicaragua (Nic) 17
Lago de Yojoa (Hon) 373-4
Lagos de Montebello (Mex) 72
Laguna (Bel) 272
Laguna Bacalar (Mex) 65
Laguna Chicabal (Gua) 158
Laguna de Apoyeque (Nic) 447-8
Laguna de Ibans (Hon) 424
Laguna de Xiloá (Nic) 447-8
Laguna El Jocotal (El S) 347
Lagunita Creek (Gua) 183
Lamanai (Bel) 246
language 21, 743-50
language courses 219-20, 732, *see also individual locations*
Antigua (Gua) 114
Bocas del Toro Town (Pan) 683
Boquete (Pan) 675
Copán Ruinas (Hon) 380
Estelí (Nic) 491
Granada (Nic) 460
Heredia (Cos) 550-1
León (Nic) 483
Managua (Nic) 443
Monterrico (Gua) 169
Monteverde 14, 576
Nebaj (Gua) 144
Panajachel (Gua) 123
Panama City 645
Playa del Carmen (Mex) 59
Playa Sámara (Cos) 599
Playa Tamarindo (Cos) 595

language courses *continued*
Quetzaltenango (Gua) 149-50
Reserva Natural Laguna de Apoyo (Nic) 466
San Cristóbal de las Casa (Mex) 73
San José (Cos) 533
San Juan del Sur (Nic) 477
Santa Elena (Cos) 576
Suchitoto (El S) 337
Lanquín (Gua) 175-6
Lars, Claudia 345
Las Fiestas de Zapote (Cos) 27, 536
Las Isletas (Nic) 457
Las Marías (Hon) 424
Las Peñitas (Nic) 489
Lempira 428
León (Nic) 482-9, **484-5**
accommodations 486-7
attractions 482-3
courses 483-4
drinking 487
entertainment 487
food 487
tours 484-6
travel to/from & within 488-9
León Viejo (Nic) 490
lesbian travelers, *see* gay & lesbian travelers
Liberia (Cos) 586-9, **586-7**
Little Corn Island (Nic) 506-7, **7**
Lívingston (Gua) 187-91
Llort, Fernando 288, 341, 346
Lobo, Porfirio 427
Lobsterfest (Bel) 26, 266
Lopez, Matilde Elena 346
Los Chiles (Cos) 583
Los Cóbanos (El S) 320
Los Planes de Renderos (El S) 303
Los Vahos (Gua) 156

M

Mahahual (Mex) 65
Mal País (Cos) 604-5
Managua (Nic) 442-54, **444-5**, **448-9**, **455-6**
accommodations 444-6
attractions 442-3
courses 443
drinking & nightlife 447-9
entertainment 449-50
food 446-7
shopping 450
travel to/from 452-4
travel within 454
Manuel Antonio (Cos) 610-11, **608**
Manzanillo (Cos) 571
maps 733
Marcala (Hon) 372-3
markets
Belén Gualcho (Hon) 390
Chichicastenango (Gua) 138, **29**
Mercado Artesanal (Cos) 542
Mercado Artesanías (Nic) 467
Mercado Central (Cos) 542
Mercado de Artesanía (Pan) 662
Mercado de Artesanías (Gua) 119, 144
Mercado de Buhonerías y Artesanías (Pan) 654
Mercado del Carmen (Gua) 119
Mercado Municipal (Nic) 458
Mercado Municipal Lucas de Gálvez (Mex) 54
Mercado Nacional de Artesanías (Pan) 654
Mercado Oriental (Nic) 450-1
Mercado Roberto Huembes (Nic) 450-1
Nahuizalco (El S) 322
San Francisco El Alto (Gua) 155
San Ignacio (Bel) 254
Martinelli, Ricardo 713
Martínez, Aurelio 431
Martínez, Denis 517
Martino, Miguel 337
Masachapa (Nic) 454-5
Masaya (Nic) 467-9, **468-9**
Matagalpa (Nic) 498-500
Mateare (Nic) 447-8
Maximón 127, 156
Maya, the
culture 96, 147, 157, 380
festivals 157
museums 43, 55, 73
history 210, 274
Menchú, Rigoberta 145
Mérida (Mex) 54-9, **56-7**
accommodations 55-7
attractions 54-5
drinking & nightlife 58
entertainment 58
food 57-8
travel to/from 58-9
Mérida (Nic) 475-6
Metapán (El S) 312-13
Meteti (Pan) 705-6
Mexico's Yucatán & Chiapas 40-90, **42**
accommodations 86
activities 86
climate 40, 86
culture 86
customs 86
embassies & consulates 87
food & drink 41
gay & lesbian travelers 87
history 85-6
itineraries 41
money 87
planning 36
resources 41
safety 86
travel to/from 89-90
travel within 90
visas & documents 89
Miami (Hon) 398
Miramundo (El S) 341
Miskito Keys (Nic) 506
Mistruk (Hon) 425
mobile phones 735
Molina, Otto Fernando Perez 209
Momostenango (Gua) 157-8
money 19, 733
Monkey Point (Nic) 506
Monterrico (Gua) 168-70
Monteverde (Cos) 14, 572-9, **574-5**
accommodations 576-8
activities 573-6
attractions 572-3
courses 576
food 578
shopping 579
travel to/from 579
Montezuma (Cos) 601-3, **602**
Monumento Nacional Arqueológico Guayabo (Cos) 556
Monumento Nacional Cañon de Somoto (Nic) 496-7
Monumento Nacional Isla Barro Colorado (Pan) 660
Morazán (El S) 333-5
motorcycle travel 739, 742
Moya, Horacio Casellanos 346
Moyogalpa (Nic) 473-4
museums, *see also* anthropology museums, archaeological museums, history museums
Centro de Exhibiciones Marinas (Pan) 644
Centro Intercultural de Quetzaltenango (Gua) 147
Cojolya Association of Maya Women Weavers (Gua) 132
Museo de Arte Popular (El S) 290
Museo de Jade (Cos) 533
Museo de la Biodiversidad (Pan) 645
Museo de Leyendas y Tradiciones (Nic) 482
Museo del Ámbar de Chiapas (Mex) 73
Museo del Folklore (Nic) 467
Museum of Butterflies & Other Insects (Hon) 399

N

Nahuizalco (El S) 322
Naïve Art 341, 346
national parks, *see also* reserves
Blue Hole National Park (Bel) 240, 261, **23**
Guanacaste National Park (Bel) 251
Parque Internacional La Amistad (Pan) 678-9
Parque Nacional Archipiélago Zapatera (Nic) 465
Parque Nacional Braulio Carrillo (Cos) 551-2
Parque Nacional Cahuita (Cos) 562
Parque Nacional Carara (Cos) 605
Parque Nacional Cerro Azul Meambar (Hon) 374
Parque Nacional Chirripó (Cos) 616-17
Parque Nacional Coiba (Pan) 34, 667
Parque Nacional Corcovado (Cos) 620-1
Parque Nacional Cusuco (Hon) 378

Parque Nacional Darién (Pan) 702
Parque Nacional El Imposible (El S) 16, 316, 321-2
Parque Nacional Jeannette Kawas (Hon) 397
Parque Nacional La Tigra (Hon) 369
Parque Nacional Laguna Lachuá (Gua) 174
Parque Nacional Las Victorias (Gua) 171
Parque Nacional Los Volcanes (El S) 308
Parque Nacional Manuel Antonio (Cos) 13, 610, **13**
Parque Nacional Marino Ballena (Cos) 613
Parque Nacional Marino Golfo de Chiriquí (Pan) 671
Parque Nacional Marino Isla Bastimentos (Pan) 690
Parque Nacional Marino Las Baulas de Guanacaste (Cos) 594
Parque Nacional Montaña de Celaque (Hon) 392-3
Parque Nacional Montaña de Comayagua (Hon) 370
Parque Nacional Montecristo-El Trifinio (El S) 313
Parque Nacional Palo Verde (Cos) 586
Parque Nacional Pico Bonito (Hon) 404
Parque Nacional Rincón de la Vieja (Cos) 589
Parque Nacional Río Dulce (Gua) 190
Parque Nacional San Lorenzo (Pa) 695
Parque Nacional Santa Bárbara (Hon) 374
Parque Nacional Soberanía (Pan) 659
Parque Nacional Tapantí-Macizo Cerro de la Muerte (Cos) 553
Parque Nacional Tortuguero (Cos) 557, **31**
Parque Nacional Volcán Arenal (Cos) 580
Parque Nacional Volcán Barú (Pan) 677-8, **30-1**
Parque Nacional Volcán Irazú (Cos) 554
Parque Nacional Volcán Masaya (Nic) 469-70
Parque Nacional Volcán Poás (Cos) 550
Parque Nacional Walter T Deininger (El S) 304
Port Royal National Park (Hon) 416
Río Blanco National Park (Bel) 273
Temash-Sarstoon National Park (Bel) 273
Nebaj (Gua) 143-5
Neily (Cos) 622-3
Nicaragua 438-527, **440-1**
accommodations 520
arts 518
climate 438
culture 517-18
disabilities, travelers with 524
embassies & consulates 521
food & drink 439, 521
gay & lesbian travelers 522
highlights 440
history 513-17
itineraries 439
landscape & wildlife 519-20
money 522-3
planning 37
safe travel 524
travel to/from 439, 525-6
travel within 526-7
women travelers 525
Nicaraguan Baseball Championship 25
Noche de Agüizotes (Nic) 27, 468
Nogapope (Pan) 27
Noriega, Colonel Manuel Antonio 712
Nueva Ocotepeque (Hon) 393

O

Oak Ridge (Hon) 416
Ocosingo (Mex) 72
Omoa (Hon) 394-5
opening hours 733, *see also individual locations*
Orange Walk (Bel) 246-8
Orinoco (Nic) 503
Orosi (Cos) 553
Ortega, Daniel 512

P

Palenque (Mex) 79-83
Palenque Ruins (Mex) 13, 80-1, **81**, **13**
Palmar (Cos) 617
Palo de Mayo (Nic) 26, 502
Panajachel (Gua) 122-30, **124-5**
accommodations 123-7
attractions & activities 123
courses 123
drinking & entertainment 129
food 128
shopping 129
travel to/from 130
Panama 637-725, **640-1**
accommodations 717
activities 717
arts 715
climate 637, 718
culture 713-14
customs regulations 718
disabilities, travelers with 722
embassies & consulates 718
food & drink 638, 718
gay & lesbian travelers 719
health 719
highlights 640-1
history 709-13
itineraries 638
landscapes & wildlife 715-25
money 720
planning 38
safe travel 721
sports 715
travel to/from 638, 723-4
travel within 724-6
women travelers 723
Panama Canal 657-9, 695, **658**
Panama City 13, 639-57, **642-3**, **646-7**, **652**, **2**, **13**
accommodations 647-50
attractions 639-45
courses 645
drinking & nightlife 651-3
entertainment 653-4
food 650-1
shopping 654
tours 645-6
travel to/from 655-6
travel within 656-7
Panama Jazz Festival 25
Panamá Viejo (Pan) 644
Panchimalco (El S) 303
Paquera (Cos) 600-1
paragliding 123
Paraíso (Cos) 553
parasailing 240
Parque Arqueológico Takalik Abaj (Gua) 164
Parque Internacional La Amistad (Pan) 678-9
Parque Nacional Braulio Carrillo (Cos) 551-2
Parque Nacional Cahuita (Cos) 562
Parque Nacional Carara (Cos) 605
Parque Nacional Chirripó (Cos) 616-17
Parque Nacional Coiba (Pan) 34, 667
Parque Nacional Corcovado (Cos) 620-1
Parque Nacional Cusuco (Hon) 378
Parque Nacional Darién (Pan) 702
Parque Nacional El Imposible (El S) 16, 316, 321-2
Parque Nacional La Tigra (Hon) 369
Parque Nacional Laguna del Tigre (Gua) 208
Parque Nacional Los Volcanes (El S) 308
Parque Nacional Manuel Antonio (Cos) 13, 610, **13**
Parque Nacional Marino Ballena (Cos) 613
Parque Nacional Marino Golfo de Chiriquí (Pan) 671
Parque Nacional Marino Isla Bastimentos (Pan) 690
Parque Nacional Montaña de Celaque (Hon) 392-3
Parque Nacional Montaña de Comayagua (Hon) 370
Parque Nacional Montecristo-El Trifinio (El S) 313
Parque Nacional Palo Verde (Cos) 586
Parque Nacional Pico Bonito (Hon) 404
Parque Nacional Rincón de la Vieja (Cos) 589
Parque Nacional San Lorenzo (Pan) 695
Parque Nacional Soberanía (Pan) 659

Parque Nacional Tortuguero (Cos) 557, **31**
Parque Nacional Volcán Arenal (Cos) 580
Parque Nacional Volcán Barú (Pan) 677-8, **30-1**
Parque Nacional Volcán Irazú (Cos) 554
Parque Nacional Volcán Masaya (Nic) 469-70
Parque Nacional Volcán Poás (Cos) 550
Parque Natural Metropolitano (Pan) 645
Parramos Grande (Gua) 144
Paso Canoas (Cos) 623
Pastores (Gua) 121
Pavones (Cos) 622
Pearl Islands (Pan), *see* Archipiélago de Las Perlas
Pearl Keys (Nic) 35, 503
Pearl Lagoon (Nic) 503-4
Pedasí (Pan) 663-5
Peña Blanca (Hon) 373
Península de Azuero (Pan) 663
Península de Nicoya (Cos) 591-604, **592-3**
Península de Osa 613-21, **614-15**
Perdomo, Guillermo 298
Perquín (El S) 34, 334-5
photography 734
Placencia (Bel) 266-9, **267**
planning
  Belize 37
  budgeting 19
  calendar of events 25-7
  Costa Rica 38
  El Salvador 37
  first time 20-1
  Guatemala 36
  Honduras 37
  internet resources 19
  itineraries 28-35
  Mexico 36
  money 19
  Nicaragua 37
  Panama 38
  responsible travel 19
  travel seasons 18, 25-7
  what to wear 20
Playa Aserradores (Nic) 489-90
Playa Avellanas (Cos) 598
Playa del Carmen (Mex) 59-61, **60**
Playa del Coco (Cos) 591-4
Playa El Coco (Nic) 481
Playa El Cuco (El S) 332
Playa El Sunzal (El S) 307
Playa El Tunco (El S) 16, 305, **16**
Playa El Zonte (El S) 307
Playa Gigante (Nic) 477
Playa Hermosa (Nic) 481
Playa Jiquilillo (Nic) 490-1
Playa Las Lajas (Pan) 672
Playa Maderas (Nic) 480
Playa Naranjo (Cos) 590, 600
Playa Negra (Cahuita, Cos) 562
Playa Negra (Puerto Viejo de Talamanca, Cos) 567
Playa Negra (Tamarindo, Cos) 598-9
Playa Popoyo (Nic) 477
Playa Sámara (Cos) 599-600
Playa Santo Domingo (Nic) 475
Playa Tamarindo (Cos) 594-8, **596**
Playa Venao (Pan) 665
Pochomil (Nic) 454-5
Poneloya (Nic) 489
Portobelo (Pan) 695-7
postal services 734
Pro-Búsqueda (El S) 344
Pueblos Blancos (Nic) 466-7
Pueblo Viejo (Bel) 273
Puerto Barrios (Gua) 185-7
Puerto Cabezas (Nic), *see* Bilwi
Puerto Cortés (Hon) 394
Puerto El Triunfo (El S) 326
Puerto Jiménez (Cos) 619-20
Puerto Lempira (Hon) 425-6
Puerto Limón (Cos) 560-1
Puerto Sandino (Nic) 490
Puerto Viejo de Sarapiquí (Cos) 584-5
Puerto Viejo de Talamanca (Cos) 566-71, **568**
Punta Allen (Mex) 35, 68
Punta Burica (Pan) 672
Punta de Manabique (Gua) 187
Punta Gorda (Bel) 269-72, **270**
Puntarenas (Cos) 605

Q

Quepos (Cos) 607-10
Quetzaltenango (Gua) 145-55, **146**, **148-9**
  accommodations 151
  activities 147-9
  attractions 145
  courses 149-50
  entertainment 153
  food 152
  shopping 153
  tours 150
  travel to/from 154
  travel within 155
Quiriguá (Gua) 180-1

R

Rabin Ajau (Gua) 27
Rabinal (Gua) 170
Raista (Hon) 424
Rama Cay (Nic) 501
Rancho Frío (Pan) 707
Refugio de Vida Silvestre Cuero y Salado (Hon) 405-6
Refugio de Vida Silvestre La Flor (Nic) 481
Reserva Biológica Río Indio-Maíz (Nic) 511
Reserva de Biosfera Bosawás (Nic) 498
Reserva de la Biosfera del Río Plátano (Hon) 424-5
Reserva de la Biosfera Sian Ka'an (Mex) 68
Reserva Natural Absoluta Cabo Blanco (Cos) 603-4
Reserva Natural Isla Juan Venado (Nic) 489
Reserva Natural Laguna de Apoyo (Nic) 466
Reserva Natural Punta Patiño (Pan) 707
Reserva Natural Volcán Mombacho (Nic) 465-6
Reserva Silvestre Greenfields (Nic) 502
reserves, *see also* national parks
  Área Protegida Cerro Tisey-Estanzuela (Nic) 495-6
  Área Protegida Miraflor (Nic) 495
  Biotopo Cerro Cahuí (Gua) 199
  Biotopo Chocón Machaca (Gua) 190
  Biotopo del Quetzal (Gua) 171
  Biotopo Monterrico-Hawaii (Gua) 168
  Bosque Eterno de los Niños (Cos) 572
  Cayos Cochinos (Hon) 405
  Celestún (Mex) 55
  Cloudbridge Nature Reserve (Cos) 615
  Columbia Forest Reserve (Bel) 272
  Isla de Cañas (Pan) 664
  La Montañona (El S) 340
  Lancetilla Jardín Botánico (Hon) 397
  Parque Hawaii (Gua) 168
  Parque Punta Sur (Mex) 63
  Refugio de Vida Punta Izopo (Hon) 397
  Refugio de Vida Silvestre Bocas del Polochic (Gua) 185
  Refugio de Vida Silvestre Cuero y Salado (Hon) 405-6
  Refugio de Vida Silvestre Isla Iguana (Pan) 664
  Refugio de Vida Silvestre La Flor (Nic) 481
  Refugio de Vida Silvestre los Guatuzos (Nic) 509
  Refugio Nacional de Vida Silvestre Caño Negro (Cos) 35, 584
  Refugio Nacional de Vida Silvestre Gandoca-Manzanillo (Cos) 571
  Reserva Biológica Bosque Nuboso Monteverde (Cos) 14, 572, **14**
  Reserva Biológica Río Indio-Maíz (Nic) 511
  Reserva de Biosfera Bosawás (Nic) 498
  Reserva de la Biosfera del Río Plátano (Hon) 424
  Reserva de la Biosfera la Encrucijada (Mex) 72
  Reserva de la Biosfera Sian Ka'an (Mex) 68
  Reserva Esperanza Verde (Nic) 509
  Reserva Natural Absoluta Cabo Blanco (Cos) 603-4
  Reserva Natural Atitlán (Gua) 123
  Reserva Natural Estero Padre Ramos (Nic) 490

Reserva Natural Isla Juan Venado (Nic) 489
Reserva Natural Laguna de Apoyo (Nic) 466
Reserva Natural Pilas-El Hoyo (Nic) 490
Reserva Natural Punta Patiño (Pan) 707
Reserva Natural Volcán Mombacho (Nic) 465-6
Reserva Privada El Quebracho (Nic) 511
Reserva Silvestre Greenfields (Nic) 502
Reserva Silvestre Privada Domitila (Nic) 465
Roatán Marine Park (Hon) 411
Sendero Ecológico El Aprisco (Gua) 156
Shipstern Nature Reserve (Bel) 251
Tawahka Asangni Biosphere Reserve (Hon) 433
Retalhuleu (Gua) 163-4
Río Cangrejal (Hon) 403-4
Río Coco (Nic) 506
Río Dulce (Gua) 181-4, 190
Río Lagartos (Mex) 66
Río Orosi Valley (Cos) 553-4
Río San Juan (Nic) 510-12
Rivas (Nic) 470-1
river-tubing 256
Roatán (Hon) 12, 410-17, **412**, **4**
Ruinas de Tazumal (El S) 314
ruins, *see* archaeological sites
Ruta de las Flores (El S) 16, 316-20, **16**
Ruta de los Conventos (Mex) 66

S

safety 734, *see also individual locations*
sailing 182, 241
Salamá (Gua) 170
Sambo Creek (Hon) 405
Sambú (Pan) 35, 709
San Andrés Xecul (Gua) 156
San Antonio (Bel) 272-3
San Antonio Palopó (Gua) 131
San Carlos (Nic) 508-10
San Cristóbal de las Casas (Mex) 72-9, **76-7**
accommodations 75
attractions 72-3
courses 73
drinking 78
entertainment 78
food 75-8
tours 73
travel to/from 78-9
travel within 79
San Felipe de Lara (Gua) 184
San Francisco El Alto (Gua) 155-6
San Gerardo de Rivas (Cos) 615-16
San Ignacio (Bel) 254-8, **255**
San Ignacio (El S) 341
San Isidro de El General (Cos) 613-15
San Jacinto (Nic) 490
San Jorge (Nic) 471
San Jose (Bel) 273
San José (Cos) 532-46, **534-5**
accommodations 536-9
attractions 532-3
courses 533
drinking & nightlife 540-1
entertainment 541
food 539-40
gay & lesbian travelers 541
safety 542
shopping 542
tours 533-6
travel to/from 543-4
travel within 544-6
San Jose Succotz (Bel) 260
San Juan (Hon) 393
San Juan Chamula (Mex) 79
San Juan de Oriente (Nic) 467
San Juan del Norte (Nic) 511
San Juan del Sur (Nic) 476-80, **478**, **32-3**
San Juan La Laguna (Gua) 136
San Lorenzo Zinacantán (Mex) 79
San Manuel Colohete (Hon) 392
San Marcos (Nic) 467
San Marcos La Laguna (Gua) 15, 135-7
San Miguel (Bel) 272
San Miguel (El S) 327-30, **328**
San Miguel Totonicapán (Gua) 156-7
San Pedro (Bel) 240-5, **242**
San Pedro Columbia (Bel) 272
San Pedro La Laguna (Gua) 133-5
San Pedro Sula (Hon) 374-8
San Ramón (Nic) 475-6, 499
San Salvador (El S) 285-302, **289-90**, **292**, **294**, **296**
accommodations 290-3
attractions 285-90
drinking & nightlife 297
entertainment 298
food 295-7
shopping 298
travel to/from 300
travel within 300-2
San Sebastián (El S) 323
San Simón, *see* Maximón
San Vicente (El S) 323-4
Sánchez, Oscar Arias 626
Sandy Bay (Hon) 416
Santa Ana (El S) 309-12, **310**
Santa Catalina (Pan) 666-8
Santa Catarina Palopó (Gua) 131
Santa Cruz del Quiché (Gua) 142-3
Santa Cruz La Laguna (Gua) 137-8
Santa Elena (Bel) 273
Santa Elena (Cos) 572-9, **574-5**
accommodations 577-8
activities 576
attractions 572-3, 573-6
courses 576
food 578
shopping 579
travel to/from 579
Santa Elena (Gua), *see* Flores & Santa Elena
Santa Fé (Pan) 668
Santa Lucía (Hon) 369
Santa Lucía Cotzumalguapa (Gua) 165-7
Santa Rosa (Cos) 589-90
Santa Rosa de Aguán (Hon) 408
Santa Rosa de Copán (Hon) 388-90
Santa Tecla (El S) 299
Santa Teresa (Cos) 604-5
Santamaría, Juan 546
Santiago Atitlán (Gua) 15, 130-3
Sarteneja (Bel) 35, 251
Sayaxché (Gua) 191
sea travel 740, 741, *see also individual locations*
Semana Santa (El S) 320
Semana Santa (Gua) 26, 115, 188
Semuc Champey (Gua) 176
sharks, *see* whale sharks
Sierpe (Cos) 617
Sima de las Cotorras (Mex) 72
Sipacate (Gua) 167
Sixaola (Cos) 571
Smithsonian Tropical Research Institute (Pan) 660
snorkeling 22, 729, *see also* diving
Archipiélago de Las Perlas (Pan) 661
Caye Caulker (Bel) 236
Cayos Cochinos (Hon) 405
Great Corn Island (Nic) 504
Hopkins (Bel) 264
Isla Bastimentos (Pan) 691
Isla Colón (Pan) 680
Isla Cozumel (Mex) 63
Isla del Caño (Cos) 617
Isla Grande (Pan) 697
Isla Mujeres (Mex) 49
Isla Taboga (Pan) 660
Montezuma (Cos) 601
Panama 717
Parque Nacional Cahuita (Cos) 562
Parque Nacional Jeannette Kawas (Hon) 397
Playa del Carmen (Mex) 59
Playa Ocotal (Cos) 591
Puerto Viejo de Talamanca (Cos) 567
Refugio Nacional de Vida Silvestre Gandoca-Manzanillo (Cos) 571
Roatán (Hon) 12, 411
Sarteneja (Bel) 251
Tobacco Caye (Bel) 265
Tulum (Mex) 65
Utila (Hon) 12, 420
Uvita (Cos) 613
Sololá (Gua) 131
Somoto (Nic) 496-7
Sonis (Nic) 497
Sonsonate (El S) 320-1
Suchitoto (El S) 336-9
Sun Jam (Hon) 27
surfing 24, 730
Dominical (Cos) 611
El Salvador 349

surfing *continued*
Isla Carenero (Pan) 689
Isla Colón (Pan) 681
Jacó (Cos) 606
Las Flores (El S) 332
Mal País (Cos) 604
Masachapa (Nic) 454-5
Nicaragua 523
Ollie's Point (Cos) 590
Panama 717
Pavones (Cos) 622
Playa Avellanas (Cos) 598-9
Playa El Sunzal (El S) 307
Playa El Tunco (El S) 16, 305, **16**
Playa Grande (Cos) 594
Playa Hermosa (Cos) 606
Playa Hermosa (Nic) 481
Playa Maderas (Nic) 480-1
Playa Naranjo (Cos) 590
Playa Negra (Cos) 598-9
Playa Sámara (Cos) 599
Playa Tamarindo (Cos) 594-8
Pochomil (Nic) 454-5
Punta Roca (El S) 304
Salsa Brava (Cos) 567
San Juan del Sur (Nic) 476-480, **478**, **32-3**
Santa Catalina (Pan) 666-8
Sipacate (Gua) 167
Witch's Rock (Cos) 590
swimming 735
Balneario La Nueva Barranca (Pan) 670
Guatemala 176
Isla de Ometepe (Nic) 472
Laguna de Xiloá (Nic) 447-8
Monkey Point (Nic) 506
Perquín (El S) 335
Playa Cocalito (Cos) 618
Playa Marsella (Nic) 480
Playa Platanares (Cos) 619
Reserva Natural Laguna de Apoyo (Nic) 466

T

Tacuba (El S) 16, 316
Tamarindo (Cos), *see* Playa Tamarindo
Tawahka Asangni Biosphere Reserve (Hon) 433
Tegucigalpa (Hon) 357-68, **360-1**, **364**
accommodations 362-3
attractions 357-62
drinking & nightlife 365
entertainment 365-6
food 363-5
safety 366
shopping 366
travel to/from 367-8
travel within 368
Tela (Hon) 395-6
telephone services 735
Ticul (Mex) 66
Tihosuco (Mex) 66
Tikal (Gua) 10, 200-7, **11**, **202-3**
travel to/from 82
Tilapita (Gua) 166
Tilarán (Cos) 579-80
tipping 21
Tobacco Caye (Bel) 265
toilets 735
Tola (Nic) 477
Toledo (Bel) 272-4
Toledo Cacao Festival (Bel) 26
Tornabé (Hon) 398
Tortuguero (Cos) 557-60
tourist information 735, *see also individual locations*
train travel 742
transportation 18, 738-42
Trujillo (Hon) 406-8, **407**
Tulate (Gua) 166
Tulum (Mex) 64-7
Tulum Ruins (Mex) 65
Turrialba (Cos) 554-7
turtles
Biotopo Monterrico-Hawaii (Gua) 168
Isla de Cañas (Pan) 664
Isla Mujeres (Mex) 49
Parque Hawaii (Gua) 168
Playa Grande (Cos) 594
Playa Larga (Pan) 690
Raista (Hon) 424
Refugio de Vida Silvestre La Flor (Nic) 481
Santa Rosa (Cos) 590
Tortuguero (Cos) 557
Western Azuero (Pan) 665

U

Uaxactún (Gua) 207-8
Unesco World Heritage Sites
Antigua (Gua) 108-21, **110-11**, **2**
Campeche (Mex) 68-72, **70-1**
Casco Viejo (Pan) 639-44
Chichén Itzá (Mex) 15, 51-4, **15**, **52-3**
Copán Archaeological Site (Hon) 16, 384-8, **385**, **16**
Joya de Cerén (El S) 303
Panamá Viejo (Pan) 644
Parque Nacional Coiba (Pan) 34, 667
Parque Nacional Darién (Pan) 702
Quiriguá (Gua) 180
Tikal (Gua) 10, 200-7, **11**, **202-3**
Urban Maeztro 431
Uspantán (Gua) 145
Usulután (El S) 325-6
Utila (Hon) 12, 417-23, **418**
Uvita (Cos) 613

V

Valladolid 50-1
Velásquez, José Antonio 431
video 734
visas & documents 19, 736, *see also individual countries*
Visquerra, Julio 431
volcanoes 24
Acatenango (Gua) 113
Agua (Gua) 113
Cerro Negro (Nic) 490
Cerro Verde (El S) 308
Chichontepec (El S) 323
Fuego (Gua) 113
Pacaya (Gua) 113
Quezaltepeque (Volcán San Salvador) 303
Volcán Arenal (Cos) 580
Volcán Barú (Pan) 677, **30-1**
Volcán Barva (Cos) 551
Volcán Concepción (Nic) 472
Volcán Cosigüina (Nic) 490
Volcán de Usulután (El S) 325
Volcán Irazú (Cos) 554
Volcán Izalco (El S) 308
Volcán Maderas (Nic) 471
Volcán Masaya (Nic) 469
Volcán Mombacho (Nic) 465
Volcán Momotombo (Nic) 490
Volcán Poás (Cos) 550
Volcán Rincón de la Vieja (Cos) 589
Volcán Santa Ana (El S) 308
Volcán Santa María (Gua) 147
Volcán Santiaguito (Gua) 147
Volcán Santo Tomás (Gua) 155
Volcán Tajumulco (Gua) 147
Volcán Zunil (Gua) 155
Volcano Chaparrastique (El S) 328-9
volunteering 736-7
Costa Rica 633
El Salvador 290, 337, 352
Guatemala 113, 149, 223
Honduras 436
Mexico 89
Nicaragua 473, 525

W

Walker, William 406, 514, 625
walking, *see* hiking
waterfalls
Agua Azul (Mex) 72
Biotopo del Quetzal (Gua) 171
Cascada de los Ensueños (Hon) 370
Cascada los Tercios (El S) 337
Cascada San Ramón (Nic) 476
Cascada Zacate (Hon) 404
Catarata La Cangreja (Cos) 589
El Bejuco (Hon) 405
El Gavilán (Hon) 370
El Salto (El S) 334
Five Sisters Falls (Bel) 259
Hidden Valley (Thousand Foot) Falls (Bel) 259
Isla de Ometepe (Nic) 17, 472
La Cascada de los Duendes (Hon) 393
La Cascada del Chorreron (El S) 334

La Catarata de la Fortuna (Cos) 580
La Estanzuela (Hon) 372
Las Cataratas (Gua) 143
Los Chorros de Calera (El S) 317
Los Siete Altares (Gua) 187
Misol-Ha (Mex) 72
Montezuma (Cos) 601
Parque Internacional La Amistad (Pan) 679
Parque Nacional Braulio Carrillo (Cos) 551-2
Pulhapanzak (Hon) 374
Río Blanco Falls (Bel) 273
Río On Pools (Bel) 259
Ruta de las Seite Cascadas (El S) 317
Salto El Cubo (El S) 337
Salto El Espino (El S) 314
Salto Estanzuela (Nic) 495
Santa Fé (Pan) 668
Viento Fresco (Cos) 581
weather 18, *see also individual countries*
West Bay (Hon) 415-16
Western Belize 250-61, **252-3**
whale sharks 420
Isla Holbox (Mex) 48
Isla Mujeres (Mex) 49
Placencia (Bel) 266
Playa del Carmen (Mex) 59
Utila (Hon) 12, 419
Whale Shark & Oceanic Research Center (Hon) 420
white-water rafting 730
Apuzunga Water Park (El S) 312
Boquete (Pan) 673
Orosi (Cos) 554
Panama 717
Puerto Viejo de Sarapiquí (Cos) 584
Río Cangrejal (Hon) 403
Río Sarapiquí (Cos) 583
Turrialba (Cos) 555
wildlife-watching 22, 730, *see also* bird-watching
Aguacaliente Wildlife Sanctuary (Bel) 272
Biotopo Cerro Cahuí (Gua) 199
Biotopo Monterrico-Hawaii (Gua) 168
Bosque Eterno de los Niños (Cos) 572
Community Baboon Sanctuary (Bel) 245
Crocodile Bridge (Cos) 605
Crooked Tree Wildlife Sanctuary (Bel) 246
El Valle Amphibian Conservation Center (Pan) 662
Finca La Isla (Cos) 567
Guatemala 214-16
Iguana Research & Breeding Station (Hon) 418
Isla Barro Colorado (Pan) 660
Jaguar Centro de Rescate (Cos) 566
Laguna de Guaimoreto (Hon) 408
Monkey Bay Wildlife Sanctuary (Bel) 251
Parque Nacional Cahuita (Cos) 562
Parque Nacional Carara (Cos) 605
Parque Nacional Corcovado (Cos) 620
Parque Nacional Marino Ballena (Cos) 613
Parque Nacional Montecristo-El Trifinio (El S) 313
Parque Nacional Pico Bonito (Hon) 404
Parque Nacional Rincón de la Vieja (Cos) 589
Parque Nacional Soberanía (Pan) 659
Parque Nacional Tortuguero (Cos) 557, **31**
Parque Nacional Walter T Deininger (El S) 304
Parque Natural Metropolitano (Pan) 645
Refugio de Vida Silvestre Bocas del Polochic (Gua) 185
Refugio de Vida Silvestre Cuero y Salado (Hon) 405
Reserva Biológica Bosque Nuboso Monteverde (Cos) 572
Reserva de la Biosfera del Río Plátano (Hon) 424
Reserva Natural Punta Patiño (Pan) 707
Reserva Silvestre Privada Domitila (Nic) 465
Utila (Hon) 12, 420
Wiwili (Nic) 498
women travelers 737, *see also individual locations*
work 737

X

Xcalak (Mex) 65
Xeo (Gua) 144

Y

Yaviza (Pan) 706
Yaxchilán (Mex) 84
Yucatán 43-71, **44-5**, *see also* Mexico's Yucatán & Chiapas

Z

Zaculeu (Gua) 158
Zapatistas 85
Zelaya, José Santos 513
Zelaya, Manuel 427
zip-lining 729
Apaneca (El S) 318
Boquete (Pan) 673
Isla Bastimentos (Pan) 691
Isla de Ometepe (Nic) 17, 475
La Campa (Hon) 392
La Fortuna (Cos) 581
Lago de Yojoa (Hon) 374
Monteverde 573
Montezuma (Cos) 601
Río Cangrejal (Hon) 404
Sambo Creek (Hon) 405
San Juan del Sur (Nic) 477
Santa Elena (Cos) 573
Tikal (Gua) 206
zoos
Belize 250
Costa Rica 572, 573
Guatemala 97, 147
Zunil (Gua) 156

Map Legend

Sights

- Beach
- Bird Sanctuary
- Buddhist
- Castle/Palace
- Christian
- Confucian
- Hindu
- Islamic
- Jain
- Jewish
- Monument
- Museum/Gallery/Historic Building
- Ruin
- Sento Hot Baths/Onsen
- Shinto
- Sikh
- Taoist
- Winery/Vineyard
- Zoo/Wildlife Sanctuary
- Other Sight

Activities, Courses & Tours

- Bodysurfing
- Diving/Snorkeling
- Canoeing/Kayaking
- Course/Tour
- Skiing
- Snorkeling
- Surfing
- Swimming/Pool
- Walking
- Windsurfing
- Other Activity

Sleeping

- Sleeping
- Camping

Eating

- Eating

Drinking & Nightlife

- Drinking & Nightlife
- Cafe

Entertainment

- Entertainment

Shopping

- Shopping

Information

- Bank
- Embassy/Consulate
- Hospital/Medical
- Internet
- Police
- Post Office
- Telephone
- Toilet
- Tourist Information
- Other Information

Geographic

- Beach
- Hut/Shelter
- Lighthouse
- Lookout
- Mountain/Volcano
- Oasis
- Park
- Pass
- Picnic Area
- Waterfall

Population

- Capital (National)
- Capital (State/Province)
- City/Large Town
- Town/Village

Transport

- Airport
- Border crossing
- Bus
- Cable car/Funicular
- Cycling
- Ferry
- Metro station
- Monorail
- Parking
- Petrol station
- Subway station
- Taxi
- Train station/Railway
- Tram
- Underground station
- Other Transport

Note: Not all symbols displayed above appear on the maps in this book

Routes

- Tollway
- Freeway
- Primary
- Secondary
- Tertiary
- Lane
- Unsealed road
- Road under construction
- Plaza/Mall
- Steps
- Tunnel
- Pedestrian overpass
- Walking Tour
- Walking Tour detour
- Path/Walking Trail

Boundaries

- International
- State/Province
- Disputed
- Regional/Suburb
- Marine Park
- Cliff
- Wall

Hydrography

- River, Creek
- Intermittent River
- Canal
- Water
- Dry/Salt/Intermittent Lake
- Reef

Areas

- Airport/Runway
- Beach/Desert
- Cemetery (Christian)
- Cemetery (Other)
- Glacier
- Mudflat
- Park/Forest
- Sight (Building)
- Sportsground
- Swamp/Mangrove